Strategic Management

9th Edition

Michael A. Hitt

Texas A&M University

R. Duane Ireland

Texas A&M University

Robert E. Hoskisson

Rice University

S. Manikutty

Indian Institute of Management, Ahmedabad

CENGAGE Learning

Andover • Melbourne • Mexico City • Stamford, CT • Toronto • Hong Kong • New Delhi • Seoul • Singapore • Tokyo

CENGAGE Learning

Strategic Management, 9th Edition

Michael A. Hitt, R. Duane Ireland
Robert E. Hoskisson,
and S. Manikutty

Cover Image: © Thinkstock

Original Edition © 2011, 2009 South-Western, a part of Cengage Learning
The Management of Strategy: Concepts and Cases, 9e
by R. Duane Ireland, Robert E. Hoskisson, and Michael Hitt
ISBN-13: 978-0-538-75319-7
ISBN-10: 0-538-75319-6

ISBN-13: 978-81-315-2038-3
ISBN-10: 81-315-2038-2

Cengage Learning India Private Limite
T-303, 3rd Floor
DAV Complex, Plot 3
Mayur Vihar Phase 1
Delhi-110091

Cengage Learning is a leading provider of customized learning solutions with office locations around the globe, including Andover, Melbourne, Mexico City, Stamford (CT), Toronto, Hong Kong, New Delhi, Seoul, Singapore, and Tokyo. Locate your local office at: **www.cengage.com/global**

Cengage Learning products are represented in Canada by Nelson Education, Ltd.

For product information, visit **www.cengage.co.in**

Printed in India
Sixteen Indian Reprint 2019

To my grandchildren who are very special to me: Ashlyn, Aubrey Mason, and Michelle
Your smiles are like sunshine—they brighten my day.
—Michael A. Hitt

To my entire family
I love each of you dearly and remain so grateful for your incredibly strong support and encouragement all these years. Your words and deeds have indeed showed me how to "keep my good eye to the sun and my blind eye to the dark".
—R. Duane Ireland

To my wonderful grandchildren (Mara, Seth, Rosalyn, Ian, Abby, Madeline, Joseph, Nadline, and Elizabeth), who are absolutely amazing and light up my life.
—Robert E. Hoskisson

To my granddaughter Madhumati with her infinite power to attract.
—S. Manikutty

Brief Contents

Contents

PART II: FORMULATION OF STRATEGIC ACTIONS 77

Preface to India Edition

Our goal in coming up with this edition of the book *Strategic Management* is to present a new, up-to-date standard for explaining the strategic management process, with special reference to the Indian context. To reach this goal with this edition of our market-leading text, we again present you with an intellectually rich yet thoroughly practical analysis of strategic management.

With each new edition, we are challenged and invigorated by the goal of establishing a new standard for presenting strategic management knowledge in a readable style. To prepare for each new edition, we carefully study the most recent academic research to ensure that the strategic management content we present to you is highly current and relevant for use in organizations. In addition, we continuously read articles appearing in many different business publications (e.g., *Wall Street Journal, Business Week, Fortune, Financial Times, Business India, Business Today, Economic Times, Mint,* and *Forbes,* to name a few); we do this to identify valuable examples of how companies are actually using the strategic management process. Though many of the hundreds of companies we discuss in the book will be quite familiar to you, some companies will likely be new to you as well. One reason for this is that we use examples of companies from around the world to demonstrate how globalized business has become. But in this Indian edition, we have sought to present many examples of Indian companies and situations so that the Indian reader and student will gain maximum value from the book. To maximize your opportunities to learn as you read and think about how actual companies use strategic management tools, techniques, and concepts (based on the most current research), we emphasize a lively and user-friendly writing style. The Indian examples also help to relate the concepts to the Indian context, so as to answer the question, how we apply these concepts in India.

Several characteristics of this edition of our book will enhance your learning opportunities:

- This book presents you with the most comprehensive and thorough coverage of strategic management that is available in the market.
- The research used in this book is drawn from the "classics" as well as the most recent contributions to the strategic management literature. The historically significant "classic" research provides the foundation for much of what is known about strategic management; the most recent contributions reveal insights about how to effectively use strategic management in the complex, global business environment in which most firms operate while trying to outperform their competitors. Our book also presents you with many up-to-date or recent examples of how firms use the strategic management tools, techniques, and concepts developed by leading researchers. Indeed, this book is strongly application oriented and presents you, our readers, with a vast number of examples and applications of strategic management concepts, techniques, and tools. In this edition, for example, we examine more than 600 companies to describe the use of strategic management. Collectively, no other strategic management book presents you with the combination of useful and insightful research and applications in a wide variety of organizations as does this text. Company examples range from the large U.S.-based firms such as Amazon.com, Wal-Mart, IBM, Johnson & Johnson, Hershey, Hewlett Packard, Dell, PepsiCo, and Cisco to major firms based in other countries such as Toyota, Nokia, British Petroleum, Ryanair, Volkswagon, and Huawei, and Indian companies such as Bajaj Auto, Tata Motors, ITC, Ballarpur Industries and Larsen & Toubro (L&T). We also include examples of successful younger and newer firms such as Dylan's Candy Bar, Facebook, Honext Tea, MySpace, Yandex, Sun Tech Power, Infosys and Cognizant Technologies and middle-sized family-owned firms such as Sargento Foods and a number of Indian companies.

- We carefully integrate two of the most popular and well-known theoretical concepts in the strategic management field: industrial-organization economics and the resource based view of the firm. Other text books usually emphasize one of these two theories (at the cost of explaining the other one to describe strategic management). However, such an approach is incomplete; research and practical experience indicate that both theories play a major role in understanding the linkage between strategic management and organizational success. No other book integrates these two theoretical perspectives effectively to explain the strategic management process and its application in all types of organizations.
- We use the ideas of prominent scholars, e.g., Raphael (Raffi) Amit, Kathy Eisenhardt, Don Hambrick, Constance (Connie) Helfat, Ming-Jer Chen, Michael Porter, C.K. Prahalad, Vijay Govindarajan, Richard Rumelt, Ken Smith, David Ţeece, Michael Tushman, Oliver Williamson, and many younger, emerging scholars such as Rajshree Agarwal, Gautam Ahuja, Javier Gimono, Amy Hillman, Michael Lennox, Yadong Luo, Jeff Reuer, Mary Tripsas, and Maurizio Zollo (along with numerous others) to shape the discussion of what strategic management is. We describe the practices of prominent executives and practitioners (e.g., Mike Duke, Jeffrey Immelt, Steven Jobs, Gianfranco Lanci, Indra Nooyi, and many others) to help us describe how strategic management is used in many types of organizations.
- We, the authors of this book, are also active scholars. We conduct research on different strategic management topics. Our interest in doing so is to contribute to the strategic management literature and to better understand how to effectively apply strategic management tools, techniques, and concepts to increase organizational performance. Thus, our own research is integrated in the appropriate chapters along with the research of numerous other scholars, some of which are noted above.

In addition to our book's characteristics, there are some specific features of this edition that we want to highlight for you:

- **New Opening Cases and Strategic Focus Segments**—we continue our tradition of providing all-new Opening Cases and Strategic Focus segments. In addition, new company-specific examples are included in each chapter. Through all of these venues, we present you with a wealth of examples of how actual organizations, most of which compete internationally as well as in their home markets, use the strategic management process to outperform rivals and increase their performance.
- **16 All-New Cases** with an effective mix of organizations headquartered or based in India, the United States and a number of other countries. Many of the cases have full financial data (the analyses of which are in the Case Notes that are available to instructors). These timely cases present active learners with opportunities to apply the strategic management process and understand organizational conditions and contexts and to make appropriate recommendations to deal with critical concerns.
- **New and Revised Experiential Exercises** to support individuals' efforts to understand the use of the strategic management process. These exercises place active learners in a variety of situations requiring application of some part of the strategic management process.
- **Strategy Right Now** is used in each chapter to highlight companies that are effectively using a strategic management concept examined in the chapter or to provide additional coverage of a particular topic. In **Chapter 5**, for example, how the three banking giants in India, ICICI Bank, HDFC Bank and State Bank of India are competing by offering financial services tailored to its customers' needs is highlighted and recommended for further study. In **Chapter 13**, the explosion of social media and networking, in particular Twitter, is examined in detail. This feature is a valuable tool for readers to quickly identify how a firm is effectively using a strategic management tool, technique, or concept. We follow up with the most current research and information about these firms by using Cengage Learning's Business & Company Resource Center (BCRC). Links to specific current news articles related to these companies and topics can be found on our website (www.cengage.com/international). Whenever you see the Strategy Right Now icon in the text, you will know that current research is available from the BCRC links posted to our website.
- **An Exceptional Balance** between current research and up-to-date applications of it in actual organizations. The content has not only the best research documentation but also the largest amount of effective real-world examples to help active learners understand the different types of strategies organizations use to achieve their vision and mission.
- **Lively, Concise Writing Style** to hold readers' attention and to increase their interest in strategic management.
- **Continuing, Updated Coverage** of vital strategic management topics such as competitive rivalry and dynamics, strategic alliances, mergers and acquisitions, internal strategies, corporate governance, and ethics. Also, we continue to be the only book in the market with a separate chapter devoted to strategic entrepreneurship.

To maintain current and up-to-date content, new concepts are explored in this edition.

In **Chapter 2**, we added the physical environment as the seventh segment of the general environment. The discussion of the physical environment emphasizes the importance of sustainability. Sustainability has become a "watchword" at many companies such as Honest Tea and Dell. For example, Dell has a goal of having a carbon neutral footprint. This discussion is integrated with the explanation in **Chapter 4** of how firms are developing a "green" strategy that is a core part of their competitive strategy. Wal-Mart is investing significant capital and effort to be a "green" firm, as are other firms such as Procter & Gamble and Target. We describe the actions a number of firms regarding the physical environment in one of the Strategic Focus segments in **Chapter 2.**

In **Chapter 6**, we explore a new strategic trend also caused by the global economic crisis. While many firms downscoped in the late 1980s and 1990s because of the performance problems caused by over-diversification, the economic recession has served as a catalyst for a new trend of diversification to help firms spread their risk across several markets (to avoid bankruptcy). In **Chapter 7**, we expand our discussion of cross-border acquisitions. In fact, cross-border acquisitions remain quite popular during the global economic crisis, largely because of the number of firms in financial trouble that have under-valued assets as a result. Indian and Chinese firms have become especially active, which is discussed in detail in **Chapter 7** in the Strategic Focus segment. **Chapter 8** includes new content exampling emerging international firms from India and China (Sun Tech Power in commercial solar power, ZTE and Huawei in network equipment, Bharti Airtel in telecommunications, Tata Motors in automobiles and Suzlon in conventional energy) and Russia (Yandex, a competitor to Google).

In **Chapter 10**, we added content related to the new actions and policies that deal with corporate governance. For example, the U.S. Securities and Exchange Commission (SEC) has implemented some new policies providing for closer oversight of companies' financial dealings. The SEC has also developed new rules to allow owners with large stakes to propose new directors. These new rules are likely to shift the balance even more in favor of outside and independent members of companies' boards of directors. As a major new global economic power with several of the world's largest firms, corporate governance in China has become an important issue. Interestingly, many of the new corporate governance practices implemented in Chinese companies resemble governance practices in the United States. The measures that have been taken to improve corporate governance in India have been included in considerable detail. Some examples that gave rise to major questions on corporate governance such as Satyam and ITC have also been included.

In **Chapter 13**, we explain how innovation has become highly important for firms to compete effectively in global markets. As such, there have been major drives to increase the innovativeness of firms in the United States and China. The importance of innovation has been heightened by the emphasis on sustainability (developing "greener" products—see Chapters 2 and 4) and by the growing demand from customers that companies provide them with "excellent" value in the form of the goods or services they are making and selling (see Chapter 2).

SUPPLEMENTS

Instructors

Case Notes Many of the cases in this edition are accompanied by succinct case notes designed for ease of use while also providing the necessary background and financial data for classroom discussion.

Instructor's Resource Manual The Instructor's Resource Manual, organized around each chapter's knowledge objectives, includes teaching ideas for each chapter and how to reinforce essential principles with extra examples. This support product includes lecture outlines, detailed answers to end-of-chapter review questions, instructions for using each chapter's experiential exercises, and additional assignments.

Test Bank Thoroughly revised and enhanced, test bank questions are linked to each chapter's knowledge objectives and are ranked by difficulty and question type. We provide an ample number of application questions throughout, and we have also retained scenario-based questions as a means of adding in-depth problem-solving questions.

PowerPoint® An all-new PowerPoint presentation, created for this edition, provides support for lectures, emphasizing key concepts, key terms, and instructive graphics. Slides can also be used by students as an aid to note-taking.

Acknowledgments

We express our appreciation for the excellent support received from our editorial and production team at Cengage Learning India. We are grateful for their dedication, commitment, and outstanding contributions to the development and publication of this book and its package of support materials.

We are grateful to The Research and Publications of Indian Institute of Management, Ahmedabad for their support of the research for this book. We thank Shruti Chopra for her contribution in locating materials for the Indian examples, preparing the short case studies and for improving the presentation of the Indian materials. We thank Anand Manikutty, then in the doctoral program in the Harvard Business School, for his suggestions on the evolving draft of this adapted edition.

We are highly indebted to the reviewers of the earlier 9th International edition in preparation for this current edition:

Erich Brockmann
University of New Orleans
Scott Elston
Iowa State University
Carol Jacobson
Purdue University
Consuelo M. Ramirez
University of Texas at San Antonio
Deepak Sethi
Old Dominion University
Len J. Trevino
Washington State University
Marta Szabo White
Georgia State University
Diana J. Wong-MingJi
Eastern Michigan University

Bruce H. Charnov
Hofstra University
Susan Hansen
University of Wisconsin-Platteville
Frank Novakowski
Davenport University
Manjula S. Salimath
University of North Texas
Manisha Singal
Virginia Tech
Edward Ward
Saint Cloud State University
Michael L Williams
Michigan State University
Wilson Zehr
Concordia University

Finally, we are very appreciative of the following people for the time and care that went into preparing of the supplements to accompany this edition:

Charles Byles
Virginia Commonwealth University
Richard H. Lester
Texas A&M University

Paul Friga
University of North Carolina
Paul Mallette
Colorado State University
Kristi L. Marshall

Michael A. Hitt
R. Duane Ireland
Robert E. Hoskisson
S. Manikutty

About the Authors

Michael A. Hitt

Michael A. Hitt is a University Distinguished Professor and holds the Joe B. Foster Chair in Business Leadership at Texas A&M University. He received his Ph.D. from the University of Colorado. He has more than 260 publications including 26 co-authored or co-edited books and was cited as one of the 10 most-cited scholars in management over a 25-year period in an article published in the 2008 volume of the *Journal of Management.* In 2010, *Times Higher Education* listed him as one of the top scholars in economics, finance and management.

Some of his books are *Downscoping: How to Tame the Diversified Firm* (Oxford University Press, 1994); *Mergers and Acquisitions: A Guide to Creating Value for Stakeholders* (Oxford University Press, 2001); *Competing for Advantage,* 2nd edition (South-Western, 2008); and *Understanding Business Strategy,* 3rd edition (South-Western Cengage Learning, 2012). He is co-editor of several books including the following: *Managing Strategically in an Interconnected World* (1998); *New Managerial Mindsets: Organizational Transformation and Strategy Implementation* (1998); *Dynamic Strategic Resources: Development, Diffusion, and Integration* (1999); *Winning Strategies in a Deconstructing World* (John Wiley & Sons, 2000); *Handbook of Strategic Management* (2001); *Strategic Entrepreneurship: Creating a New Integrated Mindset* (2002); *Creating Value: Winners in the New Business Environment* (Blackwell Publishers, 2002); *Managing Knowledge for Sustained Competitive Advantage* (Jossey-Bass, 2003); *Great Minds in Management: The Process of Theory Development* (Oxford University Press, 2005); and *The Global Mindset* (Elsevier, 2007). He has served on the editorial review boards of multiple journals, including the *Academy of Management Journal, Academy of Management Executive, Journal of Applied Psychology, Journal of Management, Journal of World Business,* and *Journal of Applied Behavioral Sciences.* Furthermore, he has served as consulting editor and editor of the *Academy of Management Journal.* He was a founding co-editor and currently a consulting editor for the *Strategic Entrepreneurship Journal.* He is a past president of the Strategic Management Society and of the Academy of Management.

He is a Fellow in the Academy of Management and in the Strategic Management Society. He received an honorary doctorate from the Universidad Carlos III de Madrid and is an Honorary Professor and Honorary Dean at Xi'an Jiao Tong University. He has been acknowledged with several awards for his scholarly research and he received the Irwin Outstanding Educator Award and the Distinguished Service Award from the Academy of Management. He has received Best Paper Awards for articles published in the *Academy of Management Journal, Academy of Management Executive,* and *Journal of Management.*

R. Duane Ireland

R. Duane Ireland is a University Distinguished Professor and holds the Conn Chair in New Ventures Leadership in the Mays Business School, Texas A&M University where he previously served as head of the management department. He teaches strategic management courses at all levels (undergraduate, masters, doctoral, and executive). He has over 200 publications including more than a dozen books. His research, which focuses on diversification, innovation, corporate entrepreneurship, and strategic entrepreneurship, has been published in a number of journals, including *Academy of Management Journal, Academy of Management Review, Academy of Management Executive, Administrative Science Quarterly, Strategic Management Journal, Journal of Management, Strategic Entrepreneurship Journal, Human Relations, Entrepreneurship Theory and Practice, Journal of Business Venturing,* and *Journal of Management Studies,* among others. His recently published books include *Understanding Business Strategy,* 3rd edition (South-Western Cengage Learning, 2012), *Entrepreneurship: Successfully Launching New Ventures,* 4th edition (Prentice-Hall, 2012), and *Competing for Advantage,* 2nd edition (South-Western, 2008). He is serving or has served as a member of the editorial review boards for a number of journals, including *Academy of Management Journal, Academy of Management Review, Academy of Management Executive, Journal of Management, Strategic Entrepreneurship Journal, Journal of Business Venturing, Entrepreneurship Theory and Practice, Journal of Business Strategy, Academy of Management Perspectives,* and *European Management Journal.* He recently completed a term as editor of the *Academy of Management Journal.* He has completed terms as an associate editor for *Academy of Management Journal,* as an associate editor for *Academy of Management Executive,* and as a consulting editor for *Entrepreneurship Theory and Practice.* He has co-edited special issues of *Academy of Management Review, Academy of Management Executive, Journal of Business Venturing, Strategic Management Journal, Journal of High Technology and Engineering Management,* and *Organizational Research Methods.* He received awards for the best article published in *Academy of Management Executive* (1999) and *Academy of Management Journal* (2000). In 2001, his co-authored article published in *Academy of Management Executive* won the Best Journal Article in Corporate Entrepreneurship Award from the U.S. Association for Small Business & Entrepreneurship (USASBE).

He is a Fellow of the Academy of Management, a Fellow of the Strategic Management Society, and a 21st Century Entrepreneurship Research Scholar. He is the current Vice President and Program Chair for the Academy of Management. He received the 1999 Award for Outstanding Intellectual Contributions to Competitiveness Research from the American Society for Competitiveness and the USASBE Scholar in Corporate Entrepreneurship Award (2004).

Robert E. Hoskisson

Robert E. Hoskisson is the George R. Brown Chair of Strategic Management at the Jesse H. Jones Graduate School of Business, Rice University. He received his Ph.D. from the University of California-Irvine. Professor Hoskisson's research topics focus on corporate governance, acquisitions and divestitures, corporate and international diversification, corporate entrepreneurship, privatization, and cooperative strategy. He teaches courses in corporate and international strategic management, cooperative strategy, and strategy consulting, among others. Professor Hoskisson's research has appeared in over 120 publications, including articles in the *Academy of Management Journal, Academy of Management Review, Strategic Management Journal, Organization Science, Journal of Management, Journal of International Business Studies, Journal of Management Studies, Organization Research Methods, Journal of Business Venturing, Entrepreneurship Theory and Practice, Academy of Management Perspectives, Academy of Management Executive, Journal of World Business, California Management Review,* and 26 co-authored books. He is currently an associate editor of the *Strategic Management Journal* and a consulting editor for the *Journal of International Business Studies,* as well as serving on the Editorial Review board of the *Academy of Management Journal.* Professor Hoskisson has served on several editorial boards for such publications as the *Academy of Management Journal* (including consulting editor and guest editor of a special issue), *Journal of Management* (including associate editor), *Organization Science, Journal of International Business Studies* (consulting editor), *Journal of Management Studies* (guest editor of a special issue) and *Entrepreneurship Theory and Practice.* He has co-authored several books including *Understanding Business Strategy,* 3rd Edition (South-Western Cengage Learning, 2012), *Competing for Advantage,* 2nd edition (South-Western, 2008), and *Downscoping: How to Tame the Diversified Firm* (Oxford University Press, 1994).

He has an appointment as a Special Professor at the University of Nottingham and as an Honorary Professor at Xi'an Jiao Tong University. He is a Fellow of the Academy of Management and a charter member of the Academy of Management

Journals Hall of Fame. He is also a Fellow of the Strategic Management Society. In 1998, he received an award for Outstanding Academic Contributions to Competitiveness, American Society for Competitiveness. He also received the William G. Dyer Distinguished Alumni Award given at the Marriott School of Management, Brigham Young University. He completed three years of service as a representative at large on the Board of Governors of the Academy of Management and currently is President-Elect of the Strategic Management Society.

S. Manikutty

Professor Manikutty is a professor in Business Policy and Strategy at the Indian Institute of Management, Ahmedabad, India. His areas of interest include strategic management and competitive strategy, leadership, global competitiveness of industries, corporate governance and strategies for family businesses. His paper (coauthored with another person) won the award for the Best Paper on Family Businesses for 2003 awarded by the Family Firm Institute, Boston, U.S.A. His paper (coauthored) also won an award for the best empirical paper presented at the Annual Conference of the Small Business Institute, Clearwater Beach, Florida, February 11–15, 2004. He was the Chief Editor of *Vikalpa*, the journal published from IIM, Ahmedabad, and is the Regional Editor, Asia and Pacific of *European Journal of International Management* (EJIM). He is a regular reviewer of papers for the Academy of Management Annual Conferences in the Business Policy and Strategy (BPS), International Management Division (IMD) and the Management Education Division (MED), and has served as a reviewer for the journals *Family Business Review* and *Vikalpa.* His recent book on leadership based on literature, *Essentials of Leadership: Explorations from Literature* (Delhi: Macmillan), co-authored with Sampath P Singh, won the award for the best management book awarded by the Indian Society for Training and Development, in 2010.

He served in the Indian Railways as a mechanical engineer for 21 years before joining academics. He has done extensive work in telecom sector. He has been a consultant to the World Bank and ODA, U.K. in the field of social development programs and has conducted training programs for several organizations some of which are Coca-Cola India, Ballarpur Industries, JSW Steel, Bharti Airtel, Bharat Sanchar Nigam Limited, The Park Group of hotels and Tata Motors, and taught in the programs for many companies, some of which are Pepsi India, GAIL, Sterlite Industries, Apollo Tyres, Idea Cellular, Vijaya Bank, Pfizer India and Zydus Pharmaceuticals.

Professor Manikutty was a visiting scholar at the Cornell University in 2000. He has written a number of cases, mostly dealing with issues in strategy, and published 13 papers in national and international journals. He is a visiting faculty at ESSEC, France, where he teaches a full-time course every year. He is a professional member of the Academy of Management and the Strategic Management Society.

Professor Manikutty has been included in *Marquis Who's Who* of the World for its 2012 issue.

PART I: Strategic Inputs

Strategic Management and Competitiveness

CHAPTER

1

Studying this chapter should provide you with the strategic management knowledge needed to

- Define strategic competitiveness, strategy, competitive advantage, above-average returns, and the strategic management process.
- Describe the competitive landscape and explain how globalization and technological changes shape it.
- Use the industrial organization (I/O) model to explain how firms can earn above-average returns.
- Use the resource-based model to explain how firms can earn above-average returns.
- Describe vision and mission and discuss their value.
- Define stakeholders and describe their ability to influence organizations.
- Describe the work of strategic leaders.
- Explain the strategic management process.

OPENING CASE
Bharti Airtel: Making of a Telecom Leader in India

Bharti Airtel Limited (previously called Bharti Tele-Ventures) is one of India's leading private sector providers of telecommunications services delivering landline, mobile, Internet including broadband, overseas, and enterprise telecom services. Popular by its brand name Airtel, it offers post-paid, pre-paid, roaming and value added services through their extensive sales and distribution channel. Its network is present in 5,091 census towns and 438,933 non-census towns and villages in India, covering approximately 84.2 per cent of the country's population. As on May 31, 2010, it commanded a customer base of over 133 million GSM mobile users, giving it a market share of 30 per cent. Bharti has come a long way since 1995 when it launched its cellular services in India. It has been the market leader for the last five years, and has profitability higher than the industry average.

Airtel has achieved all this against tremendous odds. At the time of its launch in 1995, it was pitted against incumbent state-owned telecom provider, Bharat Sanchar Nigam Limited (BSNL) and Mahanager Telephone Nigam Limited (MTNL) and a host of competitors backed by major Indian business groups such as Sterling Cellular and Essar. Though BSNL did not operate in the mobile segment, it was the monopoly provider of fixed line services, and it was also an arm of the Department of Telecommunications (DoT) which then was the policy maker as well as the regulator. By March 1998, Airtel had 56 per cent of the Delhi market where it became the first of India's cellular providers to show a profit. The company's success can be attributed to a sound strategy, excellent and fast execution, tight cost controls, and a total focus on telecom business. Despite the odds it faced, it managed to attract foreign investment from British Telecom, Singapore Telecom, and private equity investors such as Warburg Pincus. These tie-ups also provided Airtel with procurement benefits through its global vendor network and technology support in network and systems development.

In 1999, the National Telecom Policy (NTP 99) eliminated the cap on the number of cellular licenses allowed to each company; it also replaced the then prevalent fixed license fee regime to a revenue sharing model.

Airtel seized this expansion opportunity and set out on a series of acquisitions such as JT mobile's cellular operations in two category "A" circles of the southern states of Karnataka and Andhra Pradesh, and Skycell's mobile operations in Chennai, the country's fourth largest cellular market in 2000. In less than a year, Airtel more than tripled its subscriber base. In 2001, it acquired Spice Cell's network in Kolkata. These acquisitions gave Airtel a total of six cellular service areas with over a million subscribers at the close of 2001. In 2002, it became the first private operator to launch national and international long distance operations service in India. This made it more profitable and it was important, since India had the lowest telecom tariffs in the world.

Contrary to the usual emphasis on post-paid customers, Bharti went in for pre-paid customers, giving pre-paid cards of low denominations. These cards were made available through small shops, often even *paan* and *beedi* kiosks. Thus, it not only expanded its base in a billion-strong country but also established itself as a very well known brand. Subsequently, it set up a sales distribution network that was amongst the largest in the industry using exclusive showrooms and dealerships catering to premium customers and small businesses, and a network of non-exclusive sub-dealers catering to general customers. It also introduced several direct sales strategies to tap the corporate sector which provided the bulk of post-paid revenues. Airtel, thus, implemented a mass market strategy in its cellular business, offering innovative services catering to every customer class. Its large coverage area and market share afforded Airtel a competitive advantage in offering a comprehensive free roaming and low Airtel-to-Airtel calling rates.

©Indiatodayimages.com

Airtel has established itself as the market leader by differentiating itself with its focus on building a strong brand through innovations in sales, marketing, and customer service, and an innovative cost effective business model.

The company's unique business model of being profitable despite having the lowest tariffs in the world, became a benchmark for emerging markets. At that time, mobile telephony in India was experiencing the fastest growth in the world and the country was already one of the leading markets in terms of mobile subscriber base. Despite Average Revenue per User (ARPU) figures in the country being quite low compared to many other overseas markets, it was viewed as an attractive market as mobile penetration of the market, particularly in the huge rural areas, was still low. Instead of the ARPU model that was universally adopted for monitoring performance, Airtel adopted a Revenue-per-Minute model, perhaps better-suited to India, as the company moved into small and remote villages and towns.

However by 2007, Airtel was facing serious threats to its leadership position. On the one hand, there was the onslaught from global players such as Vodafone and Virgin Mobile, and on the other, the threat from established Indian companies such as Reliance Communications Ltd., Tata Teleservices Ltd., and the state-owned BSNL, which entered the mobile segment in 2003. Moreover, the market was expected to witness the entry of some more Indian and foreign companies. Airtel responded by investing heavily in expanding its network, technology, and marketing. It was trying to cover all segments of the population from the tech-savvy youth population who desired the latest value-added services (VAS) to the Bottom of the Pyramid (BoP) segment who would be satisfied with a low-cost offering and recharge vouchers of very small denominations.

Airtel's impressive performance in the recent past suggests that the firm is effectively implementing its strategy with continuous innovation. From a time when mobiles were considered a luxury to a state when auto rickshaw drivers and roadside vendors possess a mobile phone, Airtel has established itself as the market leader by differentiating itself with its focus on building a strong brand through innovations in sales, marketing, and customer service, and an innovative cost effective business model. Some examples of its recent innovations are introducing India's first ever *Family Tunes*—a call management service offering a pre-recorded "welcome message" customized to the subscriber's individual family name to greet callers instead of the conventional tone. It offers a library of more than 1000 Indian family names for customers to choose from. Airtel has also partnered with Facebook, the popular social networking site, to provide its customers to access Facebook's full mobile site faster and at no data cost (for a limited period) from their mobiles via m.facebook.com. In the 3G spectrum auction in May 2010, Airtel won 3G licenses in 13 telecom circles of India and launched the services in January 2011.

Having dominated the Indian telecom market, Airtel, made forays into overseas emerging markets with an aim to replicate its success story. In the autumn of 2010, it acquired the mobile service operations of Zain, a Kuwait-based public shareholding telecommunications company, in 15 African countries for US$ 10.7 billion, making it one of the biggest overseas acquisitions made by an Indian company. Now it is one of the top five telecom companies in the world.

Telecom being a capital intensive industry, the financial resources needed for expansion are large. Bharti reduced its capital needs by outsourcing most of its functions, except for customer management, people management, financial management, managing regulation, brand management, and strategic management to outside companies. The most notable steps were the outsourcing of its IT operations, worth $2.5 billion, to IBM, payments being on a revenue sharing basis, network equipment management to Ericsson and Nokia Siemens, paying them on erlangs (the unit of telecom traffic) used; Lucent for managing its fixed network; and Comviva to take care of the managed (value added) services.

Airtel now offers more varied services to its customers by striking strategic partnerships with other companies. It has entered into a strategic partnership with Google that will enable Google search on handsets to Airtel users. As part of the agreement, Airtel will bring Google search to the Airtel Live mobile WAP portal. Customers can type in keywords in the Google Search button, click "search" and the results will be displayed on to the customer's screen. Google will incorporate advertising through its Mobile Ads product on the Airtel Live mobile portal. The company possesses a customized version of the Google search engine which will enhance broadband services to customers. This will help advertisers reach targeted users with their products and services on a cost-per-click basis.

It has also entered into partnerships with Apple for its new i-Phone and with Blackberry. Whilst the new i-phone will be launched in India via an *Airtel* distributorship, BlackBerry from Airtel is an "always connected" wireless solution providing easy and secure access to customer's email and data. BlackBerry Personal Mail is a new version of the current BIS (Prosumer) service. BlackBerry Personal Mail is a unique offering to customers in India. The BlackBerry Personal Mail service plan offers unlimited access to the industry-leading email and instant messaging features of BlackBerry® Internet Service, allowing Airtel customers to access up to 10 supported POP3/IMAP email accounts (including most popular ISP email accounts such as Yahoo! Mail and Google Mail) as well as various instant messaging services (including Windows Live Messenger, GTalk, Yahoo! Messenger and BlackBerry® Messenger) from a single device.

According to a survey in *Voice and magazine*, Airtel was the largest Indian telecom company with revenues of ₹3880 billion in 2009-10.

Sources: C.K. Prahalad and R.A. Mashelkar, 2010 "Bharti Airtel: Making of a Telecom Leader in India", Innovation's holy grail, ***Harvard Business Review***, July-August, Company Web site, COAI.com, moneycontrol.com, business.in.com, HBS case study, "Bharti Tele-ventures" (case # 9-704-426), thehindubusinessline.com, en.wikipedia.org/wiki/bharti_airtel, http://timesofindia.indiatimes.com/business/india-business/Bharti-Airtel-number-one-telecom-company-Survey/articleshow/6265209.cms.

As we see from the Opening Case, Bharti Airtel Limited which was started in 1995 became the leading telecom company in India by 2010. Airtel's performance during this period suggests that it has become highly competitive (something we call a condition of strategic competitiveness) as it registered above-average returns in the telecom sector in India consistently. It started as an underdog against a powerful incumbent, the state-owned Bharat Sanchar Nigam Limted (BSNL), which was an arm of the Ministry of Telecommunications, which then was the regulator as well as the policy maker. How did Bharti Airtel Ltd. achieve this position? It used, to a great effect, the strategic management process (see Figure 1.1) as the foundation for its commitments, decisions, and the actions it took when pursuing strategic competitiveness and above-average terms. The strategic management process is fully explained in this book. We introduce you to this process in the following paragraphs.

Strategic competitiveness is achieved when a firm successfully formulates and implements a value-creating strategy. A **strategy** is an integrated and coordinated set of commitments and actions designed to exploit core competencies and gain a competitive advantage. When choosing a strategy, firms make choices among competing alternatives as the pathway for deciding how they will pursue strategic competitiveness.[1] In this sense, the chosen strategy indicates what the firm *will do* as well as what the firm *will not do*.

As explained in the Opening Case, BTVL/Bharti Airtel focused on a single business: telecommunications, that too in the mobile telephony segment using GSM technology, but with reinforcing presence in basic, broadband, Internet service, and international telecom businesses. Bharti's strategic leaders also decided that the firm would pursue continuous innovations to stay ahead of its competitors, and that it would not diversify into any unrelated businesses, a principle it has followed to this day. A firm's strategy also demonstrates how it differs from its competitors. Idea Cellular is solely in GSM mobiles business. BSNL also has its presence in all areas of telecom, but its dependence on basic services continues to be very high. Reliance Telecom is into both GSM and CDMA, with more strength in the latter. Thus, each of the players tries to gain competitive advantage by playing the game differently. A firm must also demonstrate how its game is different. Cognizant Technologies, one of the larger IT companies claims that its "two-in-a-box model" gives much better customer value than the models followed by its competitors such as Infosys Technologies, Tata Consultancy Services and Wipro.[2] Recently, Ford Motor Company devoted efforts to explain to stakeholders how the company differs from its competitors. In times of growing concerns over environment degradation, Ford's main idea was the claim that it is "greener" and more technically advanced than its competitors, such as General Motors and Chrysler Group LLC (an alliance between Chrysler and Fiat SpA).[3]

A firm has a **competitive advantage** when it implements a strategy competitors are unable to duplicate or find too costly to try to imitate.[4] An organization can be confident that its strategy has resulted in one or more useful competitive advantages only after competitors' efforts to duplicate its strategy have ceased or failed. In addition, firms must understand that no competitive advantage is permanent.[5] The speed with which competitors are able to acquire the skills needed to duplicate the benefits of a firm's value-creating strategy determines how long the competitive advantage will last.[6]

Above-average returns are returns in excess of what an investor expects to earn from other investments with a similar amount of risk. **Risk** is an investor's uncertainty about the economic gains or losses that will result from a particular investment.[7] The most successful companies learn how to effectively manage risk. Effectively managing risks reduces investors' uncertainty about the results of their investment.[8] Returns are often measured in terms of accounting figures, such as return on assets, return on equity, or return on sales. Alternatively, returns can be measured on the basis of stock market returns, such as monthly returns (the end-of-the-period stock price minus the beginning stock price, divided by the beginning stock price, yielding a percentage return). In smaller, new venture firms, returns are sometimes measured in terms of the amount and speed of growth (e.g., in annual sales) rather than more traditional profitability measures[9] because new ventures require time to earn acceptable returns (in the form of return on assets and so forth) on investors' investments.[10]

Understanding how to exploit a competitive advantage is important for firms seeking to earn above-average returns.[11] Firms without a competitive advantage or that are not competing in an attractive industry earn, at best, average returns. **Average returns** are returns equal to those an investor expects to earn from other investments with a similar amount of risk. In the long run, an inability to earn at least average returns results first in decline and, eventually, failure. Failure occurs because investors withdraw their investments from those firms earning less-than-average returns.

After carefully evaluating its deteriorating performance and options, Air Deccan, among the pioneers of low cost aviation in India (or more aptly, low priced aviation) was sold in December, 2007 to Kingfisher Airlines.[12] Many household names of business groups such as Dalmia, Modi, and some companies of the Birla group have lost their pre-eminent position due to the changed environment in India. The Standard Automobiles, one of the three car producers in India was liquidated long ago. The closing down of numerous textile mills in Mumbai and Ahmedabad during the mid 1980s was a dramatic demonstration of the inability to adjust to major changes in the economic environment, in this case, the emergence

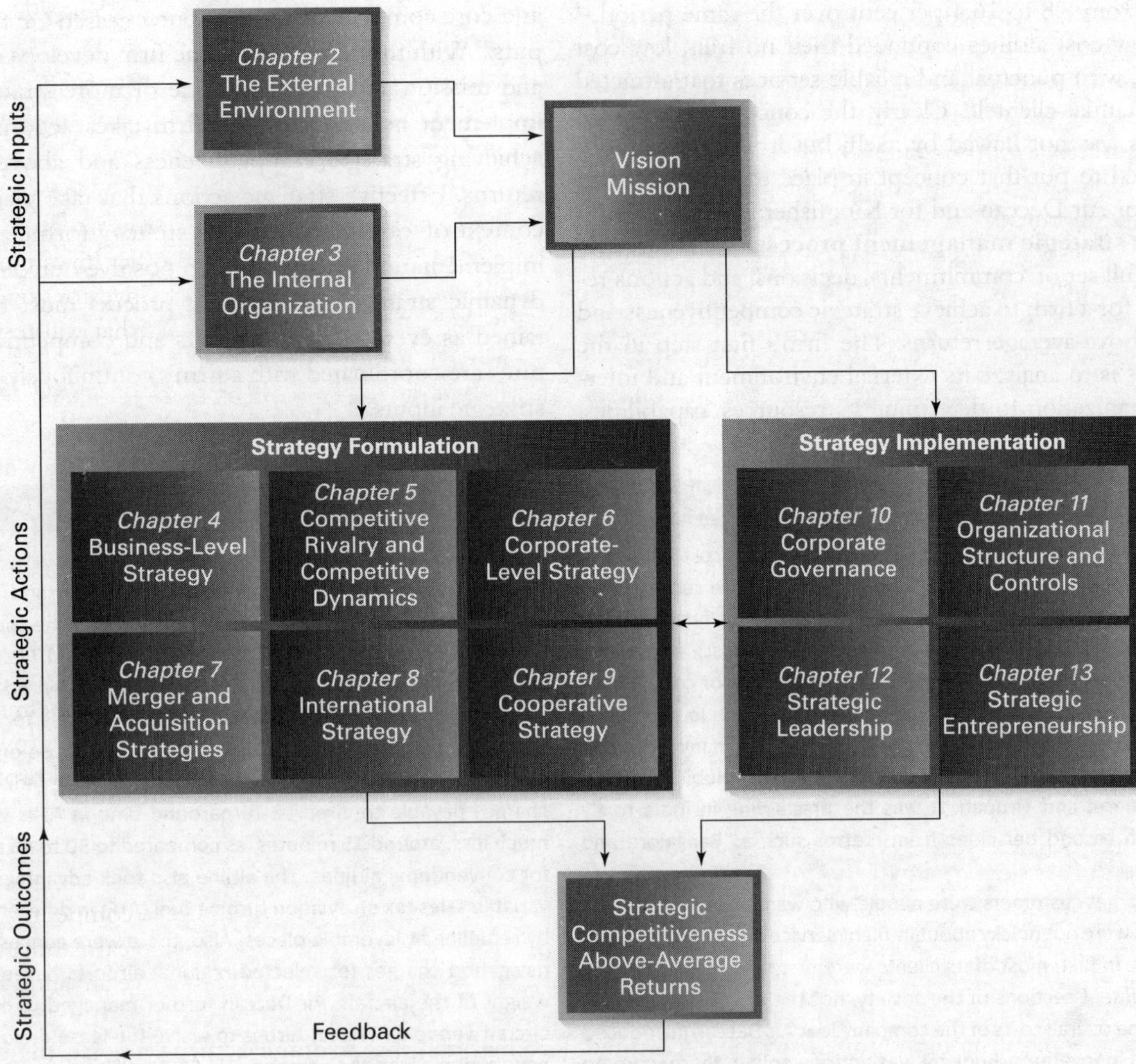

Figure 1.1 The strategic management process

of power looms on the one hand and unfavorable government policies on the other. These instances point to the difficulty of sustaining the competitive advantage during changes in environment.

As we explain, in Strategic Focus 1.1, stiff competition from other airlines and mistakes made while implementing its strategy were the primary causes of Air Deccan's failure and subsequent disappearance of its highly visible brand from the Indian skyline. Air Deccan's failure to focus on likely short-term profits was a problem. But excessive attention to short term profits also tends to have a negative effect on a firm's ability to create value in the long term.[13]

Air Deccan's demise, however, did not really benefit Kingfisher so much as it did other low cost airlines such as Spicejet and Indigo. Vijay Mallya, the owner-CEO of Kingfisher, promoted the Kingfisher brand, operating the Air Deccan flights as a low cost arm, Kingfisher Red. He also tried to augment the services. But the new positioning fell between two stools: costlier than the low cost airlines, but poorer in service than full service airlines. Hence, as C.R. Gopinath, the ex CEO of Deccan commented, (a substantial part of) the market share of Air Deccan, which was about 16 per cent at the time of its liquidation, did not go to Kingfisher; it went to other low cost airlines such as Spicejet and Indigo. Kingfisher gained only about 8 per cent of Deccan's market share; while Spicejet increased its market share from 9.2 to 13.3 per cent between 2007–08 (when Deccan was sold to Kingfisher) and 2009–10; Indigo increased its market share from 8.8 to 16.4 per cent over the same period.[14] The low cost airlines continued their no frills, low cost model, with punctual and reliable services that attracted a substantial clientele. Clearly, the concept of low cost airlines was not flawed by itself, but it was the strategy followed to put that concept in place that went wrong, both for Air Deccan and for Kingfisher.

The **strategic management process** (see Figure 1.1) is the full set of commitments, decisions, and actions required for a firm to achieve strategic competitiveness and earn above-average returns. The firm's first step in the process is to analyze its external environment and internal organization to determine its resources, capabilities, and core competencies—the sources of its "strategic inputs." With this information, the firm develops its vision and mission and formulates one or more strategies. To implement its strategies, the firm takes actions toward achieving strategic competitiveness and above-average returns. Effective strategic actions that take place in the context of carefully integrated strategy formulation and implementation efforts result in positive outcomes. This dynamic strategic management process must be maintained as ever-changing markets and competitive structures are coordinated with a firm's continuously evolving strategic inputs.[15]

STRATEGIC FOCUS

1.1 Air Deccan: Unable to Reach the Cruising Height

Air Deccan introduced the concept of low cost airlines in India in August 2003 and was initially quite successful in implementing it. It was a no frills airline (at first, they did not even serve water on board free of cost), and prices were less than half of what the full service or conventional airlines offered. It broke away from the hub and spoke system, introducing direct flights between many cities and towns, some of them quite small, such as Hubli, Madurai, Mangalore, and Tirupati. It was the first airline in India to fly to such second tier cities from metros such as Bangalore and Chennai.

Its target customers were people who wanted a cheap way to fly and were not finicky about in-flight service and other value additions. In fact, most of its clients were first time flyers from the less affluent sections of the society, not the typical "jet set". To keep the overall costs of the company low, Air Deccan introduced several innovations: Booking was entirely online, there were no paper tickets, no commissions to travel agents, no through booking of luggage, and each journey was considered separate, so that full refunds were not available if a passenger missed an onward connection. There was no free service on board, and hence the flight staff required in each flight was lower in comparison to other airlines. In fact, it did not time its flights to ensure connections with its other flights or with other airlines' flights, thereby eliminating waiting time between flights. It tried to do a quick turn around at airports. All flights were economy only, which allowed a 22 per cent increase in the number of seats in a plane (180 seats as against 154 in Indian Airlines in an A-320 aircraft).

Several innovations were brought in to increase revenue generation as well. It tried to generate revenues from on-board sales of food and beverages, and through fares saved on cancellations (only a relatively small portion of the fare was refundable in case of cancellations). Further more, it sold space on its assets (such as aircraft itself, its seats, boarding cards, etc.) for advertising. It was estimated that the company derived an additional 5 per cent revenue by these means. It installed the latest revenue management systems to enable it to quote more accurate fares depending on the demand supply balance. These innovations were widely acclaimed in the Indian aviation industry and became benchmarks for new as well as existing airlines in the country.

Air Deccan used smaller ATR aircraft (both 48 and 72 seat size) for shorter flights and regional destinations thereby reducing its infrastructure usage fees because the landing fees for smaller aircraft were almost half that of larger aircraft. Its use of smaller airports, especially for overnight parking, further reduced the charges payable to airports. Turnaround time in ATRs was also much less, around 15 minutes, as compared to 30 to 45 minutes for conventional airlines. The airline also took advantage of the variable sales tax on aviation turbine fuel (ATF) in different states by refueling at favorable places. Also, there were concessions in navigation charges for selected regional airports based on the weight of the aircraft. Air Deccan further managed to convince aircraft vendors ATR and Airbus to waive the lease deposit. This negotiation saved the company US $1.2 million deposit per aircraft. The airline also obtained the approval of the Directorate General of Civil Aviation (DGCA) to send certified tools and personnel to various local airports having access to an aircraft hangar for maintenance rather than having to fly an aircraft to its home base as most airlines in India did.

At places where the traffic levels were very low and the airline operated only one flight a day, ground handling (manning of check-in counters, ticket sales counter, supply of on-board food, beverages and in-flight magazines, and even cabin crew members) was outsourced. Air Deccan refrained from incurring expenditures on fancy offices, lounges, and frequent flyer programs. The company had created its own Internet based Centralized Reservation System (CRS), with the help of InterGlobe Technology, instead of opting for a global distribution service (GDS) such as Galileo, Sabre or Amadeus used by other airlines. Air Deccan kept its distribution costs low by selling tickets through Web sites and round the clock multilingual call centers for customers who did not have access to the Internet. It also sold tickets through airport ticketing desks, HPCL petrol retail outlets, Reliance Web World retail outlets and mobile ticket vans.

A policy of "pay and fly" (pre-paid tickets) as against "fly and pay" policy followed by the conventional airlines ensured that there were no cash flow problems. Air Deccan also opted for a single fare system instead of a multi-fare one to avoid the additional costs involved in accounting and auditing processes. In as much as it could attract a large number of new travelers, Air Deccan was successful. In fact, its brand became a household name. But it did not realize that, as an analyst put it, in India, there are only low fare airlines, not low cost ones. This was because a whole lot of costs were beyond the control of the airlines. For example, fuel is taxed heavily in India, and this constitutes about 30 per cent of the total costs. Airport charges are also heavy, and there were no cheap alternative airports as in the case of US and Europe, which charge less for parking, landing, etc. Air Deccan had no clear idea of how to meet this cost structure. To add to its woes, its competitors, Jet Airways and Indian Airlines introduced predatory fares on parallel routes, and then scheduled their flights just before or after Deccan's flights. Air Deccan had no real response to such moves. Thus, despite all its cost cutting initiatives, its overall costs were not very much less than those of its competitors even as it attempted to gain volume through steep fare cuts. This led to continuous losses right from the beginning and it could never find a way out to make a profitable business model.

In the very first year of its operations (2003–2004), it incurred a loss of ₹117.7 million, ₹352.3 million in 2004-05 and over ₹2000 million in 2005-06. Its lease charges were mounting, and it was in arrears of payment to fuel companies, to airports, and vendors. Nonetheless, Air Deccan tried to expand too fast, leading to very serious cash flow problems. It tried to raise funds through a public issue in January 2006, to offer 25 per cent of its shareholding. Unfortunately for it, that turned out to be a period of stock market downturn, and its IPO barely managed to scrape through. Due to continued financial difficulties and inability to raise the desired capital from public issue, Air Deccan eventually succumbed to pressures for consolidation.

Air Deccan could not convert its strategic innovations into business results and, in December 2007, it announced its merger with Kingfisher Airlines, which renamed its acquisition Kingfisher Red (Kingfisher has its own full service airline, Kingfisher). However, the problem did not get solved by the acquisition. Kingfisher tried to upgrade the services in Red, thus pushing up its costs; it also increased the fares substantially. The result was that the Air Deccan clientele shifted, not to Red, but to other low cost carriers such as Indigo and Spice Jet. Kingfisher Airlines is making losses, with substantial contribution from Kingfisher Red. On the other hand, both Spice Jet and Indigo are reported to be making profits. Thus, the problem with Air Deccan was not one of the basic concept (of a low cost airline), nor just its execution, but of its basic strategy.

Strategy execution led to crash landing for Air Deccan, even as other low cost airlines continue to reap above-average returns

Sources: Case study series "Air Deccan", # F&A 0481 (A) through (D), Indian Institute of Management, Ahmedabad; www.moneycontrol. Indian Institute of Management—Ahmedabad, www.moneycontrol.com;www.scribd.com; en.wikipedia.org/wiki/kingfisher_red

In the remaining chapters of this book, we use the strategic management process to explain what firms do to achieve strategic competitiveness and earn above-average returns. These explanations demonstrate why some firms consistently achieve competitive success while others fail to do so.[16] As you will see, the reality of global competition is a critical part of the strategic management process and significantly influences firms' performances, even though many Indian firms may feel that their exposure to the international markets is small and they will remain, by and large, little affected by the global goings on (the recent recession must have left far fewer firms with that feeling, though).[17] Indeed, learning how to successfully compete not only in India but in the globalized world and global firms is one of the most significant challenges for firms competing in the current century.[18] Several topics will be discussed in this chapter. First, we describe the current competitive landscape. This challenging landscape is being created primarily by the emergence of a global economy, globalization resulting from that economy, and rapid technological changes. Next, we examine two models that firms use to gather the information and knowledge required to choose and then effectively implement their strategies. The insights gained from these models also serve as the foundation for forming the firm's vision and mission. The first model (the industrial organization or I/O model) suggests that the external environment is the primary determinant of a firm's strategic actions. Identifying and then competing successfully in an attractive (i.e., profitable) industry or segment of an industry are the keys to competitive success when using this model.[19] The second model (resource-based) suggests that a firm's unique resources and capabilities are the critical link to strategic competitiveness.[20] Thus, the first model is concerned primarily with the firm's external environment while the second model is concerned primarily with the firm's internal organization. After discussing vision and mission, direction-setting statements that influence the choice and use of strategies, we describe the stakeholders that organizations serve. The degree to which stakeholders' needs can be met increases when firms achieve strategic competitiveness and earn above-average returns. Closing the chapter are introductions to strategic leaders and the elements of the strategic management process.

The Competitive Landscape

The fundamental nature of competition in many of the world's industries is changing. The reality is that financial capital is scarce and markets are increasingly volatile.[21] Because of this, the pace of change is relentless and ever-increasing. Even determining the boundaries of an industry has become challenging. Consider, for example, how advances in interactive computer networks and telecommunications have blurred the boundaries of the entertainment industry. Today, not only do cable companies and satellite networks compete for entertainment revenue from television, but telecommunication companies are moving into the entertainment business through significant improvements in fiber-optic lines.[22] After 3G becomes widely prevalent in India, it can be expected that a great deal of entertainment will be over the mobile phone. Partnerships among firms in different segments of the entertainment industry further blur industry boundaries. For example, MSNBC is co-owned by NBC Universal and Microsoft. In turn, General Electric owns 80 per cent of NBC Universal while Vivendi owns the remaining 20 per cent.[23] We can expect a similar trend in India with entertainment and media companies taking up stakes in telecom companies.

There are other examples of fundamental changes to competition in various industries. For example, many firms are looking for the most profitable and interesting way to deliver video on demand (VOD) online besides cable and satellite companies. Raketu, a voice over the Internet protocol (VoIP) phone service in the United Kingdom, is seeking to provide customers with a social experience while watching the same entertainment on a VOD using a chat feature on its phone service.[24] Raketu's vision is to "... bring together communications, information, and entertainment into one service, to remove the complexities of how people communicate with one another, make a system that is contact centric, and to make it fun and easy to use."[25] In addition, the competitive possibilities and challenges for more "traditional" communications companies that are suggested by social networking sites such as Facebook, MySpace, and Friendster appear to be endless.[26]

Other characteristics of the current competitive landscape are noteworthy. Conventional sources of competitive advantage such as economies of scale and huge advertising budgets are not as effective as they once were in terms of helping firms earn above-average returns. Moreover, the traditional managerial mind-set is unlikely to lead a firm to strategic competitiveness. Managers must adopt a new mind-set that values flexibility, speed, innovation, integration, and the challenges that evolve from constantly changing conditions.[27] The conditions of the competitive landscape result in a perilous business world, one where the investments that are required to compete on a global scale are enormous and the consequences of failure are severe.[28] Effective use of the strategic management process reduces the likelihood of failure for firms as they encounter the conditions of today's competitive landscape.

Hypercompetition is a term often used to capture the realities of the competitive landscape. Under conditions of hypercompetition, assumptions of market stability are replaced by notions of inherent instability and change.[29] Hypercompetition results from the dynamics of strategic maneuvering among global and innovative combatants.[30] It is a condition of rapidly escalating competition based on price-quality positioning, competition to create new know-how and establish first-mover advantage, and competition to protect or invade established product or geographic markets.[31] In a hypercompetitive market, firms often aggressively challenge their competitors in the hopes of improving their competitive position and ultimately their performance.[32]

Several factors create hypercompetitive environments and influence the nature of the current competitive landscape. The emergence of a global economy and technology, specifically rapid technological change, are the two primary drivers of hypercompetitive environments and the nature of today's competitive landscape. Continuous changes in government policies can change the rules of the game in competition quite suddenly. For example, in 2010, the Telecom Regulatory Authority of India has given a recommendation to charge existing operators for spectrum in excess of 6.2 MHZ. This will change the profitability of these companies, and will also usher in competition from other operators in a different form.

The Global Economy

A **global economy** is one in which goods, services, people, skills, and ideas move freely across geographic borders. Relatively unfettered by artificial constraints, such as tariffs, the global economy significantly expands and complicates a firm's competitive environment.[33]

Interesting opportunities and challenges are associated with the emergence of the global economy.[34] For example, Europe, instead of the United States, is now the world's largest single market, with 700 million potential customers. The European Union and the other Western European countries also have a gross domestic product that is more than 35 per cent higher than the GDP of the United States.[35] "In the past, China was generally seen as a low-competition market and a low-cost producer. Today, China is an extremely competitive market in which local market-seeking MNCs (multinational corporations) must fiercely compete against other MNCs and against those local companies that are more cost effective and faster in product development. While it is true that China has been viewed as a country from which to source low-cost goods, lately, many MNCs, such as P&G (Procter and Gamble), are actually net exporters of local management talent; they have been dispatching more Chinese abroad than bringing foreign expatriates to China."[36] India, the world's largest democracy, has an economy that also is growing rapidly and now ranks as the fourth largest in the world.[37] Apart from its well known advantage as a center for outsourcing, giving rise to even a slang, "being Bangalored" to denote loss of jobs in US due to their being outsourced to India), India is emerging as a base for new low cost R&D, manufacture of certain equipment, clinical outsourcing and many other services. In 2005, India accounted for 65 per cent of the global industry in offshore IT. India's leading car maker, Maruti Udyog is reported to be the main source of profit for Suzuki, which owns a majority shareholding in the former. Global companies such as IBM, GE, and Microsoft see India as a location for some of their cutting edge R&D. Many large multinational companies are also emerging as significant global competitors from these emerging economies.[38]

Imaginechina via AP Images

General Electric received a $300 million contract from China to supply turbines and compression gear that will propel natural gas from the nation's remote north-western regions to booming eastern cities such as Shanghai.

The statistics detailing the nature of the global economy reflect the realities of a hypercompetitive business environment and challenge individual firms to think seriously about the markets in which they will compete. Consider the case of General Electric (GE). Although headquartered in the United States, GE expects that as much as 60 per cent of its revenue growth between 2005 and 2015 will be generated by competing in rapidly developing economies (e.g., China and India). The decision to count on revenue growth in developing countries instead of in developed countries such as the United States and European nations seems quite reasonable in the global economy. In fact, according to an analyst, what GE is doing is not by choice but by necessity: "Developing countries are where the fastest growth is occurring and more sustainable growth."[39] Based on its analyses of world markets and their potential, GE estimates that by 2024, China will be the world's largest consumer of electricity and will be the world's largest consumer and consumer-finance market (business areas in which GE competes). GE is making strategic decisions today, such as investing significantly in China and India, in order to improve its competitive position in what the firm believes are becoming vital geographic sources of revenue and profitability.

The March of Globalization

Globalization is the increasing economic interdependence among countries and their organizations as reflected in the flow of goods and services, financial capital, and knowledge across country borders.[40] Globalization is a product of a large number of firms competing against one another in an increasing number of global economies.

In globalized markets and industries, financial capital might be obtained in one national market and used to buy raw materials in another one. Manufacturing equipment bought from a third national market can then be used to produce products that are sold in yet a fourth market. Thus, globalization increases the range of opportunities for companies competing in the current competitive landscape.[41]

Wal-Mart, for instance, is trying to achieve boundary-less retailing with global pricing, sourcing, and logistics. It has also set up shop in India through an alliance with Bharti Retail; many Indian firms are suppliers to Wal-Mart. Through boundary-less retailing, the firm seeks to make the movement of goods and the use of pricing strategies as seamless among all of its international operations as has historically been the case among its domestic stores. The firm is pursuing this type of retailing on an evolutionary basis. For example, most of Wal-Mart's original international investments were in Canada and Mexico, because it was easier for the firm to apply its global practices in countries that are geographically close to its home base, the United States. Because of the success it has had in proximate international markets, Wal-Mart is now seeking boundary-less retailing across its operations in countries such as Argentina, Brazil, Chile, China, India, Japan, and the United Kingdom. (The importance of Wal-Mart's international operations is indicated by the fact that the firm is divided into three divisions: Wal-Mart, Sam's Club, and International.[42])

Firms experiencing and engaging in globalization to the degree Wal-Mart is must make culturally sensitive decisions when using the strategic management process. Additionally, highly globalized firms must anticipate ever-increasing complexity in their operations as goods, services, people, and so forth move freely across geographic borders and throughout different economic markets.

Overall, it is important for firms to understand that globalization has led to higher levels of performance standards in many competitive dimensions, including those of quality, cost, productivity, product introduction time, and operational efficiency. In addition to firms competing in the global economy, these standards affect firms competing on a domestic-only basis. The reason is that customers will purchase from a global competitor rather than a domestic firm when the global company's good or service is superior. Because workers now flow rather more freely among global economies, and because employees are a key source of competitive advantage, firms must understand that increasingly "the best people will come from … anywhere."[43] Firms must learn how to deal with the reality that in the competitive landscape of the twenty-first century, only companies capable of meeting, if not exceeding, global standards typically have the capability to earn above-average returns.

Although globalization does offer potential benefits to firms, it is not without risks. Collectively, the risks of participating outside of a firm's domestic country in the global economy are labeled as "liability of foreignness."[44]

One risk of entering the global market is the amount of time typically required for firms to learn how to compete in markets that are new to them. A firm's performance can suffer until this knowledge is either developed locally or transferred from the home market to the newly established global location.[45] Additionally, a firm's performance may suffer with substantial amounts of globalization. In this instance, firms may over diversify internationally beyond their ability to manage these extended operations.[46] The result of over diversification can have strong negative effects on a firm's overall performance.

Thus, entry into international markets, even for firms with substantial experience in the global economy, requires effective use of the strategic management process. It is also important to note that even though global markets are an attractive strategic option for some companies, they are not the only source of strategic competitiveness. In fact, for most companies, even for those capable of competing successfully in global markets, it is critical to remain committed to and strategically competitive in both domestic and international markets by staying attuned to technological opportunities and potential competitive disruptions that innovations create.[47]

Technology and Technological Changes

Technology-related trends and conditions can be placed into three categories: technology diffusion and disruptive technologies, the information age, and increasing knowledge intensity. Through these categories, technology is significantly altering the nature of competition and contributing to unstable competitive environments as a result of doing so.

Technology Diffusion and Disruptive Technologies

The rate of technology diffusion, which is the speed at which new technologies become available and are used, has increased substantially over the past 15 to 20 years. Consider the following rates of technology diffusion:

It took the telephone 57 years to achieve a penetration of 25 per 100 population in India (reached in 2007).[48] *By 2010, this had become about 68 per cent.*[49] *The diffusion of mobile phones in India is even more striking: in just over15 years the penetration has been about 65 per 100, i.e., out of 688 million telephone subscribers, 652 million were mobile subscribers.*[50] *It took TV only about 10 years to reach 25 per 100 population, and by 2009, TV had reached 60 per cent of the households .*[51] *By 2010, that is, over a period of about 20 years, Internet penetration had reached about 8 per 100 and is expected to reach 25 per 100 by 2015, perhaps much earlier, with the opening of 3G*[52].

Perpetual innovation is a term used to describe how rapidly and consistently new, information-intensive technologies replace older ones. The shorter product life cycles resulting from these rapid diffusions of new technologies place a competitive premium on being able to quickly introduce new, innovative goods and services into the marketplace.[53]

In fact, when products become somewhat indistinguishable because of the widespread and rapid diffusion of technologies, speed to market with innovative products may be the primary source of competitive advantage (see Chapter 5).[54] Indeed, some argue that the global economy is increasingly driven by or revolves around constant innovations. Not surprisingly, such innovations must be derived from an understanding of global standards and global expectations in terms of product functionality.[55]

Another indicator of rapid technology diffusion is that it now may take only 12 to 18 months for firms to gather information about their competitors' research and development and product decisions.[56] In the global economy, competitors can sometimes imitate a firm's successful competitive actions within a few days. In this sense, the rate of technological diffusion has reduced the competitive benefits of patents. Today, patents may be an effective way of protecting proprietary technology in a small number of industries such as pharmaceuticals. Indeed, many firms competing in the electronics industry often do not apply for patents to prevent competitors from gaining access to the technological knowledge included in the patent application.

Disruptive technologies—technologies that destroy the value of an existing technology and create new markets[57]—surface frequently in today's competitive markets. Think of the new markets created by the technologies underlying the development of products such as iPods, PDAs, WiFi, and the browser. These types of products are thought by some to represent radical or breakthrough innovations.[58] (We talk more about radical innovations in Chapter 13.) A disruptive or radical technology can create what is essentially a new industry or can harm industry incumbents. Some incumbents though, are able to adapt based on their superior resources, experience, and ability to gain access to the new technology through multiple sources (e.g., alliances, acquisitions, and ongoing internal research).[59]

Reverse Innovation

Traditionally, innovations were conceived in developed countries, and then marketed, with or without adaptations, to less developed countries. In a recent article, Jeff Immelt (the CEO of GE), Vijay Govindarajan and Chris Trimble showed how a whole new process of innovation, conceived and developed in emerging economies, were "exported back" to developed countries[60]. In the traditional model, high end products were developed at "home" of the giant MNCs such as GE, and sold them, after scaling down, to less developed countries, at a lower price. This assumed a path of development for emerging economies similar to that followed by developed economies. This also assumed that products developed in emerging economies and less developed countries cannot be sold in developed markets because they would not be good enough to be sold there. These assumptions no longer hold; products and business models developed in developing countries can and do find their way into developed countries as well. These have been frugally, but functionally engineered. Examples are a $1000 handheld electro-cardiogram machine and a $15,000 PC based ultra sound machine. These are not only sold in India and China (where they were developed), but also in US and other developed economies. Aravind Eye Care System (see the case in this book on Aravind Eye Care System) has evolved a low cost model for eye surgeries that enables it to conduct 60 per cent of its surgeries free, market rates being charged to paying patients, and yet chalk up a good profit margin. These models get developed for the tough environment in less developed countries, with low capacity to pay, low skill levels, frequent power disruptions and an unsophisticated consumer set. The reverse innovations exploit high, indeed extraordinary productivity, full exploitation of the possibilities of economies of scale, borrowing best practices from other sectors, investing in critical activities but saving on frills, and, often, a deep commitment to an ideology to serve, that goes beyond a mere commercial model[61]. There is reason to believe that such reverse innovations will become a major supplement to the traditional "forward" innovation.

The Information Age

Dramatic changes in information technology have occurred in recent years. Personal computers, cellular phones, artificial intelligence, virtual reality, massive databases, and multiple social networking sites are a few examples of how information is used differently as a result of technological developments. An important outcome of these changes is that the ability to effectively and efficiently access and use information has become an important source of competitive advantage in virtually all industries. Information technology advances have given small firms more flexibility in competing with large firms, if that technology can be efficiently used.[62]

Both the pace of change in information technology and its diffusion will continue to increase. For instance, the number of personal computers in use in the United States is expected to reach 278 million by 2010. The declining costs of information technologies and the increased accessibility to them are also evident in the current competitive landscape. The global proliferation of relatively inexpensive computing power and its linkage on a global scale via computer networks combine to increase the speed and diffusion of information technologies. Thus, the competitive potential of information technologies is now available to companies of all sizes throughout the world, including those in emerging economies.

The Internet is another technological innovation contributing to hypercompetition. Available to an increasing number of people throughout the world, the Internet provides an infrastructure that allows the delivery of information to computers in any location. It enables emerging economies to compete on an equal (or at least near equal) basis with firms from developed countries; it also makes the customers in emerging economies more aware and demanding. It makes it possible for entirely new segments, at times from the bottom of the pyramid, to emerge, and it makes it possible for firms to become market savvy and obtain better prices for their products, as for example, from ITC's *e-Choupal* in India.[63] Access to the Internet on smaller devices such as cell phones is having an ever-growing impact on competition in a number of industries. However, possible changes to Internet Service Providers' (ISPs) pricing structures could affect the rate of growth of Internet-based applications. In mid-2009, ISPs such as Time Warner Cable and Verizon were "… trying to convince their customers that they should pay for their service based on how much data they download in a month."[64] ISPs in India are now offering similar service based on the data downloaded. Users downloading or streamlining high-definition movies, playing video games online, and so forth would be affected the most if ISPs were to base their pricing structure around total usage.

Increasing Knowledge Intensity

Knowledge (information, intelligence, and expertise) is the basis of technology and its application. In the competitive landscape of the twenty-first century, knowledge is a critical organizational resource and an increasingly valuable source of competitive advantage.[65] Indeed, starting in the 1980s, the basis of competition shifted from hard assets to intangible resources. For example, "Wal-Mart transformed retailing through its proprietary approach to supply chain management and its information-rich relationships with customers and suppliers."[66] Relationships with customers and suppliers are an example of an intangible resource.

Knowledge is gained through experience, observation, and inference and is an intangible resource (tangible and intangible resources are fully described in Chapter 3). The value of intangible resources, including knowledge, is growing as a proportion of total shareholder value in today's competitive landscape.[67] For consulting and legal firms, knowledge is the principal source of competitive advantage. The probability of achieving strategic competitiveness is enhanced for the firm that realizes that its survival depends on the ability to capture intelligence, transform it into usable knowledge, and diffuse it rapidly throughout the company.[68] Therefore, firms must develop (e.g., through training programs) and acquire (e.g., by hiring educated and experienced employees) knowledge, integrate it into the organization to create capabilities, and then apply it to gain a competitive advantage.[69] In addition, firms must build routines that facilitate the diffusion of local knowledge throughout the organization for use everywhere that it has value.[70] Firms are better able to do these things when they have strategic flexibility.

Strategic flexibility is a set of capabilities used to respond to various demands and opportunities existing in a dynamic and uncertain competitive environment. Thus, strategic flexibility involves coping with uncertainty and its accompanying risks.[71] Firms should try to develop strategic flexibility in all areas of their operations. However, those working within firms to develop strategic flexibility should understand that the task is not easy, largely because of inertia that can build up over time. A firm's focus and past core competencies may actually slow change and strategic flexibility.[72]

To be strategically flexible on a continuing basis and to gain the competitive benefits of such flexibility, a firm has to develop the capacity to learn. In the words of John Browne, former CEO of British Petroleum: "In order to generate extraordinary value for shareholders, a company has to learn better than its competitors and apply that knowledge throughout its businesses faster and more widely than they do."[73] Continuous learning provides the firm with new and up-to-date sets of skills, which allow it to adapt to its environment as it encounters changes.[74] Firms capable of rapidly and broadly applying what they have learned exhibit the strategic flexibility and the capacity to change in ways that will increase the probability of successfully dealing with uncertain, hypercompetitive environments.

The I/O Model of Above-Average Returns

From the 1960s through the 1980s, the external environment was thought to be the primary determinant of strategies that firms selected to be successful.[75] The industrial organization (I/O) model of above-average returns explains the external environment's dominant influence on a firm's strategic actions. The model specifies that the industry or segment of an industry in which a company chooses to compete has a stronger influence on performance than do the choices managers make inside their organizations.[76] The firm's performance is believed to be determined primarily by a range of industry properties, including economies of scale, barriers to market entry, diversification, product differentiation, and the degree of concentration of firms in the industry.[77] We examine these industry characteristics in Chapter 2.

Grounded in economics, the I/O model has four underlying assumptions. First, the external environment is assumed to impose pressures and constraints that determine the strategies that would result in above-average returns. Second, most firms competing within an industry or within a segment of that industry are assumed to control similar strategically relevant resources and to pursue similar strategies in light of those resources. Third, resources used to implement strategies are assumed to be highly mobile across firms, so any resource differences that might develop between firms will be short-lived. Fourth, organizational decision makers are assumed to be rational and committed to acting in the firm's best interests, as shown by their profit-maximizing behaviors.[78] The I/O model challenges firms to find the most attractive industry in which to compete. Because most firms are assumed to have similar valuable resources that are mobile across companies, their performance generally can be increased only when they operate in the industry with the highest profit potential and learn how to use their resources to implement the strategy required by the industry's structural characteristics.[79]

The five forces model of competition is an analytical tool used to help firms find the industry that is the most attractive for them. The model (explained in Chapter 2) encompasses several variables and tries to capture the complexity of competition. The five forces model suggests that an industry's profitability (i.e., its rate of return on invested capital relative to its cost of capital) is a function of interactions among five forces: suppliers, buyers, competitive rivalry among firms currently in the industry, product substitutes, and potential entrants to the industry.[80]

Firms can use the five forces model to identify the attractiveness of an industry (as measured by its profitability potential) as well as the most advantageous position for the firm to take in that industry, given the industry's structural characteristics.[81] Typically, the model suggests that firms can earn above-average returns by producing either standardized goods or services at costs below those of competitors (a cost leadership strategy) or by producing differentiated goods or services for which customers are willing to pay a price premium (a differentiation strategy). (The cost leadership and product differentiation strategies are discussed in Chapter 4.) The fact that "...the fast food industry is becoming a "zero-sum industry" as companies" battle for the same pool of customers"[82] suggests that McDonald's is competing in a relatively unattractive industry. Similarly, telecom industry is fast becoming more and more unattractive with reduced margins, as may be seen from the dropping of share prices of Bharti Airtel to about one third of its price two years ago[83]. However, as described in the Opening Case, by focusing on product innovations and enhancing existing services as the foundation for its strategy, Bharti is positioned in the telecom industry in a way that still allows it to earn above-average returns as compared to its competitors.

As shown in Figure 1.2, the I/O model suggests that above-average returns are earned when firms are able to effectively study the external environment as the foundation for identifying an attractive industry and implementing the appropriate strategy. Companies that develop or acquire the internal skills needed to implement strategies required by the external environment are likely to succeed, while those that do not are likely to fail. Hence, this model suggests that returns are determined primarily by external characteristics rather than by the firm's unique internal resources and capabilities.

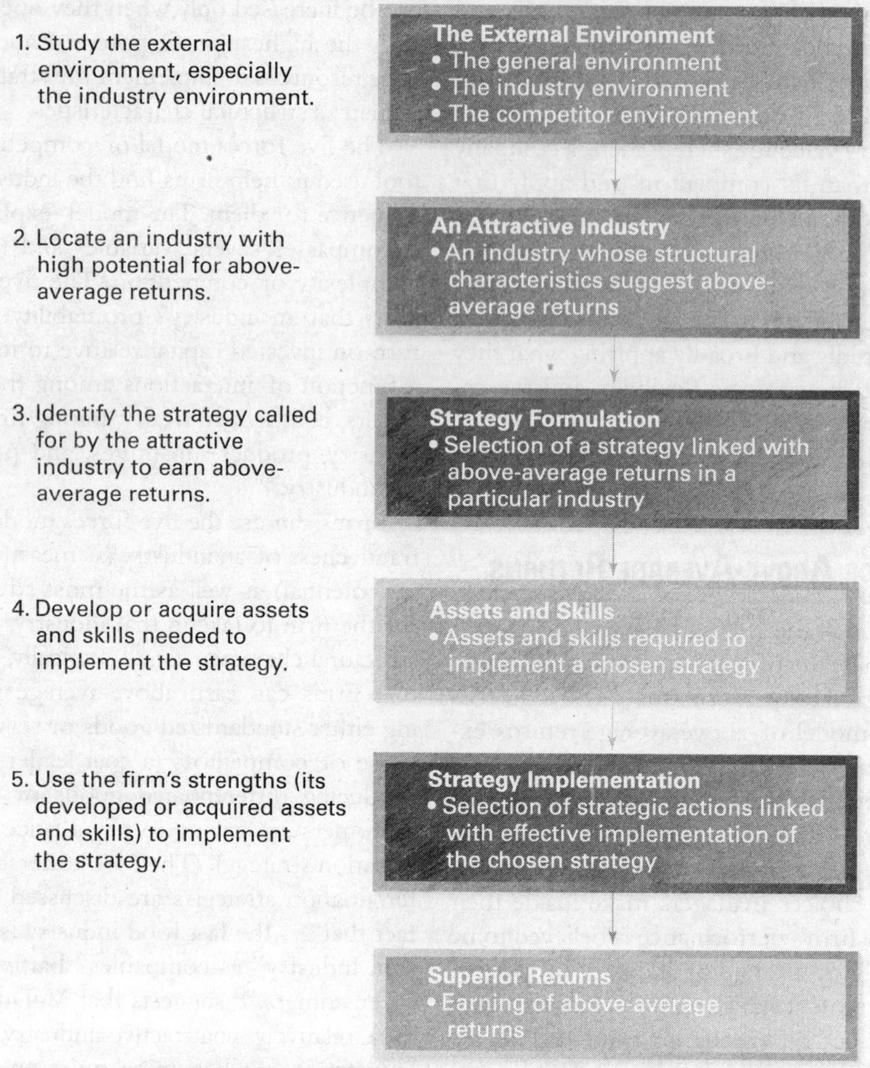

Figure 1.2 The I/O model of above-average returns

Research findings support the I/O model, in that approximately 20 per cent of a firm's profitability is explained by the industry in which it chooses to compete. However, this research also shows that 36 per cent of the variance in firm profitability can be attributed to the firm's characteristics and actions.[84] These findings suggest that the external environment and a firm's resources, capabilities, core competencies, and competitive advantages (see Chapter 3) all influence the company's ability to achieve strategic competitiveness and earn above-average returns.

As shown in Figure 1.2, the I/O model considers a firm's strategy to be a set of commitments and actions flowing from the characteristics of the industry in which the firm has decided to compete. The resource-based model, discussed next, takes a different view of the major influences on a firm's choice of strategy.

THE RESOURCE-BASED MODEL OF ABOVE-AVERAGE RETURNS

The resource-based model assumes that each organization is a collection of unique resources and capabilities. The *uniqueness* of its resources and capabilities is the basis of a firm's strategy and its ability to earn above-average returns.[85]

Resources are inputs into a firm's production process, such as capital equipment, the skills of individual employees, patents, finances, and talented managers. In general, a firm's resources are classified into three categories: physical, human, and organizational capital. Described fully in Chapter 3, resources are either tangible or intangible in nature.

Individual resources alone may not yield a competitive advantage.[86] In fact, resources have a greater likelihood of being a source of competitive advantage when they are formed into a capability. A **capability** is the capacity for a set of resources to perform a task or an activity in an integrative manner. Capabilities evolve over time and must be managed dynamically in pursuit of above-average returns.[87] **Core competencies** are resources and capabilities that serve as a source of competitive advantage for a firm over its rivals. Core competencies are often visible in the form of organizational functions. For example, Reliance Industries is building on its extensive project management skills, the ability to conceive and build large projects, often on a world scale, and a highly developed system of cost control to identify fresh areas which it can enter to meet customers' needs. Thus, it took to oil exploration on the one end and telecom at another. Tata Motors has leveraged its formidable design and manufacturing competencies to design and produce the world's cheapest car, the *Nano*. For this, it allied itself to Germany's Bosch for a new engine management system, Italy's IDEA Institute and Trilix for styling and exterior design, India's Sona Koyo for light weight steering shafts, America's Johnson Controls for seating systems, Toyo of Japan for engine cooling, Germany's Behr for heating, ventilating, and air conditioning systems, and India's Madras Rubber Factory (MRF) for new rear tyres.[88] The result was the world's cheapest fully functional car that can carry four persons; is suitable for both city and long distance driving—at an introductory price of ₹1,20,000 in March 2009.

According to the resource-based model, differences in firms' performances across time are primarily due to their unique resources and capabilities rather than the industry's structural characteristics. This model also assumes that firms acquire different resources and develop unique capabilities based on how they combine and use the resources; that resources and certainly capabilities are not highly mobile across firms; and that the differences in resources and capabilities are the basis of competitive advantage.[89] Through continued use, capabilities become stronger and more difficult for competitors to understand and imitate. As a source of competitive advantage, a capability "should be neither so simple that it is highly imitable, nor so complex that it defies internal steering and control."[90]

©Indiatodayimages.com

Tata Motors has leveraged its formidable design and manufacturing competencies to design and produce the world's cheapest car, the Nano.

The resource-based model of superior returns is shown in Figure 1.3. This model suggests that the strategy the firm chooses should allow it to use its competitive advantages in an attractive industry (the I/O model is used to identify an attractive industry).

Not all of a firm's resources and capabilities have the potential to be the foundation for a competitive advantage. This potential is realized when resources and capabilities are valuable, rare, costly to imitate, and nonsubstitutable.[91] Resources are *valuable* when they allow a firm to take advantage of opportunities or neutralize threats in its external environment. They are *rare* when possessed by few, if any, current and potential competitors. Resources are *costly to imitate* when other firms either cannot obtain them or are at a cost disadvantage in obtaining them compared with the firm that already possesses them. And they are *non-substitutable* when they have no structural equivalents. Many resources can either be imitated or substituted over time. Therefore, it is difficult to achieve and sustain a competitive advantage based on resources alone.[92] When these four criteria are met, however, resources and capabilities become core competencies.

As noted previously, research shows that both the industry environment and a firm's internal assets affect that firm's performance over time.[93] Thus, to form a vision and mission, and subsequently to select one or more strategies and to determine how to implement them, firms use both the I/O and the resource-based models.[94] In fact, these models complement each other in that one (I/O) focuses outside the firm while the other (resource-based) focuses inside the firm. Next, we discuss the forming of the firm's vision and mission—actions taken after the firm understands the realities of its external environment (Chapter 2) and internal organization (Chapter 3).

Figure 1.3 The resource-based model of above-average returns

Vision and Mission

After studying the external environment and the internal organization, the firm has the information it needs to form its vision and a mission (see Figure 1.1). Stakeholders (those who affect or are affected by a firm's performance, as explained later in the chapter) learn a great deal about a firm by studying its vision and mission. Indeed, a key purpose of vision and mission statements is to inform stakeholders of what the firm is, what it seeks to accomplish, and who it seeks to serve.

Vision

Vision is a picture of what the firm wants to be and, in broad terms, what it wants to ultimately achieve.[95] Thus, a vision statement articulates the ideal description of an organization and gives shape to its intended future. In other words, a vision statement points the firm in the direction of where it would eventually like to be in the years to come.[96] Vision is "big picture" thinking with passion that helps people *feel* what they are supposed to be doing in the organization.[97] People feel what they are to do when their firm's vision is simple, positive, and emotional. However, an effective vision stretches and challenges people as well.

It is also important to note that vision statements reflect a firm's values and aspirations and are intended to capture the heart and mind of each employee and, hopefully, many of its other stakeholders. It should be more poetry than prose, something to ignite imagination and provide inspiration. A vision statement tends to be relatively short and concise, making it easy to remember. Examples of vision statements include the following[98]:

To be a globally respected corporation that provides best-of-breed business solutions, leveraging technology, delivered by best-in-class people. (Infosys)

To be a respected world class corporation and the leader in Indian steel business in quality, productivity, profitability and customer satisfaction. (Steel Authority of India, or SAIL)

Eradication of needless blindness. (Aravind Eye Care System)

Leadership through differentiation. (The Park group of hotels)

To make the automobile accessible to every American. (Ford Motor Company's vision when established by Henry Ford)

As a firm's most important and prominent strategic leader, the CEO is responsible for working with others to form the firm's vision. Experience shows that the most effective vision statement results when the CEO involves a host of stakeholders (e.g., other top-level managers, employees working in different parts of the organization, suppliers, and customers) to develop it. In addition, to help the firm reach its desired future state, a vision statement should be clearly tied to the conditions in the firm's external environment and internal organization. Moreover, the decisions and actions of those involved with developing the vision, especially the CEO and the other top-level managers, must be consistent with that vision. At McDonald's, for example, a failure to openly provide employees with what they need to quickly and effectively serve customers would be a recipe for disaster.

Mission

The vision is the foundation for the firm's mission. A **mission** specifies the business or businesses in which the firm intends to compete and the customers it intends to serve.[99] It could also specify what impact the firm seeks to create in the broader society it serves. The firm's mission is more concrete than its vision. However, like the vision, a mission should establish a firm's individuality and should be inspiring and relevant to all stake-holders.[100] A firm's vision tends to be enduring while its mission can change in light of changing environmental conditions. Together, vision and mission provide the foundation the firm needs to choose and implement one or more strategies. The probability of forming an effective mission increases when employees have a strong sense of the ethical standards that will guide their behaviors as they work to help the firm reach its vision.[101] Thus, business ethics are a vital part of the firm's discussions to decide what it wants to become (its vision) as well as who it intends to serve and how it desires to serve those individuals and groups (its mission).[102]

Even though the final responsibility for forming the firm's mission rests with the CEO, the CEO and other top-level managers tend to involve a larger number of people in forming the mission. The main reason is that the mission deals more directly with product markets and customers, and middle- and first-level managers and other employees have more direct contact with customers and the markets in which they are served. Examples of mission statements include the following:

To achieve our objectives in an environment of fairness, honesty, and courtesy towards our clients, employees, vendors and society at large. (Infosys)

Embrace talent and harness expertise to leverage standards of excellence in the art of hospitality to grow our international presence, increase domestic dominance, and create value for all stakeholders. (Taj group of hotels)

Notice how the mission statement of Infosys flows from its vision of being a globally respected software company through technology and people. Taj's mission statement describes the business areas (domestic and international presence in the hospitality business) in which the firm intends to compete.

Some believe that vision and mission statements fail to create value for the firms forming them. One expert believes that "Most vision statements are either too vague, too broad in scope, or riddled with superlatives."[103] If this is the case, why do firms spend so much time developing these statements? As explained in Strategic Focus 1.2, vision and mission statements that are poorly developed do not provide the direction the firm needs to take appropriate strategic actions. Still, as shown in Figure 1.1, the firm's vision and mission are critical aspects of the *strategic inputs* it requires to engage in *strategic actions* as the foundation for achieving strategic competitiveness and earning above-average returns. Nucor, one of the world's largest steel manufacturers, have tied up all their strategic actions around its vision to be the world's lowest cost steel manufacturer[104]. Aravind Eye Care System have defined all their areas of action as those contributing to the quickest attainment of their vision of eradicating needless blindness[105]. Therefore, as we discuss in Strategic Focus 1.2, firms must accept the challenge of forming effective vision and mission statements.

STRATEGIC FOCUS

1.2 Effective Vision and Mission Statements: Why Firms Need Them

Some clearly believe that working on vision and mission statements is a waste of time and energy. "We have more important things to accomplish"; "We are too busy fighting daily fires to spend time thinking about the future or dreaming about what we might want to be"; and "All vision and mission statements look alike across companies—there's just no difference among them, so why bother?" Almost everyone who has been involved with or worked for an organization either on or off campus has likely heard similar comments.

Thinking about the challenges facing firms today allows us to understand the reasons for the negative perspective some have about the benefits organizations gain by forming vision and mission statements. A difficult competitive environment and the realities of globalization are but two reasons that may cause some to react less-than-positively when asked to participate in efforts to form vision and mission statements for their organization. In addition, the difficulty and challenge associated with developing *effective* or *meaningful* vision and mission statements may be the key reasons some prefer not to bother trying to do so.

A vision is a picture of what the firm wants to be and, in broad terms, what it ultimately wants to achieve. Based on the vision, a firm's mission indicates the business or businesses in which the firm will compete and the customers it will serve. An important aspect of these statements is that deep, critical, and reflective thinking is required to form them. Moreover, forming these statements requires choices to be made—about what the firm wants to be, what it wants to achieve, and the businesses it will compete in, and the specific groups of customers it will serve. Simultaneously, the firm is deciding what it won't become, won't try to achieve, where it won't compete, and who it won't serve. These are hard choices that result only from intensive thinking
Some clearly believe that working on vision and mission statements is a waste of time and energy. "We have more important things to accomplish"; "We are too busy fighting daily fires to spend time thinking about the future or dreaming about what we might want to be"; and "All vision and mission statements look alike across companies—there's just no difference among them, so why bother?" Almost everyone who has been involved with or worked for an organization either on or off campus has likely heard similar comments.

Thinking about the challenges facing firms today allows us to understand the reasons for the negative perspective some have about the benefits organizations gain by forming vision and mission statements. A difficult competitive environment and the realities of globalization are but two reasons that may cause some to react less-than-positively when asked to participate in efforts to form vision and mission statements for their organization. In addition, the difficulty and challenge associated with developing *effective* or *meaningful* vision and mission statements may be the key reasons some prefer not to bother trying to do so.

A vision is a picture of what the firm wants to be and, in broad terms, what it ultimately wants to achieve. Based on the vision, a firm's mission indicates the business or businesses in which the firm will compete and the customers it will serve. An important aspect of these statements is that deep, critical, and reflective thinking is required to form them. Moreover, forming these statements requires choices to be made—about what the firm wants to be, what it wants to achieve, and the businesses it will compete in, and the specific groups of customers it will serve. Simultaneously, the firm is deciding what it won't become, won't try to achieve, where it won't compete, and who it won't serve. These are hard choices that result only from intensive thinking and analysis. Having obtained information about the firm's external environment and its internal organization, those asked to form the firm's vision and mission statements must be willing to rigorously and thoroughly debate the realities and possibilities associated with the information that has been gathered.

CORBIS/Jupiter Images

Developing vision and mission statements is not an exercise in futility.

There are benefits for organizations willing to accept the challenge of rigorously examining and interpreting this information. Internally, the benefits include (1) providing the direction required to select the firm's strategies, (2) prioritizing how the firm's resources will be allocated, (3) providing opportunities for people to work together to deal with significant issues, (4) gaining an appreciation for the necessity of making trade-offs, and (5) learning more about the firm's culture and character. Benefits for the firm's external environment include (1) showing how the organization differs from competitors, (2) reflecting the organization's priorities, and (3) signaling aspects of the firm's culture and values. In addition, strategic leaders should be aware of research evidence suggesting that there is a positive relationship between forming vision and mission statements that is consistent with the realities of their external environment and internal organization and performance.[106] Thus, there are multiple reasons for firms to take the steps required to effectively develop a vision statement and a mission statement.

Sources: H. Ibarra & O. Obodaru, 2009, Women and the vision thing, *Harvard Business Review*, 87(1): 62–70; B. Bartkus & M. Glassman, 2008, Do firms practice what they preach? The relationship between mission statements and stakeholder management, *Journal of Business Ethics*, 83: 207–216; B. Perkins, 2008, State your purpose, *Computerworld*, May 12, 35; L. S. Williams, 2008, The mission statement, *Journal of Business Communication*, 45: 94–119; J. Davis, J. A. Ruhe, M. Lee, & U. Rajadhyaksha, 2007, Mission possible: Do school mission statements work? *Journal of Business Ethics*, 70: 99–110.

STAKEHOLDERS

Every organization involves a system of primary stakeholder groups with whom it establishes and manages relationships.[107] **Stakeholders** are the individuals and groups who can affect the firm's vision and mission, are affected by the strategic outcomes achieved, and have enforceable claims on the firm's performance.[108] Claims on a firm's performance are enforced through the stakeholders' ability to withhold participation essential to the organization's survival, competitiveness, and profitability.[109] Stakeholders continue to support an organization when its performance meets or exceeds their expectations.[110] Also, research suggests that firms that effectively manage stakeholder relationships outperform those that do not. Stakeholder relationships can therefore be managed to be a source of competitive advantage.[111]

Although organizations have dependency relationships with their stakeholders, they are not equally dependent on all stakeholders at all times;[112] as a consequence, not every stakeholder has the same level of influence.[113] The more critical and valued a stakeholder's participation, the greater a firm's dependency on it. Greater dependence, in turn, gives the stakeholder more potential influence over a firm's commitments, decisions, and actions. Managers must find ways to either accommodate or insulate the organization from the demands of stakeholders controlling critical resources.[114]

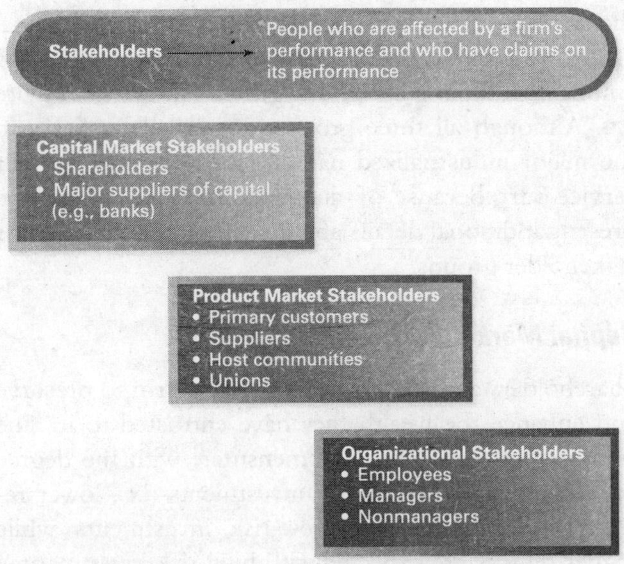

Figure 1.4 The three stakeholder groups

Classifications of Stakeholders

The parties involved with a firm's operations can be separated into at least three groups.[115] As shown in Figure 1.4, these groups are the capital market stakeholders (shareholders and the major suppliers of a firm's capital), the product market stakeholders (the firm's primary customers, suppliers, and host communities, and the organizational stakeholders (all of a firm's employees, including both non-managerial and managerial personnel).

Each stakeholder group expects those making strategic decisions in a firm to provide the leadership through which its valued objectives will be reached.[116] The objectives of the various stakeholder groups often differ from one another, sometimes placing those involved with a firm's strategic management process in situations where trade-offs have to be made. The most obvious stakeholders, at least in US organizations, are **shareholders**—individuals and groups who have invested capital in a firm in the expectation of earning a positive return on their investments. These stakeholders' rights are grounded in laws governing private property and private enterprise.

In contrast to shareholders, another group of stakeholders—the firm's customers—prefers that investors receive a minimum return on their investments. Customers could have their interests maximized when the quality and reliability of a firm's products are improved, but without a price increase. High returns to customers might come at the expense of lower returns negotiated with capital market shareholders.

Because of potential conflicts, each firm is challenged to manage its stakeholders. First, a firm must carefully identify all important stakeholders. Second, it must prioritize them, in case it cannot satisfy all of them. Power is the most critical criterion in prioritizing stakeholders. Other criteria might include the urgency of satisfying each particular stakeholder group and the degree of importance of each to the firm.[117]

When the firm earns above-average returns, the challenge of effectively managing stakeholder relationships is lessened substantially. With the capability and flexibility provided by above-average returns, a firm can more easily satisfy multiple stakeholders simultaneously. When the firm earns only average returns, it is unable to maximize the interests of all stakeholders. The objective then becomes one of at least minimally satisfying each stakeholder. Trade-off decisions are made in light of how important the support of each stakeholder group is to the firm. For example, environmental groups may be very important to firms in the energy industry but less important to professional service firms.[118] A firm earning below-average returns does not have the capacity to minimally satisfy all stakeholders. The managerial challenge in this case is to make trade-offs that minimize the amount of support lost from stakeholders. Societal values also influence the general weightings allocated among the three stakeholder groups shown in Figure 1.4. Although all three groups are served by firms in the major industrialized nations, the priorities in their service vary because of cultural differences. Next, we present additional details about each of the three major stakeholder groups.

Capital Market Stakeholders

Shareholders and lenders both expect a firm to preserve and enhance the wealth they have entrusted to it. The returns they expect are commensurate with the degree of risk accepted with those investments (i.e., lower returns are expected with low-risk investments while higher returns are expected with high-risk investments). Dissatisfied lenders may impose stricter covenants on subsequent borrowing of capital. Dissatisfied shareholders may reflect their concerns through several means, including selling their stock.

When a firm is aware of potential or actual dissatisfactions among capital market stakeholders, it may respond to their concerns. The firm's response to stakeholders who are dissatisfied is affected by the nature of its dependency relationship with them (which, as noted earlier, is also influenced by a society's values). The greater and more significant the dependency relationship is, the more direct and significant the firm's response becomes. Before its takeover by Kingfisher Airlines, Air Deccan took several actions to try to satisfy its capital market stakeholders. In part, these actions were taken because of the significance of Air Deccan's dependence on its capital market stakeholders. It had to try to renegotiate its arrears to airports and fuel companies, and the leasing charges to the leasing companies from which it had leased its aircraft. It also issued a public offering which did not do well in the market. It made desperate attempts to get fresh loans from domestic and international financiers. However, the reality is that none of these actions resulted in outcomes that allowed Air Deccan to meet the expectations of its capital market stakeholders.

Product Market Stakeholders

Some might think that product market stakeholders (customers, suppliers, and host communities) share few common interests. However, all these groups can benefit as firms engage in competitive battles. For example, depending on product and industry characteristics, marketplace competition may result in lower product prices being charged to a firm's customers and higher prices being paid to its suppliers (the firm might be willing to pay higher supplier prices to ensure delivery of the types of goods and services that are linked with its competitive success).[119]

Customers, as stakeholders, demand reliable products at the lowest possible prices. Suppliers seek loyal customers who are willing to pay the highest sustainable prices for the goods and services they receive. Host communities want companies willing to be long-term employers and providers of tax revenue without placing excessive demands on public support services. Thus, product market stakeholders are generally satisfied when a firm's profit margin reflects at least a balance between the returns to capital market stakeholders (i.e., the returns lenders and shareholders will accept and still retain their interests in the firm) and the returns in which they share.

Organizational Stakeholders

Employees—the firm's organizational stakeholders—expect the firm to provide a dynamic, stimulating, and rewarding work environment. As employees, we are usually satisfied working for a company that is growing and actively developing our skills, especially those skills required to be effective team members and to meet or exceed global work standards. Workers who learn how to use new knowledge productively are critical to organizational success. In a collective sense, the education and skills of a firm's workforce are competitive weapons affecting strategy implementation and firm performance.[120] The Unions, representing the workers, form a separate group of stakeholders. Union officials are interested in secure jobs, under highly desirable working conditions, for the employees they represent. As suggested by the following statement, strategic leaders are ultimately responsible for serving the needs of organizational stakeholders on a day-to-day basis: "The job of [strategic] leadership is to fully utilize human potential, to create organizations in which people can grow and learn while still achieving a common objective, to nurture the human spirit."[121]

Strategic Leaders

Strategic leaders are people located in different parts of the firm using the strategic management process to help the firm reach its vision and mission. Regardless of their location in the firm, successful strategic leaders are decisive, committed to nurturing those around them[122] and are committed to helping the firm create value for all stakeholder groups.[123] In this vein, research evidence suggests that employees who perceive that their CEO emphasizes the need for the firm to operate in ways that are consistent with the values of all stakeholder groups rather than focusing only on maximizing profits for shareholders identify that CEO as a visionary leader. In turn, visionary leadership is related to extra effort by employees, with employee effort leading to enhanced firm performance. These intriguing findings suggest that decision-making values "… that are oriented toward a range of stakeholders may yield more favorable outcomes for leaders than values that focus primarily on economic-based issues."[124] These findings are consistent with the argument that "To regain society's trust … business leaders must embrace a way of looking at their role that goes beyond their responsibility to the shareholder to include a civic and personal commitment to their duty as institutional custodians."[125]

When identifying strategic leaders, most of us tend to think of chief executive officers (CEOs) and other top-level managers. Clearly, these people are strategic leaders. And, in the final analysis, CEOs are responsible for making certain that their firm effectively uses the strategic management process. Indeed, the pressure on CEOs to manage strategically is stronger than ever.[126] However, many other people in today's organizations help choose a firm's strategy and then determine the actions for successfully implementing it.[127] The main reason is that the realities of twenty-first–century competition that we discussed earlier in this chapter (e.g., the global economy, globalization, rapid technological change, and the increasing importance of knowledge and people as sources of competitive advantage) are creating a need for those "closest to the action" to be the ones making decisions and determining the actions to be taken.[128] In fact, the most effective CEOs and top-level managers understand how to delegate strategic responsibilities to people throughout the firm who influence the use of organizational resources.[129]

Organizational culture also affects strategic leaders and their work. In turn, strategic leaders' decisions and actions shape a firm's culture. **Organizational culture** refers to the complex set of ideologies, symbols, and core values that are shared throughout the firm and that influence how the firm conducts business. It is the social energy that drives—or fails to drive—the organization.[130] For example, Southwest Airlines is known for having a unique and valuable culture. Its culture encourages employees to work hard but also to have fun while doing so. Moreover, its culture entails respect for others—employees and customers alike. The firm also places a premium on service, as suggested by its commitment to provide POS (Positively Outrageous Service) to each customer. The Christian Medical College, Vellore has a culture where the patients are served in "the spirit of Christ", i.e., not only with professional competence, but also compassion[131]. Aravind Eye Care System also has a similar culture (see the case on Aravind Eye Care System among the cases in this book).

Some organizational cultures are a source of disadvantage. It is important for strategic leaders to understand, however, that whether the firm's culture is functional or dysfunctional, their work takes place within the context of that culture. The relationship between organizational culture and strategic leaders' work is reciprocal in that the culture shapes how they work while their work helps shape an ever-evolving organizational culture. It is for this reason that bringing about changes in organizations with a strong culture proves to be a difficult task.

The Work of Effective Strategic Leaders

Perhaps not surprisingly, hard work, thorough analyses, a willingness to be brutally honest, a penchant for wanting the firm and its people to accomplish more, and tenacity are prerequisites to an individual's success as a strategic leader.[132] In addition, strategic leaders must be able to "think seriously and deeply … about the purposes of the organizations they head or functions they perform, about the strategies, tactics, technologies, systems, and people necessary to attain these purposes and about the important questions that always need to be asked."[133] In addition, effective strategic leaders work to set an ethical tone in their firms. For example, Kevin Thompson, IBM's Manager of Corporate Citizenship, suggests, "We don't think you can survive without integrating business and societal values."[134]

IBM's organizational culture holds that there is indeed a corporate responsibility to bettering society at large.

Strategic leaders, regardless of their location in the organization, often work long hours, and their work is filled with ambiguous decision situations.[135] However, the opportunities afforded by this work are appealing and offer exciting chances to dream and to act.[136] The following words, given as advice to the late Time Warner chair and co-CEO Steven J. Ross by his father, describe the opportunities in a strategic leader's work:

There are three categories of people—the person who goes into the office, puts his feet up on his desk, and dreams for 12 hours; the person who arrives at 5 A.M. and works for 16 hours, never once stopping to dream; and the person who puts his feet up, dreams for one hour, then does something about those dreams.[137]

The organizational term used for a dream that challenges and energizes a company is vision. Strategic leaders have opportunities to dream and to act, and the most effective ones provide a vision as the foundation for the firm's mission and subsequent choice and use of one or more strategies.

Predicting Outcomes of Strategic Decisions: Profit Pools

Strategic leaders attempt to predict the outcomes of their decisions before taking efforts to implement them, which is difficult to do. Many decisions that are a part of the strategic management process are concerned with an uncertain future and the firm's place in that future.[138]

Mapping an industry's profit pool is something strategic leaders can do to anticipate the possible outcomes of different decisions and to focus on growth in profits rather than strictly growth in revenues. A **profit pool** entails the total profits earned in an industry at all points along the value chain.[139] (We explain the value chain in Chapter 3 and discuss it further in Chapter 4.) Analyzing the profit pool in the industry may help a firm see something others are unable to see by helping it understand the primary sources of profits in an industry. There are four steps to identifying profit pools: (1) define the pool's boundaries, (2) estimate the pool's overall size, (3) estimate the size of the value-chain activity in the pool, and (4) reconcile the calculations.[140]

Let's think about how McDonald's might map the quick-service restaurant industry's profit pools. First, McDonald's would need to define the industry's boundaries and, second, estimate its size. These boundaries would include markets across the globe. The size of the US market is not currently expanding. The net result of this is that McDonald's is trying to increase its market share by taking market share away from competitors such as Burger King and Wendy's. Growth is more likely in international markets, which is why McDonald's is establishing more units internationally than it is domestically. Armed with information about its industry, McDonald's would then be prepared to estimate the amount of profit potential in each part of the value chain (step 3). In the quick-service restaurant industry, marketing campaigns and customer service are likely more important sources of potential profits than are inbound logistics' activities. With an understanding of where the greatest amount of profits are likely to be earned, McDonald's would then be ready to select the strategy to use in order to be successful where the largest profit pools are located in the value chain.[141] As this brief discussion shows, profit pools are a tool the firm's strategic leaders can use to help recognize the actions to take to increase the likelihood of increasing profits.

The Strategic Management Process

As suggested by Figure 1.1, the strategic management process is a rational approach which firms use to achieve strategic competitiveness and earn above-average returns. Figure 1.1 also features the topics we examine in this book to present the strategic management process to you.

This book is divided into three parts. In Part 1, we describe what firms do to analyze their external environment (Chapter 2) and internal organization (Chapter 3). These analyses are completed to identify marketplace opportunities and threats in the external environment (Chapter 2) and to decide how to use the resources, capabilities, core competencies, and competitive advantages in the firm's internal organization to pursue opportunities and overcome threats (Chapter 3). With knowledge about its external environment and internal organization, the firm forms its vision and mission.

The firm's strategic inputs (see Figure 1.1) provide the foundation for choosing one or more strategies and deciding how to implement them. As suggested in Figure 1.1 by the horizontal arrow linking the two types of strategic actions, formulation and implementation must be simultaneously integrated if the firm is to successfully use the strategic management process. Integration happens as decision makers think about implementation issues when choosing strategies and as they think about possible changes to the firm's strategies while implementing a currently chosen strategy.

In Part 2 of this book, we discuss the different strategies which the firms may choose to use. First, we examine business-level strategies (Chapter 4). A business-level strategy describes the actions a firm decides to take in order to exploit its competitive advantage over rivals. A company competing in a single product market (e.g., a locally owned grocery store operating in only one location) has but one business-level strategy while a diversified firm competing in multiple product markets (e.g., General Electric) forms a business-level strategy for each of its businesses. In Chapter 5, we describe the actions and reactions that occur among firms while using their strategies in marketplace competitions. As we will see, competitors respond to and try to anticipate each other's actions. The dynamics of competition affect the strategies the firms choose to use as well as how they try to implement the chosen strategies.[142]

For the diversified firm, corporate-level strategy (Chapter 6) is concerned with determining the businesses in which the company intends to compete as well as how to manage its different businesses. Other topics vital to strategy formulation, particularly in the diversified corporation, include acquiring other companies and, as appropriate, restructuring the firm's portfolio of businesses (Chapter 7) and selecting an international strategy (Chapter 8). With cooperative strategies (Chapter 9), firms form a partnership to share their resources and capabilities in order to develop a competitive advantage. Cooperative strategies are becoming increasingly important as firms seek ways to compete in the global economy's array of different markets.[143]

To examine actions taken to implement strategies, we consider several topics in Part 3 of the book. First, we examine the different mechanisms used to govern firms (Chapter 10). With demands for improved corporate governance being voiced today by many stakeholders, organizations are challenged to learn how to simultaneously satisfy their stakeholders' different interests.[144] Finally, the organizational structure and actions needed to control a firm's operations (Chapter 11), the patterns of strategic leadership appropriate for today's firms and competitive environments (Chapter 12), and strategic entrepreneurship (Chapter 13) as a path to continuous innovation are addressed.

Before closing this introductory chapter, it is important to emphasize that primarily because they are related to how a firm interacts with its stakeholders, almost all strategic management process decisions have ethical dimensions.[145] Organizational ethics are revealed by an organization's culture; that is to say, a firm's decisions are a product of the core values that are shared by most or all of a company's managers and employees. Especially in the turbulent and often ambiguous competitive landscape of the twenty-first century, those making decisions that are part of the strategic management process are challenged to recognize that their decisions affect capital market, product market, and organizational stakeholders differently and to evaluate the ethical implications of their decisions on a daily basis.[146] Decision makers failing to recognize these realities accept the risk of putting their firm at a competitive disadvantage when it comes to consistently engaging in ethical business practices.[147]

As you will discover, the strsategic management process examined in this book calls for disciplined approaches to serve as the foundation for developing a competitive advantage. These approaches provide the pathway through which firms will be able to achieve strategic competitiveness and earn above-average returns. Mastery of this strategic management process will effectively serve you, our readers, and the organizations for which you will choose to work.

SUMMARY

- Firms use the strategic management process to achieve strategic competitiveness and earn above-average returns. Strategic competitiveness is achieved when a firm has developed and learned how to implement a value-creating strategy. Above-average returns (in excess of what investors expect to earn from other investments with similar levels of risk) provide the foundation a firm needs to simultaneously satisfy all of its stakeholders.
- The fundamental nature of competition is different in the current competitive landscape. As a result, those making strategic decisions must adopt a different mind-set, one that allows them to learn how to compete in highly turbulent and chaotic environments that are producing disorder and a great deal of uncertainty. The globalization of industries and their markets and rapid and significant technological changes are the two primary factors contributing to the turbulence of the competitive landscape.
- Firms use two major models to help them form their vision and mission and then choose one or more strategies to use in pursuit of strategic competitiveness and above-average returns. The core assumption of the I/O model is that the firm's external environment has more of an influence on the choice of strategies than do the firm's internal resources, capabilities, and core competencies. Thus, the I/O model is

used to understand the effects an industry's characteristics can have on a firm when deciding what strategy or strategies to use to compete against rivals. The logic supporting the I/O model suggests that above-average returns are earned when the firm locates an attractive industry or part of an industry and successfully implements the strategy dictated by that industry's characteristics. The core assumption of the resource-based model is that the firm's unique resources, capabilities, and core competencies have more of an influence on selecting and using strategies than does the firm's external environment. Above-average returns are earned when the firm uses its valuable, rare, costly-to-imitate, and non-substitutable resources and capabilities to compete against its rivals in one or more industries. Evidence indicates that both models yield insights that are linked to successfully selecting and using strategies. Thus, firms want to use their unique resources, capabilities, and core competencies as the foundation for one or more strategies that will allow them to compete in industries they understand.

- Vision and mission are formed in light of the information and insights gained from studying a firm's internal and external environments. Vision is a picture of what the firm wants to be and, in broad terms, what it wants to ultimately achieve. Flowing from the vision, the mission specifies the business or businesses in which the firm intends to compete and the customers it intends to serve. Vision and mission provide direction to the firm and signal important descriptive information to stakeholders.
- Stakeholders are those who can affect, and are affected by, a firm's strategic outcomes. Because a firm is dependent on the continuing support of stakeholders (shareholders, customers, suppliers, employees, host communities, etc.), they have enforceable claims on the company's performance. When earning above-average returns, a firm has the resources it needs to, at minimum, simultaneously satisfy the interests of all stakeholders. However, when earning only average returns, the firm must carefully manage its stakeholders in order to retain their support. A firm earning below-average returns must minimize the amount of support it loses from unsatisfied stakeholders.
- Strategic leaders are people located in different parts of the firm using the strategic management process to help the firm reach its vision and mission. In the final analysis, though, CEOs are responsible for making certain that their firms properly use the strategic management process. Today, the effectiveness of the strategic management process is increased when it is grounded in ethical intentions and behaviors. The strategic leader's work demands decision trade-offs, often among attractive alternatives. It is important for all strategic leaders and especially the CEO and other members of the top-management team to work hard, conduct thorough analyses of situations facing the firm, be brutally and consistently honest, and ask the right questions of the right people at the right time.
- Strategic leaders predict the potential outcomes of their strategic decisions. To do this, they must first calculate profit pools in their industry that are linked to value chain activities. Predicting the potential outcomes of their strategic decisions reduces the likelihood of the firm formulating and implementing ineffective strategies.

KEY TERMS AND DEFINITIONS

Strategic leaders are people located in different parts of the firm using the strategic management process to help the firm reach its vision and mission.

Organizational culture refers to the complex set of ideologies, symbols, and core values that are shared throughout the firm and that influence how the firm conducts business.

Strategic competitiveness is achieved when a firm successfully formulates and implements a value-creating strategy.

A **strategy** is an integrated and coordinated set of commitments and actions designed to exploit core competencies and gain a competitive advantage.

A firm has a **competitive advantage** when it implements a strategy competitors are unable to duplicate or find too costly to try to imitate.

Average returns are returns equal to those an investor expects to earn from other investments with a similar amount of risk.

The **strategic management process** is the full set of commitments, decisions, and actions required for a firm to achieve strategic competitiveness and earn above-average returns.

A **global economy** is one in which goods, services, people, skills, and ideas move freely across geographic borders.

Strategic flexibility is a set of capabilities used to respond to various demands and opportunities existing in a dynamic and uncertain competitive environment.

Above-average returns are returns in excess of what an investor expects to earn from other investments with a similar amount of risk.

Risk is an investor's uncertainty about the economic gains or losses that will result from a particular investment.

Resources are inputs into a firm's production process, such as capital equipment, the skills of individual employees, patents, finances, and talented managers.

A **capability** is the capacity for a set of resources to perform a task or an activity in an integrative manner.

Core competencies are capabilities that serve as a source of competitive advantage for a firm over its rivals.

Vision is a picture of what the firm wants to be and, in broad terms, what it wants to ultimately achieve.

A **mission** specifies the business or businesses in which the firm intends to compete and the customers it intends to serve.

Stakeholders are the individuals and groups who can affect the firm's vision and mission, are affected by the strategic outcomes achieved, and have enforceable claims on the firm's performance.

A **profit pool** entails the total profits earned in an industry at all points along the value chain.

REVIEW QUESTIONS

1. What are strategic competitiveness, strategy, competitive advantage, above-average returns, and the strategic management process?
2. What are the characteristics of the current competitive landscape? What two factors are the primary drivers of this landscape?
3. According to the I/O model, what should a firm do to earn above-average returns?
4. What does the resource-based model suggest a firm should do to earn above-average returns?
5. What are vision and mission? What is their value for the strategic management process?
6. What are stakeholders? How do the three primary stakeholder groups influence organizations?
7. How would you describe the work of strategic leaders?
8. What are the elements of the strategic management process? How are they interrelated?

EXPERIENTIAL EXERCISES

Exercise 1: Business and Blogs

One element of industry structure analysis is the leverage that buyers can exert on firms. Is technology changing the balance of power between customers and companies? If so, how should business respond?

Blogs offer a mechanism for consumers to share their experiences—good or bad—regarding different companies. Bloggers first emerged in the late 1990s, and today the Technorati search engine currently monitors roughly 100 million blogs. With the wealth of this "citizen media" available, what are the implications for consumer power? One of the most famous cases of a blogger drawing attention to a company was Jeff Jarvis of the Web site http://www.buzzmachine.com. Jarvis, who writes on media topics, was having problems with his Dell computer and shared his experiences on the Web. Literally thousands of other people recounted similar experiences, and the phenomena became known as "Dell hell." Eventually, Dell created its own corporate blog in an effort to deflect this wave of consumer criticism. What are the implications of the rapid growth in blogs? Work in a group on the following exercise.

Part One

Visit a corporate blog. Only a small per centage of large firms maintain a blog presence on the Internet. *Hint:* Multiple wikis online provide lists of such companies. A Web search using the term *Fortune 500 blogs* will turn up several options. Review the content of the firm's blog. Was it updated regularly or not? Multiple contributors or just one? What was the writing style? Did it read like a marketing brochure or something more informal? Did the blog allow viewer comments or post replies to consumer questions?

Part Two

Based on the information you collected in the blog review, answer the following questions:

- Have you ever used blogs to help make decisions about something that you are considering purchasing? If so, how did the blog material affect your decision? What factors would make you more (or less) likely to rely on a blog in making your decision?
- How did the content of corporate blogs affect your perception of that company and its good and services? Did it make you more or less likely to view the company favorably, or have no effect at all?
- Why do so few large companies maintain blogs?
- Can mala fide blogs create serious problems for companies? Even destroy them? What action can companies take with regard to such blogs?

Exercise 2: Creating a Shared Vision

Drawing on an analysis of internal and external conditions, firms create a mission and vision as a cornerstone of their strategy. This exercise examines some of the challenges associated with creating a firm's shared direction.

Part One

The instructor will break the class into a set of small teams. Half of the teams will be given an "A" designation, and the other half assigned as "B." Each individual team will need to plan a time outside class to complete Part 2; the exercise should take about half an hour.

Teams given the A designation will meet in a face-to-face setting. Each team member will need paper and a pen or pencil. Your meeting location should be free from distraction. The location should have enough space so that no person can see another's notepad.

Teams given the B designation will meet electronically. You may choose to meet through text messaging or IM. Be sure to confirm everyone's contact information and meeting time beforehand.

Part Two

Each team member prepares a drawing of a real structure. It can be a famous building, a monument, museum, or even your dorm. Do not tell other team members what you drew.

- Randomly select one team member. The goal is for everyone else to prepare a drawing as similar to the selected team member as possible. That person is not allowed to show his or her drawing to the rest of the team. The rest of the group can ask questions about the drawing, but only ones that can be answered "yes" or "no."

After 10 minutes, have everyone compare their drawings. If you are meeting electronically, describe your drawings, and save them for the next time your team meets face to face.

Next, select a second team member and repeat this process again.

Part Three

- In class, discuss the following questions:
- How easy (or hard) was it for you to figure out the "vision" of your team members?
- Did you learn anything in the first iteration that made the second drawing more successful?
- What similarities might you find between this exercise and the challenge of sharing a vision among company employees?
- How did the communication structure affect your process and outcomes?

CHAPTER

2

The External Environment: Opportunities, Threats, Competition, and Competitor Analysis

Studying this chapter should provide you with the strategic management knowledge needed to

- Explain the importance of analysing and understanding the firm's external environment.
- Define and describe the general environment and the industry environment.
- Discuss the four activities of the external environmental analysis process.
- Name and describe the general environment's seven segments.
- Identify the five competitive forces and explain how they determine an industry's profit potential.
- Define strategic groups and describe their influence on the firm.
- Describe what firms need to know about their competitors and different methods (including ethical standards) used to collect intelligence about them.

OPENING CASE
ITC Limited

The Imperial Tobacco Company was incorporated in 1910 at Calcutta as a subsidiary of the British Tobacco Company, UK. It broke the "Imperial" connection in 1970 when it changed its name to India Tobacco Company Ltd. Since tobacco was seen as a somewhat unpleasant name to have on a sign board, and also with a view to project an image of a diversified company, it again changed its name to I.T.C. Ltd. in 1974 and finally to ITC Ltd. in 2001. The company pioneered the growth of cigarette industry in India. ITC Ltd. has had very strong cigarette brands such as Players Navy Cut Medium, Wills Gold Flake, Capstan, Scissors, Embassy, and Star.

Initially, the tobacco industry was discouraged by the government and was considered to be a non-priority sector in India. Foreign companies could not have a majority holding in such companies. There were also restrictions on increasing foreign equity in companies which were "dominant", and ITC fell under this category. ITC, as predominantly a foreign held company, came under the purview of the MRTP (Monopoly and Restrictive Trade Practices) Act, 1969 and the FERA (Foreign Exchange Regulations Act), 1973. With the advent of the FERA and MRTP Acts, the prospects for growth of the company's operations in the existing line of tobacco business seemed dim. This was further aggravated by fiscal measures such as excise duty on tobacco products which increased tremendously in the 1970s. The excise content of medium-priced cigarettes was about two-thirds of their selling price and was even higher for prestige brand products. Manufacturers passed on the entire excise burden to the customer but this restricted the demand growth.

During 1969–70, the management of ITC Ltd., under the leadership of its first Indian Chairman, Mr. A.N. Haksar, considered actively the strategic alternatives that were open to them in the coming decade. The central problem was being in a hostile environment. They were aware that any decision in this regard would not depend on the economic factors alone but also on a number of of important issues like social, political and regulatory factors. Consequently, the ITC management embarked on a "corporate refounding process". This meant thinking through Lines of business of the company—that they were a foreign held company operating under the constraints of FERA and MRTP Acts, and were in a non essential, non priority business. Hence, it attracted little government support. ITC realized that an organization cannot fight the economic policies of the government; rather it should partner with it in achieving its objectives, and extend its help to the government so that policies of the latter are implemented in an effective manner. The answer they found was to diversify into more core areas that would be considered as high priority by the government.

ITC's diversification thrust started with forays into paper manufacturing, deep-sea fishing (a failed project) and hospitality ventures (hotel business). It entered into many export businesses such as rice exports. Its paper business, The Bhadrachalam Paperboards Ltd., and its hotels, such as The Chola at Madras, Mughal in Agra, and Maurya in Delhi were successful. Later on, in the early 1990s, it tried to market its own Indian brands (all the brands of ITC earlier were BAT brands) of cigarettes, enter the hotel business globally, and enter significant (and likely to be profitable) sectors such as the power sector. These initiatives did not succeed, partly due to opposition from BAT and partly because ITC got involved in some scandals. It, however, succeeded in developing its tobacco leaf business, exporting to a number of countries, and entered into agri-food business, such as edible oils.

Today, ITC has transformed itself from a single-product company to one of India's largest multi-business corporate enterprises that offer a diversified product mix to enhance its brand image and reduce dependency on tobacco related products. It has become a major player in the hospitality segment, with the prestigious Maurya in Delhi having played host to many foreign heads of state. Its position in the FMCG (fast moving consumer goods) business is also on a growth curve. It has made heavy investments to strengthen its IT (information technology) segment and to compete with the big players like Infosys and Wipro. It has also become the country's foremost agri-business player pioneering rural transformation through its path-breaking e-Choupal initiative, an IT kiosk based network enabling farmers to get the best prices for their products. It has also entered into contract farming, mainly for tobacco, and to some extent, oil seeds, improving the price realization of farmers.

ITC Ltd: Transformation through diversification. Shedding colonial legacy is not all that easy. Tobacco still provides 80 per cent of revenues of the ₹100 billion company.

Its market capitalisation now tops ₹1000 billion, and the company has seen something like a 10-fold growth over the past decade, a period during which it has given much better returns to its shareholders than the Sensex and many other FMCG companies. But despite aggressive diversification, the company remains dependent on cigarettes for profits, which still depends on government policies. The company admitted in its annual report in 2010, that ITC is struggling to cope with the increasing taxation and regulations on cigarettes. "While the economic importance of tobacco has been acknowledged, the cigarette industry in India has been contending with the twin challenges of discriminatory and punitive taxation and increased regulation," it said. Diversification, which remains the keyword, was almost completely in response to the regulatory environment. Though cigarettes continue to be its main business, ITC has acquired a great reputation (independent of the tobacco business) in its hotels and restaurants business. Its *e-Choupal* has become a case study in Management expert C.K. Prahalad's book *Fortune at the Bottom of the Pyramid* and led to other such initiatives.

The company's longest-serving (present) chairman, Y.C. Deveshwar has repeatedly stressed the company's environmental record as a green company, and established a triple-bottom line objective (offering financial, environmental, and social returns) while also making the company carbon-neutral and water-positive. The corporate social responsibility activities signify a constant endeavor to shed the colonial legacy as a cigarette maker to that of a diversified multinational company earning it new respect. Although the ITC group is marketing its image as an ideal corporate citizen and a company that takes its social responsibility seriously, it still earns 80% of its revenues by selling cigarettes and other tobacco related products, and in that sense the task of transforming the company that began 100 years ago as Imperial Tobacco remains an unfinished one.

Sources: IIM-A Case Study–*ITC: Out on a No Ball?* (Case study # BP 252); IIM–A Case Study: ITC 'A', and ITC 'B' (Case studies #); ITC: Annual Report, 2010; Business-standard.com, economictimes.indiatimes.com, equitymaster.com, Macquarie Research Equities – Report, www.ibscdc.org/Case_Studies, C.K. Prahalad, 2005, ITC e-Choupal Story: Profitable Rural transformation, *Fortune at the Bottom of the Pyramid: Eradicating Poverty through Profits*. Wharton School Publishing. pp.319-357.

As described in the Opening Case and suggested by research, the external environment affects a firm's strategic actions[1]. For instance, the regulations that are a part of the **political/legal segment** of ITC's general environment affect how the company conducts its business. In general, the regulations regarding the selling of tobacco products are highly restrictive in India and tobacco, especially cigarettes have been treated as a source of excise duty by the government. It is also a non priority sector; hence in the earlier licensing era, it was difficult for a company like ITC to expand its operations. In addition to the regulatory influence, which is partly due to considerations of public health, and hence a part of the socio-cultural segment of ITC's external environment, the firm's strategic actions are affected by conditions in other segments of its general environment, such as the global and the physical environment segments. A firm must be aware of how the regulations might change in the markets it serves as well as those it may desire to serve in the future, and must prepare to deal with these changes. Aware of the possible effects of the political/legal environment on its operations in the future, Mr. A.N. Haksar, Chairman, ITC made the following public pronouncement in 1975: "I believe that every company has two balance sheets. The obvious one … is the Report and Accounts. The other, not so obvious, relates to obligations in the national interest and thus to the public good."

ITC thus sought to grow through diversification into a number of sectors, many having no relationship with its core business of tobacco and tobacco products. It entered into what were seen as priority sectors such as hotels, since that would attract foreign tourists and bring foreign exchange into the country, something very important at that time. To pursue what it believes are opportunities to export different items in the global market, it launched a series of trading activities in many commodities such as rice. It also sought to expand its hotel/restaurant activities in other countries even as it continued and enhanced its sale of tobacco to its parent company, BAT. It made profits out of its hospitality business, and its hotels are considered to be very well managed and competitive. However, it did not make such a success from its other forays; in fact, it got involved with regulatory authorities, leading even to the arrest of some of its executives. In this chapter, we explain that a firm's external environment creates both opportunities (e.g., the opportunity for ITC to enter other businesses, and threats; the possibility that additional regulations in its markets will reduce consumption of ITC's tobacco products). Collectively, opportunities and threats affect a firm's strategic actions.[2]

Regardless of the industry in which they compete, the external environment influences firms as they seek strategic competitiveness and the earning of above-average returns. This chapter focuses on how firms analyze their

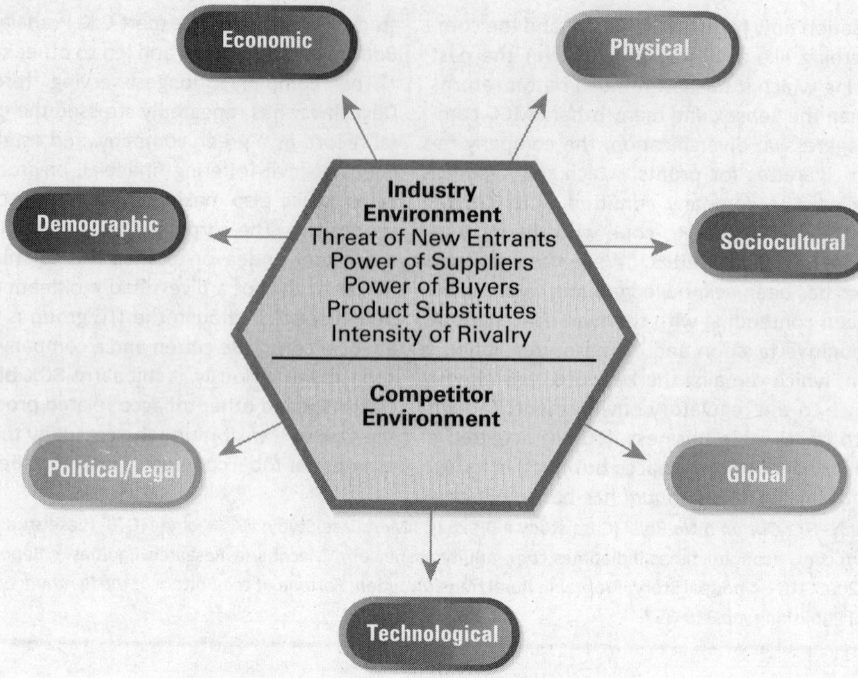

Figure 2.1 The external environment

external environment. The understanding about conditions in its external environment that the firm gains by analyzing that environment is matched with knowledge about its internal organization (discussed in the next chapter) as the foundation for forming the firm's vision, developing its mission, and identifying and implementing strategic actions (see Figure 1.1).

As noted in Chapter 1, the environmental conditions in the current global economy differ from historical conditions. For example, technological changes and the continuing growth of information gathering and processing capabilities increase the need for firms to develop effective competitive actions on a timely basis.[3] (In slightly different words, firms have little time to correct errors when implementing their competitive actions.) The rapid sociological changes occurring in many countries affect labor practices and the nature of products demanded by increasingly diverse consumers. Governmental policies and laws also affect where and how firms choose to compete.[4] In addition, changes to nations' financial regulatory systems that have been enacted recently are expected to increase the complexity of organizations' financial transactions.[5]

Viewed in their totality, the conditions that affect firms today indicate that for most organizations, their external environment is filled with uncertainty.[6] To successfully deal with this uncertainty and to achieve strategic competitiveness and thrive, firms must be aware of and fully understand the different segments of the external environment.

Firms understand the external environment by acquiring information about competitors, customers, and other stakeholders to build their own base of knowledge and capabilities.[7] On the basis of the new information, firms take actions, such as building new capabilities and core competencies, in the hope of buffering themselves from any negative environmental effects and to pursue opportunities as the basis for better serving their stakeholders' needs.[8] A firm's strategic actions are influenced by the conditions in the three parts (the general, industry, and competitor) of its external environment (see Figure 2.1).

The General, Industry, and Competitor Environments

The **general environment** is composed of dimensions in the broader society that influence an industry and the firms within it.[9] We group these dimensions into seven environmental *segments*: demographic, economic, political/legal, socio-cultural, technological, global, and physical. Examples of *elements* analyzed in each of these segments are shown in Table 2.1.

Firms cannot directly control the general environment's segments. The bankruptcy filings by General

Table 2.1 The general environment: segments and elements

Segment	Elements	Elements
Demographic Segment	• Population size • Age structure • Geographic distribution	• Ethnic mix • Income distribution
Economic Segment	• Inflation rates • Interest rates • Trade deficits or surpluses • Import controls and duties • Regulations on foreign investments • Budget deficits or surpluses	• Personal savings rate • Business savings rates • Gross domestic product
Political/Legal Segment	• Antitrust/competition laws • Taxation laws • Deregulation philosophies	• Labor training laws • Educational philosophies and policies
Sociocultural Segment	• Women in the workforce • Workforce diversity • Attitudes about the quality of work life	• Shifts in work and career preferences • Shifts in preferences regarding product and service characteristics
Technological Segment	• Product innovations • Applications of knowledge	• Focus of private and government-supported R&D expenditures • New communication technologies
Global Segment	• Important political events • Critical global markets	• Newly industrialized countries • Different cultural and institutional attributes
Physical Environment Segment	• Energy consumption • Practices used to develop energy sources • Renewable energy efforts • Minimizing a firm's environmental footprint • Anti pollution laws • Environmental clearance	• Availability of water as a resource • Producing environmentally friendly products

Motors and Chrysler Corporation in the United States during the 2008–2009 automotive crisis highlight this fact. These firms could not directly control various parts of their external environment, including the economic and political/legal segments; however, these segments are influencing the actions the firms are taking now including the forming of Chrysler's alliance with Fiat.[10] Because firms cannot directly control the segments of their external environment, successful ones learn how to gather the information needed to understand all segments and their implications for selecting and implementing the firm's strategies.

The **industry environment** is the set of factors that directly influences a firm and its competitive actions and responses:[11] the threat of new entrants, the power of suppliers, the power of buyers, the threat of product substitutes, and the intensity of rivalry among competitors. In total, the interactions among these five factors determine an industry's profit potential; in turn, the industry's profit potential influences the choices each firm makes about its strategic actions. The challenge for a firm is to locate a position within an industry where it can favorably influence the five factors or where it can successfully defend against their influence. The greater a firm's capacity to favorably influence its industry environment, the greater the likelihood that the firm will earn above-average returns.

How companies gather and interpret information about their competitors is called **competitor analysis.** Understanding the firm's competitor environment complements the insights provided by studying the general and industry environments.[12] This means, for example, that JSW Steel needs to learn as much as it can about its two major competitors— SAIL and Tata Steel—while also learning about its general and industry environments.

Analysis of the general environment is focused on environmental trends while an analysis of the industry environment is focused on the factors and conditions influencing an industry's profitability potential and an analysis of competitors is focused on predicting competitors' actions, responses, and intentions. In combination, the results of these three analyses influence the firm's vision, mission, and strategic actions. Although we discuss each analysis separately, performance improves when the firm integrates the insights provided by analyses of the general environment, the industry environment, and the competitor environment.

External Environmental Analysis

Most firms face external environments that are highly turbulent, complex, and global— conditions that make interpreting those environments difficult.[13] To cope with often ambiguous and incomplete environmental data and to increase understanding of the general environment, firms engage in external environmental analysis. This analysis has four parts: scanning, monitoring, forecasting, and assessing (see Table 2.2). Analyzing the external environment is a difficult, yet significant, activity.[14]

Identifying opportunities and threats is an important objective of studying the general environment. An **opportunity** is a condition in the general environment that if exploited effectively, helps a company achieve strategic competitiveness. For example, the success of Velvet Shampoo in sachets and Hindustan Unilever (HUL)'s own market research results suggested to HUL that there was a big opportunity in the low income segment to sell a variety of products through such small packets and still earn a good margin, and hence it created a new delivery system with independent rural women, financed through microfinance and trained by HUL to take up their selling and entrepreneurial role, through what it called *Project Shakti*.[15]

Independent rural women financed and trained by HUL to penetrate markets that were difficult through the traditional route.

A **threat** is a condition in the general environment that may hinder a company's efforts to achieve strategic competitiveness.[16] The once-revered firm Polaroid can attest to the seriousness of external threats. Polaroid was a leader in its industry and considered one of the top 50 firms in the United States. When its competitors developed photographic equipment using digital technology, Polaroid was unprepared and never responded effectively. It filed for bankruptcy in 2001. In 2002, the former Polaroid Corp. was sold to Bank One's OEP Imaging unit, which promptly changed its own name to Polaroid Corp. Jacques Nasser, a former CEO at Ford, took over as CEO at Polaroid and found that the brand had continued life. Nasser used the brand in a partnership with Petters Group to put the Polaroid name on "TVs and DVDs made in Asian factories and sell them through Wal-Mart and Target."[17] Polaroid went public again and was later sold to Petters Group in 2005. However, the firm then failed again, resulting in another bankruptcy filing in December 2008. On April 16, 2009, Polaroid was sold to a joint venture of Hilco Consumer Capital LP of Toronto and Gordon Brothers Brands LLC of Boston. At the time, the only assets remaining were the firm's name, its intellectual property, and its photography collection.[18] Similarly, in India, HMV (originally standing for His Master's Voice), with its famous and well loved symbol of a dog listening to the voice of its master in the musical record, did not meet the threat posed by, first, cassette tapes, and then by cheap, mass produced tapes selling famous film songs sung by budding artistes (thus avoiding royalty payments). The T series, pioneered by the late Gulshan Kumar, sold its cassettes for less than ₹20, while HMV was selling its cassettes for over ₹50. As a result, HMV nearly went out of existence.[19] Thus, not responding to threats in its external environment resulted in the failure of the once highly successful Polaroid Corp, and the near failure of HMV.

Table 2.2 Components of the external environmental analysis

Scanning	• Identifying early signals of environmental changes and trends
Monitoring	• Detecting meaning through ongoing observations of environmental changes and trends
Forecasting	• Developing projections of anticipated outcomes based on monitored changes and trends
Assessing	• Determining the timing and importance of environmental changes and trends for firms' strategies and their management

Firms use several sources to analyze the general environment, including a wide variety of printed materials (such as trade publications, newspapers, business publications, and the results of academic research and public polls), trade shows and suppliers, customers, and employees of public-sector organizations. People in *boundary-spanning* positions can obtain a great deal of this type of information. Salespersons, purchasing managers, public relations directors, and customer service representatives, each of whom interacts with external constituents, are examples of boundary-spanning positions.

Scanning

Scanning entails the study of all segments in the general environment. Through scanning, firms identify early signals of potential changes in the general environment and detect changes that are already underway.[20] Scanning often reveals ambiguous, incomplete, or unconnected data and information. Thus, environmental scanning is challenging but critically important for firms, especially those competing in highly volatile environments.[21] In addition, scanning activities must be aligned with the organizational context; a scanning system designed for a volatile environment is inappropriate for a firm in a stable environment.[22]

Many firms use special software to help them identify events that are taking place in the environment and that are announced in public sources. For example, news event detection uses information-based systems to categorize text and reduce the trade-off between an important missed event and false alarm rates.[23] The Internet provides significant opportunities for scanning. Amazon.com, for example, records significant information about individuals visiting its Web site, particularly if a purchase is made. Amazon then welcomes these customers by their name when they visit their Web site again. The firm sends messages to customers about specials and new products similar to those they had purchased in previous visits.

Indian banks need to continuously scan segments of their external environment to detect current conditions and to anticipate changes that might take place in different segments. For example, changes in interest rates, Cash Reserve Ratio regulations etc. need to be monitored, as also the regulations for opening new branches and customer service norms (these policies are part of the political/legal segment). The reason for this is that even small changes in these policies can affect the business of banks quite substantially.

Monitoring

When **monitoring**, analysts observe environmental changes to see if an important trend is emerging among those spotted through scanning.[24] Critical to successful monitoring is the firm's ability to detect meaning in different environmental events and trends. The recent (2008–2009) financial crisis found companies carefully monitoring the emerging trend of customers deciding to "go back to basics" when purchasing products. A reduction in brand loyalty may be an outcome of this trend. Companies selling carefully branded products should monitor this trend to determine its meaning—both in the short and long term.[25]

Effective monitoring requires the firm to identify important stakeholders as the foundation for serving their unique needs.[26] (Stakeholders' unique needs are described in Chapter 1.) Scanning and monitoring are particularly important when a firm competes in an industry with high technological uncertainty.[27] Scanning and monitoring can provide the firm with information; they also serve as a means of importing knowledge about markets and how to successfully commercialize new technologies the firm has developed.[28]

Forecasting

Scanning and monitoring are concerned with events and trends in the general environment at a point in time. When **forecasting**, analysts develop feasible projections of what might happen, and how quickly, as a result of the changes and trends detected through scanning and monitoring.[29] For example, analysts might forecast the time that will be required for a new technology to reach the marketplace, the period of time before different corporate training procedures are required to deal with anticipated changes in the composition of the workforce, or how much time will elapse before changes in governmental taxation policies affect consumers' purchasing patterns.

Forecasting events and outcomes accurately is challenging. Already in place, the trend of firms outsourcing call center work and logistics' activities to companies specializing in these activities appeared to accelerate as a result of the recent global crisis. Having noticed (through scanning) and monitored these outsourcing trends for some time, logistics companies such as DHL, FedEx and United Parcel Service are developing forecasts about possible increases in their business.[30] Indian firms depending a great deal on outsourcing by US companies are watching keenly how long the increasing trend of using their services might continue in the wake of growing American angst against outsourcing. Similarly, FMCG companies like Procter & Gamble (P&G) and Colgate-Palmolive, two firms selling carefully branded consumer products, are now forecasting the effects of the retailers' trend to "... tout their lower-priced, private-label goods and low cost Indian manufacturers of competing products (such as Babool toothpaste) and pressure their suppliers for lower prices." Thus, P&G and Colgate are forecasting the effects of the twin issues of the decisions by the retailers, to whom they sell products, to manufacture and sell their own consumer products while simultaneously seeking lower prices on the products they buy from them.[31]

Assessing

The objective of **assessing** is to determine the timing and significance of the effects of environmental changes and trends that have been identified.[32] Through scanning, monitoring, and forecasting, analysts are able to understand the general environment. Going a step further, the intent of assessment is to specify the implications of that understanding. Without assessment, the firm is left with data that may be interesting but are of unknown competitive relevance. Even if formal assessment is inadequate, the appropriate interpretation of that information is important: "Research found that how accurate senior executives are about their competitive environments is indeed less important for strategy and corresponding organizational changes than the way in which they interpret information about their environments."[33] Thus, although gathering and organizing information is important, appropriately interpreting that intelligence to determine if an identified trend in the external environment is an opportunity or threat is equally important.

As previously noted, through forecasting P&G and Colgate have identified a trend among many of the retailers to whom they sell their carefully branded products. Essentially, the trend is for these retailers to pressure firms such as P&G, Colgate, H. J. Heinz, and Kellogg's—to name a few—to reduce the prices at which they sell their products to the retailers. The ability of these retailers to produce and sell their own private-label merchandise supports their efforts to receive lower prices from branding giants such as those mentioned.

In addition, firms with well-known brands have detected a trend among consumers to receive more "value" when purchasing branded products. Having forecasted that this trend toward "wanting more value" may last beyond the current global recession, many of these firms are taking actions in response to their assessment of the significance of what may be a long-lasting trend toward value purchases. India, especially, is a highly value sensitive market, where customers are constantly searching for better value-for-money propositions. In the Strategic Focus 2.1, we describe actions that some firms with well-known brands are taking in response to an assessment that this trend may have significant effects on their operations, at least in the short run if not longer term as well.

STRATEGIC FOCUS

2.1 Consumers' Desire to Receive Additional Value When Purchasing Branded Products

In Chapter 3, we will note that *value* is measured by a product's performance characteristics and by its attributes for which customers are willing to pay. A number of companies producing brand-name products believe that the recent global crisis is producing a trend in which what customers *value* is changing. In slightly different words, through monitoring and scanning, companies are forecasting that the performance characteristics and product attributes for which today's customers are willing to pay are changing as a result of the recent global crisis. In addition, through assessment, companies producing name-brand products believe that changes in how customers define value are significant and may be long-lasting. In response, some firms are changing some of the performance characteristics and attributes of their products to create more value for customers. A comment from an analyst about this trend is: "... companies are having (under pressure) to consider their "value" equation to try to serve the millions of consumers who either can't afford premium experiences, or just don't want them anymore."

Let's consider some examples of "different" value that companies are now providing to customers. The desire for smaller homes is a trend spotted by builders of premium-priced homes. Builders of premium homes are using better designs to improve space utilization and traffic flow to create more value for customers. For example, Surya Roshni, a manufacturer of electric lamps, has introduced its T8 and T5 range of tube lights, that the company claims, will save 85 per cent energy. They are also claimed to be more environment friendly.[34] The value created by this product is twofold—reduced cost to the consumer and a reduction to energy consumption as a benefit to society as a whole. Moser Baer, the manufacturer of compact discs and legally copied movies on DVDs to sell high quality, legal movies, has come out with content loaded SD cards for use on mobile phones.[35] The cards come pre-loaded with films and music and offer anytime, anywhere entertainment to mobile users. Watching movies is highly popular in India, and so are mobile phones. Combining these two, the firm hopes, will enable it to offer a very unique value through its products.

Builders of premium homes are using better designs to improve space utilization and traffic flow to create more value for customers.

Other types of companies are also redefining the value their products provide to customers. Believing that "... value is not just cost; it's also taste, nutrition and quality," Del Monte Foods' advertising campaigns now emphasize that compared to some frozen and even fresh items, canned foods can offer better value when the customer combines cost with nutritional benefits. Frito-Lay (a division of PepsiCo) is increasing customer value by adding 20 per cent more product to selected bags of Cheetos, Fritos, and Tostitos without increasing prices. Michaels, a large chain of craft outlets, now emphasizes that when customers purchase their goods as raw materials for making various items they are becoming more sustainable in that they are "making stuff" rather than simply "buying more stuff."

As these examples suggest, all types of companies (and especially those selling brand-name products) are trying to create a different type of value for customers in response to trends they are observing in their general environment. Regardless of the good or service a firm offers, it seems that the following words from an analyst capture the challenge facing today's companies: "So here's a call to all companies: evaluate everything you are offering consumers to see how you can infuse the value of good value into your brand."

Sources: A. Athavaley, 2009, Eco-friendly—and frugal, *Wall Street Journal Online*, http://www.wsj.com, February 11; S. Elliott, 2009, Food brands compete to stretch a dollar, *New York Times Online*, http://www.nytimes.com, May 10; D. Kaplan, 2009, Value-oriented chains thrive amid recession, *Houston Chronicle Online*, http://www.chron.com, April 24; M. Penn, 2009, Value is the new green, *Wall Street Journal Online*, http://www.wsj.com, March 13; C. C. Miller, 2008, For craft sales, the recession is a help, *New York Times Online*, http://www.nytimes.com, December 23.

Segments of the General Environment

The general environment is composed of segments that are external to the firm (see Table 2.1). Although the degree of impact varies, these environmental segments affect all industries and the firms competing in them. The challenge to each firm is to scan, monitor, forecast, and assess the elements in each segment to determine their effects on the firm. Effective scanning, monitoring, forecasting, and assessing are vital to the firm's efforts to recognize and evaluate opportunities and threats.

The Demographic Segment

The **demographic segment** is concerned with a population's size, age structure, geographic distribution, ethnic mix, and income distribution.[36] Demographic segments are commonly analyzed on a global basis because of their potential effects across countries' borders and because many firms compete in global markets.

Population Size

The world's population doubled (from 3 billion to 6 billion) in the roughly 40-year period between 1959 and 1999. Current projects suggest that population growth will continue in the twenty-first century, but at a slower pace. The US Census Bureau projects that the world's population will be 9 billion by 2040.[37] By 2050, India is expected to be the most populous nation in the world (with over 1.8 billion people). In 2010, India's population was about 1.1 billion. China, the United States, Indonesia, and Pakistan are predicted to be the next four largest nations by population count in 2050. Firms seeking to find growing markets in which to sell their goods and services want to recognize the market potential that may exist for them in these five nations.

While observing the population of different nations and regions of the world, firms also want to study changes occurring within different populations to assess their strategic implications. For example, in 2006, 20 per cent of Japan's citizens were 65 or older, while the United States and China will not reach this level until 2036.[38] Aging populations are a significant problem for countries because of the need for workers and the burden of funding retirement programs. In Japan and other countries, employees are urged to work longer to overcome these problems. Interestingly, the United States has a higher birthrate and significant immigration, placing it in a better position than Japan and other European nations. India's median age is 25.9 years, significantly smaller than that of China (35.4 years), and this is expected to place India at an advantage over China in the coming years.[39] It also places it favorably as compared to UK (39.8 years) and USA (36.8 years). In fact, India has one of the youngest populations among the emerging economies, placing it at an advantage on many fronts.

Age Structure

As noted earlier, in Japan and other countries, the world's population is rapidly aging. In North America and Europe, millions of baby boomers are approaching retirement, but are postponing retirement due to the difficult economic conditions. However, even in developing countries with large numbers of people under the age of 35, birthrates have been declining sharply. In China, for example, by 2040 there will be more than 400 million people over the age of 60. On the other hand, India will push into the job market very young people, who will be better educated, and seek more skilled jobs. Thus these two countries will pose entirely different challenges.

Geographic Distribution

For decades, the Indian population has been shifting from the rural to the urban areas. There is also a steady migration from the states that have been stagnating, such as Bihar, to the more prosperous states such as Punjab, and to cities such as Mumbai and Delhi. Firms should consider the effects of this shift in demographics as well. For example, the cities will need more and different urban infrastructure such as roads, suburban transport systems, flyovers and water supply systems, and services such as waste disposal, sewage, supply of clean water, electricity, and so on. These offer immense opportunities as well as challenges. Less and less senior citizens are being cared for by their children, and they increasingly getting pushed to old age homes, or fend for themselves in smaller and quieter towns such as Rishikesh and Coimbatore. Thus, industries catering to these citizens, including food catering for older people who can no longer cook themselves, specialized medical care and house keeping services are likely to grow in future in these centers, as well as in the major cities where old age homes are likely to find greater demand.

Unlike in some other countries, the urban migration in India may not result in the need for less attention to the rural market. There is growth in purchasing power in rural areas, and the consequent increase in demand for a wide variety of goods and services. Thus, many marketers see rural markets as a huge growth market, needing their close attention.

Ethnic Mix

The ethnic mix of population in some countries changes continuously, although this is not a major problem in India. For example, with a population in excess of 40 million, Hispanics are now the largest ethnic minority in the United States. In fact, the US Hispanic market is the third largest "Latin American" economy after Brazil and Mexico. Spanish is now the dominant language in parts of the US states such as Texas, California, Florida, and New Mexico.[40] Indians also constitute a significant ethic group in some parts of USA (such as New Jersey and California) and UK (the South Hall area). Given these facts, some firms might want to assess the degree to which their goods or services could be adapted to serve the unique needs of Hispanic and Indian consumers. This is particularly appropriate for companies competing in consumer sectors such as grocery stores, movie studios, financial services, and clothing stores. "Indian" and "Chinese" grocery stores are common sights in many states in the US.

Changes in the ethnic mix also affect a workforce's composition.[41] In the United States, for example, the population and labor force will continue to diversify, as immigration accounts for a sizable part of growth. Projections are that the combined Latino and Asian population shares will increase to more than 20 per cent of the total US population by 2014[42]. Interestingly, much of this immigrant workforce is bypassing high-cost coastal cities and settling in smaller rural towns. Many of these workers are in low-wage, labor-intensive industries such as construction, food service, lodging, and landscaping.[43] For this reason, if border security is tightened, these industries will likely face labor shortages. However, that does not seem to have deterred US administration from imposing a steep hike in the fees for H 1 visas, ostensibly to finance greater protection of the US Mexico border.

Income Distribution

Understanding how income is distributed within and across populations informs firms of different groups' purchasing power and discretionary income. Studies of income distributions suggest that although living standards have improved over time, variations exist within and between nations.[44] Of interest to firms are the average incomes of households and individuals. For instance, the increase in dual-career couples has had a notable effect on average incomes. Although real income has been declining in general in some nations, the household income of dual-career couples has increased, especially in the United States; it is also an emerging trend in India. These figures yield strategically relevant information for firms. For instance, research indicates that whether an employee is part of a dual-career couple can strongly influence the willingness of the employee to accept an international assignment[45] or even transfers within the same country.

The assessment by some that in 2005 about 55 per cent of the world's population could be defined as "middle class" generates interesting possibilities for many firms. (For the purpose of this survey, **middle class** was defined as people with one third of their income left for discretionary spending after providing for basic food and shelter.) The size of this market may have "... immense implications for companies selling their products and services on a global scale."[46] Of course, the recent global financial crisis may affect the size of the world's "middle class." In India, the middle class is the focus of attention of many marketers, closely tracking their spending habits.[47]

The Economic Segment

The **economic environment** refers to the nature and direction of the economy in which a firm competes or may compete.[48] In general, firms seek to compete in relatively stable economies with strong growth potential. Because nations are interconnected as a result of the global economy, firms must scan, monitor, forecast, and assess the health of their host nation and the health of the economies outside their host nation.

As firms prepare to compete during the second decade of the twenty-first century, the world's economic environment is quite uncertain. Some businesspeople were even beginning to question the ability of economists to provide valid and reliable predictions about trends to anticipate in the world's economic environment.[49] The lack of confidence in predictions from those specializing in providing such predictions complicates firms' efforts to understand the conditions they might face during future competitive battles.

In terms of specific economic environments, companies competing in Japan or desiring to do so might carefully evaluate the meaning of the position recently taken by some that this nation's economy has ingrained flaws such as "... unwieldy corporate structures, dogged loyalty to increasingly commoditized business lines and a history of punting problems into the future."[50] Because of its acknowledged growth potential, a number of companies are evaluating the possibility of entering Russia to compete or, for those already competing in that nation, to expand the scope of their operations. However, statements by analysts in mid-2009 that "the banking crisis in Russia is in its very beginning"[51] warrant careful attention. If this prediction comes true, the Russian economy could become destabilized. In contrast, Vietnam's economy was expanding during late 2009 and being recognized as one in which opportunities might exist for companies from across the globe to pursue.[52] Needless to say, China and India are emerging as major markets, attracting investment and marketing efforts.

The Political/Legal Segment

The **political/legal segment** is the arena in which organizations and interest groups compete for attention, resources, and a voice in overseeing the body of laws and regulations guiding interactions among nations as well as between firms and various local governmental agencies.[53] Essentially, this segment represents how organizations try to influence governments and how they try to understand the influences (current and projected) of those governments on their strategic actions.

When regulations are formed in response to new laws that are legislated (e.g., the Sarbanes-Oxley Act dealing with corporate governance in USA—see Chapter 10 for more information), they often influence a firm's strategic actions. In India, the Securities and Exchange Board of India (SEBI) has been coming out with new regulations to improve corporate governance and to give a fair deal to investors. The Satyam scandal had led to demands for action against independent directors of the Board of Satyam, and this led to a fear among independent directors of their being held liable for the firm's misdeeds. In the wake of the Union Carbide case judgment in 2010, the independent directors were again reported to be "hounded" for their liability in the disaster.[54] As many as 340 independent directors were reported to have quit the Boards of different companies due this fear.[55] This has made it very hard for companies to find good and willing people for serving as independent directors. The transformation from state-owned to private firms (privatization) occurring in multiple nations, including India, has substantial implications for the competitive landscapes in a number of countries and across multiple industries.[56] The Delhi Metro, expected to cost ₹300 billion, will connect a large part of Delhi through this mass transit. This system, now on to its third phase, will require equipment and materials from different manufacturers of rail equipment all over the world: locomotives, rolling stock, signaling equipment, and so on. For global firms manufacturing high-speed rail equipment, this development requires them to forecast the demand for their products. The nuclear energy program of India, similarly, will stimulate demand for different kinds of nuclear power equipment and plant, including power plants globally.

Firms must also carefully analyze a new political administration's business-related policies and philosophies. Antitrust laws, taxation laws, industries chosen for deregulation, labor training laws, and the degree of commitment to educational institutions are areas in which an administration's policies can affect the operations and profitability of industries and individual firms across the globe. For example, the thrusts in the education sector pioneered by Union Minister, Mr. Kapil Sibal, notably his attempts to make education a right, facilitating the entry of foreign universities in India and attempts to reform the regulatory system in education are likely to change the education scenario in India significantly. Similarly, early signals from President Obama's administration that policies might be formed with the intention of reducing the amount of work US companies outsource to firms in other nations seemingly could affect information technology outsourcing firms based in countries such as India.[57] The introduction of legislation in the US Congress during the early tenure of the Obama administration suggested at least some support for these stated intentions.[58] Thus, many Indian companies might want to carefully examine the US administration's intentions to understand their potential effects. The recent emphasis on environmental impacts of major projects may impact the strategies of firms, especially those whose activities are environmentally sensitive. For example, Vedanta, the natural resources company, had plans to mine bauxite from a certain area in Orissa (Niyamgiri) to feed its aluminum smelters, but the government refused permission due to the impact it would have on environment and tribal displacement. A proposed new airport in Navi Mumbai is hanging fire for the same reasons.[59]

To deal with issues such as those we are describing, firms develop a political strategy to influence governmental policies that might affect them. Some argue that developing an effective political strategy is essential to the newly formed General Motors' efforts to achieve strategic competitiveness.[60] Reliance Industries is widely believed to have developed an ability to "manage" the political environment, and in the early years (the late 1970s and 1980s), when government control was significant, Reliance is believed to have been helped in its growth through what were seen as government policies that helped the company. In addition, the effects of global governmental policies (e.g., those related to firms in India that are engaging in IT outsourcing work) on a firm's competitive position increase the need for firms to form an effective political strategy.[61]

Firms competing in the global economy encounter an interesting array of political/legal questions and issues. For example, in mid-2009, leaders from South Korea and the European Union remained committed to developing a free trade agreement between the relevant parties. At the time, the two parties had worked for over two years to develop an agreement that many thought would benefit both by creating a host of opportunities for firms to sell their goods and services in what would be a new market for them. The key political challenge affecting the parties' efforts was the European Union's decision not to permit "… refunds South Korea pays to local companies who import parts from third countries before exporting finished goods."[62] Both South Korea and European Union firms are monitoring the progress of these talks in order to be able to forecast the effects of a possible trade agreement on their strategic actions.

The Socio-cultural Segment

The **socio-cultural segment** is concerned with a society's attitudes and cultural values. Because attitudes and values form the cornerstone of a society, they often drive demographic, economic, political/legal, and technological conditions and changes.

Societies' attitudes and cultural values appear to be undergoing possible changes at the start of the second decade of the twenty-first century. This seems to be the case in the United States and other nations as well. Attitudes and values about health care in the United States is an area where socio-cultural changes might occur. Statistics are a driving force for these potential changes. For example, while the United States "… has the highest overall health care expenditure as well as the highest expenditure per capital of any country in the world,"[63] millions of citizens there lack health insurance. Some feel that effective health care reform in the United States requires securing coverage for all citizens and lowering the cost of services.[64] Changes to the nature of health care policies and their delivery would likely to affect business firms, meaning that they must carefully monitor this possibility and future trends regarding health care in order to anticipate the effects on their operations. In India, public distribution system has long been a major corner stone of public policy, with the intention of making essential food grains and fuel (kerosene) available to the poorer sections of society, despite its major drawbacks. Similarly reservations for scheduled castes and scheduled tribes in education and jobs in government have been in existence since independence. The recent order by the government to enforce quotas also for OBCs (Other Backward Classes) as a means of giving better social justice to the people left behind in development or have been subject to discrimination in the past on the basis of their castes is an example of the government taking cognizance of the socio-cultural aspects.

STRATEGY RIGHT NOW

Read what one leading marketing consultant, Rama Bijapurkar says about changing consumer attitudes and how companies should be adapting in her book (2007), *We Are Like that Only: Understanding the Logic of Consumer India* (Penguin Books).

As the Indian labor force has increased, it has also become more diverse. A greater proportion consists of educated people; women have increased; the mix of castes has now a greater representation from the "other backward classes". In 1981, the total Indian workforce was about 245 million; in 2001, it was about 402 million. In the coming years, the Indian workforce can be expected to be composed of a greater proportion of women, a more "inclusive" representation from different castes and religions, and with significantly better education. The growing diversity in the workforce creates challenges and opportunities, including combining the best of both men's and women's traditional leadership styles. Although diversity in the workforce has the potential to improve performance, research indicates that management of diversity initiatives is required in order to reap these organizational benefits. Human resource practitioners are trained to successfully manage diversity issues to enhance positive outcomes.[65]

Another manifestation of changing attitudes toward work is the continuing growth of contract workers (part-time and temporary employees) throughout the global economy. This trend is significant in several parts of the world, including Canada, Japan, Latin America, Western Europe, and the United States. Each country and culture has unique values and trends. As suggested earlier, national cultural values affect behavior in organizations, and thus also influence organizational outcomes.[66] For example, the importance of collectivism and social relations in Chinese and Russian cultures lead to the open sharing of information and knowledge among members of an organization.[67] Knowledge sharing is important for defusing new knowledge in organizations and increasing the speed in implementing innovations. Personal relationships are especially important in China as *guanxi* (personal connections) has become a way of doing business within the country and for individuals to advance their careers in what is becoming a more open market society.[68] India is also a highly collectivistic society, with its own business groups and family businesses functioning in an interconnected manner. Understanding the importance of *guanxi* and Indian business groups and families is critical for foreign firms doing business in China and India respectively.

The Technological Segment

Pervasive and diversified in scope, technological changes affect many parts of societies. These effects occur primarily through new products, processes, and materials. The **technological segment** includes the institutions and activities involved with creating new knowledge and translating that knowledge into new outputs, products, processes, and materials.

Given the rapid pace of technological change, it is vital for firms to thoroughly study the technological segment.[69] The importance of these efforts is suggested by the finding that early adopters of new technology often achieve higher market shares and earn higher returns. Thus, both large and small firms should continuously scan the external environment to identify potential substitutes for technologies that are in current use, as well as to identify newly emerging technologies from which their firm could derive competitive advantage.[70]

Spencer Platt/Getty images

The Kindle DX, a new purpose-built reading device, features storage for up to 3,500 books. Amazon has also partnered with select major newspapers to offer readers discounts on the DX in return for long-term subscriptions.

As a significant technological development, the Internet has become a remarkable capability to provide information easily, quickly, and effectively to an ever-increasing percentage of the world's population. Companies continue to study the Internet's capabilities to anticipate how it may allow them to create more value for customers in the future and to anticipate future trends. For example, ITC's *e-Choupal* enables farmers to find out the best rates available in markets and a variety of other information. This has helped ITC's own tobacco business by reducing the power of middlemen over farmers.

In spite of the Internet's far-reaching effects, wireless communication technology is predicted to be the next significant technological opportunity for companies to apply when pursuing strategic competitiveness. Handheld devices and other wireless communications equipment are used to access a variety of network-based services. The use of handheld computers with wireless network connectivity, Web-enabled mobile phone handsets, and other emerging platforms (e.g., consumer Internet-access devices) is expected to increase substantially, soon becoming the dominant form of communication and commerce.[71] Today no taxi company would function without giving mobile phones to its drivers, nearly fulfilling Sunil Mittal's notion of every taxi driver having a mobile phone. (There are more than 50 million taxi drivers in India).[72]

Amazon.com's Kindle is an emerging wireless technology with capabilities firms should evaluate. In addition to books, customers can download an ever-increasing array of products to the Kindle. In mid-2009, over 275,000 of Amazon's books were available through the Kindle. Magazines and newspapers are available for purchase and use on the Kindle as well. The ease of reading daily newspapers on the Kindle without charge instead of waiting for the hard copy to be delivered is threatening the very existence of a host of newspapers. The Kindle can also be used to surf the Web and send e-mail messages.[73]

Currently in its second generation, there is no doubt that Amazon will continue developing more advanced versions of the Kindle with each version having additional functionalities. As a service, the Kindle creates opportunities for those wanting to distribute knowledge electronically but is a threat to companies whose strategies call for the distribution of physical "hard copies" of written words. As such, many firms should study this technology to understand its competitive implications.

Travel is an area where the Internet has made a major impact in India. After the launch of its IRCTC (Indian Railway Catering and Tourism Corporation) Web site and selling tickets through the web, purchase of tickets on Indian Railways has never been the same. Many Indian travel portals such as Makemytrip.com have been able to attract a sizeable number of customers to their sites. Makemytrip.com, which attracted 1.76 million air travel bookings at its site in 2010, has been registering a 50 per cent growth per year between 2007 and 2010.[74]

The Global Segment

The **global segment** includes relevant new global markets, existing markets that are changing, important international political events, and critical cultural and institutional characteristics of global markets.[75] There is little doubt that markets are becoming more global and that consumers as well as companies throughout the world accept this fact. Consider the automobile industry as an example of this. The global auto industry is one in which an increasing number of people believe that because "we live in a global community," consumers in multiple nations are willing to buy cars and trucks "from whatever area of the world."[76]

When studying the global segment, firms (including automobile manufacturers) should recognize that globalization of business markets may create *opportunities* to enter new markets as well as *threats* that new competitors from other economies may enter their market. This is both an opportunity and a threat for the world's automobile manufacturers—worldwide production capacity is now a potential threat to all of these global companies while entering another market to sell a company's products appears to be an opportunity. In terms of overcapacity, evidence indicated that in mid-2009, this global industry had "… the capacity to make an astounding 94 million vehicles each year (which is roughly) 34 million too many based on current sales."[77] This prediction of excess capacity suggests that most if not all automobile manufacturers may decide to enter markets that are new to them in order to try to sell more of the units they are producing.

The markets from which firms generate sales and income are one indication of the degree to which they are participating in the global economy. For example, in 2008, 53 per cent of McDonald's operating income was accounted for by its international operations.[78] Food giant H. J. Heinz earns over 60 per cent of its revenue outside the United States.[79] Consumer products giant Procter & Gamble, with operations in over 180 countries, recently generated over 56 per cent of its sales revenue in markets outside the United States.[80] All the IT firms in India have a very high percentage of their revenues from overseas operations. Thus in 2005, Infosys had just 1.7 per cent of its revenues coming from India; Tata Consultancy Services (TCS) about 12.7 per cent, Wipro about 6 per cent, and Cognizant negligible.[81] Now these firms have increased their revenues from India slightly, but still they are quite small. Thus, for these companies and so many others, understanding the conditions of today's global segment and being able to predict future conditions is critical to their success.

The global segment presents firms with both opportunities and threats or risks. Because of the threats and risks, some firms choose to take a more cautious approach to competing in international markets. These firms participate in what some refer to as **global focusing**. Global focusing often is used by firms with moderate levels of international operations and increase their internationalization by focusing on global niche markets.[82] In this way, they build on and use their special competencies and resources while limiting their risks with the niche market. Another way in which firms limit their risks in international markets is to focus their operations and sales in one region of the world.[83] In this way, they can build stronger knowledge and relationships in their markets. As they build these strengths, rivals find it more difficult to enter their markets and compete successfully.

In all instances, firms competing in global markets should recognize the different socio-cultural and institutional attributes of global markets. Earlier, we mentioned that South Korea and the European Union remain committed to developing a trade agreement that benefits both parties. If this happens, European Union companies (as well as those from other regions of the world) who choose to compete in South Korea must understand the value placed on hierarchical order, formality, and self-control, as well as on duty rather than rights. Furthermore, Korean ideology emphasizes communitarianism, a characteristic of many Asian countries. Korea's approach differs from those of Japan and China, however, in that it focuses on *inhwa,* or harmony. *Inhwa* is based on a respect of hierarchical relationships and obedience to authority. In India, this is conveyed by the term *aadar* or respect, especially for elders and for those higher in hierarchy. Alternatively, the approach in China stresses *guanxi*—personal relationships or good connections—while in Japan, the focus is on *wa,* or group harmony and social cohesion.[84] The institutional context of China suggests a major emphasis on centralized planning by the government. The Chinese government provides incentives to firms to develop alliances with foreign firms having sophisticated technology in hopes of building knowledge and introducing new technologies to the Chinese markets over time.[85]

The Physical Environment Segment

The **physical environment segment** refers to potential and actual changes in the physical environment and business practices that are intended to positively respond to and deal with those changes[86]. Concerned with trends oriented to sustaining the world's physical environment, firms recognize that ecological, social, and economic systems interactively influence what happens in this particular segment.[87]

There are many parts or attributes of the physical environment that firms should consider as they try to identify trends in this segment. Some argue that global warming is a trend firms and nations should carefully examine in efforts to predict any potential effects on the global society as well as on their business operations[88]. Energy consumption is another part of the physical environment that concerns both organizations and nations. Canada, for example, "... has formulated various strategic measures to accelerate the development of energy efficiency systems and renewable energy technologies and has made significant progress."[89]

Because of increasing concern about sustaining the quality of the physical environment, a number of companies are developing environmentally friendly policies. Pepsi India, for example, claims that during the last five years, it has reduced its requirements for water by 45 per cent and saved more than 3 billion liters of water due to its innovative programs; and that it has replenished more water than it has consumed through initiatives such as community programs, water harvesting, etc. [90] Pepsi has also initiated an award winning program to convert household waste into manure using vermiculture in South India, in partnership with an NGO, Exnora. In the process, it also generates employment to the poorer sections. [91]

As noted in the Opening Case, ITC is committed to sustainable tobacco farming and the efficient use of resources in recognition of the effects of its operations on the physical environment.

We discuss other firms' efforts to "reduce their environmental footprint" and, by doing so, to be good stewards of the physical environment. in the following Strategic Focus. As we note, the number of "green" products that companies are producing is continuously increasing.

As our discussion of the general environment shows, identifying anticipated changes and trends among external elements is a key objective of analyzing the firm's general environment. With a focus on the future, the analysis of the general environment allows firms to identify opportunities and threats. It is necessary to have a top management team with the experience, knowledge, and sensitivity required to effectively analyze this segment of the environment.[92] Also critical to a firm's choices of strategic actions to take is an understanding of its industry environment and its competitors; we consider these issues next.

Industry Environment Analysis

An **industry** is a group of firms producing products that are close substitutes. In the course of competition, these firms influence one another. Typically, industries include a rich mixture of competitive strategies that companies use in pursuing above-average returns. In part, these strategies are chosen because of the influence of an industry's characteristics.[93]

Compared with the general environment, the industry environment has a more direct effect on the firm's strategic competitiveness and ability to earn above-average returns.[94] An industry's profit potential is a function of five forces of competition: the threats posed by new entrants, the power of suppliers, the power of buyers, product substitutes, and the intensity of rivalry among competitors (see Figure 2.2).

The five forces model of competition expands the arena for competitive analysis. Historically, when studying the competitive environment, firms concentrated on companies with which they competed directly. However, firms must search more broadly to recognize current and potential competitors by identifying potential customers as well as the firms serving them. For example, the communications industry is now broadly defined as encompassing media companies, telecoms, entertainment companies, and companies producing devices such as phones and i-Pods. In such an environment, firms must study many other industries to identify firms with capabilities (especially technology-based capabilities) that might be the foundation for producing a good or a service that can compete against what they are producing.[95] Using this perspective finds firms focusing on customers and their needs rather than on specific industry boundaries to define markets.

When studying the industry environment, firms must also recognize that suppliers can become a firm's competitors (by integrating forward) as can buyers (by integrating backward). For example, several firms have integrated forward in the pharmaceutical industry by acquiring distributors or wholesalers. In addition, firms choosing to enter a new market and those producing products that are adequate substitutes for existing products can become a company's competitors. Next, we examine the five forces the firm analyzes to understand the profitability potential within the industry (or a segment of an industry) in which it competes or may choose to compete.

STRATEGIC FOCUS

2.2 Firms' Efforts to Take Care of the Physical Environment in which They Compete

The number of companies throughout the world that recognize that they compete within the confines of the physical environment and that they are expected to reduce the negative effect of their operations on the physical environment while competing continues to increase. Those concerned about the physical environment value this trend.

Producing and selling additional "green" (i.e., environmentally friendly) products is one company response to this trend. By mid-2009, for example, firms had launched almost 460 new green products such as toilet paper, diapers, and household cleaning products in the United States alone. Analysts saw these launches, which represented a threefold increase compared to launches in 2008, as more evidence that "green" is going mainstream. Most of the Indian banks and demat agencies have switched almost completely to electronic statements of accounts; many companies are making their Annual Reports available on their websites. Libraries are switching over to e-journals, eliminating the paper versions to an increasing extent; the Indian Institute of Management, Ahmedabad, for example, now gets only 50 per cent of its journals in hard paper form, besides getting a host of journals through data bases such as EBSCO.

In addition to green products, companies across the globe are committing to or increasing their commitment to environmental sustainability. McDonald's, for example, "takes its responsibility to the environment seriously." Green restaurant design, sustainable packaging and waste management, and energy efficiency are areas where McDonald's acts to reduce its environmental footprint. Dell Inc. recently announced that its operations are now "carbon neutral." Dell envisions this as an important step in the firm's quest to become "the greenest technology company on the planet." Google and Yahoo! have also pledged to become carbon neutral.

Procter & Gamble's easily shipped PUR packets have helped provide over 1 billion liters of clean drinking water since the creation of the Children's Safe Drinking Water program in 2004.

Honest Tea produces "delicious, truly healthy, organic beverages." Since its founding in 1998, the firm has had a very strong commitment to environmentally friendly business practices, including the way its new corporate headquarters was designed. In the company's words, "When came the time for a new office, we did our best to walk our talk and create an office that is environmentally friendly to both the planet and our employees." Honest Tea used reclaimed bricks, flooring, and desks when building its new facility.

Procter & Gamble (P&G) recently announced increased targets for its 2012 sustainability goals. Among the goals are the following: (1) develop and market at least $50 billion in cumulative sales of sustainable innovation products, (2) deliver a 20 per cent reduction (per unit of production) in carbon dioxide emissions, energy consumption, water usage and disposed waste from P&G plants, and (3) enable 300 million children to live, learn and thrive, and deliver three billion liters of clean water through P&G's Children's Safe Drinking Water program.' Dutch consumer products giant Unilever also has an ongoing commitment to sustainability. The firm's sustainability actions include reducing water usage in its plants, working with its suppliers to encourage sustainability practices on their parts, and improving the eco-efficiency of their manufacturing facilities.

A number of other companies mirror the commitments of these firms in response to emerging trends in the physical environment segment. In addition to positively responding to the observed trends in this segment of the general environment, there is some evidence that firms engaging in these types of behaviors outperform those failing to do so. This emerging evidence suggests that these behaviors benefit companies, their stakeholders, and the physical environment in which they operate.

Sources: 2009, Eco-friendly growth, *BusinessWeek*, May 4,5–6; 2009, Honest Tea, http://www.honesttea.com; June 12; 2009, McDonald's Corporate Responsibility, http://www.mcdonalds.com, June 12; 2009, Procter & Gamble deepens corporate commitment to sustainability, http://www.pandg.com, April 29; 2009, Introduction to Unilever, http://www .unilever.com, June 12; 2008, Procter & Gamble, Sustainability Full Report, http://www.pandg.com, May 10; J. Ball, 2008, Green goal of "carbon neutrality" has limits, *Wall Street Journal Online*, http://www.wsj.com, December 28; T. B. Porter, 2008, Managerial applications of corporate social responsibility and systems thinking for achieving sustainability outcomes, *Systems Research and Behavioral Science*, 25: 397–411.

Threat of New Entrants

Identifying new entrants is important because they can threaten the market share of existing competitors.[96] One reason why new entrants pose such a threat is that they bring additional production capacity. Unless the demand for a good or service is increasing, additional capacity holds consumers' costs down, resulting in less revenue and lower returns for competing firms. Often, new entrants have a keen interest in gaining a large market share. As a result, new competitors may force existing firms to be more efficient and to learn how to compete on new dimensions (e.g., using an Internet-based distribution channel).

The likelihood that firms will enter an industry is a function of two factors: barriers to entry and the retaliation expected from current industry participants. Entry barriers make it difficult for new firms to enter an industry and often place them at a competitive disadvantage even when they are able to enter. As such, high entry barriers tend to increase the returns for existing firms

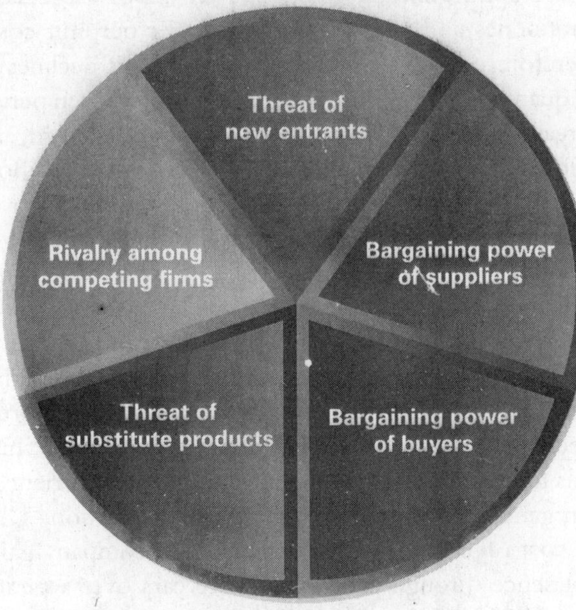

Figure 2.2 The five forces of competition model

in the industry and may allow some firms to dominate the industry.[97] Thus, firms competing successfully in an industry want to maintain high entry barriers in order to discourage potential competitors from deciding to enter the industry.

Barriers to Entry

Firms competing in an industry (and especially those earning above-average returns) try to develop entry barriers to thwart potential competitors. For example, the server market is hypercompetitive and dominated by IBM, Hewlett-Packard, and Dell. Historically, the scale economies these firms have developed by operating efficiently and effectively have created significant entry barriers, causing potential competitors to think very carefully about entering the server market to compete against them. Recently though, Oracle paid $7.4 billion to acquire Sun Microsystems, which is primarily a computer hardware company. Early evidence suggests that Oracle intends to "… focus Sun's server business on a small but promising segment of the market: computer appliances preloaded with Oracle software."[98] The degree of success Oracle will achieve as a result of its decision to enter the server market via an acquisition remains uncertain.

Several kinds of potentially significant entry barriers may discourage competitors from entering a market.

Economies of Scale These are derived from incremental efficiency improvements through operating larger plants and systems as a firm grows larger. For example, larger ships are cheaper to operate per ton of cargo; larger refineries and steel plants yield lower per unit costs. Therefore, the cost of producing each unit declines as the quantity of a product produced during a given period increases. This is the case for IBM, Hewlett-Packard, and Dell in the server market, as previously described. Both Maruti, the producer of cars, and Bajaj, the producer of scooters and motor cycles have attained unbeatable cost positions through their scale of production. Reliance Industries is an example where the management consciously went in for very large plant sizes comparable to global companies, making it nearly impossible for other Indian producers to compete based on costs. A different effect is the so called **experience curve effect**, which leads to higher efficiencies as a result of the experience a firm gains through higher cumulative production. Thus the cost of cars produced declines as a company gains experience through producing more cars over a period of time. This effect was studied first in the airplane production, and was found applicable to a large variety of situations, not merely in manufacturing, but in sales, distribution, etc.

Economies of scale can be developed in most business functions, such as marketing, advertising, manufacturing, research and development, and purchasing.[99] Increasing economies of scale enhances a firm's flexibility. For example, a firm may choose to reduce its price and capture a greater share of the market. Alternatively, it may keep its price constant to increase profits. In doing so, it will likely increase its free cash flow, which is very helpful during financially challenging times.

New entrants face a dilemma when confronting current competitors' scale economies. Small-scale entry places them at a cost disadvantage. Given the size of Sun Microsystems relative to the three major competitors in the server market, Oracle may, at least initially, be at a disadvantage in competing against them. Alternatively, large-scale entry, in which the new entrant manufactures large volumes of a product to gain economies of scale, risks strong competitive retaliation.

Some competitive conditions reduce the ability of economies of scale to create an entry barrier. Many companies now customize their products for large numbers of small customer groups. Customized products are not manufactured in the volumes necessary to achieve economies of scale. Customization is made possible by flexible manufacturing systems (this point is discussed further in Chapter 4). One good example of this is in the printing industry, where giants such as R.R. Donnelley & Sons, who basically owned large plants with long runs to be highly competitive, faced a completely different threat with the advent of digital printing. The latter was capable of infinite customization, at very little extra cost, and Donnelley set up its own digital business for catering to such businesses that could gain through customization.[100] In fact, the new manufacturing technology facilitated by advanced information systems has allowed the development of mass customization in an increasing number of industries. Although it is not appropriate for all products and implementing it can be challenging, mass customization has become increasingly common in manufacturing products.[101] In fact, online ordering has enhanced the ability of customers to obtain customized products. They are often referred to as "markets of one."[102] Companies manufacturing customized products learn how to respond quickly to customers' needs in lieu of developing scale economies.

Product Differentiation Over time, customers may come to believe that a firm's product is unique. This belief can result from the firm's service to the customer, effective advertising campaigns, or being the first to market a good or service. Currently, Ford Motor Company is seeking to differentiate its products from competitors on the basis that it is "... stronger, greener, and more technologically advanced than those other guys."[103] If successful with these efforts, Ford hopes those buying its cars today will generate the type of loyalty that results in repeat purchases.

Companies such as Hindustan Unilever (HUL), Procter & Gamble (P&G), and Colgate-Palmolive spend a great deal of money on advertising and product development to convince potential customers of their products' distinctiveness and of the value buying their brands provides.[104] Fair and Lovely has become a powerful brand, promising to improve the complexion. Customers valuing a product's uniqueness tend to become loyal to both the product and the company producing it. In turn, customer loyalty is an entry barrier for firms thinking of an entering an industry and competing against the likes of HUL, P&G, and Colgate. To compete against firms offering differentiated products to individuals who have become loyal customers, new entrants often allocate many resources to overcome existing customer loyalties. To combat the perception of uniqueness, new entrants frequently offer products at lower prices. Many firms and brands were spectacularly successful with such products, as for example, the famous Nirma detergent challenging HUL's brands, notably Surf, and Promise brand of toothpaste (and later on, Babool and a host of cheaper toothpastes) challenged the dominance of Colgate. Such entries may, however, result in lower profits or even losses.

Capital Requirements Competing in a new industry requires a firm to have resources to invest. In addition to physical facilities, capital is needed for inventories, marketing activities, and other critical business functions. Even when a new industry is attractive, the capital required for successful market entry may not be available to pursue the market opportunity. For example, steel, oil exploration, refining and marketing, fertilizers, and airlines are all industries that need a large capital to make an entry at all.

Switching Costs Switching costs are the one-time costs customers incur when they buy from a different supplier. The costs of buying new ancillary equipment and of retraining employees, and even the psychic costs of ending a relationship, may be incurred in switching to a new supplier. In some cases, switching costs are low, such as when the consumer switches to a different soft drink or when a consumer switches from Sunsilk shampoo to Head and Shoulders produced by a competitor. Switching costs can vary as a function of time. For example, in terms of credit hours toward graduation, the cost to a student to transfer from one university to another as a freshman is much lower than it is when the student is entering the senior year. Occasionally, a decision made by manufacturers to produce a new, innovative product creates high switching costs for the final consumer. Customer loyalty programs, such as airlines' frequent flyer miles, are intended to increase the customer's switching costs.

If switching costs are high, a new entrant must offer either a substantially lower price or a much better product to attract buyers. Usually, the more established the relationships between parties, the greater are switching costs.

In India, the commercial vehicles industry (buses) is an example of high switching costs. Usually, road transport corporations tend to have a fleet from a single manufacturer, such as Tata or Ashok Leyland. This enables them to achieve standardization of maintenance spares, equipment, skills, etc., and ease with which buses can be switched between routes. Hence they tend to resist the competitor's efforts to market their competing products.

Access to Distribution Channels Over time, industry participants typically develop effective means of distributing products. Once a relationship with its distributors has been built, a firm will nurture it, thus creating switching costs for the distributors. Access to distribution channels can be a strong entry barrier for new entrants, particularly in consumer nondurable goods industries (e.g., in grocery stores where shelf space is limited) and in international markets. New entrants have to persuade distributors to carry their products, either in addition to or in place of those currently distributed. Price breaks and cooperative advertising allowances may be used for this purpose; however, those practices reduce the new entrant's profit potential.

Cost Disadvantages Independent of Scale Sometimes, established competitors have cost advantages that new entrants cannot duplicate. Proprietary product technology, favorable access to raw materials, desirable locations, and government subsidies are examples. Successful competition requires new entrants to reduce the strategic relevance of these factors. Delivering purchases directly to the buyer can counter the advantage of a desirable location; new food establishments in an undesirable location often follow this practice.

Government Policy Through licensing and permit requirements, governments can also control entry into an industry. Liquor retailing, radio and TV broadcasting, and banking are examples of industries in which government decisions and actions affect entry possibilities. Also, governments often restrict entry into some industries because of the need to provide quality service or the need to protect jobs. Alternatively, deregulation of industries, exemplified by the airline industry and utilities in India, allows more firms to enter, often *too many* firms making it a case of hyper competition.[105] However, some of the most publicized government actions are those involving antitrust. In 2009, for example, the European Commission announced a fine of $1.4 billion—the largest the Commission had assessed—against Intel, the world's largest computer-chip maker. The fine was for "... breaking European antitrust rules."[106] The Commission's major conclusion was that Intel's competitive actions were blocking effective access by competitors to European markets. In response to the announcement, Intel indicated that it would appeal the fine as well as the ruling that the firm would have to change its business practices in the European Union.[107] These rulings caused other dominant firms such as Microsoft and Google to wonder about potential governmental rulings that the Commission might assess against them in the future. The law passed by Ohio State banning outsourcing of certain types of work in 2010, is expected to affect the operations of many companies in India that depend on such outsourcing.[108]

Expected Retaliation

Companies seeking to enter an industry also anticipate the reactions of firms in the industry. An expectation of swift and vigorous competitive responses reduces the likelihood of entry. Vigorous retaliation can be expected when the existing firm has a major stake in the industry (e.g., it has fixed assets with few, if any, alternative uses), when it has substantial resources, and when industry growth is slow or constrained. For example, any firm attempting to enter the airline industry at the current time can expect significant retaliation from existing competitors due to overcapacity.

Locating market niches not being served by incumbents allows the new entrant to avoid entry barriers. Small entrepreneurial firms are generally best suited for identifying and serving neglected market segments. When Honda first entered the US motorcycle market, it concentrated on small-engine motorcycles, a market that firms such as Harley-Davidson ignored. By targeting this neglected niche, Honda avoided competition. After consolidating its position, Honda used its strength to attack rivals by introducing larger motorcycles and competing in the broader market. Competitive actions and competitive responses between firms such as Honda and Harley-Davidson are discussed more fully in Chapter 5. Nirma exploited such a niche (of price conscious consumers) to produce a detergent that was substantially cheaper than Surf that appealed to a huge market of middle class consumers.[109]

Bargaining Power of Suppliers

Increasing prices and reducing the quality of their products are potential means suppliers use to exert power over firms competing within an industry. If a firm is unable to recover cost increases by its suppliers through its own pricing structure, its profitability is reduced by its suppliers' actions. A supplier group is powerful when

- It is dominated by a few large companies and is more concentrated than the industry to which it sells.
- Satisfactory substitute products are not available to industry firms.
- Industry firms are not a significant customer for the supplier group.
- Suppliers' goods are critical to buyers' marketplace success.
- The effectiveness of suppliers' products has created high switching costs for industry firms.
- It poses a credible threat to integrate forward into the buyers' industry. Credibility is enhanced when suppliers have substantial resources and provide a highly differentiated product.

The airline industry is one in which suppliers' bargaining power is changing. Though the number of suppliers is low, the demand for major aircraft is also relatively low. Boeing and Airbus aggressively compete for orders of major aircraft, creating more power for buyers in the process. India has emerged as a major market for aircraft, and the deals involve financial arrangements that are advantageous to the buyers. On the other hand, in the steel industry, firms that do not have captive mining facilities, such as JSW Steel, are at the mercy of mining companies that supply iron ore.

Bargaining Power of Buyers

Firms seek to maximize the return on their invested capital. Alternatively, buyers (customers of an industry or a firm) want to buy products at the lowest possible price—the point at which the industry earns the lowest acceptable rate of return on its invested capital. To reduce their costs, buyers bargain for higher quality, greater levels of service, and lower prices. These outcomes are achieved by encouraging competitive battles among the industry's firms. Customers (buyer groups) are powerful when

- They purchase a large portion of an industry's total output.
- The sales of the product being purchased account for a significant portion of the seller's annual revenues.
- They could switch to another product at little, if any, cost.
- The industry's products are undifferentiated or standardized, and the buyers pose a credible threat if they were to integrate backward into the sellers' industry.

ICP-UK/Alamy

With consumer access to news at their fingertips via the iPhone and other wireless devices, newspapers and other traditional news sources face increasing competition for customers.

Armed with greater amounts of information about the manufacturer's costs and the power of the Internet as a shopping and distribution alternative have increased consumers' bargaining power in many industries. One reason for this shift is that individual buyers incur virtually zero switching costs when they decide to purchase from one manufacturer to another or from one dealer as opposed to a second or third one. The Internet enables dissatisfied consumers to launch online campaigns, through Web sites, Facebook, Twitter, etc. to generate serious adverse publicity for companies. For example, the large utility vehicle, Hummer was targeted by people who felt that, with its size, it was encroaching on public spaces. They launched a Web site, www.ihumpedyourhummer.com. Similarly, a group of consumers accusing PayPal of making their terms of service unfriendly to customers launched a site, www.paypalsucks.com to give wide publicity to their allegations. HSBC had to reverse its charging graduating students 9.9% AR on their overdrafts. HSBC, in their press release, later stated that it was not too big to listen to its customers.[110]

Threat of Substitute Products

Substitute products are goods or services from outside a given industry that perform similar or the same functions as a product that the industry produces. For example, e-mail and fax machines replace postal mail and overnight deliveries, video conferencing can substitute travel (eliminating the need for face to face physical meetings), and plastic containers substitute glass containers. Newspaper firms have experienced significant circulation declines over the past decade or more. The declines are due to substitute outlets for news including Internet sources, cable television news channels, and e-mail and cell phone alerts. These products are increasingly getting popular, especially among younger, and technologically savvy people, and as product substitutes they have significant potential to continue to reduce overall newspaper circulation sales.

In general, product substitutes present a strong threat to a firm when customers face few, if any, switching costs and when the substitute product's price is lower or its quality and performance capabilities are equal to or greater than those of the competing product. Differentiating a product along dimensions that customers value (such as quality, service after the sale, and location) reduces a substitute's attractiveness.

Intensity of Rivalry Among Competitors

Because an industry's firms are mutually dependent, actions taken by one company usually invite competitive responses. In many industries, firms actively compete against one another. Competitive rivalry intensifies when a firm is challenged by a competitor's actions or when a company recognizes an opportunity to improve its market position.

Firms within industries are rarely homogeneous; they differ in resources and capabilities and seek to differentiate themselves from competitors.[111] Typically, firms seek to differentiate their products from competitors' offerings in ways that customers value and in which the firms have a competitive advantage. Common dimensions on which rivalry is based include price, service after the sale, and innovation.

The most prominent factors that, according to experience, affect the intensity of firms' rivalries are discussed in the succeeding paragraphs.

Numerous or Equally Balanced Competitors

Intense rivalries are common in industries with many companies. With multiple competitors, it is common for a few firms to believe they can act without eliciting a response. However, evidence suggests that other firms generally are aware of competitors' actions, often choosing to respond to them. At the other extreme, industries with only a few firms of equivalent size and power also tend to have strong rivalries. The large and often similar-sized resource bases of these firms permit vigorous actions and responses. The competitive battles between Pepsi and Coca-Cola exemplify intense rivalry between relatively equal competitors, and almost certainly will increase as the market for soft drinks in India becomes larger.

Slow Industry Growth

When a market is growing, firms try to effectively use resources to serve an expanding customer base. Growing markets reduce the pressure to take customers from competitors. However, rivalry in no-growth or slow-growth markets (slow change) becomes more intense as firms battle to increase their market shares by attracting competitors' customers.[112]

Typically, battles to protect market share are fierce. Certainly, this has been the case in the airline industry and in the soft drinks industry as the companies try to win each other's customers. Rivalry in power plant and equipment industry to get the orders for the new power plants being set up in emerging economies such as China and India is fierce. The instability in the market that results from these competitive engagements may reduce the profitability for all firms engaging in such competitive battles.

High Fixed Costs or High Storage Costs

When fixed costs account for a large part of total costs, companies try to maximize the use of their productive capacity. Doing so allows the firm to spread costs across a larger volume of output. However, when many firms attempt to maximize their productive capacity, excess capacity is created on an industry-wide basis. To then reduce inventories, individual companies typically cut the price of their product and offer rebates and other special discounts to customers. However, these practices, common in the US automobile manufacturing industry and the Indian telecom industry in the recent past, often intensify competition. The pattern of excess capacity at the industry level followed by intense rivalry at the firm level is observed frequently in industries with high storage costs. Perishable products, for example, lose their value rapidly with the passage of time. As their inventories grow, producers of perishable goods often use pricing strategies to sell products quickly.

Lack of Differentiation or Low Switching Costs

When buyers find a differentiated product that satisfies their needs, they frequently purchase the product loyally over time. Industries with many companies that have successfully differentiated their products have less rivalry, resulting in lower competition for individual firms. Firms that develop and sustain a differentiated product that cannot be easily imitated by competitors often earn higher returns. However, when buyers view products as commodities (i.e., as products with few differentiated features or capabilities), rivalry intensifies. In these instances, buyers' purchasing decisions are based primarily on price and, to a lesser degree, service. Personal computers are a commodity product. Thus, the rivalry between Dell, Hewlett-Packard, and other computer manufacturers is strong and these companies are always trying to find ways to differentiate their offerings (Hewlett-Packard now pursues product design and service as a means of differentiation.)

High Strategic Stakes

Competitive rivalry is likely to be high when it is important for several of the competitors to perform well in the market. For example, although it is diversified and is a market leader in other businesses, Samsung has targeted market leadership in the consumer electronics market and is doing quite well. This market is quite important to Sony and other major competitors, such as Hitachi, Matsushita, NEC, and Mitsubishi, suggesting that rivalry among these competitors will remain strong.

High strategic stakes can also exist in terms of geographic locations. For example, Japanese automobile manufacturers are committed to a significant presence in the US marketplace because it is the world's largest single market for automobiles and trucks. Because of the stakes involved in this country for Japanese and US manufacturers, rivalry among firms in the US and the global automobile industry is intense. With the excess capacity in this industry we mentioned earlier in this chapter, there is every reason to believe that the rivalry among global automobile manufacturers will become even more intense, certainly in the foreseeable future.

High Exit Barriers

Sometimes companies continue competing in an industry even though the returns on their invested capital are low or negative. Firms making this choice in all likelihood face high exit barriers, which include economic, strategic, and emotional factors causing them to remain in an industry when the profitability of doing so is questionable. Exit barriers are especially high in the airline industry. Although earning even average returns is difficult for these firms, they face substantial exit barriers, such as their ownership of specialized assets (e.g., large aircraft).[113] Due to the government regulations on closing down of firms, exit barriers are high in all industries in India. Common exit barriers include the following:

- Specialized assets (assets with values linked to a particular business or location).
- Fixed costs of exit (such as labor agreements).
- Strategic interrelationships (relationships of mutual dependence, such as those between one business and other parts of a company's operations, including shared facilities and access to financial markets).
- Emotional barriers (aversion to economically justified business decisions because of fear for one's own career, loyalty to employees, and so forth).
- Government and social restrictions (often based on government concerns for job losses and regional economic effects).

Interpreting Industry Analyses

Effective industry analyses are products of careful study and interpretation of data and information from multiple sources. A wealth of industry-specific data is available to be analyzed. Because of globalization, international markets and rivalries must be included in the firm's analyses. In fact, research shows that in some industries, international variables are more important than domestic ones as determinants of strategic competitiveness. Furthermore, because of the development of global markets, a country's borders no longer restrict industry structures. Rather, movement into international markets enhances the chances of success for new ventures as well as more established firms.[114]

Analysis of the five forces in the industry allows the firm to determine the industry's attractiveness in terms of the potential to earn adequate or superior returns. In general, the stronger competitive forces are, the lower the profit potential for an industry's firms. An unattractive industry has low entry barriers, suppliers and buyers with strong bargaining positions, strong competitive threats from product substitutes, and intense rivalry among competitors. These industry characteristics make it difficult for firms to achieve strategic competitiveness and earn above-average returns. Alternatively, an attractive industry has high entry barriers, suppliers and buyers with little bargaining power, few competitive threats from product substitutes, and relatively moderate rivalry.[115] Next, we explain strategic groups as an aspect of industry competition.

Strategic Groups

A set of firms that emphasize similar strategic dimensions and use a similar strategy is called a **strategic group.**[116] The competition between firms within a strategic group is greater than the competition between a member of a strategic group and companies outside that strategic group. Therefore, intrastrategic group competition is more intense than is interstrategic group competition. In fact, more heterogeneity is evident in the performance of firms within strategic groups than across the groups. The performance leaders within groups are able to follow strategies similar to those of other firms in the group and yet maintain strategic distinctiveness to gain and sustain a competitive advantage.[117]

The extent of technological leadership, product quality, pricing policies, distribution channels, and customer service are examples of strategic dimensions that firms in a strategic group may treat similarly. Thus, membership in a particular strategic group defines the essential characteristics of the firm's strategy.[118]

The notion of strategic groups can be useful for analyzing an industry's competitive structure. Such analyses can be helpful in diagnosing competition, positioning, and the profitability of firms within an industry.[119] High mobility barriers, high rivalry, and low resources among the firms within an industry limit the formation of strategic groups.[120] However, research suggests that after strategic groups are formed, their membership remains relatively stable over time, making analysis easier and more useful.[121] Using strategic groups to understand an industry's competitive structure requires the firm to plot companies' competitive actions and competitive responses along strategic dimensions such as pricing decisions, product quality, distribution channels, and so forth. This type of analysis shows the firm how certain companies are competing similarly in terms of how they use similar strategic dimensions.

Strategic groups have several implications. First, because firms within a group offer similar products to the same customers, the competitive rivalry among them can be intense. The more intense the rivalry, the greater the threat to each firm's profitability. Second, the strengths of the five industry forces differ across strategic groups. Third, the closer the strategic groups are in terms of their strategies, the greater is the likelihood of rivalry between the groups.

Competitor Analysis

The competitor environment is the final part of the external environment requiring study. Competitor analysis focuses on each company against which a firm directly competes. For example, Airtel, Vodafone, Reliance and BSNL; Coca-Cola and Pepsi, DHL and Fedex; and Boeing and Airbus are keenly interested in understanding their competitors' objectives, strategies, assumptions, and capabilities. Indeed, intense rivalry creates a strong need to understanding their competitors' objectives.[122] In a competitor analysis, the firm seeks to understand the following:

- What drives the competitor, as shown by its *future objectives.*
- What the competitor is doing and can do, as revealed by its *current strategy.*
- What the competitor believes about the industry, as shown by its *assumptions.*
- What the competitor's capabilities are, as shown by its *strengths* and *weaknesses.*[123]

Information about these four dimensions helps the firm prepare an anticipated response profile for each competitor (see Figure 2.3). The results of an effective competitor analysis helps a firm understand, interpret, and predict its competitors' actions and responses. Understanding the actions of competitors clearly contributes to the firm's ability to compete successfully within the industry.[124] Interestingly, research suggests that executives often fail to analyze competitors' possible reactions to competitive actions which their firm takes,[125] placing their firm at a potential competitive disadvantage as a result.

Critical to an effective competitor analysis is gathering data and information that can help the firm understand its competitors' intentions and the strategic implications resulting from them.[126] Useful data and information combine to form **competitor intelligence**: the set of data and information the firm gathers to better understand and better anticipate competitors' objectives, strategies, assumptions, and capabilities. In competitor analysis, the firm gathers intelligence not only about its competitors, but also regarding public policies in countries around the world. Such intelligence facilitates an understanding of the strategic posture of foreign competitors. Through effective competitive and public policy intelligence, the firm gains the insights needed to make effective strategic decisions about how to compete against its rivals.

When asked to describe competitive intelligence, it seems that a number of people respond with phrases such as "competitive spying" and "corporate espionage." These phrases denote the fact that competitive intelligence is an activity that appears to involve trade-offs.[127] According to some, the reason for this is that "what is ethical in one country is different from what is ethical in other countries." This position implies that the rules of engagement to follow when gathering competitive intelligence change in different contexts. However, firms avoid the possibility of legal entanglements and ethical quandaries only when their competitive intelligence gathering methods are governed by a strict set of legal and ethical guidelines.[128] This means that ethical behavior and actions as well as the mandates of relevant laws and regulations should be the foundation on which a firm's competitive intelligence-gathering process is formed. We address this matter in greater detail in the next section.

When gathering competitive intelligence, firms must also pay attention to the complementors of its products and strategy.[129] **Complementors** are companies or networks of companies that sell complementary goods or services that are compatible with the focal firm's good or service. When a complementor's good or service adds value to the sale of the focal firm's good or service it is likely to create value for the focal firm.

There are many examples of firms whose good or service complements other companies' offerings. For example, firms manufacturing affordable home photo printers complement other companies' efforts to sell digital cameras. Pen and ink manufacturers form a set of complementors. Intel and Microsoft are perhaps the most widely recognized complementors. The Microsoft slogan "Intel Inside" demonstrates the relationship between two firms who do not directly buy from or sell to each other but

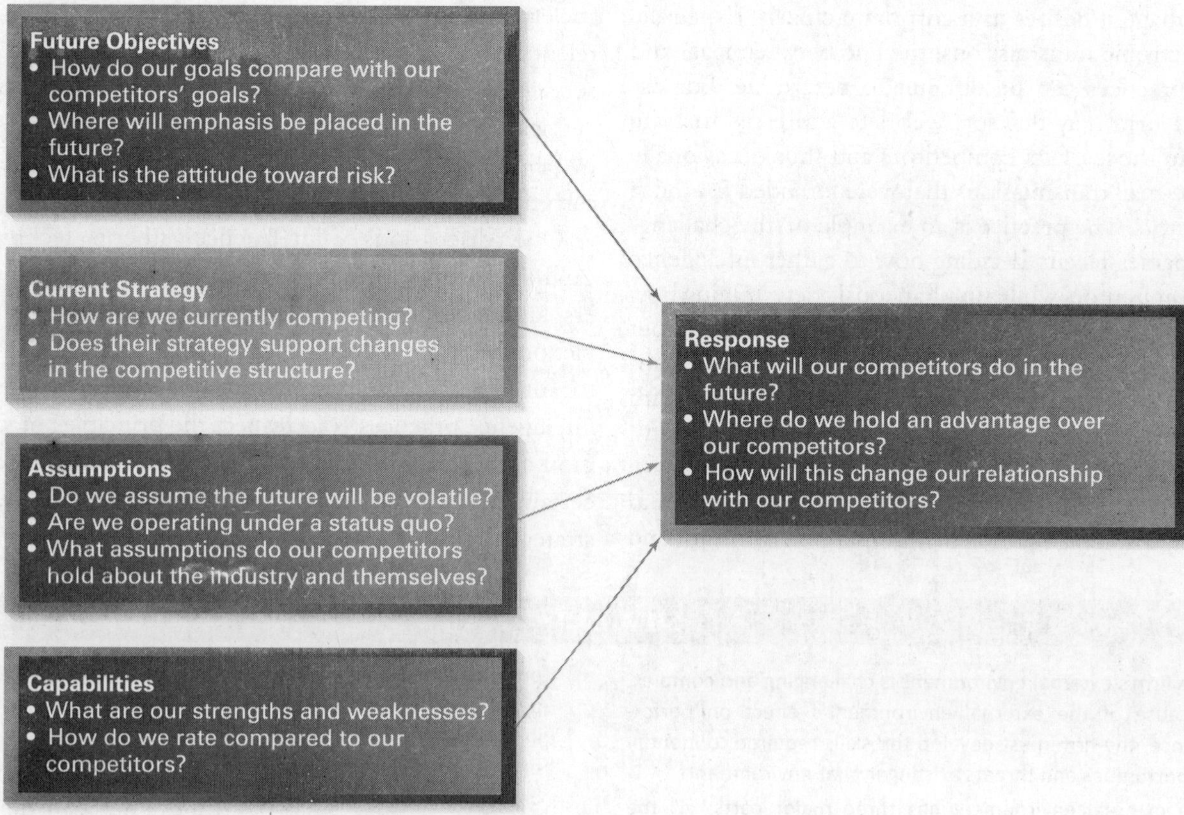

Figure 2.3 Competitor analysis components

whose products have a strong complementary relationship. Alliances among airline operations (e.g., the Star Alliance and the SkyTeam Alliance) find these companies sharing their route structures and customer loyalty programs as means of complementing each others' operations. (Each alliance is a network of complementors.) Recently, Continental Airlines announced that it was leaving the SkyTeam Alliance to join the Star Alliance. The primary reason for this change was to provide greater global coverage to Continental's customers by combining its routes with those of the other members of the Star Alliance.[130] In essence, Continental's conclusion was that the complementors of the Star Alliance created more value for its customers than did its complementors in the SkyTeam Alliance.

As our discussion shows, complementors expand the set of competitors firms must evaluate when completing a competitor analysis. For example, when Delta Airlines wants to study Continental Airlines, it must examine Continental's strategic actions as an independent company as well as its actions as a member of the Star Alliance. The same is true in reverse—Continental must study Delta's actions as an independent firm as well as its actions as a member of the SkyTeam Alliance. Similarly, Intel and Microsoft analyze each other's actions in that those actions might either help each firm gain a competitive advantage or damage each firm's ability to exploit a competitive advantage.

Ethical Considerations

Firms must follow relevant laws and regulations as well as carefully articulated ethical guidelines when gathering competitor intelligence. Industry associations often develop lists of these practices that firms can adopt. Practices considered both legal and ethical include (1) obtaining publicly available information (e.g., court records, competitors' help-wanted advertisements, annual reports, financial reports of publicly held corporations, and Uniform Commercial Code filings) and (2) attending trade fairs and shows to obtain competitors' brochures, view their exhibits, and listen to discussions about their products. In contrast, certain practices (including blackmail, trespassing, eavesdropping, and stealing drawings, samples, or documents) are widely viewed as unethical and often are illegal.

Some competitor intelligence practices may be legal, but a firm must decide whether they are also ethical, given the image it desires as a corporate citizen. Especially with electronic transmissions, the line between legal and ethical practices can be difficult to determine. For example, a firm may develop Web site addresses that are similar to those of its competitors and thus occasionally receive e-mail transmissions that were intended for those competitors. The practice is an example of the challenges companies face in deciding how to gather intelligence about competitors while simultaneously determining how to prevent competitors from learning too much about them. To deal with these challenges, firms should establish principles and take actions that are consistent with them. Infosys, the well known Indian software company, expresses the principles guiding its actions as: "to achieve our objectives in an environment of fairness, honesty, and courtesy towards their clients, employees, vendors and society at large.[131] It competes hard, but fairly: "To strive relentlessly, constantly improve ourselves, our teams, our services and products to become the best", but by being "ethical, sincere and open in all our transactions" and by being objective and transaction-oriented, and thereby earn trust and respect.

Open discussions of intelligence-gathering techniques can help a firm ensure that employees, customers, suppliers, and even potential competitors understand its convictions to follow ethical practices for gathering competitor intelligence. An appropriate guideline for competitor intelligence practices is to respect the principles of common morality and the right of competitors not to reveal certain information about their products, operations, and strategic intentions.[132]

SUMMARY

- The firm's external environment is challenging and complex. Because of the external environment's effect on performance, the firm must develop the skills required to identify opportunities and threats existing in that environment.
- The external environment has three major parts: (1) the general environment (elements in the broader society that affect industries and their firms), (2) the industry environment (factors that influence a firm, its competitive actions and responses, and the industry's profit potential), and (3) the competitor environment (in which the firm analyzes each major competitor's future objectives, current strategies, assumptions, and capabilities).
- The external environmental analysis process has four steps: scanning, monitoring, forecasting, and assessing. Through environmental analyses, the firm identifies opportunities and threats.
- The general environment has seven segments: demographic, economic, political/legal, socio-cultural, technological, global, and physical. For each segment, the firm wants to determine the strategic relevance of environmental changes and trends.
- Compared with the general environment, the industry environment has a more direct effect on the firm's strategic actions. The five forces model of competition includes the threat of entry, the power of suppliers, the power of buyers, product substitutes, and the intensity of rivalry among competitors. By studying these forces, the firm finds a position in an industry where it can influence the forces in its favor or where it can buffer itself from the power of the forces in order to achieve strategic competitiveness and earn above-average returns.
- Industries are populated with different strategic groups. A strategic group is a collection of firms following similar strategies along similar dimensions. Competitive rivalry is greater within a strategic group than between strategic groups.
- Competitor analysis informs the firm about the future objectives, current strategies, assumptions, and capabilities of the companies with which it competes directly. A thorough analysis examines complementors that sustain a competitor's strategy and major networks or alliances in which competitors participate. When analyzing competitors, the firm should also identify and carefully monitor major actions taken by firms with performance below the industry norm.
- Different techniques are used to create competitor intelligence: the set of data, information, and knowledge that allows the firm to better understand its competitors and thereby predict their likely strategic and tactical actions. Firms should use only legal and ethical practices to gather intelligence. The Internet enhances firms' capabilities to gather insights about competitors and their strategic intentions.

KEY TERMS AND DEFINITIONS

An **industry** is a group of firms producing products that are close substitutes.

An **opportunity** is a condition in the general environment that if exploited effectively, helps a company achieve strategic competitiveness.

A **threat** is a condition in the general environment that may hinder a company's efforts to achieve strategic competitiveness.

The **industry environment** is the set of factors that directly influences a firm and its competitive actions and competitive responses: the threat of new entrants, the power of suppliers, the power of buyers, the threat of product substitutes, and the intensity of rivalry among competitors.

The **demographic segment** is concerned with a population's size, age structure, geographic distribution, ethnic mix, and income distribution.

The **economic environment** refers to the nature and direction of the economy in which a firm competes or may compete.

The **political/legal segment** is the arena in which organizations and interest groups compete for attention, resources, and a voice in overseeing the body of laws and regulations guiding interactions among nations as well as between firms and various local governmental agencies.

The **sociocultural segment** is concerned with a society's attitudes and cultural values.

The **technological segment** includes the institutions and activities involved with creating new knowledge and translating that knowledge into new outputs, products, processes, and materials.

The **physical environment segment** refers to potential and actual changes in the physical environment and business practices that are intended to positively respond to and deal with those changes.

A **strategic group** is a set of firms emphasizing similar strategic dimensions to use a similar strategy.

[Comp: Marginal definitions below]

An industry is a group of firms producing products that are close substitutes.

Competitor intelligence is the set of data and information the firm gathers to better understand and better anticipate competitors' objectives, strategies, assumptions, and capabilities.

Complementors are companies or networks of companies that sell complementary goods or services that are compatible with the focal firm's good or service.

The **global segment** includes relevant new global markets, existing markets that are changing, important international political events, and critical cultural and institutional characteristics of global markets.

The **general environment** is composed of dimensions in the broader society that influence an industry and the firms within it.

REVIEW QUESTIONS

1. Why is it important for a firm to study and understand the external environment?
2. What are the differences between the general environment and the industry environment? Why are these differences important?
3. What is the external environmental analysis process (four steps)? What does the firm want to learn when using this process?
4. What are the seven segments of the general environment? Explain the differences among them.
5. How do the five forces of competition in an industry affect its profit potential? Explain.
6. What is a strategic group? Of what value is knowledge of the firm's strategic group in formulating that firm's strategy?
7. What is the importance of collecting and interpreting data and information about competitors? What practices should a firm use to gather competitor intelligence and why?

EXPERIENTIAL EXERCISES

Exercise 1: Airline Competitor Analysis

The International Air Transport Association (IATA) reports statistics on the number of passengers carried each year by major airlines. Passenger data for 2007 are reported for the top 10 carriers in three categories:

- International flights
- Domestic flights
- Combined traffic, domestic and international flights

The following table lists both passenger data and rankings for each category:

Airline	Intl Rank	Intl Passengers	Domestic Rank	Domestic Passengers	Combined Rank	Combined Passengers
Air France	3	31,549			8	50,465
All Nippon Airways			6	44,792		
American Airlines	7	21,479	2	76,687	2	98,166
British Airways	5	28,302				
Cathay Pacific	10	17,695				
China Southern Airlines			5	52,505	5	56,522
Continental Airlines			9	37,175	9	49,059
Delta Air Lines			3	61,651	3	73,086

Easyjet	4	30,173				
Emirates	8	20,448				
Japan Airlines International			10	35,583		
KLM	6	23,165				
Lufthansa	2	41,322			7	54,165
Northwest Airlines			7	44,337	6	54,696
Ryanair	1	49,030			10	49,030
Singapore Airlines	9	18,957				
Southwest Airlines			1	101,911	1	101,911
United Airlines			4	58,162	4	68,363
US Airways Inc.			8	37,560		

For this exercise, you will develop competitor profiles of selected air carriers.

Part One

Working in groups of five to seven people, each team member selects one airline from the table. The pool of selected airlines should contain roughly an even balance of three regions: North America, Europe/Middle East, and Asia. Answer the following questions:

What drives this competitor? (i.e., what are its objectives?)

What is its current strategy?

What does this competitor believe about its industry?

What are its strengths and weaknesses?

Does this airline belong to an airline alliance (e.g., Oneworld, Star, SkyTeam)?

When researching your companies, you should use multiple resources. The company's Web site is a good starting point. Public firms headquartered in the United States will also have annual reports and 10-K reports filed with the Securities and Exchange Commission.

Part Two

As a group, summarize the results of each competitor profile into a single table with columns for objectives, current strategy, beliefs, strengths, weaknesses, and alliance partner(s). Then, discuss the following topics:

Which airlines had the most similar strategies? The most different? Would you consider any of the firms you studied to be in the same strategic group (i.e., a group of firms that follows similar strategies along similar dimensions)?

Create a composite five forces model based on the firms you reviewed. How might these elements of industry structure (e.g., substitutes, or bargaining power of buyers) differ from the perspective of individual airlines?

Which airlines appear best positioned to succeed in the future? Why?

Exercise 2: What Does the Future Look Like?

A critical ingredient to studying the general environment is identifying opportunities and threats. As discussed in this chapter, an opportunity is a condition in the environment that, if exploited, helps a company achieve strategic competitiveness. In order to identify opportunities, one must be aware of current and future trends affecting the world around us.

Thomas Fry, senior futurist at the DaVinci Institute, says that the chaotic nature of interconnecting trends and the vast array of possibilities that arise from them is somewhat akin to watching a spinning compass needle. From the way we use phones and e-mail, or recruit new workers to organizations, the climate for business is changing and shifting dramatically and at rapidly increasing rates. Sorting out these changes and making sense of them provides the basis for opportunity decision making. Which ones will dominate and which will fade? Understanding this is crucial for business success.

Your challenge (either individually or as a group) is to identify a trend, technology, entertainment, or design that is likely to alter the way in which business is conducted in the future. Once you have identified your topic, be prepared to discuss:

- Which of the seven segments of the general environment will this affect? (There may be more than one.)
- Describe the impact.
- List some business opportunities that will come from this.
- Identify some existing organizations that stand to benefit.
- What, if any, are the ethical implications?

You should consult a wide variety of sources. For example, the Gartner Group and McKinsey & Company produce market research and forecasts for business. There are also many Web forecasting tools and addresses such as TED (Technology, Entertainment, Design). TED hosts an annual conference for groundbreaking ideas, and you can find videos of their discussions on their Web site. Similarly the DaVinci Institute, Institute for Global Futures, and a host of others offer their own unique vision for tomorrow's environment.

The Internal Environment: Resources, Capabilities, Competencies, and Competitive Advantages

CHAPTER

3

Studying this chapter should provide you with the strategic management knowledge needed to

- Explain why firms need to study and understand their internal organization.
- Define value and discuss its importance.
- Describe the differences between tangible and intangible resources.
- Define capabilities and discuss their development.
- Describe four criteria used to determine whether resources and capabilities are core competencies.
- Explain how value chain analysis is used to identify and evaluate resources and capabilities.
- Define outsourcing and discuss reasons for its use.
- Discuss the importance of identifying internal strengths and weaknesses.

OPENING CASE
Apple Defies Gravity with Innovative Genius

During a bad recession in 2008, Apple recorded record sales. The firm's strong performance in poor economic times is largely credited to its innovation capabilities. Apple has continued to upgrade its current products, such as its laptops, with enhancements (e.g., MacBook and MacBook Pro). Analysts believe that these innovative additions will keep Apple's "hot streak" alive and well. Furthermore, projections suggest that smartphone sales will surge over the next few years. These projections include a 200 per cent increase in the sales of high-end mobile phones by 2013, to 300 million in annual sales. The growing popularity of Web 2.0 applications such as Facebook and Twitter are increasing the desire for these phones. Such demand is very positive for the future of BlackBerry and Apple's iPhone. By 2013, analysts believe that approximately 23 per cent of all new mobile phone sales will be smartphones.

Apple has also continued to upgrade its innovative iPod with its second generation of iPod touch. One analyst gave it a perfect score for the significant enhancements made. And the iPod touch serves some similar functions as the iPhone such as providing an Internet connection, using the same touchscreen, and playing music and videos in the same way. An example of the continuous innovation is the 4-gigabyte iPod Shuffle introduced in 2009. It is less than two inches long (smaller than a double-A battery) and can store approximately 1,000 songs. This is the third-generation Shuffle—the first-generation Shuffle launched in 2005 could store approximately 240 songs. In addition to increased storage, the new Shuffle can handle songs in 14 different languages. Apple has "set the standard" for design of personal computer since the mid-1990s. Since 1996, Apple product innovations include developing a tool that created a quantum increase in the sale of digital music, creating a mobile phone—a flexible computer—that is fun to use, and, in customer service, developing a chain of unique and popular retail stores. Thus, most external observers argue that Apple's innovative products have led to their becoming one of the fastest-growing companies in the United States.

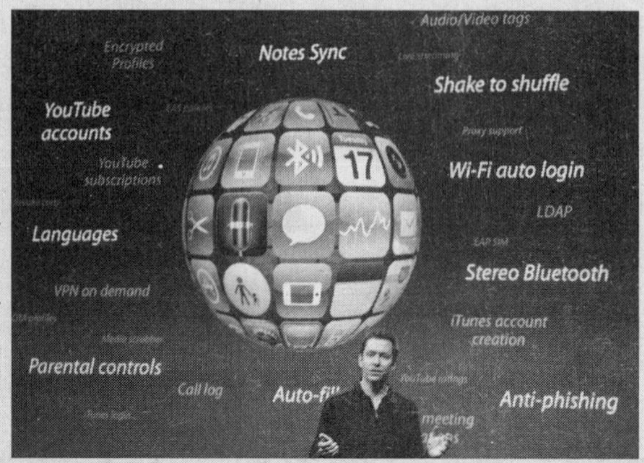

Robert Galbraith/Reuters/Landov

Apple now offers more than 50,000 applications for the iPhone, enabling their customers to continually discover new uses for their smartphone.

Coupled with its innovation, Apple is an aggressive marketer. While most firms were paring back their costs and advertising during the recession, Apple increased its marketing and advertising programs. It is the second most prolific technology advertiser, after Microsoft.

While Apple is in a positive market position, it did experience potential problems in 2009. Its charismatic leader, Steve Jobs, had to take a medical leave of absence, causing uncertainty about the company's future. It also lost a few other top managers to key positions in other firms. Thus, investors became nervous and analysts questioned whether the firm could continue to be a market innovator, especially without Jobs.

Sources: C. Wildstrom, 2008, Apple laptops: The hits keep coming, *BusinessWeek*, http://businessweek.com, November 4; C. Edwards, 2008, Apple's superlative sequel: The latest iPod touch, *BusinessWeek*, http://businessweek.com, November 20; R. Waters & C. Nutialin, 2009, Apple moves to clear up uncertainty ahead of Jobs' absence, *Financial Times,* http://www.ft.com, January 16; B. Stone, 2009, Can Apple fill the void? *The New York Times,* http://www.nytimes.com, January 16; Apple bobbing, *Financial Times,*. http://www.ft.com, January 22; N. Lomas, 2009, Smartphones set to surge, *Business Week,* http://businessweek.com, February 3; B. Stone, 2009, In campaign wars, Apple still has Microsoft's number, *The New York Times,* http://www.nytimes.com, February 4; P. Elmer-Dewitt, 2009, Apple is 14th fastest-growing tech company, *Fortune,* http://www.fortune.com, February 6; Apple launches smaller, 4-gigabyte iPod shuffle, *Houston Chronicle,* http://www.chron.com, March 11.

As discussed in the first two chapters, several factors in the global economy, including the rapid development of the Internet's capabilities[1] and of globalization in general have made it increasingly difficult for firms to find ways to develop a competitive advantage that can be sustained for any period of time.[2] As is suggested by Apple's experiences, innovation may be a vital path to efforts to develop sustainable competitive advantages.[3] Sometimes, product innovation serves simultaneously as the foundation on which a firm is started as well as the source of its competitive advantages. This occurred with Apple. Steve Jobs was one of the cofounders of the company and helped to develop the personal computer that the company introduced to the market. Later, Jobs and the board of directors of Apple felt the need for more marketing expertise. So, a new CEO with a strong marketing background was brought in to the firm. Later Jobs was forced out and Apple lost its innovative approach. However, Jobs was brought back into the firm in 1997; he is commonly believed to be the savior of the company because he was able to revitalize the firm's innovation capabilities. Thus, his departure on medical leave, announced in December 2008 (see opening case), created uncertainty and concern on the part of investors.[4]

Competitive advantages and the differences they create in firm performance are often strongly related to the resources firms hold and how they are managed.[5] "Resources are the foundation for strategy, and unique bundles of resources generate competitive advantages that lead to wealth creation."[6] As Apple's experience shows, resources must be managed to simultaneously allow production efficiency and an ability to form competitive advantages such as the consistent development of innovative products.

To identify and successfully use resources over time, those leading firms need to think constantly about how to manage them to increase the value for customers who "are arbiters of value"[7] as they compare firms' goods and services against each other before making a purchase decision. As this chapter shows, firms achieve strategic competitiveness and earn above-average returns when their unique core competencies are effectively acquired, bundled, and leveraged to take advantage of opportunities in the external environment in ways that create value for customers.[8]

People are an especially critical resource for helping organizations learn how to continuously innovate as a means of achieving successful growth.[9] In other words, "smart growth" happens when the firm manages its need to grow with its ability to successfully manage growth.[10] People are a critical resource to efforts to grow successfully at 3M, where the director of global compensation says that harnessing the innovative powers of the firm's employees is the means for rekindling growth.[11] And, people at 3M as well as virtually all other firms who know how to effectively manage resources to help organizations learn how to continuously innovate are themselves a source of competitive advantage.[12] In fact, a global labor market now exists as firms seek talented individuals to add to their fold. As Richard Florida argues, "Wherever talent goes, innovation, creativity, and economic growth are sure to follow."[13]

The fact that over time the benefits of any firm's value-creating strategy can be duplicated by its competitors is a key reason for having employees who know how to manage resources. These employees are critical to firms' efforts to perform well. Because all competitive advantages have a limited life,[14] the question of duplication is not if it will happen, but when. In general, the sustainability of a competitive advantage is a function of three factors: (1) the rate of core competence obsolescence because of environmental changes, (2) the availability of substitutes for the core competence, and (3) the imitability of the core competence.[15] The challenge for all firms, then, is to effectively manage current core competencies while simultaneously developing new ones.[16] Only when firms develop a continuous stream of capabilities that contribute to competitive advantages do they achieve strategic competitiveness, earn above-average returns, and remain ahead of competitors (see Chapter 5).

In Chapter 2, we examined the general, industry, and competitor environments. Equipped with this knowledge about the realities and conditions of their external environment, firms have a better understanding of marketplace opportunities and the characteristics of the competitive environment in which those opportunities exist. In this chapter, we focus on the firm itself. By analyzing its internal organization, a firm determines what it can do. Matching what a firm can do (a function of its resources, capabilities, core competencies, and competitive advantages) with what it might do (a function of opportunities and threats in the external environment) allows the firm to develop vision, pursue its mission, and select and implement its strategies.

We begin this chapter by briefly discussing conditions associated with analyzing the firm's internal organization. We then discuss the roles of resources and capabilities in developing core competencies, which are the sources of the firm's competitive advantages. Included in this discussion are the techniques firms use to identify and evaluate resources and capabilities and the criteria for selecting core competencies from among them. Resources and capabilities are not inherently valuable, but they create value when the firm can use them to perform certain activities that result in a competitive advantage. Accordingly, we also discuss the value chain concept and examine four criteria to evaluate core competencies that establish competitive advantage.[17] The chapter closes with cautionary comments about the need for firms to prevent their core competencies from becoming core rigidities. The existence of core rigidities indicates that the firm is too anchored to its past, which prevents it from continuously developing new competitive advantages.

Analyzing the Internal Organization

The Context of Internal Analysis

In the global economy, traditional factors such as labor costs, access to financial resources and raw materials, and protected or regulated markets remain sources of competitive advantage, but to a lesser degree.[18] One important reason is that competitors can apply their resources to successfully use an international strategy (discussed in Chapter 8) as a means of overcoming the advantages created by these more traditional sources. For example, Volkswagen began establishing production facilities in Slovakia "shortly after the Russians moved out" as part of its international strategy. Volkswagen is thought to have a competitive advantage over rivals such as France's Peugeot Citroen and South Korea's Kia Motors, firms that are now investing in Slovakia in an effort to duplicate the competitive advantage that has accrued to Volkswagen. In 2008, a total of 770,000 automobiles were manufactured in Slovakia[19]

© AP Photo/CTK, Jan Koller

Using a global mind-set, Volkswagen's leaders decided that the firm should open facilities in Slovakia. Opening these facilities long before their competitors has led to a distinct competitive advantage for VW in Slovakia and surrounding countries.

Increasingly, those who analyze their firm's internal organization should use a **global mind-set** to do so. A global mind-set is the ability to analyze, understand, and manage (if in a managerial position) an internal organization in ways that are not dependent on the assumptions of a single country, culture, or context.[20] Because they are able to span artificial boundaries,[21] those with a global mind-set recognize that their firms must possess resources and capabilities that allow understanding of and appropriate responses to competitive situations that are influenced by country-specific factors and unique societal cultures. Firms populated with people having a global mind-set have a "key source of long-term competitive advantage in the global marketplace."[22]

Finally, analysis of the firm's internal organization requires that evaluators examine the firm's portfolio of resources and the *bundles* of heterogeneous resources and capabilities managers have created.[23] This perspective suggests that individual firms possess at least some resources and capabilities that other companies do not—at least not in the same combination. Resources are the source of capabilities, some of which lead to the development of a firm's core competencies or its competitive advantages.[24] Understanding how to *leverage* the firm's unique bundle of resources and capabilities is a key outcome decision makers seek when analyzing the internal organization.[25] Figure 3.1 illustrates the relationships among resources, capabilities, and core competencies and shows how firms use them to create strategic competitiveness. Before examining these topics in depth, we describe value and its creation.

Creating Value

By exploiting their core competencies to meet if not exceed the demanding standards of global competition, firms create value for customers.[26] **Value** is measured by a product's performance characteristics and by its attributes for which customers are willing to pay. Customers of Udupi restaurants, for example, pay for meals that are value-priced, generally healthy, and served quickly in a casual setting, like Luby Cafétarias in the West.[27]

Firms with a competitive advantage offer value to customers that is superior to the value competitors provide.[28] Firms create value by innovatively bundling and leveraging their resources and capabilities.[29] Firms unable to creatively bundle and leverage their resources and capabilities in ways that create value for customers suffer performance declines. Sometimes, it seems that these declines may happen because firms fail to understand what customers value. For example, after learning that General Motors (GM) intended to focus on visual design to create value for buyers, one former GM customer said that

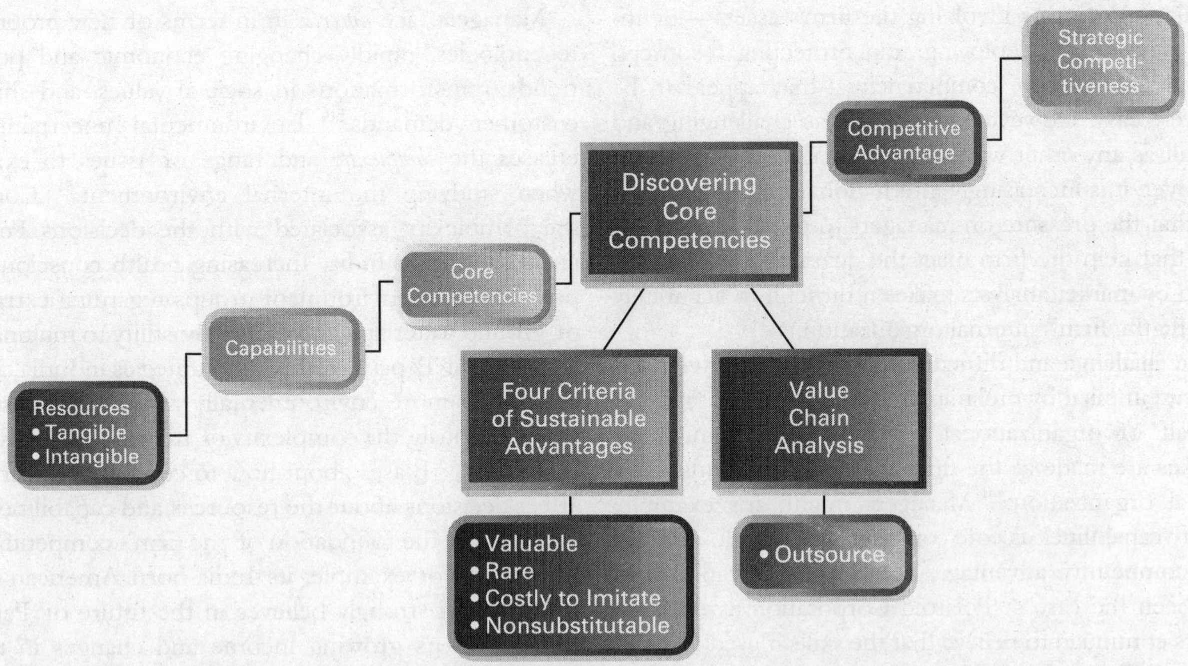

Figure 3.1 Components of internal analysis leading to competitive advantage and strategic competitiveness

in his view, people buying cars and trucks valued durability, reliability, good fuel economy, and a low cost of operation more than visual design.[30]

Ultimately, creating value for customers is the source of above-average returns for a firm. What the firm intends regarding value creation affects its choice of business-level strategy (see Chapter 4) and its organizational structure (see Chapter 11).[31] In Chapter 4's discussion of business-level strategies, we note that value is created by a product's low cost, by its highly differentiated features, or by a combination of low cost and high differentiation, compared with competitors' offerings. A business-level strategy is effective only when it is grounded in exploiting the firm's core competencies and competitive advantages. Thus, successful firms continuously examine the effectiveness of current and future core competencies and advantages.[32]

At one time, the strategic management process was concerned largely with understanding the characteristics of the industry in which the firm competed and, in light of those characteristics, determining how the firm should be positioned relative to competitors. This emphasis on industry characteristics and competitive strategy underestimated the role of the firm's resources and capabilities in developing a competitive advantage. In fact, core competencies, in combination with product-market positions, are the firm's most important sources of competitive advantage.[33] The core competencies of a firm, in addition to results of analyses of its general, industry, and competitor environments, should drive its selection of strategies. The resources held by the firm and their context are important when formulating strategy.[34] As Clayton Christensen noted, "Successful strategists need to cultivate a deep understanding of the processes of competition and progress and of the factors that undergird each advantage. Only thus will they be able to see when old advantages are poised to disappear and how new advantages can be built in their stead."[35] By emphasizing core competencies when formulating strategies, companies learn to compete primarily on the basis of firm-specific differences, but they must be aware of how things are changing in the external environment as well.[36]

The Challenge of Analyzing the Internal Organization

The strategic decisions which managers make about the components of their firm's internal organization are non-routine,[37] have ethical implications,[38] and significantly influence the firm's ability to earn above-average returns.[39] These decisions involve choices about the assets the firm needs to collect and how to best use those assets. "Managers make choices precisely because they believe these contribute substantially to the performance and survival of their organizations."[40]

Making decisions involving the firm's assets—identifying, developing, deploying, and protecting resources, capabilities, and core competencies—may appear to be relatively easy. However, this task is as challenging and difficult as any other with which managers are involved; moreover, it is increasingly internationalized.[41] Some believe that the pressure on managers to pursue only decisions that help the firm meet the quarterly earnings expected by market analysts makes it difficult to accurately examine the firm's internal organization.[42]

The challenge and difficulty of making effective decisions are implied by preliminary evidence suggesting that one-half of organizational decisions fail.[43] Sometimes, mistakes are made as the firm analyzes conditions in its internal organization.[44] Managers might, for example, identify capabilities as core competencies that do not create a competitive advantage. This misidentification may have been the case at Polaroid Corporation as decision makers continued to believe that the skills it used to build its instant film cameras were highly relevant at the time its competitors were developing and using the skills required to introduce digital cameras.[45] When a mistake occurs, such as one that occurred at Polaroid, decision makers must have the confidence to admit it and take corrective actions.[46] A firm can still grow through well-intended errors; the learning generated by making and correcting mistakes can be important to the creation of new competitive advantages.[47] Moreover, firms and those managing them can learn from the failure resulting from a mistake—that is, what not to do when seeking competitive advantage.[48] Thus, difficult managerial decisions concerning resources, capabilities, and core competencies are characterized by three conditions: uncertainty, complexity, and intraorganizational conflicts (see Figure 3.2).[49]

Managers face *uncertainty* in terms of new proprietary technologies, rapidly changing economic and political trends, transformations in societal values, and shifts in customer demands.[50] Environmental uncertainty increases the *complexity* and range of issues to examine when studying the internal environment.[51] Consider the complexity associated with the decisions Pepsi is encountering in India. Increasing health consciousness, pressure from environment groups regarding extraction of ground water and an inherent hostility to multinationals is forcing Pepsi to rethink its strategies in India, and to move into more environmentally responsible businesses.[52] Obviously, the complexity of these decisions is quite significant.[53] Biases about how to cope with uncertainty affect decisions about the resources and capabilities that will become the foundation of the firm's competitive advantage.[54] For example, its India-born American CEO Indra Nooyi strongly believes in the future of Pepsi in India, with its growing income and changes in tastes. Finally, *intraorganizational conflict* surfaces when decisions are made about the core competencies to nurture as well as how to nurture them.

In making decisions affected by these three conditions, judgment is required. **Judgment** is the capability of making successful decisions when no obviously correct model or rule is available or when relevant data are unreliable or incomplete. In this type of situation, decision makers must be aware of possible cognitive biases. Overconfidence, for example, can often lower value when a correct decision is not obvious, such as making a judgment as to whether an internal resource is a strength or a weakness.[55]

When exercising judgment, decision makers often take intelligent risks. In the current competitive landscape, ex-

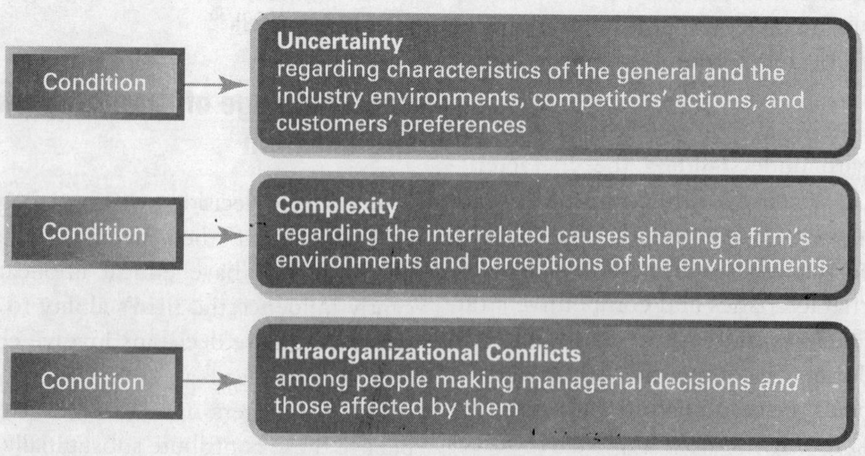

Figure 3.2 Conditions affecting managerial decisions about resources, capabilities, and core competencies

ecutive judgment can be a particularly important source of competitive advantage. One reason is that, over time, effective judgment allows a firm to build a strong reputation and retain the loyalty of stakeholders whose support is linked to above-average returns.[56] It is important even to have the judgment to see the need for an external view, as for example, of a consultant, and be willing to be challenged on the CEO's existing world views.

As explained in Strategic Focus 3.1, GE's managers build their capabilities in its executive leadership program. This program, which is recognized as one of the best in the world, helps GE's managers develop the capabilities to deal with uncertainty, complexity, and intraorganizational conflict. As such, they learn to use their judgment to make decisions that help GE navigate effectively in an uncertain and complex competitive landscape. The effectiveness of GE's managers and their ability to exercise good judgment in making strategic decisions is shown in the value GE has created for its shareholders and the number of former GE managers who are now CEOs of other major companies.

In the next section, we discuss how resources (such as young professionals and low-level managers) are developed and bundled to create capabilities.

STRATEGIC FOCUS

3.1 GE Builds Management Capabilities and Shares Them with Others

For many years, GE was considered one of the best organizations for management talent in the world. For the period, 1993–2002, GE was ranked first or second in market value added among the Stern Stewart 1,000 firms. In fact, GE was one of the top producers of shareholder value through the more than 20 years of Jack Welch's tenure as CEO. Most analysts attribute this phenomenal record to GE's exceptional leadership development program.

Approximately 9,000 managers participated in programs annually at GE's Leadership Center in Crotonville, New York. Managers received extensive leadership and team-based training in these programs. They even provided internal consulting by working on major GE projects, such as evaluating joint venture partners and analyzing opportunities for the use of artificial intelligence. Its world-class management development programs provided GE with an inventory of successors for almost any management position in the company. In fact, many analysts believe that the management development programs helped GE achieve a competitive advantage. Some argue that the management development process has the characteristics of a core competence; it is valuable, rare, difficult to imitate, and non-substitutable.

Jack Welch was often quoted as saying that people came first and strategy second. He actively participated in the management development program, sharing his expertise with other GE managers. Welch's successor, Jeff Immelt, does the same. Immelt believes that effective leaders learn constantly and help others in the firm to learn as well. GE's leadership development program is so good that many companies look for talent among GE's management team because the program produces more leaders than it can usefully absorb. Thus, there are many company CEOs who are former GE managers. A study of these CEOs found they outperformed non-GE CEOs by a significant margin.

GE is experiencing problems in the economic malaise of 2008–2009. This is partly because of problems in its major financial services business (similar to the whole financial services industry). However, it is also partly due to the current CEO's emphasis on innovation for the future of the company. To innovate effectively requires that the firm invest now for returns several years later, which involves taking risks. As such, shorter-term returns are likely to suffer with high costs and lower returns awaiting the major longer-term payoffs of important innovations. Only time will tell if these investments to create innovations with long-term payoffs (as opposed to short-term returns) will work.

AP Photo/Mark Lennihan

GE CEO Jeff Immlet, like his predecessor Jack We!ch, believes the development of leaders within the organization is an essential investment.

Sources: G. Spotts, 2006, GE's Immelt may have "ecomagination," but he needs project managers for jumbo-sized ideas, *FastCompany*, http://www.fastcompany.com, June 11; Things leaders do, *FastCompany,* http://www.fastcompany.com, December 19; S. Hamm, 2008, Tech innovations for tough times, ADNetAsia, http://www.zdnetasia.com, December 26; E. Smith, 2009, At GE, management development is a continuous process. Aprendia Corp, http://www.aprendiacorp.com, February 15; G. Rowe, R. E. White, D. Lehmbert, and J. R. Phillips, 2009, General Electric: An outlier in CEO talent development, *IVEY Business Journal,* http://www.iveybusinessjournal.com/article, January/February; P. Eavis & L. Denning, 2009, GE needs a circuit breaker, *Wall Street Journal,* http://www.wsj.com, March 5; P. Eaves, 2009, GE paper cut is greeted with relief, *Wall Street Journal,* http://www.wsj.com, March 13; D. Lehmberg, W. G. Rowe, R. E. White, and R. R. Phillips, 2009, The GE paradox: Competitive advantage through tangible non-firm-specific investment, *Journal of Management,* in press.

Resources, Capabilities, and Core Competencies

Resources, capabilities, and core competencies are the foundation of competitive advantage. Resources are bundled to create organizational capabilities. In turn, capabilities are the source of a firm's core competencies, which are the basis of competitive advantages.[57] Figure 3.1, depicts these relationships. Here, we define and provide examples of these building blocks of competitive advantage.

Resources

Broad in scope, resources cover a spectrum of individual, social, and organizational phenomena.[58] Typically, resources alone do not yield a competitive advantage.[59] In fact, a competitive advantage is generally based on the unique bundling of several resources.[60] For example, Amazon.com combined service and distribution resources to develop its competitive advantages. The firm started as an online bookseller, directly shipping orders to customers. It quickly grew large and established a distribution network through which it could ship "millions of different items to millions of different customers." Lacking Amazon's combination of resources, traditional bricks-and-mortar companies, such as Borders, found it difficult to establish an effective online presence. These difficulties led some of them to develop partnerships with Amazon. Through these arrangements, Amazon now handles the online presence and the shipping of goods for several firms, including Borders—which now can focus on sales in its stores.[61] These types of arrangements are useful to the brick-and-mortar companies because they have little experience in shipping large amounts of diverse merchandise directly to individuals.

Some of a firm's resources (defined in Chapter 1 as inputs to the firm's production process) are tangible while others are intangible. **Tangible resources** are assets that can be observed and quantified. Production equipment, manufacturing facilities, distribution centers, and formal reporting structures are examples of tangible resources. Intangible resources are assets that are rooted deeply in the firm's history and have accumulated over time. Because they are embedded in unique patterns of routines, **intangible resources** are relatively difficult for competitors to analyze and imitate. Knowledge, trust between managers and employees, managerial capabilities, organizational routines (the unique ways people work together), scientific capabilities, the capacity for innovation, brand name, and the firm's reputation for its goods or services and how it interacts with people (such as employees, customers, and suppliers) are intangible resources.[62]

The four types of tangible resources are financial, organizational, physical, and technological (see Table 3.1). The three types of intangible resources are human, innovation, and reputational (see Table 3.2).

Table 3.1 Tangible resources

Financial Resources	• The firm's borrowing capacity • The firm's ability to generate internal funds
Organizational Resources	• The firm's formal reporting structure and its formal planning, controlling, and coordinating systems
Physical Resources	• Sophistication and location of a firm's plant and equipment • Access to raw materials
Technological Resources	• Stock of technology, such as patents, trademarks, copyrights, and trade secrets

Sources: Adapted from J. B. Barney, 1991, Firm resources and sustained competitive advantage, *Journal of Management,* 17: 101; R. M. Grant, 1991, *Contemporary Strategy Analysis,* Cambridge, UK: Blackwell Business, 100–102.

Table 3.2 Intangible resources

Human Resources	• Knowledge • Trust • Managerial capabilities • Organizational routines
Innovation Resources	• Ideas • Scientific capabilities • Capacity to innovate
Reputational Resources	• Reputation with customers • Brand name • Perceptions of product quality, durability, and reliability • Reputation with suppliers • For efficient, effective, supportive, and mutually beneficial interactions and relationships

Sources: Adapted from R. Hall, 1992, The strategic analysis of intangible resources, *Strategic Management Journal,* 13: 136–139; R. M. Grant, 1991, *Contemporary Strategy Analysis,* Cambridge, UK: Blackwell Business, 101–104.

Tangible Resources

As tangible resources, a firm's borrowing capacity and the status of its physical facilities are visible. The value of many tangible resources can be established through financial statements, but these statements do not account for the value of all the assets of the firm, because they disregard some intangible resources.[63] The value of tangible resources is also constrained because they are hard to leverage—it is difficult to derive additional business or value from a tangible resource. For example, an airplane is a tangible resource, but "You can't use the same airplane on five different routes at the same time. You can't put the same crew on five different routes at the same time. And the same goes for the financial investment you've made in the airplane."[64]

Although production assets are tangible, many of the processes necessary to use these assets are intangible. Thus, the learning and potential proprietary processes associated with a tangible resource, such as manufacturing facilities, can have unique intangible attributes, such as quality control processes, unique manufacturing processes, and technology that develop over time and create competitive advantage.[65]

Intangible Resources

Compared to tangible resources, intangible resources are a superior source of core competencies.[66] In fact, in the global economy, "the success of a corporation lies more in its intellectual and systems capabilities than in its physical assets. [Moreover], the capacity to manage human intellect—and to convert it into useful products and services—is fast becoming the critical executive skill of the age.[67]

Because intangible resources are less visible and more difficult for competitors to understand, purchase, imitate, or substitute, firms prefer to rely on them rather than on tangible resources as the foundation for their capabilities and core competencies. In fact, the more unobservable (i.e., intangible) a resource is, the more sustainable will be the competitive advantage that is based on it.[68] Another benefit of intangible resources is that, unlike most tangible resources, their use can be leveraged. For instance, sharing knowledge among employees does not diminish its value for any one person. To the contrary, two people sharing their individualized knowledge sets often can be leveraged to create additional knowledge that, although new to each of them, contributes to performance improvements for the firm. This is especially true when members of the top management team share knowledge with each other to make more effective decisions. The new knowledge created is then often shared with managers and employees in each of the units managed by executives in the top management team.[69] With intangible resources, the larger the network of users, the greater the benefit to each party.

As shown in Table 3.2, the intangible resource of reputation is an important source of competitive advantage. Indeed, some argue that "a firm's reputation is widely considered to be a valuable resource associated with sustained competitive advantage."[70] Earned through the firm's actions as well as its words, a value-creating reputation is a product of years of superior marketplace competence as perceived by stakeholders.[71] A reputation indicates the level of awareness a firm has been able to develop among stakeholders and the degree to which they hold the firm in high esteem.[72]

A well-known and highly valued brand name is an application of reputation as a source of competitive advantage.[73] A continuing commitment to innovation and aggressive advertising facilitate firms' efforts to take advantage of the reputation associated with their brands.[74] Because of the desirability of its reputation, the Harley-Davidson brand name, for example, has such status that it adorns a limited edition Barbie doll, a popular restaurant in New York City, and a line of cologne. Additionally, the firm offers a broad range of clothing items, from black leather jackets to fashions for tots through Harley-Davidson MotorClothes.[75] The Tata Group has leveraged its reputation to a number of new businesses such as telecom, insurance and financial services.[76] However, even established firms need to build their reputations in new markets that they enter. For example, Ford hired a well-respected Indian actor, Sunil Shetty, to serve as the brand ambassador for the Ford Endeavor launch in India. The Endeavor had the highest sales of SUVs in 2008.[77]

Capabilities

Capabilities exist when resources have been purposely integrated to achieve a specific task or set of tasks. These tasks range from human resource selection to product marketing and research and development activities.[78] Critical to the building of competitive advantages, capabilities are often based on developing, carrying, and exchanging information and knowledge through the firm's human capital.[79] Client-specific capabilities often develop from repeated interactions with clients and the learning about their needs that occur from the use of the firm's products or services. As a result, capabilities often evolve and develop over time.[80] The foundation of many

Table 3.3 Examples of firms' capabilities

Functional Areas	Capabilities	Examples of Firms
Distribution	Effective use of logistics management techniques	Wal-Mart, Hindustan Unilever (HUL)
Human Resources	Motivating, empowering, and retaining employees	Microsoft, Infosys
Management Information Systems	Effective and efficient control of inventories through point-of-purchase data collection methods	Wal-Mart, HUL, ITC
Marketing	Effective promotion of brand-name products Effective customer service Innovative merchandising	Procter & Gamble HUL ITC McKinsey & Co. Bharti Airtel, Cavincare
Management	Ability to envision the future of clothing Effective organizational structure	Hugo Boss PepsiCo
Manufacturing	Design and production skills yielding reliable products Product and design quality Miniaturization of components and products	Komatsu Tata Motors Sony
Research & Development	Innovative technology Development of sophisticated elevator control solutions Rapid transformation of technology into new products and processes Digital technology	Caterpillar Otis Elevator Co. Chaparral Steel Thomson Consumer Electronics

capabilities lies in the unique skills and knowledge of a firm's employees and, often, their functional expertise. Hence, the value of human capital in developing and using capabilities and, ultimately, core competencies cannot be overstated.[81]

While global business leaders increasingly support the view that the knowledge possessed by human capital is among the most significant of an organization's capabilities and may ultimately be at the root of all competitive advantages,[82] firms must also be able to utilize the knowledge they have and transfer it among their business units.[83] Given this reality, the firm's challenge is to create an environment that allows people to integrate their individual knowledge with that held by others in the firm so that, collectively, the firm has significant organizational knowledge.[84] As noted in Strategic Focus 3.1, GE has been effective in developing its human capital and in promoting the transfer of their knowledge throughout the company. Building important capabilities is critical to achieving high firm performance.[85]

As illustrated in Table 3.3, capabilities are often developed in specific functional areas (such as manufacturing, R&D, and marketing) or in a part of a functional area (e.g., advertising). Table 3.3 shows a grouping of organizational functions and the capabilities that some companies are thought to possess in terms of all or parts of those functions.

Core Competencies

Defined in Chapter 1, core competencies are capabilities that serve as a source of competitive advantage for a firm over its rivals. Core competencies distinguish a company competitively and reflect its personality. Core competencies emerge over time through an organizational process of accumulating and learning how to deploy different resources and capabilities.[86] As the capacity to take action, core competencies are "crown jewels of a company," the activities the company performs especially well compared with competitors and through which the firm adds unique value to its goods or services over a long period of time.[87]

Innovation is thought to be a core competence at Xerox today. It is not surprising because this firm was built on a world-changing innovation—xerography. And even though Xerox was the first firm to integrate the mouse with the graphical user interface of a PC, it was Apple Computer that initially recognized the value of this innovation and derived value from it. In 2000, then-CEO Paul Allaire admitted that Xerox's business model no longer worked and that the firm had lost its innovative ability. Some nine-plus years later, things have changed for the better at Xerox. Using the capabilities of its scientists, engineers, and researchers, Xerox has reconstituted innovation as a core competence. For example, Xerox received more than 230 industry awards for the attributes of a range of products and services including image quality, performance, and technical innovation. One example of a recent focus of Xerox's research is on identifying products and services that help customers deal with the information explosion, according to Xerox's Chief Technology Officer, Sophie Vandebroek.[88]

How many core competencies are required for the firm to have a sustained competitive advantage? Responses to this question vary. McKinsey & Co. recommends that its clients identify no more than three or four competencies around which their strategic actions can be framed. Supporting and nurturing more than four core competencies may prevent a firm from developing the focus it needs to fully exploit its competencies in the marketplace. At Xerox, services expertise, employee talent, and technological skills are thought to be core competencies along with innovation.[89]

Building Core Competencies

Two tools help firms identify and build their core competencies. The first consists of four specific criteria of sustainable competitive advantage that firms can use to determine those capabilities that are core competencies. Because the capabilities shown in Table 3.3 have satisfied these four criteria, they are core competencies. The second tool is the value chain analysis. Firms use this tool to select the value-creating competencies that should be maintained, upgraded, or developed and those that should be outsourced.

Four Criteria of Sustainable Competitive Advantage

As shown in Table 3.4, capabilities that are valuable, rare, costly to imitate, and non-substitutable are core competencies. In turn, core competencies are sources of competitive advantage for the firm over its rivals. Capabilities failing to satisfy the four criteria of sustainable competitive advantage are not core competencies, meaning that although every core competence is a capability, not every capability is a core competence. In slightly different words, for a capability to be a core competence, it must be valuable and unique from a customer's point of view. For a competitive advantage to be sustainable, the core competence must be inimitable and non-substitutable by competitors.[90]

A sustained competitive advantage is achieved only when competitors cannot duplicate the benefits of a firm's strategy or when they lack the resources to attempt imitation. For some period of time, the firm may earn a competitive advantage by using capabilities that are, for example, valuable and rare, but imitable. For example, some firms are trying to gain an advantage by out-greening their competitors. Wal-Mart initiated a major sustainability program that helped to reduce the use of containers, saving approximately 1,000 barrels of oil and thousands of trees while simultaneously saving $2 million. GE's ecomanagement system, through which it has developed and introduced new, "greener" products to meet growing demand, is another example.[91] The length of time a firm can expect to retain its competitive advantage is a function of how quickly competitors can successfully imitate a good, service, or process. Sustainable competitive advantage results only when all four criteria are satisfied.

Valuable

Valuable capabilities allow the firm to exploit opportunities or neutralize threats in its external environment. By effectively using capabilities to exploit opportunities, a firm creates value for customers. Under former CEO Jack Welch's leadership, GE built a valuable competence in financial services. It built this powerful competence largely through acquisitions and its core competence in integrating newly acquired businesses. In addition, making such competencies as financial services highly successful required placing the right people in the right jobs. As noted in the opening case, Welch emphasized human capital because it is important in creating value for customers. That emphasis has continued in the company after Welch retired.

Table 3.4 The four criteria of sustainable competitive advantage

Valuable Capabilities	• Help a firm neutralize threats or exploit opportunities
Rare Capabilities	• Are not possessed by many others
Costly-to-Imitate Capabilities	• Historical: A unique and a valuable organizational culture or brand name • Ambiguous cause: The causes and uses of a competence are unclear • Social complexity: Interpersonal relationships, trust, and friendship among managers, suppliers, and customers
Non-substitutable Capabilities	• No strategic equivalent

Rare

Rare capabilities are capabilities that few, if any, competitors possess. A key question to be answered when evaluating this criterion is, "How many rival firms possess these valuable capabilities?" Capabilities possessed by many rivals are unlikely to be sources of competitive advantage for anyone of them. Instead, valuable but common (i.e., not rare) resources and capabilities are sources of competitive parity.[92] Competitive advantage results only when firms develop and exploit valuable capabilities that differ from those shared with competitors.

Costly to Imitate

Costly-to-imitate capabilities are capabilities that other firms cannot easily develop. Capabilities that are costly to imitate are created because of one reason or a combination of three reasons (see Table 3.4). First, a firm sometimes is able to develop capabilities because of **unique historical conditions**. As firms evolve, they often acquire or develop capabilities that are unique to them.[93]

A firm with a unique and valuable **organizational culture** that emerged in the early stages of the company's history "may have an imperfectly imitable advantage over firms founded in another historical period;"[94] one in which less valuable or less competitively useful values and beliefs strongly influenced the development of the firm's culture. Briefly discussed in Chapter 1, organizational culture is a set of values that are shared by members in the organization. This will be explained in more detail in Chapter 12. An organizational culture is a source of advantage when employees are held together tightly by their belief in it.[95]

For example, culture is a competitive advantage for The Park group of hotels. The Park group of hotels are boutique hotels, with an informal culture and it attempts to differentiate itself from other five star hotels by holding different kinds of exciting events aimed at the relatively young, through a personal touch towards its guests and an encouraging and informal culture towards Its employees.[96] The Aravind Eye Care System also derives its high effectiveness in eye care through a service oriented culture, where even the poorest patients are treated with respect.[97]

A second condition of being costly to imitate occurs when the link between the firm's capabilities and its competitive advantage is **causally ambiguous**.[98] In these instances, competitors can't clearly understand how a firm uses its capabilities as the foundation for competitive advantage. As a result, firms are uncertain about the capabilities they should develop to duplicate the benefits of a competitor's value-creating strategy. For years, firms tried to imitate Southwest Airlines' low-cost strategy but most have been unable to do so, primarily because they can't replicate Southwest's unique culture. Of all Southwest imitators, Ryanair, an Irish airline headquartered in Dublin, is the most successful. However, Ryanair is also a controversial company, praised by some, criticized by others. Ryanair's core competence is its capability to keep its costs excessively low and to generate alternative sources of revenue.

Social complexity is the third reason that capabilities can be costly to imitate. Social complexity means that at least some, and frequently many, of the firm's capabilities are the product of complex social phenomena. Interpersonal relationships, trust, friendships among managers and between managers and employees, and a firm's reputation with suppliers and customers are examples of socially complex capabilities. Southwest Airlines is careful to hire people who fit with its culture. This complex interrelationship between the culture and human capital adds value in ways that other airlines cannot, such as jokes on flights by the flight attendants or the cooperation between gate personnel and pilots.

Non-substitutable

Non-substitutable capabilities are capabilities that do not have strategic equivalents. This final criterion for a capability to be a source of competitive advantage "is that there must be no strategically equivalent valuable resources that are themselves either not rare or imitable. Two valuable firm resources (or two bundles of firm resources) are strategically equivalent when they each can be separately exploited to implement the same strategies."[99] In general, the strategic value of capabilities increases as they become more difficult to substitute. The more invisible the capabilities are, the more difficult it is for firms to find substitutes and the greater the challenge is to competitors trying to imitate a firm's value-creating strategy. Firm-specific knowledge and trust-based working relationships between managers and nonmanagerial personnel, such as existed for years at Southwest Airlines, are examples of capabilities that are difficult to identify and for which finding a substitute is challenging. However, causal ambiguity may make it difficult for the firm to learn as well and may stifle progress, because the firm may not know how to improve processes that are not easily codified and thus are ambiguous.[100]

STRATEGIC FOCUS

3.2 Ryanair: The Passionate Cost Cutter that Is both Loved and Hated

Ryanair is the leading low-cost airline in Europe. It has achieved a high market share by relentlessly holding down costs and thereby offering the lowest prices on its routes. To attract new customers, it once offered flights for one penny to selected destinations. It sold almost 500,000 tickets with the promotion. While Michael O'Leary, Ryanair CEO, is known to be cheap (he will not provide employees with pens; he recommends that they get them from hotels where they stay overnight), the primary reason for Ryanair's lowest cost status is that it has the fastest turnarounds in the industry (their speed resembles that of an auto racing pit crew). O'Leary is also constantly identifying new revenue streams such as charges for use of airport check-in facilities, charging for each piece of luggage, offering rental cars at the destination, charging to use the toilet on the plane, etc.

To obtain free publicity, O'Leary or other executives often make outrageous statements and roundly criticize their competitors to get Ryanair's name in the news. The firm uses multiple marketing gimmicks such as advertising that directly criticizes competitors and even some "off-color" advertising slogans. The firm's core competence is the capability to maintain the lowest costs in the industry and to generate alternative revenues. Because of its very low fares, its passenger load grew at an annual rate of approximately 25 per cent until the economic crisis that began in 2008, but the company remained profitable in 2008.

Despite its success, Ryanair receives a significant amount of criticism. In 2006, for example, it was voted as the least favorite airline (despite its popularity evidenced in passenger numbers). Critics have also accused Ryanair of poor customer service, an unfriendly, uncaring staff, and hidden charges. Yet O'Leary believes that Ryanair may be one of the few airlines in Europe left standing after the latest severe economic recession. He is planning growth (although the airline announced some small reductions in service and staff in 2009) and is negotiating with Boeing and Airbus to buy as many as 400 new aircraft. With its decided strengths and acknowledged weaknesses, the future of Ryanair will be interesting to witness.

Ulrich Perrey/Dpa /Landov

Michael O'Leary, CEO of low-cost airline Ryanair, poses with a model of an aircraft during a press conference in Hamburg, Germany.

Sources: 2005, Ryanair exercises options on five Boeing 737s, *Wikinews*, http://en.wikinews.org, June 13; M. Scott, 2007, Ryanair flying high, *BusinessWeek,* http://www.businessweek.com, July 31; A. Davidson, 2008, Michael O'Leary: Ryanair's rebel with a cause, *The Sunday Times,* http://business.timesonline.co.uk, December 7; K. Done, 2009, Ryanair in talks to buy 400 aircraft, *Financial Times,* http://www.ft.com, February 2; K. Done, 2009, Virgin and Ryanair to cut jobs, *Financial Times,* http://www.ft.com, February 12; 2009, Ryanair Holdings PLC, http://www.answers.com, March 13; 2009, Ryanair, *Wikipedia*, http://www.wikipedia.org, March 13.

Table 3.5 Outcomes from combinations of the criteria for sustainable competitive advantage

Is the Resource or Capability Valuable?	Is the Resource or Capability Rare?	Is the Resource or Capability Costly to Imitate?	Is the Resource or Capability Non-substitutable?	Competitive Consequences	Performance Implications
No	No	No	No	Competitive disadvantage	Below-average returns
Yes	No	No	Yes/no	Competitive parity	Average returns

Is the Resource or Capability Valuable?	Is the Resource or Capability Rare?	Is the Resource or Capability Costly to Imitate?	Is the Resource or Capability Non-substitutable?	Competitive Consequences	Performance Implications
Yes	Yes	No	Yes/no	Temporary competitive advantage	Average returns to above-average returns
Yes	Yes	Yes	Yes/no	Sustainable competitive advantage	Above-average returns

In summary, only using valuable, rare, costly-to-imitate, and non-substitutable capabilities creates sustainable competitive advantage. Table 3.5 shows the competitive consequences and performance implications resulting from combinations of the four criteria of sustainability. The analysis suggested by the table helps managers determine the strategic value of a firm's capabilities. The firm should not emphasize capabilities that fit the criteria described in the first row in the table (i.e., resources and capabilities that are neither valuable nor rare and that are imitable and for which strategic substitutes exist). Capabilities yielding competitive parity and either temporary or sustainable competitive advantage, however, will be supported. Some competitors such as Coca-Cola and PepsiCo may have capabilities that result in competitive parity. In such cases, the firms will nurture these capabilities while simultaneously trying to develop capabilities that can yield either a temporary or sustainable competitive advantage.

Value Chain Analysis

Value chain analysis allows the firm to understand the parts of its operations that create value and those that do not.[101] Understanding these issues is important because the firm earns above-average returns only when the value it creates is greater than the costs incurred to create that value.[102]

The value chain is a template that firms use to analyze their cost position and to identify the multiple means that can be used to facilitate implementation of a chosen business-level strategy.[103] Today's competitive landscape demands that firms examine their value chains in a global rather than a domestic-only context.[104] In particular, activities associated with supply chains should be studied within a global context.[105]

As shown in Figure 3.3, a firm's value chain is segmented into primary and support activities. **Primary activities** are involved with a product's physical creation, its sale and distribution to buyers, and its service after the sale. **Support activities** provide the assistance necessary for the primary activities to take place.

The value chain shows how a product moves from the raw-material stage to the final customer. For individual firms, the essential idea of the value chain is to create additional value without incurring significant costs while doing so and to capture the value that has been created. In a globally competitive economy, the most valuable links on the chain are people who have knowledge about customers. This locus of value-creating possibilities applies just as strongly to retail and service firms as to manufacturers. Moreover, for organizations in all sectors, the effects of e-commerce make it increasingly necessary for companies to develop value-adding knowledge processes to compensate for the value and margin that the Internet strips from physical processes.[106]

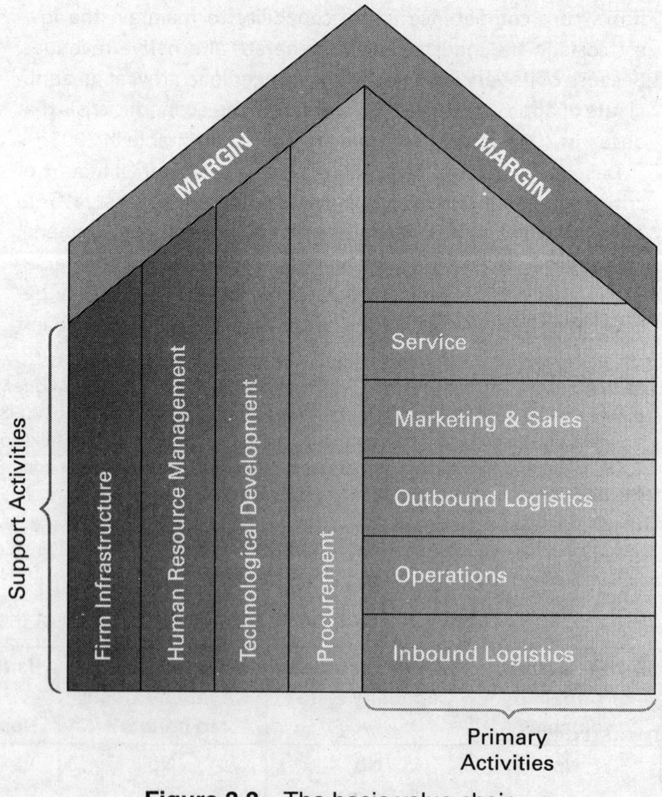

Figure 3.3 The basic value chain

What are the Value Creating Potentials of Primary Activities?

In *inbound logistics* as well as in *outbound logistics*, one can change the materials handling systems, warehousing, inventory control systems, and the way materials are handled and stored. In *operations*, changes can be made by altering the production processes, materials used, machines, quality control systems, packaging, maintenance and quality of labor involved in producing them. In *marketing and sales*, which customersare purchasing the product (and see whether you can alter their profile to create more value), the needed advertising strategies, selection of distribution channels, sales force quality and product features that can lead to enhanced value, can be considered. In *service*, the level and quality of service, frequency of service needed, warranty terms, quality of repair and the quality of service personnel are variables in the firm's control.

It may be noted that before considering alteration of these parameters, it may be useful to benchmark each parameter vis-à-vis what is offered or done by major competitors and see where the firm is likely to derive maximum value by alterations.

In *procurement*, activities to be examined could be the procurement systems, the quickness of response, the inventory policies and the credit policies toward vendors. This is not regarding what materials are to be used (that comes under operations above) but the way materials, including capital equipment are procured. In *technology development*, one could look at the R&D labs, process equipment design, basic vs. applied research, criteria for selection of products for R&D and policies relating R&D to production. In *human resources management*, the policies relating to hiring, training, promotion and compensation need to be looked at and benchmarked. Finally, the firm could look at the *infrastructure* that includes a whole lot of things such as general management, planning, finance, accounting, legal support and management of relations with the government. It also includes physical infrastructure, provision of standby power, adequate water supply and systems for recycling and conservation of water, internal roads and quality of maintenance of this infrastructure.

Again, these have no significance in themselves except in comparison with the competition.

Creating value through the value chain activities often requires building effective alliances with suppliers (and sometimes others to which the firm outsources activities, as discussed in the next section) and developing strong positive relationships with customers. When firms have such strong positive relationships with suppliers and customers, they are said to have "social capital."[107] The relationships themselves have value because they produce knowledge transfer and access to resources that a firm may not hold internally.[108] To build social capital whereby resources such as knowledge are transferred across organizations requires trust between the parties. The partners must trust each other in order to allow their resources to be used in such a way that both parties will benefit over time and neither party will take advantage of the other.[109] Trust and social capital usually evolve over time with repeated interactions but firms can also establish special means to jointly manage alliances that promote greater trust with the outcome of enhanced benefits for both partners.[110]

Sometimes start-up firms create value by uniquely reconfiguring or recombining parts of the value chain. FedEx changed the nature of the delivery business by reconfiguring outbound logistics (a primary activity) and human resource management (a support activity) to provide overnight deliveries, creating value in the process. As shown in Figure 3.4, the Internet has changed many aspects of the value chain for a broad range of firms. A key reason is that the Internet affects how people communicate, locate information, and buy goods and services.

Evaluating a firm's capability to execute its primary and support activities is challenging. Earlier in the chapter, we noted that identifying and assessing the value of a firm's resources and capabilities requires judgment. Judgment is equally necessary when using value chain analysis, because no obviously correct model or rule is universally available to help in the process.

What should a firm do about primary and support activities in which its resources and capabilities are not a source of core competence and, hence, of competitive advantage? Outsourcing is one solution to consider.

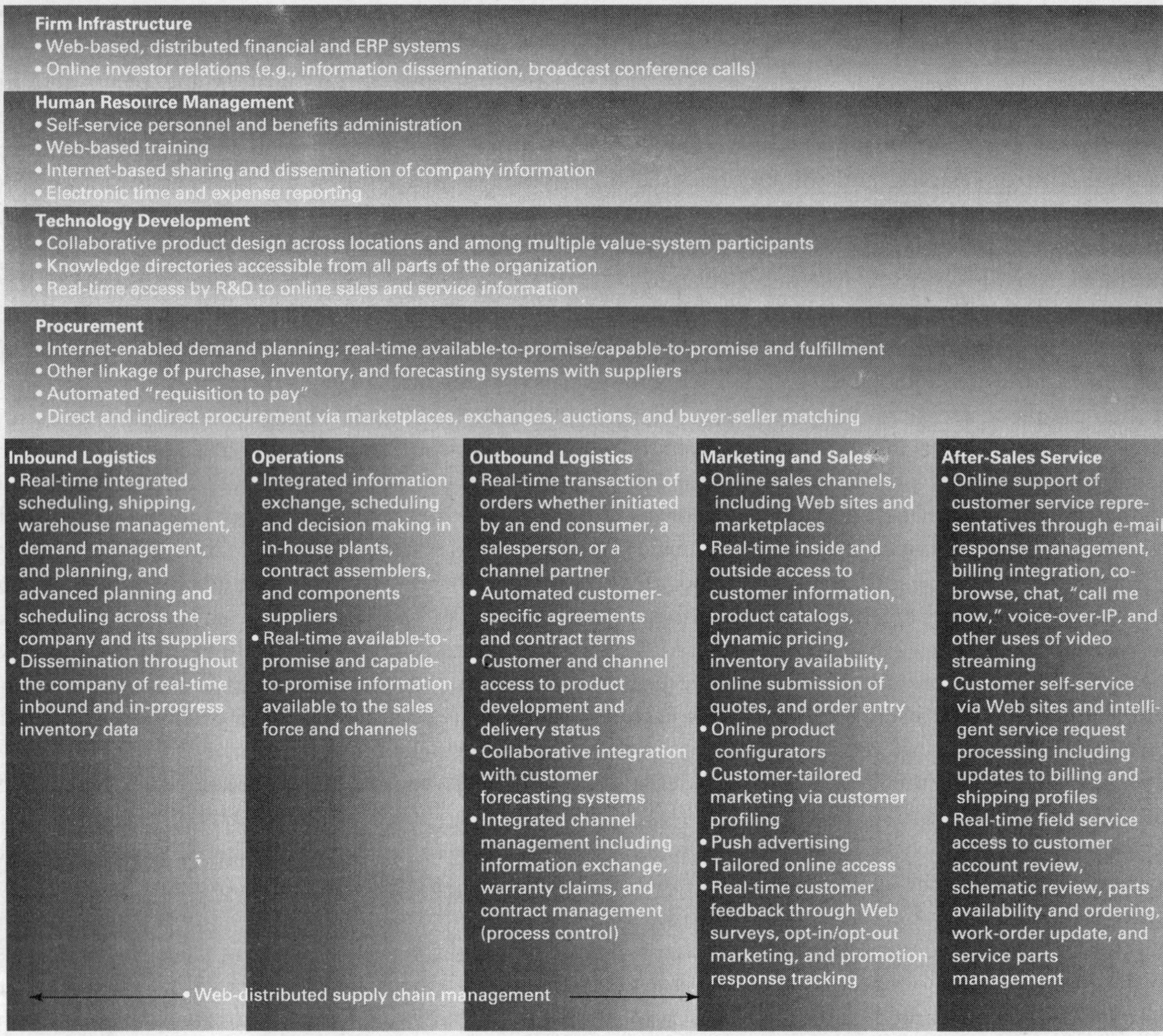

Figure 3.4 Prominent applications of the Internet in the value chain

OUTSOURCING

Concerned with how components, finished goods, or services will be obtained, **outsourcing** is the purchase of a value-creating activity from an external supplier.[111] Not-for-profit agencies as well as for-profit organizations actively engage in outsourcing.[112] Firms engaging in effective outsourcing increase their flexibility, mitigate risks, and reduce their capital investments.[113] In multiple global industries, the trend toward outsourcing continues at a rapid pace.[114] Moreover, in some industries virtually all firms seek the value that can be captured through effective outsourcing. As with other strategic management process decisions, careful analysis is required before the firm decides to engage in outsourcing.[115]

Outsourcing can be effective because few, if any, organizations possess the resources and capabilities required to achieve competitive superiority in all primary and support activities. For example, research suggests that few companies can afford to develop internally all the technologies that might lead to competitive advantage.[116] By nurturing a smaller number of capabilities, a firm increases the probability of developing a competitive advantage because it does not become overextended. In addition, by outsourcing activities in which it lacks competence, the firm can fully concentrate on those areas in which it can create value.

Firms must outsource only activities where they cannot create value or where they are at a substantial disadvantage compared to competitors.[117] To verify that the appropriate primary and support activities are outsourced, managers should have four skills: strategic thinking, deal making, partnership governance, and change management.[118] Managers need to understand whether and how outsourcing creates competitive advantage within their company—they need to think strategically. To complete effective outsourcing transactions, these managers must also be deal makers, able to secure rights from external providers that can be fully used by internal managers. They must be able to oversee[119] and govern appropriately the relationship with the company to which the services were outsourced. Because outsourcing can significantly change how an organization operates, managers administering these programs must also be able to manage that change, including resolving employee resistance that accompanies any significant change effort.[120]

The consequences of outsourcing cause additional concerns.[121] For the most part, these concerns revolve around the potential loss in firms' innovative ability and the loss of jobs within companies that decide to outsource some of their work activities to others. Thus, innovation and technological uncertainty are two important issues to consider in making outsourcing decisions. However, firms can also learn from outsource suppliers how to increase their own innovation capabilities.[122] Companies must be aware of these issues and be prepared to fully consider the concerns about opportunities from outsourcing suggested by different stakeholders (e.g., employees). The opportunities and concerns may be especially great when firms outsource activities or functions to a foreign supply source (often referred to as offshoring).[123] Bangalore and Belfast are the newest hotspots for technology outsourcing, competing with major operations in China and India.[124] Yet, IBM recently made the decision to keep outsourced activities in the United States instead of moving them to a foreign location.[125]

Outsourcing has become, of late, a sensitive topic in developed countries, especially US, since it is seen as "taking away" local jobs. Whatever may be the economic arguments, it has become primarily a political issue. Firms that depend on such outsourcing evidently have to worry about this trend and what it portends.

STRATEGY RIGHT NOW

Read how Boeing's experience with the 787 Dreamliner highlights many of the benefits and concerns associated with outsourcing. www.cengage.com/management/hitt

As is true with all strategic management tools and techniques, criteria should be established to guide outsourcing decisions. Outsourcing is big business, but not every outsourcing decision is successful. For example, amid delays and cost overruns, Electronic Data Systems abandoned a $1 billion opportunity to run Dow Chemical Co.'s phone and computer networks. These less-than-desirable outcomes indicate that firms should carefully study outsourcing opportunities to verify that they will indeed create value that exceeds the cost incurred.

Competencies, Strengths, Weaknesses, and Strategic Decisions

At the conclusion of the internal analysis, firms must identify their strengths and weaknesses in resources, capabilities, and core competencies. For example, if they have weak capabilities or do not have core competencies in areas required to achieve a competitive advantage, they must acquire those resources and build the capabilities and competencies needed. Alternatively, they could decide to outsource a function or activity where they are weak in order to improve the value that they provide to customers.[126]

Therefore, firms need to have the appropriate resources and capabilities to develop the desired strategy and create value for customers and other stakeholders such as shareholders.[127] Managers should understand that having a significant quantity of resources is not the same as having the "right" resources. Moreover, decision makers sometimes become more focused and productive when their organization's resources are constrained.[128] Managers must help the firm obtain and use resources, capabilities, and core competencies in ways that generate value-creating competitive advantages.

Tools such as outsourcing help the firm focus on its core competencies as the source of its competitive advantages. However, evidence shows that the value-creating ability of core competencies should never be taken for granted. Moreover, the ability of a core competence to be a permanent competitive advantage can't be assumed. The reason for these cautions is that all core competencies have the potential to become **core rigidities**. Thus, a core competence is usually a strength because it is a source of competitive advantage. If emphasized when it is no longer competitively relevant, it can become a weakness, a seed of organizational inertia.

Noel Vasquez/Getty Images here

The Ford Flex, which the company launched in fall 2008, was designed to turn heads and excite consumers interested in crossover vehicles. Could the Flex represent a shift toward more customer-centered product development?

Inertia embedded in the organizational culture may be a problem at Ford Motor Company, where some argue that the firm's culture has become a core rigidity that is constraining efforts to improve performance. In one writer's words: "One way or another, the company will have to figure out how to produce more vehicles that consumers actually want. And doing that will require addressing the most fundamental problem of all: Ford's dysfunctional, often defeatist culture."[129] In contrast, Toyota constantly reexamines product planning, customer service, sales and marketing, and employee training practices to prevent "being spoiled by success."[130] A leading cement company in India found the way of thinking, procedures and culture such a source of rigidity that it sought to have a series of management development programmes with one of the authors of this book to change the outlook of its managers.

Events occurring in the firm's external environment create conditions through which core competencies can become core rigidities, generate inertia, and stifle innovation. "Often the flip side, the dark side, of core capabilities is revealed due to external events when new competitors figure out a better way to serve the firm's customers, when new technologies emerge, or when political or social events shift the ground underneath."[131] However, in the final analysis, changes in the external environment do not cause core competencies to become core rigidities; rather, strategic myopia and inflexibility on the part of managers are the causes.

After studying its external environment to determine what it might choose to do (as explained in Chapter 2) and its internal organization to understand what it can do (as explained in this chapter), the firm has the information required to select a business-level strategy that will help it reach its vision and mission. We describe different business-level strategies in the next chapter.

SUMMARY

- In the global business environment, traditional factors (e.g., labor costs and superior access to financial resources and raw materials) can still create a competitive advantage. However, these factors are less often a source of competitive advantage in the current competitive landscape. In the current landscape, the resources, capabilities, and core competencies in the firm's internal organization likely have a stronger influence on its performance than do conditions in the external environment. The most effective organizations recognize that strategic competitiveness and above-average returns result only when core competencies (identified by studying the firm's internal organization) are matched with opportunities (determined by studying the firm's external environment).
- No competitive advantage lasts forever. Over time, rivals use their own unique resources, capabilities, and core competencies to form different value-creating propositions that duplicate the value-creating ability of the firm's competitive advantages. In general, the Internet's capabilities are reducing the sustainability of many competitive advantages. Because competitive advantages are not permanently sustainable, firms must exploit their current advantages while simultaneously using their resources and capabilities to form new advantages that can lead to future competitive success.
- Effectively managing core competencies requires careful analysis of the firm's resources (inputs to the production process) and capabilities (resources that have been purposely integrated to achieve a specific task or set of tasks). The knowledge possessed by human capital is among the most significant of an organization's capabilities and ultimately provides the base for most competitive advantages. The firm must create an environment that allows people to integrate their individual knowledge with that held by others so that, collectively, the firm has significant organizational knowledge.
- Individual resources are usually not a source of competitive advantage. Capabilities are a more likely source of competitive advantages, especially more sustainable ones. The firm's nurturing and support of core competencies that are based on capabilities are less visible to rivals and, as such, they are more difficult to understand and imitate.
- Only when a capability is valuable, rare, costly to imitate, and non-substitutable is it a core competence and a source of competitive advantage. Over time, core competencies must be supported, but they cannot be allowed to become core rigidities. Core competencies are a source of competitive advantage only when they allow the firm to create value by exploiting opportunities in its external environment. When

it can no longer do so, the company shifts its attention to selecting or forming other capabilities that satisfy the four criteria of a sustainable competitive advantage.

- Value chain analysis is used to identify and evaluate the competitive potential of resources and capabilities. By studying their skills relative to those associated with primary and support activities, firms can understand their cost structure and identify the activities through which they can create value.
- When the firm cannot create value in either an internal primary or support activity, outsourcing is considered. Used commonly in the global economy, outsourcing is the purchase of a value-creating activity from an external supplier. The firm should outsource only to companies possessing a competitive advantage in terms of the particular primary or support activity under consideration. In addition, the firm must continuously verify that it is not outsourcing activities from which it could create value.

KEY TERMS AND DEFINITIONS

Valuable capabilities allow the firm to exploit opportunities or neutralize threats in its external environment.

Rare capabilities are capabilities that few, if any, competitors possess.

Costly-to-imitate capabilities are capabilities that other firms cannot easily develop.

Non-substitutable capabilities are capabilities that do not have strategic equivalents.

Primary activities are involved with a product's physical creation, its sale and distribution to buyers, and its service after the sale.

Support activities provide the assistance necessary for the primary activities to take place.

A **global mind-set** is the ability to analyze, understand, and manage an internal organization in ways that are not dependent on the assumptions of a single country, culture, or context.

Tangible resources are assets that can be observed and quantified.

Intangible resources include assets that are rooted deeply in the firm's history, accumulate over time, and are relatively difficult for competitors to analyze and imitate.

Value is measured by a product's performance characteristics and by its attributes for which customers are willing to pay.

Outsourcing is the purchase of a value-creating activity from an external supplier.

REVIEW QUESTIONS

1. Why is it important for a firm to study and understand its internal organization?
2. What is value? Why is it critical for the firm to create value? How does it do so?
3. What are the differences between tangible and intangible resources? Why is it important for decision makers to understand these differences? Are tangible resources linked more closely to the creation of competitive advantages than are intangible resources, or is the reverse true? Why?
4. What are capabilities? How do firms create capabilities?
5. What are the four criteria used to determine which of a firm's capabilities are core competencies? Why is it important for firms to use these criteria in developing capabilities?
6. What is value chain analysis? What does the firm gain when it successfully uses this tool?
7. What is outsourcing? Why do firms outsource? Will outsourcing's importance grow as we progress in the twenty-first century? If so, why?
8. How do firms identify internal strengths and weaknesses? Why is it vital that managers have a clear understanding of their firm's strengths and weaknesses?

EXPERIENTIAL EXERCISES

Exercise 1: What Makes a Great Outsourcing Firm?

The focus of this chapter is on understanding how firm resources and capabilities serve as the cornerstone for competencies, and, ultimately, a competitive advantage. However, when firms cannot create value in either a primary or support activity, outsourcing becomes a potential strategy. Yet with the recession that began in 2007 there seems to be a shift occurring. According to the International Association of Outsourcing Professionals (IAOP) at their 2008 annual conference, nearly 75 per cent of organizations will do the same or more outsourcing in response to the financial crisis and that greater contract flexibility is their top need. However, 25 per cent of organizations reported lower volumes and 19 per cent said they have renegotiated lower prices on existing contracts. In addition, the IAOP reports more than 53 per cent of respondents say they are doing more due diligence and also favor working with larger providers.

During that same 2008 conference, the IAOP announced their Global Outsourcing 100, a ranking of the world's best outsourcing service providers. The evaluation process mirrors that employed by many top customers and considers four key criteria: (1) size and growth in revenue, employees, centers, and countries served; (2) customer experience as demonstrated through the value being created for the company's top customers; (3) depth and breadth of competencies as demonstrated through industry recognition, relevant certifications, and investment in the development of people, processes, and technologies; and (4) management capabilities as reflected in the experience and accomplishments of the business's top leaders and investments in management systems that ensure outsourcing success. Below are the top 10 for 2008.

1. Accenture
2. IBM
3. Infosys Technologies
4. Sodexo
5. Capgemini
6. Tata Consultancy Services
7. Wipro Technologies
8. Hewlett-Packard
9. Genpact
10. Tech Mahindra

Split up into groups and pick one of the Global Outsourcing 100 to analyze. The complete list can be found on the IAOP website at http://www.outsourcingprofessional.org/. (A new list is published annually in *Fortune* magazine and updated on the IAOP website.) Prepare a brief presentation using your research and the contents of this chapter that addresses at a minimum the following questions:

- Why was this company chosen? What has been their history as regards outsourcing as a source of revenue?
- How does the firm describe, or imply, its value proposition?
- What unique competitive advantage does the firm exhibit?
- Do you consider this to be a sustainable competitive advantage? Utilize the four sources of sustainable competitive advantage as your guide.

Exercise 2: Competitive Advantage and Pro Sports

What makes one team successful while another team struggles? At first glance, a National Football League franchise or Women's National Basketball Association team may not seem like a typical business. However, professional sports have been around for a long time: pro hockey in the United States emerged around World War I, and pro basketball shortly after World War II; both could be considered newcomers relative to the founding of baseball leagues. Pro sports are big business as well, as evidenced by the Boston Red Sox's 2009 opening day payroll of $121,745,999.

With this exercise, we will use tools and concepts from the chapter to analyze factors underlying the success or failure of different sports teams. Working as a group, pick two teams that play in the same league. For each team, address the following questions:

- How successful are the two teams you selected? How stable has their performance been over time?
- Make an inventory of the characteristics of the two teams. Characteristics you might choose to identify include reputation, coaching, fan base, playing style and tactics, individual players, and so on. For each characteristic you describe:
- Decide if it is best characterized as tangible, intangible, or a capability.
- Apply the concepts of value, rarity, imitation, and sustainability to analyze its value-creating ability.
- Is there evidence of bundling in this situation (i.e., the combination of different resources and capabilities)?
- What would it take for these two teams to substantially change their competitive position over time? For example, if a team is successful, what types of changes in resources and capabilities might affect it negatively? If a team is below average, what changes would you recommend to its portfolio of resources and capabilities?

PART II: Formulation of Strategic Actions

CHAPTER 4

Business-Level Strategy

Studying this chapter should provide you with the strategic management knowledge needed to

- Define business-level strategy.
- Discuss the relationship between customers and business-level strategies in terms of who, what, and how.
- Explain the differences among business-level strategies.
- Use the five forces of competition model to explain how above-average returns can be earned through each business-level strategy.
- Describe the risks of using each of the business-level strategies.

OPENING CASE
Bajaj Auto Ltd.: Cost Leadership Through Volume and Market Leadership

Bajaj Auto Limited (BAL) was established in 1945. It started operations as an importer of two- and three-wheelers from Piaggio (the Italian manufacturer of Vespa). In 1959, the company was granted a license from the Indian government to produce 6000 scooters and three wheelers annually. In 1960, it forged a technical collaboration with Piaggio to manufacture its products in India and set up a manufacturing unit at Akurdi in Pune. It also went public that year. Bajaj Auto Limited (BAL) started assembling scooters and three-wheeler vehicles using Piaggio designs and components. During the 1960s, the company concentrated on indigenization of components and establishing a dealer network in India. It also developed a network of vendors who could produce quality components at reasonable prices. Initially, the local component content was as low as 26 per cent but it was gradually increased to total indigenous supply of components. By 1966, BAL had become the largest Indian producer of two wheelers and product demand far exceeded supply. It became by far the dominant market leader—a position it retained for the next twenty-five years.

When its collaboration with Piaggio concluded in 1971, BAL started manufacturing scooters under the Bajaj brand. *Chetak*, BAL's first scooter model under this brand, was introduced in 1972. Throughout the 1970s and 1980s, scooters dominated the Indian two-wheeler market, and the introduction of its own model enabled Bajaj to retain its leadership. According to Rajiv Bajaj, Managing Director, BAL, the company had produced about 10 million *Chetak* scooters before the model was discontinued.

In 1970, the company was limited to producing just 20,000 units a year. Supply and demand were completely out of sync, with waiting lists for Bajaj Auto vehicles averaging 10 years. To lower costs while improving the price and quality of its products, BAL needed economies of scale. The company increased its production steadily and, by the beginning of the 1980s, Bajaj Auto's annual production had reached 172,000 vehicles. By 1988 it was producing 510,000 units a year and 800,000 units by 1990.

Till about 1990, Bajaj's business strategy had centered on four objectives: keeping costs and prices low, improving product quality; focusing on two-and three-wheeler vehicles, and striving for economies of scale. In other words, it was a pure cost leadership strategy. Used to market leadership, Rahul Bajaj, the chairman of the group, once famously remarked that he did not need a marketing department. Innovation, design orientation, and service orientation were low consistent with the almost monopolistic market position of Bajaj Auto. It attained the position of a cost leader through multiple sources of advantage: economies through volume, through highly efficient production processes, supply of components from its own production as well as a network of vendors it had developed, a wide dealer and service network, and very little by way of marketing and R&D expenses.

In 1984, government policy permitted companies to become full product range manufacturers and to establish foreign collaborations, resulting in major global two wheeler manufacturers such as Honda, Suzuki, Yamaha, and Piaggio entering the Indian market through collaborations or joint ventures. The entry of foreign companies posed a tough competition to Bajaj as they had more sophisticated technologies compared to BAL's low-end technology. It needed to differentiate as well. Through a technological collaboration with Japanese bike manufacturer Kawasaki, BAL entered both the motorcycle and moped (smaller, gearless two-wheeler vehicles) segments of the two-wheeler market. The technical collaboration with Kawasaki centered on the development and production of a 2-stroke and 4-stroke motorcycle that gave BAL access to Kawasaki motorcycle design and expertise enabling it to improve variety and quality of its motorcycles.

Bajaj continued with its cost leadership strategy. To keep its costs low, the company relied on using as much of its old machinery and equipment as possible; it also altered its supply-chain management, turning to outsourcing for almost every component used in the assembly line and relying on just-in-time deliveries several times a day. Major suppliers were reduced from 900 to 200. It developed a core theme, "Build technology inside and parts outside". About 60 per cent by value of a Bajaj vehicle was outsourced. Virtually no components were imported, 20 per cent of its requirements were single sourced and most components were procured from three or less vendors. Many suppliers were completely or largely dedicated to BAL. This enabled the vendors also to reap economies of scale. The company bought raw material in bulk for itself and for some of its vendors, thus enabling them also to reduce their costs. For most two wheeler companies, material costs accounted for about 70 per cent of operating income but in Bajaj's case it was only 57 per cent (in FY 98), the lowest in the industry. This also led to its manpower productivity becoming much higher: while earlier it used to take 1.9 man days to make a scooter, due to outsourcing it came down to about 1.4 man days.

After the liberalization in the early '90s, there emerged broad changes in demographic patterns and consumer preferences. Motor cycles emerged as the preference to scooters. The new entrants positioned their motorcycles according to consumer preferences by emphasizing their fuel efficiency and their life style appeal. To reach the younger generation, Bajaj replaced its age-old slogan, "Hamara Bajaj", which positioned the scooter as a vehicle for the family for almost a life time, with a new tagline "Definitely Male" for its motorcycle, Pulsar, showing men in jeans and sunglasses, shirts unbuttoned, sharing the motorcycle seat with scantily clad women. Bajaj also began emphasizing the company's technology. The Pulsar, it claimed, had 52 per cent lower emissions than what was on the market and was 20 per cent more fuel efficient.

In 1993, BAL became the largest manufacturer of scooters and the third largest manufacturer of two-and three-wheeler vehicles in the world. It produced several models that matched the competitors in various segments: five in scooters, three in motorcycles, one moped model, and three three-wheeler models. BAL leveraged on its experience in low cost, highly efficient production, and, by offering products at very competitive prices, was able to retrieve its market position. It also emerged as the only company manufacturing a full range of two-and three-wheeler products.

Bajaj Auto Ltd. Achieving market leadership by managing costs diligently

To leverage further on its economies of scale, BAL set up its own Research and Development department. The department concentrated on modifying the existing designs and adapting the vehicles for Indian conditions, improving their fuel efficiencies, and trying out new materials. This saved on labor hours and raw materials. BAL's R&D enhanced its digital computational capabilities along with the ability to prototype and test the products to even higher standards, thereby enabling the company to reduce its development cycle. Advanced machines were installed in the prototype shop to enable quick and precise building and inspection of parts.

Man power productivity in terms of number of vehicles per man-year improved by 88 per cent in the decade 1988–98. Lower costs were designed into new models, and further enhanced in the manufacturing process.

A major advantage Bajaj had was its dealer and service network. Here again, Bajaj's economies of scope were put into effect. Besides, Bajaj Auto also began working with dealers to increase their customer friendliness and service and helped them to modernize their workshops in order to increase productivity and reduce service time. The company believed that this would encourage customers to come to authorized workshops and service centers where they were ensured good service and genuine spare parts. This was a value addition to the customers.

Today, Bajaj Auto, the country's second-largest two-wheeler maker continues to surprise the market with a strong volume growth and tight control on operational costs. The strategy has helped the company to grow aggressively without sacrificing margins. Cost leadership and customization were two contrary things. But that is where manufacturing technology counts; even if you are producing slightly different versions for different segments of the market, you can derive economies of scale.

Sources: www,rediff.com, 2009, A peek into Bajaj Auto's illustrious journey, http://business.rediff.com/slide-show/2009/dec/11/slide-show-1-auto-bajajs-illustrious-journey.htm#contentTop, December 11; Bajaj Auto Ltd.: Overtaken in the Indian Scooter Market, 2006, IBS Centre for Market Research, http://www.icmrindia.org/casestudies/catalogue/business%20strategy/Bajaj%20Auto%20Ltd-Overtaken%20in%20the%20Indian%20Scooter%20Market.htm; Bajaj Auto Ltd, :Case study # N9-593-097 of Harvard Business School (1993); Bajaj Auto Limited (A) (Case study of Indian Institute of Management, Ahmedabad (1987); Rahul Bajaj –Aumni Achievement Awards, 2005, http://www.alumni.hbs.edu/awards/2005/bajaj.html; Shally Seth, 2010, Bajaj Auto gains from outsourced non-critical manufacturing, www.livemint.com, April 13, http://www.livemint.com/2010/04/13001557/Bajaj-Auto-gains-from-outsourc.html; Gita Piramal, Sumantra Ghoshal & Sudeep Budhiraja, 2003, Transformation of Bajaj Auto Ltd., Case study on Lessons on Excellence Series, http://alltimenews.net/bajaj-auto-finance-limited-becomes-bajaj-finance-limited/; http://www.iitk.ac.in/techkriti/2004/events/olymbiz/LessonsInExcellenceCase.pdf, http://www.iitk.ac.in/techkriti/2004/events/olymbiz/LessonsInExcellenceCase.pdf ; *Economic Times*, 2010, Bajaj: Rising Auto Sales to Drive Growth, 23 July; Forbes Asia; 10/2/2006, Vol. 2 Issue 16 – Biker Bajaj: link http://web.ebscohost.com/ehost/detail?vid=1&hid=12&sid=5bb19a9e-355e-4a64-9458-a3f8bb9b0a33%40sessionmgr11&bdata=JnNpdGU9ZWhvc3QtbGl2ZQ%3d%3d#db=bth&AN=22735555.

Increasingly important to the firm's success,[1] strategy is concerned with making choices among two or more alternatives.[2] As we noted in Chapter 1, when choosing a strategy, the firm decides to pursue one course of action instead of others. The choices are influenced by opportunities and threats in the firm's external environment[3] (see Chapter 2) as well as the nature and quality of the resources, capabilities, and core competencies in its internal organization[4] (see Chapter 3). As we see in the Opening Case, Bajaj Auto Limited tries to drive its costs lower and lower as the foundation for how it competes in India's two wheeler market. Recently, it has been producing motor cycles for different segments at a highly competitive cost that its competitors find difficult to match.

The fundamental objective of using any type of strategy (see Figure 1.1) is to gain strategic competitiveness and earn above-average returns.[5] Strategies are purposeful, precede the actions to which they apply, and demonstrate a shared understanding of the firm's vision and mission.[6]

An effectively formulated strategy marshals, integrates, and allocates the firm's resources, capabilities, and competencies so that it will be properly aligned with its external environment.[7] A properly developed strategy also rationalizes the firm's vision and mission along with the actions taken to achieve them.[8] Information about a host of variables including markets, customers, technology, worldwide finance, and the changing world economy must be collected and analyzed to properly form and use strategies. In the final analysis, sound strategic choices that reduce uncertainty regarding outcomes[9] are the foundation for building successful strategies.[10]

Business-level strategy, this chapter's focus, is an integrated and coordinated set of commitments and actions which the firm uses to gain a competitive advantage by exploiting core competencies in specific product markets.[11] Business-level strategy indicates the choices the firm has made about how it intends to compete in individual product markets. The choices are important because long-term performance is linked to a firm's strategies.[12] Given the complexity of successfully competing in the global economy, the choices about how the firm will compete can be difficult.[13] It might involve divesting from a business in which the firm had been for a number of years (Bajaj discontinuing its scooter line), entering into new segments (motor cycles and mopeds) and entering into altogether new businesses (Larsen & Toubro getting into IT software). For example, during the downturn in 2008, Tata Steel offered an early separation scheme for its employees over 50 years of age. By this scheme, Tata Steel hoped to reduce the strength of its work force by about 2100, from its strength of 34,000.[14] IBM laid off 700 employees from its Indian offices, and TCS, the venerable software giant, asked 500 employees to leave. TCS also reduced the variable pay or the incentives of its employees for the first quarter of 2008 by 1.5%.[15] Reliance Industries sought to "outplace" around 400 employees to reduce the pain of severance. Wipro, the other venerable software giant, found creative ways of handling its costs during the downturn. It launched a scheme, in April 2009, named "Project Enrich" to give an alternative to its employees by allowing them to work 10 days a month, with a pay that was 50 per cent of their cost to company (CTC). They were to be absorbed back into projects once deployment opportunities came up. The scheme had already enrolled 1000 of their employees, according to the daily, *Mint*.[16] Another innovative scheme, "Project Rejuvenate", allowed some benched staff and senior executives to take leave for one to one-and-a-half years to augment their skills and knowledge at 25 per cent of their CTC.[17] Another way to cut costs by IT firms such as Wipro, TCS, and HCL, without any significant impact on quality has been to hire more number of non engineering graduates (who come for a lower salary): it was estimated that 20–25 per cent of their core workforce would be non engineering personnel.[18] Every firm must form and use a business-level strategy. However, every firm may not use all the strategies—corporate-level, merger and acquisition, international, and cooperative—that we will examine in Chapters 6–9. A firm competing in a single-product market area in a single geographic location does not need a corporate-level strategy to deal with product diversity or an international strategy to deal with geographic diversity. In contrast, a diversified firm will use one of the corporate-level strategies as well as a separate business-level strategy for each product market area in which it competes. Every firm—from the local dry cleaner to the multinational corporation—chooses at least one business-level strategy. Thus business-level strategy is the **core** strategy—the strategy that the firm forms to describe how it intends to compete in a product market.[19]

We discuss several topics to examine business-level strategies. Because customers are the foundation of successful business-level strategies and should never be taken for granted,[20] we present information about customers that is relevant to business-level strategies. In terms of customers, when selecting a business-level strategy the firm determines (1) *who* will be served, (2) *what* needs those target customers have that it will satisfy, and (3) *how* those needs will be satisfied. Selecting customers and deciding which of their needs the firm will try to satisfy, as well as how it will do so, are challenging tasks. Global competition has created many attractive options for customers, thus making it difficult to determine the strategy to best serve them. Effective global competitors have become adept at identifying the needs of customers in different cultures and geographic regions as well as learning how to quickly and successfully adapt the functionality of a firm's good or service to meet those needs.

Descriptions of the purpose of business-level strategies—and of the five business-level strategies—follow the discussion of customers. The five strategies we examine are called **generic** because they can be used in any organization competing in any industry.[21] Our analysis describes how effective use of each strategy allows the firm to favorably position itself relative to the five competitive forces in the industry (see Chapter 2). In addition, we use the value chain (see Chapter 3) to show examples of the primary and support activities necessary to implement specific business-level strategies. Because no strategy is risk-free,[22] we also describe the different risks the firm may encounter when using these strategies. In Chapter 11, we explain the organizational structures and controls linked with the successful use of each business-level strategy.

Customers: Their Relationship with Business-Level Strategies

Strategic competitiveness results only when the firm satisfies a group of customers by using its competitive advantages as the basis for competing in individual product markets.[23] A key reason firms must satisfy customers with their business-level strategy is that returns earned from relationships with customers are the lifeblood of all organizations.[24]

The most successful companies try to find new ways to satisfy current customers and/or to meet the needs of new customers. Being able to do this can be even more difficult when firms and consumers face challenging economic conditions. During such times, firms may decide to reduce their workforce to control costs. Bajaj Auto did that, as we have seen in the Opening Case. This can lead to problems, however, when having fewer employees makes it harder for companies to meet individual customers' needs and expectations. In these instances, some suggest that firms should follow several courses of action, including "babying their best customers" by paying extra attention to them and developing a flexible workforce by cross-training employees so they can fill a variety of responsibilities on their jobs. Amazon.com, insurer USAA, and Lexus were recently identified as "customer service champs" because they devote extra care and attention to customer service during challenging economic times.[25]

Effectively Managing Relationships with Customers

The firm's relationships with its customers are strengthened when it delivers superior value to them. Strong interactive relationships with customers often provide the foundation for the firm's efforts to profitably serve customers' unique needs.

As may be seen from the Strategic Focus later on in this chapter, The Park group of hotels is committed to providing superior and a unique value and experience to its customers. Importantly, as The Park appears to anticipate, delivering superior value often results in increased customer loyalty. The IT Company, Cognizant Technologies has a narrow base of customers compared to its competitors such as Infosys and TCS, but due to an intimate relationship with its customers over a long period of time, it has developed an ability to anticipate how to create value for its customers, most of whom are loyal to the company.[26] In turn, customer loyalty has a positive relationship with profitability. However, more choices and easily accessible information about the functionality of firms' products are creating increasingly sophisticated and knowledgeable customers, making it difficult to earn their loyalty.[27]

A number of companies have become skilled at the art of *managing* all aspects of their relationship with their customers.[28] For example, Amazon.com is widely recognized for the quality of information it maintains about its customers, the services it renders, and its ability to anticipate customers' needs. Using the information it has, Amazon tries to serve what it believes are the unique needs of each customer; and it has a strong reputation for being able to successfully do this.[29]

As we discuss next, firms' relationships with customers are characterized by three dimensions. Companies such as Amazon.com understand these dimensions and manage their relationships with customers in light of them.

Reach, Richness, and Affiliation

The **reach** dimension of relationships with customers is concerned with the firm's access and connection to customers. In general, firms seek to extend their reach, adding customers in the process of doing so.

Reach is an especially critical dimension for social networking sites such as Facebook and MySpace in that the value these firms create for users is to connect them with others. In mid-2009, traffic to MySpace was falling; at the same time, data showed that Facebook had matched MySpace in monthly US visitors for the first time. Specifically, in May 2009, "MySpace attracted 70.2 million unique US visitors ... down 4.7% from a year ago while Facebook's US audience nearly doubled to 70.3 million, according to comScore Media Metrix."[30] Reach is also important to telecom firms such as Bharti Airtel. Fortunately for this firm, recent results indicate that its reach continues to expand: "Bharti Airtel ended the first quarter of 2010 with 139.77 million total subscribers, representing a 33 per cent year-over-year growth from 105.2 million subscribers at the end of the first quarter of 2009 and a 7 per cent sequential growth from 130.69 million subscribers at the end of the fourth quarter of 2009."[31]

AP Photo/Press Association

Facebook's reach continues to grow rapidly. In July 2009, it had surpassed 250 million users worldwide.

Richness, the second dimension of firms' relationships with customers, is concerned with the depth and detail of the two-way flow of information between the firm and the customer. The potential of the richness dimension to help the firm establish a competitive advantage in its relationship with customers leads many firms to offer online services in order to better manage information exchanges with their customers. Broader and deeper information-based exchanges allow firms to better understand their customers and their needs. Such exchanges also enable customers to become more knowledgeable about how the firm can satisfy them. Internet technology and e-commerce transactions have substantially reduced the costs of meaningful information exchanges with current and potential customers. As we have noted, Amazon is a leader in using the Internet to build relationships with customers. In fact, it bills itself as the most "customer-centric company" on earth. The firm's decision in June 2009 to launch "Your Amazon Ad Contest" demonstrates its belief in and focus on its customers. This contest asked Amazon customers to submit their vision of an Amazon television commercial to the firm. The winning entry was to receive $20,000 in Amazon.com gift cards.[32]

Affiliation, the third dimension, is concerned with facilitating useful interactions with customers. Viewing the world through the customer's eyes and constantly seeking ways to create more value for the customer have positive effects in terms of affiliation. Internet navigators such as Microsoft's MSN Autos helps online clients find and sort information. MSN Autos provides data and software to prospective car buyers that enable them to compare car models along multiple objective specifications. A prospective buyer who has selected a specific car based on comparisons of different models can then be linked to dealers that meet the customer's needs and purchasing requirements. Information about other relevant issues such as financing and insurance and even local traffic patterns is also available at the site. Because its revenues come not from the final customer or end user but from other sources (such as advertisements on its Web site, hyperlinks, and associated products and services), MSN Autos represents the customer's interests, a service that fosters affiliation.[33]

As we discuss next, effectively managing customer relationships (along the dimensions of reach, richness, and affiliation) helps the firm answer questions related to the issues of *who, what,* and *how.*

Who: Determining the Customers to Serve

Deciding *who* the target customer is that the firm intends to serve with its business-level strategy is an important decision.[34] Companies divide customers into groups based on differences in the customers' needs (needs are discussed further in the next section) to make this decision. Dividing customers into groups based on their needs is called **market segmentation**, which is a process that clusters people with similar needs into individual and identifiable groups. Soft drink manufacturers such as Coca-Cola and Pepsi segment their customers in terms of age, income, rural vs. urban, socio economic status, and so on. Remarkably, these two major brands selling beverages that are hard to distinguish in blind tests, position their products quite differently, with the Pepsi famously declaring that there is "nothing official about it" when Coca-Cola became the official drinks supplier for the 1996 Wills World Cup in cricket. Consistently, Pepsi has positioned its drink as a youthful drink as compared to Coca-Cola.[35]

Almost any identifiable human or organizational characteristic can be used to subdivide a market into segments that differ from one another on a given characteristic. Common characteristics on which customers' needs vary are illustrated in Table 4.1.

In light of what it learned about its customers, Arihant Retail, a small retailing firm in garments and textiles in Chennai, used **shopping experience** as a characteristic to subdivide its customers into different segments as a basis for serving their unique needs. Specifically, Arihant learned from its experience that its female and male customers want different shopping experiences. Men generally wanted to make their purchases quickly, while women looked at many textiles and garments be-

Table 4.1 Basis for customer segmentation

Consumer Markets	Industrial Markets
1. Demographic factors (age, income, sex, etc.)	1. End-use segments (identified by SIC code)
2. Socioeconomic factors (social class, stage in the family life cycle)	2. Product segments (based on technological differences or production economics)
3. Geographic factors (cultural, regional, and national differences)	3. Geographic segments (defined by boundaries between countries or by regional differences within them)
4. Psychological factors (lifestyle, personality traits)	4. Common buying factor segments (cut across product market and geographic segments)
5. Consumption patterns (heavy, moderate, and light users)	5. Customer size segments
6. Perceptual factors (benefit segmentation, perceptual mapping)	

Source: Adapted from S. C. Jain, 2000, *Marketing Planning and Strategy,* Cincinnati: South-Western College Publishing, 120.

fore making their choice. In light of these research results, women's sections in Arihant stores are organized more spaciously and with greater number of staff helping them to choose, while the men's sections of Arihant stores are more straightforward, with clothing items that are commonly stacked by size. It also employs five tailors to stitch women's garments such as *salvaar kameez* sets to ensure a better fit, since good tailors are becoming difficult to come by. Arihant believes that this provides it with a competitive advantage.[36]

What: Determining Which Customer Needs to Satisfy

After the firm decides *who* it will serve, it must identify the targeted customer group's needs that its goods or services can satisfy. In a general sense, *needs (what)* are related to a product's benefits and features.[37] Successful firms learn how to deliver to customers what they want and when they want it.[38] Having close and frequent interactions with both current and potential customers helps the firm identify those individuals' and groups' current and future needs.[39]

From a strategic perspective, a basic need of all customers is to buy products that create value for them. The generalized forms of value that goods or services provide are either low cost with acceptable features or highly differentiated features with acceptable cost. In the recent global financial crisis, companies across industries recognized their customers' need to feel as secure as possible when making purchases. Allowing customers to return their cars if they lose their job within 12 months of the purchase is how Hyundai Motors decided to address this consumer need, creating value in the form of security.[40]

The most effective firms continuously strive to anticipate changes in customers' needs. The firm that fails to anticipate and certainly to recognize changes in its customers' needs may lose its customers to competitors whose products can provide more value to the focal firm's customers. For example, Ford Motor Company concluded that customers' needs across the global automobile market were becoming more similar. In response, the firm decided to build the Fiesta as a world car. While the car will be tailored somewhat to the needs of different customers in different markets, analysts believe that the firm "… is betting that it has figured out what has bedeviled mass-market automakers for decades, which is hitting a home run in every market with the same car."[41] Ford believes that changes have occurred resulting in more similarity in customers' needs for automotive transportation across multiple markets. If this assessment is correct, the firm may take customers away from automobile manufacturers failing to see the trend toward similarity rather than differences in customers' needs within multiple market segments.

Though there are exceptions like the perceived market for Ford's Fiesta, consumers' needs within individual market segments often vary a great deal.[42] Chennai's Grand Sweets tries to address consumers' desires for high-quality, fresh sweets and savories, and it has become a sort of legend in that city. Its emphasis on fresh food is such that it donates all is leftovers each day to feed the poor. This raises its costs, but its popularity with its clientele desiring fresh and tasty food is such that often they patiently wait for some time in a queue to get the items from Grand Sweets. In contrast, many large fast-food companies satisfy customer needs for lower-cost food items with acceptable quality that are delivered quickly, as is the case with many of the so called *Udupi* restaurants. Diversified food and soft-drink producer PepsiCo believes that "any one consumer has different needs at different times of the day." Through its soft drinks (Pepsi products), snacks (Frito-Lay), juices (Tropicana), and cereals (Quaker), PepsiCo is developing new products from breakfast bars to healthier potato chips "to make certain that it covers all those needs."[43]

How: Determining Core Competencies Necessary to Satisfy Customer Needs

After deciding *who* the firm will serve and the specific *needs* of those customers, the firm is prepared to determine how to use its capabilities and competencies to develop products that can satisfy the needs of its target customers. As explained in Chapters 1 and 3, *core competencies* are resources and capabilities that serve as a source of competitive advantage for the firm over its rivals. Firms use core competencies (*how*) to implement value-creating strategies and thereby satisfy customers' needs. Only those firms with the capacity to continuously improve, innovate, and upgrade their competencies can expect to meet and hopefully exceed customers' expectations across time.[44]

Companies draw from a wide range of core competencies to produce goods or services that can satisfy customers' needs. ProEnergy Services is an integrated service company operating seven business units in the energy industry. Superior client satisfaction is a core competence the firm relies on in competition with its rivals.[45]

SAS Institute is the world's largest privately owned software company and is the leader in business intelligence and analytics. Customers use SAS's programs for data warehousing, data mining, and decision support purposes. Allocating approximately 22 per cent of revenues to research and development (R&D), a percentage that exceeds percentages allocated by its competitors, SAS relies on its core competence in R&D to satisfy the data-related needs of such customers as the US Census Bureau and a host of consumer goods firms (e.g., hotels, banks, and catalog companies).[46] HDFC, the housing finance company, relies on the capabilities of its sales force as well as desk staff to help its customers to select the right house and the right financing options, and thus creates value for its customers.

Sometimes, firms may find it necessary to use their core competencies as the foundation for producing new goods or services for new customers. This may be the case for some small automobile parts suppliers in the United States. Given that US auto production in recent years declined about a third from more typical levels, a number of these firms are seeking to diversify their operations, perhaps exiting the auto parts supplier industry as a result of doing so. Some analysts believe that the first rule for these small manufacturers is to determine how their current capabilities and competencies might be used to produce value-creating products for different customers. One analyst gave the following example of how this might work: "There may be no reason that a company making auto door handles couldn't make ball-and-socket joints for artificial shoulders."[47]

Our discussion about customers shows that all organizations must use their capabilities and core competencies (the *how*) to satisfy the needs (the *what*) of the target group of customers (the *who*) the firm has chosen to serve. Next, we describe the different business-level strategies that are available to firms to use to satisfy customers as the foundation for earning above-average returns.

The Purpose of a Business-Level Strategy

The purpose of a business-level strategy is to create differences between the firm's position and those of its competitors.[48] To position itself differently from competitors, a firm must decide whether it intends to *perform activities differently* or to *perform different activities*. In fact, "choosing to perform activities differently or to perform different activities than rivals" is the essence of business-level strategy.[49] Thus, the firm's business-level strategy is a deliberate choice about how it will perform the value chain's primary and support activities to create unique value. Indeed, in the complex twenty-first century competitive landscape, successful use of a business-level strategy results only when the firm learns how to integrate the activities it performs in ways that create superior value for customers.

Firms develop an activity map to show how they integrate the activities they perform. We show Southwest Airlines' activity map in Figure 4.1. The manner in which Southwest has integrated its activities is the foundation for the successful use of its cost leadership strategy (this strategy is discussed later in the chapter). The tight integration among Southwest's activities is a key source of the firm's ability to at least historically operate more profitably than its competitors.

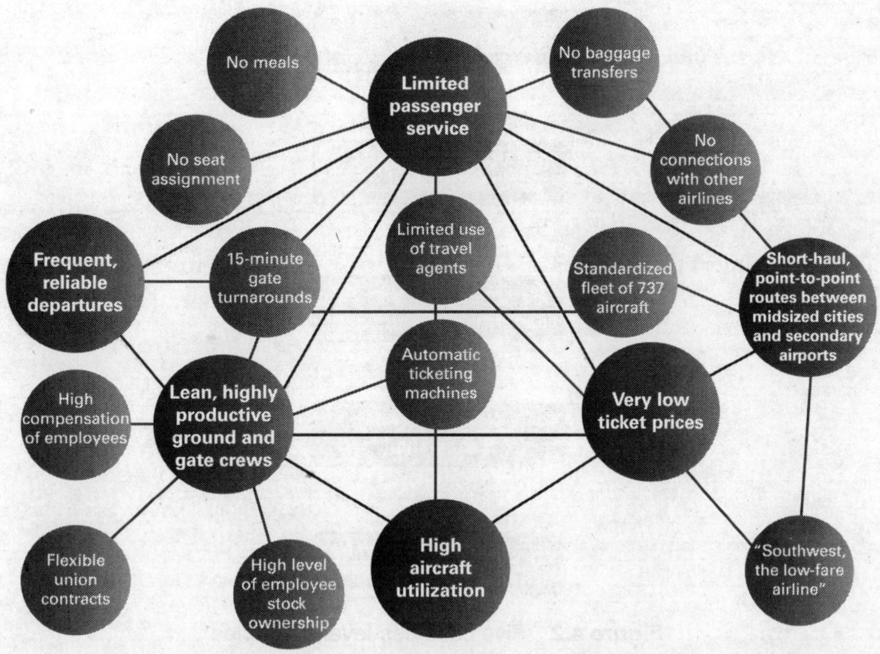

Figure 4.1 Southwest airlines activity system

As shown in Figure 4.1, Southwest Airlines has configured the activities it performs into six strategic themes—limited passenger service; frequent, reliable departures; lean, highly productive ground and gate crews; high aircraft utilization; very low ticket prices; and short-haul, point-to-point routes between mid-sized cities and secondary airports. Individual clusters of tightly linked activities make it possible for the outcome of a strategic theme to be achieved. For example, no meals, no seat assignments, and no baggage transfers form a cluster of individual activities that support the strategic theme of limited passenger service (see Figure 4.1).

Southwest's tightly integrated activities make it difficult for competitors to imitate the firm's cost leadership strategy. The firm's unique culture and customer service, both of which are sources of competitive advantages, are features that rivals have been unable to imitate, although some have tried. US Airways' MetroJet subsidiary, United Airlines' United Shuttle, Delta's Song, and Continental Airlines' Continental Lite—all failed in their attempts to imitate Southwest's strategy. Hindsight shows that these competitors offered low prices to customers, but weren't able to operate at costs close to those of Southwest or to provide customers with any notable sources of differentiation, such as a unique experience while in the air. The key to Southwest's success has been its ability to continuously reduce its costs while providing customers with *acceptable* levels of differentiation such as an engaging culture. Firms using the cost leadership strategy must understand that in terms of sources of differentiation that accompany the cost leader's product, the customer defines *acceptable*.

Fit among activities is a key to the sustainability of competitive advantage for all firms, including Southwest Airlines. As Michael Porter comments, "Strategic fit among many activities is fundamental not only to competitive advantage but also to the sustainability of that advantage. It is harder for a rival to match an array of interlocked activities than it is merely to imitate a particular sales-force approach, match a process technology, or replicate a set of product features. Positions built on systems of activities are far more sustainable than those built on individual activities."[50]

Types of Business-Level Strategies

Firms choose from among five business-level strategies to establish and defend their desired strategic position against competitors: **cost leadership, differentiation, focused cost leadership, focused differentiation,** and **integrated cost leadership/differentiation** (see Figure 4.2). Each business-level strat-

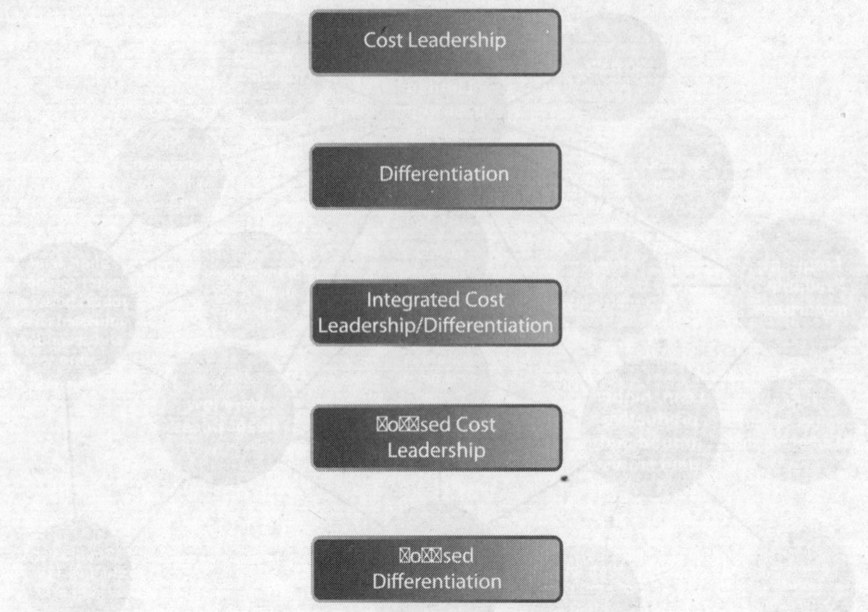

Figure 4.2 Five business-level strategies

egy helps the firm to establish and exploit a particular **competitive advantage** within a particular **competitive scope**. How firms integrate the activities they perform within each different business-level strategy demonstrates how they differ from one another.[51] For example, firms have different activity maps, and thus, a Southwest Airlines activity map differs from those of competitors JetBlue, Continental, American Airlines, and so forth. Superior integration of activities increases the likelihood of being able to gain an advantage over competitors and to earn above-average returns.

When selecting a business-level strategy, firms evaluate two types of potential competitive advantages: "lower cost than rivals, or the ability to differentiate and command a premium price that exceeds the extra cost of doing so."[52] Having lower cost derives from the firm's ability to perform activities differently than rivals; being able to differentiate indicates the firm's capacity to perform different (and valuable) activities.[53] Thus, based on the nature and quality of its internal resources, capabilities, and core competencies, a firm seeks to form either a cost competitive advantage or a uniqueness competitive advantage as the basis for implementing its business-level strategy.

Two types of competitive scopes are broad target and narrow target (see Figure 4.2). Firms serving a broad target market seek to use their competitive advantage on an industry-wide basis. A narrow competitive scope means that the firm intends to serve the needs of a narrow target customer group. With focus strategies, the firm "selects a segment or group of segments in the industry and tailors its strategy to serving them to the exclusion of others."[54] Buyers with special needs and buyers located in specific geographic regions are examples of narrow target customer groups.[55] As shown in Figure 4.2, a firm could also strive to develop a combined cost/uniqueness competitive advantage as the foundation for serving a target customer group that is larger than a narrow segment but not as comprehensive as a broad (or industry-wide) customer group. In this instance, the firm uses the integrated cost leadership/differentiation strategy.

None of the five business-level strategies shown in Figure 4.2 is inherently or universally superior to the others.[56] The effectiveness of each strategy is contingent both on the opportunities and threats in a firm's external environment and on the strengths and weaknesses derived from the firm's resource portfolio. It is critical, therefore, for the firm to select a business-level strategy that is based on a match between the opportunities and threats in its external environment and the strengths of its internal organization as shown by its core competencies.[57] Once the firm chooses its strategy, it should consistently emphasize actions that are required to successfully use it. Wal-Mart's continuous emphasis on driving its costs lower is thought to be a key to the firm's effective cost leadership strategy.[58]

Cost Leadership Strategy

The **cost leadership strategy** is an integrated set of actions taken to produce goods or services with features that are acceptable to customers at the lowest cost, relative to that of competitors.[59] Firms using the cost leadership strategy commonly sell standardized goods or services (but with competitive levels of differentiation) to the industry's most typical customers. Process innovations, which are newly designed production and distribution methods and techniques that allow the firm to operate more efficiently, are critical to the successful use of the cost leadership strategy.[60]

As noted, cost leaders' goods and services must have competitive levels of differentiation that create value for customers. The Indian car market leader, Maruti, had traditionally relied on its cost advantage, especially in its small car, Maruti 800. It produced this model for over two decades, and, through its learning curve, depreciated but continuously modernized plants, and low cost derived from its volume, attained an unassailable cost position. Recently, however, Maruti has decided to emphasize the design and variety of its cars in the Indian market as a source of differentiation while implementing its cost leadership strategy. It has also built a differentiation based on its unbeatable dealer and service networks. We saw Bajaj Auto also taking a similar approach. It is important for firms using the cost leadership strategy, such as Maruti and Bajaj Auto, to do so in this way because concentrating only on reducing costs could result in the firm efficiently producing products that no customer wants to purchase. In fact, such extremes could lead to limited potential for all-important process innovations, employment of lower-skilled workers, poor conditions on the production line, accidents, and a poor quality of work life for employees.[61]

As shown in Figure 4.2, the firm using the cost leadership strategy targets a broad customer segment or group. Cost leaders concentrate on finding ways to lower their costs relative to competitors by constantly rethinking how to complete their primary and support activities to reduce costs still further while maintaining competitive levels of differentiation.[62]

For example, cost leader Greyhound Lines Inc., one of USA's leading bus operators, continuously seeks ways to reduce the costs it incurs to provide bus service while offering customers an acceptable level of differentiation. Greyhound is offering new services to customers as a way of improving the quality of the experience customers have when paying the firm's low prices for its services. Changes in the economic segment of the general environment (see Chapter 2) are creating an opportunity for Greyhound to do this. Specifically, the recent recession found more people seeking to travel by bus instead of by planes and trains. However, these new customers "... insist on certain amenities they've grown accustomed to on planes and trains—such as Internet access and cushier seats, not to mention cleanliness." To maintain competitive levels of differentiation while using the cost leadership strategy, Greyhound recently starting using over 100 "motor coaches" that have leather seats, additional legroom, Wi-Fi access, and power outlets in every row.[63]

Greyhound enjoys economies of scale by serving more than 25 million passengers annually with about 2,300 destinations in the United States and operating approximately 1,250 buses. These scale economies allow the firm to keep its costs low while offering some of the differentiated services today's customers seek from the company.

Demonstrating the firm's commitment to the physical environment segment of the general environment is the fact that "one Greyhound bus takes an average of 34 cars off the road."[64]

India's Bharti Airtel is another such example. It is the market leader and has been so for a number of years, although competitors are fast catching up. Its investments in scale economies, cost reduction through outsourcing of many of its activities and a lean and efficient management has resulted in its able to get an EBIDTA of almost 40 per cent[65], while being able to offer its services at one paisa per second, among the lowest in the world. Yet it seeks to also differentiate through innovative schemes, a fairly good customer service, and a portfolio of services including broadband and 3G.

As primary activities, inbound logistics (e.g., materials handling, warehousing, and inventory control), and outbound logistics (e.g., collecting, storing, and distributing products to customers) often account for significant portions of the total cost to produce some goods and services. Research suggests that having a competitive advantage in terms of logistics creates more value when using the cost leadership strategy than when using the differentiation strategy.[66] Thus, cost leaders seeking competitively valuable ways to reduce costs may want to concentrate on the primary activities of inbound logistics and outbound logistics. In doing so many firms choose to outsource their manufacturing operations to low-cost firms with low-wage employees (e.g., China).[67]

Cost leaders also carefully examine all support activities to find additional sources of potential cost reductions. Developing new systems for finding the optimal combination of low cost and acceptable levels of differentiation in the raw materials required to produce the firm's goods or services is an example of how the procurement support activity can facilitate successful use of the cost leadership strategy.

India's largest organized retailer Big Bazaar uses essentially the cost leadership strategy. With its credo of "Rewrite the Rules, Retain the Values" and its vision of being the retail that aims to "Deliver Everything, Everywhere, Every time to Every Indian Consumer in the most profitable manner",[68] it operates in over 70 cities with a total floor space of over 6 million sq. ft. recording sales of ₹60,000 million for the Pantaloon Group.[69] For Big Bazaar, closeout goods "are the same first-quality, brand-name products found at other retailers, but at substantially lower prices."[70] The firm relies on a disciplined merchandise cost and inventory management system to continuously drive its costs lower.[71] The firm's stores sell name-brand products at prices that are 10–15 per cent below those of other retailers. Big Bazaar's buyers search for goods priced well below the prices in other stores, and they do not mind the inconvenience of being jostled about in non air conditioned stores with ramps between floors, and hardly any lifts. The firm continuously seeks low cost suppliers and enters into long term contracts to ensure a steady supply. Big Bazaar satisfies the customers' need to access the differentiated features of brand-name products also, but at a substantially lower cost. Tightly integrating its purchasing and inventory management activities across its stores is a core competence Big Bazaar uses to satisfy its customers' needs.

Big Bazaar's buyers search for goods priced well below the prices in other stores, and they do not mind the inconvenience of being jostled about in non air conditioned stores with ramps between floors, and hardly any lifts.

As described in Chapter 3, firms use value-chain analysis to identify the parts of the company's operations that create value and those that do not.

Cost leadership involves a clear approach to each element of a form's value chain. In inbound logistics, it needs to set up highly efficient systems to link suppliers' products with the firm's production processes; in operations, it involves use of economies of scale and scope in production; in outbound logistics, efficient delivery systems including transport; in marketing and sales, a small highly trained sales force, products priced in such a way that they attract volumes; and in service, it involves efficient and proper product and service centers, quick availability of spare parts and reduction for need of service in the first place.

In firm infrastructure, it involves cost effective management information systems, small hierarchy, quick decision making and simplified planning procedures. Its HR policies need to focus on reducing turnover costs, and training programs to improved worker efficiency. Its manufacturing technologies need to be easy to use and maintain, and the R&D tend to be oriented toward incremental innovation to reduce costs rather than disruptive or fundamental innovation. The procurement systems need to lead to low costs of inventories, prevention of write-offs through deterioration and systems to evaluate vendor performance.

In short, a cost leader would tend to focus all the attention toward this objective of reducing costs in each and every element of the firm value chain.

Bargaining Power of Suppliers

The cost leader operates with margins greater than those of competitors. Cost leaders want to constantly increase their margins by driving their costs lower. Big Bazaar's net profit after tax increased from 2.2 per cent in 2008-09 to 3.0 percent in 2009-10, despite recession and a consequent drop in sales by 7 per cent,[73] an indication the firm was effectively using the cost leadership strategy. Among other benefits, higher gross margins relative to those of competitors make it possible for the cost leader to absorb its suppliers' price increases. When an industry faces substantial increases in the cost of its supplies, only the cost leader may be able to pay the higher prices and continue to earn either average or above-average returns. Alternatively, a powerful cost leader may be able to force its suppliers to hold down their prices, which would reduce the suppliers' margins in the process.

Firms such as Wal-Mart and Big Bazaar use their power with suppliers (gained because they buy such large quantities from many suppliers) to extract lower prices from them. These savings are then passed on to customers in the form of lower prices, which further strengthens their position relative to competitors lacking the power to extract lower prices from suppliers. The fact that Wal-Mart is the largest retailer in North America is a key reason the firm has a great deal of power with its suppliers. Another indicator of this power is that with 25 per cent of the total market, Wal-Mart is the largest supermarket operator in the United States; and its Sam's Club division is the second largest warehouse club in the United States. Collectively, this sales volume and the market penetration it suggests (over 100 million people visit a Wal-Mart store each week) create the ability for Wal-Mart to gain access to low prices from its suppliers. The scope for Big Bazaar to do this in India is much less, due to the cost structure of many of the suppliers; besides its volumes are not yet big enough to extract much lower prices from its key suppliers, who themselves are big companies, but the retail scene in India is also shifting towards such a model.

Potential Entrants

Through continuous efforts to reduce costs to levels that are lower than competitors', a cost leader becomes highly efficient. Because ever-improving levels of efficiency (e.g., economies of scale) enhance profit margins, they serve as a significant entry barrier to potential competitors.[74] New entrants must be willing and able to accept no-better-than-average returns until they gain the experience required to approach the cost leader's efficiency. To earn even average returns, new entrants must have the competencies required to match the cost levels of competitors other than the cost leader. The low profit margins (relative to margins earned by firms implementing the differentiation strategy) make it necessary for the cost leader to sell large volumes of its product to earn above-average returns. However, firms striving to be the cost leader must avoid pricing their products so low that their ability to operate profitably is reduced, even though volume increases.

In India, many new MNC entrants are able to leverage their advantages to offer products at lower prices, lower quality, or both. Hence the entry of an MNC is almost always viewed with a certain degree of alarm by the incumbent domestic companies. Even some of the large groups such as Reliance can enter the market "with a bang" challenging the incumbents, as it did when it entered the telecom market with rates much lower than those prevailing. Some new entrants could also enter with new technologies, with collaboration from foreign firms, as was the case in the two wheeler market, with firms such as Hero Honda and TVS Suzuki entering with very different propositions such as the design, look, and fuel efficiency.

Product Substitutes

Compared with its industry rivals, the cost leader also holds an attractive position in terms of product substitutes. A product substitute becomes an issue for the cost leader when its features and characteristics, in terms of cost and differentiated features, are potentially attractive to the firm's customers. When faced with possible substitutes, the cost leader has more flexibility than its competitors. To retain customers, it can reduce the price of its good or service. With still lower prices and competitive levels of differentiation, the cost leader increases the probability that customers will prefer its product rather than a substitute.

Competitive Risks of the Cost Leadership Strategy

The cost leadership strategy is not risk free. One risk is that the processes used by the cost leader to produce and distribute its good or service could become obsolete because of competitors' innovations. These innovations may allow rivals to produce at costs lower than those of the original cost leader, or to provide additional differentiated features without increasing the product's price to customers.

A second risk is that too much focus by the cost leader on cost reductions may occur at the expense of trying to understand customers' perceptions of "competitive levels of differentiation." Wal-Mart, for example, has been criticized for having too few salespeople available to help customers and too few individuals at checkout registers. These complaints suggest that there might be a discrepancy between how Wal-Mart's customers define "minimal levels of service" and the firm's attempts to drive its costs lower and lower. Bajaj Auto was reluctant at first to enter into the motor cycle segment in a big way because of its unassailable position in the scooter segment thanks to its low costs.

Imitation is a final risk of the cost leadership strategy. Using their own core competencies, competitors sometimes learn how to successfully imitate the cost leader's strategy. When this happens, the cost leader must increase the value its good or service provides to customers. Commonly, value is increased by selling the current product at an even lower price or by adding differentiated features that create value for customers while maintaining price. Nirma, for example, which entered the market in the 1980s challenging the market leader, Hindustan Lever in detergents and washing powders with a much lower cost product, found itself being imitated by numerous competitors who managed even lower costs than Nirma.

Differentiation Strategy

The **differentiation strategy** is an integrated set of actions taken to produce goods or services (at an acceptable cost) that customers perceive as being different in ways that are important to them.[75] While cost leaders serve a typical customer in an industry, differentiators target customers for whom value is created by the manner in which the firm's products differ from those produced and marketed by competitors. Product innovation, which is "the result of bringing to life a new way to solve the customer's problem—through a new product or service development—that benefits both the customer and the sponsoring company"[76] is critical to successful use of the differentiation strategy.[77]

Firms must be able to produce differentiated products at competitive costs to reduce upward pressure on the price that customers pay. When a product's differentiated features are produced at noncompetitive costs, the price for the product can exceed what the firm's target customers are willing to pay. When the firm has a thorough understanding of what its target customers value, the relative importance they attach to the satisfaction of different needs, and for what they are willing to pay a premium, the differentiation strategy can be effective in helping it earn above-average returns. Finding this sweet spot, however, is a challenge.

Through the differentiation strategy, the firm produces non-standardized (that is, unique) products for customers who value differentiated features more than they value low cost. For example, superior product reliability, durability and high-performance sound systems are among the differentiated features of Toyota Motor Corporation's luxury vehicle division Lexus' products. The Lexus promotional statement—"We pursue perfection, so you can pursue living"—suggests a strong commitment to overall product quality as a source of differentiation. However, Lexus offers its vehicles to customers at a competitive purchase price. As with Lexus products, a good's or service's unique attributes, rather than its purchase price, provide the value for which customers are willing to pay.

Continuous success with the differentiation strategy results when the firm consistently upgrades differentiated features that customers value and/or creates new valuable features (innovates) without significant cost increases.[78] This approach requires firms to constantly change their product lines.[79] These firms may also offer a portfolio of products that complement each other, thereby enriching the differentiation for the customer and perhaps satisfying a portfolio of consumer needs.[80] Because a differentiated product satisfies customers' unique needs, firms following the differentiation strategy are able to charge premium prices. Customers are willing to pay a premium price for a product only when a "firm (is) truly unique at something or be(ing) perceived as unique".[81] The ability to sell a good or service at a price that substantially exceeds the cost of creating its differentiated features allows the firm to outperform rivals and earn above-average returns. For example, shirt and neckwear manufacturer Robert Talbott follows stringent standards of craftsmanship and pays meticulous attention to every detail of production. The firm imports exclusive fabrics from the world's finest mills to make men's dress shirts and neckwear. Single-needle tailoring is used, and precise collar cuts are made to produce shirts. According to the company, customers purchasing one of its products can be assured that they are being provided with the finest fabrics available.[82] Thus, Robert Talbott's success rests on the firm's ability to produce and sell its differentiated products at a price exceeding the costs of imported fabrics and its unique manufacturing processes.

Rather than costs, a firm using the differentiation strategy always concentrates on investing in and developing features that differentiate a product in ways that create value for customers. Robert Talbott uses the finest silks from Europe and Asia to produce its "Best of Class" collection of ties. Overall, a firm using the differentiation strategy seeks to be different from its competitors on as many dimensions as possible. The less similarity between a firm's goods or services and those of competitors, the more buffered it is from rivals' actions. Commonly recognized differentiated goods include

Toyota's Lexus, Ralph Lauren's wide array of product lines, Mont Blanc's writing instruments, and Caterpillar's heavy-duty earth-moving equipment. McKinsey & Co. is a well-known example of a firm that offers differentiated services.

A good or service can be differentiated in many ways. Unusual features, responsive customer service, rapid product innovations and technological leadership, perceived prestige and status, different tastes, and engineering design and performance are examples of approaches to differentiation.[83] While the number of ways to reduce costs may be finite, virtually anything a firm can do to create real or perceived value is a basis for differentiation. Consider product design as a case in point. Because it can create a positive experience for customers, design is becoming an increasingly important source of differentiation (even for cost leaders seeking to find ways to add functionalities to their low-cost products as a way of differentiating their products from competitors) and hopefully, for firms emphasizing it, of competitive advantage.[84] As we noted, design is a way Maruti is now trying to create some uniqueness for its products that are manufactured and sold as part of the firm's cost leadership strategy. Apple is often cited as the firm that sets the standard in design, with the iPod and the iPhone demonstrating Apple's product design capabilities.[85] Industrial products, their packaging, display in the show rooms, the design of the ambience of the show rooms, designing suitable themes and logos, etc. are assuming greater importance. IKEA, a giant in the home furnishing and décor area, uses design in its products to give better value to consumers at a lower cost. To be effective, design has to be integrated with the strategy of the company.[86] Organizations such as the National Institute of Design (NID) are getting involved in the design of products and themes of companies and this trend is expected to increase as a result of the quest for differentiation by companies. The value chain can be analyzed to determine if a firm is able to link the activities required to create value by using the differentiation strategy. Examples of primary and support activities that are commonly used to differentiate a good or service are shown in. Companies without the skills needed to link these activities cannot expect to successfully use the differentiation strategy. Next, we explain how firms using the differentiation strategy can successfully position themselves in terms of the five forces of competition (see Chapter 2) to earn above-average returns.

Differentiation strategy also involves a clear approach to each element in a firm's value chain, but its approach needs to be different from that of a cost leader. In inbound logistics, the firm would set up handling and storage systems that would lead to minimization of damage, in operations, rapid response to customer needs would take priority over long and efficient production runs, in outbound logistics, the firm would focus on packaging to improve appearance, handling to avoid damages in transit and timely deliveries to the customers. In service, it would focus on extensive customer training to assure high quality product installations, quick and efficient service and adequate stocking of spare parts.

Its information systems would focus on customer needs and preferences, and quality of infrastructure to produce consistent high quality products. Its HR would focus on creativity and innovation, and ability to respond to new customer needs. Selection of better personnel and giving them better training would be priorities. Its technology development would focus more on basic research as compared to cost leaders, and it would invest in technologies that would lead to identification and production of innovative, cutting edge products. Lastly, its procurement policies would focus on use of high quality raw materials, replacement parts and good quality control systems at the supplier end also.

In short, the emphasis of a differentiator would be on enhancing the potential for value for customer through superior features, quality and continuous innovation.

Rivalry with Existing Competitors

Customers tend to be loyal purchasers of products differentiated in ways that are meaningful to them. As their loyalty to a brand increases, customers' sensitivity to price increases is reduced. The relationship between brand loyalty and price sensitivity insulates a firm from competitive rivalry. Thus, Robert Talbott's "Best of Class" neckwear line is insulated from competition, even on the basis of price, as long as the company continues to satisfy the differentiated needs of its target customer group with the unique qualities of this line of ties. Likewise, Bose is insulated from intense rivalry as long as customers continue to perceive that its stereo equipment offers superior sound quality at a competitive purchase price. Both Robert Talbott and Bose have strong positive reputations for the high-quality and unique products that they provide. Thus, reputations can sustain the competitive advantage of firms following a differentiation strategy.[87]

Bargaining Power of Buyers (Customers)

The uniqueness of differentiated goods or services reduces customers' sensitivity to price increases. Customers are willing to accept a price increase when a product still satisfies their perceived unique needs better than a competitor's offering does. Thus, the users of Nike and Adidas shoes whose needs are uniquely satisfied by these shoes will likely continue buying those products even if their prices increase. Similarly, the customer who has been highly satisfied with a Mont Blanc pen will probably replace that pen with another one made by the same company even though the purchase price is higher than the original one. Purchasers of brand-name food items such as Kissan ketchup and Amul butter, will accept price increases in those products as long as they continue to perceive that the product satisfies their unique needs at an acceptable cost. In all of these instances, the customers are relatively insensitive to price increases because they do not think that an acceptable product alternative exists.

Suppliers of heavy equipment such as locomotives and power plant equipment tend to supply to large buyers, typically big utilities and governments. These buyers bargain hard, and firms can build differentiation through various means. General Motors, for example, builds differentiation through their excellent spare part supply system. Service support is another means used by companies such as GE.

Bargaining Power of Suppliers

Because the firm using the differentiation strategy charges a premium price for its products, suppliers must provide high-quality components, driving up the firm's costs. However, the high margins the firm earns in these cases partially insulate it from the influence of suppliers in that higher supplier costs can be paid through these margins. Alternatively, because of buyers' relative insensitivity to price increases, the differentiated firm might choose to pass the additional cost of supplies on to the customer by increasing the price of its unique product. Manufacturers of good wines provide a good example of this kind of reduction of the suppliers' bargaining power (in this case, the grape growers).

Potential Entrants

Customer loyalty and the need to overcome the uniqueness of a differentiated product present substantial barriers to potential entrants. Entering an industry under these conditions typically demands significant investments of resources and patience while seeking customers' loyalty. Soft drinks are a good example of this sort of entry barriers.

Product Substitutes

Firms selling brand-name goods and services to loyal customers are positioned effectively against product substitutes. In contrast, companies without brand loyalty face a higher probability of their customers switching either to products that offer differentiated features that serve the same function (particularly if the substitute has a lower price) or to products that offer more features and perform more attractive functions. For example, manufacturers of precision mechanical watches and high quality fountain pens have insulated themselves against the substitutes (quartz watches and ball point pens).

Competitive Risks of the Differentiation Strategy

One risk of the differentiation strategy is that customers might decide that the price differential between the differentiator's product and the cost leader's product is too large. In this instance, a firm may be offering differentiated features that exceed target customers' needs. The firm then becomes vulnerable to competitors that are able to offer customers a combination of features and price that is more consistent with their needs.

This risk is generalized across a number of companies producing different types of products during the recent (2008–2009) global economic crisis—a time when forecasters suggested that "sales of luxury goods, everything from apparel, to jewelry and leather goods, could plunge globally by 10% ..." [88] in 2009. The decline was expected to be more severe in the United States compared to Europe and Japan. A decision made during this time by Coach Inc., a maker of high-quality, luxurious accessories and gifts for women and men, demonstrates one firm's reaction to the predicted decline in the sales of luxury goods. With an interest of providing products to increasingly cost-conscious customers without "cheapening" the firm's image, Coach chose to introduce a new line of its products called "Poppy"; the average price of items in this line is approximately 20 per cent lower than the average price of Coach's typical products.[89] Another example is the introduction of low cost services by airlines such as Jet Konnect by Jet Airways and Air India Express by Air India as a response to the greater consciousness of value among air travelers. The trap to guard against is that these lower cost versions do not affect the image of the core brand itself, something that seems to be happening to Jet Airways.

Another risk of the differentiation strategy is that a firm's means of differentiation may cease to provide value for which customers are willing to pay. A differentiated product becomes less valuable if imitation by rivals causes customers to perceive that competitors offer essentially the same good or service, but at a lower price.[90] A third risk of the differentiation strategy is that experience can narrow customers' perceptions of the value of a product's differentiated features. For example, customers having positive experiences with generic tissues may decide that the differentiated features of the Kleenex product are not worth the extra cost. Similarly, while a customer may be impressed with the quality of a Robert Talbott "Best of Class" tie, positive experiences with less expensive ties may lead to a conclusion that the price of the "Best of Class" tie exceeds the benefit. To counter this risk, firms must continue to meaningfully differentiate their product for customers at a price they are willing to pay.

Counterfeiting is the differentiation strategy's fourth risk. "Counterfeits are those products bearing a trademark that is identical to or indistinguishable from a trademark registered to another party, thus infringing the rights of the older of the trademark."[91] We describe actions companies such as Moser Baer take to deal with the problems counterfeit goods create for firms whose rights are infringed upon in the Strategic Focus.

Focus Strategies

The **focus strategy** is an integrated set of actions taken to produce goods or services that serve the needs of a particular competitive segment. Thus, firms use a focus strategy when they utilize their core competencies to serve the needs of a particular industry segment or niche to the exclusion of others. Examples of specific market segments that can be targeted by a focus strategy include (1) a particular buyer group (e.g., youths or senior citizens), (2) a different segment of a product line (e.g., products for professional painters or the do-it-yourself group), or (3) a different geographic market (e.g., northern or southern Italy).[92]

There are many specific customer needs firms can serve by using a focus strategy. For example, the cooperative banks (such as Kalupur Commercial Cooperative Bank in Gujarat) position themselves to the needs of smaller industrial units and farmers. Their staff mostly speak in the local language, and they run their operations with much less overheads so that they are able to give higher interest rates to their depositors. Their working hours and even working days are suited to the needs of their clients. Many of the Indian food manufacturers such as MTR and Haldirams have developed a niche clientele of Indians living in foreign countries, especially USA and UK, who crave for the Indian aroma. By successfully using a focus strategy, firms such as these gain a competitive advantage in specific market niches or segments, even though they do not possess an industry-wide competitive advantage.

Although the breadth of a target is clearly a matter of degree, the essence of the focus strategy "is the exploitation of a narrow target's differences from the balance of the industry."[93] Firms using the focus strategy intend to serve a particular segment of an industry more effectively than can industry-wide competitors. They succeed when they effectively serve a segment whose unique needs are so specialized that broad-based competitors choose not to serve that segment or when they satisfy the needs of a segment being served poorly by industry-wide competitors.[94]

STRATEGIC FOCUS

4.1 Handling Piracy: The Moser Baer Way

Piracy is a universal issue. Most of us watch movies, and we may buy DVDs/VCDs for our personal collection also. In India, a customer could buy a pirated copy of a movie from ₹30–100. In the early 2000s, the price advantage pirates had over the original content was so large that most customers preferred the pirated versions, the original creators got short shrift.

Moser Baer is India's largest and the world's second largest manufacturer of optical storage media. It was originally a manufacturer of blank CDs. It then entered the recorded video industry in 2006 forming The Moser Baer Home Videos. It saw an opportunity to sell good quality, fully licensed DVDs and VCDs at reasonable prices. This would also deal a blow to the piracy industry. The DVD/VCD industry was a fragmented indus-

Moser Baer Home Videos: Dealing a blow to the video piracy industry with its fully licensed pre recorded DVDs.

try, with many small players producing VCDs and DVDs at low costs. They used cheap blank discs, their recording was poor and they could even damage the audio equipment of the users. But due to their not having to pay royalties, their products were cheap and they developed a huge distribution network, selling these movies even at *paan* shops and traffic signals. Often, these pirated movies would arrive within a few days of the release of the movies. While the legitimate content came in disks priced at ₹300–500 each, the pirated ones were available at ₹30–40 per disk. Moser Baer shifted the entire price-performance curve and set a new standard for the industry by applying its technology developed for other purposes. This company could use its own blank discs, and copy the discs in high quality machines. Moser Baer was, however, clear on one thing: they would sell only licensed versions. They hoped to significantly reduce the retail price of high quality movie VCD and DVDs through volume and through releasing movies in all major regional languages. Moser Baer retailed their high-quality VCDs/DVDs at prices up to 80 per cent less than those charged by established "legitimate" players, bringing them close to the prices of the pirated ones.

Moser Baer established a national distribution network to offer their DVDs and VCDs. It began selling DVDs and VCDs of old Hindi movies and then started adding the latest Hindi as well as regional movies. It acquired copyrights, marketing and distribution rights of around 10,000 titles in all major Indian languages constituting over 45 per cent of mainstream cinema in India. Within a short span of six months, it emerged as a market leader in this segment due to its widespread presence in India (offering home video copyrighted titles in multiple languages) and a nationwide distribution network, coupled with aggressive marketing. Moser Baer set up 456 distributors across the country by 2007. By 2008, the company planned to reach 150,000–175,000 retail outlets across the country by having their DVDs/VCDs available at grocery stores and *paan–beedi* shops which would stock all the latest films. The company was also setting up its own retail outlets. By 2008, the company planned to open 400–500 exclusive stores across India. Moser Baer was clearly going beyond others and was attempting to be an end-to-end player, right from producing a film to selling it at the customer's doorstep.

Typically, a movie is released on video six-eight weeks after it opens in movie theatres, by which time video pirates have already made thousands of illegal copies. Moser Baer entered into a tie-up with regular content producers like UTV to release their productions on home videos shortly after theatrical release. Moser Baer was able to reduce the time between theatrical and DVD releases from six-eight weeks to about two weeks (10 days in some cases) as against several months earlier.

When the prices of blank DVDs fell sharply in late 2008, pirates were able to bundle four or five movies of low resolution into a single disk at a low cost. For Moser Baer, more content per disk would have meant higher cost. So, it started innovating to reach new audiences. It created an extended offering with collections (like the "Shah Rukh Khan 6 pack" of six movies of the Bollywood superstar) priced at a premium and aimed at high-end customers. It also created a brand "Super DVD" priced at ₹27-30 with three movies to cater to the rural markets and take the pirates head on.

Despite Moser Baer's obvious advantages and continuous efforts to counter piracy, the pirated content still commands a significant market share. The gigantic numbers involved in the business model is another challenge. Therefore, in addition to its physical distribution model, it has also put in place an online sales model. It also plans to take its model overseas.

Also, Moser Baer Entertainment Limited, another subsidiary of the company, has formed the Indian Cinema Rights Association along with Eros Entertainment, Yashraj Films, and Reliance, among others, to keep an eye on the market and conduct raids on those indulging in piracy. With this, the company feels it will be able to fulfill its vision, which is to wean consumers away from pirated products to original products, and to offer quality DVDs and VCDs at price points that help eliminate piracy. The strategy is to beat piracy by simply offering the discs at prices not much above those offered by pirated discs, but at significantly higher quality. Its outlets also offer a wide choice.

Sources: Business Today, May 30, 2010, Taking on Piracy Profitably, http:BusinessToday.intoday/bt/story/5619/1/taking-on-piracy-profitably.html.; May 30; Govindkrishna Seshan, 2007, Home entertainment won't be same again, *Business Standard* at http://www.rediff.com/money/2007/apr/19spec1.htm; www.techshout.com, 2007, Moser Baer acquires over 800 ultra video Hindi, Gujarati, Movie Titles, October 8, http://www.techshout.com/general/2007/08/moser-baer-acquires-over-800-ultra-video-hindi-gujarati-movie-titles/; businesstoday.intoday.in - innovation article. BT Cover story: Hello Movies–Oct, 2008;

Firms can create value for customers in specific and unique market segments by using the focused cost leadership strategy or the focused differentiation strategy.

Focused Cost Leadership Strategy

Based in Sweden, IKEA, a global furniture retailer with locations in 24 countries and territories and sales revenue of 21.1 billion euros in 2008, uses the focused cost leadership strategy. Young buyers desiring style at a low cost are IKEA's target customers.[95] For these customers, the firm offers home furnishings that combine good design, function, and acceptable quality with low prices. According to the firm, "Low cost is always in focus. This applies to every phase of our activities."[96]

IKEA emphasizes several activities to keep its costs low. For example, instead of relying primarily on third-party manufacturers, the firm's engineers design low-cost, modular furniture ready for assembly by customers. To eliminate the need for sales associates or decorators, IKEA positions the products in its stores so that customers can view different living combinations (complete with sofas, chairs, tables, etc.) in a single room-like setting, which helps the customer imagine how a grouping of furniture will look in the home. A third practice that helps keep IKEA's costs low is requiring customers to transport their own purchases rather than providing delivery service.

Although it is a cost leader, IKEA also offers some differentiated features that appeal to its target customers, including its unique furniture designs, in-store playrooms for children, wheelchairs for customer use, and extended hours. IKEA believes that these services and products "are uniquely aligned with the needs of [its] customers, who are young, are not wealthy, are likely to have children (but no nanny), and, because they work, have a need to shop at odd hours."[97] Thus, IKEA's focused cost leadership strategy also includes some differentiated features with its low-cost products.

Focused Differentiation Strategy

Other firms implement the focused differentiation strategy. As noted earlier, there are many dimensions on which firms can differentiate their good or service. For example, As can be seen from Strategic Focus, The Park group of hotels use a boutique concept, and focus on customers who are young, trendy and different. They try to combine the luxury and exclusiveness of a five star hotel with a certain degree of informality and friendliness to its customers. They organize events where younger customers can enjoy, and make their pubs and discos the best in the town, fun places to be in. In this process, they may lose out on some older and more conservative customers, but the focused differentiation strategy invariability leads to a decision not only on whom to have as customers, but also whom not to have.

Denver-based Kazoo Toys uses the focused differentiation strategy to create value for parents and children interested in purchasing unique toys while simultaneously having access to unique services. Continuously concentrating on ways to create unique value for its customers seems to be the foundation of the firm's continuing success.

With a focus strategy, firms such as The Park Hotels and Kazoo Toys must be able to complete various primary and support activities in a competitively superior manner to develop and sustain a competitive advantage and earn above-average returns. The activities required to use the focused cost leadership strategy are virtually identical to those of the industry-wide cost leadership strategy, and activities required to use the focused differentiation strategy are largely identical to those of the industry-wide differentiation strategy. Similarly, the manner in which each of the two focus strategies allows a firm to deal successfully with the five competitive forces parallels those of the two broad strategies. The only difference is in the firm's competitive scope; the firm focuses on a narrow industry segment. Thus, and the text regarding the five competitive forces also describe the relationship between each of the two focus strategies and competitive advantage.

STRATEGIC FOCUS

4.2 The Park Group of Hotels

India's first collection of luxury, boutique hotels and, for quite some time, a member of Small Luxury Hotels of the World, The Park Hotels are a part of the Apeejay Surrendra Group, a diversified industrial conglomerate. But the hotel business is managed as an independent business by Ms. Priya Paul. The Park Hotels are located in Kolkata, Bangalore, Chennai, New Delhi, Navi Mumbai, and Visakhapatnam. The chain has achieved global standards of product quality and service excellence. A destination of choice for corporate and leisure travelers from India and abroad, these hotels, due to their downtown location, give easy access to key commercial entertainment districts.

The company started in 1967 with their first property in Kolkata with 150 rooms. It had a highly attractive location, on the Park Street very near the busy Chourangee Road. Subsequently properties were purchased at Visakhapatnam (1968), New Delhi (1987), Bangalore (2000), Chennai (2002), Navi Mumbai (2007), Hyderabad (2010), and near Vembanad Lake, Kerala (2010). The last is a small hotel and has a luxury lake cruiser, the Apsara, with eight bedrooms. None of the properties are very large, the biggest ones having less than 300 rooms. They are all boutique hotels.

Ms. Priya Paul took over the management of the hotel in 1990 under tragic circumstances, when her father was killed by rebels in Assam. She had no prior experience in managing hotels, and she had no idea of how to revamp these hotels which had gone into a state of neglect. The property in Kolkata was constrained due to its location, and she had to compete with the likes of the Taj and Oberoi groups. She thought of positioning the hotels under what she called the "boutique concept", which was not well known in India (but there were boutique hotels in US and Europe). This was to be the differentiation for the hotels. It was a risky concept, but "I had nothing to lose", said Ms. Paul. She was joined by Mr. Vijay Dewan, who had worked in Iraq with the Oberoi Group. Together, they developed and promoted the boutique concept in India.

Boutique hotel is a hotel with a "classy" feel and touch in everything it does. Rooms are designed with the same attention to detail that one would find in a specialized store or boutique; the furnishings are also classy; the service is distinctively different and more personalized. Smaller than the usual five star luxury hotels, they offer a friendlier service, homelier so to speak, but otherwise they have all the features and facilities of a large five star hotel. They are classy, stylish, design driven, trendy, sophisticated, upmarket, and exclusive. A boutique hotel, thus, offers the guests an "experience" not a "product".

©Indiatodayimages.com

The Park: Seeking differentiation to succeed. It is credited with pioneering the concept of Boutique hotels in India

To achieve the classiness, international designers were roped in to tastefully decorate rooms; many new paintings were purchased; renowned artists were commissioned to paint murals. The furnishings were changed more often than in regular hotels. Being a boutique hotel also meant that The Park had to communicate the image of being young and trendy. It had to promote individualism and innovation. These hotels were not only for in-house guests but also had local and other guests who were invited for events, fashion shows, and for celebrating occasions such as Deepavali, New Year, etc. The hotels give excellent ambience in its cafés, and the cuisine is also quite exotic. Market leadership has been attained through constant upgradation of products and services to bring a truly cutting edge international experience. It also runs a bakery, named Flurry's, in Kolkata, which is more of an institution than a mere cake café, famed for its afternoon tea boasting of visits by many leading personalities.

The hotel operates a pub, a night club and two bars, one of them very exclusive, all providing different kinds of experience to its in-house as well as local guests. Its pub, "Some Place Else" is one of the top spots in Kolkata with high patronage of outside members. Its exclusive bar attracts the cream of society in Kolkata.

The company's business processes are also modernized by state-of-the-art IT systems to give its guests a different experience. For example, it keeps track of the preferences of its customers, including the room arrangement, and strive to spring pleasant surprises on their guests on their repeat visits by anticipating their preferences. The system introduced by The Park also ensures that the complaints registered by a guest are also fed into the database of the guest's history such that the concerned departments are informed and careful during the person's repeat visit.

Due to its sharp differentiation, The Park was affected much less during the 2008–2009 recession. While most of the other hotels were facing the heat, The Park turned in a profit. This was also because the Park has a tight control on its costs, and uses IT to achieve efficiencies on every front.

By positioning "The Park" as a collection of luxury boutique hotels, the group is trying to create a niche through differentiation and innovation. Each hotel of the Park Group is different, and provides a different customer experience. This is in sharp contrast to the generally accepted norm in the industry, that all hotels in a chain must provide a near similar experience to the customer. But the customers are kept informed of all events in all properties, and, at a broad level, a high standard of nuanced personalized and informal service is maintained. How your customers feel when they interact with your company and its offering can be a powerful source of differentiation that creates a long lasting emotional attachment. Pioneers of the boutique concept in India, the Park Hotels are differentiated by their constant innovations, designs, new experiences, creating landmark nightspots, and excellent customer service.

Sources: The Web site of The Park, http://www.theparkhotels.com/; Case "The Park, Calcutta", Case # BP 267 of the Indian Institute of Management, Ahmedabad (2001).

Competitive Risks of Focus Strategies

With either focus strategy, the firm faces the same general risks as does the company using the cost leadership or the differentiation strategy, respectively, on an industry-wide basis. However, focus strategies have three additional risks.

First, a competitor may be able to focus on a more narrowly defined competitive segment and "outfocus" the focuser. This would happen to IKEA if another firm found a way to offer IKEA's customers (young buyers interested in stylish furniture at a low cost) additional sources of differentiation while charging the same price or to provide the same service with the same sources of differentiation at a lower price. Second, a company competing on an industry-wide basis may decide that the market segment served by the firm using a focus strategy is attractive and worthy of competitive pursuit. For example, Hindustan Lever decided, as a response to Nirma's entry into the detergent market, to enter the low price segment with new products such as the Wheel brand of soap and detergent. The third risk involved with a focus strategy is that the needs of customers within a narrow competitive segment may become more similar to those of industry-wide customers as a whole over time. As a result, the advantages of a focus strategy are either reduced or eliminated. At some point, for example, in India, the cheap assembled computers lost their market when branded computers started becoming cheaper and within the budgets of most buyers. Even though the assembled computers were still cheaper than branded ones, the price differential was no longer enough to induce the customers to go in for the unbranded ones.

Integrated Cost Leadership/Differentiation Strategy

Most consumers have high expectations when purchasing a good or service. In general, it seems that most consumers want to pay a low price for products with somewhat highly differentiated features. Because of these customer expectations, a number of firms engage in primary and support activities that allow them to simultaneously pursue low cost and differentiation. Firm seeking to do this use the **integrated cost leadership/differentiation strategy**. The objective of using this strategy is to efficiently produce products with some differentiated features. Efficient production is the source of maintaining low costs while differentiation is the source of creating unique value. Firms that successfully use the integrated cost leadership/differentiation strategy usually adapt quickly to new technologies and rapid changes in their external environments. Simultaneously concentrating on developing two sources of competitive advantage (cost and differentiation) increases the number of primary and support activities in which the firm must become competent. Such firms often have strong networks with external parties that perform some of the primary and support activities.[98] In turn, having skills in a larger number of activities makes a firm more flexible.

Concentrating on the needs of its core customer group (higher-income, fashion-conscious discount shoppers), Target Stores uses an integrated cost leadership/differentiation strategy as shown by its "Expect More. Pay Less" brand promise. Target's annual report describes this strategy: "To ensure our guests understand our unique ability to meet their desire for everyday essentials and affordable indulgences, we elevated the prominence of the "Pay Less" half of our brand promise in both our merchandising and marketing through in-store signing and presentation as well as new campaigns that emphasize our outstanding value. At the same time, we continued to deliver differentiation and newness on the "Expect More" side of our brand promise with the introduction of Converse One Star in apparel and shoes, the launch of upscale beauty brands, an expanded owned brand presence and a continuous flow of designer collections at exceptional prices."[99] To implement this strategy, Target relies on its relationships with various companies to offer differentiated products at discounted prices. Collections from eco-conscious Rogan Gregory in apparel, Anya Hindmarch in handbags, Sigerson Morrison in shoes, and John Derian and Sami Hayek in home décor are some of the products available in Target's stores. While implementing its strategy, "Target strives to be a responsible steward of the environment."[100] To protect the physical environment, the firm takes several actions annually including recycling 47,600 broken shopping carts, 2.1 million pounds of plastic, and 153,000 pounds of metal from broken hangers.

Maruti uses a twin strategy of low cost and differentiation to gain a competitive advantage. Maruti was the market leader in cars for over two decades, producing mainly a small car, Maruti 800. But as competition increased, it entered into all segments of cars, and leveraged its cost advantage derived from experience, parts of the plant that could be shared and dealer networks with the other segments. In these segments, Maruti could offer a lower priced car, and yet differentiate itself through its superior dealer and service network, and availability of cheap and easily available spare parts. The result is that Maruti has a strong presence in every segment except the ultra luxury segment.

©Indiatodayimages.com

Maruti has used a twin strategy of low cost and differentiation to gain competitive advantage. It has a strong presence in every segment except the ultra luxury one

Flexibility is required for firms to complete primary and support activities in ways that allow them to use the integrated cost leadership/differentiation strategy in order to produce somewhat differentiated products at relatively low costs. Flexible manufacturing systems, information networks, and total quality management systems are three sources of flexibility that are particularly useful for firms trying to balance the objectives of continuous cost reductions and continuous enhancements to sources of differentiation as called for by the integrated strategy.

Flexible Manufacturing Systems

A flexible manufacturing system (FMS) increases the "flexibilities of human, physical, and information resources"[101] that the firm integrates to create relatively differentiated products at relatively low costs. A significant technological advance, FMS is a computer-controlled process used to produce a variety of products in moderate, flexible quantities with a minimum of manual intervention.[102] Often the flexibility is derived from modularization of the manufacturing process (and sometimes other value chain activities as well).[103]

The goal of an FMS is to eliminate the "low cost versus product variety" trade-off that is inherent in traditional manufacturing technologies. Firms use an FMS to change quickly and easily from making one product to making another. Used properly, an FMS allows the firm to respond more effectively to changes in its customers' needs, while retaining low-cost advantages and consistent product quality.[104] Because an FMS also enables the firm to reduce the lot size needed to manufacture a product efficiently, the firm's capacity to serve the unique needs of a narrow competitive scope is higher. In industries of all types, effective mixes of the firm's tangible assets (e.g., machines) and intangible assets (e.g., people's skills) facilitate implementation of complex competitive strategies, especially the integrated cost leadership/differentiation strategy.[105]

STRATEGY RIGHT NOW

Following similar principles to the integrated cost leadership/differentiation strategy, read how companies are creating uncontested market space employing the Blue Ocean Strategy. www.cengage.com/management/hitt

Information Networks

By linking companies with their suppliers, distributors, and customers, information networks provide another source of flexibility. These networks, when used effectively, help the firm satisfy customer expectations in terms of product quality and delivery speed.[106]

Earlier, we discussed the importance of managing the firm's relationships with its customers in order to understand their needs. Customer relationship management (CRM) is one form of an information-based network process that firms use for this purpose.[107] An effective CRM system provides a 360-degree view of the company's relationship with its customers, encompassing all contact points, business processes, and communication media and sales channels.[108] The firm can then use this information to determine the trade-offs its customers are willing to make between differentiated features and low cost—an assessment that is vital for companies using the integrated cost leadership/differentiation strategy.

Thus, to make comprehensive strategic decisions with effective knowledge of the organization's context, good information flow is essential. Better quality managerial decisions require accurate information on the firm's environment.[109]

Total Quality Management Systems

Total quality management (TQM) is a "managerial innovation that emphasizes an organization's total commitment to the customer and to continuous improvement of every process through the use of data-driven, problem-solving approaches based on empowerment of employee groups and teams."[110] Firms develop and use TQM systems in order to (1) increase customer satisfaction, (2) cut costs, and (3) reduce the amount of time required to introduce innovative products to the marketplace.[111]

Firms able to simultaneously reduce costs while enhancing their ability to develop innovative products increase their flexibility, an outcome that is particularly helpful to firms implementing the integrated cost leadership/differentiation strategy. Exceeding customers' expectations regarding quality is a differentiating feature, and eliminating process inefficiencies to cut costs allows the firm to offer that quality to customers at a relatively low price. Thus, an effective TQM system helps the firm develop the flexibility needed to spot opportunities to simultaneously increase differentiation and reduce costs. Yet, TQM systems are available to all competitors. So they may help firms maintain competitive parity, but rarely alone will they lead to a competitive advantage.[112]

Competitive Risks of the Integrated Cost Leadership/ Differentiation Strategy

The potential to earn above-average returns by successfully using the integrated cost leadership/differentiation strategy is appealing. However, it is a risky strategy, because firms find it difficult to perform primary and support activities in ways that allow them to produce relatively inexpensive products with levels of differentiation that create value for the target customer. Moreover, to properly use this strategy across time, firms must be able to simultaneously reduce costs incurred to produce products (as required by the cost leadership strategy) while increasing products' differentiation (as required by the differentiation strategy).

Firms that fail to perform the primary and support activities in an optimum manner become "stuck in the middle."[113] Being stuck in the middle means that the firm's cost structure is not low enough to allow it to attractively price its products and that its products are not sufficiently differentiated to create value for the target customer. These firms will not earn above-average returns and will earn average returns only when the structure of the industry in which it competes is highly favorable.[114] Thus, companies implementing the integrated cost leadership/differentiation strategy must be able to perform the primary and support activities in ways that allow them to produce products that offer the target customer some differentiated features at a relatively low cost/price.

Firms can also become stuck in the middle when they fail to successfully implement *either* the cost leadership *or* the differentiation strategy. In other words, industry-wide competitors too can become stuck in the middle.

Trying to use the integrated strategy is costly in that firms must pursue both low costs and differentiation. Firms may need to form alliances with other firms to achieve differentiation, yet alliance partners may extract prices for the use of their resources that make it difficult to meaningfully reduce costs.[115] Firms may be motivated to make acquisitions to maintain their differentiation through innovation or to add products to their portfolio not offered by competitors.[116] Recent research suggests that firms using "pure strategies," either cost leadership or differentiation, often outperform firms attempting to use a "hybrid strategy" (i.e., integrated cost leadership/ differentiation strategy). This research suggests the risky nature of using an integrated strategy.[117] However, the integrated strategy is becoming more common and perhaps necessary in many industries because of technological advances and global competition.

SUMMARY

- A business-level strategy is an integrated and coordinated set of commitments and actions the firm uses to gain a competitive advantage by exploiting core competencies in specific product markets. Five business-level strategies (cost leadership, differentiation, focused cost leadership, focused differentiation, and integrated cost leadership/differentiation) are examined in the chapter.
- Customers are the foundation of successful business-level strategies. When considering customers, a firm simultaneously examines three issues: *who, what,* and *how.* These issues, respectively, refer to the customer groups to be served, the needs those customers have that the firm seeks to satisfy, and the core competencies the firm will use to satisfy customers' needs. Increasing segmentation of markets throughout the global economy creates opportunities for firms to identify more unique customer needs they can serve with one of the business-level strategies.
- Firms seeking competitive advantage through the cost leadership strategy produce no-frills, standardized products for an industry's typical customer. However, these low-cost products must be offered with competitive levels of differentiation. Above-average returns are earned when firms continuously emphasize efficiency such that their costs are lower than those of their competitors, while providing customers with products that have acceptable levels of differentiated features.
- Competitive risks associated with the cost leadership strategy include (1) a loss of competitive advantage to newer technologies, (2) a failure to detect changes in customers' needs, and (3) the ability of competitors to imitate the cost leader's competitive advantage through their own unique strategic actions.
- Through the differentiation strategy, firms provide customers with products that have different (and valued) features. Differentiated products must be sold at a cost that customers believe is competitive relative to the product's features as compared to the cost/feature combinations available from competitors' goods. Because of their uniqueness, differentiated goods or services are sold at a premium price. Products can be differentiated along any dimension that some customer group values. Firms using this strategy seek to differentiate their products from competitors' goods or services along as many dimensions as possible. The less similarity to competitors' products, the more buffered a firm is from competition with its rivals.
- Risks associated with the differentiation strategy include (1) a customer group's decision that the differences between the differentiated product and the cost leader's goods or services are no longer worth a premium price, (2) the inability of a differentiated product to create the type of value for which customers are willing to pay a premium price, (3) the ability of competitors to provide customers with products that have features similar to those of the differentiated product, but at a lower cost, and (4) the threat of counterfeiting, whereby firms produce a cheap "knockoff" of a differentiated good or service.
- Through the cost leadership and the differentiated focus strategies, firms serve the needs of a narrow competitive segment (e.g., a buyer group, product segment, or geographic area). This strategy is successful when firms have the core competencies required to provide value to a specialized market segment that exceeds the value available from firms serving customers on an industry-wide basis.
- The competitive risks of focus strategies include (1) a competitor's ability to use its core competencies to "outfocus" the focuser by serving an even more narrowly defined market segment, (2) decisions by industry-wide competitors to focus on a customer group's specialized needs, and (3) a reduction in differences of the needs between customers in a narrow market segment and the industry-wide market.
- Firms using the integrated cost leadership/differentiation strategy strive to provide customers with relatively low-cost products that also have valued differentiated features. Flexibility is required for the firm to learn how to use primary and support activities in ways that allow them to produce differentiated products at relatively low costs. The primary risk of this strategy is that a firm might produce products that do not offer sufficient value in terms of either low cost or differentiation. In such cases, the company is "stuck in the middle." Firms stuck in the middle compete at a disadvantage and are unable to earn more than average returns.

KEY TERMS AND DEFINITIONS

A **business-level strategy** is an integrated and coordinated set of commitments and actions the firm uses to gain a competitive advantage by exploiting core competencies in specific product markets.

The **differentiation strategy** is an integrated set of actions taken to produce goods or services (at an acceptable cost) that customers perceive as being different in ways that are important to them.

The **focus strategy** is an integrated set of actions taken to produce goods or services that serve the needs of a particular competitive segment.

The **integrated cost leadership/differentiation strategy** involves engaging in primary and support activities that allow a firm to simultaneously pursue low cost and differentiation.

Market segmentation is a process used to cluster people with similar needs into individual and identifiable groups.

The **cost leadership strategy** is an integrated set of actions taken to produce goods or services with features that are acceptable to customers at the lowest cost, relative to that of competitors.

Total quality management (TQM) is a managerial innovation that emphasizes an organization's total commitment to the customer and to continuous improvement of every process through the use of data-driven, problem-solving approaches based on empowerment of employee groups and teams.

REVIEW QUESTIONS

1. What is a business-level strategy?
2. What is the relationship between a firm's customers and its business-level strategy in terms of *who, what,* and *how*? Why is this relationship important?
3. What are the differences among the cost leadership, differentiation, focused cost leadership, focused differentiation, and integrated cost leadership/differentiation business-level strategies?
4. How can each one of the business-level strategies be used to position the firm relative to the five forces of competition in a way that helps the firm earn above-average returns?
5. What are the specific risks associated with using each business-level strategy?

EXPERIENTIAL EXERCISES

Exercise 1: Customer Needs and Stock Trading

The motor cycle market in India is large and growing continuously with the aspirational levels of people in general, and the younger generation in particular. Scooters, the dream of every middle class Indian in the 1970s and 1980s, are no longer the vehicles in demand; the venerable Bajaj Auto, which ruled this market for over thirty years, finally called it a day for their scooters. Scooters were really a means of transportation. Motorcycles are much more than that: they are also a fashion statement. Good and reliable performance, easy maintainability, fuel economy and ruggedness are still important, but they are also expressions of status and preferences.

Motor cycles may have ousted scooters, but they are facing competition from low priced cars such as the Nano. The government is also becoming aware of the need for public transportation due to increasing congestion on the roads and pollution.

Part One

After forming small teams, the instructor will ask the teams to count off by threes. The teams will study three manufacturers of motor cycles: Bajaj, Hero Honda, and TVS , with team 1 examining Bajaj, team 2 studying Hero Honda, and team 3 examining TVS. They follow quite different strategies.

Part Two

Each team should research its target company to answer the following questions:

- Describe the "who, what, and how" for your firm. How stable is this focus? How much have these elements changed in the last five years?
- Describe your firm's strategy.
- How does your firm's strategy offer protection against each of the five forces?

Part Three

In class, the instructor will ask two teams for each firm to summarize their results. Next, the whole class will discuss which firm is likely to be the most effective at meeting the needs of its customer base. Learning is also provided by the answers to the questions, Do firms in the same industry need to follow the same generic strategy? Are generic strategies mainly a function of the industry the firm is in? For example, compare commodities and cosmetics. How does the motor cycle industry fit in?

Exercise 2: Create a Business-Level Strategy

This assignment brings together elements from the previous chapters. Accordingly, you and your team will create a business-level strategy for a firm of your own creation. The instructor will assign you an industry for which you will create an entry strategy using one of the five business-level strategies.

Each team is assigned one of the business-level strategies described in the chapter:

- Cost leadership
- Differentiation
- Focused cost leadership
- Focused differentiation
- Integrated cost leadership/differentiation

Part One

Research your industry and describe the general environment. Using the segments of the general environment, identify some factors for each segment that are influential for your industry. Next, describe the industry environment using Porter's five-forces model. Database services like CMIE can be helpful in this regard. If those are not available, consult your local librarian for assistance. After this, you should be able to clearly articulate the opportunities and the threats that exist.

Part Two

Create on a poster the business-level strategy assigned to your team. Be prepared to describe the following:

- Vision statement and mission statement
- Description of your target customer
- Picture of your business—for example, where is it located (downtown, suburb, rural, etc)?
- Describe trends that provide opportunities and threats for your intended strategy.
- List the resources, both tangible and intangible, required to compete successfully in this market.
- How will you go about creating a sustainable competitive advantage?

CHAPTER

5

Competitive Rivalry and Dynamics

Studying this chapter should provide you with the strategic management knowledge needed to

- Define competitors, competitive rivalry, competitive behavior, and competitive dynamics.
- Describe market commonality and resource similarity as the building blocks of a competitor analysis.
- Explain awareness, motivation, and ability as drivers of competitive behaviors.
- Discuss factors affecting the likelihood a competitor will take competitive actions.
- Describe factors affecting the likelihood a competitor will respond to actions taken against it.
- Explain the competitive dynamics in each of slow-cycle, fast-cycle, and standard-cycle markets.

OPENING CASE
Coca-Cola vs. Pepsi in India

Leaving no stone unturned to upstage one another to capture the Indian market

Coca-Cola and Pepsi are arch rivals across the globe. Pepsi first introduced their aerated soft drinks in India in 1956 but did not quite succeed in their their efforts at developing the Indian market. So, they withdrew in 1961. Thereafter, Coca-Cola entered India and did well. A number of Indian soft drink manufacturers such as Parle Industries with its Thums-up brand, and Pure Drinks with its brand Campa Cola, as well as several local brands also had their places under the sun. In 1977, Coca-Cola was asked to leave the country in the wake of political opposition to multinationals and the field was open for Indian brands who made the most of the situation.

In 1986, Pepsi staged a comeback by way of a tie up with an Indian agro-company, and introduced its products in 1991. It established an excellent network of bottlers and distributors. Coca-Cola followed suit and re-entered India in 1993 but struggled to find its feet. It bought out all the brands of Parle industries, such as Thums-up, besides brands in other segments such as Fanta in the orange, Limca in the clouded lime and Citra in the clear lime segments. It opted for a franchisee bottler model, unlike Pepsi, which opted for a Company Owned Bottlers (COBO) model for most of its operations. On the whole, Pepsi had much smoother relationships with its bottlers and distributors than Coca-Cola.

Also, Coca-Cola had a number of country managers who did not understand the Indian market. Pepsi, on the other hand, had Indians who were homegrown and knew the market inside out. Moreover, Coca-Cola faced a peculiar problem of having two sets of brands to manage: its own, and those acquired from Parle. The latter were well known, well recognized in the country and commanded great brand equity, but Coca-Cola decided to promote its own brands and suppress those of Parle's by cutting down on advertising and promotion. Parle brands, however, held ground, since Indian customers seemed to have a hook with Thums-up and its sister brand Limca. Such share that was lost by these brands in fact went to Pepsi.

In terms of sales of individual brands, Pepsi led Coca-Cola in India, one of the few countries in the world where Coca-Cola was not the leader (though if all the brands owned by Coca-Cola, including those of Parle were added and compared to the Pepsi brands, Coca-Cola company had a leading market share). Pepsi, from the very beginning, adapted to Indian needs and practices. Instead of projecting its global lineage, Pepsi used vernacular phrases, associated itself with local festivals, and coined or adapted its jingles to suit the Indian market. For example, it adapted its famous US campaign line "You've got the right one baby, Uh-Huh" sung by Ray Charles to "Yehi hai right choice baby, Aha". It positioned itself as a drink for the youth. When Pepsi failed in its bid for the official drink for the Wills World Cup in 1996 to Coca-Cola, which touted its "official" status, Pepsi turned the tables on Coke with its famous campaign, "Nothing official about it", featuring the then emerging youth cricket icon, Sachin Tendulkar. Coca-Cola took sometime to recover from this advertisement onslaught.

Pepsi installed a large number of fountains and built a good number of high image clients. Coca-Cola seemed to be driven by its Atlanta Head Office which sought to project a global image of

Coke. Pepsi had a decentralized organization, with considerable freedom given both to its Indian unit and the different units in regions and states in the country. Coca-Cola, on the other hand, tended to install the same systems that it adopted globally.

The portfolio strategies of Coca-Cola and Pepsi were also different. Coca-Cola depended basically on its soft drink business, while Pepsi also had other products such as snacks. Apart from its Frito-Lay potato chips, it developed a number of items suited to the Indian palate such as Kurkure. Pepsi also tied up with local growers to producing potatoes of good and consistent quality.

Coca-Cola had its share of controversies, especially over its usage practices for water, while Pepsi seems to have avoided adverse publicity. Pepsi managed to develop better public relations and tied up with Indian organizations on a number of fronts, as we saw in Chapter 2.

Sources: Case, "Coca-Cola versus Pepsi in India: The Battle for the Bottle Continues"; *Business India,* 1996, Leading the Way, January 15-28; *Business India*, 1998, Adding a Lemon, May 7; *Business Today,* 1997, Why Coke Should be more Like Pepsi, August 7–21; *Business India,* 1998, Turning on the Heat, June 29–July 12; *Business Today,* 1998, The Cola Warriors' Indian Summer, September 7#, Case #BP 0251 of the Indian Institute of Management, Ahmedabad.

Firms operating in the same market, offering similar products, and targeting similar customers are **competitors**.[1] Air India, Jet Airways, Kingfisher, Spicejet, etc., are competitors, as are PepsiCo and Coca Cola Company, or ICICI Bank, State Bank of India, and HDFC Bank. As described in the Opening Case, PepsiCo and Coca-Cola are constantly engaged in a neck to neck competition in the market for soft drinks with the two companies trying to maintain or increase their market share in India. Despite selling very similar products, the two firms are adopting different strategies. Competing firms must not only understand their environment and their own strengths and weaknesses, but also those of their competitors.

Firms interact with their competitors as part of the broad context within which they operate while attempting to earn above-average returns.[2] The decisions firms make about their interactions with their competitors significantly affect their ability to earn above-average returns.[3] Because 80 to 90 per cent of new firms fail, learning how to select the markets in which to compete and how to best compete within them is highly important.[4]

Competitive rivalry is the ongoing set of competitive actions and competitive responses that occur among firms as they maneuver for an advantageous market position.[5] Especially in highly competitive industries, firms constantly jockey for advantage as they launch strategic actions and respond or react to rivals' moves.[6] It is important for those leading organizations to understand competitive rivalry, in that "the central, brute empirical fact in strategy is that some firms outperform others,"[7] meaning that competitive rivalry influences an individual firm's ability to gain and sustain competitive advantages.[8]

A sequence of firm-level moves, rivalry results from firms initiating their own competitive actions and then responding to actions taken by competitors.[9] **Competitive behavior** is the set of competitive actions and responses the firm takes to build or defend its competitive advantages and to improve its market position.[10] Through competitive behavior, the firm tries to successfully position itself relative to the five forces of competition (see Chapter 2) and to defend current competitive advantages while building advantages for the future (see Chapter 3). Increasingly, competitors engage in competitive actions and responses in more than one market.[11] Firms competing against each other in several product or geographic markets are engaged in **multimarket competition.**[12] All competitive behavior—that is, the total set of actions and responses taken by all firms competing within a market—is called **competitive dynamics**. The relationships among these key concepts are shown in Figure 5.1.

This chapter focuses on competitive rivalry and competitive dynamics. A firm's strategies are dynamic in nature because actions taken by one firm elicit responses from competitors that, in turn, typically result in responses from the firm that took the initial action.[13] As explained in the Opening Case, Coca-Cola and PepsiCo are constantly changing how they compete. Similarly, in India, DHL India, formerly a division of Air freight Ltd. (AFL) competed against Blue Dart by concentrating on international consignments and documents while Blue Dart sought to become the dominant player in the domestic market, and in parcels. They had to constantly rework their strategies due to constant and quick changes in the environment.[14] Competitive rivalry's effect on the firm's strategies is shown by the fact that a strate-

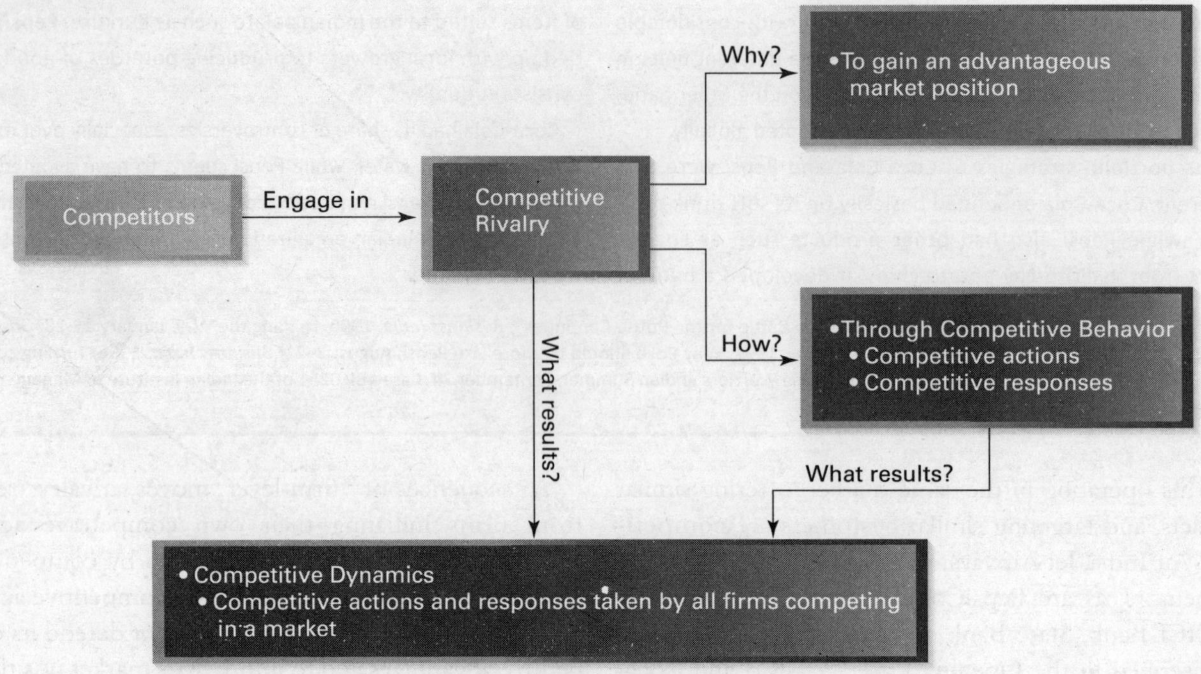

Figure 5.1 From competitors to competitive dynamics

Source: Adapted from M. J. Chen, 1996, Competitor analysis and interfirm rivalry: Toward a theoretical integration, *Academy of Management Review*, 21: 100–134.

gy's success is determined not only by the firm's initial competitive actions but also by how well it anticipates competitors' responses to them and by how well the firm anticipates and responds to its competitors' initial actions (also called attacks).[15] Although competitive rivalry affects all types of strategies (e.g., corporate-level, acquisition, and international), its dominant influence is on the firm's business-level strategy or strategies. Indeed, firms' actions and responses to those of their rivals are the basic building blocks of business-level strategies.[16] Recall from Chapter 4 that business-level strategy is concerned with what the firm does to successfully use its competitive advantages in specific product markets. In the global economy, competitive rivalry is intensifying[17] meaning that the significance of its effect on firms' business-level strategies is increasing. However, firms that develop and use effective business-level strategies tend to outperform competitors in individual product markets, even when experiencing intense competitive rivalry that price cuts bring about.[18]

A Model of Competitive Rivalry

Competitive rivalry evolves from the pattern of actions and responses as one firm's competitive actions have noticeable effects on competitors, eliciting competitive responses from them.[19] This pattern suggests that firms are mutually interdependent, that they are affected by each other's actions and responses, and that marketplace success is a function of both individual strategies and the consequences of their use.[20] Increasingly, too, executives recognize that competitive rivalry can have a major effect on the firm's financial performance.[21] Research shows that intensified rivalry within an industry results in decreased average profitability for the competing firms.[22]

Figure 5.2 presents a straightforward model of competitive rivalry at the firm level; this type of rivalry is usually dynamic and complex.[23] The competitive actions and responses the firm takes are the foundation for successfully building and using its capabilities and core competencies to gain an advantageous market position.[24] The model in Figure 5.2 presents the sequence of activities commonly involved in competition between a particular firm and each of its competitors. Companies can use the model to understand how to be able to predict competitors' behavior (actions and responses) and reduce the uncertainty associated with competitors' actions.[25] Being able to predict competitors' actions and responses has a positive effect on the firm's market position and its subsequent financial performance.[26] The sum of all the individual rivalries, modeled in Figure 5.2, that occur in a particular market reflects the competitive dynamics in that market.

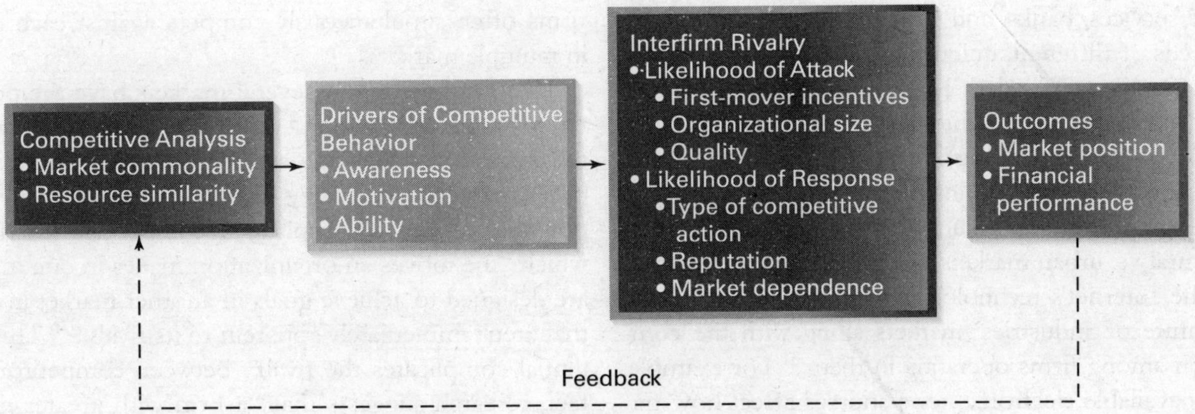

Figure 5.2 A model of competitive rivalry

Source: Adapted from M. J. Chen, 1996, Competitor analysis and interfirm rivalry: Toward a theoretical integration, *Academy of Management Review*, 21: 100–134.

The remainder of the chapter explains components of the model shown in Figure 5.2. We first describe market commonality and resource similarity as the building blocks of a competitor analysis. Next, we discuss the effects of three organizational characteristics—awareness, motivation, and ability—on the firm's competitive behavior. We then examine competitive rivalry between firms, or interfirm rivalry, in detail by describing the factors that affect the likelihood a competitive action firm will take and the factors that affect the likelihood a firm will respond to a competitor's action. In the chapter's final section, we turn our attention to competitive dynamics to describe how market characteristics affect competitive rivalry in slow-cycle, fast-cycle, and standard-cycle markets.

Competitor Analysis

As previously noted, a competitor analysis is the first step the firm takes to be able to predict the extent and nature of its rivalry with each competitor. The number of markets in which firms compete against each other (called market commonality, defined in the following pages) and the similarity in their resources (called resource similarity, also defined in the following section) determine the extent to which the firms are competitors. Firms with high market commonality and highly similar resources are "clearly direct and mutually acknowledged competitors."[27] The drivers of competitive behavior—as well as factors influencing the likelihood that a competitor will initiate competitive actions and will respond to its competitor's actions—influence the intensity of rivalry, even for direct competitors.[28]

In Chapter 2, we discussed competitor analysis as a technique which firms use to understand their competitive environment. Together, the general, industry, and competitive environments comprise the firm's external environment. We also described how competitor analysis is used to help the firm understand its competitors. This understanding results from studying competitors' future objectives, current strategies, assumptions, and capabilities (see Figure 2.3). In this chapter, the discussion of competitor analysis is extended to describe what firms study to be able to *predict* competitors' behavior in the form of their competitive actions and responses. The discussions of competitor analysis in Chapter 2 and in this chapter are complementary in that firms must first understand competitors (Chapter 2) before their competitive actions and competitive responses can be predicted (this chapter). These analyses are highly important because they help managers to avoid "competitive blind spots," in which managers are unaware of specific competitors or their capabilities. If managers have competitive blind spots, they may be surprised by a competitor's actions, thereby allowing the competitor to increase its market share at the expense of the manager's firm.[29] Competitor analyses are especially important when a firm enters a foreign market. Managers need to understand the local competition and foreign competitors currently operating in the market.[30] Without such analyses, they are less likely to be successful.

Market Commonality

Each industry is composed of various markets. The financial services industry has markets for insurance, brokerage services, banks, and so forth. To concentrate on the needs of different, unique customer groups, markets can be further subdivided. The insurance market, for example, could be broken into market segments (such as commercial and consumer), product segments (such as health insurance, general insurance, and life insurance), and geographic markets (such as India and overseas markets; rural vs. urban markets). In general, the capabilities that the Internet's technologies generate help to shape the nature of industries' markets along with the competition among firms operating in them.[31] For example, widely available electronic news sources affect how traditional print news distributors such as newspapers conduct their business.

Competitors tend to agree about the different characteristics of individual markets that form an industry.[32] For example, in the passenger transportation industry, the commercial air travel market differs from the ground transportation market, which is served by Railways and bus services; in the cargo sector, the dominant Railways differs from road logistics providers such as Gati. Although differences exist, many industries' markets are partially related in terms of technologies used or core competencies needed to develop a competitive advantage. For example, different types of transportation companies need to provide reliable and timely service. Commercial air carriers such as Air India, Jet Airways, etc., must therefore, develop service competencies to satisfy their passengers, while Railways, Blue Dart, Gati, etc., must develop such competencies to serve the needs of those using their fleets to ship goods.

Firms sometimes compete against each other in several markets that are in different industries. As such these competitors interact with each other several times, a condition called market commonality. More formally, **market commonality** is concerned with the number of markets with which the firm and a competitor are jointly involved and the degree of importance of the individual markets to each.[33] When firms produce similar products and compete for the same customers, the competitive rivalry is likely to be high.[34] Firms competing against one another in several or many markets engage in multimarket competition.[35] Coca-Cola and PepsiCo compete across a number of products (e.g., soft drinks, bottled water) and geographic markets (throughout the United States, India and in many foreign markets). Even smaller firms, such as Amul, are likely to compete with some competitors in several geographic markets as they enter new cities. Airlines, chemicals, pharmaceuticals, and consumer foods are examples of other industries in which firms often simultaneously compete against each other in multiple markets.

Firms competing in several markets have the potential to respond to a competitor's actions not only within the market in which the actions are taken, but also in other markets where they compete with the rival. This potential creates a complicated competitive mosaic in which "the moves an organization makes in one market are designed to achieve goals in another market in ways that aren't immediately apparent to its rivals."[36] This potential complicates the rivalry between competitors. In fact, research suggests that "a firm with greater multimarket contact is less likely to initiate an attack, but more likely to move (respond) aggressively when attacked."[37] Thus, in general, multimarket competition reduces competitive rivalry, but some firms will still compete when the potential rewards (e.g., potential market share gain) are high.[38]

Michael Urban/AFP Getty Images.

In order to grow, DHL Express is tasked with competing against UPS and FEDEX, much larger rivals with similar resources.

Resource Similarity

Resource similarity is the extent to which the firm's tangible and intangible resources are comparable to those of a competitor's in terms of both type and amount.[39] Firms with similar types and amounts of resources are likely to have similar strengths and weaknesses and use similar strategies.[40] The competition between FedEx and DHL in using information technology to improve the efficiency of their operations and to reduce costs demonstrates these expectations. Pursuing similar strategies that are supported by similar resource profiles, personnel in these firms work at a feverish pace to receive, sort, and ship packages. At a UPS hub, for example, "workers have less than four hours (on a peak night) to process more than a million packages from at least 100 planes and probably 160 trucks."[41] FedEx and UPS are both spending more than $1 billion annually on research and development (R&D) to find ways to improve efficiency and reduce costs. Rival DHL Express is trying to compete with the two global giants supported by the privatized German postal service, Deutsche Post World Net, which acquired it in 2002. Blue Dart has to struggle to compete against its stronger rivals such as DHL. To survive, it has negotiated a partnership agreement with FedEx in which Blue Dart will handle Fedex's shipments within India. Such arrangements are often referred to as "coopetition" (cooperation between competitors).[42]

When performing a competitor analysis, a firm analyzes each of its competitors in terms of market commonality and resource similarity. The results of these analyses can be mapped for visual comparisons. In Figure 5.3, we show different hypothetical intersections between the firm and individual competitors in terms of market commonality and resource similarity. These intersections indicate the extent to which the firm and those with which it is compared are competitors. For example, the firm and its competitor displayed in quadrant I have similar types and amounts of resources (i.e., the two firms have a similar portfolio of resources). The firm and its competitor in quadrant I would use their similar resource portfolios to compete against each other in many markets that are important to each. These conditions lead to the conclusion that the firms modeled in quadrant I are direct and mutually acknowledged competitors (e.g., FedEx and UPS). In contrast, the firm and its competitor shown in quadrant III share few markets and have little similarity in their resources, indicating that they aren't direct and mutually acknowledged competitors. Thus, a small local, family-owned Udupi restaurant does not compete directly against Taj or Oberoi Hotels, nor does it have resources that are similar to those of the latter. The firm's mapping of its competitive relationship with rivals is fluid as firms enter and exit markets and as companies' resources change in type and amount. Thus, the companies with which the firm is a direct competitor change across time.

Drivers of Competitive Actions and Responses

As shown in Figure 5.2 market commonality and resource similarity influence the drivers (awareness, motivation, and ability) of competitive behavior. In turn, the drivers influence the firm's competitive behavior, as shown by the actions and responses it takes while engaged in competitive rivalry.[43]

Awareness, which is a prerequisite to any competitive action or response taken by a firm, refers to the extent to which competitors recognize the degree of their mutual interdependence that results from market commonality and resource similarity.[44] Awareness tends to be greatest when firms have highly similar resources (in terms of types and amounts) to use while competing against each

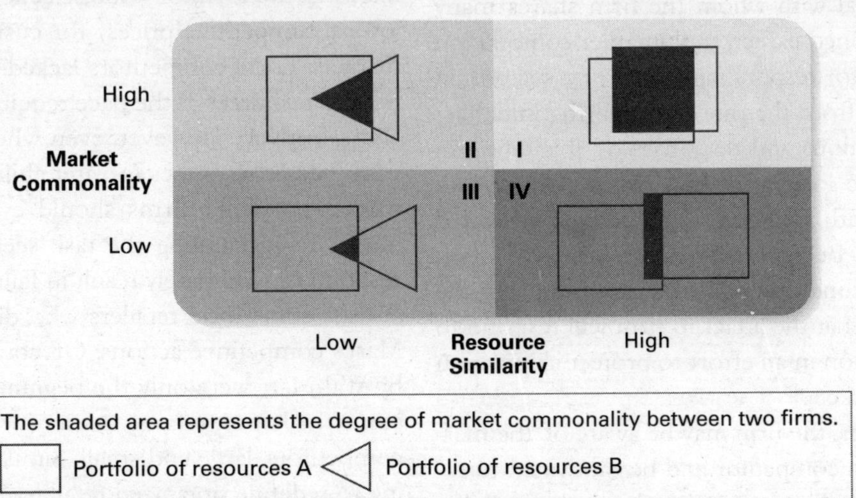

Figure 5.3 A framework of competitor analysis

Source: Adapted from M. J. Chen, 1996, Competitor analysis and interfirm rivalry: Toward a theoretical integration, *Academy of Management Review*, 21: 100–134.

other in multiple markets. Komatsu Ltd., Japan's top construction machinery maker and US-based Caterpillar Inc. have similar resources and are certainly aware of each other's actions.[45] The same is true for ICICI and HDFC banks. The last two firms' joint awareness has increased as they use similar resources to compete against each other for dominant positions in multiple markets in India such as banking, insurance, depository services, and online trading. Awareness affects the extent to which the firm understands the consequences of its competitive actions and responses. A lack of awareness can lead to excessive competition, resulting in a negative effect on all competitors' performance.[46]

Motivation, which is about the firm's incentive to take action or to respond to a competitor's attack, relates to perceived gains and losses. Thus, a firm may be aware of competitors but may not be motivated to engage in rivalry with them if it perceives that its position will not improve or that its market position won't be damaged if it doesn't respond.[47] In some cases, firms may locate near competitors in order to more easily access suppliers and customers. For example, Indian banks have located operations in Europe, US, and Middle East, to reach Indian customers settled there or working in those countries.

Market commonality affects the firm's perceptions and resulting motivation. For example, the firm is generally more likely to attack the rival with whom it has low market commonality than the one with whom it competes in multiple markets. The primary reason is the high stakes involved in trying to gain a more advantageous position over a rival with whom the firm shares many markets. As mentioned earlier, multimarket competition can find a competitor responding to the firm's action in a market different from the one in which the initial action was taken. Actions and responses of this type can cause both firms to lose focus on core markets and to battle each other with resources that had been allocated for other purposes. Because of the high stakes of competition under the condition of market commonality, the probability is high that the attacked firm will respond to its competitor's action in an effort to protect its position in one or more markets.[48]

In some instances, the firm may be aware of the markets it shares with a competitor and be motivated to respond to an attack by that competitor, but lack the ability to do so. **Ability** relates to each firm's resources and the flexibility they provide. Without available resources (such as financial capital and people), the firm lacks the ability to attack a competitor or respond to its actions. For example, smaller and newer firms tend to be more innovative but generally have fewer resources to attack their larger and established competitors. Likewise, foreign firms often are at a disadvantage against local firms because of the latters' social capital (relationships) with consumers, suppliers, and government officials.[49] However, similar resources suggest similar abilities to attack and respond. When a firm faces a competitor with similar resources, careful study of a possible attack before initiating it is essential because the similarly resourced competitor is likely to respond to that action.[50]

STRATEGY RIGHT NOW

Study how ICICI, HDFC, and State Bank of India are competing against one another. See on how many different fronts they are competing, and see whether they derive any advantage by such portfolios.

Resource **dissimilarity** also influences competitive actions and responses between firms, in that "the greater is the resource imbalance between the acting firm and competitors or potential responders, the greater will be the delay in response"[51] by the firm with a resource disadvantage. For example, Wal-Mart initially used a focused cost leadership strategy to compete only in small communities (those with a population of 25,000 or less). Using sophisticated logistics systems and extremely efficient purchasing practices, among others, to gain competitive advantages, Wal-Mart created a new type of value (primarily in the form of wide selections of products at the lowest competitive prices) for customers in small retail markets. Local competitors lacked the ability to marshal needed resources at the pace required to respond quickly and effectively. However, even when facing competitors with greater resources (greater ability) or more attractive market positions, firms should eventually respond, no matter how daunting the task seems. Choosing not to respond can ultimately result in failure, as happened with at least some local retailers who didn't respond to Wal-Mart's competitive actions. Of course, the actions taken by Wal-Mart were only the beginning. Wal-Mart has become the largest retailer in the world and is feared by all competitors, large and small. Similarly, Big Bazaar is trying to redefine organized retailing in India, with its concept of a supermarket offering low prices, yet with the look and feel of a chaotic Indian bazaar or *mandi* as they are called in Hindi), as explained in the Strategic Focus.

STRATEGIC FOCUS

5.1 Big, But a Bazaar all the Same

The Future Group, run by Kishore Biyani, is one of India's leading business houses with multiple businesses spanning across the consumption space. The company follows a multi-format strategy that captures almost the entire consumption basket of Indian consumers. Big Bazaar is a hypermarket format of the group that combines the look, touch, and feel of Indian bazaars with the choice and convenience of modern retail. Like Wal-Mart, it offers only one feature: low prices. Big Bazaar was inspired by Saravana Store located in T-Nagar, Chennai, a family-run 25-year-old store, whose philosophy was "low margin, high turnover". In that store, food, groceries, clothes, everything had a separate section. With about 120 people managing the crowds, the shop was doing annual business of more than ₹2000 million. This shop was the template for Big Bazaar. Foraying into retail with The Pantaloon Shoppe in mid 1990s, Kishore Biyani launched his discount hypermarkets concept in 2001, with the opening of the first Big Bazaar on the ground floor of a residential building in Kolkata. It was the first departmental store that offered regulated parking services, apparel, steel vessels, and electronics under one roof, and all at the most competitive prices! But Biyani also had another idea: they would look and feel like the crowded, chaotic mandis (traditional markets) of India; so items were stocked not always neatly on aisles, but are often dumped together, like in an Indian market. The stores were not air conditioned. The floors were connected by ramps rather than elevators. The stores are quite crowded, not just because a lot of people shop there due to the low prices, but also because the store space provided is deliberately less than needed. Biyani once commented that his customers in fact prefer crowded stores, since they give an appearance of being very highly patronized, and second, they reflected the look and feel of a traditional *mandi* or bazaar. The format got bigger and better with the introduction of fresh food and vegetables—Food Bazaar, introduced as a shop in shop concept, which then went on to become a very successful stand alone chain of stores across India. Eventually the format became a huge hit with the middle and lower middle class. Kishore Biyani is reported to have said that the word "bazaar" was mandatory for the name as they wanted to replicate the Indian mandi or market feel, and "big" came about because this was a much larger concept than just a regular market.

The Big Bazaar was launched as a totally *desi* (Indian) store to reach out to all Indian consumers. Simplicity was the essence of character and the idea was to bring all grocery and food items under one roof at the cheapest possible prices, which was conveyed through the tagline of the store "Is Se Sasta Aur Kuch Nahin" (There is nothing cheaper than this), placing the store at the top of consumers' minds. The immediate objective was not to make money but to have the widest reach in large cities and small towns.

To get maximum customers to visit the stores and overcome any inhibitions that most small town people have against visiting large stores, the store was localized in smaller towns. The stores also carry stocks of items that are likely to be patronized by the people in that township. For example, in Sangli district in western Maharashtra, the goods stocked are visibly different than other stores. It is also the only company outlet to sell oil loosely. For customers to experience the store, Big Bazaar organized a "kumkum" ceremony at its outlet at Sangli, where any married woman invited for kumkum could not turn it down. Also, Srimati Sangli (Mrs Sangli) contest, *bhakti sangeet* functions for the elderly etc. were organized to strike a cord with rural clientele. Biyani, recalls in his autobiography, *It happened in India*, a customer from Sangli, Mohan Jadhav, who lives with his extended family of 127 members. He shopped till his bill was 14 feet long and totaled a whopping ₹137,367. According to Biyani, Jadhav has been his biggest customer thus far!

To reach closer to customers, Big Bazaar has constantly been coming up with new and innovative sales strategies.

To reach closer to customers, Big Bazaar has constantly been coming up with new and innovative sales strategies. For instance, coinciding with Republic Day, it organizes its "*Maha*" or grand savings offer at all the Big Bazaar stores across the country. The event popular as *"Sabse Saste Teen Din,"* (The three cheapest days) puts on offer merchandise across categories at very cheap prices. These concessions are made possible with the active support of several apparel, appliances, and other manufacturers. Yet another unique initiative to attract greater footfalls on a "traditionally lean" week day was to begin the Wednesday Bazaar by advertising it as "hafte ka sabse sasta din" (The cheapest day of the week). The company announced higher discounts than other days for homemakers to make the most of the "best bargains" on the offer. Further, to counter the effect of the recent recession in 2008, it announced a month long "The Great Exchange Offer" from 16 February. The offer, with a "Bring anything old and take anything new" tagline, entailed giving customers "value" (discount) coupons for old junk such as newspapers, clothes, footwear, plastics, electronics, or furniture. The value coupons could then be "exchanged" at any Big Bazaar store while purchasing a fresh item. This offer was also extended to corporate offices and various housing societies to off-load junk items ranging from computers, stationery and printouts waiting to be disposed of.

Regular customer feedback is also an influential factor for the success of Big Bazaar. The Big Bazaar has a separate team that studies customers' purchasing pattern including their likes and dislikes and how they approach particular products. For example, Indian women generally prefer to purchase pulses, rice, grains, sugar, etc., after touching them to ensure the quality of these products, so Big Bazaar sells these items loose. One can thus touch and feel the quality of grains and pulses and get the desired quantity packed to get a feel of the traditional grocer within the super market format. There is no cheating on weights, as is the perceived norm in Indian mandis. These loose items are also slightly cheaper than the packed ones. This is a trend seen in rival stores such as Vishal, Easy Day, etc., as well. Also, unlike other stores where the most expensive and catchy item is placed at the front display, Big Bazaar places the "Value for Money" items at entrance and exit points. They also ensure that no other *kirana* store/departmental stores are offering any bigger discount compared to its own price.

Big Bazaar also refrains from high-end locations for its stores, although it does not locate the stores far from the city. The objective is to reduce its rental budget and thus provide competitive advantage over competitors. For a retailer, location is one of the most important decisions. According to Kishore Biyani, real estate cost should be less than 5% of total sales of store in order to provide maximum benefits to customer. The strategic decisions to secure spaces before other retailers join in have resulted in cost-saving. Also, it has created early presence in market.

Shopping in India is witnessing a gradual revolution with the phenomenal rise and exponential growth of the retail industry that employs around 8 per cent of the country's work force and contributes to over 10 per cent of the GDP. The largely untapped organized retail arena is now viewed as a multibillion dollar proposition by Indian and foreign players. With improving infrastructure facilities, especially in cities, and with government moving in the direction of relaxing rules for foreign brands, the organized retail sector in the country has seen the entry of large domestic business conglomerates such as Reliance Group, Tatas, Aditya Birla Group, and Bharti Enterprises in a big way. Foreign chains are also seeking a share in the Indian retail market by way of collaboration with domestic players. A little over a decade after a clutch of players like Pantaloon, Trent and Shoppers' Stop took their first tentative steps in organized retail, plenty has changed. After years of experimenting with various formats, the serious players are beginning to settle down. And they're settling down in the categories that matter—basically food and beverages and personal care, which constitute some two-thirds of the market for organized retail. As Raghu Pillai, President and CEO (Retail Operations and Strategy), Reliance Retail, observes: "Incremental private consumption will be in the range of $40–60 billion annually. That's why large players with strong balance sheets are busy putting their stakes on the ground to seize this developing opportunity." "We are now in phase II of the retail story, when companies have figured out (or are close to figuring out) what works and what doesn't. The moves of the larger players with strong balance sheets could well deter the smaller players from proceeding," says Biyani.

Today, consumer preferences in the country are changing and they are moving from traditional *kirana* stores to modern retail outlets. The main challenge to these modern retailers is to wean the customers from that of competitors as well as the neighborhood *kirana* stores. The phenomenal growth of retail in India is reflected in the rapid increase in number of supermarkets, departmental stores and hypermarkets in the country. The recent economic slowdown, however, had raised a fear of dip in consumption and slowdown of growth for organized retailers. At a time when consumer spending is yet to emerge from the impact of that slowdown, success will lie with those retailers who would be able to drive customer loyalty by responding to the demands of the discerning consumers.

Sources: Business Today, 2008, Retail Wars, June 15, http://businesstoday.intoday.in/story/retail-wars.html/1/2288.html; Deepika Mittal, http://www.chillibreeze.com/articles/Big-Bazaar.asp; Kishore BIyani, 2010, Big Bazaar: the Brand Building Challenge, March 18, http://www.articlesbase.com/advertising-articles/big-bazaar-the-brand-building-challenge-2008037.html#ixzz10J66jZOt; Raul Bailay, 2010, Slowdown Teaches Retailers to Renew Business Models, April 2, http://www.livemint.com/2010/04/02230227/Slowdown-teaches-retailers-to.html; *Journal of Retail & Leisure Property*, 2010; Customer expectations of store attributes: A study of organized retail outlets in India. February; Kishore Biyani, *It happened in India.* Delhi: Rupa; *BusinessToday*, 2007, Coffee, tea or bhajan, July 1.

Competitive Rivalry

The ongoing competitive action/response sequence between a firm and a competitor affects the performance of both firms;[52] thus it is important for companies to carefully analyze and understand the competitive rivalry present in the markets they serve to select and implement successful strategies.[53] Understanding a competitor's awareness, motivation, and ability helps the firm to predict the likelihood of an attack by that competitor and the probability that a competitor will respond to actions taken against it.

As we described earlier, the predictions drawn from studying competitors in terms of awareness, motivation, and ability are grounded in market commonality and resource similarity. These predictions are fairly general. The value of the final set of predictions the firm develops about each of its competitors' competitive actions and responses is enhanced by studying the "Likelihood of Attack" factors (such as first-mover incentives and organizational size) and the "Likelihood of Response" factors (such as the actor's reputation) that are shown in Figure 5.2. Evaluating and understanding these factors allow the firm to refine the predictions it makes about its competitors' actions and responses.

Strategic and Tactical Actions

Firms use both strategic and tactical actions when forming their competitive actions and competitive responses in the course of engaging in competitive rivalry.[54] A **competitive action** is a strategic or tactical action the firm takes to build or defend its competitive advantages or improve its market position. A **competitive response** is a strategic or tactical action the firm takes to counter the effects of a competitor's competitive action. A **strategic action** or a **strategic response** is a market-based move that involves a significant commitment of organizational resources and is difficult to implement and reverse. A **tactical action** or a **tactical response** is a market-based move that is taken to fine-tune a strategy; it involves fewer resources and is relatively easy to implement and reverse.

The decision a few years ago by Priya Paul to position The Park group of hotels is an example of a strategic response[55] and Boeing's decision to commit the resources required to build the super-efficient 787 midsized jetliner with its first deliveries in 2007 and 2008[56] demonstrates a strategic action. Changes in airfares are somewhat frequently announced by airlines. As tactical actions that are easily reversed, pricing decisions are often taken by these firms to increase demand in certain markets during certain periods. Most garment manufacturers as well as dealers in white goods such as TVs, washing machines, etc. offer "diwali discounts" purely for that season, another example of a tactical decision.

As discussed in Strategic Focus 5.1, Big Bazaar prices aggressively as a means of increasing revenues and gaining market share at the expense of competitors as also the more famous Wal-Mart. But discounted prices with high expenses (as implemented by Carrefour) weigh on margins and slow profit growth (or possibly even produce losses). Although pricing aggressively is at the core of what Wal-Mart is and how it competes, can the tactical action of aggressive pricing continue to lead to the competitive success the firm has enjoyed historically? Are Wal-Mart and Big Bazaar achieving the type of balance between strategic and tactical competitive actions and competitive responses that is a foundation for all firms' success in marketplace competitions in the long run?

When engaging rivals in competition, firms must recognize the differences between strategic and tactical actions and responses and should develop an effective balance between the two types of competitive actions and responses. Airbus, Boeing's major competitor in commercial airliners, is aware that Boeing is strongly committed to taking actions it believes are necessary to successfully launch the 787 jetliner, because deciding to design, build, and launch the 787 is a major strategic action. In fact, many analysts believe that Boeing's development of the 787 airliner was a strategic response to Airbus's new A380 aircraft.

Likelihood of Attack

In addition to market commonality, resource similarity, and the drivers of awareness, motivation, and ability, there are other factors that affect the likelihood a competitor will use strategic actions and tactical actions to attack its competitors. Three of these factors—first-mover incentives, organizational size, and quality—are discussed next.

First-Mover Incentives

A **first mover** is a firm that takes an initial competitive action in order to build or defend its competitive advantages or to improve its market position. The first-mover concept has been influenced by the work of the famous economist Joseph Schumpeter, who argued that firms achieve competitive advantage by taking innovative actions[57] (innovation is defined and described in detail in Chapter 13). In general, first movers "allocate funds for product innovation and development, aggressive advertising, and advanced research and development."[58] The benefits of being a successful first mover can be substantial.[59] Especially in fast-cycle markets (discussed later in the chapter), where changes occur rapidly and where it is virtually impossible to sustain a competitive advantage for any length of time, a first mover can experience many times the valuation and revenue of a second mover.[60] This evidence suggests that although first-mover benefits are never absolute, they are often critical to a firm's success in industries experiencing rapid technological developments and relatively short product life cycles.[61] In addition to earning above-average returns until its competitors respond to its successful competitive action, the first mover can gain (1) the loyalty of customers who may become committed to the goods or services of the firm that first made them available, and (2) market share that can be difficult for competitors to take during future competitive rivalry.[62] The general evidence that first movers have greater survival rates than later market entrants[63] is perhaps the culmination of first-mover benefits.

The firm trying to predict its competitors' competitive actions might conclude that they will take aggressive strategic actions to gain first movers' benefits. However, even though a firm's competitors might be motivated to be first movers, they may lack the ability to do so. First movers tend to be aggressive and willing to experiment with innovation and take higher, yet reasonable, levels of risk.[64] To be a first mover, the firm must have readily available the resources required to significantly invest in R&D as well as to rapidly and successfully produce and market a stream of innovative products.[65]

Organizational slack makes it possible for firms to have the ability (as measured by available resources) to be first movers. **Slack** is the buffer or cushion provided by actual or obtainable resources that are not currently in use and are in excess of the minimum resources needed to produce a given level of organizational output.[66] As a liquid resource, slack can quickly be allocated to support competitive actions, such as R&D investments and aggressive marketing campaigns that lead to first-mover advantages. This relationship between slack and the ability to be a first mover allows the firm to predict that a first mover competitor likely has available slack and will probably take aggressive competitive actions to continuously introduce innovative products. Furthermore, the firm can predict that as a first mover, a competitor will try to rapidly gain market share and customer loyalty in order to earn above-average returns until its competitors are able to effectively respond to its first move.

Firms evaluating their competitors should realize that being a first mover carries risk. For example, it is difficult to accurately estimate the returns that will be earned from introducing product innovations to the marketplace.[67] Additionally, the first mover's cost to develop a product innovation can be substantial, reducing the slack available to support further innovation. Thus, the firm should carefully study the results a competitor achieves as a first mover. Continuous success by the competitor suggests additional product innovations, while lack of product acceptance over the course of the competitor's innovations may indicate less willingness in the future to accept the risks of being a first mover.[68]

A **second mover** is a firm that responds to the first mover's competitive action, typically through imitation. More cautious than the first mover, the second mover studies customers' reactions to product innovations. In the course of doing so, the second mover also tries to find any mistakes the first mover has made so that it can avoid them and the problems arising from them. Often, successful imitation of the first mover's innovations allows the second mover to avoid the mistakes and the major investments required of the pioneers (first movers).[69] Second movers also have the time to develop processes and technologies that are more efficient than those used by the first mover or that create additional value for consumers.[70] The most successful second movers rarely act too fast (so they can fully analyze the first mover's actions) nor too slow (so they do not give the first mover time to correct its mistakes and "lock in" customer loyalty).[71] Overall, the outcomes of the first mover's competitive actions may provide an effective blueprint for second and even late movers (discussed below) as they determine the nature and timing of their competitive responses.[72] Determining whether a competitor is an effective second mover (based on its past actions) allows a first-mover firm to predict that the competitor will respond quickly to successful, innovation-based market entries. The first mover can expect a successful second-mover competitor to study its market entries and to respond with a new entry into the market within a short time period. As a second mover, the competitor will try to respond with a product that provides greater customer value than does the first mover's product. The most successful second movers are able to rapidly and meaningfully interpret market feedback to respond quickly, yet successfully, to the first mover's successful innovations.

A **late mover** is a firm that responds to a competitive action a significant amount of time after the first mover's action and the second mover's response. Typically, a late response is better than no response at all, although any success achieved from the late competitive response tends to be considerably less than that achieved by first and second movers. However, on occasion, late movers can be successful if they develop a unique way to enter the market and compete.[73] The firm competing against a late mover can predict that the competitor will likely enter a particular market only after both the first and second movers have achieved success in that market. Moreover, on a relative basis, the firm can predict that the late mover's competitive action will allow it to earn average returns only after the considerable time required for it to understand how to create at least as much customer value as that offered by the first and second movers' products.

Organizational Size

An organization's size affects the likelihood it will take competitive actions as well as the types and timing of those actions.[74] In general, small firms are more likely than large companies to launch competitive actions and tend to do it more quickly. Smaller firms are thus perceived as nimble and flexible competitors who rely on speed and surprise to defend their competitive advantages or develop new ones while engaged in competitive rivalry, especially with large companies, to gain an advantageous market position.[75] Small firms' flexibility and nimbleness allow them to develop variety in their competitive actions; large firms tend to limit the types of competitive actions used.[76]

Large firms, however, are likely to initiate more competitive actions along with more strategic actions during a given period.[77] Thus, when studying its competitors in terms of organizational size, the firm should use a measurement such as total sales revenue or total number of employees. The competitive actions the firm is likely to encounter from competitors larger than itself will be different from the competitive actions it will encounter from smaller competitors.

The organizational size factor adds another layer of complexity. When engaging in competitive rivalry, the firm often prefers a large number of unique competitive actions. Ideally, the organization has the amount of slack resources held by a large firm to launch a greater number of competitive actions and a small firm's flexibility to launch a greater variety of competitive actions. Herb Kelleher, cofounder and former CEO of Southwest Airlines, addressed this matter: "Think and act big and we'll get smaller. Think and act small and we'll get bigger."[78]

In the context of competitive rivalry, Kelleher's statement can be interpreted to mean that relying on a limited number or types of competitive actions (which is the large firm's tendency) can lead to reduced competitive success across time, partly because competitors learn how to effectively respond to the predictable. In contrast, remaining flexible and nimble (which is the small firm's tendency) in order to develop and use a wide variety of competitive actions contributes to success against rivals.

Life Insurance Corporation of India (LIC) is a huge company and generates annual sales revenue that makes it by far the country's largest insurance company. Because of its size, scale, and resources, LIC has the flexibility required to take many types of competitive actions that few—if any—of its competitors can undertake. Demonstrating this type of flexibility in terms of competitive actions may prove critical to LIC's battles with competitors such as ICICI Pru, Tata AIG, and Bajaj-Allianz, among others.

Quality

Quality has many definitions, including well-established ones relating it to the production of goods or services with zero defects[79] and as a cycle of continuous improvement.[80] From a strategic perspective, we consider quality to be the outcome of how a firm completes primary and support activities (see Chapter 3). Thus, **quality** exists when the firm's goods or services meet or exceed customers' expectations. Some evidence suggests that quality may be the most critical component in satisfying the firm's customers.[81]

In the eyes of customers, quality is about doing the right things relative to performance measures that are important to them.[82] Customers may be interested in measuring the quality of a firm's goods and services against a broad range of dimensions. Sample quality dimensions in which customers commonly express an interest are shown in Table 5.1. Quality is possible only when top-level managers support it and when its importance is institutionalized throughout the entire organization and its value chain.[83] When quality is institutionalized and valued by all, employees and managers alike become vigilant about continuously finding ways to improve quality.[84]

Quality is a universal theme in the global economy and is a necessary but not sufficient condition for competitive success.[85] Without quality, a firm's products lack credibility, meaning that customers don't think of them as viable options. Indeed, customers won't consider buying a product until they believe that it can satisfy at least their base-level expectations in terms of quality dimensions that are important to them. Boeing's new 787 aircraft may have problems in the marketplace because of quality concerns. For example, Chi Zhou, Chairman of Shanghai Airlines, suggested that the 787 does not "fully meet the quality that Boeing touted earlier." As such Zhou stated that his airline may cancel or postpone delivery of its order for nine aircraft.[86]

Quality affects competitive rivalry. The firm evaluating a competitor whose products suffer from poor quality can predict declines in the competitor's sales revenue until the quality issues are resolved. In addition, the firm can predict that the competitor likely won't be aggressive in its competitive actions until the quality problems are corrected in order to gain credibility with customers. However, after the problems are corrected, that competitor is likely to take more aggressive competitive actions.

Table 5.1 Quality dimensions of goods and services

Product Quality Dimensions
1. *Performance*—Operating characteristics
2. *Features*—Important special characteristics
3. *Flexibility*—Meeting operating specifications over some period of time
4. *Durability*—Amount of use before performance deteriorates
5. *Conformance*—Match with pre-established standards
6. *Serviceability*—Ease and speed of repair
7. *Aesthetics*—How a product looks and feels
8. *Perceived quality*—Subjective assessment of characteristics (Product image)
Service Quality Dimensions
1. *Timeliness*—Performed in the promised period of time
2. *Courtesy*—Performed cheerfully
3. *Consistency*—Giving all customers similar experiences each time
4. *Convenience*—Accessibility to customers
5. *Completeness*—Fully serviced, as required
6. *Accuracy*—Performed correctly each time

Source: Adapted from J. Evans, 2008, *Managing for Quality and Performance*, 7th ed., Mason, OH: Thomson Publishing.

Likelihood of Response

The success of a firm's competitive action is affected by the likelihood that a competitor will respond to it as well as by the type (strategic or tactical) and effectiveness of that response. As noted earlier, a competitive response is a strategic or tactical action the firm takes to counter the effects of a competitor's competitive action. In general, a firm is likely to respond to a competitor's action when (1) the action leads to better use of the competitor's capabilities to gain or produce stronger competitive advantages or an improvement in its market position, (2) the action damages the firm's ability to use its capabilities to create or maintain an advantage, or (3) the firm's market position becomes less defensible.[87]

In addition to market commonality and resource similarity and awareness, motivation, and ability, firms evaluate three other factors—type of competitive action, reputation, and market dependence—to predict how a competitor is likely to respond to competitive actions (see Figure 5.2).

Type of Competitive Action

Competitive responses to strategic actions differ from responses to tactical actions. These differences allow the firm to predict a competitor's likely response to a competitive action that has been launched against it. Strategic actions commonly receive strategic responses and tactical actions receive tactical responses. In general, strategic actions elicit fewer total competitive responses because strategic responses, such as market-based moves, involve a significant commitment of resources and are difficult to implement and reverse.[88]

Another reason that strategic actions elicit fewer responses than tactical actions do is that the time needed to implement a strategic action and to assess its effectiveness can delay the competitor's response to that action.[89] In contrast, a competitor likely will respond quickly to a tactical action, such as when an airline company almost immediately matches a competitor's tactical action of reducing prices in certain markets. Either strategic actions or tactical actions that target a large number of a rival's customers are likely to elicit strong responses.[90] In fact, if the effects of a competitor's strategic action on the focal firm are significant (e.g., loss of market share, loss of major resources such as critical employees), a response is likely to be swift and strong.[91]

Actor's Reputation

In the context of competitive rivalry, an **actor** is the firm taking an action or a response while **reputation** is "the positive or negative attribute ascribed by one rival to another based on past competitive behavior."[92] A positive reputation may be a source of above-average returns, especially for consumer goods producers.[93] Thus, a positive corporate reputation is of strategic value[94] and affects competitive rivalry. To predict the likelihood of a competitor's response to a current or planned action, firms evaluate the responses that the competitor has taken previously when attacked—past behavior is assumed to be a predictor of future behavior.

AP Photo/Ng Han Guan

While IBM's initial success in the PC market may have inspired a host of competitors, the competitive landscape has continued to shift with the acquisitions of Gateway by Acer, Compaq by HP, and IBM's PC division by Lenovo.

Competitors are more likely to respond to strategic or tactical actions when they are taken by a market leader.[95] In particular, evidence suggests that commonly successful actions, especially strategic actions, will be quickly imitated. For example, although a second mover, IBM committed significant resources to enter the PC market. When IBM was immediately successful in this endeavor, competitors such as Dell, Compaq, HP, and Gateway responded with strategic actions to enter the market. IBM's reputation as well as its successful strategic action strongly influenced entry by these competitors. However, the competitive landscape has changed dramatically over time. For example, Lenovo, a Chinese firm, paid $1.75 billion in 2005 to buy IBM's PC division.

In contrast to a firm with a strong reputation such as IBM, competitors are less likely to take responses against a company with a reputation for competitive behavior that is risky, complex, and unpredictable. The firm with a reputation as a price predator (an actor that frequently reduces prices to gain or maintain market share) generates few responses to its pricing tactical actions because price predators, which typically increase prices once their market share objective is reached, lack credibility with their competitors.[96] Occasionally, a firm with a minor reputation can sneak up on larger, more resourceful competitors and take market share from them. In recent years, for example, firms from emerging markets have taken market share from major competitors based in developed markets.[97]

Dependence on the Market

Market dependence denotes the extent to which a firm's revenues or profits are derived from a particular market.[98] In general, competitors with high market dependence are likely to respond strongly to attacks threatening their market position.[99] Interestingly, the threatened firm in these instances may not always respond quickly, even though an effective response to an attack on the firm's position in a critical market is important.

Gujarat Co-operative Milk Marketing Federation (GCMMF), which owns the famous Amul brand, is a farmers' co-operative based at Anand, Gujarat. The firm is a leading packager and marketer of milk and milk products, including cheese, milk based sweets and chocolates, that are sold under the Amul brand. With sales exceeding ₹80 billion in 2009-10[100], GCMMF's business is founded on a passion for dairy products. Because its business operations revolve strictly around diary products, it is totally dependent on the market for these products. As such, any competitor that chooses to attack GCMMF and its market positions can anticipate a strong response to its competitive actions.

Competitive Dynamics

Whereas competitive rivalry concerns the ongoing actions and responses between a firm and its direct competitors for an advantageous market position, competitive dynamics concern the ongoing actions and responses among all firms competing within a market for advantageous positions. Building and sustaining competitive advantages are at the core of competitive rivalry, in that advantages are the key to creating value for shareholders.[101]

To explain competitive dynamics, we explore the effects of varying rates of competitive speed in different markets (called slow-cycle, fast-cycle, and standard-cycle markets) on the behavior (actions and responses) of all competitors within a given market. Competitive behaviors as well as the reasons for taking them are similar within each market type, but differ across types of markets.[102] Thus, competitive dynamics differ in slow-cycle, fast-cycle, and standard-cycle markets. The sustainability of the firm's competitive advantages differs across the three market types.

As noted in Chapter 1, firms want to sustain their competitive advantages for as long as possible, although no advantage is permanently sustainable. The degree of sustainability is affected by how quickly competitive advantages can be imitated and how costly it is to do so.

Slow-Cycle Markets

Slow-cycle markets are those in which the firm's competitive advantages are shielded from imitation commonly for long periods of time and where imitation is costly.[103] Thus, competitive advantages are sustainable over longer periods of time in slow-cycle markets.

Building a unique and proprietary capability produces a competitive advantage and success in a slow-cycle market. This type of advantage is difficult for competitors to understand. As discussed in Chapter 3, a difficult-to-understand and costly-to-imitate resource or capability usually results from unique historical conditions, causal ambiguity, and/or social complexity. Copyrights, geography, patents, and ownership of an information resource are examples of resources.[104] After a proprietary advantage is developed, the firm's competitive behavior in a slow-cycle market is oriented to protecting, maintaining, and extending that advantage. Thus, the competitive dynamics in slow-cycle markets usually concentrate on competitive actions and responses that enable firms to protect,

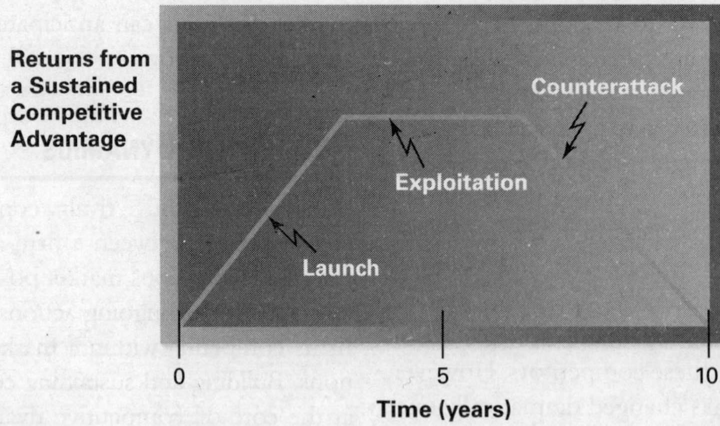

Figure 5.4 Gradual erosion of a sustained competitive advantage

Source: Adapted from I. C. MacMillan, 1988, Controlling competitive dynamics by taking strategic initiative, *Academy of Management Executive*, II(2): 111–118.

maintain, and extend their competitive advantage. Major strategic actions in these markets, such acquisitions, usually carry less risk than in faster-cycle markets.[105]

Walt Disney Co. continues to extend its proprietary characters, such as Mickey Mouse, Minnie Mouse, and Goofy. These characters have a unique historical development as a result of Walt and Roy Disney's creativity and vision for entertaining people. Products based on the characters seen in Disney's animated films are sold through Disney's theme park shops as well as freestanding retail outlets called Disney Stores. Because copyrights shield it, the proprietary nature of Disney's advantage in terms of animated character trademarks protects the firm from imitation by competitors.

Consistent with another attribute of competition in a slow-cycle market, Disney protects its exclusive rights to its characters and their use. As with all firms competing in slow-cycle markets, Disney's competitive actions (such as building theme parks in France, Japan, and China) and responses (such as lawsuits to protect its right to fully control use of its animated characters) maintain and extend its proprietary competitive advantage while protecting it.

Patent laws and regulatory requirements such as those in the United States requiring FDA (Food and Drug Administration) approval to launch new products shield pharmaceutical companies' positions. Competitors in this market try to extend patents on their drugs to maintain advantageous positions that the patents provide. However, after a patent expires, the firm is no longer shielded from competition, allowing generic imitations and usually leading to a loss of sales. For a long time, Indian drug manufacturers were protected under Indian patent laws that granted only process patents and not product patents. This meant that a manufacturer could produce the same drug, so long it was produced by a different process. In 2005, a new Act was passed, amending the patent laws substantially. This was done to conform to the WTO requirements. Even though Western companies still were not satisfied with its provisions, it would change the rules of the game for the Indian drug manufacturers: while original drug molecule research would be rewarded through patents, copying generic manufacturers would find it more difficult.[106]

The competitive dynamics generated by firms competing in slow-cycle markets are shown in Figure 5.4. In slow-cycle markets, firms launch a product (e.g., a new drug) that has been developed through a proprietary advantage (e.g., R&D) and then exploit it for as long as possible while the product is shielded from competition. Eventually, competitors respond to the action with a counterattack. In markets for drugs, this counterattack commonly occurs as patents expire or are broken through legal means, creating the need for another product launch by the firm seeking a protected market position.

Fast-Cycle Markets

Fast-cycle markets are markets in which the firm's capabilities that contribute to competitive advantages aren't shielded from imitation and where imitation is often rapid and inexpensive. Thus, competitive advantages aren't sustainable in fast-cycle markets. Firms competing in fast-cycle markets recognize the importance of speed; these companies appreciate that "time is as precious a business resource as money or head count—and that the costs of hesitation and delay are just as steep as going over budget or missing a financial forecast."[107] Such high-velocity environments place considerable pressures on top managers to quickly make strategic decisions that are also effective.[108] The often substantial competition and technology-based strategic focus make the strategic decision complex, increasing the need for a comprehensive approach integrated with decision speed, two often-conflicting characteristics of the strategic decision process.[109]

Reverse engineering and the rate of technology diffusion in fast-cycle markets facilitate rapid imitation. A competitor uses reverse engineering to quickly gain the knowledge required to imitate or improve the firm's products. Technology is diffused rapidly in fast-cycle markets, making it available to competitors in a short period. The technology often used by fast-cycle competitors isn't proprietary, nor is it protected by patents as is the technology used by firms competing in slow-cycle markets. For example, only a few hundred parts, which are readily available in the open market, are required to build a PC. Patents protect only a few of these parts, such as microprocessor chips.[110]

Fast-cycle markets are more volatile than slow-cycle and standard-cycle markets. Indeed, the pace of competition in fast-cycle markets is almost frenzied, as companies rely on innovations as the engines of their growth. Because prices often decline quickly in these markets, companies need to profit quickly from their product innovations. Imitation of many fast-cycle products is relatively easy, as demonstrated by Dell and HP, along with many other PC vendors that have partly or largely imitated the original PC design to create their products. Continuous reductions in the costs of parts, as well as the fact that the information required to assemble a PC isn't especially complicated and is readily available, make it possible for additional competitors to enter this market without significant difficulty.[111]

The fast-cycle market characteristics just described make it virtually impossible for companies in this type of market to develop sustainable competitive advantages. Recognizing this reality, firms avoid "loyalty" to any of their products, preferring to cannibalize their own before competitors learn how to do so through successful imitation. This emphasis creates competitive dynamics that differ substantially from those found in slow-cycle markets. Instead of concentrating on protecting, maintaining, and extending competitive advantages, as in slow-cycle markets, companies competing in fast-cycle markets focus on learning how to rapidly and continuously develop new competitive advantages that are superior to those they replace. They commonly search for fast and effective means of developing new products. For example, it is common in some industries for firms to use strategic alliances to gain access to new technologies and thereby develop and introduce more new products into the market.[112] In recent years, many of these alliances have been offshore (with partners in foreign countries) in order to access appropriate skills while maintaining lower costs to compete.[113]

The competitive behavior of firms competing in fast-cycle markets is shown in Figure 5.5. As suggested by the figure, competitive dynamics in this market type entail actions and responses that are oriented to rapid and continuous product introductions and the development of a stream of ever-changing competitive advantages. The firm launches a product to achieve a competitive advantage and then exploits the advantage for as long as possible. However, the firm also tries to develop another temporary competitive advantage before competitors can respond to the first one (see Figure 5.5). Thus, competitive dynamics in fast-cycle markets often result in rapid product upgrades as well as quick product innovations.[114]

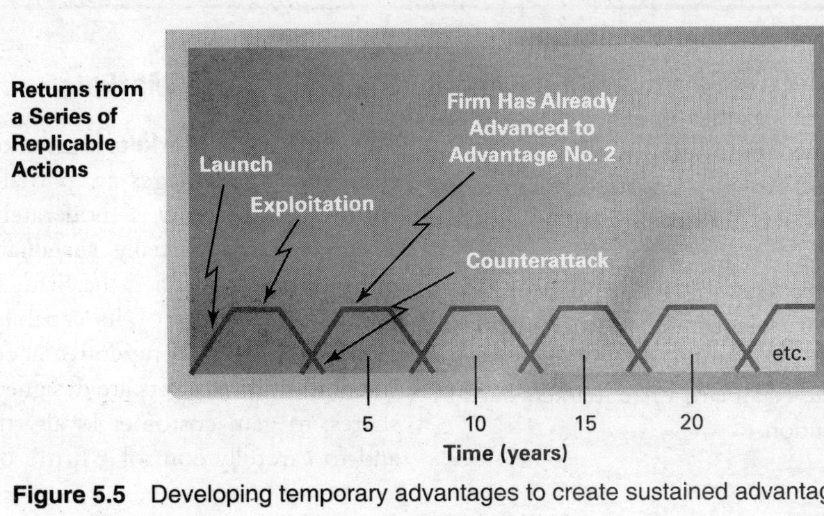

Figure 5.5 Developing temporary advantages to create sustained advantage

Source: Adapted from I. C. MacMillan, 1988, Controlling competitive dynamics by taking strategic initiative, *Academy of Management Executive*, II(2): 111–118.

STRATEGIC FOCUS

5.2 Soothing the Soul with Kisses—Candy Kisses That Is

Candy seems to be recession proof. For example, in the depression of the 1930s, candy companies actually performed well. In fact, several candy products that remain popular today were developed and introduced during the 1930s. For example, Snickers was introduced in 1930, Tootsie Roll Pops in 1931, and Mars Bars in 1932. During tough economic times, people spend more time at home and look for ways they can reduce their stress. Eating candy is an enjoyable way to relax and it is inexpensive compared to many other outlets one may seek. It is an affordable luxury. Eating candy makes people think of better times and may even remind them of enjoyable times as a child. One person who works in his father's candy store on the weekend says that he likes to do so because people are happy when they are buying candy.

For these reasons, the performance of candy manufacturers has been one of the few bright spots in the recession of 2008–2009. For example, the Hershey Company experienced a 3.8 per cent sales increase in 2008 compared to 2007 as well as an increase in profits. Few companies in other industries had such a positive experience. In fact, Hershey announced plans to increase its advertising by almost 17 per cent in 2009. Many of the best-selling candies during the recession are cheaper and old fashioned, which has also helped Hershey. However, even some of the more exclusive candy companies had performance gains during the recession. Godiva Chocolatier, Inc., expects continued growth, while Lindt & Sprungli AG, maker of premium candies, had a 5.8 per cent increase in sales during 2008. Cadbury achieved a 30 per cent increase in its annual profits. Nestle's profits were 10.9 per cent higher in 2008 as well.

Hershey took several actions in recent years that have aided its performance gains. For example, it finally responded to its competitors' premium product lines (e.g., Godiva, Cadbury) with a premium line of its own, Bliss Chocolates. In addition, it developed a line of chocolates for Starbucks that are sold as premium candies. However, Hershey's best sales have come from its basic product lines such as Hershey Bars, Kisses, and Reese's Peanut Butter Cups. Thus, Hershey placed a renewed emphasis on these product lines. Hershey also experienced increased sales through discount retailers and at convenience stores (especially after the price of gasoline declined significantly).

Mark Savage/CORBIS

Not only have candy manufacturers seen sales increase during the recession, brands such as Hershey are investing more in marketing and launching new product lines to take on more upscale competitors.

Sources: S. Grimmett, 2008, Hershey (HSY): Kisses sweeten the recession, *Today's Financial News,* http://www.todaysfinancialnews.com, October 8; J. Gordon, 2008, Prospecting in the recession? Think chocolate, The Customer Collective, http://www.thecustomercollective.com, November 3; D. Hockens, 2009, Hershey's profits rise as economy slumps, *Pennlive Blog,* http://www.pennlive.com/blogs, January 27; J. Jargon & A. Cordeiro, 2009, Recession puts Hershey in sweet spot, *The Wall Street Journal,* http://www.wsj.com, January 28; 2009, Cadbury chocolate sales soar in recession, *YumSugar,* http://www.yumsugar.com, February 26; C. Haughney, 2009, When economy sours, tootsie rolls soothe souls, *The New York Times,* http://www.nytimes.com, March 24.

As our discussion suggests, innovation plays a critical role in competitive dynamics in fast-cycle markets. For individual firms, then, innovation is a key source of competitive advantage. Through innovation, the firm can cannibalize its own products before competitors successfully imitate them.

Candy products represent a standard-cycle market. The firms in the industry take actions to build customer loyalty, seek high market shares and try to build positive brand names. We discuss standard-cycle markets such as this one in the next section.

Standard-Cycle Markets

Standard-cycle markets are markets in which the firm's competitive advantages are partially shielded from imitation and imitation is moderately costly. Competitive advantages are partially sustainable in standard-cycle markets, but only when the firm is able to continuously upgrade the quality of its capabilities to stay ahead of competitors. The competitive actions and responses in standard-cycle markets are designed to seek large market shares, to gain customer loyalty through brand names, and to carefully control a firm's operations in order to consistently provide the same positive experience for customers.[115]

Standard-cycle companies serve many customers in competitive markets. Because the capabilities and core competencies on which their competitive advantages are based are less specialized, imitation is faster and less costly for standard-cycle firms than for those competing in slow-cycle markets. However, imitation is slower and more expensive in these markets than in fast-cycle markets. Thus, competitive dynamics in standard-cycle markets rest midway between the characteristics of dynamics in slow-cycle and fast-cycle markets. Imitation comes less quickly and is more expensive for standard-cycle competitors when a firm is able to develop economies of scale by combining coordinated and integrated design and manufacturing processes with a large sales volume for its products.

Because of large volumes, the size of mass markets, and the need to develop scale economies, the competition for market share is intense in standard-cycle markets. This form of competition is readily evident in the battles among consumer foods' producers, such as the candy makers described in Strategic Focus 5.2. Hershey competes in different market segments with Mars, Cadbury, Nestle, and Godiva. In addition, similar to other consumer food manufacturers, some candy makers have kept prices constant selling downsized packages (others, like Hershey, have increased their prices). Package design and ease of availability are the competitive dimensions on which these firms sometimes compete to outperform their rivals in this market.

Innovation can also drive competitive actions and responses in standard-cycle markets, especially when rivalry is intense. Some innovations in standard-cycle markets are incremental rather than radical in nature (incremental and radical innovations are discussed in Chapter 13). For example, consumer foods' producers are innovating in terms of healthy products. Overall, many firms are relying on innovation as a means of competing in standard-cycle markets and to earn above-average returns.

Overall, innovation has a substantial influence on competitive dynamics as it affects the actions and responses of all companies competing within a slow-cycle, fast-cycle, or standard-cycle market. We have emphasized the importance of innovation to the firm's strategic competitiveness in earlier chapters and do so again in Chapter 13. These discussions highlight the importance of innovation in most types of markets.

SUMMARY

- Competitors are firms competing in the same market, offering similar products, and targeting similar customers. Competitive rivalry is the ongoing set of competitive actions and competitive responses occurring between competitors as they compete against each other for an advantageous market position. The outcomes of competitive rivalry influence the firm's ability to sustain its competitive advantages as well as the level (average, below average, or above average) of its financial returns.
- The set of competitive actions and responses that an individual firm takes while engaged in competitive rivalry is called competitive behavior. Competitive dynamics is the set of actions and responses taken by all firms that are competitors within a particular market.
- Firms study competitive rivalry in order to predict the competitive actions and responses that each of their competitors likely will take. Competitive actions are either strategic or tactical in nature. The firm takes competitive actions to defend or build its competitive advantages or to improve its market position. Competitive responses are taken to counter the effects of a competitor's competitive action. A strategic action or a strategic response requires a significant commitment of organizational resources, is difficult to successfully implement, and is difficult to reverse. In contrast, a tactical action or a tactical response requires fewer organizational resources and is easier to implement and reverse. For example, for an airline company, entering major new markets is an example of a strategic action or a strategic response; changing its prices in a particular market is an example of a tactical action or a tactical response.
- A competitor analysis is the first step the firm takes to be able to predict its competitors' actions and responses. In Chapter 2, we discussed what firms do to *understand* competitors. This discussion was extended in this chapter to describe what the firm does to *predict* competitors' market-based actions. Thus, understanding precedes prediction. Market commonality (the number of markets with which competitors are jointly involved and their importance to each) and resource similarity (how comparable competitors' resources are in terms of type and amount) are studied to complete a competitor analysis. In general, the greater the market commonality and resource similarity, the more firms acknowledge that they are direct competitors.
- Market commonality and resource similarity shape the firm's awareness (the degree to which it and its competitors understand their mutual interdependence), motivation (the firm's incentive to attack or respond), and ability (the quality of the resources available to the firm to attack and respond). Having

knowledge of these characteristics of a competitor increases the quality of the firm's predictions about that competitor's actions and responses.

- In addition to market commonality and resource similarity and awareness, motivation, and ability, three more specific factors affect the likelihood a competitor will take competitive actions. The first of these concerns first-mover incentives. First movers, those taking an initial competitive action, often gain loyal customers and earn above-average returns until competitors can successfully respond to their action. Not all firms can be first movers in that they may lack the awareness, motivation, or ability required to engage in this type of competitive behavior. Moreover, some firms prefer to be a second mover (the firm responding to the first mover's action). One reason for this is that second movers, especially those acting quickly, can successfully compete against the first mover. By evaluating the first mover's product, customers' reactions to it, and the responses of other competitors to the first mover, the second mover can avoid the early entrant's mistakes and find ways to improve upon the value created for customers by the first mover's good or service. Late movers (those that respond a long time after the original action was taken) commonly are lower performers and are much less competitive.
- Organizational size, the second factor, tends to reduce the variety of competitive actions that large firms launch while it increases the variety of actions undertaken by smaller competitors. Ideally, the firm would prefer to initiate a large number of diverse actions when engaged in competitive rivalry. The third factor, quality, is a base denominator to competing successfully in the global economy. It is a necessary prerequisite to achieve competitive parity. Although necessary, yet it is an insufficient condition for gaining an advantage.
- The type of action (strategic or tactical) the firm took, the competitor's reputation for the nature of its competitor behavior, and that competitor's dependence on the market in which the action was taken are studied to predict a competitor's response to the firm's action. In general, the number of tactical responses taken exceeds the number of strategic responses. Competitors respond more frequently to the actions taken by the firm with a reputation for predictable and understandable competitive behavior, especially if that firm is a market leader. In general, the firm can predict that when its competitor is highly dependent for its revenue and profitability in the market in which the firm took a competitive action, that competitor is likely to launch a strong response. However, firms that are more diversified across markets are less likely to respond to a particular action that affects only one of the markets in which they compete.
- In slow-cycle markets, where competitive advantages can be maintained for at least a period of time, the competitive dynamics often include firms taking actions and responses intended to protect, maintain, and extend their proprietary advantages. In fast-cycle markets, competition is substantial as firms concentrate on developing a series of temporary competitive advantages. This emphasis is necessary because firms' advantages in fast-cycle markets aren't proprietary and, as such, are subject to rapid and relatively inexpensive imitation. Standard-cycle markets have a level of competition between that in slow-cycle and fast-cycle markets; firms are moderately shielded from competition in these markets as they use capabilities that produce competitive advantages that are moderately sustainable. Competitors in standard-cycle markets serve mass markets and try to develop economies of scale to enhance their profitability. Innovation is vital to competitive success in each of the three types of markets. Companies should recognize that the set of competitive actions and responses taken by all firms differs by type of market.

KEY TERMS AND DEFINITIONS

Competitors are firms operating in the same market, offering similar products, and targeting similar customers.

Competitive rivalry is the ongoing set of competitive actions and competitive responses that occur among firms as they maneuver for an advantageous market position.

Competitive behavior is the set of competitive actions and competitive responses the firm takes to build or defend its competitive advantages and to improve its market position.

Multimarket competition occurs when firms compete against each other in several product or geographic markets.

Competitive dynamics refer to all competitive behaviors—that is, the total set of actions and responses taken by all firms competing within a market.

A **first mover** is a firm that takes an initial competitive action in order to build or defend its competitive advantages or to improve its market position.

A **second mover** is a firm that responds to the first mover's competitive action, typically through imitation.

A **late mover** is a firm that responds to a competitive action a significant amount of time after the first mover's action and the second mover's response.

Market commonality is concerned with the number of markets with which the firm and a competitor are jointly involved and the degree of importance of the individual markets to each.

Resource similarity is the extent to which the firm's tangible and intangible resources are comparable to a competitor's in terms of both type and amount.

A **competitive action** is a strategic or tactical action the firm takes to build or defend its competitive advantages or improve its market position.

A **competitive response** is a strategic or tactical action the firm takes to counter the effects of a competitor's competitive action.

A **strategic action** or a **strategic response** is a market-based move that involves a significant commitment of organizational resources and is difficult to implement and reverse.

A **tactical action** or a **tactical response** is a market-based move that is taken to fine-tune a strategy; it involves fewer resources and is relatively easy to implement and reverse.

Quality exists when the firm's goods or services meet or exceed customers' expectations.

Slow-cycle markets are those in which the firm's competitive advantages are shielded from imitation commonly for long periods of time and where imitation is costly.

Fast-cycle markets are markets in which the firm's capabilities that contribute to competitive advantages aren't shielded from imitation and where imitation is often rapid and inexpensive.

Standard-cycle markets are markets in which the firm's competitive advantages are moderately shielded from imitation and where imitation is moderately costly.

REVIEW QUESTIONS

1. Who are competitors? How are competitive rivalry, competitive behavior, and competitive dynamics defined in the chapter?
2. What is market commonality? What is resource similarity? What does it mean to say that these concepts are the building blocks for a competitor analysis?
3. How do awareness, motivation, and ability affect the firm's competitive behavior?
4. What factors affect the likelihood a firm will take a competitive action?
5. What factors affect the likelihood that a firm will initiate a competitive response to the action taken by a competitor?
6. What competitive dynamics can be expected among firms competing in slow-cycle markets? In fast-cycle markets? In standard-cycle markets?

EXPERIENTIAL EXERCISES

Exercise 1: Win-Win, Win-Lose, or Lose-Lose?

A key aspect of company strategy concerns the interactions between two or more firms. When a new market segment emerges, should a firm strive for a first-mover advantage or wait to see how the market takes shape? Diversified firms compete against one another in multiple market segments and must often consider how actions in one market might be subject to retaliation by a competitor in another segment. Similarly, when a competitor initiates a price war, a firm must decide whether it should respond in kind or not.

Game theory is helpful for understanding the strategic interaction between firms. Game theory uses assumptions about the behavior of rivals to help a company choose a specific strategy that maximizes its return. In this exercise, you will use game theory to help analyze business decisions.

Individual

One of the classic illustrations of game theory can be found in the prisoner's dilemma. Two criminals have been apprehended by the police for suspicion of a robbery. The police separate the thieves and offer them the same deal: Inform on your peer and receive a lesser sentence. Let your peer inform on you, and receive a harsher sentence. What should you tell the police?

Visit http://www.gametheory.net where you can play the prisoner's dilemma against a computer. Play the dilemma using different parameters, and make notes of your experience.

Groups

There are many examples of game theory in popular culture, from the reality show *Survivor* to episodes of *The Simpsons*. Revisit http://www.gametheory.net and select either a television or movie illustration. Discuss the applications of game theory with your team.

As a group, prepare a one-page summary of how game theory can be applied to competitive interactions between firms.

Exercise 2: Does the First Mover Truly Have an Advantage?

Henry Ford is often credited with saying that he would rather be the first person to be second. This is strange coming from the innovator of the mass-produced automobile in the United States. So is the first-mover advantage a myth, or is it something that every firm should strive for?

First movers are considered to be the ones that initially introduce an innovative product or service into a market segment. The theory is that doing so creates an almost impenetrable competitive advantage that later entrants find difficult to overcome. However, history is replete with situations where second or later movers find success. If the best way to succeed in the future is to understand the past, then an understanding of why certain first movers succeeded and others failed should be instructive. This exercise requires you to investigate a first mover and identify specifically why, or why not, it was able to hold onto its first-mover advantage.

Part One

Pick an industry that you find of interest. This assignment can be done individually or in a team. Research that industry and identify one or two instances of a first mover—the introduction of new offering into new market segments. For example, you might pick consumer electronics and look for firms that initiated new products in new market segments. Your choice of industry must be approved in advance by your instructor as duplication of industry is to be avoided.

Part Two

- Each individual or team is to present their findings with the discussion centering on the following:
- Provide a brief history and description of the industry chosen. Was this a fast-, standard-, or slow-cycle market at the time the first mover initiated its strategic action?
- How has innovation of new products been accomplished traditionally in this industry: through new firms entering the market or existing firms launching new offerings?
- Identify one or two first movers and provide a review of what happened when they entered that industry. Describe why the product or offering has been successful or why it failed.
- What did you learn as a result of this exercise? Do you consider the first mover a wise strategy; is your answer dependent on industry, timing, or luck?

CHAPTER 6

Corporate-Level Strategy

Studying this chapter should provide you with the strategic management knowledge needed to

- Define corporate-level strategy and discuss its purpose.
- Describe different levels of diversification with different corporate-level strategies.
- Explain three primary reasons why firms diversify.
- Describe how firms can create value by using a related diversification strategy.
- Explain the two ways value can be created with an unrelated diversification strategy.
- Discuss the incentives and resources that encourage diversification.
- Describe motives that can encourage managers to over diversify a firm.

OPENING CASE
Foster's Group Diversification into the Wine Business

Foster's Group's slogan "Australian for beer" is fitting, given that it produces some of Australia's top beers, including Foster's Lager and Victoria beer. However, in 2008, wine contributed 76 per cent of the company's sale earnings. Although Foster's was traditionally a brewer and distributor of beer products, it foresaw more growth prospects with the sales of wine than beer. It also perceived an opportunity to commingle the marketing and distribution of these two spirit products to create economies of scope (a concept defined later in the chapter). In 2001, Foster's bought Beringer Wine Estates, a leading California winery with approximately $1.2 billion in sales. Then in 2005, Foster's acquired another premium winemaker, Southcorp; the acquisition of these companies made Foster's one of the world's biggest wine companies.

Christian Heeb/laif/Redux

Despite perceived opportunities to leverage their existing brewery-focused marketing and distribution operations, Foster's encountered numerous problems in the integration of the Beringer and Southcorp wineries.

In order to create synergy between the beer and wine assets, Foster's used one sales force to focus on the mass marketing of beer and cheap spirits, as well as selling high-priced wine to specialized restaurants and liquor stores selling to wine connoisseurs with more sophisticated tastes. The sharing of these activities between businesses that focus on low-cost mass marketing and focused differentiation (premium wines) turned out to be a significant mistake. Furthermore, the assets, especially Southcorp, were purchased at a distinct premium. Although the higher growth rate potential for wine sales seemed like the perfect strategic fit with the low growth rate of beer sales, the synergy between these two businesses was apparently not realized. Furthermore, currency problems contributed to the performance problem; the Southcorp assets were devalued as the US dollar depreciated relative to the Australian dollar. One analyst said "they [Foster's] paid too much and they bought at the wrong time in the cycle."

To correct the problem, Foster's has recently been separating these businesses and creating a new marketing group for the wine business while maintaining its current expertise in the brewing and distribution of beer. Because the separation of these businesses is crucial for Foster's to remain profitable, it may be willing to divest one of these businesses, most likely the wine segment because its basic expertise among the key leaders and other personnel is in the beer business.

This is an example of related constrained diversification being poorly executed. Interestingly, a new CEO was appointed after the strategic mistakes occurred. Related constrained diversification, as defined later in the chapter, focuses on managing different businesses, which are potentially highly related in regard to the manufacturing, sales, and distribution activities among the firm's related business portfolio. Unfortunately, Foster's focused on the growth cycle differences and not the detailed implementation differences related to the sharing of actual activities between beer and premium wine, which were not as great a fit as earlier suspected.

Sources: C. Koons, 2009, Earnings: Foster's to retain, revamp struggling wine business, *Wall Street Journal*, February 18, B6; 2009, Foster's Company limited, 2009, *Hoovers Company Records*, http://www.hoovers.com, March 15, 42414; E. Ellis, 2008, What'll you have mate? *Barron's*, October 27, 34–36; S. Murdoch, 2008, Corporate news: Foster's Group names Johnston to be CEO, *Wall Street Journal*, September 27, D6; G. Charles, 2007, Foster's Group plans global wine brands relaunch, *Marketing*, November 29, 3.

Our discussions of business-level strategies (Chapter 4) and the competitive rivalry and competitive dynamics associated with them (Chapter 5) concentrate on firms competing in a single industry or product market.[1] In this chapter, we introduce you to corporate-level strategies, which are strategies firms use to *diversify* their operations from a single business competing in a single market into several product markets and, most commonly, into several businesses. Thus, a **corporate-level strategy** specifies the actions a firm takes to gain a competitive advantage by selecting and managing a group of different businesses competing in different product markets. Corporate-level strategies help companies select new strategic positions—positions that are expected to increase the firm's value.[2] As explained in the Opening Case, Foster's Group Ltd., an Australian beverage company, competes in several different beverage segments dominated by beer and wine brands.

Another example is Interpublic Group, a marketing and advertising firm. It is taking advantage of the economic downturn to acquire companies at a decreased price and increase its portfolio of businesses. It is currently seeking to acquire firms in the digital and mobile sector to grow its Media Brands operations to help achieve its goal of being one of the top three players in its respective market by the year 2011.[3]

As is the case with Foster's, firms use corporate-level strategies as a means to grow revenues and profits. But there can be different strategic intents beside growth. Firms can pursue defensive or offensive strategies that realize growth but have different strategic intents. Firms can also pursue market development by moving into different geographic markets (this approach will be discussed in Chapter 8). Firms can acquire competitors (horizontal integration) or buy a supplier or customer (vertical integration). These strategies will be discussed in Chapter 7. The basic corporate strategy, the topic of this chapter, focuses on diversification.

The decision to take actions to pursue growth is never a risk-free choice for firms. Indeed, as the Opening Case illustrated, Foster's Group experienced difficulty in integrating the beer and wine marketing and sales operations to share these activities. Also, Luxottica Group, a leader in the fashion sunglasses industry, has faced risks associated with its acquisition of Oakley, a firm focused on producing sporty sunglasses. Can a luxury goods manufacturer successfully integrate a sporting goods manufacturing company?[4] Effective firms carefully evaluate their growth options (including the different corporate-level strategies) before committing firm resources to any of them.[5]

Because the diversified firm operates in several different and unique product markets and likely in several businesses, it forms two types of strategies: corporate-level (or company-wide) and business-level (or competitive).[6] Corporate-level strategy is concerned with two key issues: in what product markets and businesses the firm should compete and how corporate headquarters should manage those businesses.[7] For the diversified corporation, a business-level strategy (see Chapter 4) must be selected for each of the businesses in which the firm has decided to compete. In this regard, each of Foster's product divisions uses different business-level strategies; while both focus on differentiation, the beer business is focused more on differentiation by a mass market approach while the high-end of the wine business targets unique customers based on individual tastes desired by marketing "its pricey wines to chic restaurants and liquor stores catering to connoisseurs."[8]

As is the case with a business-level strategy, a corporate-level strategy is expected to help the firm earn above-average returns by creating value.[9] Some suggest that few corporate-level strategies actually create value.[10] As the Opening Case indicates, realizing value through a corporate strategy can be difficult to achieve. In fact, the degree to which corporate-level strategies create value beyond the sum of the value created by all of a firm's business units remains an important research question.[11]

Evidence suggests that a corporate-level strategy's value is ultimately determined by the degree to which "the businesses in the portfolio are worth more under the management of the company than they would be under any other ownership."[12] Thus, an effective corporate-level strategy creates, across all of a firm's businesses, aggregate returns that exceed what those returns would be without the strategy[13] and contributes to the firm's strategic competitiveness and its ability to earn above-average returns.[14]

Product diversification, a primary form of corporate-level strategies, concerns the scope of the markets and industries in which the firm competes as well as "how managers buy, create and sell different businesses to match skills and strengths with opportunities presented to the firm."[15] Successful diversification is expected to reduce variability in the firm's profitability as earnings are generated from different businesses.[16] Because firms incur development and monitoring costs when diversifying, the ideal portfolio of businesses balances the costs and benefits of diversification. CEOs and their top-management teams are responsible for determining the ideal portfolio for their company.[17]

We begin this chapter by examining different levels of diversification (from low to high). After describing the different reasons why firms diversify their operations, we focus on two types of related diversification (related diversification signifies a moderate to high level of diversification for the firm). When properly used, these strategies help create value in the diversified firm, either through the sharing of resources (the related constrained strategy) or the transferring of core competencies across the firm's different businesses (the related linked strategy). We then discuss unrelated diversification, which is another corporate-level strategy that can create value. The chapter then shifts to the topic of incentives and resources that may stimulate diversification which is value neutral. However, managerial motives to diversify, the final topic in the chapter, can actually destroy some of the firm's value.

While discussing diversification, it is important to understand the unit of analysis. This is especially true in many emerging economies such as India, where "Business Groups", controlled by the same family or management control a number of legally different companies. We shall discuss this point in detail later. For various reasons, while entering into different businesses, the groups often float different companies such that even though the companies themselves may not be diversified, the group as a whole is.

Levels of Diversification

Diversified firms vary according to their level of diversification and the connections between and among their businesses. Figure 6.1 lists and defines five categories of businesses according to increasing levels of diversification. The single- and dominant-business categories denote relatively low levels of diversification; more fully diversified firms are classified into related and unrelated categories. A firm is related through its diversification when its businesses share several links; for example, businesses may share products (goods or services), technologies, or distribution channels. The more links among businesses, the more "constrained" is the relatedness of diversification. Unrelatedness refers to the absence of direct links between businesses.

Low Levels of Diversification

A firm pursuing a low level of diversification uses either a single or a dominant business, corporate-level diversification strategy. A single-business diversification strategy is a corporate-level strategy wherein the firm generates 95 per cent or more of its sales revenue from its core business area.[18] For example, Tata Steel, Tata Motors, Bajaj Auto, Infosys, Ballarpur Industries, etc. have all historically pursued single business or single-business diversified strategy, with one dominant product: steel, automobile (cars, bus and trucks chassis, two wheelers and three wheelers, software and paper products respectively). In 1969–70, ITC, which till then was a focused company dealing in tobacco products, diversified into many businesses, as we have already seen in Chapter 2.

With the **dominant-business diversification strategy,** the firm generates between 70 and 95 per cent of its total revenue within a single business area. ITC, over the years, has come into this category, with tobacco products accounting for about 75 per cent of its business as on 2010, the rest being in the agri-foods and hotels businesses. Though the tobacco business currently generates the largest percentage of ITC's sales revenue, the firm anticipates that in the future its other two businesses will account for the majority of revenue growth, due to the continuous pressure on the tobacco business on many

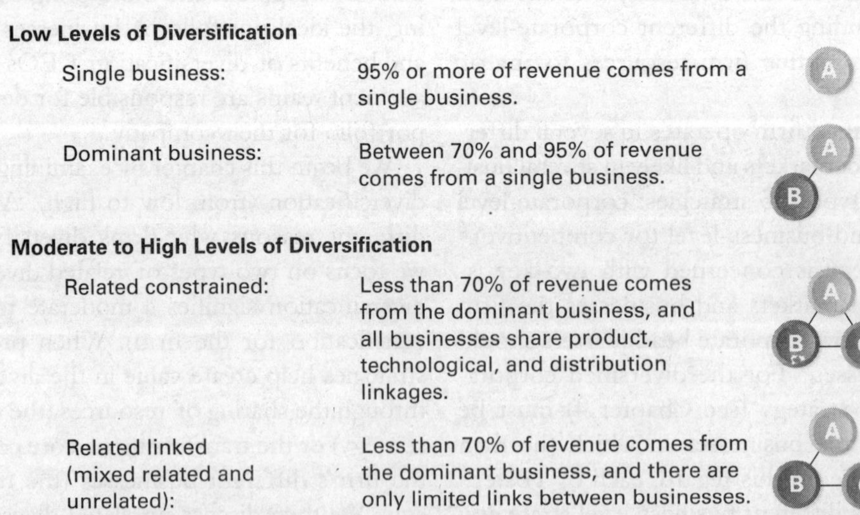

Figure 6.1 Levels and types of diversification

Source: Adapted from R. P. Rumelt, 1974, *Strategy, Structure and Economic Performance*, Boston: Harvard Business School.

fronts such as taxation, and health consciousness against smoking and tobacco chewing among people at large. This expectation suggests that ITC may become more diversified, both in terms of its goods and services.

Moderate and High Levels of Diversification

A firm generating more than 30 per cent of its revenue outside a dominant business and whose businesses are related to each other in some manner uses a related diversification corporate-level strategy. When the links between the diversified firm's businesses are rather direct, a **related constrained diversification strategy** is being used. Nestlé, Procter & Gamble, Hindustan Unilever and Larsen & Toubro all use a related constrained strategy[19]. With a related constrained strategy, a firm shares resources and activities between its businesses.

The diversified company with a portfolio of businesses that have only a few links between them is called a **mixed related** and **unrelated firm** and is using the **related linked diversification strategy** (see Figure 6.1). General Electric (GE) uses this corporate-level diversification strategy. Compared with related constrained firms, related linked firms share fewer resources and assets between their businesses, concentrating instead on transferring knowledge and core competencies between the businesses. As with firms using each type of diversification strategy, companies implementing the related linked strategy constantly adjust the mix in their portfolio of businesses as well as make decisions about how to manage these businesses.

A highly diversified firm that has no relationships between its businesses follows an **unrelated diversification strategy**. Videocon, Samsung, Godrej, and Sanmar Group are examples of firms using this type of corporate-level strategy. Godrej, for example, is in the businesses of locks, steel cupboards, cosmetics, refrigerators, etc. Videocon and Samsung are different kinds of consumer durables. (We have not included Wipro here, since though it is also in software, cosmetics, and vanaspati businesses, the software business has now become by far the dominant business). Commonly, firms using this strategy are called **conglomerates**.

GE, 3M, etc. are examples of companies committed to innovation and technology with businesses spanning the globe. GE's businesses span across a wide spectrum, ranging from medical diagnostic equipment, aero engines, and locomotives. 3M also has a huge variety of businesses ranging from abrasive papers, post it notes, and optical equipment. These businesses are not related to each other, and function independently as distinct business entities, but the corporate offices of these firms manage their financial function, and make some efforts to share knowledge and some competencies between or among them.

REASONS FOR DIVERSIFICATION

A firm uses a corporate-level diversification strategy for a variety of reasons (see Table 6.1). Typically, a diversification strategy is used to increase the firm's value by improving its overall performance. Value is created either through related diversification or through unrelated diversification when the strategy allows a company's businesses to increase revenues or reduce costs while implementing their business-level strategies.

Table 6.1 Reasons for diversification

Value-Creating Diversification
• Economies of scope (related diversification)
■ Sharing activities
■ Transferring core competencies
• Market power (related diversification)
■ Blocking competitors through multipoint competition
■ Vertical integration
• Financial economies (unrelated diversification)
■ Efficient internal capital allocation
■ Business restructuring
Value-Neutral Diversification
• Antitrust regulation
• Tax laws
• Low performance
• Uncertain future cash flows
• Risk reduction for firm
• Tangible resources
• Intangible resources
Value-Reducing Diversification
• Diversifying managerial employment risk
• Increasing managerial compensation

Other reasons for using a diversification strategy may have nothing to do with increasing the firm's value; in fact, diversification can have neutral effects or even reduce a firm's value. Value-neutral reasons for diversification include a desire to match and thereby neutralize a competitor's market power (such as to neutralize another firm's advantage by acquiring a similar distribution outlet). Decisions to expand a firm's portfolio of businesses to reduce managerial risk can have a negative effect on the firm's value. Greater amounts of diversification reduce managerial risk in that if one of the businesses in

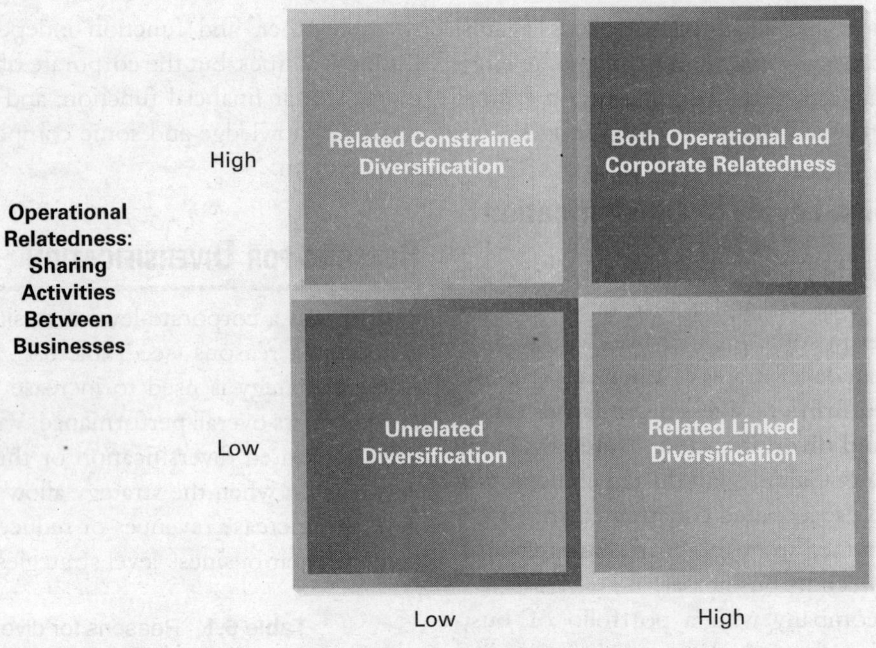

Figure 6.2 Value-creating diversification strategies: operational and corporate relatedness

a diversified firm fails, the top executive of that business does not risk total failure by the corporation. As such, this reduces the top executives' employment risk. In addition, because diversification can increase a firm's size and thus managerial compensation, managers have motives to diversify a firm to a level that reduces its value.[20] Diversification rationales that may have a neutral or negative effect on the firm's value are discussed later in the chapter.

Operational relatedness and corporate relatedness are two ways by which diversification strategies can create value (see Figure 6.2). Studies of these independent relatedness dimensions show the importance of resources and key competencies.[21] The figure's vertical dimension depicts opportunities to share operational activities between businesses (operational relatedness) while the horizontal dimension suggests opportunities for transferring corporate-level core competencies (corporate relatedness). The firm with a strong capability in managing operational synergy, especially in sharing assets between its businesses, falls in the upper left quadrant, which also represents vertical sharing of assets through vertical integration. The lower right quadrant represents a highly developed corporate capability for transferring one or more core competencies across businesses. This capability is located primarily in the corporate headquarters office. Unrelated diversification is also illustrated in Figure 6.2 in the lower left quadrant. Financial economies (discussed later), rather than either operational or corporate relatedness, are the source of value creation for firms using the unrelated diversification strategy.

Value-Creating Diversification: Related Constrained and Related Linked Diversification

With the related diversification corporate-level strategy, the firm builds upon or extends its resources and capabilities to create value.[22] The company using the related diversification strategy wants to develop and exploit economies of scope between its businesses.[23] Available to companies operating in multiple product markets or industries,[24] **economies of scope** are cost savings that the firm creates by successfully sharing some of its resources and capabilities or transferring one or more corporate-level core competencies that were developed in one of its businesses to another of its businesses.

As illustrated in Figure 6.2, firms seek to create value from economies of scope through two basic kinds of operational economies: *sharing activities* (operational relatedness) and *transferring corporate-level core competencies* (corporate relatedness). The difference between sharing activities and transferring competencies is based on how separate resources are jointly used to create economies of scope. To create economies of scope, tangible resources, such as plant and equipment or other business-unit physical assets, often must be shared. Less tangible resources, such as manufacturing know-how, can also be shared. However, know-how transferred between separate activities with no physical or tangible resource involved is a transfer of a corporate-level core competence, not an operational sharing of activities.[25]

©Indiatodayimages.com

©Indiatodayimages.com

HUL's distinct businesses such as cosmetics, detergents, and food businesses can share logistics, distribution facilities, and relationships with the supermarkets.

Operational Relatedness: Sharing Activities

Firms can create operational relatedness by sharing either a primary activity (such as inventory delivery systems) or a support activity (such as purchasing practices)—see discussion of the value chain in Chapter 3. Firms using the related constrained diversification strategy share activities in order to create value. Procter & Gamble (P&G) uses this corporate-level strategy. P&G's paper towel business and baby diaper business both use paper products as a primary input to the manufacturing process. The firm's paper production plant produces inputs for both businesses and is an example of a shared activity. In addition, because they both produce consumer products, these two businesses are likely to share distribution channels and sales networks. Similarly, HUL's distinct businesses such as cosmetics, detergents, and food businesses can share logistics, distribution facilities, and relationships with the supermarkets.

As noted in the Opening Case, Foster's Group sought to create operational relatedness between the beer and wine business. Firms expect activity sharing among units to result in increased strategic competitiveness and improved financial returns. Through its shared product approach, Foster's Group was unable to improve its market share position, especially in the wine business. As previously mentioned, pursuing operational relatedness is not easy, and often synergies are not realized as planned.

Activity sharing is also risky because ties among a firm's businesses create links between outcomes. For instance, if demand for one business' product is reduced, it may not generate sufficient revenues to cover the fixed costs required to operate the shared facilities. These types of organizational difficulties can reduce activity-sharing success. This problem occurred in the Foster's Group in the Opening Case because there were problems in the sharing of activities between the beer and wine businesses, especially in the marketing and distribution.

Activity sharing can lead to friction between the units sharing the activities, necessitating frequent coordination from the top. Two products from different profit centers or SBUs may share a machine, for example, but the machine has to be kept under the control of one of the activity managers. In this situation, the others may feel, rightly or wrongly, that they are not getting the needed priority. This problem became serious, for example, in the case of British Railways when, after its restructuring, the different business groups created, such as the passenger business and parcels businesses, had to share common facilities such as the track and signaling. Finding equitable rules for allocation of assets proved to be a constant problem for British Rail.

Although activity sharing across businesses is not risk-free, research shows that it can create value. For example, studies that acquisitions of firms in the same industry (horizontal acquisitions), such as the banking industry and software, found that sharing resources and activities and thereby creating economies of scope contributed to post acquisition increases in performance and higher returns to shareholders.[26] Additionally, firms that sold off related units in which resource sharing was a possible source of economies of scope have been found to produce lower returns than those that sold off businesses unrelated to the firm's core business.[27] Still other research discovered that firms with closely related businesses have lower risk.[28] These results suggest that gaining economies of scope by sharing activities across a firm's businesses may be important in reducing risk and in creating value. Further, more attractive results are obtained through activity sharing when a strong corporate headquarters office facilitates it.[29]

Corporate Relatedness: Transferring of Core Competencies

Over time, the firm's intangible resources, such as its know-how, become the foundation of core competencies. **Corporate-level core competencies** are complex sets of resources and capabilities that link different businesses, primarily through managerial and technological knowledge, experience, and expertise.[30] Firms seeking to create value through corporate relatedness use the related linked diversification strategy.

In at least two ways, the related linked diversification strategy helps firms to create value.[31] First, because the expense of developing a core competence has already been incurred in one of the firm's businesses, transferring this competence to a second business eliminates the need for that business to allocate resources to develop it. Such is the case at Hewlett-Packard (HP), where the firm transferred its competence in ink printers to high-end copiers. Rather than the standard laser printing technology in most high-end copiers, HP is using ink-based technology. One manager liked the product because, according to him, "We are able to do a lot better quality at less price."[32] This capability will also give HP the opportunity to sell more ink products, which is how it has been able to create higher profit margins.

Resource intangibility is a second source of value creation through corporate relatedness. Intangible resources are difficult for competitors to understand and imitate. Because of this difficulty, the unit receiving a transferred corporate-level competence often gains an immediate competitive advantage over its rivals.[33]

A number of firms have successfully transferred one or more corporate-level core competencies across their businesses. Virgin Group Ltd. transfers its marketing core competence as well as its brand equity across airlines, cosmetics, music, drinks, mobile phones, health clubs, and a number of other businesses.[34] Honda has developed and transferred its competence in engine design and manufacturing among its businesses making products such as motorcycles, lawnmowers, and cars and trucks. Company officials indicate that "Honda is the world's largest manufacturer of engines and has earned its reputation for unsurpassed quality, performance and reliability."[35]

One way managers facilitate the transfer of corporate-level core competencies is by moving key people into new management positions.[36] However, the manager of an older business may be reluctant to transfer key people who have accumulated knowledge and experience critical to the business' success. Thus, managers with the ability to facilitate the transfer of a core competence may come at a premium, or the key people involved may not want to transfer. Additionally, the top-level managers from the transferring business may not want the competencies transferred to a new business to fulfill the firm's diversification objectives. Research also suggests too much dependence on outsourcing can lower the usefulness of core competencies and thereby reduce their useful transferability to other business units in the diversified firm.[37]

Market Power

Firms using a related diversification strategy may gain market power when successfully using their related constrained or related linked strategy. **Market power** exists when a firm is able to sell its products above the existing competitive level or to reduce the costs of its primary and support activities below the competitive level, or both.[38] JSW Steel's acquisition of Ispat Industries, another steel manufacturer by buying 41.3 per cent of the equity of Ispat is expected to enable JSW steel to overtake SAIL and become India's second largest steel producer. JSW had a capacity of 7.5 million tons in 2009, to be increased to 11 million tons by 2011 when its expansion projects go on stream. Ispat is an ailing producer, with 3.3 million tons capacity, which JSW hopes to turn

STRATEGIC FOCUS

6.1 Cognizant's Diversification Strategy

Cognizant, a New Jersey, US based firm with large operations in India, is in the software business. It is in four "verticals", namely, financial, health, telecom, and manufacturing. Within the financial vertical, it is in the capital market, banking and insurance; in the health care vertical, it is in healthcare and life sciences; in the telecom vertical, it is in telecommunications, media and information services; and in manufacturing, it is in retail and logistics. While the vast majority of its revenues come from outside India, mainly from US, its staff are largely located in India, though as compared to other Indian IT companies, it employs a greater proportion of its staff in locations. Its top management are all Indians, and it is always included as an Indian IT company while analysts write about the Indian IT sector. Its growth—about 55 per cent per year and profit growth at about 60 per cent per year—has consistently been above many other Indian IT majors. All the same, its margins are lower than the other IT companies, due to the model it employs to ensure a high degree of customer satisfaction. Its major strong point is the customer satisfaction, which results in retention of its customers over long periods of time, and highly positive referrals to other clients.

Cognizant has diversified into new areas in software, but very carefully (in software, the domain knowledge needed in each vertical is high, and hence the different verticals are as good as different businesses). In deciding into a new vertical, the potential of the market and the stage of maturity it is in are the dominant considerations. Cognizant first employs a core staff to develop expertise in a proposed new vertical, and only after developing this expertise, does it move into the new vertical. This applies to acquisitions also where it does not proceed without acquiring its own strength. It also looks very carefully at the cultural fit of the acquired company. It never makes a hostile acquisition, since the employees of the acquired company may not integrate well into Cognizant.

Cognizant pursues both operational as well as corporate relatedness in its businesses

In its businesses, Cognizant pursues both operational as well as corporate relatedness, and hence would be in the northeast quadrant in Figure 6.2. It is usually difficult to link the different verticals, which tend to operate independently, but Cognizant has devised mechanisms for getting synergies across the verticals also, and they call these "horizontals". These are basically competencies such as data warehousing, business intelligence, customer relationship management, ERP, testing, etc. and these horizontals are organizational units themselves developing expertise in their own areas, and lending it to the verticals. The operational relatedness is derived from common training programs, movement of personnel, and sharing of infrastructure. Knowledge management is a key device by which the organization derives its synergies, with knowledge management officers at each project level and a central integration team.

Sources: "Cognizant: Managing Growth", unregistered case of Indian Institute of Management, Ahmedabad; "Cognizant: Preparing for a Global Footprint", Case # IIMA/BP0328 of the Indian Institute of Management, Ahmedabad; SEC filing of Cognizant (Form 10K) by Cognizant in various years; Karvey Analyst Reports, 2009; Cognizant Annual Reports of different years.

around and integrate with JSW. With its combined capacity of 14.3 million tons, JSW will overtake SAIL (capacity: 13.9 million tons) and be second only to Tata Steel (capacity: 26.5 million tons).[39]

In addition to efforts to gain scale as a means of increasing market power, as JSW did when it acquired Ispat, firms can create market power through multipoint competition and vertical integration. **Multipoint competition** exists when two or more diversified firms simultaneously compete in the same product areas or geographic markets.[40] The actions taken by LIC and banks such as State Bank of India and ICICI Bank in two markets, insurance and financial services, illustrate multipoint competition. LIC has moved into financial services including home loans and mutual funds, the stronghold of Banks and financial institutions; State Bank of India and ICICI Bank have moved into insurance, LIC's stronghold. Moreover, geographic competition for markets increases. The strongest shipping company in Europe is DHL. All three competitors (UPS, FedEx, and DHL) are trying to move into large foreign markets to either gain a stake or to expand their existing share. For instance, because the area of China that is close to Hong Kong is becoming a top destination for shipping throughout Asia, competition is raging among these three international shippers.[41] If one of these firms successfully gains strong positions in several markets while competing against its rivals, its market power may increase. Interestingly, DHL had to exit the US market because it was too difficult to compete against UPS and FedEx, which are dominant there.

Some firms using a related diversification strategy engage in vertical integration to gain market power. **Vertical integration** exists when a company produces its own inputs (backward integration) or owns its own source of output distribution (forward integration). In some instances, firms partially integrate their operations, producing and selling their products by using company businesses as well as outside sources.[42]

Vertical integration is commonly used in the firm's core business to gain market power over rivals. Market power is gained as the firm develops the ability to save on its operations, avoid market costs, improve product quality, and, possibly, protect its technology from imitation by rivals.[43] Market power also is created when firms have strong ties between their assets for which no market prices exist. Establishing a market price would result in high search and transaction costs, so firms seek to vertically integrate rather than remain separate businesses.[44]

Vertical integration has its limitations. For example, an outside supplier may produce the product at a lower cost. As a result, internal transactions from vertical integration may be expensive and reduce profitability relative to competitors.[45] Also, bureaucratic costs may occur with vertical integration. And, because vertical integration can require substantial investments in specific technologies, it may reduce the firm's flexibility, especially when technology changes quickly. Finally, changes in demand create capacity balance and coordination problems. If one business is building a part for another internal business but achieving economies of scale requires the first division to manufacture quantities that are beyond the capacity of the internal buyer to absorb, it would be necessary to sell the parts outside the firm as well as to the internal business. Thus, although vertical integration can create value, especially through market power over competitors, it is not without risks and costs.[46]

Reliance Industries is a good example of vertical integration leading to the creation of independent businesses over a period of time. It started as a textile mill marketing high quality polyester fabrics. To produce these fabrics, it integrated backward into the production of the polyester "chips" and further into the production of petrochemicals. Then it integrated backwards further into the production and refining of oil itself, setting up large refineries. Finally it entered into exploration of oil and gas. The scales required for the economic production of these are very different; for example, refining requires a huge scale, as compared to textiles or even petrochemicals. The production from Reliance's refineries cannot be absorbed by their own petrochemical business, thus necessitating Reliance to get into the retail business of petroleum products. Today, its oil business is vastly bigger than the original textile business, which has in fact become a fringe business. The case of Nirma, on the other hand, illustrates the problems caused by vertical integration. Nirma started as a detergent manufacturer. It went into production of soda ash and Linear Alkyl Benzene (LAB), essential raw materials for the production of detergents. Since salt is a byproduct of soda ash, it went into the marketing of salt as well. These forays, besides its other diversification plans, increased its debt to a much higher level than that of its competitors. Its EPS and stock price has been below the market for the last five years. Recently, it has expanded its soda ash business, and has proposed buying back its shares from its shareholders, making it an unlisted company. It was reported to be unsure of the non promoter shareholders' support for its ventures, all of which are capital intensive and will increase its debt still further.[47] Each of its vertical integration forays seem to have led to entry into another business, with its own logic.

Many manufacturing firms have been reducing vertical integration as a means of gaining market power.[48] In fact, de-integration is the focus of most manufacturing firms, such as Intel and Dell, and even some large auto companies, such as Ford and General Motors, as they develop independent supplier networks.[49] We have noted, in an earlier chapter, how Bajaj Auto has outsourced many of its manufacturing activities. India's premier forging company, Bharat Forge, on the other hand, is *taking advantage* of the outsourcing in the automobile industry, many of whose manufacturers are closing their in house forging units, by becoming a prime forging supplier to many automobile companies all over the world. It is also moving up the value chain by supplying machined components rather than raw forgings.[50] Flextronics, an electronics contract manufacturer, represents a new breed of large contract manufacturers that is helping to foster this revolution in supply-chain management.[51] Such firms often manage their customers' entire product lines and offer services ranging from inventory management to delivery and after-sales service. Conducting business through e-commerce also allows vertical integration to be changed into "virtual integration."[52] Thus, closer relationships are possible with suppliers and customers through virtual integration or electronic means of integration, allowing firms to reduce the costs of processing transactions while improving their supply-chain management skills and tightening the control of their inventories. Much of the BPO business is of this nature. This evidence suggests that **virtual integration** rather than **vertical integration** may be a more common source of market power gains for firms today.

Simultaneous Operational Relatedness and Corporate Relatedness

As Figure 6.2 suggests, some firms simultaneously seek operational and corporate relatedness to create economies of scope.[53] The ability to simultaneously create economies of scope by sharing activities (operational relatedness) and transferring core competencies (corporate relatedness) is difficult for competitors to understand and learn how to imitate. However, if the cost of realizing both types of relatedness is not offset by the benefits created, the result is diseconomies because the cost of organization and incentive structure is very expensive.[54]

As the Strategic Focus on Johnson & Johnson illustrates, this company uses a strategy that combines operational and corporate relatedness with some success. Likewise, Walt Disney Co. uses a related diversification strategy to simultaneously create economies of scope through operational and corporate relatedness. Within the firm's Studio Entertainment business, for example, Disney can gain economies of scope by sharing activities among its different movie distribution companies such as Touchstone Pictures, Hollywood Pictures, and Dimension Films. Broad and deep knowledge about its customers is a capability on which Disney relies to develop corporate-level core competencies in terms of advertising and marketing. With these competencies, Disney is able to create economies of scope through corporate relatedness as it cross-sells products that are highlighted in its movies through the distribution channels that are part of its Parks and Resorts and Consumer Products businesses. Thus, characters created in movies become figures that are marketed through Disney's retail stores (which are part of the Consumer Products business). In addition, themes established in movies become the source of new rides in the firm's theme parks, which are part of the Parks and Resorts business and provide themes for clothing and other retail business products.[55]

As we described, Johnson & Johnson and Walt Disney Co. have been able to successfully use related diversification as a corporate-level strategy through which they create economies of scope by sharing some activities and by transferring core competencies. However, it can be difficult for investors to actually observe the value created by a firm (such as Walt Disney Co.) as it shares activities and transfers core competencies. For this reason, the value of the assets of a firm using a diversification strategy to create economies of scope in this manner tends to be discounted by investors. For example, analysts have complained that both Citibank and UBS, two large multiplatform banks, have underperformed their more focused counterparts in regard to stock market appreciation. In fact, both banks have heard calls for breaking up their separate businesses in insurance, hedge funds, consumer lending, and investment banking.[56] One analyst speaking of Citigroup suggested that "creating real synergy between its divisions has been hard," implying that Citigroup's related diversification strategy suffered from some possible diseconomies of scale.[57] Due to its diseconomies and other losses related to the economic downturn, Citigroup has recently considered selling some of its foreign divisions, such as its Japanese investment bank and brokerage service.[58] USB is changing its strategy as well. The bank's three divisions—private banking, investment banking, and asset management—will be reorganized into a more centralized unit to reduce costs. Previously each segment was given more autonomy over its operations; this model proved too costly and the new CEO, Oswald Grubel, is seeking to reduce possible diseconomies of scale through the centralization, especially in regard to information technology.[59]

Unrelated Diversification

Firms do not seek either operational relatedness or corporate relatedness when using the unrelated diversification corporate-level strategy. An unrelated diversification strategy (see Figure 6.2) can create value through two types of financial economies. **Financial economies** are cost savings realized through improved allocations of financial resources based on investments inside or outside the firm.[60]

Efficient internal capital allocations can lead to financial economies. Efficient internal capital allocations reduce risk among the firm's businesses—for example, by leading to the development of a portfolio of businesses with different risk profiles. The second type of financial economy concerns the restructuring of acquired assets. Here, the diversified firm buys another company, restructures that company's assets in ways that allow it to operate more profitably, and then sells the company for a profit in the external market.[61] Next, we discuss the two types of financial economies in greater detail.

STRATEGIC FOCUS

6.2 Johnson & Johnson Uses Both Operational and Corporate Relatedness

Johnson & Johnson (J&J) is a widely diversified company. It is the world's seventh largest pharmaceutical company, fourth largest biologics company, the premier consumer health products company, and the largest medical devices and diagnostics company. These businesses are combined into three main groups: consumer health care, medical devices and diagnostics, and pharmaceuticals. The consumer health care business produces products for hair, skin, teeth, and babies. The medical devices and diagnostics business develops stents and many other products focused on cardiovascular care and equipment for surgical settings. The pharmaceutical business is focused on the central nervous system and internal medicines for helping with such disorders as schizophrenia, epilepsy, diabetes, and cardiovascular and infectious diseases. Within the pharmaceutical business, another unit focuses on biotechnology to treat autoimmune disorders such as rheumatoid arthritis, psoriasis, and Crohn's disease. Yet another unit, the neurology unit, focuses on developing drugs for HIV/AIDS, hepatitis C, and tuberculosis. Traditionally these businesses were managed with a mixed related and unrelated strategy. Associated with this strategy was a definite approach focused on decentralization.

More recently, J&J aspired to not only have relatedness within the major businesses, but also to have corporate relatedness across all of its business units. CEO William Bolden has sought to propel growth by getting autonomous divisions to work more closely together. "The move suggests the desire to increase interaction to squeeze more value from areas where they overlap." The integrated approach aims to harness expertise from various units to harness and use its diagnostics testing equipment in diagnosing disease earlier than other products in the market. It is also seeking to harness expertise to better assist its glucose monitoring segment to more effectively monitor diabetes.

Other drug companies have been focused on either pharmaceuticals or consumer products and have been reducing the overlap. J&J has taken advantage of both positions and as a result has been more profitable during the current economic downturn than the more focused pharmaceutical or principal products companies. One major innovation between the pharmaceuticals and the device business was the drug-coated stent, which was originally created by Cordis, a division of its medical equipment business. This spurred competition in this industry with other stent makers, including Boston Scientific and Abbott Laboratories. J&J also increased the competition with its new device, Nevo, "a totally redesigned product" in the stent business.

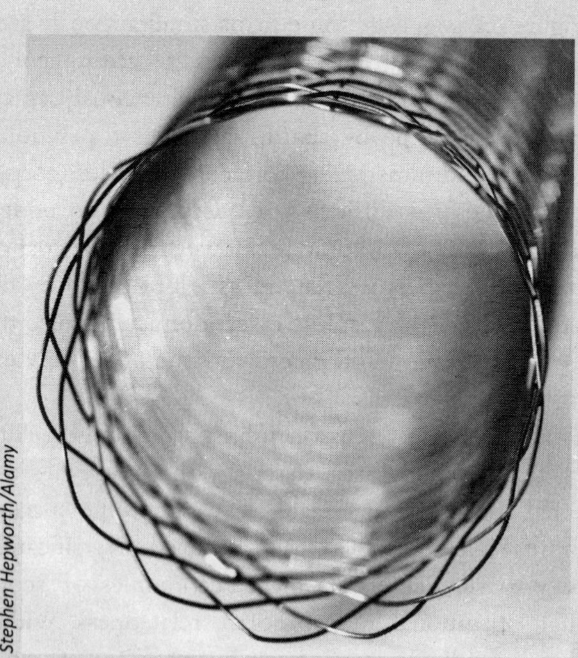
Stephen Hepworth/Alamy

Johnson & Johnson's development of the drug-coated stent was made possible through the coordinated efforts of both their pharmaceutical and medical device businesses.

Besides innovation where the expertise of previously decentralized businesses is combined, J&J is seeking to pursue corporate relatedness in regard to marketing by completing a massive consolidation of its contracted media and advertising agencies. It has settled on a large involvement of several companies such as WPP and Interpublic Group. It is therefore pursuing a single brand according to market and channels and is forcing a consolidation of marketing across its businesses. The purpose for this strategic change is to create a more unified brand and decrease the high costs that are associated with each business unit handling its own media and advertising concepts.

In summary, J&J moved from a related linked strategy focused only on operational relatedness to a strategy that is focused more on pursuing both operational relatedness (with its separate businesses sharing operation activities) and corporate relatedness across its business units. It has strived to achieve greater innovation and management of the regulatory process as well as much better coordination across its businesses in marketing. There are other areas in which it is trying to develop more efficiencies, such as the production process. As such, it is pursuing both operational and corporate relatedness.

Sources: M. Arnold, 2009, J&J shows the way, *Medical Marketing and Media*, January, 39, 41, 43; 2008, J&J perks up, *Financial Times*, http://www.ft.com, December 1; J. Bennett, 2008, J&J: A balm for your portfolio, *Barron's*, October 27, 39; C. Bowe, 2008, Cautious chief with an impulse for innovation, *Financial Times*, http://www.ft.com, January 14, 14; P. Loftus & S. Wang, 2008, Earnings digest—pharmaceuticals: Diversified strategy buoys J&J's results, *Wall Street Journal*, July 16, B4; S. Wang, 2008, Corporate news: J&J acquires wellness firm, widening scope, *Wall Street Journal*, October 28, B3; A. Johnson, 2007, J&J realigns managers, revamps units; move calls for divisions to integrate their work, *Wall Street Journal*, November 16, A10.

Efficient Internal Capital Market Allocation

In a market economy, capital markets are thought to efficiently allocate capital. Efficiency results as investors take equity positions (ownership) with high expected future cash-flow values. Capital is also allocated through debt as shareholders and debt holders try to improve the value of their investments by taking stakes in businesses with high growth and profitability prospects.

In large diversified firms, the corporate headquarters office distributes capital to its businesses to create value for the overall corporation. The nature of these distributions may generate gains from internal capital market allocations that exceed the gains that would accrue to shareholders as a result of capital being allocated by the external capital market.[62] Because those in a firm's corporate headquarters generally have access to the detailed and accurate information regarding the actual and prospective performance of the company's portfolio of businesses, they have the best information to make capital distribution decisions.

Compared to corporate office personnel, external investors have relatively limited access to internal information and can only estimate the performances of individual businesses as well as their future prospects. Moreover, although businesses seeking capital must provide information to potential suppliers (such as banks or insurance companies), firms with internal capital markets may have at least two informational advantages. First, information provided to capital markets through annual reports and other sources may not include negative information, instead emphasizing positive prospects and outcomes. External sources of capital have limited ability to understand the operational dynamics of large organizations. Even external shareholders who have access to information have no guarantee of full and complete disclosure.[63] Second, although a firm must disseminate information, that information also becomes simultaneously available to the firm's current and potential competitors. With insights gained by studying such information, competitors might attempt to duplicate a firm's value-creating strategy. Thus, an ability to efficiently allocate capital through an internal market may help the firm protect the competitive advantages it develops while using its corporate-level strategy as well as its various business-unit level strategies.

STRATEGY RIGHT NOW

Read more about the corporate-level strategies that guide decision-making at Johnson & Johnson.
www.cengage.com/management/hitt

If intervention from outside the firm is required to make corrections to capital allocations, only significant changes are possible, such as forcing the firm into bankruptcy or changing the top management team. Alternatively, in an internal capital market, the corporate headquarters office can fine-tune its corrections, such as choosing to adjust managerial incentives or suggesting strategic changes in one of the firm's businesses. Thus, capital can be allocated according to more specific criteria than is possible with external market allocations. Because it has less accurate information, the external capital market may fail to allocate resources adequately to high-potential investments. The corporate headquarters office of a diversified company can more effectively perform such tasks as disciplining underperforming management teams through resource allocations.[64]

Large, highly diversified businesses often face what is known as the "conglomerate discount." This discount results from analysts not knowing how to value a vast array of large businesses with complex financial reports. For instance, one analyst suggested in regard to figuring out GE's financial results in its quarterly report, "Rubik's cube may in fact be easier to figure out."[65] To overcome this discount, many unrelated diversified or industrial conglomerates have sought to establish a brand for the parent company. For instance, recent advertisements by GE "moved its focus from customer comfort and convenience ("We Bring Good Things to Life") to a more future-oriented mantra ("Imagination at Work") that promises creative and innovative products."[66] On assumption of the stewardship of the Tata Group, Mr. Ratan Tata required that all the members of the Tata Group, in which the holding company, Tata Sons had a stake, should promote the Tata brand, and also pay a "contribution" (he avoided the term "royalty") to Tata Sons for the use of the brand name. He sought to derive value from the Tata name, which stood for good quality, probity in dealings and trust, across its different businesses: steel, automobiles and cars, chemicals, insurance and financial services, etc.[67] It is hoping that the "umbrella" brand advertisement will raise its PE to a level comparable to its competitors.[68] He wanted to create a strong equity that would benefit all the group companies.[69]

In spite of the challenges associated with it, a number of corporations continue to use the unrelated diversification strategy, especially in Europe and in emerging markets. Siemens, for example, is a large German conglomerate with a highly diversified approach. Its former CEO argued that "When you are in an up-cycle and the capital markets have plenty of opportunities to invest in single-industry companies … investors savor those opportunities. But when things change pure plays go down faster than you can look."[70] In the current downturn, diversification is helping some companies improve future performance,[71] as was the case with Oracle.

The Achilles' heel for firms using the unrelated diversification strategy in a developed economy is that competitors can imitate financial economies more easily than they can replicate the value gained from the economies of scope developed through operational relatedness and corporate relatedness. This issue is less of a problem in emerging economies, where the absence of a "soft infrastructure" (including effective financial intermediaries, sound regulations, and contract laws) supports and encourages use of the unrelated diversification strategy.[72] In fact, in emerging economies such as those in Korea, India, and Chile, research has shown that diversification increases the performance of firms affiliated with large diversified business groups.[73]

Restructuring of Assets

Financial economies can also be created when firms learn how to create value by buying, restructuring, and then selling the restructured companies' assets in the external market.[74] As in the real estate business, buying assets at low prices, restructuring them, and selling them at a price that exceeds their cost generates a positive return on the firm's invested capital.

As the ensuing Strategic Focus on unrelated diversified companies that pursue this strategy suggests, creating financial economies by acquiring and restructuring other companies' assets involves significant trade-offs. For example, the continued success of the Siva group requires a very fine sense of the market and timing. Siva avoids high-technology businesses, because resource allocation decisions become too complex, creating information-processing overload on the small corporate headquarters offices that are common in unrelated diversified firms. High-technology businesses are often human-resource dependent; these people can leave or demand higher pay and thus appropriate or deplete the value of an acquired firm.[75]

Buying and then restructuring service-based assets so that they can be profitably sold in the external market is also difficult. Sales in such instances are often a product of close personal relationships between a client and the representative of the firm being restructured. Thus, for both high-technology firms and service-based companies, relatively few tangible assets can be restructured to create value and sell profitably. It is difficult to restructure intangible assets such as human capital and effective relationships that have evolved over time between buyers (customers) and sellers (firm personnel). As the Strategic Focus Segment also indicates, care must be taken in a downturn to restructure and buy and sell at appropriate times. The downturn can also present opportunities. Ideally, executives will follow a strategy of buying businesses when prices are lower, such as in the midst of a recession and selling them at later stages in an expansion.[76]

STRATEGIC FOCUS

6.3 SIVA GROUP: Serial Acquirers of Diversified Industrial Manufacturing Businesses

Chinnakannan Sivasankaran, "Siva": The maverick businessman with the "Midas touch".

Chinnakannan Sivasankaran (popularly known as Siva) is known for spotting business opportunities well ahead of time and way before others. Dubbed as a "maverick businessman" whose moves are as unpredictable as they are unconventional, Siva focuses on buying, running, and turning around unprofitable businesses and almost unfailingly making a substantial profit when he exits the acquisitions. The Chennai-based Siva Group which Sivasankaran founded in 1986, has the credit of pioneering new concepts and introducing paradigm shifts in the way business is shaped and grown in India. From a modest fabrication contractor of Chennai Petroleum Corporation (CPCL) to the head of a multi-billion dollar diversified business conglomerate, Siva has indeed come a long way. Today, the group has global operations in high growth industries like telecom, project engineering, shipping & logistics, renewable energy, commodity trading, hospitality & realty, agro business, and e-education/software.

Siva pioneered the concept of low-cost computers way back in the 1980s with the acquisition of a small computer company, Sterling Computers, and virtually changed the rules of the PC business forever. He sold PCs for as low as ₹33,000 in an era when computers were still a luxury, priced at more than ₹100,000. His strategy was simple: drop PC prices by half and introduce the product in March—the peak season for computer sales by companies seeking to take advantage of depreciation allowance for tax purposes by the end of the financial year (31 March). He also offered a free printer along with a computer —a practice unheard-of in the PC business then. Thereafter, in a masterstroke, Siva tied up with Computer Point, the country's first computer retail mart, to ensure that he had an all-India distribution. This strategy catapulted him amongst the top three in the PC business. Siva, however, soon realized that competitors were also beginning to drop prices, hence he decided to quit the PC business. Siva is reported to have said in an interview: "You are in the business to make money. If it doesn't, close it and get into a profitable venture."

Siva has a signature operating style. First, he identifies a broad line of business. Then, he enters companies by acquiring major stakes in them. Once invested, he plays two distinct roles: In some cases, he plays an active role in management while in others, he is content with a more passive role. The Siva model has certainly worked. Between 1995 and 2005, he made gains of about $1billion from his entry and exits in telecom: Aircel, RPG Cellular, and Dishnet. In the 1990s, when mobile telephony was launched, he acquired the Tamil Nadu circle, launched Aircel Cellular in 1997–98 and built it into a significant player in the South, buying along the way 79 per cent in RPG Cellular in Chennai for about ₹2500 million in 2003. In 1998, he incorporated Dishnet, India's first DSL internet provider, which he later sold to Videsh Sanchar Nigam limited (VSNL) for ₹2700 million, in 2004. In 2006, Siva sold Aircel to Malaysia's Maxis Communications for $1.08 billion and divested 33 per cent in Tamil Nadu Mercantile Bank for ₹1300 billion.

Barista (a coffee shop format) is another prominent acquisition by Siva and is a good example of his strategy. In 2004, Siva acquired 65.4 per cent stake in Barista Coffee Company from Turner Morrison Group for ₹300 million and 34.3 per cent stake from the Tatas for ₹650 million. After the acquisition, 90 outlets were added to the existing stable, taking the total to 175 outlets in India and 12 outlets across the UAE, Sri Lanka, and Oman. The additional investments amounted to ₹1200 million. In 2007, Siva sold the coffee business of the Sterling Group, comprising Fresh & Honest Café (which focuses on vending filter coffee and other beverages) and Barista to the Italian company Lavassa for about ₹5000 million. While Barista provided the brand and perhaps the entry interest for Lavazza, Fresh & Honest gave it an existing platform of profits.

There is always an element of surprise in Siva's business deals. Whether it was the acquisition of RPG Cellular or sale of Dishnet DSL to VSNL, "like his entry, his exit is well timed and the valuations he got are more than he could have asked for," says an analyst at a leading brokerage. He started off with ventures in the telecom space and then expanded to a range of diverse business. After making a windfall through the sale of Aircel, Siva created an investment company, Siva Ventures Limited, and entered new businesses through a mix of organic and inorganic growth strategies. In 2008, the group ventured into packaged mineral water business by acquiring a 50 per cent stake in the Norwegian glacial natural mineral water company Isklar for $22 million. The deal was a 50:50 joint venture with Sabco, a premier water brand in the Middle East. Isklar is currently sold with retailers like Tesco, Sainsbury's and Waitrose, and few other Norway major retail chains. Mineral water business in India is dominated by well known MNCs like PepsiCo (Aquafina), Coca-Cola (Kinley), Nestle (PureLife), and the home grown Bisleri.

Siva is a consummate deal maker. He holds on to his investments till he gets the target value. He held on to his Aircel business for a long time and did not yield to lesser offers. He also does not shy away from selling and buying stakes back, like Barista or TMB. He might strike another goldmine in the water business too.

Sources: Siva Group Web site, http://www.svl.oc.in/Open/SIVAGrp.aspx; Manoj Govindassamy, 2010, Siva venturing into the mineral water business—buys 50% stake in Isklar, www.moneymint.com, March 11,http://www.moneymint.in/deals/sivasankaran-venturing-into-mineral-water-business-buys-50-stake-in-isklar; Sabarinath M, and V Balasubramanian, 2010, Serial Entrepreneur Sivasankaran bets on edible oil, *Economic Times*, October 4, http://economictimes.indiatimes.com/markets/stocks/stocks-in-news/Serial-entrepreneur-Sivasankaran-bets-on-edible-oil/articleshow/6680147.cms; http://connect.in.com/sivasankaran/biography-354390.html; 2007, Nitya Varadarajan, Bucks for Beans, *Business Today*, April 8, http://archives.digitaltoday.in/businesstoday/20070408/current4.html; N Madhavan, 2008, Deal Meister, *Business Today*, August 10, http://businesstoday.intoday.in/bt/story/2648/1/deal-meister.html; 2007, *Times of India*, Italian Lavazza buys Barista for ₹ 480 Crore, March 10, http://findarticles.com/p/news-articles/times-of-india-the/mi_8012/is_20070310/italian-lavazza-acquires-barista-rs/ai_n39437766/; Sahad P V, 2006, Sivasankaran scouting for strategic investors for Barista, www.vccircle.com, August 31, http://www.vccircle.com/2006/08/31/sivasankaran-scouting-for-strategic-investors-for-barista.

Value-Neutral Diversification: Incentives and Resources

The objectives firms seek when using related diversification and unrelated diversification strategies all have the potential to help the firm create value by using a corporate-level strategy. However, these strategies, as well as single- and dominant-business diversification strategies, are sometimes used with value-neutral rather than value-creating objectives in mind. As we discuss next, different incentives to diversify sometimes exist, and the quality of the firm's resources may permit only diversification that is value neutral rather than value creating.

Incentives to Diversify

Incentives to diversify come from both the external environment and a firm's internal environment. External incentives include antitrust regulations and tax laws. Internal incentives include low performance, uncertain future cash flows, and the pursuit of synergy and reduction of risk for the firm.

Regulation, Tax Laws, and Diversification Strategies

The pattern of development of the Indian industry was a direct outcome of the regulatory framework operating from time to time. After Independence, a socialistic dream led to the attempt to curb monopoly and concentration of powers in the private sector; State enterprises were seen as the engines for growth. Hence, a number of laws were passed, such as the Industrial Regulation Act, Monopoly and Restricted Trade Practices Act (MRTP), and Foreign Exchange Regulations Act (FERA). Licenses were needed to set up industries, expand capacities and to change lines of business. These licenses were given for specific capacities only, and excess production was penalized. The result was a severely restricted growth rate, but the companies which had licenses could thrive and make huge profits in the capacity constrained economy. Nonetheless their expansion was restricted, and the areas they could get into were also specified by the government. Companies which had large surpluses in cash found it necessary to diversify into whatever sectors they could procure licenses, thus leading to a totally unrelated diversification pattern.

Tax rates were very high. This led to large tax evasions, and the development of unaccounted money or the black economy. The money had to be invested in sectors that thrived on an informal basis, such as the real estate and construction sector. These diversifications also had no relationship with the core strengths of the companies, but that did not matter in a capacity constrained economy; a firm had to just produce, and the product would sell.

The progressive liberalization in the 1980s, which gathered momentum in the early 1990s led to many new firms entering the industry. The old companies, thus, had to refocus on their core businesses. Many, however, continued with their conglomerate structure and even derived strengths from their brand name and group affiliation. In an interesting article, Khanna and Palepu argued that focused strategies may be *wrong* in emerging markets.[77] They argued that in such markets, the capital market systems are weak, often illiquid or with a narrow floating stock; the labor market is not well developed producing people with good skills; the product markets are also characterized by low enforcement of intellectual property rights, distorted liability laws and few activist consumers; the regulation is weak in enforcement and corruption driven; and contract enforcement is weak. The group affiliation can overcome at least to some extent these problems, and creating a number of unrelated industries enables the group to overcome the risk of being narrowly focused, without the disadvantages of operating in a multiplicity of industries.

Thus, capital markets can be substituted by internal resource allocation among the businesses and the group companies can act in effect as venture capitalists. Groups can create value by developing skilled labor and capable managers through group training programs (such as the Tata Administrative Service); they can develop skills at managing the regulation for the group as a whole; they can develop their own products and protect them through strong brands that provide a degree of assurance to a customer that is otherwise not possible; and can even set norms of their own for others to follow. Indeed these advantages seem to prevail in not only India, but in other developing countries in Latin America as well.

But as India became an "emerging" economy, many of these points of logic seemed to be withering away. Now many large companies have come up (such as Infosys) with no group affiliation; indeed many of the old big industrial houses have gone into a decline. As India gets into an "emerged" state, probably, these advantages of a group affiliation and the need for opportunistic diversification would decline.

Low Performance

Some research shows that low returns are related to greater levels of diversification.[78] If "high performance eliminates the need for greater diversification,"[79] then low performance may provide an incentive for diversification. In 2005, eBay acquired Skype for $3.1 billion in hopes that it would create synergies and improve communication between buyers and sellers. However, in 2008, eBay announced that it would sell Skype if the opportunity presents itself because it has failed to increase cash flow for its core e-commerce business and the synergies have not been realized. Some critics have even urged eBay to rid itself of PayPal in order to boost its share price.[80] Similarly, Larsen & Toubro (L&T) which had diversified into cement and other businesses in the late 1960s and early 1970s due to the regulatory issues at that time (see ITC Opening case in Chapter 2) sold its cement business to the Birla group in May, 2004[81]. The stock of L&T went up from ₹580 in May 2004 to ₹760 in August 2004. This was because the cement business was seen as a drag on L&T.[82]

Research evidence and the experience of a number of firms suggest that an overall curvilinear relationship, as illustrated in Figure 6.3, may exist between diversification and performance.[83] Although low performance can be an incentive to diversify, firms that are more broadly diversified compared to their competitors may have overall lower performance. Further, broadly based banks, such as Citigroup and UBS as noted earlier, have been under pressure to "break up" because they seem to underperform compared to their peers. Following liberalization, Indian companies have tried to get rid of their unrelated businesses and focus on their core business. Besides managing businesses they know, they also release resources from unfamiliar and non-core businesses to the businesses in which they are strong. For example, the Tata Group decided to focus on steel, motor vehicles, and IT/software businesses and divested its cement, soap and toiletry, and tapered roller bearings businesses. The Thapar Group divested its edible oils, glass, leather, aquaculture, bricks, china clay, and adhesive tapes businesses, and decided to focus on paper, pulp, and chemicals businesses. The Mahindra Group decided to concentrate on its automobiles and related businesses, and divested its elevator and EAC Graphics businesses.[84]

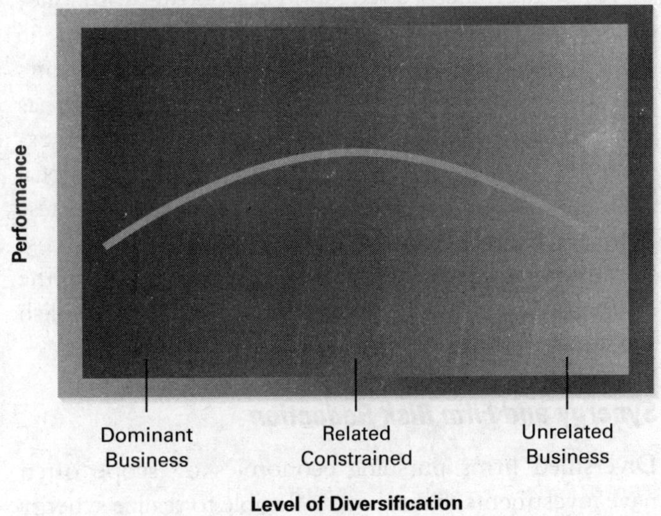

Figure 6.3 The curvilinear relationship between diversification and performance

Uncertain Future Cash Flows

As a firm's product line matures or is threatened, diversification may be an important defensive strategy.[85] Small firms and companies in mature or maturing industries sometimes find it necessary to diversify for long-term survival.[86] For example, auto-industry suppliers in USA have been slowly diversifying into other more promising ventures such as "green" businesses and medical supplies as the auto industry has declined. Dephi, for instance, once part of General Motors, has been expanding its electric car battery expertise into residential energy systems. Abbott Workholding Products, Inc. has been expanding its industrial tools business into tools for making artificial knee and bone replacements.[87]

Diversifying into other product markets or into other businesses can reduce the uncertainty about a firm's future cash flows. Dr. Reddy's Laboratories (DRL) looked to expand into the biosimilars business (production of drugs which are similar to approved drugs). DRL launched its first biosimilar product, Grafeel (filgrastim), in 2001 in India. Subsequently, its second biosimilar product, Reditux (biosimilar version of Rituximab) which is the world's first monoclonal anti-body based anti-cancer drug, was launched in the domestic market in 2007. DRL has launched its biosimilars in the Indian market at a much lower price than the original products, often patented and marketed by multinationals.[88] On expiry of the patents, the biosimilars are available at a much lower price. Thus Grafeel which is a biotech equivalent of Roche's Neupogen, was launched at a steep discount in 2001; in August 2010, DRL's Cresp—an equivalent of Amgen's Aranesp, a red blood cell booster for kidney disease patients—made a debut claiming savings of 55 per cent for patients who were on Johnson & Johnson's Eprex (a precursor to Aranesp). The company now has many more biosimilars in the pipeline, which are expected to be launched in the next few years in the local Indian market. It hopes to expand its domestic business by being highly competitive both due to its lower cost position as compared to overseas companies, as also the much easier regulatory requirements in India to establish bio-equivalence.[89]

Synergy and Firm Risk Reduction

Diversified firms pursuing economies of scope often have investments that are too inflexible to realize synergy between business units. As a result, a number of problems may arise. **Synergy** exists when the value created by business units working together exceeds the value that those same units create working independently. But as a firm increases its relatedness between business units, it also increases its risk of corporate failure, because synergy produces joint interdependence between businesses that constrains the firm's flexibility to respond. This threat may force two basic decisions.

First, the firm may reduce its level of technological change by operating in environments that are more certain. This behavior may make the firm risk averse and thus uninterested in pursuing new product lines that have potential, but are not proven. Alternatively, the firm may constrain its level of activity sharing and forgo synergy's potential benefits. Either or both decisions may lead to further diversification.[90] The former would lead to related diversification into industries in which more certainty exists. The latter may produce additional, but unrelated, diversification.[91] Research suggests that a firm using a related diversification strategy is more careful in bidding for new businesses, whereas a firm pursuing an unrelated diversification strategy may be more likely to overprice its bid, because an unrelated bidder may not have full information about the acquired firm.[92] However, firms using either a related or an unrelated diversification strategy must understand the consequences of paying large premiums.[93] In the situation with eBay, former CEO Meg Whitman received heavy criticism for paying such a high price for Skype, especially when the firm did not realize the synergies it was seeking.

Resources and Diversification

As already discussed, firms may have several value-neutral incentives as well as value-creating incentives (such as the ability to create economies of scope) to diversify. However, even when incentives to diversify exist, a firm must have the types and levels of resources and capabilities needed to successfully use a corporate-level diversification strategy.[94] Although both tangible and intangible resources facilitate diversification, they vary in their ability to create value. Indeed, the degree to which resources are valuable, rare, difficult to imitate, and nonsubstitutable (see Chapter 3) influences a firm's ability to create value through diversification. For instance, free cash flows are a tangible financial resource that may be used to diversify the firm. However, compared with diversification that is grounded in intangible resources, diversification based on financial resources only is more visible to competitors and thus more imitable and less likely to create value on a long-term basis.[95]

Tangible resources usually include the plant and equipment necessary to produce a product and tend to be less-flexible assets. Any excess capacity often can be used only for closely related products, especially those requiring highly similar manufacturing technologies. For example, Acer Inc. hopes to benefit during the current economic downturn and build market share through a related diversification move. Acer believes that large computer makers such as Dell and Hewlett-Packard have underestimated the demand for mini-notebook or "netbook" computers. Acer diversified into these compact machines and now has about 30 per cent of the market share. These smaller and less expensive machines are expected to become 15–20 per cent of the overall PC market. It has also expanded into "smart phones" and at the same time has created seamless integration between such phones and PCs for data transfer. There are obvious manufacturing and sales integration opportunities between its basic tangible assets and these related diversification moves.[96]

GIPhotoStock Z/Alamy

The small "EEE" Acer notebook computer (shown here in white) facilitates Acer's related diversification strategy.

Excess capacity of other tangible resources, such as a sales force, can be used to diversify more easily. Again, excess capacity in a sales force is more effective with related diversification, because it may be utilized to sell similar products. The sales force would be more knowledgeable about related-product characteristics, customers, and distribution channels.[97] Tangible resources may create resource interrelationships in production, marketing, procurement, and technology, defined earlier as activity sharing. Intangible resources are more flexible than tangible physical assets in facilitating diversification. Although the sharing of tangible resources may induce diversification, intangible resources such as tacit knowledge could encourage even more diversification.[98]

Sometimes, however, the benefits expected from using resources to diversify the firm for either value-creating or value-neutral reasons are not gained.[99] For example, as noted in the Opening Case, implementing operational relatedness has been difficult for the Foster's Group in integrating the wine and beer businesses; the joint marketing operation was a failure. Similarly, Ballarpur Industries' attempts to get some synergies between its paper and pulp businesses has met with only very limited success[100]

Value-Reducing Diversification: Managerial Motives to Diversify

Managerial motives to diversify can exist independent of value-neutral reasons (i.e., incentives and resources) and value-creating reasons (e.g., economies of scope). The desire for increased compensation and reduced managerial risk are two motives for top-level executives to diversify their firm beyond value-creating and value-neutral levels.[101] In slightly different words, top-level executives may diversify a firm in order to diversify their own employment risk, as long as profitability does not suffer excessively.[102]

Diversification provides additional benefits to top-level managers that shareholders do not enjoy. Research evidence shows that diversification and firm size are highly correlated, and as firm size increases, so does executive compensation.[103] Because large firms are complex, difficult-to-manage organizations, top-level managers commonly receive substantial levels of compensation to lead them.[104] Greater levels of diversification can increase a firm's complexity, resulting in still more compensation for executives to lead an increasingly diversified organization. Governance mechanisms, such as the board of directors, monitoring by owners, executive compensation practices, and the market for corporate control, may limit managerial tendencies to over-diversify. These mechanisms are discussed in more detail in Chapter 10.

In some instances, though, a firm's governance mechanisms may not be strong, resulting in a situation in which executives may diversify the firm to the point that it fails to earn even average returns.[105] The loss of adequate internal governance may result in poor relative performance, thereby triggering a threat of takeover. Although takeovers may improve efficiency by replacing ineffective managerial teams, managers may avoid takeovers through defensive tactics, such as "poison pills," or may reduce their own exposure with "golden parachute" agreements.[106] Therefore, an external governance threat, although restraining managers, does not flawlessly control managerial motives for diversification.[107]

Most large publicly held firms are profitable because the managers leading them are positive stewards of firm resources, and many of their strategic actions, including those related to selecting a corporate-level diversification strategy, contribute to the firm's success.[108] As mentioned, governance mechanisms should be designed to deal with exceptions to the managerial norms of making decisions and taking actions that will increase the firm's ability to earn above-average returns. Thus, it is overly

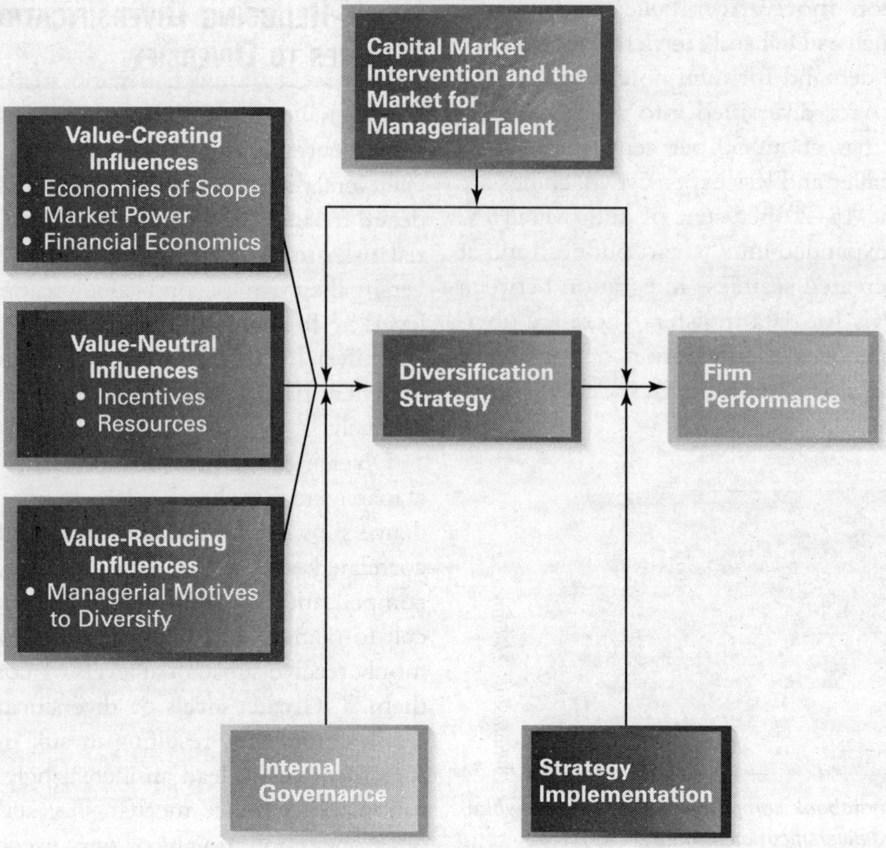

Figure 6.4 Summary model of the relationship between diversification and firm performance

Source: Adapted from R. E. Hoskisson & M. A. Hitt, 1990, Antecedents and performance outcomes of diversification: A review and critique of theoretical perspectives, *Journal of Management*, 16: 498.

pessimistic to assume that managers usually act in their own self-interest as opposed to their firm's interest.[109]

Top-level executives' diversification decisions may also be held in check by concerns for their reputation. If a positive reputation facilitates development and use of managerial power, a poor reputation may reduce it. Likewise, a strong external market for managerial talent may deter managers from pursuing inappropriate diversification.[110] In addition, a diversified firm may police other firms by acquiring those that are poorly managed in order to restructure its own asset base. Knowing that their firms could be acquired if they are not managed successfully encourages executives to use value-creating, diversification strategies.

As shown in Figure 6.4, the level of diversification that can be expected to have the greatest positive effect on performance is based partly on how the interaction of resources, managerial motives, and incentives affects the adoption of particular diversification strategies. As indicated earlier, the greater the incentives and the more flexible the resources, the higher the level of expected diversification. Financial resources (the most flexible) should have a stronger relationship to the extent of diversification than either tangible or intangible resources. Tangible resources (the most inflexible) are useful primarily for related diversification.

As discussed in this chapter, firms can create more value by effectively using diversification strategies. However, diversification must be kept in check by corporate governance (see Chapter 10). Appropriate strategy implementation tools, such as organizational structures, are also important (see Chapter 11).

We have described corporate-level strategies in this chapter. In the next chapter, we discuss mergers and acquisitions as prominent means for firms to diversify and to grow profitably. These trends toward more diversification through acquisitions, which have been partially reversed due to restructuring (see Chapter 7), indicate that learning has taken place regarding corporate-level diversification strategies.[111] Accordingly, firms that diversify should do so cautiously, choosing to focus on relatively few, rather than many, businesses. In fact, research suggests that although unrelated diversification has decreased, related diversification has increased, possibly due to the restructuring that continued into the 1990s and early twenty-first century. This sequence of diversification followed by restructuring is now taking place in Europe and other places such as Korea, mirroring actions of firms in the United States and the United Kingdom.[112] Firms can improve their strategic competitiveness when they pursue a level of diversification that is appropriate for their resources (especially financial resources) and core competencies and the opportunities and threats in their country's institutional and competitive environments.[113]

SUMMARY

- The primary reason a firm uses a corporate-level strategy to become more diversified is to create additional value. Using a single- or dominant-business corporate-level strategy may be preferable to seeking a more diversified strategy, unless a corporation can develop economies of scope or financial economies between businesses, or unless it can obtain market power through additional levels of diversification. Economies of scope and market power are the main sources of value creation when the firm diversifies by using a corporate-level strategy with moderate to high levels of diversification.
- The related diversification corporate-level strategy helps the firm create value by sharing activities or transferring competencies between different businesses in the company's portfolio.
- Sharing activities usually involves sharing tangible resources between businesses. Transferring core competencies involves transferring core competencies developed in one business to another business. It also may involve transferring competencies between the corporate headquarters office and a business unit.
- Sharing activities is usually associated with the related constrained diversification corporate-level strategy. Activity sharing is costly to implement and coordinate, may create unequal benefits for the divisions involved in the sharing, and may lead to fewer managerial risk-taking behaviors.
- Transferring core competencies is often associated with related linked (or mixed related and unrelated) diversification, although firms pursuing both sharing activities and transferring core competencies can also use the related linked strategy.
- Efficiently allocating resources or restructuring a target firm's assets and placing them under rigorous financial controls are two ways to accomplish successful unrelated diversification. Firms using the unrelated diversification strategy focus on creating financial economies to generate value.
- Diversification is sometimes pursued for value-neutral reasons. Incentives from tax and antitrust government policies, performance disappointments, or uncertainties about future cash flow are examples of value-neutral reasons that firms may choose to become more diversified.
- Managerial motives to diversify (including to increase compensation) can lead to over diversification and a subsequent reduction in a firm's ability to create value. Evidence suggests, however, that the majority of top-level executives seek to be good stewards of the firm's assets and avoid diversifying the firm in ways and amounts that destroy value.
- Managers need to pay attention to their firm's internal organization and its external environment when making decisions about the optimum level of diversification for their company. Of course, internal resources are important determinants of the direction that diversification should take. However, conditions in the firm's external environment may facilitate additional levels of diversification, as might unexpected threats from competitors.

KEY TERMS AND DEFINITIONS

A **corporate-level strategy** specifies actions a firm takes to gain a competitive advantage by selecting and managing a group of different businesses competing in different product markets.

Economies of scope are cost savings that the firm creates by successfully sharing some of its resources and capabilities or transferring one or more corporate-level core competencies that were developed in one of its businesses to another of its businesses.

Corporate-level core competencies are complex sets of resources and capabilities that link different businesses, primarily through managerial and technological knowledge, experience, and expertise.

Market power exists when a firm is able to sell its products above the existing competitive level or to reduce the costs of its primary and support activities below the competitive level, or both.

Multipoint competition exists when two or more diversified firms simultaneously compete in the same product areas or geographical markets.

Vertical integration exists when a company produces its own inputs (backward integration) or owns its own source of output distribution (forward integration).

Financial economies are cost savings realized through improved allocations of financial resources based on investments inside or outside the firm.

Synergy exists when the value created by business units working together exceeds the value that those same units create working independently.

REVIEW QUESTIONS

1. What is corporate-level strategy and why is it important?
2. What are the different levels of diversification firms can pursue by using different corporate-level strategies?
3. What are three reasons firms choose to diversify their operations?
4. How do firms create value when using a related diversification strategy?
5. What are the two ways to obtain financial economies when using an unrelated diversification strategy?
6. What incentives and resources encourage diversification?
7. What motives might encourage managers to over diversify their firm?

EXPERIENTIAL EXERCISES

Exercise 1: Comparison of Diversification Strategies

The use of diversification varies both across and within industries. In some industries, most firms may follow a single- or dominant-product approach. Other industries are characterized by a mix of both single-product and heavily diversified firms. The purpose of this exercise is to learn how the use of diversification varies across firms in an industry, and the implications of such use.

Part One

Working in small teams of four to seven people, choose an industry to research. You will then select two firms in that industry for further analysis. Many resources can aid you in identifying specific firms in an industry for analysis. Data bases such as CMIE can give you some ideas on which firms to choose. Identify two public firms based in India.

Identify the businesses they are in and get a rough idea of the size of each of these businesses. If data is available, get the exact data for each business segment.

Next, based on your reading of the company data, determine whether the firm is best classified as:

- Single product
- Dominant product
- Related diversified
- Unrelated diversified

Part Two

Prepare a brief PowerPoint presentation for use in class discussion. Address the following in the presentation:

- Describe the extent and nature of diversification used at each firm.
- Can you provide a motive for the firm's diversification strategy, given the rationales for diversification put forth in the chapter?
- Which firm's diversification strategy appears to be more effective? Try to justify your answer by explaining why you think one firm's strategy is more effective than the other.

Exercise 2: How Does the Firm's Portfolio Stack Up?

The BCG (Boston Consulting Group) product portfolio matrix has been around for decades and was introduced by the BCG as a way

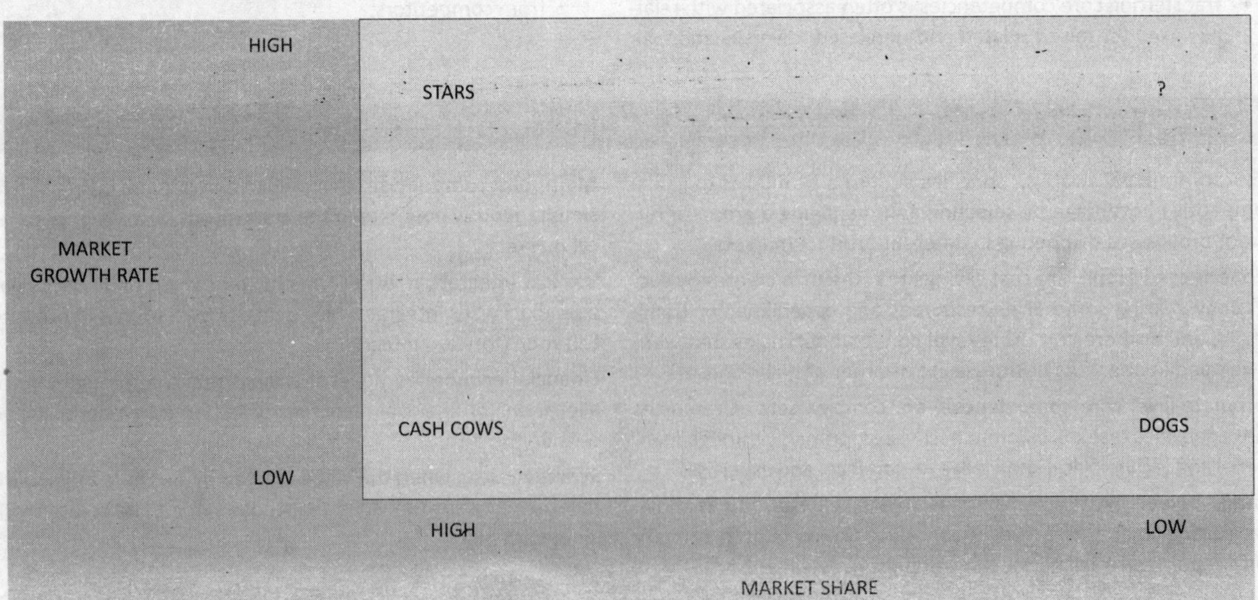

for firms to understand the priorities that should be given to the various segments within their mix of businesses. It is based on a matrix with two vertices: firm market share and projected market growth rate, as shown below:

Each firm therefore can categorize its business units as follows:

- **Stars**: High growth and high market share. These business units generate large amounts of cash but also use large amounts of cash. These are often the focus of the firm's priorities as these segments have a potentially bright future.
- **Cash Cows**: Low market growth coupled with high market share. Profits and cash generated are high; the need for new cash is low. Provides a foundation for the firm from which it can launch new initiatives.
- **Dogs**: Low market growth and low market share. This is usually a situation firms seek to avoid. This is quite often the target of a turnaround plan or liquidation effort.
- **Question Marks**: High market growth but low market share. Creates a need to move strategically because of high demands on cash due to market needs yet low cash returns because of the low firm market share.

This way to analyze a firm's corporate level strategy or the way in which it rewards and prioritizes its business units has come under some criticism. For one, market share is not the only way in which a firm should view success or potential success; second, market growth is not the only indicator for the attractiveness of a market; and third, sometimes "dogs" can earn as much cash as "cows."

Part One

Pick a publicly traded firm that has a diversified corporate-level strategy. The more unrelated the segments the better.

Part Two

Analyze the firm using the BCG matrix. In order to do this you will need to develop market share ratings for each operating unit and assess the overall market attractiveness for that segment. You could develop the matrix for GCMMF (see the case Gujarat Milk Marketing Federation in the book).

Strategic Acquisition and Restructuring

CHAPTER

7

Studying this chapter should provide you with the strategic management knowledge needed to

- Explain the popularity of merger and acquisition strategies in firms competing in the global economy.
- Discuss reasons why firms use an acquisition strategy to achieve strategic competitiveness.
- Describe seven problems that work against achieving success when using an acquisition strategy.
- Name and describe the attributes of effective acquisitions.
- Define the restructuring strategy and distinguish among its common forms.
- Explain the short- and long-term outcomes of the different types of restructuring strategies.

OPENING CASE
Merger and Acquisition Activity During a Global Crisis: Global and in India

Mergers and acquisitions (M&A) are a primary means of firm growth. We define these terms and discuss a number of reasons why firms use merger and acquisition strategies in this chapter.

Cross-border M&A activity (activity involving firms headquartered in different nations) increased during the 1990s and into the early part of the twenty-first century, largely because of the continuing globalization of the world's markets. A key advantage of mergers and acquisitions is that they can help firms grow rapidly in both domestic and international markets. For societies, mergers and acquisitions can be beneficial in that they "... are a critical tool for eliminating weaker players and wringing out excess capacity."

Merger and acquisition activity tends to be cyclical in nature flowing and ebbing in light of the opportunities and threats associated with a firm's external environment. In the very recent past, the global financial crisis has contributed to a sharp decline in M&A activity. The fact that "merger and acquisition volume worldwide dropped to $29 trillion in 2008, from $42 trillion the year before," demonstrates the caution firms exercised during 2008 in terms of using merger and acquisition strategies.

Evidence from the first part of 2009 suggests that the decline observed in 2008 continued, certainly with respect to cross-border M&A activity. "Global flows of foreign direct investment halved during the first three months of 2009 as the value of cross-border mergers and acquisitions plummeted." Indeed, the value of cross-border M&A activity declined by 77 per cent in the first quarter of 2009 as compared to the same quarter a year earlier. The size of individual mergers and acquisitions also declined during 2008 and early 2009. In the first half of 2009, Pfizer's proposed $68 billion acquisition of Wyeth was the largest transaction. According to Dealogic, which tracks M&A activity, the US federal government's $25 billion stake in Citigroup ranked as the fifth largest transaction during this six-month period. Uncertainty in the world's credit markets and possible political changes in different nations' orientation to M&A activity were among the causes of decline in global M&A activity during the recent financial crisis.

In spite of the recent declines in M&A activity both globally and domestically, merger and acquisition strategies are still a very viable source of firm growth; as a result, they remain popular with many of the world's corporations. In the foreseeable future, M&A opportunities seem strong in several sectors such as energy and health care. In response to pushes toward greener, renewable energy sources, for example, major oil companies "... are eyeing players in alternative energy..." Fuel refiner Valero's purchase of ethanol producer VeraSun is an example of M&A activity taking place in this sector. Some of the major corporations in the health care industry have large amounts of cash that can be used to gain access to promising drugs and other firm's research and development skills. Pfizer's $68 billion acquisition of Wyeth demonstrates the type of activity taking place in this sector. (We further discuss this acquisition in a Strategic Focus in this chapter.) However, as is true for all strategies, firms in these two sectors and all other companies must carefully evaluate the "deal" (either a merger or an acquisition) they are contemplating to verify that completing the transaction will facilitate the firm's efforts to achieve strategic competitiveness and create value for stakeholders as a result of doing so.

AP Photo/Eric Landwehr

Despite adverse economic conditions, in early 2009 Valero Energy became the first oil company to purchase a major ethanol producer when it bought the seven plants from the bankruptcy inventory of VeraSun.

The Indian scenario

In India, M&A activities have become a major component of the strategies of companies. Driven by Bharti Airtel's $10.7 billion takeover deal for the African assets of Kuwait's Zain Telecom, the total value of merger and acquisition deals in the country in the calendar year 2010 nearly quadrupled to a whopping $50 billion over the corresponding figures for 2009. In 2010, the total number of M&A deals in India was 623, with a total value of $50 billion. Of these, 350 were domestic deals, 187 were outbound international deals, and 86 were inbound international deals, with values of $19.59 billion, $21.31 billion, and $8.88 billion respectively. These were comparable with the figures for 2007, while 2008 and 2009 saw sharp drop in numbers, due to the global recession. The number of deals in 2007, 2008, and 2009 were 676, 454, and 330 respectively, with values of $51, $31, and $12 billion respectively.

The number of domestic transactions in India increased from 174 deals worth $6.7 billion in 2009 to 350 deals worth $19.59 billion in 2010. There were 187 outbound deals in 2010, while the figure stood at 82 a year ago. In terms of value, the increase was more than fifteen times, primarily due to the Bharti–Zain deal. The number of inbound deals also rose from 74 deals in 2009 to 86 in 2010.

Apart from Bharti Airtel's Zain acquisition deal, the other top two deals in 2010 were the $5.48 billion acquisition of Mundra Port and Special Economic Zone (SEZ) by Adani Enterprises and the acquisition of Piramal Healthcare by Abbot Laboratories for $3.72 billion. The attempt to acquire Cairn India by Vedanta for $8.5 million has not yet been approved. Other major deals in the period under consideration include Fortis Healthcare $685-million investment in Parkway Holdings, Essar Group's $600 million acquisition of Trinity Coal Corporation and Telenor ASA's $433 million stake buy in Unitech Wireless. The five major deals in the first quarter of 2010 accounted for over 71 per cent of the total M&A deals.

A sector wise analysis shows that telecommunication services, energy, and healthcare were the most targeted sectors as these segments attracted deals worth $14.03 billion, $1.17 billion, and $ 961 million respectively. Big ticket deals dominated the M&A space as large deals worth $100 million and above accounted for as much as 90 per cent of total capital invested in the first quarter of 2010. Public sector Oil and Natural Gas Corporation's (ONGC) acquisition of Russia based Imperial Energy for $2.8 billion marked the beginning of the Indian hunt for for natural reserves in competition with China. Essar Group's acquisition of 100 per cent of Trinity Coal for $600 million follows the steps taken by other Indian power companies, such as Tata Power Co. and Reliance Power Ltd., to secure coal assets overseas in order to supply the surging power consumption in India (over 75 percent of India's power generation is coal-fired). In the pharmaceuticals sector, Dr. Reddy's Laboratories acquired Betapharm, USA for $597 million, apart from the Piramal acquisition by US based Abbott Laboratories. .

Going forward, the value and volume of Indian M&A activity is likely to increase as investor confidence and liquidity returns to the market. "Strategic investors will try to take advantage of lower valuations in the midst of the crisis and strengthen their position across various sectors," according to VCC Edge, a financial research agency.

Sources: P. Hannon, 2009, Foreign investing decreased by half earlier this year, *Wall Street Journal Online*, http://www.wsj.com, June 25; S. Jung-a, 2009, Mergers & Acquisitions: Ambitious companies with war-chests look for value, *Financial Times Online*, http://www.ft.com, May 20; Z. Kouwe, 2009, Deals on ice in first half, with 40% drop in M.&A., *New York Times Online*, http://www.nytimes.com, July 1; J. Silver-Greenberg, 2009, Dealmakers test the waters, *BusinessWeek*, March 2, 18–20; 2008, Global M&A falls in 2008, *New York Times Online*, http://www.nytimes.com, December 22; L. Saigoi, 2008, Record number of M&A deals cancelled in 2008, *Financial Times Online*, http://www.ft.com, December 22; *Deccan Herald*, 2010, India Inc's M&A deal touches $19 b in Q1 of 2010, April 4, http://www.deccanherald.com/content/ 62113/india-incs-mampa-deal-touches.html; *Economic Times,* 2011, Being Force Merger, 16 January, p.7; Joydeep, 2010, Top 10 Valuable Global Acquistions by Indian Companies, February 18, retrieved from http://apac.globalthoughtz.com/index.php/top-10-valuable-global-acquisitions-by-indian-companies/.

We examined corporate-level strategy in Chapter 6, focusing on types and levels of product diversification strategies that firms derive from their core competencies to create competitive advantages and value for stakeholders. As noted in that chapter, diversification allows a firm to create value by productively using excess resources.[1] In this chapter, we explore merger and acquisition strategies. Firms throughout the world use these strategies, often in concert with diversification strategies, to become more diversified. As noted in the Opening Case, even though the amount of merger and acquisition activity completed in 2008 and through mid-2009 fell short of such activity in previous years, merger and acquisition strategies remain popular as a source of firm growth and hopefully, of above-average returns.

Most corporations are very familiar with merger and acquisition strategies. For example, the latter half of the twentieth century found major companies using these strategies to grow and to deal with the competitive challenges in their domestic markets as well as those emerging from global competitors. Today, smaller firms also use merger and acquisition strategies to grow in their existing markets and to enter new markets.[2]

Not unexpectedly, some mergers and acquisitions fail to reach their promise.[3] Accordingly, explaining how firms can successfully use merger and acquisition strategies to create stakeholder value[4] is a key purpose of this chapter. To do this, we first explain the continuing popularity of merger and acquisition strategies as a choice firms evaluate when seeking growth and strategic competitiveness. As part of this explanation, we describe the differences between mergers, acquisitions, and takeovers. We next discuss specific reasons firms choose to use acquisition strategies and some of the problems organizations may encounter when implementing them. We then describe the characteristics associated with effective acquisitions before closing the chapter with a discussion of different types of restructuring strategies. Restructuring strategies are commonly used to correct or deal with the results of ineffective mergers and acquisitions.

The Popularity of Merger and Acquisition Strategies

Merger and acquisition strategies have been popular among US firms for many years. Some believe that these strategies played a central role in the restructuring of US businesses during the 1980s and 1990s and that they continue generating these types of benefits in the twenty-first century.[5] After liberalization, M&A have become very popular in India also. Studies have shown that the liberalized policy regime and greater access to financial markets have impacted the M&A activities in the country.[6]

Although popular and appropriately so as a means of growth with the potential to lead to strategic competitiveness, it is important to emphasize that changing conditions in the external environment influence the type of M&A activity firms pursue. During the recent financial crisis for example, tightening credit markets made it more difficult for firms to complete "megadeals" (those costing $10 billion or more). As a result, "… many acquirers are focusing on smaller targets with a niche focus that complements their existing business."[7] Additionally, when a currency weakens, it becomes cheaper to acquire firms in that country, unless there are regulatory hurdles. For example, the relatively weak US dollar increased the interest of firms from other nations to acquire US companies. Perhaps the lower valuations of European companies during the current financial crisis prompted increased acquisition activities in Europe by Indian companies.

In the final analysis, firms use merger and acquisition strategies to improve their ability to create more value for all stakeholders including shareholders. As suggested by Figure 1.1, this reasoning applies equally to all of the other strategies (e.g., business-level, corporate-level, international and cooperative) a firm may formulate and then implement.

However, evidence suggests that using merger and acquisition strategies in ways that consistently create value is challenging. This is particularly true for acquiring firms in that some research results indicate that shareholders of acquired firms often earn above-average returns from acquisitions while shareholders of acquiring firms typically earn returns that are close to zero.[8] Moreover, in approximately two-thirds of all acquisitions, the acquiring firm's stock price falls immediately after the intended transaction is announced. This negative response reflects investors' skepticism about the likelihood that the acquirer will be able to achieve the synergies required to justify the premium.[9] Premiums can sometimes be excessive, as appears to be the case with Tata's acquisition of Corus for $12.4 billion in January 2007. Corus had a turnover of £10.1 (₹808) billion and profits of £450 million (₹36 billion) after tax. The enterprise value to EBITDA ratio for Corus was around 9, while it was around 4.6 for Tata Steel. The stock market reaction was decidedly negative: Tata Steel lost more than 10 per cent in stock price and a billion dollars in market capitalization. *The Hindu Businessline* commented that three elements were stacked against the deal, at least in the short run: equity dilution that will be needed, drop in margins due to the lower margins earned by Corus, and the likely downturn in the steel industry[10]. Obviously, creating the amount of value required to account for this type of premium would be extremely difficult. Overall then, those leading firms that are using merger and acquisition strategies must recognize that creating more value for their stakeholders by doing so is indeed difficult.[11]

Mergers, Acquisitions, and Takeovers: What Are the Differences?

A **merger** is a strategy through which two firms agree to integrate their operations on a relatively coequal basis. Recently, Towers Perrin Forster & Crosby Inc. and Watson Wyatt Worldwide Inc., two large human-resources consulting firms, agreed to merge. Shareholders of each firm will own 50 per cent of the newly formed company, which will be "…the world's biggest employee-benefits consultancy…."[12]

Even though the transaction between Towers Perrin and Watson Wyatt appears to be a merger, the reality is that few true mergers actually take place. The main reason for this is that one party to the transaction is usually dominant in regard to various characteristics such as market share, size, or value of assets. The transaction proposed between Xstrata and Anglo American appears to be an example of this. An exception is the merger between two companies belonging to the same group. For example, an Anil Dhirubhai Ambani Group's (ADAG's) gas transportation company, Reliance Natural Resources Ltd (RNRL), merger with its sister firm Reliance Power (R-Power) for $ 10686 million. But this was in a sense, more a consolidation than a merger. However, the shareholders of the two companies being different, issues did arise on the exchange value of shares of the two companies.[13]

In 2009, Swiss-based Xstrata (a global diversified mining group) proposed a friendly merger with London-based Anglo American (a diversified mining and natural resource group). While some analysts thought that the proposed merger of equals "should create some value," they also concluded that the "...friendly merger with Anglo American (was) a pretty aggressive bear hug" given the terms Xstrata was seeking and its potential inability to pay the premium Anglo's shareholders expected. In this case too some felt that Anglo's assets were of higher quality, reducing the likelihood that the transaction was actually one of "equals."[14]

An **acquisition** is a strategy through which one firm buys a controlling, or 100 per cent, interest in another firm with the intent of making the acquired firm a subsidiary business within its portfolio. After completing the transaction, the management of the acquired firm reports to the management of the acquiring firm.

In spite of the situation we described dealing with Xstrata and Anglo American, most of the mergers that are completed are friendly in nature. However, acquisitions can be friendly or unfriendly. A **takeover** is a special type of acquisition wherein the target firm does not solicit the acquiring firm's bid; thus, takeovers are unfriendly acquisitions. Research evidence showing "...that hostile acquirers deliver significantly higher shareholder value than friendly acquirers" for the acquiring firm[15] is a reason some firms are willing to pursue buying another company even when that firm is not interested in being bought. Often, determining the price that the acquiring firm is willing to pay to "take over" the target firm is the core issue in these transactions. In the case of the Tata Corus deal, for example, the initial offer of Tata was 455 pence (₹364) per share. This was challenged by the Brazilian steel maker Compendia Siderúrgica Nacional (CSN) which offered 475 pence (₹380) per share. The auction went on for nine rounds, and the final offer of Tata was 608 pence (₹486.40) per share, as compared to 603 pence (₹482.40) by CSN.[16] Such competitive bidding sometimes leads to a high price being eventually being paid, and its becoming a millstone around the neck of the acquirer, the so called "winner's curse".

On a comparative basis, acquisitions are more common than mergers and takeovers. Accordingly, we focus the remainder of this chapter's discussion on acquisitions.

Reasons for Acquisitions

In this section, we discuss reasons which firms decide to acquire another company. Although each reason can provide a legitimate rationale, acquisitions are not always as successful as the involved parties want the case to be. Later in the chapter, we examine problems firms may encounter when seeking growth and strategic competitiveness through acquisitions.

Increased Market Power

Achieving greater market power is a primary reason for acquisitions.[17] Defined in Chapter 6, **market power** exists when a firm is able to sell its goods or services above competitive levels or when the costs of its primary or support activities are lower than those of its competitors. Market power usually is derived from the size of the firm and its resources and capabilities to compete in the marketplace.[18] It is also affected by the firm's share of the market. Therefore, most acquisitions that are designed to achieve greater market power entail buying a competitor, a supplier, a distributor, or a business in a highly related industry to allow the exercise of a core competence and to gain competitive advantage in the acquiring firm's primary market.

If a firm achieves enough market power, it can become a market leader, which is the goal of many firms. For example, having already acquired Gateway and Packard Bell, Acer is contemplating acquiring other firms (perhaps Asustek of Taiwan or Lenovo of China) as a means of getting closer to its goal of being the leading maker and seller of personal computers.[19] Mahindra & Mahindra acquired 90 per cent stakes of Schoneweiss, a leading company in the forging sector in Germany. The deal took place in 2007, and consolidated Mahindra's position in the global market.[20] JSW Steel's acquisition of Ispat was meant to increase the market power of JSW by making it the largest steel producer in India. Its capacity of 11 million tons, combined with that of Ispat (3.3 million tons) will make JSW the market share leader.[21]

Next, we discuss how firms use horizontal, vertical, and related types of acquisitions to increase their market power.

Horizontal Acquisitions

The acquisition of a company competing in the same industry as the acquiring firm is a **horizontal acquisition**. Horizontal acquisitions increase a firm's market power by exploiting cost-based and revenue-based synergies.[22] For example, JSW's acquisition of Ispat was meant to increase the former's market share and power in the Indian market. Holcım, the Swiss cement manufacturer, acquired ACC and Gujarat Ambuja Cement enabling it to gain a quick entry into the Indian market with a market share of 23 per cent and a capacity of 33 million tons[23]. The acquisition of Patni Computers by iGate Corporation, for $1.2 billion is expected to enable iGate to increase its scale, widen its client base, and reduce its dependence on a few clients, said Mr. Phaneesh Murthy, CEO of iGate. While iGate has its revenues coming from banking and finance sectors, Patni is strong in insurance sector.[24]

Research suggests that horizontal acquisitions result in higher performance when the firms have similar characteristics[25] such as strategy, managerial styles, and resource allocation patterns. Similarities in these characteristics support efforts to integrate the acquiring and the acquired firm. The similarity in the strategies they use should facilitate the integration of Patni's and iGate's businesses. Holcim's acquisition of Gujarat Ambuja was also considered successful due to the similarity of strategies of the two companies: In India, Gujarat Ambuja was the cost leader thanks to its modern plants, an exclusive jetty for its exports, and access to raw materials. Horizontal acquisitions are often most effective when the acquiring firm integrates the acquired firm's assets with its own assets, but only after evaluating and divesting excess capacity and assets that do not complement the newly combined firm's core competencies.[26]

Vertical Acquisitions

A **vertical acquisition** refers to a firm acquiring a supplier or distributor of one or more of its goods or services.[27] Through a vertical acquisition, the newly formed firm controls additional parts of the value chain (see Chapters 3 and 6),[28] which is how vertical acquisitions lead to increased market power.

The acquisition of Indian Petrochemicals Corporation Limited (IPCL) by Reliance Industries Limited (RIL) was hailed as a landmark vertical acquisition when it happened in May, 2002. RIL was a large petroleum company with large refineries. Though it was already in petrochemicals business, the acquisition of IPCL was important as a downstream processing unit for RIL, enabling it to increase its presence in the value added petrochemicals. A media analysis of the deal observed: It will be a dominant player in the domestic petrochemicals industry with a market share exceeding 70 per cent across most product categories. It will be a near monopoly in some products such as mono-ethylene glycol and ethylene oxide…There are immense synergies in feedstock sourcing and transportation, because, the complexes of Reliance and IPCL are located in the same region. There would be bigger gains on the marketing side where Reliance and IPCL were the two biggest competitors hitherto… With the two operating under a single umbrella now (and maybe even a single brand in the near future), the perils of competition such as discounts can be avoided…Over and above all these benefits is a strategic one—the denial of strategic space to competition for which a premium has to be paid. By acquiring IPCL, Reliance has effectively denied IOC the opportunity to get a foothold in the domestic petrochemicals industry.[29]

Related Acquisitions

Acquiring a firm in a highly related industry is called a **related acquisition**. Through a related acquisition, firms seek to create value through the synergy that can be generated by integrating some of their resources and capabilities. For example, Nicholas Piramal, later renamed as Piramal Healthcare, grew, since its incorporation in 1988, through acquisitions of different companies, specifically for certain synergies. Thus it acquired, during its history, the Indian operations of Roche Products Ltd., Boehringer Mannheim India Ltd., Hoechst Marrion Roussel Ltd,'s Research Centre, Rhone Poulenc India Ltd., ICI India Ltd's Pharma Division, and Aventis' Research facilities.[30] Ballarpur Industries acquired an ailing Andhra Pradesh Rayons for its pulp capacity, it's access to raw materials, and possible integration with its paper business (rayon pulp is different from paper pulp).

Sometimes, firms fail to create value through a related acquisition. This was the case with the acquisition of Neycer by Spartek Ceramics in 1988. The synergies appeared to be enormous but they were companies with very different cultures and integration proved to be a big problem.[31] The acquisition of Rasi Cement and Vishnu Cement by India Cements went wrong due to the non materialization of the benefits and the inability of India Cements to convert the initial debt incurred for the acquisition into equity.[32] Horizontal, vertical, and related acquisitions that firms complete to increase their market power are subject to regulatory review as well as to analysis by financial markets.[33] For example, Procter & Gamble (P&G) completed a horizontal acquisition of Gillette Co. in 2006. In announcing the transaction, P&G noted that integrating Gillette into P&G's operations would result in between $1 and $1.2 billion in annual cost synergies and a 1 per cent incremental annual sales growth from revenue synergies for the first three years following the acquisition. However, before being finalized, this acquisition was subjected to a significant amount of government scrutiny as well as close examination by financial analysts. Ultimately, P&G had to sell off several businesses to gain the Federal Trade Commission's approval to acquire Gillette.[34] The recent attempt by Vedanta Resources, a London based metals company, to acquire the Indian stake of Cairn Energy went into regulatory hurdles due to a variety of reasons.[35] The government's concern was the entry of a metals refining and marketing company into the oil sector. It involved the terms under which the oil filed exploration was granted to Cairn and whether Cairn could sell its stake without public sector giant, ONGC, having a right for first refusal. Thus, firms seeking growth and market power through acquisitions must understand the political/legal segment of the general environment (see Chapter 2) in order to successfully use an acquisition strategy.

Overcoming Entry Barriers

Barriers to entry (introduced in Chapter 2) are factors associated with a market or with the firms currently operating in it that increase the expense and difficulty new firms encounter when trying to enter that particular market. For example, well-established competitors may have economies of scale in the manufacture or service of their products. In addition, enduring relationships with customers often create product loyalties that are difficult for new entrants to overcome. When facing differentiated products, new entrants typically must spend considerable resources to advertise their products and may find it necessary to sell at prices below competitors' to entice new customers.

Facing the entry barriers that economies of scale and differentiated products create, a new entrant may find acquiring an established company to be more effective than entering the market as a competitor offering a product that is unfamiliar to current buyers. In fact, the higher the barriers to market entry, the greater the probability that a firm will acquire an existing firm to overcome them.

As this discussion suggests, a key advantage of using an acquisition strategy to overcome entry barriers is that the acquiring firm gains immediate access to a market. This advantage can be particularly attractive for firms seeking to overcome entry barriers associated with entering international markets.[36] Large multinational corporations from developed economies seek to enter emerging economies such as Brazil, Russia, India, and China (BRIC) because they are among the fastest-growing economies in the world.[37] As discussed next, completing a cross-border acquisition of a local target allows a firm to quickly enter fast-growing economies such as these.

Cross-Border Acquisitions

Acquisitions made between companies with headquarters in different countries are called **cross-border acquisitions.**[38] The purchase of UK carmakers Jaguar and Land Rover by India's Tata Motors is an example of a cross-border acquisition. We discuss this acquisition further later in this chapter.

We noted in the Opening Case that global M&A activity declined during the recent global financial crisis. The declines continued throughout the first half of 2009 largely because "… shrinking economies, volatile markets and scarce debt hammered corporate confidence."[39] This decline was in stark contrast to the significant increase in cross-border M&A activity during the 1990s. Nonetheless, cross-border acquisitions remain popular as a viable path to firm growth and strategic competitiveness.

There are other interesting changes taking place in terms of cross-border acquisition activity. Historically, North American and European companies were the most active acquirers of companies outside their domestic markets. However, the current global competitive landscape is one in which firms from other nations may use an acquisition strategy more frequently than their counterparts in North America and Europe. In this regard, some believe that "… the next wave of cross-border M&A may be led out of Asia. Chinese companies, in particular, are well positioned for cross-border acquisitions. Relative to their overseas peers, Chinese corporates are well capitalized with strong balance sheets and cash reserves."[40] In the Strategic Focus, we describe some cross-border acquisitions that some Chinese and Indian companies have recently completed or are evaluating. As you will see, in the case of Chinese firms, the acquisitions we will discuss involve natural resource companies and many are horizontal acquisitions through which the acquiring companies seek to increase their market power.

Firms headquartered in India are also completing more cross-border acquisitions than in the past. The weakening US dollar and more favorable government policies toward cross-border acquisitions are supporting Indian companies' desire to rapidly become "global powerhouses."[41] In addition to rapid market entry, Indian companies typically seek access to product innovation capabilities and new brands and distribution channels when acquiring firms outside their domestic market. The acquisitions by Indian companies cover a much wider spectrum as compared to Chinese companies.

Firms using an acquisition strategy to complete cross-border acquisitions should understand that these transactions are not risk free. For example, firms seeking to acquire companies in China must recognize that "... China remains a challenging environment for foreign investors. Cultural, regulatory, due diligence, and legal obstacles make acquisitions in China risky and difficult."[42] Thus, firms must carefully study the risks as well as the potential benefits when contemplating cross-border acquisitions.

STRATEGY RIGHT NOW
Learn more about how the recent global economic crisis changed the cross-border acquisition environment. www.cengage.com/management/hitt

Cost of New Product Development and Increased Speed to Market

Developing new products internally and successfully introducing them into the marketplace often requires significant investment of a firm's resources, including time, making it difficult to quickly earn a profitable return.[43] Because an estimated 88 percent of innovations fail to achieve adequate returns, firm managers are also concerned with achieving adequate returns from the capital invested to develop and commercialize new products. Potentially contributing to these less-than-desirable rates of return is the successful imitation of approximately 60 per cent of innovations within four years after the patents are obtained. These types of outcomes may lead managers to perceive internal product development as a high-risk activity.[44]

Acquisitions are another means a firm can use to gain access to new products and to current products that are new to the firm. Compared with internal product development processes, acquisitions provide more predictable returns as well as faster market entry. Returns are more predictable because the performance of the acquired firm's products can be assessed prior to completing the acquisition.[45]

Recently, America Online (AOL) acquired two online media companies, Patch Media Corp. and Going Inc. AOL acquired these firms to move more rapidly into the relatively fast-growing local online and advertising market. Patch operates Web sites to help local communities publish news and information while Going makes it possible for users to share information about local events. Access to these new products and services supports AOL's other products in the local online and advertising market space such as MapQuest and social networking site Bebo.[46]

A number of pharmaceutical firms use an acquisition strategy because of the cost of new product development. Acquisitions can enable firms to enter markets quickly and to increase the predictability of returns on their investments. To expand on these points, we discuss Pfizer's recently announced horizontal acquisition of Wyeth in Strategic Focus 7.2.

STRATEGIC FOCUS

7.1 The Increasing Use of Acquisition Strategies by Chinese and Indian Firms as a Means of Gaining Market Power in a Particular Industry

Taking advantage of depressed prices for oil and gas assets, and through the access to credit in their home country, Chinese state-owned companies have begun to use acquisitions as the path to securing "the resources needed to power China's growing economy" and to secure access to energy in future. The belief that the recent global financial crisis has created an "unmatched buying opportunity" is also driving Chinese firms to acquire companies to gain access to their assets and to increase their market power.

The pace of Chinese firms' cross-border acquisitions gathered momentum in 2009. By mid-2009, Chinese companies had completed 10 transactions in the oil and gas sector compared to just 14 transactions in the sector in 2008. Moreover, if outstanding bids were accepted by target companies, the amount Chinese firms will have spent on acquisitions would be 80 per cent greater than the amount spent previously on a year-to-year basis.

Completed in mid-2009, state-owned Sinopec Group's acquisition of oil exploration company Addax Petroleum Corp. for $8.27 billion Canadian dollars was at the time the largest cross-border acquisition by a Chinese company. Calling the acquisition a "transformational transaction" that would accelerate its international growth, Sinopec paid a 16 per cent premium for Addax. Based in Switzerland and listed in London and Toronto, Addax is one of the world's largest independent oil producers in West Africa and the Middle East on the basis of volume. Around the same time, CNOCC, China's top offshore oil and gas producer, hired Goldman Sachs to advise it on bidding to acquire a stake in Kosmos Energy, an Africa-focused oil and gas exploration company. CNOCC hired an investment advisory firm in anticipation of a bidding war breaking out for Kosmos, largely because of the attractiveness of the firm's assets.

Analysts studying these acquisitions and others that likely will be completed conclude that Chinese energy companies are becoming more confident in their ability to create value and gain market power through acquisitions. Business writers describe this confidence as follows: "... deals like the Addax acquisition show (that) they are gradually growing into international oil companies, capable of striking high-profile, cross-border deals. They are even expanding into countries, such as Syria, deemed too risky by Western oil companies."

AP Photo/Imaginechina

The 2009 acquisition of Addax Petroleum Corp. with its holdings in Africa and the Middle East by the state-owned Sinopec Group represented at the time the largest Chinese cross-border oil and gas acquisition in history.

But not all of the cross-border acquisitions attempted by Chinese companies have been successful. For example, Anglo-American mining giant Rio Tinto Ltd. rejected Aluminum Corp. of China's (Chinalco) $19.5 billion bid to buy 18 per cent of the company. Rio was attractive to Chinalco because it was then the world's third-largest miner and owned rich iron-ore and copper mines across the world, including major facilities in Australia. This acquisition would have given Chinalco a direct stake in mining assets—assets that were important to China's growth. In particular, iron ore is a crucial ingredient in China's steelmaking operations. Although disappointing, the rejection by Rio Tinto was not expected to slow China's commitment to allow its state-owned companies to pursue cross-border acquisitions as a means of improving their competitiveness in the global economy and as a means of gaining ownership of natural resources the nation believes are vital to its long-term growth.

Acquisitions by Indian Corporate

The major overseas acquisitions by Indian companies may said to have started in 2000, when Tata Tea took over a UK company twice its size. Since then there have been several acquisitions by Indian companies, many of which are quite large in size. The most important acquisitions among them were: Tata Steel's acquisition of the Anglo Dutch steel major Corus in 2006 for $7.6 billion; Hindalco's acquisition of Canadian aluminum company Novalis in 2007 for $6 billion; Tata Motors' acquisition of Jaguar and Land Rover in 2008 for $2.3 billion; Ranbaxy's acquisition of three European pharmaceutical companies in 2006: Allen S.p.A, a division of GlaxoSmithKline (GSK) in Italy, Romania's largest independent generic drug producer Terapia and drug maker Ethimed NV in Belgium; Wockhart's acquisition of the French drug company Negma in 2007 for $265 million; the acquisition of the Virgin Radio by India's largest media group, The Times Group in 2008 for £53 million; Sterlite's acquisition of the copper mining company Asarco in 2008 for $2.6 billion; ONGC's acquisition of Imperial Energy in 2009 for $1.9 billion; and Bharti Airtel's acquisition of Zain's African operations in 2010 for $10.7 billion. Besides these, there have been other acquisitions across a number of sectors, of value over $1 billion: RE Power, Germany by Suzlon, Algoma Steel, Canada by Essar, Whyte & Mackay (UK) by United Spirits, PT Kaltim Prima Coal; PT Arutmin Indonesia (30 per cent Stake—Indonesia) by Tata Power, InterGen NV, Netherlands by GMR Infrastructure, General Chemical (USA) by Tata Chemicals. A study undertaken by the Associated Chambers of Commerce and Industry of India (ASSOCHAM) says that the first nine months of 2010-11 (April–December) have witnessed more than a three-fold increase in value terms in the Merger & Acquisitions (M&A) growing from US$ 13.54 billion in the corresponding period to US$ 58.73 billion. It further says the number of deals also rose to 222 from 129 during the same period. During the first nine months of FY 2010, the telecom sector topped the list with 28.26 per cent share of the total valuation of M&A deals that took place in India. It was followed by the energy sector accounting for 23.59 per cent, metal & mining sector 23.19 per cent, while pharmaceutical and BFSI sector accounted for 8.20 per cent and 5.74 per cent respectively.

Sources: 2009, Is China Inc. overpaying in its merger deals? *Wall Street Journal Online*, http://www.wsj.com, June 25; R. Carew, 2009, Chinalco acts to preserve its stake in Rio Tinto, *Wall Street Journal Online*, http://www.wsj.com, July 1; G. Chazan & S. Oster, 2009, Sinopec pact for Addax boosts China's buying binge, *Wall Street Journal Online*, http://www.wsj.com, June 25; E. Fry, 2009, Chinalco buys $1.5 bn Rio Tinto shares, *Financial Times Online*, http://www.ft.com, July 2; K. Maxwell, 2009, Shinsei and Aozora still talking, *Wall Street Journal Online*, http://www.wsj.com, June 26; S. Tucker, 2009, CNOCC considers Kosmos stake bid, *Financial Times Online*, http://www.ft.com, June 20; 2010, Top 10 Outbound Merger and Acquisitions(M&A) deals in India All Time, April, http://layman-blog.blogspot.com/2010/04/top-10-outbound-merger-and.html; 2011, Assocham, M&A increases three-fold from April-December 2010: Assocham, January, 5, http://www.assocham.org/prels/shownews.php?id=2706; Joydeep, 2010, www.buzzom.com, Top 10 Valuable Global Acquisitions by Indian Companies, February, http://www.buzzom.com/2010/02/top-10-valuable-global-acquisitions-by-indian-companies/ http://apac.globalthoughtz.com/index.php/top-10-valuable-global-acquisitions-by-indian-companies/; 2010, www.blogspot.com, Top 10 biotechnologypharmaceuticals, May http://layman-blog.blogspot.com/2010/05/top-10-biotechnologypharmaceutical-eals.html; 2010, *Financial Affairs*, Airtel-Zain second largest M&A ever in India!, March 25, http://financialaffairs.in/2010/03/25/airtel-gets-close-to-the-second-largest-ma/.

STRATEGY RIGHT NOW

Compare the Chinese pattern of acquisitions to the Indian pattern. Do you think Indian companies are following a fundamentally different path as compared to Chinese companies? (please look up for more data on Chinese companies). If yes, what could be the reasons?

Lower Risk Compared to Developing New Products

Because the outcomes of an acquisition can be estimated more easily and accurately than the outcomes of an internal product development process, managers may view acquisitions as being less risky.[47] However, firms should exercise caution when using acquisitions to reduce their risks relative to the risks the firm incurs when developing new products internally. Indeed, even though research suggests acquisition strategies are a common means of avoiding risky internal ventures (and therefore risky R&D investments), acquisitions may also become a substitute for innovation. Accordingly, acquisitions should always be strategic rather than defensive in nature. Thus, Pfizer's acquisition of Wyeth should be driven by strategic factors (e.g., cost and revenue synergies) instead of by defensive reasons (e.g., to gain sales revenue in the short term that will compensate for the revenue that will be lost when Lipitor goes off patent). Moreover, Pfizer should not reduce its emphasis on increasing the productivity from its R&D expenditures as a result of acquiring Wyeth.

Increased Diversification

Acquisitions are also used to diversify firms. Based on experience and the insights resulting from it, firms typically find it easier to develop and introduce new products in markets they are currently serving. In contrast, it is difficult for companies to develop products that differ from their current lines for markets in which they lack experience.[48] Thus it is relatively uncommon for a firm to develop new products internally to diversify its product lines.[49]

Cisco Systems is an example of a firm that uses acquisitions to become more diversified. Historically, these acquisitions have helped the firm build its network components business that is focused on producing hardware. Recently, however, Cisco purchased IronPort Systems Inc., a company focused on producing security software for networks. This acquisition will help Cisco diversify its operations beyond its original expertise in network hardware and basic software. Cisco previously acquired technology in the security area through its purchase of Riverhead Networks Inc., Protego Networks Inc., and Perfigo Inc. However, the IronPort deal provides software service in networks that can help guard against spam and viruses that travel through e-mail and Web-based traffic.[50] In 2009, Cisco IronPort announced its "… new managed, hosted and hybrid hosted e-mail security systems that provide the industry's most versatile set of e-mail protection offerings."[51] Thus, the IronPort acquisition seems to be successful in terms of helping Cisco diversify its operations in ways that create value.

STRATEGIC FOCUS

7.2 Pfizer's Proposed Acquisition of Wyeth: Will this Acquisition be Successful?

Pharmaceutical companies allocate significant amounts of money to research and development (R&D) in efforts to successfully develop new drugs. Pfizer Inc., for example, spends 15 per cent of its sales revenue on R&D. As is the case for most, if not all, of its major competitors, Pfizer is committed to upholding the highest ethical standards when engaging in R&D. According to Pfizer, the firm is "… committed to the safety of patients who take part in our trials and uphold the highest ethical standards in all of (its) research initiatives."

In the words of a scholar who studies innovation: "R&D dollars by definition lead to uncertain outcomes." Because of the high levels of uncertainty associated with efforts to develop products internally, a number of pharmaceutical companies use acquisitions to gain access to new products and to target a firm's capabilities. At this time, some believe that the acquisitions taking place among these firms are "… reconfiguring the entire pharmaceutical sector."

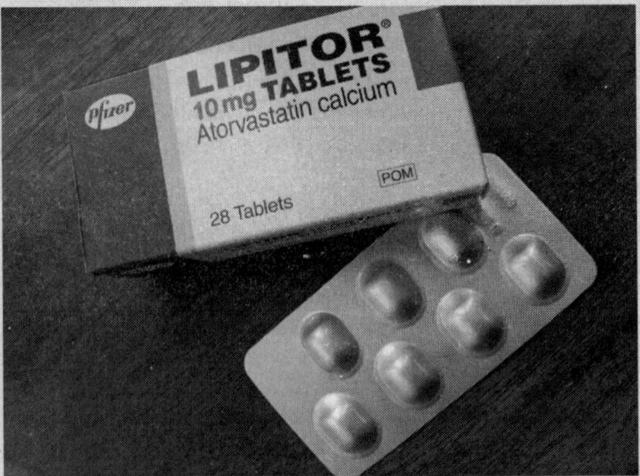

Libby Welch/Alamy

With the patent on Lipitor due to expire in 2011 and generic competitors lining up, Pfizer's acquisition of Wyeth and its pipeline of new products could help replace anticipated lost revenue.

Announced in early 2009, Pfizer's horizontal acquisition of Wyeth for roughly $ 68 billion was the largest transaction in the pharmaceutical industry in almost a decade. The purchase price meant that Pfizer would pay a premium of approximately 29 per cent to acquire Wyeth. As a horizontal acquisition, this price suggested that Pfizer felt that the transaction would result in cost and revenue synergies that at least equaled the amount of the premium it was willing to pay.

Why did Pfizer conclude that this acquisition was in the best interests of its stakeholders—including its shareholders? A key reason was that Wyeth had been investing heavily in biotechnology and vaccines for about three decades. In fact, Wyeth had become the third-largest biotechnology company after Amgen Inc. and Genentech Inc. Pfizer wanted to gain access to the new products that might flow from Wyeth's biotechnology-oriented R&D investments. Equally important is the contribution Wyeth would make to Pfizer's sales revenue—revenue that was expected to decline significantly after November 2011 when its hugely successful Lipitor drug (a drug for patients to control their high cholesterol) is scheduled to come off-patent. The impact of generic drugs being produced to compete against Lipitor was potentially huge for Pfizer in that this drug alone generates about 25 per cent of the firm's total revenue.

Analysts' reactions to this acquisition were mixed to negative. Some said that the core problem is that although Wyeth's sales revenue would help Pfizer replace the revenue it will lose after Lipitor goes off patent, it does not deal with the fact that Pfizer is struggling to develop new products in-house. One analyst said that "Pfizer is spending $7.5 billion a year in research and producing almost nothing and now it has to buy Wyeth. If its pipeline were producing it wouldn't need to buy Wyeth."

Evidence suggests that acquisitions in the pharmaceutical industry do tend to generate cost savings through operational synergies. Accordingly, Pfizer's intended acquisition of Wyeth may achieve one of the benefits of a horizontal acquisition. Simultaneously though, Pfizer seeks to rely on Wyeth's capabilities in the biotechnology space to develop new products that the newly formed firm can quickly introduce to the market.

Sources: 2009, Pfizer's acquisition of Wyeth brings scale but will fail to deliver sustainable sales growth, *Trading Markets.com*, http://www.tradingmarkets.com, January 28; C. Arnst, 2009, The drug mergers' harsh side effects, *BusinessWeek Online*, http://www.businessweek.com, March 12; R. Jana, 2009, Do ideas cost too much? *BusinessWeek,* April 20, 46–58; J. Jannarone, 2009, Pfizer treatment is no cure, *Wall Street Journal Online*, http://www.wsj.com, January 24; S. Pettyprice, T. Randall, & Z. Mider, 2009, Pfizer's $68 billion Wyeth deal eases Lipitor loss, *Bloomberg.com*, http://www.bloomberg.com, January 26.

Acquisition strategies can be used to support use of both unrelated and related diversification strategies (see Chapter 6).[52] For example, United Technologies Corp. (UTC) uses acquisitions as the foundation for implementing its unrelated diversification strategy. Since the mid-1970s it has been building a portfolio of stable and noncyclical businesses including Otis Elevator Co. (elevators, escalators, and moving walkways) and Carrier Corporation (heating and air conditioning systems) in order to reduce its dependence on the volatile aerospace industry. Pratt & Whitney (aircraft engines), Hamilton Sundstrand (aerospace and industrial systems), Sikorsky (helicopters), UTC Fire & Security (fire safety and security products and services), and UTC Power (fuel cells and power systems) are the other businesses in which UTC competes as a result of using its acquisition strategy. While each business which UTC acquires, manufactures industrial and/or commercial products, many have a relatively low focus on technology (e.g., elevators, air conditioners, and security systems).[53] In contrast to UTC, Procter & Gamble (P&G) uses acquisitions to implement its related diversification strategy. Beauty, Health & Well-Being, and Household Care are P&G's core business segments. Gillette's products are included in the Beauty segment, where they are related to other products in this segment such as cosmetics, hair care, and skin care. As noted earlier in the chapter, P&G completed a horizontal acquisition of Gillette in 2006.

Firms using acquisition strategies should be aware that in general, the more related the acquired firm is to the acquiring firm, the greater is the probability the acquisition will be successful.[54] Thus, horizontal acquisitions and related acquisitions tend to contribute more to the firm's strategic competitiveness than do acquisitions of companies operating in product markets that are quite different from those in which the acquiring firm competes.[55]

Reshaping the Firm's Competitive Scope

As discussed in Chapter 2, the intensity of competitive rivalry is an industry characteristic that affects the firm's profitability.[56] To reduce the negative effect of an intense rivalry on their financial performance, firms may use acquisitions to lessen their dependence on one or more products or markets. Reducing a company's dependence on specific markets shapes the firm's competitive scope.

Each time UTC enters a new business (such as UTC Power, the firm's latest business segment), the corporation reshapes its competitive scope. In a more subtle manner, P&G's acquisition of Gillette reshaped its competitive scope by giving P&G a stronger presence in some products for which men are the target market. By merging their operations, Towers Perrin and Watson Wyatt reshaped the scope of their formerly independent firms' operations in that Towers was stronger in health care consulting while Watson Wyatt was stronger in pension consulting. Thus, using an acquisition strategy reshaped the competitive scope of each of these firms.

Learning and Developing New Capabilities

Firms sometimes complete acquisitions to gain access to capabilities they lack. For example, acquisitions may be used to acquire a special technological capability. Research shows that firms can broaden their knowledge base and reduce inertia through acquisitions.[57] For example, research suggests that firms increase the potential of their capabilities when they acquire diverse talent through cross-border acquisitions.[58] Of course, firms are better able to learn these capabilities if they share some similar properties with the firm's current capabilities. Thus, firms should seek to acquire companies with different but related and complementary capabilities in order to build their own knowledge base.[59]

A number of large pharmaceutical firms are acquiring the ability to create "large molecule" drugs, also known as biological drugs, by buying bio-technology firms. Thus, these firms are seeking access to both the pipeline of possible drugs and the capabilities that these firms have to produce them. Such capabilities are important for large pharmaceutical firms because these biological drugs are more difficult to duplicate by chemistry alone (the historical basis on which most pharmaceutical firms have expertise). These capabilities will allow generic drug makers to be more successful after chemistry-based drug patents expire. To illustrate the difference between these types of drugs, David Brennen, CEO of British drug maker AstraZeneca, suggested, "Some of these [biological-based drugs] have demonstrated that they're not just symptomatic treatments but that they actually alter the course of the disease."[60] Furthermore, biological drugs must clear more regulatory barriers or hurdles which, when accomplished, add more to the advantage the acquiring firm develops through successful acquisitions.

Problems in Achieving Acquisition Success

Acquisition strategies based on reasons described in this chapter can increase strategic competitiveness and help firms earn above-average returns. However, even when pursued for value-creating reasons, acquisition strategies are not problem-free. Reasons for the use of acquisition strategies and potential problems with such strategies are shown in Figure 7.1.

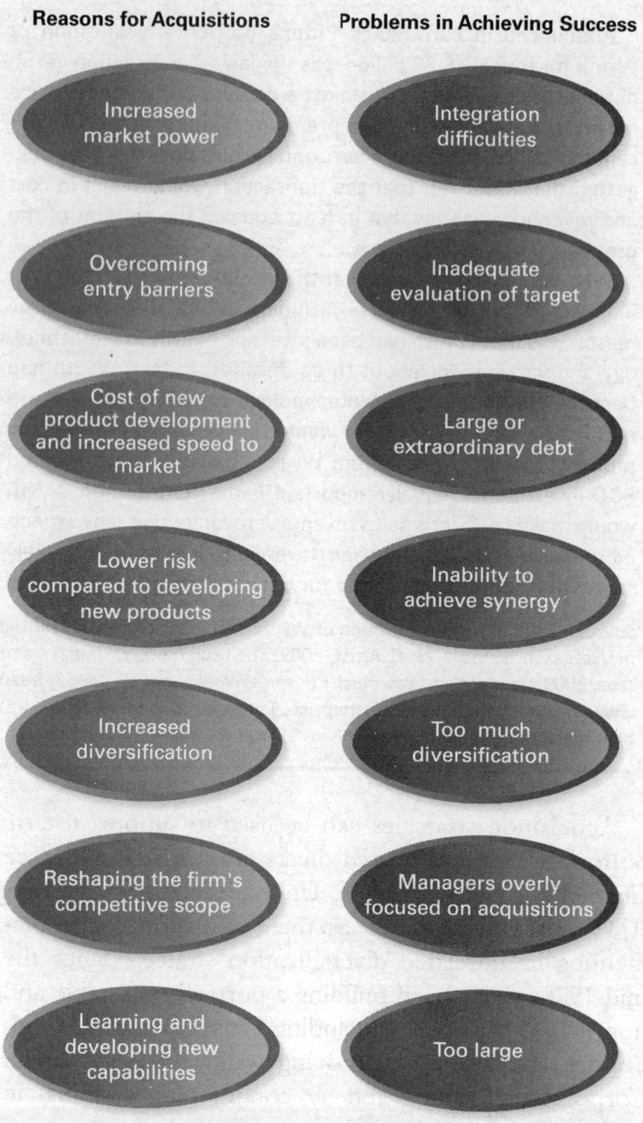

Figure 7.1 Reasons for acquisitions and problems in achieving success

Research suggests that perhaps 20 per cent of all mergers and acquisitions are successful, approximately 60 per cent produce disappointing results, and the remaining 20 percent are clear failures.[61] In general, though, companies appear to be increasing their ability to effectively use acquisition strategies. An investment banker representing acquisition clients describes this improvement in the following manner: "I've been doing this work for 20-odd years, and I can tell you that the sophistication of companies going through transactions has increased exponentially."[62] Greater acquisition success accrues to firms able to (1) select the "right" target, (2) avoid paying too high a premium (doing appropriate due diligence), and (3) effectively integrate the operations of the acquiring and target firms.[63] In addition, retaining the target firm's human capital is basic to efforts by employees of the acquiring firm to fully understand the target firm's operations and the capabilities on which those operations are based.[64] As shown in Figure 7.1, several problems may prevent successful acquisitions.

Integration Difficulties

The importance of a successful integration should not be underestimated.[65] As suggested by a researcher studying the process, "Managerial practice and academic writings show that the post-acquisition integration phase is probably the single most important determinant of shareholder value creation (and equally of value destruction) in mergers and acquisitions."[66]

Although critical to acquisition success, firms should recognize that integrating two companies following an acquisition can be quite difficult. Blending two corporate cultures, linking different financial and control systems, building effective working relationships (particularly when management styles differ), and resolving problems regarding the status of the newly acquired firm's executives are examples of integration challenges firms often face.[67]

Integration is complex and involves a large number of activities, which if overlooked can lead to significant difficulties. For example, when Air India and Indian Airlines were merged on March 1, 2007, it appeared to be a merger that would generate benefits for both firms. But even nearly three years after this merger, the integration is far from complete, and the two airlines function virtually as two different companies. The problems of integration have been many: their aircraft are different; there is only a limited possibility of merging the routes; the terms and conditions of service of the employees are very different, and the financial situations of the two companies at the time were quite different. It has been such a problem that the Parliamentary Committee on Public Undertakings, in March 2010, described it as "a marriage of incompatibles" and called the decision "whimsical".[68] As late as 2009, even the schedules of the two airlines were not shared, and passengers of one airline could not get information on the flights of the other airline. On a query by a journalist, a staff member of Air India at the airport replied that "though the merger has been completed, we are updated with only details of Air India flights".[69] Furthermore, a culture clash surfaced between the two organizations following which the Union Minister for Civil Aviation remarked that the merger was being sabotaged "from within".[70]

Inadequate Evaluation of Target

Due diligence is a process through which a potential acquirer evaluates a target firm for acquisition. In an effective due diligence process, hundreds of items are examined in areas as diverse as the financing for the intended transaction, differences in cultures between the acquiring and target firm, tax consequences of the transaction, and actions that would be necessary to successfully meld the two workforces. Due diligence is commonly performed by investment bankers such as Deutsche Bank, Goldman Sachs, and Morgan Stanley, as well as accountants, lawyers, and management consultants specializing in that activity, although firms actively pursuing acquisitions may form their own internal due-diligence team.[71]

The failure to complete an effective due-diligence process may easily result in the acquiring firm paying an excessive premium for the target company. Interestingly, research shows that in times of high or increasing stock prices due diligence is relaxed; firms often overpay during these periods and long-run performance of the newly formed firm suffers.[72] Research also shows that without due diligence, "the purchase price is driven by the pricing of other "comparable" acquisitions rather than by a rigorous assessment of where, when, and how management can drive real performance gains. [In these cases], the price paid may have little to do with achievable value."[73]

In addition, firms sometimes allow themselves to enter a "bidding war" for a target, even though they realize that their current bids exceed the parameters identified through due diligence. Earlier, we mentioned Tata Steel's acquisition of Corus and the acquisitions of India Cements, and pointed out the problem of "the winner's curse."[74] Rather than entering a bidding war, firms should only extend bids that are consistent with the results of their due diligence process. But all too often, the bidding becomes a matter of ego, and a high price, once paid, becomes a permanent drag on companies' finances.

Large or Extraordinary Debt

To finance a number of acquisitions completed during the 1980s and 1990s, some companies significantly increased their levels of debt. A financial innovation called junk bonds helped make this possible. **Junk bonds** are a financing option through which risky acquisitions are financed with money (debt) that provides a large potential return to lenders (bondholders). Because junk bonds are unsecured obligations that are not tied to specific assets for collateral, interest rates for these high-risk debt instruments sometimes reached between 18 and 20 per cent during the 1980s.[75] Some prominent financial economists viewed debt as a means to discipline managers, causing them to act in the shareholders' best interests.[76] Managers holding this view are less concerned about the amount of debt their firm assumes when acquiring other companies.

Junk bonds are now used less frequently to finance acquisitions, and the conviction that debt disciplines managers is less strong. Nonetheless, firms sometimes still take on what turns out to be too much debt when acquiring companies. This may be the case for Tata Motors. Some analysts describe Tata's problems with debt this way: "Tata Motors' troubles began last year when it paid $2.3bn for Jaguar and Land Rover and borrowed $3bn to finance the transaction and provide additional working capital."[77] Because of this, some felt that the firm was less capable of providing the capital its various units required to remain competitive.

High debt can have several negative effects on the firm. For example, because high debt increases the likelihood of bankruptcy, it can lead to a downgrade in the firm's credit rating by agencies such as Moody's and Standard & Poor's.[78] In other instances, a firm may have to divest some assets to relieve its debt burden, or even go back on the merger. We have mentioned the case of acquisition of Rasi Cements and Vishnu Cements by India Cements, which, to manage its debt burden had to demerge the two companies. Thus, firms using an acquisition strategy must be certain that their purchases do not create a debt load that overpowers the company's ability to remain solvent.

Inability to Achieve Synergy

Derived from *synergos,* a Greek word that means "working together," **synergy** exists when the value created by units working together exceeds the value those units could create by working independently (see Chapter 6). That is, synergy exists when assets are worth more when used in conjunction with each other than when they are used separately. For shareholders, synergy generates gains in their wealth that they could not duplicate or exceed through their own portfolio diversification decisions.[79] Synergy is created by the efficiencies derived from economies of scale and economies of scope and by sharing resources (e.g., human capital and knowledge) across the businesses in the merged firm.[80]

A firm develops a competitive advantage through an acquisition strategy only when a transaction generates private synergy. **Private synergy** is created when combining and integrating the acquiring and acquired firms' assets yield capabilities and core competencies that could not be developed by combining and integrating either firm's assets with another company. Private synergy is possible when the participating firms' assets are complementary in unique ways; that is, the unique type of asset complementarity is not possible by combining either company's assets with another firm's assets.[81] Because of its uniqueness, private synergy is difficult for competitors to understand and imitate. However, private synergy is difficult to create.

A firm's ability to account for costs that are necessary to create anticipated revenue- and cost-based synergies affects its efforts to create private synergy. Firms experience several expenses when trying to create private synergy through acquisitions. Called transaction costs, these expenses are incurred when firms use acquisition strategies to create synergy.[82] Transaction costs may be direct or indirect. Direct costs include legal fees and charges from investment bankers who complete due diligence for the acquiring firm. Indirect costs include managerial time to evaluate target firms and then to complete negotiations, as well as the loss of key managers and employees following an acquisition.[83] Firms tend to underestimate the sum of indirect costs when the value of the synergy that may be created by combining and integrating the acquired firm's assets with the acquiring firm's assets is calculated.

Too Much Diversification

As explained in Chapter 6, diversification strategies can lead to strategic competitiveness and above-average returns. In general, firms using related diversification strategies outperform those employing unrelated diversification strategies. However, conglomerates formed by using an unrelated diversification strategy also can be successful, as demonstrated by the Siva Group.

At some point, however, firms can become over-diversified. The level at which overdiversification occurs varies across companies because each firm has different capabilities to manage diversification. Recall from Chapter 6 that related diversification requires more information processing than does unrelated diversification. Because of this additional information processing, related diversified firms become overdiversified with a smaller number of business units than do firms using an unrelated diversification strategy.[84] Regardless of the type of diversification strategy implemented, however, over-diversification leads to a decline in performance, after which business units are often divested.[85] Commonly, such divestments, which tend to reshape a firm's competitive scope, are part of a firm's restructuring strategy. (We discuss the strategy in greater detail later in the chapter.)

Even when a firm is not over-diversified, a high level of diversification can have a negative effect on its long-term performance. For example, the scope created by additional amounts of diversification often causes managers to rely on financial rather than strategic controls to evaluate business units' performance (we define and explain financial and strategic controls in Chapters 11 and 12). Top-level executives often rely on financial controls to assess the performance of business units when they do not have a rich understanding of business units' objectives and strategies. Using financial controls, such as return on investment (ROI), causes individual business-unit managers to focus on short-term outcomes at the expense of long-term investments. When long-term investments are reduced to increase short-term profits, a firm's overall strategic competitiveness may be harmed.[86]

Another problem resulting from too much diversification is the tendency for acquisitions to become substitutes for innovation. As we noted earlier, pharmaceutical firms such as Pfizer must be aware of this tendency as they acquire other firms to gain access to their products and capabilities. Typically, managers have no interest in acquisitions substituting for internal R&D efforts and the innovative outcomes that they can produce. However, a reinforcing cycle evolves. Costs associated with acquisitions may result in fewer allocations to activities, such as R&D, that are linked to innovation. Without adequate support, a firm's innovation skills begin to atrophy. Without internal innovation skills, the only option available to a firm to gain access to innovation is to complete still more acquisitions. Evidence suggests that a firm using acquisitions as a substitute for internal innovations eventually encounters performance problems.[87]

Managers Overly Focused on Acquisitions

Typically, a considerable amount of managerial time and energy is required for acquisition strategies to be used successfully. Activities with which managers become involved include (1) searching for viable acquisition candidates, (2) completing effective due-diligence processes, (3) preparing for negotiations, and (4) managing the integration process after completing the acquisition.

Top-level managers do not personally gather all of the data and information required to make acquisitions. However, these executives do make critical decisions on the firms to be targeted, the nature of the negotiations, and so forth. Company experiences show that participating in and overseeing the activities required for making acquisitions can divert managerial attention from other matters that are necessary for long-term competitive success, such as identifying and taking advantage of other opportunities and interacting with important external stakeholders.[88]

Both theory and research suggest that managers can become overly involved in the process of making acquisitions.[89] One observer suggested, "Some executives can become preoccupied with making deals—and the thrill of selecting, chasing and seizing a target."[90] The over-involvement can be surmounted by learning from mistakes and by not having too much agreement in the boardroom. Dissent is helpful to make sure that all sides of a question are considered (see Chapter 10).[91] When failure does occur, leaders may be tempted to blame the failure on others and on unforeseen circumstances rather than on their excessive involvement in the acquisition process.

Actions taken at Liz Claiborne Inc. demonstrate the problem of being overly focused on acquisitions. Over time, Claiborne acquired a number of firms in sportswear apparel, growing from 16 to 36 brands in the process of doing so. However, while its managers were focused on making acquisitions, changes were taking place in the firm's external environment, including industry consolidation. Specifically, while most Claiborne sales were focused on traditional department stores, consolidation through acquisitions in this sector left less room for as many brands, given the purchasing practices of the large department stores. Additionally, competitors were gaining favor with customers, leaving fewer sales for Claiborne's products. In response to these problems, CEO William McComb announced in July 2007 a "... framework of a new organizational structure that was a crucial step in making Liz Claiborne Inc. a more brand-focused and cost-effective business that (could) successfully navigate a rapidly changing retail environment." As a result of these actions, Claiborne is less diversified in terms of brands and less focused on acquisitions. Today, the firm has three distinct brand segments—domestic-based direct brands, international-based direct brands, and partnered brands.[92]

Too Large

Most acquisitions create a larger firm, which should help increase its economies of scale. These economies can then lead to more efficient operations—for example, two sales organizations can be integrated using fewer sales representatives because such sales personnel can sell the products of both firms (particularly if the products of the acquiring and target firms are highly related).[93]

Many firms seek increases in size because of the potential economies of scale and enhanced market power (discussed earlier). At some level, the additional costs required to manage the larger firm will exceed the benefits of the economies of scale and additional market power. The complexities generated by the larger size often lead managers to implement more bureaucratic controls to manage the combined firm's operations. **Bureaucratic controls** are formalized supervisory and behavioral rules and policies designed to ensure consistency of decisions and actions across different units of a firm. However, through time, formalized controls often lead to relatively rigid and standardized managerial behavior. Certainly, in the long run, the diminished flexibility that accompanies rigid and standardized managerial behavior may produce less innovation. Because of innovation's importance to competitive success, the bureaucratic controls resulting from a large organization (i.e., built by acquisitions) can have a detrimental effect on performance. As one analyst noted, "Striving for size per se is not necessarily going to make a company more successful. In fact, a strategy in which acquisitions are undertaken as a substitute for organic growth has a bad track record in terms of adding value."[94]

Effective Acquisitions

Earlier in the chapter, we noted that acquisition strategies do not always lead to above-average returns for the acquiring firm's shareholders.[95] Nonetheless, some companies are able to create value when using an acquisition strategy.[96] The probability of success increases when the firm's actions are consistent with the "attributes of successful acquisitions" shown in Table 7.1.

Cisco Systems is an example of a firm that appears to pay close attention to Table 7.1's attributes when using its acquisition strategy. In fact, Cisco is admired for its ability to complete successful acquisitions. A number of other network companies pursued acquisitions to build up their ability to sell into the network equipment binge, but only Cisco retained much of its value in the post-bubble era. Many firms, such as Lucent, Nortel, and Ericsson, teetered on the edge of bankruptcy after the dot-com bubble burst. When it makes an acquisition, "Cisco has gone much further in its thinking about integration. Not only is retention important, but Cisco also works to minimize the distractions caused by an acquisition. This is important, because the speed of change is so great, that even if the target firm's product development teams are distracted, they will be slowed, contributing to acquisition failure. So, integration must be rapid and reassuring."[97] For example, Cisco facilitates acquired employees' transitions to their new organization through a link on its Web site called "Connection for Acquired Employees." This Web site has been specifically designed for newly acquired employees and provides up-to-date materials tailored to their new jobs.[98] Most of Cisco's acquisitions are friendly acquisitions, with the acquired company management itself seeking to be acquired, and in all cases, Cisco makes sure the staff of the acquired company do not feel "acquired".[99]

Table 7.1 Attributes of successful acquisitions

Attributes	Results
1. Acquired firm has assets or resources that are complementary to the acquiring firm's core business	1. High probability of synergy and competitive advantage by maintaining strengths
1. Acquisition is friendly	2. Faster and more effective integration and possibly lower premiums
3. Acquiring firm conducts effective due diligence to select target firms and evaluate the target firm's health (financial, cultural, and human resources)	3. Firms with strongest complementarities are acquired and overpayment is avoided
4. Acquiring firm has financial slack (cash or a favorable debt position)	4. Financing (debt or equity) is easier and less costly to obtain
5. Merged firm maintains low to moderate debt position	5. Lower financing cost, lower risk (e.g., of bankruptcy), and avoidance of trade-offs that are associated with high debt
6. Acquiring firm has sustained and consistent emphasis on R&D and innovation	6. Maintain long-term competitive advantage in markets
7. Acquiring firm manages change well and is flexible and adaptable	7. Faster and more effective integration facilitates achievement of synergy

Results from a research study shed light on the differences between unsuccessful and successful acquisition strategies and suggest that a pattern of actions improves the probability of acquisition success.[100] The study shows that when the target firm's assets are complementary to the acquired firm's assets, an acquisition is more successful. With complementary assets, the integration of two firms' operations has a higher probability of creating synergy. In fact, integrating two firms with complementary assets frequently produces unique capabilities and core competencies. With complementary assets, the acquiring firm can maintain its focus on core businesses and leverage the complementary assets and capabilities from the acquired firm. In effective acquisitions, targets are often selected and "groomed" by establishing a working relationship prior to the acquisition.[101] As discussed in Chapter 9, strategic alliances are sometimes used to test the feasibility of a future merger or acquisition between the involved firms.[102]

The study's results also show that friendly acquisitions facilitate integration of the firms involved in an acquisition. This is the reason why Cisco generally makes friendly acquisitions. Through friendly acquisitions, firms work together to find ways to integrate their operations to create synergy.[103] In hostile takeovers, animosity often results between the two top-management teams, a condition that in turn affects working relationships in the newly created firm. As a result, more key personnel in the acquired firm may be lost, and those who remain may resist the changes necessary to integrate the two firms.[104] With effort, cultural clashes can be overcome, and fewer key managers and employees will become discouraged and leave.[105]

Additionally, effective due-diligence processes involving the deliberate and careful selection of target firms and an evaluation of the relative health of those firms (financial health, cultural fit, and the value of human resources) contribute to successful acquisitions.[106] Financial slack in the form of debt equity or cash, in both the acquiring and acquired firms, also frequently contributes to acquisition success. Even though financial slack provides access to financing for the acquisition, it is still important to maintain a low or moderate level of debt after the acquisition to keep debt costs low. When substantial debt was used to finance the acquisition, companies with successful acquisitions reduced the debt quickly, partly by selling off assets from the acquired firm, especially noncomplementary or poorly performing assets. For these firms, debt costs do not prevent long-term investments such as R&D, and managerial discretion in the use of cash flow is relatively flexible.

Another attribute of successful acquisition strategies is an emphasis on innovation, as demonstrated by continuing investments in R&D activities. Significant R&D investments show a strong managerial commitment to innovation, a characteristic that is increasingly important to overall competitiveness in the global economy as well as to acquisition success.

Flexibility and adaptability are the final two attributes of successful acquisitions. When executives of both the acquiring and the target firms have experience in managing change and learning from acquisitions, they will be more skilled at adapting their capabilities to new environments.[107] As a result, they will be more adept at integrating the two organizations, which is particularly important when firms have different organizational cultures.

As we have learned, firms use an acquisition strategy to grow and achieve strategic competitiveness. Sometimes, though, the actual results of an acquisition strategy fall short of the projected results. When this happens, firms consider using restructuring strategies.

Restructuring

Restructuring is a strategy through which a firm changes its set of businesses or its financial structure.[108] Restructuring is a global phenomenon.[109] From the 1970s into the 2000s, divesting businesses from company portfolios and downsizing accounted for a large percentage of firms' restructuring strategies. Commonly, firms focus on a fewer number of products and markets following restructuring. The words of an executive describe this typical outcome: "Focus on your core business, but don't be distracted, let other people buy assets that aren't right for you."[110]

Although restructuring strategies are generally used to deal with acquisitions that are not reaching expectations, firms sometimes use these strategies because of changes they have detected in their external environment. For example, opportunities sometimes surface in a firm's external environment that a diversified firm can pursue because of the capabilities it has formed by integrating firms' operations. In such cases, restructuring may be appropriate to position the firm to create more value for stakeholders, given the environmental changes.[111]

As discussed next, firms use four types of restructuring strategies: pure restructuring, downsizing, downscoping, and leveraged buyouts.

Pure Restructuring

In this restructuring, the company does not alter its business portfolio, or the size of its businesses, but changes the status of its businesses, or alters the reporting relationships. Often, new subsidiaries are formed, defining the scope of their businesses. For example, L&T restructured itself in January 2011 by turning itself into nine business verticals: Civil Engineering, Mechanical Engineering, Electrical Engineering, Engineering and Construction, Hydrocarbons & Chemicals, Heavy Engineering, Electrical & Automation products, Mechanical & Industrial products and power equipment. Each of these businesses would be an independent company, with its own board of directors, and its own profitability responsibility. Each would have a turnover of $1 billion, or has the potential to reach there very soon. L&T had been a company doing well anyway: Its net profit rose 31.80 per cent to ₹7.6 billion, while its net sales increased by 17.70 per cent to ₹92.6 billion in Q2 September 2010 over Q2 September 2009.[112] L&T would form a hybrid holding company, with both subsidiaries and independent operating businesses, said Mr. A.M. Naik, Chairman, L&T. The reorganization was expected to yield a four fold increase in revenue by 2015, from ₹469 billion, according to Mr. Naik. The stockmarket gained about 0.82 percent consequent on this announcement, indicating its favorable expectation.[113]

Sometimes, companies may rearrange their businesses for better control. This was done, for example, by the Ballarpur Industries with regard to its Andhra Pradesh Rayons.[114] The idea here is to unlock synergies better through bringing different businesses under a common management. In February, 2011, Wipro restructured its operations, hitherto decentralized with a CEO for each business, bringing them together under a common CEO. The Chairman, Mr. Azim Premjee was reported to have felt that under the old structure, fast growing areas such as banking, financial services and insurance (BFSI), and healthcare were not realizing their full potential, especially when compared to their competitors such as TCS, Cognizant, and Infosys.[115]

Lastly, companies also restructure for tax considerations. This may consist of spinning off a subsidiary, or merging a subsidiary back with the parent. Since this is essentially a financial move, rather than strategic, we are not discussing this further.

Downsizing

Downsizing is a reduction in the number of a firm's employees and, sometimes, in the number of its operating units, but it may or may not change the composition of businesses in the company's portfolio. Thus, downsizing is an intentional proactive management strategy whereas "decline is an environmental or organizational phenomenon that occurs involuntarily and results in erosion of an organization's resource base."[116] Downsizing is often a part of acquisitions that fail to create the value anticipated when the transaction was completed. Downsizing is often used when the acquiring firm paid too high of a premium to acquire the target firm.[117] Once thought to be an indicator of organizational decline, downsizing is now recognized as a legitimate restructuring strategy.

Reducing the number of employees and/or the firm's scope in terms of products produced and markets served occurs in firms to enhance the value being created as a result of completing an acquisition. When integrating the operations of the acquired firm and the acquiring firm, managers may not at first appropriately downsize. This is understandable in that "no one likes to lay people off or close facilities."[118] However, downsizing may be necessary because acquisitions often create a situation in which the newly formed firm has duplicate organizational functions such as sales, manufacturing, distribution, human resource management, and so forth. Failing to downsize appropriately may lead to too many employees doing the same work and prevent the new firm from realizing the cost synergies it anticipated. This has been a major problem with the merger of Air India and Indian Airlines. Managers should remember that as a strategy, downsizing will be far more effective when they consistently use human resource practices that ensure procedural justice and fairness in downsizing decisions.[119]

Downscoping

Downscoping refers to divestiture, spin-off, or some other means of eliminating businesses that are unrelated to a firm's core businesses. Downscoping has a more positive effect on firm performance than does downsizing[120] because firms commonly find that downscoping causes them to refocus on their core business.[121] Managerial effectiveness increases because the firm has become less diversified, allowing the top management team to better understand and manage the remaining businesses.[122]

Motorola Inc. is a firm that has struggled recently. With an interest of refocusing on "technologies that can grow its business" as one path to reversing the firm's fortunes, Motorola is divesting assets that are not related to its core businesses. The recent sale of its fiber-to-the-node product line to Communications Test Design Inc., an engineering, repair, and logistics company, is an example of Motorola's use of a downscoping strategy.[123] L&T divested its cement business; Ballarpur Industries divested their glass business and in certain chemicals to enable them to focus on their core business of paper; the Tata Group divested their roller bearing business. In mid-2009, the McGraw-Hill Companies indicated that it was seeking a buyer for *BusinessWeek* magazine. This magazine was one of the products in McGraw's Information and Media business unit (the firm has two other business units). As was the case with many other magazines during the global financial crisis, *BusinessWeek* was being hurt "... by defections of readers and advertisers to the Internet." as well as by the oversupply of business magazine titles.[124] Divesting *BusinessWeek* would allow those leading McGraw's Information & Media unit to refocus on its other businesses, such as J.D. Power and Associates and the Aviation Week Group. Previous to the announcement, McGraw had already divested most of its periodicals.[125]

Firms often use the downscoping and the downsizing strategies simultaneously. However, when doing this, firms avoid layoffs of key employees, in that such layoffs might lead to a loss of one or more core competencies. Instead, a firm that is simultaneously downscoping and downsizing becomes smaller by reducing the diversity of businesses in its portfolio.[126].

Generally, the downscoping as well as downsizing releases funds to be used in their core business to strengthen it. In general, US firms use downscoping as a restructuring strategy more frequently than do European and Indian companies—in fact, the trend in Europe, Latin America, and Asia has been to build conglomerates. In Latin America, these conglomerates are called **grupos**. Many Asian and Latin American conglomerates have begun to adopt Western corporate strategies in recent years and have been refocusing on their core businesses. This downscoping has occurred simultaneously with increasing globalization and with more open markets that have greatly enhanced competition. By downscoping, these firms have been able to focus on their core businesses and improve their competitiveness.[127]

Colin Young-Wolff/PhotoEdit

In response to increasingly negative sales trends in print periodicals and to allow for more internal focus on growth-oriented services, McGraw-Hill is selling BusinessWeek which has been in publication since 1929.

Leveraged Buyouts

A **leveraged buyout** (LBO) is a restructuring strategy whereby a party (typically a private equity firm) buys all of a firm's assets in order to take the firm private. Once the transaction is completed, the company's stock is no longer traded publicly. Traditionally, leveraged buyouts were used as a restructuring strategy to correct for managerial mistakes or because the firm's managers were making decisions that primarily served their own interests rather than those of shareholders.[128] However, some firms use buyouts to build firm resources and expand rather than simply restructure distressed assets.[129]

Significant amounts of debt are commonly incurred to finance a buyout; hence, the term *leveraged* buyout. To support debt payments and to downscope the company to concentrate on the firm's core businesses, the new owners may immediately sell a number of assets.[130] It is not uncommon for those buying a firm through an LBO to restructure the firm to the point that it can be sold at a profit within a five- to eight-year period.

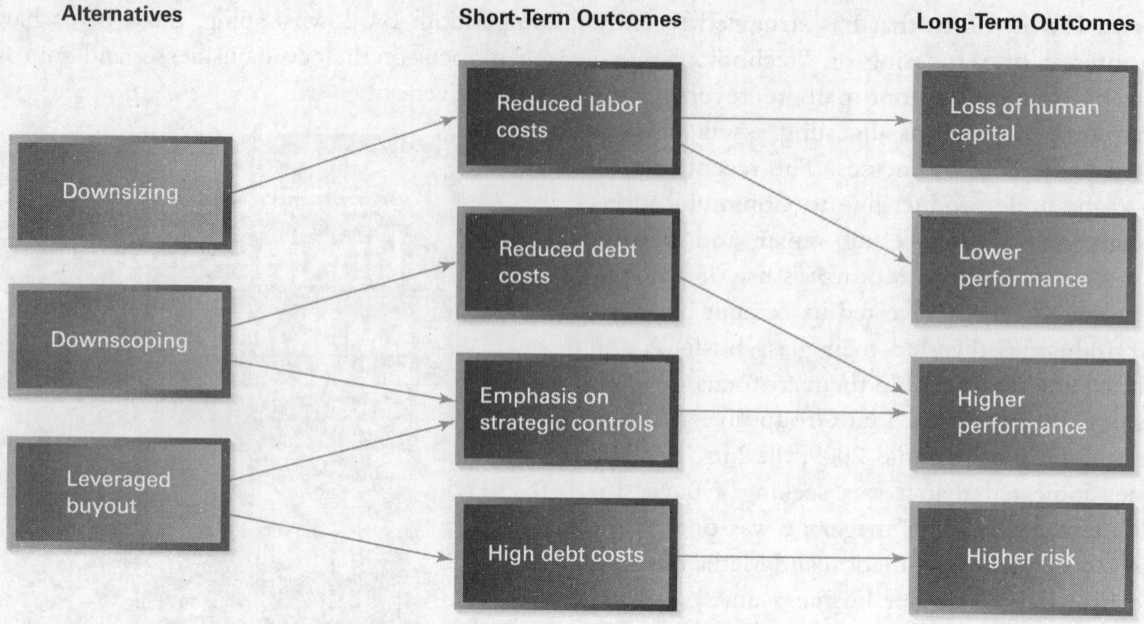

Figure 7.2 Restructuring and outcomes

Management buyouts (MBOs), employee buyouts (EBOs), and whole-firm buyouts, in which one company or partnership purchases an entire company instead of a part of it, are the three types of LBOs. In part because of managerial incentives, MBOs, more so than EBOs and whole-firm buyouts, have been found to lead to downscoping, increased strategic focus, and improved performance.[131] Research shows that management buyouts can lead to greater entrepreneurial activity and growth.[132] As such, buyouts can represent a form of firm rebirth to facilitate entrepreneurial efforts and stimulate strategic growth.[133]

Levaraged buyouts have not been popular in India.

Restructuring Outcomes

The short- and long-term outcomes associated with the three restructuring strategies are shown in Figure 7.2. As indicated, downsizing typically does not lead to higher firm performance.[134] In fact, some research results show that downsizing contributes to lower returns for both US and Japanese firms. The stock markets in the firms' respective nations evaluated downsizing negatively, believing that it would have long-term negative effects on the firm's efforts to achieve strategic competitiveness. Investors also seem to conclude that downsizing occurs as a consequence of other problems in a company.[135] This assumption may be caused by a firm's diminished corporate reputation when a major downsizing is announced.[136]

The loss of human capital is another potential problem of downsizing (see Figure 7.2). Losing employees with many years of experience with the firm represents a major loss of knowledge. As noted in Chapter 3, knowledge is vital to competitive success in the global economy. Thus, in general, research evidence and corporate experience suggest that downsizing may be of more tactical (or short-term) value than strategic (or long-term) value,[137] meaning that firms should exercise caution when restructuring through downsizing. Nucor, for example, never resorts to downsizing even on a downturn because it lays great emphasis on the knowledge base of its employees.[138]

Downscoping generally leads to more positive outcomes in both the short-and long-term than does downsizing or a leveraged buyout. Downscoping's desirable long-term outcome of higher performance is a product of reduced debt costs and the emphasis on strategic controls derived from concentrating on the firm's core businesses. In doing so, the refocused firm should be able to increase its ability to compete.[139]

Although whole-firm LBOs have been hailed as a significant innovation in the financial restructuring of firms, they can involve negative trade-offs.[140] First, the resulting large debt increases the firm's financial risk, as is evidenced by the number of companies that filed for bankruptcy in the 1990s after executing a whole-firm LBO. Sometimes, the intent of the owners to increase the efficiency of the bought-out firm and then sell it within five to eight years creates a short-term and risk-averse managerial focus.[141] As a result, these firms may fail to invest adequately in R&D or take other major actions designed to maintain or improve the company's core competence.[142] Research also suggests that in firms with an entrepreneurial mind-set, buyouts can lead to greater innovation, especially if the debt load is not too great.[143] However, because buyouts more often result in significant debt, most LBOs have been completed in mature industries where stable cash flows are possible.

SUMMARY

- Although the number of mergers and acquisitions completed declined in 2008 and early 2009, largely because of the global financial crisis, merger and acquisition strategies remain popular as a path to firm growth and earning of strategic competitiveness. Globalization and deregulation of multiple industries in many economies are two of the factors making mergers and acquisitions attractive to large corporations and small firms. With progressive liberalization, M&A has become a vital component of strategy of Indian companies.
- Firms use acquisition strategies to (1) increase market power, (2) overcome entry barriers to new markets or regions, (3) avoid the costs of developing new products and increase the speed of new market entries, (4) reduce the risk of entering a new business, (5) become more diversified, (6) reshape their competitive scope by developing a different portfolio of businesses, and (7) enhance their learning as the foundation for developing new capabilities.
- Among the problems associated with using an acquisition strategy are (1) the difficulty of effectively integrating the firms involved, (2) incorrectly evaluating the target firm's value, (3) creating debt loads that preclude adequate long-term investments (e.g., R&D), (4) overestimating the potential for synergy, (5) creating a firm that is too diversified, (6) creating an internal environment in which managers devote increasing amounts of their time and energy to analyzing and completing the acquisition, and (7) developing a combined firm that is too large, necessitating extensive use of bureaucratic, rather than strategic, controls.
- Effective acquisitions have the following characteristics: (1) the acquiring and target firms have complementary resources that are the foundation for developing new capabilities; (2) the acquisition is friendly, thereby facilitating integration of the firms' resources; (3) the target firm is selected and purchased based on thorough due diligence; (4) the acquiring and target firms have considerable slack in the form of cash or debt capacity; (5) the newly formed firm maintains a low or moderate level of debt by selling off portions of the acquired firm or some of the acquiring firm's poorly performing units; (6) the acquiring and acquired firms have experience in terms of adapting to change; and (7) R&D and innovation are emphasized in the new firm.
- Restructuring is used to improve a firm's performance by correcting for problems created by ineffective management. Restructuring by downsizing involves reducing the number of employees and hierarchical levels in the firm. Although it can lead to short-term cost reductions, they may be realized at the expense of long-term success, because of the loss of valuable human resources (and knowledge) and overall corporate reputation.
- The goal of restructuring through downscoping is to reduce the firm's level of diversification. Often, the firm divests unrelated businesses to achieve this goal. Eliminating unrelated businesses makes it easier for the firm and its top-level managers to refocus on the core businesses.
- Through an LBO, a firm is purchased so that it can become a private entity. LBOs usually are financed largely through debt. Management buyouts (MBOs), employee buyouts (EBOs), and whole-firm LBOs are the three types of LBOs. Because they provide clear managerial incentives, MBOs have been the most successful of the three. Often, the intent of a buyout is to improve efficiency and performance to the point where the firm can be sold successfully within five to eight years.
- Commonly, restructuring's primary goal is to gain or re-establish effective strategic control of the firm. Of the three restructuring strategies, downscoping is aligned most closely with establishing and using strategic controls and usually improves performance more on a comparative basis.

KEY TERMS AND DEFINITIONS

A **merger** is a strategy through which two firms agree to integrate their operations on a relatively coequal basis.

An **acquisition** is a strategy through which one firm buys a controlling, or 100 per cent, interest in another firm with the intent of making the acquired firm a subsidiary business within its portfolio.

A **takeover** is a special type of acquisition wherein the target firm does not solicit the acquiring firm's bid; thus, takeovers are unfriendly acquisitions.

Restructuring is a strategy through which a firm changes its set of businesses or its financial structure.

A **global strategy** is an international strategy through which the firm offers standardized products across country markets, with competitive strategy being dictated by the home office.

REVIEW QUESTIONS

1. Why are merger and acquisition strategies popular in many firms competing in the global economy? Are the reasons the same in the case of India?
2. What reasons account for firms' decisions to use acquisition strategies as a means to achieve strategic competitiveness?
3. What are the seven primary problems that affect a firm's efforts to successfully use an acquisition strategy?
4. What are the attributes associated with a successful acquisition strategy?
5. What is restructuring strategy, and what are its common forms?
6. What are the short- and long-term outcomes associated with the different restructuring strategies?

EXPERIENTIAL EXERCISES

Exercise 1: How Did the Deal Work Out?

The text argues that mergers and acquisitions are a popular strategy for businesses. However, returns for acquiring firms do not always live up to expectations. This exercise seeks to address this notion by analyzing, pre and post hoc, the results of actual acquisitions. By looking at the notifications of a deal beforehand, categorizing that deal, and then following it for a year, you will be able to learn about actual deals and their implications for strategic leaders and their firms.

Working in teams, identify a merger or acquisition that was completed in the last few years. This may be a cross-border acquisition or one centered in India. Each team must have its M&A choice approved in advance so as to avoid duplicates.

To complete this assignment you should be prepared to answer the following questions:

1. Describe the environment for the merger or acquisition you identified at the time it was completed. Using concepts discussed in the text, focus on management's representation to shareholders, industry environment, and the overall rationale for the transaction.
2. Did the acquirer pay a premium for the target firm? If so, how much? In addition, search for investor comments regarding the wisdom of the transaction. Attempt to identify how the market reacted at the announcement of the transaction (Go through the stock prices for a period prior to and after the acquisition announcement).
3. Describe the transaction going forward. Use concepts from the text such as, but not limited to:
   - The reason for the transaction (i.e., market power, overcoming entry barriers, etc.).
   - Any problems in achieving acquisition success.
   - Whether the transaction has been a success or not and why.
   - Prepare a 10—15 minute presentation for the class describing your findings. Organize the presentation as if you were updating the shareholders of the newly formed firm.

Exercise 2: L&T—DEMERGER OF ITS CEMENT BUSINESS

Indian engineering major, Larsen & Toubro Ltd. (L&T) was established in 1942. It was basically in the engineering and construction business. In 1983, the company established a cement plant with an installed capacity 1 million tons per annum in Chandrapur district in Maharashtra and commenced commercial production of cement. With three major business segments—engineering and construction (ECC), electrical business group (EBG) and cement, the cement division was India's largest cement producer with a manufacturing capacity of 16 MTPA. The sales turnover of the company rose from ₹53.88 billion in the year 1996/1997 to ₹115.25 billion in the year 2003/2004.

From the year 2000, L&T was planning to restructure some of its business divisions through demerger and consolidation in order to concentrate more on its infrastructure and turnkey businesses. In 2004, its shareholders approved the demerger of the cement division into a separate company named UltraTech CemCo Ltd. (UCL) and divest 8.5 per cent of its stake to Aditya Birla group's flagship company, Grasim Industries. This group held only a minority stake in the new company, but could acquire additional stakes through a public offer.

Grasim, a company belonging to the Birla Group, was incorporated in 1947 as Gwalior Rayon Silk Manufacturing (Weaving) Co. Ltd. It commenced operations as a textile manufacturing mill in 1948, and later backward integrated to produce a number of raw materials and manufacture of textile equipment. Thereafter, Grasim diversified into cement manufacturing with a single plant in central India in the mid-1980s when the sector was opened for private players. The taking over of the management of UltraTech made sense to Grasim, since with this merger, it would become the market leader in cement in India, with almost a quarter of the market share and 22 per cent of installed capacity, and world's seventh largest producer of cement.

ICICI direct.com, which is the electronic brokerage house of ICICI Bank, commented that:

The company will now be a focused engineering player with substantial improvement in various parameters. The new L&T would be a low gearing, high-RoCE and free cash generating operation.

The outlook for all the engineering divisions is encouraging. In the E&C segment, L&T has a robust order pipeline with orders expected in the oil and gas sector (both upstream and down stream) and infrastructure spending. The current order book at ₹18,7 billion implies a book-to-bill ratio of 2.4:1, the best in the history of the company.

In FY04, the engineering business, on a like-for-like basis, registered a 31 per cent year-on-year (YoY) rise in sales, while operating profit rose 38 per cent. Overall order inflows are up 22 per cent in FY04 and order backlog rose 21 per cent.

L&T has given a guidance of 20 per cent top line growth and margin improvement of 100–150 bps. This coupled with the order book will give the company good earning visibility over the next year and keep it on the investment radar.

Sources: "L&T: Restructuring the Cement Business", *Asian Case Research Journal,* 9(1): 83-115, which may be accessed at: http://www.worldscinet.com/acrj/09/preserved-docs/0901/S0218927505000629.pdf; http://content.icicidirect.com/ULFiles/UploadFile_2004611162658.asp; http://entrepreneur.com/tradejournals/article/204480539_2.html.

1. Why did L&T decide to divest itself of the cement business?
2. What does it mean that L&T listed the separation as a demerger?
3. Do you feel that both the construction and cement businesses are better or worse off being separated (Construction is an activity consuming a great deal of cement)?

Please access other Web sites on this topic before making your presentation/submission.

CHAPTER 8

Global Strategy

Studying this chapter should provide you with the strategic management knowledge needed to

- Explain traditional and emerging motives for firms to pursue international diversification.
- Identify the four major benefits of an international strategy.
- Explore the four factors that provide a basis for international business-level strategies.
- Describe the three international corporate-level strategies: multidomestic, global, and transnational.
- Discuss the environmental trends affecting international strategy, especially liability of foreignness and regionalization.
- Name and describe the five alternative modes for entering international markets.
- Explain the effects of international diversification on firm returns and innovation.
- Name and describe two major risks of international diversification.

OPENING CASE
Entry into India and China by Foreign Firms and Indian/Chinese Firms Reaching for Global Markets

Case of the Indian Firms

In recent years, there has been a sea change in the business trend regarding the entry of foreign companies into India as also of Indian companies going abroad. This is a major move away from the days of self sufficiency, when India was essentially a closed economy. There are many reasons why foreign companies choose to come to India. A very important reason is, of course, the sheer size of the market, and its much higher growth rates as compared to most of the developed economies. For example, while US growth rate is still languishing (in early 2011) at around 2 per cent, India is expected to end the year 2011 with a growth rate of about 8.6 per cent.

General Motors, which entered India some 14 years ago, plans to move away from its present position of being a bit player in the Indian car market (market share: 4.6%). GM now manufactures the Chevrolet Spark, Chevrolet U-Va , Chevrolet Aveo, Chevrolet SRV, Chevrolet Optra Magnum, Chevrolet Cruze, Chevrolet Tavera and Chevrolet Captiva at its two facilities in Halol in Gujarat and Talegaon in Maharashtra. It also operates R&D, engineering and design centers in Bangalore. Its engine plant at Talegaon would be commissioned by next year-end.

General Motors is reportedly looking at introducing an entry-level car to be positioned below the Chevrolet Spark, to drive up volumes in the Indian market. The Indian car market is dominated by the small car segment, which constitutes nearly 70 per cent of passenger vehicle sales, and grew by a third between April and December 2010. In collaboration with one of the top state-owned Chinese automakers Shanghai Automotive Industry Corporation (SAIC), General motors' is attempting to challenge Maruti Suzuki's Alto, the largest selling small car globally in 2010. GM intends to treble sales to 300,000 units in India by 2013 and has planned to launch six new vehicles in association with SAIC over the next two years. This would include two light commercial vehicles, a sports utility vehicle, a sedan, a hatchback, and a notchback.

Tim Lee, president, international operations, GM, said, "We are looking at having products strategically across segments to boost sales in the Indian market. We are working closely with SAIC and looking at opportunities to introduce a product priced lower than the Spark in future." The Chevrolet Spark is priced between ₹323,000 and ₹424,000 (ex-showroom), while the Alto is tagged between ₹231,000 and ₹327,000.

"India and the rest of the emerging markets are very important to us. The business model after the IPO (Initial Public Offering, of GM shares) is to focus on and leverage on these growth markets," added Lee.

The company recently launched a powertrain engine, developed exclusively for the Indian market at its technical center in Bangalore, and to be manufactured at its factory in Talegaon, Pune. The 1.2 liter engine would be first fitted on the Chevrolet Beat from February 1, and then to other models. The locally developed engine would help optimize costs and enable the company to price products competitively.

SAIC and GM run a series of successful JVs in China, and had, in December 2009, formed an all-new 50:50 JV in Hong Kong to support expansion into emerging markets. The new JV had also got charge of GM India, which till then was a wholly-owned subsidiary of GM (US). Lee said that SAIC would play a "major role" in the development and launch of new products in India, including light commercial vehicles and cars. "The frugal element (in design and production of car) is added by SAIC, while GM helps with its branding, distribution set-up and existing products."

The Indian market is attracting foreign companies in the service sector also. UK-based retail major and leading mother and baby care retailer, Mothercare, has received government approval to invest ₹258.7 million in a retail joint venture. The speciality retailer of maternity garments, baby clothes and equipment, will pick up a 30 per cent stake in a joint venture with DLF Brands, the retail management arm of realty giant DLF. Mothercare had announced the JV in 2009 through its subsidiary, Mothercare UK, and has already set up two single-brand stores in the country. Mothercare also operates in India through an agreement with Shoppers Stop, under which it runs around two dozen outlets at the Raheja Group promoted large format stores. Mothercare, plans to open 70 stores in India by March 2011, growing to at least 200 by March 2015 as part of its overseas expansion plans.

France's Carrefour, the world's second-largest retailer after Wal Mart, announced its entry into the Indian market by opening its first cash and carry store for wholesale distribution in December, 2010 ("Cash and Carry Stores" means that technically they are the suppliers to a separate Joint Venture, with an Indian partner. This is needed due to the retail sector in India presently not being open to foreign retailers, more specifically, to multi-brand retailers). Carrefour tied up with the country's largest retailer Future Group for its India entry. The new store—Carrefour Wholesale Cash & Carry—will house over 10,000 stock keeping units and cater to professional businesses, institutions, restaurants, and local retailers. The development is in line with the group's strategy to be present in major emerging markets that offer significant expansion and medium and long-term growth opportunities. Carrefour is already present in China, Indonesia, Malaysia, and several other Asian countries. India's estimated $500-billion retail sector is seen as having high growth potential but it remains tightly regulated with large retailers accounting for around 6% of industry sales.

Existing players Bharti Wal-Mart and Metro Cash & Carry are scaling up operations even as Carrefour and Tesco are drawing out rollout plans. The world's largest retailer, Wal-Mart, has a joint venture with Bharti Enterprises since 2007 and has set up the "Best Price Modern Wholesale" cash and carry store in Amritsar in May, 2009. The Bharti Wal-Mart joint venture, so far confined to Punjab, plans to build a national presence over the next 18 months with outlets in Karnataka, Andhra Pradesh, MP,

Uttar Pradesh, and Haryana. Tesco, which has partnered with Tata Group's retail firm Trent, plans to invest £60 (₹4800) million in the country. German company Metro made an entry into the Indian market even earlier, in 2003. It currently operates six cash-and-carry stores in Hyderabad, Bangalore, Mumbai, and Kolkata.

DHL Global Forwarding, the freight division of leading global logistics player DHL, plans to set up facilities in five free trade warehousing zones (FTWZ) in the country by 2013. These will be in addition to the $10 million (₹450 million) facility in the country's first FTWZ in Chennai. "We plan to set up facilities in five FTWZs here in next two to three years to cater to the growing need of the trade as well as expand our footprint," DHL Global, South Asia Pacific CEO Amadou Diallo said. He said DHL Global Forwarding will be the first global logistics company to operate a facility within the FTWZ that offers customers the benefits of a duty free zone with high quality infrastructure, and a one-stop-shop for all logistics requirements of customers. On investments so far in India, Diallo said, "DHL Forwarding has so far invested around $315 million (₹150 billion) in India". The logistics market in India is expected to grow to $120 billion in 2014 from about $90 billion at present. "We are well positioned to capitalize on this fast growing market with India poised for a 9 per cent growth," Diallo added. Also, the company is looking at public-private-partnership projects in logistics in India.

DHL Global Forwarding is also looking at outsourcing some of its back-office work to India and is running a pilot project for this. It will move certain segments of operations to the country and utilize the trained manpower and infrastructure developed in India. The company has set up the DHL Fashion and Apparel Centre for Excellence in Tirupur in Tamil Nadu to facilitate trade within the SAARC region, Europe and North America, and to take a share of the $3.9 billion per annum market for apparel logistics in South Asia. Diallo said that DHL believes there are opportunities for Indian suppliers in European countries, especially in Eastern Europe, where a lot of small and medium enterprises need to be serviced.

Costa Coffee, one of the major players in the ₹10 billion organized coffee business in India, aims to consolidate its position in the market through brisk expansion. The UK-based coffee retailer, which entered India in 2005 and operates 70 outlets through its franchisee Devyani International, has invested "300–350 million for setting up 50–60 Costa cafe's across India, by the end of 2011. Santosh Unni, CEO, Costa Coffee said, "There's a spurt in the coffee retailing business in India, with new entrants in the market and changes in consumption patterns. The entry of Starbucks will bring about a healthy competition." The organized coffee segment in India is estimated to be growing at 40%. There are about 1400 branded coffee shops, dominated by Café Coffee Day, while Barista, Costa Coffee, and Gloria Jeans Coffee are other important players.

Many foreign firms see India as an excellent source for getting their R&D done cheaply and efficiently. For example, DuPont opened a large research facility in Hyderabad in 2008 and is expanding the scope of its work at the Knowledge Center by adding research & development capabilities to support local customer needs for various businesses that serve the safety & protection, construction, transportation and packaging markets in India, ASEAN and other emerging markets in the region. "The expansion at the DuPont Knowledge Center demonstrates DuPont's focus on growing in emerging markets, such as India, by addressing local market needs," said Mark Vergnano, DuPont executive vice president. DuPont also plans to have headcount of 600 scientists and engineers in two years (At present, the Knowledge Centre has about 250 scientists and engineers). Homi C. Bhedwar, director at DuPont Knowledge Center said, "This expansion will help us in developing products such as life protection equipments. We are also developing technology that will limit emissions and provide clean technology." DuPont India anticipates exceeding $1 billion in sales by 2014. DuPont sees India not only as a key growth market, but also as a strategic partner particularly in the areas of the company's R&D and knowledge initiatives. The company has six production facilities in India in three locations (Vadodara, Madurai, and Hyderabad) for Crop Protection, Pioneer Hi-Bred, Performance Polymers, Performance Coatings, and Chemicals and Fluoroprod. DKC also will conduct research on emerging technologies such as bio-based materials and agriculture biotechnology to improve rice yields and drought tolerance capabilities.

Indian companies are moving overseas too, in a big way. With its growth rate, India's needs for energy and raw materials will go up considerably in the coming years, and ensuring the sources of supply has become a priority for Indian companies (just as with Chinese companies). The Prime Minister, Dr. Manmohan Singh himself urged Indian companies to move overseas for oil sources, since India's own domestic production is still not high.

Indian conglomerates are shifting their manufacturing bases overseas. The relative ease in doing business, need for local presence and availability of cheaper raw materials and other assets are driving this phenomenon. Companies are also using the acquisition route to expand overseas, as we have seen in the previous chapter. The quest to go global in the absence of good acquisition opportunities at home, diversifying the revenue base and lowering risks and looking for feedstock like coal and iron ore which power domestic businesses are also major factors making companies opting for overseas acquisitions where it fits their business plans.

Gradually, a larger percentage of revenues of many Indian firms (especially the large ones) are coming from their overseas businesses. The trend is visible across sectors from auto to infrastructure to pharma and telecom. According to the latest available figures, 65.6 per cent of the total revenues of Bharat Forge, an auto ancillary major, come from outside India. After the acquisition of Jaguar-Land Rover (JLR), 59.2 per cent of revenues of Tata Motors come from overseas. Same is the case with another Tata group company, Tata Steel. After acquisition of Anglo-Dutch steel maker, Corus, Thailand's Millennium Steel and Singapore's NatSteel, 73.5 per cent of the group's revenues come from outside the country. With the acquisition of the Canadian aluminium firm Novelis in 2007, AV Birla group's Hindalco Industries too now earns 70.1 per cent of its revenues overseas. With the acquisition of the African operations of Zain Telecom last year, Bharti Airtel's share of overseas revenues has gone up to 26 per cent. One interesting exception is India's largest provate sector company, Reliance Industries, which does not have a significant revenue stream from overseas, but even here, with the recent acquisition of shale gas assets abroad, things are bound to change.

African consumer spending will nearly double to $1.4 trillion by 2020, while the number of households in Africa with discretionary income will rise by 50 per cent to 128 million over the same period, a recent McKinsey and Co. report predicted. Indian consumer goods makers are actively buying assets in Africa, applying their knowledge of challenging, lower-income markets to a continent where spending power is on the rise. A sizeable population of Africans of Indian origin in eastern and southern Africa give Indian companies an advantage over global competitors, including China. Indian companies accounted for the most acquisitions in sub-Saharan Africa in 2010, accounting for a third of the total value of deals done in the region, according to Thomson Reuters data. Tapping Africa opens up new growth avenues for cash-rich Indian makers of personal care products such as soaps, shampoos, hair and skin care products, with rising costs and fierce competition squeezing profits at home. "We are a homegrown multinational from a developing economy," said Jimmy Anklesaria, executive vice president for international operations at Godrej Consumer Products. "Our ability to understand consumers in developing economies is sharp." Whereas global players sometimes sell one-size-fits all products, Indian manufacturers often adjust their offerings to suit local tastes and spending habits. "The product portfolios of Indian companies are tweaked to suit local needs," said Debashish Mukherjee, principal with consultancy AT Kearney.

Godrej bought Nigerian personal care products maker Tura in 2009 for around $33 million, according to analysts, and has also bought hair care brands Rapidol and Kinky in South Africa over the past two years and is on the hunt for more acquisitions. We have already mentioned the acquisition of Zain by Bharti Airtel. Indian makers of consumer goods such as Dabur India, Marico and Emami also have been among those buying up assets in Africa.

Risks to Indian firms making acquisitions in Africa include overpaying in the competition for scarce attractive targets, vulnerability to input costs, especially in commodities in a highly price sensitive market, political uncertainties, and the ability to compete against much larger companies both from developed countries and from China, in fact, more from the latter. Yet, Indian consumer goods firms active in Africa expect growth of between 25–30 per cent from their operations there, and expect opportunities to move beyond personal care to household care and over-the-counter healthcare products in coming years.

Peter Parks/AFP/Getty Images

Models pose next to a Porsche Panamera, a new four-door sports car making its international debut at Auto Shanghai, China's largest auto show.

Case of the Chinese Firms

As in the case of India, many foreign firms choose to operate in the Chinese market because it is very large and important. This is certainly the case for automobile firms that have used China as a base to both produce cars more cheaply and expand their market by selling in China. In particular, GM, through its partnership with SAIC, has created successful joint ventures. Because this venture continues to be successful, Fritz Henderson, GM's CEO since its bankruptcy filing, has indicated that none of GM's operations in China are for sale. In fact, GM is seeking to extend its operations in China, possibly with new ventures. Volkswagen also has a joint venture with SAIC. Recently SAIC has sought to introduce its own automobiles domestically and plans to participate in global markets when possible. Similarly, another GM partner in China, Liuzhou Wuling Motors Co., is planning to develop its own vehicles rather than through a GM brand such as Chevrolet.

Because the US auto market and other auto markets elsewhere in the world are experiencing substantially lower sales, the Chinese market is becoming more important. Porsche AG now owns 50.76 per cent of Volkswagen and launched the first exposure of its new model, the Panamera, in a Shanghai auto show in April 2009. Although the US market still counts as the most important sale zone for Porsche, China is expected to have the largest auto market by sales volume in 2009.

The Chinese market is not only important for manufacturing such as the automobile industry, but also for service industries. For example, Google recently launched a music service supported by the world's four largest music labels: Warner Music Group Corp., Vivendi SA's Universal Music, EMI Group Ltd., and Sony Corp.'s Music Entertainment. Google and its partners hope to draw users away from Google's main Chinese competitors, especially Baidu Inc. Baidu is the dominant market share holder, with approximately 62 per cent of the search market for Web downloads in China. Google increased its search engine market in China to 28 per cent in 2008, up from 23 per cent in 2007, but Baidu dominance increased from 59 per cent in 2007 to 62 per cent market share in the same period.

Interestingly, some Chinese firms are more successful abroad than they are in their home market. Huawei Technologies Co. Ltd. is making inroads in the US market. Huawei, a Chinese telecom equipment supplier, recently won a contract with Cox Communications, a US TV cable provider. Huawei is also in the running for a potentially bigger contract with Clearwire Corporation. Clearwire is in the process of helping to build a wireless broadband network that would serve 120 million people in the United States by 2010. Other finalists for the contract include Motorola Inc., Samsung Electronics Co., and Nokia Siemens Networks. More generally, other competitors include Alcatel-Lucent and Telefon AB L.M. Ericsson. Another Chinese company, ZTE, competes with these firms as well. Although Huwaei and ZTE have had more success in developing regions of the world, Huawei has become a major vendor in Europe, where it has won numerous contracts with significant telecom providers such as Vodaphone Group PLC, and France Telecom SA's Orange. Huawei also has a foothold in Canada, where it is building a third-generation (3G) network for BCE Inc.'s partners Bell Canada and Telus Corp.

Additionally, Huawei and ZTE were laggards in selling telephone equipment in their home market against Telefon AB L.M. Ericsson, Alcatel-Lucent, and Nokia Siemens Networks (a joint venture of Nokia Corp. and Siemens AG), mainly because they were an unknown company when the first wireless networks were developed in China. However, thanks to government support for new wireless technology and an aggressive strategy of deeply undercutting competitors' prices, these two firms are beating out their rivals for an estimated $59 billion of spending over the next three years for new 3G wireless networks. China has approximately 659 million mobile subscribers, and the rollout of 3G is making sales growth for these markets even more important. It is expected that Huawei and ZTE will double their combined market share for 3G revenue with current wireless network growth. Although Ericsson's market share is remaining stable, market shares for Alcatel-Lucent and Nokia Siemens are expected to decline in China. Historically, Ericsson won the lion's share because Huawei and ZTE, as noted, were small when the existing network was built in the 1990s. Both companies have access to large credit lines from China's state-owned banks and other perks such as low cost land. This has allowed them to have more flexibility in pricing and to operate with lower margins without shareholder pressure. It will be interesting to see what happens when the fourth-generation (4G) networks are rolled out in a few years.

Sources: Pankaj Doval, 2011, GM plans rival to Alto with Chinese Partner, *Times of India*, January 28, http://timesofindia.indiatimes.com/business/india-business/GM-plans-rival-to-Alto-with-Chinese-partner/articleshow/7375411.cms; Sharmishta Mukherjee, 2011, GM plans small car to take on Alto, *Business Standard,* http://business-standard.com/india/news/gm-plans-small-car-to-takealto/423260/; www.money.oneindia.in, 2011, GM plans rival to Alto with Chinese Partner, January 28, http://money.oneindia.in/news/2011/01/28/general-motors-plans-rival-alto-chinese.html; Shewta Bhanot, Rajat Guha, 2009, GM's 800 cc Spark to take Alto head on, *Financial Express*, December 23, http://www.financialexpress.com/news/gms-800cc-spark-to-take-alto-head-on/557913/; http://economictimes.indiatimes.com/news/news-by-industry/cons-products/durables/indian-consumer-firms-eye-africa-as-next-growth-driver/articleshow/7371481.cms; *Retail-guru.com*, 2010, Mothercare gets FDI nod, to partner DLF, February 24, http://retail-guru.com/mothercare-gets-fdi-nod-to-partner-dlf/; *Retail-guru.com,* 2010, Mothercare to open 70 centres in India by March 2011, December 13, http://retail-guru.com/mothercare-to-open-70-stores-in-india-by-march-2011/; retail-guru.com, Carrefour to enter India with an Indian Partner, February 21, http://retail-guru.com/carrefour-to-enter-indian-in-2010-with-an-indian-partner/; *Times of India*, 2010, Carrefour opens first cash and carry store in India, December 30, http://timesofindia.indiatimes.com/business/india-business/Carrefour-opens-first-cash-and-carry-store-in-India-/articleshow/7189921.cms; Guvleen Aulakh and Writankar Mukherjee, 2010, Cash and carry gets ready for national roll out, August 4, http://economictimes.indiatimes.com/news/news-by-industry/services/retailing/cash--carry-gets-ready-for-national-rollout/articleshow/6254001.cms; Archana Shukla, 2009, DHL's Back office work will be shifted to India, *Daily News and Analysis,* February 20, http://www.dnaindia.com/money/report_dhls-back-office-work-will-be-shifted-to-india_1232525; *Business Standard*, 2010, DHL set for Expansion, eyes logistics market, November 18, http://www.business-standard.com/india/news/dhl-set-for-expansion-eyes-logistics-market/415311/; Sohini Mitter, 2011, Costa Coffee brews growth plan, menu churn, *Financial Express,* January 27, http://www.financialexpress.com/news/costa-coffee-brews-growth-plan-menu-churn/742431/; Pallavi Gogoi, 2010, Many US companies are hiring ... Overseas, December 28, *Associated Press,* http://www.msnbc.msn.com/id/40827123/ns/business-us_business/; Urvashi Jha, 2010, DuPont to expand R and D work in India, *Financial Chronicle,* February 1, http://www.mydigitalfc.com/opportunities/dupont-expand-rd-work-india-006; DuPont information from company Web site, 2010, http://www2.dupont.com/India_Country_Site/en_IN/Media_Center/2010/Indian_Press_1Feb2010.html, http://www2.dupont.com/Media_Room/en_US/assets/downloads/fact_sheet/Fact_Sheet_Emerging_Markets.pdf; Voanews.com, 2010, India urges state-owned oil companies to expand overseas, November 1, http://www.voanews.com/english/news/India-Urges-State-Owned-Oil-Companies-to-Expand-Overseas-106441968.html; http://news.in.msn.com/business/article.aspx?cp-documentid=4854656.

Chinese section: A. Back & L. Chao, 2009, Google begins China music service; Partnership with record labels gives users free access to licensed tracks, *Wall Street Journal,* March 30, B3; L. Chao, 2009, China's telecom-gear makers, once laggards at home, pass foreign rivals, *Wall Street Journal*, April 10, B1; K. Hille & A. Parker, 2009, Upwardly mobile Huawei, *Financial Times*, http://www.ft.com, March 20; K. Li, 2009, Google launches China service, *Financial Times*, March 31, 20; C. Rauwald, 2009, Porsche chooses the China road; four-door Panamera's Shanghai debut signals focus on emerging markets, *Wall Street Journal,* April 20, B2; A. Sharma & S. Silver, 2009, Huawei tries to crack US market; Chinese telecom supplier wins Cox contract, is finalist for Clearwire deal, *Wall Street Journal*, March 26, B2; N. Shirouzu, P. J. Ho, & K. Rapoza, 2009, Corporate news: GM plans to retain China, Brazil units. *Wall Street Journal* June 3, B2; J. D. Stoll, 2009, Corporate news: GM pushes the throttle in China—affiliate's plan to expand into cars is seen as a key to growth in Asia, *Wall Street Journal,* April 27, B3; M. B. Teagarden & D. H. Cai, 2009, Learning from dragons who are learning from us; developmental lessons from China's global companies, *Organizational Dynamics*, 38(1): 73; C.-C. Tschang, 2009, Search engine squeeze? *BusinessWeek*, January 12, 21; E. Woyke, 2009, ZTE's smart phone ambitions, *Forbes,* http://www.forbes.com, March 16; B. Einhorn, 2008, Huawei, *BusinessWeek*, December 22, 51; S. Tucker, 2008, Case study: Huawei of China takes stock after frustrating year, *Financial Times*, http://www.ft.com, November 25.

As the Opening Case indicates, firms are entering India and China because of their large markets, lower costs, and of an excellent technology infrastructure and scientific manpower, but Indian and Chinese firms are also building their competitive capabilities and seeking to enter foreign markets. China's entry into the World Trade Organization (WTO) brought change not only to China and its trading partners but also to industries and firms throughout the world. Despite their developing market and institutional environments, Chinese firms such as Huawei Technologies Co. and India's Hero Honda are taking advantage of the growing sizes of the Chinese and Indian markets; they had previously learned new technologies and managerial capabilities from foreign partners and are now competing more strongly in domestic as well as foreign markets.[1]

Many firms choose direct investment in assets in foreign countries (e.g., establishing new subsidiaries, making acquisitions, or building joint ventures) over indirect investment because it provides better protection for their assets.[2] Indian and Chinese firms are developing their manufacturing capabilities and building their own branded products (e.g., Bharti Airtel, Huawei, and ZTE Corporation). As such, the potential global market power of Indian and Chinese firms is astounding.[3]

As foreign firms enter India and China and as Indian and Chinese firms enter into other foreign markets, both opportunities and threats for firms competing in global markets are magnified. This chapter examines opportunities facing firms as they seek to develop and exploit core competencies by diversifying into global markets. In addition, we discuss different problems, complexities, and threats that might accompany a firm's international strategy.[4] Although national boundaries, cultural differences, and geographic distances all pose barriers to entry into many markets, significant opportunities motivate businesses to enter international markets. A business that plans to operate globally must formulate a successful strategy to take advantage of these global opportunities.[5] Furthermore, to mould their firms into truly global companies, managers must develop global mind-sets.[6] As firms move into international markets, they develop relationships with suppliers, customers, and partners and learning from these relationships. For example, as the Opening Case illustrates, SAIC learned new capabilities from its partnerships with GM and Volkswagen, while Hero Honda did the same with Honda. India's largest car manufacturer, Maruti Suzuki introduced many systems of production and management from its Japanese partner, Suzuki, and itself became a model for Suzuki, so much so that the chief of Suzuki, Mr. Osamu Suzuki flew in 2,000 of his Japanese dealers to show how Maruti functioned in India.[7]

As illustrated in Figure 1.1, we discuss the importance of international strategy as a source of strategic competitiveness and above-average returns. This chapter focuses on the incentives to internationalize. After a firm decides to compete internationally, it must select its strategy and choose a mode of entry into international markets. It may enter international markets by exporting from domestic-based operations, licensing some of its products or services, forming joint ventures with international partners,

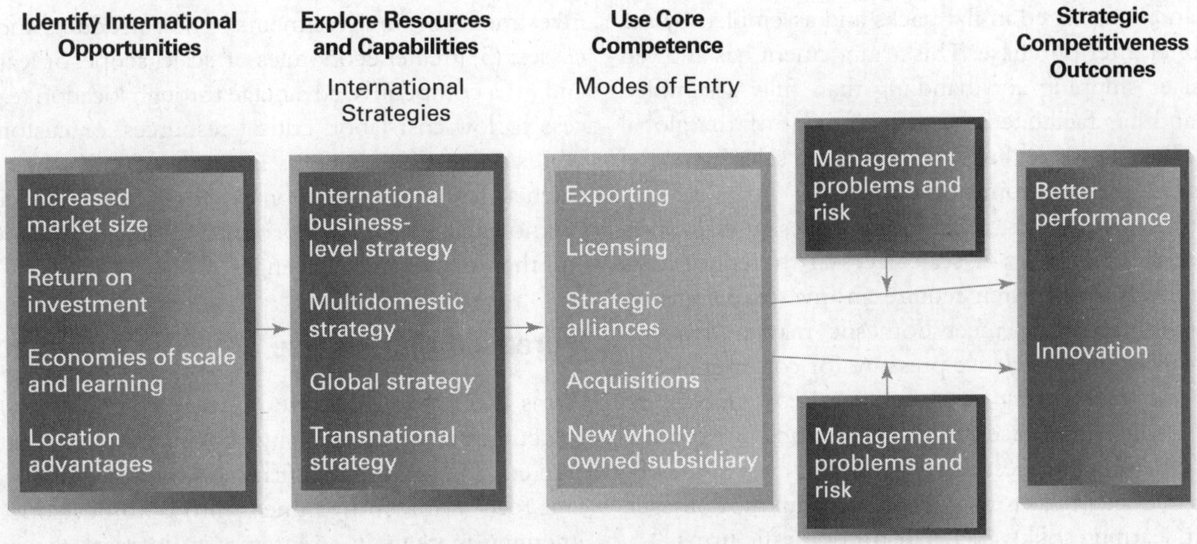

Figure 8.1 Opportunities and outcomes of international strategy

acquiring a foreign-based firm, or establishing a new subsidiary. Such international diversification can extend product life cycles, provide incentives for more innovation, and produce above-average returns. These benefits are tempered by political and economic risks and the problems of managing a complex international firm with operations in multiple countries.

Figure 8.1 provides an overview of the various choices and outcomes of strategic competitiveness. The relationships among international opportunities, the resources and capabilities that result from such strategies, and the modes of entry that are based on core competencies are explored in this chapter.

Identifying International Opportunities: Incentives to Use an International Strategy

An **international strategy** is a strategy through which the firm sells its goods or services outside its domestic market.[8] One of the primary reasons for implementing an international strategy (as opposed to a strategy focused on the domestic market) is that international markets yield potential new opportunities.[9]

Raymond Vernon captured the classic rationale for international diversification.[10] He suggested that typically a firm discovers an innovation in its home-country market, especially in an advanced economy such as that of the United States. Often demand for the product then develops in other countries, and exports are provided by domestic operations. Increased demand in foreign countries justifies making investments in foreign operations, especially to fend off foreign competitors. Vernon, therefore, observed that one reason why firms pursue international diversification is to extend a product's life cycle.

Another traditional motive for firms to become multinational is to secure needed resources. Key supplies of raw material—especially minerals and energy—are important in some industries. Other industries, such as clothing, electronics, and watch making, have moved portions of their operations to foreign locations in pursuit of lower production costs. Clearly one of the reasons for Chinese firms to expand internationally is to gain access to important resources, and the recent acquisitions by energy firms in India indicate that they may also be moving in this direction.[11] In Chapter 7, we have already discussed some of these acquisitions, such as ONGC's acquisition of Imperial Energy, Essar's acquisition of Trinity Coal, and Indonesian coal companies by Tata Steel.

Although these traditional motives persist, other emerging motivations also drive international expansion (see Chapter 1). For instance, pressure has increased for a global integration of operations, mostly driven by more universal product demand. As nations industrialize, the demand for some products and commodities appears to become more similar. This borderless demand for globally branded products may be due to similarities in lifestyle in developed nations. Increases in global communication media also facilitate the ability of people in different countries to visualize and model lifestyles in different cultures.[12] IKEA, for example, has become a global brand by selling furniture in 44 countries through more than 300 stores that it owns and operates through franchisees. All of its furniture is sold in components that can be packaged in flat packs and assembled by the consumer after purchase. This arrangement has allowed for easier shipping and handling than fully assembled units and has facilitated the development of the global brand. Because of its low-cost approach, sales increased even during the economic downturn.[13]

In some industries, technology drives globalization because the economies of scale necessary to reduce costs to the lowest level often require an investment greater than that needed to meet domestic market demand. Companies also experience pressure for cost reductions, achieved by purchasing from the lowest-cost global suppliers. For instance, research and development expertise for an emerging business startup may not exist in the domestic market, but as foreign firms locate in the domestic market, learning spillovers occur for domestic firms.[14]

New large-scale, emerging markets, such as China and India, provide a strong internationalization incentive based on their high potential demand for consumer products and services.[15] Because of currency fluctuations, firms may also choose to distribute their operations across many countries, including emerging ones, in order to reduce the risk of devaluation in one country.[16] However, the uniqueness of emerging markets presents both opportunities and challenges.[17] Even though India, for example, differs from Western countries in many respects, including culture, politics, and the precepts of its economic system, it also offers a huge potential market and its government is becoming more supportive of foreign direct investment.[18] However, the differences between China, India, and Western countries pose serious challenges to Western competitive paradigms that emphasize the skills needed to manage financial, economic, and political risks.[19]

Employment contracts and labor forces differ significantly in international markets. For example, it is more difficult to lay off employees in Europe than in the United States because of employment contract differences. In many cases, host governments demand joint ownership with a local company in order to invest in local operations; this allows the foreign firm to avoid tariffs. Also, host governments frequently require a high percentage of procurements, manufacturing, and R&D to use local sources.[20] These issues increase the need for local investment and responsiveness as opposed to seeking global economies of scale.

We have discussed incentives that influence firms to use international strategies. When these strategies are successful, firms can derive four basic benefits: (1) increased market size; (2) greater returns on major capital investments or on investments in new products and processes; (3) greater economies of scale, scope, or learning; and (4) a competitive advantage through location (e.g., access to low-cost labor, critical resources, or customers). We examine these benefits in terms of both their costs (such as higher coordination expenses and limited access to knowledge about host country political influences)[21] and their managerial challenges.

Increased Market Size

Firms can expand the size of their potential market—sometimes dramatically—by moving into international markets. Pharmaceutical firms have been doing significant foreign direct investment into both developed and emerging markets in an attempt to increase the market potential for new drugs. For example, when Japanese pharmaceutical firms made acquisitions of international rivals in 2008, one analyst noted: "One factor [driving the trend for outbound M&A] is that there are limited domestic growth opportunities... [These Japanese] companies are cash-rich and are in a good position to conduct acquisitions."[22] Indeed, Japan's large pharmaceutical firms collectively paid more than $20 billion during 2008 to buy overseas firms.

Although seeking to manage different consumer tastes and practices linked to cultural values or traditions is not simple, following an international strategy is a particularly attractive option to firms competing in domestic markets that have limited growth opportunities. For example, firms in the domestic soft drink industry have been searching for growth in foreign markets for some time now. Major competitors Pepsi and Coca-Cola have had relatively stable market shares in the United States for several years. Most of their sales growth has come from foreign markets. Coke, for instance, has used a strategy of buying overseas bottlers or expanding into other beverages such as fruit juice. For example, Coca-Cola bought out the then reigning Parle drinks with its brands, bottler relationships and distribution systems.[23] However, a recent acquisition attempt of China's largest fruit-juice producer, China Huiyuan Juice Group Ltd., was turned down by Beijing regulators claiming that it would crowd out smaller players and increase consumer prices. China is Coke's fourth largest market by volume after the United States, Mexico, and Brazil. As with other emerging markets, it is growing faster than the US market.[24]

The size of an international market also affects a firm's willingness to invest in R&D to build competitive advantages in that market. Larger markets usually offer higher potential returns and thus pose less risk for a firm's investments. The strength of the science base of the country in question also can affect a firm's foreign R&D investments.[25] Most firms prefer to invest more heavily in those countries with the scientific knowledge and talent to produce value-creating products and processes from their R&D activities.[26] This may be a good opportunity for India to attract many R&D intensive companies to set up their R&D centers. Already, Intel, GE and some other companies have some of their R&D done in India.

For example, GM has tied up with 21 Indian educational institutions, including the Indian Institutes of Technology (IITSs) and the Indian Institute of Science, Bangalore (IISc). It conducts research with IISc on fuel alternatives and light-weight engine materials. Texas Instruments has set up its Digital Signal Processing (DSP) laboratory at IISc and five IITs. Samsung undertakes designing of color televisions, washing machines, and air conditioners in collaboration with IIT Delhi's Industrial Design Department and has a consumer laboratory at IIT Delhi that undertakes usability studies. Hewlett Packard and IIT Chennai run a joint laboratory at the IITs campus to develop technologies for emerging economies and to do research to help HP's global efforts. The R&D arm of automobile major Toyota Motor Company has joined hands with the Indian Institute of Chemical Technology (IICT) to develop chemicals for use in light harvesting devices in the vehicle. Claimed to be first of its kind in India, the multinational company is jointly working with the IICT to develop high breed chemicals, which can be used for running air conditioners, lights and other devices inside and outside the vehicle, thereby slowly replacing petrol with solar power to run the devices. IBM has partnered with IIT Mumbai for collaborative research on different technologies; Intel has partnered with IIT Madras for research on speech technology; Wipro has partnered with Wollongong University, Australia in the area of education and research in IT service. Besides, Intel, Microsoft, GE, HP, and a host of other companies conduct some of their research in India due to their cost effectiveness and the excellent research manpower available.[27]

Return on Investment

Large markets may be crucial for earning a return on significant investments, such as plant and capital equipment or R&D. Therefore, most R&D-intensive industries such as electronics are international. In addition to the need for a large market to recoup heavy investment in R&D, the development pace for new technology is increasing. New products become obsolete more rapidly, and therefore, investments need to be recouped more quickly. Moreover, firms' abilities to develop new technologies are expanding, and because of different patent laws across country borders, imitation by competitors is more likely. Through reverse engineering, competitors are able to disassemble a product, learn the new technology, and develop a similar product. Because competitors can imitate new technologies relatively quickly, firms need to recoup new product development costs even more rapidly. Consequently, the larger markets provided by international expansion are particularly attractive in many industries such as pharmaceutical firms, because they expand the opportunity for the firm to recoup significant capital investments and large-scale R&D expenditures.[28]

Regardless of other motives however, the primary reason for investing in international markets is to generate above-average returns on investments. Still, firms from different countries have different expectations and use different criteria to decide whether to invest in international markets, such as industry conditions and the potential for knowledge transfer.[29]

Economies of Scale and Learning

By expanding their markets, firms may be able to enjoy economies of scale, particularly in their manufacturing operations. To the extent that a firm can standardize its products across country borders and use the same or similar production facilities, thereby coordinating critical resource functions, it is more likely to achieve optimal economies of scale.[30]

Economies of scale are critical in the global auto industry. China's decision to join the World Trade Organization has allowed carmakers from other countries to enter their market and for lower tariffs to be charged (in the past, Chinese carmakers have had an advantage over foreign carmakers due to tariffs). Ford, Honda, General Motors, and Volkswagen are each producing an economy car to compete with the existing cars in China. Because of global economies of scale (allowing them to price their products competitively) and local investments in China, all of these companies are likely to obtain significant market share in China. Alternatively, SAIC is developing its own branded vehicles to compete with the foreign automakers. SAIC's joint ventures with both GM and Volkswagen have been highly successful (as explained in the Opening Case). However, as also explained in the Opening Case, Porsche is seeking to market its vehicles in China to extend its scale economies, while Chinese firms are seeking to begin exporting vehicles overseas and perhaps enter foreign markets in other ways, such as through acquisitions.[31]

Firms may also be able to exploit core competencies in international markets through resource and knowledge sharing between units and network partners across country borders.[32] This sharing generates synergy, which helps the firm produce higher-quality goods or services at lower cost. In addition, working across international markets provides the firm with new learning opportunities.[33] Multinational firms have substantial occasions to learn from the different practices they encounter in separate international markets. However, research finds that to take advantage of international R&D investments, firms need to already have a strong R&D system in place to absorb the knowledge.[34]

Location Advantages

Firms may locate facilities in other countries to lower the basic costs of the goods or services they provide. These facilities may provide easier access to lower-cost labor, energy, and other natural resources. Other location advantages include access to critical supplies and to customers. Once positioned favorably with an attractive location, firms must manage their facilities effectively to gain the full benefit of a location advantage.[35]

Such location advantages can be influenced by costs of production and transportation requirements as well as by the needs of the intended customers.[36] Cultural influences may also affect location advantages and disadvantages. If there is a strong match between the cultures in which international transactions are carried out, the liability of foreignness is lower than if there is high cultural distance.[37] Research also suggests that regulation distances influence the ownership positions of multinational firms as well as their strategies for managing local and expatriate human resources.[38]

As suggested in the Opening Case, General Motors (GM) entered international markets to expand its market size. While GM has lost its position as the world's largest automaker after 76 years, even in bankruptcy it has expansion plans for its China ventures,[39] and as discussed in the Opening Case, in India as well. Still, GM faces a number of challenges from domestic Chinese competitors, such as its partners, SAIC and Liuzhou Wuling Motors Co., and from foreign competitors, such as Toyota and Volkswagen. It will have to formulate and implement a successful strategy for the Chinese market to maintain a competitive advantage there. Interestingly, given the downturn in sales, China may overtake the United States in domestic sales. An article in the *Wall Street Journal* noted: "China is expected to become the world's number one vehicle producer this year [2009], surpassing Japan. Mr. Young [chief financial officer of GM] said he is starting to think China could outmuscle the United States this year as the number one market for vehicle sales. GM had been predicting China would surpass the United States in 2015, but Chinese sales leapfrogged those in the United States in the first quarter [2009]."[40]

International Strategies

Firms choose to use one or both of two basic types of international strategies: business-level international strategy and corporate-level international strategy. At the business level, firms follow generic strategies: cost leadership, differentiation, focused cost leadership, focused differentiation, or integrated cost leadership/differentiation. The three corporate-level international strategies are multi-domestic, global, or transnational (a combination of multi-domestic and global). To create competitive advantage, each strategy must utilize a core competence based on difficult-to-imitate resources and capabilities.[41] As discussed in Chapters 4 and 6, firms expect to create value through the implementation of a business-level strategy and a corporate-level strategy.

International Business-Level Strategy

Each business must develop a competitive strategy focused on its own domestic market. We discussed business-level strategies in Chapter 4 and competitive rivalry and competitive dynamics in Chapter 5. International business-level strategies have some unique features. In an international business-level strategy, the home country of operation is often the most important source of competitive advantage.[42] The resources and capabilities established in the home country frequently allow the firm to pursue the strategy into markets located in other countries.[43] However, research indicates that as a firm continues its growth into multiple international locations, the country of origin is less important for competitive advantage.[44]

Michael Porter's model, illustrated in Figure 8.2, describes the factors contributing to the advantage of

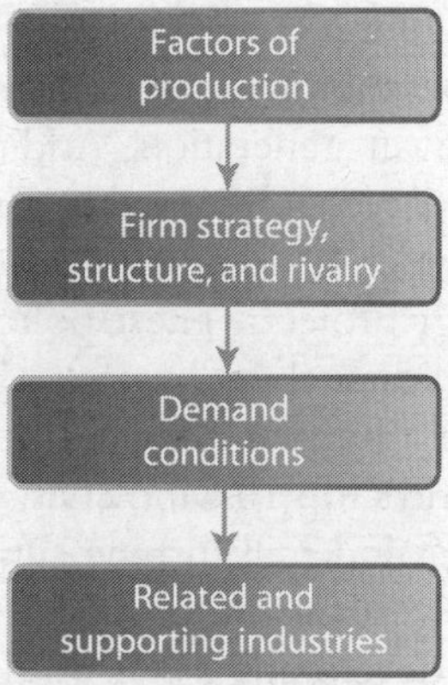

Figure 8.2 Determinants of national advantage

firms in a dominant global industry and associated with a specific home country or regional environment.[45] The first dimension in Porter's model is the factors of production. This dimension refers to the inputs necessary to compete in any industry—labor, land, natural resources, capital, and infrastructure (such as transportation, postal, and communication systems). There are basic factors (for example, natural and labor resources) and advanced factors (such as digital communication systems and a highly educated workforce). Other production factors are generalized (highway systems and the supply of debt capital) and specialized (skilled personnel in a specific industry, such as the workers in a port that specialize in handling bulk chemicals). If a country has both advanced and specialized production factors, it is likely to serve an industry well by spawning strong home-country competitors that also can be successful global competitors. Indian BPO and education industries offer excellent examples of taking advantage of favorable factor conditions in India.

Ironically, countries often develop advanced and specialized factors because they lack critical basic resources. For example, some Asian countries, such as South Korea, lack abundant natural resources but offer a strong work ethic, a large number of engineers, and systems of large firms to create an expertise in manufacturing. Similarly, Germany developed a strong chemical industry, partially because Hoechst and BASF spent years creating a synthetic indigo dye to reduce their dependence on imports, unlike Britain, whose colonies provided large supplies of natural indigo.[46]

The second dimension in Porter's model, demand conditions, is characterized by the nature and size of buyers' needs in the home market for the industry's goods or services. A large market segment can produce the demand necessary to create scale-efficient facilities.

Chinese manufacturing companies have spent years focused on building their businesses in China, but are now beginning to look at markets beyond their borders, as described in the Opening Case about SAIC. As mentioned, SAIC (along with other Chinese firms) has begun the challenging process of building its brand equity in China but especially in other countries. In doing so, most Chinese firms begin in the Far East with the intention to move into Western markets when ready. Companies such as SAIC have been helped by China's entry to the World Trade Organization. Of course, companies such as SAIC are interested in entering international markets to increase their market share and profits. The strong demand conditions in the telecom industry in India have enabled companies such as Bharti Airtel to grow[47] and then move overseas to extend their reach.

Related and supporting industries are the third dimension in Porter's model. Italy has become the leader in the shoe industry because of related and supporting industries; a well-established leather-processing industry provides the leather needed to construct shoes and related products. Also, many people travel to Italy to purchase leather goods, providing support in distribution. Supporting industries in leather-working machinery and design services also contribute to the success of the shoe industry. In fact, the design services industry supports its own related industries, such as ski boots, fashion apparel, and furniture. In Japan, cameras and copiers are related industries. Similarly, it is argued that the creative resources associated with "popular cartoons such as Manga and the animation sector along with technological knowledge from the consumer electronics industry facilitated the emergence of a successful video game industry in Japan."[48] In India, the clusters of industries in areas such as automobile components in and around Pune, Chennai and Delhi; electronic and software industries in Bangalore and the knitted garments in Tirupur point to the existence of such strong effects of related and supporting industries.

Firm strategy, structure, and rivalry make up the final country dimension and also foster the growth of certain industries. The types of strategy, structure, and rivalry among firms vary greatly from nation to nation. The excellent technical training system in Germany fosters a strong emphasis on continuous product and process improvements. In Japan, unusual cooperative and competitive systems have facilitated the cross-functional management of complex assembly operations. In Italy, the national pride of the country's designers has spawned strong industries in sports cars, fashion apparel, and furniture. In the United States, competition among computer manufacturers and software producers has contributed to the development of these industries.

The four basic dimensions of the "diamond" model in Figure 8.2 emphasize the environmental or structural attributes of a national economy that contribute to national advantage. Government policy also clearly contributes to the success and failure of many firms and industries. For example, as illustrated in the Strategic Focus 8.1, the Chinese government has provided incentives for SunTech, a Chinese firm focused on creating solar power for utilities around the world, particularly in Europe.[49] SunTech is a "born global" firm that went directly into international markets that were emerging within the solar power industry. It has been successful so far because of the low-cost manufacturing and the high levels of engineering talent available in China. In India, both the Union and the state governments have been supporting the development of non conventional energy through various incentives. For example, the wind power program in India, initiated in 1983–84, includes wind resource assessment activities, research and development support, implementation of demonstration projects to create awareness, opening up of new sites, involvement of utilities and industry, growth of infrastructure capability and capacity for manufacture, installation, operation and maintenance of Wind Turbine Generators (WTGs) and policy support. India's Electricity Act of 2003, requires all state-level energy regulatory commissions to encourage electricity distributors to procure a specified minimum percentage of power generation from renewable energy sources. This has led to support from various state governments as well. For example, Maharashtra offers an accelerated depreciation benefit of 80 per cent, capital subsidies, and exemption from income, excise, import, and concessional taxes for wind power projects. The government incentives were partially supported by a "Clean Energy Fund" funded by taxes on conventional energy. Support for investments in wind power is also provided through fiscal incentive schemes or public grants to the owners of wind power systems, for example, through preferential tariffs on power generated by WTGs or tax incentives promoting investments in wind power. The Wind Energy industry enjoys special tax benefits from government and subsidies from regulatory bodies, and better tariff rates from the purchasing Electricity Boards. The budget for 2010–11 encouraged private solar companies by reducing customs duty on solar panels by 5 per cent and exempting excise duty on solar photovoltaic panels. This is expected to reduce the roof-top solar panel installation by 15–20 per cent. The budget also proposed a coal tax of $1 per metric ton on domestic and imported coal used for power generation. Additionally, the government has initiated a Renewable Energy Certificate (REC) scheme which is designed to drive investment in low-carbon energy projects. These policies led to the creation of companies such as Suzlon, a nonconventional energy firm with emphasis on wind powered energy. It is among the world's top 10 wind energy companies, and the third leading wind mill turbine supplier. Suzlon has become a highly vertically integrated wind turbine technology supplier, developing a full wind turbine technology supply chain in-house.[50]

The Wind Energy industry enjoys special tax benefits from government and subsidies from regulatory bodies, and better tariff rates from the purchasing Electricity Boards.

Likewise, Yandex in Russia (see the Strategic Focus 8.1) was successful because it found a way to meet the complexities of developing a search tool for the complex Russian language, which turned out to be an advantage in global competition.[51] Also, Yandex had strong demand conditions in Russia for Internet service and has been able to maintain its market share against strong competition from Google. Yandex is now entering the US market and establishing a research base near Google's headquarters.

Although each firm must create its own success, not all firms will survive to become global competitors—not even those operating with the same country factors that spawned other successful firms. The actual strategic choices managers make may be the most compelling reasons for success or failure. Accordingly, the factors illustrated in Figure 8.2 are likely to produce competitive advantages only when the firm develops and implements an appropriate strategy that takes advantage of distinct country factors. Thus, these distinct country factors must be given thorough consideration when making a decision regarding the business-level strategy to use (i.e., cost leadership, differentiation, focused cost leadership, focused differentiation, and integrated cost leadership/differentiation, discussed in Chapter 4) in an international context. However, pursuing an international strategy leads to more adjustment and learning as the firm adjusts to competition in the host country. Such adjustments are continuous as illustrated by SunTech's operations, given the steep decline in demand for solar facilities in the economic downturn. It must adapt to the increasing competition from other startups and its major competitors in global markets.

International Corporate-Level Strategy

The international business-level strategies are based at least partially on the type of international corporate-level strategy the firm has chosen. Some corporate strategies give individual country units the authority to develop their own business-level strategies; other corporate strategies dictate the business-level strategies in order to standardize the firm's products and sharing of resources across countries.[52] International corporate-level strategy focuses on the scope of a firm's operations through both product and geographic diversification.[53] International corporate-level strategy is required when the firm operates in multiple industries and multiple countries or regions.[54] The headquarters unit guides the strategy, although business- or country-level managers can have substantial strategic input, depending on the type of international corporate-level strategy followed. The three international corporate-level strategies are multidomestic, global, and transnational, as shown in Figure 8.3.

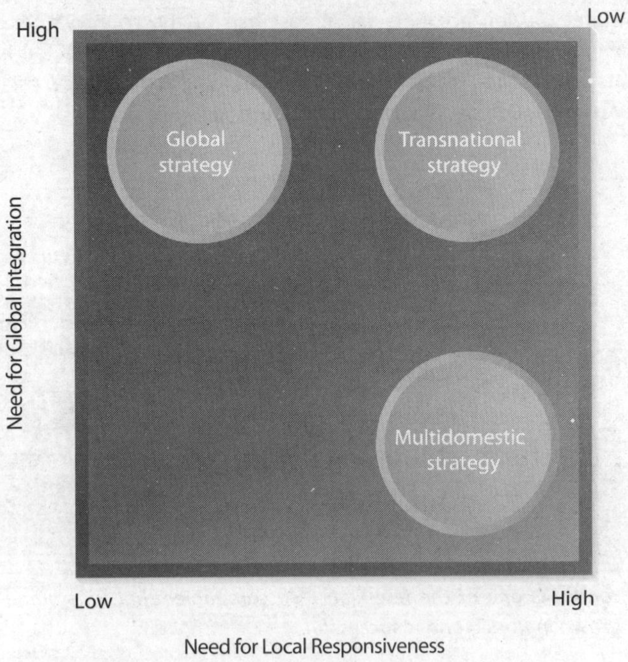

Figure 8.3 International corporate-level strategies

STRATEGIC FOCUS

8.1 Country Conditions Spawn Successful High Tech Firms in Emerging Markets

Few firms from large emerging economies have been more successful than SunTech Power Holdings, which manufactures solar panels in China for the global electric utilities industry. It was a "born global" firm founded in China and quickly began competing with large firms that dominated the industry such as Sharpe, Siemens, and BP Solar. It was initiated by Shi Zhengrong and he is still the CEO. He was allocated $6 million startup money from the government of Wuxi in China's Jiangsu province. Shi was trained in Australia at the University of New South Wales in Sydney, where he earned his Ph.D.

SunTech's biggest markets for solar panels and modules are in Europe, with German companies providing its largest amount of revenue. It is listed on the US stock exchange with an all-time stock price high of $85 in 2007. There was overcapacity in the industry in 2009, partly because SunTech spawned lots of imitators; however, iSuppli, a research company that provides analytical data for the solar industry, suggests that there will be 11.1 gigawatts of panels produced in 2009, which is up 62 per cent from 7.7 gigawatts in 2008. SunTech itself produces one gigawatt and hoped to produce 1.4 gigawatts by the end of 2009 and two gigawatts by 2010. However, SunTech's expansion plans are currently on hold until the financial crisis is over and the markets improve; in fact, SunTech had to lay off 800 employees in 2008.

The big advantage that SunTech has is its low-cost production system in China. It aims to have "grid parity," which means that the cost of producing solar energy is at the point where there is no difference between competing fossil fuels such as coal and natural gas relative to that produced by solar panels. Currently SunTech is producing at a cost of $0.35 per kilowatt hour whereas the grid parity cost is near $0.14. Although this suggests that the firm has a long way to go to realize grid parity, Shi believes it can be realized in several years given its low cost of production and improvements in technological efficiency. The company has improved the collective power of its solar panels primarily through advancements in silicon technology. Shi predicts that subsidies will improve and stimulate demand under the Obama administration, and that striving to reach grid parity will also help the company as it moves toward a "post carbon" future.

India's Suzlon has become a major player in the world due to a combination of favorable government policies, focus on a narrow set of businesses, primarily on wind energy, and an aggressive push abroad in terms of acquisition and alliances (We shall discuss more on Suzlon's alliances in Chapter 9). In 2010, Suzlon Energy Limited installed 1,500 WTGs across India with a combined capacity of 5,000 megawatts or 5 gigawatts, which will contribute to the country's low-carbon targets while ensuring energy security and rural development. According to the company, the combined capacity will electrify four million homes and reduce carbon emissions by about 8.5 million metric tons annually. With over 1,000 megawatts installed in three major Indian states, Suzlon accounts for almost half of the country's total wind installations. The company's global spread is reflected in its projects and markets portfolio—extending across Africa, Asia, Australia, Europe, and North and South America.

Fomichev Mikhail/Itar-Tass/Landov

Yandex is one of the few high tech companies that was home-grown in Russia and is successful.

Russia's largest online search company, Yandex, is equivalent to Google in the United States. Interestingly, Yandex started in the 1980s, long before Google's founders Sergey Brin and Larry Page had envisioned their company. Yandex arguably has superior search technology because of the peculiarities of the Russian language. Russian words often have 20 different endings that indicate their relationship to one another and make the language much more precise, but at the same time it makes searching for Russian words much more difficult than searching for English words. However, Yandex found a way to catch all of this phraseology and as such it controls 56 per cent of the search engine market share in Russia compared to Google's 23 per cent. More impressively, it has two thirds of all of the revenue from the search ads and draws three billion hits a month. Because of this FireFox has dropped Google as its default search engine in Russia in favor of Yandex.

Nonetheless, Yandex realizes that it must continue to innovate. For instance, it has an image search engine that eliminates repeated images and filters out faces, thus it provides better search capabilities for imaging. In addition, as mentioned in the chapter, Yandex has opened labs not far from Google's headquarters in Mountain View, California, with a staff of 20 or more engineers who not only index pages for a Russian audience but also keep abreast of technology developments that surface near Silicone Valley. According to Arkady Volozh, CEO of Yandex, Yahoo!, Microsoft, and Google have made repeated buyout offers for Yandex. Such offers suggest that Google and other companies would be interested in increasing their market share in Russia. One reason for this interest is that Russia has the fastest-growing Internet population in Europe. Google has increased its market share from 6 per cent in 2001 to 23 per cent in 2009; most likely because it hired engineers who understand the Russian language. One analyst indicated that due to the high demand for Internet service "Russia is a pivotal country for Google."

Yandex is one of the few high tech companies that was home-grown in Russia and is successful. The Russians are proud of this fact. The company hopes to continue to be successful and possibly even compete for market share in the United States. Yandex has been given the opportunity to list on the Nasdaq Exchange; however, it has put off doing an IPO because of the financial crisis.

Sources: J. Ioffe, 2009, The Russians are coming, Fortune, February 16, 36–38; B. Powell, 2009, China's new king of solar, Fortune, February 16, 94–97; G. L. White, 2009, Russia Web firm negotiates autonomy, *Wall Street Journal*, April 22, A10; 2008, China-based SunTech plans to triple US sales through acquisitions, residential sales, FinancialWire, http://www.financialwire.net, October 2; J. Bush, 2008, Where Google isn't Goliath: Russia's Yandex—set to go public on Nasdaq—is innovating in a hurry to hold off the US giant, *BusinessWeek*, http://www.businessweek.com, June 26; P. Ghemawat & T. Hout, 2008, Tomorrow's global giants: Not the usual suspects, Harvard Business Review, 86(11): 80–88; Suzlon information from company knowledge book and Web site www.suzlon.com; http://www.suzlon.com/pdf/Knowledge%20Book.pdf http://en.wikipedia.org/wiki/Wind_power_in_India; SEBI, 2005, Red herring prospectus of Suzlon, September 12, http://www.sebi.gov.in/dp/suz.pdf; Rowena F. Caronan, 2010, Suzlon reaches 5000 MW in home country and wind hotspot in India, www.ecoseed.org, September 29, http://www.ecoseed.org/en/business/renewable-energy/article/95-renewable-energy/8079-suzlon-reaches-5-000-mw-in-home-country-and-wind-hotspot-india; Joanna I. Lewis, 2007, A comparison of Wind Power Industry Development Strategies in India, Spain, and China, www.newenergyindia.org, July 19, http://www.newenergyindia.org/Comparison%20of%20Wind%20Energy%20Power%20Industry%20in%20India,%20China,%20and%20Spain.pdf; www.iloveindia.com, 2007, Suzlon energy Limited, July 21, http://www.iloveindia.com/economy-of-india/top-50-companies/suzlon.html.

Multidomestic Strategy

A **multidomestic strategy** is an international strategy in which strategic and operating decisions are decentralized to the strategic business unit in each country so as to allow that unit to tailor products to the local market.[55] A multidomestic strategy focuses on competition within each country. It assumes that the markets differ and therefore, are segmented by country boundaries. The multidomestic strategy uses a highly decentralized approach, allowing each division to focus on a geographic area, region, or country.[56] In other words, consumer needs and desires, industry conditions (e.g., the number and type of competitors), political and legal structures, and social norms vary by country. With multidomestic strategies, the country managers have the autonomy to customize the firm's products as necessary to meet the specific needs and preferences of local customers. Therefore, these strategies should maximize a firm's competitive response to the idiosyncratic requirements of each market.[57]

The use of multidomestic strategies usually expands the firm's local market share because the firm can pay attention to the needs of the local clientele.[58] However, the use of these strategies results in less knowledge sharing for the corporation as a whole because of the differences across markets, decentralization, and the different strategies employed by local country units.[59] Moreover, multidomestic strategies do not allow the development of economies of scale and thus can be more costly. As a result, firms employing a multidomestic strategy decentralize their strategic and operating decisions to the business units operating in each country. Historically, Unilever, a large European consumer products firm, has had a highly decentralized approach to managing its international operations. This approach allows regional managers considerable autonomy to adapt the product offerings to fit the market needs. However, more recently it has sought to have better coordination between its independent country subsidiaries and develop a strong global brand presence.[60]

Two companies that are in the same industry, are direct competitors worldwide and yet adopt different strategies are Unilever and Proctor & Gamble (P&G). Unilever believes strongly in a multidomestic strategy, with local products, local advertisements, and local methods of management. Some of its famous brands such as Dalda and Liril were developed solely for India. P&G, on the other hand, tends to adopt more uniform products, advertisements and practices all over the world, and introduces its products as worldwide brands. For example Tide detergent powder. Similarly, while Pepsi allows a great deal of adaptive freedom in the countries it operates in, Coca-Cola tends to adopt more uniform policies across different countries in the world. It must be noted that most of the FMCG and soft drinks products really do not have any global economies of scale in production, and the advantages of adaptation often outweigh those of global standardization.

Global Strategy

In contrast to a multidomestic strategy, a global strategy assumes more standardization of products across country markets.[61] As a result, a global strategy is centralized and controlled by the home office. The strategic business units operating in each country are assumed to be interdependent, and the home office attempts to achieve integration across these businesses.[62] The firm uses a **global strategy** to offer standardized products across country markets, with competitive strategy being dictated by the home office. Thus, a global strategy emphasizes economies of scale and offers greater opportunities to take innovations developed at the corporate level or in one country and utilize them in other markets.[63] Improvements in global accounting and financial reporting standards are facilitating this strategy.[64]

Although a global strategy produces lower risk, it may cause the firm to forego growth opportunities in local markets, either because those markets are less likely to be identified as opportunities or because the opportunities require that products be adapted to the local market.[65] The global strategy is not as responsive to local markets and is difficult to manage because of the need to coordinate strategies and operating decisions across country borders. Yahoo! and eBay experienced these challenges when they moved into specific Asian markets. For example, eBay was unsuccessful in both the Japanese and Chinese markets when attempting to export its business model and approach from North America to these two countries. It has reentered China but Meg Whitman, former CEO of eBay, suggested that she had no plans to reenter the Japanese market. Yahoo! has had rough times in China, going through several CEOs and trying to find the right formula to compete effectively in the Chinese market.[66] Also, as the Opening Case indicates, Google has had difficulty penetrating foreign markets such as China and competing against local competitors such as Baidu.

Achieving efficient operations with a global strategy requires sharing resources and facilitating coordination and cooperation across country boundaries, which in turn require centralization and headquarters control. Furthermore, research suggests that the performance of the global strategy is enhanced if it is deployed in areas where regional integration among countries is occurring, such as the European Union.[67] Many Japanese firms have successfully used the global strategy.[68]

CEMEX is the third largest cement company in the world, behind France's Lafarge and Switzerland's Holcim, and is the largest producer of ready mix, a prepackaged product that contains all the ingredients needed to make localized cement products.

CEMEX has strong market power in the Americas as well as in Europe. CEMEX serves customers in more than 50 countries with more than 50,000 employees globally. Because CEMEX pursues a global strategy effectively, its centralization process has facilitated the integration of several businesses it acquired in the United States, Europe, and Asia. To integrate its businesses globally, CEMEX uses the Internet to improve logistics and manage an extensive supply network, thereby increasing revenue and reducing costs. Connectivity between the operations in different countries and universal standards dominates its approach. However, because of its recent acquisition of Ringer, a large Australian cement producer, it took on too much debt during the downturn and has had a very difficult time meeting its debt obligations.[69] Because of increasing global competition and the need to be cost efficient while simultaneously providing high-quality differentiated products, a number of firms have begun to pursue the transnational strategy, which is described next.

Transnational Strategy

A **transnational strategy** is an international strategy through which the firm seeks to achieve both global efficiency and local responsiveness. Realizing these goals is difficult: One requires close global coordination while the other requires local flexibility. "Flexible coordination"—building a shared vision and individual commitment through an integrated network—is required to implement the transnational strategy. Such integrated networks allow a firm to manage its connections with customers, suppliers, partners, and other parties more efficiently rather than using arm's-length transactions.[70] The transnational strategy is difficult to use because of its conflicting goals (see Chapter 11 for more on the implementation of this and other corporate-level international strategies). On the positive side, the effective implementation of a transnational strategy often produces higher performance than does the implementation of either the multidomestic or global international corporate-level strategies, although it is difficult to accomplish.[71]

Transnational strategies are challenging to implement but are becoming increasingly necessary to compete in international markets. The growing number of global competitors heightens the requirement to hold costs down. However, the increasing sophistication of markets with greater information flow (e.g., based on the diffusion of the Internet) and the desire for specialized products to meet consumers' needs pressures firms to differentiate and even customize their products in local markets. Differences in culture and institutional environments also require firms to adapt their products and approaches to local environments. However, some argue that most multinationals pursue more regional strategies and as such transnational strategies and structures may not be as necessary as once thought.[72]

To help decide the degree of integration and adaptation needed for a global strategy, Prahalad and Doz developed a simple model, named Integration-Responsiveness (IR) framework. It maps the degree of integration needed for each *activity*, such as R&D, production, marketing etc. The point here is that the degree of adaptation required may differ across functions: thus, while a firm may completely centralize R&D, it may decentralize production. Managers can analyze, function by function, which activities are best decentralized to each country and which to be centralized, depending on the advantages and disadvantages of each.[73]

Environmental Trends

Although the transnational strategy is difficult to implement, emphasis on global efficiency is increasing as more industries begin to experience global competition. To add to the problem, an increased emphasis on local requirements means that global goods and services often demand some customization to meet government regulations within particular countries or to fit customer tastes and preferences. In addition, most multinational firms desire coordination and sharing of resources across country markets to hold down costs, as illustrated by the CEMEX example.[74] Furthermore, some products and industries may be more suited than others for standardization across country borders.

As a result, some large multinational firms with diverse products employ a multidomestic strategy with certain product lines and a global strategy with others. Many multinational firms may require this type of flexibility if they are to be strategically competitive, in part due to trends that change over time. Two important trends are the liability of foreignness, which has increased since the terrorist attacks and the war in Iraq, and regionalization.

Liability of Foreignness

The dramatic success of Japanese firms such as Toyota and Sony in the United States and other international markets in the 1980s was a powerful jolt to the US managers and awakened them to the importance of international competition in markets that were rapidly becoming global. In the twenty-first century, China, India, Brazil, and Russia represent major international market opportunities for firms from many countries, including the United States, Japan, Korea, and the European Union.[75] However, there are legitimate concerns about the relative attractiveness of global strategies, due to the extra costs incurred to pursue internationalization, or the liability of foreignness relative to domestic competitors in a host country.[76] This is illustrated by the experience of Walt Disney Company in opening theme parks in foreign countries. For example, Disney suffered "lawsuits in France, at Disneyland Paris, because of the lack of fit between its transferred personnel policies and the French employees charged to enact them."[77] Disney executives learned from this experience in building the firm's newest theme park in Hong Kong.

Research shows that global strategies are not as prevalent as they once were and are still difficult to implement, even when using Internet-based strategies.[78] In addition, the amount of competition vying for a limited amount of resources and customers can limit firms' focus to regional rather than global markets. A regional focus allows firms to marshal their resources to compete effectively in regional markets rather than spreading their limited resources across many international markets.[79]

As such, firms may focus less on truly global markets and more on regional adaptation. Although parallel developments in the Internet and mobile telecommunication facilitate communications across the globe, as noted earlier, the implementation of Web-based strategies also requires local adaptation. The globalization of businesses with local strategies is demonstrated by the strategy that Google is using (see the Opening Case) by developing an online music download business in China.

Regionalization

Regionalization is a second trend that has become more common in global markets. Because a firm's location can affect its strategic competitiveness,[80] it must decide whether to compete in all or many global markets, or to focus on a particular region or regions. Competing in all markets provides economies that can be achieved because of the combined market size. Research suggests that firms that compete in risky emerging markets can also have higher performance.[81]

However, a firm that competes in industries where the international markets differ greatly (in which it must employ a multidomestic strategy) may wish to narrow its focus to a particular region of the world. In doing so, it can better understand the cultures, legal and social norms, and other factors that are important for effective competition in those markets. For example, a firm may focus on Far East markets only rather than competing simultaneously in the Middle East, Europe, and the Far East. Or the firm may choose a region of the world where the markets are more similar and some coordination and sharing of resources would be possible. In this way, the firm may be able not only to better understand the markets in which it competes, but also to achieve some economies, even though it may have to employ a multidomestic strategy. For instance, research suggests that most large retailers are better at focusing on a particular region rather than being truly global.[82] Firms commonly focus much of their international market entries into countries adjacent to their home country, which might be referred to as their home region.[83]

Countries that develop trade agreements to increase the economic power of their regions may promote regional strategies. The European Union (EU) and South America's Organization of American States (OAS) are country associations that developed trade agreements to promote the flow of trade across country boundaries within their respective regions.[84] Many European firms acquire and integrate their businesses in Europe to better coordinate pan-European brands as the EU creates more unity in European markets. With this process likely to continue as new countries are added to the agreement, some international firms may prefer to pursue regional strategies versus global strategies because the size of the market is increasing.[85]

The North American Free Trade Agreement (NAFTA), signed by the United States, Canada, and Mexico, facilitates free trade across country borders in North America. NAFTA loosens restrictions on international strategies within this region and provides greater opportunity for regional international strategies.[86] NAFTA does not exist for the sole purpose of US businesses moving across its borders. In fact, Mexico is the number two trading partner of the United States, and NAFTA greatly increased Mexico's exports to the United States. Research suggests that managers of small- and medium-sized firms are influenced by the strategy they implement (those with a differentiation strategy are more positively disposed to the agreement than are those pursuing a cost leadership strategy) and by their experience and rivalry with exporting firms.[87] SAARC (South Asian Association for Regional Cooperation) is an example of a regional group of countries in Asia trying to get mutual cooperation.

SAARC (South Asian Association for Regional Cooperation) is an example of a regional group of countries in Asia trying to get mutual cooperation.

Most firms enter regional markets sequentially, beginning in markets with which they are more familiar. They also introduce their largest and strongest lines of business into these markets first, followed by their other lines of business once the first lines achieve success. They also usually invest in the same area as their original investment location.[88] However, research also suggests that the size of the market and industry characteristics can influence this decision.[89]

After the firm selects its international strategies and decides whether to employ them in regional or world markets, it must choose a market entry mode.[90]

Choice of International Entry Mode

International expansion is accomplished by exporting products, participating in licensing arrangements, forming strategic alliances, making acquisitions, and establishing new wholly owned subsidiaries. These means of entering international markets and their characteristics are shown in Table 8.1. Each means of market entry has its advantages and disadvantages. Thus, choosing the appropriate mode or path to enter international markets affects the firm's performance in those markets.

Exporting

Many industrial firms begin their international expansion by exporting goods or services to other countries.[91] Exporting does not require the expense of establishing operations in the host countries, but exporters must establish some means of marketing and distributing their products. Usually, exporting firms develop contractual arrangements with host-country firms.

The disadvantages of exporting include the often-high costs of transportation and tariffs placed on some incoming goods. Furthermore, the exporter has less control over the marketing and distribution of its products in the host country and must either pay the distributor or allow the distributor to add to the price to recoup its costs and earn a profit.

As a result, it may be difficult to market a competitive product through exporting or to provide a product that is customized to each international market.[92] However, evidence suggests that cost leadership strategies enhance the performance of exports in developed countries, whereas differentiation strategies with larger scale are more successful in the emerging economies.[93] Most exports from India to developed countries are based on their cost advantage, which translates into a lower price.

Firms export mostly to countries that are closest to their facilities because of the lower transportation costs and the usually greater similarity between geographic neighbors. For example, United States' NAFTA partners Mexico and Canada account for more than half of the goods exported from Texas. The Internet has also made exporting easier. Even small firms can access critical information about foreign markets, examine a target market, research the competition, and find lists of potential customers.[94] Governments also use the Internet to facilitate applications for export and import licenses. Although terrorist threat is likely to slow its progress, high-speed technology is still the wave of the future.[95]

Small businesses are most likely to use the exporting mode of international entry; up to 50 per cent of small US firms will be involved in international trade by 2018, most of them through export.[96] Currency exchange rates are one of the most significant problems faced by small businesses. The United States in recent years has supported a weak dollar against the euro, which makes imports to the United States more expensive to US consumers and US goods less costly to foreign buyers, thus providing some economic relief for US exporters.[97]

Much has been made of the so called flat world, with progressively reducing trade barriers, a thesis put forward by Thomas Friedman. But, as Ghemawat has argued and supported by his extensive research, the vast majority of international trade takes place among adjacent countries, and countries that are similar in their stages of development and culture.[98] Thus, the world without barriers is largely a myth. Exporters from the developing world have experienced numerous barriers to entry from developed markets.

Licensing

Licensing is an increasingly common form of organizational network, particularly among smaller firms.[99] A licensing arrangement allows a foreign company to purchase the right to manufacture and sell the firm's products within a host country or set of countries.[100] The licensor is normally paid a royalty on each unit produced and sold. The licensee takes the risks and makes the monetary investments in facilities for manufacturing, marketing, and distributing the goods or services. As a result, licensing is possibly the least costly form of international expansion.

Table 8.1 Global market entry: choice of entry

Type of Entry	Characteristics
Exporting	High cost, low control
Licensing	Low cost, low risk, little control, low returns
Strategic alliances	Shared costs, shared resources, shared risks, problems of integration (e.g., two corporate cultures)
Acquisition	Quick access to new market, high cost, complex negotiations, problems of merging with domestic operations
New wholly owned subsidiary	Complex, often costly, time consuming, high risk, maximum control, potential above-average returns

China is a large and growing market for cigarettes, while the US market is shrinking due to health concerns. But US cigarette firms have had trouble entering the Chinese market because state-owned tobacco firms have lobbied against such entry. As such, cigarette company Philip Morris International (PMI), which was separated from its former parent company Altria, had an incentive to form a deal with these state-owned firms. Such an agreement provides the state-owned firms access to the most famous brand in the world, Marlboro. Accordingly, both the Chinese firms and PMI have formed a licensing agreement to take advantage of the opportunity as China opens its markets more fully.[101] Because it is a licensing agreement rather than a foreign direct investment by PMI, China maintains control of the distribution. However, the Chinese state-owned tobacco monopoly, as part of the agreement, also gets to have PMI's help to distribute its own brands in select foreign markets. "The question is whether it can pluck three cigarette brands—RGD, Harmony and Dubliss—from relative obscurity and elevate them to an international, or at least regional, presence."[102]

Licensing is also a way to expand returns based on prior innovations.[103] Even if product life cycles are short, licensing may be a useful tool. For instance, because the toy industry faces relentless change and unpredictable buying patterns, licensing is used and contracts are often completed in foreign markets where labor may be less expensive.[104] Google, as the Opening Case illustrates, facilitated license agreements with the top four music producers in support of its strategy to gain more market share from Baidu in China.

Licensing also has disadvantages. For example, it gives the firm little control over the manufacture and marketing of its products in other countries. Thus, license deals must be structured properly.[105] In addition, licensing provides the least potential returns, because returns must be shared between the licensor and the licensee. Additionally, the international firm may learn the technology and produce and sell a similar competitive product after the license expires. Komatsu, for example, first licensed much of its technology from International Harvester, Bucyrus-Erie, and Cummins Engine to compete against Caterpillar in the earthmoving equipment business. Komatsu then dropped these licenses and developed its own products using the technology it had gained from the US companies.[106] Bajaj Auto had its teeth cut through licensing from Piaggio of Italy, and produced Vespa scooters, but developed its own capability to develop independent models, and the licensing from Vespa was stopped. Tata Motors, in its earlier years, made its trucks through licensing from Mercedes-Benz of Germany, but discontinued its licensing to not only produce, but export its own vehicles. Franchising is a particular kind of licensing, and certain companies such as McDonalds and some hotels have used this strategy for expansion. Starwood Hotels & Resorts Worldwide Inc., for example, uses a franchise licensing arrangement and does not own most of its hotels. This, however, has its own hazards. While focusing on other brands, Starwood has let its Sheraton brand slip in quality. Given the current economic downturn, it is going to be difficult to get the owners to invest in needed design improvements and upgrades, especially given the owner differences in varying geographic markets.[107] Thus licensing can also lead to inflexibilities, and as such it is important that a firm think ahead and consider the consequences of each entry, especially in international markets.[108]

Strategic Alliances

In recent years, strategic alliances have become a popular means of international expansion.[109] Strategic alliances allow firms to share the risks and the resources required to enter international markets.[110] Moreover, strategic alliances can facilitate the development of new core competencies that contribute to the firm's future strategic competitiveness.[111]

As explained in the Opening Case, GM formed a joint venture with SAIC. This venture produced Buick and Cadillac automobiles for the Chinese market. The alliance has been highly successful for both firms. Similar to this example, most international strategic alliances are formed with a host-country firm that knows and understands the competitive conditions, legal and social norms, and cultural idiosyncrasies of the country, which helps the expanding firm manufacture and market a competitive product. Often, firms in emerging economies want to form international alliances and ventures to gain access to sophisticated technologies that are new to them. Gaining access to new technologies and markets is one of ZTE's goals in seeking alliances with the mobile phone systems of Sprint, AT&T, and Verizon. ZTE, as introduced in the Opening Case, is a telecommunications network gear producer; it also produces mobile phones. It now is working on agreements with these three phone companies to produce "smartphones" for 3G and 4G systems to advance its product portfolio.[112] This type of arrangement can also benefit the non-emerging economy firm, in that it gains access to a new market and does not have to pay tariffs to do so (because it is partnering with a local company). In return, the host-country firm may find its new access to the expanding firm's technology and innovative products attractive.

Each partner in an alliance brings knowledge or resources to the partnership. Indeed, partners often enter an alliance with the purpose of learning new capabilities.[113] Common among those desired capabilities are technological skills. However, for technological knowledge to be transferred in an alliance usually requires trust between the partners.[114] Managing these expectations can facilitate improved performance.

The alliance between GM and SAIC has been successful over the years because of the way it is managed. In fact, both firms are pleased with the outcomes. Research suggests that company executives need to know their own firm well, understand factors that determine the norms in different countries, know how the firm is seen by other partners in the venture, and learn to adapt while remaining consistent with their own company cultural values. Such a multifaceted and versatile approach has helped the GM and SAIC alliance succeed.

Mario Tama/Getty Images

ZTE Corporation, one of the largest Chinese telecommunication equipment manufacturers, has set the goal of becoming the third largest global provider of handsets by 2014 based on sales of its newly unveiled portfolio of smartphones and other wireless devices.

Not all alliances are successful; in fact, many fail.[115] The primary reasons for failure include incompatible partners and conflict between the partners. International strategic alliances are especially difficult to manage. Several factors may cause a relationship to sour. Trust between the partners is critical and is affected by at least four fundamental issues: the initial condition of the relationship, the negotiation process to arrive at an agreement, partner interactions, and external events.[116] Trust is also influenced by the country cultures involved in the alliance or joint venture.[117]

Research has shown that equity-based alliances, over which a firm has more control, tend to produce more positive returns.[118] (Strategic alliances are discussed in greater depth in Chapter 9.) However, if trust is required to develop new capabilities in a research collaboration, equity can serve as a barrier to the necessary relationship building. If conflict in a strategic alliance or joint venture is not manageable, an acquisition may be a better option.[119] Alliances can also lead to acquisitions, which is discussed next.

Acquisitions

As free trade has continued to expand in global markets, cross-border acquisitions have also been increasing significantly. In 2008, cross-border acquisitions comprised about 40 per cent of all acquisitions completed worldwide, down from 45 per cent in previous years.[120] As explained in Chapter 7, acquisitions can provide quick access to a new market. In fact, acquisitions often provide the fastest and the largest initial international expansion of any of the alternatives.[121] Thus, entry is much quicker than by other modes. For example, while Wal-Mart entered India through an alliance with Bharti group (due to the regulatory regime in India regarding entry of foreign firms in the retail sector), in Germany and the United Kingdom it did so by acquiring local firms. Later, Wal-Mart withdrew from Germany.[122]

Although acquisitions have become a popular mode of entering international markets, they are not without costs. International acquisitions carry some of the disadvantages of domestic acquisitions (see Chapter 7). In addition, they can be expensive and also often require debt financing, which carries an extra cost. International negotiations for acquisitions can be exceedingly complex and are generally more complicated than domestic acquisitions. For example, acquisitions are being used by firms in emerging economies to enter developed economies. China has been buying firms in foreign countries that have assets in natural resources. For instance, China Minmetals, a state-owned mining firm, tried to acquire Oz Minerals, the world's second largest zinc miner based in Australia. However, this acquisition, like many others, has been opposed by the government because of the potential for a sovereign power to take control of important natural resources.[123] We have seen in Chapter 7 how Indian firms such as ONGC acquired foreign companies for their resources.

Interestingly, acquirers make fewer acquisitions in countries with significant corruption. They choose to use international joint ventures instead. However, these ventures fail more often, although this is moderated by the acquiring firms' past experience with such deals. When acquisitions are made in such countries, acquirers commonly pay smaller premiums to buy the target firms.[124]

Dealing with the legal and regulatory requirements in the target firm's country and obtaining appropriate information to negotiate an agreement are frequent problems. Finally, the merging of the new firm into the acquiring firm is often more complex than in domestic acquisitions. The acquiring firm must deal not only with different corporate cultures, but also with potentially different social cultures and practices.[125] These differences make the integration of the two firms after the acquisition more challenging; it is difficult to capture the potential synergy when integration is slowed or stymied because of cultural differences.[126] Therefore, while international acquisitions have been popular because of the rapid access to new markets they provide, they also carry with them important costs and multiple risks.

SAIC acquired assets of the MG Rover Group, the British auto producer, which was insolvent at the time. This acquisition gave the Chinese firm an entry point into Europe and an opportunity to establish its own brand through the MG Rover label. SAIC previously considered a joint venture but decided to make the acquisition bid, worth $1.04 million. However, SAIC experienced formidable government opposition in the United Kingdom and had to clear extra regulatory hurdles to receive approval. By 2008 it had not produced one of the MG roadsters that it had intended because of "quality issues."[127]

Tata Motors' acquisition of Jaguar and Land Rover (JLR) units from the US-based auto manufacturer Ford Motor Company for $2.3 billion, on a cash free-debt free basis in 2008, created considerable difficulties for Tata Motors. The acquisition was intended to reduce Tata Motors' dependence on the Indian market, which accounted for 90 per cent of its sales and also provide it with the unique opportunity to move into premium segment with access to world class iconic brands and build a comprehensive product portfolio with a global footprint immediately. Tata Motors had to incur a huge capital expenditure as it needed to invest another $1 billion in JLR in addition to the amount spent on the acquisition. With the onset of recession, market conditions were extremely tough, especially in the key US and European market, making the investment look somewhat mistimed. Tata Motors also had to invest a lot in brand building. Along with retaining present customers and developing new customers, they needed to instill confidence in distributors worldwide that the Tata's are moving to add value to the brand market value.

A big challenge for the Tata's was to make sure that they can enhance both Jaguar and Land Rover in their own terms by not diluting the brand names of Jaguar and Land Rover with a lower-cost image as there is a huge gap between the Tata domestic products and these luxury brands. They needed to ensure that Land Rover and Jaguar achieve their potential and manage them as if they were luxury manufacturers themselves. They do value engineering on the backend but should also give the resources necessary for maintaining and enhancing the brands. Also, there were differences in terms of how you produce a very high-end automobile and a medium-priced automobile. To make the business profitable, especially with Jaguar, cost reduction was essential. The focus needed to be on adding innovative processes and using cheaper material.

According to Harbir Singh, a Wharton Management professor, "I think what the Tatas can do differently is to manage the supply chain effectively and take advantage of their experience in managing manufacturing companies in England and in Europe, specifically with Corus, that they have had some experience with. And to preserve the sources of value where they are and enhance them where they are, they should try that and not integrate quite as much as Ford and Jaguar did with the Jaguar X type and the Ford Lincoln counterpart."[128]

But Tata Motors seem to have met these challenges well. The third quarter of year 2010 year ended with the JLR making a good profit, largely due to sale of luxury cars in emerging markets, especially China.[129]

New Wholly Owned Subsidiary

The establishment of a new wholly owned subsidiary is referred to as a **greenfield venture.** The process of creating such ventures is often complex and potentially costly, but it affords maximum control to the firm and has the most potential to provide above-average returns. This potential is especially true of firms with strong intangible capabilities that might be leveraged through a greenfield venture.[130] A firm maintains full control of its operations with a greenfield venture. More control is especially advantageous if the firm has proprietary technology. Research also suggests that "wholly owned subsidiaries and expatriate staff are preferred" in service industries where "close contacts with end customer" and "high levels of professional skills, specialized know-how, and customization" are required.[131] Other research suggests that greenfield investments are more prominent where physical capital-intensive plants are planned and that acquisitions are more likely preferred when a firm is human capital intensive—that is, where a strong local degree of unionization and high cultural distance would cause difficulty in transferring knowledge to a host nation through a greenfield approach.[132]

The risks are also high, however, because of the costs of establishing a new business operation in a new country. The firm may have to acquire the knowledge and expertise of the existing market by hiring either host-country nationals, possibly from competitors, or through consultants, which can be costly. Still, the firm maintains control over the technology, marketing, and distribution of its products. Furthermore, the company must build new manufacturing facilities, establish distribution networks, and learn and implement appropriate marketing strategies to compete in the new market.[133] Research also suggests that when the country risk is high, firms prefer to enter with joint ventures instead of greenfield investments in order to manage the risk. However, if they have previous experience in a country, they prefer to use a wholly owned greenfield venture rather than a joint venture.[134]

The globalization of the air cargo industry has implications for companies such as UPS and FedEx. The impact of this globalization is especially pertinent to China and the Asia Pacific region. China's air cargo market is expected to grow 11 per cent per year through 2023. Accordingly, in 2008, both UPS and FedEx opened new hub operations in Shanghai and Gangzhou, respectively; each firm has about 6,000 employees in China. These hubs facilitated their distribution and logistics business during the Olympics in Beijing. These investments are wholly owned because these firms need to maintain the integrity of their IT and logistics systems in order to maximize efficiency. Greenfield ventures also help the firms to maintain the proprietary nature of their systems.[135]

Dynamics of Mode of Entry

A firm's mode of entry into international markets is affected by a number of factors.[136] Initially, market entry is often achieved through export, which requires no foreign manufacturing expertise and investment only in distribution. Licensing can facilitate the product improvements necessary to enter foreign markets, as in the Komatsu example. Strategic alliances have been popular because they allow a firm to connect with an experienced partner already in the targeted market. Strategic alliances also reduce risk through the sharing of costs. Therefore, all three modes—export, licensing, and strategic alliance—are good tactics for early market development. Also, the strategic alliance is often used in more uncertain situations, such as an emerging economy where there is significant risk, such as Venezuela or Colombia.[137] However, if intellectual property rights in the emerging economy are not well protected, the number of firms in the industry is growing fast, and the need for global integration is high, a joint venture or wholly owned subsidiary entry mode is preferred.[138]

To secure a stronger presence in international markets, acquisitions or greenfield ventures may be required. Aerospace firms Airbus and Boeing have used joint ventures, especially in large markets, to facilitate entry, while military equipment firms such as Thales SA have used acquisitions to build a global presence. Japanese auto manufacturers, such as Toyota, have gained a presence in the United States through both greenfield ventures and joint ventures. Because of Toyota's highly efficient manufacturing process, it wants to maintain control over its auto manufacturing when possible. It has engaged in a joint venture in the United States with General Motors,[139] but most of its manufacturing facilities are greenfield investments. It opened a new plant in Canada in 2008 and planned opening a new plant in Mississippi in 2010, although this project may be delayed or postponed given the economic downturn.[140] Therefore, Toyota uses some form of foreign direct investment (e.g., greenfield ventures and joint ventures) rather than another mode of entry (although it may use exporting in new markets as it did in China). Car manufacturers Ford and General Motors have set up greenfield ventures in India, while Honda preferred a joint venture with the Hero group to produce its motorcycles. Recently that alliance has come to an end, and Honda seems to be planning to set up a greenfield venture to produce its motorcycles. Both acquisitions and greenfield ventures are likely to come at later stages in the development of an international strategy.

Large diversified business groups, often found in emerging economies, not only gain resources through diversification but also have specialized abilities in managing differences in inward and outward flows of foreign direct investment.[141] For instance, in India such groups have facilitated the development of a thriving pharmaceutical industry.[142]

Thus, to enter a global market, a firm selects the entry mode that is best suited to the situation at hand. In some instances, the various options will be followed sequentially, beginning with exporting and ending with greenfield ventures. In other cases, the firm may use several, but not all, of the different entry modes, each in different markets. The decision regarding which entry mode to use is primarily a result of the industry's competitive conditions, the country's situation and government policies, and the firm's own unique set of resources, capabilities, and core competencies.

Strategic Competitive Outcomes

After its international strategy and mode of entry have been selected, the firm turns its attention to implementation issues (see Chapter 11). Implementation is highly important, because international expansion is risky, making it difficult to achieve a competitive advantage (see Figure 8.1). The probability the firm will be successful with an international strategy increases when it is effectively implemented.

International Diversification and Returns

Firms have numerous reasons to diversify internationally.[143] **International diversification** is a strategy through which a firm expands the sales of its goods or services across the borders of global regions and countries into different geographic locations or markets. Because of its potential advantages, international diversification should be related positively to firms' returns. Research has shown that, as international diversification increases, firms' returns decrease initially but then increase quickly as firms learn to manage international expansion.[144] In fact, the stock market is particularly sensitive to investments in international markets. Firms that are broadly diversified into multiple international markets usually achieve the most positive stock returns, especially when they diversify geographically into core business areas.[145] Many factors contribute to the positive effects of international diversification, such as private versus government ownership, potential economies of scale and experience, location advantages, increased market size, and the opportunity to stabilize returns. The stabilization of returns helps reduce a firm's overall risk.[146] All of these outcomes can be achieved by smaller and newer ventures, as well as by larger and established firms.

Toyota has found that international diversification allows, it to better exploit its core competencies, because sharing knowledge resources across subsidiaries can produce synergy. Also, a firm's returns may affect its decision to diversify internationally. For example, poor returns in a domestic market may encourage a firm to expand internationally in order to enhance its profit potential. In addition, internationally diversified firms may have access to more flexible labor markets, as the Japanese do in the United States, and may thereby benefit from scanning international markets for competition and market opportunities. Also, through global networks with assets in many countries, firms can develop more flexible structures to adjust to changes that might occur. "Offshore outsourcing" has created significant value-creation opportunities for firms engaged in it, especially as firms move into markets with more flexible labor markets. Furthermore, offshoring increases exports to firms that receive the offshoring contract.[147]

International Diversification and Innovation

In Chapter 1, we indicated that the development of new technology is at the heart of strategic competitiveness. As noted in Porter's model (see Figure 8.2), a nation's competitiveness depends, in part, on the capacity of its industry to innovate. Eventually and inevitably, competitors outperform firms that fail to innovate and improve their operations and products. Therefore, the only way to sustain a competitive advantage is to upgrade it continually.[148]

International diversification provides the potential for firms to achieve greater returns on their innovations (through larger or more numerous markets) and reduces the often substantial risks of R&D investments. Therefore, international diversification provides incentives for firms to innovate. Additionally, the firm uses its primary resources and capabilities to diversify internationally and thus earn further returns on these capabilities (e.g., capability to innovate).[149]

In addition, international diversification may be necessary to generate the resources required to sustain a large-scale R&D operation. An environment of rapid technological obsolescence makes it difficult to invest in new technology and the capital-intensive operations necessary to compete in this environment. Firms operating solely in domestic markets may find such investments difficult because of the length of time required to recoup the original investment. If the time is extended, it may not be possible to recover the investment before the technology becomes obsolete. However, international diversification improves a firm's ability to appropriate additional returns from innovation before competitors can overcome the initial competitive advantage created by the innovation. In addition, firms moving into international markets are exposed to new products and processes. If they learn about those products and processes and integrate this knowledge into their operations, further innovation can be developed. To incorporate the learning into their own R&D processes, firms must manage those processes effectively in order to absorb and use the new knowledge to create further innovations.[150]

The relationship among international diversification, innovation, and returns is complex. Some level of performance is necessary to provide the resources to generate international diversification, which in turn provides incentives and resources to invest in research and development. The latter, if done appropriately, should enhance the returns of the firm, which then provides more resources for continued international diversification and investment in R&D. Of course, these relationships have to be managed well by a firm's top level managers. Evidence suggests that more culturally diverse top management teams often have a greater knowledge of international markets and their idiosyncrasies, but their orientation to expand internationally can be affected by the nature of their compensation.[151] (Top management teams are discussed further in Chapter 12.) Moreover, managing the diverse business units of a multinational firm requires skill, not only in managing a decentralized set of businesses, but also coordinating diverse points of view derived from regionalized businesses without descending into chaos. Firms that are able to do this will challenge the best global industry incumbents.[152] This topic will be addressed next.

Complexity of Managing Multinational Firms

Although firms can realize many benefits by implementing an international strategy, doing so is complex and can produce greater uncertainty.[153] For example, multiple risks are involved when a firm operates in several different countries. Firms can grow only so large and diverse before becoming unmanageable, or before the costs of managing them exceed their benefits. Managers are constrained by the complexity and sometimes by the culture and institutional systems within which they must operate.[154] The complexities involved in managing diverse international operations are shown in the problems experienced by even high-performing firms such as Toyota. Toyota became overly focused on sales in the North American market and began to experience quality problems (i.e., increased number of recalls) and reduced customer satisfaction. It was also late in entering the Chinese market with manufacturing and as a result, it was behind the market leaders, Volkswagen and GM. However, by 2008 it had recovered and actually was outselling both firms in China, but only in passenger cars.[155] Other complexities include the highly competitive nature of global markets, multiple cultural environments, potentially rapid shifts in the value of different currencies, and the instability of some national governments.

Risks in an International Environment

International diversification carries multiple risks. Because of these risks, international expansion is difficult to implement and manage. The chief risks are political and economic. Specific examples of political and economic risks are shown in Figure 8.4.

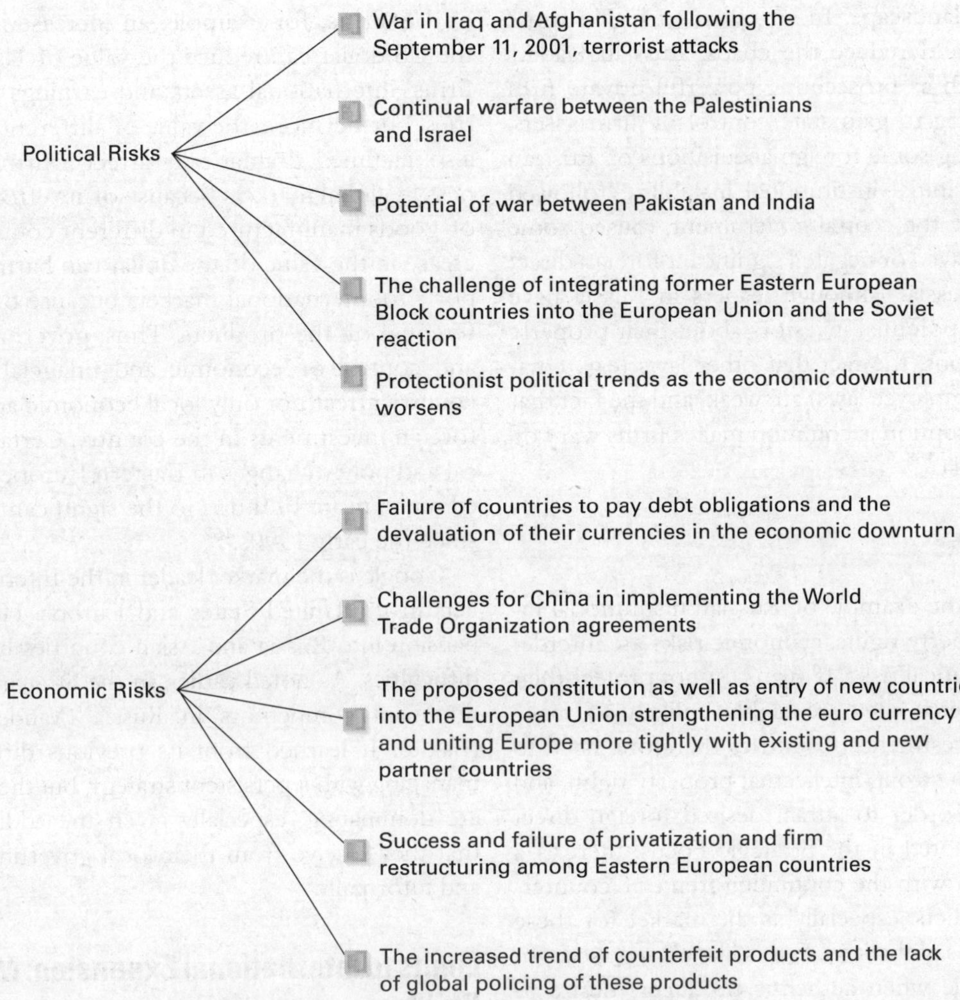

Figure 8.4 Risk in the international environment

Sources: 2009, Euro-Zone PPI posts biggest annual drop in 22 years, Wall Street Journal, http://www.online.wsj.com, May 5; 2009, The nuts and bolts come apart: As global demand contracts, trade is slumping and protectionism rising, Economist, http://www.economist.com, March 26; 2009, New fund, old fundamentals: Has the IMF changed or has the world? Economist, http://www.economist.com, April 30; 2009, Competitive devaluations, Financial Times, http://www .ft.com, March 14; D. Bilefsky, 2009, A crisis is separating Eastern Europe's strong from its weak, New York Times, http://www.nytimes.com, February 23; I. Dreyer, 2009, Mending EU-China trade ties, Wall Street Journal, http://www.online.wsj.com, May 6; J. Garten, 2009, The dangers of turning inward, Wall Street Journal, http://www.online.wsj.com, March 5; S. Levine, 2009, Emergency loans for European banks: Three international development banks pledged nearly $30 billion to shore up the troubled Eastern European banking system, BusinessWeek, http://www.businessweek.com, February 28; M. Singh, 2009, India launches a toy trade war with China, Time, http://www.time.com, February 6; 2008, The best way to do business with Russia, Financial Times, http:// www.ft.com, August 21; 2008, Strong dollar, weak dollar, Russia Today, http://www.russiatoday.com, October 28; J. Barnham, 2008, China's pirates move up value chain, Security Management, June 44; L. Burkitt, 2008, Fighting fakes, Forbes, August 11, 44; B. Szlanko, 2008, Will the crisis spur Hungary to reform? BusinessWeek, http://www.businessweek.com, November, 13; B. Szlanko, Europe: Tougher than it looks on Russia, BusinessWeek, http://www.businessweek .com, September 4; C.-C. Tschang, 2008, Currency stalemate at US-China meeting, BusinessWeek, http://www.businessweek.com, December 5.

Political Risks

Political risks are risks related to instability in national governments and to war, both civil and international. Instability in a national government creates numerous problems, including economic risks and uncertainty created by government regulation; the existence of many, possibly conflicting, legal authorities or corruption; and the potential nationalization of private assets.[156] Foreign firms that invest in another country may have concerns about the stability of the national government and the effects of unrest and government instability on their investments or assets.[157]

Russia has experienced a relatively high level of institutional instability in the years following its revolutionary transition to a more democratic government. Decentralized political control and frequent changes in policies created chaos for many, but especially for those in the business landscape. In an effort to regain more central control and reduce the chaos, Russian leaders took actions such as prosecuting powerful private firm executives, seeking to gain state control of firm assets, and not approving some foreign acquisitions of Russian businesses. The initial institutional instability, followed by the actions of the central government, caused some firms to have delayed or negated significant foreign direct investment in Russia. Although leaders in Russia have tried to reassure potential investors about their property rights, prior actions, the fact that other laws (e.g., environmental and employee laws) are weak, and the fact that government corruption is common makes firms wary of investing in Russia.[158]

Economic Risks

As illustrated in the example of Russian institutional instability and property rights, economic risks are interdependent with political risks. If firms cannot protect their intellectual property, they are highly unlikely to make foreign direct investments. Countries therefore, need to create and sustain strong intellectual property rights and enforce them in order to attract desired foreign direct investment. As noted in the Strategic Focus, there is a growing problem with the continuing trend of counterfeit or fake products, especially as the market for these products becomes globalized. Firms like eBay get caught up in the struggle when authentic producers desire to punish the counterfeit producers for selling products on the Internet.

Another economic risk is the perceived security risk of a foreign firm acquiring firms that have key natural resources or firms that may be considered strategic in regard to intellectual property. For instance, many Chinese and Indian firms have been buying natural resource firms in Europe, Australia and Latin America as well as manufacturing assets in the United States. This has made the governments of the key resource firms nervous about such strategic assets falling under the control of state-owned Chinese firms, although Indian firms do not seem to evoke such concern perhaps because of the smaller scales of their acquisition.[159] Terrorism has also been of concern. Indonesia has difficulty competing for investment against China and India, countries that are viewed to have fewer security risks.

As noted earlier, foremost among the economic risks of international diversification are the differences and fluctuations in the value of different currencies.[160] The value of the dollar relative to other currencies determines the value of the international assets and earnings of US firms; for example, an increase in the value of the US dollar can reduce the value of US multinational firms' international assets and earnings in other countries. Furthermore, the value of different currencies can also, at times, dramatically affect a firm's competitiveness in global markets because of its effect on the prices of goods manufactured in different countries.[161] An increase in the value of the dollar can harm US firms' exports to international markets because of the price differential of the products. Thus, government oversight and control of economic and financial capital in the country affect not only local economic activity, but also foreign investments in the country. Certainly, the political and policy changes in Eastern Europe have stimulated much more FDI due to the significant changes there since the early 1990s.[162]

Google is the market leader in the Internet search markets in the United States and Europe. However, its expansion into Russia and Asian countries has experienced difficulties. As noted earlier, in the Strategic Focus, it has dominant competitors in Russia (Yandex) and China (Baidu). It learned from its previous difficulties and is managing with a persistent strategy, but these competitors are dominating, especially given the additional support that they receive from their local governments, formally and informally.

Limits to International Expansion: Management Problems

After learning how to operate effectively in international markets, firms tend to earn positive returns on international diversification. But, the returns often level off and become negative as the diversification increases past a certain point.[163] Several reasons explain the limits to the positive effects of international diversification. First, greater geographic dispersion across country borders increases the costs of coordination between units and the distribution of products. Second, trade barriers, logistical costs, cultural diversity, and other differences by country (e.g., access to raw materials and different employee skill levels) greatly complicate the implementation of an international diversification strategy.

Institutional and cultural factors can present strong barriers to the transfer of a firm's competitive advantages from one country to another. Marketing programs often have to be redesigned and new distribution networks established when firms expand into new countries. In addition, firms may encounter different labor costs and capital charges. In general, it is difficult to effectively implement, manage, and control a firm's international operations.

STRATEGIC FOCUS

8.2 The Continuing Threat to Legitimate Companies from Counterfeit or Fake Products

The International Anti-Counterfeiting Coalition has estimated that counterfeit or fake products make up 7 per cent of the world's goods. This is an issue of growing importance, especially for firms competing on a more global basis and for firms that have significant profit margins associated with intellectual property rights, such as software makers, entertainment content businesses (i.e., music producers), and branded products. As businesses or governments implement solutions to overcome counterfeit products, the "pirates" often move up the value chain to copy more high-tech, high-margin products. China's rock bottom production costs have turned it into the "world's workshop and [have] empowered an economic boom;" however, China's environment, because of lax legal enforcement, creates an incentive for counterfeit product makers to create fake products and software and also to supply "nonstandard" electronic components, which are less traceable.

For example, Philip Morris has filed a compliant with the International Trade Commission (ITC) to stop illegal import of "gray market" cigarettes from China and other regions bearing Philip Morris USA's trademarks, including Marlboro. Charlie Whitaker, the vice president of compliance and brand integrity for Philip Morris USA, suggests that "our brands are among our company's most valuable assets and we take many steps to protect them." The firm complains that Internet-based cigarette vendors are selling Philip Morris–labeled products in violation of US intellectual property laws and the Lanham Act.

Many of the counterfeit products are sold on the Internet, similar to the cigarette example. French perfume producer L'Oréal has mounted a legal challenge to eBay for sales of fake products using its brand. L'Oréal argues that by failing to police fake products, eBay is in fact acting in concert with the sellers of those goods. Of course, eBay denies the claim saying that it is simply providing a trading platform and that the responsibility for looking after L'Oréal's trademarks should rest with L'Oréal. Interestingly, luxury good manufacturers LVMH and Hermes have won rulings in French courts on similar issues against eBay, but eBay has triumphed in other cases, such as one in a Belgium court.

Some counterfeit products are more than just a nuisance—they are dangerous. One firm identified bogus pesticides used to treat crops that could create health risks and reduce farmers' livelihoods. Additionally, the US military is facing a growing threat from fatal equipment failures and even foreign espionage through computer components that might be embedded in war planes, ships, and communication networks. For instance, BEA Systems experienced field failures of some military equipment with bogus parts, and some defense contractors have traced Chinese producers to fake microchips as well as tiny electronic circuits found in computer equipment and other electric gear. Because of these threats, the Pentagon has established more secure buying procedures to prevent the spread of counterfeit military-grade chips as aging equipment needs updating.

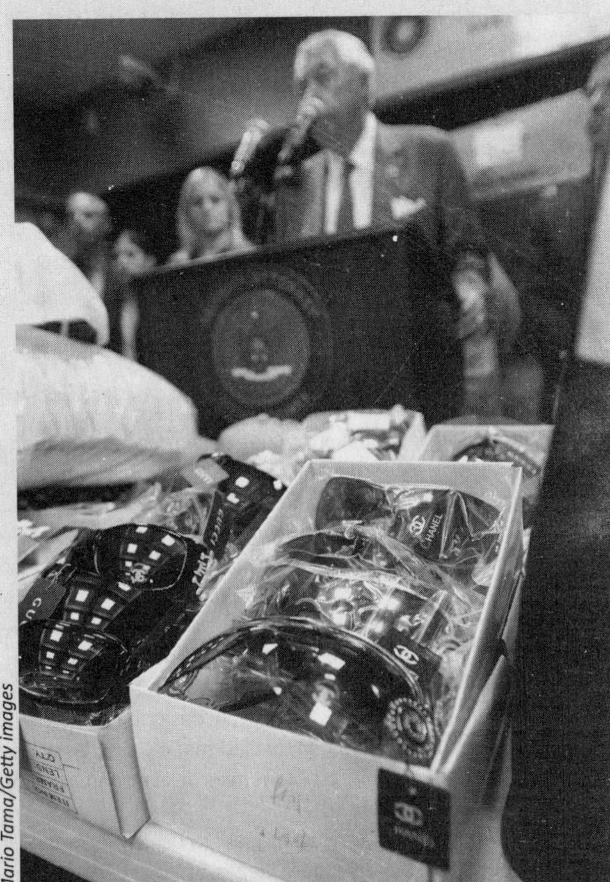

Mario Tama/Getty images

Brooklyn district attorney displays seized counterfeit goods as evidence for court proceedings.

These and other problems illustrate the importance of protecting intellectual property and the risks associated with pursuing global trade and production. Firms might pursue legal challenges, but this is often difficult in emerging economies such as China and Russia, where there is weak legal protection. Some products such as fashion and clothing items can be protected with more sophisticated labels that guard against counterfeiters. As firms pursue international strategies by using strategies based on intellectual property and which require significant R&D investments, the loss of such intellectual property to counterfeiting increases and proactive strategies must be taken to protect against significant losses.

Sources: M. Murphy & N. Tait, 2009, L'Oréal mounts legal challenges over eBay sales, *Financial Times*, March 10, 4; J. Barnham, 2008, China's pirates move up value chain, *Security Management*, June 44; L. Burkitt, 2008, Fighting fakes, *Forbes*, August 11, 44; M. Fairley, 2008, Brand protection: Label makers become vital security link in anti-counterfeiting, *Converting Magazine*, August, 20; B. Grow, C.-C. Tschang, B. Burnsed, & K. Epstein, 2008, Dangerous fakes, *BusinessWeek*, October 13, 34–37; J. Slota & M. Humphreys, 2008, Connect the dots, *Pharmaceutical Executive*, July 67–70; 2008, Alarm at flood of bogus pesticides, *Financial Times*, May 20, 12.

> **STRATEGY RIGHT NOW**
>
> Learn how leading companies such as Unilever are using information technologies to help manage international diversification You can choose any other company; Unilever is only a suggestion). www.cengage.com/management/hitt

The amount of international diversification that can be managed varies from firm to firm and according to the abilities of each firm's managers. The problems of central coordination and integration are mitigated if the firm diversifies into more friendly countries that are geographically close and have cultures similar to its own country's culture. In that case, the firm is likely to encounter fewer trade barriers, the laws and customs are better understood, and the product is easier to adapt to local markets.[164] For example, US firms may find it less difficult to expand their operations into Mexico, Canada, and Western European countries than into Asian countries.

Management must also be concerned with the relationship between the host government and the multinational corporation.[165] Although government policy and regulations are often barriers, many firms, such as Toyota and General Motors, have turned to strategic alliances, as they did in China, to overcome those barriers. By forming interorganizational networks, such as strategic alliances (see Chapter 9), firms can not only share resources and risks but also build flexibility. However, large networks can become difficult to manage.[166]

SUMMARY

- The use of international strategies is increasing. Traditional motives include extending the product life cycle, securing key resources, and having access to low-cost labor. Emerging motives include the integration of the Internet and mobile telecommunications, which facilitates global transactions. Also, firms experience increased pressure for global integration as the demand for commodities becomes borderless, and yet they feel simultaneous pressure for local country responsiveness.
- An international strategy is commonly designed primarily to capitalize on four benefits: increased market size; earning a return on large investments; economies of scale and learning; and advantages of location.
- International business-level strategies are usually grounded in one or more home-country advantages, as Porter's model suggests. Porter's model emphasizes four determinants: factors of production; demand conditions; related and supporting industries; and patterns of firm strategy, structure, and rivalry.
- There are three types of international corporate-level strategies. A multidomestic strategy focuses on competition within each country in which the firm competes. Firms using a multidomestic strategy decentralize strategic and operating decisions to the business units operating in each country, so that each unit can tailor its goods and services to the local market. A global strategy assumes more standardization of products across country boundaries; therefore, a competitive strategy is centralized and controlled by the home office. A transnational strategy seeks to integrate characteristics of both multidomestic and global strategies to emphasize both local responsiveness and global integration and coordination. This strategy is difficult to implement, requiring an integrated network and a culture of individual commitment.
- Although the transnational strategy's implementation is a challenge, environmental trends are causing many multinational firms to consider the need for both global efficiency and local responsiveness. Many large multinational firms, particularly those with many diverse products, use a multidomestic strategy with some product lines and a global strategy with others.
- The threat of wars and terrorist attacks increases the risks and costs of international strategies. Furthermore, research suggests that the liability of foreignness is more difficult to overcome than once thought.
- Some firms decide to compete only in certain regions of the world, as opposed to viewing all markets in the world as potential opportunities. Competing in regional markets allows firms and managers to focus their learning on specific markets, cultures, locations, resources, and other factors.
- Firms may enter international markets in any of several ways, including exporting, licensing, forming strategic alliances, making acquisitions, and establishing new wholly owned subsidiaries, often referred to as greenfield ventures. Most firms begin with exporting or licensing, because of their lower costs and risks, but later they might use strategic alliances and acquisitions to expand internationally. The most expensive and risky means of entering a new international market is through the establishment of a new wholly owned subsidiary. On the other hand, such subsidiaries provide the advantages of maximum control by the firm and, if it is successful, the greatest returns.
- International diversification facilitates innovation in a firm, because it provides a larger market to gain more and faster returns from investments in innovation. In addition, international diversification may generate the resources necessary to sustain a large-scale R&D program.
- In general, international diversification is related to above-average returns, but this assumes that the diversification is effectively implemented and that the firm's international operations are well managed. International diversification provides greater economies of scope and learning which, along with greater innovation, help produce above-average returns.
- Several risks are involved with managing multinational operations. Among these are political risks (e.g., instability of

national governments) and economic risks (e.g., fluctuations in the value of a country's currency).

- Some limits also constrain the ability to manage international expansion effectively. International diversification increases coordination and distribution costs, and management problems are exacerbated by trade barriers, logistical costs, and cultural diversity, among other factors.

KEY TERMS AND DEFINITIONS

A **multidomestic strategy** is an international strategy in which strategic and operating decisions are decentralized to the strategic business unit in each country so as to allow that unit to tailor products to the local market.

A **global strategy** is an international strategy through which the firm offers standardized products across country markets, with competitive strategy being dictated by the home office.

A **transnational strategy** is an international strategy through which the firm seeks to achieve both global efficiency and local responsiveness.

The establishment of a new wholly owned subsidiary is referred to as a **greenfield venture.**

International diversification is a strategy through which a firm expands the sales of its goods or services across the borders of global regions and countries into different geographic locations or markets.

An **international strategy** is a strategy through which the firm sells its goods or services outside its domestic market.

REVIEW QUESTIONS

1. What are the traditional and emerging motives that cause firms to expand internationally?
2. What are the four primary benefits of an international strategy?
3. What four factors provide a basis for international business-level strategies?
4. What are the three international corporate-level strategies? How do they differ from each other? What factors lead to their development?
5. What environmental trends are affecting international strategy?
6. What five modes of international expansion are available, and what is the normal sequence of their use?
7. What is the relationship between international diversification and innovation? How does international diversification affect innovation? What is the effect of international diversification on a firm's returns?
8. What are the risks of international diversification? What are the challenges of managing multinational firms?

EXPERIENTIAL EXERCISES

Exercise 1: McDonald's: Global, Multicountry, or Transnational Strategy?

McDonald's is one of the world's best-known brands: the company has approximately 31,000 restaurants located in more than 118 countries and serves 58 million customers *every day*. McDonald's opened its first international restaurant in Japan in 1971. Its Golden Arches are featured prominently in two former bastions of communism: Puskin Square in Moscow and Tiananmen Square in Beijing, China. It has become quite a presence in India as well, at least in the metros.

What strategy has McDonald's used to achieve such visibility? For this exercise, each group will be asked to conduct some background research on the firm and then make a brief presentation to identify the international strategy (i.e., global, multidomestic, or transnational) McDonald's is implementing. Is there a difference in the extent to which McDonald's has been adapting to the tastes of particular countries (see in the case of India)? Is it the general strategy for McDonald's, or is it adapting to particular countries (such as India) as exception?

Individual

Use the Internet to find examples of menu variations in different countries. How much do menu items differ for a McDonald's in the United States from other locations outside the United States?

Groups

Review the characteristics of global, multidomestic, and transnational strategies. Conduct additional research to assess what strategy best describes the one McDonald's is using. Prepare a flip chart with a single page of bullet points to explain your reasoning.

Whole Class

Each group should have five to seven minutes to explain its reasoning. Following Q&A for each group, ask class members to vote for the respective strategy choices.

Exercise 2: Does the World Need More SARAVANA BHAVANS?

Saravana Bhavan restaurants are a chain of restaurants with its headquarters in Chennai, India and with 30 outlets in 10 countries across the globe. It was founded in 1981 by Mr. P. Rajagopal, primarily to bridge the gap of non-existence of quality vegetarian restaurants at reasonable prices without compromising on high quality of hygiene and standrard of cooking. The highly recognizable brand is prolific in South India, with 25 outlets in the southern states, two in North India and 30 overseas locations. It operates in USA, Canada, Malaysia, Singapore, UK, France, UAE, Bahrain, Qatar, and Oman. It caters primarily to the ethinc Indian population, and prides itself on its authentic Indian cuisine peppered with traditional spices. They also emphasize a friendly approach to customers. The product range includes fast food, takeaways, home delivery, outdoor and party catering. Recently, it launched (in India) a new ice cream under the brand "Real fruits", and is planning to launch a pizza line also. Even though there are quite a few Indian states in which the chain has no locations, the management team has been seriously considering further international expansion program and an expansion in its product range.

For purposes of this exercise, assume you have been retained by the top management team of Saravana Bhavan to evaluate its international and product range expansion options. Management has concluded that the following options are the most promising:

1. Continue expansion throughout India into other states.
2. Expand into SAARC countires such as Sri Lanka, Nepal, Bhutan, Pakistan, Bangladesh etc.
3. Increase expansion in the Middle East, where there are a sizeable number of Indians.
4. Expand to other countries of Europe, Australia, and Asia-Pacific including China.

Part One

Working in teams, select one of the four options above as approved by the instructor. Next, with Porter's determinates of national advantage as a foundation, identify the factors that work either in favor of or against your strategy.

To begin this assignment, each team must prepare a strategy for expansion. Using information gleaned from different sources, identify Saravana Bhavan's main strategies for growth. For instance, what is their position on franchise vs. company-owned stores (this helps determine cash needs)? What are their most significant needs for expansion regarding resources?

Conduct research on your team's selected area for expansion on the following criteria:

- Economic characteristics: Gross national product, wages, unemployment, inflation, and so on. Trend analysis of these data (e.g., are wages rising or falling, rate of change in wages, etc.) is preferable to single point-in-time snapshots.
- Social characteristics: Life expectancy, education norms, income distributions, literacy, and so on.
- Risk factors: Economic and political risk assessment.

The following Internet resources may be useful in your research:

- http://www.saravanabhavan.com/index.php, the company's Web site.
- BBC News offers country profiles online.
- *The Economist Intelligence Unit* (http://www.eiu.com) offers country profiles.
- Both the United Nations and International Monetary Fund provide statistics and research reports.
- The *CIA World Factbook* has profiles of different regions.
- *The Global Entrepreneurship Monitor* provides reports with detailed information about economic conditions and social aspects for a number of countries.
- Links can be found at http://www.countryrisk.com to a number of resources that assess both political and economic risk for individual countries.

Part Two

Based on your research, each team is to prepare a presentation (10 to 15 minutes) highlighting the strategic advantages and disadvantages of their assigned country's opportunities and threats as regards expansion potential. Each team must also decide which corporate level strategy should be utilized if their country expansion were chosen and why.

Next, as a class, be prepared to discuss what the overall consensus would be if you were making the decision at Saravana Bhavan.

CHAPTER

9

Cooperative Implications for Strategy

Studying this chapter should provide you with the strategic management knowledge needed to

- Define cooperative strategies and explain why firms use them.
- Define and discuss three types of strategic alliances.
- Name the business-level cooperative strategies and describe their use.
- Discuss the use of corporate-level cooperative strategies in diversified firms.
- Understand the importance of cross-border strategic alliances as an international cooperative strategy.
- Explain cooperative strategies' risks.
- Describe two approaches used to manage cooperative strategies.

OPENING CASE
Using Cooperative Strategies at IBM

A company widely known throughout the world, IBM has over 350,000 employees working in design, manufacturing, sales, and service advanced information technologies such as computer systems, storage systems, software, and microelectronics. The firm's extensive lineup of products and services is grouped into three core business units—Systems and Financing, Software, and Services.

As is true for all companies, IBM uses three means to grow—internal developments (primarily through innovation), mergers and acquisitions (such as the recent purchase of France-based ILOG, which produces software tools to automate and speed up a firm's decision-making process), and cooperative strategies. Interestingly, IBM had a ten-year partnership with ILOG before making the acquisition. By cooperating with other companies, IBM is able to leverage its core competencies to grow and improve its performance.

IBM works in collaboration with several companies in Europe such as CEA, a French public research and technology organization focused on semiconductor and nano-electronics technology.

Through cooperative strategies (e.g., strategic alliances and joint ventures, both of which are defined and discussed in this chapter), IBM finds itself working with a variety of firms in order to deliver products and services. However, IBM has specific performance-related objectives it wants to accomplish as it engages in an array of cooperative arrangements. For example, with regard to its systems business, IBM works to develop leading-edge chip technology. In order to do this it has formed five separate alliances to develop the most advanced semiconductor research and expand its facilities by purchasing the latest chip-making equipment. These allies provide brainpower, including more than 250 scientists and engineers who work along with IBM's engineers and scientists to foster innovation. Some of these innovations come through new advances in materials and chemistry. For instance, IBM signed an agreement with Japan's JSR, a Japanese firm engaged in materials science, to develop materials and processes for circuitry necessary to advance futuristic semiconductors.

Even during the economic downturn, IBM's business analytics business is growing. The ILOG acquisition, noted previously, is an example of IBM's thrust into this area. IBM has created a new unit called IBM Business Analytics and Optimization Services. This business provides software solutions to help a firm better analyze data and make smarter decisions. It has 4,000 consultants who examine IBM's research and software divisions for algorithms, applications, and other innovations to help provide solutions to companies. This is just one aspect of the services business that IBM pursues with its consulting services. Of course, it needs software to produce the solutions. Many of these solutions come through partnerships with small providers that IBM manages through cooperative agreements and often these cooperative agreements lead to an acquisition as in the case of ILOG mentioned earlier.

However, other firms are entering into this space through their own acquisitions or alliances. For instance, Sun Microsystems had an alliance with IBM to produce software in competition with Hewlett-Packard. IBM bid for Sun in an acquisition attempt but was bested by Oracle, which won with a $7.3 billion bid. Thus the competition for the solutions service and network business has heated up through acquisitions and especially through partnerships, which IBM has used to facilitate its change from solely producing hardware to adding solution services and software. One study concluded that IBM was able to make this significant shift by managing its alliance of networks according to three principles. First, that company alliance networks may be used not just for individual projects but to facilitate strategic change inside a company; second, that two principal mechanisms can bring about this change: (1) increasing speed of change through partners and (2) finding partners in areas outside existing competencies; and finally, that companies can shape their alliance networks by conscious actions. Other firms are observing IBM's actions and learning and seeking to catch up fast through their own partnerships, as illustrated by a recent partnership between Cisco and the Japanese firm Fujitsu. These two firms are traditionally hardware firms that build networks, such as for phone companies, but are moving to increase their service options, especially among mobile telephone providers.

As one might anticipate, a firm as large and diverse as IBM is involved with a number of cooperative relationships. Given the challenges associated with achieving and maintaining superior performance, and in light of its general success with cooperative relationships, IBM will likely continue to use cooperative strategies as a path toward growth and enhanced performance.

Sources: R. Agarwal & C. E. Helfat, 2009, Strategic renewal of organizations, *Organization Science,* 20(2): 281–293; W. M. Bulkeley, 2009, Corporate news: IBM buoyed by its balance of business, *Wall Street Journal*, April 20, B3; W. M. Bulkeley, 2009, IBM results are clouded by Oracle's deal for Sun, *Wall Street Journal*, April 21, B1; S. Hamm, 2009, Big blue goes into analysis, *BusinessWeek*, April 27, 16; J. Menn, 2009, IBM focuses on software and services to meet targets, *Financial Times*, April 21, 19; J. M. O'Brien, 2009, IBM's grand plan to save the planet, *Fortune*, May 4, 84–91; 2009, IBM completes acquisition of ILOG, *2009 Journal OR-MS Today*, 36(1): 60; W. M. Bulkeley, 2008, Business technology, A service rival looms for IBM; H-P deal for EDS to pose challenge for big blue unit, *Wall Street Journal*, May 20, B6; K. Dittrich, G. Duysters, & A.-P. de Man, 2007, Strategic repositioning by means of alliance networks: The case of IBM, *Research Policy*, 36: 1496–1511; S. Hamm, 2007, Radical collaboration: Lessons from IBM's innovation factory, *BusinessWeek*, September 10, 16.

As noted in the Opening Case, firms use three means to grow and improve their performance—internal development, mergers and acquisitions, and cooperation. In each of these cases, the firm seeks to use its resources in ways that will create the greatest amount of value for stakeholders.[1]

Recognized as a viable engine of firm growth,[2] a **cooperative strategy** is a means by which firms work together to achieve a shared objective.[3] Thus, cooperating with other firms is another strategy firms use to create value for a customer at a lower cost than it would to do it by the firm itself and thereby establish a favorable position relative to competition.[4]

As explained in the Opening Case, IBM is involved with a number of cooperative arrangements. The intention of serving customers better than its competitors serve them, and of gaining an advantageous position relative to competitors drive this firm's use of cooperative strategies. IBM's corporate-level cooperative strategy in services and software finds it seeking to deliver server technologies in ways that maximize customer value while improving the firm's position relative to competitors. For example, Hewlett-Packard recently bought EDS to battle IBM for the leadership position in the global services market.[5] IBM has many business-level alliances with partner firms focusing on what they believe are better ways to improve services for customer firms, such as the cooperative agreements that IBM has through its new division in business analytics.[6] The objectives IBM and its various partners seek by working together highlight the reality that in the twenty-first century landscape, firms must develop the skills required to successfully use cooperative strategies as a complement to their abilities to grow and improve performance through internally developed strategies and mergers and acquisitions.[7]

We examine several topics in this chapter. First, we define and offer examples of different strategic alliances as primary types of cooperative strategies. Next, we discuss the extensive use of cooperative strategies in the global economy and reasons for them. In succession, we describe business-level (including collusive strategies), corporate-level, international, and network cooperative strategies. The chapter closes with discussion of the risks of using cooperative strategies as well as how effective management of them can reduce those risks.

As you will see, we focus on strategic alliances in this chapter because firms use them more frequently than other types of cooperative relationships. Although not frequently used, collusive strategies are another type of cooperative strategy discussed in this chapter. In a **collusive strategy**, two or more firms cooperate to increase prices above the fully competitive level.[8]

Strategic Alliances as a Primary Type of Cooperative Strategy

A **strategic alliance** is a cooperative strategy in which firms combine some of their resources and capabilities to create a competitive advantage.[9] Thus, strategic alliances involve firms with some degree of exchange and sharing of resources and capabilities to co-develop, sell, and service goods or services.[10] Strategic alliances allow firms to leverage their existing resources and capabilities while working with partners to develop additional resources and capabilities as the foundation for new competitive advantages.[11] To be certain, the reality today is that "strategic alliances have become a cornerstone of many firms' competitive strategy."[12]

Consider the case of Kodak. CEO Antonio Perez stated, "Kodak today is involved with partnerships that would have been unthinkable a few short years ago."[13] His comment suggests the breadth and depth of cooperative relationships with which the firm is involved. Each of the cooperative relationships is intended to lead to a new competitive advantage as a source of growth and performance improvement. Kodak has changed from a firm rooted in film and imaging into a digital technology-oriented company.[14]

After the life insurance sector was opened up in the late 1990s, many Indian firms entered this market, but most had alliances with some well known foreign firms. For example, ICICI linked up with Prudential; Max linked up with New York Life; Bajaj with Alliance, and so on. A feature of the insurance industry is that the service (settlement of claims) takes place long after the payment is made (of premia). So an important consideration for a purchaser of an insurance policy is the confidence he/she can place in the company. Unknown new entrants have a huge problem getting this assurance. A well known foreign firm can increase the confidence level of a consumer. Besides, the insurance industry depends on the actuarial models and hence though the actuary statistics in India may be different from the West, the models and management of data may have much in common. Thus the incidence of cooperative joint ventures in this segment (regulations on the entry of foreign firms on their own also contributed to the formation of these joint ventures). However, the fact remains that hardly any Indian company has ventured into this field on its own.

> **STRATEGY RIGHT NOW**
>
> Read about the cooperative strategy formed between any of the Indian insurance companies and their foreign partners and assess its benefits and costs.

A competitive advantage developed through a cooperative strategy often is called a **collaborative** or **relational** advantage.[15] As previously discussed, particularly in Chapter 4, competitive advantages enhance the firm's marketplace success. Rapid technological changes and the global economy are examples of factors challenging firms to constantly upgrade current competitive advantages while they develop new ones to maintain strategic competitiveness.[16]

Many firms, especially large global competitors, establish multiple strategic alliances. Although we discussed only a few of them in the Opening Case, the reality is that IBM has formed hundreds of partnerships through cooperative strategies. IBM is not alone in its decision to frequently use cooperative strategies as a means of competition. Focusing on developing advanced technologies, Lockheed Martin has formed more than 250 alliances with firms in more than 30 countries as it concentrates on its primary business of defense modernization and serving the needs of the air transportation industry. For instance, Lockheed Martin recently entered into an alliance with Northrop Grumman Corp. and Alliant Techsystems Inc. These three firms are contracted to develop multirole missiles which have both air-to-air and air-to-ground capabilities. This missile would give the aircraft much more flexibility in pursuing either air or ground targets and thus boost the target efficiency of each flight sortie.[17] Indian Space Research Organization has alliances with other countries and agencies whereby its own advanced satellites (such as INSAT) are launched by companies such as Arianne, while ISRO launches satellites for other countries which do not have the capability to launch satellites through its PSLV. India is one of the few countries in the world that have satellite launch capability. For all cooperative arrangements, including those we are describing here, success is more likely when partners behave cooperatively. Actively solving problems, being trustworthy, and consistently pursuing ways to combine partners' resources and capabilities to create value are examples of cooperative behavior known to contribute to alliance success.[18]

Three Types of Strategic Alliances

The three major types of strategic alliances include joint venture, equity strategic alliance, and nonequity strategic alliance. These alliance types are classified by their ownership arrangements; later, we classify alliances by strategic categorizations.

A **joint venture** is a strategic alliance in which two or more firms create a legally independent company to share some of their resources and capabilities to develop a competitive advantage. Joint ventures, which are often formed to improve firms' abilities to compete in uncertain competitive environments,[19] are effective in establishing long-term relationships and in transferring tacit knowledge. Because it can't be codified, tacit knowledge is learned through experiences such as those taking place when people from partner firms work together in a joint venture.[20] As discussed in Chapter 3, tacit knowledge is an important source of competitive advantage for many firms.[21]

Typically, partners in a joint venture own equal percentages and contribute equally to the venture's operations. Germany's Siemens AG and Japan's Fujitsu Ltd. equally own the joint venture Fujitsu Siemens Computers. Although the joint venture has been losing money, Fujitsu has decided that it wants to increase its market share from 4–10 per cent, so it is taking over the joint venture. The new entity will be called Fujitsu Technology Solutions.[22] Overall, evidence suggests that a joint venture may be the optimal type of cooperative arrangement when firms need to combine their resources and capabilities to create a competitive advantage that is substantially different from any they possess individually and when the partners intend to enter highly uncertain markets.[23] These conditions influenced the two independent companies' decision to form Fujitsu Siemens Computers.

One of the most successful joint ventures in India has been that of Maruti Suzuki, the market leader in passenger cars in India. It was a JV between the Government of India and Suzuki of Japan. It started as a JV with the Government of India having a marginally majority stake; later some of the GoI shares were offloaded to the public; and later Suzuki acquired majority control. India benefitted from the technology and management practices of Suzuki; Suzuki, not a major world player in cars, benefitted from the large Indian market. Today, Suzuki gets a major portion of its sales and profits from its Indian partner, Maruti.

An **equity strategic alliance** is an alliance in which two or more firms own different percentages of the company they have formed by combining some of their resources and capabilities to create a competitive advantage. Many foreign direct investments, such as those made by Japanese and US companies in China, are completed through equity strategic alliances.[24]

Interestingly, as many banks have suffered poor results in the United States, foreign banks have been creating equity alliances to provide US banks with the necessary capital to survive and expand. For instance, 21 per cent of Morgan Stanley's ownership was sold to Mitsubishi UFJ Financial Group in 2008. As a result, Nobuyuki Hirano, a senior executive for Mitsubishi, took a seat on the board of directors of Morgan Stanley. This will enhance Mitsubishi's understanding of Morgan Stanley's US strategy. The relationship may move towards combining Mitsubishi's and Morgan Stanley Japan's Securities Corporation into a single entity in Japan.[25]

A **nonequity strategic alliance** is an alliance in which two or more firms develop a contractual relationship to share some of their unique resources and capabilities to create a competitive advantage.[26] In this type of alliance, firms do not establish a separate independent company and therefore, do not take equity positions. For this reason, nonequity strategic alliances are less formal and demand fewer partner commitments than do joint ventures and equity strategic alliances, though research evidence indicates that they create value for the firms involved.[27] The relative informality and lower commitment levels characterizing nonequity strategic alliances make them unsuitable for complex projects where success requires effective transfers of tacit knowledge between partners.[28]

Forms of nonequity strategic alliances include licensing agreements, distribution agreements, and supply contracts. Hewlett-Packard (HP), which actively "partners to create new markets … and new business models," licenses some of its intellectual property through strategic alliances.[29] Typically, outsourcing commitments are specified in the form of a nonequity strategic alliance. (Discussed in Chapter 3, **outsourcing** is the purchase of a value-creating primary or support activity from another firm.) Dell Inc. and most other computer firms outsource most or all of their production of laptop computers and often form nonequity strategic alliances to detail the nature of the relationship with firms to whom they outsource. Interestingly, many of these firms that outsource introduce modularity that prevents the contracting partner or outsourcee from gaining too much knowledge or from sharing certain aspects of the business the outsourcing firm does not want revealed.[30]

Reasons Firms Develop Strategic Alliances

As our discussion to this point implies, cooperative strategies are an integral part of the competitive landscape and are quite important to many companies and even to educational institutions. In fact, many firms are cooperating with educational institutions to help commercialize ideas coming from basic research at universities.[31] In for-profit organizations, many executives believe that strategic alliances are central to their firm's success.[32] One executive's position that "you have to partner today or you will miss the next wave … and that … you cannot possibly acquire the technology fast enough, so partnering is essential"[33] highlights this belief.

Among other benefits, strategic alliances allow partners to create value that they couldn't develop by acting independently and to enter markets more quickly and with greater market penetration possibilities.[34] Moreover, most (if not all) firms lack the full set of resources and capabilities needed to reach their objectives, which indicates that partnering with others will increase the probability of reaching firm-specific performance objectives.[35] Dow Jones & Co., the publisher of *Wall Street Journal* and owned by News Corp., is forming a joint venture with SBI Holdings Inc. to create a Japanese edition of the *Wall Street Journal*'s Web site. It will primarily feature Japanese translations of news articles, videos, multimedia print, and other features of online editions of the *Wall Street Journal*. In particular this venture will develop mobile products and services in conjunction with the Web site. This is the second news Web site launched by Dow Jones in Asia; the first was launched in China in 2002.[36]

The effects of the greater use of cooperative strategies—particularly in the form of strategic alliances—are noticeable. In large firms, for example, alliances can account for 25 per cent or more of sales revenue. Many executives believe that alliances are a prime vehicle for firm growth.[37] In some industries, alliance versus alliance is becoming more prominent than firm versus firm as a point of competition. In the global airline industry, for example, competition is increasingly between large alliances rather than between airlines.[38]

In summary, we can note that firms form strategic alliances to reduce competition, enhance their competitive capabilities, gain access to resources, take advantage of opportunities, build strategic flexibility, and innovate. To achieve these objectives, they must select the right partners and develop trust.[39] Thus, firms attempt to develop a network portfolio of alliances in which they create social capital that affords them flexibility.[40] Because of the social capital, they can call on their partners for help when needed. Of course, social capital means reciprocity exists: Partners can ask them for help as well (and they are expected to provide it).[41]

The individually unique competitive conditions of slow-cycle, fast-cycle, and standard-cycle markets[42] find firms using cooperative strategies to achieve slightly different objectives (see Table 9.1). We discussed these three market types in Chapter 5 while examining competitive rivalry and competitive dynamics. **Slow-cycle markets** are markets where the firm's competitive advantages are shielded from imitation for relatively long periods of time and where imitation is costly. These markets are close to monopolistic conditions. Railroads and, historically, telecommunications, utilities, and financial services are examples of industries characterized as slow-cycle markets. In **fast-cycle markets**, the firm's competitive advantages are not shielded from imitation, preventing their long-term sustainability. Competitive advantages are moderately shielded from imitation in **standard-cycle markets**, typically allowing them to be sustained for a longer period of time than in fast-cycle market situations, but for a shorter period of time than in slow-cycle markets.

Table 9.1 Reasons for strategic alliances by market type

Market	Reason
Slow-Cycle	• Gain access to a restricted market • Establish a franchise in a new market • Maintain market stability (e.g., establishing standards)
Fast-Cycle	• Speed up development of new goods or services • Speed up new market entry • Maintain market leadership • Form an industry technology standard • Share risky R&D expenses • Overcome uncertainty
Standard-Cycle	• Gain market power (reduce industry overcapacity) • Gain access to complementary resources • Establish better economies of scale • Overcome trade barriers • Meet competitive challenges from other competitors • Pool resources for very large capital projects • Learn new business techniques

Slow-Cycle Markets

Firms in slow-cycle markets often use strategic alliances to enter restricted markets or to establish franchises in new markets. For example, because of consolidating acquisitions that have occurred over the last dozen or so years, the American steel industry has only two remaining major players: US Steel and Nucor. To improve their ability to compete successfully in the global steel market, these companies are forming cooperative relationships. They have formed strategic alliances in Europe and Asia and are investing in ventures in South America and Australia. Most recently Nucor has established a 50/50 joint venture with Duferco Group's subsidiary Duferdofin to produce steel joists and beams in Italy and then to distribute these products in Europe and North Africa. Duferco has been seeking alliances with major players in order to continue operating on a global basis.[43] Simultaneously however, companies around the world, especially in China, are forming or expanding alliances in order to establish supply sources that are important for steelmaking, in particular coal and iron ore. In 2008 Sinosteel Corp., a Chinese state-owned steelmaker, boosted its ownership in Midwest Corp. to 44 per cent. Midwest Corp. is an Australian iron ore producer. The reason for this is that the raw materials account for 50 per cent of the selling price whereas a decade ago iron ore accounted for about 15 per cent of the selling price.[44] Although 2009 commodity prices were depressed due to the economic downturn, it is expected that commodity prices will go higher as the economy improves and the partnering and joint venturing pace will increase.

The truth of the matter is that slow-cycle markets are becoming rare in the twenty-first century competitive landscape for several reasons, including the privatization of industries and economies, the rapid expansion of the Internet's capabilities for quick dissemination of information, and the speed with which advancing technologies make possible quick imitation of even complex products.[45] Firms competing in slow-cycle markets, including steel manufacturers, should recognize the future likelihood that they'll encounter situations in which their competitive advantages become partially sustainable (in the instance of a standard-cycle market) or unsustainable (in the case of a fast-cycle market). Cooperative strategies can be helpful to firms transitioning from relatively sheltered markets to more competitive ones.[46]

Fast-Cycle Markets

Fast-cycle markets are unstable, unpredictable, and complex; in a word, "hypercompetitive" (a concept that was discussed in Chapter 5).[47] Combined, these conditions virtually preclude establishing long-lasting competitive advantages, forcing firms to constantly seek sources of new competitive advantages while creating value by using current ones. "You are looking at the future, when US companies will be competing not only with European, Japanese, South Korean, and Chinese companies but also with highly competitive companies from every corner of the world: Argentina, Brazil, Chile, Egypt, Hungary, India, Indonesia, Malaysia, Mexico, Poland, Russia, Thailand, Turkey, Vietnam, and places you'd never expect."[48] Alliances between firms with current excess resources and capabilities and those with promising capabilities help companies compete in fast-cycle markets to effectively transition from the present to the future and to gain rapid entry into new markets. As such a "collaboration mindset" is paramount.[49]

The rapidly evolving media landscape lead competitors ABC, FOX, and NBC Universal to be cooperative in the development and launch of Hulu.com where many of their top rated shows can be watched online.

The entertainment business is fast becoming a new digital marketplace as television content is now available on the Web. This has led the entertainment business into a fast-cycle market where collaboration is important not only to succeed but to survive. Many of the firms that have digital video content have also sought to make a profit through digital music and have had difficulties in extracting profits from their earlier ventures. In 2007 GE's NBC Universal and News Corp.'s FOX formed a new Web site named http://www.Hulu.com. Walt Disney Corporation in 2009 became a third partner contributing content and capital in this joint venture along with an investment stake held by private equity firm Providence Equity Partners. Thus this Web site will be co-owned by direct competitors. ABC (owned by Disney) will shift much of its content to the Hulu site and viewers will be able to stream ABC TV shows such as *Lost* and *Grey's Anatomy*. CBS will be the only major network not participating in the Hulu venture with NBC Universal, FOX, and ABC. As digital video content moves onto the Web, it will be interesting to see how the competition and cooperation between all of these firms evolve.[50]

Standard-Cycle Markets

In standard-cycle markets, alliances are more likely to be made by partners with complementary resources and capabilities. Even though airline alliances were originally set up to increase revenue,[51] airlines have realized that they can also be used to reduce costs. SkyTeam (chaired by Delta and Air France) developed an internal Web site to speed up joint purchasing and to swap tips on pricing. Managers at Oneworld (American Airlines and British Airways) say the alliance's members have already saved more than $200 million through joint purchasing, and Star Alliance (United and Lufthansa) estimates that its member airlines save up to 25 per cent on joint orders.

Given the geographic areas where markets are growing, these global alliances are adding partners from Asia. In recent years, China Southern Airlines joined the SkyTeam alliance, Air China and Shanghai Airlines were added to the Star Alliance, and Dragonair joined as an affiliate of Oneworld. One of the competitive difficulties with the airline alliances is that major partners often switch between airlines. For instance, Continental Airlines, which was part of SkyTeam, recently switched to the Star Alliance with United Airlines, Air Canada, and Lufthansa. Although this move has been approved by the US Department of Transportation, it still lacks approval from the European Union regulators.[52] The fact that Oneworld, SkyTeam, and Star Alliance account for more than 60 per cent of the world's airline capacity suggests that firms participating in these alliances have gained scale economies.

Business-Level Cooperative Strategy

A firm uses a **business-level cooperative strategy** to grow and improve its performance in individual product markets. As discussed in Chapter 4, business-level strategy details what the firm intends to do to gain a competitive advantage in specific product markets. Thus, the firm forms a business-level cooperative strategy when it believes that combining its resources and capabilities with those of one or more partners will create competitive advantages that it can't create by itself and will lead to success in a specific product market. The four business-level cooperative strategies are listed in Figure 9.1.

Complementary Strategic Alliances

Complementary strategic alliances are business-level alliances in which firms share some of their resources and capabilities in complementary ways to develop competitive advantages.[53] Vertical and horizontal are the two types of complementary strategic alliances (see Figure 9.1).

- Complementary strategic alliances
  - Vertical
  - Horizontal
- Competition response strategy
- Uncertainty-reducing strategy
- Competition-reducing strategy

Figure 9.1 Business-level cooperative strategies

Vertical Complementary Strategic Alliance

In a **vertical complementary strategic alliance**, firms share their resources and capabilities from different stages of the value chain to create a competitive advantage (see Figure 9.2).[54] Many a time, vertical complementary alliances are formed to adapt to environmental changes;[55] sometimes the changes represent an opportunity for partnering firms to innovate while adapting.[56]

The Strategic Focus on complementary alliances discusses what is happening with vertical alliances given the downturn in the world economy. In particular, it points out that economic pressures are creating stress in the vertical alliance relationships between buyers and suppliers

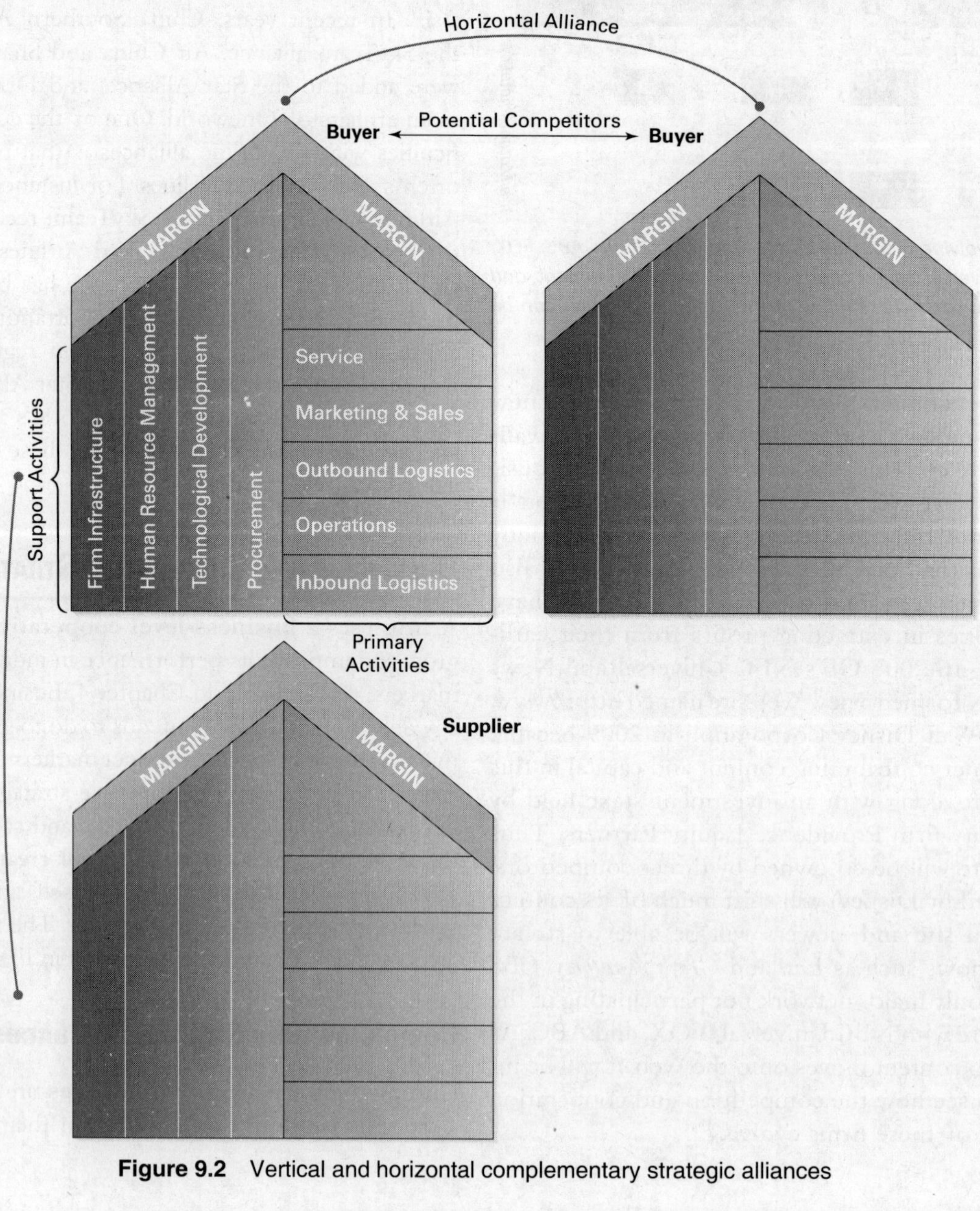

Figure 9.2 Vertical and horizontal complementary strategic alliances

in the grocery and apparel retail industry supply chains. However, in other industries it is leading to new partnerships where complementary strategic alliances are more likely to increase, such as in the steelmaking industry.

Another example of a vertical complementary alliance is Nintendo and its need for additional software and games for its Wii game console. To fulfill this need Nintendo has developed a partnership with Electronic Arts. Through this partnership, it will release two sports games prior to the release of its brand new hardware: *Tiger Woods PGA Tour 10* and *Grand Slam Tennis.* Nintendo is allowing these games to be sold even before it releases more of its own games. Previously, Nintendo trailed other game platforms in its production of new releases because it stressed its own games over those of other game software producers and would not release its hardware details to them in advance. It has changed its policy to encourage more vertical relationships with game software producing firms such as Electronic Arts and Activision Blizzard, Inc.[57]

STRATEGIC FOCUS

9.1 How Complementary Alliances Are Affected by the Global Economic Downturn

Supply chain management principles have changed over the last decade as suppliers have sought to work more closely with buyers. Traditionally a company's purchasing office dealt with a relatively small group of suppliers and had the overall goal of obtaining as many price cuts as possible. This, however, changed because as globalization and outsourcing increased the supply chain decision-making process involved a greater network of partners around the world. This drove companies to collaborate with suppliers and develop stronger relationships to reduce waste and develop products more quickly. As such, supply chain managers have had to shoulder a lot more responsibility, which has required much more emphasis on collaborative skills.

In the economic downturn, however, many of these collaborative relationships and partnerships—which are complementary by nature, especially in the vertical supply chain—have been strained. Large retailers have been squeezing their vendors in order to survive the requirement for heavy sales promotions and lower prices to sell their apparel products. This strategy has affected firms like Liz Claiborne, Phillips-Van Heusen, and Jones Apparel Group. Marks and Spencer sources many of its products from India; Wal-Mart also sources some of its products from India. During downturns, these large retailers have squeezed the margins of the Indian companies which have struggled to survive. Because large stores such as Marks and Spencer and Wal-Mart have many vendors to choose from, and they buy in large volumes, they have power to force price cuts from their suppliers. However, this has strained their relationships because both companies "require long-term, healthy partners to operate efficiently." Hartmarx Corp., a men's clothing producer whose main customers are Dillard's, Nordstrom, and Bloomingdale's (owned by Macy's), has been forced to file for Chapter 11 bankruptcy court protection due to the pressure. On the other hand, JCPenney has had long-term relationships with its vendors and its spokesperson noted, "We don't view 'squeezing' of vendors to protect our bottom line as a viable long-term strategy."

Similar events are happening in the grocery industry. For example, Unilever has been trying to stop its price margins from shrinking by forcing price increases on retailers such as the Belgian supermarket chain Delhaize Group SA. Delhaize operates the Food Lion chain and other grocery stores in the United States. In 2008, Unilever pushed worldwide price increases of more than 9 per cent. Because of the price increases forced on Delhaize, it banished products by Unilever such as Dove soap and Axe deodorant from its US stores. At the same time, commodity prices dropped and British retailer Tesco PLC urged suppliers to pass onto stores the recent drops in prices for commodities and oil that are used to produce food products. In response, firms like Wal-Mart (Great Value) have started to freshen up their in-house brands. As such, when large food producers such as Unilever do not respond appropriately, Wal-Mart can cut back on stocking national brands.

AP Photo/Shoun Hill

Shoppers at Food Lion found Axe and other Unilever products off the shelves as Delhaize, operator of the supermarket, responded to price increases passed on from the manufacturer.

While the downturn has put stress on some vertical alliances as previously noted, it has also created opportunities for new partnerships in other areas. For example, many private equity firms have experienced a significant decrease in the amount of funds invested in the United States. Blackstone Group has formed global joint ventures to increase its fund supply. It has formed a joint venture with Bank Larrain Vial in Latin America and Och-Ziff Capital Management. In Latin America in particular there is a large opportunity in Chile, where private pension funds hold $82 billion in assets due to a pioneering program that places 12.3 per cent of all payroll into private pension accounts. This complementary alliance would most likely not have occurred if the economy did not turn for the worse. Blackstone Group will also help diversify pension funds by investing in private equity and hedge funds. South and Central America have almost $200 billion in assets under management, which is comparable to the California Public Employees Retirement System (CalPERS). This is a significant opportunity for private equity funds such as the Blackstone Group to increase their supply of capital.

Sources: M. Arnold, 2009, Private equity boost for Latin America, *Financial Times*, May 12, 6; L. C. Gunipero, R. V. Handfield, & D. L. Johansen, 2008, Beyond buying: Supply chain managers used to have one main job: Purchasing stuff cheaply, *Wall Street Journal*, March 10, R8; P. Lattman, 2009, Schwarzman's Latin sojourn, *Wall Street Journal*, May 22, C2; S. Pignal, 2009, Delhaize shrugs off Unilever clash, *Financial Times*, March 13, 18; C. Rohwedder, A. O. Patrick, & T. W. Martin, 2009, Big grocers pulls Unilever items over pricing, *Wall Street Journal*, February 11, D1, B5l; K. Talley, 2009, Retailers, apparel firms tussle over tough deals, *Wall Street Journal*, February 11, B6.

Horizontal Complementary Strategic Alliance

A **horizontal complementary strategic alliance** is an alliance in which firms share some of their resources and capabilities from the same stage (or stages) of the value chain to create a competitive advantage (see Figure 9.2). Commonly, firms use complementary strategic alliances to focus on joint long-term product development and distribution opportunities.[58] As previously noted in the example regarding www.Hulu.com, GE's Universal Pictures, Disney's ABC, and News Corp's FOX Video Production have formed a joint Web site to distribute video content. Recently, pharmaceutical companies have been pursuing horizontal alliances as well. As healthcare reform takes place in the United States, large pharmaceutical firms are seeking relationships with generic drug producers. For example, Pfizer has reached marketing agreements with two Indian makers of generic drugs: Aurobindo Pharma Ltd. and Claris Lifesciences Ltd. These two firms produce and sell 60 and 15 off-patent drugs and injectables, respectively. Similarly, Novartis AG is acquiring Ebewe Pharma, an Austrian drugmaker, which will partner with the Novartis generic drug subsidiary, Sandoz. These moves are targeted to tap into the growing generic drug market, which was $3.5 billion in 2008 and is expected to be $9 billion by 2015.[59] In January 2011, Zydus Cadila, a ₹39 billion pharmaceuticals company, located in Ahmedabad, signed an agreement with the €15.9 (₹1000) billion company Bayer AG's subsidiary, Bayer HealthCare to jointly market pharmaceuticals in India. According to the agreement, a 50:50 Joint Venture (JV), Bayer Zydus Pharma would be formed. Bayer would transfer its marketing and sales activities in India to the new company, and Zydus would contribute through its women's products, diagnostic imaging, and other products. Bayer would market its existing products as well as future products that were in the pipeline. "We will leverage the strengths of Bayer Zydus Pharma for optimized product portfolio and distribution capabilities for launching new products and the sales of existing brands", said Bayer HealthCare AG CEO, Dr. JVRG Reinhardt. The manufacturing activities would continue with the respective companies.[60]

The automotive manufacturing industry is one in which many horizontal complementary strategic alliances are formed. In fact, virtually all global automobile manufacturers use cooperative strategies to form scores of cooperative relationships. The Renault-Nissan alliance, signed in March 1999, is a prominent example of a horizontal complementary strategic alliance. Maruti Suzuki alliance has been one of the most successful automotive industry alliances in the world. Other successful alliances in this industry in India have been TVS & Suzuki, Hero & Honda and Kinetic and Honda (for two wheelers). In all these alliances, the challenge is to integrate the partners' operations to create value while maintaining their unique cultures.

Competition Response Strategy

As discussed in Chapter 5, competitors initiate competitive actions to attack rivals and launch competitive responses to their competitors' actions. Strategic alliances can be used at the business level to respond to competitors' attacks. Because they can be difficult to reverse and expensive to operate, strategic alliances are primarily formed to take strategic rather than tactical actions and to respond to competitors' actions in a like manner.

Many complementary horizontal alliances are created in response to heavy competition. For instance, digital music producers have been trying to extract more value from their products beyond what they can collect through middle-men such as Apple's iTunes distribution outlet. Many music producers have sought to develop their own distribution outlets through joint partnership, in response to Apple's success, such as Blue Matter Press, Jimmy and Doug's Farmclub, and eMusic, but most have failed. Now many of them are seeking online advertisements through Web sites that distribute music and video. For instance, Warner Music has invested in LaLa Media and a startup company called imeem, Inc. because MySpace

Music, a joint venture among four major labels and News Corp., was not generating enough advertising revenue. In response to the focus on advertising, Universal Music, a division of Vivendi SA, through a joint venture with Google has created a new online site for music videos called VEVO. Most of these actions are attempts to bolster revenue because digital music downloads are increasing, but not quickly enough to offset the steep decline in CD sales.[61]

Uncertainty-Reducing Strategy

Some firms use business-level strategic alliances to hedge against risk and uncertainty, especially in fast-cycle markets.[62] These strategies are also used where uncertainty exists, such as in entering new product markets or emerging economies.

As large global auto firms manufacture more hybrid vehicles, there is insufficient capacity in the battery industry to meet future demand. Volkswagen AG is partnering with China's BYD Co. to produce hybrid and electric vehicles powered by lithium batteries. BYD is the one of the world's largest cell phone battery producers and is also a fledgling auto producer as it moves to launch a plug-in car before more established rival firms. Volkswagen has also made agreements with Samuel Electric and Toshiba Corp. of Japan to reduce the uncertainty about the insufficient capacity for lithium-ion batteries used in hybrid vehicles.[63]

Competition-Reducing Strategy

Used to reduce competition, collusive strategies differ from strategic alliances in that collusive strategies are often an illegal type of cooperative strategy. Two types of collusive strategies are explicit collusion and tacit collusion.

When two or more firms negotiate directly with the intention of jointly agreeing about the amount to produce and the price of the products that are produced, **explicit collusion** exists.[64] Explicit collusion strategies are illegal in the United States and most developed economies (except in regulated industries). They are illegal in India as well, and the law is expected to be more stringently enforced in the coming years with the Competition Commission getting a mandate to play a more active regulatory role.

Firms that use explicit collusion strategies may find others challenging their competitive actions. In early 2009, for example, the US Department of Justice joined forces with European officials to investigate alleged "price coordination" among three air cargo carriers. Luxembourg's Cargolux, Japan's Nippon Cargo Airlines, and Korea's Asiana Airlines plead guilty and paid criminal fines of $214 million for their role in a global conspiracy to fix prices on air freight. This investigation began in 2001 and prosecution began in 2006. Throughout the history of the investigation more than 15 air cargo airlines have been prosecuted and fined over $1.6 billion. The investigation continues in the air freight industry and is one of the world's biggest cartel probes by competition officials around the world.[65] As this example suggests, any firm that may use explicit collusion as a strategy should recognize that competitors and regulatory bodies might challenge the acceptability of their competitive actions. In India, many of the industries follow the leader in pricing, although explicit price collusion may be hard to prove. For example, both in the airline industry and the telecom industry, the leaders set the price trends and the others simply match the prices. Some of these practices do attract government attention, and the general practice seems to be quiet arm twisting by the government. Thus, collusion in India may be more of a tacit collusion.

Tacit collusion exists when several firms in an industry indirectly coordinate their production and pricing decisions by observing each other's competitive actions and responses.[66] Tacit collusion results in production output that is below fully competitive levels and above fully competitive prices. Unlike explicit collusion, firms engaging in tacit collusion do not directly negotiate output and pricing decisions. However, research suggests that joint ventures or cooperation between two firms can lead to less competition in other markets in which both firms operate.[67]

Tacit collusion tends to be used as a business-level, competition-reducing strategy in highly concentrated industries, such as airlines and breakfast cereals. Research in the airline industry suggests that tacit collusion reduces service quality and on-time performance.[68] Firms in these industries recognize that they are interdependent and that their competitive actions and responses significantly affect competitors' behavior toward them. Understanding this interdependence and carefully observing competitors can lead to tacit collusion.

Four firms (Kellogg's, General Mills, Post, and Quaker) have accounted for as much as 80 per cent of sales volume in the ready-to-eat segment of the US cereal market.[69] Some believe that this high degree of concentration results in "prices for branded cereals that are well above [the] costs of production."[70] The *Wall Street Journal* reported in 2008 that prices for breakfast cereals were among the easiest to inflate when there are commodity shortages.[71] Prices above the competitive level in this industry suggest the possibility that the dominant firms use a tacit collusion cooperative strategy.

Discussed in Chapter 6, **mutual forbearance** is a form of tacit collusion in which firms do not take competitive actions against rivals they meet in multiple markets. Rivals learn a great deal about each other when engaging in multimarket competition, including how to deter the effects of their rival's competitive attacks and responses. Given what they know about each other as a competitor, firms choose not to engage in what could be destructive competitions in multiple product markets.[72]

In general, governments in free-market economies need to determine how rivals can collaborate to increase their competitiveness without violating established regulations.[73] However, this task is challenging when evaluating collusive strategies, particularly tacit ones. For example, regulation of pharmaceutical and biotech firms who collaborate to meet global competition might lead to too much price fixing and, therefore, regulation is required to make sure that the balance is right, although sometimes the regulation gets in the way of efficient markets.[74] Individual companies must analyze the effect of a competition-reducing strategy on their performance and competitiveness.

Assessment of Business-Level Cooperative Strategies

Firms use business-level strategies to develop competitive advantages that can contribute to successful positions and performance in individual product markets. To develop a competitive advantage using an alliance, the resources and capabilities that are integrated through the alliance must be valuable, rare, imperfectly imitable, and nonsubstitutable (see Chapter 3).

Evidence suggests that complementary business-level strategic alliances, especially vertical ones, have the greatest probability of creating a sustainable competitive advantage.[75] Horizontal complementary alliances are sometimes difficult to maintain because they are often between rival competitors. In this instance, firms may feel a "push" toward and a "pull" from alliances. Airline firms, for example, want to compete aggressively against others serving their markets and target customers. However, the need to develop scale economies and to share resources and capabilities (such as scheduling systems) dictates that alliances be formed so the firms can compete by using cooperative actions and responses while they simultaneously compete against one another through competitive actions and responses. As noted previously, this has led to many changes in the large airline alliances—for instance, with Continental recently aligning with United and Lufthansa rather than Delta and AirFrance-KLM.[76] The challenge in these instances is for each firm to find ways to create the greatest amount of value from both their competitive and cooperative actions. It seems that Nissan and Renault have learned how to achieve this balance.

Although strategic alliances designed to respond to competition and to reduce uncertainty can also create competitive advantages, these advantages often are more temporary than those developed through complementary (both vertical and horizontal) strategic alliances. The primary reason is that complementary alliances have a stronger focus on creating value than do competition-reducing and uncertainty-reducing alliances, which are formed to respond to competitors' actions or reduce uncertainty rather than to attack competitors.

Of the four business-level cooperative strategies, the competition-reducing strategy has the lowest probability of creating a sustainable competitive advantage. For example, research suggests that firms following a foreign direct investment strategy using alliances as a follow-the-leader imitation approach may not have strong strategic or learning goals. Thus, such investment could be attributable to tacit collusion among the participating firms instead of forming a competitive advantage (which should be the core objective).

Corporate-Level Cooperative Strategy

A firm uses a **corporate-level cooperative strategy** to help it diversify in terms of products offered or markets served, or both. Diversifying alliances, synergistic alliances, and franchising are the most commonly used corporate-level cooperative strategies (see Figure 9.3).

Firms use diversifying alliances and synergistic alliances to grow and improve performance by diversifying their operations through a means other than a merger or an acquisition.[77] When a firm seeks to diversify into markets in which the host nation's government prevents mergers and acquisitions, alliances become an especially appropriate option. Corporate-level strategic alliances are also attractive as compared to mergers and, particularly acquisitions, because they require fewer resource commitments[78] and permit greater flexibility in terms of efforts to diversify partners' operations.[79] An alliance can be used as a way to determine whether the partners might benefit from a future merger or acquisition between them. This "testing" process often characterizes alliances formed to combine firms' unique technological resources and capabilities.[80]

Diversifying Strategic Alliance

A **diversifying strategic alliance** is a corporate-level cooperative strategy in which firms share some of their resources and capabilities to diversify into new product or market areas. The spread of high-speed wireless networks and devices with global positioning chips and the popularity of Web site applications running on Apple's iPhone and Research in Motion's BlackBerry (and other smartphones) shows that consumers are increasingly accessing mobile information. Equipped with this knowledge, Alcatel-Lucent is entering the market through mobile advertising, which will allow a cell phone carrier to alert customers about the location of a favorite store or the closest ATM. It is pursuing this diversification alliance with 1020 Placecast, a California-based developer of cell phone online ads associated with user locations. Hyatt, FedEx, and Avis are especially interested in using the service. The ads will also include a link to coupons or other promotions. Other mobile phone producers have started to sell mobile phone display ads in other metropolitan areas through Nokia Phones. These networks are trying to gain a share of the profits that would normally be out of their reach through revenue-sharing models with companies that are advertising as well as the ad-producing service companies.[81]

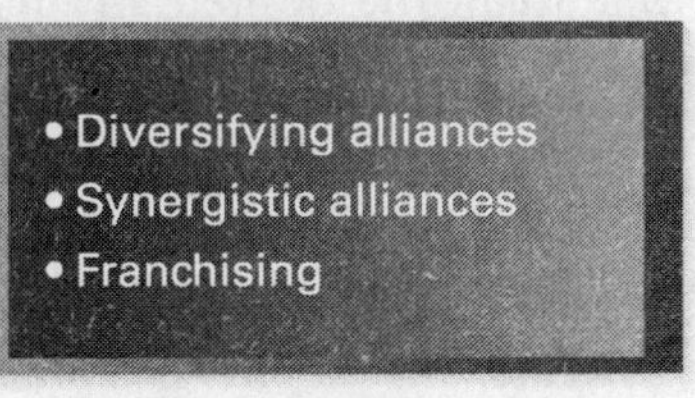

Figure 9.3 Corporate-level cooperative strategies

It should be noted that highly diverse networks of alliances can lead to poorer performance by partner firms.[82] However, cooperative ventures are also used to reduce diversification in firms that have overdiversified.[83] Japanese chipmakers Fujitsu, Mitsubishi Electric, Hitachi, NEC, and Toshiba have been using joint ventures to consolidate and then spin off diversified businesses that were performing poorly. For example, Fujitsu, realizing that memory chips were becoming a financial burden, dumped its flash memory business into a joint venture company controlled by Advanced Micro Devices. This alliance helped Fujitsu refocus on its core businesses.[84]

Synergistic Strategic Alliance

A **synergistic strategic alliance** is a corporate-level cooperative strategy in which firms share some of their resources and capabilities to create economies of scope. Similar to the business-level horizontal complementary strategic alliance, synergistic strategic alliances create synergy across multiple functions or multiple businesses between partner firms. The most recent development for Disney's media segment, and ABC in particular, is a partnership with Google's YouTube that will allow it to advertise its movies and products by showing short clips and selling ads.[85] This is an example of a synergistic diversification alliance.

AP Photo/M. Spencer Green

With apps like the Slacker personalized radio and hundreds of others available for the BlackBerry and iPhone, companies are already looking at these devices as a means of conveying personalized advertising as well.

In recent years, there has been much more competitive interaction between hardware and software firms. Cisco, traditionally a network telecommunications equipment manufacturer, is moving into computers—in particular, servers. After HP moved into selling network equipment, Cisco decided to move more fully into developing its server business. To drive its computer business Cisco needs to develop a service segment, although it is not trying to upset its historical partners, HP and IBM, which have large service businesses. Both IBM and HP have large service businesses. As such, Cisco developed partnership agreements with Accenture Ltd. and India-based Tata Consulting Services Ltd. to help market Cisco's products to businesses around the world. These were synergistic alliances to foster this diversification move by Cisco into services.[86]

Franchising

Franchising is a corporate-level cooperative strategy in which a firm (the franchisor) uses a franchise as a contractual relationship to describe and control the sharing of its resources and capabilities with partners (the franchisees).[87] A **franchise** is a "contractual agreement between two legally independent companies whereby the franchisor grants the right to the franchisee to sell the franchisor's product or do business under its trademarks in a given location for a specified period of time."[88] Success is often determined in these strategic alliances by how well the franchisor can replicate its success across multiple partners in a cost-effective way.[89] Research suggests that too much innovation results in difficulties for replicating this success.[90]

Franchising is a popular strategy. In the United States alone, more than 2,500 franchise systems are located in more than 75 industries; and those operating franchising outlets generate roughly one-third of all US retail sales.[91] Already frequently used in developed nations, franchising is also expected to account for significant portions of growth in emerging economies in the twenty-first century.[92] As with diversifying and synergistic strategic alliances, franchising is an alternative to pursuing growth through mergers and acquisitions. McDonald's, Hilton International, Marriott International, Mrs. Fields Cookies, Subway, and Ace Hardware are well-known examples of firms using the franchising corporate-level cooperative strategy. In India, Amul, the dairy products giant, and Vadilal Icecream have used franchises to spread their network quickly. An interesting application of the franchising concept in India on a very large scale has been the educational institutions such as NIIT, ICFAI (Institute of Chartered Financial Analysts of India), and IIPM (Indian Institute of Planning and Management). The people running these "branches" are independent entrepreneurs, who conform to certain requirements and standards laid down by the franchisor.

Franchising is a particularly attractive strategy to use in fragmented industries, such as retailing, hotels and motels, and commercial printing. In fragmented industries, a large number of small and medium-sized firms compete as rivals; no firm or small set of firms has a dominant share, making it possible for a company to gain a large market share by consolidating independent companies through contractual relationships.

In the most successful franchising strategy, the partners (the franchisor and the franchisees) work closely together.[93] A primary responsibility of the franchisor is to develop programs to transfer to the franchisees the knowledge and skills that are needed to successfully compete at the local level.[94] In return, franchisees should provide feedback to the franchisor regarding how their units could become more effective and efficient.[95] Working cooperatively, the franchisor and its franchisees find ways to strengthen the core company's brand name, which is often the most important competitive advantage for franchisees operating in their local markets.[96]

Assessment of Corporate-Level Cooperative Strategies

Costs are incurred with each type of cooperative strategy.[97] Compared to those at the business level, corporate-level cooperative strategies commonly are broader in scope and more complex, making them relatively more costly. Those forming and using cooperative strategies, especially corporate-level ones, should be aware of alliance costs and carefully monitor them.

In spite of these costs, firms can create competitive advantages and value when they effectively form and use corporate-level cooperative strategies.[98] When successful alliance experiences are internalized, it is more likely that the strategy will attain the desired advantages. In other words, those involved with forming and using corporate-level cooperative strategies can also use them to develop useful knowledge about how to succeed in the future. To gain maximum value from this knowledge, firms should organize it and verify that it is always properly distributed to those involved with forming and using alliances.[99]

We explained in Chapter 6 that firms answer two questions to form a corporate-level strategy—in which businesses will the diversified firm compete and how will those businesses be managed? These questions are also answered as firms form corporate-level cooperative strategies. Thus, firms able to develop corporate-level cooperative strategies and manage them in ways that are valuable, rare, imperfectly imitable, and nonsubstitutable (see Chapter 3) develop a competitive advantage that is in addition to advantages gained through the activities of individual cooperative strategies. (Later in the chapter, we will further describe alliance management as another potential competitive advantage.)

International Cooperative Strategy

A **cross-border strategic alliance** is an international cooperative strategy in which firms with headquarters in different nations decide to combine some of their resources and capabilities to create a competitive advantage. Taking place in virtually all industries, the number of cross-border alliances continues to increase.[100] These alliances too are sometimes formed instead of mergers and acquisitions (which can be riskier).[101] Even though cross-border alliances can themselves be complex and hard to manage,[102] they have the potential to help firms use their resources and capabilities to create value in locations outside their home market.

IMG Worldwide, Inc. is one of the largest producers and distributors of sports entertainment in the world. It pursues its strategy through international joint ventures with other broadcasting firms. The events that it currently broadcasts include two tennis Grand Slam events, Wimbledon, and the Australian Open. In an effort to expand into emerging economies, IMG signed a 20-year sporting event partnership with China Central Television, the main Chinese broadcasting organization. A national broadcast of this size could have an audience of 740 million viewers daily. The first two events to be broadcast through this venture included the China Open Tennis Tournament in Beijing and the Chengdu Open Tennis Tournament in 2009. The top 50 women players in the world were expected to play in the China Open tournament. Through this strategic alliance, IMG aimed at substantially broadening its international reach.[103]

As may be seen from the Strategic Focus below, Suzlon, an energy firm focusing mainly on wind mills and wind turbines, has expanded its reach worldwide through a series of alliances with different companies. Some of these are manufacturing alliances; some for technology; and some for marketing.

STRATEGIC FOCUS

9.2 Suzlon: Windy Alliances

Incorporated in 1995 and owned by a family that diversified into wind energy business from the textile industry, within five years, Suzlon has made it to the list of top ten wind companies worldwide, proving itself to be a worthy competitor among the more established wind turbine manufacturers. Ranked as the world's third leading wind turbine supplier in terms of market share in 2009, the company's global spread is reflected in its projects and markets portfolio—extending across Africa, Asia, Australia, Europe, and North and South America. Suzlon is a highly vertically integrated wind turbine technology supplier, developing a full wind turbine technology supply chain in-house. Its varied services are offered by its associated company subsidiaries, which have also been established to cover specific regional markets. Suzlon's licensing arrangements with Sudwind, Aerpac, and Enron Wind provided it with the necessary base of technical knowledge needed to enter the wind turbine manufacturing business. As the largest Indian-owned wind turbine manufacturer in India, Suzlon has access to local networks that foreign companies lack, especially manufacturers. It has been able to build its Indian supply chain through a network of subsidiaries, allowing it to retain control of the intellectual property associated with its turbine designs. Also, building on the knowledge gained through international technology transfers in the form of licenses, Suzlon formed many overseas subsidiaries. It did this jointly with foreign-owned companies, either to manufacture a specific component such as its gearbox company in Austria, or to undertake collaborative R&D such as its Netherlands-based blade design center, and its Germany-based gearbox research center. Suzlon's wholly-owned subsidiaries include technological development centers in Germany and the Netherlands, a rotor blade manufacturing company (Suzlon Energy B.V) in the Netherlands, a US market subsidiary (SWECO), and an Australian market subsidiary (Suzlon Energy Australia Pty Limited).

In 2004, Suzlon Wind Energy A/S, a wholly-owned subsidiary was established in Denmark, the origin of the utility-scale wind turbine industry, to supervise Suzlon's international marketing activities, and head Suzlon´s activities within the regions: Europe, Middle East and Africa. As of May 2009, the company signed contracts totaling 400 MW for the delivery of wind turbines to European markets such as Portugal, Spain, Italy, Turkey, and Romania and is expanding into other European markets such as Ukraine, Bulgaria, Greece, and Sweden. This demonstrates that European customers have begun to appreciate the added value that Suzlon's experienced teams bring from the development phase of a wind park, through the construction and commissioning to its life-time maintenance. A representative office in Beijing and manufacturing facility in Tianjin have also been set up in China to expand Suzlon's presence in the Chinese market.

The company's true prowess as a global giant was highlighted with two major acquisitions bids: Suzlon acquired Hansen Transmissions NV—the world's second leading wind gearbox maker—in 2006, completing its quest to integrate all critical component technologies into its value chain and create a strong, extendible supply chain to support high growth in a global supply-restricted environment. Suzlon made Hansen grow, increasing fourfold the capacity in China and India, and also brought down the cost of gearbox. In addition, the company, in 2007, succeeded in its bid to acquire a stake in German wind turbine maker RE power Systems AG, giving it immediate access to the mature

European market which is the largest WTG market in terms of volumes. Recently, the company, through its 90 per cent subsidiary REpower bagged an order for 25 turbines totaling 51 MW from EverPower Wind Holdings in the US. Suzlon and REpower, if taken together, stand as the world's third leading wind turbine supplier group in terms of market share. With this acquisition, Suzlon, marked the first major contested acquisition in the wind energy space. To strengthen its research base, Suzlon has entered into an agreement with REpower, founding the Joint Venture "Renewable Energy Technology Center GmbH" (RETC) in Hamburg, in which each firm holds a 50 per cent stake. With the aim to combine forces and cooperate strategically in the field of research and technical training in the future, the facility will function as a hub and integrator for Suzlon's R&D efforts around the world.

Suzlon, the largest wind turbine manufacturer, formed many overseas subsidiaries.

Sources: Suzlon information from company knowledge book and website www.suzlon.com; http://www.suzlon.com/pdf/Knowledge%20Book.pdf http://en.wikipedia.org/wiki/Wind_power_in_India; SEBI, 2005, Red herring prospectus of Suzlon, September 12, http://www.sebi.gov.in/dp/suz.pdf; Rowena F. Caronan, 2010, Suzlon reaches 5000 MW in home country and wind hotspot in India, www.ecoseed.org, September 29, http://www.ecoseed.org/en/business/renewable-energy/article/95-renewable-energy/8079-suzlon-reaches-5-000-mw-in-home-country-and-wind-hotspot-in-dia; Joanna I. Lewis, 2007, A comparison of Wind Power Industry Development Strategies in India, Spain, and China, www.newenergyindia.org, July 19, http://www.newenergyindia.org/Comparison%20of%20Wind%20Energy%20Power%20Industry%20in%20India,%20China,%20and%20Spain.pdf; www.iloveindia.com, 2007, Suzlon energy Limited, July 21, http://www.iloveindia.com/economy-of-india/top-50-companies/suzlon.html.

Several reasons explain the increasing use of cross-border strategic alliances, including the fact that in general, multinational corporations outperform domestic-only firms.[104] What takes place with a cross-border alliance is that a firm leverages core competencies that are the foundation of its domestic success in international markets.[105] Nike provides an example as it leverages its core competence with celebrity marketing to expand globally with its diverse line of athletic goods and apparel. With a $2 billion celebrity endorsement budget, Nike has formed relationships with athletes who have global appeal. Tiger Woods, Michael Phelps, and LeBron James are recent endorsers, while seven-time Tour de France winner Lance Armstrong, Michael Jordan, and Magic Johnson are historic examples of these types of individuals. In addition, Nike has endorsement relationships with star athletes and organizations outside the United States, such as Brazilian soccer star Ronaldo and Manchester United, the world's most popular soccer team.[106] Coupling these alliances with Nike's powerful global brand name helps the firm apply its marketing competencies in foreign markets. However, the downturn in the economy is causing problems such that even these relationships are not protecting sales declines.[107]

Limited domestic growth opportunities and foreign government economic policies are additional reasons firms use cross-border alliances. As discussed in Chapter 8, local ownership is an important national policy objective in some nations. In India and China, for example, governmental policies reflect a strong preference to license local companies. Thus, in some countries, the full range of entry mode choices that we described in Chapter 8 may not be available to firms seeking to diversify internationally. Indeed, investment by foreign firms in these instances may be allowed only through a partnership with a local firm, such as in a cross-border alliance. Especially important, strategic alliances with local partners can help firms overcome certain liabilities of moving into a foreign country, such as lack of knowledge of the local culture or institutional norms.[108] A cross-border strategic alliance can also be helpful to foreign partners from an operational perspective, because the local partner has significantly more information about factors contributing to competitive success such as local markets, sources of capital, legal procedures, and politics.[109] Interestingly, recent research suggests that firms with foreign operations have longer survival rates than domestic-only firms, although this is reduced if there are competition problems between foreign subsidiaries.[110]

In general, cross-border alliances are more complex and risky than domestic strategic alliances, especially in emerging economies.[111] However, the fact that firms competing internationally tend to outperform domestic-only competitors suggests the importance of learning how to diversify into international markets. Compared with mergers and acquisitions, cross-border alliances may be a better way to learn this process, especially in the early stages of the firms' geographic diversification efforts. Starbucks is a case in point.

When Starbucks sought overseas expansion, it wanted to do so quickly as a means of supporting its strong orientation to continuous growth. Thus, it agreed to a complex series of joint ventures in many countries in the interest of speed. While the company receives a percentage of the revenues and profits as well as licensing fees for supplying its coffee, controlling costs abroad is more difficult than in the United States. Starbucks is learning from the results achieved from the collaborative relationships it initially established. In light of what it has learned, the firm continues to collaborate with others in different countries including China. At Starbuck's 10-year anniversary mark in China, one analyst noted that "China, conventionally a coffee exporter, may become a net importer in 2009 with demand outpacing supply, as Starbucks Coffee Co. and other coffee chains mushroom around the country."[112] Among other actions, Starbucks is taking larger equity positions in some of the joint ventures with which it is now involved in different countries (such as China).

Network Cooperative Strategy

In addition to forming their own alliances with individual companies, a growing number of firms are joining forces in multiple networks.[113] A **network cooperative strategy** is a cooperative strategy wherein several firms agree to form multiple partnerships to achieve shared objectives. As noted, Cisco has multiple cooperative arrangements with IBM and HP, and with service providers Accenture Ltd. and Tata Consulting Services Ltd. Demonstrating the complexity of network cooperative strategies is the fact that Cisco has a set of unique collaborations with both IBM and HP, but is also competing with them as they move into servers. The fact is that the number of network cooperative strategies being formed today continues to increase as firms seek to find the best ways to create value by offering multiple goods and services in multiple geographic (domestic and international) locations.

A network cooperative strategy is particularly effective when it is formed by geographically clustered firms,[114] as in California's Silicon Valley (where "the culture of Silicon Valley encourages collaborative webs"[115]) and Singapore's Biopolis (in the bio-medical sciences) and the new fusionopolis (collaborations in "physical sciences and engineering to tackle global science and technology challenges").[116] Effective social relationships and interactions among partners while sharing their resources and capabilities make it more likely that a network cooperative strategy will be successful,[117] as does having a productive **strategic center firm** (we discuss strategic center firms in detail in Chapter 11). Firms involved in networks gain information and knowledge from multiple sources. They can use these heterogeneous knowledge sets to produce more and better innovation. As a result, firms involved in networks of alliances tend to be more innovative.[118] However, there are disadvantages to participating in networks as a firm can be locked into its partnerships, precluding the development of alliances with others. In certain types of networks, such as Japanese *keiretsus,* firms in the network are expected to help other firms in the network whenever they need aid. Such expectations can become a burden and reduce the focal firm's performance over time.[119]

Alliance Network Types

An important advantage of a network cooperative strategy is that firms gain access to their partners' other partners. Having access to multiple collaborations increases the likelihood that additional competitive advantages will be formed as the set of shared resources and capabilities expands.[120] In turn, being able to develop new capabilities further stimulates product innovations that are critical to strategic competitiveness in the global economy.[121]

The set of strategic alliance partnerships resulting from the use of a network cooperative strategy is commonly called an **alliance network**. The alliance networks that companies develop vary by industry conditions. A **stable alliance network** is formed in mature industries where demand is relatively constant and predictable. Through a stable alliance network, firms try to extend their competitive advantages to other settings while continuing to profit from operations in their core, relatively mature industry. Thus, stable networks are built primarily to *exploit* the economies (scale and/or scope) that exist between the partners such as in the airline industry.[122] **Dynamic alliance networks** are used in industries characterized by frequent product innovations and short product life cycles.[123] For instance, the pace of innovation in the information technology (IT) industry (as well as other industries that are characterized by fast-cycle markets) is too fast for any one company to be successful across time if it only competes independently. Another example is the movie industry, which has a lot of collaborative ventures and networked firms to produce and distribute movies.[124] In dynamic alliance networks, partners typically *explore* new ideas and possibilities with the potential to lead to product innovations, entries to new markets, and the development of new markets.[125] Often, large firms in such industries as software and pharmaceuticals create networks of relationships with smaller entrepreneurial startup firms in their search for innovation-based outcomes.[126] An important outcome for small firms successfully partnering with larger firms in an alliance network is the credibility they build by being associated with their larger collaborators.[127]

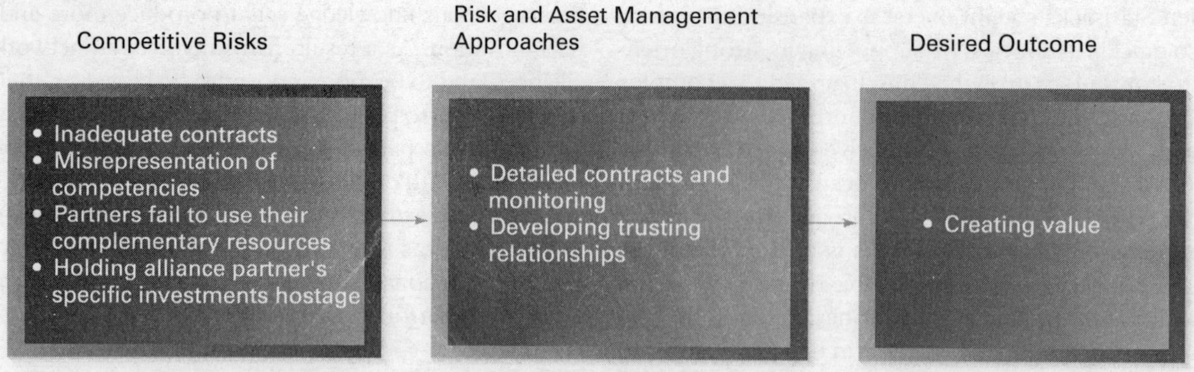

Figure 9.4 Managing competitive risks in cooperative strategies

Competitive Risks with Cooperative Strategies

Stated simply, many cooperative strategies fail. In fact, evidence shows that two-thirds of cooperative strategies have serious problems in their first two years and that as many as 50 per cent of them fail. This failure rate suggests that even when the partnership has potential complementarities and synergies, alliance success is elusive.[128] Although failure is undesirable, it can be a valuable learning experience, meaning that firms should carefully study a cooperative strategy's failure to gain insights with respect to how to form and manage future cooperative arrangements.[129] We show prominent cooperative strategy risks in Figure 9.4.

One cooperative strategy risk is that a partner may act opportunistically. Opportunistic behaviors surface either when formal contracts fail to prevent them or when an alliance is based on a false perception of partner trustworthiness. Not infrequently, the opportunistic firm wants to acquire as much of its partner's tacit knowledge as it can.[130] Full awareness of what a partner wants in a cooperative strategy reduces the likelihood that a firm will suffer from another's opportunistic actions.[131] The Strategic Focus on the Proctor & Gamble–Godrej Alliance, a 51/49 joint venture between the US FMCG gaint, Proctor & Gamble (P&G) and the Indian business group of Godrej , demonstrates potential opportunistic actions by parties involved and some of the potential risks of joint ventures, especially in an emerging economy like India.

Some cooperative strategies fail when it is discovered that a firm has misrepresented the competencies it can bring to the partnership. The risk of competence misrepresentation is more common when the partner's contribution is grounded in some of its intangible assets. Superior knowledge of local conditions is an example of an intangible asset that partners often fail to deliver. An effective way to deal with this risk may be to ask the partner to provide evidence that it does possess the resources and capabilities (even when they are largely intangible) it will share in the cooperative strategy.[132]

Another risk is a firm failing to make available to its partners the resources and capabilities (such as brands, distribution systems and sophisticated technologies) that it committed to the cooperative strategy. For example, as may be seen from the Strategic Focus 9.3, P&G and Godrej did not fulfill their parts of the agreement, at least in the eyes of the other party, and this put the alliance in a situation of weakness relative to its main competitor, Hindustan Lever (HLL; now Hindustan Unilever or HUL). This risk surfaces most commonly when firms form an international cooperative strategy, especially in emerging economies.[133] In these instances, different cultures and languages can cause misinterpretations of contractual terms or trust-based expectations. Some times, in the euphoria at the time of entering the agreement, both parties fail to specify the terms adequately, leading to unnecessary recriminations later. Trust breaks down and the alliance slides down the path of doom.

A final risk is that one firm may make investments that are specific to the alliance while its partner does not. For example, the firm might commit resources and capabilities to develop manufacturing equipment that can be used only to produce items coming from the alliance. If the partner isn't also making alliance-specific investments, the firm is at a relative disadvantage in terms of returns earned from the alliance compared with investments made to earn the returns. This was certainly an issue in the alliance between British Petroleum (BP) and three Russian tycoons, known as the TNK BP Alliance. In this, BP felt that it was continuing to make most of the investments, although it was losing control in managing those investments.

Managing Cooperative Strategies

Although cooperative strategies are an important means of firm growth and enhanced performance, managing these strategies is challenging. However, learning how to effectively manage cooperative strategies is important such that it can be a source of competitive advantage.[134] Because the ability to effectively manage cooperative strategies is unevenly distributed across organizations in general, assigning managerial responsibility for a firm's cooperative strategies to a high-level executive or to a team improves the likelihood that the strategies will be well managed.

Those responsible for managing the firm's set of cooperative strategies should take the actions necessary to coordinate activities, categorize knowledge learned from previous experiences, and make certain that what the firm knows about how to effectively form and use cooperative strategies is in the hands of the right people at the right time. Firms must also learn how to manage both the tangible and intangible assets (such as knowledge) that are involved with a cooperative arrangement. Too often, partners concentrate on managing tangible assets at the expense of taking action to also manage a cooperative relationship's intangible assets.[135]

Alliances are essentially marriages of convenience, or, more aptly, live-in relationships, and it is not likely that they last for a long time. Often, it is better to specify the terms of termination of the contract, and even its duration, so that the parting is smooth. Also, conditions change very fast, and the conditions under which the agreements were reached could change drastically enough to warrant a relook at the agreement after a certain period of time. If a termination and review clause is there in the contract, the renegotiation can be done more smoothly.

Two primary approaches are used to manage cooperative strategies—cost minimization and opportunity max-

STRATEGIC FOCUS

9.3 Troubles in the Godrej–P&G Alliance

In 1992, Godrej, a diversified Indian company with a major consumer products business, and Proctor and Gamble (P&G) entered into a marketing alliance (JV). The JV was named P&G Godrej (PGG). P&G had 51 per cent stake in it; Godrej had 49. By late 1996, it was all over, and the parties parted with a considerable amount of bitterness. The case illustrates the common pitfalls in alliances.

The JV had P&G's Indian country head as its CEO, while Mr. Adi Godrej, the head of the Godrej group was its chairman. P&G paid about ₹500 million to Godrej to acquire its detergents brands such as Key and Ezee, fairly well known brands in India, though by no means market leaders. Godrej had a number of good soap brands such as Cinthol, and these were leased to the alliance. Godrej became the sole supplier of soaps and detergents to the JV on a cost plus basis. P&G seems to have given some sort of a commitment to utilize the soap manufacturing capacity of Godrej, some 80,000 tons per annum; certainly it would not procure from elsewhere. Godrej had a problem utilizing its capacity on its own, since basically most of its brands were weak and would not sell. It seemed that utilizing its capacity better was the main motivation for Godrej to enter into the alliance. Godrej was allowed to complete its existing commitments to other companies, but could not take up any new supply contract. Godrej transferred some 400 of its sales people to this venture as well.

P&G's motivation to enter into this alliance seems to have been the excellent distribution network of Godrej in India, and its excellent overall corporate reputation. P&G was new to India (its predecessor, Richardson Hindustan was mainly an OTC drugs company selling such remedies as Vicks), and Godrej's local knowledge, including its knowhow of making soaps with vegeta-

©Indiatodayimages.com

ble oils (rather than tallow) was also valuable. The ready manufacturing capacity was also perhaps an attraction.

By 1995, the JV ran into serious problems. P&G had already raised its shareholding to 65 per cent. The soap off-take was nowhere near projections; in 1995, the off-take was only about 40,000 tons. This pushed up the costs. P&G felt that Godrej was taking advantage of the cost plus conditions of the contract, and was not making adequate efforts to bring down its costs. Godrej blamed the lack of marketing efforts of P&G, especially the former's old brands, which it felt were getting killed by P&G. Certainly, these brands did not see any increase in their sales.

The cultures and operating systems of the two partners were quite different, and though this did not pose problems during the honeymoon period, they soon posed major issues. P&G was a "systems based" company, and concentrated on developing and sustaining long term brands. Godrej, on the other hand, was somewhat more informal in its decision making style. P&G, in the meanwhile learnt enough about India, and the local knowledge of Godrej was no longer as valuable as it was two years ago. The distribution was also firmly in P&G's hands. However, the manufacturing agreement was a major irritant.

In late 1996, the alliance was formally terminated. P&G retained the detergent brands but returned the soap brands, which were taken on lease, to Godrej. PGG was taken over by P&G, including most of the erstwhile Godrej salespeople. But Godrej's detergent brands did not make much headway; brands were not well known in India. P&G's own soap portfolio was also not well known in India. Thus both Godrej and P&G were left in a weaker position than before, and perhaps HLL, the market leader of FMCG in India gained form the whole episode.

One problem was the poor drafting of the terms and conditions in the agreement, which left room for both the parties to behave in an opportunistic manner. Trust certainly seemed to have been a casualty.

Sources: A.V. Vedpuriswar, *Global CEO,* Chapter 7, 2001, retrieved from http://www.vedpuriswar.org/BookWritten_CEO.htm; *Business India*, 1996, Why P&G and Godrej broke up, July 15–28; *www.thefreelibrary.com, Business*; *PR Newswire,* 1996, Godrej, P&G agree to terminate their alliance, July 3.

imization[136] (see Figure 9.4). In the **cost minimization** management approach, the firm develops formal contracts with its partners. These contracts specify how the cooperative strategy is to be monitored and how partner behavior is to be controlled. The goal of the cost-minimization approach is to minimize the cooperative strategy's cost and to prevent opportunistic behavior by a partner. The focus of the second managerial approach—**opportunity maximization**—is on maximizing a partnership's value-creation opportunities. In this case, partners are prepared to take advantage of unexpected opportunities to learn from each other and to explore additional marketplace possibilities. Less formal contracts, with fewer constraints on partners' behaviors, make it possible for partners to explore how their resources and capabilities can be shared in multiple value-creating ways.

Firms can successfully use both approaches to manage cooperative strategies. However, the costs to monitor the cooperative strategy are greater with cost minimization, in that writing detailed contracts and using extensive monitoring mechanisms is expensive, even though the approach is intended to reduce alliance costs. Although monitoring systems may prevent partners from acting in their own best interests, they also often preclude positive responses to new opportunities that surface to use the alliance's competitive advantages. Thus, formal contracts and extensive monitoring systems tend to stifle partners' efforts to gain maximum value from their participation in a cooperative strategy and require significant resources to be put into place and used.[137]

The relative lack of detail and formality that is a part of the contract developed by firms using the second management approach of opportunity maximization means that firms need to trust each other to act in the partnership's best interests. The psychological state of *trust* in the context of cooperative arrangements is "the expectation held by one firm that another will not exploit its vulnerabilities when faced with the opportunity to do so."[138] When partners trust each other, there is less need to write detailed formal contracts to specify each firm's alliance behaviors,[139] and the cooperative relationship tends to be more stable.[140] On a relative basis, trust tends to be more difficult to establish in international cooperative strategies compared with domestic ones. Differences in trade policies, cultures, laws, and politics that are part of cross-border alliances account for the increased difficulty. When trust exists, monitoring costs are reduced and opportunities to create value are maximized. Essentially, in these cases, the firms have built social capital.[141] According to company officials, the alliance between Renault and Nissan is built on "mutual trust between the two partners ... together with operating and confidentiality rules."[142]

Research showing that trust between partners increases the likelihood of alliance success seems to highlight the benefits of the opportunity-maximization approach to managing cooperative strategies. Trust may also be the most efficient way to influence and control alliance partners' behaviors. Research indicates that trust can be a capability that is valuable, rare, imperfectly imitable, and often nonsubstitutable.[143] Thus, firms known to be trustworthy can have a competitive advantage in terms of how they develop and use cooperative strategies.[144] One reason is that it is impossible to specify all operational details of a cooperative strategy in a formal contract. Confidence that its partner can be trusted reduces the firm's concern about the inability to contractually control all alliance details.

SUMMARY

- A cooperative strategy is one in which firms work together to achieve a shared objective. Strategic alliances, where firms combine some of their resources and capabilities to create a competitive advantage, are the primary form of cooperative strategies. Joint ventures (where firms create and own equal shares of a new venture that is intended to develop competitive advantages), equity strategic alliances (where firms own different shares of a newly created venture), and non-equity strategic alliances (where firms cooperate through a contractual relationship) are the three basic types of strategic alliances. Outsourcing, discussed in Chapter 3, commonly occurs as firms form non-equity strategic alliances.
- Collusive strategies are the second type of cooperative strategies (with strategic alliances being the other). In many economies, explicit collusive strategies are illegal unless sanctioned by government policies. Increasing globalization has led to fewer government-sanctioned situations of explicit collusion. Tacit collusion, also called mutual forbearance, is a cooperative strategy through which firms tacitly cooperate to reduce industry output below the potential competitive output level, thereby raising prices above the competitive level.
- The reasons firms use cooperative strategies vary by slow-cycle, fast-cycle, and standard-cycle market conditions. To enter restricted markets (slow cycle), to move quickly from one competitive advantage to another (fast cycle), and to gain market power (standard cycle) are among the reasons why firms choose to use cooperative strategies.
- Four business-level cooperative strategies are used to help the firm improve its performance in individual product markets. (1) Through vertical and horizontal complementary alliances, companies combine their resources and capabilities to create value in different parts (vertical) or the same parts (horizontal) of the value chain. (2) Competition-responding strategies are formed to respond to competitors' actions, especially strategic ones. (3) Competition-reducing strategies are used to avoid excessive competition while the firm marshals its resources and capabilities to improve its competitiveness. (4) Uncertainty-reducing strategies are used to hedge against the risks created by the conditions of uncertain competitive environments (such as new product markets). Complementary alliances have the highest probability of yielding a sustainable competitive advantage; competition-reducing alliances have the lowest probability.
- Firms use corporate-level cooperative strategies to engage in product and/or geographic diversification. Through diversifying strategic alliances, firms agree to share some of their resources and capabilities to enter new markets or produce new products. Synergistic alliances are ones where firms share resources and capabilities to develop economies of scope. This alliance is similar to the business-level horizontal complementary alliance where firms try to develop operational synergy, except that synergistic alliances are used to develop synergy at the corporate level. Franchising is a corporate-level cooperative strategy where the franchisor uses a franchise as a contractual relationship to specify how resources and capabilities will be shared with franchisees.
- As an international cooperative strategy, a cross-border alliance is used for several reasons, including the performance superiority of firms competing in markets outside their domestic market and governmental restrictions on growth through mergers and acquisitions. Commonly, cross-border alliances are riskier than their domestic counterparts, particularly when partners aren't fully aware of each other's purpose for participating in the partnership.
- In a network cooperative strategy, several firms agree to form multiple partnerships to achieve shared objectives. A primary benefit of a network cooperative strategy is the firm's opportunity to gain access "to its partner's other partnerships." When this happens, the probability greatly increases that partners will find unique ways to share their resources and capabilities to form competitive advantages. Network cooperative strategies are used to form either a stable alliance network or a dynamic alliance network. Used in mature industries, partners use stable networks to extend competitive advantages into new areas. In rapidly changing environments where frequent product innovations occur, dynamic networks are primarily used as a tool of innovation.
- Cooperative strategies aren't risk free. If a contract is not developed appropriately, or if a partner misrepresents its competencies or fails to make them available, failure is likely. Furthermore, a firm may be held hostage through asset-specific investments made in conjunction with a partner, which may be exploited.
- Trust is an increasingly important aspect of successful cooperative strategies. Firms recognize the value of partnering with companies known for their trustworthiness. When trust exists, a cooperative strategy is managed to maximize the pursuit of opportunities between partners. Without trust, formal contracts and extensive monitoring systems are used to manage cooperative strategies. In this case, the interest is to minimize costs rather than to maximize opportunities by participating in a cooperative strategy.

KEY TERMS AND DEFINITIONS

A **cooperative strategy** is a strategy in which firms work together to achieve a shared objective.

A **strategic alliance** is a cooperative strategy in which firms combine some of their resources and capabilities to create a competitive advantage.

A **joint venture** is a strategic alliance in which two or more firms create a legally independent company to share some of their resources and capabilities to develop a competitive advantage.

An **equity strategic alliance** is an alliance in which two or more firms own different percentages of the company they have formed by combining some of their resources and capabilities to create a competitive advantage.

A **nonequity strategic alliance** is an alliance in which two or more firms develop a contractual relationship to share some of their unique resources and capabilities to create a competitive advantage.

A firm uses a **business-level cooperative strategy** to grow and improve its performance in individual product markets.

Complementary strategic alliances are business-level alliances in which firms share some of their resources and capabilities in complementary ways to develop competitive advantages.

A firm uses a **corporate-level cooperative strategy** to help it diversify in terms of products offered or markets served, or both.

A **diversifying strategic alliance** is a corporate-level cooperative strategy in which firms share some of their resources and capabilities to diversify into new product or market areas.

A **synergistic strategic alliance** is a corporate-level cooperative strategy in which firms share some of their resources and capabilities to create economies of scope.

Franchising is a corporate-level cooperative strategy in which a firm (the franchisor) uses a franchise as a contractual relationship to describe and control the sharing of its resources and capabilities with partners (the franchisees).

A **cross-border strategic alliance** is an international cooperative strategy in which firms with headquarters in different nations decide to combine some of their resources and capabilities to create a competitive advantage.

A **network cooperative strategy** is a cooperative strategy wherein several firms agree to form multiple partnerships to achieve shared objectives.

REVIEW QUESTIONS

1. What is the definition of cooperative strategy, and why is this strategy important to firms competing in the twenty-first century competitive landscape?
2. What is a strategic alliance? What are the three types of strategic alliances firms use to develop a competitive advantage?
3. What are the four business-level cooperative strategies, and what are the differences among them?
4. What are the three corporate-level cooperative strategies? How do firms use each one to create a competitive advantage?
5. Why do firms use cross-border strategic alliances?
6. What risks are firms likely to experience as they use cooperative strategies?
7. What are the differences between the cost-minimization approach and the opportunity-maximization approach to managing cooperative strategies?

EXPERIENTIAL EXERCISES

Exercise 1: What Is It: TV, Internet, or Both?

Hulu (http://www.hulu.com) is a Web site and a cooperative alliance that offers commercially supported content of TV (video on demand) shows through the Internet. The name is derived from a Chinese word which when translated means "holder of precious things." The alliance has many different partners related in interesting ways. In addition, the alliance includes firms and partners from very different market types.

Working in groups, answer the following questions:

1. How would you describe the alliance partners? Characterize the market type for each (slow cycle, fast cycle, standard cycle).
2. What type of strategic alliance has Hulu become?
3. In what type of market is Hulu competing?
4. Why did this alliance form? List some competitive pressures that made this alliance a necessity for its partners.
5. What does the future hold for this alliance?

Exercise 2: The Swatchmobile

Swatch is well known for its line of stylish, affordable wristwatches. In the early 1990s, Swatch CEO Nicholas Hayek had a novel idea to diversify his company's product offerings: a stylish, affordable automobile. His vision was to create a two-seat car with minimal storage space. Hayek expected these fuel-efficient cars would be highly attractive to younger European car buyers. Drawing on the company's watch designs, the Swatch car was intended to have removable body panels so that owners could change the car's look on a whim.

Swatch initially partnered with Volkswagen, but the alliance never reached production. In 1994, Swatch partnered with Mercedes-Benz. The vehicle was named SMART, which stood for "Swatch Mercedes Art."

Using Internet resources, answer the following questions:

1. What resources did each partner bring to the partnership?
2. How successful has the partnership been for each company?
3. Which company seems to be deriving the greatest benefit from the partnership and why?

PART III: Implementation of Strategic Actions

Corporate Governance and Ethics

CHAPTER

10

Studying this chapter should provide you with the strategic management knowledge needed to

- Define corporate governance and explain why it is used to monitor and control managers' strategic decisions.
- Explain why ownership has been largely separated from managerial control in the corporation.
- Define an agency relationship and managerial opportunism and describe their strategic implications.
- Explain how three internal governance mechanisms—ownership concentration, the board of directors, and executive compensation—are used to monitor and control managerial decisions.
- Discuss the types of compensation executives receive and their effects on strategic decisions.
- Describe how the external corporate governance mechanism—the market for corporate control—acts as a restraint on top-level managers' strategic decisions.
- Discuss the use of corporate governance in international settings, especially in Germany, Japan, and China.
- Describe how corporate governance fosters ethical strategic decisions and the importance of such behaviors on the part of top level managers.

OPENING CASE
Is CEO Pay Outrageous, Irresponsibile, Or Greedy?

In 2008, the ten most highly paid CEOs earned a total of $472.2 million in USA. Furthermore, seven of these CEOs who worked at the same companies in 2007 received an increase in pay of approximately 26 per cent over the previous year. Placing this in perspective, an average of $47.22 million was paid to these CEOs in a year when most large firms—including theirs—lost significant market value, and many experienced net losses. In 2008, we learned that the US economy and, indeed, much of the rest of the world, was in a deep recession. In fact, it is perhaps the worst since the Great Depression in the 1930s. Many believe that this recession was largely caused by irresponsible and greedy strategies followed by top-level managers in the financial services and real estate industries. In addition, the corporate governance system failed to rein in these managers, who took extreme risks causing billions of dollars in losses. Real estate values plummeted in many parts of the country, there were a substantial number of mortgage foreclosures, unemployment increased substantially, and the stock market took a nosedive.

Julia Hiebaum/Alamy

In 2008, seven of ten most highly paid CEOs took home 26 per cent more than what they did in the preceding year. This when their firms lost significant market value and experienced net losses as the world plunged in deep recession.

In this context, top executive pay came under intense criticism. In recent years, supposedly knowledgeable people argued that top-level managers were being paid for performance. If so, how could they earn such high compensation when their companies were performing poorly? Many CEOs earn more than 100 times the amount received by their firm's lowest-paid employee. Despite the average increases for the highest-paid CEOs, the median salary and bonuses for CEOs of the largest 200 US firms decreased by 8.5 per cent in 2008, but their total direct compensation only fell by 3.4 per cent. The decline in the financial services industry was much greater, as could be expected. Still, the median value of perks provided to CEOs in 2008 increased by about 7 per cent. "Perks" include many possible benefits, such as club memberships, free personal travel in company jets, bodyguards, and chauffeured cars. In fact, the CEO of Occidental Petroleum received $400,000 worth of financial planning. This was a part of his compensation in 2008, which totaled $30 million. While this benefit for financial planning is only 1.33 per cent of his total pay for the year, $400,000 is greater than the total annual household income for most US citizens.

In a survey conducted by *The Financial Times*, respondents from France, Germany, Italy, Spain, the United Kingdom, and the United States stated that they believed that business leaders were paid too much. The lowest percentage believing that top-level managers were overpaid was about 75 per cent in France, while almost 90 per cent in Germany felt they were overpaid. When the feelings of the general public are combined with the poor performance of companies in a weak economy, pundits often blame an inadequate system of corporate governance. This concern is amplified by reports of bad strategic decisions of business leaders blamed for creating the economic crisis. Thus, governments and others have begun to explore the governance mechanisms including compensation systems, boards of directors, ownership, and disciplining from the markets. It is likely that new regulations will be proposed and adopted to control what the public perceives to be irresponsibility and greed on the part of business leaders.

The Indian Scenario

Compared to the CEOs in US, Indian CEOs' compensation packages may seem puny. In 2008-09, the top earners were the Marans of the Sun TV group in Tamil Nadu. Kalanithi Maran and his wife Kaveri Kalanithi (₹370 million each); and Anil Ambani (₹520 million). Some exercised voluntary restraint, as for example, Mukesh Ambani, who was eligible for more than ₹300 million but actually took ₹50 million. Other companies that paid at least ₹10 million (one crore, as it is called in India) in 2010 to their top executives were Ranbaxy, JSW Steel, HDFC Bank, Infosys, ACC, HDFC Bank, ICICI Bank, and many others. But compared to the general salary levels and the per capita GDP in PPP terms, these figures are also high, high enough to attract comments from the Prime Minister Mr. Manmohan Singh and then Union Minister for Corporate Affairs, Mr. Salman Kurshid. In India, many of the large firms are in fact family firms, with a high stake in the companies, hence the promoters also get dividend from their shares, which are distinct from the salaries reported. In the year ending 2010, the hike in pay of Indian CEOs was around 33 per cent, as compared to about 16 per cent increase in profits in their companies. In certain sectors such as engineering and finance, the hikes were even higher. There have been debates on whether there should be any government control on top management compensation, and the opinion is sharply divided.

Sources: V. Tong, 2009, As pay falls, CEOs get more perks, *YAHOO! News*, http://news.yahoo.com, May 1; 2009, The pay at the top, *The New York Times*, http://www.nytimes.com, April 16; R. Milne, 2009, Sharp divide on executive pay, *Financial Times*, http://www.ft.com, April 13; J. S. Lublin, 2009, CEO pay sinks along with profits, *Wall Street Journal*, http://www.wsj.com, April 6; T. Carr, 2008, An ethical analysis of CEO compensation, Fast Company, http://www.fastcompany.com, November 28; A. Cohen, 2008, CEO pay; outrageous—and bad for MBA programs, Fast Company, http://www.fastcompany.com, April 6; Suniet Bexbaroowa, 2010, Does CEO compensation in India need a rethink?, March 2, www.paycheck.in, http://www.paycheck.in/main/work-and-pay/paycheck-articles-archives/does-ceo-compensation-in-india-need-a-rethink; *Economic Times*, 2010, India Inc. CEOs draw bigger pay packets despite slowdown, 3 May; *Press Trust of India*, 2010, ₹.one crore CEO salary is no big Indian deal, June 13, retrieved from http://ibnlive.in.com/news/rs-onecrore-ceo-salary-is-no-big-indian-deal/124130-7.html.

As the Opening Case illustrates, governance mechanisms designed to ensure effective leadership of firms to develop and implement strategies that create value for stakeholders is challenging. However, corporate governance is critical to firms' success and thus has become an increasingly important part of the strategic management process.[1] If the board makes the wrong decisions in selecting, governing, and compensating the firm's strategic leader (e.g., CEO), the shareholders and the firm suffer. When CEOs are motivated to act in the best interests of the firm—in particular, the shareholders—the firm's value should increase.

As suggested in the Opening Case, many people now believe that CEOs in the United States (and in India) are paid too much; the hefty increases in their incentive compensation in recent years ostensibly come from trying to link pay to their firms' performance (bonus etc.). However, research also suggests that firms with a smaller pay gap between the CEO and other top level managers perform better, especially when collaboration among top management team members is more important.[2] The performance improvement in these cases is due to better cooperation among the top management team members. Other research suggests that CEOs receive excessive compensation when corporate governance is the weakest.[3]

Corporate governance is the set of mechanisms used to manage the relationship among stakeholders and to determine and control the strategic direction and performance of organizations.[4] At its core, corporate governance is concerned with identifying ways to ensure that strategic decisions are made effectively.[5] Governance can also be thought of as a means to establish harmony between parties (the firm's owners and its top-level managers) whose interests may conflict. In modern corporations—especially those in the United States and the United Kingdom—a primary objective of corporate governance is to ensure that the interests of top-level managers are aligned with the interests of the shareholders. Corporate governance involves oversight in areas where owners, managers, and members of boards of directors may have conflicts of interest. These areas include the election of directors, the general supervision of CEO pay and more focused supervision of director pay, and the corporation's overall structure and strategic direction.[6]

Recent emphasis on corporate governance stems mainly from the failure of corporate governance mechanisms to adequately monitor and control top-level managers' decisions. This situation results in changes in governance mechanisms in corporations throughout the world, especially with respect to efforts intended to improve the performance of boards of directors. A second and more positive reason for this interest comes from evidence that a well-functioning corporate governance and control system can create a competitive advantage for an individual firm.[7] Thus, in this chapter, we describe actions designed to implement strategies that focus on monitoring and controlling mechanisms that are designed to ensure that top-level managerial actions contribute to the firm's strategic competitiveness and its ability to earn above-average returns.

Effective corporate governance is also of interest to nations.[8] Although corporate governance reflects company standards, it also collectively reflects country societal standards.[9] As with these firms and their boards, nations that effectively govern their corporations may gain a competitive advantage over rival countries. In a range of countries, but especially in the United States and the United Kingdom, the fundamental goal of business organizations is to maximize shareholder value.[10] Indian companies also seem to be falling in line with this line of thinking. The underlying logic is simple. Shareholders are treated as the firm's key stakeholders, because they are the company's legal owners. The firm's owners expect top-level managers and others influencing the corporation's actions (e.g., the board of directors) to make decisions that will maximize the company's value and, hence, the owners' wealth.[11] Research shows that national models of corporate governance influence firms' decisions to invest and operate in different countries.[12]

In the first section of this chapter, we describe the relationship that is the foundation on which the modern corporation is built: the relationship between owners and managers. The majority of this chapter is used to explain various mechanisms owners use to govern managers and to ensure that they comply with their responsibility to maximize shareholder value.

Three internal governance mechanisms and a single external one are used in the modern corporation. The three internal governance mechanisms we describe in this chapter are (1) ownership concentration, represented by types of shareholders and their different incentives to monitor managers; (2) the board of directors; and (3) executive compensation. We then consider the market for corporate control, an external corporate governance mechanism. Essentially, this market is a set of potential owners seeking to acquire undervalued firms and earn above-average returns on their investments by replacing ineffective top-level management teams.[13] The chapter's focus then shifts to the issue of international corporate governance. We briefly describe governance approaches used in German, Japanese, Chinese, and Indian firms whose traditional governance structures are being affected by the realities of global competition. In part, this discussion suggests that the structures used to govern global companies in many different countries, including Germany, Japan, the United Kingdom, and the United States, as well as emerging economies such as China and India, are becoming more, rather than less, similar. Closing our analysis of corporate governance is a consideration of the need for these control mechanisms to encourage and support ethical behavior in organizations.

Importantly, the mechanisms discussed in this chapter can positively influence the governance of the modern corporation, which has placed significant responsibility and authority in the hands of top-level managers. With multiple governance mechanisms operating simultaneously, however, it is also possible for some of the governance mechanisms to be in conflict.[14] Later, we review how these conflicts can occur.

Separation of Ownership and Managerial Control

Historically, US as well as Indian firms were managed by the founder-owners and their descendants. In these cases, corporate ownership and control resided in the same persons. As firms grew larger, "the managerial revolution led to a separation of ownership and control in most large corporations, where control of the firm shifted from entrepreneurs to professional managers while ownership became dispersed among thousands of unorganized stockholders who were removed from the day-to-day management of the firm."[15] These changes created the modern public corporation, which is based on the efficient separation of ownership and managerial control. Supporting the separation is a basic legal premise suggesting that the primary objective of a firm's activities is to increase the corporation's profit and, thereby, the financial gains of the owners (the shareholders).[16]

The separation of ownership and managerial control allows shareholders to purchase stock, which entitles them to income (residual returns) from the firm's operations after paying expenses. This right, however, requires that they also take a risk that the firm's expenses may exceed its revenues. In order to manage this investment risk, shareholders maintain a diversified portfolio by investing in several companies to reduce their overall risk.[17] The poor performance or failure of any one firm in which they invest has less overall effect on the value of the entire portfolio of investments. Thus, shareholders specialize in managing their investment risk.

In small firms, managers often are high percentage owners, which means less separation between ownership and managerial control. In fact, in a large number of family-owned firms (as is the case in India), ownership and managerial control are not separated. In the United States, at least one-third of the S&P 500 firms have substantial family ownership, holding on average about 18 per cent of the outstanding equity. In India, this percentage is likely to be higher. And family-owned firms perform better when a member of the family is the CEO than when the CEO is an outsider.[18] In many countries outside the United States, such as in Latin America, Asia, and some European countries, family-owned firms represent the dominant form.[19] The primary purpose of most of these firms is to increase the family's wealth, which explains why a family CEO often is better than an outside CEO.

Family-controlled firms face at least two critical issues. First, as they grow, they may not have access to all of the skills needed to effectively manage the firm and maximize its returns for the family. Thus, they may need outsiders. Also, as they grow, they may need to seek outside capital and thus give up some of the ownership. In these cases, protection of the minority owners' rights becomes important.[20] To avoid these potential problems, when these firms grow and become more complex, their owner-managers may contract with managerial specialists. These managers make major decisions in the owners' firm and are compensated on the basis of their decision-making skills. As such, recent research suggests that firms in which families own enough equity to have influence without major control tend to make the best strategic decisions.[21]

Without owner (shareholder) specialization in risk bearing and management specialization in decision making, a firm may be limited by the abilities of its owners to manage and make effective strategic decisions. Thus, the separation and specialization of ownership (risk bearing) and managerial control (decision making) should produce the highest returns for the firm's owners.

Shareholder value is reflected by the price of the firm's stock. As stated earlier, corporate governance mechanisms, such as the board of directors, or compensation based on the performance of a firm is the reason that CEOs show general concern about the firm's stock price.

Agency Relationships

The separation between owners and managers creates an agency relationship. An **agency relationship** exists when one or more persons (the principal or principals) hire another person or persons (the agent or agents) as decision-making specialists to perform a service.[22] Thus, an agency relationship exists when one party delegates decision-making responsibility to a second party for compensation (see Figure 10.1).[23] In addition to shareholders and top-level managers, other examples of agency relationships are consultants and clients and insured and insurer. Moreover, within organizations, an agency relationship exists between managers and their employees, as well as between top level managers and the firm's owners.[24] However, in this chapter, we focus on the agency relationship between the firm's owners (the principals) and top-level managers (the principals' agents) because these managers formulate and implement the firm's strategies, which have major effects on firm performance.[25]

The separation between ownership and managerial control can be problematic. Research evidence documents a variety of agency problems in the modern corporation.[26] Problems can surface because the principal and the agent have different interests and goals, or because shareholders lack direct control of large publicly traded corporations. Problems also arise when an agent makes decisions that result in the pursuit of goals that conflict with those of the principals. Thus, the separation of ownership and control potentially allows divergent interests (between principals and agents) to surface, which can lead to managerial opportunism.

Managerial opportunism is the seeking of self-interest with guile (i.e., cunning or deceit).[27] Opportunism is both an attitude (e.g., an inclination) and a set of behaviors (i.e., specific acts of self-interest).[28] It is not possible for principals to know beforehand which agents will

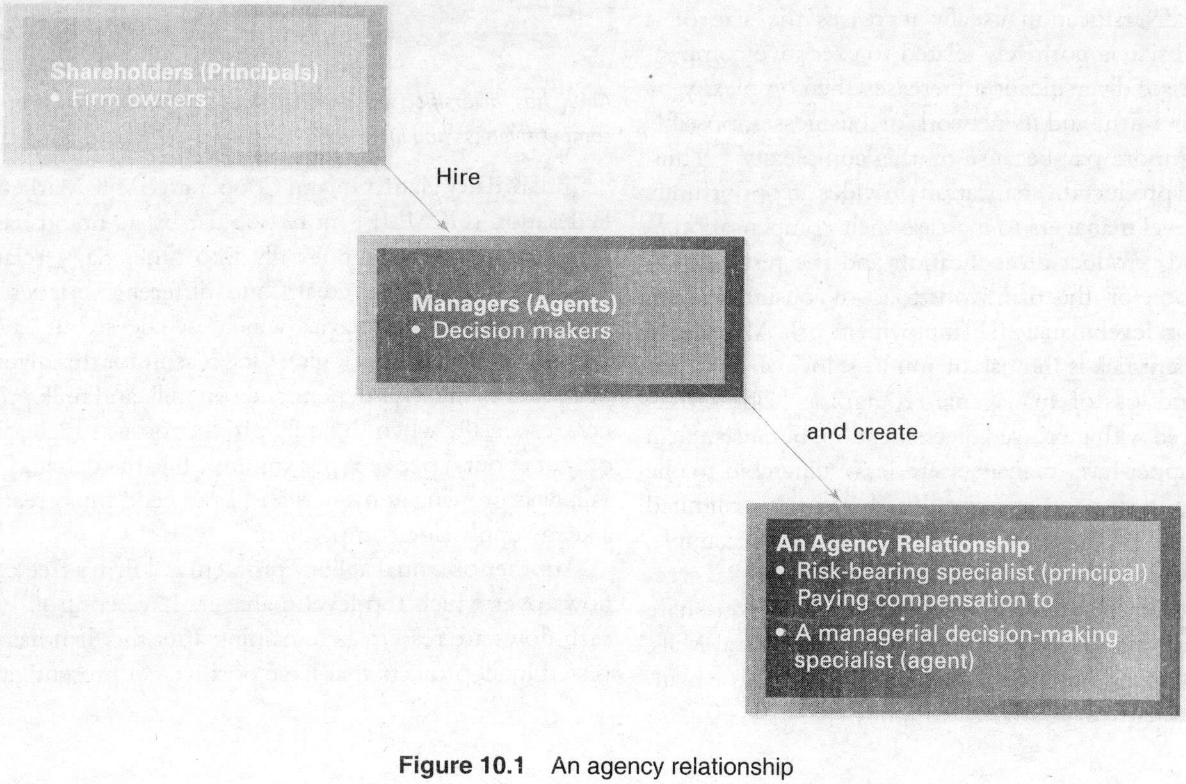

Figure 10.1 An agency relationship

or will not act opportunistically. The reputations of top level managers are an imperfect predictor, and opportunistic behavior cannot be observed until it has occurred. Thus, principals establish governance and control mechanisms to prevent agents from acting opportunistically, even though only a few are likely to do so. Interestingly, research suggests that when CEOs feel constrained by governance mechanisms, they are more likely to seek external advice that in turn helps them to make better strategic decisions.[29] Whenever principals delegate decision-making responsibilities to agents, the opportunity for conflicts of interest exists. Top-level managers, for example, may make strategic decisions that maximize their personal welfare and minimize their personal risk.[30] Decisions such as these prevent the maximization of shareholder wealth. Decisions regarding product diversification demonstrate this alternative.

Product Diversification as an Example of an Agency Problem

As explained in Chapter 6, a corporate-level strategy to diversify the firm's product lines can enhance a firm's strategic competitiveness and increase its returns, both of which serve the interests of shareholders and the top-level managers. However, product diversification can result in two benefits to managers that shareholders do not enjoy, so top level managers may prefer product diversification more than shareholders do.[31]

First, diversification usually increases the size of a firm, and size is positively related to executive compensation. Also, diversification increases the complexity of managing a firm and its network of businesses, possibly requiring more pay because of this complexity.[32] Thus, increased product diversification provides an opportunity for top-level managers to increase their compensation.[33]

Second, product diversification and the resulting diversification of the firm's portfolio of businesses can reduce top-level managers' employment risk. Managerial employment risk is the risk of job loss, loss of compensation, and loss of managerial reputation.[34] These risks are reduced with increased diversification, because a firm and its upper-level managers are less vulnerable to the reduction in demand associated with a single or limited number of product lines or businesses. For example, Kellogg Co. was almost entirely focused on breakfast cereal in 2001 when it suffered its first-ever market share leadership loss to perennial number two, General Mills, Inc. Upon appointing Carlos Gutierrez, a longtime manager at Kellogg, to the CEO position, the company embarked on a new strategy to overcome its poor performance. A *BusinessWeek* article outlined his strategy results as follows: "To drive sales, Gutierrez unveiled such novel products as Special K snack bars, bought cookie maker Keebler Co., and ramped up Kellogg's health-foods presence by snapping up Worthington Foods Inc., a maker of soy and vegetarian products, and cereal maker Kashi. He pushed net earnings up 77 per cent, to $890.6 million, from 1998 to 2004, as sales rose 42 per cent, to $9.6 billion."[35] Kellogg's revenues continued to increase to approximately $13 billion a year in 2008, which was almost 8 per cent higher than 2007.[36] This is a remarkable accomplishment during a recessionary economy. Kellogg's diversified scope increased, yet it was accomplished in highly related businesses that provided synergy. Through this strategy, the CEO's risk of job loss was substantially reduced. Recent research shows that this type of diversification can be profitable.[37]

Amul has diversified its product lines, enhancing its strategic competitiveness and increasing its returns.

India's dairy giant, Gujarat Cooperative Milk Marketing Federation (GCMMF) more popular by its brand name Amul, has diversified not only into other dairy related products such as ice cream and different varieties of cheese, but also into pizzas (which use cheese but have a very different business logic). One reason for this diversification was the over dependence on milk and milk products, especially when the milk production was increasing only at about 6 per cent per annum while the demand for milk was growing at more than 11 per cent, thus creating a keen supply side competition.[38]

Another potential agency problem is a firm's free cash flows over which top-level managers have control. Free cash flows are resources remaining after the firm has invested in all projects that have positive net present value

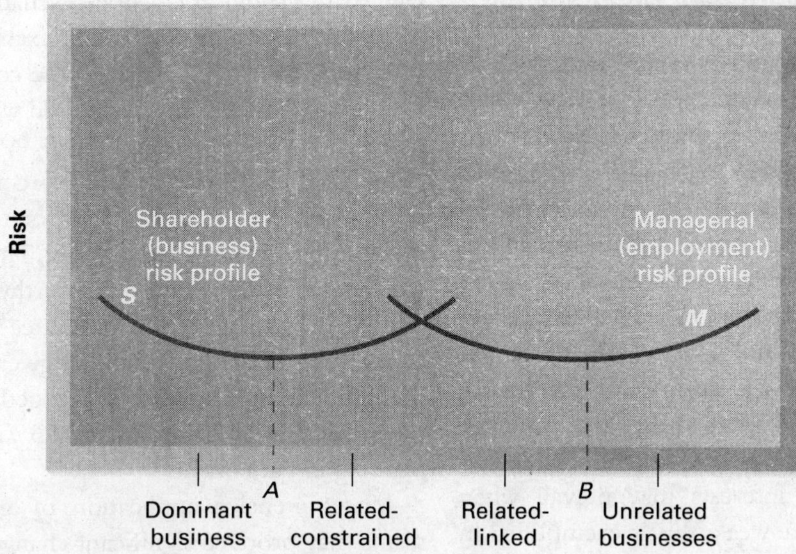

Figure 10.2 Manager and shareholder risk and diversification

within its current businesses.[39] In anticipation of positive returns, managers may decide to invest these funds in products that are not associated with the firm's current lines of business to increase the firm's level of diversification. The managerial decision to use free cash flows to over-diversify the firm is an example of self-serving and opportunistic managerial behavior. In contrast to managers, shareholders may prefer that free cash flows be distributed to them as dividends, so they can control how the cash is invested.[40]

Curve *S* in Figure 10.2 depicts the shareholders' optimal level of diversification. Owners seek the level of diversification that reduces the risk of the firm's total failure while simultaneously increasing the company's value through the development of economies of scale and scope (see Chapter 6). Of the four corporate-level diversification strategies shown in Figure 10.2, shareholders likely prefer the diversified position noted by point *A* on curve *S*—a position that is located between the dominant business and related-constrained diversification strategies. Of course, the optimum level of diversification owners seek varies from firm to firm.[41] Factors that affect shareholders' preferences include the firm's primary industry, the intensity of rivalry among competitors in that industry, and the top management team's experience with implementing diversification strategies and its effects on other firm strategies, such as its entry into international markets (see Chapter 8).[42]

As do principals, top level managers—as agents—also seek an optimal level of diversification. Declining performance resulting from too much product diversification increases the probability that corporate control of the firm will be acquired in the market. After a firm is acquired, the employment risk for the firm's top-level managers increases substantially. Furthermore, a manager's employment opportunities in the external managerial labor market (discussed in Chapter 12) are affected negatively by a firm's poor performance. Therefore, top level managers prefer diversification, but not to a point that it increases their employment risk and reduces their employment opportunities.[43] Curve *M* in Figure 10.2 shows that top level managers prefer higher levels of product diversification than do shareholders. Top-level managers might prefer the level of diversification shown by point *B* on curve *M*.

In general, shareholders prefer riskier strategies and more focused diversification. They reduce their risk through holding a diversified portfolio of equity investments. Alternatively, managers cannot balance their employment risk by working for a diverse portfolio of firms, and therefore, may prefer a level of diversification that maximizes firm size and their compensation while also reducing their employment risk. Product diversification, therefore, is a potential agency problem that could result in principals incurring costs to control their agents' behaviors.

Agency Costs and Governance Mechanisms

The potential conflict illustrated by Figure 10.2, coupled with the fact that principals cannot easily predict which managers might act opportunistically, demonstrates why principals establish governance mechanisms. However, the firm incurs costs when it uses one or more governance mechanisms. **Agency costs** are the sum of incentive costs, monitoring costs, enforcement costs, and individual financial losses incurred by principals because governance mechanisms cannot guarantee total compliance by the agent. If a firm is diversified, governance costs increase because it is more difficult to monitor what is going on inside the firm.[44]

In general, managerial interests may prevail when governance mechanisms are weak; this is exemplified in situations where managers have a significant amount of autonomy to make strategic decisions. If, however, the board of directors controls managerial autonomy, or if other strong governance mechanisms are used, the firm's strategies should better reflect the interests of the shareholders. More recently, governance observers have been concerned about more egregious behavior beyond inefficient corporate strategy.

Due to fraudulent behavior such as that found at Enron and WorldCom, concerns regarding corporate governance continue to grow. In 2002, the US Congress enacted the Sarbanes-Oxley (SOX) Act, which increased the intensity of corporate governance mechanisms.[45] Furthermore, the serious problems experienced in the financial services industry can be attributed to the result of poor governance and top-level managers making very bad strategic decisions. In fact, the bonuses paid to Merrill Lynch executives after extremely poor performance (described in the Opening Case) are reflective of managerial opportunism.

While the implementation of the Sarbanes-Oxley Act in 2002 has been controversial to some, most believe that the results of it have been generally positive. Section 404 of SOX, which prescribes significant transparency improvement on internal controls associated with accounting and auditing, has arguably improved the internal auditing scrutiny and thereby trust in such financial reporting. A recent study indicated that internal controls associated with Section 404 increased shareholder value.[46] However, some argue that the Act, especially Section 404, creates excessive costs for firms. In addition, a decrease in foreign firms listing on US stock exchanges occurred at the same time as listing on foreign exchanges increased. In part, this shift may be due to the costs associated with listing on US exchanges associated with requirements of SOX.

In India also, a number of committees were set up to look into issues of corporate governance. The most important of these were: The Naresh Chandra Committee[47], the Narayana Murthy Committee[48], the Kumar Mangalam Birla Committee[49], and the J.J. Irani Committee[50]. The last one had given a number of recommendations that were put together by the government in the form of a *Companies Bill* in 2008, and is now pending in Parliament.

More intensive application of governance mechanisms may produce significant changes in strategies. For example, because of more intense governance, firms may take on fewer risky projects and thus decrease potential shareholder wealth. Next, we explain the effects of different governance mechanisms on the decisions managers make about the choice and the use of the firm's strategies.

Ownership Concentration

Both the number of large-block shareholders and the total percentage of shares they own define **ownership concentration. Large-block shareholders** typically own at least 5 per cent of a corporation's issued shares. Ownership concentration as a governance mechanism has received considerable interest because large-block shareholders are increasingly active in their demands that corporations adopt effective governance mechanisms to control managerial decisions.[51]

In general, diffuse ownership (a large number of shareholders with small holdings and few, if any, large-block shareholders) produces weak monitoring of managers' decisions. For example, diffuse ownership makes it difficult for owners to effectively coordinate their actions. Diversification of the firm's product lines beyond the shareholders' optimum level can result from ineffective monitoring of managers' decisions. Higher levels of monitoring could encourage managers to avoid strategic decisions that harm shareholder value. In fact, research evidence shows that ownership concentration is associated with lower levels of firm product diversification.[52] Thus, with high degrees of ownership concentration, the probability is greater that managers' strategic decisions will be designed to maximize shareholder value.[53]

As noted, such concentration of ownership has an influence on strategies and firm value, mostly positive but perhaps not in all cases. For example, when large shareholders have a high degree of wealth, they have power relative to minority shareholders in extracting wealth from the firm, especially when they are in managerial positions. The importance of boards of directors in mitigating expropriation of minority shareholder value has been found in firms with strong family ownership wherein family members have incentive to appropriate shareholder wealth, especially in the second generation after the founder has departed.[54] Such expropriation is often found in countries such as Korea where minority shareholder rights are not as protected as they are in the United States.[55] However, in the United States much of the ownership concentration has come from increasing equity ownership by institutional investors.

The Growing Influence of Institutional Owners

A classic work published in the 1930s argued that the "modern" corporation was characterized by a separation of ownership and control.[56] The change occurred primarily because growth prevented founders-owners from maintaining their dual positions in their increasingly complex companies. More recently, another shift has occurred: Ownership of many modern corporations is now concentrated in the hands of institutional investors rather than individual shareholders.[57]

Institutional owners are financial institutions such as stock mutual funds and pension funds that control large-block shareholder positions. In India, these consist of institutions such as Life Insurance Corporation of India (LIC) and Unit Trust of India (UTI), banks such as State Bank of India, ICICI Bank, and HDFC Bank, and development banks such as IDBI and NABARD. Many of them were originally lenders to the firms, providing the capital, and their loans were converted to equity at some point in time, so that they became shareholders. Because of their prominent ownership positions, institutional owners, as large-block shareholders, are a powerful governance mechanism. They have their nominees in companies in which they have a significant stake. Institutions of these types now own more than 60 per cent of the stock in large US corporations. In India, they would be much less, around 30 per cent, since the promoters' shares tend to be larger. In US, pension funds alone control at least one-half of corporate equity.[58]

These ownership percentages suggest that as investors, institutional owners have both the size and the incentive to discipline ineffective top-level managers and can significantly influence a firm's choice of strategies and overall strategic decisions.[59] Research evidence indicates that institutional and other large-block shareholders are becoming more active in their efforts to influence a corporation's strategic decisions, unless they have a business relationship with the firm. Initially, these shareholder activists and institutional investors concentrated on the performance and accountability of CEOs and contributed to the dismissal of a number of them. They often target the actions of boards more directly via proxy vote proposals that are intended to give shareholders more decision rights because they believe board processes have been ineffective.[60] In fact, a new rule recently proposed and approved by the US Securities and Exchange Commission allows large shareholders (owning 1 to 5 per cent of a company's stock) to nominate up to 25 per cent of a company's board of directors.[61]

While the nomination of these directors on the boards has led to an increase in the so called institutional activism, with the institutions aggressively promoting governance decisions, in India, the institutions have tended to play a much more passive role. In fact, many of these institutions are controlled by the government, and hence, wary of being seen as taking sides, prefer to play a neutral role, or supporting company managements.[62]

Even though it might appear, at first sight, that the presence of these "independent" institutional representatives would lead to better corporate governance, in reality, it may not happen. These institutions may be more interested in protecting their own interests than the company's interests. This can happen, for example, if an issue comes up vis-à-vis a firm in which they have a substantial exposure.

Board of Directors

Typically, shareholders monitor the managerial decisions and actions of a firm through the board of directors. Shareholders elect members to their firm's board. Those who are elected are expected to oversee managers and to ensure that the corporation is operated in ways that will maximize its shareholders' wealth. Even with large institutional investors having major equity ownership in

US firms, diffuse ownership continues to exist in most firms, which means that in large corporations, monitoring and control of managers by individual shareholders is limited. Furthermore, large financial institutions, such as banks, are prevented in US from directly owning stock in firms and from having representatives on companies' boards of directors, although this restriction is not the case in Europe and elsewhere.[63] These conditions highlight the importance of the board of directors for corporate governance. Unfortunately, over time, boards of directors have not been highly effective in monitoring and controlling top management's actions.[64] Given the recent problems with top-level managers making less than ethical decisions, boards are experiencing increasing pressure from shareholders, lawmakers, and regulators to become more forceful in their oversight role to prevent inappropriate actions by top-level managers. Furthermore, boards not only serve a monitoring role, but they also provide resources to firms. These resources include their personal knowledge and expertise as well as their access to resources of other firms through their external contacts and relationships.[65]

The **board of directors** is a group of elected individuals whose primary responsibility is to act in the owners' best interests by formally monitoring and controlling the corporation's top-level managers.[66] Boards have the power to direct the affairs of the organization, punish and reward managers, and protect shareholders' rights and interests. Thus, an appropriately structured and effective board of directors protects owners from managerial opportunism such as that found at Enron and WorldCom and at financial services firms including AIG and Merrill Lynch, where shareholders and employees encountered significant losses. Board members are seen as stewards of their company's resources, and the way they carry out these responsibilities affects the society in which their firm operates. For instance, research suggests that better governance produces more effective strategic decisions, which lead to higher firm performance.[67]

Generally, board members (often called **directors**) are classified into one of three groups (see Table 10.1). **Insiders** are active top-level managers in the corporation who are elected to the board because they are a source of information about the firm's day-to-day operations.[68] **Related outsiders** have some relationship with the firm, contractual or otherwise, that may create questions about their independence, but these individuals are not involved with the corporation's day-to-day activities. **Outsiders** provide independent counsel to the firm and may hold top-level managerial positions in other companies or may have been elected to the board prior to the beginning of the current CEO's tenure.[69]

Historically, boards of directors were primarily dominated by inside managers. A widely accepted view is that a board with a significant percentage of its membership from the firm's top-level managers provides relatively weak monitoring and control of managerial decisions.[70] Managers have sometimes used their power to select and compensate directors and exploit their personal ties with them. In response to the SEC's proposal to require audit committees to be composed of outside directors, in 1984, the New York Stock Exchange implemented a rule requiring outside directors to head the audit committee. Subsequently, other rules required important committees such as the compensation committee and the nomination committee to be headed by independent outside directors.[71] These other requirements were instituted after the Sarbanes-Oxley Act was passed, and policies of the New York Stock Exchange now require companies to maintain boards of directors that are composed of a majority of outside independent directors and to maintain full independent audit committees. Thus, corporate governance is becoming more intense especially with the oversight of the board of directors.

The Indian Companies Bill seeks to provide for at least one third of the board to consist of independent directors. This is not much different from the present conditions to be listed in the stock exchange, i.e., one third if the chairperson of the board and the chief executive (managing director) are two different persons, and half, if they are one and the same person. This is expected to lead to better governance, though, ironically, India may face a shortage of good independent directors willing to serve on boards. The Audit Committee is envisaged to consist of only a majority of independent directors, unlike in many countries where the Audit Committees consist solely of independent directors.

The fundamental problem lies in the independence of the so called independent directors. They are, on paper, appointed by the board, but it is the CEO who really identifies and recommends the persons (unless they are institutional nominees). Thus, they actually serve in the board at the pleasure of the CEO, and to what extent they can really take tough stances against CEO's points of view is any one's guess.

Table 10.1 Classifications of board of director members

Classification
Insiders • The firm's CEO and other top-level managers
Related outsiders • Individuals not involved with the firm's day-to-day operations, but who have a relationship with the company
Outsiders • Individuals who are independent of the firm in terms of day-to-day operations and other relationships

Critics advocate reforms to ensure that independent outside directors represent a significant majority of the total membership of a board, which research suggests has been accomplished in US.[72] On the other hand, others argue that having outside directors is not enough to resolve the problems; it depends on the power of the CEO. One proposal to reduce the power of the CEO is to separate the chairperson's role and the CEO's role on the board so that the same person does not hold both positions.[73] Yet, having a board that actively monitors top executive decisions and actions does not ensure high performance. The value that the directors bring to the company also influences the outcomes. For example, boards with members having significant relevant experience and knowledge are the most likely to help the firm formulate effective strategies and to implement them successfully.[74]

Alternatively, having a large number of outside board members can also create some problems. Outsiders do not have contact with the firm's day-to-day operations and typically do not have easy access to the level of information about managers and their skills so as to effectively evaluate managerial decisions and initiatives.[75] Outsiders can, however, obtain valuable information through frequent interactions with inside board members, during board meetings, and otherwise. Insiders possess such information by virtue of their organizational positions. Thus, boards with a critical mass of insiders typically are better informed about intended strategic initiatives, the reasons for the initiatives, and the outcomes expected from them.[76] Without this type of information, outsider-dominated boards may emphasize the use of financial, as opposed to strategic, controls to gather performance information to evaluate managers' and business units' performances. A virtually exclusive reliance on financial evaluations shifts risk to top-level managers, who, in turn, may make decisions to maximize their interests and reduce their employment risk. Reductions in R&D investments, additional diversification of the firm, and the pursuit of greater levels of compensation are some of the results of managers' actions to achieve financial goals set by outsider-dominated boards.[77] Additionally, boards can make mistakes in CEO succession decisions because of the lack of important information about candidates as well as specific needs of the firm. As you would expect, knowledgeable and balanced boards are likely to be the most effective over time.[78]

Enhancing the Effectiveness of the Board of Directors

As explained in the Strategic Focus 10.1, because of the importance of boards of directors in corporate governance and as a result of increased scrutiny from shareholders—in particular, large institutional investors—the performances of individual board members and of entire boards are being evaluated more formally and with greater intensity.[79] Given the demand for greater accountability and improved performance, many boards have initiated voluntary changes. Among these changes are (1) increases in the diversity of the backgrounds of board members (e.g., a greater number of directors from public service, academic, and scientific settings); (2) the strengthening of internal management and accounting control systems; and (3) the establishment and consistent use of formal processes to evaluate the board's performance.[80] Additional changes include (4) the creation of a "lead director" role that has strong powers with regard to the board agenda and oversight of non-management board member activities, and (5) modification of the compensation of directors, especially reducing or eliminating stock options as a part of the package.

Boards are increasingly involved in the strategic decision-making process, so they must work collaboratively. Some argue that improving the processes used by boards to make decisions and monitor managers and firm outcomes is important for board effectiveness.[81] Moreover, because of the increased pressure from owners and the potential conflict among board members, procedures are necessary to help boards function effectively in facilitating the strategic decision-making process.

STRATEGIC FOCUS

10.1 Where Have All the Good Directors Gone?

The global economic crisis, largely the result of extremely poor strategic decisions made by top-level managers in the financial services industry, laid bare the holes in the US corporate governance system. In particular, the crisis showed that many boards of directors were very weak. In the early 2000s, boards of directors suffered significant criticism for the failures in monitoring executive actions at Enron, Tyco, WorldCom, and other companies. With more recent failures, boards are now experiencing substantial public animosity. Many people do not understand how top-level managers were allowed to take the extreme risks that have melted away corporate value when the debt became too heavy for most of the firms.

The weakness of corporate boards is exemplified by the fact that the President of the United States had to fire a highly ineffective CEO because the board of General Motors had failed to act in recent years.

As a result of the economic meltdown, the obviously poor strategic decisions leading to it, and the inability of previous boards to prevent the problems, many boards are now changing. Old board members are resigning or being replaced and many new members are joining boards. For example, in 2009, Citigroup, one of the major contributors to the problems in the financial services industry, nominated four new independent directors. Boardroom shakeups are also occurring outside of the financial services industry. For example, EasyJet announced that it had appointed a new chairman of its board to replace the current chairman, Colin Chandler. The new chairman, Michael Rake, formerly headed the BT Group.

In an industry challenged by technology developments and the recession, Borders has suffered the most. Its poor financial results are the outcome of its inability to keep pace. Thus, in 2009, Borders made major changes in the top management team and announced that seven of its ten directors were departing. Only five of them will be replaced, thereby shrinking the number of members on the board to eight. The former executive team and board tried unsuccessfully to sell the firm. The new team will focus on restructuring the firm.

Rick Wagoner is the former CEO of GM, who was asked to resign by President Obuma.

Interestingly, research suggests that smaller boards are more effective in governing companies than are larger boards. Thus, Borders' decision to downsize its board may be a good one. Changes are being made in the processes used by many boards in order to improve their monitoring function. These changes extend to the balance of independent and inside members, renewed emphasis on audit and compensation committees, and ensuring that outside board members spend an adequate amount of time on board business so that they can make informed decisions. Furthermore, there are other moves afoot to change the governance practices in firms. These include new rules and a renewed scrutiny by the US Securities and Exchange Commission and other governmental agencies. In addition, the chairman of the Financial Reporting Council in the United Kingdom announced a complete review of the Combined Code, a template of corporate governance used by investors and listed companies. In fact, the code is commonly used by institutional investors to evaluate the boards of companies. In India, the Institute of Company Secretaries announced plans to strengthen the norms for corporate governance practices.

In India, many committees have been constituted to look at the issues in corporate governance, as was pointed out earlier, the latest being the J.J. Irani Committee, whose recommendations have been instrumental in shaping the draft of the new Companies Bill. It should be borne in mind that whereas in US, the main concern has been the alignment of shareholders' interests to those of the Board and the managers, in India the concerns seem to be different. First, most of the large companies are still dominated in terms of effective control (though not necessarily in terms of shareholdings) by the promoters, and the boards are largely selected by these promoters themselves. The kind of overhaul of boards that we saw in US are unusual in India, unless the board members had problems with the promoters, generally at a personal level, or in very unusual cases like Satyam. Second, a main concern in India is the fair treatment of minority shareholders, who are often taken for a ride by the promoters. This is done through a variety of means, such as allotment of large shares by the promoters to themselves at prices very different from those prevailing in the market, entering into transactions with companies in which they have a higher or complete holding, and delisting of shares from the markets, after offering the minority shareholders the repurchase of their shares at discounted prices. The Companies Bill and the recommendations of the different committees are to be seen in this light.

As mentioned earlier, the Bill proposes a proportion of at least one third independent directors in a company. This is considered by some experts as insufficient. The Irani Committee thought that the nominee directors of institutions will represent their constituents' interests rather than the interest of the company on whose boards they sit. This is seen as untenable. The nomination of independent directors is left to the board as a whole rather than a committee consisting wholly of existing independent directors, thus enabling the incumbent management to control who become the independent directors.

There have been numerous outcries regarding the accountability of the board members. In the case of the Bhopal disaster, for example, the Chairman and the board were held also responsible. These well intentioned efforts, however, have made people wary of taking up independent directorships in companies, making it more difficult to find quality independent directors. This will become more acute if prosecutions are launched against all directors, including independent directors, for any accidents, financial misdeeds etc. arising out of decisions the detailed facts of which at least the independent directors could have not known.

Sources: J. A. Trachtenberg, 2009, Borders plans to install new board, *Wall Street Journal,* http://www.wsj.com, April 16; K. Shwiff, 2009, Egan-Jones urges vote against Citi directors, *Wall Street Journal,* http://www.wsj.com, April 13; J. Espinoza, 2009, EasyJet shakes up boardroom, *Forbes,* http://www.forbes.com, April 6; 2009, ICSI plans governance norms, *Business Standard,* http://www.business-standard.com, April 5; D. Serchuk, 2009, Where are Wall Street's directors? *Forbes,* http://www.forbes.com, March 31; M. Costello, 2009, New boardroom code to "draw on lessons" from bank crisis, *The Times,* http://www.business.timesonline.co.uk, March 18; 2009, Directors under fire, *Stuff,* http://www.stuff.co.nz, March 10; N Balasubramanian, 2010, *Corporate Governance and Stewardship*, New Delhi, Tata Mc Graw Hill.

Increasingly, outside directors are being required to own significant equity stakes as a prerequisite to holding a board seat. In fact, some research suggests that firms perform better if outside directors have such a stake; the trend is toward higher pay for directors with more stock ownership, but with fewer stock options.[82] Compensating independent directors through strong incentives such as equity, stock options, performance based bonus, and large sitting fees for board meetings may appear at first sight to ensure better quality membership in boards, and in their devoting more time to ensure better quality decisions. In fact, the experience of Barings Bank, Enron, and Satyam seem to suggest that when the incentives are too strong, the incentive to question the figures may come down, especially if they are good, and results that seem to be too good to be true may go unchallenged. This seems to have happened in the case of Barings Bank, whose Board of Directors did not question the extraordinary results returned by their rogue trader, Nick Leeson, partly because their own bonuses were good, thanks to the "profits" shown by Leeson. Research also suggests that too much ownership can lead to lower independence for board members.[83] In addition, other research suggests that diverse boards help firms make more effective strategic decisions and perform better over time.[84] Although questions remain about whether more independent and diverse boards enhance board effectiveness, the trends for greater independence and increasing diversity among board members are likely to continue. Clearly, the corporate failures in the first decade of the 21st century suggest the need for more effective boards.

STRATEGY RIGHT NOW

Read further about the Bhopal tragedy and discuss to what extent the members of the board of directors of Union Carbide, India could be assigned responsibility. Plenty of materials are available on this case.
www.cengage.com/management/hitt

Executive Compensation

As the Opening Case illustrates, the compensation of top-level managers, and especially of CEOs, generates a great deal of interest and strongly held opinions. One reason for this widespread interest can be traced to a natural curiosity about extremes and excesses. For example, the *Los Angeles Times* reported that "CEO compensation tripled from 1990 to 2004, rising at more than three times the rate of corporate earnings. CEOs at 11 of the largest US companies received $865 million in a five-year period while presiding over losses in shareholder value."[85] As stated in the Opening Case, the ten highest-paid executives in 2008, during a strong recession, earned an average of $47.22 million. Some consider this excessive pay, especially for those whose firms suffered net losses during this year, because most firms lost market value in 2008. Another stems from a more substantive view that CEO pay is tied in an indirect but tangible way to the fundamental governance processes in large corporations. Some believe that while highly paid, CEOs are not overpaid.[86] Others argue that not only are they highly paid, they are overpaid. These critics are especially concerned that compensation is not as strongly related to performance as some believe.[87]

Executive compensation is a governance mechanism that seeks to align the interests of managers and owners through salaries, bonuses, and long-term incentive compensation, such as stock awards and options.[88] Long-term incentive plans have become a critical part of compensation packages in US firms. The use of longer-term pay theoretically helps firms cope with or avoid potential agency problems by linking managerial wealth to the wealth of common shareholders.[89]

Sometimes the use of a long-term incentive plan prevents major stockholders (e.g., institutional investors) from pressing for changes in the composition of the board of directors, because they assume the long-term incentives will ensure that top executives will act in shareholders' best interests. Alternatively, stockholders largely assume that top-executive pay and the performance of a firm are more closely aligned when firms have boards that are dominated by outside members. However, research shows that fraudulent behavior can be associated with stock option incentives, such as earnings manipulation.[90]

Effectively using executive compensation as a governance mechanism is particularly challenging to firms implementing international strategies. For example, the interests of owners of multinational corporations may be best served by less uniformity among the firm's foreign subsidiaries' compensation plans.[91] Developing an array of unique compensation plans requires additional monitoring and increases the firm's potential agency costs. Importantly, levels of pay vary by regions of the world. For example, managerial pay is highest in the United States and much lower in Asia. Compensation is lower in India partly because many of the largest firms have strong family ownership and control.[92] As corporations acquire firms in other countries, the managerial compensation puzzle for boards becomes more complex and may cause additional governance problems.[93]

The Effectiveness of Executive Compensation

Executive compensation—especially long-term incentive compensation—is complicated for several reasons. First, the strategic decisions made by top-level managers are typically complex and non-routine, so direct supervision of executives is inappropriate for judging the quality of their decisions. The result is a tendency to link the compensation of top-level managers to measurable outcomes, such as the firm's financial performance. Second, an executive's decision often affects a firm's financial outcomes over an extended period, making it difficult to assess the effect of current decisions on the corporation's performance. In fact, strategic decisions are more likely to have long-term, rather than short-term, effects on a company's strategic outcomes. Third, a number of other factors affect a firm's performance besides top-level managerial decisions and behavior. Unpredictable economic, social, or legal changes (see Chapter 2) make it difficult to identify the effects of strategic decisions. Thus, although performance-based compensation may provide incentives to top management teams to make decisions that best serve shareholders' interests, such compensation plans alone cannot fully control managers. Still, incentive compensation represents a significant portion of many executives' total pay.

Although incentive compensation plans may increase the value of a firm in line with shareholder expectations, such plans are subject to managerial manipulation.[94] Additionally, annual bonuses may provide incentives to pursue short-run objectives at the expense of the firm's long-term interests. Although in long-term, performance-based incentives may reduce the temptation to under-invest in the short run, they increase executive exposure to risks associated with uncontrollable events, such as market fluctuations and industry decline. The longer the focus of incentive compensation, the greater are the long-term risks borne by top-level managers. Also, because long-term incentives tie a manager's overall wealth to the firm in a way that is inflexible, such incentives and ownership may not be valued as highly by a manager as by outside investors who have the opportunity to diversify their wealth in a number of other financial investments.[95] Thus, firms may have to overcompensate for managers using long-term incentives.

A P Photo/M. Spencer Green

Merrill Lynch's acquisition by Bank of America has not been without controversy, including the awarding of large bonuses to Merrill Lynch managers after the acquisition despite enormous losses.

Even though some stock option–based compensation plans are well designed with option strike prices substantially higher than current stock prices, some have been designed with the primary purpose of giving executives more compensation. Research of stock option re-pricing where the strike price value of the option has been lowered from its original position suggests that action is taken more frequently in high-risk situations.[96] However, re-pricing also happens when firm performance is poor, to restore the incentive effect for the option. Evidence also suggests that politics are often involved, which has resulted in "option backdating."[97] While this evidence shows that no internal governance mechanism is perfect, some compensation plans accomplish their purpose. For example, recent research suggests that long-term pay designed to encourage managers to be environmentally friendly has been linked to higher success in preventing pollution.[98]

Stock options became highly popular as a means of compensating top executives and linking pay with performance, but they also have become controversial of late as indicated in the Opening Case. Because all internal governance mechanisms are imperfect, external mechanisms are also needed. One such governance device is the market for corporate control.

Market for Corporate Control

The **market for corporate control** is an external governance mechanism that becomes active when a firm's internal controls fail.[99] The market for corporate control is composed of individuals and firms that buy ownership positions in or take over potentially undervalued corporations so they can form new divisions in established diversified companies or merge two previously separate firms. Because the undervalued firm's top-level managers are assumed to be responsible for formulating and implementing the strategy that led to poor performance, they are usually replaced. Thus, when the market for corporate control operates effectively, it ensures that managers who are ineffective or act opportunistically are disciplined.[100]

The takeover market as a source of external discipline is used only when internal governance mechanisms are relatively weak and have proven to be ineffective. Alternatively, other research suggests that the rationale for takeovers as a corporate governance strategy is not as strong as the rationale for takeovers as an ownership investment in target candidates where the firm is performing well and does not need discipline.[101] A study of active corporate raiders in the 1980s showed that takeover attempts often were focused on above-average performance firms in an industry.[102] Taken together, this research suggests that takeover targets are not always low performers with weak governance. As such, the market for corporate control may not be as efficient as a governance device as theory suggests.[103] At the very least, internal governance controls are much more precise relative to this external control mechanism.

Hedge funds have become a source of activist investors as noted in Chapter 7. An enormous amount of money has been invested in hedge funds, and because it is significantly more difficult to gain high returns in the market, hedge funds turned to activism. Likewise in a competitive environment characterized by a greater willingness on part of investors to hold underperforming managers accountable, hedge funds have been given license for increased activity.[104] Traditionally, hedge funds are a portfolio of stocks or bonds, or both, managed by an individual or a team on behalf of a large number of investors. Activism allows them to influence the market by taking a large position in seeking to drive the stock price up in a short period of time and then sell. Most hedge funds have been unregulated relative to the Securities and Exchange Commission because they represent a set of private investors. However, the recent economic crisis has increased the scrutiny of hedge funds' actions by government regulatory bodies.

Although the market for corporate control may be a blunt instrument for corporate governance, the takeover market continues to be active even in the economic crisis. In fact, the more intense governance environment has fostered an increasingly active takeover market. Certainly, the government has played a highly active role in the acquisitions of major US financial institutions (e.g., Merrill Lynch's acquisition by the Bank of America). Target firms earn a substantial premium over the acquiring firm.[105] At the same time, managers who have ownership positions or stock options are likely to gain in making a transaction with an acquiring firm. Even more evidence indicates that this type of gain may be the case, given the increasing number of firms that have golden parachutes that allow up to three years of additional compensation plus other incentives if a firm is taken over. These compensation contracts reduce the risk for managers if a firm is taken over. Private equity firms often seek to obtain a lower price in the market through initiating friendly takeover deals. The target firm's top-level managers may be amenable to such "friendly" deals because not only do they get the payout through a golden parachute, but at their next firm they may get a "golden hello" as a signing bonus to work for the new firm.[106] Golden parachutes help them leave, but "golden hellos are increasingly needed to get them in the door" of the next firm.[107] Although the 1980s had more defenses put up against hostile takeovers, the more recent environment has been much friendlier. However, the recent economic crisis has led to significant criticism of golden parachutes, especially for executives of poorly performing firms. For example, there was significant criticism of the large bonuses paid to Merrill Lynch managers after the acquisition by Bank of America. This is because of the huge loss suffered by Merrill Lynch because of poor strategic decisions executed by these managers. Furthermore, there were issues with AIG, which received billions of dollars in government support to stay afloat yet paid huge managerial bonuses. As a result of the criticism, the firm cancelled its $10 million golden parachute for its departing CFO, Steven Bensinger.[108]

The market for corporate control governance mechanisms should be triggered by a firm's poor performance relative to industry competitors. A firm's poor performance, often demonstrated by the firm's below-average returns, is an indicator that internal governance mechanisms have failed; that is, their use did not result in managerial decisions that maximized shareholder value. Yet, although these acquisitions often involve highly underperforming firms and the changes needed may appear obvious, there are no guarantees of success. The acquired firm's assets still must be integrated effectively into the acquiring firm's operation to earn positive returns from the takeover. Also, integration is an exceedingly complex challenge.[109] Even active acquirers often fail to earn positive returns from some of their acquisitions, but some acquirers are successful and earn significant returns from the assets they acquire.[110]

Target firm managers and members of the boards of directors are commonly sensitive about hostile takeover bids. It frequently means that they have not done an effective job in managing the company. If they accept the offer, they are likely to lose their jobs; the acquiring firm will insert its own management. If they reject the offer and fend off the takeover attempt, they must improve the performance of the firm or risk losing their jobs as well.[111]

Managerial Defense Tactics

Hostile takeovers are the major activity in the market for corporate control governance mechanism. Not all hostile takeovers are prompted by poorly performing targets, and firms targeted for hostile takeovers may use multiple defense tactics to fend off the takeover attempt. Historically, the increased use of the market for corporate control has enhanced the sophistication and variety of managerial defense tactics that are used in takeovers. The market for corporate control tends to increase risk for managers. As a result, managerial pay is often augmented indirectly through golden parachutes (wherein, a CEO can receive up to three years' salary if his or her firm is taken over). Golden parachutes, similar to most other defense tactics, are controversial.

Among other outcomes, takeover defenses increase the costs of mounting a takeover, causing the incumbent management to become entrenched while reducing the chances of introducing a new management team.[112] One takeover defense is traditionally known as a "poison pill." This defense mechanism usually allows shareholders (other than the acquirer) to convert "shareholders' rights" into a large number of common shares if anyone acquires more than a set amount of the target's stock (typically 10–20 percent). This move dilutes the percentage of shares that the acquiring firm must purchase at a premium and in effect raises the cost of the deal for the acquiring firm.

Table 10.2 lists a number of additional takeover defense strategies. Some defense tactics necessitate only changes in the financial structure of the firm, such as repurchasing shares of the firm's outstanding stock.[113] Some tactics (e.g., reincorporation of the firm in another state) require shareholder approval, but the greenmail tactic, wherein money is used to repurchase stock from a corporate raider to avoid the takeover of the firm, does not require shareholder approval. Some firms use rotating board member elections as a defense tactic where only one third of members are up for reelection each year. Research shows that this results in managerial entrenchment and reduced vulnerability to hostile takeovers.[114]

Most institutional investors oppose the use of defense tactics. TIAA-CREF and CalPERS have taken actions to have several firms' poison pills eliminated. Many institutional investors also oppose severance packages (golden parachutes), and the opposition is growing significantly in Europe as well.[115] However, as previously noted, an advantage to severance packages is that they may encourage top level managers to accept takeover bids that are attractive to shareholders.[116] Alternatively, recent research has shown that the use of takeover defenses reduces pressure experienced by managers for short-term performance gains. As such, managers engage in longer-term strategies and pay more attention to the firm's stakeholders. When they do this, the firm's market value increases, which rewards the shareholders.[117]

A potential problem with the market for corporate control is that it may not be totally efficient. A study of several of the most active corporate raiders in the 1980s showed that approximately 50 per cent of their takeover attempts targeted firms with above-average performance in their industry—corporations that were neither undervalued nor poorly managed.[118] The targeting of high-performance businesses may lead to acquisitions at premium prices and to decisions by managers of the targeted firm to establish what may prove to be costly takeover defense tactics to protect their corporate positions.[119]

Table 10.2 Hostile takeover defense strategies

Defense strategy	Category	Popularity among firms	Effectiveness as a defense	Stockholder wealth effects
Poison pill Preferred stock in the merged firm offered to shareholders at a highly attractive rate of exchange.	Preventive	High	High	Positive
Corporate charter amendment An amendment to stagger the elections of members to the board of directors of the attacked firm so that all are not elected during the same year, which prevents a bidder from installing a completely new board in the same year.	Preventive	Medium	Very low	Negative
Golden parachute Lump-sum payments of cash that are distributed to a select group of senior executives when the firm is acquired in a takeover bid.	Preventive	Medium	Low	Negligible
Litigation Lawsuits that help a target company stall hostile attacks; areas may include antitrust, fraud, inadequate disclosure.	Reactive	Medium	Low	Positive
Greenmail The repurchase of shares of stock that have been acquired by the aggressor at a premium in exchange for an agreement that the aggressor will no longer target the company for takeover.	Reactive	Very low	Medium	Negative
Standstill agreement Contract between the parties in which the pursuer agrees not to acquire any more stock of the target firm for a specified period of time in exchange for the firm paying the pursuer a fee.	Reactive	Low	Low	Negative
Capital structure change Dilution of stock, making it more costly for a bidder to acquire; may include employee stock option plans (ESOPs), recapitalization, new debt, stock selling, share buybacks.	Reactive	Medium	Medium	Inconclusive

Source: J. A. Pearce II & R. B. Robinson, Jr., 2004, Hostile takeover defenses that maximize shareholder wealth, *Business Horizons*, 47(5): 15–24.

Although the market for corporate control lacks the precision of internal governance mechanisms, the fear of acquisition and influence by corporate raiders is an effective constraint on the managerial-growth motive. The market for corporate control has been responsible for significant changes in many firms' strategies and, when used appropriately, has served shareholders' interests. But this market and other means of corporate governance vary across regions of the world and also by country. Accordingly, we next address the topic of international corporate governance.

International Corporate Governance

Understanding the corporate governance structure of the United Kingdom and the United States is inadequate for a multinational firm in the current global economy.[120] The stability associated with German and Japanese governance structures has historically been viewed as an asset, but the governance systems in these countries are changing, similar to other parts of the world. The importance of these changes has been heightened by the global economic crisis.[121] These changes are partly the result of multinational firms operating in many different countries and attempting to develop a more global governance system.[122] Although the similarity among national governance systems is increasing, significant differences remain evident, and firms employing an international strategy must understand these differences in order to operate effectively in different international markets.[123]

Corporate Governance in Germany and Japan

In many private German firms, the owner and manager may still be the same individual. In these instances, agency problems are not present.[124] Even in publicly traded German corporations, a single shareholder is often dominant. Thus, the concentration of ownership is an important means of corporate governance in Germany, as it is in the United States.[125]

Historically, banks occupied the center of the German corporate governance structure, as is also the case in many other European countries, such as Italy and France. As lenders, banks become major shareholders when companies they financed earlier seek funding on the stock market or default on loans. Although the stakes are usually less than 10 per cent, banks can hold a single ownership position up to but not exceeding 15 per cent of the bank's capital. Shareholders can tell the banks how to vote their ownership position, they generally do not do so. The banks monitor and control managers, both as lenders and as shareholders, by electing representatives to supervisory boards.

German firms with more than 2,000 employees are required to have a two-tiered board structure that places the responsibility for monitoring and controlling managerial (or supervisory) decisions and actions in the hands of a separate group.[126] All the functions of strategy and management are the responsibility of the management board (the Vorstand), but appointment to the Vorstand is the responsibility of the supervisory tier (the Aufsichtsrat). Employees, union members, and shareholders appoint members to the Aufsichtsrat. Proponents of the German structure suggest that it helps prevent corporate wrongdoing and rash decisions by "dictatorial CEOs" However, critics maintain that it slows decision making and often ties a CEO's hands. The corporate governance framework in Germany has made it difficult to restructure companies as quickly as can be done in the United States when performance suffers. Because of the role of local government (through the board structure) and the power of banks in Germany's corporate governance structure, private shareholders rarely have major ownership positions in German firms. Large institutional investors, such as pension funds and insurance companies, are also relatively insignificant owners of corporate stock. Thus, at least historically, German executives generally have not been dedicated to the maximization of shareholder value that occurs in many countries.[127]

However, corporate governance in Germany is changing, at least partially, because of the increasing globalization of business. Many German firms are beginning to gravitate toward the US system. Recent research suggests that the traditional system produced some agency costs because of a lack of external ownership power. Interestingly, German firms with listings on the US stock exchange have increasingly adopted executive stock option compensation as a long-term incentive pay policy.[128]

Attitudes toward corporate governance in Japan are affected by the concepts of obligation, family, and consensus.[129] In Japan, an obligation "may be to return a service for one rendered or it may derive from a more general relationship, for example, to one's family or old alumni, or one's company (or Ministry), or the country. This sense of particular obligation is common elsewhere but it feels stronger in Japan."[130] As part of a company family, individuals are members of a unit that envelops their lives; families command the attention and allegiance of parties throughout corporations. Moreover, a *keiretsu* (a group of firms tied together by cross-shareholdings) is more than an economic concept; it, too, is a family. Consensus, an important influence in Japanese corporate governance, calls for the expenditure of significant amounts of energy to win the hearts and minds of people whenever possible, as opposed to top executives issuing edicts.[131] Consensus is highly valued, even when it results in a slow and cumbersome decision-making process.

As in Germany, banks in Japan play an important role in financing and monitoring large public firms.[132] The bank owning the largest share of stocks and the largest amount of debt—the main bank—has the closest relationship with the company's top executives. The main bank provides financial advice to the firm and also closely monitors managers. Thus, Japan has a bank-based financial and corporate governance structure, whereas the United States has a market-based financial and governance structure.[133]

Apart from lending money, a Japanese bank can hold up to 5 per cent of a firm's total stock; a group of related financial institutions can hold up to 40 per cent. In many cases, main-bank relationships are part of a horizontal *keiretsu*. A *keiretsu* firm usually owns less than 2 per cent of any other member firm; however, each company typically has a stake of that size in every firm in the *keiretsu*. As a result, somewhere between 30 and 90 per cent of a firm is owned by other members of the *keiretsu*. Thus, a keiretsu is a system of relationship investments.

As is the case in Germany, Japan's structure of corporate governance is changing. For example, because of Japanese banks' continuing development as economic organizations, their role in the monitoring and control of managerial behavior and firm outcomes is less significant than in the past.[134] Also, deregulation in the financial sector reduced the cost of mounting hostile takeovers.[135] As such, deregulation facilitated more activity in Japan's market for corporate control, which was nonexistent in past years.[136] Interestingly, however, recent research shows that CEOs of both public and private companies in Japan receive similar levels of compensation and their compensation is tied closely to observable performance goals.[137]

Corporate Governance in China

Corporate governance in China has changed dramatically in the past decade, as has the privatization of business and the development of the equity market. The stock markets in China are young. In their early years, these markets were weak because of significant insider trading. However, research has shown that they have improved with stronger governance in recent years.[138] The Chinese institutional environment is unique. While there has been a gradual decline in the equity held in state-owned enterprises and the number and percentage of private firms have grown, the state still dominates the strategies employed by most firms through direct or indirect controls.

Recent research shows that firms with higher state ownership tend to have lower market value and more volatility in those values over time. This is because of agency conflicts in the firms and because the executives do not seek to maximize shareholder returns. They also have social goals they must meet placed on them by the government.[139] This suggests a potential conflict between the principals, particularly the state owner and the private equity owners of the state-owned enterprises.[140]

The Chinese governance system has been moving toward the Western model in recent years. For example, China YCT International recently announced that it was strengthening its corporate governance, with the establishment of an audit committee within its board of directors, and appointing three new independent directors.[141] In addition, recent research shows that the compensation of top executives of Chinese companies is closely related to prior and current financial performance of the firm.[142] While state ownership and indirect controls complicate governance in Chinese companies, research in other countries suggests that some state ownership in recently privatized firms provides some benefits. It signals support and temporarily buoys stock prices, but over time continued state ownership and involvement tend to have negative effects on the stock price.[143] Thus, the corporate governance system in China and the heavy oversight of the Chinese government will need to be observed to determine the long-term effects.

Global Corporate Governance

As noted in the Strategic Focus 10.1, corporate governance is becoming an increasingly important issue in economies around the world, even in emerging economies. The problems with Satyam in India (see Strategic Focus 10.2) could be repeated in other parts of the world if diligence in governance is not exercised. This concern is stronger because of the globalization in trade, investments, and equity markets. Countries and major companies based in them want to attract foreign investment. To do so, the foreign investors must be confident of adequate corporate governance. Effective corporate governance is also required to attract domestic investors. Although many a time domestic shareholders will vote with management, as activist foreign investors enter a country it gives domestic institutional investors the courage to become more active in shareholder proposals, which will increase shareholder welfare.

For example, Steel Partners, LLC, focused its attention on Korean cigarette maker KT&G. Warren Lichtenstein of Steel Partners and Carl Icahn pressured KT&G to increase its market value. Lichtenstein and Icahn began their activism in February 2006, by nominating a slate of board directors as well as pushing KT&G to sell off its lucrative Ginseng unit, which manufactures popular herbal products in Korea. They also demanded that the company sell off its real estate assets, raise its dividends, and buy back common shares. Lichtenstein and Icahn threatened a hostile tender offer if their demands were not met. Shareholders showed support for Steel Partners' activism such that they elected Lichtenstein to KT&G's board. In 2008, Lichtenstein resigned from the board with the election of four new independent directors. During his service on the board, KT&G's market value increased and its corporate governance improved.[144] Steel Partners recently targeted Aderans Holdings Company Limited in Japan for major changes. Steel Partners is Aderans's largest shareholder with about 27 per cent of the outstanding stock. Steel Partners is unhappy with Aderans's efforts to turnaround its performance and has proposed replacing most of its board members and undergoing a major restructuring.[145] Research suggests that foreign investors are likely to focus on critical strategic decisions and their input tends to increase a firm's movement into international markets.[146] Thus, foreign investors are playing major roles in the governance of firms in many countries.

STRATEGIC FOCUS

10.2 The Satyam Truth: CEO Fraud and Corporate Governance Failure

In 2008, Satyam was India's fourth largest IT company with clients around the world. The firm provided IT services to more than one third of the *Fortune 500* companies. The company and its founder and CEO, Ramalinga Raju, were well known and respected. In September 2008, Raju was named the Ernst & Young Entrepreneur of the Year. On December 16, 2008, he was given the Golden Peacock Award for Corporate Governance and Compliance. But then his term as CEO started to unravel.

On December 17, 2008, Raju announced plans to acquire two companies, Maytas Infra and Maytas Properties, both owned by members of his family. The rationale was to diversify Satyam's business portfolio to avoid being tied to the IT services market. However, the stockholders strongly protested these acquisitions. They believed that only Raju and his family would benefit from the acquisition but Satyam would not.

On December 23, 2008, the World Bank announced that Satyam was barred from doing business with the bank because of alleged malpractices in securing previous contracts (e.g., paying bribes). In turn, Satyam requested an apology from the World Bank. Shortly thereafter, the price of Satyam's stock declined to a four-year low. Then, on December 26 three major outside directors resigned from Satyam's board of directors.

Worst of all, on January 7, 2009, Raju sent a letter to the Satyam board of directors and India's Securities and Exchange Commission. In this letter, he admitted his involvement in overstating the amount of cash held by Satyam on its balance sheet. The overstatement was approximately $1 billion. Furthermore, Satyam had a liability for $253 million arranged for his personal use, and he overstated Satyam's September 2008 quarterly revenues by 76 per cent and its quarterly profits by 97 per cent. This announcement sent shockwaves through corporate India and through India's stock market. Not only did Satyam's stock price suffer greatly (78 per cent decline) but the overall market decreased by 7.3 per cent on the day of the announcement.

James Leynse/Documentary Value/CORBIS

Ramalinga Raju, Satyam's chairman quit after admitting the company's profits had been doctored for several years, shaking faith in the country's corporate giants as shares of the software services provider plunged nearly 80 per cent.

Ironically, Satyam means "truth" in Sanskrit. While the CEO has been arrested and charged, others are working hard to save the company—and it appears that Satyam will be saved. Tech Mahindra outbid two other firms to acquire an eventual 51 per cent of Satyam and thus will have controlling interest in the company. The sale was due partly to swift government intervention to arrange a sale and save the company. Even though Satyam has been saved, corporate governance in India has taken a big hit and its reputation has been tarnished.

Sources: P. G. Thakurta, 2009, Satyam scam questions corporate governance, *IPS Inter Press Service*, http://www.ipsnews.net. April 21; G. Anand, 2009, How Satyam was saved, *Wall Street Journal*, http://www.wsj.com, April 14; 2009, Satyam-chronology, *Trading Markets*, http://www.tradingmarkets.com, April 7; H. Timmons & B. Wassener, 2009, Satyam chief admits huge fraud, *New York Times*, http://nytimes.com, January 8; H. Arakali, 2009, Satyam chairman resigns after falsifying accounts, *Bloomberg*, http://bloomberg.com, January 7; M. Kripalani, 2009, India's Madoff? Satyam scandal rocks outsourcing industry, *BusinessWeek*, http://www.businessweek.com, January 7; J. Riberiro, 2008, Satyam demands apology from World Bank, *Network World*, http://www.networkworld.com, December 26.

Not only has the legislation that produced the Sarbanes-Oxley Act in 2002 increased the intensity of corporate governance in the United States,[147] but other governments across the world are seeking to increase the transparency and intensity of corporate governance to prevent the types of scandals found in the United States and other places in the world. For example, the British government in 2003 implemented the findings of the Derek Higgs report, which increased governance intensity mandated by the United Kingdom's Combined Code on Corporate Governance, a template of corporate governance used by investors and listed companies. Also, as reported in the earlier Strategic Focus 10.1, in 2009 the chairman of the Financial Reporting Council in the United Kingdom announced a complete review of the Combined Code. In addition, the European Union enacted what is known as the "Transparency Directive," which is aimed at enhancing reporting and the disclosure of financial reports by firms within the European capital markets. Another European Union initiative labeled "Modernizing Company Law and Enhancing Corporate Governance" is designed to improve the responsibility and liability of executive officers, board members, and others to important stakeholders such as shareholders, creditors, and members of the public at large.[148] Thus, governance is becoming more intense around the world.

Some Interesting Situations in Corporate Governance

Even though the theory of corporate governance as matching the interests of the owners with the Board and management appears neat, it can pose tricky problems when applied in some concrete situations. Two such situations are described as follows:

Local Subsidiaries of Multinationals

Often, MNCs establish their subsidiaries in other countries, with a variety of objectives. These may be fully owned, in which case there is no problem. But what if they are partly owned? Suppose the MNC has a substantial minority shareholding, with the balance with the local shareholders: then the subsidiary will have its own board, in which only some of the members would be from the MNC. If there is a conflict of interests between the MNC and the local subsidiary, whose objectives and interests should be served by the subsidiary board? Who are the real "owners"? This tricky situation was faced by ITC in the 1990s. The case is highlighted in the Strategic Focus 10.3.

STRATEGIC FOCUS

10.3 ITC in a Turbulent Period

We are already familiar with the Indian company, ITC in Chapter 2. This well respected company had a murky period in the mid 1990s. It was a fully owned subsidiary of British American Tobacco (BAT) till 1954. Due to the requirements of regulation (see the Opening Case in Chapter 2), ITC had to dilute its foreign holdings, its core business of tobacco not being in a priority sector. By 1976, BAT's holdings had come down to 40 per cent, and by 1985, to 32.8 per cent. We had already seen in Chapter 2 that due to the new regulations, ITC undertook some diversifications into the hospitality industry and trading. Due to its near monopoly position in cigarettes in India, ITC was a well performing company financially, and BAT did not take much interest in it; it let its Indian managers run the company in their own way. The company increasingly took pains to project itself as an Indian company rather than a subsidiary of an MNC.

In 1991, Mr. K.L. Chugh took over as the CEO of ITC. His background was quite different from that of his predecessors: He came from a middle class background, had worked in a State enterprise before joining ITC, and, most of all, had little background of the core business of tobacco (he had worked for quite some time at a paper plant in Bhadrachalam). He was an ambitious person, and perceived ITC as a global entity in its own right, with its own brands of tobacco, cigarettes, and hotels all over the world.

Just at that time the Indian government was liberalizing its economy, and BAT was considering introduction of its own brands of cigarettes in the country. BAT also indicated its interest in raising its holdings to 51 per cent. Though overtly Mr. Chugh did not oppose this proposal, he effectively forestalled the move by managing to get the support of independent nominee directors of financial institutions and the Indian government. These institutions had 38 per cent of share holdings, the Indian public had 24 per cent while, BAT had only 32 per cent stake.

In 1995, Mr. Chugh submitted a proposal at the Board meeting to enter the power sector in India. This was a core sector and huge growth was possible. But this would need further investments. If BAT did not invest further, it was required to dilute its holdings further. BAT, however, opposed this move saying ITC had no business to be in the power sector. It also accused ITC of having taken certain decisions without informing BAT and, in turn, demanded the resignation of Mr. Chugh in a private one to one meeting. Mr. Chugh reportedly refused to resign "at a gun point".

In this board meeting, BAT got the composition of the Nominations Committee (to the members of the Board) altered, with no executive director of the company being a member, except Mr. Chugh. Thus, if the independent directors remained neutral, BAT would have full control over the nominations.

To resolve the issue of diversification into power, Mr. Chugh convened an extraordinary General Body Meeting (GBM) of its shareholders. In this stormy meeting, the public shareholders vocally supported the move, but, despite the request by BAT, the motions were not put to vote. BAT rejected the motion as invalid. The independent directors took a neutral stance.

In the meanwhile, BAT alleged major irregularities and "lack of professionalism" against Mr. Chugh and demanded his resignation again. It got a special Audit Committee to go into the affairs of ITC. This Committee, however, found major FERA (Foreign Exchange Regulation Act) violations in the decisions taken by the ITC board. Now the institutions were alarmed that they would themselves be held responsible and withdrew their support to Mr. Chugh. He resigned in August 1995. The proposal to get into the power sector was also dropped quietly.

In September 1995, Mr. Chugh was exonerated of all the charges by the Special Audit Committee. But he was not allowed to return to ITC.

Sources: ITC: Out on a no ball?, Case # BP 252, Indian Institute of Management, Ahmedabad; A.N. Haksar, 1993, *Bite the Bullet*, New Delhi: Viking; *Business India*, 1996, Shame at ITC, November 4–17; *Business India*, 1995, Exit Chugh, September 11–24; *Business India*, 1995, The K.L. Chugh Interview, October 7–21; Arun Chaudhuri, 1997, *ITC vs. BAT: A Case for Indian Corporate PR*, New Delhi: Wheeler Publications; *Business Today*, 1996, The Inside Story of ITC, November 7–21; *Business Standard*, 1995, Chugh vs. BAT: A tale with many twists, March 24; *Economic Times*, 1995, BAT seeks ITC chief's resignation, March 23; *Economic Times*, 1995, Is to back Chugh at today's EGM, March 23; *Economic Times*, 1995, Chugh wins but BAT won't accept the verdict, March 25; *Economic Times*, 1995, Chugh agrees to quit: An announcement most likely at AGM, August 10; *Financial Express*, 1995, FIs firm on not playing ball with BAT, October 19.

Family Businesses

Family businesses, in which the family holds a dominant but not total or near total percentage of shares presents another tricky area. The family members may have other businesses, in which they have a 100 per cent interest. Clearly, if the first business has major dealings with the 100 per cent business, it has to be on terms fair to the main business. It can be, however, that the fully owned business is given lucrative contracts at inflated prices, thus depriving the shareholders of the main business of their legitimate dues. They can be acquired at terms highly favorable to the fully owned firm. The decisions can be taken in Board meetings, and even be ratified in a General Body Meeting of the shareholders, using the voting power of the family. In a way, the problem at Satyam was of this category. The problem in both the situations projected above is that outwardly, it complies with the requirement of company governance the majority shareholders decide. But this should not be at the expense of the minority shareholders, or even a group of shareholders who own a substantial, though not a majority of the shares. It seems that at the end, whereas the governance mechanisms provide a structural protection against mismanagement, ultimately it is the ethical orientation and behavior of the management that counts, and there is no substitute for this.

Governance Mechanisms and Ethical Behavior

The governance mechanisms described in this chapter are designed to ensure that the agents of the firm's owners—the corporation's top-level managers—make strategic decisions that best serve the interests of the entire group of stakeholders, as described in Chapter 1. In the United States, shareholders are recognized as the company's most significant stakeholders. Thus, governance mechanisms focus on the control of managerial decisions to ensure that shareholders' interests will be served, but product market stakeholders (e.g., customers, suppliers, and host communities) and organizational stakeholders (e.g., managerial and nonmanagerial employees) are important as well.[149] Therefore, at least the minimal interests or needs of all stakeholders must be satisfied through the firm's actions. Otherwise, dissatisfied stakeholders will withdraw their support from one firm and provide it to another (e.g., customers will purchase products from a supplier offering an acceptable substitute).

The firm's strategic competitiveness is enhanced when its governance mechanisms take into consideration the interests of all stakeholders. Although the idea is subject to debate, some believe that ethically responsible companies design and use governance mechanisms that serve all stakeholders' interests. The more critical relationship, however, is found between ethical behavior and corporate governance mechanisms. The Enron disaster and the sordid saga of Satyam (described in the Strategic Focus 10.2) illustrate the devastating effect of poor ethical behavior not only on a firm's stakeholders, but also on other firms. This issue is being taken seriously in other countries. The trend toward increased governance scrutiny continues to spread around the world.[150]

In addition to Enron, scandals at WorldCom, HealthSouth, Tyco, and Satyam along with the questionable behavior of top-level managers in several of the major US financial services firms such as Merrill Lynch, AIG, etc. show that all corporate owners are vulnerable to unethical behavior and very poor judgments exercised by their employees, including top-level managers—the agents who have been hired to make decisions that are in shareholders' best interests. The decisions and actions of a corporation's board of directors can be an effective deterrent to these behaviors. In fact, some believe that the most effective boards participate actively to set boundaries for their firms' business ethics and values.[151] Once formulated, the board's expectations related to ethical decisions and actions of all of the firm's stakeholders must be clearly communicated to its top-level managers. Moreover, as shareholders' agents, these managers must understand that the board will hold them fully accountable for the development and support of an organizational culture that allows unethical decisions and behaviors. As will be explained in Chapter 12, CEOs can be positive role models for improved ethical behavior.

Only when proper corporate governance is exercised can strategies be formulated and implemented that will help the firm achieve strategic competitiveness and earn above-average returns. While there are many examples of poor governance, Cummins Inc. is a positive example. In 2009 it was given the highest possible rating for its corporate governance by GovernanceMetrics International. The rating is based on careful evaluation of board accountability and financial disclosure, executive compensation, shareholder rights, ownership base, takeover provisions, corporate behavior, and overall responsibility exhibited by the company.[152] In India, Tatas are often seen as example of sound governance practices. As the discussion in this chapter suggests, corporate governance mechanisms are a vital, yet imperfect, part of firms' efforts to select and successfully use strategies.

SUMMARY

- Corporate governance is a relationship among stakeholders that is used to determine a firm's direction and control its performance. How firms monitor and control top-level managers' decisions and actions affects the implementation of strategies. Effective governance that aligns managers' decisions with shareholders' interests can help produce a competitive advantage.
- Three internal governance mechanisms in the modern corporation include (1) ownership concentration, (2) the board of directors, and (3) executive compensation. The market for corporate control is the single external governance mechanism influencing managers' decisions and the outcomes resulting from them.
- Ownership is separated from control in the modern corporation. Owners (principals) hire managers (agents) to make decisions that maximize the firm's value. As risk-bearing specialists, owners diversify their risk by investing in multiple corporations with different risk profiles. As decision-making specialists, owners expect their agents (the firm's top-level managers) to make decisions that will help to maximize the value of their firm. Thus, modern corporations are characterized by an agency relationship that is created when one party (the firm's owners) hires and pays another party (top-level managers) to use its decision-making skills.
- Separation of ownership and control creates an agency problem when an agent pursues goals that conflict with principals' goals. Principals establish and use governance mechanisms to control this problem.
- Ownership concentration is based on the number of large-block shareholders and the percentage of shares they own. With significant ownership percentages, such as those held by large mutual funds and pension funds, institutional investors often are able to influence top-level managers' strategic decisions and actions. Thus, unlike diffuse ownership, which tends to result in relatively weak monitoring and control of managerial decisions, concentrated ownership produces more active and effective monitoring. Institutional investors are a powerful force in corporate America and actively use their positions of concentrated ownership to force managers and boards of directors to make decisions that maximize a firm's value.
- In the United States and the United Kingdom, a firm's board of directors, composed of insiders, related outsiders, and outsiders, is a governance mechanism expected to represent shareholders' collective interests. The percentage of outside directors on many boards now exceeds the percentage of inside directors. Through the implementation of the SOX Act, outsiders are expected to be more independent of a firm's top-level managers compared with directors selected from inside the firm. New rules imposed by the US Securities and Exchange Commission to allow owners with large stakes to propose new directors are likely to change the balance even more in favor of outside and independent directors.
- Executive compensation is a highly visible and often criticized governance mechanism. Salary, bonuses, and long-term incentives are used to strengthen the alignment between managers' and shareholders' interests. A firm's board of directors is responsible for determining the effectiveness of the firm's executive compensation system. An effective system elicits managerial decisions that are in shareholders' best interests.
- In general, evidence suggests that shareholders and boards of directors have become more vigilant in their control of managerial decisions. Nonetheless, these mechanisms are insufficient to govern managerial behavior in many large companies as shown in the latest economic crisis brought on by poor strategic decisions made by top-level managers in financial services firms. Therefore, the market for corporate control is an important governance mechanism. Although it, too, is imperfect, the market for corporate control has been effective in causing corporations to combat inefficient diversification and to implement more effective strategic decisions.
- Corporate governance structures used in Germany, Japan, and China differ from each other and from the structure used in the United States. Historically, the US governance structure focused on maximizing shareholder value. In Germany, employees, as a stakeholder group, take a more prominent role in governance. By contrast, until recently, Japanese shareholders played virtually no role in the monitoring and control of top-level managers. However, now Japanese firms are being challenged by "activist" shareholders. China's governance system is the youngest and has a number of characteristics that mirror those in the United States. However, the central government still plays a major role in governance in China as well. Internationally, all these systems are becoming increasingly similar, as are many governance systems both in developed countries, such as France and Spain, and in transitional economies, such as Russia and India.
- Effective governance mechanisms ensure that the interests of all stakeholders are served. Thus, long-term strategic success results when firms are governed in ways that permit at least minimal satisfaction of capital market stakeholders (e.g., shareholders), product market stakeholders (e.g., customers and suppliers), and organizational stakeholders (managerial and nonmanagerial employees; see Chapter 2). Moreover, effective governance produces ethical behavior in the formulation and implementation of strategies.

KEY TERMS AND DEFINITIONS

Corporate governance is the set of mechanisms used to manage the relationship among stakeholders and to determine and control the strategic direction and performance of organizations.

An **agency relationship** exists when one or more persons (the principal or principals) hire another person or persons (the agent or agents) as decision-making specialists to perform a service.

Managerial opportunism is the seeking of self-interest with guile (i.e., cunning or deceit).

Institutional owners are financial institutions such as stock mutual funds and pension funds that control large-block shareholder positions.

The **market for corporate control** is an external governance mechanism that becomes active when a firm's internal controls fail.

Agency costs are the sum of incentive costs, monitoring costs, enforcement costs, and individual financial losses incurred by principals because governance mechanisms cannot guarantee total compliance by the agent.

The **board of directors** is a group of elected individuals whose primary responsibility is to act in the owners' interests by formally monitoring and controlling the corporation's top-level managers.

Executive compensation is a governance mechanism that seeks to align the interests of managers and owners through salaries, bonuses, and long-term incentive compensation, such as stock awards and options.

Both the number of large-block shareholders and the total percentage of shares they own define **ownership concentration.**

Large blockshareholders typically own at least 5 per cent of a corporation's issued shares.

REVIEW QUESTIONS

1. What is corporate governance? What factors account for the considerable amount of attention corporate governance receives from several parties, including shareholder activists, business press writers, and academic scholars? Why is governance necessary to control managers' decisions?
2. What is meant by the statement that ownership is separated from managerial control in the corporation? Why does this separation exist?
3. What is an agency relationship? What is managerial opportunism? What assumptions do owners of corporations make about managers as agents?
4. How is each of the three internal governance mechanisms—ownership concentration, boards of directors, and executive compensation—used to align the interests of managerial agents with those of the firm's owners?
5. What trends exist regarding executive compensation? What is the effect of the increased use of long-term incentives on executives' strategic decisions?
6. What is the market for corporate control? What conditions generally cause this external governance mechanism to become active? How does the mechanism constrain top-level managers' decisions and actions?
7. What is the nature of corporate governance in Germany, Japan, and China?
8. How can corporate governance foster ethical strategic decisions and behaviors on the part of managers as agents?

EXPERIENTIAL EXERCISES

Exercise 1: INDIAN COMPANIES BILL, 2009

As described in the chapter, the introduction of Companies Bill, 2009 marks a new attempt by the Government to clean up the governance of Indian companies. It can be accessed from http://www.mca.gov.in/Ministry/actsbills/pdf/Companies_Bill_2009_24Aug2009.pdf.

Access and Read the Entire Bill

Working in small groups, prepare a short (two to three pages, single-spaced) bullet-point evaluation of the Bill, based on the discussion in this chapter. Be sure to include the following topics in your analysis:

- How are the provisions in the Bill structured? Do they consist of rules (i.e., required) or recommendations (i.e., suggestions)? What mechanism is included to monitor or enforce the guidelines?
- What board roles are addressed? (such as monitoring, oversight, and reporting) How does it see the Boards' role in supporting strategy, or their contribution to firm performance and shareholder wealth?
- What aspects of board composition and structure are covered in theBill? For instance, please look for the balance of insiders and outsiders, important committees such as the Audit Committee, Nomination Committee, Compensation Committee etc., whether the CEO also serves as board chair, director education, and/or evaluation, compensation of officers and directors, and ownership by board members.

Exercise 2: Governance: Does It Matter Competitively?

Governance mechanisms are considered to be effective if they meet the needs of all stakeholders, including shareholders.

Governance mechanisms are also an important way to ensure that strategic decisions are made effectively. As a potential employee, how would you go about investigating a firm's governance structure and would that investigation weigh in your decision to become an employee or not? Identify a firm that you would like to join or one that you just find interesting. Working individually, complete the following research on your target firm:

- Find a copy of the company's most recent Annual Report. The Annual Reports would contain detailed information about the company's governance and present issues.
- Identify one of the company's main competitors for comparison purposes.

Some of the topics that you should examine include:

- Compensation plans (for both the CEO and board members; be sure to look for any difference between fixed and incentive compensation).
- Board composition (e.g., board size, insiders and outsiders, interlocking directorates, functional experience, how many active CEOs, how many retired CEOs, what is the demographic makeup, age diversity, etc.)
- Committees (how many, composition, compensation).
- Stock ownership by officers and directors—identify beneficial ownership from stock owned (you will need to look through the notes sections of the ownership tables to comprehend this).
- Ownership concentration. How much of the firm's outstanding stock is owned by institutions, individuals, and insiders? How many large-block shareholders are there (owners of 5 percent or more of stock)?
- Does the firm utilize a duality structure for the CEO?
- Activities by activist shareholders regarding corporate governance issues of concern.
- Are there any managerial defense tactics employed by the firm? For example, what does it take for a shareholder proposal to come to a vote and be adopted?
- List the firm's code of conduct.

Prepare a double-spaced memo summarizing the results of your findings with a side-by-side comparison of your target and its competitor. Your memo should include the following topics:

- Summarize what you consider to be the key aspects of the firm's governance mechanisms.
- Attach to your memo a single graph covering the last 10-year historical stock performance for both companies. If applicable, find a representative index to compare both with, such as the NSE stock price, or other applicable industry index.
- Highlight key differences between your target firm and its competitor.
- Based on your review of the firm's governance, did you change your opinion of the firm's desirability as an employer? How does the competitor stack up, governance wise? Why or why not?

Structure and Controls with Organizations

CHAPTER

11

Studying this chapter should provide you with the strategic management knowledge needed to

- Define organizational structure and controls and discuss the difference between strategic and financial controls.
- Describe the relationship between strategy and structure.
- Discuss the functional structures used to implement business-level strategies.
- Explain the use of three versions of the multidivisional (M-form) structure to implement different diversification strategies.
- Discuss the organizational structures used to implement three international strategies.
- Define strategic networks and discuss how strategic center firms implement such networks at the business, corporate, and international levels.

OPENING CASE
CISCO's Evolution of Strategy and Structure

Cisco's focus traditionally has been on producing network equipment that enables voice, video, and data to travel across computer networks. Accordingly, its products are at the heart of allowing the Internet and intranets to function across most corporate, public, and educational institutions around the world. Because Cisco's rapid growth was influenced by the Internet, it focused on three semi-autonomous lines of business with distinct customers: Internet service providers, large enterprises, and small and medium-sized businesses. Within each of these three lines of business was a self-contained organization with separate marketing and operational groups. This allowed the firm to grow rapidly by focusing on the idiosyncratic needs of different customer segments.

This structure worked because the market was expanding quickly. However, in 2001, the explosive growth ceased when the Internet bubble burst. Thus, on August 23, 2001, Cisco announced a reorganization. The restructuring created 11 technology groups or divisions, all of which had previously been in the three separate business organizations. The sales groups, however, maintained their focus on the three particular customer segments. The integration across technologies allowed for more efficient cost reduction, which was necessary given the external environment change. Despite the many changes, Cisco emphasized its constant focus on customers because of the informal organization and previous personal interconnections between people in the reorganized engineering groups and the marketing segments.

Over time, Cisco has also evolved its approach with the external environment. As networks matured, Cisco focused more on large-firm data centers. Therefore, Cisco has changed from a pure networking player focused on routers and switches to an overall information technology (IT) supplier. Thus, it needed to build new software businesses as well as service collaborations. Furthermore, it has expanded through acquisitions of software and hardware firms to create the necessary capabilities to develop a more integrated support system necessary to serve large corporate data centers. It also developed a consumer strategy by acquiring Linksys for home network systems and Scientific-Atlanta for television network boxes to facilitate cable systems. Likewise, it purchased software firms such as WebEx and IronPort to facilitate its corporate communication business and network security business, respectively. In addition, it has been collaborating with Accenture and Tata Consulting Services to provide an overall solutions business (as discussed in Chapter 9). Accordingly, not only is Cisco changing its focus on large and small customers, but it is offering software and consulting solution services.

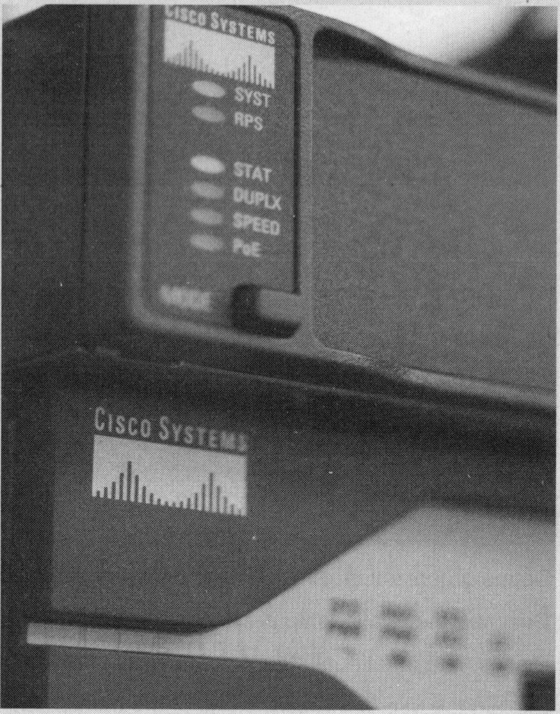

Terry Smith Images/Alamy

Cisco has changed from a pure networking player focused on routers and switches to an overall information technology (IT) supplier.

The current downturn in the economy is forcing Cisco and other major firms to reposition and expand into nontraditional businesses in order to gain revenues lost in other areas. Most recently, it moved into servers, which have been the traditional business of its former partners Hewlett-Packard and IBM. To manage this expansion and the integration process, Cisco needs to change its structure again. It is more likely that a corporate M-form will be necessary (this structure will be defined later in the chapter) because Cisco will need to not only have a large group of separate businesses, but it will need to integrate these businesses in a cooperative way such that all of the services are bundled and sold together to large IT centers. It will probably develop different structural approaches to manage its consumer businesses. It remains to be seen whether Cisco can make these changes effectively. Cisco does have one thing going for it—its strong culture focused on customer satisfaction. As stated earlier, customer focus is even embedded in its engineering divisions. But it will need more than a strategy—it will need a finely tuned organization to make it all work. Only time will tell whether Cisco is successful with this new strategy and the necessary structural adaptation.

Sources: R. Gulati & P. Puranam, 2009, Renewal through reorganization: The value of inconsistencies between formal and informal organization, *Organizational Science,* 20(2): 422–440; S. Lohr, 2009, In Sun, Oracle sees a software gem, *The New York Times,* http://www.nytimes.com, April 20; S. H. Wildstrom, 2009, Meet Cisco, the consumer company, *BusinessWeek*, May 4, 73; B. Worthen & J. Scheck, 2009, As growth slows, ex-allies square off in a turf war, *Wall Street Journal*, March 16, A1; J. Duffy, 2008, Cisco accelerates shift to software, data center, *Network World*, January 7, 12; J. Duffy, 2008, Cisco plans data center product overhaul, *Network World*, December 15, 1–2; B. Novak, 2008, Cisco connects the dots; aligning leaders with new organizational structure, *Global Business and Organizational Excellence*, 27(5): 22–32.

As we learnt in Chapter 4, all firms use one or more business-level strategies. In Chapters 6–9, we discussed other strategies which firms may choose to use (corporate-level, international, and cooperative). Once selected, strategies are not implemented in a vacuum. Organizational structure and controls, this chapter's topic, provide the framework within which strategies are used in both for-profit organizations and not-for-profit agencies.[1] However, separate structures and controls are required to successfully implement different strategies. In all organizations, top-level managers have the final responsibility for ensuring that the firm has matched each of its strategies with the appropriate organizational structure and that both change when necessary. Thus, John Chambers, the CEO of Cisco, is responsible for changing its organizational structure if the firm decides to use a different business or corporate-level strategy. The match or degree of fit between strategy and structure influences the firm's attempts to earn above-average returns.[2] Thus, the ability to select an appropriate strategy and match it with the appropriate structure is an important characteristic of effective strategic leadership.[3]

This chapter opens with an introduction to organizational structure and controls. We then provide more details about the need for the firm's strategy and structure to be properly matched. Affecting firms' efforts to match strategy and structure is their influence on each other.[4] As we discuss, strategy has a more important influence on structure, although once in place, structure influences strategy.[5] Next, we describe the relationship between growth and structural change successful firms experience. We then discuss the different organizational structures firms use to implement the separate business-level, corporate-level, international, and cooperative strategies. A series of figures highlights the different structures firms match with strategies. Across time and based on their experiences, organizations, especially large and complex ones, customize these general structures to meet their unique needs.[6] Typically, the firm tries to form a structure that is complex enough to facilitate the use of its strategies but simple enough for all parties to understand and implement.[7] When strategies become more diversified as with Cisco's in the Opening Case, a firm must adjust its structure to deal with the increased complexity.[8]

Organizational Structure and Controls

Research shows that organizational structure and the controls that are a part of the structure affect firm performance.[9] In particular, evidence suggests that performance declines when the firm's strategy is not matched with the most appropriate structure and controls.[10] Even though mismatches between strategy and structure do occur, research indicates that managers try to act rationally when forming or changing their firm's structure.[11] His record of success at General Electric (GE) suggests that CEO Jeffrey Immelt pays close attention to the need to make certain that strategy and structure remain matched, as evidenced by restructuring alignments in GE Capital, GE's financial service group, during the economic downturn.[12]

Organizational Structure

Organizational structure specifies the firm's formal reporting relationships, procedures, controls, and authority and decision-making processes.[13] Developing an organizational structure that effectively supports the firm's strategy is difficult, especially because of the uncertainty (or unpredictable variation[14]) about cause-effect relationships in the global economy's rapidly changing and dynamic competitive environments.[15] When a structure's elements (e.g., reporting relationships, procedures, etc.) are properly aligned with one another, the structure facilitates effective use of the firm's strategies.[16] Thus, organizational structure is a critical component of effective strategy implementation processes.[17]

A firm's structure specifies the work to be done and how to do it, given the firm's strategy or strategies.[18] Thus, organizational structure influences how managers work and the decisions resulting from that work.[19] Supporting the implementation of strategies, structure is concerned with processes used to complete organizational tasks.[20] Having the right structure and process is important. For example, many product-oriented firms have been moving to develop service businesses associated with those products. This has been a strategy used by many of GE's businesses, such as medical equipment. However, research suggests that developing a separate division for such services in product-oriented companies, rather than managing the service business within the product divisions, leads to additional growth and profitability in the service business.[21]

Effective structures provide the stability that a firm needs to successfully implement its strategies and maintain its current competitive advantages while simultaneously providing the flexibility to develop the advantages it will need in the future.[22] **Structural stability** provides the capacity the firm requires to consistently and predictably manage its daily work routines[23], while **structural flex-**

ibility provides the opportunity to explore competitive possibilities and then allocate resources to activities that will shape the competitive advantages the firm will need to be successful in the future.[24] An effectively flexible organizational structure allows the firm to *exploit* current competitive advantages while *developing* new ones that can potentially be used in the future.[25] For example, the management system at Cisco is said to provide "speed, skill, and flexibility."[26] Cisco is able to accomplish this by using team-based processes as an overlay to its basic structure, allowing it to exploit its current advantages while exploring new ones.

Modifications to the firm's current strategy or selection of a new strategy call for changes in its organizational structure. However, research shows that once in place, organizational inertia often inhibits efforts to change structure, even when the firm's performance suggests that it is time to do so.[27] In his pioneering work, Alfred Chandler found that organizations change their structures when inefficiencies force them to.[28] Chandler's contributions to our understanding of organizational structure and its relationship to strategies and performance are quite significant. Indeed, some believe that Chandler's emphasis on "organizational structure" so transformed the field of business history that some call the period before Dr. Chandler's publications "B.C.," meaning "before Chandler."[29]

Firms seem to prefer the structural status quo and its familiar working relationships until the firm's performance declines to the point where change is absolutely necessary.[30] For example, necessity is obviously the case for General Motors given that it went into bankruptcy to force the required restructuring.[31]

In addition to the issues we already mentioned, it is important to note that top-level managers hesitate to conclude that the firm's structure (or its strategy, for that matter) are the problem, in that doing so suggests that their previous choices were not the best ones. Because of these inertial tendencies, structural change is often induced instead by actions from stakeholders (e.g., those from the capital market and customers—see Chapter 2) who are no longer willing to tolerate the firm's performance. Evidence shows that appropriate timing of structural change happens when top-level managers recognize that a current organizational structure no longer provides the coordination and direction needed for the firm to successfully implement its strategies.[32] Interestingly, many organizational changes are taking place in the current economic downturn, apparently because poor performance reveals organizational weaknesses. As we discuss next, effective organizational controls help managers recognize when it is time to adjust the firm's structure.

Organizational Controls

Organizational controls are an important aspect of structure.[33] **Organizational controls** guide the use of strategy, indicate how to compare actual results with expected results, and suggest corrective actions to take when the difference is unacceptable. When fewer differences separate actual from expected outcomes, the organization's controls are more effective.[34] It is difficult for the company to successfully exploit its competitive advantages without effective organizational controls.[35] Properly designed organizational controls provide clear insights regarding behaviors that enhance firm performance.[36] Firms use both strategic controls and financial controls to support using their strategies.

Strategic controls are largely subjective criteria intended to verify that the firm is using appropriate strategies for the conditions in the external environment and the company's competitive advantages. Thus, strategic controls are concerned with examining the fit between what the firm *might do* (as suggested by opportunities in its external environment) and what it *can do* (as indicated by its competitive advantages). Effective strategic controls help the firm understand what it takes to be successful.[37] Strategic controls demand rich communications between managers responsible for using them to judge the firm's performance and those with primary responsibility for implementing the firm's strategies (such as middle and first-level managers). These frequent exchanges are both formal and informal in nature.[38]

Strategic controls are also used to evaluate the degree to which the firm focuses on the requirements to implement its strategies. For a business-level strategy, for example, the strategic controls are used to study primary and support activities (see Tables 3.6 and 3.7) to verify that the critical activities are being emphasized and properly executed.[39] With related corporate-level strategies, strategic controls are used by corporate strategic leaders to verify the sharing of appropriate strategic factors such as knowledge, markets, and technologies across businesses. To effectively use strategic controls when evaluating related diversification strategies, headquarter executives must have a deep understanding of each unit's business-level strategy.[40]

As we described in the Opening Case, Cisco's executives allocate a great deal of time and energy to issues related to strategic control. Constantly challenged to meet the demands of an ever-changing market, John Chambers, Cisco's CEO, was able to implement a revised strategic controls system where he "was able to surrender his role as a command-and-control CEO and institute a collaborative decision-making model that allows the company to respond speedily to emerging transitions."[41] Using this system on strategic control allowed Cisco to move to open source software development before competitors such as Microsoft. They also were one of the first companies to move to Web-based customer service centers from call centers having foreseen this change through their strategic control system.

Financial controls are largely objective criteria used to measure the firm's performance against previously established quantitative standards. Accounting-based measures such as return on investment (ROI) and return on assets (ROA) as well as market-based measures such as economic value added are examples of financial controls. Partly because strategic controls are difficult to use with extensive diversification,[42] financial controls are emphasized to evaluate the performance of the firm using the unrelated diversification strategy. The unrelated diversification strategy's focus on financial outcomes (see Chapter 6) requires using standardized financial controls to compare performances between business units and associated managers.[43]

When using financial controls, firms evaluate their current performance against previous outcomes as well as against competitors' performance and industry averages. In the global economy, technological advances are being used to develop highly sophisticated financial controls, making it possible for firms to more thoroughly analyze their performance results and to assure compliance with regulations. Companies such as Oracle and SAP sell software tools that automate processes firms use to meet the financial reporting requirements specified by the Sarbanes-Oxley Act. (As noted in Chapter 10, this Act requires a firm's principal executive and financial officers to certify corporate financial and related information in quarterly and annual reports submitted to the Securities and Exchange Commission.)

Both strategic and financial controls are important aspects of each organizational structure, and as we noted previously, any structure's effectiveness is determined by using a combination of strategic and financial controls. However, the relative use of controls varies by type of strategy. For example, companies and business units of large diversified firms using the cost leadership strategy emphasize financial controls (such as quantitative cost goals), while companies and business units using the differentiation strategy emphasize strategic controls (such as subjective measures of the effectiveness of product development teams).[44] As previously explained, a corporate-wide emphasis on sharing among business units (as called for by related diversification strategies) results in an emphasis on strategic controls, while financial controls are emphasized for strategies in which activities or capabilities are not shared (e.g., in an unrelated diversification strategy).

As firms consider controls, the important point is to properly balance the use of strategic and financial controls. Indeed, overemphasizing one at the expense of the other can lead to performance declines. According to Michael Dell, an overemphasis on financial controls to produce attractive short-term results contributed to performance difficulties at Dell Inc. In addressing this issue, Dell said the following: "The company was too focused on the short term, and the balance of priorities was way too leaning (inclined) toward things that deliver short-term results."[45] Executives at Dell have now achieved a more appropriate emphasis on the long-term as well as the short-term due a reemphasis on strategic controls, although Dell is still playing catch up to Hewlett-Packard.[46]

STRATEGY RIGHT NOW
For another example of how organizations use both strategic and financial controls, read about L&T's recent restructuring to split the organization into nine independent entities.

Relationships between Strategy and Structure

Strategy and structure have a reciprocal relationship.[47] This relationship highlights the interconnectedness between strategy formulation (Chapters 4, 6–9) and strategy implementation (Chapters 10–13). In general, this reciprocal relationship finds structure flowing from or following selection of the firm's strategy. Once in place though, structure can influence current strategic actions as well as choices about future strategies. Consider, for example, the possible role of Cisco's structure and control system in influencing its strategy as illustrated in the Opening Case.

The general nature of the strategy/structure relationship means that changes to the firm's strategy create the need to change how the organization completes its work. In the "structure influences strategy" direction, firms must be vigilant in their efforts to verify that how their structure calls for work to be completed remains consistent with the implementation requirements of chosen strategies. Research shows, however, that "strategy has a much more important influence on structure than the reverse."[48]

Regardless of the strength of the reciprocal relationships between strategy and structure, those choosing the firm's strategy and structure should be committed to matching each strategy with a structure that provides the stability needed to use current competitive advantages as well as the flexibility required to develop future advantages. Therefore, when changing strategies, the firm should simultaneously consider the structure that will be needed to support use of the new strategy; properly matching strategy and structure can create a competitive advantage.[49]

Evolutionary Patterns of Strategy and Organizational Structure

Research suggests that most firms experience a certain pattern of relationships between strategy and structure. Chandler[50] found that firms tend to grow in somewhat predictable patterns: first by volume, then by geography, then integration (vertical, horizontal), and finally through product/business diversification[51] (see Figure 11.1). Chandler interpreted his findings as an indication that firms' growth patterns determine their structural form.

As shown in Figure 11.1, sales growth creates coordination and control problems the existing organizational structure cannot efficiently handle. Organizational growth creates the opportunity for the firm to change its strategy to try to become even more successful. However, the existing structure's formal reporting relationships, procedures, controls, and authority and decision-making processes lack the sophistication required to support the use or implementation of the new strategy.[52] A new structure is needed to help decision makers gain access to the knowledge and understanding required to effectively integrate and coordinate actions to implement the new strategy.[53]

Firms choose from among three major types of organizational structures—simple, functional, and multidivisional—to implement strategies. Across time, successful firms move from the simple to the functional to the multidivisional structure to support changes in their growth strategies.[54]

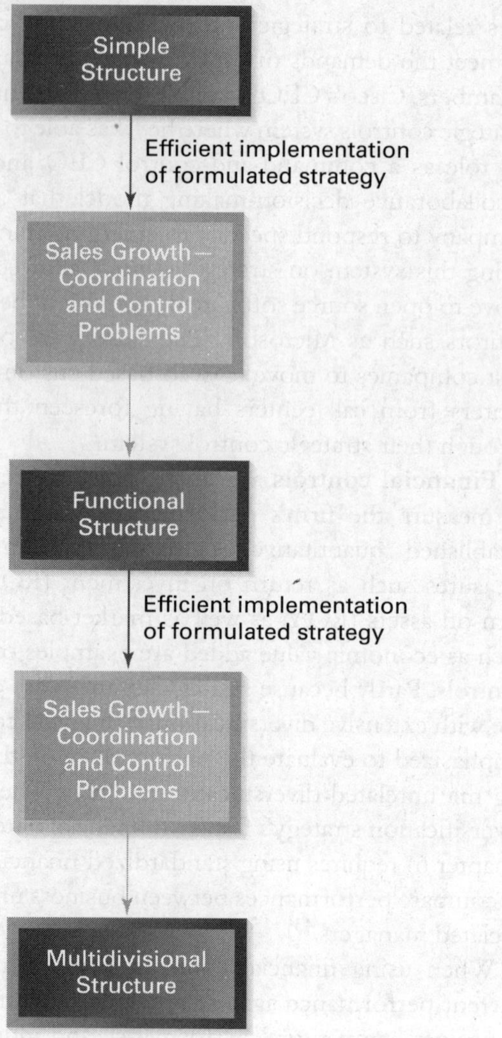

Figure 11.1 Strategy and structure growth pattern

Simple Structure

The **simple structure** is a structure in which the owner-manager makes all major decisions and monitors all activities while the staff serves as an extension of the manager's supervisory authority.[55] Typically, the owner-manager actively works in the business on a daily basis. Informal relationships, few rules, limited task specialization, and unsophisticated information systems characterize this structure. Frequent and informal communications between the owner-manager and employees make coordinating the work to be done relatively easy. The simple structure is matched with focus strategies and business-level strategies, as firms implementing these strategies commonly compete by offering a single product line in a single geographic market. Local restaurants, repair businesses, and other specialized enterprises are examples of firms using the simple structure.

As the small firm grows larger and becomes more complex, managerial and structural challenges emerge. For example, the amount of competitively relevant information requiring analysis substantially increases, placing significant pressure on the owner-manager. Additional growth and success may cause the firm to change its strategy. Even if the strategy remains the same, the firm's larger size dictates the need for more sophisticated workflows and integrating mechanisms. At this evolutionary point, firms tend to move from the simple structure to a functional organizational structure.[56]

Functional Structure

The **functional structure** consists of a chief executive officer and a limited corporate staff, with functional line managers in dominant organizational areas such as production, accounting, marketing, R&D, engineering, and human resources.[57] This structure allows for functional specialization,[58] thereby facilitating active sharing of knowledge within each functional area. Knowledge sharing facilitates career paths as well as professional development of functional specialists. However, a functional orientation can negatively affect communication and coordination among those representing different organizational functions. For this reason, the CEO must work hard to verify that the decisions and actions of individual business functions promote the entire firm rather than a single function. The functional structure supports implementing business-level strategies and some corporate-level strategies (e.g., single or dominant business) with low levels of diversification. When changing from a simple to a functional structure, firms want to avoid introducing value-destroying bureaucratic procedures, particularly those failing to promote innovation and creativity.[59]

Multidivisional Structure

With continuing growth and success, firms often consider greater levels of diversification. Successfully using a diversification strategy requires analyzing substantially greater amounts of data and information when the firm offers the same products in different markets (market or geographic diversification) or offers different products in several markets (product diversification). In addition, trying to manage high levels of diversification through functional structures creates serious coordination and control problems,[60] a fact that commonly leads to a new structural form.[61]

The **multidivisional (M-form) structure** consists of a corporate office and operating divisions, each operating division representing a separate business or profit center in which the top corporate officer delegates responsibilities for day-to-day operations and business-unit strategy to division managers. Each division represents a distinct, self-contained business with its own functional hierarchy.[62] As initially designed, the M-form was thought to have three major benefits: "(1) it enabled corporate officers to more accurately monitor the performance of each business, which simplified the problem of control; (2) it facilitated comparisons between divisions, which improved the resource allocation process; and (3) it stimulated managers of poorly performing divisions to look for ways of improving performance."[63] Active monitoring of performance through the M-form increases the likelihood that decisions made by managers heading individual units will be in stakeholders" best interests. Because diversification is a dominant corporate-level strategy used in the global economy, the M-form is a widely adopted organizational structure.[64]

Used to support implementation of related and unrelated diversification strategies, the M-form helps firms successfully manage diversification's many demands.[65] Chandler viewed the M-form as an innovative response to coordination and control problems that surfaced during the 1920s in the functional structures then used by large firms such as DuPont and General Motors.[66] Research shows that the M-form is appropriate when the firm grows through diversification.[67] Partly because of its value to diversified corporations, some consider the multidivisional structure to be one of the twentieth century's most significant organizational innovations.[68]

No one organizational structure (simple, functional, or multidivisional) is inherently superior to the others.[69] Management guru Peter Drucker says the following about this matter: "There is no one right organization. .. Rather the task … is to select the organization for the particular task and mission at hand."[70] In our context, Drucker is saying that the firm must select a structure that is "right" for successfully using the chosen strategy. As no single structure is optimal in all instances, managers concentrate on developing proper matches between strategies and organizational structures rather than searching for an "optimal" structure. This matching of structure and strategy is taking place at Cisco. As noted in the Opening Case, John Chambers is increasing the firm's level of diversification and as such is adjusting its structure to match.

We now describe the strategy/structure matches that, evidence shows, positively contribute to firm performance.

Matches between Business-Level Strategies and the Functional Structure

Firms use different forms of the functional organizational structure to support implementing the cost leadership, differentiation, and integrated cost leadership/differentiation strategies. The differences in these forms are accounted for primarily by different uses of three important structural characteristics: **specialization** (concerned with the type and number of jobs required to complete work[71]), **centralization** (the degree to which decision-making authority is retained at higher managerial levels[72]), and **formalization** (the degree to which formal rules and procedures govern work[73]).

Using the Functional Structure to Implement the Cost Leadership Strategy

Firms using the cost leadership strategy sell large quantities of standardized products to an industry's typical customer. Simple reporting relationships, few layers in the decision-making and authority structure, a centralized corporate staff, and a strong focus on process improvements through the manufacturing function rather than the development of new products by emphasizing product R&D characterize the cost leadership form of the functional structure[74] (see Figure 11.2). This structure contributes to the emergence of a low-cost culture—a culture in which employees constantly try to find ways to reduce the costs incurred to complete their work.[75]

In terms of centralization, decision-making authority is concentrated in a staff function to maintain a cost-reducing emphasis within each organizational function (engineering, marketing, etc.). While encouraging continuous cost reductions, the centralized staff also verifies that further cuts in costs in one function won't adversely affect the productivity levels in other functions.[76]

Jobs are highly specialized in the cost leadership functional structure; work is divided into homogeneous subgroups. Organizational functions are the most common subgroup, although work is sometimes batched on the basis of products manufactured or clients served. Specializing in their work allows employees to increase their efficiency, resulting in reduced costs. Guiding individuals' work in this structure are highly formalized rules and procedures, which often emanate from the centralized staff.

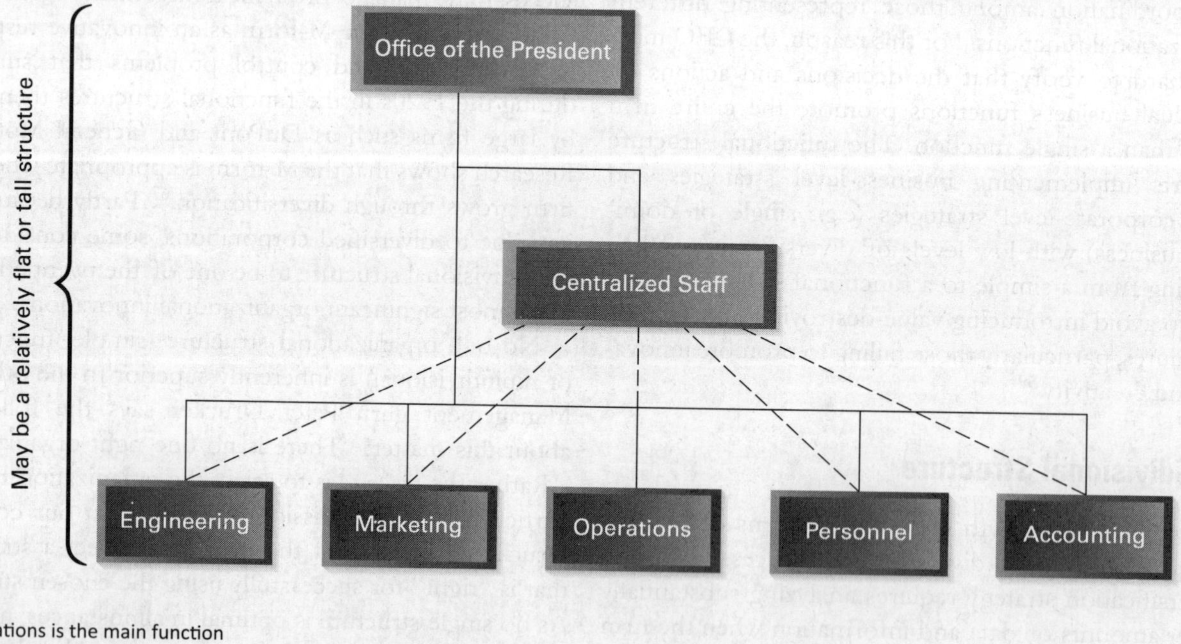

Notes:
- Operations is the main function
- Process engineering is emphasized rather than new product R&D
- Relatively large centralized staff coordinates functions
- Formalized procedures allow for emergence of a low-cost culture
- Overall structure is mechanistic; job roles are highly structured

Figure 11.2 Functional structure for implementing a cost leadership strategy

Wal-Mart Stores Inc. uses the functional structure to implement cost leadership strategies in each of its three segments (Wal-Mart Stores, Sam's Clubs, and International). In the Wal-Mart Stores segment (which generates the largest share of the firm's total sales), the cost leadership strategy is used in the firm's Supercenter, Discount, and Neighborhood Market retailing formats.[77] Long known for its "Always Low Prices" slogan (which was used for 19 years), Wal-Mart recently changed to a new slogan—"Save Money, Live Better".[78] Although the slogan is new, Wal-Mart continues using the functional organizational structure in its divisions to drive costs lower. As discussed in Chapter 4, competitors' efforts to duplicate the success of Wal-Mart's cost leadership strategies have generally failed, partly because of the effective strategy/structure matches in each of the firm's segments.

Using the Functional Structure to Implement the Differentiation Strategy

Firms using the differentiation strategy make products which customers perceive as being different in ways that create value for them. With this strategy, the firm wants to sell non-standardized products to customers with unique needs. Relatively complex and flexible reporting relationships, frequent use of cross-functional product development teams, and a strong focus on marketing and product R&D rather than manufacturing and process R&D (as with the cost leadership form of the functional structure) characterize the differentiation form of the functional structure (see Figure 11.3). From this structure emerges a development-oriented culture in which employees try to find ways to further differentiate current products and to develop new, highly differentiated products.[79]

Continuous product innovation demands that people throughout the firm interpret and take action based on information that is often ambiguous, incomplete, and uncertain. Following a strong focus on the external environment to identify new opportunities, employees often gather this information from people outside the firm (e.g., customers and suppliers). Commonly, rapid responses to the possibilities indicated by the collected information are necessary, suggesting the need for decentralized decision-making responsibility and authority. To support creativity and the continuous pursuit of new sources of differentiation and new products, jobs in this structure are not highly specialized. This lack of specialization means that workers have a relatively large number of tasks in their job descriptions. Few formal rules and procedures also characterize this structure. Low formalization, decentralization of decision-making authority and responsibility, and low specialization of work tasks combine to create a structure in which people interact frequently to exchange ideas about how to further differ-

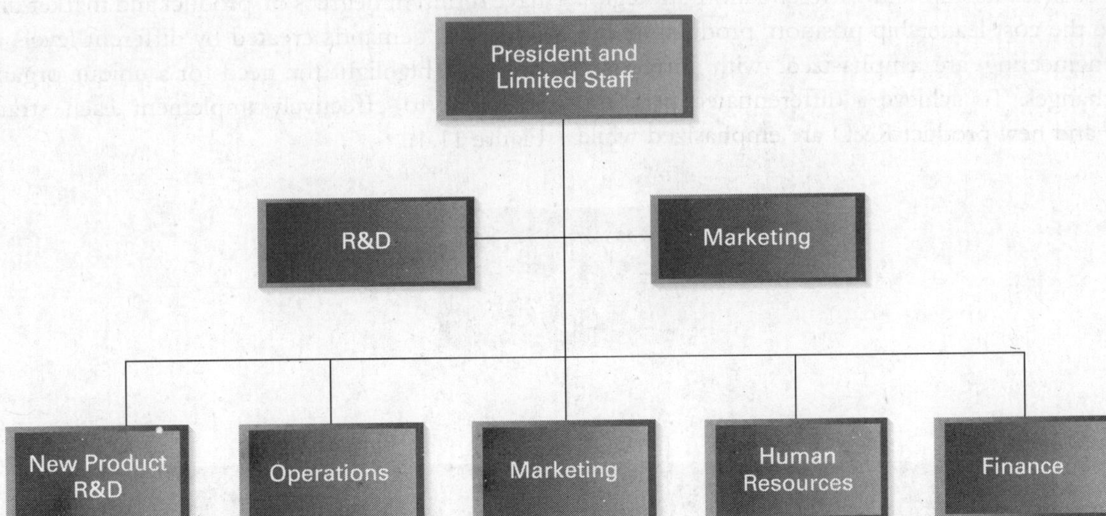

Notes:

- Marketing is the main function for keeping track of new product ideas
- New product R&D is emphasized
- Most functions are decentralized, but R&D and marketing may have centralized staffs that work closely with each other
- Formalization is limited so that new product ideas can emerge easily and change is more readily accomplished
- Overall structure is organic; job roles are less structured

Figure 11.3 Functional structure for implementing a differentiation strategy

entiate current products while developing ideas for new products that can be crisply differentiated.

Under Armour has used a differentiation strategy and matching structure to create success in the sports apparel market. Under Armour's objective was to create improved athletic performance through innovative design, testing, and marketing, especially to professional athletes and teams, and translate that perception to the broader market. With a strong match between strategy and structure, it has successfully created innovative sports performance products and challenged Nike and other sports apparel competitors.[80]

Using the Functional Structure to Implement the Integrated Cost Leadership/Differentiation Strategy

Firms using the integrated cost leadership/differentiation strategy sell products that create value because of their relatively low cost and reasonable sources of differentiation. The cost of these products is low "relative" to the cost leader's prices while their differentiation is "reasonable" when compared with the clearly unique features of the differentiator's products.

Although challenging to implement, the integrated cost leadership/differentiation strategy is used frequently in the global economy. The challenge of using this structure is due largely to the fact that different primary and support activities (see Chapter 3) are emphasized when using the cost leadership and differentiation strategies. To achieve the cost leadership position, production and process engineering are emphasized, with infrequent product changes. To achieve a differentiated position, marketing and new product R&D are emphasized while production and process engineering are not. Thus, effective use of the integrated strategy depends on the firm's successful combination of activities intended to reduce costs with activities intended to create additional differentiation features. As a result, the integrated form of the functional structure must have decision-making patterns that are partially centralized and partially decentralized. Additionally, jobs are semi-specialized, and rules and procedures call for some formal and some informal job behavior.

Matches between Corporate-Level Strategies and the Multidivisional Structure

As explained earlier, Chandler's research shows that the firm's continuing success leads to product or market diversification or both.[81] The firm's level of diversification is a function of decisions about the number and type of businesses in which it will compete as well as how it will manage the businesses (see Chapter 6). Geared to managing individual organizational functions, increasing diversification eventually creates information processing, coordination, and control problems that the functional structure cannot handle. Thus, using a diversification strategy requires the firm to change from the functional structure to the multidivisional structure to develop an appropriate strategy/structure match.

As defined in Figure 6.1, corporate-level strategies have different degrees of product and market diversification. The demands created by different levels of diversification highlight the need for a unique organizational structure to effectively implement each strategy (see Figure 11.4).

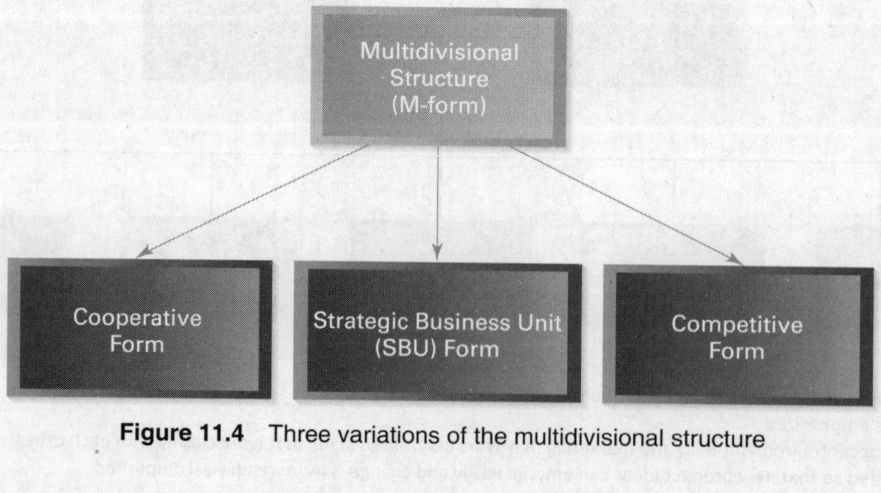

Figure 11.4 Three variations of the multidivisional structure

Using the Cooperative Form of the Multidivisional Structure to Implement the Related Constrained Strategy

The **cooperative form** is an M-form structure in which horizontal integration is used to bring about interdivisional cooperation. Divisions in a firm using the related constrained diversification strategy commonly are formed around products, markets, or both. In Figure 11.5, we use product divisions as part of the representation of the cooperative form of the multidivisional structure, although market divisions could be used instead of, or in addition to product divisions to develop the figure.

Using this structure, Hewlett-Packard (HP) has implemented the related constrained strategy as described in the Strategic Focus 11. 1. HP's intent is to sell integrated solutions to corporate data centers, so it has placed an emphasis on creating more relationships among its products (servers, storage, mobile computing, and high-speed printers) and coordinating these products through value-added services. This has required the implementation of the cooperative M-form and more centralization among the various business units to foster cooperation and synergy.

Sharing divisional competencies facilitates the corporation's efforts to develop economies of scope. As explained in Chapter 6, economies of scope (cost savings resulting from the sharing of competencies developed in one division with another division) are linked with successful use of the related constrained strategy. Interdivisional sharing of competencies depends on cooperation, suggesting the use of the cooperative form of the multidivisional structure.[82] HP seems to have developed the structure and processes well to accomplish this.

The cooperative structure uses different characteristics of structure (centralization, standardization, and formalization) as integrating mechanisms to facilitate interdivisional cooperation. Frequent, direct contact between division managers, another integrating mechanism, encourages and supports cooperation and the sharing of competencies or resources that could be used to create new advantages. Sometimes, liaison roles are established in each division to reduce the time division managers spend integrating and coordinating their unit's work with the work occurring in other divisions. Temporary teams or task forces may be formed around projects whose success depends on sharing competencies that are embed-

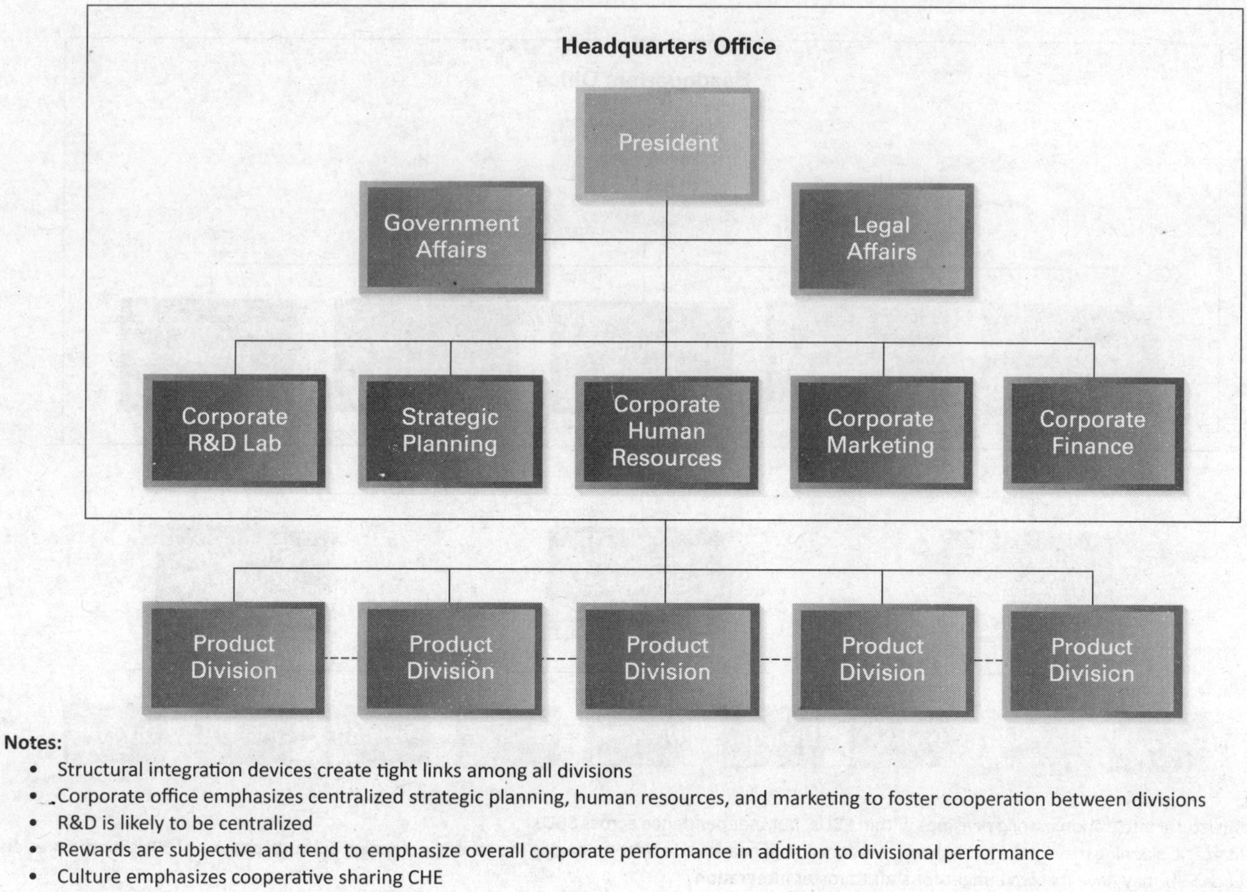

Figure 11.5 Cooperative form of the multidivisional structure for implementing a related constrained strategy

ded within several divisions. Cisco has used these devices to develop new cooperative strategies, as illustrated in the Opening Case. Formal integration departments might be established in firms frequently using temporary teams or task forces.

Ultimately, a matrix organization may evolve in firms implementing the related constrained strategy. A **matrix organization** is an organizational structure in which there is a dual structure combining both functional specialization and business product or project specialization.[83] Although complicated, an effective matrix structure can lead to improved coordination among a firm's divisions.[84]

The success of the cooperative multidivisional structure is significantly affected by how well divisions process information. However, because cooperation among divisions implies a loss of managerial autonomy, division managers may not readily commit themselves to the type of integrative information-processing activities that this structure demands. Moreover, coordination among divisions sometimes results in an unequal flow of positive outcomes to divisional managers. In other words, when managerial rewards are based at least in part on the performance of individual divisions, the manager of the division that is able to benefit the most by the sharing of corporate competencies might be viewed as receiving relative gains at others' expense. Strategic controls are important in these instances, as divisional managers' performance can be evaluated at least partly on the basis of how well they have facilitated interdivisional cooperative efforts. In addition, using reward systems that emphasize overall company performance, besides outcomes achieved by individual divisions, helps overcome problems associated with the cooperative form.

Using the Strategic Business Unit Form of the Multidivisional Structure to Implement the Related Linked Strategy

Firms with fewer links or less constrained links among their divisions use the related linked diversification strategy. The strategic business unit form of the multidivisional structure supports implementation of this strategy. The **strategic business unit (SBU) form** is an M-form structure consisting of three levels: corporate headquarters, strategic business units (SBUs), and SBU divisions (see Figure 11.6). The SBU structure is used by

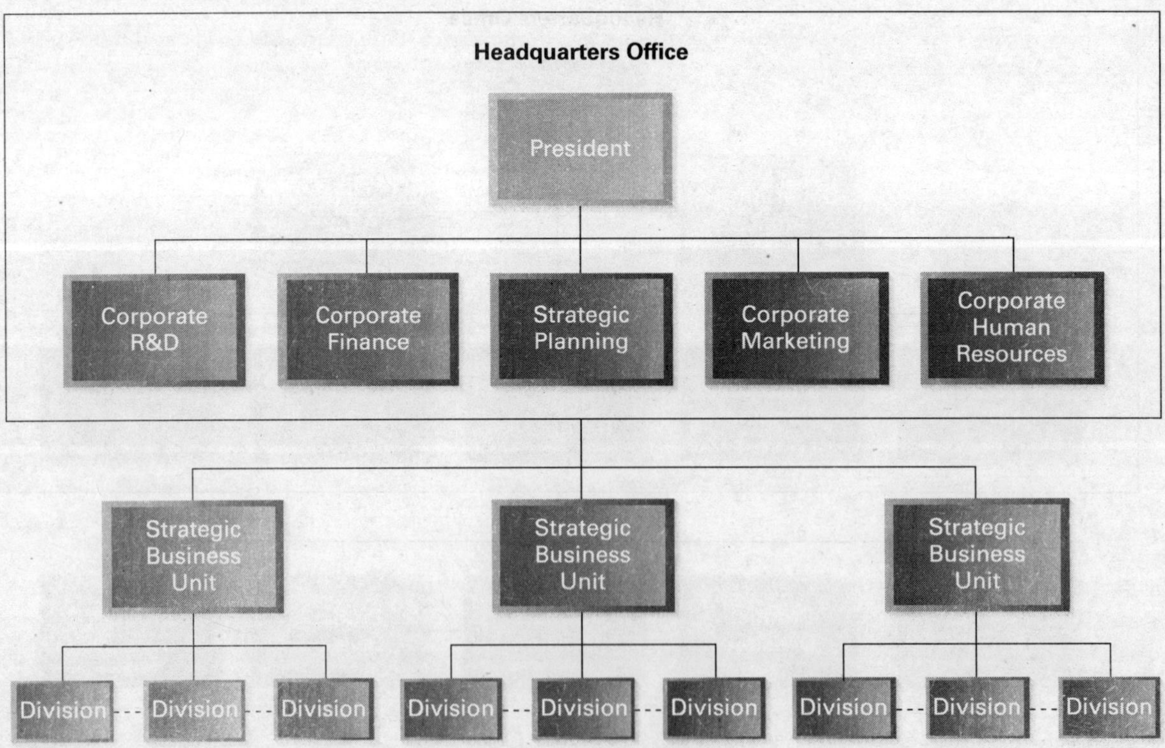

Notes:

- Structural integration among divisions within SBUs, but independence across SBUs
- Strategic planning may be the most prominent function in headquarters for managing the strategic planning approval process of SBUs for the president
- Each SBU may have its own budget for staff to foster integration
- Corporate headquarters staff members serve as consultants to SBUs and divisions, rather than having direct input to product strategy, as in the cooperative form

Figure 11.6 SBU form of the multidivisional structure for implementing a related linked strategy

STRATEGIC FOCUS

11.1 Hewlett-Packard Implements the Related Constrained Strategy through the Cooperative M-form Structure

Hewlett-Packard (HP) has three main related businesses through which it pursues industry leadership and technology development. First, it has the Personal Systems Group, including business and consumer PCs, mobile computing, and workstation devices. Second, it has a complementary business with a very large market share in Imaging and Printing, which includes inkjet and laserjet printers, commercial printing, printing supplies, digital photography, and entertainment products and support. Finally, it has a Technology Service Solutions Group, which includes business products focused on servers and storage, managed services and software, and services solutions. This group has been augmented through its recent acquisition of Electronic Data Systems (EDS). HP stood number nine in the 2009 Fortune 500 ranking with more than $118 billion in total revenue for fiscal year 2008.

Its main focus for customers is on corporate data centers that allow connected mobile computing, printing, and imaging delivery. HP pursues a related constrained strategy (as discussed in Chapter 6) by using the cooperative M-form structure. As firms pursue diversified growth and the economy becomes more Internet based, corporate data centers are increasingly important to help firms pursue improved top-line and bottom-line growth. HP's three main businesses allow the related strategy to work well by focusing on the growing importance of corporate data centers. Firms that seek to deliver the products and services necessary to the centers are required to have interrelated services and businesses to sell integrated solutions.

David Paul Morris/Getty Images News/Getty Images

Mark Hurd, President and CEO of Hewlett-Packard, has increased efficiency and reduced costs at HP through the implementation of the cooperative M-form structure.

This is driving firms that have a dominant focus on one product category to move into the other categories. For instance, Cisco, as noted in the Opening Case, is moving toward a corporate data center approach but coming at it from a traditional focus on network equipment. For this reason it is now moving into servers, which has been one of HP's dominant businesses (Cisco previously partnered with HP in this area). Like Cisco, HP has moved away from its formerly decentralized structure toward a related constrained strategy by seeking to implement the cooperative M-form organization structure. The cooperative M-form requires more centralization to make it function appropriately and to foster cooperation between the separate divisions within and across business unit divisions. This requires distinctive leadership and focus on improved execution to function properly.

Mark Hurd, the current CEO who succeeded Carly Fiorina in 2005, has been able to fine-tune HP's structural approach through his 'get things done' mentality. One security analyst describes Hurd as someone who is, '... all about execution and has an uncanny ability to get things done.' Furthermore, this same analyst suggests, 'He is the most adept at taking costs out of the system than any executive I know.' His no-nonsense style has led to increasing operational efficiency by realizing a strong implementation of the cooperative M-form structure. For instance, through the $13 billion acquisition of the consulting services firm EDS in 2008, Hurd cut 15,000 jobs or 10 per cent of the workforce to create the synergistic effect needed across all businesses. In 2009, this led HP to project a decline of 5 per cent in revenues, but to still be able to project a 6 per cent growth in profits, all despite the economic downturn.

Although the cooperative structure implementation has created wealth and efficiency, there are those who speculate that Hurd's approach has an Achilles heel because it lacks an emphasis on breakthrough innovation such as Apple's iPod and iPhone. Robert Burgelman, a Stanford professor who has studied Hurd, says, "He will not tell them we should do this project or that project. He helps them think more clearly about the space in which they are operating." While these actions have made HP's R&D operations more efficient, Hurd may need to give employees more creative license if he wants breakthrough innovations that would allow HP to compete more effectively with IBM and Apple.

Sources: J. Brodkin, 2009, HP BladeSystem, Matrix takes aim at Cisco, Network World, April 20, 34; A. Lashinsky, 2009, Mark Hurd's moment, *Fortune*, March 16, 90–100; J. Scheck, 2009, Corporate news: HP chief sees more pain ahead, trims more jobs, *Wall Street Journal*, May 20, B3; B. Worthen & J. Scheck, 2009, H-P to step up fight in market for servers, *Wall Street Journal*, April 16, B5; C. Edwards, 2008, How HP got the wow! back, *BusinessWeek*, December 20, 60; J. Fortt, 2008, Mark Hurd, superstar, *Fortune*, June 29, 35; J. Jain, 2008, Decision sciences: A story of excellence at Hewlett-Packard, OR-MS Today, 35(2): 20; L. Lee, 2008, HP's Hurd is about to be tested: After a sterling three-year run, the company's CEO faces a weaker PC market and a stronger Dell, *BusinessWeek*, February 14, 59–60; 2008, Business: Now services; Hewlett-Packard, *Economist*, May, 78; D. M. Zell, A. M. Glassman, & S. A. Duron, 2007, Strategic management in turbulent times: The short and glorious history of accelerated decision making at Hewlett-Packard, *Organizational Dynamics*, 36(1): 93–104.

large firms and can be complex, given associated organization size and product and market diversity.

The divisions within each SBU are related in terms of shared products or markets or both, but the divisions of one SBU have little in common with the divisions of the other SBUs. Divisions within each SBU share product or market competencies to develop economies of scope and possibly economies of scale. The integrating mechanisms used by the divisions in this structure can be equally well used by the divisions within the individual strategic business units that are part of the SBU form of the multidivisional structure. In this structure, each SBU is a profit center that is controlled and evaluated by the headquarters office. Although both financial and strategic controls are important, on a relative basis financial controls are vital to headquarters' evaluation of each SBU; strategic controls are critical when the heads of SBUs evaluate their divisions' performances. Strategic controls are also critical to the headquarters' efforts to determine whether the company has formed an effective portfolio of businesses and whether those businesses are being successfully managed.

Sears Holdings changed to the SBU form in 2008 by dividing into five strategic business units (with multiple divisions as parts of each SBU): brands, real estate, support, online, and store operations.[85] This allowed for related businesses to work together (such as Sears and K-Mart) to focus on their distinct customer sets, but also provided for better control for headquarters in order to evaluate performance of each strategic business unit and division within the SBU.

Sharing competencies among units within an SBU is an important characteristic of the SBU form of the multidivisional structure (see the notes to Figure 11.6). A drawback to the SBU structure is that multifaceted businesses often have difficulties in communicating this complex business model to stockholders.[86] Furthermore, if coordination between SBUs is needed, problems can arise because the SBU structure, similar to the competitive form discussed next, does not readily foster cooperation across SBUs. A typical case in point in this context is the organizational structure of the Indian Railways, which is discussed in the following Strategic Focus.

STRATEGIC FOCUS

11.2 Indian Railways: Is the Present Structure Good Enough?

Indian Railways has faced the problem of its structure for a long time. It is the largest single employer in the country. It is run as a department of the Central Government, although it is essentially a commercial activity rather than one of public administration. It has about 65,000 route kilometers, making it one of the largest railway systems in the world. It has an investment of about ₹2 trillion, with about 9,000 locomotives, 60,000 coaches, and 220,000 wagons. It has mainly two businesses: freight business, earning about two thirds of its revenues earning about ₹570 billion, and passenger traffic grossing about ₹234 billion. There is also a small parcels business.

Indian Railways is divided into 16 zones, each under a General Manager. Besides, there are some other production units such as Chittaranjan Locomotive Works, Integral Coach Factory, etc., each again under a General Manager.

How to structure this vast organization has been the subject of debate in many committees. IR is essentially a functional organization, with a Board consisting of members from different functional departments. Each zone is also functionally organized, with Heads of different functional departments reporting operationally to the respective GMs, and functionally to the respective member of the Board. This not only results in a double reporting relationship, but it also becomes difficult to exact accountability from any one.

At first, it might seem that the Railways can be reorganized with each zone being a profit center. But this overlooks an important feature of the Railways, i.e., its close interconnectivity. This means that decision taken in one zone will affect other zones, and since most the important freight and passenger trains run on more than one zone, the decisions become those of the Board and its office, making the decision making highly centralized. The zonal GMs can hardly take any pricing decisions, since the tariffs need to be uniform over the entire system; they cannot decide investments on their own, nor can they take any marketing initiatives of any consequence.

Indian Railways: Is the structure/strategy mix optimal?

The British Rail, after privatization by Margaret Thatcher, was split into different business units, such as passenger, freight, etc., and that too for different zones, each of which became an independent unit. The track and signaling were put under another entity. This restructuring does not appear to have yielded much results, mainly due to the interdependency of these businesses.

Can such an approach be adopted for the Indian Railways? Should it be restructured, splitting it into different business units, each accountable for its own bottom line? Will it enable the units to become more customer-centric? These questions are still discussed by some subcommittees constituted under the National Transport Policy Committee in 2010.

Sources: Brian Wadsworth (1995), British Railways Case Study, in Ron Kopicki and Louis S Thomson, *Best Methods of Railway Restructuring and Privatization*, CFS Discussion Paper Series, Number 111, 1995; ; http://www.indianrailways.gov.in/railwayboard/uploads/directorate/stat_econ/Stat_0910/Summery_Sheet_Final-English_2009-10.pdf.

Using the Competitive Form of the Multidivisional Structure to Implement the Unrelated Diversification Strategy

Firms using the unrelated diversification strategy want to create value through efficient internal capital allocations or by restructuring, buying, and selling businesses.[87] The competitive form of the multidivisional structure supports implementation of this strategy.

The **competitive form** is an M-form structure characterized by complete independence among the firm's divisions which compete for corporate resources (see Figure 11.7). Unlike the divisions included in the cooperative structure, divisions that are part of the competitive structure do not share common corporate strengths. Because strengths are not shared, integrating devices are not developed for use by the divisions included in the competitive structure.

The efficient internal capital market that is the foundation for using the unrelated diversification strategy requires organizational arrangements emphasizing divisional competition rather than cooperation.[88] Three benefits are expected from the internal competition. First, internal competition creates flexibility (e.g., corporate headquarters can have divisions working on different technologies and projects to identify those with the greatest potential). Resources can then be allocated to the division appearing to have the most potential to fuel the entire firm's suc-

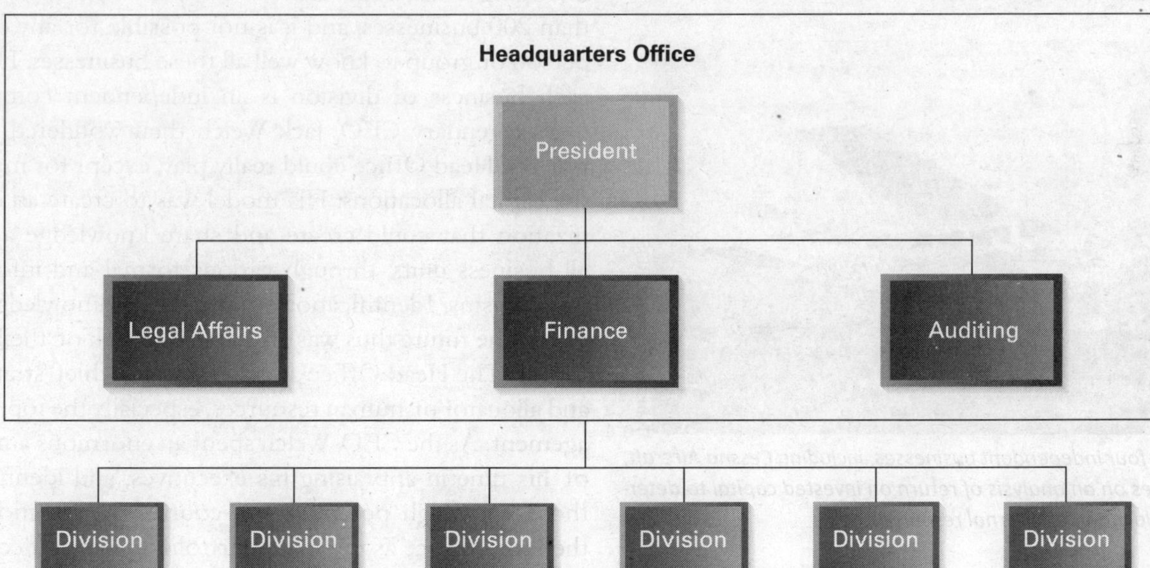

Notes:

- Corporate headquarters has a small staff
- Finance and auditing are the most prominent functions in the headquarters office to manage cash flow and assure the accuracy of performance data coming from divisions
- The legal affairs function becomes important when the firm acquires or divests assets
- Divisions are independent and separate for financial evaluation purposes
- Divisions retain strategic control, but cash is managed by the corporate office
- Divisions compete for corporate resources

Figure 11.7 Competitive form of the multidivisional structure for implementing an unrelated strategy

cess. Second, internal competition challenges the status quo and inertia, because division heads know that future resource allocations are a product of excellent current performance as well as superior positioning in terms of future performance. Last, internal competition motivates effort in that the challenge of competing against internal peers can be as great as the challenge of competing against external rivals.[89] In this structure, organizational controls (primarily financial controls) are used to emphasize and support internal competition among separate divisions and as the basis for allocating corporate capital based on divisions' performances.

Textron Inc., a large "multi-industry" company seeks "to identify, research, select, acquire and integrate companies, and has developed a set of rigorous criteria to guide decision making." Textron continuously looks "to enhance and reshape its portfolio by divesting non-core assets and acquiring branded businesses in attractive industries with substantial long-term growth potential." Textron operates four independent businesses—Bell Helicopter (20 per cent of revenue), Cessna Aircraft (40 per cent), Textron Systems (15 per cent), Finance (5 per cent), and Industrial (20 per cent). The firm uses return on invested capital (ROIC) as a way to evaluate the contribution of its diversified set of businesses as they compete internally for resources.[90]

Transtock/Terra/CORBIS

Made of up four independent businesses, including Cessna Aircraft, Textron relies on an analysis of return on invested capital to determine the allocation of internal resources.

To emphasize competitiveness among divisions, the headquarters office maintains an arm's-length relationship with them, intervening in divisional affairs only to audit operations and discipline managers whose divisions perform poorly. In emphasizing competition between divisions, the headquarters office relies on strategic controls to set rate-of-return targets and financial controls to monitor divisional performance relative to those targets. The headquarters office then allocates cash flow on a competitive basis, rather than automatically returning cash to the division that produced it. Thus, the focus of the headquarters' work is on performance appraisal, resource allocation, and long-range planning to verify that the firm's portfolio of businesses will lead to financial success.[91]

The three major forms of the multidivisional structure should each be paired with a particular corporate-level strategy. Table 11.1 shows these structures' characteristics. Differences exist in the degree of centralization, the focus of the performance appraisal, the horizontal structures (integrating mechanisms), and the incentive compensation schemes. The most centralized and most costly structural form is the cooperative structure. The least centralized, with the lowest bureaucratic costs, is the competitive structure. The SBU structure requires partial centralization and involves some of the mechanisms necessary to implement the relatedness between divisions. Also, the divisional incentive compensation awards are allocated according to both SBUs and corporate performance.

GE offers an interesting study of the complexities of managing a widely diversified company. GE is in more than 200 businesses, and it is not possible for any single person or group to know well all these businesses. Hence each business or division is an independent company. GE's legendary CEO, Jack Welch then wondered what role the Head Office could really play, except for making the capital allocations. His model was to create an organization that could create and share knowledge across all business units, through various formal and informal mechanisms. Identification of the crucial knowledge areas of the future thus was an important task of the Head Office. The Head Office also became the chief strategist and allocator of human resources, especially the top management. As the CEO, Welch spent an enormous amount of his time in appraising his executives, and identifying those with high potential. Of course, the function of the Head Office as the main portfolio manager, deciding which businesses should continue, which to be weeded out, and which to be promoted, continued. The result of these initiatives has been the wide acknowledgement of GE as the leadership factory that produces more leaders than it can use and these leaders in fact head many other major corporations in the United States.[92]

Table 11.1 Characteristics of the structures necessary to implement the related constrained, related linked, and unrelated diversification strategies

	Overall structural form		
Structural characteristics	Cooperative M-Form (Related Constrained Strategy)[a]	SBU M-Form (Related Linked Strategy)[a]	Competitive M-Form (Unrelated Diversification Strategy)[a]
Centralization of operations	Centralized at corporate office	Partially centralized (in SBUs)	Decentralized to divisions
Use of integration mechanisms	Extensive	Moderate	Nonexistent
Divisional performance appraisals	Emphasize subjective (strategic) criteria	Use a mixture of subjective (strategic) and objective (financial) criteria	Emphasize objective (financial) criteria
Divisional incentive compensation	Linked to overall corporate performance	Mixed linkage to corporate, SBU, and divisional performance	Linked to divisional performance

[a]Strategy implemented with structural form.

Matches between International Strategies and Worldwide Structure

As explained in Chapter 8, international strategies are becoming increasingly important for long-term competitive success[93] in what continues to become an increasingly borderless global economy.[94] Among other benefits, international strategies allow the firm to search for new markets, resources, core competencies, and technologies as part of its efforts to outperform competitors.[95]

As with business-level and corporate-level strategies, unique organizational structures are necessary to successfully implement the different international strategies.[96] Forming proper matches between international strategies and organizational structures facilitates the firm's efforts to effectively coordinate and control its global operations. More importantly, research findings confirm the validity of the international strategy/structure matches we discuss here.[97]

Using the Worldwide Geographic Area Structure to Implement the Multidomestic Strategy

The **multidomestic strategy** decentralizes the firm's strategic and operating decisions to business units in each country so that product characteristics can be tailored to local preferences. Firms using this strategy try to isolate themselves from global competitive forces by establishing protected market positions or by competing in industry segments that are most affected by differences among local countries. The worldwide geographic area structure is used to implement this strategy. The **worldwide geographic area structure** emphasizes national interests and facilitates the firm's efforts to satisfy local differences (see Figure 11.8).

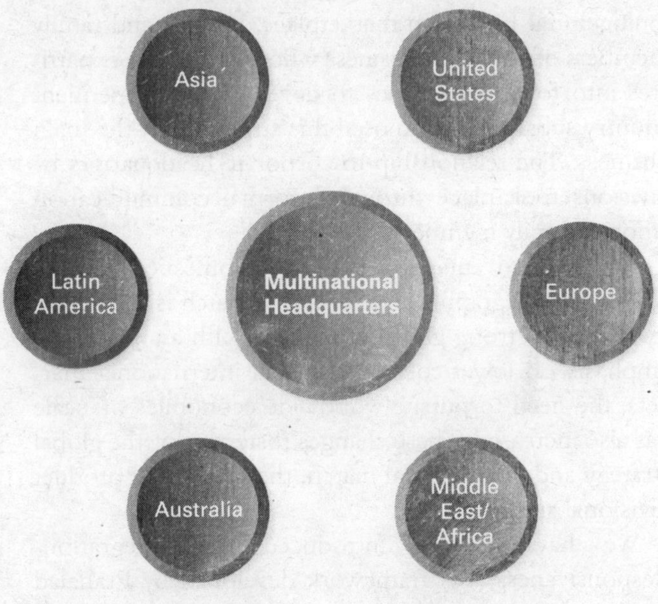

Notes:
- The perimeter circles indicate decentralization of operations
- Emphasis is on differentiation by local demand to fit an area or country culture
- Corporate headquarters coordinates financial resources among independent subsidiaries
- The organization is like a decentralized federation

Figure 11.8 Worldwide geographic area structure for implementing a multidomestic strategy

Although the automobile industry is doing poorly in global markets, on a relative basis Ford of Europe is doing better than other auto firms in the continent within the same middle market segment strategy. This is due to the fact that Ford implemented the worldwide geographic area structure more than a decade ago to give local European managers more autonomy to manage their operations. One analysis called Ford "the most efficient volume carmaker in Europe."[98] Furthermore, they have an efficient set of designs matched responsively to the European market. They have kept costs down by partnering with European automakers such as Fiat and France's PSA Peugeot Citroen on chassis and engines. The timing of the release of their new models was also good to take advantage of the European "cash for clunkers' program, although the underlying market is still weak.

Using the multidomestic strategy requires little coordination between different country markets, meaning that integrating mechanisms among divisions around the world are not needed. Coordination among units in a firm's worldwide geographic area structure is often informal.

The multidomestic strategy/worldwide geographic area structure match evolved as a natural outgrowth of the multicultural European marketplace. Friends and family members of the main business who were sent as expatriates into foreign countries to develop the independent country subsidiary often used this structure for the main business. The relationship to corporate headquarters by divisions took place through informal communication among "family members."[99]

A key disadvantage of the multidomestic strategy/worldwide geographic area structure match is the inability to create strong global efficiency. With an increasing emphasis on lower-cost products in international markets, the need to pursue worldwide economies of scale has also increased. These changes foster use of the global strategy and its structural match, the worldwide product divisional structure.

We have already introduced the Integration-Responsiveness (IR) framework developed by Prahalad and Doz, Bartlett and Ghoshal in Chapter 8. In terms of structure, this framework also indicates the need for identifying not merely a formal structure, but also the kind of centralization and decentralization needed to execute a global strategy effectively.

The Worldwide Product Divisional Structure to Implement the Global Strategy

With the corporation's home office dictating competitive strategy, the **global strategy** is one through which the firm offers standardized products across country markets. The firm's success depends on its ability to develop economies of both scope and scale on a global level. Decisions to outsource or maintain integrated subsidiaries may in part depend on the country risk and institutional environment in which the firm is entering.[100]

The worldwide product divisional structure supports use of the global strategy. In the **worldwide product divisional structure**, decision-making authority is centralized in the worldwide division headquarters to coordinate and integrate decisions and actions among divisional business units (see Figure 11.9). This structure is often used in rapidly growing firms seeking to manage their diversified product lines effectively. Avon Products, Inc. is an example of a firm using the worldwide product divisional structure.

Avon is a global brand leader in cosmetics and personal care products for women such as lipsticks, fragrances, and anti-aging skin care. Committed to "empowering women all over the world since 1886," Avon relies on product innovation to be a first-mover in its markets. For years, Avon used the multidomestic strategy. However, the firm's growth came to a screeching halt in 2006. Contributing to this decline were simultaneous stumbles in sales revenues in emerging markets (e.g., Russia and Central Europe), the United States, and Mexico. To cope with its problems, the firm changed to a global strategy and to the worldwide product divisional structure to support its use. Commenting on this change, CEO Andrea Jung noted that, "Previously, Avon managers from Poland to Mexico ran their own plants, developed new products, and created their own ads, often relying as much on gut as numbers."[101] Today, Avon is organized around product divisions including Avon Color, the firm's "flagship global color cosmetics brand, which offers a variety of color cosmetics, including foundations, powders, lip, eye, and nail products, skincare, bath & body, hair care, wellness, and fragrance. The analysis of these product divisions" performances is conducted by individuals in the firm's New York headquarters. One of the purposes of changing strategy and structure is for Avon to control its costs and gain additional scale economies as paths to performance improvements. Avon has announced the success of this restructuring program and vowed to cut costs even further; the original program is "expected to result in annual savings of about $430 million by 2011-12," while the new changes will result in "another $450 million expected to be saved beginning in 2010."[102]

Notes:

- The headquarters'circle indicates centralization to coordinate information flow among worldwide products
- Corporate headquarters uses many intercoordination devices to facilitate global economies of scale and scope
- Corporate headquarters also allocates financial resources in a cooperative way
- The organization is like a centralized federation

Figure 11.9 Worldwide product divisional structure for implementing a global strategy

Integrating mechanisms are important in the effective use of the worldwide product divisional structure. Direct contact between managers, liaison roles between departments, and temporary task forces as well as permanent teams are examples of these mechanisms. One researcher describes the use of these mechanisms in the worldwide structure: "There is extensive and formal use of task forces and operating committees to supplement communication and coordination of worldwide operations."[103] The disadvantages of the global strategy/worldwide structure combination are the difficulty involved with coordinating decisions and actions across country borders and the inability to quickly respond to local needs and preferences.

To deal with these types of disadvantages, Avon has a vast set of local salespeople who are committed to the organization and who help the company to become locally responsive. Another solution is to develop a regional approach in addition to the product focus, which might be similar to the combination structure discussed next.[104]

Using the Combination Structure to Implement the Transnational Strategy

The **transnational strategy** calls for the firm to combine the multidomestic strategy's local responsiveness with the global strategy's efficiency. Firms using this strategy are trying to gain the advantages of both local responsiveness and global efficiency. The combination structure is used to implement the transnational strategy. The **combination structure** is a structure drawing characteristics and mechanisms from both the worldwide geographic area structure and the worldwide product divisional structure. The transnational strategy is often implemented through two possible combination structures: a global matrix structure and a hybrid global design.[105]

The global matrix design brings together both local market and product expertise into teams that develop and respond to the global marketplace. The global matrix design (the basic matrix structure was defined earlier) promotes flexibility in designing products and responding to customer needs. However, it has severe limitations in that it places employees in a position of being accountable to more than one manager. At any given time, an employee may be a member of several functional or product group teams. Relationships that evolve from multiple memberships can make it difficult for employees to be simultaneously loyal to all of them. Although the matrix places authority in the hands of managers who are most able to use it, it creates problems in regard to corporate reporting relationships that are so complex and vague that it is difficult and time-consuming to receive approval for major decisions.

We illustrated the hybrid structure in Figure 11.10. In this design, some divisions are oriented toward products while others are oriented toward market areas. Thus, in some cases when the geographic area is more important, the division managers are area-oriented. In other divisions where worldwide product coordination and efficiencies are more important, the division manager is more product-oriented. The Strategic Focus on PepsiCo illustrates the hybrid design. Although PepsiCo is generally focused on geographic areas like most consumer product companies, as it has diversified into snacks and other foods, it also has product divisions to build better worldwide efficiencies.

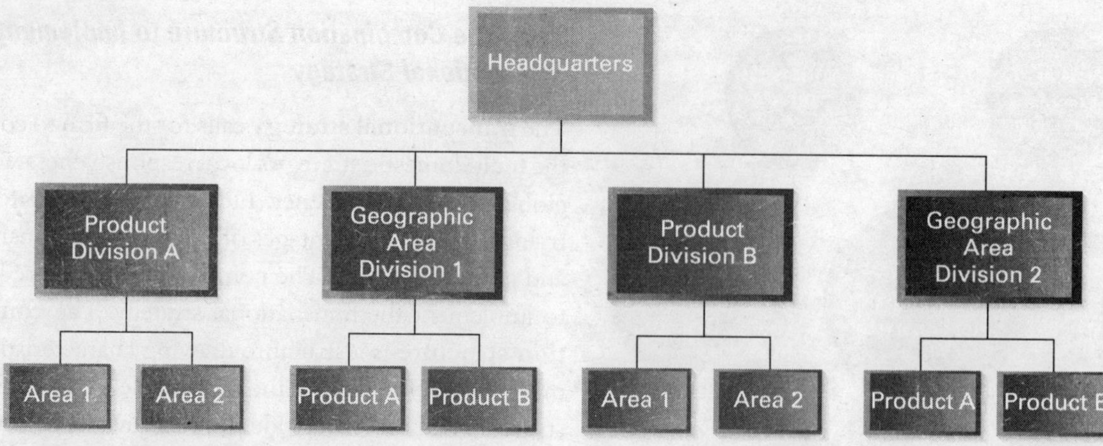

Figure 11.10 Hybrid form of the combination structure for implementing a transnational strategy

The fits between the multidomestic strategy and the worldwide geographic area structure and between the global strategy and the worldwide product divisional structure are apparent. However, when a firm wants to implement the multi-domestic and global strategies simultaneously through a combination structure, the appropriate integrating mechanisms are less obvious. The structure used to implement the transnational strategy must be simultaneously centralized and decentralized; integrated and nonintegrated; formalized and non-formalized.

IKEA has done a good job of balancing these organization aspects in implementing the transnational strategy.[106] IKEA is a global furniture retailer with outlets in more than 35 countries. IKEA focuses on lowering its costs and also understanding its customers' needs, especially younger customers. It has been able to manage these seemingly opposite characteristics through its structure and management process. It has also been able to encourage its employees to understand the effects of cultural and geographic diversity on firm operations. IKEA's system also has internal network attributes, which will be discussed next in regard to the external inter-organizational networks.

Matches between Cooperative Strategies and Network Structures

As discussed in Chapter 9, a network strategy exists when partners form several alliances in order to improve the performance of the alliance network itself through cooperative endeavors.[107] The greater levels of environmental complexity and uncertainty facing companies in today's competitive environment are causing more firms to use cooperative strategies such as strategic alliances and joint ventures.[108]

The breadth and scope of firms' operations in the global economy create many opportunities for firms to cooperate.[109] In fact, a firm can develop cooperative relationships with many of its stakeholders, including customers, suppliers, and competitors. When a firm becomes involved with combinations of cooperative relationships, it is part of a strategic network, or what others call an alliance constellation or portfolio.[110]

A **strategic network** is a group of firms that has been formed to create value by participating in multiple cooperative arrangements. An effective strategic network facilitates discovering opportunities beyond those identified by individual network participants.[111] A strategic network can be a source of competitive advantage for its members when its operations create value that is difficult for competitors to duplicate and that network members can't create by themselves.[112] Strategic networks are used to implement business-level, corporate-level, and international cooperative strategies.

Commonly, a strategic network is a loose federation of partners participating in the network's operations on a flexible basis. At the core or center of the strategic network, the **strategic center firm** is one around which the network's cooperative relationships revolve (see Figure 11.11).

Because of its central position, the strategic center firm is the foundation for the strategic network's structure. Concerned with various aspects of organizational structure, such as formal reporting relationships and procedures, the strategic center firm manages what are often complex, cooperative interactions among network partners. To perform the tasks, discussed next, the strategic

STRATEGIC FOCUS

11.3 PepsiCo: Moving from the Geographic Area Structure toward the Combined Structure Implementing the Transnational Strategy

PepsiCo has organized its businesses into three groups: PepsiCo North American Beverages (PNAB), PepsiCo Americas Foods (PAF), and PepsiCo International (PI). PNAB focuses on the Pepsi brand that includes carbonated soft drinks, juices and juice drinks, ready-to-drink tea and coffee, and isotonic sports drinks (Gatorade). It also has Aquafina water, Sierra Mist, Mug root beer, Tropicana juice drinks, Propel, SoBe, Slice, Dole, Tropicana Twister, and Tropicana Season's Best. Some of these drinks are through joint ventures such as with the Thomas J. Lipton Company (tea) and Starbucks coffee (Frappuccino). Gatorade became part of PepsiCo through a 2001 acquisition of Quaker Oats Company.

PAF is focused on food and snacks in North and South America including the products of Frito-Lay, Quaker Oats, Sabritas (Mexican snacks and fun food), and Gamesa (one of Mexico's top brands for cookies, pastries, oats, and cereals).

PepsiCo International includes the PepsiCo businesses in Europe, Asia, Africa, and Australia. Originally, this segment focused on distribution of beverages, but in 2003 it combined food and beverages to form PepsiCo International.

As you can see from these descriptions of its business segments, PepsiCo is primarily organized geographically—beverages in North America, food in North America, and food and beverages internationally by region. Accordingly, like most consumer product firms, it has traditionally implemented the multidomestic strategy with a regional focus, using the worldwide geographic area structure to better create a marketing approach that is adaptable to various languages, cultures, and lifestyles. However, as it has diversified into a variety of beverages and snack foods, it has consequently organized into product divisions as well to gain greater efficiencies in managing these products worldwide. Although it is still predominately area focused through the management structure, it has additional structures that allow the product divisions to be managed more efficiently. Accordingly, PepsiCo is moving toward implementing the transnational strategy through the combination structure.

Neville Elder/CORBIS

PepsiCo's geographic organization and move toward the implementation of a transnational strategy are supported by a highly diverse leadership team, headed by CEO and chairman of the board, Indra Nooyi, who is originally from India.

Interestingly, PepsiCo has one of the most diverse leadership teams. Its CEO and chairman of the board, Indra Nooyi, is originally from India. A large number of board members possess significant international experience, including the ability to speak several languages. These board members allow a broad understanding of cultures and buying habits within geographic regions outside of the United States. The diversity on the board supports the geographic focus maintained by the company and has added to the success of marketing PepsiCo brands and products throughout the world.

Sources: 2009, The PepsiCo family, http://www.pepsico.com, June 25; H. Ehein, 2009, Internal relations, *Brand Week*, February 16, 8–9; D. Morris, 2008, The Pepsi challenge, *Fortune*, March 3, 54; M. Useem, 2008, America's best leaders: Indra Nooyi, PepsiCo CEO, *US News & World Report*, http://www.usnews.com, November 19; 2008, Global companies with global boards, *Directorship*, 34(5): 28–30; 2008, Pepsi versus Coke: An unhealthy obsession: They are global, but are they relevant? *Strategic Direction*, 24(1): 6–8.

center firm must make sure that incentives for participating in the network are aligned so that network firms continue to have a reason to remain connected.[113] The strategic center firm is engaged in the following four primary tasks as it manages the strategic network and controls its operations:[114]

Strategic outsourcing The strategic center firm outsources and partners with more firms than other network members. At the same time, the strategic center firm requires network partners to be more than contractors. Members are expected to find opportunities for the network to create value through its cooperative work.

Competencies To increase network effectiveness, the strategic center firm seeks ways to support each member's efforts to develop core competencies with the potential of benefiting the network.

Technology The strategic center firm is responsible for managing the development and sharing of technology-based ideas among network members. The structural requirement that members submit formal reports detailing the technology-oriented outcomes of their efforts to the strategic center firm facilitates this activity.[115]

Race to learn The strategic center firm emphasizes that the principal dimensions of competition are be-

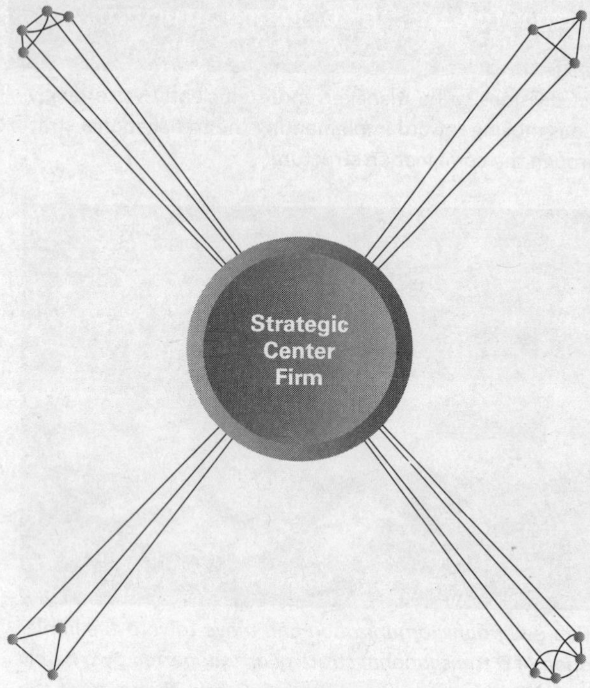

Figure 11.11 A strategic network

tween value chains and between networks of value chains. Because of this interconnection, the strategic network is only as strong as its weakest value-chain link. With its centralized decision-making authority and responsibility, the strategic center firm guides participants in efforts to form network-specific competitive advantages. The need for each participant to have capabilities that can be the foundation for the network's competitive advantages encourages friendly rivalry among participants seeking to develop the skills needed to quickly form new capabilities that create value for the network.[116]

Interestingly, strategic networks are being used more frequently, partly because of the ability of a strategic center firm to execute a strategy that effectively and efficiently links partner firms. Improved information systems and communication capabilities (e.g., the Internet) make such networks possible.[117]

Implementing Business-Level Cooperative Strategies

As noted in Chapter 9, the two types of business-level complementary alliances are vertical and horizontal. Firms with competencies in different stages of the value chain form a vertical alliance to cooperatively integrate their different, but complementary, skills. Firms combining their competencies to create value in the same stage of the value chain are using a horizontal alliance. Vertical complementary strategic alliances such as those developed by Toyota Motor Company are formed more frequently than horizontal alliances.[118]

A strategic network of vertical relationships such as the network in Japan between Toyota and its suppliers often involves a number of implementation issues.[119] First, the strategic center firm encourages subcontractors to modernize their facilities and provides them with technical and financial assistance to do so, if necessary. Second, the strategic center firm reduces its transaction costs by promoting longer-term contracts with subcontractors, so that supplier-partners increase their long-term productivity. This approach is diametrically opposed to that of continually negotiating short-term contracts based on unit pricing. Third, the strategic center firm enables engineers in upstream companies (suppliers) to have better communication with those companies with whom it has contracts for services. As a result, suppliers and the strategic center firm become more interdependent and less independent.[120]

The lean production system (a vertical complementary strategic alliance) pioneered by Toyota and others has been diffused throughout the global auto industry.[121] However, no auto company has learned how to duplicate the manufacturing effectiveness and efficiency Toyota derives from the cooperative arrangements in its strategic network.[122] A key factor accounting for Toyota's manufacturing-based competitive advantage is the cost other firms would incur to imitate the structural form used to support Toyota's application. In part, then, the structure of Toyota's strategic network that it created as the strategic center firm facilitates cooperative actions among network participants that competitors can't fully understand or duplicate.

In vertical complementary strategic alliances, such as the one between Toyota and its suppliers, the strategic center firm is obvious, as is the structure that the firm establishes. However, the same is not always true with horizontal complementary strategic alliances where firms try to create value in the same part of the value chain, as with airline alliances that are commonly formed to create value in the marketing and sales primary activity segment of the value chain (see Table 3.6). Because air carriers commonly participate in multiple horizontal complementary alliances such as the Star Alliance between Lufthansa, United, Continental, US Airways, Thai, Air Canada, SAS, and others, it is difficult to determine the strategic center firm. Moreover, participating in several alliances can cause firms to question partners' true loyalties and intentions. Also, if rivals band together in too many collaborative activities, one or more governments may suspect the possibility of illegal collusive activities. For these reasons, horizontal complementary alliances are used less often and less successfully than their vertical counterpart, although there are examples of success, for instance, among auto and aircraft manufacturers.[123]

Implementing Corporate-Level Cooperative Strategies

Corporate-level cooperative strategies (such as franchising) are used to facilitate product and market diversification. As a cooperative strategy, franchising allows the firm to use its competencies to extend or diversify its product or market reach, but without completing a merger or an acquisition.[124] Research suggests that knowledge embedded in corporate-level cooperative strategies facilitates synergy.[125] For example, McDonald's Corporation pursues a franchising strategy, emphasizing a limited value-priced menu in more than 100 countries. The McDonald's franchising system is a strategic network. McDonald's headquarters serves as the strategic center firm for the network's franchisees. The headquarters office uses strategic and financial controls to verify that the franchisees' operations create the greatest value for the entire network.

An important strategic control issue for McDonald's is the location of its franchisee units. Because it believes that its greatest expansion opportunities are outside the United States, the firm has decided to continue expanding in countries such as China and India, where it might need to adjust its menu according to the local culture. For example, "McDonald's adapts its restaurants in India to local tastes; in a nation that is predominantly Hindu and reveres the cow, beef isn't on the menu. It stands replaced by chicken burgers and vegetable patties."[126] It plans on expanding the number of restaurants in India by 40 in 2009 bringing the total to 200; it expanded by 25 restaurants in 2008. Accordingly, as the strategic center firm around the globe for its restaurants, McDonald's is devoting the majority of its capital expenditures to develop units in non–US markets.

Implementing International Cooperative Strategies

Strategic networks formed to implement international cooperative strategies result in firms competing in several countries.[127] Differences among countries' regulatory environments increase the challenge of managing international networks and verifying that at a minimum, the network's operations comply with all legal requirements.[128]

Distributed strategic networks are the organizational structure used to manage international cooperative strategies. As shown in Figure 11.12, several regional strategic center firms are included in the distributed network to manage partner firms' multiple cooperative arrangements.[129]

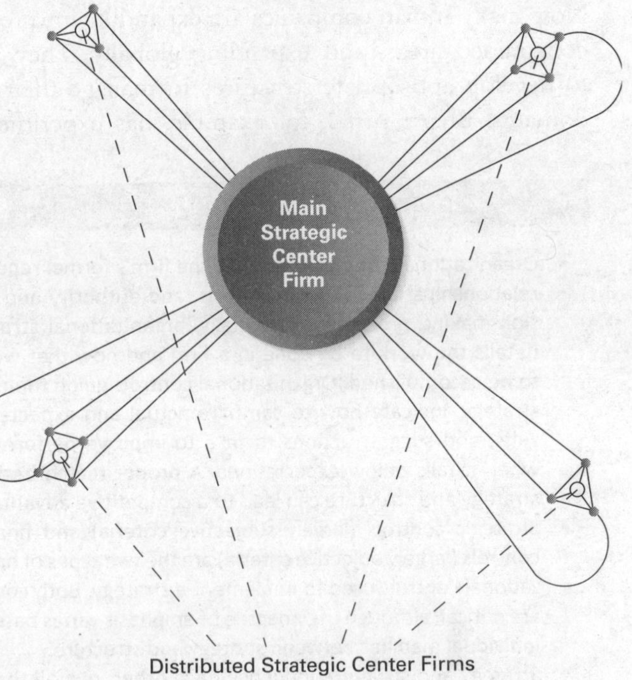

Figure 11.12 A distributed strategic network

Hewlett-Packard recently acquired EDS, a large information technology consulting firm. One of EDS' assets is the EDS Agility Alliance, its distributed strategic network. The Agility Alliance is EDS "premiere" partner program bringing together industry-leading technology providers to build and deliver end-to-end IT solutions.[130] EDS is the main strategic center firm in this alliance and has two dedicated centers that are the hubs for jointly developing initiatives with its partners. Cisco, SAP, Sun, Xerox, Oracle, EMC, and Microsoft are members of this distributed strategic network. Symantec, an Internet antivirus and security firm, was recently added as a partner to respond to clients' needs "for more innovative security products and solutions that help them better secure their mission-critical business data and address specific enterprise security issues."[131] EDS' partners each work with their own networks to complete projects that are a part of the Agility Alliance. As this example demonstrates, the structure used to implement the international cooperative strategy is complex and demands careful attention to be used successfully.

Indian companies have grown in a protected environment, where either they went into a wide variety of industries, or stuck to just one business. When they went into a number of industries, generally, the businesses were treated as independent businesses, under different companies, with only an overall direction from the top. Now many Indian companies are expanding into related constrained areas, and expanding globally. They need to develop appropriate structures to manage their new domains. Bharti Airtel, for example, has experimented with a number of organization structures to manage its different businesses in telecom: basic services including long distance, international services, broad band, media, and the business enterprise solutions. It also has a reach spanning virtually the whole country, and hence, a geographical structure is also needed. Thus, it has to operate in a matrix structure, constantly deriving synergies across its businesses. Tata Motors, Tata Steel, Essar, and many other companies have operations and plants in multiple countries, and by and large, they have adopted a multidomestic strategy. But the need for cost reduction, deriving value from brands, etc., would compel the firms to rethink their structures so as to get the maximum value from their operations.

SUMMARY

- Organizational structure specifies the firm's formal reporting relationships, procedures, controls, and authority and decision-making processes. Essentially, organizational structure details the work to be done in a firm and how that work is to be accomplished. Organizational controls guide the use of strategy, indicate how to compare actual and expected results, and suggest actions to take to improve performance when it falls below expectations. A proper match between strategy and structure can lead to a competitive advantage.
- Strategic controls (largely subjective criteria) and financial controls (largely objective criteria) are the two types of organizational controls used to implement a strategy. Both controls are critical, although their degree of emphasis varies based on individual matches between strategy and structure.
- Strategy and structure influence each other; overall though, strategy has a stronger influence on structure. Research indicates that firms tend to change structure when declining performance forces them to do so. Effective managers anticipate the need for structural change and quickly modify structure to better accommodate the firm's strategy when evidence calls for that action.
- The functional structure is used to implement business-level strategies. The cost leadership strategy requires a centralized functional structure—one in which manufacturing efficiency and process engineering are emphasized. The differentiation strategy's functional structure decentralizes implementation-related decisions, especially those concerned with marketing, to those involved with individual organizational functions. Focus strategies, often used in small firms, require a simple structure until such time that the firm diversifies in terms of products and/or markets.
- Unique combinations of different forms of the multidivisional structure are matched with different corporate-level diversification strategies to properly implement these strategies. The cooperative M-form, used to implement the related constrained corporate-level strategy, has a centralized corporate office and extensive integrating mechanisms. Divisional incentives are linked to overall corporate performance to foster cooperation among divisions. The related linked SBU M-form structure establishes separate profit centers within the diversified firm. Each profit center or SBU may have divisions offering similar products, but the SBUs are often unrelated to each other. The competitive M-form structure, used to implement the unrelated diversification strategy, is highly decentralized, lacks integrating mechanisms, and utilizes objective financial criteria to evaluate each unit's performance.
- The multi-domestic strategy, implemented through the worldwide geographic area structure, emphasizes decentralization and locates all functional activities in the host country or geographic area. The worldwide product divisional structure is used to implement the global strategy. This structure is centralized in order to coordinate and integrate different functions' activities so as to gain global economies of scope and economies of scale. Decision-making authority is centralized in the firm's worldwide division headquarters.
- The transnational strategy—a strategy through which the firm seeks the local responsiveness of the multi-domestic strategy and the global efficiency of the global strategy—is implemented through the combination structure. Because it must be simultaneously centralized and decentralized, integrated and nonintegrated, and formalized and non-formalized, the combination structure is difficult to organize and successfully manage. However, two structural designs are suggested: the matrix and the hybrid structure with both geographic and product-oriented divisions.
- Increasingly important to competitive success, cooperative strategies are implemented through organizational structures framed around strategic networks. Strategic center firms play a critical role in managing strategic networks. Business-level strategies are often employed in vertical and horizontal alliance networks. Corporate-level cooperative strategies are used to pursue product and market diversification. Franchising is one type of corporate strategy that uses a strategic network to implement this strategy. This is also true for international cooperative strategies, where distributed networks are often used.

KEY TERMS AND DEFINITIONS

Organizational structure specifies the firm's formal reporting relationships, procedures, controls, and authority and decision-making processes.

Organizational controls guide the use of strategy, indicate how to compare actual results with expected results, and suggest corrective actions to take when the difference is unacceptable.

Strategic controls are largely subjective criteria intended to verify that the firm is using appropriate strategies for the conditions in the external environment and the company's competitive advantages.

Financial controls are largely objective criteria used to measure the firm's performance against previously established quantitative standards.

The **multidivisional (M-form) structure** consists of a corporate office and operating divisions, each operating division representing a separate business or profit center in which the top corporate officer delegates responsibilities for day-to-day operations and business-unit strategy to division managers.

The **simple structure** is a structure in which the owner-manager makes all major decisions and monitors all activities while the staff serves as an extension of the manager's supervisory authority.

The **functional structure** consists of a chief executive officer and a limited corporate staff, with functional line managers in dominant organizational areas such as production, accounting, marketing, R&D, engineering, and human resources.

The **competitive form** is an M-form structure characterized by complete independence among the firm's divisions which compete for corporate resources.

The **worldwide geographic area structure** emphasizes national interests and facilitates the firm's efforts to satisfy local differences.

In the **worldwide product divisional structure**, decision-making authority is centralized in the worldwide division headquarters to coordinate and integrate decisions and actions among divisional business units.

The **combination structure** is a structure drawing characteristics and mechanisms from both the worldwide geographic area structure and the worldwide product divisional structure.

The **strategic business unit (SBU) form** is an M-form consisting of three levels: corporate headquarters, strategic business units (SBUs), and SBU divisions.

The **cooperative form** is an M-form structure in which horizontal integration is used to bring about interdivisional cooperation.

REVIEW QUESTIONS

1. What is organizational structure and what are organizational controls? What are the differences between strategic controls and financial controls? What is the importance of these differences?
2. What does it mean to say that strategy and structure have a reciprocal relationship?
3. What are the characteristics of the functional structures used to implement the cost leadership, differentiation, integrated cost leadership/differentiation, and focused business-level strategies?
4. What are the differences among the three versions of the multidivisional (M-form) organizational structures that are used to implement the related constrained, the related linked, and the unrelated corporate-level diversification strategies?
5. What organizational structures are used to implement the multi-domestic, global, and transnational international strategies?
6. What is a strategic network? What is a strategic center firm? How is a strategic center used in business-level, corporate-level, and international cooperative strategies?

EXPERIENTIAL EXERCISES

Exercise 1: Organizational Structure and Business-Level Strategy

The purpose of this exercise is to apply the concepts introduced in this chapter to live examples of business-level strategies and how various firms actually structure their organizations to compete. In teams, your instructor will assign a business-level strategy such as differentiation or cost leader. You are to identify a firm that exemplifies this strategy and pictorially draw out its corporate structure. You will need to present the results of your investigation by comparing your firm's organizational chart with that in your text identified for your particular business-level strategy. (See text for figures labeled "Functional Structure for Implementing a Differentiation [or Cost Leadership] Strategy.") Be prepared to address the following issues:

1. Describe your firm's business-level strategy. Why do you consider it to be a cost leader or a differentiator?
2. What is the mission statement and/or vision statement of this firm? Is this firm targeting specific strategic goals?
3. Using the text examples for a functional structure, how does your firm match those structures or differ, if it does?
4. Summarize your conclusions. Does your team believe that this firm is structured appropriately considering its current and future strategic goals?

CHAPTER 12

Leadership Implications for Strategy

Studying this chapter should provide you with the strategic management knowledge needed to

- Define strategic leadership and describe top-level managers' importance.
- Explain what top management teams are and how they affect firm performance.
- Describe the managerial succession process using internal and external managerial labor markets.
- Discuss the value of strategic leadership in determining the firm's strategic direction.
- Describe the importance of strategic leaders in managing the firm's resources.
- Define organizational culture and explain what must be done to sustain an effective culture.
- Explain what strategic leaders can do to establish and emphasize ethical practices.
- Discuss the importance and use of organizational controls.

OPENING CASE
Selecting a New CEO: The Importance of Strategic Leaders

Evidence in US shows that the shelf life of a CEO is not long, and it continues to get shorter. In 2005, the average CEO tenure was 7.3 years. Today, it is even shorter at (about 6 years). In India, where many firms are controlled by families, this may not be true, but where the CEO is a "professional" appointed by the family, their accountability also seems to be on the increase, as may be seen from the recent change of CEO in Wipro.

The brevity of CEOs and top-level managers' tenure means that planning for and selecting new leaders should be continuous processes. Furthermore, the importance of strategic leaders to a firm's overall health and success makes selecting effective leaders critical. In India, as in US, the departure of CEOs, especially non family ones has become quite a common feature. Despite the high number of strategic leader departures, boards of directors are rarely effective in planning for and completing the succession. A survey of boards in US found that over 40 per cent of the firms had no succession plan, and Indian boards may not be better. In another survey in US, more than 50 per cent of directors rated the boards at their firms as ineffective in succession planning. Changes in the CEO often occur without warning. For example, in 2009 the CEOs at Toyota, Lenovo, and Ranbaxy unexpectedly resigned or were replaced, and so were Wipro's CEOs (it had a joint two CEO system) in 2011. In the cases of Toyota, Lenovo, and Wipro, poor firm performance was the reason for change. Both Toyota and Lenovo suffered net losses in 2008 and Lenovo's market share declined from third to fourth place in the PC industry. Wipro also saw an erosion in its market share and profits in 2010, and it being overtaken by Cognizant.

Mr. Ratan Tata, CEO of TATA group, will retire in December 2012.

The importance of CEOs and planning for succession is clearly evident with Steve Jobs at Apple. Jobs took time off from the CEO role in 2009 due to illness. Analysts expressed major concerns about his ability to continue because of his importance to the success of the firm. He is believed to be especially important to Apple's innovation capability. While he does not design new products, he reviews each new project and serves as an internal champion for those he feels are worthy. For example, Jobs supported the work on the iPod in its early stages despite the skepticism of several others in the company. Furthermore, Jobs will not accept compromises; he pushes project teams to do everything possible to make the product right.

Jobs is a co-founder of Apple but left the company for 12 years. During that time, the company floundered. He returned in 1997 and Apple has had a number of market successes since that time. This is why many wonder if Jobs can be replaced. One analyst referred to Apple without Jobs as similar to a John Wayne movie without John Wayne. Another stated that Apple without Jobs is Sony. While Jobs has trained and delegated authority over innovation at Apple, few believe that he can be adequately replaced. Thus, the selection of a new CEO for Apple whenever Jobs departs will be critical for the company.

Infosys was closely identified with its legendary founder CEO, Mr. Narayana Murthy, and when he decided to step down, there were speculations about the future of Infosys. But thanks to its effective succession plan, it carried on without any discontinuity or adverse effects.

Companies can develop effective succession plans. Usually such plans call for selecting one or more potential successors and helping them to build the capabilities necessary to be effective CEOs. For example, they may be given challenging assignments where they can build valuable knowledge of critical markets and/or establish relationships with important stakeholders. They can receive mentoring and 360-degree feedback to identify positive traits and work on negative ones. For example, Mr. Nandan Nilekani was identified as the successor to Mr. Murthy, well before he handed over the reins; though Mr. Nilekani quit in 2007 to head India's Unique Card Identification Project, his successor, Mr. S. Gopalakrishnan was also indentified very quickly. Both Mr. Nilekani and Mr. Gopalakrishnan were the co-founders of Infosys along with Mr. Murthy, and hence they were fully prepared for the task. In other companies, the identified successor would be mentored before he/she becomes ready for the role. Identifying potential CEOs is a difficult assignment because of the many and varied capabilities needed for the job. Recent efforts to identify potential successors for CEOs focused on people who were innovative and championed innovation, had vision and could gain others commitment to that vision, nurtured important human capital, and built relationships with critical constituencies such as customers and suppliers. These precisely are the considerations for the appointment of the successor to Mr. Ratan Tata who is to retire in December 2012. A nine member search panel has been formed with a mandate to formulate criteria "for identifying the most suitable candidate taking into account the global nature and complexity of the group's business."

Sources: S. Tobak, 2009, What happens when Steve Jobs leaves Apple? *BNET*, http://www.blogs.bnet.com, May 26; L. Whipp, 2009, Ranbaxy chief to step down, *Financial Times*, http://www.ft.com, May 24; J. Soble, 2009, Toyota plans top-level overhaul, *Financial Times*, http://www.ft.com, May 14; M. Boyle, 2009, The art of succession, *BusinessWeek*, May 11, 30–37; M. Boyle, 2009, The art of CEO succession, *BusinessWeek*, http://www.businessweek.com, April 30; F. Balfour and B. Einhorn, 2009, Lenovo CEO is out; Chinese execs return, *BusinessWeek*, http://www.businessweek.com, February 5; J. Scheck & N. Wingfield, 2008, How Apple could survive without Steve Jobs, *Wall Street Journal*, http://www.wsj.com, December 19; B. Behan, 2008; Shareholder proposals on CEO succession planning, *BusinessWeek*, http://www.businessweek.com, January 24; 2011, wipro appoints new CEO, posts weak Q3 Profits, www.informationweek.in, http://www.informationweek.in/IT_ITES/ 11-01-21/ Wipro_appoints_new_CEO_posts_weak_Q3_profits.aspx, January 21; 2009, Nilekani bids adieu to Infosys, www.sify.com, http://www.sify.com/ finance/nandan-nilekani-bids-adieu-to-infosys-news-corporate-jhkhRVigdfb.html, July 10; 2010, *The Times of India*, 5-member panel to pick Tata's successor, http://articles.timesofindia.indiatimes.com/ 2010-08-05/india-business/28313336_1_ratan-tata-tata-sons-pallonji-mistry, August 5.

As the Opening Case implies, strategic leaders' work is demanding, challenging, and may last for a long period of time. Regardless of how long they remain in their positions, strategic leaders (and most prominently CEOs) can make a major difference in how a firm performs.[1] If a strategic leader can create a strategic vision for the firm using forward thinking, they may be able to energize the firm's human capital and achieve positive outcomes. However, the challenge of strategic leadership is significant. For example, replacing Steve Jobs at Apple will be difficult because of his special skills in identifying and nurturing creative new products that have significant market potential. On the other hand, the transition at Infosys was smooth because a person was identified early, had intimate knowledge of the company and was ready to take over the CEO role when change was necessary.

A major message in this chapter is that effective strategic leadership is the foundation for successfully using the strategic management process. As is implied in Figure 1.1, strategic leaders guide the firm in ways that result in forming a vision and mission (see Chapter 1). Often, this guidance finds leaders thinking of ways to create goals that stretch everyone in the organization to improve performance.[2] Moreover, strategic leaders facilitate the development of appropriate strategic actions and determine how to implement them. As we see in Figure 12.1, these actions are the path to strategic competitiveness and above-average returns.[3]

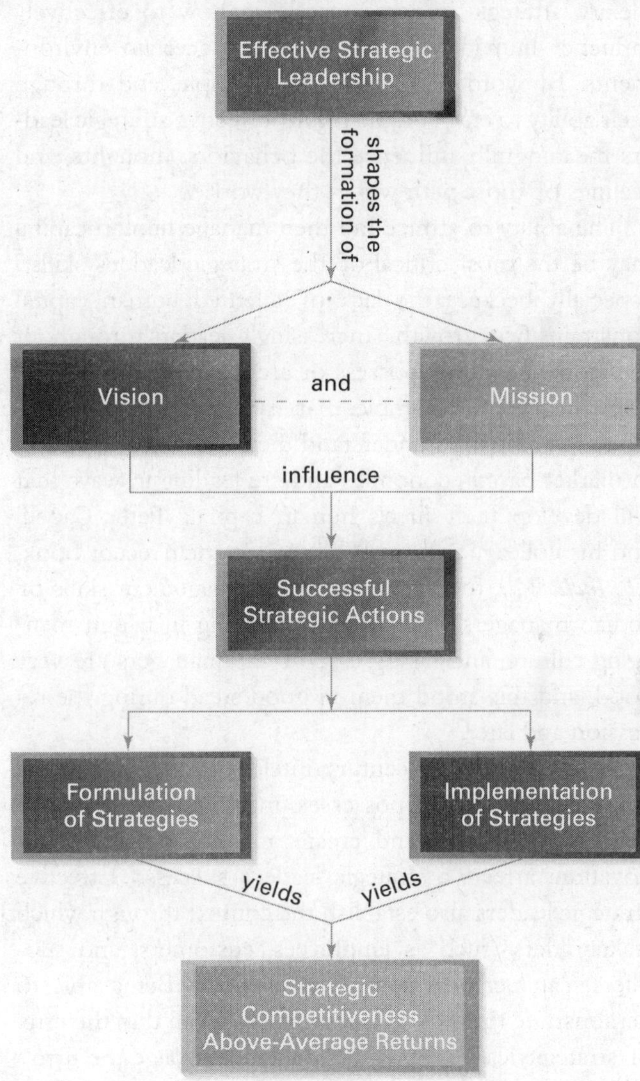

Figure 12.1 Strategic leadership and the strategic management process

We begin this chapter with a definition of strategic leadership; we then discuss its importance as a potential source of competitive advantage as well as effective strategic leadership styles. Next, we examine top management teams and their effects on innovation, strategic change, and firm performance. Following this discussion, we analyze the internal and external managerial labor markets from which strategic leaders are selected. Closing the chapter are descriptions of the five key components of effective strategic leadership: determining a strategic direction, effectively managing the firm's resource portfolio (which includes exploiting and maintaining core competencies along with developing human capital and social capital), sustaining an effective organizational culture, emphasizing ethical practices, and establishing balanced organizational controls.

Strategic Leadership and Style

Strategic leadership is the ability to anticipate, envision, maintain flexibility, and empower others to create strategic change as necessary. Multifunctional in nature, strategic leadership involves managing through others, managing an entire enterprise rather than a functional subunit, and coping with change that continues to increase in the global economy. Because of the global economy's complexity, strategic leaders must learn how to effectively influence human behavior, often in uncertain environments. By word or by personal example, and through their ability to envision the future, effective strategic leaders meaningfully influence the behaviors, thoughts, and feelings of those with whom they work.[4]

The ability to attract and then manage human capital may be the most critical of the strategic leader's skills,[5] especially because the lack of talented human capital constrains firm growth.[6] Increasingly, leaders throughout the global economy possess or are developing this skill. Some believe, for example, that leaders now surfacing in Chinese companies understand the rules of competition in market-based economies and are leading in ways that will develop their firm's human capital.[7] Peter Capelli and his colleagues from Wharton, in their recent book, *The India Way*, found that the HR management skills of Indian managers, especially in investing in talent, managing culture, and taking care of the managers are very good, and this stood them in good stead during the recession and later.[8]

In the twenty-first century, intellectual capital that the firm's human capital possesses, including the ability to manage knowledge and create and commercialize innovation, affects a strategic leader's success.[9] Effective strategic leaders also establish the context through which stakeholders (such as employees, customers, and suppliers) can perform at peak efficiency.[10] Being able to demonstrate these skills is important, given that the crux of strategic leadership is the ability to manage the firm's operations effectively and sustain high performance over time.[11]

A firm's ability to achieve a competitive advantage and earn above-average returns is compromised when strategic leaders fail to respond appropriately and quickly to changes in the complex global competitive environment. The inability to respond or to identify the need for change in the competitive environment is one of the reasons some CEOs fail, as shown by the replacement of CEOs in Toyota and Lenovo described in the Opening Case. Therefore, strategic leaders must learn how to deal with diverse and complex environmental situations. Individual judgment is an important part of learning about and analyzing the firm's competitive environment.[12] In particular, effective strategic leaders build strong ties with external stakeholders to gain access to information and advice on the events in the external environment.[13]

The primary responsibility for effective strategic leadership rests at the top, in particular with the CEO. Other commonly recognized strategic leaders include members of the board of directors, the top management team, and divisional general managers. In truth, any individual with responsibility for the performance of human capital and/or a part of the firm (e.g., a production unit) is a strategic leader. Regardless of their title and organizational function, strategic leaders have substantial decision-making responsibilities that cannot be delegated.[14] Strategic leadership is a complex but critical form of leadership. Strategies cannot be formulated and implemented for the purpose of achieving above-average returns without effective strategic leaders.[15]

The styles used to provide leadership often affect the productivity of those being led. Transformational leadership is the most effective strategic leadership style. This style entails motivating followers to exceed the expectations others have of them, to continuously enrich their capabilities, and to place the interests of the organization above their own.[16] Transformational leaders develop and communicate a vision for the organization and formulate a strategy to achieve the vision. They make followers aware of the need to achieve valued organizational outcomes and encourage them to continuously strive for higher levels of achievement. These types of leaders have a high degree of integrity (J.N. Tata, founder of Tata Steel, and his successor, Mr. J.R.D. Tata were strategic leaders valued for their high degree of integrity)[17] and character. Dwelling on character, a CEO said, "Leaders are shaped and defined by character. Leaders inspire and enable others to do excellent work and realize their potential. As a result, they build successful, enduring organizations."[18] Additionally, transformational leaders have emotional intelligence. Emotionally intelligent leaders understand themselves well, have strong motivation, are empathetic with others, and have effective interpersonal skills.[19] As a result of these characteristics, transformational leaders are especially effective in promoting and nurturing innovation in firms.[20]

The Role of Top-Level Managers

Comstock Images/Jupiter Images

Top-level management decisions influence the culture of firms as well as how organizations are structured and how goals are set and achieved.

Top-level managers play a critical role in that they are charged to make certain their firm is able to effectively formulate and implement strategies.[21] Top-level managers' strategic decisions influence how the firm is designed and goals will be achieved. Thus, a critical element of organizational success is having a top management team with superior managerial skills.[22]

Managers often use their discretion (or latitude for action) when making strategic decisions, including those concerned with effectively implementing strategies.[23] Managerial discretion differs significantly across industries. The primary factors that determine the amount of decision-making discretion held by a manager (especially a top-level manager) are (1) external environmental sources such as the industry structure, the rate of market growth in the firm's primary industry, and the degree to which products can be differentiated; (2) characteristics of the organization, including its size, age, resources, and culture; and (3) characteristics of the manager, including commitment to the firm and its strategic outcomes, tolerance for ambiguity, skills in working with different people, and aspiration levels (see Figure 12.2). Because strategic leaders' decisions are intended to help the firm gain a competitive advantage, how managers exercise discretion when determining appropriate strategic actions is critical to the firm's success.[24]

In addition to determining new strategic initiatives, top-level managers develop a firm's organizational structure and reward systems. Top executives also have a major effect on a firm's culture. Evidence suggests that managers' values are critical in shaping a firm's cultural values.[25] Accordingly, top-level managers have an important effect on organizational activities and performance.[26] Because of the challenges top executives face, they often are more effective when they operate as top management teams.

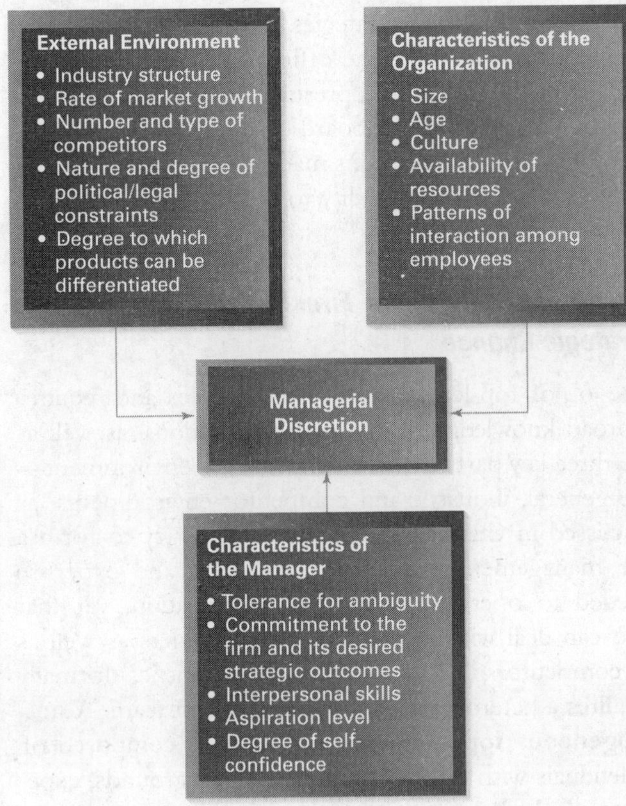

Figure 12.2 Factors affecting managerial discretion

Top Management Teams

In most firms, the complexity of challenges and the need for substantial amounts of information and knowledge require strategic leadership by a team of executives. Using a team to make strategic decisions also helps to avoid another potential problem when these decisions are made by the CEO alone: managerial hubris. Research evidence shows that when CEOs begin to believe glowing press accounts and to feel that they are unlikely to make errors, they are more likely to make poor strategic decisions.[27] Top executives need to have self-confidence but must guard against allowing it to become arrogance and a false belief in their own invincibility.[28] To guard against CEO overconfidence and poor strategic decisions, firms often use the top management team to consider strategic opportunities and problems and to make strategic decisions. The **top management team** is composed of the key individuals who are responsible for selecting and implementing the firm's strategies. Typically, the top management team includes the officers of the corporation, defined by the title of vice president and above or by service as a member of the board of directors.[29] The quality of the strategic decisions made by a top management team affects the firm's ability to innovate and engage in effective strategic change.[30]

Top Management Team, Firm Performance, and Strategic Change

The job of top-level executives is complex and requires a broad knowledge of the firm's operations, as well as the three key parts of the firm's external environment—the general, industry, and competitor environments, as discussed in Chapter 2. Therefore, firms try to form a top management team with knowledge and expertise needed to operate the internal organization, yet that also can deal with all the firm's stakeholders as well as its competitors.[31] To have these characteristics normally requires a heterogeneous top management team. A **heterogeneous top management team** is composed of individuals with different functional backgrounds, experience, and education.

Members of a heterogeneous top management team benefit from discussing the different perspectives advanced by team members.[32] In many cases, these discussions increase the quality of the team's decisions, especially when a synthesis emerges within the team after evaluating the diverse perspectives.[33] The net benefit of such actions by heterogeneous teams has been positive in terms of market share and above-average returns. Research shows that more heterogeneity among top management team members promotes debate, which often leads to better strategic decisions. In turn, better strategic decisions produce higher firm performance.[34]

It is also important for top management team members to function cohesively. In general, the more heterogeneous and larger the top management team is, the more difficult it is for the team to effectively implement strategies.[35] Comprehensive and long-term strategic plans can be inhibited by communication difficulties among top executives who have different backgrounds and different cognitive skills.[36] Alternatively, communication among diverse top management team members can be facilitated through electronic communications, sometimes reducing the barriers before face-to-face meetings.[37] However, a group of top executives with diverse backgrounds may inhibit the process of decision making if it is not effectively managed. In these cases, top management teams may fail to comprehensively examine threats and opportunities, leading to a suboptimal strategic decision. Thus, the CEO must attempt to achieve behavioral integration among the team members.[38]

Having members with substantive expertise in the firm's core functions and businesses is also important to a top management team's effectiveness.[39] In a high-technology industry, it may be critical for a firm's top management team members to have R&D expertise, particularly when growth strategies are being implemented. Yet their eventual effect on strategic decisions depends not only on their expertise and the way the team is managed but also on the context in which they make the decisions (the governance structure, incentive compensation, etc.).[40]

The characteristics of top management teams are related to innovation and strategic change.[41] For example, more heterogeneous top management teams are positively associated with innovation and strategic change. The heterogeneity may force the team or some of its members to "think outside of the box, and thus be more creative in making decisions."[42] Therefore, firms that need to change their strategies are more likely to do so if they have top management teams with diverse backgrounds and expertise. When a new CEO is hired from outside the industry, the probability of strategic change is greater than if the new CEO is from inside the firm or inside the industry.[43] Although hiring a new CEO from outside the industry adds diversity to the team, the top management team must be managed effectively to use the diversity in a positive way. Thus, to successfully create strategic change, the CEO should exercise transformational leadership.[44] A top management team with various areas of expertise is more likely to identify environmental changes (opportunities and threats) or changes within the firm, suggesting the need for a different strategic direction.

In the current competitive environment, an understanding of international markets is vital. However, recent research suggests that only about 15 per cent of the top executives in *Fortune* 500 firms have global leadership expertise.[45] In India, probably it is even lower. Executives generally gain this knowledge by working in one of the firm's international subsidiaries but can also gain some knowledge by working with international alliance partners.[46] The executives who have such experience are therefore, much in demand.

The CEO and Top Management Team Power

As noted in Chapter 10, the board of directors is an important governance mechanism for monitoring a firm's strategic direction and for representing stakeholders' interests, especially those of shareholders.[47] In fact, higher performance normally is achieved when the board of directors is more directly involved in shaping a firm's strategic direction.[48]

Boards of directors, however, may find it difficult to direct the strategic actions of powerful CEOs and top management teams.[49] Often, a powerful CEO appoints a number of sympathetic outside members to the board or may have inside board members who are also on the top management team and report to her or him.[50] In either case, the CEO may significantly influence the board's actions. Thus, the amount of discretion a CEO has in making strategic decisions is related to the board of directors and how it chooses to oversee the actions of the CEO and the top management team.[51]

STRATEGY RIGHT NOW

Read more about the role of the board of directors in a firm's top management dynamic.
www.cengage.com/management/hitt

CEOs and top management team members can achieve power in other ways. A CEO who also holds the position of chairperson of the board usually has more power than the CEO who does not.[52] Some analysts and corporate "watchdogs" criticize the practice of CEO duality (when the CEO and the chairperson of the board are the same) because it can lead to poor performance and slow response to change.[53]

Although it varies across industries, CEO duality occurs most commonly in larger firms. It is almost the rule in India. Increased shareholder activism, however, has brought CEO duality under scrutiny and attack in both US and European firms. As reported in Chapter 10, an independent board leadership structure in which the same person did not hold the positions of CEO and chair is commonly believed to enhance a board's ability to monitor top-level managers' decisions and actions, particularly with respect to financial performance.[54] On the other hand, if a CEO acts as a steward, holding the dual roles facilitates effective decisions and actions. In these instances, the increased effectiveness gained through CEO duality accrues from the individual who wants to perform effectively and desires to be the best possible steward of the firm's assets. It is true that in many firms, the tussle between the Chairperson and the CEO creates difficult situations, holding up critical decisions. A CEO-cum-chairperson can effect positive change quicker. Because of this person's positive orientation and actions, extra governance and the coordination costs resulting from an independent board leadership structure would be unnecessary.[55]

Top management team members and CEOs who have long tenure—on the team and in the organization—have a greater influence on board decisions. CEOs with greater influence may take actions in their own best interests, the outcomes of which increase their compensation from the company.[56] As reported in Chapter 10, many people are angry about excessive top executive compensation, especially during poor economic times when others are losing their jobs because of ineffective strategic decisions made by the same managers.

In general, long tenure is thought to constrain the breadth of an executive's knowledge base. Some evidence suggests that with the limited perspectives associated with a restricted knowledge base, long-tenured top executives typically develop fewer alternatives to evaluate in making strategic decisions.[57] However, long-tenured managers also may be able to exercise more effective strategic control, thereby obviating the need for board members' involvement because effective strategic control generally produces higher performance.[58] Intriguingly, recent findings suggest that "the liabilities of short tenure ... appear to exceed the advantages, while the advantages of long tenure—firm-specific human and social capital, knowledge, and power—seem to outweigh the disadvantages of rigidity and maintaining the status quo."[59] Overall then the relationship between CEO tenure and firm performance is complex, indicating that to strengthen the firm, boards of directors, it is necessary to develop an effective relationship with the top management team.

In summary, the relative degrees of power held by the board and top management team members should be examined in light of an individual firm's situation. For example, the abundance of resources in a firm's external environment and the volatility of that environment may affect the ideal balance of power between the board and the top management teams. Moreover, a volatile and uncertain environment may create a situation where a powerful CEO is needed to move quickly, but a diverse top management team may create less cohesion among team members and prevent or stall necessary strategic actions. With effective working relationships, boards, CEOs, and other top management team members have the foundation required to select arrangements with the highest probability of best serving stakeholders' interests.[60]

Managerial Succession

The choice of top executives—especially CEOs—is a critical decision with important implications for the firm's performance.[61] Many companies use leadership screening systems to identify individuals with managerial and strategic leadership potential as well as to determine the criteria individuals should satisfy to be candidates for the CEO position.[62]

The most effective of these systems assesses people within the firm and gains valuable information about the capabilities of other companies' managers, particularly their strategic leaders.[63] Based on the results of these assessments, training and development programs are provided for current individuals in an attempt to preselect and shape the skills of people who may become tomorrow's leaders. Because of the quality of its programs, General Electric "is famous for developing leaders who are dedicated to turning imaginative ideas into leading products and services."[64]

Organizations select managers and strategic leaders from two types of managerial labor markets—internal and external.[65] An **internal managerial labor market** consists of a firm's opportunities for managerial positions and the qualified employees within that firm. An **external managerial labor market** is the collection of managerial career opportunities and the qualified people who are external to the organization in which the opportunities exist.

Several benefits are thought to accrue to a firm when the internal labor market is used to select an insider as the new CEO. Because of their experience with the firm and the industry environment in which it competes, insiders are familiar with company products, markets, technologies, and operating procedures. Also, internal hiring produces lower turnover among existing personnel, many of whom possess valuable firm-specific knowledge. When the firm is performing well, internal succession is favored to sustain high performance. It is assumed that hiring from inside keeps the important knowledge necessary to sustain performance.

Results of work completed by management consultant Jim Collins support the value of using the internal labor market when selecting a CEO. Collins found that high-performing firms almost always appoint an insider to be the new CEO. He argues that bringing in a well-known outsider, to whom he refers as a "white knight," is a recipe for mediocrity.[66] For example, given the phenomenal success of General Electric (GE) during Jack Welch's tenure as CEO and the firm's highly effective management and leadership development programs, insider Jeffrey Immelt was chosen to succeed Welch. However, shareholders have become disgruntled because GE's stock values have decreased in recent years; GE has suffered along with many other firms in the global economic crisis experienced in 2008 and 2009. Thus, GE under Immelt's leadership is not experiencing the returns achieved by his predecessor. In India, Hindustan Unilever (HUL) has always had an insider as its CEO, and so have ITC and L&T. Japanese firms usually have insiders as CEOs and rarely bring in an outsider at the CEO level.

Hindustan Unilever is regarded as the leadership factory in India, producing many well-known leaders who joined other companies. For example, Mr. Prakash Tandon, who headed the Punjab National Bank was the CEO of Hindustan Lever (HLL), in fact its first Indian CEO. Mr. R. Gopalakrishnan of Tata Sons is an ex HLL person. It grooms so many leaders through a rigorous internal training and mentoring process and by giving responsibilities to the fast track people, rather than through structured training programmes in management institutes (though it does get its executives trained in top management institutes also).

Employers commonly prefer the internal managerial labor market when selecting top management team members and a new CEO. In the past, companies have also had a preference for insiders to fill top-level management positions because of a desire for continuity and a continuing commitment to the firm's current vision, mission, and chosen strategies.[67] However, because of a changing competitive landscape and varying levels of performance, an increasing number of boards of directors are turning to outsiders to succeed CEOs. Although the circumstances are rather unique, Ed Whitacre, former CEO of AT&T was chosen to be the new chairman for GM. Of course, he will have to help GM come out of bankruptcy.[68] A firm often has valid reasons to select an outsider as its new CEO. In some situations, long tenure with a firm may reduce strategic leaders' level of commitment to pursue innovation. Given innovation's importance to firm success (see Chapter 13), this hesitation could be a liability for a strategic leader. The Tata Group has traditionally chosen the successors from within the Tata family, but for the succession of Mr. Ratan Tata who retires in December 2012, the search has already begun, and it is believed that many outsiders (who are in no way connected with the Tata Group) are in the list of persons being considered. The names do-

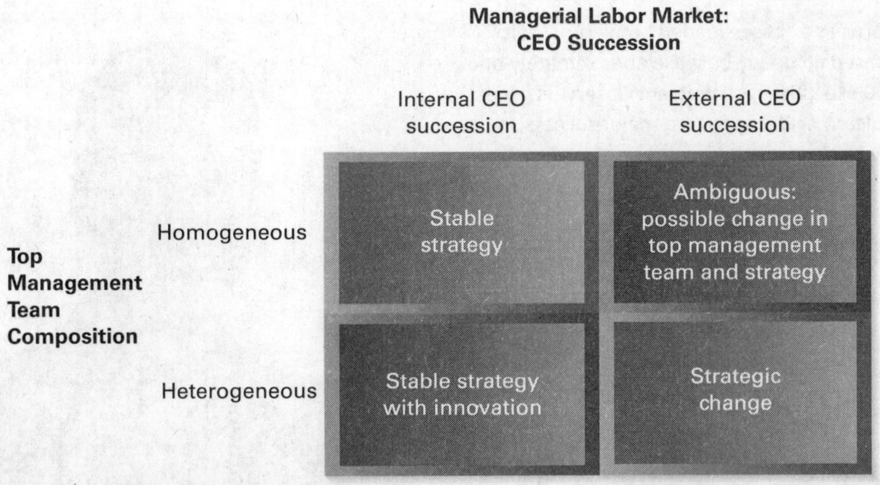

Figure 12.3 Effects of CEO succession and top management team composition on strategy

ing the round reportedly include Arun Sarin (formerly of Vodaphone), Indira Nooyi (Pepsi), Keki Dadiseth (Unilever), and Carlos Ghosn (Renault).[69]

In Figure 12.3, we show how the composition of the top management team and the CEO succession (managerial labor market) interact to affect strategy. For example, when the top management team is homogeneous (its members have similar functional experiences and educational backgrounds) and a new CEO is selected from inside the firm, the firm's current strategy is unlikely to change. Alternatively, when a new CEO is selected from outside the firm and the top management team is heterogeneous, the probability is high that strategy will change. When the new CEO is from inside the firm and a heterogeneous top management team is in place, the strategy may not change, but innovation is likely to continue. An external CEO succession with a homogeneous team creates a more ambiguous situation. The selection of Sir Howard Stringer as CEO of Sony signaled major changes in that firm's future. He is not only an outsider but also a foreigner. He is making major changes in the hopes of turning around Sony's poor performance. His intent is to have Sony regain its traditional excellence in innovative products.[70]

An unwelcome side effect of an insider succession is that unsuccessful contenders for the post may leave, following which the company may suffer serious talent erosion. This happened in the case of GE and HUL. Such erosion could happen if an outsider CEO is brought in also, but the chances seem to be less.

STRATEGIC FOCUS

12.1 The Model Succession at Xerox

Anne Mulcahy became CEO of Xerox in 2001 and is credited with restoring the company's profitability and market leadership during her tenure. She championed innovation and built a strong relationship with customers. In fact, the firm was close to bankruptcy when she became the CEO. She told Xerox shareholders that the company's business model at the time was not sustainable. She was advised to declare bankruptcy but refused to do so. To gain the support needed for changes, she had personal meetings with the top 100 managers at Xerox. She refused to cut R&D or sales but did reduce costs significantly in other areas. The lead independent director, N.J. Nicholas, believes she created a major turnaround that built Xerox into an innovative technology and services company. Her work as CEO has earned her recognition as one of America's best leaders.

The succession process she has used reinforces that recognition. Ursula Burns was selected as heir apparent and given the job as president to "learn the ropes" for a couple of years before Mulcahy decided to take early retirement (Mulcahy was only 56 years old in 2009). Actually, Burns played a major role in Xerox's turnaround. She served as Mulcahy's lieutenant and managed most of the day-to-day operations. She also helped to identify gaps in Xerox's product portfolio and found products to fill those gaps. With the largest product portfolio in Xerox's history, it became a major competitor in marketing products to small and medium-sized businesses. Interestingly, Burns is the first African-American woman to head a major US corporation. Burns (CEO) and Mulcahy (Chairman) are planning to work as a team for a couple of years. This is probably good because Xerox faces multiple challenges given the negative economic environment. Burns receives praise from insiders and external analysts for her deep knowledge of the industry and business and her technological expertise. She is also known for her willingness to take risks. One observer called the selection of Burns and model transition between Mulcahy and Burns as a "bases-loaded home run." Xerox is a unique technology-based company because approximately one third of its almost 4,000 executives are women. Observers expect the transition from Mulcahy to Burns to be a major success.

Jeff Weiner/Courtesy of Xerox Corporation.

Anne Mulcahy, Chairman of Xerox.

Nik Rocklin/Courtesy of Xerox Corporation

Ursula Burns, CEO of Xerox.

Sources: N. Byrnes and R. O. Crockett, 2009, An historic succession at Xerox, *BusinessWeek,* June 8, 18–22; W. M. Bulkeley, 2009, Xerox names Burns chief as Mulcahy retires early, *Wall Street Journal,* http://www.wsj.com, May 22; 2009, Chief executive is retiring at Xerox, *New York Times,* http://www.nytimes.com, May 22; 2009, Anne Mulcahy to retire as Xerox CEO; Ursula Burns named successor, *FreshNews,* http://www.freshnews.com, May 21; E. White, 2009, Xerox succession a 'model' case, *Wall Street Journal,* http://www.wsj.com, May 21; D. Gelles, 2009, Burns to replace Mulcahy at Xerox, *Financial Times,* http://www.ft.com, May 21; 2008, Women CEOs, Xerox, *Financial Times,* http://www.ft.com, December 31; B. George, 2008, America's best leaders: Anne Mulcahy, Xerox CEO, *US News,* http://www.usnews.com, November 19.

Including talent from all parts of both the internal and external labor markets increases the likelihood that the firm will be able to form an effective top-management team. Evidence suggests that women are a qualified source of talent as strategic leaders that have been somewhat overlooked. In light of the success of a growing number of female executives, the foundation for change may be established. Trailblazers such as Catherine Elizabeth Hughes (the first African-American woman to head a firm that was publicly traded on a US stock exchange), Muriel Siebert (the first woman to purchase a seat on the New York Stock Exchange), and publisher Judith Regan have made important contributions as strategic leaders. Recent years have produced several prominent female CEOs, such as Indira Nooyi of Pepsi, Anne Mulcahy (Xerox Corporation), Meg Whitman (eBay), and Andrea Jung (Avon Products). As noted in the Strategic Focus 12.1, Anne Mulcahy stepped out of the role of CEO and became chairman of the board for Xerox in 2009. Ursula Burns succeeded her as the CEO. In India, too, many women CEOs head large organizations: Chanda Kochar of ICICI Bank; Shikha Sharma of Axis Bank; Naina Lal Kidwai of HSBC India; Kiran Mazumdar Shaw of Biocon; Mallika Srinivasan of TAFE; Kalpana Morparia of JP Morgan India; Priya Paul of The Park Hotels, Chitra Ramakrishnan of National Stock Exchange, and Preetha Reddy of Apollo Hospitals Group.

Managerial talent is critical to a firm's success as noted earlier. And, one area in which managerial talent is crucial is in the integration of an acquired firm into the acquiring business. In fact, the top management team of an acquired firm is vital to a successful integration process because they play a critical role in helping the change be implemented and accepted by the acquired firm's employees.[71] However, it is common that there is a major turnover among the top management team of acquired firms. Sometimes it occurs because the acquiring firm unwisely replaces them. In other cases, the managers depart voluntarily to seek other top management positions. Research shows that high turnover among the acquired firm's top managers often produces poor performance and perhaps even leads to a failed acquisition.[72] Therefore, acquiring firms should work hard to avoid successions during the integration process and thereafter.

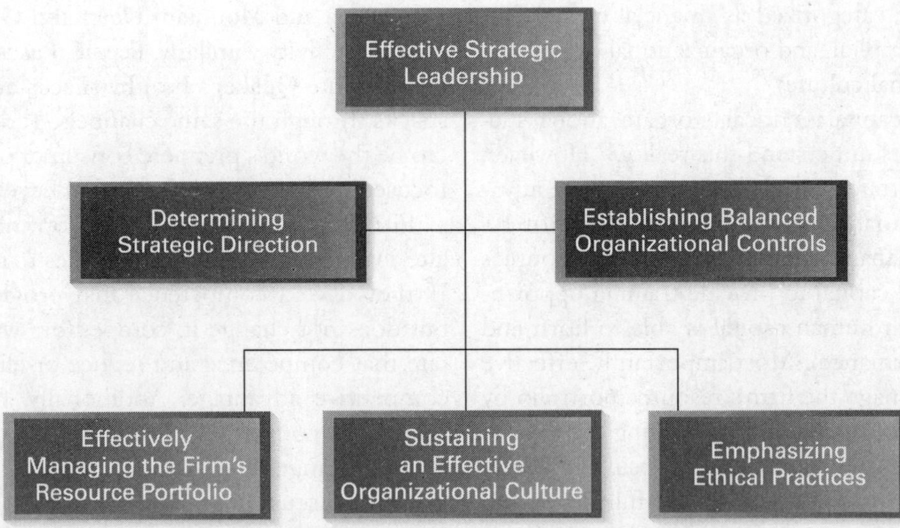

Figure 12.4 Exercise of effective strategic leadership

Key Strategic Leadership Actions

Certain actions characterize effective strategic leadership; we present the most important ones in Figure 12.4. Many of the actions interact with each other. For example, managing the firm's resources effectively includes developing human capital and contributes to establishing a strategic direction, fostering an effective culture, exploiting core competencies, using effective organizational control systems, and establishing ethical practices. The most effective strategic leaders create viable options in making decisions regarding each of the key strategic leadership actions.[73]

Determining Strategic Direction

Determining strategic direction involves specifying the image and character the firm seeks to develop over time.[74] The strategic direction is framed within the context of the conditions (i.e., opportunities and threats) strategic leaders expect their firm to face in roughly the next three to five years.

The ideal long-term strategic direction has two parts: a core ideology and an envisioned future. The core ideology motivates employees through the company's heritage, but the envisioned future encourages employees to stretch beyond their expectations of accomplishment and requires significant change and progress to be realized.[75] The envisioned future serves as a guide to many aspects of a firm's strategy implementation process, including motivation, leadership, employee empowerment, and organizational design. The strategic direction could include such actions as entering new international markets and developing a set of new suppliers to add to the firm's value chain.[76]

Most changes in strategic direction are difficult to design and implement; however, CEO Jeffrey Immelt has an even greater challenge at GE. GE performed exceptionally well under Jack Welch's leadership. Although change is necessary because the competitive landscape has shifted significantly, stakeholders accustomed to Jack Welch and high performance are experiencing problems in accepting Immelt's changes (e.g., changes to the firm's corporate-level strategy and structure). His challenges are made even more difficult because GE is experiencing performance problems partly the result of the difficult economic climate.[77] Additionally, information regarding the firm's strategic direction must be consistently and clearly communicated to all affected parties.[78]

A charismatic CEO may foster stakeholders' commitment to a new vision and strategic direction. Nonetheless, it is important not to lose sight of the organization's strengths when making changes required by a new strategic direction. Immelt, for example, needs to use GE's strengths to ensure continued positive performance. The goal is to pursue the firm's short-term need to adjust to a new vision and strategic direction while maintaining its long-term survivability by effectively managing its portfolio of resources.

Effectively Managing the Firm's Resource Portfolio

Effectively managing the firm's portfolio of resources may be the most important strategic leadership task. The firm's resources are categorized as financial capital, human capital, social capital, and organizational capital (including organizational culture).[79]

Clearly, financial capital is critical to organizational success; strategic leaders understand this reality.[80] However, the most effective strategic leaders recognize the equivalent importance of managing each remaining type of resource as well as managing the integration of resources (e.g., using financial capital to provide training opportunities through which human capital is able to learn and maximize its performance). Most importantly, effective strategic leaders manage the firm's resource portfolio by organizing them into capabilities, structuring the firm to facilitate using those capabilities, and choosing strategies through which the capabilities are successfully leveraged to create value for customers.[81] Exploiting and maintaining core competencies and developing and retaining the firm's human and social capital are actions taken to reach these important objectives.

Exploiting and Maintaining Core Competencies

Examined in Chapters 1 and 3, **core competencies** are capabilities that serve as a source of competitive advantage for a firm over its rivals. Typically, core competencies relate to an organization's functional skills, such as manufacturing, finance, marketing, and research and development. Strategic leaders must verify that the firm's competencies are emphasized when implementing strategies. Intel, for example, has core competencies of **competitive agility** (an ability to act in a variety of competitively relevant ways) and **competitive speed** (an ability to act quickly when facing environmental and competitive pressures).[82] Capabilities are developed over time as firms learn from their actions and enhance their knowledge about specific actions needed. For example, through repeated interactions, some firms have formed a capability allowing them to fully understand customers' needs as they change.[83] Firms with capabilities in R&D that develop into core competencies are rewarded by the market because of the critical nature of innovation in many industries.[84]

In many large firms, and certainly in related diversified ones, core competencies are effectively exploited when they are developed and applied across different organizational units (see Chapter 6). For example, PepsiCo purchased Quaker Oats (now called Quaker Foods), which makes the sports drink Gatorade. PepsiCo uses its competence in distribution systems to exploit the Quaker assets. In this instance, Pepsi soft drinks (e.g., Pepsi Cola and Mountain Dew) and Gatorade share the logistics activity. Similarly, PepsiCo uses this competence to distribute Quaker's healthy snacks and Frito-Lay salty snacks through the same channels. Today, PepsiCo seeks "to be the world's premiere consumer products company focused on convenient foods and beverages."[85]

Firms must continuously develop and, when appropriate, change their core competencies to outperform rivals. If they have a competence that provides an advantage but does not change it, competitors will eventually imitate that competence and reduce or eliminate the firm's competitive advantage. Additionally, firms must guard against the competence becoming a liability, thereby preventing change.

As we discuss next, human capital is critical to a firm's success. One reason it's so critical is that human capital is the resource through which core competencies are developed and used.

Developing Human Capital and Social Capital

Human capital refers to the knowledge and skills of a firm's entire workforce. From the perspective of human capital, employees are viewed as a capital resource requiring continuous investment.[86] At Hindustan Unilever (HUL), people are identified as the key to the firm's continuing success. Given the need to "sustain its talent," HUL invests in its human capital in the form of a host of programs and development-oriented experiences. It has a rigorous and result oriented training program for its newly inducted management trainees, which is considered to be one of the best such initiatives. It also follows up with periodic training of its people at all levels, so much so that, as mentioned earlier, it has supplied leaders not only for itself, but for many other Indian companies.

Investments such as those being made at HUL are productive, in that much of the development of Indian industry can be attributed to the effectiveness of its human capital. This fact suggests that "as the dynamics of competition accelerate, people are perhaps the only truly sustainable source of competitive advantage."[87] In all types of organizations—large and small, new and established, and so forth—human capital's increasing importance suggests a significant role for the firm's human resource management activities.[88] As a support activity (see Chapter 3), human resource management practices facilitate people's efforts to successfully select and especially use the firm's strategies.[89]

Effective training and development programs increase the probability of individuals becoming successful strategic leaders.[90] These programs are increasingly linked to firm success as knowledge becomes more integral to gaining and sustaining a competitive advantage.[91] Additionally, such programs build knowledge and skills, inculcate a common set of core values, and offer a systematic view of the organization, thus promoting the firm's vision and organizational cohesion. For example, HUL's development programs emphasize its "performance with purpose," which focuses on building shareholder value while simultaneously ensuring human, environmental, and talent sustainability.

Effective training and development programs also contribute positively to the firm's efforts to form core competencies.[92] Furthermore, they help strategic leaders improve skills that are critical to completing other tasks associated with effective strategic leadership, such as determining the firm's strategic direction, exploiting and maintaining the firm's core competencies, and developing an organizational culture that supports ethical practices. Thus, building human capital is vital to the effective execution of strategic leadership. Indeed, some argue that the world's 'best companies are realizing that no matter what business they're in, their real business is building leaders.'[93]

Dave & Les Jacobs/Cultura/Getty Images

Training and development programs can provide the means by which new strategic leaders are cultivated within an organization.

Strategic leaders must acquire the skills necessary to help develop human capital in their areas of responsibility.[94] When human capital investments are successful, the result is a workforce capable of learning continuously. Continuous learning and leveraging the firm's expanding knowledge base are linked with strategic success.[95]

Learning also can preclude making errors. Strategic leaders tend to learn more from their failures than their successes because they sometimes make the wrong attributions for the successes.[96] For example, the effectiveness of certain approaches and knowledge can be context specific.[97] Thus, some "best practices" may not work well in all situations. We know that using teams to make decisions can be effective, but sometimes it is better for leaders to make decisions alone, especially when the decisions must be made and implemented quickly (e.g., in crisis situations).[98] Thus, effective strategic leaders recognize the importance of learning from success and from failure.

Learning and building knowledge are important for creating innovation in firms.[99] Innovation leads to competitive advantage. Overall, firms that create and maintain greater knowledge usually achieve and maintain competitive advantages. However, as noted with core competencies, strategic leaders must guard against allowing high levels of knowledge in one area to lead to myopia and overlooking knowledge development opportunities in other important areas of the business.[100]

When facing challenging conditions, firms sometimes decide to lay off some of their human capital. Strategic leaders must recognize though that layoffs can result in a significant loss of the knowledge possessed by the firm's human capital. Research evidence shows that moderate-sized layoffs may improve firm performance, but large layoffs produce stronger performance downturns in firms because of the loss of human capital.[101] Although it is also not uncommon for restructuring firms to reduce their expenditures on or investments in training and development programs, restructuring may actually be an important time to increase investments in these programs. The reason for increased focus on training and development is that restructuring firms have less slack and cannot absorb as many errors; moreover, the employees who remain after layoffs may find themselves in positions without all the skills or knowledge they need to perform the required tasks effectively.

Viewing employees as a resource to be maximized rather than as a cost to be minimized facilitates successful implementation of a firm's strategies as does the strategic leader's ability to approach layoffs in a manner that employees believe is fair and equitable.[102] A critical issue for employees is the fairness in the layoffs and in treatment in their jobs.[103]

As is well known, Japanese management generally included a no layoffs policy. Even when confronted with the challenges posed by the Great Depression, Konosuke Matsushita refused to lay off any of his employees; instead he reduced the factory hours to half days and asked the factory workers to spend their time selling the company's products[104]. This earned him not only the loyalty for his staff, but also made him one of the most admired business leaders of the world, prompting the famous Harvard professor, John Kotter to research

Matsushita's life and write a book titled *The Matsushita Leadership*.[105] Indian companies also avoid layoffs to the extent possible, certainly the older ones.[106] Tatas, for example, long followed a strict no layoffs policy, but in the recent years, they have also laid off people; they also gave the severed workers excellent plans by way of retirement schemes.[107]

Social capital involves relationships inside and outside the firm that help the firm accomplish tasks and create value for customers and shareholders.[108] Social capital is a critical asset for a firm. Inside the firm, employees and units must cooperate to get the work done. In multinational organizations, employees often must cooperate across country boundaries on activities such as R&D to achieve performance objectives (e.g., developing new products).[109]

External social capital is increasingly critical to firm success. The reason for this is that few, if any, companies have all of the resources they need to successfully compete against their rivals. Firms can use cooperative strategies such as strategic alliances (see Chapter 9) to develop social capital. Social capital can develop in strategic alliances as firms share complementary resources. Resource sharing must be effectively managed, though, to ensure that the partner trusts the firm and is willing to share the desired resources.[110]

Research evidence suggests that the success of many types of firms may partially depend on social capital. Large multinational firms often must establish alliances in order to enter new foreign markets. Likewise, entrepreneurial firms often must establish alliances to gain access to resources, venture capital, or other types of resources (e.g., special expertise that the entrepreneurial firm cannot afford to maintain in-house).[111] Retaining quality human capital and maintaining strong internal social capital can be affected strongly by the firm's culture.

Sustaining an Effective Organizational Culture

In Chapter 1, we defined **organizational culture** as a complex set of ideologies, symbols, and core values that are shared throughout the firm and influence the way business is conducted. Evidence suggests that a firm can develop core competencies in terms of both the capabilities it possesses and the way the capabilities are leveraged when implementing strategies to produce desired outcomes. In other words, because the organizational culture influences how the firm conducts its business and helps regulate and control employees' behavior, it can be a source of competitive advantage[112] and is a "critical factor in promoting innovation."[113] Given its importance, it may be that a vibrant organizational culture is the most valuable competitive differentiator for business organizations. Thus, shaping the context within which the firm formulates and implements its strategies—that is, shaping the organizational culture—is an essential strategic leadership action.[114]

According to Management expert Peter Drucker, the chief objective of leadership is to create a human community held together by a bond for a common purpose[115]. This purpose is more than a mundane one: the purpose needs a strong and energizing vision; the bondage requires developing a sense of purpose in their followers. It is this sense of purpose that enables followers to develop a commitment, and continue their commitment through trying times. This may be articulated as a vision and has to be supplemented by a dedicated passion for the vision, for without passion, there can be no energy. Developing passion, vision, commitment, and character are most essential aspects of leadership.[116]

Entrepreneurial Mind-Set

Especially in large organizations, an organizational culture often encourages (or discourages) strategic leaders from pursuing (or not pursuing) entrepreneurial opportunities.[117] This issue is important because entrepreneurial opportunities are a vital source of growth and innovation.[118] Therefore, a key role of strategic leaders is to encourage and promote innovation by pursuing entrepreneurial opportunities.[119]

One way to encourage innovation is to invest in opportunities as real options—that is, invest in an opportunity in order to provide the potential option of taking advantage of the opportunity at some point in the future.[120] For example, a firm might buy a piece of land to have the option to build on it at some time in the future should the company need more space and should that location increase in value to the company. Firms might enter strategic alliances for similar reasons. In this instance, a firm might form an alliance to have the option of acquiring the partner later or of building a stronger relationship with it (e.g., developing a joint new venture).[121]

In Chapter 13, we describe how large firms use strategic entrepreneurship to pursue entrepreneurial opportunities and to gain first-mover advantages. Small and medium-sized firms also rely on strategic entrepreneurship when trying to develop innovations as the foundation for profitable growth. In firms of all sizes, strategic entrepreneurship is more likely to be successful when employees have an entrepreneurial mind-set.[122]

Five dimensions characterize a firm's entrepreneurial mind-set: autonomy, innovativeness, risk taking, proactiveness, and competitive aggressiveness.[123] In combination, these dimensions influence the actions a firm takes to be innovative and launch new ventures. In sum, strategic leaders with an entrepreneurial mind-set are committed to pursuing profitable growth.[124]

Autonomy, the first of an entrepreneurial orientation's five dimensions, allows employees to take actions that are free of organizational constraints and permits individuals and groups to be self-directed. The second dimension, **innovativeness**, "reflects a firm's tendency to engage in and support new ideas, novelty, experimentation, and creative processes that may result in new products, services, or technological processes."[125] Cultures with a tendency toward innovativeness encourage employees to think beyond existing knowledge, technologies, and parameters to find creative ways to add value. **Risk taking** reflects a willingness by employees and their firm to accept risks when pursuing entrepreneurial opportunities. Assuming significant levels of debt and allocating large amounts of other resources (e.g., people) to projects that may not be completed are examples of these risks. The fourth dimension of an entrepreneurial orientation, **proactiveness**, describes a firm's ability to be a market leader rather than a follower. Proactive organizational cultures constantly use processes to anticipate future market needs and to satisfy them before competitors learn how to do so. Finally, **competitive aggressiveness** is a firm's propensity to take actions that allow it to consistently and substantially outperform its rivals.[126]

Changing the Organizational Culture and Restructuring

Changing a firm's organizational culture is more difficult than maintaining it; however, effective strategic leaders recognize when change is needed. Incremental changes to the firm's culture typically are used to implement strategies.[127] More significant and sometimes even radical changes to organizational culture support selecting strategies that differ from those the firm has implemented historically. Regardless of the reasons for change, shaping, and reinforcing a new culture require effective communication and problem solving, along with selecting the right people (those who have the values desired for the organization), engaging in effective performance appraisals (establishing goals and measuring individual performance toward goals that fit in with the new core values), and using appropriate reward systems (rewarding the desired behaviors that reflect the new core values).[128]

Evidence suggests that cultural changes succeed only when the firm's CEO, other key top management team members, and middle-level managers actively support them.[129] To effect change, middle-level managers in particular need to be highly disciplined to energize the culture and foster alignment with the strategic vision.[130] In addition, managers must be sensitive to the effects of other major strategic changes on organizational culture. For example, major downsizings can have negative effects on an organization's culture, especially if it is not implemented in accordance with the dominant organizational values.[131]

Emphasizing Ethical Practices

The effectiveness of processes used to implement the firm's strategies increases when they are based on ethical practices. Ethical companies encourage and enable people at all organizational levels to act ethically when doing what is necessary to implement strategies. In turn, ethical practices and the judgment on which they are based create "social capital" in the organization, increasing the "goodwill available to individuals and groups" in the organization.[132] Alternatively, when unethical practices evolve in an organization, they may become acceptable to many managers and employees.[133] One study found that in these circumstances, managers were particularly likely to engage in unethical practices to meet their goals when current efforts to meet them were insufficient.[134]

To properly influence employees' judgment and behavior, ethical practices must shape the firm's decision-making process and must be an integral part of organizational culture. In fact, research evidence suggests that a value-based culture is the most effective means of ensuring that employees comply with the firm's ethical requirements.[135] As we explained in Chapter 10, managers may act opportunistically, making decisions that are in their own best interests but not in the firm's best interests when facing lax expectations regarding ethical behavior. In other words, managers acting opportunistically take advantage of their positions, making decisions that benefit themselves to the detriment of the firm's stakeholders.[136] But strategic leaders are most likely to integrate ethical values into their decisions when the company has explicit ethics codes, the code is integrated into the business through extensive ethics training, and shareholders expect ethical behavior.[137]

Firms should employ ethical strategic leaders—leaders who include ethical practices as part of their strategic direction for the firm, who desire to do the right thing, and for whom honesty, trust, and integrity are important.[138] Strategic leaders who consistently display these qualities inspire employees as they work with others to develop and support an organizational culture in which ethical practices are the expected behavioral norms.[139]

Strategic leaders can take several actions to develop an ethical organizational culture. Examples of these actions include (1) establishing and communicating specific goals to describe the firm's ethical standards (e.g., developing and disseminating a code of conduct); (2) continuously revising and updating the code of conduct, based on inputs from people throughout the firm and from other stakeholders (e.g., customers and suppliers); (3) disseminating the code of conduct to all stakeholders to inform them of the firm's ethical standards and practices; (4) developing and implementing methods and procedures to use in achieving the firm's ethical standards (e.g., using internal auditing practices that are consistent with the standards); (5) creating and using explicit reward systems that recognize acts of courage (e.g., rewarding those who use proper channels and procedures to report observed wrongdoings); and (6) creating a work environment in which all people are treated with dignity.[140] The effectiveness of these actions increases when they are taken simultaneously and thereby are mutually supportive. The most important determinant, however, is the example set by the leader, and the way he/she actually deals with an ethical situation. Jack Welch identified four types of managers: those who have neither the right values nor the competence. Dealing with them is easy—out they go. Managers who have both are the gems to be retained in the organization at all costs. Those without the competence but with the right values can be trained or given a suitable assignment that matches their competencies. The hardest to deal with are those who are very competent, produce results every time, but do not share the values and/or are unethical. It is difficult to deal with them, especially when they occupy crucial positions, and the leader needs to take a tough call on such persons.[141] When strategic leaders and others throughout the firm fail to take actions such as these—perhaps because an ethical culture has not been created—problems are likely to occur.

The Strategy Leadership Intersection

The above may leave the readers wondering how strategic leadership is different from strategy formulation itself. Strategy formulation is an important task of the leader, but not the only job. The leadership element consists in generating an inspiring vision, articulating it effectively so as to generate the needed commitment and involvement of the people, and enabling other leaders to come up in the organization. The true test of leadership is the degree of commitment and involvement of the organization members, rather than mere results in the short run. This needs authenticity, generation of trust, providing the example for others to see and follow, and making people feel a sense of ownership in the organization.

This requires not only analytical skills, but also an ability to understand the context, interpersonal skills, and a highly developed moral compass. It is felt that today the problem with business schools is that they produce people who have a high degree of analytical skills, without the other skills, and who see themselves more as providing the intellectual leadership rather than human and ethical leadership, a concern articulated by very eminent academics and managers.[143] Sumantra Ghoshal has argued that theories such as the agency theory and concepts such as maximization of shareholder value have led to a crisis in the teaching and practice of management.[144]

We discuss next how formal organizational controls can help prevent problems and reinforce better ethical practices.

Establishing Balanced Organizational Controls

Organizational controls are basic to a capitalistic system and have long been viewed as an important part of strategy implementation processes.[145] Controls are necessary to help ensure that firms achieve their desired outcomes.[146] Defined as the "formal, information-based ... procedures used by managers to maintain or alter patterns in organizational activities," controls help strategic leaders build credibility, demonstrate the value of strategies to the firm's stakeholders, and promote and support strategic change.[147] Most critically, controls provide the parameters for implementing strategies as well as the corrective actions to be taken when implementation-related adjustments are required.

In this chapter, we focus on two organizational controls—strategic and financial—that were introduced in Chapter 11. Our discussion of organizational controls here emphasizes strategic and financial controls because strategic leaders, especially those at the top of the organization, are responsible for their development and effective use.

As we explained in Chapter 11, financial control focuses on short-term financial outcomes. In contrast, strategic control focuses on the *content* of strategic actions rather than their *outcomes*. Some strategic actions can be correct but still result in poor financial outcomes because of external conditions such as a recession in the economy, unexpected domestic or foreign government actions, or natural disasters. Therefore, emphasizing financial controls often produces more short-term and risk-averse managerial decisions, because financial outcomes may be caused by events beyond managers' direct control. Alternatively, strategic control encourages lower-level managers to make decisions that incorporate moderate and acceptable levels of risk because outcomes are shared between the business-level executives making strategic proposals and the corporate-level executives evaluating them.

The challenge strategic leaders face is to verify that their firm is emphasizing financial and strategic controls so that firm performance improves. The Balanced Scorecard is a tool that helps strategic leaders assess the effectiveness of the controls.

The Balanced Scorecard

The **balanced scorecard** is a framework firms can use to verify that they have established both strategic and financial controls to assess their performance.[148] This technique is most appropriate for use when dealing with business-level strategies; however, it can also be used with the other strategies firms may choose to implement (e.g., corporate level, international, and cooperative).

The underlying premise of the balanced scorecard is that firms jeopardize their future performance possibilities when financial controls are emphasized at the expense of strategic controls,[149] in that financial controls provide feedback about outcomes achieved from past actions, but do not communicate the drivers of future performance.[150] Thus, an overemphasis on financial controls has the potential to promote managerial behavior that sacrifices the firm's long-term, value-creating potential for short-term performance gains.[151] An appropriate balance of strategic controls and financial controls, rather than an overemphasis on either, allows firms to effectively monitor their performance.

Four perspectives are integrated to form the balanced scorecard framework: **financial** (concerned with growth, profitability, and risk from the shareholders' perspective), **customer** (concerned with the amount of value customers perceive was created by the firm's products), **internal business processes** (with a focus on the priorities for various business processes that create customer and shareholder satisfaction), and **learning and growth** (concerned with the firm's effort to create a climate that supports change, innovation, and growth). Thus, using the balanced scorecard framework allows the firm to understand how it looks to shareholders (financial perspective), how customers view it (customer perspective), the processes it must emphasize to successfully use its competitive advantage (internal perspective), and what it can do to improve its performance in order to grow (learning and growth perspective).[152] Generally speaking, strategic controls tend to be emphasized when the firm assesses its performance relative to the learning and growth perspective, whereas financial controls are emphasized when assessing performance in terms of the financial perspective.

Firms use different criteria to measure their standing relative to the scorecard's four perspectives. We show sample criteria in Figure 12.5. The firm should select the number of criteria that will allow it to have both a strategic understanding and a financial understanding of its performance without becoming immersed in too many details.[153] For example, we know from research that a firm's innovation, quality of its goods and services, growth of its sales, and its profitability are all interrelated.[154]

Strategic leaders play an important role in determining a proper balance between strategic controls and financial controls, whether they are in single-business firms or large diversified firms. A proper balance between controls is important, in that "wealth creation for organizations where strategic leadership is exercised is possible because these leaders make appropriate investments for future viability (through strategic control), while maintaining an appropriate level of financial stability in the present (through financial control)."[155] In fact, most corporate restructuring is designed to refocus the firm on its core businesses, thereby allowing top executives to reestablish strategic control of their separate business units.[156]

Successfully using strategic control frequently is integrated with appropriate autonomy for the various subunits

Perspectives	Criteria
Financial	• Cash flow • Return on equity • Return on assets
Customer	• Assessment of ability to anticipate customers' needs • Effectiveness of customer service practices • Percentage of repeat business • Quality of communications with customers
Internal Business Processes	• Asset utilization improvements • Improvements in employee morale • Changes in turnover rates
Learning and Growth	• Improvements in innovation ability • Number of new products compared to competitors • Increases in employees' skills

Figure 12.5 Strategic controls and financial controls in a balanced scorecard framework

so that they can gain a competitive advantage in their respective markets.[157] Strategic control can be used to promote the sharing of both tangible and intangible resources among interdependent businesses within a firm's portfolio. In addition, the autonomy provided allows the flexibility necessary to take advantage of specific marketplace opportunities. As a result, strategic leadership promotes simultaneous use of strategic control and autonomy.[158]

The balanced scorecard is being used by car manufacturer Porsche. After this manufacturer of the much sought-after sports cars regained its market-leading position, it implemented a balanced scorecard approach in an effort to maintain this position. In particular, Porsche used the balanced scorecard to promote learning and continuously improve the business. For example, knowledge was collected from all Porsche dealerships throughout the world. The instrument used to collect the information was referred to as "Porsche Key Performance Indicators." The fact that Porsche is now the world's most profitable automaker suggests the value the firm gained and is gaining by using the balanced scorecard as a foundation for simultaneously emphasizing strategic and financial controls.[159] Balanced Score Card has become a widely used tool in India as well.

As we have explained, strategic leaders are critical to a firm's ability to successfully use all parts of the strategic management process. For instance, the new CEO for Wal-Mart, Mike Duke, has the strategic leadership skills to position himself and his company for future success. Certainly, the future for strategic leaders similar to Duke is likely to be challenging; but he is leading a highly successful company that is increasing its market share and is likely to grow in international markets, where he has significant experience and knowledge. He appears to emphasize balanced organizational controls and uses many of the principles of the Balanced Scorecard. Similarly, we see in Strategic Focus that the Chairman and CEOs of Tata Steel struck the balance between strategic vision and financial controls to bring about a turn around in the century old steel plant at Jamshedpur. With people like Mike Duke, Ratan Tata, J.J. Irani, and B. Muthuraman in these roles, the work of strategic leaders will remain exciting and has a strong possibility of creating positive outcomes for all of a firm's stakeholders.

STRATEGIC FOCUS

12.2 Rejuvenating Tata Steel

Tata Iron and Steel Company Ltd. (TISCO or Tata Steel) is one of the India's oldest companies. It was established in 1907, though actual operations commenced only in 1911. Its visionary founder was Mr. J.N. Tata. For a long time, TISCO was the only steel producer in India.

In the late 1980s and early 1990s, TISCO was doing quite well although due to the protected environment in India complacency had set in the organization. Its performance was mediocre and questions on its further viability were beginning to be raised. The company had many legacy problems, among which was its "no lay-offs" policy (in fact, it was said that once a person was an employee of Tata Steel, not only that person, but also their children would be employees of the company). Other problems included its responsibility for running a huge township, an old plant, old technology and a huge workforce. However, a silver lining was that Tata Steel had started a plan of modernization in the 1980s, and this could be accelerated.

In 1992, Mr. Ratan Tata took over as the Chairman of the Tata Group, and Mr. J.J. Irani was the CEO of TISCO. They embarked on a program to reduce costs and improve revenues. They introduced certain technological improvements such as utilization of fine iron ore (the so called "blue dust"), that otherwise was wasted; a new technology to make coke; optimization of the blast furnaces; and reducing energy costs. TISCO also embarked on a massive program to reduce its workforce from 83,000 to 45,000, over a number of years. This was done in consultation with the labor unions in such a way that did not lead to any industrial relations problems.

A change in work culture was needed. At this time, a new cold rolling plant was on the anvil. This was used as a place to develop a new culture. The new plant was physically separated from the old plant, and was given its own rules and norms. By the turn of the century, the modernization of the plant was complete, and the labor force had become much leaner. A new quality control system was also put in place. However, by then the company faced fresh challenges: The world steel prices crashed, and the domestic demand for steel also registered a fall. Post liberalization, import of steel was easy, thus, Tata Steel had to compete against imported steel, often dumped by large producers. The company responded by further cost cutting and efficiency enhancement measures, the main being the Total Operational Improvement Program (TOP). Many areas were tackled simultaneously, and as per an estimate, about ₹6 billion were saved over the years.

In mid 2001, another Tata Steel veteran, B. Muthuraman took over as CEO. He gave a new direction to the company by installing a formidable knowledge management system and imbibing a new entrepreneurial spirit in the company. The company became the second lowest cost steel producer in the world, giving it a cushion to tide over the fluctuations in steel prices globally. It became so comfortable in its cash position that it took over a much bigger Corus in 2006, as we have read in an earlier chapter.

TISCO: On The Path Of Becoming A Global Steel Producer

Sources: Cases "Tata Steel" (A) through (E), Indian Institute of Management, Bangalore.

SUMMARY

- Effective strategic leadership is a prerequisite to successfully using the strategic management process. Strategic leadership entails the ability to anticipate events, envision possibilities, maintain flexibility, and empower others to create strategic change.
- Top-level managers are an important resource for firms to develop and exploit competitive advantages. In addition, when they and their work are valuable, rare, imperfectly imitable, and non-substitutable, strategic leaders are also a source of competitive advantage.
- The top management team is composed of key managers who play a critical role in selecting and implementing the firm's strategies. Generally, they are officers of the corporation and/or members of the board of directors.
- The top management team's characteristics, a firm's strategies, and its performance are all interrelated. For example, a top management team with significant marketing and R&D knowledge positively contributes to the firm's use of a growth strategy. Overall, having diverse skills increases most top management teams' effectiveness.
- Typically, performance improves when the board of directors is involved in shaping a firm's strategic direction. However, when the CEO has a great deal of power, the board may be less involved in decisions about strategy formulation and implementation. By appointing people to the board and simultaneously serving as CEO and chair of the board, CEOs increase their power.
- In managerial succession, strategic leaders are selected from either the internal or the external managerial labor market. Because of their effect on firm performance, selection of strategic leaders has implications for a firm's effectiveness. Companies use a variety of reasons for selecting the firm's strategic leaders either internally or externally. In most instances, the internal market is used to select the CEO; but the number of outsiders chosen is increasing. Outsiders often are selected to initiate major changes in strategy.
- Effective strategic leadership has five major components: determining the firm's strategic direction, effectively managing the firm's resource portfolio (including exploiting and maintaining core competencies and managing human capital and social capital), sustaining an effective organizational culture, emphasizing ethical practices, and establishing balanced organizational controls.
- Strategic leaders must develop the firm's strategic direction. The strategic direction specifies the image and character the firm wants to develop over time. To form the strategic direction, strategic leaders evaluate the conditions (e.g., opportunities and threats in the external environment) they expect their firm to face over the next three to five years.
- Strategic leaders must ensure that their firm exploits its core competencies, which are used to produce and deliver products that create value for customers, when implementing its strategies. In related diversified and large firms in particular, core competencies are exploited by sharing them across units and products.
- The ability to manage the firm's resource portfolio and manage the processes used to effectively implement the firm's strategy are critical elements of strategic leadership. Managing the resource portfolio includes integrating resources to create capabilities and leveraging those capabilities through strategies to build competitive advantages. Human capital and social capital are perhaps the most important resources.
- As a part of managing the firm's resources, strategic leaders must develop a firm's human capital. Effective strategic leaders view human capital as a resource to be maximized—not as a cost to be minimized. Such leaders develop and use programs designed to train current and future strategic leaders to build the skills needed to nurture the rest of the firm's human capital.
- Effective strategic leaders also build and maintain internal and external social capital. Internal social capital promotes cooperation and coordination within and across units in the firm. External social capital provides access to resources the firm needs to compete effectively.
- Shaping the firm's culture is a central task of effective strategic leadership. An appropriate organizational culture encourages the development of an entrepreneurial orientation among employees and an ability to change the culture as necessary.
- In ethical organizations, employees are encouraged to exercise ethical judgment and to always act ethically. Improved ethical practices foster social capital. Setting specific goals to meet the firm's ethical standards, using a code of conduct, rewarding ethical behaviors, and creating a work environment where all people are treated with dignity are actions that facilitate and support ethical behavior.
- Developing and using balanced organizational controls are the final components of effective strategic leadership. The balanced scorecard is a tool that measures the effectiveness of the firm's strategic and financial controls. An effective balance between strategic and financial controls allows for flexible use of core competencies, but within the parameters of the firm's financial position.

KEY TERMS AND DEFINITIONS

Strategic leadership is the ability to anticipate, envision, maintain flexibility, and empower others to create strategic change as necessary.

An **internal managerial labor market** consists of a firm's opportunities for managerial positions and the qualified employees within that firm.

An **external managerial labor market** is the collection of managerial career opportunities and the qualified people who are external to the organization in which the opportunities exist.

An **organizational culture** consists of a complex set of ideologies, symbols, and core values that are shared throughout the firm and influence the way business is conducted.

The **top management team** is composed of the key individuals who are responsible for selecting and implementing the firm's strategies.

A **heterogeneous top management team** is composed of individuals with different functional backgrounds, experience, and education.

The **balanced scorecard** is a framework firms can use to verify that they have established both strategic and financial controls to assess their performance.

Human capital refers to the knowledge and skills of a firm's entire workforce.

Social capital involves relationships inside and outside the firm that help the firm accomplish tasks and create value for customers and shareholders.

Determining strategic direction involves specifying the image and character the firm seeks to develop over time.

REVIEW QUESTIONS

1. What is strategic leadership? In what ways are top executives considered important resources for an organization?
2. What is a top management team, and how does it affect a firm's performance and its abilities to innovate and design and implement effective strategic changes?
3. How do the internal and external managerial labor markets affect the managerial succession process?
4. What is the effect of strategic leadership on determining the firm's strategic direction?
5. How do strategic leaders effectively manage their firm's resource portfolio to exploit its core competencies and leverage the human capital and social capital to achieve a competitive advantage?
6. What is organizational culture? What must strategic leaders do to develop and sustain an effective organizational culture?
7. As a strategic leader, what actions could you take to establish and emphasize ethical practices in your firm?
8. What are organizational controls? Why are strategic controls and financial controls important aspects of the strategic management process?

EXPERIENTIAL EXERCISE

Exercise 1: Executive Succession

For this exercise, you will identify and analyze a case of CEO succession. Working in small groups, find a publicly held firm that has changed CEOs. The turnover event must have happened at least twelve months ago, but no more than twenty four months ago. Use a combination of company documents and news articles to answer the following questions:

1. Why did the CEO leave? Common reasons for CEO turnover include death or illness, retirement, accepting a new position, change in ownership or control, or termination. In cases of termination, there is often no official statement as to why the CEO departed. Consequently, you may have to rely on news articles that speculate why a CEO was fired or forced to resign.
2. Did the replacement CEO come from inside the organization, or outside?
3. What are the similarities and differences between the new CEO and the CEO who was replaced? Possible comparison items could include functional experience, industry experience, etc. If your library has a subscription to *Hoover's Online*, you can find information on top managers through this resource.
4. At the time of the succession event, how did the firm's financial performance compare to industry norms? Has the firm's standing relative to the industry changed since the new CEO took over?
5. Has the firm made major strategic changes since the succession event? Has the firm made major acquisitions or divestitures? Launched or closed down product lines?

Create a PowerPoint presentation that presents answers to each of the above questions. Your presentation should be brief, consisting of no more than five to seven slides.

Exercise 2: Strategic Leadership is Tough!

Your textbook defines strategic leadership as "The ability to anticipate, envision, maintain flexibility, and empower others...." Accordingly, this exercise combines the practical elements of leadership in an experiential exercise. You are asked to replicate leaders and followers in the attainment of a defined goal.

First, the class is divided into teams of three to five individuals. Next, each team chooses a leader, which also dictates who the followers will be. It is important to choose your leader wisely. The classroom instructor will then assign the task to be completed.

Students should be prepared to debrief the assignment when completed. Your instructor will guide this discussion.

Entrepreneurial Implications for Strategy

CHAPTER

13

Studying this chapter should provide you with the strategic management knowledge needed to

- Define strategic entrepreneurship and corporate entrepreneurship.
- Define entrepreneurship and entrepreneurial opportunities and explain their importance.
- Define invention, innovation, and imitation, and describe the relationship among them.
- Describe entrepreneurs and the entrepreneurial mind-set.
- Explain international entrepreneurship and its importance.
- Describe how firms internally develop innovations.
- Explain how firms use cooperative strategies to innovate.
- Describe how firms use acquisitions as a means of innovation.
- Explain how strategic entrepreneurship helps firms create value.

OPENING CASE
The Continuing Innovation Revolution at Amazon: The Kindle and E-Books

Jeff Bezos led the Internet retailing revolution with his entry into the book retail market in 1995. Since then Amazon.com has significantly expanded its product lines and implemented several innovations, especially in processes and approaches to marketing their products. Recently, Bezos and Amazon are leading a potential revolution in the book market with the Kindle, which provides easy access to store and read many e-books. Let's be clear—Amazon did not create the digital book. E-books have been available for several years, but access to and use of e-books has not been necessarily easy. However, with the development of the Kindle e-reader, access to and ease of reading e-books has been simplified and it is predicted to revolutionize the book publishing business within the next five years.

The Kindle was first introduced in 2007, and two newer and improved versions were introduced in 2009. The Kindle 2 was introduced in February 2009 and according to market analysts, it literally "flew off the shelves" at a time when consumers were curtailing purchases of most other products. Then in May 2009, Amazon introduced a large-screen version of the Kindle 2, the Kindle DX, which has a 9.7-inch screen. While the DX appears to be a little cumbersome, it provides larger screen access to graphics-heavy publications common in college textbooks. The Kindle currently can be used to download any of the 285,000 e-books available in Amazon's inventory. Amazon's new Kindles are thinner than a pencil and offer a feature allowing text to be translated into voice. This means that it can read to you! Bezos demonstrated this feature at the introduction by having the computer-generated voice read the Gettysburg Address.

Amazon's success in the first quarter of 2009 (e.g., a 24 per cent increase in earnings from the first quarter 2008) was largely attributed to the Kindle. It is predicted to be wildly successful. Barclays Capital has predicted that it will reach annual sales of $3.7 billion in 2012 with a profit of $840 million. This amount would account for approximately 20 per cent of Amazon's predicted sales that year. Amazon also earns a return by selling content for use on the Kindle in the form of e-books and other electronic content. For example, Amazon sells subscriptions to 37 different newspapers for the Kindle at $10 per month. This set includes such respected newspapers as the *New York Times, Boston Globe,* and *Washington Post.* It also has an agreement for a pilot program at five major universities, hoping that students will soon be carrying all of their textbooks on the Kindle in their backpacks.

AP Photo/Mark Lennihan

The new Kindle 2 electronic reader "flew off the shelves" at a time when consumers were curtailing purchases of most other products.

Clearly, Amazon's biggest potential challenge may come from competitors. The Kindle technology is likely imitable and Sony already has a competitor e-reader on the market. Thus, Amazon must entrench the Kindle quickly and continue to enrich its features (the Kindle currently only provides "black-and-white" content even though it is said to provide better resolution than can be obtained in print copies). While the Kindle may help Amazon become the Apple of the e-reader market, the Kindle is likely to revolutionize all publishing industries (e.g., book publishers, newspapers).

Sources: S. Stein, 2009, Old, real book vs. Kindle alternative: Which will win? CNET.com, http://www.cnet.com, June 12; J. M. O'Brien, 2009, Amazon's next revolution, *Fortune,* June 8, 68–76; B. Stone & M. Rich, 2009, Amazon introduces big-screen Kindle, *New York Times,* http://www.nytimes.com, May 7; D. MacMillan, 2009, Amazon's widescreen Kindle DX: Winners and losers, *BusinessWeek,* http://businessweek.com, May 7; C. Dannen, 2009, Amazon CEO Jeff Bezos unveils Kindle DX in New York, *Fast Company,* http://www.fastcompany.com, May 6; D. Darlin, 2009, First impressions of the new Kindle DX, *New York Times,* http://www.gadgetwise.blogs.nytimes.com, May 6; C. Gallo, 2009, How Amazon's Bezos sparked demand for Kindle 2, *BusinessWeek,* http://businessweek.com, February, 24.

In Chapter 1, we indicated that **organizational culture** refers to the complex set of ideologies, symbols, and core values that are shared throughout the firm and that influence how the firm conducts business. Thus, culture is the social energy that drives—or fails to drive—the organization. The Opening Case explains Amazon's new innovation, the Kindle, that is expected to revolutionize the publishing industries (any businesses which provide products printed with ink on paper). Increasingly, a firm's ability to engage in innovation makes the difference in gaining and maintaining a competitive advantage and achieving performance targets.[1]

Amazon is clearly an entrepreneurial and innovative company. It is the leading Internet retailer in the world and also consistently produces innovations. Not all of them are successful, but the Kindle appears to be on the verge of being highly successful. From reading this chapter, you will understand that Amazon's ability to innovate shows that it successfully practices strategic entrepreneurship.

Strategic entrepreneurship is taking entrepreneurial actions using a strategic perspective. In this process, the firm tries to find opportunities in its external environment that it can try to exploit through innovations. Identifying opportunities to exploit through innovations is the **entrepreneurship** dimension of strategic entrepreneurship, while determining the best way to manage the firm's innovation efforts is the **strategic** dimension. Thus, firms engaging in strategic entrepreneurship integrate their actions to find opportunities and to successfully innovate in order to pursue them.[2] In the twenty-first century competitive landscape, firm survival and success depend on a firm's ability to continuously find new opportunities and quickly produce innovations to pursue them.[3]

To examine strategic entrepreneurship, we consider several topics in this chapter. First, we examine entrepreneurship and innovation in a strategic context. Definitions of entrepreneurship, entrepreneurial opportunities, and entrepreneurs as those who engage in entrepreneurship to pursue entrepreneurial opportunities are presented. We then describe international entrepreneurship, a phenomenon reflecting the increased use of entrepreneurship in economies throughout the world. After this discussion, the chapter shifts to descriptions of the three ways firms innovate. Internally, firms innovate through either autonomous or induced strategic behavior. We then describe actions firms take to implement the innovations resulting from those two types of strategic behaviors.

In addition to innovating within the firm, firms can develop innovations by using cooperative strategies, such as strategic alliances, and by acquiring other companies to gain access to their innovations and innovative capabilities.[4] Most large, complex firms use all three methods to innovate. The chapter closes with summary comments about how firms use strategic entrepreneurship to create value and earn above-average returns.

As emphasized in this chapter, innovation and entrepreneurship are vital for young and old, and for large and small firms, for service companies as well as manufacturing firms, and for high-technology ventures.[5] In the global competitive landscape, the long-term success of new ventures and established firms is a function of their ability to meld entrepreneurship with strategic management.[6]

A major portion of the material in this chapter is on innovation and entrepreneurship within established organizations. This phenomenon is called **corporate entrepreneurship**, which is the use or application of entrepreneurship within an established firm.[7] Corporate entrepreneurship has become critical to the survival and success of established organizations.[8] Indeed, established firms use entrepreneurship to strengthen their performance and to enhance growth opportunities.[9] Of course, innovation and entrepreneurship play a critical role in the degree of success achieved by startup entrepreneurial ventures as well. Much of the content examined in this chapter is equally important in entrepreneurial ventures (sometimes called "startups") and established organizations.[10]

Entrepreneurship and Entrepreneurial Opportunities

Entrepreneurship is the process by which individuals, teams, or organizations identify and pursue entrepreneurial opportunities without being immediately constrained by the resources they currently control.[11] **Entrepreneurial opportunities** are conditions in which new goods or services can satisfy a need in the market. These opportunities exist because of competitive imperfections in markets and among the factors of production used to produce them or because they were independently developed by entrepreneurs.[12] Entrepreneurial opportunities come in many forms such as the chance to develop and sell a new product and the chance to sell an existing product in a new market.[13] Firms should be receptive to pursuing entrepreneurial opportunities whenever and wherever they may surface.[14]

As these two definitions suggest, the essence of entrepreneurship is to identify and exploit entrepreneurial opportunities—that is, opportunities others do not see or for which they do not recognize the commercial potential.[15] As a process, entrepreneurship results in the "creative destruction" of existing products (goods or services) or methods of producing them and replaces them with new products and production methods.[16] Thus, firms engaging in entrepreneurship place high value on individual innovations as well as the ability to continuously innovate across time.[17]

We study entrepreneurship at the level of the individual firm. However, evidence suggests that entrepreneurship is the economic engine driving many nations' economies in the global competitive landscape.[18] Thus, entrepreneurship, and the innovation it spawns, is important for companies competing in the global economy and for countries seeking to stimulate economic climates with the potential to enhance the living standard of their citizens.[19] A recent study conducted by the Boston Consulting Group and the Small Business Division of Intuit found that 10 million people in the United States were considering starting a new business. About one-third of those who do will expand into international markets. The study suggested that by 2017 the number of entrepreneurs will increase, and the entrepreneurs will be younger and include more women and immigrants. Thus, even though the importance of entrepreneurship continues to grow, the "face" of those who start new ventures is also changing.[20] The increasing importance attached to entrepreneurship is also reflected in the larger number of MBAs from Indian business schools to opt out of regular placement and start on their own ventures. In the Indian Institue of Management, Ahmedabad, for example, about 5–10 per cent of graduates are now opting for entrepreneurship. The well known dot com firms, Naukri.com and Makemytrip.com were started by IIMA alumni, and so were Mastek and Orchard Chemicals. The attraction of the concept is reflected in the huge success of Rashmi Bansal's book, *Stay Hungry, Stay Foolish*.[21]

INNOVATION

Peter Drucker argued that "innovation is the specific function of entrepreneurship, whether in an existing business, a public service institution, or a new venture started by a lone individual."[22] Moreover, Drucker suggested that innovation is "the means by which the entrepreneur either creates new wealth-producing resources or endows existing resources with enhanced potential for creating wealth."[23] Thus, entrepreneurship and the innovation resulting from it are critically important for all firms. The realities of competition in the competitive landscape of the twenty-first century suggest that to be market leaders, companies must regularly develop innovative products desired by customers. This means that innovation should be an intrinsic part of virtually all of a firm's activities.[24]

Innovation is a key outcome firms seek through entrepreneurship and is often the source of competitive success, especially in turbulent, highly competitive environments.[25] For example, research results show that firms competing in global industries that invest more in innovation also achieve the highest returns.[26] In fact, investors often react positively to the introduction of a new product, thereby increasing the price of a firm's stock. Furthermore, "Innovation may be required to maintain or achieve competitive parity, much less a competitive advantage in many global markets."[27] Investing in the development of new technologies can increase the performance of firms that operate in different but related product markets (refer to the discussion of related diversification in Chapter 6). In this way, the innovations can be used in multiple markets, and return on the investments is earned more quickly.[28]

In his classic work, Schumpeter argued that firms engage in three types of innovative activities.[29] **Invention** is the act of creating or developing a new product or process. **Innovation** is the process of creating a commercial product from an invention. Innovation begins after an invention is chosen for development.[30] Thus, an invention brings something new into being, while an innovation brings something new into use. Accordingly, technical criteria are used to determine the success of an invention, whereas commercial criteria are used to determine the success of an innovation.[31] Finally, **imitation** is the adoption of a similar innovation by different firms. Imitation usually leads to product or process standardization, and products based on imitation often are offered at lower prices, but without as many features. Entrepreneurship is critical to innovative activity in that it acts as the linchpin between invention and innovation.[32]

In the United States in particular, innovation is the most critical of the three types of innovative activities. Many companies are able to create ideas that lead to inventions, but commercializing those inventions has, at times, proved difficult.[33] This difficulty is suggested by the fact that approximately 80 per cent of R&D occurs in large firms, but these same firms produce fewer than 50 per cent of the patents.[34] Patents are a strategic asset and the ability to regularly produce them can be an important source of competitive advantage, especially for firms competing in knowledge-intensive industries (e.g., pharmaceuticals).[35]

A fascinating new concept that has caught on is reverse innovation, a term coined by V. Govindarajan and Jeff Immelt. This refers to the innovative ideas that emanate in the less developed world and that are adopted in developed countries, thus reversing the traditional innovation sequence, where innovations originate in developed countries and are adopted or adapted in less developed countries.[36]

ENTREPRENEURS

Entrepreneurs are individuals, acting independently or as part of an organization, who perceive an entrepreneurial opportunity and then take risks to develop an innovation to pursue it. Entrepreneurs can be found throughout an organization—from top-level managers to those working to produce a firm's goods or services. Entrepreneurs are found throughout Amazon, for example. Many Amazon employees must devote at least a portion of their time to develop innovations. Entrepreneurs tend to demonstrate several characteristics: They are highly motivated, willing to take responsibility for their projects, self-confident, and often optimistic.[37] In addition, entrepreneurs tend to be passionate and emotional about the value and importance of their innovation-based ideas.[38] They are able to deal with uncertainty and are more alert to opportunities than others.[39] Interestingly, recent research found that genetic factors partly influence people to engage in entrepreneurship.[40] To be successful, entrepreneurs often need to have good social skills and to plan exceptionally well (e.g., to obtain venture capital).[41] Entrepreneurship entails much hard work to be successful but it can also be highly satisfying. As noted by Mary Kay Ash, founder of Mary Kay Cosmetics, "It is far better to be exhausted from success than to be rested from failure."[42]

Evidence suggests that successful entrepreneurs have an entrepreneurial mind-set. The person with an **entrepreneurial mind-set** values uncertainty in the marketplace and seeks to continuously identify opportunities with the potential to lead to important innovations.[43] Because it has the potential to lead to continuous innovations, an individual's entrepreneurial mind-set can be a source of competitive advantage for a firm.[44] Entrepreneurial mind-sets are fostered and supported when knowledge is readily available throughout a firm. Indeed, research has shown that units within firms are more innovative when they have access to new knowledge.[45] Transferring knowledge, however, can be difficult, often because the receiving party must have adequate absorptive capacity (or the ability) to learn the knowledge.[46] Learning requires that the new knowledge be linked to the existing knowledge. Thus, managers need to develop the capabilities of their human capital to build on their current knowledge base while incrementally expanding that knowledge.[47]

Some companies are known for their entrepreneurial culture. For example, in 2008, Apple was ranked as the most innovative company for the fourth year in a row. The rest of the top 10 most innovative companies were Google, Toyota, General Electric, Microsoft, Tata Group, Nintendo, Procter & Gamble, Sony, and Nokia. Yet, there are other companies known as the antithesis of innovative. For example, GM was known for sacrificing innovation for profits. Of course, this approach eventually led to GM's demise.[48]

International Entrepreneurship

International entrepreneurship is a process in which firms creatively discover and exploit opportunities that are outside their domestic markets in order to develop a competitive advantage.[49] As the practices suggested by this definition show, entrepreneurship is a global phenomenon.[50] As noted earlier, approximately one-third of new ventures move into international markets early in their life cycle. Most large established companies have significant foreign operations and often start new ventures in domestic and international markets. Large multinational companies, for example, generate approximately 54 per cent of their sales outside their domestic market, and more than 50 per cent of their employees work outside of the company's home country.[51]

A key reason that entrepreneurship has become a global phenomenon is that in general, internationalization leads to improved firm performance.[52] Nonetheless, decision makers should recognize that the decision to internationalize exposes their firms to various risks, including those of unstable foreign currencies, problems with market efficiencies, insufficient infrastructures to support businesses, and limitations on market size.[53] Thus, the decision to engage in international entrepreneurship should be a product of careful analysis.

Because of its positive benefits, entrepreneurship is at the top of public policy agendas in many of the world's countries, including Finland, Ireland, Israel, and the United States. Entrepreneurship has become a particularly important public agenda item with the global economic crisis, which began in late 2007. For example, the US government and the Michigan state government are emphasizing entrepreneurial activity to revitalize the Detroit area hurt seriously by the loss of jobs due to the US auto companies' decline.[54]

Even though entrepreneurship is a global phenomenon, the rate of entrepreneurship differs across countries. A study of 43 countries found that the percentage of adults involved in entrepreneurial activity ranged from a high of more than 45 per cent in Bolivia to a low of approximately 4.4 per cent in Russia. The United States had a rate of almost 19 per cent. Importantly, this study also found a strong positive relationship between the rate of entrepreneurial activity and economic development in a country.[55] The study found that in economies that are at an early stage of development, the percentage of entrepreneurs to the total population was high, these consisting of tiny self managed businesses. As the economy picks up, there is consolidation, and larger firms emerge, and people tend to gravitate to these larger firms that offer security and a decent pay and benefits. As the economy develops still further, however, the opportunities increase, and the disposable incomes also increase, so that people feel it fine to take a greater risk in their careers and opt for entrepreneurship, thus showing a moderate increase in the percentage of people who opt for entrepreneurship, thus, producing a spoon shaped curve.

Culture is one of the reasons for the differences in rates of entrepreneurship among different countries. The research suggests that a balance between individual initiative and a spirit of cooperation and group ownership of innovation is needed to encourage entrepreneurial behavior. For firms to be entrepreneurial, they must provide appropriate autonomy and incentives for individual initiative to surface, and also promote cooperation and group ownership of an innovation if it is to be implemented successfully. Thus, international entrepreneurship often requires teams of people with unique skills and resources, especially in cultures that highly value individualism or collectivism. In addition to a balance of values for individual initiative and cooperative behaviors, firms must build the capabilities to be innovative and acquire the resources needed to support innovative activities.[56]

The level of investment outside of the home country made by young ventures is also an important dimension of international entrepreneurship. In fact, with increasing globalization, a greater number of new ventures have been "born global."[57] Research has shown that new ventures that enter international markets increase their learning of new technological knowledge and thereby enhance their performance.[58]

The probability of entering international markets increases when the firm has top executives with international experience, which increases the likelihood of the firm successfully competing in those markets.[59] Because of the learning and economies of scale and scope afforded by operating in international markets, both young and established internationally diversified firms often are stronger competitors in their domestic market as well. Additionally, as research has shown, internationally diversified firms are generally more innovative.[60]

As explained in the Strategic Focus 13.1, innovation has become highly important in the global competitive landscape. Thus, the ability of firms to gain and sustain a competitive advantage may be based partly or largely on the capability to produce innovations. Thus, we next discuss different types of innovations.

Internal Innovation

In established organizations, most innovation comes from efforts in research and development (R&D). Effective R&D often leads to firms' filing for patents to protect their innovative work. Increasingly, successful R&D results from integrating the skills available in the global workforce. Thus, the ability to have a competitive advantage based on innovation is more likely to accrue to firms capable of integrating the talent of human capital from countries around the world.[61]

Both Intel and Nokia have been innovative firms and market leaders. In 2009, they announced an agreement to jointly develop new mobile computing products that provide functions beyond the current smartphones and netbooks. The new products likely will integrate features of both phones and computers. Thus, the two companies can combine and integrate their current knowledge and capabilities of both types of products and the markets for them. While Intel has not yet "cracked" the smartphone market with its memory chips, Nokia has been successful with smartphones but was caught off guard when Apple introduced its now highly popular iPhone. Therefore, the marriage between the two should help each to overcome its weaknesses by integrating their strengths. In addition to the development of new products from their joint R&D efforts, they also plan to develop software for devices using the Linux operating system.[62] Interestingly, HTC Corporation of Taiwan is considered to be a highly innovative company which produced many smart phones, including a cheaper "the other iPhone", and several Android based devices. It seems to have betted on the Android system becoming the system of the future, with a high potential for innovation due to the open system it adopts.[63]

Increasingly, it seems possible that in the twenty-first century competitive landscape, R&D may be the most critical factor in gaining and sustaining a competitive advantage in some industries, such as pharmaceuticals. Larger, established firms, certainly those competing globally, often try to use their R&D labs to create competence-destroying new technologies and products. Being able to innovate in this manner can create a competitive advantage for firms in many industries.[64] Although critical to long-term corporate success, the outcomes of R&D investments are uncertain and often not achieved in the short-term, meaning that patience is required as firms evaluate the outcomes of their R&D efforts.[65]

STRATEGIC FOCUS

13.1 Competitiveness and Innovation: Are We Experiencing a Paradigm Shift?

In 2009, the United States continued to be ranked as the most competitive nation. This top ranking and those of some other developed countries are based on the quality of infrastructures, educational systems, and laws regarding business operations. It is also due to their advanced levels of innovation over the years. Yet, the major economic crisis beginning in late 2007 and early 2008 has shown some "cracks" in the economic leadership of these countries. In the twenty-first century, economic power has begun to shift to major emerging economies such as China and India.

However, the shift may be even more fundamental, as many believe that innovation is the most critical factor in a nation's competitiveness over time. In fact, the United States' competitiveness is likely to be based on the significant innovative capabilities and innovative output of its businesses. While certain business leaders in the United States understand the importance of innovation (e.g., members of the US Council on Competitiveness), the country is no longer ranked as the most innovative nation. In fact, the United States ranked eighth in the 2009 International Innovation Index (among the 110 countries ranked). Singapore was ranked first. In a report issued by the Information Technology and Innovation Foundation, the United States was ranked sixth among 40 countries and regions around the world. Singapore was also ranked first in this report. Singapore developed a strategy to promote specific programs by investing heavily in attracting major technologies and recruiting top scientists to develop more innovation. That strategy is now paying substantial dividends. Firms based in the United States have focused too much on producing short-term returns, leading to an overemphasis on incremental innovations. As a result, the country is now in danger of losing its lead in science and technology. Perhaps one of the most prominent examples is ExxonMobil, which receives approximately $756,000 in revenue per minute. Rather than focusing on developing new sources of energy, it seeks to enhance its ability to gain access to and extract with greater efficiency black gold or oil.

Corbis/PhotoLibrary

With forward-thinking investments in the recruitment of top scientists and attraction of key technologies, Singapore is the world leader in innovation.

According to a 2009 report in *BusinessWeek*, technological breakthroughs in a number of fields have been few in number since 1998 (e.g., medical science, drugs, information technology, etc.). The leadership in these fields is largely represented by firms based in the United States. However, future technological breakthroughs in these fields are likely to be produced by firms based in other countries. Regaining this lead will require a major change in mind-set, investments, and promotion of entrepreneurial endeavors. Efforts have been implemented to encourage and develop more entrepreneurial activities in a number of industries and geographic regions to stop the economic decline and facilitate economic growth in the United States. It is unclear if these efforts will be successful in the short or long-term.

Sources: M. Mandel, 2009, Innovation interrupted, *BusinessWeek,* June 15, 034-040; 2009, International innovation index, *Wikipedia*, http://www.answers.com, June 13; B. Ott, 2009, Top companies can tame bear markets, *Yahoo News*, http://www.yahoo.com, June 11; A. S. Choi, 2009, Can entrepreneurs save this town? *BusinessWeek,* http://www.businessweek.com, June 5; M. Scott, 2009, Competitiveness: The U.S. and Europe are tops, *BusinessWeek,* http://www.businessweek.com, May 19; M. Richtel & J. Wortham, 2009, Weary of looking for work, some create their own, *New York Times,* http://www.nytimes.com, March 14; S. Lohr, 2009, In innovation, U.S. said to be losing competitive edge, *New York Times,* http://www.nytimes.com, February 25; J. Rae-Dupree, 2009, Innovation should mean more jobs, not less, *New York Times,* http://www.nytimes.com, January 4; R. Empson, 2008, Encouraging innovation: How can we do it better? *Fast Company,* http://www.fastcompany.com, August 1.

Incremental and Radical Innovation

Firms produce two types of internal innovations—incremental and radical innovations—when using their R&D activities. Most innovations are **incremental**—that is, they build on existing knowledge bases and provide small improvements in the current product lines. Incremental innovations are evolutionary and linear in nature.[66] "The markets for incremental innovations are well-defined, product characteristics are well understood, profit margins tend to be lower, production technologies are efficient, and competition is primarily on the basis of price."[67] Adding a different kind of whitening agent to a soap detergent is an example of an incremental innovation, as are improvements in televisions over the last few decades. Companies launch far more incremental innovations than radical innovations because they are cheaper, easier and faster to produce, and involve less risk.[68]

In contrast to incremental innovations, **radical innovations** usually provide significant technological breakthroughs and create new knowledge.[69] Radical innovations, which are revolutionary and nonlinear in nature, typically use new technologies to serve newly created markets. The development of the original personal computer (PC) was a radical innovation at the time. Reinventing the computer by developing a "radically new computer-brain chip" (e.g., with the capability to process a trillion calculations per second) is an example of a radical innovation. Obviously, such a radical innovation would seem to have the capacity to revolutionize the tasks computers could perform. Perhaps some of the new products to be produced by the joint venture between Intel and Nokia integrating smartphones and computers will be considered to be radical innovations.

Because they establish new functionalities for users, radical innovations have strong potential to lead to significant growth in revenue and profits.[70] Developing new processes is a critical part of producing radical innovations. Both types of innovations can create value, meaning that firms should determine when it is appropriate to emphasize either incremental or radical innovation. However, radical innovations have the potential to contribute more significantly to a firm's efforts to earn above-average returns.

Radical innovations are rare because of the difficulty and risk involved in developing them. The value of the technology and the market opportunities are highly uncertain.[71] Because radical innovation creates new knowledge and uses only some or little of a firm's current product or technological knowledge, creativity is required. However, creativity does not produce something from nothing. Rather, creativity discovers, combines, or synthesizes current knowledge, often from diverse areas.[72] This knowledge is then used to develop new products that can be used in an entrepreneurial manner to move into new markets, capture new customers, and gain access to new resources.[73] Such innovations are often developed in separate business units that start internal ventures.[74]

Internally developed incremental and radical innovations result from deliberate efforts. These deliberate efforts are called **internal corporate venturing**, which is the set of activities firms use to develop internal inventions and especially innovations.[75] As shown in Figure 13.1, autonomous and induced strategic behaviors are the two types of internal corporate venturing. Each venturing type facilitates incremental and radical innovations. However, a larger number of radical innovations spring from autonomous strategic behavior while the greatest percentage of incremental innovations come from induced strategic behavior.

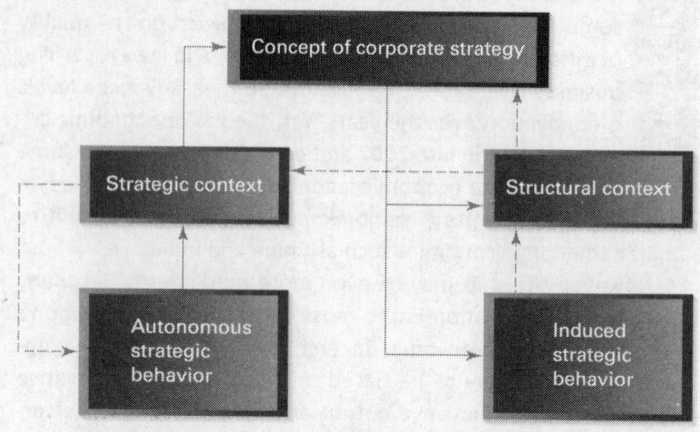

Source: Adapted from R.A. Burgelman, 1983, A model of the interactions of strategic behavior, corporate context, and the concept of strategy, *Academy of Management Review*, 8: 65.

Figure 13.1 Model of internal corporate venturing

Autonomous Strategic Behavior

Autonomous strategic behavior is a bottom-up process in which product champions pursue new ideas, often through a political process, by means of which they develop and coordinate the commercialization of a new good or service until it achieves success in the marketplace. A **product champion** is an organizational member with an entrepreneurial vision of a new good or service who seeks to create support for its commercialization. Product champions play critical roles in moving innovations forward. Indeed, in many corporations, "champions are widely acknowledged as pivotal to innovation speed and success."[76] Champions are vital to sell the ideas to others in the organization so that the innovations will be commercialized. Commonly, product champions use their social capital to develop informal networks within the firm. As progress is made, these networks become more formal as a means of pushing an innovation to the point of successful commercialization.[77] Internal innovations springing from autonomous strategic behavior frequently differ from the firm's current strategy, taking it into new markets and perhaps new ways of creating value for customers and other stakeholders.

Autonomous strategic behavior is based on a firm's wellspring of knowledge and resources that are the sources of the firm's innovation. Thus, a firm's technological capabilities and competencies are the basis for new products and processes.[78] As described in the Strategic Focus, Exxon-Mobil does not appear to use autonomous strategic behavior to identify new technologies and products that can better serve its customers. Alternatively, the iPod is likely to have been resulted from autonomous strategic behavior in Apple, though the development of the iPhone was more the result of induced strategic behavior discussed in the next section.

Changing the concept of corporate-level strategy through autonomous strategic behavior results when a product is championed within strategic and structural contexts (see Figure 13.1). Such a transformation occurred with the development of the iPod and introduction of iTunes at Apple. The strategic context is the process used to arrive at strategic decisions (often requiring political processes to gain acceptance). The best firms keep changing their strategic context and strategies because of the continuous changes in the current competitive landscape. Thus, some believe that the most competitively successful firms reinvent their industry or develop a completely new one across time as they compete with current and future rivals.[79]

To be effective, an autonomous process for developing new products requires that new knowledge be continuously diffused throughout the firm. In particular, the diffusion of tacit knowledge is important for development of more effective new products.[80] Interestingly, some of the processes important for the promotion of autonomous new product development behavior vary by the environment and country in which a firm operates. For example, the Japanese culture is high on uncertainty avoidance. As such, research has found that Japanese firms are more likely to engage in autonomous behaviors under conditions of low uncertainty.[81]

Induced Strategic Behavior

The second of the two forms of internal corporate venturing, **induced strategic behavior**, is a top-down process whereby the firm's current strategy and structure foster innovations that are closely associated with that strategy and structure.[82] In this form of venturing, the strategy in place is filtered through a matching structural hierarchy. In essence, induced strategic behavior results in internal innovations that are highly consistent with the firm's current strategy. Thus, the top management team plays a key role in induced strategic behavior, suggesting that the composition and the effectiveness of the team are important.[83]

Nokia's joint venture with Intel is an example of induced innovation. The two firms have specific goals in the development of new products to support their strategies. Intel has had a strategic interest in the smartphone market, and Nokia is trying to overcome Apple's lead in this market with the iPhone. The strategic intent of these firms is to develop a market leading product in the smartphone market that incorporates more features of the personal computer and sophisticated software to enrich the functionality of the product. These actions and approaches are intended to ensure that both firms are number one in the global market.

Vivek Prakash/Reuters/Landov

Nokia is trying to overcome the iPhone's lead in the smartphone market through a joint venture with Intel.

Implementing Internal Innovations

An entrepreneurial mind-set is required to be innovative and to develop successful internal corporate ventures. Because of environmental and market uncertainty, individuals and firms must be willing to take risks to commercialize innovations. Although they must continuously attempt to identify opportunities, they must also select and pursue the best opportunities and do so with discipline. Employing an entrepreneurial mind-set entails not only developing new products and markets but also execution in order to do these things effectively. Often, firms provide incentives to managers to be entrepreneurial and to commercialize innovations.[84]

Having processes and structures in place through which a firm can successfully implement the outcomes of internal corporate ventures and commercialize the innovations is critical. Indeed, the successful introduction of innovations into the marketplace reflects implementation effectiveness.[85] In the context of internal corporate ventures, managers must allocate resources, coordinate activities, communicate with many different parties in the organization, and make a series of decisions to convert the innovations resulting from either autonomous or induced strategic behaviors into successful market entries.[86] As described in Chapter 11, organizational structures are the sets of formal relationships that support the processes managers use to commercialize innovations.

Effective integration of the various functions involved in innovation processes—from engineering to manufacturing and, ultimately, market distribution—is required to implement the incremental and radical innovations resulting from internal corporate ventures.[87] Increasingly, product development teams are being used to integrate the activities associated with different organizational functions. Such integration involves coordinating and applying the knowledge and skills of different functional areas in order to maximize innovation.[88] Teams must help to make decisions as to which projects should be commercialized and which ones should be dropped. Although dropping a project is difficult, sometimes because of emotional commitments to innovation-based projects, effective teams recognize when conditions change such that the innovation cannot create value as originally anticipated.

Cross-Functional Product Development Teams

Cross-functional teams facilitate efforts to integrate activities associated with different organizational functions, such as design, manufacturing, and marketing. These teams may also include representatives from major suppliers because they can facilitate the firm's innovation processes.[89] In addition, new product development processes can be completed more quickly and the products more easily commercialized when cross-functional teams work effectively.[90] Using cross-functional teams, product development stages are grouped into parallel or overlapping processes to allow the firm to tailor its product development efforts to its unique core competencies and to the needs of the market.

Horizontal organizational structures support the use of cross-functional teams in their efforts to integrate innovation-based activities across organizational functions.[91] Therefore, instead of being designed around vertical hierarchical functions or departments, the organization is built around core horizontal processes that are used to produce and manage innovations. Some of the core horizontal processes that are critical to innovation efforts are formal; they may be defined and documented as procedures and practices. More commonly, however, these processes are informal: "They are routines or ways of working that evolve over time."[92] Often invisible, informal processes are critical to successful innovations and are supported properly through horizontal organizational structures more so than through vertical organizational structures.

Two primary barriers that may prevent the successful use of cross-functional teams as a means of integrating organizational functions are independent frames of reference of team members and organizational politics.[93] Team members working within a distinct specialization (e.g., a particular organizational function) may have an independent frame of reference typically based on common backgrounds and experiences. They are likely to use the same decision criteria to evaluate issues such as product development efforts as they do within their functional units. Research suggests that functional departments vary along four dimensions: time orientation, interpersonal orientation, goal orientation, and formality of structure.[94] Thus, individuals from different functional departments having different orientations on these dimensions can be expected to perceive product development activities in different ways. For example, a design engineer may consider the characteristics that make a product functional and workable to be the most important of the product's characteristics. Alternatively, a person from the marketing function may hold characteristics that satisfy customer needs as most important. These different orientations can create barriers to effective communication across functions and even produce conflict in the team at times.[95]

Organizational politics is the second potential barrier to effective integration in cross-functional teams. In some organizations, considerable political activity may center on allocating resources to different functions. Interunit conflict may result from aggressive competition for resources among those representing different organizational functions. This dysfunctional conflict between functions creates a barrier to their integration.[96] Methods must be found to achieve cross-functional integration without excessive political conflict and without changing the basic structural characteristics necessary for task specialization and efficiency.

Facilitating Integration and Innovation

Shared values and effective leadership are important for achieving cross-functional integration and implementing innovation.[97] Highly effective shared values are framed around the firm's vision and mission and become the glue that promotes integration between functional units. Thus, the firm's culture promotes unity and internal innovation.[98]

Strategic leadership is also highly important for achieving cross-functional integration and promoting innovation. Leaders set the goals and allocate resources. The goals include integrated development and commercialization of new goods and services. Effective strategic leaders also ensure a high-quality communication system to facilitate cross-functional integration. A critical benefit of effective communication is the sharing of knowledge among team members. Effective communication thus helps create synergy and gains team members' commitment to an innovation throughout the organization. Shared values and leadership practices shape the communication systems that are formed to support the development and commercialization of new products.[99]

Creating Value from Internal Innovation

Figure 13.2 shows how firms can create value from the internal corporate venturing processes they use to develop and commercialize new goods and services. An entrepreneurial mind-set is necessary so that managers and employees will consistently try to identify entrepreneurial opportunities the firm can pursue by developing new goods and services and new markets. Cross-functional teams are important for promoting integrated new product design ideas and commitment to their subsequent implementation. Effective leadership and shared values promote integration and vision for innovation and commitment to it. The end result for the firm is the creation of value for the customers and shareholders by developing and commercializing new products.[100] We should acknowledge that not all entrepreneurial efforts succeed, even with effective management. Sometimes managers must exit the market as well to avoid value decline.[101]

In the next two sections, we discuss the other ways firms innovate—by using cooperative strategies and by acquiring companies.

Innovation through Cooperative Strategies

Virtually all firms lack the breadth and depth of resources (e.g., human capital and social capital) in their R&D activities needed to internally develop a sufficient number of innovations to meet the needs of the market and remain competitive. As such, firms must be open to using external resources to help produce innovations.[102] Alliances with other firms can contribute to innovations in several ways. First, they provide information on new business opportunities and how to exploit them.[103] In other instances, firms use cooperative strategies to align what they believe are complementary assets with the potential to lead to future innovations.[104]

The rapidly changing technologies of the twenty-first century competitive landscape, globalization, and the need to innovate at world-class levels are primary influ-

Figure 13.2 Creating value through internal innovation processes

ences on firms' decisions to innovate by cooperating with other companies. Evidence shows that the skills and knowledge contributed by firms forming a cooperative strategy to innovate tend to be technology-based, a fact suggesting how technologies and their applications continue to influence the choices firms make while competing in the twenty-first century competitive landscape.[105] Indeed, some believe that because of these conditions, firms are becoming increasingly dependent on cooperative strategies as a path to successful competition in the global economy.[106] Even venerable old firms such as Intel and Nokia have learned that they need help to create innovations necessary to be competitive in a twenty-first century environment. Their agreement to jointly develop products that integrate functions of the smartphones and personal computers is based on their realization that they need great capabilities to develop market-leading products in the dynamic and highly competitive markets in which they participate.

Both entrepreneurial firms and established firms use cooperative strategies (e.g., strategic alliances and joint ventures) to innovate. An entrepreneurial firm, for example, may seek investment capital as well as established firms' distribution capabilities to successfully introduce one of its innovative products to the market.[107] Alternatively, more-established companies may need new technological knowledge and can gain access to it by forming a cooperative strategy with entrepreneurial ventures.[108] Alliances between large pharmaceutical firms and biotechnology companies increasingly have been formed to integrate the knowledge and resources of both to develop new products and bring them to market.[109]

Because of the importance of strategic alliances, particularly in the development of new technology and in commercializing innovations, firms are beginning to build networks of alliances that represent a form of social capital to them.[110] Building social capital in the form of relationships with other firms provides access to the knowledge and other resources necessary to develop innovations.[111] Knowledge from these alliances helps firms develop new capabilities.[112] Some firms now even allow other companies to participate in their internal new product development processes. It is not uncommon, for example, for firms to have supplier representatives on their cross-functional innovation teams because of the importance of the suppliers' input to ensure quality materials for any new product developed.[113]

However, alliances formed for the purpose of innovation are not without risks. In addition to conflict that is natural when firms try to work together to reach a mutual goal,[114] cooperative strategy participants also take a risk that a partner will appropriate a firm's technology or knowledge and use it to enhance its own competitive abilities.[115] To prevent or at least minimize this risk, firms, particularly new ventures, need to select their partners carefully. The ideal partnership is one in which the firms have complementary skills as well as compatible strategic goals.[116] However, because companies are operating in a network of firms and thus may be participating in multiple alliances simultaneously, they encounter challenges in managing the alliances.[117] Research has shown that firms can become involved in too many alliances, which can harm rather than facilitate their innovation capabilities.[118] Thus, effectively managing a cooperative strategy to produce innovation is critical.

As explained in the Strategic Focus 13.2, the social networking Internet sites have become highly popular with the general public and with professionals as well. Furthermore, entrepreneurs have begun to use them in ways to facilitate their businesses. These sites provide many opportunities for businesses and especially for gaining access to ideas and information. Therefore, they can facilitate innovation. Firms can use them to identify unique product ideas, to do market research, and to access new markets and new customers. As a result the social networking sites are highly valuable business mechanisms.

STRATEGIC FOCUS

13.2 All in a Twitter about My Space in order to be Linked in to the Book of Faces: The Social Networking Phenomenon

Social networks are one of the major innovations in the first decade of the twenty-first century. Perhaps the most popular and important social networking Internet sites are Facebook, MySpace, Twitter, and LinkedIn. In 2009, Facebook reached a level of approximately 1.2 million visits per month. MySpace was second with slightly more than 800,000 monthly visits, followed by Twitter in third place. LinkedIn was fifth but growing rapidly among professionals. While these are all largely used for personal social networking, their potential uses are much greater. For example, Facebook is used by approximately 150 million people globally with more than 50 million unique visitors monthly. Facebook is used in 170 different countries and territories and appears in 35 different languages. The access to people for many different reasons is substantial—perhaps larger than through any other single means other than television. In addition, MySpace has 76 million members with the average user spending about 4.4 hours per month on the site, about 1.7 hours longer than users on the site of its nearest competitor. The "rage" most recently has been Twitter, which is a micro-blogging Web site. Its use grew by 752 per cent in 2008 alone. It has attracted a more educated young adult audience.

Smart entrepreneurs are identifying ways to use these social networking sites for business purposes. For example, they may be useful to access markets. Gary Vaynerchuk used Twitter to grow his wine distribution business from $5 million (when he took over the business from his father) to $50 million within three years. He performed an experiment using a direct mail advertisement, a billboard, and a Twitter announcement to determine which would bring in more new customers (at the lowest cost). The direct mail ad brought in 200 new customers (at a cost of $75 each); the billboard brought in 300 new customers (at a cost of $25 each) and the Twitter announcement brought in 1,800 new customers (at no additional cost). He now produces short videos on wine for use on Twitter.

Social networking sites are also being used to identify potential new employees and to make all types of professional and business contacts. They provide access to new ideas and information that can be useful for solving problems and even for making strategic decisions. The access to information and ideas makes these sites excellent sources in the innovation process. For example, the use of cross-functional teams and an occasional outsider to develop new products has been valuable because of the integration of diverse ideas incorporating multiple and important perspectives. Yet, social networking sites provide access to many more and diverse perspectives and ideas. In addition, the opportunity to perform virtual market tests with a large sample from the market exists with these sites. Finally, they provide the opportunity to identify new and different markets for existing and new product ideas. Therefore, if managed properly, they could be highly valuable in the innovation process, from the identification of new product ideas, through market research to market reach (many, many potential customers).

davidbleekerphotography.com/Alamy

The demographics of social media usage are shifting quickly, with adults rapidly coming online and driving the growth of newer services such as Twitter.

Sources: L. Safko, 2009, The twitter about Twitter, *Fast Company,* http://fastcompany.com, June 13; M. Conlin & D. MacMillan, 2009, Managing the tweets, *BusinessWeek,* June 1, 20–21; A. Yee, 2009, Social network rankings: Who's hot and who's not, *ebiz,* http://www.ebizq.net, April 13; J. F. Rayport, 2009, Social networks are the new web portals, *BusinessWeek,* http://www.businessweek.com, January 21; J. Owyang, 2009, A collection of social network stats for 2009, *Web Strategist,* http://www.web-strategist.com, January 11; K. E. Klein, 2008, Are social networking sites useful for business? *BusinessWeek,* http://www.businessweek.com, August 6.

Innovation through Acquisitions

Firms sometimes acquire companies to gain access to their innovations and to their innovative capabilities. One reason companies make these acquisitions is that the capital market values growth; acquisitions provide a means to rapidly extend one or more product lines and increase the firm's revenues.[119] Acquisitions pursued for this reason should, nonetheless, have a strategic rationale. For example, several large pharmaceutical firms have made acquisitions in recent years for several reasons, such as enhancing growth. However, a primary reason for acquisitions in this industry has been to acquire innovation—new drugs that can be commercialized. In this way they strengthen their new product pipeline.[120]

Similar to internal corporate venturing and strategic alliances, acquisitions are not a risk-free approach to innovating. A key risk of acquisitions is that a firm may substitute an ability to buy innovations for an ability to produce innovations internally. In support of this contention, research shows that firms engaging in acquisitions introduce fewer new products into the market.[121] This substitution may take place because firms lose strategic control and focus instead on financial control of their original and, especially, of their acquired business units. Yet, careful selection of companies to acquire—

ones with complementary science and technology knowledge—can enhance innovation if the knowledge acquired is used effectively.[122]

We note in Chapter 7 that companies can also learn new capabilities from firms they acquire. Thus, firms may gain capabilities to produce innovation from an acquired company. Additionally, firms that emphasize innovation and carefully select companies for acquisition that also emphasize innovation are likely to remain innovative.[123] Likewise, firms must manage well the integration of the acquired firms' technical capabilities so that they remain productive and continue to produce innovation after the acquired firm is merged into the acquiring firm.[124] Cisco has been highly successful with the integration of acquired technology firms. Cisco managers take great care not to lose key personnel in the acquired firm, realizing they are the source of many innovations.

STRATEGY RIGHT NOW

Learn more about emerging Twitter business applications, including best practices and potential pitfalls. www.cengage.com/management/hitt

This chapter closes with an assessment of how strategic entrepreneurship helps firms create value for stakeholders through its operations.

Creating Value through Strategic Entrepreneurship

Newer entrepreneurial firms often are more effective than larger established firms in the identification of entrepreneurial opportunities.[125] As a consequence, entrepreneurial ventures often produce more radical innovations than do their larger, more established counterparts. Entrepreneurial ventures' strategic flexibility and willingness to take risks at least partially account for their ability to identify opportunities and then develop radical innovations to exploit them.

Alternatively, larger and well-established firms often have more resources and capabilities to exploit identified opportunities.[126] Younger, entrepreneurial firms generally excel in the opportunity-seeking dimension of strategic entrepreneurship while more established firms generally excel in the advantage-seeking dimension. However, to compete effectively in the twenty-first century competitive landscape, firms must not only identify and exploit opportunities but do so while achieving and sustaining a competitive advantage.[127] Thus, on a relative basis, newer entrepreneurial firms must learn how to gain a competitive advantage (advantage-seeking behaviors), and older, more established firms must relearn how to identify entrepreneurial opportunities (opportunity-seeking skills).

In some large organizations, action is being taken to deal with these matters. For example, an increasing number of large firms have created a new, top-level managerial position commonly called president or executive vice president of emerging brands. The essential responsibility for people holding these positions is to find entrepreneurial opportunities for their firms. If a decision is made to pursue one or more of the identified opportunities, this person also leads the analysis to determine whether the innovations should be internally developed, pursued through a cooperative venture, or acquired. The objective is to help firms develop successful incremental and radical innovations.

To be entrepreneurial, firms must develop an entrepreneurial mind-set among their managers and employees. Managers must emphasize the management of their resources, particularly human capital and social capital.[128] The importance of knowledge to identify and exploit opportunities as well as to gain and sustain a competitive advantage suggests that firms must have strong human capital.[129] Social capital is critical for access to complementary resources from partners in order to compete effectively in domestic and international markets.[130]

Many entrepreneurial opportunities continue to surface in international markets, a reality that is contributing to firms' willingness to engage in international entrepreneurship. By entering global markets that are new to them, firms can learn new technologies and management practices and diffuse this knowledge throughout the entire enterprise. Furthermore, the knowledge firms gain can contribute to their innovations. Research has shown that firms operating in international markets tend to be more innovative.[131] Entrepreneurial ventures and large firms now regularly enter international markets. Both types of firms must also be innovative to compete effectively. Thus, by developing resources (human and social capital), taking advantage of opportunities in domestic and international markets, and using the resources and knowledge gained in these markets to be innovative, firms achieve competitive advantages.[132] In so doing, they create value for their customers and shareholders.

Firms practising strategic entrepreneurship contribute to a country's economic development. In fact, some countries have made dramatic economic progress by changing the institutional rules for businesses operating in the country. This approach could be construed as a form of institutional entrepreneurship. Likewise, firms that seek to establish their technology as a standard, also representing institutional entrepreneurship, are engaging in strategic entrepreneurship because creating a standard produces a competitive advantage for the firm.[133]

Research shows that because of its economic importance and individual motives, entrepreneurial activity is increasing around the globe. Furthermore, more women are becoming entrepreneurs because of the economic opportunity entrepreneurship provides and the individual independence it affords. Recent research showed that about one-third of all entrepreneurs are now women.[134] In the United States, for example, women are the nation's fastest-growing group of entrepreneurs.[135] In the future, entrepreneurial activity may increase the wealth of less-affluent countries and continue to contribute to the economic development of the more-affluent countries. Regardless, the entrepreneurial ventures and large, established firms that choose to practice strategic entrepreneurship are likely to be the winners in the twenty-first century.[136]

After identifying opportunities, entrepreneurs must develop capabilities that will become the basis of their firm's core competencies and competitive advantages. The process of identifying opportunities is entrepreneurial, but this activity alone is not sufficient to create maximum wealth or even to survive over time.[137] As we learned in Chapter 3, to successfully exploit opportunities, a firm must develop capabilities that are valuable, rare, difficult to imitate, and non-substitutable. When capabilities satisfy these four criteria, the firm has one or more competitive advantages to exploit the identified opportunities (as described in Chapter 3). Without a competitive advantage, the firm's success will be only temporary (as explained in Chapter 1). An innovation may be valuable and rare early in its life, if a market perspective is used in its development. However, competitive actions must be taken to introduce the new product to the market and protect its position in the market against competitors to gain a competitive advantage.[138] These actions combined represent strategic entrepreneurship.

SUMMARY

- Strategic entrepreneurship is taking entrepreneurial actions using a strategic perspective. Firms engaging in strategic entrepreneurship simultaneously engage in opportunity-seeking and advantage-seeking behaviors. The purpose is to continuously find new opportunities and quickly develop innovations to exploit them.
- Entrepreneurship is a process used by individuals, teams, and organizations to identify entrepreneurial opportunities without being immediately constrained by the resources they control. Corporate entrepreneurship is the application of entrepreneurship (including the identification of entrepreneurial opportunities) within ongoing, established organizations. Entrepreneurial opportunities are conditions in which new goods or services can satisfy a need in the market. Increasingly, entrepreneurship positively contributes to individual firms' performance and stimulates growth in countries' economies.
- Firms engage in three types of innovative activities: (1) invention, which is the act of creating a new good or process, (2) innovation, or the process of creating a commercial product from an invention, and (3) imitation, which is the adoption of similar innovations by different firms. Invention brings something new into being while innovation brings something new into use.
- Entrepreneurs see or envision entrepreneurial opportunities and then take actions to develop innovations to exploit them. The most successful entrepreneurs (whether they are establishing their own venture or are working in an ongoing organization) have an entrepreneurial mind-set, which is an orientation that values the potential opportunities available because of marketplace uncertainties.
- International entrepreneurship, or the process of identifying and exploiting entrepreneurial opportunities outside the firm's domestic markets, is important to firms around the globe. Evidence suggests that firms capable of effectively engaging in international entrepreneurship outperform those competing only in their domestic markets.
- Three basic approaches are used to produce innovation: (1) internal innovation, which involves R&D and forming internal corporate ventures, (2) cooperative strategies such as strategic alliances, and (3) acquisitions. Autonomous strategic behavior and induced strategic behavior are the two forms of internal corporate venturing. Autonomous strategic behavior is a bottom-up process through which a product champion facilitates the commercialization of an innovative good or service. Induced strategic behavior is a top-down process in which a firm's current strategy and structure facilitate the development and implementation of product or process innovations. Thus, induced strategic behavior is driven by the organization's current corporate strategy and structure while autonomous strategic behavior can result in a change to the firm's current strategy and structure arrangements.
- Firms create two types of innovations—incremental and radical—through internal innovation that takes place in the form of autonomous strategic behavior or induced strategic behavior. Overall, firms produce more incremental innovations but radical innovations have a higher probability of significantly increasing sales revenue and profits. Cross-functional

integration is often vital to a firm's efforts to develop and implement internal corporate venturing activities and to commercialize the resulting innovation. The cross-functional teams now commonly include representatives from external organizations such as suppliers. Additionally, integration and innovation can be facilitated by developing shared values and effectively using strategic leadership.

- To gain access to the specialized knowledge commonly required to innovate in the complex global economy, firms may form a cooperative relationship such as a strategic alliance with other companies, some of which may be competitors.
- Acquisitions are another means firms use to obtain innovation. Innovation can be acquired through direct acquisition, or firms can learn new capabilities from an acquisition, thereby enriching their internal innovation abilities.
- The practice of strategic entrepreneurship by all types of firms, large and small, new and more established, creates value for all stakeholders, especially for shareholders and customers. Strategic entrepreneurship also contributes to the economic development of countries.

KEY TERMS AND DEFINITIONS

Entrepreneurship is the process by which individuals, teams, or organizations identify and pursue entrepreneurial opportunities without being immediately constrained by the resources they currently control.

Entrepreneurial opportunities are conditions in which new goods or services can satisfy a need in the market.

Strategic entrepreneurship is taking entrepreneurial actions using a strategic perspective.

Corporate entrepreneurship is the use or application of entrepreneurship within an established firm.

Invention is the act of creating or developing a new product or process.

Innovation is the process of creating a commercial product from an invention.

Imitation is the adoption of a similar innovation by different firms.

Entrepreneurs are individuals, acting independently or as part of an organization, who perceive an entrepreneurial opportunity and then take risks to develop an innovation to exploit it.

The person with an **entrepreneurial mind-set** values uncertainty in the marketplace and seeks to continuously identify opportunities with the potential to lead to important innovations.

International entrepreneurship is a process in which firms creatively discover and exploit opportunities that are outside their domestic markets in order to develop a competitive advantage.

REVIEW QUESTIONS

1. What is strategic entrepreneurship? What is corporate entrepreneurship?
2. What is entrepreneurship, and what are entrepreneurial opportunities? Why are they important for firms competing in the twenty-first century competitive landscape?
3. What are invention, innovation, and imitation? How are these concepts interrelated?
4. What is an entrepreneur, and what is an entrepreneurial mind-set?
5. What is international entrepreneurship? Why is it important?
6. How do firms develop innovations internally?
7. How do firms use cooperative strategies to innovate and to have access to innovative capabilities?
8. How does a firm acquire other companies to increase the number of innovations it produces and improve its capability to produce innovations?
9. How does strategic entrepreneurship help firms to create value?

EXPERIENTIAL EXERCISES

Exercise 1: Do You Want to Be an Entrepreneur?

Would you make a good entrepreneur? In this exercise, we will explore how individual attributes and characteristics contribute to entrepreneurial success. If you believe that you have the traits of a successful entrepreneur, would you be more effective working within a large firm or starting your own business? Complete the first stage of the exercise individually, then meet in small groups to discuss your answers.

Individual

Brainstorm a list of personal attributes or characteristics that could help (or hinder) in a person's success as an entrepreneur. Next, evaluate the importance of each item on your list. Finally, compare your prioritized list against your personal characteristics. Do you think that you are a good candidate to be an entrepreneur? Why or why not?

Group

First, compare each person's list of attributes and characteristics. Combine similar items and create a composite list. Second, as a group, evaluate the importance of each item on the list. It is not important to rank order the characteristics. Rather, sort them into the categories "very important," "somewhat important," and "minimally important." Then, discuss within your group which team member seems to be the best suited to be an entrepreneur.

Create a brief profile of how to describe that person if he or she were applying for a job at an innovative company such as Google, Intel, or Motorola.

Whole Class

The instructor will ask for student volunteers to present their interview profiles.

Exercise 2: The Social Nature of Entrepreneurship

Entrepreneurship is said to be as much about social connections and networks as it is about the fundamentals of running a new venture. The relationships that an entrepreneur can count upon are also a key resource for financial capital, human capital, mentoring, and legal advice.

A popular blog covering social media and Web 2.0, http://mashable.com, recently identified what it considered to be the top 10 social networks for entrepreneurs (http://mashable.com, March 12, 2009):

1. Entrepreneur Connect
2. PartnerUp
3. StartupNation
4. LinkedIn
5. Biznik
6. Perfect Business
7. Go Big Network
8. Cofoundr
9. The Funded
10. Young Entrepreneur

In teams, choose one of the sites from the list; each team must select a different site. Then, spend some time reading the posts on that site to get a feel for the types of information that is presented. After your review, prepare a 10-minute presentation to the class on your network site, paying attention to address the following, at a minimum:

1. Provide an overview of the site—what it is used for, how popular is it, features, types of conversations, etc.
2. What is unique about this site? Why does it attract followers? What technologies are enabled here—RSS, Twitter, etc.?
3. Describe the target audience for this site. Who would use it and what types of information are available to entrepreneurs?
4. How do you think this site maintains it presence? Does it support itself with ad revenue, corporate sponsor, a not-for-profit sponsor, etc.?
5. Would this site be useful for corporate entrepreneurs as well as startup entrepreneurs? If so, how?

Endnotes

CHAPTER 1

1. J. McGregor, 2009, Smart management for tough times, *BusinessWeek*, http://www.businessweek.com, March 12.
2. M. Angur, S. Manikutty and P. Nukala, Cognizant: Preparing for a Global Footprint, Case # IIM Ahmedabad case # 328.
3. D. Kiley, 2009, Ford heats out on a road of its own, *BusinessWeek*, January 19, 47–49.
4. H. R. Greve, 2009, Bigger and safer: The diffusion of competitive advantage, *Strategic Management Journal*, 30: 1–23; D. G. Sirmon, M. A. Hitt, & R. D. Ireland, 2007, Managing firm resources in dynamic environments to create value: Looking inside the black box, *Academy of Management Review*, 32: 273–292.
5. R. D. Ireland & J. W. Webb, 2009, Crossing the great divide of strategic entrepreneurship: Transitioning between exploration and exploitation, *Business Horizons*, in press; D. Lei & J. W. Slocum, 2005, Strategic and organizational requirements for competitive advantage, *Academy of Management Executive*, 19(1): 31–45.
6. J. A. Lamberg, H. Tikkanen, T. Nokelainen, & H. Suur-Inkeroinen, 2009, Competitive dynamics, strategic consistency, and organizational survival, *Strategic Management Journal*, 30: 45–60; G. Pacheco-de-Almeida & P. Zemsky, 2007, The timing of resource development and sustainable competitive advantage, *Management Science*, 53: 651–666.
7. K. D. Miller, 2007, Risk and rationality in entrepreneurial processes, *Strategic Entrepreneurship Journal*, 1: 57–74.
8. R. M. Stulz, 2009, 6 ways companies mismanage risk, *Harvard Business Review*, 87(3): 86–94.
9. P. Steffens, P. Davidsson, & J. Fitzsimmons, 2009, Performance configurations over time: Implications for growth- and profit-oriented strategies, *Entrepreneurship Theory and Practice*, 33: 125–148.
10. J. C. Short, A. McKelvie, D. J. Ketchen, Jr., & G. N. Chandler, 2009, Firm and industry effects on firm performance: A generalization and extension for new ventures, *Strategic Entrepreneurship Journal*, 3: 47–65; T. Bates, 2005, Analysis of young, small firms that have closed: Delineating successful from unsuccessful closures, *Journal of Business Venturing*, 20: 343–358.
11. K. D. Miller, F. Fabian, & S.-J. Lin, 2009, Strategies for online communities, *Strategic Management Journal*, 30: 305–322; A. M. McGahan & M. E. Porter, 2003, The emergence and sustainability of abnormal profits, *Strategic Organization*, 1: 79–108.
12. 2009, Kingfisher to Merge with Deccan, *Business Standard*, December 20.
13. D. Marginson & L. McAulay, 2008, Exploring the debate on short-termism: A theoretical and empirical analysis, *Strategic Management Journal*, 29: 273–292.
14. The Director General of Civil Aviation Web site, http://dgca.nic.in/reports/mar-ind.htm; http://business.mapsofindia.com/aviation
15. T. R. Crook, D. J. Ketchen, Jr., J. G. Combs, & S. Y. Todd, 2008, Strategic resources and performance: A meta-analysis, *Strategic Management Journal*, 29: 1141–1154; J. T. Mahoney & A. M. McGahan, 2007, The field of strategic management within the evolving science of strategic organization, *Strategic Organization*, 5: 79–99.
16. J. Barthelemy, 2008, Opportunism, knowledge, and the performance of franchise chains, *Strategic Management Journal*, 29: 1451–1463.
17. J. Li, 2008, Asymmetric interactions between foreign and domestic banks: Effects on market entry, *Strategic Management Journal*, 29: 873–893.
18. P. Ghemawat & T. Hout, 2008, Tomorrow's global giants, *Harvard Business Review*, 86(11): 80–88.
19. M. A. Delmas & M. W. Toffel, 2008, Organizational responses to environmental demands: Opening the black box, *Strategic Management Journal*, 29: 1027–1055; A. M. McGahan & M. E. Porter, 1997, How much does industry matter, really? *Strategic Management Journal*, 18 (Special Issue): 15–30.

20. T. R. Holcomb, R. M. Holmes, Jr., & B. L. Connelly, 2009, Making the most of what you have: Managerial ability as a source of resource value creation, *Strategic Management Journal*, 30: 457–485; J. Acedo, C. Barroso, &J. L. Galan, 2006, The resource-based theory: Dissemination and main trends, *Strategic Management Journal,* 27: 621–636.
21. E. Thornton, 2009, The new rules, *BusinessWeek*, January 19, 30–34;T. Friedman, 2005, *The World Is Flat:A Brief History of the 21st Century*, New York: Farrar, Strauss and Giroux.
22. D. Searcey, 2006, Beyond cable. Beyond DSL. *Wall Street Journal*, July 24, R9.
23. 2009, NBC Universal company overview, http://www.nbcuniversal.com, April 23.
24. P. Taylor, 2007, Tools to bridge the divide: Raketu aims to outperform Skype in Internet telephony while throwing in a range of information and entertainment services, *Financial Times*, May 11, 16.
25. 2009, Be entertained, http://www.raketu.com, April 22.
26. 2009, Social networking Web sites review, http://www.socialnetworking-Web sites-review.toptenreivews.com, April 22.
27. D. F. Kuratko & D. B. Audretsch, 2009, Strategic entrepreneurship: Exploring different perspectives of an emerging concept, *Entrepreneurship Theory and Practice*, 33: 1–17.
28. J. Hagel, III, J. S. Brown, & L. Davison, 2008, Shaping strategy in a world of constant disruption, *Harvard Business Review*, 86(10): 81–89; G. Probst & S. Raisch, 2005, Organizational crisis: The logic of failure, *Academy of Management Executive*, 19(1): 90–105.
29. J. W. Selsky, J. Goes, & O. N. Babüroglu, 2007, Contrasting perspectives of strategy making: Applications in"Hyper" environments, *Organization Studies*, 28(1): 71–94; G. McNamara,P. M. Vaaler, & C. Devers, 2003, Same as it ever was: The search for evidence of increasing hypercompetition, *Strategic Management Journal*, 24: 261–278.
30. A. V. Izosimov, 2008, Managing hypergrowth, *Harvard Business Review*, 86(4): 121–127.
31. R. A. D'Aveni, 1995, Coping with hypercompetition: Utilizing the new 7S's framework, *Academy of Management Executive*, 9(3): 46.
32. D. J. Bryce & J. H. Dyer, 2007, Strategies to crack well-guarded markets, *Harvard Business Review* 85(5): 84–92; R. A. D'Aveni, 2004, Corporate spheres of influence, *MIT Sloan Management Review*, 45(4): 38–46; W. J. Ferrier, 2001, Navigating the competitive landscape: The drivers and consequences of competitive aggressiveness, *Academy of Management Journal*, 44: 858–877.
33. S. H. Lee & M. Makhija, 2009, Flexibility in internationalization: Is it valuable during an economic crisis? *Strategic Management Journal*, 30: 537–555; S. J. Chang & S. Park, 2005, Types of firms generating network externalities and MNCs' co-location decisions, *Strategic Management Journal*, 26: 595–615.
34. S. E. Feinberg & A. K. Gupta, 2009, MNC subsidiaries and country risk: Internalization as a safeguard against weak external institutions, *Academy of Management Journal*, 52: 381–399; R. Belderbos & L. Sleuwaegen, 2005, Competitive drivers and international plant configuration strategies: A product-level test, *Strategic Management Journal*, 26: 577–593.
35. 2005, Organisation for Economic Cooperation and Development,OCED Statistical Profile of the United States—2005, http://www.oced.org; S. Koudsi & L. A. Costa, 1998, America vs. the new Europe: By the numbers, *Fortune*, December 21, 149–156.
36. Y. Luo, 2007, From foreign investors to strategic insiders: Shifting parameters, prescriptions and paradigms for MNCs in China, *Journal of World Business*, 42(1): 14–34.
37. M. A. Hitt & X. He, 2008, Firm strategies in a changing global competitive landscape, *Business Horizons,* 51:363–369; A. Ratanpal, 2008, Indian economy and Indian private equity, *Thunderbird International Business Review*, 50: 353–358.
38. Y. Gorodnichenko, J. Svejnar, & K. Terrell, 2008, Globalization and innovation in emerging markets, NBER Working Paper No. w14481. Available at SSRN: http://ssrn.com/abstract=1301929.
39. K. Kranhold, 2005, GE pins hopes on emerging markets, *Wall Street Journal*, http://www.wsj.com, March 2.
40. C. H. Oh, 2009, The international scale and scope of European multinationals, *European Management Journal*, inpress; G. D. Bruton, G. G. Dess &J. J. Janney, 2007, Knowledge management in technology-focused firms in emerging economies: Caveats on capabilities, networks, and real options, *Asia Pacific Journal of Management*, 24(2): 115–130.
41. A. Ciarione, P. Piselli, & G. Trebeschi, 2009, Emerging markets' spreads and global financial conditions, *Journal of International Financial Markets, Institutions and Money*, 19: 222–239.
42. 2009, Wal-Mart Stores Inc., *Standard & Poor's Stock Reports*, http://www.standardandpoors.com, April 18.
43. M. A. Prospero, 2005, The march of war, *Fast Company,* May, 14.
44. B. Elango, 2009, Minimizing effects of "liability of foreignness": Response strategies of foreign firms in the United States, *Journal of World Business*, 44: 51–62.
45. D. J. McCarthy & S. M. Puffer, 2008, Interpreting the ethicality of corporate governance decisions in Russia: Utilizing integrative social contracts theory to evaluate the relevance of agency theory norms, *Academy of Management Review*, 33: 11–31.
46. M. A. Hitt, R. E. Hoskisson, & H. Kim, 1997, International diversification: Effects on innovation and firm performance in product-diversified firms, *Academy of Management Journal,* 40: 767–798.
47. R. D. Ireland & J. W. Webb, 2007, Strategic entrepreneurship: Creating competitive advantage through streams of innovation, *Business Horizons,* 50(1): 49–59; G. Hamel, 2001, Revolution vs. evolution: You need both, *Harvard Business Review,* 79(5): 150–156.
48. http://www.diehardindian.com/infra/telecom.htm.
49. http://en.wikipedia.org/wiki/Communications_in_India.
50. http://en.wikipedia.org/wiki/Communications_in_India.
51. http://www.pwc.com/en_IN/in/assets/pdfs/Publications-2010/E_M_Report_2010.pdf.

52. http://trak.in/tags/business/2010/04/07/internet-usage-india-report-2010; http://trak.in/tags/business/2009/07/15/india-can-have-500-million-internet-users-by-2012-is-that-a-pipe-dream.
53. B. Peters, 2009, Persistence of innovation: Stylised facts and panel data evidence, *The Journal of Technology Transfer*, 34: 226–243.
54. J. L. Boyd & R. K. F. Bresser, 2008, Performance implications of delayed competitive responses: Evidence from the U.S. retail industry, *Strategic Management Journal*, 29: 1077–1096; T. Talaulicar, J. Grundei, & A. V. Werder, 2005, Strategic decision making in startups: The effect of top management team organization and processes on speed and comprehensiveness, *Journal of Business Venturing,* 20: 519–541.
55. J. Kao, 2009, Tapping the world's innovation hot spots, *Harvard Business Review*, 87(3): 109–117.
56. C. W. L. Hill, 1997, Establishing a standard: Competitive strategy and technological standards in winner-take-all industries, *Academy of Management Executive*, 11(2): 7–25.
57. J. L. Funk, 2008, Components, systems and technological discontinuities: Lessons from the IT sector, *Long Range Planning*, 41: 555–573; C. M. Christensen, 1997, *The Innovator's Dilemma,* Boston: Harvard Business School Press.
58. C. M. Christensen, 2006, The ongoing process of building a theory of disruption, *Journal of Product Innovation Management,* 23(1): 39–55; R. Adner, 2002, When are technologies disruptive? A demand-based view of the emergence of competition, *Strategic Management Journal*, 23: 667–688; G. Ahuja & C. M. Lampert, 2001, Entrepreneurship in the large corporation: A longitudinal study of how established firms create breakthrough inventions, *Strategic Management Journal,* 22 (Special Issue): 521–543.
59. C. L. Nichols-Nixon & C. Y. Woo, 2003, Technology sourcing and output of established firms in a regime of encompassing technological change, *Strategic Management Journal,* 24: 651–666; C. W. L. Hill & F. T. Rothaermel, 2003, The performance of incumbent firms in the face of radical technological innovation, *Academy of Management Review,* 28: 257–274.
60. Jeffrey R. Immelt; Vijay Govindarajan, & Chris Trimble, 2009, How GE is disrupting itself, *Harvard Business Review,* October, pp.32-41.
61. V. Govindarajan, & S. Manikutty, 2010, What Poor Countries Can Teach Rich Ones about Healthcare, *Harvard blog*: http://blogs.hbr.org/cs/2010/04/how_poor_countries_can_help_so.html.
62. K. Celuch, G. B. Murphy, & S. K. Callaway, 2007, More bang for your buck: Small firms and the importance of aligned information technology capabilities and strategic flexibility, *Journal of High Technology Management Research,* 17: 187–197.
63. C.K. Prahalad, 2005, ITC e-Choupal Story: Profitable Rural transformation, *Fortune at the Bottom of the Pyramid: Eradicating Poverty through Profits*. Wharton School Publishing. pp.319–357.
64. V. Godinez, 2009, Broadband ISPs test download caps, face resistance from more data-heavy users, *The Dallas Morning News*, http://www.dallasnews.com, April 26.
65. C. F. Fey & P. Furu, 2008, Top management incentive compensation and knowledge sharing in multinational corporations, *Strategic Management Journal*, 29: 1301–1323.
66. M. Gottfredson, R. Puryear, & S. Phillips, 2005, Strategic sourcing: From periphery to the core, *Harvard Business Review,* 83(2): 132–139.
67. L. F. Mesquita, J. Anand, & T. H. Brush 2008, Comparing the resource-based and relational views: Knowledge transfer and spillover in vertical alliances, *Strategic Management Journal*, 29: 913–941; K. G. Smith, C. J. Collins, & K. D. Clark, 2005, Existing knowledge, knowledge creation capability, and the rate of new product introduction in high-technology firms, *Academy of Management Journal,* 48: 346–357.
68. A. Capaldo, 2007, Network structure and innovation: The leveraging of a dual network as a distinctive relational capability, *Strategic Management Journal,* 28: 585–608; S. K. Ethirau, P. Kale, M. S. Krishnan, & J. V. Singh, 2005, Where do capabilities come from and how do they matter? *Strategic Management Journal,* 26: 25–45.
69. Sirmon, Hitt, & Ireland, Managing firm resources.
70. A. C. Inkpen, 2008, Knowledge transfer and international joint ventures: The case of NUMMI and General Motors, *Strategic Management Journal*, 29: 447–453; P. L. Robertson & P. R. Patel, 2007, New wine in old bottles: Technological diffusion in developed economies, *Research Policy,* 36(5): 708–721; K. Asakawa & M. Lehrer, 2003, Managing local knowledge assets globally: The role of regional innovation relays, *Journal of World Business,* 38: 31–42.
71. R. E. Hoskisson, M. A. Hitt, & R. D. Ireland, 2008, *Competing for Advantage,* 2nd ed., Cincinnati: Thomson South-Western; K. R. Harrigan, 2001, Strategic flexibility in old and new economies, in M. A. Hitt, R. E. Freeman, & J. S. Harrison (eds.), *Handbook of Strategic Management,* Oxford, UK: Blackwell Publishers, 97–123.
72. S. Nadkarni & V. K. Narayanan, 2007, Strategic schemas, strategic flexibility, and firm performance: The moderating role of industry clockspeed, *Strategic Management Journal,* 28: 243–270.
73. L. Gratton & S. Ghoshal, 2005, Beyond best practice, *MIT Sloan Management Review,* 46(3): 49–55.
74. A. C. Edmondson, 2008, The competitive imperative of learning, *Harvard Business Review*, 86(7/8): 60–67; K. Shimizu & M. A. Hitt, 2004, Strategic flexibility: Organizational preparedness to reverse ineffective strategic decisions, *Academy of Management Executive,* 18(4): 44–59; K. Uhlenbruck, K. E. Meyer, & M. A. Hitt, 2003, Organizational transformation in transition economies: Resource-based and organizational learning perspectives, *Journal of Management Studies,* 40: 257–282.
75. R. E. Hoskisson, M. A. Hitt, W. P. Wan, & D. Yiu, 1999, Swings of a pendulum: Theory and research in strategic management, *Journal of Management,* 25: 417–456.
76. E. H. Bowman & C. E. Helfat, 2001, Does corporate strategy matter? *Strategic Management Journal,* 22: 1–23.
77. M. A. Delmas & M. W. Toffel, 2008, Organizational responses to environmental demands: Opening the black box, *Strategic*

Management Journal, 29: 1027–1055; J. Shamsie, 2003, The context of dominance: An industry-driven framework for exploiting reputation, *Strategic Management Journal*, 24: 199–215.

78. J. Galbreath & P. Galvin, 2008, Firm factors, industry structure and performance variation: New empirical evidence to a classic debate, *Journal of Business Research*, 61: 109–117.
79. M. B. Lieberman & S. Asaba, 2006, Why do firms imitate each other? *Academy of Management Journal*, 31: 366–385;L. F. Feldman, C. G. Brush, & T. Manolova, 2005, Co-alignment in the resource-performance relationship: Strategy as mediator, *Journal of Business Venturing*, 20: 359–383.
80. M. E. Porter, 1985, *Competitive Advantage*, New York: Free Press; M. E. Porter, 1980, *Competitive Strategy*, New York: Free Press.
81. J. C. Short, D. J. Ketchen, Jr.,T. B. Palmer, & G. T. M. Hult, 2007,Firm, strategic group, and industry influences on performance, *Strategic Management Journal*, 28: 147–167.
82. P. Ziobro, 2009, McDonald's pounds out good quarter, *Wall Street Journal*, http://www.wsj.com, April 23.
83. The share price was ₹490 on January 4, 2008 and it had come down to ₹264 on July 2, 2010.
84. A. M. McGahan, 1999, Competition, strategy and business performance, *California Management Review*, 41(3): 74–101; McGahan & Porter, How much does industry matter, really?
85. S. L. Newbert, 2008, Value, rareness, competitive advantage, and performance: A conceptual-level empirical investigation of the resource-based view of the firm, *Strategic Management Journal*, 29:745–768; F. J. Acedo, C. Barroso, & J. L. Galan, 2006, The resource-based theory: Dissemination and main trends, *Strategic Management Journal*, 27: 621–636.
86. E. Verwall, H. Commandeur, & W. Verbeke, 2009, Value creation and value claiming in strategic outsourcing decisions: A resource contingency perspective, *Journal of Management*, 35: 420–444; B.-S. Teng & J. L. Cummings, 2002, Trade-offs in managing resources and capabilities, *Academy of Management Executive*, 16(2): 81–91.
87. S. Kaplan, 2008, Cognition, capabilities, and incentives: Assessing firm response to the fiber-optic revolution, *Academy of Management Journal*, 51: 672–694; S. A. Zahra, H. Sapienza, & P. Davidsson, 2006, Entrepreneurship and dynamic capabilities: A review, model and research agenda, *Journal of Management Studies*, 43(4): 927–955; M. Blyler & R. W. Coff, 2003, Dynamic capabilities, social capital, and rent appropriation: Ties that split pies, *Strategic Management Journal*, 24: 677–686.
88. C.K. Prahalad & R.A. Mashelkar, 2010, Innovation's Holy Grail, *Harvard Business Review*, July-August: 119.
89. S. L. Newbert, 2007, Empirical research on the resource-based view of the firm: An assessment and suggestions for future research, *Strategic Management Journal*, 28: 121–146; P. Bansal, 2005, Evolving sustainability: A longitudinal study of corporate sustainable development, *Strategic Management Journal*, 26: 197–218.
90. P. J. H. Schoemaker & R. Amit, 1994, Investment in strategic assets: Industry and firm-level perspectives, in P. Shrivastava, A. Huff, & J. Dutton (eds.), *Advances in Strategic Management*, Greenwich, CT: JAI Press, 9.
91. A. A. Lado, N. G. Boyd, P. Wright, & M. Kroll, 2006, Paradox and theorizing within the resource-based view, *Academy of Management Review*, 31: 115–131;D. M. DeCarolis, 2003, Competencies and imitability in the pharmaceutical industry: An analysis of their relationship with firm performance, *Journal of Management*, 29: 27–50.
92. C. Zott, 2003, Dynamic capabilities and the emergence of intraindustry differential firm performance: Insights from a simulation study, *Strategic Management Journal*, 24: 97–125.
93. E. Levitas & H. A. Ndofor, 2006, What to do with the resource-based view: A few suggestions for what ails the RBV that supporters and opponents might accept, *Journal of Management Inquiry*, 15(2): 135–144; G. Hawawini, V. Subramanian, & P. Verdin, 2003, Is performance driven by industry- or firm-specific factors? A new look at the evidence, *Strategic Management Journal*, 24: 1–16.
94. M. Makhija, 2003, Comparing the resource-based and market-based views of the firm: Empirical evidence from Czech privatization, *Strategic Management Journal*, 24: 433–451; T. J. Douglas & J. A. Ryman, 2003, Understanding competitive advantage in the general hospital industry: Evaluating strategic competencies, *Strategic Management Journal*, 24: 333–347.
95. R. D. Ireland, R. E. Hoskisson, & M. A. Hitt. 2009, *Understanding Business Strategy*, 2nd Edition, Cincinnati: South-Western Cengage Learning, 6.
96. S. Ward, 2009, Vision statement, *About.com*, http://www.sbinfocanada.about.com, April 22; R. Zolli, 2006, Recognizing tomorrow's hot ideas today, *BusinessWeek*, September 25: 12.
97. 2005, The CEO's secret handbook, *Business 2.0*, July, 69–76.
98. All the vision and mission statements taken from the company Web sites.
99. S. Kemp & L. Dwyer, 2003, Mission statements of international airlines: A content analysis, *Tourism Management*, 24: 635–653; R. D. Ireland & M. A. Hitt, 1992, Mission statements: Importance, challenge, and recommendations for development, *Business Horizons*, 35(3): 34–42.
100. J. I. Siciliano, 2008, A comparison of CEO and director perceptions of board involvement in strategy, *Nonprofit and Voluntary Sector Quarterly*, 27: 152–162; W. J. Duncan, 1999, *Management: Ideas and Actions*, New York: Oxford University Press, 122–125.
101. J. H. Davis, J. A. Ruhe, M. Lee, & U. Rajadhyaksha, 2007, Mission possible: Do school mission statements work? *Journal of Business Ethics*, 70: 99–110.
102. L. W. Fry & J. W. Slocum, Jr., 2008, Maximizing the triple bottom line through spiritual leadership, *Organizational Dynamics*, 37: 86–96; A. J. Ward, M. J. Lankau, A. C. Amason, J. A. Sonnenfeld, & B. A. Agle, 2007, Improving the performance of top management teams, *MIT Sloan Management Review*, 48(3): 85–90.

103. M. Rahman, 2009, Why strategic vision statements *won't* measure up, *Strategic Direction*, 25: 3–4.
104. Nucor at a Crossroads, 1998, Case # 9-793-039, Harvard Business School.
105. Aravind Eyecare System: Giving the Most Precious Gift, 2003, Case # BP 0299, Indian Institute of Management, Ahmedabad.
106. R. Kaufman, 2006, *Change, Choices, and Consequences: A Guide to Mega Thinking and Planning,* Amherst, MA: HRD Press; J. Humphreys, 2004, The vision thing, *MIT Sloan Management Review,* 45(4): 96.
107. K. Basu & G. Palazzo, 2008, Corporate social responsibility: A process model of sensemaking, *Academy of Management Review,* 33: 122–136.
108. D. A. Bosse, R. A. Phillips, & J. S. Harrison, 2009, Stakeholders, reciprocity, and firm performance, *Strategic Management Journal*, 30: 447–456; J. P. Walsh & W. R. Nord, 2005, Taking stock of stakeholder management, *Academy of Management Review,* 30: 426–438; T. M. Jones & A. C. Wicks, 1999, Convergent stakeholder theory, *Academy of Management Review,* 24: 206–221.
109. G. Donaldson & J. W. Lorsch, 1983, *Decision Making at the Top: The Shaping of Strategic Direction,* New York: Basic Books, 37–40.
110. S. Sharma & I. Henriques, 2005, Stakeholder influences on sustainability practices in the Canadian Forest products industry, *Strategic Management Journal,* 26: 159–180.
111. A. Mackey, T. B. Mackey, & J. B. Barney, 2007, Corporate social responsibility and firm performance: Investor preferences and corporate strategies, *Academy of Management Review,* 32: 817–835; A. J. Hillman & G. D. Keim, 2001, Shareholder value, stakeholder management, and social issues: What's the bottom line? *Strategic Management Journal,* 22: 125–139.
112. G. Van der Laan, H. Van Ees, & A. Van Witteloostuijn, 2008, Corporate social and financial performance: An extended stakeholder theory, and empirical test with accounting measures, *Journal of Business Ethics*, 79: 299–310; J. M. Stevens, H. K. Steensma, D. A. Harrison, & P. L. Cochran, 2005, Symbolic or substantive document? The influence of ethics codes on financialexecutives' decisions, *Strategic Management Journal,* 26: 181–195.
113. M. L. Barnett & R. M. Salomon, 2006, Beyond dichotomy: The curvilinear relationship between social responsibility and financial performance, *Strategic Management Journal,* 27: 1101–1122.
114. T. Kuhn, 2008, A communicative theory of the firm: Developing an alternative perspective on intra-organizational power and stakeholder relationships, *Organization Studies*, 29: 1227–1254; L. Vilanova, 2007, Neither shareholder nor stakeholder management: What happens when firms are run for their short-term salient stakeholder? *European Management Journal,* 25(2): 146–162.
115. J. L. Murrillo-Luna, C. Garces-Ayerbe, & P. Rivera-Torres, 2008, Why do patterns of environmental response differ? A stakeholders' pressure approach, *Strategic Management Journal*, 29: 1225–1240; R. E. Freeman & J. McVea, 2001, A stakeholder approach to strategic management, in M. A. Hitt, R. E. Freeman, & J. S. Harrison (eds.), *Handbook of Strategic Management*, Oxford, UK: Blackwell Publishers, 189–207.
116. R. Boutilier, 2009, *Stakeholder Politics: Social Capital, Sustainable Development, and the Corporation*, Sheffield, United Kingdom, Greenleaf Publishing; C. Caldwell & R. Karri, 2005, Organizational governance and ethical systems: A conventional approach to building trust, *Journal of Business Ethics,* 58: 249–267.
117. F. G. A. de Bakker & F. den Hond, 2008, Introducing the politics of stakeholder influence, *Business & Society*, 47: 8–20; C. Hardy, T. B. Lawrence, & D. Grant, 2005, Discourse and collaboration: The role of conversations and collective identity, *Academy of Management Review,* 30: 58–77.
118. P. Berrone & L. R. Gomez-Meija, 2009, Environmental performance and executive compensation: An integrated agency-institutional perspective, *Academy of Management Journal*, 52: 103–126; S. Maitlis, 2005, The social process of organizational sensemaking, *Academy of Management Journal,* 48: 21–49.
119. L. Pierce, 2009, Big losses in ecosystems niches: How core firm decisions drive complementary product shakeouts, *Strategic Management Journal*, 30: 323–347; B. A. Neville & B. Menguc, 2006, Stakeholder multiplicity: Toward an understanding of the interactions between stakeholders, *Journal of Business Ethics,* 66: 377–391.
120. D. A. Ready, L. A. Hill, & J. A. Conger, 2008, Winning the race for talent in emerging markets, *Harvard Business* Review, 86(11): 62–70; A. M. Grant,J. E. Dutton, & B. D. Rosso, 2008, Giving commitment: Employee support programs and the prosocial sensemaking process, *Academy of Management Journal*, 51: 898–918; T. M. Gardner, 2005, Interfirm competition for human resources: Evidence from the software industry, *Academy of Management Journal,* 48: 237–256.
121. J. A. Byrne, 2005, Working for the boss from hell, *Fast Company,* July, 14.
122. J. Welch & S. Welch, 2009, An employee bill of rights, *BusinessWeek,* March 16, 72.
123. J. P. Jansen, D. Vera, & M. Crossan, 2008, Strategic leadership for exploration and exploitation: The moderating role of environmental dynamism, *The Leadership Quarterly*, 20: 5–18; E. T. Prince, 2005, The fiscal behavior of CEOs, *MIT Sloan Management Review,* 46(3): 23–26.
124. M. S. de Luque, N. T. Washburn, D. A. Waldman, & R. J. House, 2008, Unrequited profit: How stakeholder and economic values related to subordinates' perceptions of leadership and firm performance, *Administrative Science Quarterly*, 53: 626–654.
125. R. Khurana & N. Nohria, 2008, It's time to make management a true profession, *Harvard Business Review*, 86(10): 70–77.
126. N. Byrnes, 2009, Executives on a tightrope, *BusinessWeek,* January 19, 43; D. C. Hambrick, 2007, Upper echelons theory: An update, *Academy of Management Review,* 32: 334–339.

127. J. C. Camillus, 2008, Strategy as a wicked problem, *Harvard Business Review* 86(5): 99–106; A. Priestland & T. R. Hanig, 2005, Developing first-level managers, *Harvard Business Review,* 83(6): 113–120.
128. R. J. Harrington & A. K. Tjan, 2008, Transforming strategy one customer at a time, *Harvard Business Review*, 86(3): 62–72; R. T. Pascale & J. Sternin, 2005, Your company's secret change agent, *Harvard Business Review,* 83(5): 72–81.
129. Y. L. Doz & M. Kosonen, 2007, The new deal at the top, *Harvard Business Review,* 85(6): 98–104.
130. B. Stevens, 2008, Corporate ethical codes: Effective instruments for influencing behavior, *Journal of Business Ethics,* 78: 601–609; D. Lavie, 2006, The competitive advantage of interconnected firms: An extension of the resource-based view, *Academy of Management Review,* 31: 638–658.
131. Christian Medical College and Hospital, Vellore, Case # -----, case material of Indian Institute of Management, Ahmedabad.
132. H. Ibarra & O. Obodru, 2009, Women and the vision thing, *Harvard Business Review*, 87(1): 62–70; M. Crossan, D. Vera, & L. Nanjad, 2008, Transcendent leadership: Strategic leadership in dynamic environments, *The Leadership Quarterly*, 19: 569–581.
133. T. Leavitt, 1991, *Thinking about Management,* New York: Free Press, 9.
134. 2007, 100 best corporate citizens for 2007, *CRO Magazine,* http://www.thecrocom, June 19.
135. C. A. Montgomery, 2008, Putting leadership back into strategy, *Harvard Business Review*, 86(1): 54–60; D. C. Hambrick, S. Finkelstein, & A. C. Mooney, 2005, Executive job demands: New insights for explaining strategic decisions and leader behaviors, *Academy of Management Review,* 30: 472–491; J. Brett & L. K. Stroh, 2003, Working 61 plus hours a week: Why do managers do it? *Journal of Applied Psychology,* 88: 67–78.
136. J. A. Byrne, 2005, Great work if you can get it, *Fast Company,* April, 14.
137. M. Loeb, 1993, Steven J. Ross, 1927–1992, *Fortune,* January 25, 4.
138. K. M. Green, J. G. Covin, & D. P. Slevin, 2008, Exploring the relationship between strategic reactiveness and entrepreneurial orientation: The role of structure-style fit, *Journal of Business Venturing*, 23: 356–383.
139. O. Gadiesh & J. L. Gilbert, 1998, Profit pools: A fresh look at strategy, *Harvard Business Review,* 76(3): 139–147.
140. O. Gadiesh & J. L. Gilbert, 1998, How to map your industry's profit pool, *Harvard Business Review,* 76(3): 149–162.
141. C. Zook, 2007, Finding your next CORE business, *Harvard Business Review,* 85(4): 66–75; M. J. Epstein & R. A. Westbrook, 2001, Linking actions to profits in strategic decision making, *Sloan Management Review,* 42(3): 39–49.
142. T. Yu, M. Subramaniam, & A. A. Cannella, Jr., 2009, Rivalry deterrence in international markets: Contingencies governing the mutual forbearance hypothesis, *Academy of Management Journal*, 52: 127–147; D. J. Ketchen, C. C. Snow, & V. L. Street, 2004, Improving firm performance by matching strategic decision-making processes to competitive dynamics, *Academy of Management Executive,* 18(4): 29–43.
143. P. Ozcan & K. M. Eisenhardt, 2009, Origin of alliance portfolios: Entrepreneurs, network strategies, and firm performance, *Academy of Management Journal*, 52: 246–279.
144. S. D. Julian, J. C. Ofori-Dankwa, & R. T. Justis, 2008, Understanding strategic responses to interest group pressures, *Strategic Management Journal*, 29: 963–984; C. Eesley & M. J. Lenox, 2006, Firm responses to secondary stakeholder action, *Strategic Management Journal,* 27: 765–781.
145. Y. Luo, 2008, Procedural fairness and interfirm cooperation in strategic alliances, *Strategic Management Journal*, 29: 27–46; S. J. Reynolds, F. C. Schultz, & D. R. Hekman, 2006, Stakeholder theory and managerial decision-making: Constraints and implications of balancing stakeholder interests, *Journal of Business Ethics,* 64: 285–301; L. K. Trevino & G. R. Weaver, 2003, *Managing Ethics in Business Organizations,* Stanford, CA: Stanford University Press.
146. D. Pastoriza, M. A. Arino, & J. E. Ricart, 2008, Ethical managerial behavior as an antecedent of organizational social capital, *Journal of Business Ethics*, 78: 329–341.
147. B. W. Heineman Jr., 2007, Avoiding integrity land mines, *Harvard Business Review,* 85(4): 100–108.

CHAPTER 2

1. D. A. Bosse, R. A. Phillips, & J. S. Harrison, 2009, Stakeholders, reciprocity, and firm performance, *Strategic Management Journal*, 30: 447–456.
2. P. Berrone & L. R. Gomez-Mejia, 2009, Environmental performance and executive compensation: An integrated agency-institutional perspective, *Academy of Management Journal*, 52: 103–126; P. Chattopadhyay, W. H. Glick, & G. P. Huber, 2001, Organizational actions in response to threats and opportunities, *Academy of Management Journal,* 44: 937–955.
3. C. Weigelt & M. B. Sarkar, 2009, Learning from supply-side agents: The impact of technology solution providers' experiential diversity on clients' innovation adoption, *Academy of Management Journal*, 52: 37–60; D. G. Sirmon, S. Gove, & M. A. Hitt, 2008, Resource management in dyadic competitive rivalry: The effects of resource bundling and deployment, *Academy of Management Journal*, 51: 919–935.
4. J. P. Bonardi, G. I. F. Holburn, & R. G. Vanden Bergh, 2006, Nonmarket strategy performance: Evidence from US electric utilities, *Academy of Management Journal,* 49: 1209–1228.
5. S. Labaton, 2009, Obama plans fast action to tighten financial rules, *New York Times Online*, http://www.nytimes.com, January 25.
6. J. Welch & S. Welch, 2009, The economy: A little clarity, *BusinessWeek*, May 4, 80.
7. J. Uotila, M. Maula, T. Keil, & S. A. Zahra, 2009, Exploration, exploitation, and financial performance: Analysis of S&P 500

corporations, *Strategic Management Journal*, 30: 221–231; J. L. Murillo-Luna, C. Garces-Ayerbe, & P. Rivera-Torres, 2008, Why do patterns of environmental response differ? A stakeholder's pressure approach, *Strategic Management Journal*, 29: 1225–1240.

8. A. Kacperczyk, 2009, With greater power comes greater responsibility? Takeover protection and corporate attention to stakeholders, *Strategic Management Journal*, 30: 261–285; C. Eesley & M. J. Lenox, 2006, Firm responses to secondary stakeholder action, *Strategic Management Journal*, 27: 765–781.
9. L. Fahey, 1999, *Competitors,* New York: John Wiley & Sons; B. A. Walters & R. L. Priem, 1999, Business strategy and CEO intelligence acquisition, *Competitive Intelligence Review,* 10(2): 15–22.
10. A. P. Kellogg & J. Bennett, 2009, Chrysler' bankruptcy deals blow to affiliates, *Wall Street Journal Online*, http://www.wsj.com, May 2.
11. J. C. Short, D. J. Ketchen, Jr., T. B. Palmer, & G. T. Hult, 2007, Firm, strategic group, and industry influences on performance, *Strategic Management Journal,* 28: 147–167.
12. K. P. Coyne & J. Horn, 2009, Predicting your competitor's reaction, *Harvard Business Review*, 87(4): 90–97.
13. D. Sull, 2009, How to thrive in turbulent markets, *Harvard Business Review*, 87(2): 78–88; J. Hagel, III, J. S. Brown, & L. Davison, 2008, Shaping strategy in a world of constant disruption, *Harvard Business Review* 86(10): 80–89.
14. J. A. Lamberg, H. Tikkanen, T. Nokelainen, & H. Suur-Inkeroinen, 2009, Competitive dynamics, strategic consistency, and organizational survival, *Strategic Management Journal*, 30: 45–60.
15. C. K. Prahalad, 2005, *The Fortune at The Bottom of The Pyramid: Eradicating Poverty through Profits*, Wharton: Wharton School Publishing, pp.193–198.
16. W. B. Gartner, K. G. Shaver, & J. Liao, 2008, Opportunities as attributions: Categorizing strategic issues from an attributional perspective, *Strategic Entrepreneurship Journal*, 2: 301–315.
17. P. Lattman, 2005, Rebound, *Forbes,* March 28, 58.
18. P. Lattman & J. McCracken, 2009, Vultures vie in auction for the remains of Polaroid, *Wall Street Journal*, http://www.wsj.com, April 17.
19. S.B. Budhiraja and M.B. Athreya, 1996, Grammaphone Company of India Limited, case in *Cases in Strategic Management*, New Delhi: Tata McGraw Hill.
20. W. H. Stewart, R. C. May, & A. Kalla, 2008, Environmental perceptions and scanning in the United States and India: Convergence in entrepreneurial information seeking? *Entrepreneurship Theory and Practice*, 32:83–106; K. M. Patton & T. M. McKenna, 2005, Scanning for competitive intelligence, *Competitive Intelligence Magazine,* 8(2): 24–26.
21. J. O. Schwarz, 2008, Assessing the future of futures studies in management, *Futures*, 40: 237–246; K. M. Eisenhardt, 2002, Has strategy changed? *MIT Sloan Management Review,* 43(2): 88–91.
22. J. R. Hough & M. A. White, 2004, Scanning actions and environmental dynamism: Gathering information for strategic decision making, *Management Decision,* 42: 781–793; V. K. Garg, B. A. Walters, & R. L. Priem, 2003, Chief executive scanning emphases, environmental dynamism, and manufacturing firm performance, *Strategic Management Journal,* 24: 725–744.
23. C. P. Wei & Y. H. Lee, 2004, Event detection from online news documents for supporting environmental scanning, *Decision Support Systems,* 36: 385–401.
24. Fahey, *Competitors,* 71–73.
25. S. M. Kalita, 2009, Companies world-wide rethink strategies, *Wall Street Journal Online*, http://www.wsj.com, April 29.
26. T. M. Jones, W. Felps, & G. A. Bigley, 2007, Ethical theory and stakeholder-related decisions: The role of stakeholder culture, *Academy of Management Review*, 32: 137–155.
27. M. J. Leiblein & T. L. Madsen, 2009, Unbundling competitive heterogeneity: Incentive structures and capability influences on technological innovation, *Strategic Management Journal*, 30: 711–735.
28. D. Matten & J. Moon, 2008, Implicit and explicit CSR: A conceptual framework for a comparative understanding of corporate social responsibility, *Academy of Management Review*, 33: 404–424; F. Sanna-Randaccio & R. Veugelers, 2007, Multinational knowledge spillovers with decentralized R&D: A game theoretic approach, *Journal of International Business Studies,* 38: 47–63.
29. Fahey, *Competitors.*
30. S. Lohr, 2009, How crisis shapes the corporate model, *Wall Street Journal Online*, http://www.wsj.com, March 29.
31. E. Byron, 2009, P&G investors need a little pampering, *Wall Street Journal Online*, http://www.wsj.com, April 30.
32. P. E. Bierly, III, F. Damanpour, & M. D. Santoro, 2009, The application of external knowledge: Organizational conditions for exploration and exploitation, *Journal of Management Studies*, 46: 481–509; Fahey, *Competitors,* 75–77.
33. K. M. Sutcliffe & K. Weber, 2003, The high cost of accurate knowledge, *Harvard Business Review,* 81(5): 74–82.
34. *Business Daily,* 2010, New Lamps from Surya Roshni, February 5.
35. *Business Daily*, 2010, Moser Baer Launches its Content-Loaded Micro SD cards, January 19.
36. E. K. Foedermayr & A. Diamantopoulos, 2008, Market segmentation in practice: Review of empirical studies, methodological assessment, and agenda for future research, *Journal of Strategic Marketing*, 16: 223–265; L. Fahey & V. K. Narayanan, 1986, *Macroenvironmental Analysis for Strategic Management,* St. Paul, MN: West Publishing Company, 58.
37. US Census Bureau, 2009, International data base, http://www.census.gov/pic/www/idb/worldpopgraph.html, May 24.
38. S. Moffett, 2005, Fast-aging Japan keeps its elders on the job longer, *Wall Street Journal,* June 15, A1, A8.
39. The World Fact Book, https://www.cia.gov/library/publications.
40. 2009, *Strictly Spanish*, The growing Hispanic market in the United States, http://www.strictlyspanish.com, June 5.
41. J. A. Chatman & S. E. Spataro, 2005, Using self-categorization theory to understand relational demography-based varia-

tions in people's responsiveness to organizational culture, *Academy of Management Journal,* 48: 321–331.
42. 2006, Characteristics of the civilian labor force, 2004 and 2014, US Department of Labor, Bureau of Labor Statistics data, http://www.bls.gov, May.
43. J. Millman, 2005, Low-wage US jobs get "Mexicanized," but there's a price, *Wall Street Journal,* May 2, A2.
44. A. K. Fosu, 2008, Inequality and the growth-poverty nexus: Specification empirics using African data, *Applied Economics Letters*, 15: 563–566; A. McKeown, 2007, Periodizing globalization, *History Workshop Journal*, 63(1): 218–230.
45. O. Sullivan, 2008, Busyness, status distinction and consumption strategies of the income rich, time poor, *Time & Society*, 17: 5–26.46. 2009, Half the world is middle class???, http:///www.edwardsglobal.com, May 10.
47. Pavan K. Varma, 1998, *The Great Indian Middle Class*, New Delhi: Viking.
48. D. Vrontis & P. Pavlou, 2008, *Journal for International Business and Entrepreneurship Development*, 3: 289–307; A. Jones & N. Ennis, 2007, Bringing the environment into economic development, *Local Economy*, 22(1): 1–5; Fahey & Narayanan, *Macroenvironmental Analysis,* 105.
49. P. Coy, 2009, What good are economists anyway? *BusinessWeek*, April 27, 26–31.
50. J. Simms, 2009, Losses at Japan's electronics companies are no shock, *Wall Street Journal Online*, http://www.wsj.com, February 4.
51. J. Bush, 2009, The worries facing Russia's banks, *Wall Street Journal Online*, http://www.wsj.com, April 13.
52. A. Peaple & N. P. Muoi, 2009, Vietnam's market—the fizz is deliberate, *Wall Street Journal Online*, http://www.wsj.com, June 11.
53. R. H. Lester, A. Hillman, A. Zardkoohi, & A. A. Cannella, Jr., 2008, Former government officials as outside directors: The role of human and social capital, *Academy of Management Journal*, 51; 999–1013; C. Oliver & I. Holzinger, 2008, The effectiveness of strategic political management: A dynamic capabilities framework, *Academy of Management Review*, 33: 496–520.
54. *Times of India,* 2010, Government Shouldn't Hound Independent Directors, quoting the views of Mr. Deepak Parikh, Chairman, HDFC, June 18.
55. *Expressindia* story, May 14, 2009. http://www.expressindia.com/story.php?storyId=459282.
56. J. W. Spencer, 2008, The impact of multinational enterprise strategy on indigenous enterprises: Horizontal spillovers and crowding out in developing countries, *Academy of Management Review*, 33: 341–361; W. Chen, 2007, Does the colour of the cat matter? The red hat strategy in China's private enterprises, *Management and Organizational Review*, 3: 55–80.
57. M. Srivastava, 2009, The sudden chill at an Indian hot spot, *BusinessWeek*, May 4, 59.
58. 2009, Taking aim at outsources on US soil, *BusinessWeek*, June 15, 10.
59. "Environment Ministry stalls Vedanta's Niyamgiri project in Orissa", *Economic Times,* 10 August, 2010.
60. H. W. Jenkins, Jr., 2009, GM needs a political strategy, *Wall Street Journal Online*, http://www.wsj.com, June 10.
61. G. L. F. Holburn & R. G. Vanden Bergh, 2008, The effectiveness of strategic political management: A dynamic capabilities framework, *Academy of Management Review*, 33: 521–540; M. A. Hitt, L. Bierman, K. Uhlenbruck, & K. Shimizu, 2006, The importance of resources in the internationalization of professional service firms: The good, the bad, and the ugly, *Academy of Management Journal,* 49: 1137–1157.
62. K. Olsen, 2009, S. Korea, EU call for early conclusion of trade pact, *Houston Chronicle Online*, http://www.chron.com, May 23.
63. L. Manchikanti, 2008, Health care reform in the United States: Radical surgery needed now more than ever, *Pain Physician*, 11: 13–42.
64. S. A. Burd, 2009, How Safeway is cutting health-care costs, *Wall Street Journal Online*, http://www.wsj.com, June 12.
65. E. S. W. Ng, 2008, Why organizations choose to manage diversity: Toward a leadership-based theoretical framework, *Human Resource Development Review*, 7: 58–78.
66. F. Moore & C. Rees, 2008, Culture against cohesion: Global corporate strategy and employee diversity in the UK plant of a German MNC, *Employee Relations*, 30: 176–189; B. L. Kirkman, K. B. Lowe, & C. B. Gibson, 2006, A quarter of a century of culture's consequences: A review of old empirical research incorporating Hofstede's cultural values framework, *Journal of International Business Studies,* 37: 285–320.
67. S. Michailova & K. Hutchings, 2006, National cultural influences on knowledge sharing: A comparison of China and Russia, *Journal of Management Studies,* 43: 384–405.
68. J. B. Knight & L. Yueh, 2008, The role of social capital in the labour market in China, *Economics of Transition*, 16: 389–414; P. J. Buckley, J. Clegg, & H. Tan, 2006, Cultural awareness in knowledge transfer to China—The role of guanxi and mianzi, *Journal of World Business,* 41: 275–288.
69. R. K. Sinha & C. H. Noble, 2008, The adoption of radical manufacturing technologies and firm survival, *Strategic Management Journal*, 29: 943–962.
70. K. H. Tsai & J.-C. Wang, 2008, External technology acquisition and firm perfor-mance: A longitudinal study, *Journal of Business Venturing*, 23: 91–112; D. Lavie, 2006, Capability reconfiguration: An analysis of incumbent responses to technological change, *Academy of Management Review,* 31: 153–174.
71. S. A. Brown, 2008, Household technology adoption, use, and impacts: Past, present, and future, *Information Systems Frontiers*, 10: 397–402.
72. Edna Fernandes, "The Race to Serve a Subcontinent", *Financial Times,* June 20, 2002, p.13.
73. W. S. Mossberg, 2009, The latest Kindle: Bigger, not better, than its sibling, *Wall Street Journal Online*, http://www.wsj.com, June 11.
74. 2010, www.makemytrip.com, SEC filings on August 12.

75. L. F. Mesquita & S. G. Lazzarini, 2008, Horizontal and vertical relationships in developing economies: Implications for SMEs' access to global markets, *Academy of Management Journal*, 51: 359–380; W. P. Wan, 2005, Country resource environments, firm capabilities, and corporate diversification strategies, *Journal of Management Studies,* 42: 161–182.
76. J. R. Healey, 2009, Penske-Saturn deal could change how cars are sold, *USA Today*, June 8, B2.
77. D. Welch, 2009, A hundred factories too many, *BusinessWeek*, January 12, 42–43.
78. 2009, McDonald's Corp, *Standard & Poor's Stock Report*, http://www.standardandpoors.com, May 16.
79. G. Marcial, 2009, Heinz: The time may be ripe, *BusinessWeek*, May 11, 67.
80. 2009, Procter & Gamble Co, *Standard & Poor's Stock Report*, http://www.standardandpoors.com, May 16.
81. Karvey Analyst Reports, Annual Reports 2005 of TCS, Infosys, Wipro & Cognizant.
82. K. E. Meyer, 2009, Uncommon common sense, *Business Strategy Review*, 20: 38–43; K. E. Meyer, 2006, Globalfocusing: From domestic conglomerates to global specialists, *Journal of Management Studies,* 43: 1110–1144.
83. C. H. Oh & A. M. Rugman, 2007, Regional multinationals and the Korean cosmetics industry, *Asia Pacific Journal of Management,* 24: 27–42.
84. P. K. Ong & Y. Kathawala, 2009, Competitive advantage through good Guanxi in the marine industry, *International Journal of Chinese Culture and Management*, 2: 28–55; X.-P. Chen & S. Peng, 2008, Guanxi dynamics: Shifts in the closeness of ties between Chinese coworkers, *Management and Organizational Review*, 4: 63–80; M. A. Hitt, M. T. Dacin, B. B. Tyler, & D. Park, 1997, Understanding the differences in Korean and US executives' strategic orientations, *Strategic Management Journal,* 18: 159–167.
85. M. A. Hitt, D. Ahlstrom, M. T. Dacin, E. Levitas, & L. Svobodina, 2004, The institutional effects on strategic alliance partner selection: China versus Russia, *Organization Science,* 15: 173–185.
86. L. Berchicci & A. King, 2008, Postcards from the edge: A review of the business and environment literature, in J. P. Walsh & A. P. Brief (eds.) *Academy of Management Annals,* New York: Lawrence Erlbaum Associates, 513–547.
87. M. J. Hutchins & J. W. Sutherland, 2008, An exploration of measures of social sustainability and their application to supply chain decisions, *Journal of Cleaner Production*, 16: 1688–1698.
88. P. K. Dutta & R. Radner, 2009, A strategic analysis of global warming: Theory and some numbers, *Journal of Economic Behavior & Organization*, in press.
89. H. Liming, E. Haque, & S. Barg, 2008, Public policy discourse, planning and measure toward sustainable energy strategies in Canada, *Renewable and Sustainable Energy Reviews*, 12: 91–115.
90. http://pepsicoindia.co.in/CSR/replenishingwater.aspx.
91. http://pepsicoindia.co.in/CSR/CorporateSocialResponsibility/wastetowealth.aspx.
92. C. A. Bartlett & S. Ghoshal, 2003, What is a global manager? *Harvard Business Review,* 81(8): 101–108; M. A. Carpenter & J. W. Fredrickson, 2001, Top management teams, global strategic posture and the moderating role of uncertainty, *Academy of Management Journal,* 44: 533–545.
93. J. Galbreath & P. Galvin, 2008, Firm factors, industry structure and performance variation: New empirical evidence to a classic debate, *Journal of Business Research*, 61: 109–117; B. R. Koka & J. E. Prescott, 2008, Designing alliance networks: The influence of network position, environmental change, and strategy on firm performance, *Strategic Management Journal*, 29: 639–661.
94. V. F. Misangyl, H. Elms, T. Greckhamer, & J. A. Lepine, 2006, A new perspective on a fundamental debate: A multilevel approach to industry, corporate, and business unit effects, *Strategic Management Journal,* 27: 571–590; G. Hawawini, V. Subramanian, & P. Verdin, 2003, Is performance driven by industry or firm-specific factors? A new look at the evidence, *Strategic Management Journal,* 24: 1–16.
95. D. Bonnet & G. S. Yip, 2009, Strategy convergence, *Business Strategy Review*, 20: 50–55; E. Nelson, R. van den Dam, & H. Kline, 2008, A future in content(ion): Can telecom providers win a share of the digital content market? *Journal of Telecommunications Management*, 1: 125–138.
96. K. E. Kushida & J. Zysman, 2009, The services transformation and network policy: The new logic of value creation, *Review of Policy Research*, 26: 173–194; E. D. Jaffe, I. D. Nebenzahl, & I. Schorr, 2005, Strategic options of home country firms faced with MNC entry, *Long Range Planning,* 38: 183–196.
97. M. R. Peneder, 2008, Firm entry and turnover: The nexus with profitability and growth, *Small Business Economics*, 30: 327–344; A. V. Mainkar, M. Lubatkin, & W. S. Schulze, 2006, Toward a product-proliferation theory of entry barriers, *Academy of Management Review,* 31: 1062–1075; J. Shamsie, 2003, The context of dominance: An industry-driven framework for exploiting reputation, *Strategic Management Journal,* 24: 199–215.
98. S. Hamm, 2009, Oracle faces its toughest deal yet, *BusinessWeek*, May 4, 24.
99. S. K. Ethiraj & D. H. Zhu, 2008, Performance effects of imitative entry, *Strategic Management Journal*, 29: 797–817; R. Makadok, 1999, Interfirm differences in scale economies and the evolution of market shares, *Strategic Management Journal,* 20: 935–952.
100. Case "R R Donnelley & Sons", Boston, MA.: Harvard Business School, Case # 9-396-154.
101. M. J. Rungtusanatham & F. Salvador, 2008, From mass production to mass customization: Hindrance factors, structural inertia, and transition hazard, *Production and Operations Management*, 17: 385–396; F. Salvador & C. Forza, 2007, Principles for efficient and effective sales configuration design, *International Journal of Mass Customisation,* 2(1,2): 114–127.
102. F. Keenan, S. Holmes, J. Greene, & R. O. Crockett, 2002, A mass market of one, *BusinessWeek,* December 2, 68–72.

103. D. Kiley, 2009, Ford heads out on a road of its own, *BusinessWeek*, January 19, 47–49.

104. E. Byron, 2009, P&G, Colgate hit by consumer thrift, *Wall Street Journal Online, http*://www.wsj.com, May 1.

105. M. A. Hitt, R. M. Holmes, T. Miller, &M. P. Salmador, 2006, Modeling country institutional profiles: The dimensions and dynamics of institutional environments, presented at the Strategic Management Society Conference, October.

106. P. Kiviniem, 2009, Intel to get EU antitrust fine, *Wall Street Journal Online*, http://www.wsj.com, May 14.

107. C. Forelle & D. Clark, 2009, Intel fine jolts tech sector, *Wall Street Journal Online*, http://www.wsj.com, May 14.

108. *Economic Times*, 2010, Ohio Bans Offshoring of IT Projects by Govt Depts., September 8.

109. Kotler, Keller, Koshy & Jha, 2009, *Marketing Management*, Delhi: Pearson, pps.5,211.

110. Richard Reeves & John Knell, 2009, *The 80 Minute MBA*, London: Headline Publishing Group, pp.113-115.

111. D. G. Sirmon, S. Gove, & M. H. Hitt, 2008, Resource management in dyadic competitive rivalry: The effects of resource bundling and deployment, *Academy of Management Journal*, 51: 919–935.

112. S. Nadkarni & V. K. Narayanan, 2007, Strategic schemas, strategic flexibility, and firm performance: The moderating role of industry clockspeed, *Strategic Management Journal,* 28: 243–270.

113. P. Prada & M. Esterl, 2009, Airlines predict more trouble, broaden cuts, *Wall Street Journal Online*, http://www.wsj.com, June 12.

114. S. E. Feinberg & A. K. Gupta, 2009, MNC subsidiaries and country risk: Internalization as a safeguard against weak external institutions, *Academy of Management Journal*, 52: 381–399.

115. M. E. Porter, 1980, *Competitive Strategy,* New York: Free Press.

116. B. Kabanoff & S. Brown, 2008, Knowledge structures of prospectors, analyzers, and defenders: Content, structure, stability, and performance, *Strategic Management Journal*, 29: 149–171; M. S. Hunt, 1972, Competition in the major home appliance industry, 1960–1970 (doctoral dissertation, Harvard University); Porter, *Competitive Strategy,* 129.

117. G. McNamara, D. L. Deephouse, & R. A. Luce, 2003, Competitive positioning within and across a strategic group structure: The performance of core, secondary, and solitary firms, *Strategic Management Journal,* 24: 161–181.

118. F. Zen & C. Baldan, 2008, The strategic paths and performance of Italian mutual banks: A nonparametric analysis, *International Journal of Banking, Accounting and Finance*, 1: 189–214; M. W. Peng, J. Tan, & T. W. Tong, 2004, Ownership types and strategic groups in an emerging economy, *Journal of Management Studies,* 41: 1105–1129.

119. W. S. DeSarbo & R. Grewal, 2008. Hybrid strategic groups, *Strategic Management Journal*, 29: 293–317; M. Peteraf & M. Shanley, 1997, Getting to know you: A theory of strategic group identity, *Strategic Management Journal,* 18(Special Issue): 165–186.

120. J. Lee, K. Lee, & S. Rho, 2002, An evolutionary perspective on strategic group emergence: A genetic algorithm-based model, *Strategic Management Journal,* 23: 727–746.

121. J. A. Zuniga-Vicente, J. M. de la Fuente Sabate, & I. S. Gonzalez, 2004, Dynamics of the strategic group membership-performance linkage in rapidly changing environments, *Journal of Business Research,* 57: 1378–1390.

122. T. Yu, M. Subramaniam, & A. A. Cannella, Jr., 2009, Rivalry deterrence in international markets: Contingencies governing the mutual forbearance hypothesis, *Academy of Management Journal*, 52: 127–147.

123. Porter, *Competitive Strategy,* 49.

124. L. Capron & O. Chatain, 2008, Competitors' resource-oriented strategies: Acting on competitors' resources through interventions in factor markets and political markets, *Academy of Management Review*, 33: 97–121; M. B. Lieberman & S. Asaba, 2006, Why do firms imitate each other? *Academy of Management Journal,* 31: 366–385.

125. D. B. Montgomery, M. C. Moore, & J. E. Urbany, 2005, Reasoning about competitive reactions: Evidence from executives, *Marketing Science,* 24: 138–149.

126. S. Jain, 2008, Digital piracy: A competitive analysis, *Marketing Science*, 27: 610–626.

127. J. G. York, 2009, Pragmatic sustainability: Translating environmental ethics into competitive advantage, *Journal of Business Ethics*, 85: 97–109.

128. K. A. Sawka, 2008, The ethics of competitive intelligence, *Kiplinger Business Resource Center Online*, http://www.kiplinger.com, March.

129. T. Mazzarol & S. Reboud, 2008, The role of complementary actors in the development of innovation in small firms, *International Journal of Innovation Management*, 12: 223–253; A. Brandenburger & B. Nalebuff, 1996, *Co-opetition,* New York: Currency Doubleday.

130. 2009, Continental to join Star alliance, *Continental Airlines Homepage*, http://www.continental.com, June 12.

131. Infosys Technologies, the Mission Statement as given in the company's Web site, http://www.infosys.com/about/who-we-are/Pages/index.aspx.

132. C. S. Fleisher & S. Wright, 2009, Examining differences in competitive intelligence practice: China, Japan, and the West, *Thunderbird International Business Review*, 51: 249–261; A. Crane, 2005, In the company of spies: When competitive intelligence gathering becomes industrial espionage, *Business Horizons*, 48(3): 233–240.

CHAPTER 3

1. M. E. Mangelsdorf, 2007, Beyond enterprise 2.0, *MIT Sloan Management Review,* 48(3): 50–55.

2. J. G. Covin & M. P. Miles, 2007, Strategic use of corporate venturing, *Entrepreneurship Theory and Practice*, 31: 183–207; R. R. Wiggins & T. W. Ruefli, 2002, Sustained competitive advantage: Temporal dynamics and the incidence of per-

sistence of superior economic performance, *Organization Science*, 13: 82–105.

3. W. M. Becker & V. M. Freeman, 2006, Going from global trends to corporate strategy, *McKinsey Quarterly*, Number 3:17–27; S. K. McEvily, K. M. Eisenhardt, & J. E. Prescott, 2004, The global acquisition, leverage, and protection of technological competencies, *Strategic Management Journal*, 25: 713–722.
4. J. Schenck & N. Wingfield, 2008, How Apple could survive without Steve Jobs, *Wall Street Journal*, http://www.wsj.com, December 8.
5. R. T. Crook, D. J. Ketchen, J. G. Combs, & S. Y. Todd, 2008, Strategic resources and performance: A meta-analysis, *Strategic Management Journal*, 29: 1141–1154; N. T. Sheehan & N. J. Foss, 2007, Enhancing the prescriptiveness of the resource-based view through Porterian activity analysis, *Management Decision*, 45: 450-461; S. Dutta, M. J. Zbaracki, & M. Bergen, 2003, Pricing process as a capability: A resource-based perspective, *Strategic Management Journal*, 24: 615–630.
6. C. G. Brush, P. G. Greene, & M. M. Hart, 2001, From initial idea to unique advantage: The entrepreneurial challenge of constructing a resource base, *Academy of Management Executive*, 15(1): 64–78.
7. L. Priem, 2007, A consumer perspective on value creation, *Academy of Management Review*, 32: 219–235.
8. D. G. Sirmon, M. A. Hitt, & R. D. Ireland, 2007, Managing firm resources in dynamic markets to create value: Looking inside the black box, *Academy of Management Review*, 32: 273–292.
9. A. Leiponen, 2008, Control of intellectual assets in client relationships: Implications for innovation, *Strategic Management Journal*, 29: 1371–1394; S. C. Kang, S. S. Morris, & S. A. Snell, 2007, Relational archetypes, organizational learning, and value creation: Extending the human resource architecture, *Academy of Management Review*, 32: 236–256.
10. S. Raisch & G. von Krog, 2007, Navigating a path to smart growth, MIT *Sloan Management Review*, 48(3): 65–72.
11. D. DePass, 2006, Cuts in incentives upset 3M supervisors, *Star Tribune*, December 16.
12. C. D. Zatzick & R. D. Iverson, 2007, High-involvement management and work force reduction: Competitive advantage or disadvantage? *Academy of Management Journal*, 49: 999–1015.
13. R. Florida, 2005, *The Flight of the Creative Class*, New York: HarperBusiness.
14. A. W. King, 2007, Disentangling interfirm and intrafirm causal ambiguity: A conceptual model of causal ambiguity and sustainable competitive advantage, *Academy of Management Review*, 32: 156–178; J. Shamsie, 2003, The context of dominance: An industry-driven framework for exploiting reputation, *Strategic Management Journal*, 24: 199–215.
15. U. Ljungquist, 2007, Core competency beyond identification: Presentation of a model, *Management Decision*, 45: 393–402; M. Makhija, 2003, Comparing the resource-based and market-based view of the firm: Empirical evidence from Czech privatization, *Strategic Management Journal*, 24: 433–451.
16. R. D. Ireland & J. W. Webb, 2007, Strategic entrepreneurship: Creating competitive advantage through streams of innovation, *Business Horizons*, 50: 49–59.
17. M. A. Peteraf & J. B. Barney, 2003, Unraveling the resource-based tangle, *Managerial and Decision Economics*, 24: 309–323; J. B. Barney, 2001, Is the resource-based "view" a useful perspective for strategic management research? Yes, *Academy of Management Review*, 26: 41–56.
18. D. P. Lepak, K. G. Smith, & M. Susan Taylor, 2007, Value creation and value capture: A multilevel perspective, *Academy of Management Review*, 32: 180–194.
19. T. Papot, 2009, Slovakia's headache as carsales fall, Radio Netherlands Worldwide,http://www.radionetherlands.nl, March 5; Z. Vilikovska, 2008, Slovak factories manufactured around 770,000 cars in 2008, *Flash News*, http://www.spector.sk; G. Katz. 2007, Assembling a future, *Houston Chronicle*, July 5, D1, D4.
20. M. Javidan, R. M. Steers, & M. A. Hitt (eds.), 2007, *The Global Mindset*, Amsterdam: Elsevier Ltd; T. M. Begley & D. P. Boyd, 2003, The need for a corporate global mindset, *MIT Sloan Management Review*, 44(2): 25–32.
21. L. Gratton, 2007, Handling hot spots, *Business Strategy Review*, 18(2): 9–14.
22. O. Levy, S. Beechler, S. Taylor, & N. A. Boyacigiller, 2007, What we talk about when we talk about "global mindset": Managerial cognition in multinational corporations, *Journal of International Business Studies*, 38: 231–258.
23. Sirmon, Hitt, & Ireland, Managing resources in a dynamic environment.
24. E. Danneels, 2008, Organizational antecedents of second-order competences, *Strategic Management Journal*, 29: 519–543; Barney, Is the resource-based "view" a useful perspective for strategic management research? Yes.
25. S. Kaplan, 2008, Cognition, capabilities, and incentives: Assessing firm response to the fiber-optic revolution, *Academy of Management Journal*, 51: 672–695; K. J. Mayer & R. M. Salomon, 2006, Capabilities, contractual hazards, and governance: Integrating resource-based and transaction cost perspectives, *Academy of Management Journal*, 49: 942–959.
26. S. K. McEvily & B. Chakravarthy, 2002, The persistence of knowledge-based advantage: An empirical test for product performance and technological knowledge, *Strategic Management Journal*, 23: 285–305.
27. D. Kaplan, 2007, A new look for Luby's, *Houston Chronicle*, July 4, D1, D5.
28. J. Barthelemy, 2008, Opportunism, knowledge, and the performance of franchise chains, *Strategic Management Journal*, 29: 1451–1463; J. L. Morrow, Jr., D. G. Sirmon, M. A. Hitt, & T. R. Holcomb, 2007, Creating value in the face of declining performance: Firm strategies and organizational recovery, *Strategic Management Journal*, 28: 271–283.
29. D. G. Sirmon, S. Gove, & M. A. Hitt, 2008, Resource management in dyadic competitive rivalry: The effects of resource

bundling and deployment, *Academy of Management Journal*, 51: 919–935; E. Danneels, 2007, The process of technological competence leveraging, *Strategic Management Journal*, 28: 511–533.

30. Putting co-creation to work for you: Build more value by co-creating with your customers, 2009, Internetviz, http://www.intemetviz-newsletters.com. J.J. Neff, 2007, What drives consumers not to buy cars, *BusinessWeek*, July 9, 16.
31. K. Chaharbaghi, 2007, The problematic of strategy: A way of seeing is also a way of not seeing, *Management Decision*, 45: 327–339.
32. V. Shankar & B. L. Bayus, 2003, Network effects and competition: An empirical analysis of the home video game industry, *Strategic Management Journal*, 24: 375–384.
33. Morrow, Sirmon, Hitt, & Holcomb, Creating value in the face of declining performance; G. Hawawini, V. Subramanian, & P. Verdin, 2003, Is performance driven by industry- or firm-specific factors? A new look at the evidence, *Strategic Management Journal*, 24: 1–16.
34. J. Woiceshyn & L. Falkenberg, 2008, Value creation in knowledge-based firms: Aligning problems and resources, *Academy of Management Perspectives,* 22 (2): 85–99; M. R. Haas & M. T. Hansen, 2005, When using knowledge can hurt performance: The value of organizational capabilities in a management consulting company, *Strategic Management Journal*, 26: 1–24.
35. C. M. Christensen, 2001, The past and future of competitive advantage, *Sloan Management Review*, 42(2): 105–109.
36. O. Gottschalg & M. Zollo, 2007, Interest alignment and competitive advantage, *Academy of Management Review*. 32: 418–437.
37. D. P. Forbes, 2007, Reconsidering the strategic implications of decision comprehensiveness, *Academy of Management Review*, 32: 361–376; J. R. Hough & M. A. White, 2003, Environmental dynamism and strategic decision-making rationality: An examination at the decision level, *Strategic Management Journal*, 24: 481–489.
38. T. M. Jones, W. Felps, & G. A. Bigley, 2007, Ethical theory and stakeholder-related decisions: The role of stakeholder culture, *Academy of Management Review*, 32: 137–155; D. C. Kayes, D. Stirling, & T. M. Nielsen, 2007, Building organizational integrity, *Business Horizons*, 50: 61–70.
39. Y. Deutsch, T. Keil, & T. Laamanen, 2007, Decision making in acquisitions: The effect of outside directors' compensation on acquisition patterns, *Journal of Management*, 33: 30–56.
40. M. De Rond & R. A. Thietart, 2007, Choice, chance, and inevitability in strategy, *Strategic Management Journal*, 28: 535–551.
41. A. Phene & P. Almieda, 2008, Innovation in multinational subsidiaries: The role of knowledge assimilation and subsidiary capabilities, *Journal of International Business Studies,* 39: 901–919; C. C. Miller & R. D. Ireland, 2005, Intuition in strategic decision making: Friend or foe in the fast-paced 21st century? *Academy of Management Executive*, 19(1): 19–30.
42. L. M. Lodish & C. F. Mela, 2007, If brands are built over years, why are they managed over quarters? *Harvard Business Review*, 85(7/8): 104–112; H. J. Smith, 2003, The shareholders vs. stakeholders debate, *MIT Sloan Management Review*, 44(4): 85–90.
43. P. C. Nutt, 2002. *Why Decisions Fail*, San Francisco: Berrett-Koehler Publishers.
44. R. Martin, 2007. How successful leaders think, *Harvard Business Review*, 85(6): 61–67.
45. Polaroid Corporation, 2007, *Wikipedia*, http://en.wikipedia.org/wiki/Polaroid_Corporation, July 5.
46. J. M. Mezias & W. H. Starbuck, 2003, What do managers know, anyway? *Harvard Business Review,* 81 (5): 16–17.
47. I. Mitroff, 2008, Knowing: How we know is as important as what we know, *Journal of Business Strategy,* 29 (3): 13–22; P. G. Audia, E. Locke, & K. G. Smith, 2000, The paradox of success: An archival and a laboratory study of strategic persistence following radical environmental change, *Academy of Management Journal*, 43: 837–853.
48. C. O. Longenecker, M. J. Neubert, & L. S. Fink, 2007, Causes and consequences of managerial failure in rapidly changing organizations, *Business Horizons*, 50:145–155; G. P. West III & J. DeCastro, 2001, The Achilles' heel of firm strategy: Resource weaknesses and distinctive inadequacies, *Journal of Management Studies*, 38: 417–442; G. Gavetti & D. Levinthal, 2000, Looking forward and looking backward: Cognitive and experimental search, *Administrative Science Quarterly*, 45: 113–137.
49. R. Arnit & P. J. H. Schoemaker, 1993, Strategic assets and organizational rent, *Strategic Management Journal*, 14: 33–46.
50. S. J. Carson, A. Madhok, & T. Wu, 2006, Uncertainty, opportunism, and governance: The effects of volatility and ambiguity on formal and relational contracting, *Academy of Management Journal*. 49: 1058–1077; R. E. Hoskisson & L. W. Busenitz, 2001, Market uncertainty and learning distance in corporate entrepreneurship entry mode choice, in M. A. Hitt, R. D. Ireland, S. M. Camp, & D. L. Sexton (eds.), *Strategic Entrepreneurship: Creating a New Integrated Mindset*, Oxford, UK: Blackwell Publishers, 151–172.
51. C. M. Fiol & E. J. O'Connor, 2003, Waking up! Mindfulness in the face of bandwagons, *Academy of Management Review,* 28: 54–70.
52. http://pepsicoindia.co.in/CSR/replenishingwater.aspx.
53. P. Davidson, Coal king Peabody cleans up, *USA Today,* http://www.usatoday.com, August 18; J. Pasternak, 2008, Global warming has a new battleground: Coal plants, *Chicago Tribune,* http://www.chicagotribune.com, April 14.
54. G. P. West, III, 2007, Collective cognition: When entrepreneurial teams, not individuals, make decisions, *Entrepreneurship Theory and Practice*, 31: 77–102.
55. N. J. Hiller & D. C. Hambrick, 2005, Conceptualizing executive hubris: The role of (hyper-) core self-evaluations in strategic decision making, *Strategic Management Journal*, 26: 297–319.

56. C. Stadler, 2007, The four principles of enduring success, *Harvard Business Review*, 85(7/8): 62–72.
57. Mayer & Salomon, Capabilities, contractual hazards, and governance; D. M. De Carolis, 2003, Competencies and imitability in the pharmaceutical industry: An analysis of their relationship with firm performance, *Journal of Management*, 29: 27–50.
58. R. H. Lester, A. Hillman, A. Zardkoohi, & A. A. Cannella, 2008, Former government officials as outside directors: The role of human and social capital, *Academy of Management Journal*, 51: 999–1013; G. Ahuja & R. Katila, 2004, Where do resources come from? The role of idiosyncratic situations, *Strategic Management Journal*, 25: 887–907.
59. K. Meyer, S. Estrin, S. K. Bhaumik, & M. W. Peng, 2009, Institutions, resources, and entry strategies in emerging economies, *Strategic Management Journal*, 30: 61–80; J. McGee & H. Thomas, 2007, Knowledge as a lens on the jigsaw puzzle of strategy, *Management Decision*, 45: 539–563.
60. Sirmon, Hitt, & Ireland, Managing firm resources in dynamic environments; S. Berman, J. Down, & C. Hill, 2002, Tacit knowledge as a source of competitive advantage in the National Basketball Association, *Academy of Management Journal*, 45: 13–31.
61. 2007, Borders teamed with Amazon.com, http://www.amazon.com, July 7.
62. K. G. Smith, C. J. Collins, & K. D. Clark, 2005, Existing knowledge, knowledge creation capability, and the rate of new product introduction in high-technology firms, *Academy of Management Journal*, 48: 346–357; S. G. Winter, 2005, Developing evolutionary theory for economics and management, in K. G. Smith and M. A. Hitt (eds.), *Great Minds in Management: The Process of Theory Development*, Oxford, UK: Oxford University Press, 509–546.
63. J. A. Dubin, 2007, Valuing intangible assets with a nested logit market share model, *Journal of Econometrics*, 139: 285–302.
64. A. M. Webber, 2000, New math for a new economy, *Fast Company*, January/February, 214–224.
65. F. T. Rothaermel & W. Boeker, 2008, Old technology meets new technology: Complementarities, similarities, and alliance formation, *Strategic Management Journal*, 29: 47–77; M. Song, C. Droge, S. Hanvanich, & R. Calantone, 2005, Marketing and technology resource complementarity: An analysis of their interaction effect in two environmental contexts, *Strategic Management Journal*, 26: 259–276.
66. M. A. Hitt & R. D. Ireland, 2002, The essence of strategic leadership: Managing human and social capital, *Journal of Leadership and Organization Studies*, 9(1): 3–14.
67. J. B. Quinn, P. Anderson, & S. Finkelstein, 1996, Making the most of the best, *Harvard Business Review*, 74(2): 71–80.
68. N. Stieglitz & K. Heine, 2007, Innovations and the role of complementarities in a strategic theory of the firm, *Strategic Management Journal*, 28: 1–15.
69. S. A. Fernhaber, B. A. Gilbert, & P. P. McDougal, 2008, International entrepreneurship and geographic location: An empirical examination of new venture internationalization, *Journal of International Business Studies*, 39: 267–290; R. D. Ireland, M. A. Hitt, & D. Vaidyanath, 2002, Managing strategic alliances to achieve a competitive advantage, *Journal of Management*, 28: 416–446.
70. E. Fischer & R. Reuber, 2007, The good, the bad, and the unfamiliar: The challenges of reputation formation facing new firms, *Entrepreneurship Theory and Practice*, 31: 53–75.
71. D. L. Deephouse, 2000. Media reputation as a strategic resource: An integration of mass communication and resource-based theories, *Journal of Management*, 26: 1091–1112.
72. P. Engardio & M. Arndt, 2007, What price reputation? *BusinessWeek*, July 9, 70–79.
73. P. Berthon, M. B. Holbrook, & J. M. Hulbert, 2003, Understanding and managing the brand space, *MIT Sloan Management Review*, 44(2): 49–54; D. B. Holt, 2003, What becomes an icon most? *Harvard Business Review*, 81(3): 43–49.
74. J. Song & J. Shin, 2008, The paradox of technological capabilities: A study of knowledge sourcing from host countries of overseas R&D operations, *Journal of International Business Studies*, 39: 291–303; J. Blasberg & V. Vishwanath, 2003, Making cool brands hot, *Harvard Business Review*, 81(6): 20–22.
75. 2007, Harley-Davidson Motor Clothes Merchandise, July 7, http://www.harley-davidson.com.
76. "House of Tata, 1995: The Next Generation", 1998, # 9-798-037, Harvard Business School.
77. S. Kalepu, 2009, Ford names Sunil Shetty as its brand ambassador, *CaretradeIndia*, http://www.cartradeindia.com, January 22.
78. T. Isobe, S. Makino, & D. B. Montgomery, 2008, Technological capabilities and firm performance: The case of small manufacturing firms in Japan, *Asia Pacific Journal of Management*, 25: 413–425; S. Dutta, O. Narasimhan, & S. Rajiv, 2005, Conceptualizing and measuring capabilities: Methodology and empirical application, *Strategic Management Journal*, 26: 277–285.
79. M. Kroll, B. A. Walters, & P. Wright, 2008, Board vigilance, director experience and corporate outcomes, *Strategic Management Journal*, 29: 363–282; J. Bitar & T. Hafsi, 2007, Strategizing through the capability lens: Sources and outcomes of integration, *Management Decision*, 45: 403–419.
80. S. K. Ethiraj, P. Kale, M. S. Krishnan, & J. V. Singh, 2005, Where do capabilities come from and do they matter? A study in the software services industry, *Strategic Management Journal*, 26: 25–45; M. G. Jacobides & S. G. Winter, 2005, The co-evolution of capabilities and transaction costs: Explaining the institutional structure of production, *Strategic Management Journal*, 26: 395–413.
81. T. A. Stewart & A. P. Raman, 2007, Lessons from Toyota's long drive, *Harvard Business Review*, 85(7/8): 74–83.
82. Y. Uu, J. G. Combs, D. J. Ketchen, Jr., & R. D. Ireland, 2007, The value of human resource management for organizational performance, *Business Horizons*, 50: 503–511.
83. B. Connelly, M. A. Hitt, A. S. DeNisi, & R. D. Ireland, 2007, Expatriates and corporate-level international strategy:

Governing with the knowledge contract, *Management Decision*, 45: 564–581.

84. M. J. Tippins & R. S. Sohi, 2003, IT competency and firm performance: Is organizational learning a missing link? *Strategic Management Journal*, 24: 745–761.
85. M. B. Neeley & R. Jacobson, 2008, The recency of technological inputs and financial performance, *Strategic Management Journal*, 29: 723–744.
86. Meyer, Estrin, Bhaumik, & Peng, Institutions, resources, and entry strategies in emerging markets; C. Zott, 2003, Dynamic capabilities and the emergence of intraindustry differential firm performance: Insights from a simulation study, *Strategic Management Journal*, 24:97–125.
87. H. R. Greve, 2009, Bigger and safer: The diffusion of competitive advantage, *Strategic Management Journal*, 30: 1–23; C. K. Prahalad & G. Hamel, 1990, The core competence of the corporation, *Harvard Business Review*, 68(3): 79–93.
88. D. Bidleman, 2009, Xerox innovation shines through industry recognition, *YAHOO!Finance,* http://finance.yahoo.com, January 26.
89. D. K. Taft, 2009, Microsoft, Xerox invest in innovation, *eWeek,* http://www.eweek.com, March 5; 2006, Xerox Annual Report, December, http://www.xerox.com.
90. S. Newbert, 2008, Value, rareness, competitive advantage, and performance: A conceptual-level empirical investigation of the resource-based view of the firm, *Strategic Management Journal*, 29: 745–768.
91. D. Seidman, 2008, Out-greening delivers sustainable competitive advantage, *BusinessWeek,* http://www.businessweek.com, December 5.
92. S. A. Zahra, 2008, The virtuous cycle of discovery and creation of entrepreneurial opportunities, *Strategic Entrepreneurship Journal*, 2: 243–257; J. B. Barney, 1995, Looking inside for competitive advantage, *Academy of Management Executive*, 9(4): 49–60.
93. G. Pacheco-de-Almeida, J. E. Henderson, & K. O. Cool, 2008, Resolving the commit-ment versus flexibility trade-off: The role of resource accumulation lags, *Academy of Management Journal,* 51: 517–536.
94. J. B. Barney, 1991, Firm resources and sustained competitive advantage, *Journal of Management*, 17: 99–120.
95. L. E. Tetrick & N. Da Silva, 2003, Assessing the culture and climate for organizational learning, in S. E. Jackson, M. A. Hitt, & A. S. DeNisi (eds.), *Managing Knowledge for Sustained Competitive Advantage*, San Francisco: Jossey-Bass, 333–359.
96. "The Park, Calcutta", 2001, Case # BP 267, Indian Institute of Management, Ahmedabad.
97. "Aravind Eye Care System: Giving the Most Precious Gift", 2003, Case # BP 299, Indian Institute of Management, Ahmedabad.
98. A. W. King & C. P. Zeithaml, 2001, Competencies and firm performance: Examining the causal ambiguity paradox, *Strategic Management Journal*, 22: 75–99.
99. Barney, Firm resources, 111.
100. A. K. Chatterjee, 2009, Spawned with a silver spoon? Entrepreneurial performance and innovation in the medical device industry, *Strategic Management Journal*, 30: 185–206; S. K. McEvily, S. Das, & K. McCabe, 2000, Avoiding competence substitution through knowledge sharing, *Academy of Management Review*, 25: 294–311.
101. D. J. Ketchen, Jr., & G. T. M. Hult, 2007, Bridging organization theory and supply chain management: The case of best value supply chains, *Journal of Operations Management*, 25: 573–580.
102. M. E. Porter, 1985, *Competitive Advantage*, New York: Free Press, 33–61.
103. J. Alcacer, 2006, Location choices across the value chain: How activity and capability influence co-location, *Management Science*, 52: 1457–1471.
104. H. U. Lee & J.-H. Park, 2008, The influence of top management team international exposure on international alliance formation, *Journal of Management Studies,* 45: 961–981; 2007, Riding the global value chain, *Chief Executive Online*, January/February, http://www.chiefexecutive.net.
105. R. Locke & M. Romis, 2007, Global supply chain, *MIT Sloan Management Review*, 48(2): 54–62.
106. R. Amit & C. Zott, 2001, Value creation in e-business, *Strategic Management Journal*, 22 (Special Issue): 493–520; M. E. Porter, 2001, Strategy and the Internet, *Harvard Business Review*, 79(3): 62–78.
107. C. L. Luk, O. H. M. Yau, L. Y. M. Sin, A. C. B. Tse, R. P. M. Chow, & J.S. Y. Lee, 2008, The effects of social capital and organizational innovativeness in different institutional contexts, *Journal of International Business Studies,* 39: 589–612.
108. L .F. Mesquita, J. Anand, & T. H. Brush, 2008, Comparing the resource-based and relational views: Knowledge transfer and spillover in vertical alliances, *Strategic Management Journal*, 29: 913–941; A. Azadegan, K. J. Dooley, P. L. Carter, & J .R. Carter, 2008, Supplier innovativeness and the role of interorganizational learning in enhancing manufacturer capabilities, *Journal of Supply Chain Management,* 44(4): 14–35.
109. A. A. Lado, R. R. Dant, & A. G. Tekleab, 2008, Trust-opportunism paradox, relationalism, and performance in interfirm relationships: Evidence from the retail industry, *Strategic Management Journal*, 29: 401–423; S. N. Wasti & S. A. Wasti, 2008, Trust in buyer-supplier relations: The case of the Turkish automotive industry, *Journal of International Business Studies,* 39:118–131.
110. D. Faems, M. Janssens, A. Madhok, & B. Van Looy, 2008, Toward an integrative perspective on alliance governance: Connecting contract design, trust dynamics and contract application, *Academy of Management Journal,* 51:1053–1078.
111. M. J. Power, K. C. DeSouze, & C. Bonifazi, 2006, *The Outsourcing Handbook: How to Implement a Successful Outsourcing Process*, Philadelphia: Kogan Page.
112. P. W. Tam, 2007, Business technology: Outsourcing finds new niche, *Wall Street Journal*, April 17, B5.
113. S. Nambisan & M. Sawhney, 2007, A buyer's guide to the innovation bazaar, *Harvard Business Review*, 85(6): 109–118.
114. Y. Shi, 2007, Today's solution and tomorrow's problem: The business process outsourcing risk management puzzle, *California Management Review*, 49(3): 27–44.

115. C. C. De Fontenay & J. S. Gans, 2008, A bargaining perspective on strategic outsourcing and supply competition, *Strategic Management Journal*, 29: 819–839; A. Tiwana & M. Keil, 2007, Does peripheral knowledge complement control? An empirical test in technology outsourcing alliances, *Strategic Management Journal*, 28: 623–634.
116. A. Tiwana, 2008, Does interfirm modularity complement ignorance? A field study of software outsourcing alliances, *Strategic Management Journal*, 29: 1241–1252; J. C. Linder, S. Jarvenpaa, & T. H. Davenport, 2003, Toward an innovation sourcing strategy, *MIT Sloan Management Review*, 44(41): 43–49.
117. S. Lohr, 2007, At IBM, a smarter way to outsource, *New York Times Online*, July 5, http://nytimes.com.
118. C. Horng & W. Chen, 2008, From contract manufacturing to own brand management: The role of learning and cultural heritage identity, *Management and Organization Review,* 4: 109–133; M. Useem & J. Harder, 2000, Leading laterally in company outsourcing, *Sloan Management Review*, 41(2): 25–36.
119. R. C. Insinga & M. J. Werle, 2000, Linking outsourcing to business strategy, *Academy of Management Executive*, 14(41): 58–70.
120. B. Arrunada & X. H. Vazquez, 2006, When your contract manufacturer becomes your competitor, *Harvard Business Review*, 84(9): 135–144.
121. C. S. Katsikeas, D. Skarmeas, & D. C. Bello, 2009, Developing successful trust-based international exchange relationships, *Journal of International Business Studies,* 40: 132–155; E. Perez & J. Karp, 2007, U.S. to probe outsourcing after ITT case, *Wall Street Journal* (Eastern Edition), March 28, A3, A6.
122. C. Weigelt & M. B. Sarkar, 2009, Learning from supply-side agents: The impact of technology solution providers' experiential diversity on clients' innovation adoption, 52: 37–60; M. J. Mol, P. Pauwels, P. Matthyssens, & L. Quintens, 2004, A technological contingency perspective on the depth and scope of international outsourcing, *Journal of International Management*, 10: 287–305.
123. K. Couke & L. Sleuwaegen, 2008, Offshoring as a survival strategy: Evidence from manufacturing firms in Belgium, *Journal of International Business Studies,* 39: 1261–1277.
124. N. Heath, 2009, Outsourcing: The new hot spots, *BusinessWeek,* http://www.businessweek.com, February 20.
125. S. Hamm, 2009, IBM: Outsourcing at home, *BusinessWeek,* http://www.businessweek.com, January 16.
126. M. H. Safizadeh, J. M. Field, & L. P. Ritzman, 2008, Sourcing practices and boundaries of the firm in the financial services industry, *Strategic Management Journal*, 29: 79–91; M. A. Hitt, D. Ahlstrom, M. T. Dacin, E. Levitas, & L. Svobodina, 2004, The institutional effects on strategic alliance partner selection in transition economies: China versus Russia, *Organization Science,* 15: 173–185.
127. T. Felin & W. S. Hesterly, 2007, The knowledge-based view, nested heterogeneity, and new value creation: Philosophical considerations on the locus of knowledge, *Academy of Management Review,* 32: 195–218; Y. Mishina, T. G. Pollock, & J. F. Porac, 2004, Are more resources always better for growth? Resource stickiness in market and product expansion, *Strategic Management Journal*, 25: 1179–1197.
128. M. Gibbert, M. Hoegl, & L. Valikangas, 2007, In praise of resource constraints, *MIT Sloan Management Review,* 48(3): 15–17. 126; D. S. Elenkov & I. M. Manev, 2005, Top management leadership and influence in innovation: The role of sociocultural context, *Journal of Management*, 31: 381–402.
129. D. Kiley, 2007, The new heat on Ford, *BusinessWeek*, June 4, 32–37.
130. D. Welch, 2007, Staying paranoid at Toyota, *BusinessWeek*, July 2, 80–82.
131. L. Barton, Wellsprings of knowledge, 30–31.

CHAPTER 4

1. D. J. Collis & M. G. Rukstad, 2008, Can you say what your strategy is? *Harvard Business Review,* 86(4): 82–90.
2. H. Greve, 2009, Bigger and safer: The diffusion of competitive advantage, *Strategic Management Journal*, 30: 1–23.
3. M. A. Delmas & M. W. Toffel, 2008, Organizational responses to environmental demands: Opening the black box, *Strategic Management Journal*, 29: 1027–1055; S. Elbanna & J. Child, 2007, The influence of decision, environmental and firm characteristics on the rationality of strategic decision-making, *Journal of Management Studies*, 44: 561–591; T. Yu & A. A. Cannella, Jr., 2007, Rivalry between multinational enterprises: An event history approach, *Academy of Management Journal,* 50: 665–686.
4. S. L. Newbert, 2008, Value, rareness, competitive advantage, and performance: A conceptual-level empirical investigation of the resource-based view of the firm, *Strategic Management Journal*, 29: 745–768.
5. N. A. Morgan & L. L. Rego, 2009, Brand portfolio strategy and firm performance, *Journal of Marketing*, 73: 59–74; C. Zott & R. Amit, 2008, The fit between product market strategy and business model: Implications for firm performance, *Strategic Management Journal*, 29: 1–26.
6. S. Kaplan, 2008, Framing contests: Strategy making under uncertainty, *Organization Science*, 19: 729–752.
7. S. Maxfield, 2008, Reconciling corporate citizenship and competitive strategy: Insights from economic theory, *Journal of Business Ethics*, 80: 367–377; K. Shimizu & M. A. Hitt, 2004, Strategic flexibility: Organizational preparedness to reverse ineffective strategic decisions, *Academy of Management Executive,* 18(4): 44–59.
8. B. Chakravarthy & P. Lorange, 2008, Driving renewal: The entrepreneur-manager, *Journal of Business Strategy*, 29: 14–21.
9. R. Oriani & M. Sobrero, 2008, Uncertainty and the market valuation of R&D within a real options logic, *Strategic Management Journal*, 29: 343–361.
10. J. A. Lamberg, H. Tikkanen, T. Nokelainen, & H. Suur-Inkeroinen, 2009, Competitive dynamics, strategic consistency, and organizational survival, *Strategic Management Journal*, 30: 45–60; R. D. Ireland & C. C. Miller, 2005, Decision-making and firm success, *Academy of Management Executive,* 18(4): 8–12.

11. I. Goll, N. B. Johnson, & A. A. Rasheed, 2008, Top management team demographic characteristics, business strategy, and firm performance in the US airline industry: The role of managerial discretion, *Management Decision*, 46: 201–222; J. R. Hough, 2006, Business segment performance redux: A multilevel approach, *Strategic Management Journal,* 27: 45–61.
12. P. Ozcan & K. M. Eisenhardt, 2009, Origin of alliance portfolios: Entrepreneurs, network strategies, and firm performance, *Academy of Management Journal*, 52: 246–279; B. Choi, S. K. Poon, & J. G. Davis, 2008, Effects of knowledge management strategy on organizational performance: A complementarity theory-based approach, *Omega*, 36: 235–251.
13. J. W. Spencer, 2008, The impact of multinational enterprise strategy on indigenous enterprises: Horizontal spill-overs and crowding out in developing countries, *Academy of Management Review*, 33: 341–361.
14. 2008, "Indian Markets Thursday wrap-up", December 4, http://seekingalpha.com/article/109193-indian-markets-thursday-wrap-up-lower-inflation-news-cheers-the-markets
15. Naukrihub.com, Indian Industry and Increasing Layoffs, http://www.naukrihub.com/hr-today/layoffs-in-indian-itcos.html Rajeshwari Sharma, 2008, Layoffs can be less painful, www.livemint.com, November 17, http://www.livemint.com/2008/11/16222306/Layoffs-can-be-less-painful.html
16. 2009, *SiliconIndia News*, Wipro Asks Employees to Work Two Days a Week, Siliconindia.com, http://www.siliconindia.com/shownews/Wipro_asks_employees_to_work_2_days_a_week-nid-55807.html
17. Ibid.
18. 2010, "IT Cos hire non-techies to Cut Costs", Current Market.net, May11, http://www.currentitmarket.net/2010/05/it-cos-hire-non-techies-to-cut-costs.html
19. D. Lei & J. W. Slocum, 2009, The tipping points of business strategy: The rise and decline of competitiveness, *Organizational Dynamics*, 38: 131–147.
20. R. J. Harrington & A. K. Tjan, 2008, Transforming strategy one customer at a time, *Harvard Business Review*, 86(3): 62–72; R. Priem, 2007, A consumer perspective on value creation, *Academy of Management Review*, 32: 219–235.
21. M. E. Porter, 1980, *Competitive Strategy,* New York: Free Press.
22. M. Baghai, S. Smit, & P. Viguerie, 2009, Is your growth strategy flying blind? *Harvard Business Review*, 87(5): 86–96.
23. D. G. Sirmon, S. Gove, & M. A. Hitt, 2008, Resource management in dyadic competitive rivalry: The effects of resource bundling and deployment, *Academy of Management Journal*, 51: 919–935; D. G. Sirmon, M. A. Hitt, & R. D. Ireland, 2007, Managing firm resources in dynamic environments to create value: Inside the black box, *Academy of Management Review,* 32: 273–292.
24. A. Wetergins & R. Boschma, 2009, Does spatial proximity to customers matter for innovative performance? Evidence from the Dutch software sector, *Research Policy*, 38: 746–755.
25. J. McGregor, 2009, When service means survival, *BusinessWeek*, March 2: 26–33.
26. 2009, "Cognizant: Preparing for a Global Footprint", Case # BP 0238 of IIMA.
27. Y. Liu & R. Yang, 2009, Competing loyalty programs: Impact of market saturation, market share, and category expandability, *Journal of Marketing*, 73: 93–108; P. R. Berthon, L. F. Pitt, I. McCarthy, & S. M. Kates, 2007, When customers get clever: Managerial approaches to dealing with creative customers, *Business Horizons,* 50(1): 39–47.
28. P. E. Frown & A. F. Payne, 2009, Customer relationship management: A strategic perspective, *Journal of Business Market Management*, 3: 7–27.
29. H. Green, 2009, How Amazon aims to keep you clicking, *BusinessWeek*, March 2: 34–35.30. E. Steel, 2009, MySpace slashes jobs as growth slows down, *Wall Street Journal Online*, http://www.wsj.com, June 17.
30. Y. Liu & R. Yang, 2009, Competing loyalty programs: Impact of market saturation, market share, and category expandability, *Journal of Marketing*, 73: 93–108; P. R. Berthon, L. F. Pitt, I. McCarthy, & S. M. Kates, 2007, When customers get clever: Managerial approaches to dealing with creative customers, *Business Horizons,* 50(1): 39–47.
31. Sources of data: http://www.trai.gov.in/WriteReadData/trai/upload/Reports/52/5octoblerindicatorreporton13oct.pdf - Pg 23; http://www.trai.gov.in/WriteReadData/trai/upload/Reports/48/IndicatorReport1oct09.pdf - pg 19; http://www.trai.gov.in/WriteReadData/trai/upload/Reports/51/finalperformanceindicatorReport9agust.pdf - Pg 20 respectively for the three data.
32. 2009, Amazon turns to customers for new TV advertising campaign, http://www.amazon.com, June 8.
33. 2009, http://www.autos.msn.com, June 17.
34. I. C. MacMillan & L. Selden, 2008, The incumbent's advantage, *Harvard Business Review*, 86(10): 111–121; G. Dowell, 2006, Product-line strategies of new entrants in an established industry: Evidence from the U. S. bicycle industry, *Strategic Management Journal,* 27: 959–979.
35. Case "Coca Cola versus Pepsi in India: The Battle for the Bottle Continues", Case # BP 251 of IIMA.
36. Case, "Arihant Retail" written by S. Manikutty for IIMA (2010).
37. S. French, 2009, Re-framing strategic thinking: The research-aims and outcomes, *Journal of Management Development*, 28: 205–224.
38. R. J. Brodie, J. R. M. Whittome, & G. J. Brush, 2009, Investigating the service brand: A customer value perspective, *Journal of Business Research*, 62: 345–355; P. D. Ellis, 2006, Market orientation and performance: A meta-analysis and cross-national comparisons, *Journal of Management Studies,* 43: 1089–1107.
39. L. A. Bettencourt & A. W. Ulwick, 2008, The customer-centered innovation map, *Harvard Business Review*, 86(5): 109–114.
40. A. Feldman, 2009, Wooing the worried, *BusinessWeek*, April 27, 24.
41. D. Kiley, 2009, One Ford for the whole wide world, *BusinessWeek*, June 15, 58–59.

42. E. A. Borg, 2009, The marketing of innovations in high-technology companies: A network approach, *European Journal of Marketing*, 43: 364-–70.
43. D. Foust, F. F. Jespersen, F. Katzenberg, A. Barrett, & R. O. Crockett, 2003, The best performers, *BusinessWeek Online*, http://www.businessweek.com, March 24.
44. T. Y. Eng & J. G. Spickett-Jones, 2009, An investigation of marketing capabilities and upgrading performance of manufacturers in Mainland China and Hong Kong, *Journal of World Business*, in press; M. B. Heeley & R. Jacobson, 2008, The recency of technological inputs and financial performance, *Strategic Management Journal*, 29: 723–744.
45. 2009, Experience our energy, http://www.proenergyservices.com, June 17.
46. 2009, SAS honored with 2009 Asia Pacific Forst & Sullivan ICT aware for business intelligence, http://www.sas.com, June 9.
47. K. E. Klein, 2009, Survival advice for auto parts suppliers, *Wall Street Journal Online*, http://www.wsj.com, June 16.
48. M. E. Porter, 1985, *Competitive Advantage,* New York: Free Press, 26.
49. M. E. Porter, 1996, What is strategy? *Harvard Business Review,* 74(6): 61–78.
50. Porter, What is strategy?
51. M. Reitzig & P. Puranam, 2009, Value appropriation as an organizational capability: The case of IP protection through patents, *Strategic Management Journal*, 30: 765–789; C. Zott, 2003, Dynamic capabilities and the emergence of intraindustry differential firm performance: Insights from a simulation study, *Strategic Management Journal,* 24: 97–125.
52. M. E. Porter, 1994, Toward a dynamic theory of strategy, in R. P. Rumelt, D. E. Schendel, & D. J. Teece (eds.), *Fundamental Issues in Strategy,* Boston: Harvard Business School Press: 423–461.
53. Porter, What is strategy? 62.
54. Porter, *Competitive Advantage*, 15.
55. S. Sun, 2009, An analysis on the conditions and methods of market segmentation, *International Journal of Business and Management*, 4: 63–70.
56. J. Gonzales-Benito & I. Suarez-Gonzalez, 2009, A study of the role played by manufacturing strategic objectives and capabilities in understanding the relationship between Porter's generic strategies and business performance, *British Journal of Management*, in press.
57. G. B. Voss, D. Sirdeshmukh, & Z. G. Voss, 2008, The effects of slack resources and environmental threat on product exploration and exploitation, *Academy of Management Journal*, 51: 147–158.
58. S. McKee, 2009, Customers your company doesn't want, *Wall Street Journal Online*, http://www.wsj.com, June 12.
59. Porter, *Competitive Strategy*, 35–40.
60. M. J. Gehlhar, A. Regmi, S. E. Stefanou, & B. L. Zoumas, 2009, Brand leadership and product innovation as firm strategies in global food markets, *Journal of Product & Brand Management*, 18: 115–126.
61. D. Mehri, 2006, The dark side of lean: An insider's perspective on the realities of the Toyota production system, *Academy of Management Perspectives,* 20(2): 21–42.
62. N. T. Sheehan & G. Vaidyanathan, 2009, using a value creation compass to discover "Blue Oceans," *Strategy & Leadership*, 37: 13-20; D. F. Spulber, 2004, *Management Strategy,* New York: McGraw Hill/Irwin, 175.
63. A. M. Chaker, 2009, Planes, trains ... and buses? *Wall Street Journal Online*, http://www.wsj.com, June 18.
64. 2009, About Greyhound, http://www.greyhound.com, June 17.
65. Bharti Airtel, *Annual Report,* 2009-10.
66. M. Kotabe & R. Mudambi, 2009, Global sourcing and value creation: Opportunities and challenges, *Journal of International Management*, 15: 121–125; D. F. Lynch, S. B. Keller, & J. Ozment, 2000, The effects of logistics capabilities and strategy on firm performance, *Journal of Business Logistics,* 21(2): 47–68.
67. J. Hatonen & T. Erikson, 2009, 30+ years of research and practice of outsourcing—Exploring the past and anticipating the future, *Journal of International Management*, 15: 142–155; P. Edwards & M. Ram, 2006, Surviving on the margins of the economy: Working relationships in small, low-wage firms, *Journal of Management Studies*, 43: 895–916.
68. 2010, information from company's official Web site, http://www.pantaloonretail.in/corporate_state.asp.
69. 2010, information taken from company official Web site, http://www.pantaloonretail.in/PRIL_FY10_Results.pdf. Separate information for Big Bazaar itself a=is not available.
70. 2009, What is a closeout? http://www.biglots.com, June 18.
71. 2009, Big Lots, *Standard & Poor's Stock Reports,* http://www.standardandpoors.com, June 13.
72. J. Morehouse, B. O'Mera, C. Hagen, & T. Huseby, 2008, Hitting back: Strategic responses to low-cost rivals, *Strategy & Leadership*, 36: 4–13; L. K. Johnson, 2003, Dueling pricing strategies, *The McKinsey Quarterly,* 44(3): 10–11.
73. 2010, Taken from the Annual Report of the Group, http://www.pantaloonretail.in/PRIL_FY10_Results.pdf.
74. O. Ormanidhi & O. Stringa, 2008, Porter's model of generic competitive strategies, *Business Economics*, 43: 55–64; J. Bercovitz & W. Mitchell, 2007, When is more better? The impact of business scale and scope on long-term business survival, while controlling for profitability, *Strategic Management Journal,* 28: 61–79.
75. Porter, *Competitive Strategy*, 35–40.
76. 2009, Product innovation, http://www.1000ventures.com, June 19.
77. R. Cowan & N. Jonard, 2009, Knowledge portfolios and the organization of innovation networks, *Academy of Management Review*, 34: 320–342.
78. D. Ashmos Plowman, L. T. Baker, T. E. Beck, M. Kulkarni, S. Thomas-Solansky, & D. V. Travis, 2007, Radical change accidentally: The emergence and amplification of small change, *Academy of Management Journal,* 50: 515–543; A. Wadhwa & S. Kotha, 2006, Knowledge creation through external venturing: Evidence from the telecommunications equipment

manufacturing industry, *Academy of Management Journal*, 49: 819–835.

79. D. W. Baack & D. J. Boggs, 2008, The difficulties in using a cost leadership strategy in emerging markets, *International Journal of Emerging Markets*, 3: 125–139; M. J. Benner, 2007, The incumbent discount: Stock market categories and response to radical technological change, *Academy of Management Review,* 32: 703–720.
80. F. T. Rothaermel, M. A. Hitt, & L. A. Jobe, 2006, Balancing vertical integration and strategic outsourcing: Effects on product portfolio, product success and firm performance, *Strategic Management Journal,* 27: 1033–1056; A. V. Mainkar, M. Lubatkin, & W. S. Schulze, 2006, Toward a product-proliferation theory of entry barriers, *Academy of Management Review,* 31: 1062–1075.
81. Porter, *Competitive Advantage*, 14.
82. 2009, History, http://www.roberttalbott.com, June 19.
83. L. A. Bettencourt & A. W. Ulwick, 2008, The customer-centered innovation map, *Harvard Business Review*, 86(5): 109–114; W. C. Bogner & P. Bansal, 2007, Knowledge management as a basis for sustained high performance, *Journal of Management Studies,* 44:165–188; M. Semadeni, 2006, Minding your distance: How management consulting firms use service marks to position competitively, *Strategic Management Journal,* 27: 169–187.
84. M. Abbott, R. Holland, J. Giacomin, & J. Shackleton, 2009, Changing affective content in brand and product attributes, *Journal of Product & Brand Management*, 18: 17–26; P. Best, Using design to drive innovation, *BusinessWeek Online*, http://www.businessweek.com, June 29.
85. B. Charny & J. A. Dicolo, 2009, Apple debuts new iPhones to long lines, *Wall Street Journal Online*, http://www.wsj.com, June 19.
86. Ashwani Kumar, 2010, Design: The new mantra, *Economic Times,* 16 October, p.8.
87. M. Jensen & A. Roy, 2008, Staging exchange partner choices: When do status and reputation matter? *Academy of Management Journal*, 51: 495–516; V. P. Rindova, T. G. Pollock, & M. A. Hayward, 2006, Celebrity firms: The social construction of market popularity, *Academy of Management Review,* 31: 50–71.
88. V. O'Connell, 2009, Sales of luxury goods seen falling by 10%, *Wall Street Journal Online*, http://www.wsj.com, April 11.
89. S. Berfield, 2009, Coach's new bag, *BusinessWeek*, June 29: 41–43; S. Berfield, 2009, Coach's Poppy line is luxury for recessionary times, *BusinessWeek Online*, http://www.wsj.com, June 18.
90. D. G. Sirmon, J.-L. Arregle, M. A. Hitt, & J. W. Webb, 2008, The role of family influence in firms' strategic responses to threat of imitation, *Entrepreneurship Theory and Practice*, 32: 979–998; F. K. Pil & S. K. Cohen, 2006, Modularity: Implications for imitation, innovation, and sustained advantage, *Academy of Management Review,* 31: 995–1011.
91. X. Bian & L. Moutinho, 2009, An investigation of determinants of counterfeit purchase consideration, *Journal of Business Research*, 62: 368–378.
92. Porter, *Competitive Strategy*, 98.
93. Porter, *Competitive Advantage*, 15.
94. Ibid., 15–16.
95. K. Kling & I. Goteman, 2003, IKEA CEO Andres Dahlvig on international growth and IKEA's unique corporate culture and brand identity, *Academy of Management Executive,* 17(1): 31–37.
96. 2009, About IKEA, http://www.ikea.com, June 21.
97. G. Evans, 2003, Why some stores strike me as special, *Furniture Today,* 27(24): 91; Porter, What is strategy?, 65.
98. O. Furrer, D. Sudharshan, H. Thomas, & M. T. Zlexandre, 2008, Resource configurations, generic strategies, and firm performance: Exploring the parallels between resource-based and competitive strategy theories in a new industry, *Journal of Strategy and Management*, 1: 15–40; J. H. Dyer & N. W. Hatch, 2006, Relation-specific capabilities and barriers to knowledge transfers: Creating advantage through network relationships, *Strategic Management Journal,* 27: 701–719.
99. 2008, Letter to our shareholders, http://www.target.com, June 20.
100. 2009, Environment, http://www.target.com, June 21.
101. R. Sanchez, 1995, Strategic flexibility in product competition, *Strategic Management Journal,* 16 (Special Issue): 140.
102. M. I. M. Wahab, D. Wu, and C.-G. Lee, 2008, A generic approach to measuring the machine flexibility of manufacturing systems, *European Journal of Operational Research*, 186: 137–149.
103. M. Kotabe, R. Parente, & J. Y. Murray, 2007, Antecedents and outcomes of modular production in the Brazilian automobile industry: A grounded theory approach, *Journal of International Business Studies,* 38: 84–106.
104. T. Raj, R. Shankar, & M. Sunhaib, 2009, An ISM approach to analyse interaction between barriers of transition to Flexible Manufacturing Systems, *International Journal of Manufacturing Technology and Management*, 16: 417–438. E. K. Bish, A. Muriel, & S. Biller, 2005, Managing flexible capacity in a make-to-order environment, *Management Science,* 51: 167–180.
105. S. M. Iravani, M. P. van Oyen, & K. T. Sims, 2005, Structural flexibility: A new perspective on the design of manufacturing and service operations, *Management Science,* 51: 151–166.
106. P. Theodorou & G. Florou, 2008, Manufacturing strategies and financial performance—the effect of advanced information Technology: CAD/CAM systems, *Omega*, 36: 107–121.
107. N. A. Morgan & L. L. Rego, 2009, Brand portfolio strategy and firm performance, *Journal of Marketing*, 73: 59–74.
108. D. Elmuti, H. Jia, & D. Gray, 2009, Customer relationship management strategic application and organizational effectiveness: An empirical investigation, *Journal of Strategic Marketing*, 17: 75–96.
109. D. P. Forbes, 2007, Reconsidering the strategic implications of decision comprehensiveness, *Academy of Management Review,* 32: 361–376.
110. J. D. Westphal, R. Gulati, & S. M. Shortell, 1997, Customization or conformity: An institutional and network perspec-

tive on the content and consequences of TQM adoption, *Administrative Science Quarterly,* 42: 366–394.

111. S. Modell, 2009, Bundling management control innovations: A field study of organisational experimenting with total quality management and the balanced scorecard, *Accounting, Auditing & Accountability Journal*, 22: 59–90.
112. A. Keramati & A. Albadvi, 2009, Exploring the relationship between use of information technology in total quality management and SMEs performance using canonical correlation analysis: A survey on Swedish car part supplier sector, *International Journal of Information Technology and Management*, 8: 442–462; R. J. David & S. Strang, 2006, When fashion is fleeting: Transitory collective beliefs and the dynamics of TQM consulting, *Academy of Management Journal,* 49: 215–233.
113. Porter, *Competitive Advantage*, 16.
114. Ibid., 17.
115. M. A. Hitt, L. Bierman, K. Uhlenbruck, & K. Shimizu, 2006, The importance of resources in the internationalization of professional service firms: The good, the bad, and the ugly, *Academy of Management Journal,* 49: 1137–1157.
116. P. Puranam, H. Singh, & M. Zollo, 2006, Organizing for innovation: Managing the coordination-autonomy dilemma in technology acquisitions, *Academy of Management Journal,* 49: 263–280.
117. S. Thornhill & R. E. White, 2007, Strategic purity: A multi-industry evaluation of pure vs. hybrid business strategies, *Strategic Management Journal,* 28: 553–561.

CHAPTER 5

1. D. F. Spulber, 2004, *Management Strategy,* Boston: McGraw-Hill/Irwin, 87–88; M.-J. Chen, 1996, Competitor analysis and interfirm rivalry: Toward a theoretical integration, *Academy of Management Review,* 21: 100–134.
2. M. Schrage, 2007, The myth of commoditization, *MIT Sloan Management Review*, 48(2): 10–14; T. Galvin, 2002, Examining institutional change: Evidence from the founding dynamics of U.S. health care interest associations, *Academy of Management Journal,* 45: 673–696.
3. R. D. Ireland & J. W. Webb, 2007, Strategic entrepreneurship: Creating competitive advantage through streams of innovation, *Business Horizons*, 50: 49–59.
4. B. R. Barringer & R. D. Ireland, 2008, *Entrepreneurship: Successfully Launching New Ventures,* 2nd ed., Upper Saddle River, NJ: Prentice Hall; A. M. Knott &H. E. Posen, 2005, Is failure good? *Strategic Management Journal,* 26: 617–641.
5. P. J. Derfus, P. G. Maggitti, C. M. Grimm, &K. G. Smith, 2008, The red queen effect: Competitive actions and firm performance, *Academy of Management Journal,* 51; 61–80; C. M. Grimm, H. Lee, & K. G. Smith, 2006, *Strategy as Action: Competitive Dynamics and Competitive Advantage*, New York: Oxford University Press.
6. J. W. Selsky, J. Goes, & O. N. Baburoglu, 2007, Contrasting perspectives of strategy making: Applications in "hyper" environments, *Organization Studies,* 28(1): 71–94; A. Nair & L. Filer, 2003, Cointegration of firm strategies within groups: A long-run analysis of firm behavior in the Japanese steel industry, *Strategic Management Journal,* 24: 145–159.
7. T. C. Powell, 2003, Varieties of competitive parity, *Strategic Management Journal,* 24: 61–86.
8. D. G. Sirmon, S. Gove, & M. A. Hitt, 2008, Resource management in dyadic competitive rivalry: The effects of resource bundling and deployment, *Academy of Management Journal,* 51: 919–935; J. Rodriguez-Pinto, J. Gutierrez-Cillan, & A. I. Rodriguez-Escudero, 2007, Order and scale market entry, firm resources, and performance, *European Journal of Marketing*, 41: 590–607.
9. S. K. Ethitaj & D. H. Zhu, 2008, Performance effects of imitative entry, *Strategic Management Journal,* 29: 797–817.
10. Grimm, Lee, & Smith, *Strategy as Action*; G. Young, K. G. Smith, C. M. Grimm, & D. Simon, 2000, Multimarket contact and resource dissimilarity: A competitive dynamics perspective, *Journal of Management,* 26: 1217–1236.
11. E. I. Rose & K. Ito, 2008, Competitive interactions: The international investment patterns of Japanese automobile manufacturers, *Journal of International Business Studies,* 39: 864–879; T. L. Sorenson, 2007, Credible collusion in multimarket oligopoly, *Managerial and Decision Economics*, 28(2): 115–128.
12. T. Yu, M. Subramaniam, & A. A. Cannella, 2009, Rivalry deterrence in international markets: Contingencies governing the mutual forbearance hypothesis, *Academy of Management Journal,* 52*:* 127–147; K. G. Smith, W. J. Ferrier, & H. Ndofor, 2001, Competitive dynamics research: Critique and future directions, inM. A. Hitt, R. E. Freeman, & J. S. Harrison (eds.), *Handbook of Strategic Management,* Oxford, UK: Blackwell Publishers, 326.
13. G. Young, K. G. Smith, & C. M. Grimm,1996, "Austrian" and industrial organization perspectives on firm-level competitive activity and performance, *Organization Science,* 73: 243–254.
14. 2003, "DHL Worldwide Express: The DHL division of Airfreight Limited", Case # BP-293 of IIMA .
15. H. D. Hopkins, 2003, The response strategies of dominant U.S. firms to Japanese challengers, *Journal of Management,* 29: 5–25; G. S. Day & D. J. Reibstein, 1997, The dynamic challenges for theory and practice, inG. S. Day & D. J. Reibstein (eds.), *Wharton on Competitive Strategy,* New York: John Wiley & Sons, 2.
16. J. J. Li, K. Z. Zhou, & A. T. Shao, 2009, Competitive position, managerial ties &profitability of foreign firms in China: An interactive perspective, *Journal of International Business Studies,* 40: 339–352; M.-J. Chen & D. C. Hambrick, 1995, Speed, stealth, and selective attack: How small firms differ from large firms in competitive behavior, *Academy of Management Journal,* 38: 453–482.
17. T. Dewett & S. David, 2007, Innovators and imitators in novelty-intensive markets: A research agenda, *Creativity and Innovation Management*, 16(1): 80–92.
18. A. Sahay, 2007, How to reap higher profits with dynamic pricing, *MIT Sloan Management Review*, 48(4): 53–60; T. J. Douglas & J. A. Ryman, 2003, Understanding competi-

tive advantage in the general hospital industry: Evaluating strategic competencies, *Strategic Management Journal,* 24: 333–347.

19. T. Yu & A. A. Cannella, Jr., 2007, Rivalry between multinational enterprises: An event history approach, *Academy of Management Journal*, 50: 665–686; W. J. Ferrier, 2001, Navigating the competitive landscape: The drivers and consequences of competitive aggressiveness, *Academy of Management Journal,* 44: 858–877.
20. Smith, Ferrier, & Ndofor, Competitive dynamics research, 319.
21. E. G. Olson & D. Sharma, 2008, Beating the commoditization trend: A framework from the electronics industry, *Journal of Business Strategy*, 29(4): 22–28; J. Shamsie, 2003, The context of dominance: An industry-driven framework for exploiting reputation, *Strategic Management Journal,* 24: 199–215.
22. J. Li, 2008, Asymmetric interactions between foreign and domestic banks: Effects on market entry, *Strategic Management Journal,* 29: 873–893;K. Cool, L. H. Roller, & B. Leleux, 1999, The relative impact of actual and potential rivalry on firm profitability in the pharmaceutical industry, *Strategic Management Journal,* 20: 1–14.
23. G. Leask & D. Parker, 2007, Strategic groups, competitive groups and performance within the U.K. pharmaceutical industry: Improving our understanding of the competitive process, *Strategic Management Journal*, 28: 723–745; D. R. Gnyawali & R. Madhavan, 2001, Cooperative networks and competitive dynamics: A structural embeddedness perspective, *Academy of Management Review,* 26: 431–445.
24. V. La, P. Patterson & C. Styls, 2009, Client-perceived performance and value in professional B2B services: An international perspective, *Journal of International Business Studies,* 40: 274–300; Y. Y. Kor & J. T. Mahoney, 2005, How dynamics, management, and governance of resource deployments influence firm-level performance, *Strategic Management Journal,* 26: 489–496.
25. R. L. Priem, L. G. Love, & M. A. Shaffer, 2002, Executives' perceptions of uncertainty scores: A numerical taxonomy and underlying dimensions, *Journal of Management,* 28: 725–746.
26. J. C. Bou & A. Satorra, 2007, The persistence of abnormal returns at industry and firm levels: Evidence from Spain, *Strategic Management Journal*, 28: 707–722.
27. Chen, Competitor analysis, 108.
28. Chen, Competitor analysis, 109.
29. D. Ng, R. Westgren, & S. Sonka, 2009, Competitive blind spots in an institutional field, *Strategic Management Journal,* 30: 349–369.
30. S. J. Chang & D. Xu, 2008, Spillovers and competition among foreign and local firms in China, *Strategic Management Journal,* 29: 495–518.
31. K. Uhlenbruck, M. A. Hitt, & M. Semadeni, 2005, Market value effects of acquisitions of Internet firms: A resource-based analysis, working paper, University of Montana; A. Afuah, 2003, Redefining firm boundaries in the face of the Internet: Are firms really shrinking? *Academy of Management Review,* 28: 34–53.
32. H. Gebauer, 2007, Entering low-end markets: A new strategy for Swiss companies, *Journal of Business Strategy*, 27(5): 23–31.
33. Chen, Competitor analysis, 106.
34. A. Kachra & R. E. White, 2008, Know-how transfer: The role of social, economic/competitive, and firm boundary factors, *Strategic Management Journal,* 29: 425–445.
35. M. J. Chen, K.-H. Su, & W. Tsai, 2007, Competitive tension: The awareness-motivation-capability perspective, *Academy of Management Journal*, 50: 101–118; J. Gimeno & C. Y. Woo, 1999, Multimarket contact, economies of scope, and firm performance, *Academy of Management Journal,* 42: 239–259.
36. I. C. MacMillan, A. B. van Putten, & R. S. McGrath, 2003, Global gamesmanship, *Harvard Business Review*, 81(5): 62–71.
37. Young, Smith, Grimm, & Simon, Multimarket contact, 1230.
38. H. R. Greve, 2008, Multimarket contact and sales growth: Evidence from insurance, *Strategic Management Journal,* 29: 229–249; J. Gimeno, 1999, Reciprocal threats in multimarket rivalry: Staking out "spheres of influence" in the U.S. airline industry, *Strategic Management Journal,* 20: 101–128.
39. S. Jayachandran, J. Gimeno, & P. R. Varadarajan, 1999, Theory of multimarket competition: A synthesis and implications for marketing strategy, *Journal of Marketing*, 63: 49–66; Chen, Competitor analysis, 107.
40. H. Schiele, 2008, Location, location:The geography of industry clusters, *Journal of Business Strategy,* 29(3): 29–36; J. Gimeno & C. Y. Woo, 1996, Hypercompetition in a multimarket environment: The role of strategic similarity and multimarket contact on competitive de-escalation, *Organization Science,* 7: 322–341.
41. C. H. Deutsch, 2007, UPS embraces high-tech delivery methods, *New York Times Online*, http://www.nytimes.com, July 12.
42. S. MacMillan, 2008, The issue: DHL turns to rival UPS, *BusinessWeek,* http://www.businessweek.com, June.
43. Chen, Su, & Tsai, Competitive tension; Chen, Competitor analysis, 110.
44. Ibid.; W. Ocasio, 1997, Towards an attention-based view of the firm, *Strategic Management Journal,* 18 (Special Issue): 187–206; Smith, Ferrier, & Ndofor, Competitive dynamics research, 320.
45. 2007, Komatsu lifts outlook, outdoes rival Caterpillar, *New York Times Online*, http://www.nytimes.com, July 30.
46. S. Tallman, M. Jenkins, N. Henry, & S. Pinch, 2004, Knowledge, clusters and competitive advantage, *Academy of Management Review,* 29: 258–271;J. F. Porac & H. Thomas, 1994, Cognitive categorization and subjective rivalry among retailers in a small city, *Journal of Applied Psychology,* 79: 54–66.
47. S. H. Park & D. Zhou, 2005, Firm heterogeneity and competitive dynamics in alliance formation, *Academy of Management Review,* 30: 531–554.
48. Chen, Competitor analysis, 113.

49. M. Leiblein & T. Madsen, 2009, Unbundling competitive heterogeneity: Incentive structures and capability influences on technological innovation, *Strategic Management Journal,* 30: in press; J. J. Li, L. Poppo, & K. Z. Zhou, 2008, Do managerial ties in China always produce value? Competition, uncertainty and domestic vs. foreign competition, *Strategic Management Journal,* 29: 383–400.
50. R. Belderbos & L. Sleuwaegen, 2005, Competitive drivers and international plant configuration strategies: A product-level test, *Strategic Management Journal,* 26: 577–593.
51. C. M. Grimm & K. G. Smith, 1997, *Strategy as Action: Industry Rivalry and Coordination,* Cincinnati: South-Western Publishing Co., 125.
52. B. Webber, 2007, Volatile markets, *Business Strategy Review*, 18(2): 60–67;K. G. Smith, W. J. Ferrier, & C. M. Grimm, 2001, King of the hill: Dethroning the industry leader, *Academy of Management Executive,* 15(2): 59–70.
53. S. E. Jackson, 2008, Grow your business without leaving your competitive stronghold, *Journal of Business Strategy,* 29(4): 60–62.
54. W. J. Ferrier & H. Lee, 2003, Strategic aggressiveness, variation, and surprise: How the sequential pattern of competitive rivalry influences stock market returns, *Journal of Managerial Issues,* 14: 162–180.
55. 2001, Case: "The Park, Calcutta", Case # BP 267 .
56. S. Holmes, 2007, Better living at 30,000 feet, *BusinessWeek*, August 6, 76–77.
57. J. Schumpeter, 1934, *The Theory of Economic Development,* Cambridge, MA: Harvard University Press.
58. J. L. C. Cheng & I. F. Kesner, 1997, Organizational slack and response to environmental shifts: The impact of resource allocation patterns, *Journal of Management,* 23: 1–18.
59. F. F. Suarez & G. Lanzolla, 2007, The role of environmental dynamics in building a first mover advantage theory, *Academy of Management Review*, 32: 377–392.
60. G. M. McNamara, J. Haleblian, & B. J. Dykes, 2008, The performance implications of participating in an acquisition wave: Early mover advantages, bandwagon effects, and the moderating influence of industry characteristics and acquirer tactics, *Academy of Management Journal,* 51, 113–130; F. Wang, 2000, Too appealing to overlook, *America's Network,* December, 10–12.
61. R. K. Sinha & C. H. Noble, 2008, The adoption of radical manufacturing technologies and firm survival, *Strategic Management Journal,* 29: 943–962; D. P. Forbes, 2005, Managerial determinants of decision speed in new ventures, *Strategic Management Journal,* 26: 355–366.
62. H. R. Greve, 2009, Bigger and safer: The diffusion of competitive advantage, *Strategic Management Journal,* 30: 1–23; W. T. Robinson & S. Min, 2002, Is the first to market the first to fail? Empirical evidence for industrial goods businesses, *Journal of Marketing Research,* 39: 120–128.
63. T. Cottrell & B. R. Nault, 2004, *Strategic Management Journal,* 25: 1005–1025; R. Agarwal, M. B. Sarkar, & R. Echambadi, 2002, The conditioning effect of time on firm survival: An industry life cycle approach, *Academy of Management Journal,* 45: 971–994.
64. A. Srivastava & H. Lee, 2005, Predicting order and timing of new product moves: The role of top management in corporate entrepreneurship, *Journal of Business Venturing*, 20: 459–481.
65. M. S. Giarratana & A. Fosfuri, 2007, Product strategies and survival in Schumpeterian environments: Evidence from the U.S. security software industry, *Organization Studies*, 28(6): 909–929;J. W. Spencer & T. P. Murtha, 2005, How do governments matter to new industry creation? *Academy of Management Review,* 30: 321–337.
66. Z. Simsek, J. F. Veiga, & M. H. Lubatkin, 2007, The impact of managerial environmental perceptions on corporate entrepreneurship: Toward understanding discretionary slack's pivotal role, *Journal of Management Studies*, 44:1398–1424; S. W. Geiger & L. H. Cashen, 2002, A multidimensional examination of slack and its impact on innovation, *Journal of Managerial Issues,* 14: 68–84.
67. B. S. Teng, 2007, Corporate entrepreneurship activities through strategic alliances: A resource-based approach toward competitive advantage, *Journal of Management Studies*,44: 119–142; M. B. Lieberman & D. B. Montgomery, 1988, First-mover advantages, *Strategic Management Journal*, 9: 41–58.
68. D. Lange, S. Boivie, & A. D. Henderson, 2009, The parenting paradox: How multibusiness diversifiers endorse disruptive technologies while their corporate children struggle, *Academy of Management Journal,* 52: 179–198.
69. S. Jonsson & P. Regner, 2009, Normative barriers to imitation: Social complexity of core competences in a mutual fund industry, *Strategic Management Journal,* 30: 517–536; 2001, Older, wiser, webbier, *The Economist,* June 30, 10.
70. M. Shank, 2002, Executive strategyreport, IBM business strategy consulting, http://www.ibm.com, March 14; W. Boulding & M. Christen, 2001, First-mover disadvantage, *Harvard Business Review,* 79(9): 20–21.
71. J. L. Boyd & R. K. F. Bresser, 2008, Performance implications of delayed competitive responses: Evidence from the U.S. retail industry, *Strategic Management Journal,* 29: 1077–1096.
72. J. Gimeno, R. E. Hoskisson, B. B. Beal, & W. P. Wan, 2005, Explaining the clustering of international expansion moves: A critical test in the U.S. telecommunications industry, *Academy of Management Journal,* 48: 297–319; K. G. Smith, C. M. Grimm, & M. J. Gannon, 1992, *Dynamics of Competitive Strategy,* Newberry Park, CA.: Sage Publications.
73. J. Li & R. K. Koxhikode, 2008, Knowledge management and innovation strategy: The challenge for latecomers in emerging economies, *Asia Pacific Journal of Management,* 25: 429–450.
74. S. D. Dobrev & G. R. Carroll, 2003, Size (and competition) among organizations: Modeling scale-based selection among automobile producers in four major countries, 1885–1981, *Strategic Management Journal,* 24: 541–558.
75. L. F. Mesquita & S. G. Lazzarini, 2008, Horizontal and vertical relationships in developing economies: Implications for SMEs access to global markets, *Academy of Management Journal,* 51: 359–380; F. K. Pil & M. Hoiweg, 2003, Exploring scale:

The advantage of thinking small, *The McKinsey Quarterly,* 44(2): 33–39.

76. M. A. Hitt, L. Bierman, & J. D. Collins, 2007, The strategic evolution of U.S. law firms, *Business Horizons*, 50: 17–28;D. Miller & M. J. Chen, 1996, The simplicity of competitive repertoires: An empirical analysis, *Strategic Management Journal,* 17: 419–440.
77. Young, Smith, & Grimm, "Austrian" and industrial organization perspectives.
78. B. A. Melcher, 1993, How Goliaths can act like Davids, *BusinessWeek,* Special Issue, 193.
79. P. B. Crosby, 1980, *Quality Is Free,* New York: Penguin.
80. W. E. Deming, 1986, *Out of the Crisis,* Cambridge, MA: MIT Press.
81. D. A. Mollenkopf, E. Rabinovich,T. M. Laseter, & K. K. Boyer, 2007, Managing Internet product returns:A focus on effective service operations, *Decision Sciences*, 38: 215–250; L. B. Crosby, R. DeVito, & J. M. Pearson, 2003, Manage your customers' perception of quality, *Review of Business,* 24(1): 18–24.
82. K. Watanabe, 2007, Lessons fromToyota's long drive, *Harvard Business Review*, 85(7/8): 74–83; R. S. Kaplan &D. P. Norton, 2001, *The Strategy-Focused Organization,* Boston: Harvard Business School Press.
83. A. Azadegan, K. J. Dooley, P. L. Carter, & J. R. Carter, 2008, Supplier innovativeness and the role of interorganizational learning in enhancing manufacturing capabilities, *Journal of Supply Chain Management,* 44(4): 14–5; O. Bayazit & B. Karpak, 2007, An analytical network process-based framework for successful total quality management (TQM): An assessment of Turkish manufacturing industry readiness, *International Journal of Production Economics*, 105(1) 79–96.
84. K. E. Weick & K. M. Sutcliffe, 2001, *Managing the Unexpected,* San Francisco: Jossey-Bass, 81–82.
85. G. Macintosh, 2007, Customer orientation, relationship quality, and relational benefits to the firm, *Journal of Services Marketing*, 21(3): 150–159; G. Yeung & V. Mok, 2005, What are the impacts of implementing ISOs on the competitiveness of manufacturing industry in China, *Journal of World Business,* 40: 139–157.
86. J Wallace, 2009, Boeing at risk of losing more 787 orders, *Seattle-Post-Intelligencer,* http://www.seattlepi.nwsource.com, March 13.
87. T. R. Cook, D. J. Ketchen, J. G. Combs, & S. Y. Todd, 2008, Strategic resources and performance: A meta-analysis, *Strategic Management Journal,* 29: 1141–1154; Smith, Ferrier, & Ndofor, Competitive dynamics research, 323.
88. M. J. Chen & I. C. MacMillan, 1992, Nonresponse and delayed response to competitive moves, *Academy of Management Journal,* 35: 539–570; Smith, Ferrier, & Ndofor, Competitive dynamics research, 335.
89. M. J. Chen, K. G. Smith, & C. M. Grimm, 1992, Action characteristics as predictors of competitive responses, *Management Science,* 38: 439–455.
90. M. J. Chen & D. Miller, 1994, Competitive attack, retaliation and performance: An expectancy-valence framework, *Strategic Management Journal,* 15: 85–102.
91. T. Gardner, 2005, Interfirm competition for human resources: Evidence from the software industry, *Academy of Management Journal,* 48: 237–258; N. Huyghebaert & L. M. van de Gucht, 2004, Incumbent strategic behavior in financial markets and the exit of entrepreneurial start-ups, *Strategic Management Journal,* 25: 669–688.
92. Smith, Ferrier, & Ndofor, Competitive dynamics research, 333.
93. V. P. Rindova, A. P. Petkova, & S. Kotha, 2007, Standing out: How firms in emerging markets build reputation, *Strategic Organization*, 5: 31–70; J. Shamsie, 2003, The context of dominance: An industry-driven framework for exploiting reputation, *Strategic Management Journal,* 24: 199–215.
94. A. D. Smith, 2007, Making the case for the competitive advantage of corporate social responsibility, *Business Strategy Series*, 8(3): 186–195; P. W. Roberts & G. R. Dowling, 2003, Corporate reputation and sustained superior financial performance, *Strategic Management Journal,* 24: 1077–1093.
95. W. J. Ferrier, K. G. Smith, & C. M. Grimm, 1999, The role of competitive actions in market share erosion and industry dethronement: A study of industry leaders and challengers, *Academy of Management Journal,* 42: 372–388.
96. Smith, Grimm, & Gannon, *Dynamics of Competitive Strategy*.
97. L. Li, L. Zhang, & B. Arys, 2008, The turtle–hare story revisited: Social capital and resource accumulation for firms from emerging economies, *Asia Pacific Journal of Management,* 25: 251–275.
98. A. Karnani & B. Wernerfelt, 1985, Multiple point competition, *Strategic Management Journal,* 6: 87–97.
99. Smith, Ferrier, & Ndofor, Competitive dynamics research, 330.
100. *Economic Times*, 2010, Amul posts 19 % growth in FY 09-10, August 18, http://economictimes.indiatimes.com/news/news-by-company/earnings/earnings-news/Amul-posts-19-growth-in-FY-09-10/articleshow/6331460.cms
101. S. L. Newbert, 2007, Empirical research on the resource-based view of the firm: An assessment and suggestions for future research, *Strategic Management Journal*, 28: 121–146; G. McNamara, P. M. Vaaler, & C. Devers, 2003, Same as it ever was: The search for evidence of increasing hypercompetition, *Strategic Management Journal,* 24: 261–278.
102. M. F. Wiersema & H. P. Bowen, 2008, Corporate diversification: The impact of foreign competition, industry globalization and product diversification, *Strategic Management Journal,* 29: 115–132; A. Kalnins & W. Chung, 2004, Resource-seeking agglomeration: A study of market entry in the lodging industry, *Strategic Management Journal,* 25: 689–699.
103. J. R. Williams, 1992, How sustainable is your competitive advantage? *California Management Review,* 34(3): 29–51.
104. J. A. Lamberg, H. Tikkanen, & T. Nokelainen, 2009, Competitive dynamics, strategic consistency and organizational survival, *Strategic Management Journal,* 30: 45–60; D. A. Chmielewski & A. Paladino, 2007, Driving a resource orientation: Reviewing the role of resources and capability characteristics, *Management Decision*, 45: 462–483.

105. N. Pangarkar & J. R. Lie, 2004, The impact of market cycle on the performance of Singapore acquirers, *Strategic Management Journal,* 25: 1209–1216.
106. Eric Langer, 2008, Understanding India's New patent Laws. Did the 2005 Patents Act engender a Western Intellectual Property Rights in the country, April, http://www.bioplanassociates.com/publications/articles/BPI_0408_Indiatoday_IPIssues.pdf
107. 2003, How fast is your company? *Fast Company,* June, 18.
108. D. P. Forbes, 2007, Reconsidering the strategic implications of decision comprehensiveness, *Academy of Management Review*, 32: 361–376; T. Talaulicar, J. Grundei, & A. V. Werder, 2005, Strategic decision making in startups: The effect of top management team organization and processes on speed and comprehensiveness, *Journal of Business Venturing,* 20: 519–541.
109. A. H. Ang, 2008, Competitive intensity and collaboration: Impact on firm growth across technological environments, *Strategic Management Journal,* 29: 1057–1075; M. Song, C. Droge, S. Hanvanich, & R. Calantone, 2005, Marketing and technology resource complementarity: An analysis of their interaction effect in two environmental contexts, *Strategic Management Journal,* 26: 259–276.
110. R. Williams, 1999, Renewable advantage: Crafting strategy through economic time, New York: Free Press, 8.
111. Ibid.
112. D. Li, L. E. Eden, M. A. Hitt, & R. D. Ireland, 2008, Friends, acquaintances or strangers? Partner selection in R&D alliances, *Academy of Management Journal,* 51: 315–334; D. Gerwin, 2004, Coordinating new product development in strategic alliances, *Academy of Management Review,* 29: 241–257.
113. K. Coucke & L. Sleuwaegen, 2008, Offshoring as a survival strategy: Evidence from manufacturing firms in Belgium, *Journal of international Business Studies,* 39: 1261–1277.
114. P. Carbonell & A. I. Rodriguez, 2006, The impact of market characteristics and innovation speed on perceptions of positional advantage and new product performance, *International Journal of Research in Marketing,* 23(1): 1–12; R. Sanchez, 1995, Strategic flexibility in production competition, *Strategic Management Journal,* 16 (Special Issue): 9–26.
115. R. Adner & D. Levinthal, 2008, Doing versus seeing: Acts of exploitation and perceptions of exploration, *Strategic Entrepreneurship Journal,* 2: 43–52; Williams, *Renewable Advantage*, 7.

CHAPTER 6

1. M. E. Porter, 1980, *Competitive Strategy,* New York: The Free Press, xvi.
2. M. D. R. Chari, S. Devaraj, & P. David, 2008, The impact of information technology investments and diversification strategies on firm performance, *Management Science,* 54: 224–234; A. Pehrsson, 2006, Business relatedness and performance: A study of managerial perceptions, *Strategic Management Journal,* 27: 265–282.
3. A. Hargrave-Silk, 2008, Media Brands moves to diversify, Media 3, November.
4. S. Walters & R. Stone, 2007, The trouble with rose-colored glasses, *Barron's*, June 25, M10.
5. A. O'Connell, 2009, Lego CEO Jørgen Vig Knudstorp on leading through survival and growth, *Harvard Business Review,* 87(1): 1–2.
6. M. E. Porter, 1987, From competitive advantage to corporate strategy, *Harvard Business Review,* 65(3): 43–59.
7. Ibid.; M. E. Raynor, 2007, What is corporate strategy, really? *Ivey Business Journal*, 71(8): 1–3.
8. E. Ellis, 2008, What'll you have, mate? *Barron's*, October 27, 34–36.
9. A. A. Calart & J. E. Ricart, 2007, Corporate strategy: An agent-based approach, *European Management Review*, 4: 107–120; M. Kwak, 2002, Maximizing value through diversification, *MIT Sloan Management Review,* 43(2): 10.
10. K. Lee, M. W. Peng, & K. Lee, 2008, From diversification premium to diversification discount during institutional transitions, *Journal of World Business*, 43(1): 47–65; M. Ammann & M. Verhofen, 2006, The conglomerate discount: A new explanation based on credit risk, *International Journal of Theoretical & Applied Finance*, 9(8): 1201–1214; S. A. Mansi & D. M. Reeb, 2002, Corporate diversification: What gets discounted? *Journal of Finance,* 57: 2167–2183.
11. N. M. Schmid & I. Walter, 2009, Do financial conglomerates create or destroy economic value? *Journal of Financial Intermediation*, 18(2): 193–216; C.E. Helfat & K.M. Eisenhardt, 2004, Intertemporal economies of scope organizational modularity, and the dynamics of diversification, *Strategic Management Journal,* 25: 1217–1232.
12. A. Campbell, M. Goold, & M. Alexander, 1995, Corporate strategy: The question for parenting advantage, *Harvard Business Review,* 73(2): 120–132.
13. D. Collis, D. Young, & M. Goold, 2007, The size, structure, and performance of corporate headquarters, *Strategic Management Journal,* 28: 283–405; M. Goold & A. Campbell, 2002, Parenting in complex structures, *Long Range Planning,* 35(3): 219–243; T. H. Brush, P. Bromiley, & M. Hendrickx, 1999, The relative influence of industry and corporation on business segment performance: An alternative estimate, *Strategic Management Journal,* 20: 519–547.
14. H. Chesbrough, 2007, The market for innovation: Implications for corporate strategy, *California Management Review,* 49(3): 45–66; D. Miller, 2006, Technological diversity, related diversification, and firm performance, *Strategic Management Journal,* 27: 601–619; D. J. Miller, 2004, Firms' technological resources and the performance effects of diversification: A longitudinal study, *Strategic Management Journal,* 25: 1097–1119.
15. D. D. Bergh, 2001, Diversification strategy research at a crossroads: Established, emerging and anticipated paths, in M. A. Hitt, R. E. Freeman, & J. S. Harrison (eds.), *Handbook of Strategic Management,* Oxford, UK: Blackwell Publishers, 363–383.
16. H. C. Wang & J. B. Barney, 2006, Employee incentives to make firm-specific investments: Implications for resource-based theories of corporate diversification, *Academy of Management Journal,* 31: 466–476.

17. J. J. Marcel, 2009, Why top management team characteristics matter when employing a chief operating officer: A strategic contingency perspective, *Strategic Management Journal,* 30(6): 647–658; A. J. Ward, M. J. Lankau, A. C. Amason, J. A. Sonnenfeld, & B. R. Agle, 2007, Improving the performance of top management teams, *MIT Sloan Management Review,* 48(3): 85–90.
18. R. P. Rumelt, *Strategy, Structure, and Economic Performance,* Boston: Harvard Business School, 1974; L. Wrigley, 1970, *Divisional Autonomy and Diversification* (Ph.D. dissertation), Harvard Business School.
19. For the first three companies, we refer to their Indian subsidiaries.
20. M. A. Williams, T. B. Michael, & E. R. Waller, 2008, Managerial incentives and acquisitions: A survey of the literature. *Managerial Finance*, 34(5): 328–341; S. W. Geiger & L. H. Cashen, 2007, Organizational size and CEO compensation: The moderating effect of diversification in downscoping organizations, *Journal of Managerial Issues,* 9(2): 233–252; R. K. Aggarwal & A. A. Samwick, 2003, Why do managers diversify their firms? Agency reconsidered, *Journal of Finance,* 58: 71–118.
21. D. J. Miller, M. J. Fern, & L. B. Cardinal, 2007, The use of knowledge for technological innovation within diversified firms, *Academy of Management Journal,* 50: 308–326.
22. H. Tanriverdi & C. -H. Lee, 2008, Within-industry diversification and firm performance in the presence of network externalities: Evidence from the software industry, *Academy of Management Journal*, 51(2): 381–397; H. Tanriverdi & N. Venkatraman, 2005, Knowledge relatedness and the performance of multibusiness firms, *Strategic Management Journal,* 26: 97–119.
23. M. D. R. Chari, S. Devaraj, & P. David, 2008, The impact of information technology investments and diversification strategies on firm performance, *Management Science*, 54(1): 224–234; H. Tanriverdi, 2006, Performance effects of information technology synergies in multibusiness firms, *MIS Quarterly,* 30(1): 57–78.
24. M. E. Porter, 1985, *Competitive Advantage,* New York: Free Press, 328.
25. N. Shin, 2009, Information technology and diversification: How their relationship affects firm performance. *International Journal of E-Collaboration*, 5(1): 69–83; D. Miller, 2006, Technological diversity, related diversification, and firm performance, *Strategic Management Journal,* 27: 601–619.
26. Tanriverdi & Lee, Within-industry diversification and firm performance in the presence of network externalities: Evidence from the software industry; P. Puranam & K. Srikanth, 2007, What they know vs. what they do: How acquirers leverage technology acquisitions, *Strategic Management Journal,* 28: 805–825; C. Park, 2003, Prior performance characteristics of related and unrelated acquirers, *Strategic Management Journal,* 24: 471–480; G. Delong, 2001, Stockholder gains from focusing versus diversifying bank mergers, *Journal of Financial Economics,* 2: 221–252; T. H. Brush, 1996, Predicted change in operational synergy and post-acquisition performance of acquired businesses, *Strategic Management Journal,* 17.
27. D. D. Bergh, 1995, Size and relatedness of units sold: An agency theory and resource-based perspective, *Strategic Management Journal,* 16: 221–239.
28. M. Lubatkin & S. Chatterjee, 1994, Extending modern portfolio theory into the domain of corporate diversification: Does it apply? *Academy of Management Journal,* 37: 109–136.
29. E. Dooms & A. A. Van Oijen, 2008, The balance between tailoring and standardizing control, *European Management Review*, 5(4): 245–252; T. Kono, 1999, A strong head office makes a strong company, *Long Range Planning,* 32(2): 225.
30. I. -C. Hsu & Y.-S. Wang, 2008, A model of intraorganizational knowledge sharing: Development and initial test. *Journal of Global Information Management*, 16(3): 45–73; Puranam & Srikanth, What they know vs. what they do; F. T. Rothaermel, M. A. Hitt, & L. A. Jobe, 2006, Balancing vertical integration and strategic outsourcing: Effects on product portfolio, product success, and firm performance, *Strategic Management Journal,* 27: 1033–1056; S. Chatterjee & B. Wernerfelt, 1991, The link between resources and type of diversification: Theory and evidence, *Strategic Management Journal,* 12: 33–48.
31. A. Rodríguez-Duarte, F. D. Sandulli, B. Minguela-Rata, & J. I. López-Sánchez, 2007, The endogenous relationship between innovation and diversification, and the impact of technological resources on the form of diversification, *Research Policy,* 36: 652–664; L. Capron & N. Pistre, 2002, When do acquirers earn abnormal returns? *Strategic Management Journal,* 23: 781–794.
32. C. Lawton, 2007, H-P begins push into high-end copiers, *Wall Street Journal,* April 24, B3.
33. Miller, Fern, & Cardinal, The use of knowledge for technological innovation within diversified firms; J. W. Spencer, 2003, Firms' knowledge-sharing strategies in the global innovation system: Empirical evidence from the flat panel display industry, *Strategic Management Journal,* 24: 217–233.
34. J. Thottam, 2008, Branson's flight plan, *Time,* April 28, 40.
35. 2009, Honda engines, Honda motor company, http://www.honda.com, March 30.
36. L. C. Thang, C. Rowley, T. Quang, & M. Warner, 2007, To what extent can management practices be transferred between countries?: The case of human resource management in Vietnam, *Journal of World Business,* 42(1): 113–127; G. Stalk Jr., 2005, Rotate the core, *Harvard Business Review,* 83(3): 18–19.
37. S. Gupta, A. Woodside, C. Dubelaar, & D. Bradmore, 2009, Diffusing knowledge-based core competencies for leveraging innovation strategies: Modeling outsourcing to knowledge process organizations (KPOs) in pharmaceutical networks, *Industrial Marketing Management*, 38(2): 219–227.
38. S. Chatterjee & J. Singh, 1999, Are trade-offs inherent in diversification moves? A simultaneous model for type of diversification and mode of expansion decisions, *Management Science,* 45: 25–41.
39. *Economic Times*, 2010, JSW to pick uo 41% of Ispat in #3 b deal, 22 December, p.1; *Mint Money,* 2010, JSW's acumen to be tested at Ispat, 22 December, p.17; http://en.wikipedia.org/wiki/List_of_steel_producers
40. L. Fuentelsaz & J. Gomez, 2006, Multi-point competition, strategic similarity and entry into geographic markets,

Strategic Management Journal, 27: 477–499; J. Gimeno & C. Y. Woo, 1999, Multimarket contact, economies of scope, and firm performance, *Academy of Management Journal,* 42: 239–259.

41. B. P. Biederman, 2008, Preparing for take-off, *Journal of Commerce*, July 28; R. Kwong, 2007, Big four hope expansion will deliver the goods, *Financial Times,* May 23, 15.
42. T. A. Shervani, G. Frazier, & G. Challagalla, 2007, The moderating influence of firm market power on the transaction cost economics model: An empirical test in a forward channel integration context, *Strategic Management Journal,* 28: 635–652; R. Gulati, P. R. Lawrence, & P. Puranam, 2005, Adaptation in vertical relationships: Beyond incentive conflict, *Strategic Management Journal,* 26: 415–440.
43. P. Broedner, S. Kinkel, & G. Lay, 2009, Productivity effects of outsourcing: New evidence on the strategic importance of vertical integration decisions, *International Journal of Operations & Production Management*, 29(2): 127–150; D. A. Griffin, A. Chandra, & T. Fealey, 2005, Strategically employing natural channels in an emerging market, *Thunderbird International Business Review,* 47(3): 287–311.
44. R. Carter & G. M. Hodgson, 2006, The impact of empirical tests of transaction cost economics on the debate on the nature of the firm, *Strategic Management Journal,* 27: 461–476; O. E. Williamson, 1996, Economics and organization: A primer, *California Management Review,* 38(2): 131–146.
45. S. Novak & S. Stern, 2008, How does outsourcing affect performance dynamics? Evidence from the automobile industry, *Management Science*, 54(12): 1963–1979.
46. C. Wolter & F. M. Veloso, 2008, The effects of innovation on vertical structure: Perspectives on transaction costs and competences, *Academy of Management Review*, 33(3): 586–605; M. G. Jacobides, 2005, Industry change through vertical disintegration: How and why markets emerged in mortgage banking, *Academy of Management Journal,* 48: 465–498.
47. *Times of India*, 2010, Nirma Bid to Unlock Value via Delisting, 14 October.
48. L. R. Kopczak & M. E. Johnson, 2003, The supply-chain management effect, *MIT Sloan Management Review,* 3: 27–34; K.R. Harrigan, 2001, Strategic flexibility in the old and new economies, in M. A. Hitt, R. E. Freeman, & J. S. Harrison (eds.), *Handbook of Strategic Management,* Oxford, UK: Blackwell Publishers, 97–123.
49. T. Hutzschenreuter & F. Gröne, 2009, Changing vertical integration strategies under pressure from foreign competition: The case of U.S. and German multinationals, *Journal of Management Studies*, 46(2): 269–307.
50. http://www.rediff.com/money/2005/jun/13spec1.htm, "Can Bharat Forge Beat Infosys?", Rediff.com, June 13. 2005.
51. 2009, Flextronics International Ltd., http://www.hoovers.com, March 15.
52. P. Kothandaraman & D. T. Wilson, 2001, The future of competition: Value-creating networks, *Industrial Marketing Management,* 30: 379–389.
53. K. M. Eisenhardt & D. C. Galunic, 2000, Coevolving: At last, a way to make synergies work, *Harvard Business Review,* 78(1): 91–111.
54. J. A. Nickerson & T. R. Zenger, 2008, Envy, comparison costs, and the economic theory of the firm, *Strategic Management Journal*, 13: 1429–1449.
55. L Greene, 2009, Adult nostalgia for childhood brands, *Financial Times*. http://www.ft.com, February 14; M. Marr, 2007, The magic kingdom looks to hit the road, *Wall Street Journal*, http://www.wsj.com, February 8.
56. E. Taylor & J. Singer, 2007, New UBS chief keeps strategy intact, *Wall Street Journal,* July 7, A3.
57. 2009, Breaking up the Citi, *Wall Street Journal*, January 14, A12; 2007, http://www.breakingviews.com: Citi to world: Drop "group," *Wall Street Journal,* January 17, C16.
58. 2009, Citigroup may sell Japanese units to raise cash, *Business 24-7*, http://www.business24-7.ae, February 26.
59. K. Bart, 2009, International finance: He cut costs at Credit Suisse; now he'll do it at UBS, *Wall Street Journal*, April 2, C2.
60. D. W. Ng, 2007, A modern resource based approach to unrelated diversification. *Journal of Management Studies*, 44(8): 1481–1502; D. D. Bergh, 1997, Predicting divestiture of unrelated acquisitions: An integrative model of ex ante conditions, *Strategic Management Journal*, 18: 715–731; C. W. L. Hill, 1994, Diversification and economic performance: Bringing structure and corporate management back into the picture, in R. P. Rumelt, D. E. Schendel, & D. J. Teece (eds.), *Fundamental Issues in Strategy,* Boston: Harvard Business School Press, 297–321.
61. Porter, *Competitive Advantage*.
62. S. Lee, K. Park, H. H. Shin, 2009, Disappearing internal capital markets: Evidence from diversified business groups in Korea. *Journal of Banking & Finance*, 33(2): 326–334; D. Collis, D. Young, & M. Goold, 2007, The size, structure, and performance of corporate headquarters, *Strategic Management Journal,* 28: 283–405; O. E. Williamson, 1975, *Markets and Hierarchies: Analysis and Antitrust Implications,* New York: Macmillan Free Press.
63. R. Aggarwal & N. A. Kyaw, 2009, International variations in transparency and capital structure: Evidence from european firms. *Journal of International Financial Management & Accounting*, 20(1): 1–34; R. J. Indjejikian, 2007, Discussion of accounting information, disclosure, and the cost of capital, *Journal of Accounting Research,* 45(2): 421–426.
64. A. Mackey, 2008, The effect of CEOs on firm performance, *Strategic Management Journal*, 29(12): 1357–1367; Dooms & Van Oijen, The balance between tailoring and standardizing control; D. Miller, R. Eisenstat, & N. Foote, 2002, Strategy from the inside out: Building capability-creating organizations, *California Management Review,* 44(3): 37–54; M. E. Raynor & J. L. Bower, 2001, Lead from the center: How to manage divisions dynamically, *Harvard Business Review,* 79(5): 92–100.
65. K. Kranhold, 2007, GE report raises doubts, *Wall Street Journal*, January 20–21, A3.
66. R. Ettenson & J. Knowles, 2008, Don't confuse reputation with brand. *MIT Sloan Management Review*, 49(2): 21.
67. "The House of Tata", case # 9-798-037, Harvard Business School, p.6.
68. P. Engardio & M. Arndt, 2007, What price reputation: Many savvy companies are starting to realize that a good name can be their most important asset—and actually boost the stock price. *Business Week*, July 8, 70–79; J. Lunsford & B.

Steinberg, 2006, Conglomerates' conundrum, *Wall Street Journal,* B1, B7.

69. "The House of Tata", case # 9-798-037, Harvard Business School, p.6.
70. F. Guerrera, 2007, Siemens chief makes the case for conglomerates, *Financial Times,* http://www.ft.com, February 5.
71. B. Quint, 2009, Companies deal with tough times through diversification. *Information Today*, 26(3): 7–8.
72. A. Delios, D. Xu, & P. W. Beamish, 2008, Within-country product diversification and foreign subsidiary performance, *Journal of International Business Studies*, 39(4): 706–724; M. W. Peng & A. Delios, 2006, What determines the scope of the firm over time and around the world? An Asia Pacific perspective, *Asia Pacific Journal of Management,* 23: 385–405; T. Khanna, K. G. Palepu, & J. Sinha, 2005, Strategies that fit emerging markets, *Harvard Business Review,* 83(6): 63–76.
73. Lee, Park, Shin, Disappearing internal capital markets: Evidence from diversified business groups in Korea; A. Chakrabarti, K. Singh, & I. Mahmood, 2006, Diversification and performance: Evidence from East Asian firms, *Strategic Management Journal,* 28: 101–120; T. Khanna & K. Palepu, 2000, Is group affiliation profitable in emerging markets? An analysis of diversified Indian business groups, *Journal of Finance,* 55: 867–892; T. Khanna & K. Palepu, 2000, The future of business groups in emerging markets: Long-run evidence from Chile, *Academy of Management Journal,* 43: 268–285.
74. D. D. Bergh, R. A. Johnson, & R. L. Dewitt, 2008, Restructuring through spin-off or sell-off: Transforming information asymmetries into financial gain, *Strategic Management Journal,* 29(2): 133–148; C. Decker & M. Mellewigt, 2007, Thirty years after Michael E. Porter: What do we know about business exit? *Academy of Management Perspectives,* 2: 41–55; S. J. Chang & H. Singh, 1999, The impact of entry and resource fit on modes of exit by multibusiness firms, *Strategic Management Journal,* 20: 1019–1035.
75. R. Coff, 2003, Bidding wars over R&D-intensive firms: Knowledge, opportunism, and the market for corporate control, *Academy of Management Journal,* 46: 74–85.
76. P. Navarro, 2009, Recession-proofing your organization, *MIT Sloan Management Review*, 50(3): 45–51.
77. T. Khanna and K. Palepu, "Why Focused Strategties May Be Wrong for Emerging Markets", *Harvard Business Review*, July August, 1997, pp.41–51.
78. T. Afza, C. Slahudin, & M. S. Nazir, 2008, Diversification and corporate performance: An evaluation of Pakistani firms, *South Asian Journal of Management*, 15(3): 7–18; J. M. Shaver, 2006, A paradox of synergy: Contagion and capacity effects in mergers and acquisitions, *Academy of Management Journal,* 31: 962–976; C. Park, 2002, The effects of prior performance on the choice between related and unrelated acquisitions: Implications for the performance consequences of diversification strategy, *Journal of Management Studies,* 39: 1003–1019.
79. Rumelt, *Strategy, Structure and Economic Performance,* 125.
80. R. Waters, 2008, eBay ready to sell Skype if strong synergies prove elusive, *Financial Times,* April 18, 17; A. Lashinsky, 2008, Is Skype on sale at eBay? *Fortune,* October 27, 158(8): 48.
81. *The Hindu*, 2004, L&T's Three Step Demerger, 5 February; *The Times of India*, 2004, L&T's Cement Business Demerger Comes into Effect, May 14, retrieved from http://timesofindia.indiatimes.com/business/india-business/LT-cement-business-demerger-comes-into-effect/articleshow/675137.cms.
82. *Hindu Businessline*, 2004, Larsen & Toubro: Buy, 15 August, retrieved from http://www.blonnet.com/iw/2004/08/15/stories/2004081500161100.htm.
83. L. E. Palich, L. B. Cardinal, & C. C. Miller, 2000, Curvilinearity in the diversification-performance linkage: An examination of over three decades of research, *Strategic Management Journal*, 21: 155–174.
84. S. Manikutty (2000), Family Business groups in India: A Resource-Based View of the Emerging Trends, *Family Business Review,* 13(4):279–292.
85. D. G. Sirmon, M. A. Hitt, & R. D. Ireland, 2007, Managing firm resources in dynamic environments to create value: Looking inside the black box, *Academy of Management Review,* 32: 273–292; A. E. Bernardo & B. Chowdhry, 2002, Resources, real options, and corporate strategy, *Journal of Financial Economics*, 63: 211–234.
86. W. H. Tsai, Y. C. Kuo, J.-H. Hung, 2009, Corporate diversification and CEO turnover in family businesses: Self-entrenchment or risk reduction? *Small Business Economics, 32*(1): 57–76; N. W. C. Harper & S. P. Viguerie, 2002, Are you too focused? *McKinsey Quarterly,* Mid-Summer, 29–38; J. C. Sandvig & L. Coakley, 1998, Best practices in small firm diversification, *Business Horizons,* 41(3): 33–40.
87. T. Aeppel, 2009, Auto suppliers attempt reinvention, *Wall Street Journal*, June 15, B1-B2.
88. N Suresh, 2008, Dr Reddy's aims to be a biosimilar leader, *Biospectrum,* 11 March, retrieved from http://biospectrumindia.ciol.com/content/IndustryInsights/10803114.asp; Syamala Ariyanchira, 2010, The opportunity for India in the global biosimilars market, 21 June, www.pharmaphorum.com, retrieved from http://www.pharmaphorum.com/2010/06/21/the-opportunity-for-india-in-the-global-biosimilars-market/.
89. *Businessworld*, 2010, Biology not Chemistry, 10 September, retrieved from http://www.businessworld.in/bw/storyContent/ 2010_10_09_Biology_Not_Chemistry.html.
90. T. B. Folta & J. P. O'Brien, 2008, Determinants of firm-specific thresholds in acquisition decisions, *Managerial and Decision Economics*, 29(2/3): 209–225.
91. N. M. Kay & A. Diamantopoulos, 1987, Uncertainty and synergy: Towards a formal model of corporate strategy, *Managerial and Decision Economics,* 8: 121–130.
92. R. W. Coff, 1999, How buyers cope with uncertainty when acquiring firms in knowledge-intensive industries: Caveat emptor, *Organization Science,* 10: 144–161.
93. P. B. Carroll & C. Muim 2008, 7 ways to fail big, *Harvard Business Review*, 86(9): 82–91.
94. D. G. Sirmon, S. Gove, & M. A. Hitt, 2008, Resource management in dyadic competitive rivalry: The effects of resource bundling and deployment, *Academy of Management Journal*, 51(5): 919–935; S. J. Chatterjee & B. Wernerfelt,

1991, The link between resources and type of diversification: Theory and evidence, *Strategic Management Journal,* 12: 33–48.

95. E. N. K. Lim, S. S. Das, & A. Das, 2009, Diversification strategy, capital structure, and the Asian financial crisis (1997–1998): Evidence from Singapore firms, *Strategic Management Journal*, 30(6): 577–594; W. Keuslein, 2003, The Ebitda folly, *Forbes,* March 17, 165–167.
96. T.-I.Tsai & I. Johnson, 2009, Acer hopes to thrive in downturn, *Wall Street Journal,* February 17, B7.
97. L. Capron & J. Hulland, 1999, Redeployment of brands, sales forces, and general marketing management expertise following horizontal acquisitions: A resource-based view, *Journal of Marketing,* 63(2): 41–54.
98. M. V. S. Kumar, 2009, The relationship between product and international diversification: The effects of short-run constraints and endogeneity. *Strategic Management Journal,* 30(1): 99–116; C. B. Malone & L. C. Rose, 2006. Intangible assets and firm diversification, *International Journal of Managerial Finance*, 2(2): 136–153; A. M. Knott, D. J. Bryce, & H. E. Posen, 2003, On the strategic accumulation of intangible assets, *Organization Science,* 14: 192–207.
99. Bergh, Johnson, & Dewitt, Restructuring through spin-off or sell-off: Transforming information asymmetries into financial gain; K. Shimizu & M. A. Hitt, 2005, What constrains or facilitates divestitures of formerly acquired firms? The effects of organizational inertia, *Journal of Management,* 31: 50–72.
100. Case "Andhra Pradesh Rayons: Quo Vadis?", Case material of the Indian Institute of Management, Ahmedabad.
101. M. A. Williams, T. B. Michael, & E. R. Waller, 2008, Managerial incentives and acquisitions: a survey of the literature. *Managerial Finance*, 34(5): 328–341; J. G. Combs & M. S. Skill, 2003, Managerialist and human capital explanation for key executive pay premiums: A contingency perspective, *Academy of Management Journal,* 46: 63–73; M. A. Geletkanycz, B. K. Boyd, & S. Finkelstein, 2001, The strategic value of CEO external directorate networks: Implications for CEO compensation, *Strategic Management Journal,* 9: 889–898; W. Grossman & R. E. Hoskisson, 1998, CEO pay at the crossroads of Wall Street and Main: Toward the strategic design of executive compensation, *Academy of Management Executive*, 12(1): 43–57.
102. R. E. Hoskisson, M. W. Castleton, & M. C. Withers, 2009, Complementarity in monitoring and bonding: More intense monitoring leads to higher executive compensation, *Academy of Management Perspectives*, 23(2): 57–74; Kaplan, S. N. 2008a. Are CEOs overpaid? *Academy of Management Perspectives*, 22(2): 5–20.
103. Geiger & Cashen, Organizational size and CEO compensation; J. J. Cordeiro &R. Veliyath, 2003, Beyond pay for performance: A panel study of the determinants of CEO compensation, *American Business Review,* 21(1): 56–66; Wright, Kroll, & Elenkov, Acquisition returns, increase in firm size, and chief executive officer compensation;S. R. Gray & A. A. Cannella Jr., 1997, The role of risk in executive compensation, *Journal of Management*, 23: 517–540.
104. Kaplan, Are CEOs overpaid?; R. Bliss & R. Rosen, 2001, CEO compensation and bank mergers, *Journal of Financial Economics,* 1: 107–138; W. G. Sanders & M. A. Carpenter, 1998, Internationalization and firm governance: The roles of CEO compensation, top team composition, and board structure, *Academy of Management Journal,* 41: 158–178.
105. J. Bogle, 2008, Reflections on CEO compensation, *Academy of Management Perspectives*, 22(2): 21–25; J.J. Janney, 2002, Eat or get eaten? How equity ownership and diversification shape CEO risk-taking, *Academy of Management Executive,* 14(4): 157–158; J. W. Lorsch, A. S. Zelleke, & K. Pick, 2001, Unbalanced boards, *Harvard Business Review,* 79(2): 28–30; R. E. Hoskisson & T. Turk, 1990, Corporate restructuring: Governance and control limits of the internal market, *Academy of Management Review,* 15: 459–477.
106. M. Kahan & E. B. Rock, 2002, How I learned to stop worrying and love the pill: Adaptive responses to takeover law, *University of Chicago Law Review,* 69(3): 871–915.
107. R. C. Anderson, T. W. Bates, J. M. Bizjak, & M. L. Lemmon, 2000, Corporate governance and firm diversification, *Financial Management*, 29(1): 5–22; J. D. Westphal, 1998, Board games: How CEOs adapt to increases in structural board independence from management, *Administrative Science Quarterly,* 43: 511–537; J. K. Seward & J. P. Walsh, 1996, The governance and control of voluntary corporate spin offs, *Strategic Management Journal,* 17: 25–39; J. P. Walsh & J. K. Seward, 1990, On the efficiency of internal and external corporate control mechanisms, *Academy of Management Review,* 15: 421–458.
108. S. M. Campbell, A. J. Ward, J. A. Sonnenfeld, & B. R. Agle, 2008, Relational ties that bind: Leader-follower relationship dimensions and charismatic attribution. *Leadership Quarterly*, 19(5): 556–568; M. Wiersema, 2002, Holes at the top: Why CEO firings backfire, *Harvard Business Review,* 80(12): 70–77.
109. J. M. Bizjak, M. L. Lemmon, & L. Naveen, 2008, Does the use of peer groups contribute to higher pay and less efficient compensation? *Journal of Financial Economics*, 90(2): 152–168; N. Wasserman, 2006, Stewards, agents, and the founder discount: Executive compensation in new ventures, *Academy of Management Journal,* 49: 960–976; V. Kisfalvi & P. Pitcher, 2003, Doing what feels right: The influence of CEO character and emotions on top management team dynamics, *Journal of Management Inquiry,* 12(10): 42–66; W. G. Rowe, 2001, Creating wealth in organizations: The role of strategic leadership, *Academy of Management Executive,* 15(1): 81–94.
110. E. F. Fama, 1980, Agency problems and the theory of the firm, *Journal of Political Economy,* 88: 288–307.
111. M. Y. Brannen & M. F. Peterson, 2009, Merging without alienating: Interventions promoting cross-cultural organizational integration and their limitations, *Journal of International Business Studies*, 40(3): 468–489; M. L. A. Hayward, 2002, When do firms learn from their acquisition experience? Evidence from 1990–1995, *Strategic Management Journal,* 23: 21–39; L. Capron, W. Mitchell, & A. Swaminathan, 2001, Asset divestiture following horizontal acquisitions: A dynamic view, *Strategic Management Journal,* 22: 817–844.
112. R. E. Hoskisson, R. A. Johnson, L. Tihanyi, & R. E. White, 2005, Diversified business groups and corporate refocusing in emerging economies, *Journal of Management,* 31: 941–965.

113. C. N. Chung & X. Luo, 2008, Institutional logics or agency costs: The influence of corporate governance models on business group restructuring in emerging economies, *Organization Science*, 19(5): 766–784; Chakrabarti, Singh, & Mahmood, Diversification and performance: Evidence from East Asian firms; W. P. Wan & R. E. Hoskisson, 2003, Home country environments, corporate diversification strategies, and firm performance, *Academy of Management Journal*, 46: 27–45.

CHAPTER 7

1. M. L. McDonald, J. D. Westphal, & M. E. Graebner, 2008, What do they know? The effects of outside director acquisition experience on firm acquisition performance, *Strategic Management Journal*, 29: 1155–1177; K. Uhlenbruck, M. A. Hitt, & M. Semadeni, 2006, Market value effects of acquisitions involving Internet firms: A resource-based analysis, *Strategic Management Journal,* 27: 899–913.
2. J. Wiklund & D. A. Shepherd, 2009, The effectiveness of alliances and acquisitions: The role of resource combination activities, *Entrepreneurship Theory and Practice*, 33: 193–212; C.-C. Lu, 2006, Growth strategies and merger patterns among small and medium sized enterprises: An empirical study, *International Journal of Management*, 23: 529–547.
3. M. A. Hitt, D. King, H. Krishnan, M. Makri, M. Schijven, K. Shimizu, & H. Zhu, 2009, Mergers and acquisitions: Overcoming pitfalls, building synergy and creating value, *Business Horizons*, in press.
4. G. M. McNamara, J. Haleblian, & B. J. Dykes, 2008, The performance implications of participating in an acquisition wave: Early mover advantages, bandwagon effects, and the moderating influence of industry characteristics and acquirer tactics, *Academy of Management Journal*, 51: 113–130; J. Haleblian; J. Y. Kim, & N. Rajagopalan, 2006, The influence of acquisition experience and performance on acquisition behavior: Evidence from the U.S. commercial banking industry, *Academy of Management Journal,* 49: 357–370; M. A. Hitt, J. S. Harrison, & R. D. Ireland, 2001, *Mergers and Acquisitions: A Guide to Creating Value for Stakeholders,* New York: Oxford University Press.
5. R. Dobbs & V. Tortorici, 2007, Cool heads will bring in the best deals; Boardroom discipline is vital if the M&A boom is to benefit shareholders, *Financial Times,* February 28, 6.
6. J.P. Pradhan, 2004, The determinants of outward foreign direct investment: A firm level analysis of Indian manufacturing, *Oxford Development Studies*, 32(4):619-639; J.P. Pradhan, 2007, Trends and patterns of overseas acquisitions by Indian multinationals, Unpublished working paper, Institute of Studies in Industrial Development; S. Gubbi, 2010, Strategic leap to multinationality: Study of international acquisitions by emerging multinationals from India, Unpublished doctoral dissertation, Indian Institute of Management, Calcutta.
7. J. Silver-Greenberg, 2009, Dealmakers test the waters, *BusinessWeek*, March 2, 18–20.
8. J. Y. Kim & S. Finkelstein, 2009, The effects of strategic and market complementarity on acquisition performance: Evidence from the U.S. commercial banking industry, 1989–2001; *Strategic Management Journal*, 30: 617–646; J. J. Reuer, 2005, Avoiding lemons in M&A deals, *MIT Sloan Management Review,* 46(3).
9. M. Baker, X. Pan, & J. Wurgler, 2009, The psychology of pricing in mergers and acquisitions, Working Paper: http://www.papers.ssrn.com/so13/papers.cfm?abstract_id=1364152; K. Cool & M. Van de Laar, 2006, The performance of acquisitive companies in the U.S. In L. Renneboog (ed.), *Advances in Corporate Finance and Asset Pricing,* Amsterdam, Netherlands: Elsevier Science, 77–105.
10. Krishnan Thiagarajan, 2007, Tata Corus Deal Should investors join the chorus?, *The Hindu Businessline*, February 4, http://www.thehindubusinessline.com/iw/2007/02/04/stories/ 200702 0401300700.htm; http://en.wikipedia.org/wiki/Tata_Corus_acquisition; http://www.businessworld.in/index.php/TATA-CORUS.html.
11. K. J. Martijn Cremers, V. B. Nair, & K. John, 2009, Takeovers and the cross-section of returns, *Review of Financial Studies*, 22: 1409–1445; C. Tuch & N. O'Sullivan, 2007, The impact of acquisitions on firm performance: A review of the evidence, *International Journal of Management Review,* 9(2): 141–170.
12. J. McCracken & J. S. Lublin, 2009, Towers Perrin and Watson Wyatt to merge, *Wall Street Journal Online*, http://www.wsj.com, June 29.
13. Assocham, 2010, "M&A increases three-fold from April-December 2010: Assocham", http://www.assocham.org/prels/shownews.php?id=2706.
14. M. Curtin, 2009, Xstrata's well-timed bear hug, *Wall Street Journal Online*, http://www.wsj.com, June 22.
15. S. Sudarsanam & A. A. Mahate, 2006, Are friendly acquisitions too bad for shareholders and managers? Long-term value creation and top management turnover in hostile and friendly acquirers, *British Journal of Management: Supplement,* 17(1): S7–S30.
16. http://en.wikipedia.org/wiki/Tata_Corus_acquisition.
17. E. Akdogu, 2009, Gaining a competitive edge through acquisitions: Evidence from the telecommunications industry, *Journal of Corporate Finance*, 15: 99–112; E. Devos, P.-R. Kadapakkam, & S. Krishnamurthy, 2009, How do mergers create value? A comparison of taxes, market power, and efficiency improvements as explanations for synergies, *Review of Financial Studies*, 22: 1179–1211.
18. J. Haleblian, C. E. Devers, G. McNamara, M. A. Carpenter, & R. B. Davison, 2009, Taking stock of what we know about mergers and acquisitions: A review and research agenda, *Journal of Management*, 35: 469–502; P. Wright, M. Kroll, & D. Elenkov, 2002, Acquisition returns, increase in firm size and chief executive officer compensation: The moderating role of monitoring, *Academy of Management Journal,* 45: 599–608.
19. A. Vance, 2009, Acer's chief urges more consolidation of the PC industry, *New York Times Online*, http://www.nytimes.com, July 7.
20. *Moneycontrol.com*, 2007, Mahindra & Mahindra acquisition of German based Schoneweiss, February 1, http://www.moneycontrol.com/news/business/mahindra-acquires-schoneweiss_265042.html; http://autonews.indiacar.com/news/n55798.htm; *Business Standard*, Mahindra acquires

leading Forging firm Schoneweiss, January 29, http://www.business-standard.com/ india/news/mahindra-buys-leading-forging-firm-schoneweiss/272932/; http://www.indiaprwire.com/pressrelease/machinery/ 200701291719.htm.

21. *Mydigitalfc.com*, 2010, JSW buys control of Ispat for Rs.2157 crore, December 21, http://www.mydigitalfc.com/companies/jsw-buys-control-ispat-rs-2157-cr-884.
22. K. E. Meyer, S. Estrin, S. K. Bhaumik, & M. W. Peng, 2009, Institutions, resources, and entry strategies in emerging economies, *Strategic Management Journal*, 30: 61–80; D. K. Oler, J. S. Harrison, & M. R. Allen, 2008, The danger of misinterpreting short-window event study findings in strategic management research: An empirical illustration using horizontal acquisitions, *Strategic Organization*, 6: 151–184.
23. Crisil, 2006, Impact Analysis: Holcim's stake acquisition in GACL, CRISIL report, retrieved from http://www.scribd.com/doc/37444702/Gujarat-Ambuja-Holcim-Deal.
24. *Times of India*, 2011, Finally, iGate seals Patni acquisition, January 11.
25. C. E. Fee & S. Thomas, 2004, Sources of gains in horizontal mergers: Evidence from customer, supplier, and rival firms, *Journal of Financial Economics*, 74: 423–460.
26. T. Ushijima, 2009, R&D intensity and acquisition and divestiture of corporate assets: Evidence from Japan, *Journal of Economics and Business*, 61(5): 415–433; L. Capron, W. Mitchell, & A. Swaminathan, 2001, Asset divestiture following horizontal acquisitions: A dynamic view, *Strategic Management Journal*, 22: 817–844.
27. B. Gulbrandsen, K. Sandvik, & S. A. Haugland, 2009, Antecedents of vertical integration: Transaction cost economics and resource-based explanations, *Journal of Purchasing and Supply Management*, 15: 89–102; F. T. Rothaermel, M. A. Hitt, & L. A. Jobe, 2006, Balancing vertical integration and strategic outsourcing: Effects on product portfolio, product success, and firm performance, *Strategic Management Journal*, 27: 1033–1056.
28. A. Parmigiani, 2007, Why do firms both make and buy? An investigation of concurrent sourcing, *Strategic Management Journal*, 28: 285–311.
29. *The Hindu Business Line*, 2002, Reliance makes it big with IPCL, May 20.
30. http://en.wikipedia.org/wiki/Piramal_Healthcare.
31. Case "Spartek Ceramics India Limited (B), Case # F&A 412, Indian Institute of management, Ahmedabad.
32. Takeover of Raasi Cement by India Cements, retrieved from http://www.scribd.com/doc/29032968/The-Takeover-of-Raasi-Cement; "Acquisition Gone Wrong", retrieved from http://www.kgsepg.com/project-id/3304-acquisition-gone-wrong.
33. J. W. Brock & N. P. Obst, 2009, Market concentration, economic welfare, and antitrust policy, *Journal of Industry, Competition and Trade*, 9: 65–75; M. T. Brouwer, 2008, Horizontal mergers and efficiencies: Theory and antitrust practice, *European Journal of Law and Economics*, 26: 11–26.
34. 2008, Procter & Gamble Annual Report, http://www.pg.com, July.
35. Veral Dholakia, 2010, Is Vedanta-Cairn deal on a slippery path?, August 18, http://trak.in/tags/business/2010/08/18/vedanta-cairn-india-deal/; *India Today*, 2010, Vedanta to face government hurdle in Cairn buy, August 24.
36. K. E. Meyer, M. Wright, & S. Pruthi, 2009, Managing knowledge in foreign entry strategies: A resource-based analysis, *Strategic Management Journal*, 30: 557–574; S.-F. S. Chen & M. Zeng, 2004, Japanese investors' choice of acquisitions vs. startups in the U.S.: The role of reputation barriers and advertising outlays, *International Journal of Research in Marketing*, 21(2): 123–136.
37. C. Y. Tseng, 2009, Technological innovation in the BRIC economies, *Research-Technology Management*, 52: 29–35; S. McGee, 2007, Seeking value in BRICs, *Barron's*, July 9, L10–L11.
38. R. Chakrabarti, N. Jayaraman, & S. Mukherjee, 2009, Mars-Venus marriages: Culture and cross-border M&A, *Journal of International Business Studies*, 40: 216–237.
39. S. Jessop, 2009, "Brave" post-Lehman M&A rewarded by market—Study, *New York Times Online*, http://www.nytimes.com, July 5.
40. E. Zabinski, D. Freeman, & X. Jian, 2009, Navigating the challenges of cross-border M&A, *The Deal Magazine*, http://www.thedeal.com, May 29.
41. N. Kumar, 2009, *The Economic Times*, http://www.economictimes.indiatimes.com, March 27.
42. J. Chapman & W. Xu, 2008, Ten strategies for successful cross-border acquisitions in China, Nixon Peabody LLP Special Report, Mergers & Acquisitions, September, 30–35.
43. M. Makri, M. A. Hitt, & P. J. Lane, 2009, Complementary technologies, knowledge relatedness, and invention outcomes in high technology M&As, *Strategic Management Journal*, in press; C. Homburg & M. Bucerius, 2006, Is speed of integration really a success factor of mergers and acquisitions? An analysis of the role of internal and external relatedness, *Strategic Management Journal*, 27: 347–367.
44. H. K. Ellonen, P. Wilstrom, & A. Jantunen, 2009, Linking dynamic-capability portfolios and innovation outcomes, *Technovation*, in press; M. Song & C. A. De Benedetto, 2008, Supplier's involvement and success of radical new product development in new ventures, *Journal of Operations Management*, 26: 1–22; S. Karim, 2006, Modularity in organizational structure: The reconfiguration of internally developed and acquired business units, *Strategic Management Journal*, 27: 799–823.
45. R. E. Hoskisson & L. W. Busenitz, 2002, Market uncertainty and learning distance in corporate entrepreneurship entry mode choice, in M. A. Hitt, R. D. Ireland, S. M. Camp, & D. L. Sexton (eds.), *Strategic Entrepreneurship: Creating a New Mindset*, Oxford, UK: Blackwell Publishers, 151–172; M. A. Hitt, R. E. Hoskisson, R. A. Johnson, & D. D. Moesel, 1996, The market for corporate control and firm innovation, *Academy of Management Journal*, 39: 1084–1119.
46. E. Steel, 2009, AOL buys two companies specializing in local online media, *Wall Street Journal Online*, http://www.wsj.com, June 11.
47. W. P. Wan & D. W Yiu, 2009, From crisis to opportunity: Environmental jolt, corporate acquisitions, and firm performance, *Strategic Management Journal*, 30: 791–801; L. F. Hsieh & Y.-T. Tsai, 2005, Technology investment mode of innovative technological corporations: M&A strat-

egy intended to facilitate innovation, *Journal of American Academy of Business,* 6(1): 185–194; G. Ahuja & R. Katila, 2001, Technological acquisitions and the innovation performance of acquiring firms: A longitudinal study, *Strategic Management Journal,* 22: 197–220.

48. F. Damanpour, R. M. Walker, & C. N. Avellaneda, 2009, Combinative effects of innovation types and organizational performance: A longitudinal study of service organizations, *Journal of Management Studies*, 46: 650–675.
49. F. Vermeulen, 2005, How acquisitions can revitalize companies, *MIT Sloan Management Review,* 46(4): 45–51; M. A. Hitt, R. E. Hoskisson, R. D. Ireland, & J. S. Harrison, 1991, Effects of acquisitions on R&D inputs and outputs, *Academy of Management Journal,* 34: 693–706.
50. B. White, 2007, Cisco to buy IronPort, a network-security firm, *Wall Street Journal,* January 4, A10.
51. 2009, Cisco breaks new ground in e-mail security, http://www.cisco.com, March 3.
52. H. Prechel, T. Morris, T. Woods, & R. Walden, 2008, Corporate diversification revisited: The political-legal environment, the multilayer-subsidiary form, and mergers and acquisitions, *The Sociological Quarterly*, 49: 849–878; C. E. Helfat & K. M. Eisenhardt, 2004, Inter-temporal economies of scope, organizational modularity, and the dynamics of diversification, *Strategic Management Journal,* 25: 1217–1232.
53. J. L. Lunsford, 2007, Boss talk: Transformer in transition; He turned UTC into giant; now, CEO George David carefully prepares successor, *Wall Street Journal,* May 17, B1.
54. T. Laamanen & T. Keil, 2008, Performance of serial acquirers: Toward an acquisition program perspective, *Strategic Management Journal*, 29: 663–672; D. J. Miller, M. J. Fern, & L. B. Cardinal, 2007, The use of knowledge for technological innovation within diversified firms, *Academy of Management Journal,* 50: 308–326.
55. J. Anand & H. Singh, 1997, Asset redeployment, acquisitions and corporate strategy in declining industries, *Strategic Management Journal,* 18 (Special Issue): 99–118.
56. T. Yu, M. Subramaniam, & A. A. Cannella, Jr., 2009, Rivalry deterrence in international markets: Contingencies governing the mutual forbearance hypothesis, *Academy of Management Journal*, 52: 127–147; D. G. Sirmon, S. Gove, & M. A. Hitt, 2008, Resource management in dyadic competitive rivalry: The effects of resource bundling and deployment, *Academy of Management Journal,* 51: 919–933.
57. H. Rui & G. S. Yip, 2008, Foreign acquisitions by Chinese firms: A strategic intent perspective, *Journal of World Business*, 43: 213–226; P. Puranam & K. Srikanth, 2007, What they know vs. what they do: How acquirers leverage technology acquisitions, *Strategic Management Journal,* 28: 805–825.
58. S. A. Zahra & J. C. Hayton, 2008, The effect of international venturing on firm performance: The moderating influence of absorptive capacity, *Journal of Business Venturing*, 23: 195–220.
59. J. S. Harrison, M. A. Hitt, R. E. Hoskisson, & R. D. Ireland, 2001, Resource complementarity in business combinations: Extending the logic to organizational alliances, *Journal of Management,* 27: 679–690.
60. J. Whalen, 2007, AstraZeneca thinks bigger; new chief increases commitment to "large molecule" biological drugs, *Wall Street Journal,* May 22, A7.
61. J. A. Schmidt, 2002, Business perspective on mergers and acquisitions, in J. A. Schmidt (ed.), *Making Mergers Work*, Alexandria, VA: Society for Human Resource Management, 23–46.
62. Jessop, "Brave" post-Lehman M&A rewarded by market.
63. M. Cording, P. Christmann, & D. R. King, 2008, Reducing causal ambiguity in acquisition integration: Intermediate goals as mediators of integration decisions and acquisition performance, *Academy of Management Journal*, 51: 744–767; M. Zollo & H. Singh, 2004, Deliberate learning in corporate acquisitions: Post-acquisition strategies and integration capability in U.S. bank mergers, *Strategic Management Journal,* 25: 1233–1256.
64. N. Kumar, 2009, How emerging giants are rewriting the rules of M&A, *Harvard Business Review*, 87(5): 115–121; M. C. Sturman, 2008, The value of human capital specificity versus transferability, *Journal of Management*, 34: 290–316.
65. K. M. Ellis, T. H. Reus, & B. T. Lamont, 2009, The effects of procedural and informational justice in the integration of related acquisitions, *Strategic Management Journal*, 30: 137–161; F. Vermeulen, 2007, Business insight (a special report); bad deals: Eight warning signs that an acquisition may not pay off, *Wall Street Journal,* April 28, R10.
66. M. Zollo, 1999, M&A—The challenge of learning to integrate: Mastering strategy (part eleven), *Financial Times,* December 6, 14–15.
67. H. G. Barkema & M. Schijven, 2008, Toward unlocking the full potential of acquisitions: The role of organizational restructuring, *Academy of Management Journal*, 51: 696–722; J. Harrison, 2007, Why integration success eludes many buyers, *Mergers and Acquisitions,* 42(3): 18–20.
68. *Times of India*, 2010, Air India-Indian Airlines merger marriage of incompatible individuals: Panel, March 12.
69. Bipin Kumar Singh, 2009, Air India & Indian airlines still operating as distant cousins?, Midday, September 28, http://www.mid-day.com/news/2009/sep/280909-Air-India-Indian-Airlines-Sharjah.htm.
70. *The Hindu,* 2010,Air India-Indian Airlines merger faces opposition from within: Patel, May 29, http://www.thehindu.com/business/article441168.ece.
71. Z. Kouwe, 2009, Deals on ice in first half, with 40% drop in M&A, *New York Times Online*, http://www.nytimes.com, July 1.
72. T. B. Folta & J. P. O'Brien, 2008, Determinants of firm-specific thresholds in acquisition decisions, *Managerial and Decision Economics*, 29: 209–225; R. J. Rosen, 2006, Merger momentum and investor sentiment: The stock market reaction to merger announcements, *Journal of Business,* 79: 987–1017.
73. A. Rappaport & Sirower, Stock or cash? *Harvard Business Review*, 77(6): 149.
74. Peers, NetApp should end Data Domain chase.
75. G. Yago, 1991, *Junk Bonds: How High Yield Securities Restructured Corporate America,* New York: Oxford University Press, 146–148.
76. M. C. Jensen, 1986, Agency costs of free cash flow, corporate finance, and takeovers, *American Economic Review,* 76: 323–329.
77. J. Leahy & J. Reed, 2009, Tata strained by UK acquisitions, *Financial Times Online*, http://www.ft.com, May 21.

78. T. H. Noe & M. J. Rebello, 2006, The role of debt purchases in takeovers: A tale of two retailers, *Journal of Economics & Management Strategy,* 15 (3): 609–648; M. A. Hitt & D. L. Smart, 1994, Debt: A disciplining force for managers or a debilitating force for organizations? *Journal of Management Inquiry,* 3: 144–152.
79. S. W. Bauguess, S. B. Moeller, F. P. Schlingemann, & C. J. Zutter, 2009, Ownership structure and target returns, *Journal of Corporate Finance*, 15: 48–65; H. Donker & S. Zahir, 2008, Takeovers, corporate control, and return to target shareholders, *International Journal of Corporate Governance*, 1: 106–134.
80. A. B. Sorescu, R. K. Chandy, & J. C. Prabhu, 2007, Why some acquisitions do better than others: Product capital as a driver of long-term stock returns, *Journal of Marketing Research,* 44(1): 57–72; T. Saxton & M. Dollinger, 2004, Target reputation and appropriability: Picking and deploying resources in acquisitions, *Journal of Management,* 30: 123–147.
81. J. B. Barney, 1988, Returns to bidding firms in mergers and acquisitions: Reconsidering the relatedness hypothesis, *Strategic Management Journal*, 9 (Special Issue): 71–78.
82. O. E. Williamson, 1999, Strategy research: Governance and competence perspectives, *Strategic Management Journal,* 20: 1087–1108.
83. S. Chatterjee, 2007, Why is synergy so difficult in mergers of related businesses? *Strategy & Leadership,* 35(2): 46–52.
84. J. Santalo & M. Becerra, 2009, Competition from specialized firms and the diversification-performance linkage, *Journal of Finance*, 63: 851–883; C. W. L. Hill & R. E. Hoskisson, 1987, Strategy and structure in the multiproduct firm, *Academy of Management Review,* 12: 331–341.
85. M. L. A. Hayward & K. Shimizu, 2006, De-commitment to losing strategic action: Evidence from the divestiture of poorly performing acquisitions, *Strategic Management Journal,* 27: 541–557; R. A. Johnson, R. E. Hoskisson, & M. A. Hitt, 1993, Board of director involvement in restructuring: The effects of board versus managerial controls and characteristics, *Strategic Management Journal,* 14 (Special Issue): 33–50; C. C. Markides, 1992, Consequences of corporate refocusing: Ex ante evidence, *Academy of Management Journal,* 35: 398–412.
86. D. Marginso & L. McAulay, 2008, Exploring the debate on short-termism: A theoretical and empirical analysis, *Strategic Management Journal*, 29: 273–292; R. E. Hoskisson & R. A. Johnson, 1992, Corporate restructuring and strategic change: The effect on diversification strategy and R&D intensity, *Strategic Management Journal,* 13: 625–634.
87. T. Keil, M. V. J. Maula, H. Schildt, & S. A. Zahra, 2008, The effect of governance modes and relatedness of external business development activities on innovative performance, *Strategic Management Journal*, 29: 895–907; K. H. Tsai & J. C. Wang, 2008, External technology acquisition and firm performance: A longitudinal study, *Journal of Business Venturing*, 23: 91–112.
88. A. Kacperczyk, 2009, With greater power comes greater responsibility? Takeover protection and corporate attention to stakeholders, *Strategic Management Journal*, 30: 261–285; L. H. Lin, 2009, Mergers and acquisitions, alliances and technology development: An empirical study of the global auto industry, *International Journal of Technology Management*, 48: 295–307; M. L. Barnett, 2008, An attention-based view of real options reasoning, *Academy of Management Review*, 33: 606–628.
89. M. L. A. Hayward & D. C. Hambrick, 1997, Explaining the premiums paid for large acquisitions: Evidence of CEO hubris, *Administrative Science Quarterly* 42: 103–127; R. Roll, 1986, The hubris hypothesis of corporate takeovers, *Journal of Business,* 59: 197–216.
90. Vermeulen, Business insight (a special report); bad deals: Eight warning signs that an acquisition may not pay off.
91. L. A. Nemanich & D. Vera, 2009, Transformational leadership and ambidexterity in the context of an acquisition, *The Leadership Quarterly*, 20: 19–33.
92. 2009, Our company, http://www.lizclaiborne.com, July 12; R. Dobbs, 2007, Claiborne seeks to shed 16 apparel brands, *Wall Street Journal,* July 11, B1, B2.
93. V. Swaminathan, F. Murshed, & J. Hulland, 2008, Value creation following merger and acquisition announcements: The role of strategic emphasis alignment, *Journal of Marketing Research*, 45: 33–47.
94. Vermeulen, Business insight (a special report); bad deals: Eight warning signs that an acquisition may not pay off.
95. H. G. Barkema & M. Schijven, 2008, How do firms learn to make acquisitions? A review of past research and an agenda for the future, *Journal of Management*, 34: 594–634.
96. S. Chatterjee, 2009, The keys to successful acquisition programmes, *Long Range Planning*, 42: 137–163; C. M. Sanchez & S. R. Goldberg, 2009, Strategic M&As: Stronger in tough times? *Journal of Corporate Accounting & Finance*, 20: 3–7; C. Duncan & M. Mtar, 2006, Determinants of international acquisition success: Lessons from FirstGroup in North America, *European Management Journal,* 24: 396–410.
97. D. Mayer & M. Kenney, 2004, Economic action does not take place in a vacuum: Understanding Cisco's acquisition and development strategy, *Industry and Innovation,* 11(4): 299–325.
98. 2009, Connection for acquired employees, http://www.cisco.com, July 12.
99. "CISCO: Are You Ready?", Case # 9-901-002, Boston: Harvard Business School Case. It also describes at length Cisco's philosophy of acquisitions.
100. M. A. Hitt, R. D. Ireland, J. S. Harrison, & A. Best, 1998, Attributes of successful and unsuccessful acquisitions of U.S. firms, *British Journal of Management*, 9: 91–114.
101. Uhlenbruck, Hitt, & Semadeni, Market value effects of acquisitions involving Internet firms: A resource-based analysis; J. Hagedoorn & G. Dysters, 2002, External sources of innovative capabilities: The preference for strategic alliances or mergers and acquisitions, *Journal of Management Studies,* 39: 167–188.
102. J. J. Reuer & R. Ragozzino, 2006, Agency hazards and alliance portfolios, *Strategic Management Journal,* 27: 27–43; P. Porrini, 2004, Can a previous alliance between an acquirer and a target affect acquisition performance? *Journal of Management,* 30: 545–562.
103. D. J. Kisgen, J. Qian, & W. Song, 2009, Are fairness opinions fair? The case of mergers and acquisitions, *Journal of Financial Economics*, 91: 179–207; R. J. Aiello & M. D.

Watkins, 2000, The fine art of friendly acquisition, *Harvard Business Review,* 78(6): 100–107.

104. S. Chatterjee, 2009, Does increased equity ownership lead to more strategically involved boards? *Journal of Business Ethics*, 87: 267–277; D. D. Bergh, 2001, Executive retention and acquisition outcomes: A test of opposing views on the influence of organizational tenure, *Journal of Management,* 27: 603–622; J. P. Walsh, 1989, Doing a deal: Merger and acquisition negotiations and their impact upon target company top management turnover, *Strategic Management Journal,* 10: 307–322.
105. D. A. Waldman & M. Javidan, 2009, Alternative forms of charismatic leadership in the integration of mergers and acquisitions, *The Leadership Quarterly*, 20: 130–142; F. J. Froese, Y. S. Pak, & L. C. Chong, 2008, Managing the human side of cross-border acquisitions in South Korea, *Journal of World Business*, 43: 97–108.
106. M. E. Graebner, 2009, Caveat Venditor: Trust asymmetries in acquisitions of entrepreneurial firms, *Academy of Management Journal*, 52: 435–472; N. J. Morrison, G. Kinley, & K. L. Ficery, 2008, Merger deal breakers: When operational due diligence exposes risk, *Journal of Business Strategy*, 29: 23–28.
107. J. M. Shaver & J. M. Mezias, 2009, Diseconomies of managing in acquisitions: Evidence from civil lawsuits, *Organization Science*, 20: 206–222; M. L. McDonald, J. D. Westphal, & M. E. Graebner, What do they know? The effects of outside director acquisition experience on firm acquisition performance, *Strategic Management Journal*, 29: 1155–1177.
108. D. D. Bergh & E. N.-K. Lim, 2008, Learning how to restructure: Absorptive capacity and improvisational views of restructuring actions and performance, *Strategic Management Journal*, 29: 593–616; J. K. Kang, J. M. Kim, W. L. Liu, & S. Yi, 2006, Post-takeover restructuring and the sources of gains in foreign takeovers: Evidence from U.S. targets. *Journal of Business,* 79(5): 2503–2537.
109. Y. G. Suh & E. Howard, 2009, Restructuring retailing in Korea: The case of Samsung-Tesco, *Asia Pacific Business Review*, 15: 29–40; Z. Wu & A. Delios, 2009, The emergence of portfolio restructuring in Japan, *Management International Review*, 49: 313–335; R. E. Hoskisson, A. A. Cannella, L. Tihanyi, & R. Faraci, 2004. Asset restructuring and business group affiliation in French civil law countries, *Strategic Management Journal*, 25: 525–539.
110. S. Thurm, 2008, Who are the best CEOs of 2008, *Wall Street Journal Online*, http://www.wsj.com, December 15.
111. J. L. Morrow Jr., D. G. Sirmon, M. A. Hitt, & T. R. Holcomb, 2007, Creating value in the face of declining performance: Firm strategies and organizational recovery, *Strategic Management Journal,* 28: 271–283; J. L. Morrow Jr., R. A. Johnson, & L. W. Busenitz, 2004, The effects of cost and asset retrenchment on firm performance: The overlooked role of a firm's competitive environment, *Journal of Management,* 30: 189–208.
112. *Oneindianews*, 2011, L and T to split into nine independent companies, January 5, http://news.oneindia.in/2011/01/05/l-and-t-split-into-nine-companies.html.
113. *Mint*, 2011, L&T to turn itself into 9 biz verticals, January 25.
114. "Andhra Pradesh Rayons: Quo Wadis?", unregistered case, Indian Institute of Management, Ahmedabad.
115. *Mint*, 2011, Wipro revamps stand-alone business units, February 8.
116. G. J. Castrogiovanni & G. D. Bruton, 2000, Business turnaround processes following acquisitions: Reconsidering the role of retrenchment, *Journal of Business Research,* 48: 25–34; W. McKinley, J. Zhao, & K. G. Rust, 2000, A sociocognitive interpretation of organizational downsizing, *Academy of Management Review,* 25: 227–243.
117. J. D. Evans & F. Hefner, 2009, Business ethics and the decision to adopt golden parachute contracts: Empirical evidence of concern for all stakeholders, *Journal of Business Ethics*, 86: 65–79; H. A. Krishnan, M. A. Hitt, & D. Park, 2007, Acquisition premiums, subsequent workforce reductions and post-acquisition performance, *Journal of Management,* 44: 709–732.
118. K. McFarland, 2008, Four mistakes leaders make when downsizing, *BusinessWeek Online*, http://www.businessweek.com, October 24.
119. C. O. Trevor & A. J. Nyberg, 2008, Keeping your headcount when all about you are losing theirs: Downsizing, voluntary turnover rates, and the moderating role of HR practices, *Academy of Management Journal*, 51: 259–276.
120. Berg & Lim, Learning how to restructure; R. E. Hoskisson & M. A. Hitt, 1994, *Downscoping: How to Tame the Diversified Firm,* New York: Oxford University Press.
121. Ushijima, R&D intensity and acquisition and divestiture of corporate assets; G. Benou, J. Madura, & T. Ngo, 2008, Wealth creation from high-tech divestitures, *The Quarterly Review of Economics and Finance*, 48: 505–519; L. Dranikoff, T. Koller, & A. Schneider, 2002, Divestiture: Strategy's missing link, *Harvard Business Review,* 80(5): 74–83.
122. R. E. Hoskisson & M. A. Hitt, 1990, Antecedents and performance outcomes of diversification: A review and critique of theoretical perspectives, *Journal of Management,* 16: 461–509.
123. 2009, Motorola sells fiber-to-the-node product line, *New York Times Online*, http://www.nytimes.com, July 7.
124. M. Peers, 2009, Magazine business suffers shakeout, *Wall Street Journal Online*, http://www.wsj.com, July 13.
125. R. Perez-Pena, 2009, McGraw-Hill is said to be seeking a buyer for *BusinessWeek*, *New York Times Online*, http://www.nytimes.com, July 14.
126. A. Kambil, 2008, What is your recession playbook? *Journal of Business Strategy*, 29: 50–52; M. Rajand & M. Forsyth, 2002, Hostile bidders, long-term performance, and restructuring methods: Evidence from the UK, *American Business Review,* 20: 71–81.
127. D. Hillier, P. McColgan, & S. Werema, 2008, Asset sales and firm strategy: An analysis of divestitures by UK companies, *The European Journal of Finance*, 15: 71–87; R. E. Hoskisson, R. A. Johnson, L. Tihanyi, & R. E. White, 2005, Diversified business groups and corporate refocusing in emerging economies, *Journal of Management,* 31: 941–965.
128. S. N. Kaplan & P. Stromberg, 2009, Leveraged buyouts and private equity, *Journal of Economic Perspectives*, 23: 121–146; C. Moschieri & J. Mair, 2008, Research on corporate divestures: A synthesis, *Journal of Management & Organization*, 14: 399–422.

129. J. Mair & C. Moschieri, 2006, Unbundling frees business for take off, *Financial Times,* October 19, 2.
130. K. H. Wruck, 2009, Private equity, corporate governance, and the reinvention of the market for corporate control, *Journal of Applied Corporate Finance*, 20: 8–21; M. F. Wiersema & J. P. Liebeskind, 1995, The effects of leveraged buyouts on corporate growth and diversification in large firms, *Strategic Management Journal,* 16: 447–460.
131. R. Harris, D. S. Siegel, & M. Wright, 2005, Assessing the impact of management buyouts on economic efficiency: Plant-level evidence from the United Kingdom, *Review of Economics and Statistics,* 87: 148–153; A. Seth & J. Easterwood, 1995, Strategic redirection in large management buyouts: The evidence from post-buyout restructuring activity, *Strategic Management Journal,* 14: 251–274; P. H. Phan & C. W. L. Hill, 1995, Organizational restructuring and economic performance in leveraged buyouts: An ex-post study, *Academy of Management Journal,* 38: 704–739.
132. M. Meuleman, K. Amess, M. Wright, & L. Scholes, 2009, Agency, strategic entrepreneurship, and the performance of private equity-backed buyouts, *Entrepreneurship Theory and Practice*, 33: 213–239; C. M. Daily, P. P. McDougall, J. G. Covin, & D. R. Dalton, 2002, Governance and strategic leadership in entrepreneurial firms, *Journal of Management,* 3: 387–412.
133. W. Kiechel III, 2007, Private equity's long view, *Harvard Business Review,* 85(8): 18–20; M. Wright, R. E. Hoskisson, & L. W. Busenitz, 2001, Firm rebirth: Buyouts as facilitators of strategic growth and entrepreneurship, *Academy of Management Executive,* 15(1): 111–125.
134. E. G. Love & M. Kraatz, 2009, Character, conformity, or the bottom line? How and why downsizing affected corporate reputation, *Academy of Management Journal*, 52: 314–335; J. P. Guthrie & D. K. Datta, 2008, Dumb and dumber: The impact of downsizing on firm performance as moderated by industry conditions, *Organization Science*, 19: 108–123.
135. H. A. Krishnan & D. Park, 2002, The impact of work force reduction on subsequent performance in major mergers and acquisitions: An exploratory study, *Journal of Business Research,* 55(4): 285–292; P. M. Lee, 1997, A comparative analysis of layoff announcements and stock price reactions in the United States and Japan, *Strategic Management Journal,* 18: 879–894.
136. D. J. Flanagan & K. C. O'Shaughnessy, 2005, The effect of layoffs on firm reputation, *Journal of Management,* 31: 445–463.
137. D. S. DeRue, J. R. Hollenbeck, M. D. Johnson, D. R. Ilgen, & D. K. Jundt, 2008, How different team downsizing approaches influence team-level adaptation and performance, *Academy of Management Journal*, 51: 182–196; C. D. Zatzick & R. D. Iverson, 2006, High-involvement management and workforce reduction: Competitive advantage or disadvantage? *Academy of Management Journal,* 49: 999–1015; N. Mirabal & R. DeYoung, 2005, Downsizing as a strategic intervention, *Journal of American Academy of Business,* 6(1): 39–45.
138. "Nucor at a Crossroads", Case # 9-793-039. Boston: Harvard Business School.
139. K. Shimizu & M. A. Hitt, 2005, What constrains or facilitates divestitures of formerly acquired firms? The effects of organizational inertia, *Journal of Management,* 31: 50–72.
140. D. T. Brown, C. E. Fee, & S. E. Thomas, 2009, Financial leverage and bargaining power with suppliers: Evidence from leveraged buyouts, *Journal of Corporate Finance*, 15: 196–211; S. Toms & M. Wright, 2005, Divergence and convergence within Anglo-American corporate governance systems: Evidence from the US and UK, 1950–2000, *Business History,* 47(2): 267–295.
141. G. Wood & M. Wright, 2009, Private equity: A review and synthesis, *International Journal of Management Reviews*, in press; A.-L. Le Nadant & F. Perdreau, 2006, Financial profile of leveraged buy-out targets: Some French evidence, *Review of Accounting and Finance,* (4): 370–392.
142. G. D. Bruton, J. K. Keels, & E. L. Scifres, 2002, Corporate restructuring and performance: An agency perspective on the complete buyout cycle, *Journal of Business Research,* 55: 709–724; W. F. Long & D. J. Ravenscraft, 1993, LBOs, debt, and R&D intensity, *Strategic Management Journal,* 14 (Special Issue): 119–135.
143. S. A. Zahra, 1995, Corporate entrepreneurship and financial performance: The case of management leveraged buyouts, *Journal of Business Venturing,* 10: 225–248.

CHAPTER 8

1. W. He & M. A. Lyles, 2009, China's outward foreign direct investment, *Business Horizons*, 51(6): 485–491; http://www.iloveindia.com/bikes/hero-honda/index.html; 2007, Honhttp://www.venturenavigator.co.uk/content/143.
2. B.C. Kho, R. M. Stulz, & F. E. Warnock, 2009, Financial globalization, governance, and the evolution of the home bias. *Journal of Accounting Research*, 47(2): 597–635; S. Li, 2005, Why a poor governance environment does not deter foreign direct investment: The case of China and its implications for investment protection, *Business Horizons*, 48(4): 297–302.
3. G. L. Ge & D. Z. Ding, 2009, A strategic analysis of surging Chinese manufacturers: The case of Galanz. *Asia Pacific Journal of Management*, 25(4): 667–683; A. K. Gupta & H. Wang, 2007, How to get China and India right: Western companies need to become smarter—and they need to do it quickly, *Wall Street Journal*, April 28, R4.
4. D. Kronborg & S. Thomsen, 2009, Foreign ownership and long-term survival, *Strategic Management Journal*, 30(2): 207–220; H. J. Sapienza, E. Autio, G. George, & S. A. Zahra, 2006, A capabilities perspective on the effects of early internationalization on firm survival and growth, *Academy of Management Review*, 31: 914–933; W. P. Wan, 2005, Country resource environments, firm capabilities, and corporate diversification strategies. *Journal of Management Studies*, 42: 161–182.
5. P. Enderwick, 2009, Large emerging markets (LEMs) and international strategy. *International Marketing Review*, 26(1): 7–16; F. T. Rothaermel, S. Kotha, & H. K. Steensma, 2006, International market entry by U.S. Internet firms: An empirical analysis of country risk, national culture and market size, *Journal of Management*, 32: 56–82; R. E. Hoskisson, H. Kim, R. E. White, & L. Tihanyi, 2004, A framework for understanding international diversification by business groups from emerg-

ing economies, in M. A. Hitt & J. L. C. Cheng (eds.), *Theories of the Multinational Enterprise: Diversity, Complexity, and Relevance. Advances in International Management*, Oxford, UK: Elsevier/JAI Press, 137–163.

6. M. Javidan, R. Steers, & M. A. Hitt (eds.), 2007, *The Global Mindset*, Oxford, UK: Elsevier Publishing; T. M. Begley & D. P. Boyd, 2003, The need for a corporate global mind-set, *MIT Sloan Management Review*, 44(2): 25–32.
7. Gaurav Parashar, 2009, Road Ahead for Maruti Suzuki- A semi-insider's view, Business Strategy, August 30, http://strat.in/2009/08/road-ahead-for-maruti-suzuki/; 2006, Maruti is now case study for Suzuki, February 15, http://autonews.indiacaar.com/news/n23591.htm
8. M. W. Peng & E. G. Pleggenkuhle-Miles, 2009, Current debates in global strategy, *International Journal of Management Reviews*, 11(1): 51–68; M. A. Hitt, L. Tihanyi, T. Miller, & B. Connelly, 2006, International diversification: Antecedents, outcomes and moderators, *Journal of Management*, 32: 831–867.
9. Y. Luo & R. L. Tung, 2007, International expansion of emerging market enterprises: A springboard perspective, *Journal of International Business Studies* 38: 481–498; J. E. Ricart, M. J. Enright, P. Ghemawat, S. L. Hart, & T. Khanna, 2004, New frontiers in international strategy, *Journal of International Business Studies*, 35: 175–200.
10. R. Vernon, 1996, International investment and international trade in the product cycle, *Quarterly Journal of Economics*, 80: 190–207.
11. He & Lyles, China's outward foreign direct investment; P. J. Buckley, L. J. Clegg, A. R. Cross, X. Liu, H. Voss, & P. Zheng, 2006, The determinants of Chinese outward foreign direct investment, *Journal of International Business Studies*, 38: 499–518.
12. L. Yu, 2003, The global-brand advantage, *MIT Sloan Management Review*, 44(3): 13.
13. M. E. Lloyd, 2009, IKEA sees opportunity during hard times—as expansion in U.S. continues, Swedish retailer expects its value furnishings to appeal to shoppers amid economic slump, *Wall Street Journal*, February 18, B5A.
14. X. Liu & H. Zou, 2008, The impact of greenfield FDI and mergers and acquisitions on innovation in Chinese high-tech industries, *Journal of World Business*, 43(3): 352–364.
15. F. Fortanier & R. Van Tulder, 2009, Internationalization trajectories—a cross-country comparison: Are large Chinese and Indian companies different? *Industrial and Corporate Change*, 18(2 Special Issue): 223–247.
16. K. Addae-Dapaah & W. T. Y. Hwee, 2009, The unsung impact of currency risk on the performance of international real property investment, *Review of Financial Economics*, 18(1): 56–65; C. C. Y. Kwok & D. M. Reeb, 2000, Internationalization and firm risk: An upstream-downstream hypothesis, *Journal of International Business Studies*, 31: 611–629.
17. M. Wright, I. Filatotchev, R. E. Hoskisson, & M. W. Peng, 2005, Strategy research in emerging economies: Challenging the conventional wisdom, *Journal of Management Studies*, 42: 1–30; T. London & S. Hart, 2004, Reinventing strategies for emerging markets: Beyond the transnational model, *Journal of International Business Studies*, 35: 350–370; R. E. Hoskisson, L. Eden, C. M. Lau, & M. Wright, 2000, Strategy in emerging economies, *Academy of Management Journal*, 43: 249–267.
18. P. Zheng, 2009, A comparison of FDI determinants in China and India, *Thunderbird International Business Review*, 51(3): 263–279; H. Sender, 2005, The economy; the outlook: India comes of age, as focus on returns lures foreign capital, *Wall Street Journal*, June 6, A2.
19. S. Athreye & S. Kapur, 2009, Introduction: The internationalization of Chinese and Indian firms—trends, motivations and strategy, *Industrial and Corporate Change*,18(2 Special Issue): 209–221; M. A. Witt & A. Y. Lewin, 2007, Outward foreign direct investment as escape to home country institutional constraints, *Journal of International Business Studies*, 38: 579–594; M. W. Peng, S.-H. Lee, & D. Y. L. Wang, 2005, What determines the scope of the firm over time? A focus on institutional relatedness, *Academy of Management Review*, 30: 622–633.
20. J. W. Spencer, T. P. Murtha, & S. A. Lenway, 2005, How governments matter to new industry creation, *Academy of Management Review*, 30: 321–337; I. P. Mahmood & C. Rufin, 2005, Government's dilemma: The role of government in imitation and innovation, *Academy of Management Review*, 30: 338–360.
21. B. Elango, 2009, Minimizing effects of "liability of foreignness": Response strategies of foreign firms in the United States, *Journal of World Business*, 44(1), 51–62; L. Eden & S. Miller, 2004, Distance matters: Liability of foreignness, institutional distance and ownership strategy, in M. A. Hitt & J. L. Cheng (eds.), *Advances in International Management*, Oxford, UK: Elsevier/JAI Press, 187–221.
22. S. Anand, 2008, Japan M&A, Prescription for Growth, *BusinessWeek*, http://www.businessweek.com, November 17.
23. The Battle for the Bottle Continues: Coke vs. Pepsi in India, case # BP 251, Indian Institute of Management, Ahmedabad.
24. V. Bauerlein and G. Fairclough, 2009, Beijing thwarts Coke's takeover bid, *Wall Street Journal*, http://www.wsj.com, March 19.
25. H. Barnard, 2008, Uneven domestic knowledge bases and the success of foreign firms in the USA, *Research Policy*, 37(10): 1674–1683.
26. S. Shimizutani & Y. Todo, 2008, What determines overseas R&D activities? The case of Japanese multinational firms, *Research Policy*, 37(3): 530–544; J. Cantwell, J. Dunning, & O. Janne, 2004, Towards a technology-seeking explanation of U.S. direct investment in the United Kingdom, *Journal of International Management*, 10: 5–20; W. Chung & J. Alcacer, 2002, Knowledge seeking and location choice of foreign direct investment in the United States, *Management Science*, 48(12): 1534–1554.
27. Rajeshwar Chigullapalli and Feroze Zaheer, Asia: The emerging Pharma R and D hub, Pharmafocusasia.com, http://

www.pharmafocusasia.com/knowledge_bank/articles/asia_emergingpharma.htm; Thomas A Hemphill, US offshore outsourcing of R and D: Accomodating firm and national competitive perspectives, Innovation, *Management Policy and Perspectives*, Vol 7 (iv), http://www.innovation-enterprise.com/archives/vol/7/issue/4/article/1625/us-offshore-outsourcing-of-rand; Nivedan Prakash, 2009, MNC R and D in India, Express Computer, May 25, http://www.expresscomputeronline.com/20090525/1000thissue07.shtml; A K Bhardwaj and Rammi Kapoor, 2008, FDI in R and D in India, NISTADS/CSIR, retrived from http://www.nistads.res.in/indiasnt2008/t4industry/t4ind5.htm *Financial Express*, 2002, Toyota Motor ties up with IICT for Auto chemicals, April 20, http://www.financialexpress.com/news/toyota-motor-ties-up-with-iict-for-auto-chemicals/43708/0; K.B. Saji, 2004, Recent trends in globalisation of R and D: The case of Indian pharmaceutical industry, *Delhi Business Review*, Vol. 5 no 2, July – December, http://www.delhibusinessreview.org/v_5n2/dbrv5n2j.pdf; Lakshmi Kanchan, 2002, HP Labs India announces collaboration with IIT Madras, www,hpl.com, February 28, http://www.hpl.hp.com/india/press/news_items/rel_feb2802_chen-dedication1.pdf; IBEF, 2006, The Untapped Opportunity, November, http://www.ibef.org/download/document_education.pdf.

28. F. Jiang, 2005, Driving forces of international pharmaceutical firms' FDI into China, *Journal of Business Research, 22*(1): 21–39.
29. M. D. R. Chari, S. Devaraj, & P. David, 2007, International diversification and firm performance: Role of information technology investments, *Journal of World Business, 42*: 184–197; W. Chung, 2001, Identifying technology transfer in foreign direct investment: Influence of industry conditions and investing firm motives, *Journal of International Business Studies*, 32: 211–229.
30. M. V. S. Kumar, 2009, The relationship between product and international diversification: The effects of short-run constraints and endogeneity. *Strategic Management Journal*, 30(1): 99–116; K. J. Petersen, R. B. Handfield, & G. L. Ragatz, 2005, Supplier integration into new product development: Co-ordinating product process and supply chain design, *Journal of Operations Management, 23*: 371–388.
31. C. Rauwald, 2009, Porsche chooses the China road; four-door Panamera's Shanghai debut signals focus on emerging markets, *Wall Street Journal*, April 20, B2; A. Webb, 2007, China needs strong automakers—not more. *Automotive News*, http://www.autonews.com, July 20; China's SAIC says first half sales up 23 percent. 2007, *Reuters*, http://www.reuters.com, July 12; A. Taylor, 2004, Shanghai Auto wants to be the world's next great car company, *Fortune*, October 4, 103–109.
32. K. D. Brouthers, L. E., Brouthers, & S. Werner, 2008, Resource-based advantages in an international context, *Journal of Management, 34*: 189–217; N. Karra, N. Phillips, & P. Tracey, 2008, Building the born global firm developing entrepreneurial capabilities for international new venture success, *Long Range Planning*, 41(4): 440–458; L. Zhou, W.-P. Wu, & X. Luo, 2007, Internationalization and the performance of born-global SMEs: The mediating role of social networks, *Journal of International Business Studies*, 38: 673–690.
33. H. Zou & P. N. Ghauri, 2009, Learning through international acquisitions: The process of knowledge acquisition in China, *Management International Review*, 48(2), 207–226; H. Berry, 2006, Leaders, laggards, and the pursuit of foreign knowledge, *Strategic Management Journal*, 27: 151–168.
34. J. Song & J. Shin, 2008, The paradox of technological capabilities: A study of knowledge sourcing from host countries of overseas R&D operations, *Journal of International Business Studies*, 39: 291–303; J. Penner-Hahn & J. M. Shaver, 2005, Does international research increase patent output? An analysis of Japanese pharmaceutical firms, *Strategic Management Journal*, 26: 121–140.
35. D. Strutton, 2009, Horseshoes, global supply chains, and an emerging Chinese threat: Creating remedies one idea at a time, *Business Horizons*, 52(1): 31–43.
36. A. M. Rugman & A. Verbeke, 2009, A new perspective on the regional and global strategies of multinational services firms, *Management International Review*, 48(4): 397–411; R. Tahir & J. Larimo, 2004, Understanding the location strategies of the European firms in Asian countries, *Journal of American Academy of Business*, 5: 102–110.
37. R. Chakrabarti, S. Gupta-Mukherjee, & N. Jayaraman, 2009, Mars-Venus marriages: Culture and cross-border M&A, *Journal of International Business Studies*, 40(2): 216–236; D. Xu & O. Shenkar, 2004, Institutional distance and the multinational enterprise, *Academy of Management Review*, 27: 608–618.
38. C. C. J. M. Millar & C. J. Choi, 2009, Worker identity, the liability of foreignness, the exclusion of local managers and unionism: A conceptual analysis, *Journal of Organizational Change Management*, 21(4): 460–470; D. Xu, Y. Pan, & P. W. Beamish, 2004, The effect of regulative and normative distances on MNE ownership and expatriate strategies, *Management International Review*, 44(3): 285–307.
39. N. Shirouzu, P. J. Ho, & K. Rapoza, 2009, *Corporate News*, GM plans to retain China, Brazil units, June 3, B2.
40. J. D. Stoll, 2009, Corporate news: GM pushes the throttle in China—affiliate's plan to expand into cars is seen as a key to growth in Asia, *Wall Street Journal*, April 27, B3.
41. J. Li & D. R. Yue, 2009, Market size, legal institutions, and international diversification strategies: Implications for the performance of multinational firms, *Management International Review*, 48(6): 667–688; T. D. A. Griffith & M. G. Harvey, 2001, A resource perspective of global dynamic capabilities, *Journal of International Business Studies*, 32: 597–606; Y. Luo, 2000, Dynamic capabilities in international expansion, *Journal of World Business*, 35(4): 355–378.
42. R. Morck, B. Yeung, & M. Zhao, 2008, Perspectives on China's outward foreign direct investment, *Journal of International Business Studies*, 39: 337–350; J. Gimeno, R. E. Hoskisson, B.D. Beal, & W. P. Wan, 2005, Explaining the clustering of international expansion moves: A critical test in the U.S. telecommunications industry, *Academy of Management Journal*, 48: 297–319.

43. A. Cuervo-Cazurra & M. Gene, 2008, Transforming disadvantages into advantages: Developing-country MNEs in the least developed countries, *Journal of International Business Studies*, 39: 957–979; M. A. Hitt, L. Bierman, K. Uhlenbruck, & K. Shimizu, 2006, The importance of resources in the internationalization of professional service firms: The good, the bad and the ugly, *Academy of Management Journal*, 49: 1137–1157.

44. P. Dastidar, 2009, International corporate diversification and performance: Does firm self-selection matter?, *Journal of International Business Studies*, 40: 71–85; L. Nachum, 2001, The impact of home countries on the competitiveness of advertising TNCs, *Management International Review*, 41(1): 77–98.

45. M. E. Porter, 1990, *The Competitive Advantage of Nations*, New York: The Free Press.

46. Ibid, 84.

47. Bharti Televentures, Case # 9-704-426, Harvard Business School.

48. C. Storz, 2008, Dynamics in innovation systems: Evidence from Japan's game software industry. *Research Policy*, 37(9): 1480–1491; Y. Aoyama & H. Izushi, 2003, Hardware gimmick or cultural innovation? Technological, cultural, and social foundations of the Japanese video game industry, *Research Policy*, 32: 423–443.

49. B. Powell, 2009, China's new king of solar, *Fortune*, February 16, 94–97.

50. Suzlon information from company knowledge book and Web site www.suzlon.com; http://www.suzlon.com/pdf/Knowledge%20Book.pdf http://en.wikipedia.org/wiki/Wind_power_in_India; SEBI, 2005, Red herring prospectus of Suzlon, September 12, http://www.sebi.gov.in/dp/suz.pdf; Rowena F. Caronan, 2010, Suzlon reaches 5000 MW in home country and wind hotspot in India, www.ecoseed.org, September 29, http://www.ecoseed.org/en/business/renewable-energy/article/95-renewable-energy/8079-suzlon-reaches-5-000-mw-in-home-country-and-wind-hotspot-india; Joanna I. Lewis, 2007, A comparison of Wind Power Industry Development Strategies in India, Spain, and China, www.newenergyindia.org, July 19, http://www.newenergyindia.org/Comparison%20of%20Wind%20Energy%20Power%20Industry%20in%20India,%20China,%20and%20Spain.pdf; www.iloveindia.com, 2007, Suzlon energy Limited, July 21, http://www.iloveindia.com/economy-of-india/top-50-companies/suzlon.html; http://cbagleyhbs.edu.tripod.com/ cases/suzlon.pdf; http://hubpages.com/hub/suzlonenergy; http://en.wikipedia.org/wiki/Solar_power_in_India.

51. J. Ioffe, 2009, Search wars; the Russians are coming, *Fortune*, February 16, 36–38.

52. A. Tempel & P. Walgenbach, 2007, Global standardization of organizational forms and management practices? What new institutionalism and business systems approach can learn from each other, *Journal of Management Studies*, 44: 1–24.

53. Kumar, The relationship between product and international diversification; W. P. Wan & R. E. Hoskisson, 2003, Home country environments, corporate diversification strategies and firm performance, *Academy of Management Journal*, 46: 27–45; J. M. Geringer, S. Tallman, & D. M. Olsen, 2000, Product and international diversification among Japanese multinational firms, *Strategic Management Journal*, 21: 51–80.

54. Kumar, The relationship between product and international diversification; M. A. Hitt, R. E. Hoskisson, & R. D. Ireland, 1994, A mid-range theory of the interactive effects of international and product diversification on innovation and performance, *Journal of Management*, 20: 297–326.

55. D. A. Ralston, D. H. Holt, R. H. Terpstra, & Y. Kai-Cheng, 2008, The impact of national culture and economic ideology on managerial work values: A study of the United States, Russia, Japan, and China, *Journal of International Business Studies*, 39(1): 8–26; B. B. Aired & K. S. Swan, 2004, Global versus multidomestic: Culture's consequences on innovation, *Management International Review*, 44: 81–105.

56. D. Grewal, G. R. Iyer, W. A. Kamakura, A. Mehrotra, & A. Sharma, 2009, Evaluation of subsidiary marketing performance: Combining process and outcome performance metrics, *Academy of Marketing Science Journal*, 37(2): 117–120; A. Ferner, P. Almond, I. Clark, T. Colling, & T. Edwards, 2004, The dynamics of central control and subsidiary anatomy in the management of human resources: Case study evidence from U.S. MNCs in the U.K., *Organization Studies*, 25: 363–392.

57. N. Guimarães-Costa & M. P. E. Cunha, 2009, Foreign locals: A liminal perspective of international managers, *Organizational Dynamics*, 38(2): 158–166; B. Connelly, M. A. Hitt, A. S. DeNisi, & R. D. Ireland, 2007, Expatriates and corporate-level international strategy: Governing with the knowledge contract, *Management Decision*, 45: 564–581; L. Nachum, 2003, Does nationality of ownership make any difference and if so, under what circumstances? Professional service MNEs in global competition, *Journal of International Management*, 9: 1–32.

58. M. W. Hansen, T. Pedersen, & B. Petersen, 2009, MNC strategies and linkage effects in developing countries, *Journal of World Business*, 44(2): 121–139; Y. Luo, 2001, Determinants of local responsiveness: Perspectives from foreign subsidiaries in an emerging market, *Journal of Management*, 27: 451–477.

59. H. Kasper, M. Lehrer, J. Mühlbacher, & B. Müller, 2009, Integration-responsiveness and knowledge-management perspectives on the MNC: A typology and field study of cross-site knowledge-sharing practices, *Journal of Leadership & Organizational Studies*, 15(3): 287–303.

60. J. Neff, 2008, Unilever's CMO finally gets down to business, *Advertising Age*, July, 11; G. Jones, 2002, Control, performance, and knowledge transfers in large multinationals: Unilever in the United States, 1945–1980, *Business History Review*, 76(3): 435–478.

61. P. J. Buckley, 2009, The impact of the global factory on economic development, *Journal of World Business*, 44(2): 131–143; Tempel & Walgenbach, Global standardization of organizational forms and management practices; Li, Is regional

strategy more effective than global strategy in the U.S. service industries?

62. H.C. Moon & M.-Y. Kim, 2009, A new framework for global expansion: A dynamic diversification-coordination (DDC) model, *Management Decision*, 46(1): 131–151.
63. Connelly, Hitt, DeNisi, & Ireland, Expatriates and corporate-level international strategy; J. F. L. Hong, M. Easterby-Smith, & R. S. Snell, 2006, Transferring organizational learning systems to Japanese subsidiaries in China, *Journal of Management Studies,* 43: 1027–1058.
64. Kho, Stulz, & Warnock, Financial globalization, governance, and the evolution of the home bias; R. G. Barker, 2003, Trend: Global accounting is coming, *Harvard Business Review*, 81 (4): 24–25.
65. A. Yaprak, 2002, Globalization: Strategies to build a great global firm in the new economy, *Thunderbird International Business Review*, 44(2): 297–302; D. G. McKendrick, 2001, Global strategy and population level learning: The case of hard disk drives, *Strategic Management Journal*, 22: 307–334.
66. P. Komiak, S. Y. X. Komiak, & M. Imhof, 2008, Conducting international business at eBay: The determinants of success of e-stores, *Electronic Markets*, 18(2): 187–204; V. Shannon, 2007, eBay is preparing to re-enter the China auction business, *New York Times,* http://www.nytimes.com, June 22; B Einhorn, 2007, A break in Yahoo's China clouds? *BusinessWeek,* http://www.businessweek.com, June 20.
67. M. Demirbag & E. Tatoglu, 2009, Competitive strategy choices of Turkish manufacturing firms in European Union, *The Journal of Management Development*, 27(7): 727–743; K. E. Meyer, 2006, Globalfocusing: From domestic conglomerates to global specialists, *Journal of Management Studies,* 43: 1109–1144; A. Delios & P. W. Beamish, 2005, Regional and global strategies of Japanese firms, *Management International Review*, 45: 19–36.
68. A. Delios, D. Xu & P. W. Beamish, 2008, Within-country product diversification and foreign subsidiary performance, *Journal of International Business Studies*, 39(4): 706–724; S. Massini, A. Y. Lewin, T. Numagami, & A. Pettigrew, 2002, The evolution of organizational routines among large Western and Japanese firms, *Research Policy*, 31(8,9): 1333–1348.
69. J. Millman, 2008, The fallen: Lorenzo Zambrano: Hard times for cement man, *Wall Street Journal*, December 11, A1; K. A. Garrett, 2005, Cemex, *Business Mexico*, April 23.
70. B. Elango & C. Pattnaik, 2007, Building capabilities for international operations through networks: A study of Indian firms, *Journal of International Business Studies*, 38: 541–555; T. B. Lawrence, E. A. Morse, & S. W. Fowler, 2005, Managing your portfolio of connections, *MIT Sloan Management Review*, 46(2): 59–65; C. A. Bartlett & S. Ghoshal, 1989, *Managing across Borders: The Transnational Solution*, Boston: Harvard Business School Press.
71. A. M. Rugman & A. Verbeke, 2008, A regional solution to the strategy and structure of multinationals, *European Management Journal*, 26(5): 305–313. A. Abbott & K. Banerji, 2003, Strategic flexibility and firm performance: The case of U.S. based transnational corporations, *Global Journal of Flexible Systems Management*, 4(1/2): 1–7; J. Child & Y. Van, 2001, National and transnational effects in international business: Indications from Sino-foreign joint ventures, *Management International Review*, 41(1): 53–75.
72. Rugman & Verbeke, A regional solution to the strategy and structure of multinationals.
73. C.K. Prahalad & Y. Doz (1987), *The Multinational Mission: Balancing Global Integration with Local Responsiveness.* New York: Free Press; Bartlett, C.A. & S. Ghoshal (1989) *Managing Across Borders: The Transnational Solution,* Boston. M.A.: Harvard Business School Press.
74. A. M. Rugman & A. Verbeke, 2003, Extending the theory of the multinational enterprise: Internalization and strategic management perspectives, *Journal of International Business Studies*, 34: 125–137.
75. H. F. Cheng, M. Gutierrez, A. Mahajan, Y. Shachmurove, & M. Shahrokhi, 2007, A future global economy to be built by BRICs, *Global Finance Journal,* 18(2): 143–156; Wright, Filatotchev, Hoskisson, & Peng, Strategy research in emerging economies: Challenging the conventional wisdom.
76. Elango, Minimizing effects of "liability of foreignness": Response strategies of foreign firms in the United States.
77. N. Y. Brannen, 2004, When Mickey loses face: Recontextualization, semantic fit and semiotics of foreignness, *Academy of Management Review*, 29: 593–616.
78. A. M. Rugman & A. Verbeke, 2007, Liabilities of foreignness and the use of firm-level versus country-level data: A response to Dunning et al. (2007), *Journal of International Business Studies,* 38: 200–205; S. Zaheer & A. Zaheer, 2001, Market microstructure in a global B2B network, *Strategic Management Journal*, 22: 859–873.
79. Rugman & Verbeke, A new perspective on the regional and global strategies of multinational services firms; S. R. Miller & L. Eden, 2006, Local density and foreign subsidiary performance, *Academy of Management Journal*, 49: 341–355.
80. Rugman & Verbeke, A new perspective on the regional and global strategies of multinational services firms; C. H. Oh & A. M. Rugman, 2007, Regional multinationals and the Korean cosmetics industry, *Asia Pacific Journal of Management*, 24: 27–42; A. Rugman & A. Verbeke, 2004, A perspective on regional and global strategies of multinational enterprises, *Journal of International Business Studies*, 35: 3–18.
81. A. K. Bhattacharya & D. C. Michael, 2008, How local companies keep multinationals at bay, *Harvard Business Review*, 86(3): 84–95; C. Pantzalis, 2001, Does location matter? An empirical analysis of geographic scope and MNC market valuation, *Journal of International Business Studies*, 32: 133–155.
82. A. Rugman & S. Girod, 2003, Retail multinationals and globalization: The evidence is regional, *European Management Journal*, 21(1): 24–37.
83. D. E. Westney, 2006. Review of the regional multinationals: MNEs and global strategic management (book review), *Journal of International Business Studies*, 37: 445–449.

84. R. D. Ludema, 2002, Increasing returns, multinationals and geography of preferential trade agreements, *Journal of International Economics*, 56: 329–358.
85. Meyer, Globalfocusing: From domestic conglomerates to global specialists; Delios & Beamish, Regional and global strategies of Japanese firms.
86. M. Aspinwall, 2009, NAFTA-ization: Regionalization and domestic political adjustment in the North American economic area. *Journal of Common Market Studies*, 47(1): 1–24.
87. T. L. Pett & J. A. Wolff, 2003, Firm characteristic and managerial perceptions of NAFTA: An assessment of export implications for U.S. SMEs, *Journal of Small Business Management*, 41(2): 117–132.
88. Morck, Yeung, & Zhao, Perspectives on China's outward foreign direct investment; W. Chung & J. Song, 2004, Sequential investment, firm motives, and agglomeration of Japanese electronics firms in the United States, *Journal of Economics and Management Strategy*, 13: 539–560; D. Xu & O. Shenkar, 2002, Institutional distance and the multinational enterprise, *Academy of Management Review*, 27(4): 608–618.
89. A. Ojala, 2008, Entry in a psychically distant market: Finnish small and medium-sized software firms in Japan, *European Management Journal*, 26(2): 135–144.
90. K. D. Brouthers, L. E. Brouthers, & S. Werner, 2008, Real options, international entry mode choice and performance, *Journal of Management Studies*, 45(5): 936–960.
91. C. A. Cinquetti, 2009, Multinationals and exports in a large and protected developing country, *Review of International Economics*, 16(5): 904–918.
92. Luo, Determinants of local responsiveness.
93. S. Shankar, C. Ormiston, N. Bloch, & R. Schaus, 2008, How to win in emerging markets, *MIT Sloan Management Review*, 49(3): 19–23; M. A. Raymond, J. Kim, & A. T. Shao, 2001, Export strategy and performance: A comparison of exporters in a developed market and an emerging market, *Journal of Global Marketing*, 15(2): 5–29.
94. A. Haahti, V. Madupu, U. Yavas, & E. Babakus, 2005, Cooperative strategy, knowledge intensity and export performance of small and medium-sized enterprises, *Journal of World Business*, 40(2): 124–138.
95. G. R. G. Clarke, 2008, Has the internet increased exports for firms from low and middle-income countries, *Information Economics and Policy*, 20(1): 16–37; K. A. Houghton & H. Winklhofer, 2004, The effect of Web site and ecommerce adoption on the relationship between SMEs and their export intermediaries, *International Small Business Journal*, 22: 369–385.
96. M. Bandyk, 2008, Now even small firms can go global, *U.S. News & World Report*, March 10, 52.
97. J. Slater, 2008, Weak dollar hits Europe, helps emerging markets, *Wall Street Journal (Europe)*, December 29, 1.
98. Pankaj Ghemawat (2007), *Redefining Global Strategy: Crossing Borders in a World Where Differences Still Matter.* Boston, M.A.: Harvard Business School Press.
99. U. Lichtenthaler, 2008, Externally commercializing technology assets: An examination of different process stages, *Journal of Business Venturing*, 23(4): 445–664; D. Kline, 2003, Sharing the corporate crown jewels, *MIT Sloan Management Review*, 44(3): 83–88.
100. R. Bird & D. R. Cahoy, 2008, The impact of compulsory licensing on foreign direct investment: A collective bargaining approach, *American Business Law Journal*, 45(2): 283–330; A. Arora & A. Fosfuri, 2000, Wholly owned subsidiary versus technology licensing in the worldwide chemical industry, *Journal of International Business Studies*, 31: 555–572.
101. N. Byrnes & F. Balfour, 2009, Philip Morris unbound, *BusinessWeek*, May 4, 38–42; N. Zamiska, J. Ye, & V. O'Connell, 2008, Chinese cigarettes to go global, *Wall Street Journal*, January 30, B4; N. Zamiska & V. O'Connell, 2005, Philip Morris is in talks to make Marlboros in China, *Wall Street Journal*, April 21, B1, B2.
102. Zamiska, Ye, & O'Connell, Chinese cigarettes to go global, B4.
103. S. Nagaoka, 2009, Does strong patent protection facilitate international technology transfer? Some evidence from licensing contracts of Japanese firms, *Journal of Technology Transfer*, 34(2): 128–144.
104. M. Johnson, 2001, Learning from toys: Lessons in managing supply chain risk from the toy industry, *California Management Review*, 43(3): 106–124.
105. U. Lichtenthaler & H. Ernst, 2007, Business insight (a special report); Think strategically about technology licensing, *Wall Street Journal*, R4
106. C. A. Bartlett & S. Rangan, 1992, Komatsu limited, in C. A. Bartlett & S. Ghoshal (eds.), *Transnational Management: Text, Cases and Readings in Cross-Border Management*, Homewood, IL: Irwin, 311–326.
107. T. Audi, 2008, Last resort: Ailing Sheraton shoots for a room upgrade; Starwood to tackle biggest hotel brand; the "ugly stepchild," *Wall Street Journal*, March 25, A1.
108. T. W. Tong, J. J. Reuer, & M. W. Peng, 2008. International joint ventures and the value of growth options, *Academy of Management Journal*, 51: 1014–1029; A. A. Ziedonis, 2007, Real options in technology licensing, *Management Science*, 53(10): 1618–1633.
109. H. K. Steensma, J. Q. Barden, C. Dhanaraj, M. Lyles, & L. Tihanyi, 2008, The evolution and internalization of international joint ventures in a transitioning economy, *Journal of International Business Studies*, 39(3): 491–507; M. Nippa, S. Beechler, & A. Klossek, 2007, Success factors for managing international joint ventures: A review and an integrative framework, *Management and Organization Review*, 3: 277–310.
110. N. Rahman, 2008, Resource and risk trade-offs in Guanxi-based IJVs in China, *Asia Pacific Business Review*, 14(2): 233–251; J. S. Harrison, M. A. Hitt, R. E. Hoskisson, & R. D. Ireland, 2001, Resource complementarity in business combinations: Extending the logic to organization alliances, *Journal of Management*, 27: 679–690.
111. W. Zhan, R. Chen, M. K. Erramilli, & D. T, Nguyen, 2009, Acquisition of organizational capabilities and competitive advantage of IJVs in transition economies: The case

of Vietnam. *Asia Pacific Journal of Management*, 26(2): 285–308; M. A. Hitt, D. Ahlstrom, M. T. Dacin, E. Levitas, & L. Svobodina, 2004, The institutional effects on strategic alliance partner selection in transition economies: China versus Russia, *Organization Science*, 15: 173–185.

112. E. Woyke, 2009, ZTE's smart phone ambitions; The company is betting on advanced phones to crack the U.S. market, *Forbes*, http://www.forbes.com, March 16.
113. T. Chi & A. Seth, 2009, A dynamic model of the choice of mode for exploiting complementary capabilities, *Journal of International Business Studies*, 40(3): 365–387; M. A. Lyles & J. E. Salk, 2007, Knowledge acquisition from foreign parents in international joint ventures: An empirical examination in the Hungarian context, *Journal of International Business Studies*, 38: 3–18; E. W. K. Tsang, 2002, Acquiring knowledge by foreign partners for international joint ventures in a transition economy: Learning-by-doing and learning myopia, *Strategic Management Journal*, 23(9): 835–854.
114. M. J. Robson, C. S. Katsikeas, & D. C. Bello, 2008, Drivers and performance outcomes of trust in international strategic alliances: The role of organizational complexity, *Organization Science*, 19(4): 647–668; S. Zaheer & A. Zaheer, 2007, Trust across borders, *Journal of International Business Studies*, 38: 21–29.
115. M. H. Ogasavara & Y. Hoshino, 2009, The effects of entry strategy and inter-firm trust on the survival of Japanese manufacturing subsidiaries in Brazil, *Asian Business & Management*, 7(3): 353–380; M. W. Peng & O. Shenkar, 2002, Joint venture dissolution as corporate divorce, *Academy of Management Executive*, 16(2): 92–105.
116. Y. Luo, O. Shenkar, & H. Gurnani, 2008, Control-cooperation interfaces in global strategic alliances: A situational typology and strategic responses, *Journal of International Business Studies*, 9(3): 428–453; A. Madhok, 2006, Revisiting multinational firms' tolerance for joint ventures: A trust-based approach, *Journal of International Business Studies*, 37: 30–43; J. Child & Y. Van, 2003, Predicting the performance of international joint ventures: An investigation in China, *Journal of Management Studies*, 40(2): 283–320; J. P. Johnson, M. A. Korsgaard, & H. J. Sapienza, 2002, Perceived fairness, decision control, and commitment in international joint venture management teams, *Strategic Management Journal*, 23(12): 1141–1160.
117. X. Lin & C. L. Wang, 2008, Enforcement and performance: The role of ownership, legalism and trust in international joint ventures, *Journal of World Business*, 43(3): 340–351; L. Huff & L. Kelley, 2003, Levels of organizational trust in individualist versus collectivist societies: A seven-nation study, *Organization Science*, 14(1): 81–90.
118. D. Li, L. Eden, M. A. Hitt, & R. D. Ireland, 2008, Friends, acquaintances and strangers? Partner selection in R&D alliances, *Academy of Management Journal,* 51: 315–334; Y. Pan & D. K. Tse, 2000, The hierarchical model of market entry modes, *Journal of International Business Studies*, 31: 535–554.
119. J. Wiklund & D. A. Shepherd, 2009, The effectiveness of alliances and acquisitions: The role of resource combination activities, *Entrepreneurship Theory and Practice*, 33(1): 193–212; P. Porrini, 2004, Can a previous alliance between an acquirer and a target affect acquisition performance? *Journal of Management*, 30: 545–562.
120. C. M. Sanchez & S. R. Goldberg, 2009, Strategic M&As: Stronger in tough times, *Journal of Corporate Accounting & Finance*, 20(2): 3–7; K. Shimizu, M. A. Hitt, D. Vaidyanath, & V. Pisano, 2004, Theoretical foundations of cross-border mergers and acquisitions: A review of current research and recommendations for the future, *Journal of International Management*, 10: 307–353; M. A. Hitt, J. S. Harrison, & R. D. Ireland, 2001, *Mergers and Acquisitions: A Guide to Creating Value for Stakeholders,* New York: Oxford University Press.
121. A. Boateng, W. Qian, & Y. Tianle, 2008, Cross-border M&As by Chinese firms: An analysis of strategic motives and performance, *Thunderbird International Business Review*, 50(4): 259–270; M. A. Hitt & V. Pisano, 2003, The cross-border merger and acquisition strategy, *Management Research*, 1: 133–144.
122. International operational fact sheet, 2007, http://www.walmartfacts.com, July; J. Levine, 2004, Europe: Gold mines and quicksand, *Forbes*, April 12, 76.
123. B. Powell, 2009, Buying binge, *Time*, April 20, GB1.
124. P. X. Meschi, 2009, Government corruption and foreign stakes in international joint ventures in emerging economies, *Asia Pacific Journal of Management*, 26(2): 241–261; U. Weitzel & S. Berns, 2006, Cross-border takeovers, corruption, and related aspects of governance, *Journal of International Business Studies,* 37: 786–806.
125. Chakrabarti, Gupta-Mukherjee, & Jayaraman, Mars-Venus marriages: Culture and cross-border M&A; A. H. L. Slangen, 2006, National cultural distance and initial foreign acquisition performance: The moderating effect of integration, *Journal of World Business*, 41: 161–170.
126. S. F. S. Chen, 2008, The motives for international acquisitions: Capability procurements, strategic considerations, and the role of ownership structures, *Journal of International Business Studies*, 39(3): 454–471; I. Bjorkman, G. K. Stahl, & E. Vaara, 2007, Cultural differences and capability transfer in cross-border acquisitions: The mediating roles of capability complementarity, absorptive capacity, and social integration, *Journal of International Business Studies,* 38: 658–672.
127. J. Reed, 2008, SAIC plans U.K. comeback for MG TF roadster, *Financial Times*, April 21, 25; C. Buckley, 2005, SAIC to fund MG Rover bid, *The Times of London*, http://www.timesonline.co.uk, July 18.
128. India Knowledge@ Wharton, 2008, Tata's takeover of Jaguar and Land Rover Bumpy Road or Smooth Ride, April 3, http://knowledge.wharton.upenn.edu/india/article.cfm?articleid=4275; http://www.mbaknol.com/management-case-studies/case-study-of-tata-motor-acquisition-of-jaguar-and-land-rover/; Sharon Silke Carty, 2008, Tata Motors to buy Jaguar LandRover for $2.3 B, USAToday, March 26, http://www.usatoday.com/money/autos/2008-03-25-ford-sells-jaguar-land-rover-tata_N.htm.
129. *Mint*, 2011, Tata Motors net triples on JLR sales in China, February 12.

130. H. Raff, M. Ryan, F. Stähler, 2009, The choice of market entry mode: Greenfield investment, M&A and joint venture, *International Review of Economics & Finance*, 18(1): 3–10; A.-W. Harzing, 2002, Acquisitions versus greenfield investments: International strategy and management of entry modes, *Strategic Management Journal*, 23: 211–227.
131. C. Bouquet, L. Hebert, & A. Delios, 2004, Foreign expansion in service industries: Separability and human capital intensity, *Journal of Business Research*, 57: 35–46.
132. K. F. Meyer, S. Estrin, S. K. Bhaumik, & M. W. Peng, 2009, Institutions, resources, and entry strategies in emerging economies, *Strategic Management Journal*, 30(1): 61–80.
133. K. F. Meyer, M. Wright, & S. Pruthi, 2009, Managing knowledge in foreign entry strategies: a resource-based analysis, *Strategic Management Journal*, 30(5): 557–574.
134. Y. Park & B. Sternquist, 2008, The global retailer's strategic proposition and choice of entry mode, *International Journal of Retail & Distribution Management*, 36(4): 281–299; S. Mani, K. D. Antia, & A. Rindfleisch, 2007, Entry mode and equity level: A multilevel examination of foreign direct investment ownership structure, *Strategic Management Journal*, 28: 857–866.
135. A. Roth, 2008, Beijing Olympics 2008: UPS markets its delivery for China only; Company transports gear for the Games; face-off with FedEx, *Wall Street Journal* (Europe), August 11, 29.
136. D. L. Paul & R. B. Wooster, 2008, Strategic investments by U.S. firms in transition economies, *Journal of International Business Studies*, 39(2): 249–266; V. Gaba, Y. Pan, & G. R. Ungson, 2002, Timing of entry in international market: An empirical study of U.S. Fortune 500 firms in China, *Journal of International Business Studies,* 33(1): 39–55; S.-J. Chang & P. Rosenzweig, 2001, The choice of entry mode in sequential foreign direct investment, *Strategic Management Journal*, 22: 747–776.
137. Meschi, Government corruption and foreign stakes in international joint ventures in emerging economies; R. Farzad, 2007, Extreme investing: Inside Colombia, *BusinessWeek*, May 28, 50–58; K. E. Myer, 2001, Institutions, transaction costs, and entry mode choice in Eastern Europe, *Journal of International Business Studies*, 32: 357–367.
138. J. Che & G. Facchini, 2009, Cultural differences, insecure property rights and the mode of entry decision, *Economic Theory*, 38(3): 465–484; S. Li, 2004, Why are property rights protections lacking in China? An institutional explanation, *California Management Review*, 46(3): 100–115.
139. A. C. Inkpen, 2008, Knowledge transfer and international joint ventures: The case of NUMMI and General Motors, *Strategic Management Journal*, 29(4): 447–453.
140. D. Hannon, 2008, Shorter is better for Toyota's supply chain, *Purchasing*, August, 46–47; M. Zimmerman, 2007, Toyota ends GM's reign as car sales leader, *Los Angeles Times*, April 25, 2007, C1; L. J. Howell & J. C. Hsu, 2002, Globalization within the auto industry, *Research Technology Management,* 45(4): 43–49.
141. J. W. Lu & X. Ma, 2008, The contingent value of local partners' business group affiliations, *Academy of Management Journal*, 51(2): 295–314; A. Chacar & B. Vissa, 2005, Are emerging economies less efficient? Performance persistence and the impact of business group affiliation, *Strategic Management Journal*, 26: 933–946; Hoskisson, Kim, Tihanyi, & White, A framework for understanding international diversification by business groups from emerging economies.
142. R. Chittoor, M. B. Sarkar, S. Ray, & P. S. Aulakh, 2009, Third-world copycats to emerging multinationals: Institutional changes and organizational transformation in the Indian pharmaceutical industry, *Organization Science*, 20(1): 187–205.
143. M. F. Wiersma & H. P. Bowen, 2008, Corporate international diversification: The impact of foreign competition, industry globalization and product diversification, *Strategic Management Journal,* 29: 115–132.
144. Dastidar, International corporate diversification and performance; L. Li, 2007, Multinationality and performance: A synthetic review and research agenda, *International Journal of Management Reviews,* 9: 117–139; J. A. Doukas & O. B. Kan, 2006, Does global diversification destroy firm value, *Journal of International Business Studies,* 37: 352–371; J. W. Lu & P. W. Beamish, 2004, International diversification and firm performance: The S-curve hypothesis, *Academy of Management Journal*, 47: 598–609.
145. S. E. Christophe & H. Lee, 2005, What matters about internationalization: A market-based assessment, *Journal of Business Research*, 58: 536–643; J. A. Doukas & L. H. P. Lang, 2003, Foreign direct investment, diversification and firm performance, *Journal of International Business Studies,* 34: 153–172.
146. H. Zou & M. B. Adams, 2009, Corporate ownership, equity risk and returns in the People's Republic of China, *Journal of International Business Studies*, 39(7): 1149–1168; Hitt, Tihanyi, Miller, & Connelly, International diversification; Kwok & Reeb, Internationalization and firm risk.
147. A. Birnik & R. Moat, 2009, Mapping multinational operations, *Business Strategy Review*, 20(1): 30–33; T. R. Holcomb & M. A. Hitt, 2007, Toward a model of strategic outsourcing, *Journal of Operations Management*, 25: 464–481; J. P. Doh, 2005, Offshore outsourcing: Implications for international business and strategic management theory and practice, *Journal of Management Studies,* 42: 695–704.
148. Song & Shin, The paradox of technological capabilities: A study of knowledge sourcing from host countries of overseas R&D operations; J. Penner-Hahn & J. M. Shaver, 2005, Does international research and development increase patent output? An analysis of Japanese pharmaceutical firms, *Strategic Management Journal,* 26: 121–140.
149. Shimizutani & Todo, What determines overseas R&D activities? The case of Japanese multinational firms; Hitt, Bierman, Uhlenbruck, & Shimizu, The importance of resources in the internationalization of professional service firms; L. Tihanyi, R. A. Johnson, R. E. Hoskisson, & M. A. Hitt, 2003, Institutional

ownership differences and international diversification: The effects of board of directors and technological opportunity, *Academy of Management Journal*, 46:195–211.

150. Zou & Ghauri, Learning through international acquisitions; B. Ambos & B. B. Schlegelmilch, 2007, Innovation and control in the multinational firm: A comparison of political and contingency approaches, *Strategic Management Journal,* 28: 473–486.
151. E. Matta & P. W. Beamish, 2008, The accentuated CEO career horizon problem: Evidence from international acquisitions, *Strategic Management Journal*, 29(7): 683; D. S. Elenkov, W. Judge, & P. Wright, 2005, Strategic leadership and executive innovation influence: An international multi-cluster comparative study, *Strategic Management Journal,* 26: 665–682; P. Herrmann, 2002, The influence of CEO characteristics on the international diversification of manufacturing firms: An empirical study in the United States, *International Journal of Management*, 19(2): 279–289.
152. H. L. Sirkin, J. W. Hemerling, & A. K. Bhattacharya, 2009, Globality: Challenger companies are radically redefining the competitive landscape, *Strategy & Leadership*, 36(6): 36–41; M. A. Hitt, R. E. Hoskisson, & H. Kim, 1997, International diversification: Effects on innovation and firm performance in product-diversified firms, *Academy of Management Journal,* 40: 767–798.
153. E. García-Canal & M. F. Guillén, 2009, Risk and the strategy of foreign location choice in regulated industries, *Strategic Management Journal,* 29(10): 1097–1115; J. Child, L. Chung, & H. Davies, 2003, The performance of cross-border units in China: A test of natural selection, strategic choice and contingency theories, *Journal of International Business Studies*, 34: 242–254.
154. C. Crossland & D. C. Hambrick, 2007, How national systems differ in their constraints on corporate executives: A study of CEO effects in three countries, *Strategic Management Journal,* 28: 767–789; M. Javidan, P. W. Dorfman, M. S. de Luque, & R. J. House, 2006, In the eye of the beholder: Cross-cultural lessons in leadership from Project GLOBE, *Academy of Management Perspectives,* 20 (1): 67–90.
155. N. Shirouzu, 2008, Corporate news: GM's car sales slide in China; Toyota, Honda zoom ahead as buyers concentrate on fuel economy, quality, *Wall Street Journal*, September 26, B1.
156. I. Alon & T. T. Herbert, 2009, A stranger in a strange land: Micro political risk and the multinational firm, *Business Horizons*, 52(2): 127–137; P. Rodriguez, K. Uhlenbruck, & L. Eden, 2005, Government corruption and the entry strategies of multinationals, *Academy of Management Review*, 30: 383–396; J. H. Zhao, S. H. Kim, & J. Du, 2003, The impact of corruption and transparency on foreign direct investment: An empirical analysis, *Management International Review*, 43(1): 41–62.
157. F. Wu, 2009, Singapore's sovereign wealth funds: The political risk of overseas investments, *World Economics,* 9(3): 97–122; P. S. Ring, G. A. Bigley, T. D'aunno, & T. Khanna, 2005, Perspectives on how governments matter, *Academy of Management Review*, 30: 308–320; A. Delios & W. J. Henisz, 2003, Policy uncertainty and the sequence of entry by Japanese firms, 1980–1998, *Journal of International Business Studies*, 34: 227–241.
158. A. Kouznetsov, 2009, Entry modes employed by multinational manufacturing enterprises and review of factors that affect entry mode choices in Russia, *The Business Review,* Cambridge, 10(2): 316–323.
159. S. Globerman & D. Shapiro, 2009, Economic and strategic considerations surrounding Chinese FDI in the United States, *Asia Pacific Journal of Management*, 26(1): 163–183.
160. I. G. Kawaller, 2009, Hedging currency exposures by multinationals: Things to consider, *Journal of Applied Finance*, 18(1): 92–98; Addae-Dapaah & Hwee, The unsung impact of currency risk on the performance of international real property investment; T. Vestring, T. Rouse, & U. Reinert, 2005, Hedging your offshoring bets, *MIT Sloan Management Review*, 46(3): 26–29.
161. T. G. Andrews & N. Chompusri, 2005, Temporal dynamics of crossvergence: Institutionalizing MNC integration strategies in post-crisis ASEAN, *Asia Pacific Journal of Management,* 22(1): 5–22; S. Mudd, R. Grosse, & J. Mathis, 2002, Dealing with financial crises in emerging markets, *Thunderbird International Business Review*, 44(3): 399–430.
162. N. Bandelj, 2009, The global economy as instituted process: The case of Central and Eastern Europe, *American Sociological Review*, 74(1): 128–149; L. Tihanyi & W. H. Hegarty, 2007, Political interests and the emergence of commercial banking in transition economies, *Journal of Management Studies,* 44: 789–813.
163. Lu & Beamish, International diversification and firm performance: The s-curve hypothesis; Wan & Hoskisson, Home country environments, corporate diversification strategies and firm performance; Hitt, Hoskisson, & Kim, International diversification.
164. A. Ojala, 2008, Entry in a psychically distant market: Finnish small and medium-sized software firms in Japan, *European Management Journal*, 26(2): 135–144; D. W. Yiu, C. M. Lau, & G. D. Bruton, 2007, International venturing by emerging economy firms: The effects of firm capabilities, home country networks, and corporate entrepreneurship, *Journal of International Business Studies*, 38: 519–540; P. S. Barr & M. A. Glynn, 2004, Cultural variations in strategic issue interpretation: Relating cultural uncertainty avoidance to controllability in discriminating threat and opportunity, *Strategic Management Journal*, 25: 59–67.
165. M. L. L. Lam, 2009, Beyond credibility of doing business in China: Strategies for improving corporate citizenship of foreign multinational enterprises in China, *Journal of Business Ethics*: Supplement, 87: 137–146; W. P. J. Henisz & B. A. Zeiner, 2005, Legitimacy, interest group pressures and change in emergent institutions, the case of foreign investors and host country governments, *Academy of Management Review*, 30: 361–382; T. P. Blumentritt & D. Nigh, 2002, The integration of subsidiary political activities in multinational corporations, *Journal of International Business Studies*, 33: 57–77.
166. D. Lavie & S. Miller, 2009, Alliance portfolio internationalization and firm performance, *Organization Science*, 19(4): 623–646

CHAPTER 9

1. D. Lavie, 2009, Capturing value from alliance portfolios, *Organizational Dynamics*, 38(1): 26–36; J. L. Morrow, Jr., D. G. Sirmon, M. A. Hitt, & T. R. Holcomb, 2007, Creating value in the face of declining performance: Firm strategies and organizational recovery, *Strategic Management Journal*, 28: 271–283.
2. T. W. Tong, J. J. Reuer, & M. W. Peng, 2008, International joint ventures and the value of growth options, *Academy of Management Journal*, 51: 1014–1029.
3. H. Ness, 2009, Governance, negotiations, and alliance dynamics: Explaining the evolution of relational practice, *Journal of Management Studies*, 46(3): 451–480; R. C. Fink, L. F. Edelman, & K. J. Hatten, 2007, Supplier performance improvements in relational exchanges, *Journal of Business & Industrial Marketing*, 22: 29–40.
4. M. J. Chen, 2008, Reconceptualizing the competition cooperation relationship: A transparadox perspective, *Journal of Management Inquiry*, 17(4): 288–304; P. E. Bierly III & S. Gallagher, 2007, Explaining alliance partner selection: Fit, trust and strategic expediency, *Long Range Planning*, 40: 134–153; K. Singh & W. Mitchell, 2005, Growth dynamics: The bidirectional relationship between interfirm collaboration and business sales in entrant and incumbent alliances, *Strategic Management Journal*, 26: 497–521.
5. W. M. Bulkeley, 2008, Business technology, A service rival looms for IBM: H-P deal for EDS to pose challenges for big blue unit, *Wall Street Journal*, May 20, B6.
6. S. Hamm, 2009, Big blue goes into analytics, *BusinessWeek*, April 27, 16.
7. R. Agarwal & C. E. Helfat, 2009, Strategic renewal of organizations, *Organization Science*, 20(2): 281–293; P. M. Senge, B. B. Lichtenstein, K. Kaeufer, H. Bradbury, & J. Carroll, 2007, Collaborating for systemic change, *MIT Sloan Management Review*, 48(2): 44–53; R. Vassolo, J. Anand, & T. B. Folta, 2004, Non-additivity in portfolios of exploration activities: A real options-based analysis of equity alliances in biotechnology, *Strategic Management Journal*, 25: 1045–1061.
8. R. C. Marshall, L. M. Marx, & M. E. Raiff, 2008, Cartel price announcement: The vitamins industry, *International Journal of Industrial Organization*, 26(3): 762–802; T. L. Sorenson, 2007, Credible collusion in multimarket oligopoly, *Managerial and Decision Economics*, 28: 115–128.
9. C. E. Ybarra & T. A. Turk, 2009, The evolution of trust in information technology alliances, *Journal of High Technology Management Research*, 20(1): 62–74; R. D. Ireland, M. A. Hitt, & D. Vaidyanath, 2002, Alliance management as a source of competitive advantage, *Journal of Management*, 28: 413–446; J. G. Coombs & D. J. Ketchen, 1999, Exploring interfirm cooperation and performance: Toward a reconciliation of predictions from the resource-based view and organizational economics, *Strategic Management Journal*, 20: 867–888.
10. M. A. Schilling, 2009, Understanding the alliance data, *Strategic Management Journal*, 30(3): 233–260; J. J. Reuer & A. Arino, 2007, Strategic alliance contracts: Dimensions and determinants of contractual complexity, *Strategic Management Journal*, 28: 313–330;M. R. Subramani & N. Venkatraman, 2003, Safeguarding investments in asymmetric interorganizational relationships: Theory and evidence, *Academy of Management Journal*, 46(1): 46–62.
11. S. Lahiri & B. L. Kedia, 2009, The effects of internal resources and partnership quality on firm performance: An examination of Indian BPO providers, *Journal of International Management*, 15(2): 209–22; R. Krishnan, X. Martin, & N. G. Noorderhaven, 2007, When does trust matter to alliance performance? *Academy of Management Journal*, 49: 894–917; P. Kale, J. H. Dyer, & H. Singh, 2002, Alliance capability, stock market response, and long-term alliance success: The role of the alliance function, *Strategic Management Journal*, 23: 747–767.
12. K. H. Heimeriks & G. Duysters, 2007, Alliance capability as a mediator between experience and alliance performance: An empirical investigation into the alliance capability development process, *Journal of Management Studies*, 44: 25–49.
13. R. E. Hoskisson, M. A. Hitt, R. D. Ireland, & J. S. Harrison, 2008, *Competing for Advantage*, 2nd ed., Thomson/Southwestern, 184.
14. B. S. Bulik, 2009, Kodak develops as modern brand with digital shift, *Advertising Age*, April 27, 26.
15. R. Lunnan & S. A. Haugland, 2008, Predicting and measuring alliance performance: A multi-dimensional analysis, *Strategic Management Journal*, 29(5): 545–556; R. Seppanen, K. Blomqvist, & S. Sundqvist, 2007, Measuring interorganizational trust—A critical review of the empirical research in 1990–2003, *Industrial Marketing Management*, 36: 249–265; T. K. Das & B.-S. Teng, 2001, A risk perception model of alliance structuring, *Journal of International Management*, 7: 1–29.
16. L. F. Mesquita, J. Anand, & T. H. Brush, 2008, Comparing the resource-based and relational views: Knowledge transfer and spillover in vertical alliances, *Strategic Management Journal*, 29: 913–941; F. F. Suarez & G. Lanzolla, 2007, The role of environmental dynamics in building a first mover advantage theory, *Academy of Management Review*, 32: 377–392; M. A. Geletkanycz & S. S. Black, 2001, Bound by the past? Experience-based effects on commitment to the strategic status quo, *Journal of Management*, 27: 3–21.
17. A. Pasztor & A. Cole, 2008, New multirole missile is planned, *Wall Street Journal*, July 16, A13.
18. K. H. Heimeriks, E. Klijn, & J. J. Reuer, 2009, Building capabilities for alliance portfolios, *Long Range Planning*, 42(1): 96–114; D. Gerwin, 2004, Coordinating new product development in strategic alliances, *Academy of Management Review*, 29: 241–257; Ireland, Hitt, & Vaidyanath, Alliance management as a source of competitive advantage.
19. X. Lin & C. L. Wang, 2008, Enforcement and performance: The role of ownership, legalism and trust in international joint ventures, *Journal of World Business*, 43(3): 340–351; Y. Luo, 2007, Are joint venture partners more opportunistic in a more volatile environment? *Strategic Management Journal*, 28: 39–60.

20. F. Evangelista & L. N. Hau, 2008, Organizational context and knowledge acquisition in IJVs: An empirical study, *Journal of World Business*, 44(1): 63–73; S. L. Berman, J. Down, & C. W. L. Hill, 2002, Tacit knowledge as a source of competitive advantage in the National Basketball Association, *Academy of Management Journal*, 45: 13–31.
21. M. Becerra, R. Lunnan, & L. Huemer, 2008, Trustworthiness, risk, and the transfer of tacit and explicit knowledge between alliance partners, *Journal of Management Studies*, 45(4): 691–713.
22. Y. Yamaguchi, 2009, Leading the news: Fujitsu targets 10% share of markets for servers, *Asian Wall Street Journal*, March 31, 3.
23. A. Tiwana, 2008,, Do bridging ties complement strong ties? An empirical examination of alliance ambidexterity, *Strategic Management Journal*, 29(3): 251–272; R. E. Hoskisson & L. W. Busenitz, 2002, Market uncertainty and learning distance in corporate entrepreneurship entry mode choice, in M. A. Hitt, R. D. Ireland, S. M. Camp, & D. L. Sexton (eds.), *Strategic Entrepreneurship: Creating a New Mindset*, Oxford, UK: Blackwell Publishers, 151–172.
24. J. Xia, J. Tan, & D. Tan, 2008, Mimetic entry and bandwagon affect: The rise and decline of international equity joint venture in China, *Strategic Management Journal*, 29(2): 195–217.
25. A. Tudor & A. Lucchetti, 2009, MUFG's Hirano takes Morgan Stanley role, *Wall Street Journal*, March 12, C5.
26. Y. Wang & S. Nicholas, 2007, The formation and evolution of nonequity strategic alliances in China, *Asia Pacific Journal of Management*, 24: 131–150.
27. N. Garcia-Casarejos, N. Alcalde-Fradejas, & M. Espitia-Escuer, 2009, Staying close to the core: Lessons of studying the cost of unrelated alliances in Spanish banking, *Long Range Planning*, 42(2): 194–215; S. C. Chang, S.-S. Chen, & J. H. Lai, 2008, The wealth effect of Japanese-U.S. strategic alliances, *Financial Management*, 37(2): 271–301.
28. C. Weigelt, 2009, The impact of outsourcing new technologies on integrative capabilities and performance, *Strategic Management Journal*, 30(6): 595–616; S. Comino, P. Mariel, & J. Sandonis, 2007, Joint ventures versus contractual agreements: An empirical investigation, *Spanish Economic Journal*, 9: 159–175.
29. 2007, Intellectual property licensing, http://www.hp.com, August 30.
30. A. Tiwana, 2008, Does interfirm modularity complement ignorance? A field study of software outsourcing alliances, *Strategic Management Journal*, 29(11): 1241–1252.
31. L. Sherwood & J. G. Covin, 2008, Knowledge acquisition in university–industry alliances: An empirical investigation from a learning theory perspective, *Journal of Product Innovation Management*, 25: 162–179.
32. P. Beamish & N. Lupton, 2009, Managing joint ventures, *Academy of Management Perspectives*, 23(2): 75–94.
33. A. Inkpen & J. Ross, 2001, Why do some strategic alliances persist beyond their useful life? *California Management Review*, 44(1): 132–148.
34. A. Al-Laham, T. L. Amburgey, & K. Bates, 2008, The dynamics of research alliances: Examining the effect of alliance experience and partner characteristics on the speed of alliance entry in the biotech industry, *British Journal of Management*, 19(4): 343–364; F. Rothaermel & D. L. Deeds, 2006, Alliance type, alliance experience and alliance management capability in high-technology ventures, *Journal of Business Venturing*, 21: 429–460; L. Fuentelsaz, J. Gomez, & Y. Polo, 2002, Followers' entry timing: Evidence from the Spanish banking sector after deregulation, *Strategic Management Journal*, 23: 245–264.
35. Mesquita, Anand, Brush, Comparing the resource-based and relational views: Knowledge transfer and spillover in vertical alliances; B. L. Bourdeau, J. J. Cronink, Jr., & C. M. Voorhees, 2007, Modeling service alliances: An exploratory investigation of spillover effects in service partnerships, *Strategic Management Journal*, 28: 609–622.
36. J. Murphy, 2009, Dow Jones: Venture to launch site for newspaper in Japanese, *Wall Street Journal*, May 8, B3.
37. J. J. Reuer, P. Olk & A. Arino, 2010, *Entrepreneurial Alliances*, Prentice Hall, forthcoming.
38. R. Fores-Fillol, 2009, Allied alliances: Parallel or complementary? *Applied Economic Letters*, 16(6): 585–590; S. G. Lazzarini, 2007, The impact of membership in competing alliance constellations: Evidence on the operational performance of global airlines, *Strategic Management Journal*, 28: 345–367.
39. S. R. Holmberg & J. L. Cummings, 2009, Building successful strategic alliance: Strategic process and analytical tools for selecting partner industries and firms, *Long Range Planning*, 42(2): 164–193; M. A. Hitt, D. Ahlstrom, M. T. Dacin, E. Levitas, & L. Svobodina, 2004, The institutional effects of strategic alliance partner selection in transition economies: China versus Russia, *Organization Science*, 15: 173–185; P. A. Saparito, C. C. Chen, & H. J. Sapienza, 2004, The role of relational trust in bank-small firm relationships, *Academy of Management Journal*, 47: 400–410.
40. G. Padula, 2008, Enhancing the innovation performance of firms by balancing cohesiveness and bridging ties, *Long Range Planning*, 41(4): 395–419; A. C. Inkpen & E. W. K. Tsang, 2005, Social capital, networks and knowledge transfer, *Academy of Management Review*, 30: 146–165.
41. W. P. Wan, D. Yiu, R. E. Hoskisson, & H. Kim, 2008, The performance implications of relationship banking during macroeconomic expansion and contraction: A study of Japanese banks' social relationships and overseas expansion, *Journal of International Business Studies*, 39: 406–447; M. Hughes, R. D. Ireland, & R. E. Morgan, 2007, Stimulating dynamic value: Social capital and business incubation as a pathway to competitive success, *Long Range Planning*, 40(2): 154–177; T. G. Pollock, J. F. Porac, & J. B. Wade, 2004, Constructing deal networks: Brokers as network "architects" in the U.S. IPO market and other examples, *Academy of Management Review*, 29: 50–72.
42. J. R. Williams, 1998, *Renewable Advantage: Crafting Strategy Through Economic Time*, New York: Free Press.

43. 2008, Nucor, Duferco team up in foreign beam venture, *Metal Center News*, February, 84.
44. R. G. Matthews, 2008, World steel makers go prospecting; Industry plows profits into buying coal or mines to reduce vulnerability to rising commodity prices, *Wall Street Journal*, June 20, B1.
45. S. A. Zahra, R. D. Ireland, I. Gutierrez, & M. A. Hitt, 2000, Privatization and entrepreneurial transformation: Emerging issues and a future research agenda, *Academy of Management Review,* 25: 509–524.
46. H. K. Steensma, J. Q. Barden, C. Dhanaraj, M. Lyles, & L. Tihanyi, 2008, The evolution and internalization of international joint ventures in a transitioning economy, *Journal of International Business Studies*, 39(3): 491–507; I. Filatotchev, M. Wright, K. Uhlenbruck, L. Tihanyi, & R. E. Hoskisson, 2003, Governance, organizational capabilities, and restructuring in transition economies, *Journal of World Business,* 38(4): 331–347.
47. H. L. Sirkin, 2008, New world disorder, *Time*, October 27, GB1; J. Lash & F. Wellington, 2007, Competitive advantage on a warming planet, *Harvard Business Review,* 85(3): 94–102; K. M. Eisenhardt, 2002, Has strategy changed? *MIT Sloan Management Review,* 43(2): 88–91.
48. Ibid., GB1.
49. S. Lahiri, L. Perez-Nordtvedt, & R. W. Renn, 2008, Will the new competitive landscape cause your firm's decline? It depends on your mindset, *Business Horizons*, 51(4): 311–320.
50. S. Schechner & E. Holmes, 2009, Disney teams up with other networks online, buying stake in Hulu site, *Wall Street Journal*, May 1, B1.
51. C. Czipura & D. R. Jolly, 2007, Global airline alliances: Sparking profitability for a troubled industry, *Journal of Business Strategy,* 28(2): 57–64.
52. C. Conkey & P. Prada, 2009, Corporate news: Continental wins nod to join Star Alliance, *Wall Street Journal*, April 8, B4.
53. S. G. Lazzarini, D. P. Claro, & L. F. Mesquita, 2008, Buyer-supplier and supplier-supplier alliances: Do they reinforce or undermine one another? *Journal of Management Studies*, 45(3): 561–584; D. R. King, J. G. Covin, & H. Hegarty, 2003, Complementary resources and the exploitation of technological innovations, *Journal of Management,* 29: 589–606; J. S. Harrison, M. A. Hitt, R. E. Hoskisson, & R. D. Ireland, 2001, Resource complementarity in business combinations: Extending the logic to organizational alliances, *Journal of Management,* 27: 679–699.
54. T. E. Stuart, S. Z. Ozdemir, & W. W. Ding, 2007, Vertical alliance networks: The case of university-biotechnology-pharmaceutical alliance chains, *Research Policy*, 36(4): 477–498; F. T. Rothaermel, M. A. Hitt, & L. A. Jobe, 2006, Balancing vertical integration and strategic outsourcing: Effects on product portfolio, product success, and firm performance, *Strategic Management Journal,* 27: 1033–1056.
55. Y. Yan, D. Ding, & S. Mak, 2009, The impact of business investment on capability exploitation and organizational control in international strategic alliances, *Journal of Change Management*, 9(1): 49–65; R. Gulati, P. R. Lawrence, & P. Puranam, 2005, Adaptation in vertical relationships beyond incentive conflict, *Strategic Management Journal,* 26: 415–440.
56. J. Wiklund & D. A. Shepherd, 2009, The effectiveness of alliances and acquisitions: The role of resource combination activities, *Theory and Practice*, 31(1): 193–212; B.-S. Teng, 2007, Corporate entrepreneurship activities through strategic alliances: A resource-based approach toward competitive advantage, *Journal of Management Studies,* 44: 119–142.
57. Y. I. Kane & D. Wakabayashi, 2009, Nintendo looks outside the box, *Wall Street Journal*, May 27, B5.
58. F. A. Ghisi, J. A.G. da Silveira, T. Kristensen, M. Hingley, & A. Lindgreen, 2008, Horizontal alliances amongst small retailers in Brazil, *British Food Journal*, 110(4/5): 514–538; Tiwana, Do bridging ties complement strong ties? An empirical examination of alliance ambidexterity; F. T. Rothaermel & M. Thursby, 2007, The nanotech versus the biotech revolution: Sources of productivity in incumbent firm research, *Research Policy,* 36: 832–849; T. H. Oum, J. H.Park, K. Kim & C. Yu, 2004, The effect of horizontal alliances on firm productivity and profitability: Evidence from the global airline industry, *Journal of Business Research,* 57: 844–853.
59. A. Johnson & A. Greil, 2009, Pfizer, Novartis disclose separate deals in generic drugs, *Wall Street Journal*, May 21, B3.
60. *Economic Times,* 2011, "Bayer, Zydus in 50"-50 JV for Drug Marketing", *Economic Times,* 29 January, 2011.
61. E. Smith, 2009, Universal takes another stab online, *Wall Street Journal*, May 15, B8.
62. Tong, Reuer, & Peng, International joint ventures and the value of growth options; J. J. Reuer & T. W. Tong, 2005, Real options in international joint ventures, *Journal of Management,* 31: 403–423; S. Chatterjee, R. M. Wiseman, A. Fiegenbaum, & C. E. Devers, 2003, Integrating behavioral and economic concepts of risk into strategic management: The twain shall meet, *Long Range Planning,* 36(1): 61–80.
63. C. Rauwald & N. Shirouzu, 2009, Volkswagen eyes China venture, *Wall Street Journal*, May 27, B4.
64. L. Tesfatsion, 2007, Agents come to bits: Toward a constructive comprehensive taxonomy of economic entities, *Journal of Economic Behavior & Organization,* 63: 333–346.
65. K. Done, 2009, Cargo airlines fined $214 for price fixing, *Financial Times*, http://www.ft.com, April 12.
66. C. d'Aspremont, R. D. S. Ferreira & L. A.Gerard-Varet, 2007, Competition for market share or for market size: Oligopolistic equilibria with varying competitive toughness, *International Economic Review,* 48: 761–784.
67. R. W. Cooper & T. W. Ross, 2009, Sustaining cooperation with joint ventures, *Journal of Law Economics and Organization*, 25(1): 31–54.
68. J. T. Prince & D. H. Simon, 2009, Multi-market contact and service quality: Evidence from on-time performance in the U.S. airline industry, *Academy of Management Journal*, 52(2): 336–354.
69. G. K. Price & J. M. Connor, 2003, Modeling coupon values for ready-to-eat breakfast cereals, *Agribusiness,* 19(2): 223–244.

70. G. K. Price, 2000, Cereal sales soggy despite price cuts and reduced couponing, *Food Review,* 23(2): 21–28.
71. S. Kilman, 2008, Food giants race to pass rising costs to shoppers, *Wall Street Journal*, August 8, A1.
72. Kilman, Food giants race to pass rising costs to shoppers; J. Hagedoorn & G. Hesen, 2007, Contract law and the governance of interfirm technology partnerships—An analysis of different modes of partnering and their contractual implications, *Journal of Management Studies,* 44: 342–366; B. R. Golden & H. Ma, 2003, Mutual forbearance: The role of intrafirm integration and rewards, *Academy of Management Review,* 28: 479–493.
73. J. Apesteguia, M. Dufwenberg, & R. Selton, 2007, Blowing the whistle, *Economic Theory,* 31: 127–142.
74. J. D. Rockoff, 2009, Drug CEOs switch tactics on reform; Pharmaceutical companies join health-care overhaul hoping to influence where costs are cut, *Wall Street Journal*, May 27, B1, B2; J. H. Johnson & G. K. Leonard, 2007, Economics and the rigorous analysis of class certification in antitrust cases, *Journal of Competition Law and Economics,* http://jcle.oxfordjournals.org, June 26.
75. Lazzarini, Claro, & Mesquita, Buyer-supplier and supplier-supplier alliances: Do they reinforce or undermine one another?; P. Dussauge, B. Garrette, & W. Mitchell, 2004, Asymmetric performances: The market share impact of scale ad link alliances in global auto industry, *Strategic Management Journal,* 25: 701–711.
76. Conkey & Prada, Corporate news: Continental wins nod to join Star Alliance.
77. Harrison, Hitt, Hoskisson, & Ireland, Resource complementarity, 684–685.
78. L. H.Lin, 2009, Mergers and acquisitions, alliances and technology development: An empirical study of the global auto industry, *International Journal of Technology Management*, 48(3): 295–307; Wiklund & Shepherd, The effectiveness of alliances and acquisitions: The role of resource combination activities; A. E. Bernardo & B. Chowdhry, 2002, Resources, real options, and corporate strategy, *Journal of Financial Economics,* 63: 211–234.
79. J. Li, C. Dhanaraj, & R. L. Shockley, 2008, Joint venture evolution: Extending the real options approach, *Managerial and Decision Economics*, 29(4): 317–336.
80. V. Moatti, 2009, Learning to expand or expanding to learn? The role of imitation and experience in the choice among several expansion modes, *European Management Journal*, 27(1): 36–46; C. C. Pegels & Y. I. Song, 2007, Market competition and cooperation: Identifying competitive/cooperative interaction groups, *International Journal of Services Technology and Management,* 2/3: 139–154.
81. S. Silver & E. Steel, 2009, Alcatel gets into mobile ads; Service will target cell phone users based on location, *Wall Street Journal*, May 21, B9.
82. A. Goerzen & P. W. Beamish, 2005, The effect of alliance network diversity on multinational enterprise performance, *Strategic Management Journal,* 333–354.
83. M. V. Shyam Kumar, 2005, The value from acquiring and divesting a joint venture: A real options approach, *Strategic Management Journal,* 26: 321–331.
84. J. Yang, 2003, One step forward for Japan's chipmakers, *BusinessWeek Online,* http://www.businessweek.com, July 7.
85. J. E. Vascellaro & E. Holmes, 2009, YouTube seals deal on ABC, ESPN clips, *Wall Street Journal Online*, http:// www.wsj.com, March 31.
86. B. Worthen & J. Scheck, 2009, As growth slows, ex-allies square off in a turf war, *Wall Street Journal*, March 16, A1.
87. M. Doherty, 2009, Market and partner selection processes in international retail franchising, *Journal of Business Research*, 62(5): 528–534; M. Tuunanen & F. Hoy, 2007, Franchising—multifaceted form of entrepreneurship, *International Journal of Entrepreneurship and Small Business,* 4: 52–67; J. G. Combs & D. J. Ketchen Jr., 2003, Why do firms use franchising as an entrepreneurial strategy? A meta-analysis, *Journal of Management,* 29: 427–443.
88. F. Lafontaine, 1999, Myths and strengths of franchising, "Mastering Strategy" (Part Nine), *Financial Times,* November 22, 8–10.
89. A. M. Hayashi, 2008, How to replicate success, *MIT Sloan Management Review*, 49(3): 6–7.
90. G. Szulanski & R. J. Jensen, 2008, Growing through copying: The negative consequences of innovation on franchise network growth, *Research Policy*, 37(10): 1732–1741.
91. B. Barringer & R. D. Ireland, 2008, *Entrepreneurship: Successfully Launching New Ventures,* 2nd ed., Prentice Hall, 440.
92. L. Sanders, 2009, International expansion: Proven strategy during economic uncertainty, *Franchising World*, March, 16–17; B. Duckett, 2008, Business format franchising: A strategic option for business growth—at home and abroad, *Strategic Direction*, 4(2): 3–4.
93. Doherty, Market and partner selection processes in international retail franchising; R. B. DiPietro, D. H. B. Welsh, P. V. Raven, & D. Severt, 2007, A message of hope in franchises systems: Assessing franchisee, top executives, and franchisors, *Journal of Leadership & Organizational Studies,* 13(3): 59–66; S. C. Michael, 2002, Can a franchise chain coordinate? *Journal of Business Venturing,* 17: 325–342.
94. A. K. Paswan & C. M. Wittmann, 2009, Knowledge management and franchise systems, *Industrial Marketing Management*, 38(2): 173–180.
95. J. Torikka, 2007, Franchisees can be made: Empirical evidence from a follow-up study, *International Journal of Entrepreneurship and Small Business,* 4: 68–96; P. J. Kaufmann & S. Eroglu, 1999, Standardization and adaptation in business format franchising, *Journal of Business Venturing,* 14: 69–85.
96. B. Arruñada, L. Vázquez, & G. Zanarone, 2009, Institutional constraints on organizations: The case of Spanish car dealerships, *Managerial and Decision Economics*, 30(1): 15–26; J. Barthélemy, 2008, Opportunism, knowledge, and the performance of franchise chains, *Strategic Management Journal*, 29(13): 1451–1463.

97. A. Tiwana, 2008, Does technological modularity substitute for control? A study of alliance performance in software outsourcing, *Strategic Management Journal*, 29(7): 769–780; M. Zollo, J. J. Reuer, & H. Singh, 2002, Interorganizational routines and performance in strategic alliances, *Organization Science,* 13: 701–714.
98. E. Levitas & M. A. McFadyen, 2009, Managing liquidity in research-intensive firms: Signaling and cash flow effects of patents and alliance activities, *Strategic Management Journal*, 30(6): 659–678; Ireland, Hitt, & Vaidyanath, Alliance management.
99. R. Durand, O. Bruyaka, & V. Mangematin, 2008, Do science and money go together? The case of the French biotech industry, *Strategic Management Journal*, 29(12): 1281–1299; A. V. Shipilov, 2007, Network strategies and performance of Canadian investment banks, *Academy of Management Journal,* 49: 590–604; P. Almeida, G. Dokko, & L. Rosenkopf, 2003, Startup size and the mechanisms of external learning: Increasing opportunity and decreasing ability? *Research Policy,* 32(2): 301–316.
100. H. Ren, B. Gray, & K. Kim, 2009, Performance of international joint ventures: What factors really make a difference and how? *Journal of Management*, 35(3): 805–832; R. Narula & G. Duysters, 2004, Globalization and trends in international R&D alliances, *Journal of International Management,* 10: 199–218; M. A. Hitt, M. T. Dacin, E. Levitas, J.-L. Arregle, & A. Borza, 2000, Partner selection in emerging and developed market contexts: Resource-based and organizational learning perspectives, *Academy of Management Journal,* 43: 449–467.
101. W. Zhan, R. Chen, M. K. Erramilli, & D. T. Nguyen, 2009, Acquisition of organizational capabilities and competitive advantage of IJVs in transition economies: The case of Vietnam, *Asia Pacific Journal of Management*, 26(2): 285–308; Tong, Reuer, & Peng, International joint ventures and the value of growth option; J. H. Dyer, P. Kale, & H. Singh, 2004, When to ally & when to acquire, *Harvard Business Review,* 81(7/8): 109–115.
102. 1Y. Yan, D. Ding, & S. Mak, 2009, The impact of business investment on capability exploitation and organizational control in international strategic alliances, *Journal of Change Management*, 9(1): 49–65; P. Ghemawat, 2007, Managing differences: The central challenge of global strategy, *Harvard Business Review,* 85(3): 59–68.
103. L. Chao, 2009, IMG China ventureopens with tennis, *Wall Street Journal*, May 26, B10.
104. Ren, Gray, & Kim, Performance of international joint ventures: What factors really make a difference and how; L. Dong & K.W. Glaister, 2007, National and corporate culture differences in international strategic alliances: Perceptions of Chinese partners, *Asia Pacific Journal of Management,* 24: 191–205; I. M. Manev, 2003, The managerial network in a multinational enterprise and the resource profiles of subsidiaries, *Journal of International Management,* 9: 133–152.
105. P. H. Dickson, K. M. Weaver, & F. Hoy, 2006, Opportunism in the R&D alliances of SMEs: The roles of the institutional environment and SME size, *Journal of Business Venturing,* 21: 487–513; H. K. Steensma, L. Tihanyi, M. A. Lyles, & C. Dhanaraj, 2005, The evolving value of foreign partnerships in transitioning economies, *Academy of Management Journal,* 48: 213–235.
106. 2007, Branding and celebrity endorsements, *VentureRepublic,* http://venturerepublic.com, August 31.
107. 2009, Nike winded, *Financial Times*, March 20, 14.
108. B. Elango, 2009, Minimizing effects of "liability of foreignness": Response strategies of foreign firms in the United States, *Journal of World Business*, 44(1): 51–62; Y. Luo, O. Shenkar, & M.-K. Nyaw, 2002, Mitigating the liabilities of foreignness: Defensive versus offensive approaches, *Journal of International Management,* 8: 283–300.
109. T. J. Wilkinson, A. R. Thomas, & J. M. Hawes, 2009, Managing relationships with Chinese joint venture partners, *Journal of Global Marketing*, 22(2): 109–210; S. R. Miller & A. Parkhe, 2002, Is there a liability of foreignness in global banking? An empirical test of banks' x-efficiency, *Strategic Management Journal,* 23: 55–75; Y. Luo, 2001, Determinants of local responsiveness: Perspectives from foreign subsidiaries in an emerging market, *Journal of Management,* 27: 451–477.
110. D. Kronborg & S. Thomsen, 2009, Foreign ownership and long-term survival, *Strategic Management Journal*, 30(2): 207–220.
111. E. Rodríguez, 2008, Cooperative ventures in emerging economies, *Journal of Business Research*, 61(6): 640–647; D. Li, L. E. Eden, M. A. Hitt, & R. D. Ireland, 2008, Friends, acquaintances or strangers? Partner selection in R&D alliances, *Academy of Management Journal,* 51: 315–334; J. E. Oxley & R. C. Sampson, 2004, The scope and governance of international R&D alliances, *Strategic Management Journal,* 25: 723–749.
112. H. Sun, 2009, China poised to be net importer of coffee, *Wall Street Journal*, January 20, C10; 2006, Starbucks acquires control of China joint venture, *Apostille US,* http://apostille.us/, October 25.
113. D. Lavie, 2009, Capturing value from alliance portfolios, *Organizational Dynamics*, 38(1): 26–36; D. Lavie, C. Lechner, & H. Singh, 2007, The performance implications of timing of entry and involvement in multipartner alliances, *Academy of Management Journal,* 49: 569–604.
114. K. Atkins, J. Chen, V. S. A. Kumar, M. Macauley, & A. Marathe, 2009, Locational market power in network constrained markets, *Journal of Economic Behavior & Organization*, 70(1/2): 416–430; A. Nosella & G. Petroni, 2007, Multiple network leadership as a strategic asset: The Carlo Gavazzi space case, *Long Range Planning,* 40: 178–201.
115. K. Sawyer, 2007, Strength in webs, *The Conference Board,* July/August, 9–11.
116. C. Yarbrough, 2008, Singapore to open fusionopolis, *Research Technology Management*, 51(5): 4–5; A. H. Van de Ven, H. J. Sapienza, & J. Villanueva, 2007, Entrepreneurial pursuits of self- and collective interests, *Strategic Entrepreneurship Journal,* 1(3/4): 353–370.

117. Lavie, Capturing value from alliance portfolios; D. Lavie, 2007, Alliance portfolios and firm performance: A study of value creation and appropriation in the U.S. software industry, *Strategic Management Journal*, 28(12): 1187–1212; G. K. Lee, 2007, The significance of network resources in the race to enter emerging product markets: The convergence of telephony communications and computer networking, 1989–2001, *Strategic Management Journal,* 28: 17–37.

118. R. Cowan & N. Jonard, 2009, Knowledge portfolios and the organization of innovation networks, *Academy of Management Review*, 34(2): 320–342; G. G. Bell, 2005, Clusters, networks, and firm innovativeness, *Strategic Management Journal,* 26: 287–295.

119. H. Kim, R. E. Hoskisson, & W. P. Wan, 2004, Power, dependence, diversification strategy and performance in keiretsu member firms, *Strategic Management Journal,* 25: 613–636.

120. A. V. Shipilov, 2009, Firm scope experience, historic multimarket contact with partners, centrality, and the relationship between structural holes and performance, *Organization Science*, 20(1): 85–106; M. Rudberg & J. Olhager, 2003, Manufacturing networks and supply chains: An operations strategy perspective, *Omega,* 31(1): 29–39.

121. Cowan & Jonard, Knowledge portfolios and the organization of innovation networks; E. J. Kleinschmidt, U. de Brentani, & S. Salomo, 2007, Programs: A resource-based view, *Journal of Product Innovation Management,* 24: 419–441; G. J. Young, M. P. Charns, & S. M. Shortell, 2001, Top manager and network effects on the adoption of innovative management practices: A study of TQM in a public hospital system, *Strategic Management Journal,* 22: 935–951.

122. Prince & Simon, Multi-market contact and service quality: Evidence from on-time performance in the U.S. airline industry; E. Garcia-Canal, C. L. Duarte, J. R. Criado, & A. V. Llaneza, 2002, Accelerating international expansion through global alliances: A typology of cooperative strategies, *Journal of World Business,* 37(2): 91–107; F. T. Rothaermel, 2001, Complementary assets, strategic alliances, and the incumbent's advantage: An empirical study of industry and firm effects in the biopharmaceutical industry, *Research Policy,* 30: 1235–1251.

123. T. Kiessling & M. Harvey, 2008, Globalisation of internal venture capital opportunities in developing small and medium enterprises' relationships, *International Journal of Entrepreneurship and Innovation Management*, 8(3): 233–253; V. Shankar & B. L. Bayus, 2003, Network effects and competition: An empirical analysis of the home video game industry, *Strategic Management Journal,* 24: 375–384.

124. A. Schwab & A. S. Miner, 2008, Learning in hybrid-project systems: The effects of project performance on repeated collaboration, *Academy of Management Journal*, 51(6): 1117–1149.

125. A. E. Leiponen, 2008, Competing through cooperation: The organization of standard setting in wireless telecommunications, *Management Science*, 54(11): 1904–1919; Z. Simsek, M. H. Lubatkin, & D. Kandemir, 2003, Inter-firm networks and entrepreneurial behavior: A structural embeddedness perspective, *Journal of Management,* 29: 401–426.

126. H. W. Gottinger & C. L. Umali, 2008, The evolution of the pharmaceutical-biotechnology industry, *Business History*, 50(5): 583–601; F. T. Rothaermel & W. Boeker, 2008, Old technology meets new technology: Complementarities, similarities, and alliance formation, *Strategic Management Journal*, 29(1): 47–77; P. Puranam & K. Srikanth, 2007, What they know vs. what they do: How acquirers leverage technology acquisitions, *Strategic Management Journal,* 28: 805–825; M. Moensted, 2007, Strategic networking in small high-tech firms, *The International Entrepreneurship and Management Journal,* 3: 15–27.

127. P. Ozcan & K. M. Eisenhardt, 2009, Origin of alliance portfolios: Entrepreneurs, network strategies, and firm performance, *Academy of Management Journal*, 52(2): 246–279; C. T. Street & A.-F. Cameron, 2007, External relationships and the small business: A review of small business alliance and network research, *Journal of Small Business Management,* 45: 239–266.

128. M. Rod, 2009, A model for the effective management of joint ventures: A case study approach, *International Journal of Management*, 26(1): 3–17; T. K. Das & R. Kumar, 2007, Learning dynamics in the alliance development process, *Management Decision,* 45: 684–707.

129. A. Carmeli & Z. Sheaffer, 2008, How learning leadership and organizational learning from failures enhance perceived organizational capacity to adapt to the task environment, *Journal of Applied Behavioral Science*, 44(4): 468–489; J.-Y. Kim & A. S. Miner, 2007, Vicarious learning from the failures and near-failures of others: Evidence from the U.S. commercial banking industry, *Academy of Management Journal,* 49: 687–714.

130. Y. Li, Y. Liu, M. Li, & H. Wu, 2008, Transformational offshore outsourcing: Empirical evidence from alliances in China, *Journal of Operations Management*, 26(2): 257–274; P. M. Norman, 2002, Protecting knowledge in strategic alliances—Resource and relational characteristics, *Journal of High Technology Management Research,* 13(2): 177–202; P. M. Norman, 2001, Are your secrets safe? Knowledge protection in strategic alliances, *Business Horizons,* November–December, 51–60.

131. Heimeriks, Klijn, & Reuer, Building capabilities for alliance portfolios; Al-Laham, Amburgey, & Bates, The dynamics of research alliances: Examining the effect of alliance experience and partner characteristics on the speed of alliance entry in the biotech industry; J. Connell & R. Voola, 2007, Strategic alliances and knowledge sharing: Synergies or silos? *Journal of Knowledge Management,* 11: 52–66.

132. M. B. Sarkar, P. S. Aulakh, & A. Madhok, 2009, Process capabilities and value generation in alliance portfolios, *Organization Science*, 20(3): 583–600.

133. P.-X. Meschi, 2009, Government corruption and foreign stakes in international joint ventures in emerging economies, *Asia Pacific Journal of Management*, 26(2): 241–261.

134. M. H. Hansen, R. E. Hoskisson, & J. B. Barney, 2008, Competitive advantage in alliance governance: Resolving the opportunism minimization-gain maximization paradox, *Managerial and Decision Economics*, 29: 191–208; J. H. Dyer,

P. Kale, & H. Singh, 2001, How to make strategic alliances work, *MIT Sloan Management Review,* 42(4): 37–43.

135. Connell & Voola, Strategic alliances and knowledge sharing.
136. Levitas & McFadyen, Managing liquidity in research-intensive firms: Signaling and cash flow effects of patents and alliance activities; Hansen, Hoskisson, & Barney, Competitive advantage in alliance governance: Resolving the opportunism minimization-gain maximization paradox; J. H. Dyer, 1997, Effective interfirm collaboration: How firms minimize transaction costs and maximize transaction value, *Strategic Management Journal,* 18: 535–556.
137. L. Poppo, K. Z. Zhou, & S. Ryu, 2008, Alternative origins to interorganizational trust: An interdependence perspective on the shadow of the past and the shadow of the future, *Organization Science*, 19(1): 39–56; J. H. Dyer & C. Wujin, 2003, The role of trustworthiness in reducing transaction costs and improving performance: Empirical evidence from the United States, Japan, and Korea, *Organization Science,* 14: 57–69.
138. Krishnan, Martin, & Noorderhaven, When does trust matter to alliance performance?
139. K. Langfield-Smith, 2008, The relations between transactional characteristics, trust and risk in the start-up phase of a collaborative alliance, *Management Accounting Research*, 19(4): 344–364; M. Lundin, 2007, Explaining cooperation: How resource interdependence, goal congruence, and trust affect joint actions in policy implementation, *Journal of Public Administration Research and Theory,* 17(4): 651–672.
140. T. K. Das & R. Kumar, 2009, Interpartner harmony in strategic alliances: Managing commitment and forbearance, *International Journal of Strategic Business Alliances,* 1(1): 24–52; V. Perrone, A. Zaheer, & B. McEvily, 2003, Free to be trusted? Boundary constraints on trust in boundary spanners, *Organization Science,* 14: 422–439.
141. J. W. Rottman, 2008, Successful knowledge transfer within offshore supplier networks: A case study exploring social capital in strategic alliances, *Journal of Information Technology*: Special Issue: Global Sourcing, 23(1): 31–43; R. D. Ireland & J. W. Webb, 2007, A multi-theoretic perspective on trust and power in strategic supply chains, *Journal of Operations Management,* 25: 482–497.
142. 2007, The principles of the alliance, http://www.renault.com, August 26.
143. C. E. Ybarra & T. A. Turk, 2009, The evolution of trust in information technology alliances, *Journal of High Technology Management Research*, 20(1): 62–74; F. D. Schoorman, R. C. Mayer, & J. H. Davis, 2007, An integrative model of organizational trust: Past, present, and future, *Academy of Management Review,* 344–354; J. H. Davis, F. D. Schoorman, R. C. Mayer, & H. H. Tan, 2000, The trusted general manager and business unit performance: Empirical evidence of a competitive advantage, *Strategic Management Journal,* 21: 563–576.
144. Y. Luo, 2008, Procedural fairness and interfirm cooperation in strategic alliances, *Strategic Management Journal*, 29(1): 27–46; B. Hillebrand & W. G. Biemans, 2003, The relationship between internal and external cooperation: Literature review and propositions, *Journal of Business Research,* 56: 735–744.

CHAPTER 10

1. B. W. Heineman, Jr., 2009, Redefining the CEO role. *BusinessWeek,* http://www.businessweek.com, April 16; C. Thomas, D. Kidd, & C. Fernández-Aráoz, 2007, Are you underutilizing your board? *MIT Sloan Management Review*, 48(2): 71–76; D. C. Carey &, M. Patsalos-Fox, 2006, Shaping strategy from the boardroom. *McKinsey Quarterly,* 3: 90–94.
2. J. B. Wade, C. A. O'Reilly, & T. G. Pollock, 2006, Overpaid CEOs and underpaid managers: Fairness and executive compensation, *Organization Science*, 17: 527–544; A. Henderson & J. Fredrickson, 2001, Top management team coordination needs and the CEO pay gap: A competitive test of economic and behavioral views, *Academy of Management Journal,* 44: 96–117.
3. A. D. F. Penalva, 2006, Governance structure and the weighting of performance measures in CEO compensation, *Review of Accounting Studies*, 11: 463–493; S. Werner, H. L. Tosi, & L. Gomez-Mejia, 2005, Organizational governance and employee pay: How ownership structure affects the firm's compensation strategy, *Strategic Management Journal,* 26: 377–384.
4. C. Crossland & D. C. Hambrick, 2007, How national systems differ in their constraints on corporate executives: A study of CEO effects in three countries, *Strategic Management Journal*, 28:767–789; M. D. Lynall, B. R. Golden, & A. J. Hillman, 2003, Board composition from adolescence to maturity: A multitheoretic view, *Academy of Management Review,* 28: 416–431.
5. M.A. Rutherford, A. K. Buchholtz, & J. A. Brown, 2007, Examining the relationships between monitoring and incentives in corporate governance, *Journal of Management Studies* 44:414–430; C. M. Daily, D. R. Dalton, & A. A. Cannella, 2003, Corporate governance: Decades of dialogue and data, *Academy of Management Review,* 28: 371–382; P. Stiles, 2001, The impact of the board on strategy: An empirical examination, *Journal of Management Studies,* 38: 627–650.
6. D. R. Dalton, M. A. Hitt, S. T. Certo, & C. M. Dalton, 2008, The fundamental agency problem and its mitigation: Independence, equity and the market for corporate control, in J. P. Walsh andA. P. Brief (eds.), *The Academy of Management Annals*, New York: Lawrence Erlbaum Associates, 1–64; E. F. Fama &M. C. Jensen, 1983, Separation of ownership and control, *Journal of Law and Economics,* 26: 301–325.
7. I. Le Breton-Miller & D. Miller, 2006, Why do some family businesses out-compete? Governance, long-term orientations, and sustainable capability, *Entrepreneurship Theory and Practice*, 30: 731–746;M. Carney, 2005, Corporate governance and competitive advantage in family-controlled

firms, *Entrepreneurship Theory and Practice,* 29: 249–265; R. Charan, 1998, *How Corporate Boards Create Competitive Advantage,* San Francisco: Jossey-Bass.

8. X. Wu, 2005, Corporate governance and corruption: A cross-country analysis, *Governance,* 18(2): 151–170; J. McGuire &S. Dow, 2002, The Japanese keiretsu system: An empirical analysis, *Journal of Business Research,* 55: 33–40.
9. R. E. Hoskisson, D. Yiu, & H. Kim, 2004, Corporate governance systems: Effects of capital and labor market congruency on corporate innovation and global competitiveness, *Journal of High Technology Management,* 15: 293–315.
10. Crossland & Hambrick, How national systems differ in their constraints on corporate executives; R. Aguilera & G. Jackson, 2003, The cross-national diversity of corporate governance: Dimensions and determinants, *Academy of Management Review,* 28: 447–465.
11. R. P. Wright, 2004, Top managers' strategic cognitions of the strategy making process: Differences between high and low performing firms, *Journal of General Management,* 30(1): 61–78.
12. X. Luo, C. N. Chung, & M. Sobczak, 2009, How do corporate governance model differences affect foreign direct investment in emerging economies? *Journal of International Business Studies,* 40: 444–467; A. Bris & C. Cabous, 2006, In a merger, two companies come together and integrate their distribution lines, brands, work forces, management teams, strategies and cultures, *Financial Times,* October 6, 1.
13. S. Sudarsanam & A. A. Mahate, 2006, Are friendly acquisitions too bad for shareholders and managers? Long-term value creation and top management turnover in hostile and friendly acquirers, *British Journal of Management: Supplement,* 17(1): S7–S30; T. Moeller, 2005, Let's make a deal! Howshareholder control impacts merger payoffs, *Journal of Financial Economics,* 76(1): 167–190; M. A. Hitt, R. E. Hoskisson, R. A. Johnson, & D. D. Moesel, 1996, The market for corporate control and firm innovation, *Academy of Management Journal,* 39: 1084–1119.
14. R. E. Hoskisson, M. A. Hitt,R. A. Johnson, & W. Grossman, 2002, Conflicting voices: The effects of ownership heterogeneity and internal governance on corporate strategy, *Academy of Management Journal,* 45: 697–716.
15. G. E. Davis & T. A. Thompson, 1994, A social movement perspective on corporate control, *Administrative Science Quarterly,* 39: 141–173.
16. R. Bricker & N. Chandar, 2000, Where Berle and Means went wrong: A reassessment of capital market agency and financial reporting, *Accounting, Organizations, and Society,* 25: 529–554; M. A. Eisenberg, 1989, The structure of corporation law, *Columbia Law Review,* 89(7): 1461, as cited in R. A. G. Monks & N. Minow, 1995, *Corporate Governance,* Cambridge, MA: Blackwell Business, 7.
17. R. M. Wiseman & L. R. Gomez-Mejia, 1999, A behavioral agency model of managerial risk taking, *Academy of Management Review,* 23: 133–153.
18. T. Zellweger, 2007, Time horizon, costs of equity capital, and generic investment strategies of firms, *Family Business Review,* 20(1): 1–15; R. C. Anderson & D. M. Reeb, 2004, Board composition: Balancing family influence in S&P 500 firms, *Administrative Science Quarterly,* 49: 209–237.
19. Carney, Corporate governance and competitive advantage in family-controlled firms; N. Anthanassiou, W. F. Crittenden, L. M. Kelly, & P. Marquez, 2002, Founder centrality effects on the Mexican family firm's top management group: Firm culture, strategic vision and goals and firm performance, *Journal of World Business,* 37: 139–150.
20. M. Santiago-Castro & C. J. Brown, 2007, Ownership structure and minority rights: A Latin American view, *Journal of Economics and Business,* 59: 430–442; M. Carney & E. Gedajlovic, 2003, Strategic innovation and the administrative heritage of East Asian family business groups, *Asia Pacific Journal of Management,* 20: 5–26; D. Miller & I. Le Breton-Miller, 2003, Challenge versus advantage in family business, *Strategic Organization,* 1: 127–134.
21. D. G. Sirmon, J.-L. Arregle, M. A. Hitt, & J. Webb, 2008, Strategic responses to the threat of imitation, *Entrepreneurship Theory and Practice,* 32: 979–998.
22. Rutherford, Buchholtz, & Brown, Examining the relationships between monitoring and incentives in corporate governance; D. Dalton, C. Daily, T. Certo, & R. Roengpitya, 2003,Meta-analyses of financial performance and equity: Fusion or confusion? *Academy of Management Journal,* 46: 13–26; M. Jensen & W. Meckling, 1976, Theory of the firm: Managerial behavior, agency costs, and ownership structure, *Journal of Financial Economics,* 11: 305–360.
23. G. C. Rodríguez, C. A.-D. Espejo, & R. Valle Cabrera, 2007, Incentives management during privatization: An agency perspective, *Journal of Management Studies,* 44: 536–560; D. C. Hambrick, S. Finkelstein, & A. C. Mooney, 2005, Executive job demands: New insights for explaining strategic decisions and leader behaviors, *Academy of Management Review,* 30: 472–491.
24. T. G. Habbershon, 2006, Commentary: A framework for managing the familiness and agency advantages in family firms, *Entrepreneurship Theory and Practice,* 30: 879–886; M. G. Jacobides & D. C. Croson, 2001, Information policy: Shaping the value of agency relationships, *Academy of Management Review,* 26: 202–223.
25. A. Mackey, 2008, The effects of CEOs on firm performance, *Strategic Management Journal,* 29: 1357–1367; Y. Y. Kor, 2006, Direct and interaction effects of top management team and board compositions on R&D investment strategy, *Strategic Management Journal,* 27: 1081–1099.
26. Dalton, Hitt, Certo, & Dalton, 2008, The fundamental agency problem and its mitigation: Independence, equity and the market for corporate control; A. Ghosh, D. Moon, & K. Tandon, 2007, CEO ownership and discretionary investments, *Journal of Business Finance & Accounting,* 34: 819–839.
27. S. Ghoshal & P. Moran, 1996, Bad for practice: A critique of the transaction cost theory, *Academy of Management Review,* 21: 13–47; O. E. Williamson, 1996, *The Mechanisms of Governance,* New York: Oxford University Press, 6.

28. B. E. Ashforth, D. A. Gioia, S. L. Robinson, & L. K. Trevino, 2008, Reviewing organizational corruption, *Academy of Management Review,* 33: 670–684; E. Kang, 2006, Investors' perceptions of managerial opportunism in corporate acquisitions: The moderating role of environmental condition, *Corporate Governance*, 14: 377–387; R. W. Coff & P. M. Lee, 2003, Insider trading as a vehicle to appropriate rent from R&D. *Strategic Management Journal,* 24: 183–190.
29. M. L. McDonald, P. Khanna, & J. D. Westphal, 2008, Getting them to think outside the circle: Corporate governance, CEOs' external advice networks, and firm performance, *Academy of Management Journal,* 51: 453–475.
30. Fama, Agency problems and the theory of the firm.
31. P. Jiraporn, Y. Sang Kim, W. N. Davidson, & M. Singh, 2006, Corporate governance, shareholder rights and firm diversification: An empirical analysis, *Journal of Banking & Finance*, 30: 947–963; R. C. Anderson, T. W. Bates, J. M. Bizjak, & M. L. Lemmon, 2000, Corporate governance and firm diversification, *Financial Management,* 29(1): 5–22; R. E. Hoskisson & T. A. Turk, 1990, Corporate restructuring: Governance and control limits of the internal market, *Academy of Management Review,* 15: 459–477.
32. G. P. Baker & B. J. Hall, 2004, CEO incentives and firm size, *Journal of Labor Economics*, 22: 767–798; R. Bushman, Q. Chen, E. Engel, & A. Smith, 2004, Financial accounting information, organizational complexity and corporate governance systems, *Journal of Accounting & Economics,* 7: 167–201; M. A. Geletkanycz, B. K. Boyd, & S. Finkelstein, 2001, The strategic value of CEO external directorate networks: Implications for CEO compensation, *Strategic Management Journal,* 9: 889–898.
33. S. W. Geiger & L. H. Cashen, 2007, Organizational size and CEO compensation: The moderating effect of diversification in downscoping organizations, *Journal of Managerial Issues*, 9(2): 233–252; Y. Grinstein & P. Hribar, 2004, CEO compensation and incentives: Evidence from M&A bonuses, *Journal of Financial Economics,* 73: 119–143;
34. S. Rajgopal, T. Shevlin, & V. Zamora, 2006, CEOs' outside employment opportunities and the lack of relative performance evaluation in compensation contracts, *Journal of Finance*, 61: 1813–1844.
35. J. Weber, 2007, The accidental CEO (well, not really); Kellogg needed a new boss, fast. Here's how it groomed insider David Mackay, *BusinessWeek*, April 23, 65.
36. Kellogg's Annual Report, 2008. Kellogg, Michigan.
37. M. Ganco & R. Agarwal, 2009, Performance differentials between diversifying entrants and entrepreneurial start-ups: A complexity approach, *Academy of Management Review,* 34: 228–252.
38. Gujarat Cooperative Milk Marketing Federation (GCMMF), Case # BP 255, Ahmedabad: Indian Institute of Management, Ahmedabad.
39. M. S. Jensen, 1986, Agency costs of free cash flow, corporate finance, and takeovers, *American Economic Review,* 76: 323–329.
40. A. V. Douglas, 2007, Managerial opportunism and proportional corporate payout policies, *Managerial Finance,* 33(1): 26–42; M. Jensen & E. Zajac, 2004, Corporate elites and corporate strategy: How demographic preferences and structural position shape the scope of the firm, *Strategic Managemen Journal,* 25: 507–524; T. H. Brush, P. Bromiley, & M. Hendrickx, 2000, The free cash flow hypothesis for sales growth and firm performance, *Strategic Management Journal,* 21: 455–472.
41. J. Lunsford & B. Steinberg, 2006, Conglomerates' conundrum, *Wall Street Journal*, September 14, B1, B7; K. Ramaswamy, M. Li, & B. S. P. Petitt, 2004, Who drives unrelated diversification? A study of Indian manufacturing firms, *Asia Pacific Journal of Management,* 21: 403–423.
42. M. V. S. Kumar, 2009, The relationship between product and international diversification: The effects of short-run constraints and endogeneity, *Strategic Management Journal*, 30: 99–116; M. F. Wiersema & H. P. Bowen, 2008, Corporate diversification: The impact of foreign competition, industry globalization and product diversification, *Strategic Management Journal*, 29: 115–132.
43. D. D. Bergh, R. A. Johnson, & R.-L. Dewitt, 2008, Restructuring through spin-off or sell-off: Transforming information asymmetries into financial gain, *Strategic Management Journal*, 29: 133–148; K. B. Lee, M. W. Peng, & K. Lee, 2008, From diversification premium to diversification discount during institutional transitions, *Journal of World Business*, 43: 47–65.
44. T. K. Berry, J. M. Bizjak, M. L. Lemmon, & L. Naveen, 2006, Organizational complexity and CEO labor markets: Evidence from diversified firms, *Journal of Corporate Finance*, 12: 797–817; R. Rajan, H. Servaes, & L. Zingales, 2001, The cost of diversity: The diversification discount and inefficient investment, *Journal of Finance,* 55: 35–79; A. Sharma, 1997, Professional as agent: Knowledge asymmetry in agency exchange, *Academy of Management Review,* 22: 758–798.
45. V. Chhaochharia & Y. Grinstein, 2007, Corporate governance and firm value: The impact of the 2002 governance rules, *Journal of Finance*, 62: 1789–1825;A. Borrus, L. Lavelle, D. Brady, M. Arndt, & J. Weber, 2005, Death, taxes and Sarbanes-Oxley? Executives may be frustrated with the law's burdens, but corporate performance is here to stay, *BusinessWeek,* January 17, 28–31.46. D. Reilly, 2006, Checks on internal controls pay off, *Wall Street Journal*, August 10, C3.
46. D. Reilly, 2006, Checks on internal controls pay off, Wall Street Journal, August 10, C3.
47. 2002, Report of the (Naresh Chandra) Committee on Corporate Audit and Governance, accessible at the Web site of *National Foundation for Corporate Governance*, http://www.nfcgindia.org/library.htm, http://dca.nic.in/naresh/index.html.
48. 2003, Report of the SEBI (Narayana Murthy) Committee on Corporate Governance, February 8, *Securities and Exchange Board of India*, http://web.sebi.gov.in/commreport/corpgov.pdf; and the online library of *National Foundation for Corporate Governance*, http://www.nfcgindia.org/library.html.
49. 2000, Report of the SEBI (Kumar Mangalam Birla) Committee on Corporate Governance, SEBI, *www.sebi.gov.in*, http://www.sebi.gov.in/commreport/corpgov.html. and the online

library of *National Foundation for Corporate Governance*, http://www.nfcgindia.org/library.htm

50. 2005, Report of the Expert (J.J. Irani) Committee on Company Law, *National Foundation for Corporate Governance*, http://www.nfcgindia.org/library.htm; http://dca.nic.in/report_expert_comt.html.
51. F. Navissi & V. Naiker, 2006, Institutional ownership and corporate value, *Managerial Finance*, 32: 247–256; A. de Miguel, J. Pindado, & C. de la Torre, 2004, Ownership structure and firm value: New evidence from Spain, *Strategic Management Journal*, 25: 1199–1207; J. Coles, N. Sen, & V. McWilliams, 2001, An examination of the relationship of governance mechanisms to performance, *Journal of Management*, 27: 23–50.
52. Jiraporn, Kim, Davidson, & Singh, Corporate governance, shareholder rights and firm diversification; M. Singh, I. Mathur, & K. C. Gleason, 2004, Governance and performance implications of diversification strategies: Evidence from large U.S. firms, *Financial Review*, 39: 489–526; R. E. Hoskisson, R. A. Johnson, & D. D. Moesel, 1994, Corporate divestiture intensity in restructuring firms: Effects of governance, strategy, and performance, *Academy of Management Journal*, 37: 1207–1251.
53. G. Iannotta, G. Nocera, & A. Sironi, 2007, Ownership structure, risk and performance in the European banking industry, *Journal of Banking & Finance*, 31: 2127–2149.
54. B. Villalonga & R. Amit, 2006, How do family ownership, control and management affect firm value? *Journal of Financial Economics*, 80: 385–417; R. C. Anderson & D. M. Reeb, 2004, Board composition: Balancing family influence in S&P 500 firms, *Administrative Science Quarterly*, 49: 209–237.
55. M. Fackler, 2008, South Korea faces question of corporate control, *New York Times*, http://www.nytimes.com, April 24; S. J. Chang, 2003, Ownership structure, expropriation and performance of group-affiliated companies in Korea, *Academy of Management Journal*, 46: 238–253.
56. A. Berle & G. Means, 1932, *The Modern Corporation and Private Property*, New York: Macmillan.
57. M. Gietzmann, 2006, Disclosure of timely and forward-looking statements and strategic management of major institutional ownership, *Long Range Planning*, 39(4): 409–427; B. Ajinkya, S. Bhojraj, & P. Sengupta, 2005, The association between outside directors, institutional investors and the properties of management earnings forecasts, *Journal of Accounting Research*, 43: 343–376; M. P. Smith, 1996, Shareholder activism by institutional investors: Evidence from CalPERS, *Journal of Finance*, 51: 227–252.
58. K. Schnatterly, K. W. Shaw, & W. W. Jennings, 2008, Information advantages of large institutional owners, *Strategic Management Journal*, 29: 219–227; Hoskisson, Hitt, Johnson, & Grossman, Conflicting voices.
59. S. D. Chowdhury & E. Z. Wang, 2009, Institutional activism types and CEO compensation: A time-series analysis of large Canadian corporations, *Journal of Management*, 35: 5–36; M. Musteen, D. K. Datta, & P. Herrmann, 2009, Ownership structure and CEO compensation: Implications for the choice of foreign market entry modes, *Journal of International Business Studies*, 40: 321–338.
60. T. W. Briggs, 2007, Corporate governance and the new hedge fund activism: An empirical analysis. *Journal of Corporation Law*, 32(4): 681–723, 725–738; K. Rebeiz, 2001, Corporate governance effectiveness in American corporations: A survey, *International Management Journal*, 18(1): 74–80.
61. D. Brewster, 2009, U.S. investors get to nominate boards, *Financial Times*, http://www.ft.com, May 20.
62. See Strategic Focus on ITC, later in the chapter.
63. V. Krivogorsky, 2006, Ownership, board structure, and performance in continental Europe, *International Journal of Accounting*, 41(2): 176–197; S. Thomsen & T. Pedersen, 2000, Ownership structure and economic performance in the largest European companies, *Strategic Management Journal*, 21: 689–705.
64. Dalton, Hitt, Certo, & Dalton, The fundamental agency problem and its mitigation: Independence, equity and the market for corporate control; C. M. Dalton & D. R. Dalton, 2006, Corporate governance best practices: The proof is in the process, *Journal of Business Strategy*, 27(4), 5–7; R. V. Aguilera, 2005, Corporate governance and director accountability: An institutional comparative perspective, *British Journal of Management*, 16(S1), S39–S53.
65. R. H. Lester, A. Hillman, A. Zardkoohi, & A. A. Cannella, 2008, Former government officials as outside directors: The role of human and social capital, *Academy of Management Journal*, 51: 999–1013; M. L. McDonald, J. D. Westphal, & M. E. Graebner, 2008, What do they know? The effects of outside director acquisition experience on firm acquisition performance, *Strategic Management Journal*, 29: 1155–1177; Hillman & Dalziel, Boards of directors and firm performance.
66. L. Bonazzi & S. M. N. Islam, 2007, Agency theory and corporate governance: A study of the effectiveness of board in their monitoring of the CEO, *Journal of Modeling in Management*, 2(1): 7–23; Rebeiz, Corporate governance effectiveness in American corporations.
67. E. Kang, 2008, Director interlocks and spillover effects of reputational penalties from financial reporting fraud, *Academy of Management Journal*, 51: 537–555; N. Chipalkatti, Q. V. Le, & M. Rishi, 2007, Portfolio flows to emerging capital markets: Do corporate transparency and public governance matter? *Business and Society Review*, 112(2): 227–249.
68. Krivogorsky, Ownership, board structure, and performance in continental Europe; Hoskisson, Hitt, Johnson, & Grossman, Conflicting voices; B. D. Baysinger & R. E. Hoskisson, 1990, The composition of boards of directors and strategic control: Effects on corporate strategy, *Academy of Management Review*, 15: 72–87.
69. Y. Y. Kor & V. F. Misangyi, 2008, Outside directors' industry-specific experience and firms' liability of newness, *Strategic Management Journal*, 29: 1345–1355; E. E. Lawler III & D. Finegold, 2006, Who's in the boardroom and does it matter: The impact of having non-director executives attend board meetings, *Organizational Dynamics*, 35(1): 106–115.

70. E. M. Fich & A. Shivdasani, 2006, Are busy boards effective monitors? *Journal of Finance*, 61: 689–724; J. Westphal & L. Milton, 2000, How experience and network ties affect the influence of demographic minorities on corporate boards, *Administrative Science Quarterly,* 45(2): 366–398.
71. Fich & Shivdasani, Are busy boards effective monitors; S. T. Petra, 2005, Do outside independent directors strengthen corporate boards? *Corporate Governance,* 5(1): 55–65.
72. S. K. Lee & L. R. Carlson, 2007, The changing board of directors: Board independence in S & P 500 firms, *Journal of Organizational Culture, Communication and Conflict,* 11(1): 31–41.
73. R. C. Pozen, 2006, Before you split that CEO/chair, *Harvard Business Review*, 84(4): 26–28; J. W. Lorsch & A. Zelleke, 2005, Should the CEO be the chairman, *MIT Sloan Management Review,* 46(2): 71–74.
74. M. Kroll, B. A. Walters, & P. Wright, 2008, Board vigilance, director experience and corporate outcomes, *Strategic Management Journal*, 29: 363–382.
75. Fich & Shivdasani, Are busy boards effective monitors; J. Roberts, T. McNulty, &, P. Stiles, 2005, Beyond agency conceptions of the work of the non-executive director: Creating accountability in the boardroom, *British Journal of Management,* 16(S1): S5–S26.
76. Fich & Shivdasani, Are busy boards effective monitors; S. Zahra, 1996, Governance, ownership and corporate entrepreneurship among the *Fortune* 500: The moderating impact of industry technological opportunity, *Academy of Management Journal,* 39: 1713–1735.
77. Baysinger, & Hoskisson, Board composition and strategic control: The effect on corporate strategy.
78. Y. Zhang, 2008, Information asymmetry and the dismissal of newly appointed CEOs: An empirical investigation, *Strategic Management Journal*, 29: 859–872.
79. Lawler & Finegold, Who's in the boardroom and does it matter?; E. E. Lawler III & D. L. Finegold, 2005, The changing face of corporate boards, *MIT Sloan Management Review,* 46(2): 67–70; A. Conger, E. E. Lawler, & D. L. Finegold, 2001, *Corporate Boards: New Strategies for Adding Value at the Top,* San Francisco: Jossey-Bass; J. A. Conger, D. Finegold, & E. E. Lawler III, 1998, Appraising boardroom performance, *Harvard Business Review,* 76(1): 136–148.
80. A. L. Boone, L. C. Field, J. M. Karpoff, & C. G. Raheja, 2007, The determinants of corporate board size and composition: An empirical analysis, *Journal of Financial Economics*, 85(1): 66–101; J. Marshall, 2001, As boards shrink, responsibilities grow, *Financial Executive,* 17(4): 36–39.
81. T. Long, 2007, The evolution of FTSE 250 boards of directors: Key factors influencing board performance and effectiveness, *Journal of General Management*, 32(3): 45–60; S. Finkelstein & A. C. Mooney, 2003, Not the usual suspects: How to use board process to make boards better, *Academy of Management Executive,* 17: 101–113.
82. J. L. Koors, 2006 Director pay: A work in progress, *The Corporate Governance Advisor*, 14(5): 25–31; W. Shen, 2005, Improve board effectiveness: The need for incentives, *British Journal of Management,* 16(S1): S81–S89; M. Gerety, C. Hoi, & A. Robin, 2001, Do shareholders benefit from the adoption of incentive pay for directors? *Financial Management,* 30: 45–61; D. C. Hambrick & E. M. Jackson, 2000, Outside directors with a stake: The linchpin in improving governance, *California Management Review,* 42(4): 108–127.
83. Y. Deutsch, T. Keil, & T. Laamanen, 2007, Decision making in acquisitions: the effect of outside directors' compensation on acquisition patterns, *Journal of Management*, 33(1): 30–56.
84. A. J. Hillman, C. Shropshire, & A. A. Cannella, Jr. 2007, Organizational predictors of women on corporate boards, *Academy of Management Journal*, 50: 941–952; I. Filatotchev & S. Toms, 2003, Corporate governance, strategy and survival in a declining industry: A study of UK cotton textile companies, *Journal of Management Studies,* 40: 895–920.
85. 2007, Wall St. roundup; pay increases for CEOs fall below 10% in 2006, *Los Angeles Times,* April 3, C4.
86. S. N. Kaplan, 2008, Are U.S. CEOs overpaid? *Academy of Management Perspectives,* 22(2): 5–20.
87. J. P. Walsh, 2009, Are U.S. CEOs overpaid? A partial response to Kaplan, *Academy of Management Perspectives,* 23(1): 73–75; J. P. Walsh, 2008, CEO compensation and the responsibilities of the business scholar to society, *Academy of Management Perspectives,* 22(3): 26–33.
88. K. Rehbein, 2007, Explaining CEO compensation: How do talent, governance, and markets fit in? *Academy of Management Perspectives*, 21(1): 75–77; J. S. Miller, R. M. Wiseman, & L. R. Gomez-Mejia, 2002, The fit between CEO compensation design and firm risk, *Academy of Management Journal,* 45: 745–756.
89. M. Larraza-Kintana, R. M. Wiseman, L. R. Gomez-Mejia, & T. M. Welbourne, 2007, Disentangling compensation and employment risks using the behavioral agency model, *Strategic Management Journal*, 28: 1001–1019; J. McGuire & E. Matta, 2003, CEO stock options: The silent dimension of ownership, *Academy of Management Journal,* 46: 255–265.
90. X. Zhang, K. M. Bartol, K. G. Smith, M. D. Pfarrer, & D. M. Khanin, 2008, CEOs on the edge: Earnings manipulations and stock-based incentive misalignment, *Academy of Management Journal,* 51: 241–258; J. P. O'Connor, R. L. Priem, J. E. Coombs, & K. M. Gilley, 2006, Do CEO stock options prevent or promote fraudulent financial reporting? *Academy of Management Journal*, 49: 483–500.
91. S. O'Donnell, 2000, Managing foreign subsidiaries: Agents of headquarters, or an interdependent network? *Strategic Management Journal,* 21: 521–548; K. Roth & S. O'Donnell, 1996, Foreign subsidiary compensation: An agency theory perspective, *Academy of Management Journal,* 39: 678–703.
92. A. Ghosh, 2006, Determination of executive compensation in an emerging economy: Evidence from India, *Emerging Markets, Finance & Trade,* 42(3): 66–90; K. Ramaswamy, R. Veliyath, & L. Gomes, 2000, A study of the determinants of CEO compensation in India, *Management International Review,* 40(2): 167–191.

93. C. L. Staples, 2007, Board globalization in the world's largest TNCs 1993–2005, *Corporate Governance*, 15(2): 311–32.
94. P. Kalyta, 2009, Compensation transparency and managerial opportunism: A study of supplemental retirement plans, *Strategic Management Journal,* 30: 405–423.
95. L. K. Meulbroek, 2001, The efficiency of equity-linked compensation: Understanding the full cost of awarding executive stock options, *Financial Management,* 30(2): 5–44.
96. C. E. Devers, R. M. Wiseman, & R. M. Holmes Jr., 2007, The effects of endowment and loss aversion in managerial stock option valuation, *Academy of Management Journal*, 50: 191–208; J. C. Bettis, J. M. Biziak, &M. L. Lemmon, 2005, Exercise behavior, valuation and the incentive effects of employee stock options, *Journal of Financial Economics,* 76: 445–470.
97. M. Klausner, 2007, Reducing directors' legal risk, *Harvard Business Review*, 85(4), 28; T. G. Pollock, H. M. Fischer, & J. B. Wade, 2002, The role of politics in repricing executive options, *Academy of Management Journal,* 45: 1172–1182; M. E. Carter & L. J. Lynch, 2001, An examination of executive stock option repricing, *Journal of Financial Economics,* 59: 207–225; D. Chance, R. Kumar, & R. Todd, 2001, The "repricing" of executive stock options, *Journal of Financial Economics,* 59: 129–154.
98. P. Berrone & L. R. Gomez-Mejia, 2009, Environmental performance and executive compensation: An integrated agency-institutional perspective, *Academy of Management Journal,* 52: 103–126.
99. R. Sinha, 2006, Regulation: The market for corporate control and corporate governance, *Global Finance Journal*, 16(3): 264–282; R. Coff, 2002, Bidding wars over R&D intensive firms: Knowledge, opportunism and the market for corporate control, *Academy of Management Journal,* 46: 74–85; Hitt, Hoskisson, Johnson, & Moesel, The market for corporate control and firm innovation.
100. D. N. Iyer & K. D. Miller, 2008, Performance feedback, slack, and the timing of acquisitions, *Academy of Management Journal,* 51: 808–822;R. W. Masulis, C. Wang, & F. Xie, 2007, Corporate governance and acquirer returns, *Journal of Finance*, 62(4): 1851–1889; R. Sinha, 2004, The role of hostile takeovers in corporate governance, *Applied Financial Economics,* 14: 1291–1305.
101. K. Ruckman, 2009, Technology sourcing acquisitions: What they mean for innovation potential, *Journal of Strategy and Management,* 2: 56–75.
102. J. P. Walsh & R. Kosnik, 1993, Corporate raiders and their disciplinary role in the market for corporate control, *Academy of Management Journal,* 36: 671–700.
103. J. Haleblian, C. E. Devers, G. McNamara, M. A. Carpenter, & R. B. Davison, 2009, Taking stock of what we know about mergers and acquisitions: A review and research agenda, *Journal of Management,* 35: 469–502; B. Kalpic, 2008, Why bigger is not always better: The strategic logic of value creation through M&As, *Journal of Business Strategy,* 29(6): 4–13.
104. T. W. Briggs, 2007, Corporate governance and a new hedge fund activism: *Empirical Analysis*, 32(4): 681–723.
105. Thurm, When investor activism doesn't pay.
106. N. Goodway, 2009, Credit Suisse pays 25 million pounds in golden hellos, *Evening Standard,* http://www.standard.co.uk, March 24; R. B. Adams & D. Ferreira, 2007, A theory of friendly boards, *Journal of Finance*, 62: 217–250.
107. J Cresswell, 2006, Gilded paychecks: Pay packages allow executives to jump ship with less risk, *New York Times*, http://www.nyt.com, December 29.
108. C. Icahn, 2009, We're not the boss of AIG, *New York Times,* http://www.nytimes.com, March 29; G. Blain & C. Siemaszko, 2008, AIG agrees to cut golden parachute for CEO, trim spending, *New York Daily News,* http://www.nydailynews.com, October 16.
109. H. G. Barkema & M. Schjven, 2008, Toward unlocking the full potential of acquisition: The role of organizational restructuring, *Academy of Management Journal,* 51: 696–722; M. Cording, P. Chritmann, & D. R. King, 2008, Reducing causal ambiguity in acquisition integration: Intermediate goals as mediators of integration decisions and acquisition performance, *Academy of Management Journal,* 51: 744–767.
110. T. Laamanen & T. Keil, 2008, Performance of serial acquirers: Toward an acquisition program perspective, *Strategic Management Journal,* 29: 663–672; G. M. McNamara, J. Haleblian, & B. J. Dykes, 2008, The performance implications of participating in an acquisition wave: Early mover advantages, bandwagon effects, and the moderating influence of industry characteristics and acquirer tactics, *Academy of Management Journal,* 51: 113–130.
111. J. A. Krug & W. Shill, 2008, The big exit: Executive churn in the wake of M&As, *Journal of Business Strategy,* 29(4): 15–21; J. Harford, 2003, Takeover bids and target directors' incentives: The impact of a bid on directors' wealth and board seats, *Journal of Financial Economics,* 69: 51–83; S. Chatterjee, J. S. Harrison, & D. D. Bergh, 2003, Failed takeover attempts, corporate governance, and refocusing, *Strategic Management Journal,* 24: 87–96.
112. E. Webb, 2006, Relationships between board structure and takeover defenses, *Corporate Governance,* 6(3): 268–280; C. Sundaramurthy, J. M. Mahoney, & J. T. Mahoney, 1997, Board structure, antitakeover provisions, and stockholder wealth, *Strategic Management Journal,* 18: 231–246.
113. W. G. Sanders & M. A. Carpenter, 2003, Strategic satisficing? A behavioral-agency theory perspective on stock repurchase program announcements, *Academy of Management Journal,* 46: 160–178; J. Westphal & E. Zajac, 2001, Decoupling policy from practice: The case of stock repurchase programs, *Administrative Science Quarterly,* 46: 202–228.
114. O. Faleye, 2007, Classified boards, firm value, and managerial entrenchment, *Journal of Financial Economics*, 83: 501–529.
115. 2007, Leaders: Pay slips; management in Europe, *Economist*, June 23, 14: A. Cala, 2005, Carrying golden parachutes; France joins EU trend to reign in executive severance deals, *Wall Street Journal,* June 8, A13.
116. J. A. Pearce II & R. B. Robinson Jr., 2004, Hostile takeover defenses that maximize shareholder wealth, *Business Horizons,* 47(5): 15–24.

117. A. Kacperzyk, 2009, With greater power comes greater responsibility? Takeover protection and corporate attention to stakeholders, *Strategic Management Journal,* 30: 261–285.
118. Walsh & Kosnik, Corporate raiders.
119. A. Chakraborty & R. Arnott, 2001, Takeover defenses and dilution: A welfare analysis, *Journal of Financial and Quantitative Analysis,* 36: 311–334.
120. M. Wolf, 2007, The new capitalism: How unfettered finance is fast reshaping the global economy, *Financial Times*, June 19, 13: C. Millar, T. I. Eldomiaty, C. J. Choi, & B. Hilton, 2005, Corporate governance and institutional transparency in emerging markets, *Journal of Business Ethics,* 59: 163–174; D. Norburn, B. K. Boyd, M. Fox, & M. Muth, 2000, International corporate governance reform, *European Business Journal,* 12(3): 116–133.
121. China YCT International strengthens corporate governance with establishment of audit committee and appointments of three new independent directors, 2009, *Quamnet.com Stock News,* http://www.quamnet.com, April 13; P. Aldrick, 2009, RBS investors threaten to vote down pay report, *Telegraph.co.uk,* http://www.telegraph.co.uk, March 24.
122. P. Witt, 2004, The competition of international corporate governance systems—A German perspective, *Management International Review,* 44: 309–333; L. Nachum, 2003, Does nationality of ownership make any difference and if so, under what circumstances? Professional service MNEs in global competition, *Journal of International Management,* 9: 1–32.
123. Crossland & Hambrick, How national systems differ in their constraints on corporate executives; Aguilera & Jackson, The cross-national diversity of corporate governance: Dimensions and determinants.
124. Carney, Corporate governance and competitive advantage in family-controlled firms; S. Klein, 2000, Family businesses in Germany: Significance and structure, *Family Business Review,* 13: 157–181.
125. A. Tuschke & W. G. Sanders, 2003, Antecedents and consequences of corporate governance reform: The case of Germany, *Strategic Management Journal,* 24: 631–649; J. Edwards & M. Nibler, 2000, Corporate governance in Germany: The role of banks and ownership concentration, *Economic Policy,* 31: 237–268; E. R. Gedajlovic & D. M. Shapiro, 1998, Management and ownership effects: Evidence from five countries, *Strategic Management Journal,* 19: 533–553.
126. P. C. Fiss, 2006, Social influence effects and managerial compensation evidence from Germany, *Strategic Management Journal,* 27: 1013–1031; S. Douma, 1997, The two-tier system of corporate governance, *Long Range Planning,* 30(4): 612–615.
127. P. C. Fiss & E. J. Zajac, 2004, The diffusion of ideas over contested terrain: The (non) adoption of a shareholder value orientation among German firms, *Administrative Science Quarterly,* 49: 501–534.
128. W. G. Sanders & A. C. Tuschke, 2007, The adoption of the institutionally contested organizational practices: The emergence of stock option pay in Germany, *Academy of Management Journal*, 57: 33–56.
129. T. Hoshi, A. K. Kashyap, & S. Fischer, 2001, *Corporate Financing and Governance in Japan,* Boston: MIT Press.
130. J. P. Charkham, 1994. *Keeping Good Companies: A Study of Corporate Governance in Five Countries*. New York: Oxford University Press, 70.
131. M. A: Hitt, H. Lee, & E. Yucel, 2002, The importance of social capital to the management of multinational enterprises: Relational networks among Asian and Western firms, *Asia Pacific Journal of Management,* 19: 353–372.
132. W. P. Wan, D. W. Yiu, R. E. Hoskisson, & H. Kim, 2008, The performance implications of relationship banking during macroeconomic expansion and contraction: A study of Japanese banks' social relationships and overseas expansion, *Journal of International Business Studies*, 39: 406–427.
133. P. M. Lee & H. M. O'Neill, 2003, Ownership structures and R&D investments of U.S. and Japanese firms: Agency and stewardship perspectives, *Academy of Management Journal,* 46: 212–225.
134. I. S. Dinc, 2006, Monitoring the monitors: The corporate governance in Japanese banks and their real estate lending in the 1980s, *Journal of Business,* 79(6): 3057–3081; A. Kawaura, 2004, Deregulation and governance: Plight of Japanese banks in the 1990s, *Applied Economics,* 36: 479–484; B. Bremner, 2001, Cleaning up the banks—finally, *BusinessWeek,* December 17, 86; 2000, Business: Japan's corporate-governance U-turn, *The Economist,* November 18, 73.
135. N. Isagawa, 2007, A theory of unwinding of cross-shareholding under managerial entrenchment, *Journal of Financial Research*, 30: 163–179.
136. C. L. Ahmadjian & G. E. Robbins, 2005, A clash of capitalisms: Foreign shareholders and corporate restructuring in 1990s Japan, *American Sociological Review,* 70: 451–471.
137. J. M. Ramseyer, M. Nakazato, & E. B. Rasmusen, 2009, Public and private firm compensation: Evidence from Japanese tax returns, Harvard Law and Economics Discussion Paper, February 1.
138. S. R. Miller, D. Li, L. Eden, & M. A. Hitt, 2008, Insider trading and the valuation of international strategic alliances in emerging stock markets. *Journal of International Business Studies,* 39: 102–117.
139. H. Zou & M. B. Adams, 2008, Corporate ownership, equity risk and returns in the People's Republic of China, *Journal of International Business Studies,* 39: 1149–1168.
140. Y. Su, D. Xu, & P. H. Phan, 2008, Principal-principal conflict in the governance of the Chinese public corporation, *Management and Organization Review,* 4: 17–38.
141. China YCT International strengthens corporate governance with establishment of audit committee and appointments of three new independent directors, 2009.
142. T. Buck, X. Lui, & R. Skovoroda, 2008, Top executives pay and firm performance in China, *Journal of International Business Studies,* 39: 833–850.
143. P. M. Vaaler & B. N. Schrage, 2009, Residual state ownership, policy stability and financial performance following strategic

decisions by privatizing telecoms, *Journal of International Business Studies,* 40: 621–641.

144. Steel Partners issues statement on changes to KT&G's board of directors, 2008, *Reuters,* http://www.reuters.com, March 13; L. Santini, 2007, Rematch: KT&G vs. Steel Partners: Korean cigarette maker again angers an activist fund, *Wall Street Journal*, June 22, C5.
145. Steel Partners LLC, 2009, *BusinessWeek,* http://investing.businessweek.com,April 16.
146. I. Filatotchev, J. Stephan, & B. Jindra, 2008, Ownership structure, strategic controls and export intensity of foreign-invested firms in transition economies, *Journal of International Business Studies,* 39: 1133–1148.
147. T. J. Healey, 2007, Sarbox was the right medicine, *Wall Street Journal*, August 9, A13.
148. J. D. Hughes & J. H. Lee, 2007, The changing landscape of D & O liability, *Risk Management Journal*, January, 18–22.
149. C. Shropshire & A. J. Hillman, 2007, A longitudinal study of significant change in stakeholder management, *Business and Society*, 46(1): 63–87; S. Sharma & I. Henriques, 2005, Stakeholder influences on sustainability practices in the Canadian Forest products industry, *Strategic Management Journal,* 26: 159–180; A. J. Hillman, G. D. Keim, & R. A. Luce, 2001, Board composition and stakeholder performance: Do stakeholder directors make a difference? *Business and Society,* 40: 295–314.
150. D. L. Gold & J. W. Dienhart, 2007, Business ethics in the corporate governance era: Domestic and international trends in transparency, regulation, and corporate governance, *Business and Society Review*, 112(2): 163–170; N. Demise, 2005, Business ethics and corporate governance in Japan, *Business and Society,* 44: 211–217.
151. R. V. Aguilera, D. E. Rupp, C. A. Williams, & J. Ganapathi, 2007, Putting the S back in corporate social responsibility: A multilevel theory of social change in organizations, *Academy of Management Review*, 32(3): 836–863; Caldwell & Karri, Organizational governance and ethical systems: A covenantal approach to building trust; A. Felo, 2001, Ethics programs, board involvement, and potential conflicts of interest in corporate governance, *Journal of Business Ethics,* 32: 205–218.
152. Cummins achieves top ranking for corporate governance, 2009, *AEDNews,* http://www.aednet.org, March 16.

CHAPTER 11

1. P. Jarzabkowski, 2008, Shaping strategy as a structuration process, *Academy of Management Journal*, 51(4): 621–650; B. Ambos & B. B. Schlegelmilch, 2007, Innovation and control in the multinational firm: A comparison of political and contingency approaches, *Strategic Management Journal,* 28: 473–486; S. Kumar, Ş. Kant, & T. L. Amburgey, 2007, Public agencies and collaborative management approaches, *Administration & Society,* 39: 569–610.
2. R. Gulati & P. Puranam, 2009, Renewal through reorganization: The value of inconsistencies between formal and informal organization, *Organization Science*, 20(2): 422–440; R. E. Miles & C. C. Snow, 1978, *Organizational Strategy, Structure and Process,* New York: McGraw-Hill.
3. S. T. Hannah & P. B. Lester, 2009, A multilevel approach to building and leading learning organizations, *Leadership Quarterly*, 20(1): 34–48;E. M. Olson, S. F. Slater, & G. T. M. Hult, 2007, The importance of structure and process to strategy implementation, *Business Horizons,* 48(1): 47–54;D. N. Sull & C. Spinosa, 2007, Promise-based management, *Harvard Business Review,* 85(4):79–86.
4. R. Ireland, J. Covin, & D. Kuratko, 2009, Conceptualizing corporate entrepreneurship strategy, *Entrepreneurship Theory and Practice*, 33(1): 19–46; T. Amburgey & T. Dacin, 1994, As the left foot follows the right? The dynamics of strategic and structural change, *Academy of Management Journal,* 37: 1427–1452.
5. L. F. Monteiro, N. Arvidsson, &J. Birkinshaw, 2008, Knowledge flows within multinational corporations: Explaining subsidiary isolation and its performance implications, *Organization Science*, 19(1): 90–107; P. Ghemawat, 2007, Managing differences: The central challenge of global strategy, *Harvard Business Review,* 85(3): 59–68; B. Keats & H. O'Neill, 2001, Organizational structure: Looking through a strategy lens, in M. A. Hitt, R. E. Freeman, & J. S. Harrison (eds.), *Handbook of Strategic Management,* Oxford, UK: Blackwell Publishers, 520–542.
6. R. E. Hoskisson, C. W. L. Hill, & H. Kim, 1993, The multidivisional structure: Organizational fossil or source of value? *Journal of Management,* 19: 269–298.
7. Jarzabkowski, Shaping strategy as a structuration process; E. M. Olson,S. F. Slater, G. Tomas, & G. T. M. Hult, 2005, The performance implications of fit among business strategy, marketing organization structure, and strategic behavior, *Journal of Marketing,* 69(3): 49–65.
8. B. Novak, 2008, Cisco connects the dots: Aligning leaders with a new organizational structure, *Global Business and Organizational Excellence*: 27(5): 22–32.
9. T. Burns & G. M. Stalker, 1961, *The Management of Innovation,* London: Tavistok; P. R. Lawrence & J. W. Lorsch, 1967, *Organization and Environment,* Homewood, IL: Richard D. Irwin; J. Woodward, 1965, *Industrial Organization: Theory and Practice,* London: Oxford University Press.
10. A. M. Rugman & A. Verbeke, 2008, A regional solution to the strategy and structure of multinationals, *European Management Journal*, 26(5): 305–313;H. Kim, R. E. Hoskisson, L. Tihanyi, &J. Hong, 2004, Evolution and restructuring of diversified business groups in emerging markets: The lessons from chaebols in Korea, *Asia Pacific Journal of Management,* 21: 25–48.
11. R. Kathuria, M. P. Joshi, & S. J. Porth, 2007, Organizational alignment and performance: Past, present and future, *Management Decision,* 45: 503–517.
12. B. Sechler, 2008, Corporate news: General Electric's reorganization resurrects GE Capital, *Wall Street Journal*, August 1, B3.
13. A. Tempel & P. Walgenbach, 2007, Global standardization of organizational forms and management practices: What new

institutionalism and the business-systems approach can learn from each other, *Journal of Management Studies,* 44: 1–24; Keats & O'Neill, Organizational structure, 533.

14. Tieying Yu, M. S. Insead, & R. H. Lester, 2008, Misery loves company: The spread of negative impacts resulting from an organizational crisis, *Academy of Management Review*, 33(2): 452–472;R. L. Priem, L. G. Love, & M. A. Shaffer, 2002, Executives' perceptions of uncertainty sources: A numerical taxonomy and underlying dimensions, *Journal of Management,* 28: 725–746.
15. A. N. Shub & P. W. Stonebraker, 2009, The human impact on supply chains: Evaluating the importance of "soft" areas on integration and performance, *Supply Chain Management*, 14(1): 31–40; S. K. Ethiraj & D. Levinthal, 2004, Bounded rationality and the search for organizational architecture: An evolutionary perspective on the design of organizations and their evolvability, *Administrative Science Quarterly,* 49: 404–437.
16. R. Khadem, 2008, Alignment and follow-up: Steps to strategy execution, *Journal of Business Strategy,* 29(6): 29–35; J. G. Covin, D. P. Slevin, & M. B. Heeley, 2001, Strategic decision making in an intuitive vs. technocratic mode: Structural and environmental consideration, *Journal of Business Research,* 52: 51–67.
17. J. R. Maxwell, 2008, Work system design to improve the economic performance of the firm, *Business Process Management Journal*, 14(3): 432–446; E. M. Olson, S. F. Slater, & G. T. M. Hult, 2005, The importance of structure and process to strategy implementation, *Business Horizons,* 48(1): 47–54.
18. L. Donaldson, 2001, *The contingency theory of organizations,* Thousand Oaks, CA: Sage; Jenster & Hussey, *Company Analysis,* 169.
19. M. A. Schilling & H. K. Steensma, 2001, The use of modular organizational forms: An industry-level analysis, *Academy of Management Journal,* 44: 1149–1168.
20. P. Legerer, T. Pfeiffer, G. Schneider, & J. Wagner, 2009, Organizational structure and managerial decisions, *International Journal of the Economics of Business*, 16(2): 147–159; C. B. Dobni & G. Luffman, 2003, Determining the scope and impact of market orientation profiles on strategy implementation and performance, *Strategic Management Journal,* 24: 577–585.
21. H. Gebauer & F. Putz, 2009, Organizational structures for the service business in product-oriented companies, *International Journal of Services Technology and Management*, 11(1): 64–81; M. Hammer, 2007, The process audit, *Harvard Business Review,* 85(4): 111–123.
22. R. D. Ireland & J. W. Webb, 2007, Strategic entrepreneurship: Creating competitive advantage through streams of innovation, *Business Horizons,* 50: 49–59; T. J. Andersen, 2004, Integrating decentralized strategy making and strategic planning processes in dynamic environments, *Journal of Management Studies,* 41: 1271–1299.
23. J. Rivkin & N. Siggelkow, 2003, Balancing search and stability: Interdependencies among elements of organizational design, *Management Science,* 49: 290–321; G. A. Bigley & K. H. Roberts, 2001, The incident command system: High-reliability organizing for complex and volatile task environments, *Academy of Management Journal,* 44: 1281–1299.
24. Monteiro, Arvidsson, & Birkinshaw, Knowledge flows within multinational corporations; S. Nadkarni & V. K. Narayanan, 2007, Strategic schemas, strategic flexibility, and firm performance: The moderating role of industry clockspeed, *Strategic Management Journal,* 28: 243–270; K. D. Miller & A. T. Arikan, 2004, Technology search investments: Evolutionary, option reasoning, and option pricing approaches, *Strategic Management Journal,* 25: 473–485.
25. S. Raisch & J. Birkinshaw, 2008, Organizational ambidexterity: Antece-dents, outcomes, and moderators, *Journal of Management* 34: 375–409; C. Zook, 2007, Finding your next core business, *Harvard Business Review,* 85(4): 66–75.
26. M. Kimes, 2008, World's most admired companies: Cisco Systems layers it on, *Fortune*, December 8, 24.
27. S. K. Maheshwari & D. Ahlstrom, 2004, Turning around a state owned enterprise: The case of Scooters India Limited, *Asia Pacific Journal of Management,* 21(1–2): 75–101; B. W. Keats & M. A. Hitt, 1988, A causal model of linkages among environ-mental dimensions, macroorgani-zational characteristics, and performance, *Academy of Management Journal,* 31: 570–598.
28. A. Chandler, 1962, *Strategy and Structure,* Cambridge, MA: MIT Press.
29. D. Martin, 2007, Alfred D. Chandler, Jr., a business historian, dies at 88, *New York Times Online,* http://www.nytimes.com, May 12.
30. R. E. Hoskisson, R. A. Johnson, L. Tihanyi, & R. E. White, 2005, Diversified business groups and corporate refocusing inemerging economies, *Journal of Management,* 31: 941–965; J. D. Day, E. Lawson, & K. Leslie, 2003, When reorganization works, *The McKinsey Quarterly,* (2), 20–29.
31. B. Simon, 2009, Restructuring chief sees benefits in GM's maligned culture, *Financial Times,* July 4, 16.
32. S. K. Ethiraj, 2007, Allocation of inventive effort in complex product systems, *Strategic Management Journal,* 28: 563–584.
33. A. M. Kleinbaum & M. L. Tushman, 2008, Managing corporate social networks, *Harvard Business Review*, 86(7): 26–27; A. Weibel, 2007, Formal control and trustworthiness, *Group & Organization Management,* 32: 500–517; P. K. Mills &G. R. Ungson, 2003, Reassessing the limits of structural empowerment: Organizational constitution and trust as controls, *Academy of Management Review,* 28: 143–153.
34. C. Rowe, J. G. Birnberg, & M. D. Shields, 2008, Effects of organizational process change on responsibility accounting and managers' revelations of private knowledge, *Accounting, Organizations and Society*, 33(2/3): 164–198; M. Santala & P. Parvinen, 2007, From strategic fit to customer fit, *Management Decision,* 45: 582–601;R. Reed, W. J. Donoher, & S. F. Barnes, 2004, Predicting misleading disclosures: The effects of control, pressure, and compensation, *Journal of Managerial Issues,* 16: 322–336.

35. P. Greve, S. Nielsen, & W. Ruigrok, 2009, Transcending borders with international top management teams: A study of European financial multinational corporations, *European Management Journal*, 27(3): 213–224; T. Galpin, R. Hilpirt, & B. Evans, 2007, The connected enterprise: Beyond division of labor, *Journal of Business Strategy,* 28(2): 38–47; C. Sundaramurthy & M. Lewis, 2003, Control and collaboration: Paradoxes of governance, *Academy of Management Review,* 28: 397–415.

36. M. A. Desai, 2008, The finance function in a global corporation, *Harvard Business Review*, 86(7): 108–112; Y. Li, L. Li,Y. Liu, & L. Wang, 2005, Linking manage-ment control system with product devel-opment and process decisions to cope with environment complexity, *International Journal of Production Research,* 43: 2577–2591.

37. I. Filatotchev, J. Stephan, & B. Jindra, 2008, Ownership structure, strategic controls and export intensity of foreign-invested firms in transition economies, *Journal of International Business Studies*, 39(7): 1133–1148; G. J. M. Braam & E. J. Nijssen, 2004, Performance effects of using the Balanced Scorecard: A note on the Dutch experience, *Long Range Planning,* 37: 335–349; S. D. Julian & E. Scifres, 2002, An interpretive perspective on the role of strategic control in triggering strategic change, *Journal of Business Strategies,* 19: 141–159.

38. J. Kratzer, H. G. Gemünden, C. Lettl, 2008, Balancing creativity and time efficiency in multi-team R&D projects: the alignment of formal and informal networks, *R & D Management*, 38(5): 538–549; D. F. Kuratko, R. D. Ireland, & J. S. Hornsby, 2004, Corporate entrepreneurship behavior among managers: A review of theory, research, and practice, in J. A. Katz & D. A. Shepherd (eds.), *Advances in Entrepreneurship: Firm Emergence and Growth: Corporate Entrepreneurship,* Oxford, UK: Elsevier Publishing, 7–45.

39. Y. Doz & M. Kosonen, 2008, The dynamics of strategic agility: Nokia's rollercoaster experience, *California Management Review*, 50(3): 95–118.

40. Y. Liu & T. Ravichandran, 2008, A comprehensive investigation on the relationship between information technology investments and firm diversification, *Information Technology and Management*, 9(3): 169–180;K. L. Turner & M. V. Makhija, 2006, The role of organizational controls in managing knowledge, *Academy of Management Review,* 31: 197–217;M. A. Hitt, R. E. Hoskisson, R. A. Johnson, &D. D. Moesel, 1996, The market for corporate control and firm innovation, *Academy of Management Journal,* 39: 1084–1119.

41. B. Fryer & T. A. Stewart, 2008, Cisco sees the future, *Harvard Business Review*, 86(11): 72–79.

42. Desai, The finance function in a global corporation; M. A. Hitt, L. Tihanyi,T. Miller, & B. Connelly, 2006, Interna-tional diversification: Antecedents, outcomes, and moderators, *Journal of Management,* 32: 831–867; R. E. Hoskisson & M. A. Hitt, 1988, Strategic control and relative R&D investment in multiproduct firms, *Strategic Management Journal,* 9: 605–621.

43. S. Lee, K. Park, H. H. Shin, 2009, Disap-pearing internal capital markets: Evidence from diversified business groups in Korea, *Journal of Banking & Finance*, 33(2): 326–334; D. Collis, D. Young, & M. Goold, 2007, The size, structure, and performance of corporate headquarters, *Strategic Management Journal,* 28: 383–405.

44. X. S. Y. Spencer, T. A. Joiner, & S. Salmon, 2009, Differentiation strategy, performance measurement systems and organizational performance: Evidence from Australia, *International Journal of Business*, 14(1): 83–103; K. Chaharbaghi, 2007, The problematic of strategy: A way of seeing is also a way of not seeing, *Management Decision*, 45: 327–339; J. B. Barney, 2002, *Gaining and Sustaining Competitive Advantage,* 2nd ed., Upper Saddle River, NJ: Prentice Hall.

45. S. Lohr, 2007, Can Michael Dell refocus his namesake? *New York Times Online,* http://www.nytimes.com, September 9.

46. L. Lee, 2008, HP's Hurd is about to be tested: After a sterling three-year run, the company's CEO faces a weaker PC market and a stronger Dell, *BusinessWeek*, February 14, 59–60.

47. Gebauer & Putz, 2009, Organizational structures for the service business in product-oriented companies; X. Yin &E. J. Zajac, 2004, The strategy/governance structure fit relationship: Theory and evidence in franchising arrangements, *Strategic Management Journal,* 25: 365–383.

48. Keats & O'Neill, Organizational structure, 531.

49. K. Wakabayashi, 2008, Relationship between business definition and corporate growth: The effect of functional alignment, *Pacific Economic Review*, 13(5): 663–679; K. M. Green, J. G. Covin,D. P. Slevin, 2008, Exploring the relationship between strategic reactiveness and entrepreneurial orientation: The role of structure-style fit. *Journal of Business Venturing*, 23(3): 356; Olson, Slater, & Hult, The importance of structure and process to strategy implementation; D. Miller & J. O. Whitney, 1999, Beyond strategy: Configuration as a pillar of competitive advantage, *Business Horizons,* 42(3): 5–17.

50. Chandler, *Strategy and Structure.*

51. Keats & O'Neill, Organizational structure, 524.

52. E. Rawley, 2009, Diversification, coordination costs and organizational rigidity: Evidence from microdata, *Strategic Management Journal*; forth-coming; M. E. Sosa, S. D. Eppinger, & C. M. Rowles, 2004, The misalignment of product architecture and organizational structure in complex product develop-ment, *Management Science,* 50: 1674–1689.

53. J. W. Yoo, R. Reed, S. J. Shin, &D. J. Lemak, 2009, Strategic choice and performance in late movers: Influence of the top management team's external ties, *Journal of Management Studies*, 46(2): 308–335; S. Karim & W. Mitchell, 2004, Innovating through acquisition and internal development: A quarter-century of boundary evolution at Johnson & Johnson, *Long Range Planning,* 37: 525–547.

54. I. Daizadeh, 2006, Using intellectual property to map the organizational evolution of firms: Tracing a biotechnology company from startup to bureaucracy to a multidivisional firm, *Journal of Commercial Biotechnology,* 13: 28–36.

55. C. Levicki, 1999, *The Interactive Strategy Workout,* 2nd ed., London: Prentice Hall.

56. E. E. Entin, F. J. Diedrich, & B. Rubineau, 2003, Adaptive communication patterns in different organizational structures,

Human Factors and Ergonomics Society Annual Meeting Proceedings, 405–409;H. M. O'Neill, R. W. Pouder, &A. K. Buchholtz, 1998, Patterns in the diffusion of strategies across organizations: Insights from the innovation diffusion literature, *Academy of Management Review,* 23: 98–114.

57. Spencer, Joiner, & Salmon, Differentiation strategy, performance measurement systems and organizational performance; 2007, Organizational structure, *Wikipedia,* http:// en.wikipedia.org; Gallbraith, *Designing Organizations,* 25.
58. Keats & O'Neill, Organizational structure, 539.
59. C. M. Christensen, S. P. Kaufman, &W. C. Shih, 2008, Innovation killers, *Harvard Business Review*: Special HBS Centennial Issue, 86(1): 98–105; J. Welch & S. Welch, 2006, Growing up but staying young, *BusinessWeek,* December 11, 112.
60. O. E. Williamson, 1975, *Markets and Hierarchies: Analysis and Anti-Trust Implications,* New York: The Free Press.
61. S. H. Mialon, 2008, Efficient horizontal mergers: The effects of internal capital reallocation and organizational form, *International Journal of Industrial Organization*, 26(4): 861–877; Chandler, *Strategy and Structure.*
62. R. Inderst, H. M. Muller, & K. Warneryd, 2007, Distributional conflict in organi-zations, *European Economic Review,* 51: 385–402; J. Greco, 1999, Alfred P. Sloan Jr. (1875–1966): The original organizational man, *Journal of Business Strategy,* 20(5): 30–31.
63. Hoskisson, Hill, & Kim, The multidivisional structure, 269–298.
64. Mialon, Efficient horizontal mergers: The effects of internal capital reallocation and organizational form; H. Zhou, 2005, Market structure and organizational form, *Southern Economic Journal,* 71: 705–719; W. G. Rowe & P. M. Wright, 1997, Related and unrelated diversification and their effect on human resource management controls, *Strategic Management Journal,* 18: 329–338.
65. C. E. Helfat & K. M. Eisenhardt, 2004, Inter-temporal economies of scope, organizational modularity, and the dynamics of diversification, *Strategic Management Journal,* 25: 1217–1232; A. D. Chandler, 1994, The functions of the HQ unit in the multibusiness firm, in R. P. Rumelt, D. E. Schendel, & D. J. Teece (eds.), *Fundamental Issues in Strategy,* Cambridge, MA: Harvard Business School Press, 327.
66. O. E. Williamson, 1994, Strategizing, economizing, and economic organization, in R. P. Rumelt, D. E. Schendel, &D. J. Teece (eds.), *Fundamental Issues in Strategy,* Cambridge, MA: Harvard Business School Press, 361–401.
67. Hoskisson, Hill, & Kim, The multidivisional structure: Organizational fossil or source of value?; R. M. Burton & B. Obel, 1980, A computer simulation test of the M-form hypothesis, *Administrative Science Quarterly,* 25: 457–476.
68. O. E. Williamson, 1985, *The Economic Institutions of Capitalism: Firms, Markets, and Relational Contracting,* New York: Macmillan.
69. Keats & O'Neill, Organizational structure, 532.
70. M. F. Wolff, 1999, In the organization of the future, competitive advantage will be inspired, *Research Technology Management,* 42(4): 2–4.
71. R. H. Hall, 1996, *Organizations: Structures, Processes, and Outcomes,* 6th ed., Englewood Cliffs, NJ: Prentice Hall, 13; S. Baiman, D. F. Larcker, & M. V. Rajan, 1995, Organizational design for business units, *Journal of Accounting Research,* 33: 205–229.
72. L. G. Love, R. L. Priem, & G. T. Lumpkin, 2002, Explicitly articulated strategy and firm performance under alternative levels of centralization, *Journal of Management,* 28: 611–627.
73. Hall, *Organizations,* 64–75.
74. Barney, *Gaining and Sustaining Competitive Advantage,* 257.
75. H. Karandikar & S. Nidamarthi, 2007, Implementing a platform strategy for a systems business via standardization, *Journal of Manufacturing Technology Management,* 18: 267–280.
76. Olson, Slater, Tomas, & Hult, The performance implications of fit.
77. 2007, Wal-Mart Stores, Inc, *New York Times Online,* http:// www.nytimes.com, July 21.
78. 2007, Wal-Mart rolling out new company slogan, *New York Times Online,* http:// www.nytimes.com, July 12.
79. Olson, Slater, Tomas, & Hult, The performance implications of fit.
80. T. Heath, 2008, In pursuit of innovation at Under Armour: Founder Kevin Plank says Super Bowl commercial has generated "buzz," *Washington Post*, February 25, D03.
81. Chandler, *Strategy and Structure.*
82. C. C. Markides & P. J. Williamson, 1996, Corporate diversification and organizational structure: A resource-based view, *Academy of Management Journal,* 39: 340–367; C. W. L. Hill, M. A. Hitt, & R. E. Hoskisson, 1992, Cooperative versus competitive structures in related and unrelated diversified firms, *Organization Science,* 3: 501–521.
83. S. H. Appelbaum, D. Nadeau, & M. Cyr, 2008, Performance evaluation in a matrix organization: A case study (part two), *Industrial and Commercial Training*, 40(6): 295–299.
84. S. H. Appelbaum, D. Nadeau, & M. Cyr, 2009, Performance evaluation in a matrix organization: A case study (part three), *Industrial and Commercial Training,* 41(1): 9–14; M. Goold & A. Campbell, 2003, Structured networks: Towards the well designed matrix, *Long Range Planning,* 36(5): 427–439.
85. P. Eavis, 2008, The pain at Sears grows, *The Wall Street Journal Online*, www.wsj.com, May 30.
86. N. M. Schmid & I. Walter, 2009, Do financial conglomerates create or destroy economic value? *Journal of Financial Intermediation*, 18(2): 193–216; P. A. Argenti, R. A. Howell, & K. A. Beck, 2005, The strategic communication imperative, *MIT Sloan Management Review,* 46(3): 84–89.
87. M. F. Wiersema & H. P. Bowen, 2008, Corporate diversification: The impact of foreign competition, industry globalization, and product diversification, *Strategic Management Journal*, 29: 115–132; R. E. Hoskisson & M. A. Hitt, 1990, Antecedents and performance outcomes of diversification: A review and critique of theoretical perspectives, *Journal of Management,* 16: 461–509.
88. Hill, Hitt, & Hoskisson, Cooperative versus competitive structures, 512.

89. Lee, Park, & Shin, Disappearing internal capital markets: Evidence from diversified business groups in Korea; J. Birkinshaw, 2001, Strategies for managing internal competition, *California Management Review,* 44(1): 21–38.
90. 2009, Vision and strategy, http://www.textron.com, July 16.
91. M. Maremont, 2004, Leadership; more can be more: Is the conglomerate a dinosaur from a bygone era? The answer is no—with a caveat, *Wall Street Journal,* October 24, R4; T. R. Eisenmann &J. L. Bower, 2000, The entrepreneurial M-form: Strategic integration in global media firms, *Organization Science,* 11: 348–355.
92. GE's two decade transformation:Jack Welch's Leadership, Harvard Business School Case # 9-399-150; J. Welch, 2001, *Straight from the Gut*, New York, Warner Books; J. Welch & S. Welch, 2006, *Winning*, NewDelhi: Harper Collins.
93. T. Yu & A. A. Cannella, Jr., 2007, Rivalry between multinational enterprises: An event history approach, *Academy of Management Journal,* 50: 665–686;S. E. Christophe & H. Lee, 2005, What matters about internationalization: A market-based assessment, *Journal of Business Research,* 58: 636–643; Y. Luo, 2002, Product diversification in international joint ventures: Performance implications in an emerging market, *Strategic Management Journal,* 23: 1–20.
94. M. Mandel, 2007, Globalization vs. immigration reform, *BusinessWeek,* June 4, 40.
95. T. M. Begley & D. P. Boyd, 2003, The need for a corporate global mind-set, *MIT Sloan Management Review,* 44(2): 25–32; Tallman, Global strategic management, 467.
96. T. Kostova & K. Roth, 2003, Social capital in multinational corporations and a micro-macro model of its formation, *Academy of Management Review,* 28: 297–317.
97. J. Jermias & L. Gani, 2005, Ownership structure, contingent-fit, and business-unit performance: A research model and evidence, *The International Journal of Accounting,* 40: 65–85; J. Wolf & W. G. Egelhoff, 2002, A reexamination and extension of international strategy-structure theory, *Strategic Management Journal,* 23: 181–189.
98. J. Ewing, 2009, A magic moment for Ford of Europe, *BusinessWeek*, July 6, 48–49.
99. C. A. Bartlett & S. Ghoshal, 1989, *Managing Across Borders: The Transnational Solution,* Boston: Harvard Business School Press.
100. S. Feinberg, & A. Gupta, 2009, MNC subsidiaries and country risk: Internalization as a safeguard against weak external institutions, *Academy of Management Journal* 52(2): 381–399; S. T. Cavusgil, S. Yeniyurt, & J. D. Townsend, 2004, The framework of a global company: A conceptualization and preliminary validation, *Industrial Marketing Manage-ment,* 33: 711–716.
101. N. Byrnes, 2007, Avon: More than cosmetic changes, *BusinessWeek,* March 12, 62–63.
102. K. Nolan, 2009, Corporate news: Avon unveils new cost cuts, *Wall Street Journal*, February 20, B2.
103. Malnight, Emerging structural patterns, 1197.
104. Rugman & Verbeke, A regional solution to the strategy and structure of multinationals.
105. B. Connelly, M. A. Hitt, A. DeNisi, & R. D. Ireland, 2007, Expatriates and corporate-level international strategy: Governing with the knowledge contract, *Management Decision,* 45: 564–581.
106. M. E. Lloyd, 2009, IKEA sees opportunity in slump, Wall Street Journal Online, http://online.wsj.com, February 17; E. Baraldi, 2008, Strategy in industrial Networks: Experiences from IKEA, *California Management Review*, 50(4): 99–126.
107. D. Lavie, 2009, Capturing value from alliance portfolios, *Organizational Dynamics*, 38(1): 26–36; S. G. Lazzarini, 2007, The impact of membership in competing alliance constellations: Evidence on the operational performance of global airlines, *Strategic Management Journal,* 28: 345–367; Y. L. Doz &G. Hamel, 1998, *Alliance Advantage:The Art of Creating Value through Partnering,* Boston: Harvard Business School Press, 222.
108. J. Li, C. Zhou, & E. J. Zajac, 2009, Control, collaboration, and productivity in international joint ventures: Theory and evidence, *Strategic Management Journal*, 30: 865–884; Y. Luo, 2007, Are joint venture partners more opportunistic in a more volatile environment? *Strategic Management Journal,* 28: 39–60;K. Moller, A. Rajala, & S. Svahn, 2005, Strategic business nets—their type and management, *Journal of Business Research,* 58: 1274–1284.
109. D. Li, L. E. Eden, M. A. Hitt, &R. D. Ireland, 2008, Friends, acquaintances, or strangers? Partner selection in R&D alliances, *Academy of Management Journal,* 51(2): 315–334.
110. Lavie, Capturing value from alliance portfolios; B. Comes-Casseres, 2003, Competitive advantage in alliance constellations, *Strategic Organization,* 1: 327–335; T. K. Das & B. S. Teng, 2002, Alliance constellations: A social exchange perspective, *Academy of Management Review,* 27: 445–456.
111. T. Vapola, P. Tossavainen, & M. Gabrielsson, 2008, The battleship strategy: The complementing role of born globals in MNC's new opportunity creation, *Journal of International Entrepreneurship*: 6(1): 1–21; S. Tallman, M. Jenkins, N. Henry, & S. Pinch, 2004, Knowledge, clusters, and competitive advantage, *Academy of Management Review,* 29: 258–271.
112. V. Moatti, 2009, Learning to expand or expanding to learn? The role of imitation and experience in the choice among several expansion modes, *European Management Journal*, 27(1): 36–46; A. Capaldo, 2007, Network structure and innovation: The leveraging of a dual network as a distinctive relational capability, *Strategic Management Journal,* 28: 585–608; A. Zaheer & G. G. Bell, 2005, Benefiting from network position: Firm capabilities, structural holes, and performance, *Strategic Management Journal,* 26: 809–825.
113. J. Wiklund & D. A. Shepherd, 2009, The effectiveness of alliances and acquisitions: The role of resource combination activities, *Theory and Practice*, 31(1): 193–212; R. D. Ireland & J. W. Webb, 2007, A multi-theoretic perspective on trust and power in strategic supply chains, *Journal of Operations Management,* 25: 482–497; V. G. Narayanan & A. Raman, 2004, Aligning incentives in supply chains, *Harvard Business Review,* 82(11): 94–102.

114. S. Harrison, 1998, *Japanese Technology and Innovation Management*, Northampton, MA: Edward Elgar.
115. M. H. Hansen, R. E. Hoskisson, & J. B. Barney, 2008, Competitive advantage in alliance governance: Resolving the opportunism minimization-gain maximization paradox, *Managerial and Decision Economics*, 29: 191–208; T. Keil, 2004, Building external corporate venturing capability, *Journal of Management Studies*, 41: 799–825.
116. T. Vapola, & Gabrielsson, The battleship strategy: The complementing role of born globals in MNC's new opportunity creation; P. Dussauge,B. Garrette, & W. Mitchell, 2004, Learning from competing partners: Outcomes and duration of scale and link alliances in Europe, North America and Asia, *Strategic Management Journal*, 21: 99–126; G. Lorenzoni & C. Baden-Fuller, 1995, Creating a strategic center to manage a web of partners, *California Management Review*, 37(3): 146–163.
117. S. R. Holmberg & J. L. Cummings, 2009, Building successful strategic alliances: Strategic process and analytical tools for selecting partner industries and firms, *Long Range Planning*, 42(2): 164–193; B. J. Bergiel, E. B. Bergiel, & P. W. Balsmeier, 2008, Nature of virtual teams: A summary of their advantages and disadvantages, *Management Research News*, 31(2): 99–110.
118. A. C. Inkpen, 2008, Knowledge transfer and international joint ventures: The case of NUMMI and General Motors, *Strategic Management Journal*, 29(4): 447–453;T. A. Stewart & A. P. Raman, 2007, Lessons from Toyota's long drive, *Harvard Business Review*, 85(7/8): 74–83; J. H. Dyer & K. Nobeoka, 2000, Creating and managing a high-performance knowledge-sharing network: The Toyota case, *Strategic Management Journal*, 21: 345–367.
119. L. F. Mesquita, J. Anand, & J. H. Brush, 2008, Comparing the resource-based and relational views: Knowledge transfer and spillover in vertical alliances, *Strategic Management Journal*, 29: 913–941: M. Kotabe, X. Martin, & H. Domoto, 2003, Gaining from vertical partnerships: Knowledge transfer, relationship duration and supplier performance improvement in the U.S. and Japanese automotive industries, *Strategic Management Journal*, 24: 293–316.
120. T. Nishiguchi, 1994, *Strategic Industrial Sourcing: The Japanese Advantage*, New York: Oxford University Press.
121. S. G. Lazzarini, D. P. Claro, & L. F. Mesquita, 2008, Buyer-supplier and supplier-supplier alliances: Do they reinforce or undermine one another? *Journal of Management Studies*, 45(3): 561–584; P. Dussauge,B. Garrette, & W. Mitchell, 2004, Asymmetric performance: The market share impact of scale and link alliances in the global auto industry, *Strategic Management Journal*, 25: 701–711.
122. J. Shook, 2009, Toyota's secret: The A3 report, *MIT Sloan Management Review*, 50(4): 30–33; C. Dawson & K. N. Anhalt, 2005, A "China price" for Toyota, *BusinessWeek*, February 21, 50–51; W. M. Fruin, 1992, *The Japanese Enterprise System*, New York: Oxford University Press.
123. B. Garrette, X. Castañer, & P. Dussauge, 2009, Horizontal alliances as an alternative to autonomous production: Product expansion mode choice in the worldwide aircraft industry 1945–2000, *Strategic Management Journal*, 30(8): 885–894.
124. A. M. Hayashi, 2008, How to replicate success, *MIT Sloan Management Review*, 49(3): 6–7; M. Tuunanen & F. Hoy, 2007, Franchising: Multifaceted form of entrepreneurship, *International Journal of Entrepreneurship and Small Business*, 4: 52–67.
125. J. Li, C. Dhanaraj, & R. L. Shockley, 2008, Joint venture evolution: Extending the real options approach, *Managerial and Decision Economics*, 29(4): 317–336;B. B. Nielsen, 2005, The role of knowl-edge embeddedness in the creation of synergies in strategic alliances, *Journal of Business Research*, 58: 1194–1204.
126. E. Bellman, 2009, Corporate news: McDonald's plans expansion in India, *Wall Street Journal*, June 30, B4.
127. T. W. Tong, J. J. Reuer, & M. W. Peng, 2008. International joint ventures and the value of growth options, *Academy of Management Journal*, 51: 1014–1029;P. H. Andersen & P. R. Christensen, 2005, Bridges over troubled water: Suppliers as connective nodes in global supply networks, *Journal of Business Research*, 58: 1261–1273; C. Jones, W. S. Hesterly, & S. P. Borgatti, 1997, A general theory of network governance: Exchange conditions and social mechanisms, *Academy of Management Review*, 22: 911–945.
128. M. W. Hansen, T. Pedersen, & B. Petersen, 2009, MNC strategies and linkage effects in developing countries, *Journal of World Business*, 44(2): 121–139; A. Goerzen, 2005, Managing alliance networks: Emerging practices of multinational corporations, *Academy of Management Executive*, 19(2): 94–107.
129. L. H. Lin, 2009, Mergers and acquisitions, alliances and technology development: An empirical study of the global auto industry, *International Journal of Technology Management*, 48(3): 295–307; R. E. Miles, C. C. Snow, J. A. Mathews, G. Miles, & J. J. Coleman Jr., 1997, Organizing in the knowledge age: Anticipating the cellular form, *Academy of Management Executive*, 11(4): 7–20.
130. 2009, EDS Agility Alliance: Collaboration for better business outcomes, http://www.eds.com, July 16.
131. 2009, EDS Agility Alliance reaches milestone, *Wireless News*, June 3.

CHAPTER 12

1. A. Mackey, 2008, The effect of CEOs on firm performance, *Strategic Management Journal*, 29: 1357–1367.
2. E. F. Goldman, 2007, Strategic thinking at the top, *MIT Sloan Management Review*, 48(4): 75–81.
3. L. Bassi & D. McMurrer, 2007, Maximizing your return on people, *Harvard Business Review*, 85(3): 115–123;R. D. Ireland & M. A. Hitt, 2005, Achieving and maintaining strategic competitiveness in the 21st century: The role of strategic leadership, *Academy of Management Executive*, 19: 63–77.
4. J. P. Kotter, 2007, Leading change: Why transformation efforts fail, *Harvard Business Review*, 85(1): 96–103.

5. M. A. Hitt, C. Miller, & A. Collella, 2009, *Organizational Behavior: A Strategic Approach,* 2nd ed., New York: John Wiley & Sons; M. A. Hitt & R. D. Ireland, 2002, The essence of strategic leadership: Managing human and social capital, *Journal of Leadership and Organizational Studies,* 9: 3–14.
6. D. A. Ready & J. A. Conger, 2007, Make your company a talent factory, *Harvard Business Review,* 85(6): 69–77.
7. D. Roberts & C.-C. Tschang, 2007, China's rising leaders, *BusinessWeek,* October 1, 33–35.
8. P. Capelli, 2010, *The India Way: How India's Top Leaders Are Revolutionizing Management*, Boston: Harvard University Press.
9. P. A. Gloor & S. M. Cooper, 2007, The new principles of a swarm business, *MIT Sloan Management Review,* 48(3): 81–85; A. S. DeNisi, M. A. Hitt, & S. E. Jackson, 2003, The knowledge-based approach to sustainable competitive advantage, in S. E. Jackson, M. A. Hitt, & A. S. DeNisi (eds.), *Managing Knowledge for Sustained Competitive Advantage,* San Francisco: Jossey-Bass, 3–33.
10. L. Bossidy, 2007, What your leader expects of you: And what you should expect in return, *Harvard Business Review,* 85(4): 58–65; J. E. Post, L. E. Preston, & S. Sachs, 2002, Managing the extended enterprise: The new stakeholder view, *California Management Review,* 45(1): 6–28.
11. A. McKee & D. Massimilian, 2007, Resonant leadership: A new kind of leadership for the digital age, *Journal of Business Strategy,* 27(5): 45–49.
12. E. Baraldi, R. Brennan, D. Harrison, A. Tunisini, & J. Zolkiewski, 2007, Strategic thinking and the IMP approach: A comparative analysis, *Industrial Marketing Management,* 36: 879–894; C. L. Shook, R. L. Priem, & J. E. McGee, 2003, Venture creation and the enterprising individual: A review and synthesis, *Journal of Management,* 29: 379–399.
13. M. L. McDonald, P. Khanna, & J. D. Westphal, 2008, Getting them to think outside the circle: Corporate governace, CEOs' external advice networks and firm performance, *Academy of Management Journal,* 51: 453–475.
14. R. A. Burgleman & A. S. Grove, 2007, Let chaos reign, then rein in chaos—repeatedly: Managing strategic dynamics for corporate longevity, *Strategic Management Journal,* 28: 965–979.
15. T. R. Holcomb, R. M. Holmes, & B. L. Connelly, 2009, Making the most of what you have: Managerial ability as a source of resource value creation, *Strategic Management Journal,* 30: 457–485.
16. A. E. Colbert, A. L. Kristof-Brown, B. H. Bradley, & M. R. Barrick, 2008, CEO transformational leadership: The role of goal importance congruence in top management teams, *Academy of Management Journal,* 51: 81–96; S. Borener, S. A. Eisenbeliss, & D. Griesser, 2007, Follower behavior and organizational performance: The impact of transformational leaders, *Journal of Leadership & Organizational Studies,* 13(3): 15–26.
17. R.M. Lala, 2004, *Creation of Wealth: The Tatas from the 19th to 21st Century,* New Delhi: Penguin; R.M. Lala, 1993, *Beyond the Last Blue Mountain: A Life of JRD Tata,* New Delhi: Penguin.
18. H. S. Givray, 2007, When CEOs aren't leaders, *BusinessWeek,* September 3, 102.
19. D. Goleman, 2004, What makes a leader? *Harvard Business Review,* 82(1): 82–91.
20. Y. Ling, Z. Simsek, M. H. Lubatkin, & J. F. Veiga, Transformational leadership's role in promoting corporate entrepreneurship: Examining the CEO-TMT interface, *Academy of Management Journal,* 51: 557–576.
21. J. L. Morrow, Jr., D. G. Sirmon, M. A. Hitt, & T. R. Holcomb, 2007, Creating value in the face of declining performance: Firm strategies and organizational recovery, *Strategic Management Journal,* 28: 271–283; R. Castanias & C. Helfat, 2001, The managerial rents model: Theory and empirical analysis, *Journal of Management,* 27: 661–678.
22. H. G. Barkema & O. Shvyrkov, 2007, Does top management team diversity promote or hamper foreign expansion? *Strategic Management Journal,* 28: 663–680; M. Beer & R. Eisenstat, 2000, The silent killers of strategy implementation and learning, *Sloan Management Review,* 41(4): 29–40.
23. V. Santos & T. Garcia, 2007, The complexity of the organizational renewal decision: The management role, *Leadership & Organization Development Journal,* 28: 336–355; M. Wright, R. E. Hoskisson, L. W. Busenitz, & J. Dial, 2000, Entrepreneurial growth through privatization: The upside of management buyouts, *Academy of Management Review,* 25: 591–601.
24. D. G. Sirmon, J.-L. Arregle, M. A. Hitt, & J. W. Webb, 2008, The role of family influence in firms' strategic responses to threat of imitation, *Entrepreneurship Theory and Practice,* 32: 979–998; Y. L. Doz & M. Kosonen, 2007, The new deal at the top, *Harvard Business Review,* 85(6): 98–104.
25. A. S. Tsui, Z.-X. Zhang, H. Wang, K. R. Xin, & J. B. Wu, 2006, Unpacking the relationship between CEO leadership behavior and organizational culture, *The Leadership Quarterly,* 17: 113–137; J. A. Petrick & J. F. Quinn, 2001, The challenge of leadership accountability for integrity capacity as a strategic asset, *Journal of Business Ethics,* 34: 331–343.
26. D. G. Sirmon, S. Gove, & M. A. Hitt, 2008, Resource management in dyadic competitive rivalry: The effects of resource bundling and deployment, *Academy of Management Journal,* 51: 918–935; R. Martin, 2007, How successful leaders think, *Harvard Business Review,* 85(6): 60–67.
27. M. L. A. Hayward, V. P. Rindova, & T. G. Pollock, 2004, Believing one's own press: The causes and consequences of CEO celebrity, *Strategic Management Journal,* 25: 637–653.
28. K. M. Hmieleski & R. A. Baron, 2008, When does entrepreneurial self-efficacy enhance versus reduce firm performance? *Strategic Entrepreneurship Journal,* 2: 57–72; N. J. Hiller & D. C. Hambrick, 2005, Conceptualizing executive hubris: The role of (hyper-) core self-evaluations in strategic decision making, *Strategic Management Journal,* 26: 297–319.
29. A. M. L. Raes, U. Glunk, M. G. Heijitjes, &R. A. Roe, 2007, Top management team and middle managers, *Small Group*

Research, 38: 360–386; I. Goll, R. Sambharya, & L. Tucci, 2001, Top management team composition, corporate ideology, and firm performance, *Management International Review,* 41(2): 109–129.

30. J. Bunderson, 2003, Team member functional background and involvement in management teams: Direct effects and the moderating role of power and centralization, *Academy of Management Journal,* 46: 458–474; L. Markoczy, 2001, Consensus formation during strategic change, *Strategic Management Journal,* 22: 1013–1031.
31. C. Pegels, Y. Song, & B. Yang, 2000, Management heterogeneity, competitive interaction groups, and firm performance, *Strategic Management Journal,* 21: 911–923.
32. R. Rico, E. Molleman, M. Sanchez-Manzanares, & G. S. Van der Vegt, 2007, The effects of diversity faultlines and team task autonomy on decision quality and social integration, *Journal of Management,* 33: 111–132.
33. A. Srivastava, K. M. Bartol, & E. A. Locke, 2006, Empowering leadership in management teams: Effects on knowledge sharing, efficacy, and performance, *Academy of Management Journal,* 49: 1239–1251; D. Knight, C. L. Pearce, K. G. Smith, J. D. Olian, H. P. Sims, K. A. Smith, & P. Flood, 1999, Top management team diversity, group process, and strategic consensus, *Strategic Management Journal,* 20: 446–465.
34. B. J. Olson, S. Parayitam, & Y. Bao, 2007, Strategic decision making: The effects of cognitive diversity, conflict, and trust on decision outcomes, *Journal of Management,* 33: 196–222; T. Simons, L. H. Pelled, & K. A. Smith, 1999, Making use of difference, diversity, debate, and decision comprehensiveness in top management teams, *Academy of Management Journal,* 42: 662–673.
35. S. Finkelstein, D. C. Hambrick, & A. A. Cannella, Jr., 2008, *Strategic Leadership: Top Executives and Their Effects on Organizations,* New York: Oxford University Press.
36. J. J. Marcel, 2009, Why top management team characteristics matter when employing a chief operating officer: A strategic contingency perspective, *Strategic Management Journal,* 30: 647–658; S. Barsade, A. Ward, J. Turner, & J. Sonnenfeld, 2000, To your heart's content: A model of affective diversity in top management teams, *Administrative Science Quarterly,* 45: 802–836.
37. B. J. Avolio & S. S. Kahai, 2002, Adding the "e" to e-leadership: How it may impact your leadership, *Organizational Dynamics,* 31: 325–338.
38. Z. Simsek, J. F. Veiga, M. L. Lubatkin, & R. H. Dino, 2005, Modeling the multilevel determinants of top management team behavioral integration, *Academy of Management Journal,* 48: 69–84.
39. A. A. Cannella, J. H. Park, & H. U. Lee, 2008, Top management team functional background diversity and firm performance: Examining the roles of team member collocation and environmental uncertainty, *Academy of Management Journal,* 51: 768–784.
40. M. Jensen & E. J. Zajac, 2004, Corporate elites and corporate strategy: How demographic preferences and structural position shape the scope of the firm, *Strategic Management Journal,* 25: 507–524.
41. R. Yokota & H. Mitsuhashi, Attributive change in top management teams as a driver of strategic change, *Asia Pacific Journal of Management,* 25: 297–315; W. B. Werther, 2003, Strategic change and leader-follower alignment, *Organizational Dynamics,* 32: 32–45.
42. H. Li & J. Li, 2009, Top management team conflict and entrepreneurial strategy making in China, *Asia Pacific Journal of Management,* 26: 263–283; S. C. Parker, 2009, Can cognitive biases explain venture team homophily? *Strategic Entrepreneurship Journal,* 3: 67–83.
43. Y. Zhang & N. Rajagopalan, 2003, Explaining the new CEO origin: Firm versus industry antecedents, *Academy of Management Journal,* 46: 327–338.
44. T. Dvir, D. Eden, B. J. Avolio, & B. Shamir, 2002, Impact of transformational leadership on follower development and performance: A field experiment, *Academy of Management Journal,* 45: 735–744.
45. J. P. Muczyk & D. T. Holt, 2008, Toward a cultural contingency model of leadership, Journal of *Leadership and Organizational Studies,* 14: 277–286.
46. C. Bouquet, A. Morrison, & J. Birkinshaw, 2009, International attention and multinational enterprise performance, *Journal of International Business Studies,* 40: 108–131; H. U. Lee & J. H. Park, 2008, The influence of top management team international exposure on international alliance formation, *Journal of Management Studies,* 45: 961–981.
47. C. Thomas, D. Kidd, & C. Fernandez-Araoz, 2007, Are you underutilizing your board? *MIT Sloan Management Review,* 48(2): 71–76.
48. F. Adjaoud, D. Zeghal & S. Andaleeb, 2007, The effect of board's quality on performance: A study of Canadian firms, *Corporate Governance: An International Review,* 15: 623–635; L. Tihanyi, R. A. Johnson, R. E. Hoskisson, & M. A. Hitt, 2003, Institutional ownership and international diversification: The effects of boards of directors and technological opportunity, *Academy of Management Journal,* 46: 195–211.
49. B. R. Golden & E. J. Zajac, 2001, When will boards influence strategy? Inclination times power equals strategic change, *Strategic Management Journal,* 22: 1087–1111.
50. M. Carpenter & J. Westphal, 2001, Strategic context of external network ties: Examining the impact of director appointments on board involvement in strategic decision making, *Academy of Management Journal,* 44: 639–660.
51. M. A. Rutherford & A. K. Buchholtz, 2007, Investigating the relationship between board characteristics and board information, *Corporate Governance: An International Review,* 15: 576–584.
52. X. Huafang & Y. Jianguo, 2007, Ownership structure, board composition and corporate voluntary disclosure: Evidence from listed companies in China, *Managerial Auditing Journal,* 22: 604–619.
53. J. Coles, N. Sen, & V. McWilliams, 2001, An examination of the relationship of governance mechanisms to performance, *Journal of Management,* 27: 23–50; J. Coles & W. Hesterly, 2000, Independence of the chairman and board composition: Firm choices and shareholder value, *Journal of Management,* 26: 195–214.

54. C. M. Daily & D. R. Dalton, 1995, CEO and director turnover in failing firms: An illusion of change? *Strategic Management Journal,* 16: 393–400.
55. D. Miller, I. LeBreton-Miller, & B. Scholnick, 2008, Stewardship vs. stagnation: An empirical comparison of small family and non-family businesses, *Journal of Management Studies,* 51: 51–78; J. H. Davis, F. D. Schoorman, &L. Donaldson, 1997, Toward a stewardship theory of management, *Academy of Management Review,* 22: 20–47.
56. P. Kalyta, 2009, Compensation transparency and managerial opportunism: A study of supplemental retirement plans, *Strategic Management Journal,* 30: 405-423; J. G. Combs & M. S. Skill, 2003, Managerialist and human capital explanations for key executive pay premiums: A contingency perspective, *Academy of Management Journal,* 46: 63–73.
57. E. Matta & P. W. Beamish, 2008, The accentuated CEO career horizon problem: Evidence from international acquisitions, *Strategic Management Journal,* 29: 683–700; N. Rajagopalan & D. Datta, 1996, CEO characteristics: Does industry matter? *Academy of Management Journal,* 39: 197–215.
58. R. A. Johnson, R. E. Hoskisson, & M. A. Hitt, 1993, Board involvement in restructuring: The effect of board versus managerial controls and characteristics, *Strategic Management Journal,* 14 (Special Issue): 33–50.
59. Z. Simsek, 2007, CEO tenure and organizational performance: An intervening model, *Strategic Management Journal,* 28: 653–662.
60. M. Schneider, 2002, A stakeholder model of organizational leadership, *Organization Science,* 13: 209–220.
61. M. Sorcher & J. Brant, 2002, Are you picking the right leaders? *Harvard Business Review,* 80(2): 78–85; D. A. Waldman, G. G. Ramirez, R. J. House, & P. Puranam, 2001, Does leadership matter? CEO leadership attributes and profitability under conditions of perceived environmental uncertainty, *Academy of Management Journal,* 44: 134–143.
62. J. Werdigier, 2007, UBS not willing to talk about departure of chief, *New York Times Online,* http://www.nytimes.com, July 7.
63. W. Shen & A. A. Cannella, 2002, Revisiting the performance consequences of CEO succession: The impacts of successor type, postsuccession senior executive turnover, and departing CEO tenure, *Academy of Management Journal,* 45: 717–734.
64. D. Ulrich & N. Smallwood, 2007, Building a leadership brand, *Harvard Business Review,* 85(7/8): 93–100.
65. G. A. Ballinger & F. D. Schoorman, 2007, Individual reactions to leadership succession in workgroups, *Academy of Management Review,* 32: 116–136; R. E. Hoskisson, D. Yiu, & H. Kim, 2000, Capital and labor market congruence and corporate governance: Effects on corporate innovation and global competitiveness, in S. S. Cohen & G. Boyd (eds.), *Corporate Governance and Globalization,* Northampton, MA: Edward Elgar, 129–154.
66. M. Hurlbert, 2005, Lo! A white knight! So why isn't the market cheering? *New York Times Online,* http://www.nytimes.com, March 27.
67. W. Shen & A. A. Cannella, 2003, Will succession planning increase shareholder wealth? Evidence from investor reactions to relay CEO successions, *Strategic Management Journal,* 24: 191–198.
68. S. Carty and L. Cauley, 2009, AT&T's former CEO Ed Whitacre joins GM as chairman, *USA Today,* http://www.usatoday.com, June 10.
69. 2010, *www.mumbaimirror.com,*Who will succeed Ratan Tata, http://www.mumbaimirror.com/ index.aspx?page=article&sectid=5&contentid=20100805201008051225258 35b9e6196, August 5.
70. Y. Tanokura, 2009, Special interview: Sony chairman, CEO Howard Stringer, *Nikkei Electronics Asia,* http://www.techon.nikkeibp.co.jp, May 26.
71. T. Kiessling, M. Harvey & J. T. Heames, 2008, Operational changes to the acquired firm's top management team and subsequent organizational performance, *Journal of Leadership and Organizational Studies,* 14: 287–302.
72. J. A. Krug & W. Shill, 2008, The big exit: Executive churn in the wake of M&As, *Journal of Business Strategy,* 29(4): 15–21.
73. J. O'Toole & E. E. Lawler, Jr., 2006, The choices managers make—or don't make, *The Conference Board,* September/October, 24–29.
74. S. Nadkarni & P. S. Barr, 2008, Environmental context, managerial cognition, and strategic action: An integrated view, *Strategic Management Journal,* 29: 1395–1427; M. A. Hitt, B. W. Keats, & E. Yucel, 2003, Strategic leadership in global business organizations, in W. H. Mobley & P. W. Dorfman (eds.), *Advances in Global Leadership,* Oxford, UK: Elsevier Science, Ltd., 9–35.
75. I. M. Levin, 2000, Vision revisited, *Journal of Applied Behavioral Science,* 36: 91–107.
76. E. Verwaal, H. Commandeur, & W. Verbeke, 2009, Value creation and value claiming in strategic outsourcing decisions: A resource contingency perspective, *Journal of Management,* 35: 420–444; S. R. Miller, D. E. Thomas, L. Eden, & M. Hitt, 2008, Knee deep in the big muddy: The survival of emerging market firms in developed markets, *Management International Review,* 48: 645–666.
77. G. Hall, 2009, Today's outrage: GE's Immelt flip flops, *TheStreet.com,* http://www.thestreet.com, May 26.
78. J. Welch & S. Welch, 2007, When to talk, when to balk, *BusinessWeek,* April 30, 102.
79. J. Barney & A. M. Arikan, 2001, The resource-based view: Origins and implications, in M. A. Hitt, R. E. Freeman, & J. S. Harrison (eds.), *Handbook of Strategic Management,* Oxford, UK: Blackwell Publishers, 124–188.
80. E. T. Prince, 2005, The fiscal behavior of CEOs, *Managerial Economics,* 46(3): 23–26.
81. Holcomb, Holmes, & Connelly, Making the most of what you have; Sirmon, Gove, & Hitt, Resource management in dyadic competitive rivalry.
82. R. A. Burgelman, 2001, *Strategy Is Destiny: How Strategy-Making Shapes a Company's Future,* New York: The Free Press.

83. D. J. Ketchen, Jr., G. T. M. Hult, & S. F. Slater, 2007, Toward greater understanding of market orientation and the resource-based view, *Strategic Management Journal,* 28: 961–964; S. K. Ethiraj, P. Kale, M. S. Krishnan, & J. V. Singh, 2005, Where do capabilities come from and how do they matter? A study in the software services industry, *Strategic Management Journal,* 26: 25–45.
84. S. K. Ethiraj, 2007, Allocation of inventive effort in complex product systems, *Strategic Management Journal,* 28: 563–584; S. Dutta, O. Narasimhan, & S. Rajiv, 2005, Conceptualizing and measuring capabilities: Methodology and empirical application, *Strategic Management Journal,* 26: 277–285.
85. 2009, PepsiCo Mission and Vision, http://www.pepsico.com/Company/Our-Mission-and-Vision.aspx, June.
86. M. Larson & F. Luthans, 2006, Potential added value of psychological capital in predicting work attitudes, *Journal of Leadership & Organizational Studies,* 13: 45–62; N. W. Hatch & J. H. Dyer, 2004, Human capital and learning as a source of sustainable competitive advantage, *Strategic Management Journal,* 25: 1155–1178.
87. M. A. Hitt, L. Bierman, K. Uhlenbruck, &K. Shimizu, 2006, The importance of resources in the internationalization of professional service firms: The good, the bad and the ugly, *Academy of Management Journal,* 49: 1137–1157; M. A. Hitt, L. Bierman, K. Shimizu, & R. Kochhar, 2001, Direct and moderating effects of human capital on strategy and performance in professional service firms: A resource-based perspective, *Academy of Management Journal,* 44: 13–28.
88. S. E. Jackson, M. A. Hitt, & A. S. DeNisi (eds.), 2003, *Managing Knowledge for Sustained Competitive Advantage: Designing Strategies for Effective Human Resource Management,* Oxford, UK: Elsevier Science, Ltd.
89. B. E. Becker & M. A. Huselid, 2007, Strategic human resources management: Where do we go from here? *Journal of Management,* 32: 898–925.
90. R. E. Ployhart, 2007, Staffing in the 21st century: New challenges and strategic opportunities, *Journal of Management,* 32: 868–897.
91. R. A. Noe, J. A. Colquitt, M. J. Simmering, & S. A. Alvarez, 2003, Knowledge management: Developing intellectual and social capital, in S. E. Jackson, M. A. Hitt, & A. S. DeNisi (eds.), 2003, *Managing Knowledge for Sustained Competitive Advantage: Designing Strategies for Effective Human Resource Management,* Oxford, UK: Elsevier Science, Ltd., 209–242.
92. G. P. Hollenbeck & M. W. McCall Jr., 2003, Competence, not competencies: Making a global executive development work, in W. H. Mobley & P. W. Dorfman (eds.), *Advances in Global Leadership,* Oxford, UK: Elsevier Science, Ltd., 101–119; J. Sandberg, 2000, Understanding human competence at work: An interpretative approach, *Academy of Management Journal,* 43: 9–25.
93. G. Colvin, 2007, Leader machines, *Fortune,* October 1, 100–106.
94. Y. Liu, J. G. Combs, D. A. Ketchen, Jr., & R. D. Ireland, 2007, The value of human resource management for organizational performance, *Business Horizons,* 6: 503–511.
95. T. R. Holcomb, R. D. Ireland, R. M. Holmes, & M. A. Hitt, 2009, Architecture of entrepreneurial learning: Exploring the link among heuristics, Knowledge, and action, *Entrepreneurship, Theory & Practice,* 33: 173–198; J. S. Bunderson & K. M. Sutcliffe, 2003, Management team learning orientation and business unit performance, *Journal of Applied Psychology,* 88: 552–560.
96. R. J. Thomas, 2009, The leadership lessons of crucible experiences, *Journal of Business Strategy,* 30(1): 21–26; J. D. Bragger, D. A. Hantula, D. Bragger, J. Kirnan, & E. Kutcher, 2003, When success breeds failure: History, hysteresis, and delayed exit decisions, *Journal of Applied Psychology,* 88: 6–14.
97. M. R. Haas & M. T. Hansen, 2005, When using knowledge can hurt performance: The value of organizational capabilities in a management consulting company, *Strategic Management Journal,* 26: 1–24; G. Ahuja & R. Katila, 2004, Where do resources come from? The role of idiosyncratic situations, *Strategic Management Journal,* 25: 887–907.
98. Hitt, Miller, & Colella, *Organizational Behavior.*
99. A. Carmeli & B. Azeroual, 2009, How relational capital and knowledge combination capability enhance the performance of work units in a high technology industry, *Strategic Entrepreneurship Journal,* 3: 85–103; J. W. Spencer, 2003, Firms' knowledge-sharing strategies in the global innovation system: Empirical evidence from the flat-panel display industry, *Strategic Management Journal,* 24: 217–233.
100. K. D. Miller, 2002, Knowledge inventories and managerial myopia, *Strategic Management Journal,* 23: 689–706.
101. R. D. Nixon, M. A. Hitt, H. Lee, & E. Jeong, 2004, Market reactions to corporate announcements of downsizing actions and implementation strategies, *Strategic Management Journal,* 25: 1121–1129.
102. Nixon, Hitt, Lee, & Jeong, Market reactions to corporate announcements of downsizing actions.
103. T. Simons & Q. Roberson, 2003, Why managers should care about fairness: The effects of aggregate justice perceptions on organizational outcomes, *Journal of Applied Psychology,* 88: 432–443; M. L. Ambrose & R. Cropanzano, 2003, A longitudinal analysis of organizational fairness: An examination of reactions to tenure and promotion decisions, *Journal of Applied Psychology,* 88: 266–275.
104. J.P. Kotter, 1997, *Matsushita Leadership.* New York: Free Press.
105. Ibid.
106. P. Capelli, *The India Way, Op. cit.*
107. Case "Tata Steel" (B), Indian Institute of Management, Bangalore.
108. C.-L. Luk, O. H. M. Yau, L. Y. M. Sin,A. C. B. Tse, R. P .M. Chow, & J. S. Y. Lee, 2008, The effects of social capital and organizational innovativeness in different institutional contexts, *Journal of International Business Studies,* 39: 589–612; P. S. Adler & S. W. Kwon, 2002, Social capital: Prospects for a new concept, *Academy of Management Review,* 27: 17–40.
109. J. J. Li, L. Poppo, & K. Z. Zhou, 2008, Do managerial ties in China always produce value? Competition, uncertainty, and

domestic vs. foreign firms, *Strategic Management Journal,* 29: 383–400; S. Gao, K. Xu, & J. Yang, 2008, Managerial ties, Absorptive capacity & innovation, *Asia Pacific Journal of Management,* 25: 395–412.

110. P. Ozcan & K. M. Eisenhardt, 2009, Origin of alliance portfolios: Entrepreneurs, network strategies, and firm performance, *Academy of Management Journal,* 52: 246–279; W. H. Hoffmann, 2007, Strategies for managing a portfolio of alliances, *Strategic Management Journal,* 28: 827–856.
111. H. E. Aldrich & P. H. Kim 2007, Small worlds, infinite possibilities? How social networks affect entrepreneurial team formation and search, *Strategic Entrepreneurship Journal,* 1: 147–165; P. Davidsson & B. Honig, 2003, The role of social and human capital among nascent entrepreneurs, *Journal of Business Venturing,* 18: 301–331.
112. C. M. Fiol, 1991, Managing culture as a competitive resource: An identity-based view of sustainable competitive advantage, *Journal of Management,* 17: 191–211; J. B. Barney, 1986, Organizational culture: Can it be a source of sustained competitive advantage? *Academy of Management Review,* 11: 656–665.
113. 2006, Connecting the dots between innovation and leadership, *Knowledge@ Wharton,* http://www.knowledge.wharton.upenn.edu, October 4.
114. V. Govindarajan & A. K. Gupta, 2001, Building an effective global business team, *Sloan Management Review,* 42(4): 63–71; S. Ghoshal & C. A. Bartlett, 1994, Linking organizational context and managerial action: The dimensions of quality of management, *Strategic Management Journal,* 15: 91–112.
115. Quoted by Warren Bennis (1998), *On Becoming a Leader*. London: Arrow Books, p. 163.
116. S. Manikutty & S.P. Singh, 2009, *Essence of Leadership: Explorations from Literature*. New Delhi: Macmillan, p.4.
117. R. D. Ireland, J. G. Covin, & D. F. Kuratko, 2009, Conceptualizing corporate entrepreneurship strategy, *Entrepreneurship Theory and Practice,* 33(1): 19–46; D. F. Kuratko, R. D. Ireland, & J. S. Hornsby, 2001, Improving firm performance through entrepreneurial actions: Acordia's corporate entrepreneurship strategy, *Academy of Management Executive,* 15(4): 60–71.
118. J. H. Dyer, H. B. Gregersen, & C. Christensen, 2008, Entrepreneur behaviors, opportunity recognition and the origins of innovative ventures, *Strategic Entrepreneurship Journal*, 2: 317–338; R. D. Ireland & J. W. Webb, 2007, Strategic entrepreneurship: Creating competitive advantage through streams of innovation, *Business Horizons,* 50: 49–49.
119. S. A. Alvarez & J. B. Barney, 2008, Opportunities, organizations and entrepreneurship, *Strategic Entrepreneurship Journal*, 2: 171–174; D. S. Elenkov, W. Judge, & P. Wright, 2005, Strategic leadership and executive innovation influence: An international multi-cluster comparative study, *Strategic Management Journal,* 26: 665–682.
120. R. E. Hoskisson, M. A. Hitt, R. D. Ireland, & J. S. Harrison, 2008, *Competing for Advantage,* 2nd ed., Thomson Publishing; R. G. McGrath, W. J. Ferrier, & A. L. Mendelow, 2004, Real options as engines of choice and heterogeneity, *Academy of Management Review,* 29: 86–101.
121. Y. Luo, 2008, Structuring interorganizational cooperation: The role of economic integration in strategic alliances, *Strategic Management Journal,* 29: 617–637; R. S. Vassolo, J. Anand, & T. B. Folta, 2004, Non-additivity in portfolios of exploration activities: A real options analysis of equity alliances in biotechnology, *Strategic Management Journal,* 25: 1045–1061.
122. P. G. Kein, 2008, Opportunity discovery, entrepreneurial action and economic organization, *Strategic Entrepreneurship Journal,* 2: 175–190; R. D. Ireland, M. A. Hitt, & D. Sirmon, 2003, A model of strategic entrepreneurship: The construct and its dimensions, *Journal of Management,* 29: 963–989.
123. G. T. Lumpkin & G. G. Dess, 1996, Clarifying the entrepreneurial orientation construct and linking it to performance, *Academy of Management Review,* 21: 135–172; R. G. McGrath & I. MacMillan, 2000, *The Entrepreneurial Mindset,* Boston: Harvard Business School Press.
124. C. Heath & D. Heath, 2007, Leadership is a muscle, *Fast Company,* July/August, 62–63.
125. Lumpkin & Dess, Clarifying the entrepreneurial orientation construct, 142.
126. Ibid., 137.
127. D. D. Bergh, R. A. Johnson, & R. Dewitt, 2008, Restructuring through spinoff or sell-off: Transforming information asymmetries into financial gain, *Strategic Management Journal,* 29: 133–148; P. Pyoria, 2007, Informal organizational culture: The foundation of knowledge workers' performance, *Journal of Knowledge Management,* 11(3): 16–30.
128. M. Kuenzi & M. Schminke, 2009, Assembling fragments into a lens: A review, critique, and proposed research agenda for the organizational work climate literature, *Journal of Management,* 35: 634–717; C. M. Christensen & S. D. Anthony, 2007, Put investors in their place, *BusinessWeek,* May 28, 10.
129. D. D. Bergh & E. N.-K. Lim, 2008, Learning how to restructure: Absorptive capacity and improvisational views of restructuring actions and performance, *Strategic Management Journal,* 29: 593–616; J. S. Hornsby, D. F. Kuratko, & S. A. Zahra, 2002, Middle managers' perception of the internal environment for corporate entrepreneurship: Assessing a measurement scale, *Journal of Business Venturing,* 17: 253–273.
130. D. F. Kuratko, R. D. Ireland, J. G. Covin, & J. S. Hornsby, 2005, A model of middle-level managers' entrepreneurial behavior, *Entrepreneurship Theory and Practice,* 29: 699–716.
131. E. G. Love & M. Kraatz, 2009, Character, conformity, or the bottom line? How and why downsizing affected corporate reputation, *Academy of Management Journal,* 52: 314–335.
132. Adler & Kwon, Social capital.
133. J. Pinto, C. R. Leana, & F. K. Pil, 2008, Corrupt organizations or organizations of corrupt individuals? Two types of organization-level corruption, *Academy of Management Review,* 33: 685–709.
134. M. E. Scheitzer, L. Ordonez, & M. Hoegl, 2004, Goal setting as a motivator of unethical behavior, *Academy of Management Journal,* 47: 422–432.

135. D. C. Kayes, D. Stirling, & T. M. Nielsen, 2007, Building organizational integrity, *Business Horizons,* 50: 61–70; L. K. Trevino, G. R. Weaver, D. G. Toffler, & B. Ley, 1999, Managing ethics and legal compliance: What works and what hurts, *California Management Review,* 41(2): 131–151.
136. X. Zhang, K. M. Bartol, K. G. Smith, M. D. Pfaffer, & D. M. Khanin, 2008, CEOs on the edge: Earnings manipulation and stock-based incentive misalignment, *Academy of Management Journal,* 51: 241–258; M. A. Hitt & J. D. Collins, 2007, Business ethics, strategic decision making, and firm performance, *Business Horizons,* 50: 353–357.
137. J. M. Stevens, H. K. Steensma, D. A. Harrison, & P. L. Cochran, 2005, Symbolic or substantive document? Influence of ethics codes on financial executives' decisions, *Strategic Management Journal,* 26: 181–195.
138. Y. Zhang & M. F. Wiersema, 2009, Stock market reaction to CEO certification: The signaling role of CEO background, *Strategic Management Journal,* 30: 693–710; C. Driscoll & M. McKee, 2007, Restorying a culture of ethical and spiritual values: A role for leader storytelling, *Journal of Business Ethics,* 73: 205–217.
139. C. Caldwell & L. A. Hayes, 2007, Leadership, trustworthiness, and the mediating lens, *Journal of Management Development,* 26: 261–281.
140. B. E. Ashforth, D. A. Gioia, S. L. Robinson, & L. K. Trevino, 2008, Re-viewing organizational corruption, *Academy of Management Review,* 33: 670–684; M. Schminke, A. Arnaud, & M. Kuenzi, 2007, The power of ethical work climates, *Organizational Dynamics,* 36: 171–186; L. B. Ncube & M. H. Wasburn, 2006, Strategic collaboration for ethical leadership: A mentoring framework for business and organizational decision making, *Journal of Leadership & Organizational Studies,* 13: 77–92.
141. These four types of managers are described in the case, GE's two decade transformation: Jack Welch's leadership, HBS case # 9-399-150.
142. J. Welch & S. Welch, 2007, Flying solo: A reality check, *BusinessWeek,* June 4, 116.
143. Mintzberg, H., 2004, *Managers not MBAs: A hard look at the soft practice of managing and management development,* San Francisco: Berret Koehler Publishers; Datar, S.M., 2010, *Rethinking the MBA: Business education at a crossroads,* Boston: Harvard Business Press.
144. Ghoshal, S., 2005, Bad management theories are destroying good management practices, *Academy of Learning and Education,* 4(1).
145. A. Weibel, 2007, Formal control and trustworthiness, *Group & Organization Management,* 32: 500–517; G. Redding, 2002, The capitalistic business system of China and its rationale, *Asia Pacific Journal of Management,* 19: 221–249.
146. B. D. Rostker, R. S. Leonard, O. Younassi, M. V. Arena, & J. Riposo, 2009, Cost controls: How the government can get more bag for its buck, *Rand Review,* http://www.rand.org/publications/randreview/issues/spring2009; A. C. Costa, 2007, Trust and control interrelations, *Group & Organization Management,* 32: 392–406;
147. M. D. Shields, F. J. Deng, & Y. Kato, 2000, The design and effects of control systems: Tests of direct- and indirect-effects models, *Accounting, Organizations and Society,* 25: 185–202.
148. R. S. Kaplan & D. P. Norton, 2009, The balanced scorecard: Measures that drive performance (HBR OnPoint Enhanced Edition), *Harvard Business Review,* Boston, MA, March; R. S. Kaplan & D. P. Norton, 2001, The strategy-focused organization, *Strategy & Leadership,* 29(3): 41–42; R. S. Kaplan & D. P. Norton, 2000, *The Strategy-Focused Organization: How Balanced Scorecard Companies Thrive in the New Business Environment,* Boston: Harvard Business School Press.
149. B. E. Becker, M. A. Huselid, & D. Ulrich, 2001, *The HR Scorecard: Linking People, Strategy, and Performance,* Boston: Harvard Business School Press, 21.
150. Kaplan & Norton, The strategy-focused organization.
151. R. S. Kaplan & D. P. Norton, 2001, Transforming the balanced scorecard from performance measurement to strategic management: Part I, *Accounting Horizons,* 15(1): 87–104.
152. R. S. Kaplan & D. P. Norton, 1992, The balanced scorecard—measures that drive performance, *Harvard Business Review,* 70(1): 71–79.
153. M. A. Mische, 2001, *Strategic Renewal: Becoming a High-Performance Organization,* Upper Saddle River, NJ: Prentice Hall, 181.
154. H. J. Cho & V. Pucik, 2005, Relationship between innovativeness, quality, growth, profitability and market value, *Strategic Management Journal,* 26: 555–575.
155. G. Rowe, 2001, Creating wealth in organizations: The role of strategic leadership, *Academy of Management Executive,* 15(1): 81–94.
156. R. E. Hoskisson, R. A. Johnson, D. Yiu, & W. P. Wan, 2001, Restructuring strategies of diversified business groups: Differences associated with country institutional environments, in M. A. Hitt, R. E. Freeman, & J. S. Harrison (eds.), *Handbook of Strategic Management,* Oxford, UK: Blackwell Publishers, 433–463.
157. J. Birkinshaw & N. Hood, 2001, Unleash innovation in foreign subsidiaries, *Harvard Business Review,* 79(3): 131–137.
158. Ireland & Hitt, Achieving and maintaining strategic competitiveness.
159. G. Edmondson, 2007, Pedal to the metal at Porsche, *BusinessWeek,* September 3, 68; J. D. Gunkel & G. Probst, 2003, Implementation of the balanced scorecard as a means of corporate learning: The Porsche case, European Case Clearing House, Cranfield, UK.

CHAPTER 13

1. S. Sato, 2009, Beyond good: Great innovations through design, *Journal of Business Strategy,* 30(2/3): 40–49; D. J. Miller, M. J. Fern, & L. B. Cardinal, 2007, The use of knowledge for technological innovation within diversified firms, *Academy of Management Journal,* 50: 308–326.
2. R. D. Ireland & J. W. Webb, 2007, Strategic entrepreneurship: Creating competitive advantage through streams of in-

novation, *Business Horizons,* 50(4): 49–59; M. A. Hitt, R. D. Ireland, S. M. Camp, & D. L. Sexton, 2002, Strategic entrepreneurship: Integrating entrepreneurial and strategic management perspectives, in M. A. Hitt, R. D. Ireland, S. M. Camp, & D. L. Sexton (eds.), *Strategic Entrepreneurship: Creating a New Mindset,* Oxford, UK: Blackwell Publishers, 1–16; M. A. Hitt, R. D. Ireland, S. M. Camp, & D. L. Sexton,2001, Strategic entrepreneurship: Entrepreneurial strategies for wealth creation, *Strategic Management Journal,* 22 (Special Issue): 479–491.

3. R. Durand, O. Bruyaka & V. Mangematin, 2008, Do science and money go together? The case of the French biotech industry, *Strategic Management Journal,* 29: 1281–1299; R. K. Sinha & C. H. Noble, 2008, The adoption of radical manufacturing technologies and firm survival, *Strategic Management Journal,* 29: 943–962.
4. E. Levitas & M. A. McFadyen, 2009, Managing liquidity in research-intensive firms: Signalling and cash flow effects of patents and alliance activities, *Strategic Management Journal,* 30: 659–678.
5. J. L. Morrow, D. G. Sirmon, M. A. Hitt, & T. R. Holcomb, 2007, Creating value in the face of declining performance: Firm strategies and organizational recovery, *Strategic Management Journal,* 28: 271–283; K. G. Smith, C. J. Collins, & K. D. Clark, 2005, Existing knowledge, knowledge creation capability, and the rate of new product introduction in high-technology firms, *Academy of Management Journal,* 48: 346–357.
6. D. F. Kuratko, 2007, Entrepreneurial leadership in the 21st century, *Journal of Leadership and Organizational Studies,* 13(4): 1–11; R. D. Ireland, M. A. Hitt, & D. G. Sirmon, 2003, A model of strategic entrepreneurship: The construct and its dimensions, *Journal of Management,* 29: 963–989.
7. B. R. Barringer & R. D. Ireland, 2008, *Entrepreneurship: Successfully Launching New Ventures,* Upper Saddle River, NJ: Pearson Prentice Hall, 5; D. T. Holt, M. W. Rutherford, & G. R. Clohessy, 2007, Corporate entrepreneurship: An empirical look at individual characteristics, context and process, *Journal of Leadership and Organizational Studies,* 13(4): 40–54.
8. M. H. Morris, S. Coombes, & M. Schindehutte, 2007, Antecedents and outcomes of entrepreneurial and market orientations in a non-profit context: Theoretical and empirical insights, *Journal of Leadership and Organizational Studies,* 13(4): 12–39; H. A. Schildt, M. V. J. Maula, & T. Keil, 2005, Explorative and exploitative learning from external corporate ventures, *Entrepreneurship Theory and Practice,* 29: 493–515.
9. J. Uotila, M. Maula, T. Keil, & S. A. Zahra, 2009, Exploration, exploitation and financial performance: Analysis of S&P 500 corporations, *Strategic Management Journal,* 30: 221–231; G. T. Lumpkin & B. B. Lichtenstein, 2005, The role of organizational learning in the opportunity-recognition process, *Entrepreneurship Theory and Practice,* 29: 451–472.
10. B. A. Gilbert, P. P. McDougall, & D. B. Audretsch, 2006, New venture growth: A review and extension, *Journal of Management,* 32: 926–950.
11. Barringer & Ireland, *Entrepreneurship;* S. A. Zahra, H. J. Sapienza, & P. Davidsson, 2006, Entrepreneurship and dynamic capabilities: A review, model and research agenda, *Journal of Management Studies,* 43: 917–955.
12. S. A. Alvarez & J. B. Barney, 2008, Opportunities, organizations and entrepreneurship, *Strategic Entrepreneurship Journal,* 2: 265–267; S. A. Alvarez & J. B. Barney, 2005, Organizing rent generation and appropriation: Toward a theory of the entrepreneurial firm, *Journal of Business Venturing,* 19: 621–635.
13. P. G. Klein, 2008, Opportunity discovery, entrepreneurial action and economic organization, *Strategic Entrepreneurship Journal,* 2: 175–190; W. Kuemmerle, 2005, The entrepreneur's path to global expansion, *MIT Sloan Management Review,* 46(2): 42–49.
14. R. K. Mitchell, J. R. Mitchell, & J. B. Smith, 2008, Inside opportunity formation: Enterprise failure, cognition and the creation of opportunities, *Strategic Entrepreneurship Journal,* 2: 225–242; C. Marquis & M. Lounsbury, 2007, Vive la resistance: Competing logics and the consolidation of U.S. community banking, *Academy of Management Journal,* 50: 799–820.
15. S. A. Zahra, 2008, The virtuous cycle of discovery and creation of entrepreneurial opportunities, *Strategic Entrepreneurship Journal,* 2: 243–257; N. Wasserman, 2006, Stewards, agents, and the founder discount: Executive compensation in new ventures, *Academy of Management Journal,* 49: 960–976.
16. J. Schumpeter, 1934, *The Theory of Economic Development,* Cambridge, MA: Harvard University Press.
17. J. H. Dyer, H. B. Gregersen, & C. Christensen, 2008, Entrepreneur behaviors and the origins of innovative ventures, *Strategic Entrepreneurship Journal,* 2: 317–338; R. Greenwood &R. Suddaby, 2006, Institutional entrepreneurship in mature fields: The big five accounting firms, *Academy of Management Journal,* 49: 27–48.
18. W. J. Baumol, R. E. Litan, & C. J. Schramm, 2007, *Good capitalism, bad capitalism, and the economics of growth and prosperity,* New Haven: Yale University Press; R. G. Holcombe, 2003, The origins of entrepreneurial opportunities, *Review of Austrian Economics,* 16: 25–54.
19. R. D. Ireland, J. W. Webb, & J. E. Coombs, 2005, Theory and methodology in entrepreneurship research, in D. J. Ketchen Jr. & D. D. Bergh (eds.), *Research Methodology in Strategy and Management* (Vol. 2), San Diego: Elsevier Publishers, 111–141.
20. K. E. Klein, 2007, The face of entrepreneurship in 2017, *BusinessWeek,* http://www.businessweek.com, January 31.
21. Bansal, R, 2008, *Stay hungry, stay foolish: The inspiring stories of 25 IIM Ahmedabad graduates who chose to tread a path of their own making,* Ahmedabad: IIM.
22. P. F. Drucker, 1998, The discipline of innovation, *Harvard Business Review,* 76(6): 149–157.
23. Ibid.
24. A. Leiponen, 2008, Control of intellectual assets in client relationships: Implications for innovation, *Strategic Management Journal,* 29: 1371–1394; M. Subramaniam & M. A. Youndt, 2005, The influence of intellectual capital on the types of innovative capabilities, *Academy of Management Journal,* 48: 450–463.

25. F. F. Suarez & G. Lanzolla, 2007, The role of environmental dynamics in building a first mover advantage theory, *Academy of Management Review,* 32: 377–392.
26. M. J. Leiblein & T. L. Madsen, 2009, Unbundling competitive heterogeneity: Incentive structures and capability influences on technological innovation, *Strategic Management Journal,* 30: 711–735; R. Price, 1996, Technology and strategic advantage, *California Management Review,* 38(3): 38–56.
27. M. A. Hitt, R. D. Nixon, R. E. Hoskisson, &R. Kochhar, 1999, Corporate entrepreneurship and cross-functional fertilization: Activation, process and disintegration of a new product design team, *Entrepreneurship: Theory and Practice,* 23(3): 145–167.
28. R. Oriani & M. Sobero, 2008, Uncertainty and the market valuation of R&D within a real options logic, *Strategic Management Journal,* 29: 343–361; D. J. Miller, 2006, Technological diversity, related diversification, and firm performance, *Strategic Management Journal,* 27: 601–619.
29. Schumpeter, *The Theory of Economic Development.*
30. R. Katila & S. Shane, 2005, When does lack of resources make new firms innovative? *Academy of Management Journal,* 48: 814–829.
31. P. Sharma & J. L. Chrisman, 1999, Toward a reconciliation of the definitional issues in the field of corporate entrepreneurship, *Entrepreneurship: Theory and Practice,* 23(3): 11–27; R. A. Burgelman & L. R. Sayles, 1986, *Inside Corporate Innovation: Strategy, Structure, and Managerial Skills,* New York: Free Press.
32. D. G. Sirmon, J.-L. Arregle, M. A. Hitt, &J. W. Webb, 2008, The role of family influence in firms' strategic responses to the threat of imitation, *Entrepreneurship Theory and Practice,* 32: 979–998; D. K. Dutta & M. M. Crossan, 2005, The nature of entrepreneurial opportunities: Understanding the process using the 4I organizational learning framework, *Entrepreneurship Theory and Practice* 29: 425–449.
33. S. F. Latham & M. Braun, 2009, Managerial risk, innovation and organizational decline, *Journal of Management,* 35: 258–281.
34. R. E. Hoskisson & L. W. Busenitz, 2002, Market uncertainty and learning distance in corporate entrepreneurship entry mode choice, in M. A. Hitt, R. D. Ireland, S. M. Camp, & D. L. Sexton (eds.), *Strategic Entrepreneurship: Creating a New Mindset,* Oxford, UK: Blackwell Publishers, 151–172.
35. S. Thornhill, 2006, Knowledge, innovation, and firm performance in high- and low-technology regimes, *Journal of Business Venturing,* 21: 687–703; D. Somaya, 2003, Strategic determinants of decisions not to settle patent litigation, *Strategic Management Journal,* 24: 17–38.
36. J. Immelt, V. Govindarajan &C Trimble, 2009, How GE is disrupting itself, *Harvard Business Review,* October: pp.32-41.
37. K. M. Hmielski & R. A. Baron, 2009, Entrepreneurs' optimism and new venture performance: A social cognitive perspective, *Academy of Management Journal,* 52: 473–488; K. M. Hmielski & R. A. Baron, 2008, When does entrepre-neurial self-efficacy enhance versus reduce firm performance? *Strategic Entrepreneurship Journal,* 2: 57–72; D. Duffy, 2004, Corporate entrepreneurship: Entrepreneurial skills for personal and corporate success, *Center for Excellence,* http://www.centerforexcellence.net, June 14.
38. M. S. Cardon, J. Wincent, J. Singh, & M. Drovsek, 2009, The nature and experience of entrepreneurial passion, *Academy of Management Review,* 34, 511–532.
39. J. O. Fiet, 2007, A prescriptive analysis of search and discovery, *Journal of Management Studies,* 44: 592–611; J. S. McMullen & D. A. Shepherd, 2006, Entrepreneurial action and the role of uncertainty in the theory of the entrepreneur, *Academy of Management Review,* 31: 132–152.
40. N. Nicolaou, S. Shane, L. Cherkas, & T. D. Spector, 2008, The influence of sensation seeking in the heritability of entrepreneurship, *Strategic Entrepreneurship Journal,* 2: 7–21.
41. X. P. Chen, X. Yao, & S. Kowtha, 2009, Entrepreneur passion and preparedness in business plan presentations: A persuasion analysis of venture capitalists' funding decisions, *Academy of Management Journal,* 52: 199–214; S. F. Matusik, J. M. George, & M. B. Heeley, 2008, Values and judgment under uncertainty: Evidence from venture capitalist assessments of founders, *Strategic Entrepreneurship Journal,* 2: 95–115.
42. S. Allen, 2009, Entrepreneurs: Quotations from famous entrepreneurs on entrepreneurship, *About.com,* http://entrepreneurs.about.com, June 13.
43. W. Stam & T. Elfring, 2008, Entrepreneurial orientation and new venture performance: The moderating role of intra- and extraindustry social capital, *Academy of Management Journal,* 51: 97–111; R. A. Baron, 2006, Opportunity recognition as pattern recognition: How entrepreneurs "connect the dots" to identify new business opportunities, *Academy of Management Perspectives,* 20(1): 104–119; R. G. McGrath & I. MacMillan, 2000, *The Entrepreneurial Mindset,* Boston, MA: Harvard Business School Press.
44. R. D. Ireland, M. A. Hitt, & J. W. Webb, 2005, Entrepreneurial alliances and networks, in O. Shenkar and J. J. Reuer (eds.), *Handbook of Strategic Alliances,* Thousand Oaks, CA: Sage Publications, 333–352; T. M. Begley & D. P. Boyd, 2003, The need for a corporate global mind-set, *MIT Sloan Management Review,* 44(2): 25–32.
45. W. Tsai, 2001, Knowledge transfer in intraorganizational networks: Effects of network position and absorptive capacity on business unit innovation and performance, *Academy of Management Journal,* 44: 996–1004.
46. S. A. Zahra & G. George, 2002, Absorptive capacity: A review, reconceptualization, and extension, *Academy of Management Review,* 27: 185–203.
47. M. A. Hitt, L. Bierman, K. Uhlenbruck, & K. Shimizu, 2006, The importance of resources in the internationalization of professional service firms: The good, the bad and the ugly, *Academy of Management Journal,* 49: 1137–1157; M. A. Hitt, L. Bierman, K. Shimizu, & R. Kochhar, 2001, Direct and moderating effects of human capital on strategy and performance in professional service firms, *Academy of Management Journal,* 44: 13–28.
48. M. Maynard, 2008, At G.M., innovation sacrificed to profits, *New York Times,* http://www.nytimes.com, December 6; 2008, Creativity and innovation driving business—Innova-

tion index, *BusinessWeek*/Boston Consulting Group, http://www.creativityandinnovationblogspot.com, April 22.

49. M. M. Keupp & O. Gassman, 2009, The past and future of international entrepreneurship: A review and sugges-tions for developing the field, *Journal of Management,* 35: 600–633.
50. H. J. Sapienza, E. Autio, G. George, & S. A. Zahra, 2006, A capabilities perspective on the effects of early internationalization on firm survival and growth, *Academy of Management Review,* 31: 914–933;T. M. Begley, W.-L. Tan, & H. Schoch, 2005, Politico-economic factors associated with interest in starting a business: A multi-country study, *Entrepreneurship Theory and Practice,* 29: 35–52.
51. M. Javidan, R. M. Steers, & M. A. Hitt, 2007, *The Global Mindset,* Amsterdam: Elsevier Ltd.
52. S. A. Fernhaber, B. A. Gilbert, & P. P. McDougal, 2008, International entrepreneurship and geographic location: An empirical examination of new venture internationalization, *Journal of International Business Studies,* 39: 267–290; Hitt, Bierman, Uhlenbruck, & Shimizu, The importance of resources in the internationalization of professional service firm.
53. H. Ren, B. Gray, & K. Kim, 2009, Performance of international joint ventures: What factors really make a difference and how? *Journal of Management,* 35: 805–832; Q. Yang & C. X. Jiang, 2007, Location advantages and subsidiaries' R&D activities in emerging economies: Exploring the effect of employee mobility, *Asia Pacific Journal of Management,* 24: 341–358.
54. 2009, Revitalizing Detroit one business at a time, *Kauffman Foundation*, http://www.kauffman.org, June.
55. N. Bosma, Z. J. Acs, E. Autio, A. Conduras, & J. Levie, 2009, *Global Entrepreneurship Monitor: 2008 Executive Report,* Global Entrepreneurship Research Consortium, http://www.gemconsortium.org, June 23. The report does not give data about India.
56. R. A. Baron & J. Tang, 2009, Entrepreneurs' social skills and new venture performance: Mediating mechanisms and cultural generality, *Journal of Management*, 35: 282–306; D. W. Yiu, C. M. Lau, & G. D. Bruton, 2007, International venturing by emerging economy firms: The effects of firm capabilities, home country networks, and corporate entrepreneurship, *Journal of International Business Studies,* 38: 519–540.
57. N. Nummeia, S. Saarenketo, & K. Puumalainen, 2005, Rapidly with a rifle or more slowly with a shotgun? Stretching the company boundaries of internationalizing ICT firms, *Journal of International Entrepreneurship,* 2: 275–288; S. A. Zahra & G. George, 2002, International entrepreneurship: The state of the field and future research agenda, inM. A. Hitt, R. D. Ireland, S. M. Camp, &D. L. Sexton (eds.), *Strategic Entrepreneurship: Creating a New Mindset,* Oxford, UK: Blackwell Publishers, 255–288.
58. S. A. Zahra, R. D. Ireland, & M. A. Hitt, 2000, International expansion by new venture firms: International diversity, mode of market entry, technological learning and performance, *Academy of Management Journal,* 43: 925–950.
59. H. U. Lee & J.H. Park, 2008, The influence of top management team international exposure on international alliance formation, *Journal of Management Studies,* 45: 961–981; Barkema & O. Chvyrkov, 2007, Does top management team diversity promote or hamper foreign expansion? *Strategic Management Journal,* 28: 663–680.
60. T. S. Frost, 2001, The geographic sources of foreign subsidiaries' innovations, *Strategic Management Journal,* 22: 101–122.
61. J. Song & J. Shin, 2008, The paradox of technological capabilities: A study of knowledge sourcing from host countries of overseas R&D operations, *Journal of International Business Studies,* 39: 291–303.
62. A. Vance, 2009, Nokia and Intel to pair up on mobile devices, *New York Times,* http://www.nytimes.com, June 24; M. Palmer & C. Nuttall, 2009, Nokia and Intel strike research deal, *Financial Times,* http://www.ft.com, June 23.
63. Case, HTC Corporation in 2009, Harvard Business School case # 9-709-466.
64. W. Chung & S. Yeaple, 2008, International knowledge sourcing: Evidence from U.S. firms expanding abroad, *Strategic Management Journal,* 29: 1207–1224; J. Santos, Y. Doz, & P. Williamson, 2004, Is your innovation process global? *MIT Sloan Management Review,* 45(4): 31–37.
65. Y.-S. Su, E. W. K. Tsang, & M. W. Peng, 2009, How do internal capabilities and external partnerships affect innovativeness? *Asia Pacific Journal of Management,* 26: 309–331; J. A. Fraser, 2004, A return to basics at Kellogg, *MIT Sloan Management Review,* 45(4): 27–30.
66. F. K. Pil & S. K. Cohen, 2006, Modularity: Implications for imitation, innovation, and sustained advantage, *Academy of Management Review,* 31: 995–1011; S. Kola-Nystrom, 2003, Theory of conceptualizing the challenge of corporate renewal, Lappeenranta University of Technology, working paper.
67. 2005, Radical and incremental innovation styles, *Strategies 2 innovate,* http://www.strategies2innovate.com, July 12.
68. E. Xu & H. Zhang, 2008. The impact of state shares on corporate innovation strategy and performance in China, *Asia Pacific Journal of Management,* 25: 473–487; W. C. Kim & R. Mauborgne, 2005, Navigating toward blue oceans, *Optimize,* February, 44–52.
69. A. Phene & P. Almieda, 2008, Innovation in multinational subsidiaries: The role of knowledge assimilation and subsidiary capabilities, *Journal of International Business Studies,* 39: 901–919; G. Ahuja & M. Lampert, 2001, Entrepreneurship in the large corporation: A longitudinal study of how established firms create breakthrough inventions, *Strategic Management Journal,* 22 (Special Issue): 521–543.
70. 2005, Getting an edge on innovation, *BusinessWeek,* March 21, 124.
71. A. J. Chatterji, 2009, Spawned with a silver spoon? Entrepreneurial performance and innovation in the medical device industry, *Strategic Management Journal,* 30: 185–206; J. Goldenberg, R. Horowitz, A. Levav, & D. Mazursky, 2003, Finding your innovation sweet spot, *Harvard Business Review,* 81(3): 120–129.
72. C. E. Shalley & J. E. Perry-Smith, 2008, The emergence of team creative cognition: The role of diverse outside ties, sociocognitive network centrality, and team evolution, *Strategic*

Entrepreneurship Journal, 2: 1, 23–41; R. I. Sutton, 2002, Weird ideas that spark innovation, *MIT Sloan Management Review,* 43(2): 83–87.

73. K. G. Smith & D. Di Gregorio, 2002, Bisociation, discovery, and the role of entrepreneurial action, in M. A. Hitt, R. D. Ireland, S. M. Camp, & D. L. Sexton (eds.), *Strategic Entrepreneurship: Creating a New Mindset,* Oxford, UK: Blackwell Publishers, 129–150.
74. S. A. Hill, M. V. J. Maula, J. M. Birkinshaw & G. C. Murray, 2009, Transferability of the venture capital model to the corporate context: Implications for the performance of corporate venture units, *Strategic Entrepreneurship Journal,* 3: 3–27; Hoskisson & Busenitz, Market uncertainty and learning distance.
75. Hill, Maula, Birkinshaw, & Murray, Transferability of the venture capital model to the corporate context; R. A. Burgelman, 1995, *Strategic Management of Technology and Innovation,* Boston: Irwin.
76. J. M. Howell, 2005, The right stuff: Identifying and developing effective champions of innovation, *Academy of Management Executive,* 19(2): 108–119.
77. M.D. Hutt & T. W. Seph, 2009, *Business Marketing Management: B@B,* 10th ed., Mason, OH: Cengage South-Western.
78. S. K. Ethiraj, 2007, Allocation of inventive effort in complex product systems, *Strategic Management Journal,* 28: 563–584; M. A. Hitt, R. D. Ireland, & H. Lee, 2000, Technological learning, knowledge management, firm growth and performance, *Journal of Engineering and Technology Management,* 17: 231–246.
79. V. Gaba & A. D. Meyer, 2008, Crossing the organizational species barrier: How venture capital practices infiltrated the information technology sector, *Academy of Management Journal,* 51: 976–998; H. W. Chesbrough, 2002, Making sense of corporate venture capital, *Harvard Business Review,* 80(3): 90–99.
80. M. Subramaniam & N. Venkatraman, 2001, Determinants of transnational new product development capability: Testing the influence of transferring and deploying tacit overseas knowledge, *Strategic Management Journal,* 22: 359–378.
81. M. Song & M. M. Montoya-Weiss, 2001, The effect of perceived technological uncertainty on Japanese new product development, *Academy of Management Journal,* 44: 61–80.
82. B. Ambos & B. B. Schegelmilch, 2007, Innovation and control in the multinational firm: A comparison of political and contingency approaches, *Strategic Management Journal,* 28: 473–486.
83. H. Li & J. Li, 2009, Top management team conflict and entrepreneurial strategy in China, *Asia Pacific Journal of Management,* 26: 263–283; S.C. Parker, 2009, Can cognitive biases explain venture team homophily, *Strategic Entrepreneurship Journal,* 3: 67–83.
84. M. Makri, P. J. Lane, & L. R. Gomez-Mejia, 2006, CEO incentives, innovation and performance in technology-intensive firms: A reconciliation of outcome and behavior-based incentive schemes, *Strategic Management Journal,* 27: 1057–1080.
85. A. Tiwana, 2008, Does technological modularity substitute for control? A study of alliance performance in software outsourcing, *Strategic Management Journal,* 29: 769–780.
86. C. Zhou & J. Li, 2008, Product innovation in emerging market-based international joint ventures: An organizational ecology perspective, *Journal of International Business Studies,* 39: 1114–1132; E. Danneels, 2007, The process of technological competence leveraging, *Strategic Management Journal,* 28: 511–533.
87. F. T. Rothaermel & W. Boeker, 2008, Old technology meets new technology: Complementarities, similarities and alliance formation, *Strategic Management Journal,* 29: 47–77; L. Yu, 2002, Marketers and engineers: Why can't we just get along? *MIT Sloan Management Review,* 43(1): 13.
88. R. Cowan & N. Jonard, 2009, Knowledge portfolios and the organization of innovation networks, *Academy of Management Review,* 34: 320–342; A. Somech, 2006, The effects of leadership style and team process on performance and innovation in functionally hetergeneous teams, *Journal of Manage-ment,* 32: 132–157.
89. A. Azadegan, K. J. Dooley, P. L. Carter & J. R. Carter, 2008, Supplier innovativeness and the role of interorganizational learning in enhancing manufacturer capabilities, *Journal of Supply Chain Management,* 44(4): 14–34; P. Evans & B. Wolf, 2005, Collaboration rules, *Harvard Business Review,* 83(7): 96–104.
90. B. Fischer & A. Boynton, 2005, Virtuoso teams, *Harvard Business Review,* 83(7): 116–123.
91. Hitt, Nixon, Hoskisson, & Kochhar, Corporate entrepreneurship.
92. Christensen & Overdorf, Meeting the challenge of disruptive change.
93. Hitt, Nixon, Hoskisson, & Kochhar, Corporate entrepreneurship.
94. A. C. Amason, 1996, Distinguishing the effects of functional and dysfunctional conflict on strategic decision making: Resolving a paradox for top management teams, *Academy of Management Journal,* 39: 123–148; P. R. Lawrence & J. W. Lorsch, 1969, *Organization and Environment,* Homewood, IL: Richard D. Irwin.
95. M. A. Cronin & L. R. Weingart, 2007, Representational gaps, information processing, and conflict in functionally heterogeneous teams, *Academy of Management Review,* 32: 761–773; D. Dougherty, L. Borrelli, K. Muncir, &A. O'Sullivan, 2000, Systems of organizational sensemaking for sustained product innovation, *Journal of Engineering and Technology Management,* 17: 321–355.
96. Hitt, Nixon, Hoskisson, & Kochhar, Corporate entrepreneurship.
97. V. Ambrosini, N. Collier, & M. Jenkins, 2009, A configurational approach to the dynamics of firm level knowledge, *Journal of Strategy and Management,* 2: 4–30; E. C. Wenger & W. M. Snyder, 2000, Communities of practice: The organizational frontier, *Harvard Business Review,* 78(1): 139–144.

98. Gary Hamel, 2000, *Leading the Revolution,* Boston: Harvard Business School Press.

99. P. H. Kim, K. T. Dirks & C. D. Cooper, 2009, The repair of trust: A dynamic bilateral perspective and multilevel conceptualization, *Academy of Management Review,* 34: 401–422; Q. M. Roberson & J. A. Colquitt, 2005, Shared and configural justice: A social network model of justice in teams, *Academy of Management Review,* 30: 595–607.

100. N. Stieglitz & L. Heine, 2007, Innovations and the role of complementarities in a strategic theory of the firm, *Strategic Management Journal,* 28: 1–15; S. W. Fowler, A. W. King, S. J. Marsh, & B. Victor, 2000, Beyond products: New strategic imperatives for developing competencies in dynamic environments, *Journal of Engineering and Technology Management,* 17: 357–377.

101. J. C. Short, A. McKelvie, D. J. Ketchen &G. N. Chandler, 2009, Firm and industry effects on firm performance: A generalization and extension for new ventures, *Strategic Entrepreneurship Journal,* 3: 47–65; M. B. Sarkar, R. Echamabadi, R. Agarwal, & B. Sen, 2006, The effect of the innovative environment on exit of entrepreneurial firms, *Strategic Management Journal,* 27: 519–539.

102. T. Keil, M. Maula, H. Schildt, & S.A. Zahra, 2008, The effect of governance modes and relatedness of external business development activities on innovative performance, *Strategic Management Journal,* 29: 895–907; K. Larsen & A. Salter, 2006, Open for innovation: The role of openness in explaining innovation performance among U.K. manufacturing firms, *Strategic Management Journal,* 27: 131–150.

103. P. Ozcan & K. M. Eisenhardt, 2009, Origin of alliance portfolios: Entrepreneurs, network strategies, and firm performance, *Academy of Management Journal,* 52: 246–279; A. Tiwana & M. Keil, 2007, Does peripheral knowledge complement control? An empirical test in technology outsourcing alliances, *Strategic Management Journal,* 28: 623–634.

104. K. B. Whittington, J. Owen-Smith, & W. W. Powell, 2009, Networks, propinquity, and innovation in knowledge-intensive industries, *Administrative Science Quarterly,* 54: 90–122; C. Dhanaraj & A. Parkhe, 2006, Orchestrating innovation networks, *Academy of Management Review,* 31: 659–669.

105. K. Ruckman, 2009, Technology sourcing acquisitions: What they mean for innovation potential, *Journal of Strategy and Management,* 2: 56–75; F. T. Rothaermel & D. L. Deeds, 2004, Exploration and exploitation alliances in biotechnology: A system of new product development, *Strategic Management Journal,* 25: 201–221.

106. D. Li, L. Eden, M. A. Hitt, & R. D. Ireland, 2008, Friends, acquaintances, or strangers? Partner selection in R&D alliances, *Academy of Management Journal,* 51: 315–334; F. T. Rothaermel, M. A. Hitt, & L. A. Jobe, 2006, Balancing vertical integration and strategic outsourcing: Effects on product portfolio, product success and firm performance, *Strategic Management Journal,* 27: 1033–1056.

107. A. C. Cooper, 2002, Networks, alliances and entrepreneurship, in M. A. Hitt, R. D. Ireland, S. M. Camp, & D. L. Sexton (eds.), *Strategic Entrepreneurship: Creating a New Mindset,* Oxford, UK: Blackwell Publishers, 204–222.

108. B. S. Teng, 2007, Corporate entrepre-neurship activities through strategic alliances: A resource-based approach toward competitive advantage, *Journal of Management Studies,* 44: 119–142; S. A. Alvarez & J. B. Barney, 2001, How entrepreneurial firms can benefit from alliances with large partners, *Academy of Management Executive,* 15(1): 139–148.

109. F. T. Rothaermel, 2001, Incumbent's advantage through exploiting complementary assets via interfirm cooperation, *Strategic Management Journal,* 22 (Special Issue): 687–699.

110. B. R. Koka & J. E. Prescott, 2008, Designing alliance networks: The influence of network position, environmental change and strategy on firm performance, *Strategic Management Journal,* 29: 639–661; A. Capaldo, 2007, Network structure and innovation: The leveraging of a dual network as a distinctive capability, *Strategic Management Journal,* 28: 585–608.

111. C. L. Luk, O. H. M. Yau, L. Y. M. Sin, A. C. B. Tse, R. P. M. Chow, & J. S. Y. Lee, 2008, The effects of social capital and organizational innovativeness in different institutional contexts, *Journal of International Business Studies,* 39: 89–612; H. Yli-Renko, E. Autio, & H. J. Sapienza, 2001, Social capital, knowledge acquisition and knowledge exploitation in young technology-based firms, *Strategic Management Journal,* 22 (Special Issue): 587–613.

112. A. Tiwana, 2008, Do bridging ties complement strong ties? An empirical examination of alliance ambidexterity, *Strategic Management Journal,* 29: 251–272; C. Lee, K. Lee, & J. M. Pennings, 2001, Internal capabilities, external networks and performance: A study of technology-based ventures, *Strategic Management Journal,* 22 (Special Issue): 615–640.

113. Azadegan, Dooley, Carter, & Carter, Supplier innovativeness and the role of interorganizational learning in enhancing manufacturer capabilities; A. Takeishi, 2001, Bridging inter- and intra-firm boundaries: Management of supplier involvement in automobile product development, *Strategic Management Journal,* 22: 403–433.

114. R. C. Sampson, 2007, R&D alliances and firm performance: The impact of technological diversity and alliance organization on innovation, *Academy of Management Journal,* 50: 364–386; J. Weiss & J. Hughes, 2005, Want collaboration? Accept—and actively manage—conflict, *Harvard Business Review,* 83(3): 92–101.

115. R. H. Shah & V. Swaminathan, 2008, Factors influencing partner selection in strategic alliances: The moderating role of alliance context, *Strategic Management Journal,* 29: 471–494; Li, Eden, Hitt, & Ireland, Friends, acquaintances, or strangers?; R. D. Ireland, M. A. Hitt, & D. Vaidyanath, 2002, Strategic alliances as a pathway to competitive success, *Journal of Management,* 28: 413–446.

116. M. A. Hitt, M. T. Dacin, E. Levitas, J. L. Arregle, & A. Borza, 2000, Partner selection in emerging and developed market contexts: Resource-based and organizational learning perspectives, *Academy of Management Journal,* 43: 449–467.

117. J. D. Westphal & M. B. Crant, 2008, Sociopolitical dynamics in relations between top managers and security analysts: Favor rendering, reciprocity, and analyst stock recommendations, *Academy of Management Journal,* 51: 873–897.
118. J. J. Reuer, M. Zollo, & H. Singh, 2002, Post-formation dynamics in strategic alliances, *Strategic Management Journal,* 23: 135–151.
119. M. A. Hitt, D. King, H. Krishnan, M. Makri, M. Schijven, K. Shimizu, & H. Zhu, 2009, Mergers and Acquisitions: Overcoming pitfalls, building synergy and creating value, *Business Horizons,* in press; H. G. Barkema & M. Schijven, 2008, Toward unlocking the full potential of acquisitions: The role of organizational restructuring, *Academy of Management Journal*, 51: 696–722.
120. 2005, Novartis announces completion of Hexal AG acquisition, http:// www.novartis.com, June 6; 2005, Pfizer sees sustained long-term growth, http://www.pfizer.com, April 5.
121. M. A. Hitt, R. E. Hoskisson, R. A. Johnson, & D. D. Moesel, 1996, The market for corporate control and firm innovation, *Academy of Management Journal,* 39: 1084–1119.
122. M. Makri, M. A. Hitt, & P. J. Lane, 2009, Complementary technologies, knowledge relatedness, and invention outcomes in high technology M&As, *Strategic Management Journal*, in press.
123. Ruckman, 2009, Technology sourcing acquisitions; P. Puranam & K. Srikanth, 2007, What they know vs. what they do: How acquirers leverage technology acquisitions, *Strategic Management Journal,* 28: 805–825; M. A. Hitt, J. S. Harrison, & R. D. Ireland, 2001, *Mergers and Acquisitions: A Guide to Creating Value for Stakeholders*, New York: Oxford University Press.
124. M. Cording, P. Christman, & D. King, 2008. Reducing causal ambiguity in acquisition integration: Intermediate goals as mediators of integration decisions and acquisition performance, *Academy of Management Journal*, 51: 744–767; P. Puranam, H. Singh, & M. Zollo, 2006, Organizing for innovation: Managing the coordination-autonomy dilemma in technology, *Academy of Management Journal,* 49: 263–280.
125. Ireland, Hitt, & Sirmon, A model of strategic entrepreneurship.
126. A. Afuah, 2009, *Strategic Innovation: New game strategies for competitive advantage*, New York: Routledge.
127. Hitt, Ireland, Camp, & Sexton, Strategic entrepreneurship.
128. D. G. Sirmon, M. A. Hitt, & R. D. Ireland, 2007, Managing firm resources in dynamic environment to create value: Looking inside the black box, *Academy of Management Review,* 32: 273–292.
129. D. G. Sirmon, S. Gove, & M. A. Hitt, 2008, Resource management in dyadic competitive rivalry: The effects of resource bundling and deployment, *Academy of Management Journal,* 51:918–935; Hitt, Bierman, Shimizu, & Kochhar, Direct and moderating effects of human capital.
130. Tiwana, Do bridging ties complement strong ties? Hitt, Bierman, Uhlenbruck, & Shimizu, The importance of resources in the internationalization of professional service firms.
131. K. Asakawa & A. Som, 2008, International-ization of R&D in China and India: Conventional wisdom versus reality, *Asia Pacific Journal of Management,* 25: 375–394; M. A. Hitt, R. E. Hoskisson, & H. Kim, 1997, International diversification: Effects on innovation and firm performance in product diversified firms, *Academy of Management Journal,* 40: 767–798.
132. M. A. Hitt & R. D. Ireland, 2002, The essence of strategic leadership: Managing human and social capital, *Journal of Leadership and Organization Studies,* 9(1): 3–14.
133. Baumol, Litan, & Schramm, *Good capitalism, bad capitalism*; R. Garud, S. Jain, & A. Kumaraswamy, 2002, Institutional entrepreneurship in the sponsorship of common technological standards: The case of Sun Microsystems and JAVA, *Academy of Management Journal,* 45: 196–214.
134. B. Batjargal, A. Tsui, M. A. Hitt, J. L. Arregle, T. Miller, & J. Webb, 2009, How relationships matter: Women and men entrepreneurs' social networks and new venture success across cultures, paper presented at the Academy of Management Conference, Chicago, August; I. E. Allen, N. Langowitz, & M. Minniti, 2007, Global entrepreneurship monitor: 2006 report on women in entrepreneurship, Babson College, http:// www3.babson.edu/ESHIP/research-publications/gem.cfm, March 1.
135. J. D. Jardins, 2005, I am woman (I think), *Fast Company,* May, 25–26.
136. Hitt, Ireland, Camp, & Sexton, Strategic entrepreneurship.
137. C. W. L. Hill & F. T. Rothaermel, 2003, The performance of incumbent firms in the face of radical technological innovation, *Academy of Management Review,* 28: 257–274.
138. D. G. Sirmon & M. A. Hitt, 2009, Contin-gencies within dynamlc managerial capabilities: Interdependent effects of resource investment and deployment on firm performance, *Strategic Management Journal,* in press.

PART IV: Case Studies

CASE 1

Coca-Cola vs. Pepsi in India: The Battle of the Bottle Continues

S. Manikutty

Soft drinks or cool drinks, as they are known in India, refer to non-alcoholic drinks served in bottles or other packaging, to be distinguished from hot beverages such as coffee and tea, or cold beverages such as squashes and fresh lemon syrups or syrups of different flavors mixed with water. Soft drinks consist of a flavor base, a sweetener, and carbonated water. These drinks were generally not very popular in India in the 1950s and early 1960s. At homes, fresh juices and squashes were more popular, while tea or coffee were usually served in offices during meetings. Most of the bottled soft drinks at that time were local brands, packaged in semi-automatic and hand-operated plants.

INDUSTRY BACKGROUND

In 1956, Pepsi Co. introduced its aerated soft drinks in India but the efforts in developing the Indian market were not successful. Pepsi withdrew from India in 1961. Coca-Cola Company then entered India and did much better than Pepsi. Coca-Cola set up a network of franchises and bottling plants across the country. In 1977, with a change in the Central government from the Congress Party, which had ruled India since Independence to the Janata Party, Coca-Cola was asked by the new government to reduce its equity holding to 40 per cent and to share the secret behind the concentrate, enabling its local manufacture. Both these conditions were unacceptable to Coca-Cola. Hence it withdrew from India in 1977. The field thereafter was left wide open for Indian soft drinks manufacturers.

They exploited this bonanza to the hilt. Parle Industries, led by Ramesh Chauhan, made great headway and captured a market share of more than 60 per cent. The profits derived were very healthy indeed. Parley Industries had a formidable array of brands which became very powerful in the Indian market: Thums Up (cola drink), Gold Spot (orange), Limca (clouded lemon), Citra (clear lemon), Maaza (mango flavoured, non-carbonated soft drink or NCSD) and Frooti (mango flavoured NCSD in tetrapacks). Besides Parle, there was Pure Drinks Ltd., owned by Charanjit Singh, which was the main bottler for Coca-Cola before its withdrawal. It launched its own brand, Campa Cola, in cola flavor and some other brands in other flavors like Campa Orange. Pure Drinks captured about 20 per cent of the soft drinks market in the 1980s, but declined subsequently because of its inability to withstand competition mainly from Parle, and later, Pepsi (which returned to India, see later in the case). Besides Parle and Pure Drinks, there were several other smaller operators such as Duke's and Spencer but they never really made any major inroads into Chauhan's empire.

The 1980s were a decade of slow liberalization in India. It appeared that time was getting ripe for soft drink multinationals to stage a comeback in the country. The first move was made by PepsiCo in 1986, proposing a tie-up with the Indian firms Punjab Agro Industries Corporation and Voltas Ltd. The proposal included setting up of an agro research centre to develop new varieties of seeds, transfer of the state-of-the-art technology in food and beverage processing and packaging, investment in processing plants for potatoes, grains and vegetables, establishment of facilities for local manufacture of cola and fruit juice concentrates, and substantial export obligations. Against stiff opposition from Indian firms, the proposal was approved, and Pepsi launched its products in January 1991. After quite trying times, especially against Chauhan and with its own partners, Pepsi bought over the equity stakes of Voltas and Punjab Agro, and became a fully owned subsidiary of PepsiCo, USA.

Coca-Cola returned to India in 1993. By this time the rules of the game regarding investment by multinationals had changed considerably, and Coca-Cola was allowed entry on terms far easier than those for Pepsi (for example, Coca-Cola was allowed to set up a 100 per cent subsidiary in India without any research or export obligations) although it must be added that, despite the obligations laid down for Pepsi, many of these obligations were not fulfilled by Pepsi for various reasons.

The Indian "warriors", notably Ramesh Chauhan, attempted many tactics (described by some as "street smart") to keep their multinational rivals at bay. But after a valiant fight, Chauhan sold out Parle's soft drinks brands to Coca-Cola, for a tidy sum of around $40 million, it was believed. By this move, Coca-Cola got a share of about 69 per cent of the soft drinks market, commanded by Parle's brands. However, Parle continued in other businesses, as for example, soda and mineral water. It also continued to be a major bottler for Coca-Cola, and was in fact the largest bottler in the country. But in the early years, Coca-Cola and its principal bottler had a relationship far from cosy, with charges and countercharges liberally thrown at each other and made public with great effort. In the opinion of a marketing consultant, "For a company like Coke that is so heavily franchise driven, to antagonise its chief bottler was nothing short of suicidal. As a result, Coca-Cola lost one clear year."[1]

Coca-Cola India also promoted its own brands vigorously, while paying a somewhat step-motherly attention to the ex-Parle brands. This, in the opinion of industry experts, was a major error of judgement. It seemed that Coca-Cola grossly overestimated the power of its own brands as too well known all over the world, while underestimating the power of the local brands. In the opinion of one of the chief executives of Coca-Cola India, they did not realize that "Coca-Cola was a new brand launch, not a relaunch."[2] The result of this error of judgement was that the market shares of the Parle brands fell drastically, but these were gained by Pepsi rather than the Coca-Cola brands. Pepsi thus gained a lead in India, one of the few countries in the world where it has led Coca-Cola consistently.

Thus, in 1998, the soft drink market in India was shared by Coca-Cola, Pepsi, and a host of Indian manufacturers, mostly regional brands. The main brands of the major contestants, namely Coca-Cola India and Pepsi India, are shown in Table 1:

Table 1 Brands of CSDs offered by the main players

Flavor	Coca-Cola	Pepsi Co.
Cola	Coca-Cola; Thums Up*	Pepsi Cola
Clouded Lime	Fanta; Limca*	SevenUp
Clear Lime	Citra*	Teem
Orange	Fanta; Gold Spot*	Mirinda
Mango NCSD	Maaza*	
Soda	Kinley	Eversel

Note: * denotes brands taken over from Parle.

Exact market share figures are not available, but it was speculated that Coca-Cola India (including its ex-Parle brands) had about 55 per cent share of the soft drinks market while Pepsi had nearly 40 per cent. Coca-Cola brand had about 18 per cent; Thums Up about 17 per cent; Pepsi Cola about 27 per cent; Limca about 10 per cent and Teem about 1.5 per cent. Fanta and Mirinda had about 7.9 per cent each.

PRODUCTS

Soft drinks could be broadly divided into aerated drinks and non-aerated drinks. Aeration was done by mixing carbon dioxide with the base liquid, which in itself was formed by adding water and sugar to the concentrate. The aerated drinks were also known as carbonated soft drinks (CSDs). Non-aerated or non-carbonated soft drinks (NCSDs) were basically diluted fruit pulp, with sugar and preservatives added.

Soft drink concentrates were supplied by concentrate producers who possessed the secret formulae which they guarded zealously. The concentrate producers supplied these concentrates to bottlers who mixed it with water and sweetener, and carbonated the mixture (for CSDs) by adding carbon dioxide. The production of concentrates involved no high technology or major investment.

CSDs in India were largely distributed in returnable glass bottles. This was quite different from the trends in most of the countries across the world, where cans were the dominant mode of packaging. In the 1960s, in USA, glass bottles accounted for 94 per cent of the soft drinks volume, and cans, four per cent. But by 1990, cans accounted for 52 per cent of the market, plastic bottles for 30 per cent, non-returnable glass bottles for 12 per cent, and returnable glass bottles just six per cent. The reason why cans were not popular in India was the price of the drink in canned form, thanks to the high import duties on cans and the high cost of the locally manufactured cans due to poor economies of scale. In India, a bottle (300 ml.) of soft drink cost around ₹8, while a can of the same drink of the same quantity sold for about ₹15, the difference being accounted for entirely by the cost of cans. The economies involved in scale can be seen from the fact that, in USA, can manufacture was highly concentrated with five companies accounting for 98 per cent of sales of cans to the soft drinks industry. For can manufacturers, sales of cans to soft drinks manufacturers accounted for about 40 per cent of their sales. Can manufacturing involved setting up of expensive and highly automated lines, with capacities of around 600 to 1200 cans per minute.

Another important way of dispensation of CSDs was through fountains, where the concentrate, water, sugar, and carbon dioxide were stored separately and mixed just prior to the purchase and served in glasses. In some cases, the concentrate could be kept in ready mixed form and carbonation done just before the sale. Fountains required special equipment costing around ₹100,000. An ingenious outlet developed in India was the so called pouring junction, which were metal boxes containing a base of ice which chilled one litre and 1.5 litres bottles and poured out in glasses of 200 ml. at a cost of ₹5 each. These contraptions cost only about ₹10,000 and, since they needed no electricity, held great potential in rural areas and roadside shops.

NCSDs were served in bottles and in tetrapacks. There were some NCSDs which were sold in concentrate form, requiring the user to mix the concentrate with water prior to consumption. These were available in concentrated liquid and powder form. None of the soft drink manufacturers were involved in this form of selling NCSDs: they were manufactured and sold by companies specializing in this business (e.g. Rasna by Paloma Industries).

The broad breakup of sales between the three kinds of soft drinks in 1998 was as follows.

Carbonated Soft Drinks (CSDS)	61.3%
Non-Carbonated Soft Drinks (NCSDs)	19.5%
NCSD concentrates. Liquid, and powder	10.4%

Squashes and syrups accounted for the rest of the market.

Indian Soft Drinks Market

Production in 1996 of CSDs and NCSDs was above 4000 million bottles, or 166 million unit cases or U/Cs[3] of value ₹32 billion. Of this CSDs accounted for nearly 60 per cent and NCSDs for 20 per cent. According to a survey, however, CSDs and NCSDs accounted only for a small percentage of the overall "share of throat" of those identified as "drinkers" of soft drinks (i.e. those who had consumed at least once during seven days prior to the survey). The "shares of throat" of different drinks in India are given in Table 2.

Per capita consumption in India of CSDs and NCSDs was still quite low. At about 5 bottles per annum per head, India's consumption of CSDs and NCSDs was about 1/250 of that of USA, 1/100 of Mexico, 1/23 of that of Thailand, 1/5 of Pakistan, and half of Bangladesh.

Table 2 Shares of throat of different liquids

Liquid	Share of Throat
Water	75.0
Tea	13.3
Coffee	1.7
Milk	4.8
CSDs	1.8
NCSDs	0.7
Squash/Powders	0.7
Fresh lime juice (Nimbu pani)	0.9
Alcohol	0.3

However, the market had been showing a good growth of around 12 per cent per annum. It was, however, sensitive to the prices offered by competitors and the climatic pattern: in a year of long, hot summer, sales went up considerably and could be as much as 25 per cent more than in a year of short, relatively cool summer.

The soft drink market was quite cyclical, with nearly 40 per cent of sales happening in the four summer months of April to July. A general idea of the cyclical pattern can be seen from Table 3.

Table 3 Sale of CSDs and NCSDs in different months during a year (Index: January = 100)

Month	Index
January	100
February	150
March	170
April	200
May	220
June	230
July	220
August	200
September	170
October	160
November	150
December	150

This seasonality had major implications for the way a CSD company dealt with its suppliers, buyers, and competition.

The soft drink industry had a peculiar supply chain structure, which made it difficult to define its industry structure. First, there were the owners of the brands of soft drinks: The Coca-Cola Company, Pepsi Co., etc. These companies basically supplied the concentrate and owned the brands. They also bore a sizeable portion of promotion, and advertising expenditure. We call them concentrate manufacturers in this case. The next in the link were bottlers. These bottlers were companies who could be either (i) owned by concentrate manufacturers; or (ii) franchisees in which case they had the exclusive right to sell the brands of the concentrate manufacturers within a territory. Since each bottler was allocated a territory, there was no question of any competition from different bottlers for the same brand. A franchisee bottler could not bottle or market a directly competing brand, that is, a Coca-Cola bottler could not bottle or market Pepsi Cola. Usually they bottled the entire range of a brand owner, but could decline to bottle particular brands. In that case, they could market a competing brand. Thus, a Coca-Cola bottler could refuse to bottle Gold Spot or Fanta and bottle Mirinda. Such instances were rare in India, although somewhat common in other countries.

Bottlers other than those owned by concentrate producers were independent companies whose profit or loss were their own concern. Concentrate producers supplied the concentrate at an agreed-to price. But the relationship was much more complex than that: the concentrate producers also placed orders and negotiated rates for bottles on behalf of the bottlers; they designed the campaigns and promotions, and shared the expenses of advertising and promotions with the bottlers. They also devised the quality control systems for the bottlers.

Bottling plants were highly capital intensive. They were highly automated plants, involving sophisticated machinery (mostly imported), the typical filling rates being 600 to 1200 bottles a minute. Filling lines were interchangeable only for bottles of similar sizes and shapes; thus any major package changes needed new equipment. A typical bottling plant cost in India anything between ₹350 million and ₹700 million. Upgradation and modernization were also expensive, and a common complaint of concentrate producers was that the bottlers did not have the vision to invest in upgradation and modernization. Hence, in the interest of their own sales, concentrate producers assisted manufacturers by sharing the expenditure involved in modernizing and upgrading the plants.

Besides the plant and equipment, bottlers also had to invest in bottles, crates, trucks and the cooling equipment in the retailers' outlets (vissicoolers and ice boxes). These constituted about ₹100 per crate. Thus, bottling was a business for big guys, and powerful ones at that. "You just cannot talk down to bottlers," in the opinion of a marketing consultant in Mumbai, so much so that "all the bottlers have direct access to me," said Mr. P.M. Sinha, Chief Executive of Pepsi in India.[4]

There were about 100 bottling companies in India. Coca-Cola (including its ex-Parle brands) had 53 franchisees and a few company owned bottlers; Pepsi, on the other hand, had about 15 owned and 11 franchisees.

After the bottlers, came the retail outlets in the delivery chain. Many of these retail outlets either sold the final product after opening the bottles, or sold the bottles to customers who returned them later. There were also non-returnable plastic bottles of 1 and 1.5 litres capacities. About 15 per cent of consumption of soft drinks was in take-home PET bottles. Larger customers such as restaurants got their supplies directly from the bottling company. There were about 400,000 retail outlets in India selling soft drinks.

Some of the retail outlets were fountains. Fountains were considered to be growing faster than bottled drinks, mainly because of the lower price at which the drinks could be sold. There were about 4000 fountains vending Pepsi drinks and 1500 vending Coca-Cola brands. The larger number of fountains of Pepsi was mainly because of their earlier entry into the country. Coca-Cola also believed that quality problems, especially of water, was quite serious with fountains, and they would like to proceed in a big way only after sorting out this issue. Also, a number of dispensing units were established at petrol pumps. Coca-Cola tied up with Indian Oil Corporation (which had by far the largest number of outlets) while Pepsi had tied up with Bharat Petroleum. In addition to fountains, there were also pouring junctions as mentioned earlier. These were just emerging, however.

A crate of soft drinks entered the distribution system at about ₹100 a crate. The bottlers' margins were believed to be about 10 per cent; retailers' about 20 per cent; and mark up because of excise and taxes about 40 per cent.

SUPPLIERS

For the industry as a whole (i.e. bottlers and brand owners), there were a number of "suppliers" whose bargaining power varied a lot.

First, there were the manufacturers of bottles. The shape of bottles varied between brands so that the brand could be identified from the shape of the bottle itself. Coca-Cola had even patented its famous contoured bottle (the hobble skirt shape, as the company called it) all over the world. The bottle manufactures were generally manufacturers of glass containers of different kinds, and for them soft drink bottles constituted a significant source of orders. They had to invest in moulds which required fairly large order sizes, and this constituted some limitation on the variety of bottles that could be introduced or the frequency with which they could be changed. The general rule was that the bottle manufacturers bore the cost of the moulds, although in some cases the concentrate producers and bottlers would contribute a part. Since sales during the peak season depended very heavily on the availability of adequate number of bottles, the concentrate producers negotiated the orders on behalf of bottlers for price, delivery, and quantity. They kept a very close tab on the orders placed sufficiently in advance and in adequate quantity.

The capacity for bottle manufacture was considered to be adequate in the country, but not generously so. This led to the common practice of pre-empting orders for bottles for the "season" by placing orders that were somewhat larger than required. In the past, when bottle manufacturing capacities were tight, this could cripple the competitor who would find himself unable to sell because of shortage of bottles. Even at the time of writing this case, it was vital to place orders for new bottles for the coming season well on time; otherwise sales would suffer in the peak season.

Since PET bottles were coming up as a new trend, suppliers for these needed to be developed. These bottles were also in particular sizes and shapes, with Coca-Cola having a contour green colored bottle. These bottles need to be made only from first quality plastic (i.e. not recycled plastic) and with adequate quality control. In 1998, the capacity for these PET bottles was considered to be tight, but it was expected that by 1999, capacity would pose no problem.

Sugar was a vital item. Production and movement of sugar from places of production to bottling plants was governed by a maze of complex laws, but what was clear was that the effect was always sub-optimal from the point of view of consumers. The sugar suppliers held complete sway over delivery and prices. Although some discounts were available for bulk purchase, sizeable bulk purchases were not possible because of regulations.

Sugar supply was also not consistent in quality or sweetness. This led to inconsistency of taste of the product itself, something the brand owners abhorred. Backward integration into sugar manufacture was not possible at that point of time because of licensing restrictions; recently the policy had been somewhat liberalized, and setting up own sugar factories was emerging as a possibility.

Carbon dioxide (CO_2) was another important supply. There were small and widely dispersed suppliers and each bottler or fountain arranged for its own suppliers. Generally this was not a problem.

Even water was a major problem, since consistency of taste was vital. So far the bottlers had tied up with local suppliers who supplied water with satisfactory properties. Mineral water was considered a costly option.

Cooling equipment needed were somewhat specialized and required high degree of reliability. But there were a number of manufacturers of these equipment who would supply, install, and maintain them at the vendors' premises.

Soft drinks were essentially driven by brand appeal, and hence advertising was extremely vital. Both Coca-Cola and Pepsi had tied up with advertising agencies, and usually for a particular period based on competitive bids. The soft drink manufacturers were quite important to advertising agencies many of whom had significant shares of their revenues coming from soft drinks advertising: one industry source put it at as much as 50 to 60 per cent for some agencies. There were at least 8 to 10 agencies which were considered suitable from the soft drinks manufacturers' point of view. Advertising agencies were invariably engaged by the brands and the agencies also planned their campaigns nation-wide.

Event managers and promotion agencies were becoming more important.[5] These agencies essentially managed sponsored events or a particular promotion. There were numerous such agencies with quite different capabilities.

Research agencies were also important, since it was necessary to continuously monitor market share and preference trends. Since this required at least state-wide operations, these were fairly large. It was the opinion of industry experts that really good quality research agencies were difficult to come by.

BUYERS

Buyers, at one level, could be classified as institutional buyers and retail outlets. They eventually sold to final consumers. The soft drink industries classified the first as customers and the latter as consumers.

Institutional buyers comprised corporations and institutions who bought and stocked soft drinks for serving visitors, meetings, etc. and hotels and restaurants. Compared to retail channels, these were high volume, high image customers. These institutions (including hotels and restaurants) stocked a variety of other soft drinks and beverages (tea, coffee, etc.), and hotels and restaurants in most states stocked liquors also.

Retail outlets stocked for sale to consumers in relatively smaller quantities and depended on turnover. The volume of each was small but collectively, of course, they accounted for nearly 75 per cent of total business.

Hotels and restaurants usually did not display much promotional material, except perhaps logos, and that too discretely. They depended on customer pull, i.e. customers specified which drink they preferred. They generally did not mind any brand in the same flavor, however. The soft drink manufacturers tried to get exclusive arrangements in hotels and restaurants and were moderately successful. Hotels and restaurants were not governed by maximum retail price (MRP) laws and could charge higher than the marked MRP for their ambience.

Retail outlets depended heavily on promotional material, and quite often stocked competing brands. The purchase of soft drinks was generally impulse driven. Retail outlets were governed by MRP laws.

Out of 800 million population in India in the late 1990s, about 150 million could be categorized as "consumers of soft drinks" in the sense that they consumed at least one soft drink in one week prior to a survey date. Of this population, males constituted 71 per cent and accounted for 68 per cent of consumption in volume.

Soft drinks were consumed pronouncedly in urban areas: though only 28 per cent of the population were in urban areas, they accounted for 58 per cent of drinkers and 75 per cent of volume. But of the sales of about 166 million unit cases (U/Cs) in the country, 120 million U/Cs were sold in urban markets; of which 59.3 million U/Cs were sold in four metros alone. Table 4 gives the consumption pattern in terms of geographic spread, while Table 5 shows the consumer profile in terms of age and Table 6 shows the consumer profile on basis of income.

Table 4 Soft drink consumption in Indian cities

City	Drinkers (million)	Volume (million U/C)	Per capita (No. of serves p.a.)
Delhi	7.5	25.0	80
Bombay	7.2	13.4	45
Calcutta	5.2	11.6	53
Madras	3.1	9.3	73
Bangalore	2.6	4.3	40
Pune	1.4	1.9	34
Total Urban Key Markets	59.3	114.0	46

The age and income profiles of consumers of soft drinks were as follows:

Table 5 Soft drink consumption in terms of age groups

Age group	% of Population	Soft drink % consumption
12–19 years	18	20
20–29 years	23	33
30–50 years	41	38
> 50 years	18	9

Source: Data obtained from industry.

Table 6 Soft drink consumption in terms of income

Household income per annum (₹)	% of population	% of soft drink drinkers	% of volume estimate 1	% of volume estimate 2
>100,000	12	22	25	31
50–100,000	15	22	23	27
25–50,000	21	25	23	27
15–25000	21	17	16	8
<15,000	30	14	14	7

Notes: 1. Estimate 1 was made by a market research agency while Estimate 2 was made by one of the soft drink manufacturers.
2. Data shown are for male population.

Source: Data collected from industry.

CSDs were consumed more often out of home and many between meals as may be seen below:

Table 7 Pattern of CSD consumption (percentages)

	Water	Tea/Coffee	CSD
At Home	92	85	44
Out of Home	8	15	56
Total	100	100	100
With Meals	46	44	12
Between Meals	54	56	88
Total	100	100	100

Source: Data obtained from industry.

The association of CSD and other beverages/drinks with activities may be seen from Table 8.

The reasons cited by respondents in selecting a particular brand and type of beverage were (i) "rational" reasons such as being refreshed after consumption, quenching of thirst and taste, and (ii) emotion-based reasons such as image projected among friends, being popular and "in" thing and "done" thing to serve guests. It was also found that while "rational" reasons were cited only to the extent of about 30 to 40 per cent of respondents, this frequency did not vary much across seasons. On the other hand, emotion-based reasons were cited by about 50 to 80 per cent of respondents but varied considerably across seasons. In hot seasons, generally emotional reasons went up in frequency.

It was the general opinion in the industry that soft drinks had strong associations and that purchases were heavily influenced by the kind of image each drink projected. Consistently over the world, blind tests had failed to distinguish between the actual preference of consumers of at least Coca-Cola and Pepsi; in fact in some blind tests conducted by Pepsi in 1974 (and widely publicized through "Challenge Booths" set up in food stores), 58 per cent of consumers were found to prefer the taste of Pepsi.[6] That did not prevent them from still preferring Coke brands in real life, apparently. Hence a great deal of effort went in building images across the brands and sustaining them.

Table 8 What people drink and when

	CSD	Fruit Juice	Coffee/ Tea	Milk	Total
Home					
Eating a meal at home	4	9	23	63	100
Having a snack	1	2	72	25	100
Watching television	6	11	46	38	100
Relaxing	4	9	63	23	100
Away from Home					
With meals	37	19	24	20	100
With snacks	17	7	72	4	100
Meal at school/work	29	10	52	9	100
Fast food joints	59	19	15	7	100
On the move	22	23	36	19	100
Shopping	25	21	38	16	100
At movie theatres	76	11	12	2	100
Home or Away					
Working or studying	6	10	65	19	100
Socializing	14	12	54	20	100
At parties	67	18	12	3	100
Celebrating special occasions	55	22	19	4	100

Source: Data obtained from industry.

Worldwide, Coca-Cola had built up very strong associations with the American way of life. Attempts at reorienting the image had generally proved disastrous in the past. In a well known case, in 1984, Coca-Cola announced that it would change the formula of its 99 year old brand to contain more sugar. Apparently this made it taste more like Pepsi. The product met with customer resistance with formation of consumer resistance groups. On the day of the announcement, Pepsi announced a holiday for its employees, claiming it welcomed the "new Pepsi drinkers". Bottlers also added to the clamor. The noise made indicated that a substantial number of Americans regarded the traditional Coca-Cola as synonymous with motherhood and apple pie.[7] Coca-Cola had to relent and reintroduce the original product as Coca-Cola Classic. Much later, in 1994, Pepsi tried repositioning its own product, canning in new blue cans. The result was equally disastrous.

Entry Barriers

The soft drink industry involved considerable economies of scale in manufacture, especially of bottle and can manufacture and bottling operations. The scale of economies in cans, for example, was so high that, at present levels of consumption, it was not feasible to set up can manufacturing factories that were viable.

The distribution system formed another formidable entry barrier. The system needed to reach a huge number of small outlets and even in cities this was a major task. Investment in bottles as well as in other matching equipment such as chillers, vissicoolers, and ice boxes was huge. Transport vehicles were needed to transport the drinks to outlets, and these vehicles were generally owned by the bottling company and carried the logo of respective brands prominently, as did the crates and bottles themselves. Thus they could not be interchanged between different brands.

The brands themselves constituted a major entry barrier. It was very expensive to launch a new brand and sustain it.

However, there was scope for local brands to be developed and promoted. This was in fact done by many local brands which concentrated on particular areas. But even put together, they constituted less than 10 per cent of the market.

SUBSTITUTES

By their very nature, soft drinks were readily substitutable by a variety of beverages and other soft drinks. Even though many consumers had strong preferences, the preferences were not so strong that the consumers would go out of their way to get their own brands. Consumers also readily switched between different flavors. The most important parameter governing the eventual choice was availability. If this was not ensured, all the efforts spent on promotion and advertisements were of little use. This meant that the full line of products of each manufacturer needed to be stocked at retail shops that were close together. At least in this business, more was better in terms of number of retail outlets. This was expressed beautifully by Coca-Cola in its famous line that its objective was to make Coke available "within an arm's reach of desire" in every country it was in. Competitors tried various ways to make sure that their brands were available whenever consumers felt like having a soft drink: mobile trolleys, employing retired personnel to intensely push their products, and so on. Railway stations were a favorite target—out of 7056 railway stations in the country, about 3000 had soft drink outlets. Supermarkets were another target for soft drink manufacturers.

The advent of fruit juice based non-carbonated drinks, packed in tetrapacks, was considered an important development. Even earlier, squashes served as convenience drinks at homes, but their major problem was that they could not be carried around easily and could not be purchased on impulse. Things changed a great deal, however, when Frooti, a drink packed in handy 250 ml. pack, was introduced in 1985 by Parle and Jumpin by Godrej. These packs could be carried around, with no risks of breakage; kids found them fun, and mothers found them less troublesome. It also provided a health assurance—"no water of doubtful purity" so that consumers very particular about water contamination (such as foreign tourists) found this product very good value for money. Frooti had been accepted for supply in trains, aircraft, and in parties as a safe, enjoyable, tasty and healthy drink. After the success of Frooti, other manufacturers had also jumped into the fray.

Another new development in 1998 was fresh fruit juice, packed hygienically and with a long shelf life, named Onjus manufactured by Enkay Texofood Limited. This was promoted as a juice no different from juices extracted on the spot from fresh fruit. The promoters were optimistic about the prospects for this drink. In 1998, Onjus had become a ₹400 million business; with a competitor, Dabur with its Dabur Real, also entering, this market was expected to take off.

Yet another development that was not to be ignored was the advent of mineral water in the Indian market. The pioneer of this concept in the Indian market was Parle Industries with its brand "Bisleri" which had almost become a generic name. Very slow to gain acceptance at first, mainly in view of its cost (about ₹16 for a one litre bottle in 1998), the market for mineral water had grown, thanks to vigorous promotion and growing health consciousness (rather, scare about possible water contamination). It was believed that mineral water was becoming an important substitute for soft drinks, especially by travellers. Some people even thought that in the next few years, mineral water would outsell carbonated drinks.[8]

There were a host of manufacturers of mineral water in 1998 with two or three leading brands operating nationally and the rest regionally. Parle Exports, with its brand Bisleri,[9] (still controlled by Ramesh Chauhan) was the market leader with about 50 per cent market share. Another major brand was Bailley, owned by Parle Agro, a company controlled by Prakash Chauhan. Bailley commanded a market share of about 31 per cent. Worldwide, both Coca-Cola and Pepsi owned mineral water brands,

Bonaqua of Coca-Cola and H2$_0$h! by Pepsi Foods. These brands, however, had not been launched in India. The market for mineral water in India as in 1998 was estimated to be around ₹4000 million, or, at an average price of ₹12 per litre, about 330 million litres. According to Mr. Ramesh Chauhan, he aimed for a consumption of 500 million litres of Bisleri by the summer of 1999.[10]

COMPETITION

The two major players were Coca-Cola India and Pepsi Co. Their profiles and strengths and weaknesses are given below. Two more brands of any significance were Campa-Cola and Sosyo.

Coca-Cola[11]

Coca-Cola Company was a $19 billion US company based in Atlanta. Its flagship drink, Coca-Cola, was one of the five best known trademarks in the world, and was identified as the most admired trademark in the world, according to a survey conducted worldwide in 1988.

Coca-Cola was developed as a formulation in 1886 by Dr. John Pemberton, a pharmacist in Atlanta. The legend goes that Dr. Pemberton, having produced the concoction in a three legged brass pot in his backyard, took it to a local chemist, Jacob's Pharmacy (of which he was part owner), and sold it through Jacob Pharmacy as a refreshing drink. The product must have been quite pleasing to the 19th century palates, for it found instant acceptance. Dr. Pemberton's partner, Frank Robinson suggested the name thinking "two Cs would look well in advertisements" and penned the famous flowing script which is also the trademark of Coca-Cola. The real development, however, took place when Asa Candler became the sole owner of Jacob's Pharmacy (at an expense of $2,300) who introduced many innovations the most important being (i)selling the concentrate to other pharmacies for a charge, (ii) heavy advertising and promotions which were ubiquitous, and (iii) the concept of bottling franchises. The famous "hobble skirt" bottle was designed by Root Glass Company of Terre Haute, Indiana, in 1916 and the shape was patented much later in 1997, an honor accorded to only a handful of other packages. The name "Coke" was also patented as a substitute for "Coca-Cola".

In 1919, Ernest Woodruff purchased the Coca-Cola Company from Asa Candler's heirs and in 1923 his son, Robert Woodruff, took the company to great heights. His was the motto "within an arm's reach of desire", making the drink available virtually everywhere, well, if not an arm's reach, certainly within the reach of a few steps. Coca-Cola's association with Olympics began in 1928 in the Amsterdam Olympics, when the spectators witnessed the first lighting of the Olympic flame as well as the first sale of Coca-Cola at an Olympiad. The Coca-Cola Company introduced open top coolers for store keepers in 1929 (provided at low prices by the company), the coin vending machine in 1937, and its famous lifestyle advertising emphasizing the product's role in a consumer's life rather than the product's attributes. This varied from time to time, and the more memorable messages were: "The Pause that Refreshes", "The Real Thing", "Things Go Better with Coke", "Coke Adds Life", "Have a Coca-Cola and a Smile", "Always Coca-Cola", "Coke is It" and "Can't Beat the Real Thing". Every Coke-person felt nostalgic about Coca-Cola's decision to supply Coke, at the request of General Dwight Eisenhower during World War II, to "every man in uniform for 5 cents wherever he is and whatever it costs". Coca-Cola bottling plants soon followed the American troops around the world, and even though we have no idea of how much it cost, surely the benefits were many times over. Coca-Cola became a dominant symbol all over the world, with a dominant market share. Even now, Coca-Cola as a brand is a leader in most of the countries, through not in India (the reader is advised not to remind Coca-Cola India executives of this!). Worldwide, Coca-Cola held almost 70 per cent of the Cola market, and in US, about 40 per cent. Pepsi Cola was the follower with about 31 per cent share in the US International sales of Coca-Cola accounted for 62 per cent of the volume in contrast to 20 per cent of Pepsi's. Other worldwide brands were: Fanta, an orange flavored CSD, Sprite, a clear lime CSD, Tab, a lemon flavored CSD, Fresca, a grape juice flavored CSD, Diet Sprite, Diet Coke, Caffeine-free Coke, Cherry Coke, Diet Cherry Coke, and an orange juice NCSD, the Minute Maid. Worldwide, 37 per cent of Coca-Cola's production was from independently owned bottlers; 50 per cent from plants with non-controlling interest; and 13 per cent from plants with controlling interest.

Pepsi-Cola

Pepsi-Cola was formulated in 1893 in New Bern, North Carolina, by a pharmacist, Caleb Bradham. Pepsi also expanded its network through a franchised network of bottlers. But, unlike Coca-Cola, Pepsi came to near bankruptcy a number of times.

Pepsi generally competed on price. Throughout the 1950s and 1960s, Pepsi had sold its concentrate to bottlers at a price 20 per cent lower than Coca-Cola. The soft drink prices to the consumers were also correspondingly lower. Later in early 1950s, it increased its concentrate price to equal that of Coca-Cola and used the increased margins for advertisements and promotions. In 1933, Pepsi Cola was sold at 5 cents per bottle of 12 oz., the same price as a Coca-Cola bottle of six and half oz. In 1939, it beamed its famous radio jingle, which went on to become the second best known song in America (behind the *Star Spangled Banner*): "Twice as much for a nickel too, Pepsi Cola is the one for you".

Unlike, the Coca-Cola Company, Pepsi, under the leadership of Donald Kendall who took over in 1963, diversified into production of snacks (Frito-lay) and restaurants (Pizza-hut, Taco Bell, and Kentucky Fried Chicken). As a consequence of these diversifications, Pepsi-Cola Company was renamed as PepsiCo. It was of the opinion that there were synergies possible across these businesses: chips were supposed to go well with soft drinks, and new fountain outlets could be opened in restaurants.

Pepsi also had a number of powerful brands worldwide in its arsenal. It had Pepsi Free in the caffeine-free segment, Sugar Free Pepsi Free with aspartame in place of sugar, clear lemon drinks Slice and Diet Slice, Cherry Cola Slice, Cherry Pepsi, and Slice Mandarin Orange. It was also the first to introduce the three litre plastic take-home bottle.

Competitors in India

India was one of the few countries in the world where Pepsi led the Coca-Cola brand in the cola segment. But since Coca-Cola also had the Parle's old brands (Thums Up, Limca, etc.) in its stable, in terms of market shares of companies, Coca-Cola company held about 54 per cent share of the market as against Pepsi Co. India's 40 per cent. Table 9 shows the market shares of the brands of the two majors.

Table 9 Market shares of the soft drink brands of the majors (as on January 1998)

Brand	Coca-Cola Co. Brands	Pepsi Brands
Cola Segment (60%)	Coca-Cola: 17.9% Thums Up: 17.5%	Pepsi: 27.3%
Orange	Fanta: 7.9% Gold Spot: 1.0%	Mirinda: 7.9%
Clouded Lime	Limca: 9.4%	Teem: 1.5%
Clear Lime	Citra: 0.5%	7 Up: 2.5%

Source: "Adding A Lemon", *Business India*, May 7, 1998; and also data obtained from the industry.

A great strength of Coca-Cola was its array of brands—fairly powerful in each segment. Pepsi's non-cola brands were generally weak.

Pepsi had been able to build a presence in many cities. Its bastions seemed to be Mumbai, Delhi, and Ahmedabad. Coca-Cola was strong in Chennai and Kolkata; Thums Up in northern cities and in Andhra Pradesh.

From the very beginning, Pepsi chose to adapt to Indian needs and preferences. It tried to associate its brand with local festivals, events, and traditions. Instead of projecting its global lineage, it used vernacular phrases, and associated with local festivals with new slogans and people. Its strategy was to introduce campaigns made in India and specific to Indian settings, people, and idioms. For example, it adapted its famous US campaign line "You've Got the Right One Baby, Uh-Huh" sung by Ray Charles to "Yehi Hai Right Choice Baby, Aha". In Chennai, it offered a bottle of free Pepsi with idlis (a South Indian snack); in Calcutta, it linked it with local cricket tournaments; and in Delhi, with the festival of Holi. In the words of a Pepsi executive, "On-the-ground activity is critical. You have to keep generating activities and increase consumption opportunities."[12]

Pepsi had adopted an aggressive campaign, targeted at the youth. It positioned itself as a "thing for the youth". Pepsi conducted a memorable advertising campaign during the Wills World Cup in cricket in 1997, for which it bid and lost. While Coca-Cola trumpeted its drink as the "official drink" for the world cup, Pepsi conducted a campaign "Nothing Official About It" featuring celebrities such as cricketer Sachin Tendulkar and the film star Akshay Kumar. The campaign, which cashed in on the anti-establishment, anti-"official" aspirations of the youth, and the campaign was considered to be highly successful, the sour grapes element not much visible.

It was only much later, from mid 1997, that Coca-Cola also started on similar local platforms, abandoning its global ads. Till then, at least in the beginning, Coca-Cola campaigned their global low key and less aggressive. But in 1997, a new CEO, Mr. Donald Short took over, and launched an India-specific campaign, abandoning its global templates and finding much wisdom in the old adage about doing as the Romans do while in Rome. In 1998, Coca-Cola ran a series of campaigns with the theme "Eat..., Sleep...., Drink only Coca-Cola", the gaps being filled at different times by different events current at that time: such as tennis, cricket, etc. This campaign was considered to be a great success in building awareness about the Coca-Cola brands.[13] According to a survey, in August 1997, only 19.4 per cent of a sample of soft drinkers' population recalled seeing a Coke advertisement, while 37 per cent remembered Pepsi ads instantly. By March 1998, Coke seemed to have caught up: 32 per cent were aware of Pepsi ads and 30.4 per cent, of Coke ads.[14]

Pepsi continued to associate celebrities in its ad campaigns. Only in 1998 did Coca-Cola realize the need for celebrities and in September 1998, it signed up some celebrities such as cine stars Karishma Kapoor, and Amir Khan, and cricketers Srinath, Saurav Ganguly, Robin Singh, and Anil Kumble. Pepsi had in its campaigns cine star Shah Rukh Khan and cricketers Sachin Tendulkar, Ajay Jadeja, Mohammed Azharuddin, and Rahul Dravid. While Coca-Cola started sponsoring live concerts featuring Asha Bhonsle, Alisha Chinai, and Daler Mahendi, Pepsi had thrown its lot with film premieres. "And thus, the cola conflict continues, celebrity against celebrity, jingle against jingle,[15] glocalization against glocalization," commented *Business Today.*[16]

Pepsi also had been agile in getting a number of events sponsored or in which it had a major presence. For example, it was expected to be associated with about 100 music related events (Coke was to be associated with about 70); with some 60 movies (Coke: 26); and 13 or so sports events (Coke: 7). Thus, Coca-Cola was seen as a "me-too" follower of Pepsi in India. However, lately, Coca-Cola too launched an aggressive sponsoring of events and was expected to overtake Pepsi in each event in 1999.

While Pepsi positioned its cola drink clearly as the youth and fun drink, its positioning in terms of its other brands was less clear. It seemed as if most of Pepsi's energies were concentrated on its cola brand. Coca-Cola's path was chequered. At first, after acquiring Parle's brands, it tried to downplay these brands promoting its own brands. But it realized by 1997 that this was a mistake; Thums Up and Limca were too powerful indeed, and not promoting them was simply leading to their share being taken up by Pepsi's brands. In 1997, Coca-Cola began a repositioning exercise, and began promoting all its brands vigorously. Thums Up was positioned with a macho image targeting at 20 to 29 year olds; Fanta was the "fun" drink for 13 to 19 year olds; and Limca was for anyone taking a breather—or, as its catch line said, "take it easy". As for Coke, it was treated as a mother brand, which would build the foundation for the rest of the brands. Also, the advertising and promotion of each brand was directed to those cities and regions where it was strong. For example, Mumbai and Kolkata saw more of Thums Up, while Chandigarh saw more of Coke, while the South saw Citra more often[17].

Pepsi worked with one ad agency while Coca-Cola India usually had four to five agencies with whom it negotiated and got better rates. All promotions of Coca-Cola were national so far, while Pepsi went in for national and regional promotions. Pepsi generally chose a city or region and ran a high intensity campaign for about a month; then moved on to another city. This usually resulted to a gain in market share by about 5 to 10 percentage points in the short run and by about 3 to 5 points in the long run, in the absence of a counter campaign.

Pepsi and Coca-Cola both had mechanisms for tracking their market shares. Essentially this was done through questioning the retail outlets and samples of consumers. Coca-Cola, from the beginning, invested heavily in market research and intelligence and its capabilities in this respect were believed to be much better. It could identify shifts in market shares in any market within about 3–7 days of the end of the period and the data were considered to be very reliable. Coca-Cola executives claimed that this enabled them to plan their campaigns and promotions and fine tune them. Pepsi, being the first mover, had a good network of well-trained salespersons. It was also believed that Pepsi paid the salesmen better than Coca-Cola. Coca-Cola executives believed that pay itself was not a major disadvantage, but they needed to do more and better training for their salespersons.

Pepsi and Coca-Cola had built different distribution and logistic systems. Pepsi had a higher number of fountains and it had built a good number of high image clients thanks to its being the first mover compared to Coca-Cola. It operated smaller trucks which covered a shorter route while Coca-Cola had larger trucks covering longer routes. Pepsi used half depth crates (i.e., with heights covering only half the bottle) while Coca-Cola used full depth crates. The latter was believed to lead to less breakages—Coca-Cola's breakage of bottles was 0.5 per cent compared to 2.5 per cent for Pepsi.

From the beginning, Pepsi followed a strategy of owning and operating many bottling plants. It acquired controlling interests in numerous bottling operations guaranteeing the bottlers financial support. This strategy gave control over bottling operations, but it resulted in spending a lot of managerial resources in manufacturing and labor problems. According to *Business India*, one of the industry managers thought that with such big investments on the ground, Pepsi "may not be able to take its eye off the manufacturing ball" and "the moot point is whether it will be able to focus adequately on marketing at the same time, which is really the name of this game."[18]

Coca-Cola, on the other hand, started with owning as little of bottling as possible. But it seems to have followed Pepsi's footsteps buying up a number of bottling units. By the end of 1998, Coca-Cola owned 52 outlets across India, and was in the process of acquiring the remaining independent plants also or setting up joint ventures with majority stakes. There were 45 more independent bottlers and in 1997–98, Coca-Cola had signed up two joint ventures and acquired the management control of five other bottling units.

Coca-Cola operated through two holding companies in India—Hindustan Coca-Cola and Bharat Coca-Cola. They had financed four downstream joint ventures: Hindustan Coca-Cola Bottling North West (investment: ₹3450 million); Hindustan Coca-Cola Bottling South West (investment: ₹2500 million); Bharat Coca-Cola Bottling North East (investment: ₹2500 million); and Bharat Coca-Cola Bottling South West (investment: ₹3450 million).[19] It was expected that when the franchising agreements would come up for renewal (mostly in late 1998 and early 1999), the balance units would be acquired by Coca-Cola.

Coca-Cola had its plants spread out thanks to historical legacies. This made for shorter access to markets but poorer economies of scale in manufacture. On the whole, neither was believed to have a decisive advantage over other because of this factor.

One and 1.5 litre bottles were emerging as important consumer preferences. These were non-returnable PET bottles, to be taken home by consumers and served within two to three days of opening the bottle. This was becoming popular in the house segment. Only first quality (not recycled) PET bottles were used for this purpose. As in 1998, Pepsi had tied up for capacities for large bottles more than Coca-Cola.

It was believed that fountain sales would pick up steeply in the coming years. Because of its first mover advantage, Pepsi had been able to set up about 4000 fountains while Coca-Cola had about 1500. According to Vibha Rishi, Vice President, Marketing, Pepsi planned to add another 200,000 access points to the existing half a million, with around 50,000 new coolers in an year. Coca-Cola also had similar plans. But it was cautious over the issue of going into fountains in a big way, for it believed these had serious quality problems, especially with water.

Coca-Cola was extremely sensitive to the issue of quality. Quality was a problem in this industry, for much depended on how much care the bottler took in his operations and supplies, especially water. Any contamination found instant headlines in newspapers, and the concentrate manufacturers believed that it hurt them almost entirely, not the bottlers (many in the public did not even know the difference between bottlers and concentrate manufacturers). Coca-Cola believed that its quality checks were very stringent and of world class, and far superior to Pepsi's. It thought that, unless the quality issues were sorted out, it would not be a good idea to get into fountains in a big way.

It was believed that Pepsi had a very thin head office. Much of the initiatives were left to the people at the regional levels, and they could launch campaigns without reference to even the Indian head office. Thus, it was speculated that the Chennai idli campaign was done at the initiative of the Chennai people alone.[20] The New York office also left the Indian executives to plan and execute work in their own way. On the other hand, Coca-Cola had a fairly large head office in Delhi, with most of the decisions on campaigns, promotions, and pricing taken at the head office level. In turn its Atlanta office also held the Indian company on a tight leash. Recently, however, Coca-Cola also seemed to have changed its approach, and had started giving more freedom to the field personnel.

Coca-Cola executives were of the opinion that over time, as in other countries in the world, their brands would dominate, with suitable and adequate promotion and advertising support. They also believed that the market would continue to grow at the rate of at least 12 to 15 per cent a year, perhaps as much as 30 per cent a year and their market share (of Coca-Cola brands, not Parle brands) would steadily inch up.

Assignment Questions

1. Conduct an industry analysis using Porter's five forces model and identify action implications in each for Coca-Cola India.
2. Identify strategic questions facing Coca-Cola India (five at the most).
3. From the profiles of Coca-Cola and Pepsi given in the case, assess the relative strengths and weaknesses of each. It may be useful to do this under different scenarios.
4. Develop a set of recommendations for Coca-Cola India (remember to take into account Pepsi's likely offensive and defensive/retaliatory moves).

NOTES

1. "Leading the Way," *Business India*, January 15–28, 1996, p.59.
2. Donald Short, CEO, Coca-Cola India, quoted by *Business India* in "Turning on the Heat," June 29–July 12, 1998.
3. One unit case was defined as 24 bottles of 250 ml. each; recently since most of the bottles are sold with 300 ml. capacity, one unit case is referred to as 24 bottles of 300 ml. each.
4. "Leading the Way," *Business India*, January 15–28, 1996, p.59.
5. Events were a recent development in India, and referred to particular shows (such as fashion shows) organized to promote a particular brand. These were quite big affairs, with celebrities gracing the occasion, of course for a suitable fee.
6. Rebecca Wayland, "Coca-Cola versus Pepsi-Cola in the Soft Drink Industry," case material of Harvard Business School, 1991. Case # 9-391-179 (case prepared under the supervision of Prof. Michael E. Porter).
7. ibid.
8. Ramesh Chauhan, for example, is reported to have shared this view. "Can Coca-Cola Bottle Up the Chauhans?," *Business Today*, August 22, 1998.
9. The brand was owned by Acqua Mineral, a wholly owned subsidiary of Parle Exports.
10. "Bottling Up Strategies for the War of the Waters," *Business Today*, September 7–21, 1998.
11. Material in this section and the next on Pepsi are based on documents given by Coca-Cola India and the Harvard Case, "Coca-Cola versus Pepsi-Cola and the Soft Drink Industry".
12. "Why Coke Should Be more Like Pepsi," *Business Today*, August 7–21, 1997.
13. "Turning on the Heat", *Business India*, June 29–July 12, 1998.
14. ibid.
15. Coca-Cola, for instance, coined its jingle *Ala-Re-Aya* which was preempting Pepsi's *Sachin Aya Re* jingle. Both were based on the same film song, and Coca-Cola was involved in some controversy over its jingle.
16. "The Cola Warriors' Indian Summer," *Business Today*, September 7, 1998.
17. "Turning on the Heat," *Business India*, June 29–July 12, 1998.
18. "That Passion to Win," *Business India*, January 15–28, 1996, pp.65.
19. "Can Coca-Cola Bottle Up the Chauhans?," *Business Today*, August 22, 1998.
20. "Why Coke Should Be More Like Pepsi", *Business Today*, August 7–21, 1997.

Arun Ice Cream

CASE 2

Abraham Koshy and N. Venkiteswaran

On June 30, 1997, even as he signed the annual accounts of Hatsun Milk Food Limited for the year to March 1997, it was clear to R.G. Chandramogan, Chairman and Managing Director, that his company was at strategic cross-roads. The dilemma related to the strategic direction the Chennai-head-quartered makers of Arun Ice Cream had to take. This in particular involved the issue of market expansion for the ice cream manufacturers beyond South India vis-à-vis diversification into products that could leverage on the company's current strengths. Recent years had been momentous for Arun as the company itself had come to be known eponymous with its key brand. Early 1996 saw Hatsun Milk Food Limited (HMFL) going public. With the Indian stock market in the grip of a bearish phase, Hatsun's initial public offering (IPO) barely managed to sail through. But the greater visibility and emergence of a powerful stakeholder in the form of public investors meant the taciturn management of Hatsun had to play a completely unfamiliar role in managing expectations. With ice cream sales increasing by a healthy 41 per cent, the just completed fiscal, the first full year after the IPO, Chandramogan reflected, was probably satisfactory in this respect. This, he felt, however only underscored the urgency to develop a sound short-term strategy to consolidate Arun brand of ice cream in the fast-changing competitive scenario and thus establish a solid platform to launch aggressive growth initiatives and attain a critical mass and scale by the year 2000.

Arun Ice Cream: Early History and Strategy

Chandramogan, son of a vegetable wholesaler from the South Indian state of Tamil Nadu, set up Arun Ice Cream in 1970 in Chennai (now re-named Chennai), essentially motivated by the urge to "do something". After his college studies were discontinued at the pre-university stage, Chandramogan agonised over several weeks about starting some business without being quite able to narrow down to any specific line, mainly because of heavy investments entailed. While driven by an urge to succeed as a businessman, he did not quite know how to go about setting up a business. It was his maternal uncle who suggested the business of ice cream. Investing ₹15,000 as his own capital and raising another ₹21,000 by way of a bank loan, he set up a small ice candy unit in a rented premise adjacent to his uncle's retail textile outlet. From a quick survey around the Madras market it appeared to Chandramogan that there were about 350 small-time ice candy manufacturers like him competing in the low end of the market. These were offering no competition to the up- market segment dominated by leading brands

Dasaprakash, Joy and Kwality. Like the "others in the crowd", Chandramogan was also selling his Arun brand ice candies for 10 paise and 15 paise a piece predominantly through street-vendors. Thanks to its prominent location in a busy locality, Arun[1] also quickly began attracting walk-in customers. The fact that one could get "fresh" ice candies right across the factory counter was a major selling point in promoting in-factory sales. In the very first year of operations, Chandramogan recalls, Arun clocked a turnover of about ₹150,000 and profit of about ₹40,000. Over-the-counter sales probably accounted for nearly half the business. Emboldened by this early success, Chandramogan went in for a three-fold expansion in the second year of operations. In the very first summer season, typically the peak months for ice cream and candies sales, Chandramogan found that his production capacity was simply inadequate to meet the peak demand. This, and an early resolve to move away from the large pack of small-time, faceless competitors influenced his decision to expand. As the existing location was found cramped, he decided to relocate the plant in a more spacious locale in the outskirts of the city. As it turned out, Chandramogan found selling the hugely expanded volumes, particularly during off-season, quite tough. The somewhat inconspicuous location of the new factory in a rather low traffic area was also found to be inappropriate for across-the-counter sales that dropped precipitously. Though Chandramogan quickly resumed over-the-counter sales at the old premises (by sourcing from the new factory), it never regained the old volumes. The expanded facilities also meant higher capacity-related fixed costs. With sharply increased costs and sales not keeping pace, Arun fell into the red. Chandramogan financed the losses through additional borrowings, partly from his uncle. Even as he was struggling debating about various options to get out of the financial squeeze, the industry was going through a major upheaval. As the input costs were rising sharply, ice-candy manufacturers decided to increase the retail price from 10 paise to 15 paise a piece, leading to a revolt and boycott by ice-candy vendors. With manufacturers such as Arun sticking to their decision, vendors slowly began returning to the fold.

With somewhat stagnating volumes and low profitability, Chandramogan felt the business outlook was one of the same unexciting existence. As he sought to move upmarket into ice cream and increase volumes through bulk institutional sales, a leading group of hotels in Madras expressed interest to source its ice cream requirements. However the hotel group insisted that Arun upgraded the product quality and supplied homogenised ice cream and also increased the range of product offering and flavors. This would involve acquiring certain new equipment for homogenisation costing ₹7500 and recruiting a qualified and experienced person to oversee production, at a salary substantially higher than what the business could have probably then afforded. Though his fellow ice candy manufacturers' caution and his own earlier experience and the current state of his finances suggested otherwise, Chandramogan decided to take the risk. With vastly improved quality and larger number of flavors in its offering, Arun was able to break into the tough hotel market. While this did help boost his confidence, it did little to improve the finances, which continued to suffer from serious profitability and liquidity problems. Chandramogan soon realised that hotels, while providing stable volumes, were nonetheless prone to making heavy demands on their suppliers and also were extremely slow in releasing payments for the supplies made. As the typical hotel customer was not particularly brand-sensitive, hotels themselves viewed ice cream like any other provision in their weekly shopping list and were not shy of using their substantial clout vis-à-vis their small time suppliers.

In the next two years or so, even as the ice cream business was beginning to break-even, Chandramogan was searching for a winning formula for steering Arun away from other "me-too" outfits. Having learnt everything the hard way "on the job" through trial and error, Chandramogan was also beginning to feel the acute need for some kind of formal training and structured inputs on the various aspects of management. He enrolled with Davar's College, an institution offering specialised short-duration programmes for working executives, and took courses in Marketing and Personnel Management.

Market for Ice Cream in Chennai and Arun's Search for a Niche

Searching for a suitable slot to position Arun in an intensely price-sensitive commodities market with a highly fragmented competition jockeying for every little competitive space, Chandramogan found little room. Nearly 95 per cent of the primary or bulk purchases of ice cream in Madras around the time were accounted for by the following three categories:

- General provisions and departmental stores with deep freezers
- Hotels and restaurants
- Social events, mostly wedding parties.

Typically, ice cream majors (such as Dasaprakash, Joy, and Kwality) invested in deep freezers and supplied them to general stores and also to a lesser extent hotels and restaurants thereby establishing some kind of cold chains as dedicated retail outlets for their brands. (Often these general stores also stocked a variety of other items besides the ice cream of the specific principals in the freezers.) Aware of his own limitations, Chandramogan was not quite sure about the feasibility and appropriateness of this proven, cold chain model for Arun. At the same time he was also conscious of the fact that the so-called deep freezer segments represented potentially the largest and the most stable market for his product. Ice cream supplies to social events like weddings, while quite lucrative, were extremely seasonal and imposed heavy demand on Arun's limited logistics management. Moreover this segment was highly brand-conscious and Arun brand was virtually unknown at the time. (While the brand name Arun was used almost since inception, Chandramogan admitted that not much thinking had probably gone into the brand-name decision.)

Left with limited options, Chandramogan continued his search for a niche for Arun and felt that two other segments accounting for just about five per cent of the Chennai ice cream market possibly gave him some hope. These were educational institutions and supplies to ships calling at the Madras port. Run by mess secretaries who themselves were college students, typically the college canteen and the hostel mess segment was virtually ignored by the leading ice cream manufacturers such as Dasaprakash and Joy. Chandramogan, in his late teens, instantly struck a rapport with the key decision-makers of college canteens. Yet it required several visits and great perseverance before he could bag orders for supplies to a large and prestigious institution like the Indian Institute of Technology, Madras. He also felt that college students were more than willing to experiment with a new brand or new flavors. Sensing a competitive vacuum, he stepped in with vastly improved service and deliveries they were unaccustomed to and steadily captured a bulk of this segment.

Similarly ship-chandlers, who procured and supplied provisions to ships that called at the Madras port, were particular about delivery of ice cream just in time for onward transhipment to ships. Chandramogan felt that this segment, while fastidious about quality, was not that brand-driven. Most leading ice cream manufacturers were unsurprisingly unexcited about these supplies in view of the small volumes and the erratic delivery requirements. Chandramogan began meeting these agents who were procuring and supplying provisions to various shipping lines, understood their special requirements regarding packing and delivery and quickly captured most of this market as well. By 1974, Chandramogan recalls that Arun had probably captured 95 per cent of the college canteen and ship-chandler segments. However, 95 per cent of the total Chennai market, represented by the other three segments, was still outside the reach of Arun.

Having firmly established Arun in the city college campuses, Chandramogan toyed with the idea of replicating the approach in the college canteens in the interior districts of Tamil Nadu. Ice cream majors of the time practically ignored the district towns because of sheer logistics problems. Since the student community in district-level colleges included in their midst former students of Madras colleges, brand recognition for Arun was made relatively easier. Chandramogan began supplying ice cream to a few colleges in nearby districts, packed in dry-ice containers, employing sales persons for the purpose. Very soon Arun had virtually 100 per cent of the small, but growing upcountry college market.

With Arun's volumes picking up in the following months Chandramogan was able to pay off all his outstanding loans, and the business regained a semblance of financial flexibility. Despite this, Chandramogan still did not feel financially strong enough to enter the deep freezer based general stores segment in Madras. While in these early days, he did provide some advertisement support to build and enhance the brand image of Arun, very few enquiries for agency or franchisee interest followed.

As he continued to stay clear of the top three segments in the Chennai market, it was evident to Chandramogan that the business was probably entering a phase of stagnation. So he began looking out for new markets in which he could compete effectively and grow.

Breaking into the Upcountry Market

As Chandramogan saw, the greatest growth potential was seen in the upcountry mofussil towns that were completely ignored by the ice cream majors. While these markets were virgin, the cost and logistics of servicing them from a central factory in Madras were indeed daunting. If he could come up with the right marketing and distribution formulas, Chandramogan felt there was a good chance of his striking it big, particularly because of the absence of any serious competition.

Having made inroads into upcountry college canteens and hostels, Chandramogan began looking at the feasibility of supplying ice cream at weddings and other important social events in upcountry towns. While ice cream was a standard fare for such events in Madras, this concept was virtually unknown outside the city. So he went around canvassing for orders for weddings and other social events in upmarket households outside Madras. Through persistent efforts, Arun was able to achieve some measure of success. While these initiatives did help in enhancing brand awareness and additional sales, Chandramogan realised that these would not be adequate to give him stable volumes and a critical mass. And to achieve this, it was important that somehow he got into some kind of mass marketing. Around this time there were a few enquiries indicating interest in stocking and retailing Arun ice cream in some areas of the Madras provided Chandramogan supplied deep freezers. Chandramogan firmly but politely turned down the offers.

Initially, Chandramogan identified a few towns like Pondicherry (now Puducherry), Madurai, Kumbakonam, and Sivakasi in Tamil Nadu for initial foray, particularly because good quality ice cream was not available in these places. (At best a few hotels and restaurants were serving home-made, unbranded, plain-vanilla ice cream to their diners.) Chandramogan advertised through banners and hoardings in these selected towns that ice cream from Chennai would be supplied on certain pre-announced days and that those interested could book their orders with Arun agents either in person or by phone. Using local telephone directories to obtain addresses, he also had mailers posted to potential upmarket customers, referring to them as eminent persons figuring in the list of VIPs. Typically, Chandramogan had Arun ice cream supplied through the agents within four to five days of the booking.

Ice cream supplied from Chennai was the key selling point. Mailers to addressees outside the specified locality were rare at that time. As the long-ignored small town consumers felt recognized, there was tremendous response to these test-marketing forays. Even as Chandramogan was beginning to feel confident to think in terms of regular distribution arrangements in place of the ad-hoc ice cream days, the novelty factor was beginning to wear-off and customer response started declining. He also felt that fixed-day selling probably left out a large number of potential customers from places contiguous to these towns as well as walk-in customers indulging in impulse purchases.

The breakthrough came by chance. As Chandramogan recalled, "people see advertisements; but they seldom read it carefully." On the appointed days when ice cream was to be supplied as announced in advertisement mailers and hoarding, even those who had not booked ice creams came to the premises of the agent whose address appeared in the advertisements for buying ice cream. Similarly many potential customers also turned up on other days. Excited by the consumer response and seeing that, on several occasions, walk-in customers had to be turned back, an agent Kanakaraj from the temple-town of Madurai offered to invest in his own deep-freezer and sought long-term distribution arrangements. This agent provided facilities to people to sit and eat ice cream. A novel method of retailing ice cream through sit-and-eat parlour was thus born in 1981. Though Kanakaraj suggested that the price of Arun ice cream be kept low keeping in view the price-sensitivity of the local market, Chandramogan was not in favour of doing so as he felt that Arun was not the same as unbranded, low-priced ice cream served in local restaurants. Chandramogan supported this agent through joint promotions and regular advertisement campaigns. Even as this first Arun franchisee began tasting success with steadily-growing demand, other small town agents also felt emboldened to invest in their own freezers. A 400-litre freezer of reputed brand typically cost about ₹12,000–13,000 around the time.

As Chandramogan reminsces, he "accidentally hit the right button. This was not a credit-oriented market." And he did not have adequate resources to invest in his own freezers and supply them to retail outlets. As it turned out, "there was no investment, no credit, but also no competition in this market." And he was implementing the franchisee concept without even knowing the term.

From 1981 he began replicating the model by opening, on an average, two such franchisee-run parlours every month. With over 700 such outlets in Tamil Nadu, Karnataka, Kerala, and Andhra Pradesh by early 1999, Chandramogan believed that Arun franchisee network was one of the largest in South India.

In appointing his franchisees, Chandramogan typically looked at the personal profile and business background of the potential candidates. Typically, he would not offer Arun franchise to big time, successful traders, or businessmen. He also avoided, as far as possible, elderly persons or highly educated individuals for distributorship. On the other hand, he would prefer people in their mid or late twenties, who had, preferably completed schooling, with average family income and had probably failed in their early business endeavors. Very often, friends and relatives of existing franchisees approached him with requests for franchise rights to open parlors in new locations. This made Chandramogan's task easier. Once appointed, the franchisee was assured of certain exclusiveness and area protection in that another Arun franchisee was not appointed within a $1^1/_2$–2 kilometre radius. These franchised outlets were exclusive sit-and-eat ice cream parlors with good ambience and located in city centre or main roads. Unlike the general stores freezer outlets of other ice cream brands, Arun's outlets did not stock other items like butter and chocolates. Over the years Chandramogan finetuned the parlor and franchisee concepts. He had deliberately decided on the strategy of parlors selling Arun Ice Cream exclusively. On its part, the company would ensure that it distributed its products only through its franchisees' parlors and not through any other channel except direct deliveries to customers against specific orders for parties, etc. The concept of exclusive parlors, Chandramogan felt, enabled the franchisee to focus on selling Arun range of ice creams and give better customer service. By 1985, Arun emerged as the largest ice cream manufacturer in Tamil Nadu in terms of volumes. Arun's turnover, which was about ₹150,000 in 1970 and had barely inched up to about ₹425,000 by 1981, had risen to about ₹28.0 million by 1990. Even as Arun became the largest ice cream brand in Tamil Nadu by 1985 thanks to its success in the upcountry districts, it still did not have significant presence in Chennai. Chandramogan now began aggressively attacking the Chennai market initially by establishing the now successful sit-and-eat parlours in the city suburbs and only thereafter, did he move downtown. In the next 18–24 months, Arun achieved its brand leadership in Chennai as well. While he continued with the strategy of not cultivating the hotel segment, the wedding parties segment came automatically to Arun now. It was estimated that Arun had a market share of around 60 per cent in Tamil Nadu by 1999 and about 36 per cent in the four South Indian states. Chandramogan estimates that probably about 120 franchisees came to his fold as friends/relatives of existing Arun agents. One franchisee, Ganesan, was responsible for introducing as many as 32 other agents. Arun's franchisee family, Chandramogan felt, was an extremely loyal lot as most them grew with Arun. There was a strong symbiotic relationship between the company and its franchisees. At a more personal level, many of them enjoyed a very warm relationship with Chandramogan. And several of them have named their sons and grandsons Arun! Chandramogan was clear that, in any business decision he took, he would not ignore the collective interests of his extended family of franchisees.

Manufacturing Operations and Logistics

While the 1970s were a period of learning, the 1980s turned out to be one of earning for Chandramogan. He also realized that in the business of ice cream, efficient management of inward and outward logistics was extremely important. The most challenging aspect was procurement of milk, a key input in ice cream manufacture in a cost-efficient manner. The problems arose because of the seasonal demand-supply imbalance in respect of the product and its extremely short shelf-life. Summer months of March through June, though peak season for ice cream sales, also happen to be the lean season for milk supplies in southern India. Similarly the flush season for milk coincides with the period of low ice cream sales. From fairly early days, Chandramogan decided to procure milk directly from dairy farmers and for this purpose set up collection centres in major milk-producing villages close to his ice cream plant. The milk procured at these collection centres could be brought to the Arun factory within 2–3 hours of collection. He offered guaranteed procurement of certain minimum quantity of milk based on his lean season requirements. For his additional requirements of milk in the peak ice cream season, he offered to pay a higher price. Generally, the payments to the dairy farmers for the milk purchases were made once every three days at the collection centres. According to Chandramogan, Arun's ice cream sales had, on an average, exhibited the kind of seasonal pattern as given in Table 1. He sourced other inputs and ingredients such as sugar, fruits, packing materials, etc., from leading wholesalers/manufacturers.

Table 1 Arun ice cream sales figure

Months	Percentage of annual sales
April–June	34
July–September	22
October–December	19
January–March	25

For outward transport of ice cream to various franchisees located in different towns, he recognised that the low volumes to various destinations did not justify the use of expensive refrigerated transport that had to return empty with no compatible load. So he typically took advantage of the regular passenger train services of the Indian Railways for despatch of ice cream to various destinations. For this purpose, ice cream cartons were tightly packed in small wooden boxes (2'×2'×2') with thermocole lining and filled with dry ice (solid carbon dioxide) to prevent melting. Being a highly perishable product, ice cream was accorded high priority by the Railways for transportation. The franchisees would have the "boxes" collected at their respective destinations. They also returned the empty containers by return trains. And it was not until 1995 that Chandramogan purchased refrigerated vehicles for delivery of ice cream. He also felt that in the long-run transporting ice cream to long distances by train or by refrigerated vehicles might not be a viable strategy. He also reckoned that a 250–300 km. radius was probably the optimal area that could be cost-effectively serviced by a central ice cream plant. As the Chennai ice cream plant was running out of capacity thanks to Arun's rapid expansion in the 1980s, Chandramogan felt a compelling need to set up another plant both to meet the growing demand and also to improve the overall logistics. In 1991 he set up a spanking new ice cream plant in Salem, some 320 km southwest of Madras and also close to both Kerala and Karnataka borders. Moreover the new plant was located in the heart of Tamil Nadu's milk belt which facilitated procurement of high quality milk at competitive prices. (See Exhibit 1 for a map of South India.) The Salem plant involving an investment of ₹22 million was constructed in record time of about 3 months, right in time for the summer season. The plant capacity at both Chennai and Salem were designed for peak seasonal production; during off-season the plant utilisation was only partial and all annual maintenance and revamp were typically scheduled during this period. While on an average seven to 10 new flavors were introduced every year, an equal number were probably phased out. Chandramogan figured that about 30–35 flavors were on offer at any given time. (A process diagram with respect of ice cream manufacture is given in Exhibit 2.) In order to conform to the prevailing regulations restricting manufacture of ice cream only in the SSI (small scale industries) sector–explained elsewhere in the case, the Salem plant was set up as an SSI unit under a new proprietary concern, Atlantic Foods. In the following years ice cream production in the Salem factory more than met the growing demands placed on it. Chandramogan then turned his attention to the Chennai plant that required major investments in upgradation. Rather than attempting a piecemeal revamp and modernization of the decades-old plant, he decided to set up a totally new automatic facility, and for this purpose he acquired a five-acre plot in the Red Hills area on the outskirts of the city. This plant with a capacity of 15,000 litres[2] of ice cream mix a day and costing about ₹45 million (inclusive of the cost of land) became operational in July 1995. In view of the investment restrictions on individual SSI unit, the new Madras plant was set up under a separate firm, Hatsun Milk Products.

Around this time, Chandramogan found it necessary to re-vamp the distribution logistics. Recent and continuing increase in the number of franchisees on the one hand and in the variety of ice cream flavors on the other, he felt, was beginning to take a heavy toll on the factories. He thought of relieving factories of the responsibility of managing the direct distribution of ice cream to various destinations on a daily basis. As a first step he set up a depot in Madurai in 1995 with adequate cold storage facilities and the required administrative personnel to handle ice cream distribution to the franchisees located in the southern districts of Tamil Nadu. The depot would be responsible for sourcing from Arun factories, inventory and cold storage management, order taking and execution as well as collections.

With the requirements of milk steadily going up in keeping with rising ice cream sales, Chandramogan was becoming increasingly concerned about managing the expectations of the dairy farmers particularly during the lean season for ice cream. While he needed increasingly large quantity of milk during the peak summer months, failure to maintain milk procurement at a reasonably high base during off-season could lead to the farmers snapping the links with Arun and moving away to other more "dependable" customers.

Brand and Promotions Strategy

From very early days Chandramogan was keen to build and preserve a distinct brand identity for his ice cream. Almost since inception, he was spending fairly large sums of money for promotion and advertisement. Whether it was a college campus in Chennai or an upcountry high-traffic junction, brand Arun was heavily promoted through colorful banners, posters or flyers. In the early years, the main advertisement media were newspapers and magazines. When color television coverage received a big boost in the mid-eighties, Chandramogan immediately took to the popular visual medium for advertising. As the turnover went up sharply following the success of the franchise strategy, he stepped up brand-focused advertisement and began investing in technology. The fact that he did not have to invest in working capital and in deep freezers meant that his liquidity remained unim-

Exhibit 1 The map of South India

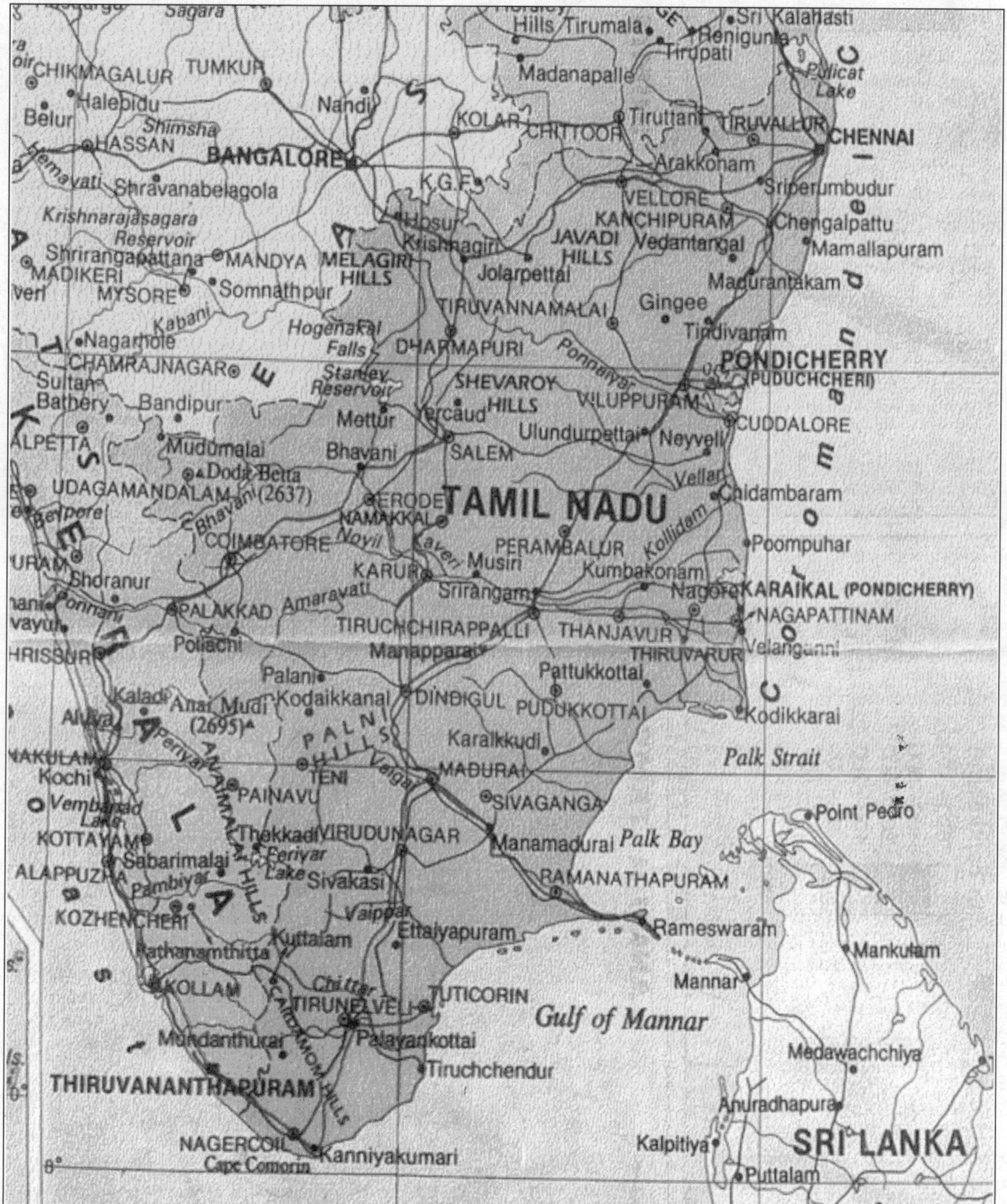

Exhibit 2 Ice cream manufacturing process

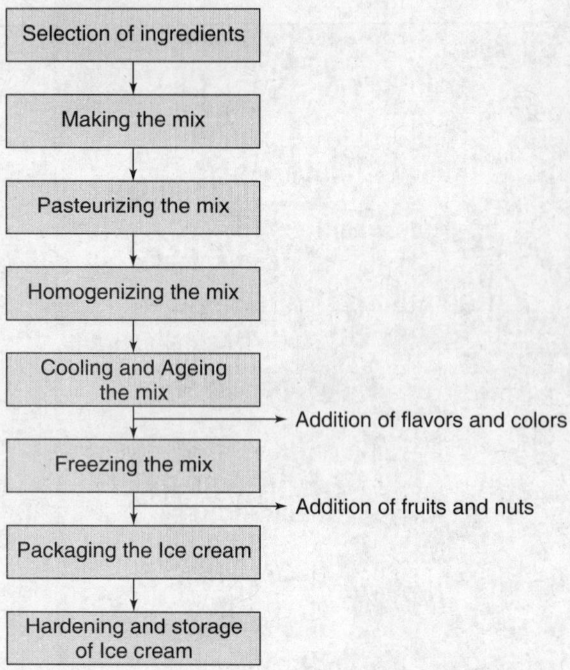

Notes on Ice cream manufacturing process

Selection of ingredients

Milk and milk products, sugar, stabiliser and emulsifier, fruits, nuts, flavour and colour.

Figuring the mix

A prior knowledge and calculation of ice cream mix is necessary in properly balancing of mix, establishing and maintaining uniform quality, and for conforming to legal standards.

Making the mix

Mixing of ingredients (i.e. liquid ingredients and dry ingredients) in a batch steam jacket vet.

Pasteurizing of mix

This process is required to destroy all pathogenic and disease-causing bacteria for safeguarding the health of the consumer. Pasteurization temperature-time combination: 68.5°C for 30 minutes.

Homogenizing the mix

Homogenization is to ensure a permanent and uniform suspension of fat by reducing the size of fat globules. Homogenization is carried out under pressurized conditions as under:
1st Stage: 2500 PSI at 60°C
2nd stage: 500 PSI at 60°C

Cooling and ageing of mix

This process, with a view to improve the body, texture etc. of the ice cream, involves keeping the mix at a low temperature (i.e. below 5°C) for a period of 3–4 hours before being frozen.

paired. This gave him considerable freedom to invest in brand building. By 1991, according to Chandramogan, Arun's advertisement spending was probably higher than the total turnover of Dasaprakash!

From 1987 Chandramogan began carrying out focused sales promotion activities. The first such promotion was "Eat All You Can" Ice Cream Mela organised in Chennai. Under this scheme, for a fixed entry fee of, say, ₹8, the participants were allowed to eat any amount of ice cream on display and the one who consumed the maximum quantity was declared winner. The specific purpose of this sales promotion campaign was to encourage consumers to try out higher-end, expensive flavors, which, in the normal course they were normally reluctant to experiment with. (Consumers normally consumed Vanilla flavor, the cheapest.) Altogether, about 4200 people participated in the campaign that probably cost about ₹270,000. Similar campaigns were repeated in other cities like Hyderabad.

Another successful scheme was "Slow Speed Driving Competition". From 1993 onwards, Arun also began conducting slow-speed driving competition for motorcycles and scooters. An intending participant typically is required to purchase ice cream worth, say, ₹15 as entry fee. Conducted in association with the local traffic police in cities like Chennai and Bengaluru (Bangalore), such competitions turned out to be a big hit with some 3400 people participating in one such event. The objective of such campaigns was again to encourage customer trial of high-end flavors that hopefully would lead to greater flow of two-wheeler traffic to Arun's parlors.

Another mode of promotion was the "Phone and Have an Ice Cream" (Dial-a-Number) campaign. It was widely advertised that anyone dialling up certain specified telephone numbers during specified time slots on a given day would win ₹100 worth Arun ice cream free. During 1993–94 the "Dial-a-Number" campaign was conducted in 20 towns attracting participation by over 12,000 callers costing an estimated at ₹1.60 million. Often such campaigns were also launched at the time of entering a new market or introducing new flavors. Sales promotion campaigns similar to these were conducted regularly in different places. Such promotional campaigns were routinely planned as the key element of the overall marketing plan. Arun also encouraged its parlors to come up with local initiatives such as the "home-delivery scheme," etc.

Approach to Pricing and Franchisee Management

Typically Chandramogan followed a cost-plus approach for setting retail price of ice cream. Franchisees were given margins 20–25 per cent of maximum retail price

(MRP), depending on factors such as their location and the costs borne by them (relating to ordering, return of empty containers, etc). This left him with 75–80 per cent of the MRP towards manufacturing and other expenses as well as profits. Chandramogan estimated that for other ice cream manufacturers, this margin was probably in the region 65 per cent of the MRP. Unlike the reported two-tier distribution structure[3] of some of the other leading ice cream players such as Vadilal, a market leader in Western India, Chandramogan decided to follow a single-tier distribution strategy, directly supplying ice cream to the point of retail customer sales. Companies like Vadilal were believed to have very large number of distribution outlets. While the turnover of these companies were 50–70 per cent higher than Arun, their profitability was believed to be significantly lower which probably impaired their ability to continuously support their brands. Their three-tier distribution structure, Chandramogan believed, added substantially to their over-all cost of distribution in areas such as packaging, transportation (in refrigerated environment), and distribution margins. According to his estimates, the overall distribution cost of Arun was about 3–4 per cent of sales (mainly outward freight), compared to 8–9 per cent for other leading ice cream manufacturers. This also gave him room for manoeuvre. In the case of other leading ice cream brands, the retailer probably enjoyed a margin of about 12–15 per cent of the MRP.

Arun's factory took orders from franchisees by phone. The number of such calls during peak seasonal months could be as high as 800 a day. Upcountry franchisees were typically expected to make advance payment by demand draft to Arun against which fresh despatches would be made. As regards the franchisees based in Chennai, Arun's franchisee control department would present the cheques collected in advance, as soon as the ice cream supplies were made. Chandramogan strongly discouraged sale of ice cream except in pre-packaged factory packs with MRP marked thereon made available in different quantities/sizes. Franchisees were required to display prominently in the parlours the price list issued by Arun. Chandramogan figures that some 60–70 franchise arrangements might have been terminated for violation of MRP guidelines or payment terms.

Management and Organization

Over the years Chandramogan had recruited a group of senior managers in various functional positions. He was of the view that for a fledgling, entrepreneur-managed organization like Arun, the CEO had to be actively involved in the personnel and human resources management function and maintain a direct line of communication with the managers. One of his earliest recruitment was Shankar, an experienced ice cream technologist, for the production function at a time when Arun could barely afford him. Another key executive during Arun's growth phase was Adinarayan who played a stellar role in completing the Salem project in record time. By the mid 1990s a professional management team was in place in key functional positions. These included R. Chandramouli as Financial Controller and Company Secretary, V. Jaganathan, an MBA, as Marketing Manager, and Prasannakumar Menta as Head of Production. While the organization was adequately staffed with most employees growing with the organization, Chandramogan recognized that in the coming years Arun would definitely need to strengthen the senior and middle management cadres, preferably with executives having experience in large, more structured organizations such as multi-national companies. Chandramogan was proud of the fact that, except for a few days of strike/lockout in 1995, employee relations remained cordial.

Emerging Competitive Scenario

The organized segment of ice cream market in India had been historically controlled by strong regional players such as Kwality in the North and the East, Kwality and Vadilal in the West, and Dasaprakash, Joy and later Arun in the South. For every Vadilal or Arun there were hundreds of small-time ice cream producers in the unorganized sector selling ice cream under local brands or private labels. Moreover, most hotels and restaurants also made a limited range of ice cream flavors in-house for their captive needs. The fact that ice cream manufacture was reserved for the small scale industry (SSI) sector meant that even the bigger players had to necessarily source their ice cream requirements from SSI units which were often specifically set up by ice cream company owners or their family members. The established brands by and large were initially confined to the metropolitan cities in their region and later expanded to service other principal towns in the region. Vadilal, for example, had a fairly wide presence in Gujarat and was steadily extending its reach to other states in the West and even beyond. In the late 1980s, the multi-national company, Cadbury India, entered the ice cream market with its brand "Dollops". After the initial surge of consumer interest created by its launch, Dollops seemed to have failed to establish itself in the market. It also appeared that Cadbury itself was somewhat wavering in its support to the brand.

The ice cream market in India was completely shaken up by the entry of the consumer product giant Unilever, through one of its Indian subsidiaries, Brooke Bond India Limited[4] (BBIL). BBIL, which has been traditionally a tea and coffee beverage company had identified ice cream and other food products as thrust area for future growth. It entered processed-fruit segment (such as jam and sauce) by acquiring the market leader Kissan from the UB Group, the leading liquor manufacturers. BBIL also entered the frozen foods segment by establishing a new, state-of-the-art plant at Nasik in Western India and launched the well-known international brand of Unilever, Walls. As part of India's economic reforms launched in 1991 several of the extant restrictions relating to entry, capacity, output and size in a variety of sectors were being phased out or relaxed. BBIL and its leading stable-mate Hindustan Lever Limited (HLL) undertook a series of transactions to consolidate and strengthen the Unilever group's presence in several product-markets. Having identified frozen desserts as growth area, BBIL took no time in acquiring Dollops from Cadbury India and other leading brands of Kwality and Milkfood. With a leading international brand such as Walls and leading Indian brands such as Kwality in its portfolio, BBIL emerged as a major player in the ice cream/frozen dessert market overnight. The entry of an international food giant with deep pockets and tremendous staying power and one who would not be content with mere regional leadership, meant that the rules of competitive game in the ice cream market were being completely re-written. In February 1997, the Indian Government announced de-reservation of ice cream manufacture from the list of products earmarked for exclusive development in the SSI sector. This meant that large companies like Hindustan Lever could restructure the supply configuration of the business by setting up world-class ice cream manufacturing facilities with Unilever's technological support. Even as Arun emerged at the top spot in the four southern states, Chandramogan had to contend with the new competitive dynamics and re-work his own strategy.

Ownership Structure and Finances

When Chandramogan entered the ice cream business in 1970, it was through a partnership firm styled Chandramohan & Co. In March 1986, a private limited company by the name of Hatsun Foods Private Limited (HFPL) was incorporated in Chennai. On April 30, 1986, HFPL took over the business of Chandramohan & Co. as a going concern. The ownership of the brand name Arun was also later transferred to HFPL whereby, the company was allowed to register the brand name Arun in its own name, subject to a royalty payment of 1 per cent on the gross ice cream sales. In August 1995 the company's name was changed to Hatsun Milk Food Private Limited (HMFPL) and was also converted into a public limited company, Hatsun Milk Food Limited (HMFL) very soon thereafter.

In January 1996, HMFL was taken public through an initial public offering of 1.80 million shares at an issue price of ₹45 per share. Following this IPO, by March 1996, HMFL paid-up capital increased to ₹38.4 million from under ₹0.50 million and its net-worth including share premium account to ₹84.0 million from about ₹11.0 million just a year before. In view of the reservation of ice cream manufacture in the SSI sector[5] which precluded HMFL from carrying out ice cream production, HMFL was conceived to be a marketing company. Actual ice cream manufacturing continued to be carried out in the two closely-held registered small scale units Atlantic Foods in Salem and Hatsun Foods Company in Chennai. HMFL sourced its ice cream requirements from these two SSI units.

The financial performance of the ice cream business over the years reflected the sharp growth in volumes arising from aggressive franchise expansion and strong promotion of the Arun brand. For example, HMFL's spending on advertisement, promotion and related items amounted to ₹21.7 million in the year to March 1997, nearly 12 per cent of its fiscal 1997 sales of ₹184.1 million. The spending in rupee terms represented a near 100 per cent increase over the previous year. As can be seen from Exhibit 3, with a net-worth of over ₹100 million as of March 1997, the company's financial position had indeed been further strengthened. While this gave substantial strategic elbowroom for Chandramogan, he was acutely aware of the fact that the competitive and regulatory scenario had changed dramatically in recent months.

Strategic Challenges and Dilemmas

The principal worrying factor for Arun's management was the dramatic developments in the market place that

Exhibit 3 Key financial figures and other information

	(₹ million)								
	1988–89	**1989–90**	**1990–91**	**1991–92**	**1992–93**	**1993–94**	**1994–95**	**1995–96**	**1996–97**
Sales	8.6	27.8	38.4	36.7	42.5	55.3	65.6	138.5	184.1
Profit before taxes	0.07	0.1	4.2	0.2	2.3	2.7	3.7	18.1	21.3
Advertisement and promotion expenses	0.7	3.8	3.6	5.6	6.1	7.3	6.5	11.1	21.7
Shareholders' funds	0.5	0.7	3.2	2.9	6.5	9.4	11.1	83.9	107.0
No. of franchisees (end of year)		157	182	250	277	355	404	453	524

could seriously undermine its growth plans. The aggressive entry of the Unilever group (through BBIL since merged with HLL) into the ice cream/frozen dessert market through a series of acquisition of well-known regional brands, as noted earlier, was indeed a pregnant pointer to the remaining independent players. The enormous array of product portfolio and financial resources at its command meant HLL could support its ₹1500 million ice cream/frozen dessert business for any length of time and aggressively seek market share, even if this meant taking eyes off the business's profitability temporarily. And unlike the regional players who were happy not to disturb the regional competitive balance, HLL would not be content with anything less than leadership position in every single market. HLL's announced strategies for its Frozen Dessert and Ice Cream product group carried in its recent annual report were ringing ominous bells for the likes of Arun.

Your Company's Frozen Products business consolidated its leadership in the Ice Cream market with its national share exceeding 50 per cent despite strong low-priced competition in key markets. Your Company's brands have been consolidated under the house name "Kwality-Walls".

Extensive consumer research has provided valuable insights into the development and application of relevant technologies in product formulation and refrigerated product handling, which have begun to set new standards in terms of delivered product quality. The standard Ice Cream portfolio was consolidated under the "Dairy Classic" brand, a new recipe having better product stability and innovative virgin board food grade packaging were established. This is a significant move for an industry, which had hitherto been using non-food grade recycled packaging.

The business strengthened its efforts on brand building and innovation, which are the key drivers for the overall development of the Ice Cream category. The key brand franchises in the impulse segment, "Cornetto" and "Feast", the cornerstone of Unilever's Ice Cream presence worldwide, and "Chocobar" were strengthened with appropriate advertising—the first individual brands to be advertised in the Ice Cream category in the country. These brands have registered significant growth in all the markets ………. ………..

A major exercise was undertaken to upgrade the manufacturing facilities of your Company's Ice Cream sourcing units. Products, marketed under the Kwality-Walls brand name, conform fully to the stringent standards specified by the Bureau of Indian Standards and also to the more exacting Unilever norms on product safety and hygiene. This is a major milestone and a key differentiator for the Kwality-Walls brand……….[6]

For Chandramogan it was clear that he had to quickly re-work the competitive strategy for Arun. The key question was whether to aggressively reinforce Arun's competitive profile and further expand its franchisee network in the face of HLL's competitive onslaught or pursue alternative business opportunities woven around Arun's limited strengths and competencies. The latter strategy, he thought, while providing an alternative platform of growth might also be necessary from the point of his ability and the need to give continued support to the ice cream business. He was certainly determined that unlike several other Indian entrepreneurs in the FMCG sector, he would not sell-out to the MNCs.

NOTES

1. The term "Arun" is often used in the case, as a matter of convenience, to refer to the business entity as well.
2. The capacity of the Salem plant, it may be noted, was 5000 litres of ice cream mix a day.
3. The two-tier distribution structure included stockists who would handle distribution to retail channels.
4. In a series of consolidation transactions, another beverages company in the Unilever fold in India, Lipton Tea India Limited, was merged with Brooke Bond India Limited to form Brooke Bond Lipton India Limited (BBLIL). BBLIL was eventually merged with HLL effective January 1, 1996, to form a single consolidated food, soaps, detergents, and personal products giant.
5. It may be noted that de-reservation of ice cream was announced by the government only in February 1997.
6. Hindustan Lever Limited, Report and Accounts, 1996

Gujarat Co-Operative Milk Marketing Federation Limited (GCMMF)

CASE 3

S. Manikutty

We have traversed a path few have dared to. We are continuing on a path still fewer have the courage to follow. We must pursue a path that even fewer can dream to pursue. Yet, we must; because we hold in trust the aims and aspirations of millions of our countrymen. I am confident–as I know you are–that with the nation's dairy farmers by our side we cannot fail! Let us, therefore, resolve that however fulfilling our first twenty five years have been, in the next twenty five years we will transform the lives of millions more, opening for them the door to an India that is the land of our dreams.

Dr. Verghese Kurien
Chairperson, Gujarat Co-operative Milk Marketing Federation[1]

Across India, every morning, millions wake up to the taste of Amul, the flagship brand name for a variety of dairy products marketed by the Gujarat Co-operative Milk Marketing Federation (GCMMF). One may start the day by boiling (as is the traditional Indian practice) one of the different varieties of liquid milk supplied in pouches and making one's morning tea or coffee. If one prefers to use creamer, one could reach for the Amulya creamer on the kitchen shelf. For breakfast, butter the toasts with Amul regular butter or, if you are calorie conscious, with Amul Lite butter. Drink a cup of Amul chocolate milk. Make sandwiches with one of the different varieties of Amul cheese and take them to the office; add Amul ghee (clarified butter) to the lunch dishes; cook up a dish with Amul paneer or cottage cheese and indulge your sweet tooth with Amul gulab jamun mix. If it is a hot day, have an Amul ice cream; and when you return home after the office, relax with tea or coffee, whitened with Amulya creamer or Amul milk. If you are a pizza fan, bake a pizza and top it with Amul mozzarella cheese, and finally retire for the day with a glass of warm Amul milk. In India, Amul was not merely the most well-known brand, way ahead of Coca-Cola or Pepsi, and even ahead of age-old brands such as Dalda, Lifebuoy and Lux, but a lifestyle range of products, consumed in some form or other by a large number of Indians of different income and social strata.

GCMMF was the sole marketing agency for the products produced by the different milk co-operative member societies in Gujarat (see Exhibit 1 for a brief note on Gujarat and Exhibit 2 for a map of India showing Gujarat) and for those of other states marketing their products under the Amul brand name.

Case prepared by Professor S. Manikutty. The case writer wishes thank the Research and Publications Committee of the Indian Institute of Management, Ahmedabad for funding the writing of this case and to the executives of GCMMF, especially Dr. V. Kurien, Mr. B.M. Vyas and Mr. K.M. Jhala. The case is also available in multimedia format on a CD, with an oral presentation by the case writer.

Exhibit 1 Gujarat—A profile

Gujarat is one of the states of India, located on the western side of the country. It lies to the north of Maharashtra, whose capital is Bombay (now Mumbai). It has an area of 196,000 sq. km. (India's total area is 3,287,590 sq. km) and a population of 41 million (India's population is 1 billion). Its capital is Gandhinagar. Gujarat is among the most industrially advanced states of India and is also one of the most prosperous. India's per capita income in 1989–99 was $1,360, while Gujarat's was $1,430 (at PPP rates[2]). Gujarat's literacy rate in 1998–99 was 73 percent for males and 49 percent for females, with an average of around 61 percent, much higher than India's average of 52 percent.

Gujarat has had a history of political non-violence (Mahatma Gandhi came from this state) as well as cooperation among its people. This made it easier to start a cooperative movement there. Even today, Gujarat is considered to be one of the best states in the country to live in.

The climate of Gujarat varies a lot. On the western side is a rain-starved region, including a desert. North Gujarat has much more rain, but many regions are semi-arid. South Gujarat is fertile and receives about 700 mm of rains per year. Fodder for cattle is naturally linked with availability of rain, and many families have milch cattle in their houses, generally as a second source of income. There are a number of people with cattle who are nomadic and migrate in search of food and fodder.

Exhibit 2 Map of India showing Gujarat

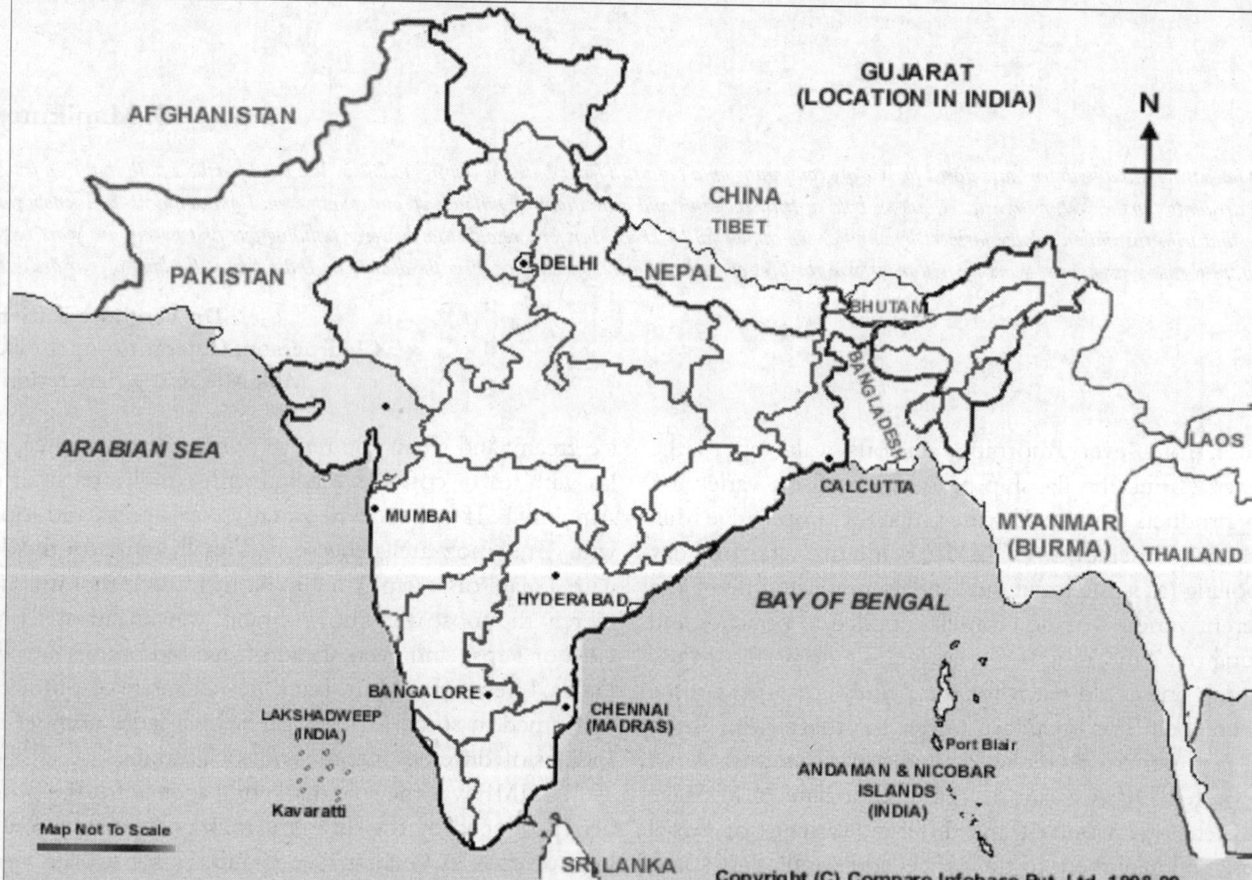

Historical Background of GCMMF

In the 1940s, in the district of Kaira in the state of Gujarat, India, a unique experiment was conducted that became one of the most celebrated success stories of India. At that time in Gujarat, milk was procured from farmers by private milk contractors and by a private company, Polson's Dairy in Anand, the headquarters of the district. The company had a virtual stranglehold on the farmers, deciding the prices of both the procured as well as the sold milk. The company arranged to collect milk, chill it and supply it to the Bombay Milk Scheme, which supplied milk to the metropolis of Bombay, and to cities in Gujarat. Polson's also extracted dairy products such as cheese and butter. Polson's used its monopoly to the maximum and the farmers were forced to accept very low prices for their products. The decisions of the company regarding the quality and even the quantity of milk supplied by the farmers were final.

In 1946, under inspiration from a leading freedom fighter, Mr. Vallabhbhai Patel (who belonged to Gujarat and who later became the Home Minister of Central Government), Mr. Tribhuvandas Patel, a local farmer, freedom fighter, and social worker, organized the farmers into co-operatives that would procure milk from the farmers, process the milk and sell it in Mumbai, including to the Bombay Milk Scheme. In 1949, purely by chance, a dairy engineer Dr. Verghese Kurien, who had just completed his studies in dairy engineering in the USA, came to India and was posted by the Government of India at the Dairy Research Institute at Anand. Settling down in Anand formed no part of his career plans. But a meeting with Tribhuvandas Patel changed his life and changed India's dairy industry.

What Mr. Patel requested to Dr. Kurien was hardly aimed to bring about such a revolution. All he wanted was help in fixing some problems about commissioning some of the equipment just purchased by his co-operative, especially the chilling and pasteurizing equipment. These items of equipment malfunctioned, leading to the rejection of large quantities of milk by the Bombay Milk Scheme.

Dr. Kurien's involvement with the Kaira District Co-operative Milk Producers' Union Limited (KDCMPUL) (that was the name of the co-operative registered) grew very rapidly from merely providing technical assistance in repairing, maintaining and ordering new equipment to the larger sociological issues involved in organizing the farmers into co-operatives and running these co-operatives efficiently. He observed the exploitation of farmers by the private milk contractors and Polson's and how the co-operatives could transform the lives of the members. The most important feature of these co-operatives was that they were run purely as farmers' cooperatives, with all the major decisions being taken by the farmers themselves. The co-operatives were not "run" by a separate bureaucracy with its own vested interests; the farmers were truly in charge of their own decisions. Any farmer could become a member by committing to supply a certain quantity of milk for a certain number of days in a year and would continue to be a member only if he kept this commitment. Each day, the farmers (or, actually, in most cases, their wives and daughters) would bring their milk to the village collection centres where the milk would be checked for the quantity in full view of all, and the quality (the fat content) would be checked through a simple hydrometer, again in full view of everyone present. The farmers would be paid in the evening for the milk supplied by them in the morning, and in the morning for the evening milk. This prompt settlement in cash was a great attraction to the farmers who were usually cash starved. Thanks to this mechanism, there were no disputes regarding the quantity or quality of milk supplied by each farmer.

It was soon clear that it was not enough to merely act as collection and selling agents for the farmers. A variety of support services were required to enable the farmers to continue selling their milk of the desired quality and to avoid disasters such as death of their cattle. For a family owning just one or two cattle and depending on its milk for their income, the death of cattle could spell disaster. The farmers were progressively given new services such as veterinary care, supply of quality cattle feed, education on better feeding of cattle and facilities for artificial insemination of their cattle[3]. All these were strictly on payment basis, none of the services were free.

This experiment of organizing farmers into co-operatives was one of the most successful interventions in India. A very loyal clientele was built up who experienced prosperity on a scale they had not dreamt of ten years earlier. With good prices being paid for their milk, raising milch cattle could become a good source of supplementary income for many households. The co-operatives were expanded to cover more and more areas of Gujarat and in each area, a network of local village level co-operatives and district level co-operatives were formed on a pattern similar to that at Anand (the so-called Anand pattern). KDCMPUL became better known by the brand name of its products (Amul) than by the name of the co-operative itself. Amul means "priceless" in Sanskrit. It was a word easily pronounceable and remembered and carried a positive connotation. This became the flagship brand for all the dairy products made by the union.

In 1954, KDCMPUL built a plant to convert surplus milk produced in the cold seasons into milk powder and butter[4]. In 1958, a plant to manufacture cheese and one to produce baby food were added. Subsequent years saw the addition of more plants to produce different products. In 1973, the milk societies/district level unions decided to set up a marketing agency to market their products. This agency was the GCMMF. It was registered as a co-operative society on July 9, 1973[5]. It had, as its members (ordinary share holders), the district level milk unions. No individual could become a shareholder in GCMMF. Starting from a daily procurement of 250 litres per day in 1946, the cooperative had become a milk giant with milk procurement at about 4 million litres per day by 1999 and 12 dairy plants all over the Gujarat.

The Structure of the Anand Pattern

The co-operative system formed under the Anand pattern had a three-tiered structure (Exhibit 3). At the base was the village-level dairy co-operative society. This was composed of the milk producers, mostly residents of the same area, who had joined the co-operative society. A typical membership figure would be about 200. A managing committee of about 8–9 members was elected, one of whom was elected as the chairperson. Care was taken to ensure that these meetings were held, and seen to be held, in an open and transparent manner. Next was the district level. This co-operative (called unions) had as its members, the village dairy co-operative societies within the district, represented by the chairpersons of the village level societies. For this co-operative, a Board of Directors consisting of 12 persons was elected from among the members (that is, the chairpersons of the village level co-operatives), with its own Chief Executive, called the Managing Director (MD). The third level was at the state level, where the co-operative (GCMMF in Gujarat) was formed with district-level milk unions (and certain other milk unions from other states) as members. The state-level organization was called a federation. The Board of Directors of the federation comprised the chairpersons of the district level co-operatives and the following ex officio members:

Exhibit 3 The Anand pattern

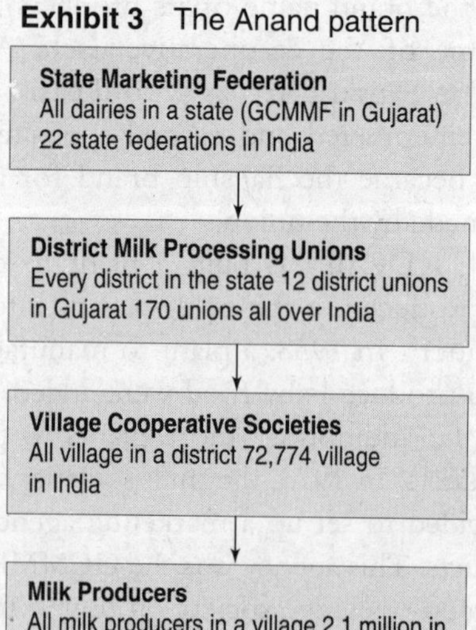

1. The registrar of co-operatives of the state concerned.
2. A representative from the National Dairy Development Board (NDDB), which was a body created by the Government of India to replicate the Anand pattern in other states of India.
3. One nominated technical expert.
4. The MD (CEO) of the state-level federation.

GCMMF was the state level federation in Gujarat.

Broadly, the village-level cooperatives did the procurement, the district level did the transportation and processing, and the federation marketed the product. The federation also handled strategic planning and investment[6].

Each of the levels had a substantial amount of autonomy. For example, the village-level societies decided entirely on their own who should be admitted as a member, and what price the farmers should be paid for their milk. Thus, the prices paid to farmers by different village societies in the state could be, and in fact were, different. The district-level unions purchased milk from the village-level societies and decided what price they would pay for the milk supplied by the village level societies. They, in turn, supplied milk to the state-level union, which decided what price it would pay the district unions. The price paid to all the district unions was the same.

In this system, GCMMF planned the type and quantity of products it would manufacture and sell each year. Milk products were produced in the state by different factories owned by the district unions. There were, for example, six butter factories and seven milk powder factories in Gujarat. GCMMF did not have its own factories as such until recently, when it set up a dairy at Gandhinagar near Ahmedabad. There was a committee, called the Programming Committee, which consisted of (i) the MD of GCMMF, (ii) MDs of the District Unions, (iii) their Head, Quality Control, GCMMF, and (iv) Head, Finance, GCMMF. This committee decided the product mix for the coming year based on the plans made by GCMMF, and translated the plans into monthly allocations to each union for the quantity of milk to be supplied.

As on April 2000, there were 10,800 village level co-operatives in Gujarat under the GCMMF umbrella with 2.1 million milk producers. Out of 25 districts in the state, there were district-level unions in 12 districts[7].

A pattern similar to the Anand pattern had also been replicated in other Indian states under the "Operation Flood" program launched by the Government of India.

The NDDB (National Dairy Development Board) was set up to coordinate the project. Dr. Kurien was the chairperson of NDDB and the main moving force behind this program. As on April 2000, there were 22 state federations in India, with 170 district-level unions, 72,774 village-level societies and 9.31 million milk producer members in the different states.

Each of the state-level federations marketed their own brands. Amul was the brand marketed by GCMMF. Vijaya was marketed by the federation in Andhra Pradesh. Interestingly, the state-level federations could market their own products under their own brands anywhere in India, thus competing against their sister federations. Thus, GCMMF could market its Amul butter in Andhra Pradesh to compete with Vijaya butter. The NDDB officials were of the conviction that such competition was healthy and would curb monopolistic tendencies.

Objectives and Business Philosophy of GCMMF

The main stakeholder of GCMMF was the farmer member for whose welfare, the GCMMF executives held, it existed. Thus, in an interesting reply, the MD of GCMMF, Mr. B. M. Vyas, told the case writer:

"Unlike other organizations, our objective is not to maximize our profit. After all, the farmers themselves are the owners of the federation. We are restricted by our bye-laws, to giving a maximum of 12 percent on the paid share capital as the dividend. So we are more interested in giving the best price to the farmers for their milk than in making a large profit. Thus, we look at the price given to our suppliers as not a cost but as an objective."

GCMMF had been, as its main objective, "carrying out activities for the economic development of agriculturists by efficiently organizing marketing of milk and dairy produce, veterinary medicines, vaccines and other animal health products, agricultural produce in raw and/or processed form and other allied produce."[8] This was to be done through

- common branding,
- centralized marketing,
- centralized quality control,
- centralized purchases, and
- pooling of milk efficiently.

GCMMF had declared as its business philosophy the following:

- To serve the interests of milk producers
- To provide quality products that offer the best value to consumers for money spent[9]

The biggest strength of GCMMF was the trust it had created in the minds of its consumers regarding the quality of its products. GCMMF and its brand Amul, explained Mr. Vyas, stood for guaranteed purity of all its products. Adulteration was simply not an option. In India, where such trust was hard to come by, this was a central anchor for GCMMF's future business plans, said Mr. Vyas.

Organization Structure of GCMMF

GCMMF was a lean organization (See Exhibit 4), which their executives believed led to a cost advantage. At its headquarters in the town of Anand, three general managers (GMs) and five assistant general managers (AGMs) assisted the MD, or the CEO. The three GMs looked after marketing, HRD, and quality assurance. The GM (marketing) was in charge of the entire marketing operations for the dairy products, liquid milk, and ice cream. This GM was assisted by one AGM (marketing, dairy products), managers (commercial, exports, liquid milk, and ice cream). The GM (HRD) also looked after edible oils, administration, legal matters and new opportunities. The whole country was divided into five zones, each

Exhibit 4 Organization structure of GCMMF

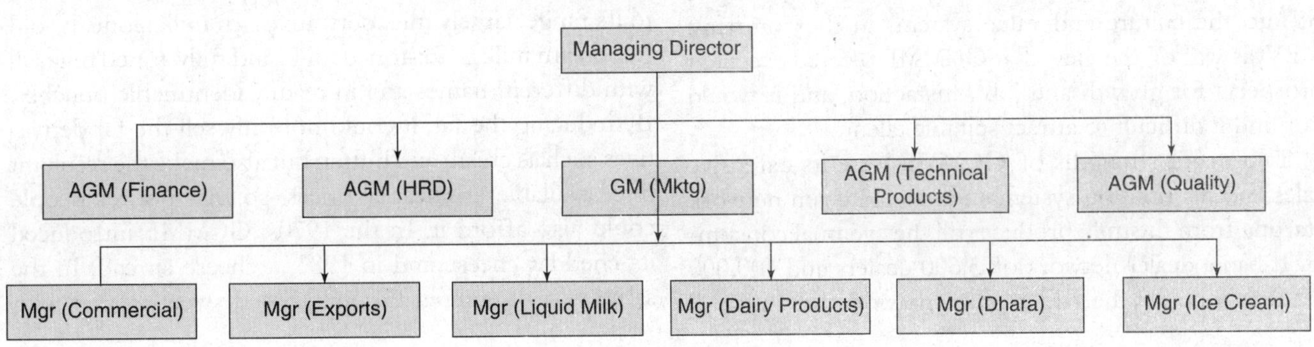

headed by a zonal manager responsible for the sales of all the products in that zone. They reported to the MD, but functionally each also reported to the various AGMs/GM at the headquarters. Under the zonal managers were the branch managers. Generally there were three product managers in each branch reporting to the branch manger: one each for edible oil, dairy products and ice cream. They were assisted by sales officers and field salespersons. There were 48 sales offices spread over the country (of which only two were in Gujarat). The entire country was represented in this structure. GCMMF had one overseas office at Dubai.

GCMMF had links with the Institute of Rural Management, Anand (IRMA), a premier management institute set up to train MBAs who would work in rural areas. It was set up under the NDDB umbrella. In the early years, IRMA charged no tuition fee at all to its students, who, in return had to furnish a bond to serve in rural areas for a specified length of time. This system did not seem to work, since many students reneged from their bond obligations and many more quit later on and took up higher-paid jobs in the private sector once their bond term was over. Hence, IRMA had given up this scheme, and the students were now charged the full fees. But a strong value orientation was given to the students of IRMA to motivate them to work in rural areas and for the poor. GCMMF drew a number of its managers from IRMA and other business schools in India, although not from the premier management schools. The salaries offered by GCMMF were decent, though nowhere close to those offered by the private sector, especially MNCs. The gap between the salaries offered by organizations such as GCMMF and the salaries expected by B-school graduates was gradually increasing. Some observers of the management job scene in India opined that even well-established and relatively well-paying organizations such as the Tatas will soon find it difficult to attract talent. For organizations like GCMMF, this could be an even more difficult situation.

Countering this perception, GCMMF executives, in interviews with the case writer, said that GCMMF had never relied on top B-school talent, since they would not fit into the culture and value systems in the company. Mr.Vyas was of the view that GCMMF offered excellent prospects for growth and job satisfaction, and it would not find it difficult to attract suitable talent.

Two major strengths of GCMMF were its extensive sales and distribution system and its cold chain network starting from the milk producer till the eventual consumer. It had a dealer network of 3,600 dealers and 400,000 retailers, one of the largest such networks in India. A cold chain had been established that linked all these dealers and retailers. It consisted of the following:

- A set of chillers near each village that could ensure chilling of milk;
- Quick transportation to the district union facilities where the milk could be further chilled and dispatched to the consumers or to the processing units for conversion into milk products;
- Refrigerated trucks to transport the milk products such as butter and cheese from the factories;
- Local chilling of milk to ensure its quick distribution to the customers through a network of trucks in many cities so that most consumers could have their milk sachets by 6 am, if not earlier;
- Deep freezers and refrigeration equipment on the dealers' premises to keep the products cold and prevent their deterioration; and
- Facilities in super markets and even larger retail stores to keep the products fresh.

This cold chain was considered by the executives of GCMMF as its major strength.

GCMMF had excellent relationships with what were called super markets in India (actually these were just large departmental stores) which stocked their products, especially cheese, butter, milk powder, sweets, and, in some cases, milk.

A remarkable innovation introduced by GCMMF in the 1970s was the movement of chilled milk from Anand all the way to Delhi and Calcutta in specially insulated railway wagons. These wagons reached their destinations overnight in the case of Delhi and the second day in the case of Calcutta, and were still fresh on their arrival. The experiment was so successful that it has continued the practice ever since.

Diversification Moves by GCMMF

Even at the time of its formation, GCMMF had three major products in its portfolio: liquid milk, butter, and milk powder. Gradually, many new products were added to its range, largely milk derivatives. In milk alone, it sold full-cream milk, semi-toned milk, and fully-toned milk, all with different names and in readily identifiable pouches. By reducing the fat, it could not only sell the fat derivatives such as cream and butter, but also make the resultant milk available at cheaper prices, so that poorer people could also afford it. In the 1970s, GCMMF introduced its cheddar cheese and in 1983, a cheese spread. In the same year, it entered the milk-based sweet market with the introduction of Amul Shrikhand (a form of yogurt). Thereafter, Amulya, a dairy whitener was introduced and was priced below the prevailing brands. It soon became the market leader. In the 1990s GCMMF introduced a lot of new products: a condensed milk called Amul Mithaimate; Amul Lite, a low fat, low cholesterol butter spread, and Amul ice cream. After 1996, it went on to introduce a still greater variety of products: pizza (mozzarella) cheese, cheese slice, cheese powder, malai paneer (a form of cottage cheese), gulab jamun mix (a sweet primer to be processed by deep frying to make a sweet called gulab jamun), buttermilk, a chocolate-based beverage called Nutramul, and chocolates.

In 1996, GCMMF launched its Amul brand of ice cream. India's ice cream market was estimated to be around ₹8 billion in 2000. GCMMF launched its ice creams in 14 flavors in the city of Mumbai and the state of Gujarat. It was priced at about 30 percent less than the prevailing prices, and it also emphasized that it did not contain any gelatin. In less than a year, Amul ice cream commanded a share of about 55 percent in Gujarat and 30 percent in Mumbai[10]; by the year 2000, its share in India as a whole had reached 30 percent. In 1997, GCMMF also scored a major achievement when it managed to get some of the co-operatives in other states of the country, trying to launch their own ice cream brands, to sell all their ice creams under the Amul brand name. This enabled GCMMF to leverage the capacity of more than 180 co-operatives in the country, with a milk procurement of more than 11 million litres per day, and located close to the markets[11].

In addition, it also diversified into non-milk products. The most important of this diversification was into edible oils in 1988. At that time, the prices of edible oils were being manipulated by oil traders with the result that the prices were shooting up to unacceptable levels. Even though oil seed growers' co-operatives existed, most of them were run badly and losing money. Edible oils have always been a very sensitive subject in India, leading to even fall of governments. Hence, the government persuaded NDDB to arrange for procurement of clean, unadulterated groundnut oil and sell it through its own outlets. Thus, it was essentially a market intervention operation. Besides, this provided NDDB to re-organize the groundnut farmers' co-operatives much as it had done with milk-producer farmers four decades earlier. Gujarat was the right state for this experiment, since more than 60 percent of the country's groundnut oil production was accounted for by Gujarat. GCMMF marketed this oil on behalf of NDDB. GCMMF launched a new brand name Dhara (literally meaning flow), not wanting to carry over the Amul brand name which was deeply associated in the public mind with milk derivatives. It sold its oil on a platform of absolute purity, a claim it could justifiably make and since much of the edible oil in India was (and continues to be) adulterated, purity could be a differentiating factor. It also coined the slogan, *Dhara, Shudh Dhara*, literally meaning, flow, pure flow. The launch was supported by an advertising campaign with a catchy jingle. Later, mustard and certain other oils were also marketed under the Dhara brand name. Even though the oil traders fought back bitterly and often violently, and used their political connections to the full, Dhara was able to hold its own and became the leading brand of packaged edible oils in the country. However, it must be said that dealing in edible oils was found to be a far more difficult task as compared to dealing in milk.

In the late 1990s, GCMMF undertook distribution of fruit-based products on behalf of NDDB. This was done under yet another brand name introduced by GCMMF: Safal (literally meaning fruitful, having achieved). Under this name were launched a mango drink sold in tetrapacks (also in small 100 ml sizes to be served in aircraft), tomato ketchup, and a mixed fruit jam. In fact, the launches of all these products were completed in a single year, 1998–99.

By the year 2000, the range of products marketed by GCMMF was truly wide: three varieties of milk, flavored milk, buttermilk, four varieties of milk powder, two varieties of butter, five varieties of cheese, two varieties of ghee clarified butter, chocolates, chocolate drink, sweets, ice creams, edible oils and fruit and vegetable-based products. Refer to Exhibit 5 for product portfolio of GCMMF as in 2000. At the time of writing this case, GCMMF was launching milk in tetrapacks in the Mumbai market.

Except in ice creams, chocolates, and chocolate-based beverages, Amul brand was the market leader in each and every one of its products. Exhibit 5 also shows the market shares of the various products of GCMMF. Its main sources of competitive advantage were seen by its executives as: (i) low costs due to the elimination of middlemen, a lean organization and relatively lower pay scales as compared to MNCs (ii) its scale and scope of operations, and (iii) its strong brand name which stood for purity and quality.

Exhibit 5 GCMMF: Product portfolio

Category	Market Share	Market Position
Liquid Milk Full-fat milk Semi-toned milk Fully-toned milk	N.A.	1
Butter Amul Butter Amul Lite, a low fat butter spread Amul Ghee and Sagar Ghee (two different brands), a highly aromatic clarified butter	 85 80 8 10	 1 1 2 1
Milk Powder Amul Spray, infant milk food Amul milk powder, instant full cream milk powder Sagar, skimmed milk powder Amulya, dairy whitener	 65 80 40 60	 1 1 1 1
Cheese Amul pasteurized processed cheddar cheese Amul cheese spreads in three flavours Amul Mozzarella Cheese, pizza cheese Amul Emmental Cheese, a form of cheese similar to Swiss cheese Amul Paneer, cottage cheese used in Indian curries Amul cheese powder	 50 90 100	 1 1
Ice Creams Amul Ice Creams	30	2
Sweets Amul Shrikhand Amul Mithai Gulab Jamun Amul Mithai Mate, condensed milk	50	1
Chocolates Amul Chocolates in a wide variety of flavours	10	3
Chocolate Drinks Nutramul	15	4
Edible Oils Dhara edible oils, groundnut, vegetable (mustard) Dhara Health, low-cholesterol oil	12	
Fruit and Vegetable based Products Safal fruit drinks Safal tomato ketchup Safal mixed fruit jam	N.A.	

Source: Data supplied by GCMMF.

Out of the total procurement of 4.6 million litres of milk per day, about 2.2 million litres were sold as liquid milk and the rest as milk products. The present per capita milk consumption in India at about 225 gms per day was still way below that in developed countries and even less than that in many developing countries. Thus, there was a need and scope for increasing the consumption of milk in its liquid form, although for every rupee spent, the nutrition value of milk was way below other high protein and fat items, both vegetarian and non-vegetarian.

Out of its total income of ₹18 billion, approximately ₹2.75 billion was accounted for by sale of liquid milk; about ₹3 billion by edible oils; ₹4 billion by butter; about ₹2.4 billion by ice creams; and the rest by the other products. The exact break-up of these products was not available. The share of processed fruits and vegetable items was still quite small.

The growth rates in different segments were quite different. The following table gives the approximate growth rates in these segments:

Table 1 Growth rates in GCMMF's businesses

			(Percent)
	1996–97	1997–98	1998–99
Liquid milk procurement	24.6	3.8	3.6
Liquid milk	N.A.	14	10
Butter	27	8	13
Cheese	N.A.	37	39
Ghee	41	31	N.A.
Milk powder	0	0	18
Ice cream	N.A.	100	100
Edible oils	13	20	18

Source: GCMMF Annual reports

The profit margin in milk was generally low. NDDB and GCMMF had as one of their important objectives, promotion of milk consumption, especially by the poor people. To achieve its objective, GCMMF tried to keep the price of liquid milk as low as it could. Edible oils were also low margin items, their sales prices being controlled rigidly by the government and input prices being essentially set by the oil traders. In the words of Mr. Kurien, they were in this business due to larger societal considerations than for the sake of profits.

Competition in Different Products

The nature of competition varied among the different products. In the case of liquid milk, competition was from private dairies and contractors. There was also competition from newly emerging private dairies that had started supplying milk to the consumers as well as sweet makers. There was intense competition for the supply of milk, which was much sought after, especially in the festival seasons, by the sweet makers who derived large profits from the sale of their sweets. Consumers were generally not very particular about the brand of liquid milk, so that the sales depended to a large extent on dealer push. However, there was scope to establish differentiation by apprising the customers of the quality not only of the initial milk itself, but also the quality of the supply chain, which ensured the stability of milk.

New entrants were making their mark in butter and cheese. Britannia, a firm engaged in manufacture and sale of biscuits, had entered into the foods business, and more particularly, in milk and milk-related products such as butter. Britannia had introduced new forms of cheese such as cheddar cheese slices, and supported its products with extensive advertising campaigns. It was believed that advertisements played a powerful role in the demand for particular brands of butter and cheese.

The sweet market was highly fragmented, with numerous small-time local operators producing their own brands and unbranded forms of sweets. The sales of sweets soared in the festival seasons, drawing milk supply by offering higher prices. Other food companies such as Hindustan Lever Limited (HLL), a subsidiary of Levers, and Nestle had also entered into the business of ready-made or near-ready sweets (such as gulab jamun) which just needed to be deep-fried to have it ready). Branded ready or near-ready sweets were advertised and heavily promoted through campaigns such as through mail orders to housewives.

Ice cream was an emerging market in India, witnessing the entry of numerous players. The national scene was dominated by HLL with its Kwality and Walls brands, accounting for about 45 percent of the market. GCMMF was the other national player, with about 30 percent of the market. There were, in addition, very powerful regional players such as Vadilal Ice Creams in Western India, which commanded a substantial share (in excess of 30 percent) of the regional market. Ice creams were largely promoted through local promotions, hoardings (billboards) and advertisements. About ice creams, Mr. Vyas said in an interview to the author:

> *In ice creams, positioning and promotions are not the only things. The Indian ice cream market is likely to expand very rapidly. The Indian consumer is changing. They will not just stick to milk. Ice creams will no longer be made at home. A large number of consumers with disposable incomes will seek value-added products, including ice cream. We shall target these consumers. Our strategy will be to manufacture and market them locally through our network. Our emphasis will be on quality. Our devotion to quality will be total and constant.*

Edible oils were of two types: loose and branded. Loose oil constituted the bulk (perhaps about 70 percent) of the total market. Among the branded oils, there were many which were just local names with little brand recall. The main branded players were Dhara and ITC's oil division, with many brands. It was believed that with increasing disposable income, the tastes of consumers would swing more to the branded end of the market. Most of the advertisements were either on the purity platform or on the health platform (zero cholesterol or low cholesterol).

In the processed fruits and vegetable foods business, there were numerous players, many regional. The largest player was HLL, which was moving away from its soaps and detergents business to the foods business. HLL was the largest fast moving consumer goods (FMCG) company in India, with a turnover of ₹101 billion and profit of ₹1 billion in the year 1998–99[12]. In the last two years, it had undertaken massive expansion through acquisitions, the most notable of them being in the tea, ready-to-cook flour, bread, and ice cream businesses. HLL was considered to be a well-run company, with aggressive marketing styles and a highly result-oriented culture. It was one of the largest ad spenders in India. It had recently announced its Millennium Plan, which envisioned a growth rate of 100 percent every four years, most of it coming from its food business. HLL owned many powerful brands such as Kissan in the ketchups and jams segment. Even though it was extremely difficult to estimate the actual size of India's processed foods market due to the proliferation of numerous local companies, it was considered a huge market with high potential for growth. Since the percentage of food that was processed was still quite small, it was expected that this sector will provide high opportunities for growth. But precisely for this reason, many MNCs were jumping into the fray, among them being, besides HLL, Nestle, and Pepsi. Thus, this emerging market was expected to be fiercely competitive.

Advertisement and Promotion by GCMMF

GCMMF had shown itself to be remarkably savvy in its advertisement and promotion campaigns. It had coined truly memorable slogans such as the one for butter: "Utterly Butterly Delicious"; for edible oils: "Dhara, Shudh Dhara", emphasizing its purity; a campaign titled "The Taste of India" for all its products, featuring Indian recipes and lifestyle; a campaign to promote drinking of milk, purely based on the nutritional value and taste. It was the first Indian company to put up advertisement hoardings (billboards) based on a topical and current news item that almost brought traffic to a stop. The hoardings, started in 1967, and handled by the advertising agency, DaCunha Associates, were changed weekly and every week it had a current and a new theme. This has continued till this day. Exhibit 6 shows some of the memorable advertisements. For example, during the Emergency in 1976–77, when forced sterilizations were done under government compulsion, the Amul hoarding read: "We have always practised compulsory sterilization". When UK was reeling under the Mad Cow Disease, GCMMF came out with an ad titled "Union Jacked by Mad Cows". These ads, topical, witty and humorous, served the purpose of high recall, powerful appeal and sustained awareness of the products.

Exhibit 6 Some interesting Amul advertisements 1976–77

On compulsory sterilization introduced during Mrs. Indira Gandhi's regime

When helmets were made compulsory in Bombay

Some Interesting Amul Advertisements 1996–97

On the mad cow disease

On the infighting within the Congress Government during the general election

On the unruly behavior of the Calcutta crowds during the 1996 World Cup Cricket

Some Interesting Amul Advertisements 1999–2000

No need for explanation

On the situation in Bihar when Mr. Laloo Prasad Yadav installed his own wife as the Chief Minister when he was disqualified to hold the position

On a bus strike in Mumbai

In ice creams, GCMMF emphasized in its advertisements that its product was entirely vegetarian, made of pure milk and that it did not have any gelatin content, unlike that made by many of its competitors (Indian ice creams usually contained vegetable oils and gelatin in addition to milk, so that in a sense, they were frozen desserts rather than ice creams). According to Mr. Vyas, the MD, the aim of the ads was not merely to stimulate interest, but also to expand the markets so that ice creams would not be seen as merely a food for the rich.

GCMMF sponsored television programmes as well. It was the sponsor, from the very beginning, of one of India's most widely watched and appreciated programmes, Surabhi, on India's national television network, Doordarshan. Doordarshan had a reach of more than 85 percent of the country's population, and its programmes commanded viewerships exceeding 60 percent, far more than any of the private channels and cable networks, which had limited reach in cities and towns. Surabhi was an hour's programme telecast at 9 pm on Sundays and showcased India's diverse culture and traditions. The programme had started the concept of posing questions at the end of each episode and inviting readers to send their replies, with handsome prizes for correct replies. The innovation was such a success that many viewers watched the programme for this feature, and their replies were so much in number that it almost choked the postal system (a typical programme drew about 50,000 to 100,000 replies!). GCMMF also sponsored a popular show, called Amul India Show on Star TV, telecast at 10 am on Sundays.

GCMMF had also sponsored two well-received feature films. The first film *Manthan* featured the exploitation of village farmers and the formation of co-operatives. It was, in a sense, the story of GCMMF itself. The second film, *Sardar*, featured the life of Sardar Vallabhbhai Patel, the first Home Minister of the country. Known as the Iron Man of India, he brought about the unification of the different princely states of India.

In addition, GCMMF has produced a number of TV campaigns of 30–60 seconds' duration, for many of its products.

GCMMF and Its Programme for Management of Change

The Government of India liberalized its dairy sector in 1991, making it possible for private players to enter the industry (it was hitherto reserved for the co-operative sector). Based on this stimulus, GCMMF looked at all its operations, strengths, weaknesses and the opportunities available, and assessed that it had to become more customer-centric (rather than merely being farmer or supplier-centric, as was the case earlier). It concluded that its strength lay in playing the volume game and hence an expansion in the customer base as well as product portfolio was essential. This required paying close attention to customer needs and quality. It realized that merely being mouthing these ideas was not enough; the entire supply chain had to function accordingly. Hence, it launched a Total Quality Management (TQM) program to ensure the high quality of products, right from the starting point (the village farmer who supplied milk), through the value chain, until it reached the consumer. This meant the need for the involvement of farmers, transporters, factory personnel, wholesalers and retailers, each of whom had a role to play. For example, if the retailer did not take care of the refrigeration, the product could deteriorate, leading to a bad name for GCMMF and its brand, Amul.

What began as a TQM movement gradually became a movement for management of change (MOC) in the entire value chain. GCMMF's MOC was launched in six areas: cleanliness of the dairy co-operative societies, planning and budgeting of the dairy co-operative society, artificial insemination service, quality testing and milk measurement by the dairy co-operatives, animal feeding and management practices, and self leadership development. Much emphasis was placed on the village-level quality control, since this was a sine quo non for subsequent consistency in quality. MOC in the factories meant close control over the operations, including cleanliness. MOC at the wholesaler level meant that their transportation and storage practices were to be closely controlled. Quality circles were formed among the wholesalers, working in tandem with the sales force. The idea was to make everyone aware of the importance of quality and the systems needed to support high quality on a continuing basis.

Growth and Financials of GCMMF

In the recent years, GCMMF had been registering an annual growth of nearly 20 percent. Exhibit 7 shows the growth rate from 1984–85 till 1998–99. Exhibit 8 gives the balance sheets and Exhibit 9 the income statements of GCMMF for the years 1993–94 to 1998–99.

Exhibit 7 Growth rates from 1984–85 till 1998–99

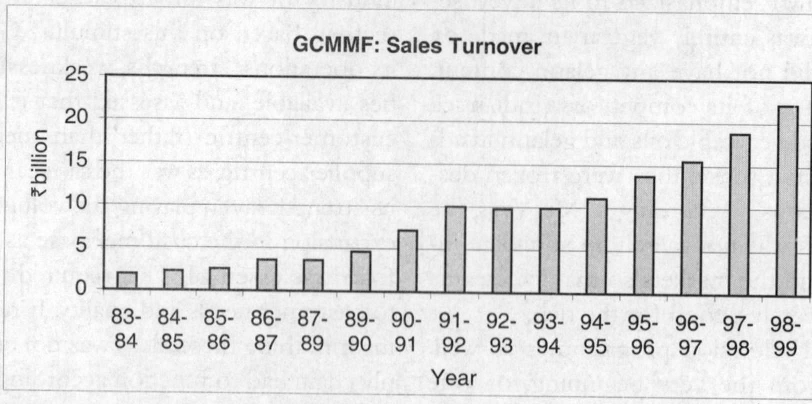

Exhibit 8 GCMMF: Balance Sheets, 1994–99

						₹ million
	31.3.1994	**31.3.1995**	**31.3.1996**	**31.3.1997**	**31.3.1998**	**31.3.1999**
LIABILITIES						
Authorized Share Capital						
200,000 shares@₹1000	200.00	200.00	200.00	200.00	500.00	500.00
Paid up Share Capital						
80,000 shares @₹1000	69.20	80.00	80.10	130.00	200.00	200.00
Reserves and Other Funds						
Reserve fund	16.65	18.62	21.98	42.43	83.09	115.62
General fund	19.96	20.18	20.90	72.37	157.75	225.04
Grant from NDDB under Operation Flood	1.04	1.04	1.04	1.04	0.01	2.04
Grant from NDDB for Gandhinagar dairy Project	243.52	300.76	314.86	321.08	177.03	150.92
Export turnover Allowance reserve	0.04	0.04	0.04	0.00	0.00	0.00
	281.20	340.64	358.82	436.92	417.88	493.62
Loans and Advances						
Cash credit			9.41		36.46	52.45
From NDDB under Operation Flood	3.75	3.75	3.73	3.70	3.51	0.00
From NDDB for Gandhinagar dairy Project	610.77	817.31	546.42	579.63	547.33	555.06
	614.53	821.06	559.56	583.33	587.30	607.51
Current Liabilities and Provisions						
Sundry creditors	574.99	310.83	212.62	271.82		
Outstanding against purchases	728.37	496.80	1185.78	1365.78	1290.81	1025.89
Outstanding against expenses	81.53	65.42	106.20	116.15		
Deposits	7.59	9.84	11.90	50.25	70.70	108.71
Provision for income tax	32.38	32.38	32.38	51.58		

Provision for dividend	5.54	9.06	9.61	14.10	21.90	30.00
For education fund	0.16	0.30	0.30	0.30	0.30	0.30
Carried to general and reserve funds	2.19	4.08	71.88	63.44		
	1432.90	929.02	1630.67	1933.42	1383.71	1164.90
Total	**2,397.67**	**2,170.41**	**2629.15**	**3083.68**	**2588.89**	**2466.03**

₹ million

	31.3.1994	31.3.1995	31.3.1996	31.3.1997	31.3.1998	31.3.1999
Fixed Assets						
Land	12.33	14.08	14.38	14.27	14.27	14.27
Buildings	16.17	100.71	155.53	177.74	204.39	213.41
Plant and machinery	---	526.99	896.33	914.07	1112.92	1245.18
Other items	28.28	57.99	78.32	158.19	107.03	133.69
	56.78	**699.77**	**1144.56**	**1264.27**	**1438.61**	**1606.55**
Less: Depreciation	24.22	95.50	202.70	306.95	568.16	733.90
	32.56	**604.27**	**941.86**	**957.32**	**870.45**	**872.64**
Work in progress	867.26	409.08	26.02	55.50	31.45	3.22
	899.82	**1013.36**	**967.88**	**1012.82**	**901.90**	**875.86**
Investments in Shares	**3.28**	**3.28**	**3.28**	**3.28**	**3.30**	**3.30**
Inventories						
Stores, spares, packing materials etc.				31.86	38.14	37.35
R.M.S.				13.57	16.48	10.89
Stock in process				7.59	11.96	6.98
FIG				1141.66	983.77	781.79
Scraps				--	0.06	0.02
	735.91	**665.64**	**762.01**	**1194.67**	**1050.41**	**837.03**
Advances & Debtors						
Sundry debtors	63.44	98.02	283.47	137.25	95.87	82.87
Advances	425.53	62.50	20.90	43.17	41.37	66.73
Advance payment of income tax less provisions	44.49	42.18	30.80	60.70	20.96	22.36
Security deposits	2.89	3.22	3.55	8.01	3.77	4.63
Balance with Government					3.19	2.11
	536.35	**205.92**	**338.72**	**249.13**	**165.16**	**178.70**
Deferred Revenue Expenditure	--	**9.12**	**6.84**	**4.56**	**2.28**	**0.00**
Cash & Bank Balance						
Cash on hand incl. Cheques	33.48	44.06	291.48	171.59	99.47	170.53
Balances with banks	166.93	172.48	236.34	420.06	314.53	357.81
Remittances in transit	21.91	56.56	22.58	27.57	51.83	42.80
	222.32	**273.11**	**550.41**	**619.22**	**465.83**	**571.14**
	2397.67	**2170.41**	**2629.15**	**3083.68**	**2588.89**	**2466.02**

Source: Annual Reports of GCMMF.

Exhibit 9 GCMMF: profit and loss accounts, 1993–94 to 1998–99

						₹. million
	1993-94	1994-95	1995-96	1996-97	1997-98	1998-99
By Sales (net of excise duty)*	7633.62	9081.92	11116.89	12529.53	15137.57	18113.01
Sales of Dhara	2255.30	2058.50	2676.00	2804.30	3698.40	4079.30
Total Turnover	9888.92	11140.42	13792.89	15333.83	18835.97	22192.31
Service charges and commission	38.96	34.85	45.74	50.31	57.59	68.46
Income from investments					0.71	0.75
Interest on loans, deposits etc.					5.22	8.72
Exchange rate differences (net)					3.54	2.86
Export incentives					1.82	1.80
Unspent liabilities and provisions no longer required to be written back**					1.41	18.59
Miscellaneous income@	1.84	3.86	13.09	34.12	5.02	14.76
Prior period adjustments				1.74		
	40.80	38.71	58.83	86.17	75.31	115.93
Closing Stock						
Finished goods					983.77	781.79
Scrap stock					0.06	0.02
Stock in progress					11.96	6.98
	735.88	635.40	735.25	1149.25	995.79	788.78
TOTAL	10665.6	11814.53	14586.97	16569.25	19907.06	23097.02

• Excludes sales of Dhara oil done on behalf of NDDB and treated as consignment sales. This is shown in the next row.

** Includes ₹12.37 million in 1998–99 towards turnover tax written back consequent to a High Court judgement.

@ Includes income from sale of scrap of ₹2.96 million in 1997–98; ₹2. 53 million in 1998–99.

GCMMF: Profit and Loss Accounts, 1993–94 to 1998–99

						₹ million
	1993–94	1994–95	1995–96	1996–97	1997–98	1998–99
To Opening Stock						
Finished goods					1141.66	983.77
Scrap stock					0.00	0.06
Stock in progress					7.59	11.96
	655.01	735.88	635.40	735.25	1149.25	995.79
Expenses						
Purchases of finished goods				10708.28	12090.38	14532.98
Raw materials, stores, spares and packing materials consumed	7349.45	8496.70	10493.62	1409.51	1963.11	2323.30

Purchases of Dhara from NDDB	2255.30	2058.50	2676.00	2804.30	3698.40	4079.30
Manufacturing expenses	--	18.50	96.95	122.28	71.20	83.60
Marketing expenses	265.41	244.77	301.03	360.56	439.82	492.47
Salaries and other benefits	41.26	47.66	56.78	69.76	92.90	113.23
Interest and bank commission	45.95	83.25	70.82	66.19	57.10	67.98
Co-operative development expenses	5.44	3.33	8.20	9.27	8.41	14.05
Charity and donations	2.90	0.00	5.00	0.00	0.63	5.00
Miscellaneous expenses	32.35	38.00	51.79	78.91	94.11	102.44
Depreciation	4.64	72.22	107.32	105.61	125.99	138.80
Deferred revenue exp. Written off	0.00	2.28	2.28	2.28	2.28	2.28
Prior period adj. (Net)					0.98	0.68
Provision for doubtful debts and advances					2.52	0.00
Provision for income tax	0.00	0.00	0.00	19.20	25.20	15.00
Total Expenses	**10002.70**	**11065.21**	**13869.79**	**15756.15**	**18673.03**	**21971.11**
Net profit carried down	**7.89**	**13.44**	**81.79**	**77.85**	**84.80**	**130.12**
TOTAL	**10665.60**	**11814.53**	**14586.98**	**16569.25**	**19907.08**	**23097.02**

Source: Annual Reports of GCMMF.

The sales of the milk and milk related products depended on the procurement of milk that could be done. Exhibit 10 shows the growth in milk procurement from 1983–84 till 1998–99. The rate of growth in milk procurement was in the region of five percent per year.

The total milk production in India was in the region of 86 million tonnes per year (see Exhibit 11 for the growth in the total milk procurement in India). It was believed that less than half (about 46 percent) of this would be procured by any organized agency, the rest being retained by farmers for their own consumption at home. With per capita availability of milk still in the region of about 225 gm per day, there was considerable scope for further increase in production of milk in the country.

Exhibit 10 GCMMF Milk procurement

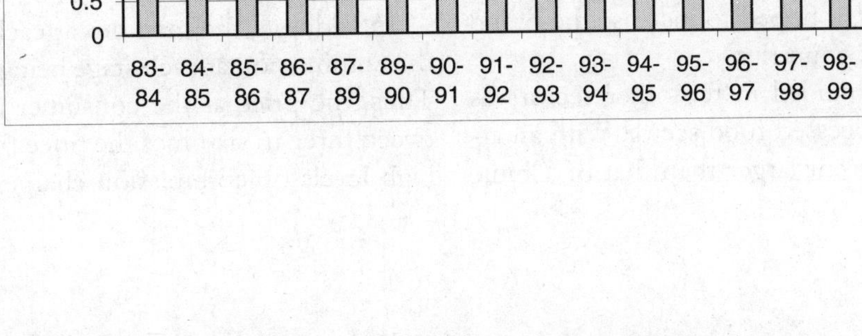

Exhibit 11 Milk production in India

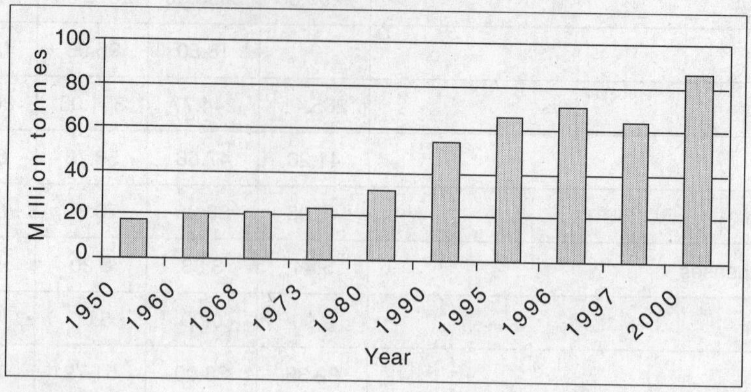

GCMMF IN THE YEAR 2000

The new millennium presented GCMMF with new opportunities as well as uncertainties. The milk market appeared to be getting saturated from the supply side. The rate of growth of milk production was around 6 percent per annum. The demand, however, could be expected to grow at 8–10 percent per annum, according to industry experts. The per capita milk consumption in India still being around 225 grams per day, as compared to more than 600 gms in many other countries, there was scope for increasing the consumption of milk still further. But the problems on the supply side were formidable. The yield of Indian cattle, at about 1000 kg per lactation per animal, was much lower than in other dairy countries such as New Zealand and Holland (about two tonnes). An increase was possible, but presented a challenge. But at least in the medium run, the supply side would pose constraints in the development of the milk market. Dr. Kurien said in an interview to the author, "In the case of milk and milk products, the limiting factor is not so much marketing, but supplies (of milk)."

Opportunities abounded in the market, both domestic as well export. GCMMF had been making major efforts to make its brand known in many countries, including the USA, where it had entered into an alliance with Kanan Dairy Products, Illinois to market its products. It had established offices and agencies in New Zealand, Gulf, Sri Lanka, and Australia. It had entered into ecommerce in a fairly big way, with all its products available for ordering through the net in India as well as abroad. Through its TV programs in Star TV, it hoped to increase the brand awareness in the SAARC countries.

But opportunities abounded in the other sectors as well, especially in the processed food sector. With an arable area of land 40 percent larger than that of China, India's food production (of about 600 million tonnes) was about 30 percent less than that of China. This situation was considered to be due to low farm productivity, lack of technology inputs, and absence of land reforms. The land holdings were small and in the hands of small families which essentially did subsistence farming. Most of these subsistence farmers cultivated basic food such as cereals, pulses, and some vegetable. But fruits and vegetables for processing did not figure among their priorities. Large farmers cultivated fruits, vegetables, and cash crops.

However, with improved per capita income and living standards, there was a general shift in the eating habits of Indians towards premium food. It was estimated that while subsistence foods would grow by 14 percent in the decade ending in the year 2005, premium food consumption would increase by 150 percent[13].

Another feature of India's food sector was a highly inefficient food logistics and distribution system. At the points of production, storage, and handling facilities were poor, so that ripening of fruit was not controlled. There were six-seven intermediaries as compared to an average of two in the USA, and these intermediaries performed the functions of transport, storage and eventual movement to the markets. The transport was extremely inefficient, packaging was poor, and temperature control was non-existent. Due to these inefficiencies, it was estimated that about 35 percent of fruit and vegetable production (estimated at about 33 million tonnes of fruits and 72 million tonnes of vegetables, of total value ₹230 billion) was wasted.

In addition, the mark-up at each stage was very high, the commission at each stage being about 25–30 percent. Thus, the price at the consumer end was anything between three to six times the price paid to the farmer. The high levels of commission charges were also related to wastage in logistics, since at each stage the intermediary had to throw away about 20 percent of the receipts due to the products having become unfit for consumption.

The Indian food chain was also poor with respect to the processing it went through. Only about 1.3 percent of India's total fruit and vegetable production was processed commercially as compared to 70 percent in the USA, Philippines and Brazil, 80 percent in Malaysia, and 30 percent in Thailand. The value addition in India was only about seven percent as compared with 23 percent in China, 45 percent in Philippines, and 188 percent in the UK.

This was a situation GCMMF was familiar with: a wasteful production system and poor prices paid to farmers. If the farmers could be organized into co-operatives, as it had done with milk, GCMMF might be able to become a truly major player in India's processed food market. This market was currently estimated to be around ₹20 billion with a total production of around 0.94 million tonnes[14]. But it was also the case that particular fruits and vegetables, especially the former, were grown in particular parts of the country. For example, mangoes were grown in Maharashtra, Andhra Pradesh, and UP, besides in Gujarat itself. Organizing farmers in theses states could be a difficult job.

The opportunities provided by this new market were, thus, quite exciting. But the magnitude of the problems in these new areas was also not to be underestimated. Competitors such as HLL and Nestle were formidable, although Mr. Vyas was confident that he and his team would be able to meet the competition. They believed that with the Amul, Dhara, and Safal names, customer-centric product offerings, good product quality and a dedicated team, meeting these challenges would be within their capability. However, not all in the competition played a fair game. As Dr. Kurien lamented in one of his speeches at the annual meeting of the shareholders:

"Most of our competitors are registered under the Companies Act, a law that in spirit and practice respects the rights of owners and observed due process. By contrast, our co-operatives operate under archaic, colonial co-operative legislation, in which the rights of owners are observed in the breach and in which due process finds scant place. For example, your federation and all the member unions are a part of the same three tier co-operative structure, yet you have to pay four percent Central sales tax when your products are transferred from your member unions to any of the branches of your federation that lie outside Gujarat. You then again pay local sales tax, when the product is sold within that state. On the other hand, if a private company transfers its product from its plant to any of its branches outside the state, it does not have to pay Central Sales Tax. ... As long as co-operatives remain in their present legal and regulatory shackles, competition can neither be free nor fair ..."[15]

During his speech to the shareholders, Dr. Kurien said:

"I find it sad that I must once again mention that co-operatives do not enjoy a level playing field in dairying, despite what the MNCs and business houses might say. Unlike private firms, co-operatives invest heavily in helping the farmers to increase their productivity. They provide breeding services, veterinary care, extension advice and inputs – often at cost or less. These are functions that, in the absence of co-operatives, would need to be played by the state. Co-operatives are committed to quality and will not compromise for the sake of easy money. Co-operatives pay their taxes and the full cost of their utilities[16]*. Most important, they operate under Co-operative Acts, which, in most states, invest the registrar of co-operatives with the power to intervene and overturn business decisions. Can you imagine the registrar of companies acting in the same fashion? At the same time, in many states private firms are eligible for tax holidays, exemption from sales tax, subsidized utilities and the like*[17]*."*

Many GCMMF officials felt that the problem was even more serious than what appeared from the above statements. Many of the private sector companies did not pay taxes, at least not fully, bribed factory and other inspectors to by-pass legislation and lower costs, and many did not even pay for electricity; with the connivance of officials of electricity boards, they simply stole electricity. Thus, GCMMF officials felt that the playing field was anything but level.

But Dr. Kurien was not daunted by these problems. He told the author: "GCMMF's strength is in its integrity. It is the honest man you cannot break."

However, it could be safely assumed that, whatever the path GCMMF took, it was not going to be a smooth one.

NOTES

1. Chairperson's speech. Annual Report of GCMMF, 1998–99, pp.14.
2. In rupee terms, India's GDP in 1998–99 was ₹19,924 while that of Gujarat was ₹18,858. In the year 2001, $1 was equivalent to around ₹48.
3. For a detailed account of the formation of the co-operatives and their early years, the reader is referred to: Heredia, Ruth (1977). *The Amul India Story*. Delhi: Tata McGraw Hill Publishing Company Limited. About the details of the nationwide program for increasing the availability of milk and forming farmers' co-operatives for milk production in other States of India as a part of a coordinated program, see: Paul, Samual (1982). *Management Development Programmes: The Lessons of Success*. Boulder, Colorado: Westview Press.
4. This was a feature of India's dairy industry. The milk output of cows varied heavily during the seasons, with heavy over-supply of milk during the winter. This naturally led to depressed prices, unless the milk was converted into other products that could be stored for a long time.
5. An organization registered as a co-operative society had certain restrictions on its operations. These will be presented in this case in due course.
6. Gandhi, Vasant (n.d.). Agro-Industry for Rural and Small Farmer Development: Issues and Lessons from India, *International Food and Agribusiness Management Review*, *2*(3/4), 331-344.
7. Some of the districts that had no district-level unions were those formed through re-organization of existing districts at different points of time.
8. Bye-law no. 5.1 of GCMMF.
9. As provided to the case writer by GCMMF.
10. Amul and India's National Dairy Development Board (1998). Case no. N9-599-060, Harvard Business School, p.8.
11. Ibid., p.8.
12. Annual Report of HLL, 1998-99.
13. Based on the findings of a study by McKinsey & Co for the Council of Indian Industries (CII).
14. Web site http://www.nic.in/mofpi/food-sectors/secfvp.html of the Department of Food Processing Industries, Ministry of Agriculture, Government of India.
15. Chairperson's speech. 26th annual report, 1996–97, p. 13.
16. It is a fact that in India, many private companies do not pay their taxes which they avoid by bribing officials.
17. Chairperson's speech. Annual report, 1997–98, p.10–11.

CASE

4

The Park, Calcutta

M.R. Dixit and S. Manikutty

In the morning of July 10, 1999 a team from the Ministry of Tourism, Government of India, visited The Park, a five star hotel in Calcutta, to consider its application for upgrading its categorization from "Five Star" to "Five Star Deluxe". The team inspected the hotel's décor, standards of service, rooms, systems and overall arrangements. In the afternoon came the verdict, not entirely unexpected: "Approved." The hotel staff went into a mood of great celebration.

The approval gave the hotel a greater recognition and status, enabled it to attract higher-class clientele and move closer to the classy image of its competitors, Taj Bengal and Oberoi. The re-categorization was another feather in the cap for the hotel, coming after its selection in May 1998 as a member of the "Small Luxury Hotels of the World"[1]. The top management of the hotel sought such recognition to strengthen the direction of its efforts to reposition the hotel as a "boutique hotel"[2] and change its image from a "comfortable and affordable hotel mainly for Public Sector executives and budget travelers" to "a classy and trendy hotel" conveying an image of youth, vitality and a place where "things happen". The management had articulated for the hotel a mission that highlighted premium status, global standards and service excellence as its key elements. It had also taken a number of steps to translate its "boutique" concept into practice.

Though the management of the hotel was very happy with the recognition as a Five Star Deluxe hotel, it did not want to rest on its laurels. It was aware that still much remained to be done. It was not sure to what extent the boutique concept was implemented and understood by its customers and employees. The scenario for the hotel industry in Calcutta was not very attractive, but the competition was increasing. Hence, it wanted to assess the competitiveness of the hotel in the changed competitive scenario of the city, develop a competitive strategy and think through the problems in implementing it.

THE INDIAN HOTEL INDUSTRY IN 2000 AD

The Players

The hotel industry, or the hospitality industry as it chose to call itself, was often seen as a component of the tourism industry, although in fact business travelers and airlines accounted for a substantial part of hotel occupancy. The industry acquired a certain status after Independence. It came to be seen as a part of an overall infrastructure for developing tourism in the country.

Prepared by Professors M.R. Dixit and S. Manikutty with the active cooperation of The Park, Calcutta and the case writers wish to thank Ms. Priya Paul, Mr. Vijay Dewan and the executives of The Park for their support. The Research and Publication Committee of the Indian Institute of Management, Ahmedabad gave the financial support for this project.

The first five star hotel in India, the Ashoka Hotel in Delhi, was set up under the State in 1957. In 1999, the hotels in the state sector accounted for about 15 percent of the five star room capacity. They were under either the Indian Tourism Development Corporation which was under the Ministry of Tourism Development, or the national airline, Air India (the Centaur Hotels). The Ministry of Tourism Development decided the policies pertaining to the industry.

The major private sector players in the five star segment were the Taj Group, the Oberoi Group, and the ITC Welcom Group. These groups owned chains of hotels in various cities. While the Oberoi Group had only five star hotels, the Taj and ITC Groups operated different categories of hotels. There were smaller groups like JayPee and Leela who owned and managed one or two five star hotels in select cities. There were also the MNC chains like Le Meridien, Holiday Inn and Hyatt, who had set up their properties either independently or through franchises. Having a chain of hotels was considered to be an advantage due to the loyalty that could be developed among customers who travel a lot. Also, facilities such as single point reservations in different cities could be offered across the hotels of the chain and commonality of standards of facilities and service could also be expected among the different hotels of the chain.

Star Ratings

The Ministry of Tourism, Government of India, assigned star ratings to hotels. It not only gave an initial certification but also renewal from time to time after an inspection. The ratings had nothing to do with tariffs as such but were based on the facilities available. "Five Star Deluxe" rating, as compared to "Five Star", was, however, based on the quality of services and on additional facilities.

The Customers of Five Star Hotels

The customers of five star hotels could be grouped under certain categories.

Tourists, Indian and foreign, constituted an important segment. Tourism was an important driving factor for this industry and fluctuations in tourist arrivals affected the earnings of hotels. Tourism was the third largest foreign exchange earner of the country (earnings: $2.735 billion in 1999) and hotels contributed considerably to these earnings, since all foreigners were required to settle their hotel bills in foreign exchange. Though India accounted for only 0.37 percent of the world tourist arrivals and 0.60 percent of revenues, the average stay of a foreign tourist in India was 30 days, as compared to three in Singapore and seven in Thailand. Due to the heat during summer and heavy rains during the monsoon, most of the tourist arrivals took place in the four months November to February. Calcutta was not among the destinations of the average foreign tourist, who generally went around the Delhi–Rajasthan circuit, with some extensions to Mumbai and the South. A few came to Orissa, and for them Calcutta constituted a transit point. Most tourists came through travel agents, and special rates were usually offered that were substantially below the advertised rates.

The second customer category was the business traveler segment. Business executives stayed in different types of hotels and again in different categories of rooms depending on their status. This segment had much less seasonality as compared to the tourist segment. Hotels negotiated rates with each company, usually for a year, and all major companies had accounts with almost all the hotels in a city. The choice of the hotel to stay in was usually done by the executives themselves so long as it was one of the hotels with which the company had an account. People working on projects stayed for long duration, even as long as three months, and gave a steady occupancy. The corporate rates could be two thirds or even half of the advertised rates which were the rates charged to the casual traveler, but usually no discounts were given in food and beverages.

The third category was the airline crew. The crew generally stayed in one hotel for the duration of a contract, usually a year. Pilots usually stayed in the best five star hotel in the city, and this might or might not be the same as the one in which the other crew stayed. Airline crew gave very steady occupancy to a hotel and hence, were much sought after; on the other hand the airlines drew hard bargains and the rates for airline crew were the lowest.

The rest of the customers were a mix of casual business travelers, casual domestic tourists, and transit passengers in need of accommodation. All these people were charged the advertised rates.

The needs of different categories of occupants were different. For a casual traveler or a tourist, links with travel agencies, airport pick up and drop, money changing information about sight seeing trips and if possible organizing such trips were important. Good restaurants providing a variety of cuisine were also considered important. For a business traveler, the business centre, facilities to entertain a group of clients, good room service and a good travel desk were important, while airline crew wanted quick check-in and check-outs, and prompt attention to their personal needs. Exhibit 1 summarizes the needs of different categories of occupants of a five star hotel.

Exhibit 1 Needs of different customer segments in the hotel industry

Service	Customer segment			
	Business travelers	International travelers	Domestic leisure travelers	Airline crew
Lobby Services				
- Airport pick up/drop	#	###	##	--
- Quick check-in	##	#	#	###
- Comfortable rooms	##	###	##	##
- Airline reservations	#	###	#	--
- Sight seeing tours	--	###	#	--
- Money changing	--	###	--	--
- Information about city, other services, etc.	--	###	##	--
Restaurants				
- Quality of food	###	###	###	###
- Quickness in service	##	#	##	###
- Variety of dishes	##	###	#	--
- Different restaurants with different cuisine	#	###	##	--
- Special food needs	#	###	##	--
- Quickness in room service	###	#	#	--
House Keeping				
- Elegance of room get up	#	###	#	--
- Promptness to attending faults (e.g. TV, telephone, air-conditioning, bathroom problems etc.)	###	##	##	###
- Quality of laundry services	##	###	#	--
- Valet service	##	#	--	--
Facilities				
- Business center	###	#	--	--
- Health club	###	###	#	#
- Shopping arcade	--	##	#	--
- Discotheque	#	#	#	#

Source: Our discussions with the executives of The Park.

The customer needs varied along many dimensions such as food and beverages, room preferences, importance given to different services, need for transportation, sports and recreation etc. and had to be taken into account in the management of a hotel. Exhibit 2 highlights the various dimensions along which guest preferences could vary. Exhibit 3 shows the drivers of satisfaction (percent impact) of guests of superior rooms (the "usual" rooms) and the Residence (the "business class") rooms, the restaurants, banquets, and night clubs.

Occupants were not the only source of revenue to hotels. Conferences and seminars were an attractive source of income. The seminars usually were accompanied by orders for food and beverages, and gave some occupancy to hotels also, unless they were purely local conferences. The second major source of revenue was the banquets and receptions, which gave revenue for food and beverages department as well as the banquet balls. Casual diners at restaurants also constituted an important source of revenue. The hotels in the town competed with one another to get these segments. Food festivals and major events around festivals like Diwali, Durga Pooja, and Christmas were organized to attract the locals. The hotels also competed to organize visits of important persons

Exhibit 2 Different types of guest preferences

1. **Room Related**: Type of room, room numbers, proximity from elevator, floor, size.
2. **In room:** Size of bed, extra fruit, bath rooms, soaps, newspapers, magazines, extra blanket, hangovers, beds, flower decoration, water, placement of jug, match box, choice of movies.
3. **F&B Preferences:** Vegetarian/non vegetarian, alcohol/teetotaler, and special type of cuisine preferred.
4. **Travel:** Car type, car agency, tele-check in, seat preference, ticketing, railway station assistance, drivers, in city car.
5. **Business:** Type of transparencies, secretary, floppies, binding, photocopying, computers, internet, fax in rooms, conference transfers, cell phones, courier needs, batteries/converters.
6. **Outside Hotel:** Golf, tennis, other sports, movie, theatre preference.
7. **Time:** For breakfast, wake-up-calls, and checkout including late checkouts.

Source: Compiled by the case writers.

Exhibit 3 Drivers of satisfaction of guests, superior and residence rooms (percent impact)

Item	Superior Rooms	Residence rooms
The room	24	
The people	17	20
Check-in	16	17
Hotel ambience	14	25
Security	12	15
Experience at the hotel restaurant	10	14
Resolution of problems		9
Ability to recognize guests	7	

Drivers of satisfaction: Restaurants

Item	Percentage
Cuisine	45
The staff	25
Ambience of the restaurant	22
Billing	8

Drivers of satisfaction: Banquets

Item	Percentage
Quality of food	31
The staff	31
Cost and flexibility	22
The banquet hall	16

Drivers of satisfaction: Night clubs

Item	Percentage
Events	32
Efficiency of service	24
Dance floor, sound, and lighting	18
Security	16
The DJ	10

Source: Data given by The Park, in turn as given to them by Gallup Organization, New Delhi.

like actors, playwrights, painters, and key business persons to add prestige to the hotel.

Organizations such as Gallup conducted customer surveys on behalf of hotels. They involved largely three dimensions: overall satisfaction, loyalty (would you come back to this hotel for your next stay?), and advocacy (would you recommend this hotel to your friends etc.?) Based on their experience, Gallup found that of the customers who rated the overall performance as 5 on a scale of 1 to 5, 75 percent were likely to come back; for a rating of 4, this percentage was 29; and for ratings of 1–3, this was close to zero percent.

Dynamics of Competition in the Hotel Industry

The metros, Delhi and Mumbai accounted for 49 percent of the premium room capacity, and the four metros, for 59 percent. Taking all rooms into account, Delhi and Mumbai accounted for 25 percent of the room capacity while 12 major cities accounted for around 60 percent capacity. The "Five Star" and the "Five Star Deluxe" categories accounted for 30 percent of the total available room capacity in the country. In recent years the percentage of three and four star categories seemed to be on the increase. Exhibit 4 gives the distribution of rooms in different categories in India between the years 1990–1993 and 1996–98.

Generally the facilities in all the five star or deluxe category of hotels were comparable. However, each hotel tried to provide some uniqueness with respect to each of its facilities. They tried to provide this uniqueness through décor, personalized service, menus, room service and customization of offerings. Since essentially the facilities, the general quality of service, the general quality of food, and sometimes even the taste of food were very similar among all the five star hotels, differentiating a hotel from its competitors was not easy. Each hotel tried to provide a certain atmosphere and a standard of service that could be called unique to it. This involved systematic training of its staff of different categories, but since turnover of staff from one hotel to another was common, the service styles etc., also tended to be more similar than dissimilar. In this situation, the following were thought to be important factors for success in this industry.

Occupancy Rates Since a very large portion of the expenses of a hotel was fixed, being (i) financial costs for the property (ii) maintenance costs (iii) establishment costs and (iv) day to day running costs, it was very im-

Exhibit 4 Distribution of room capacity in Indian hotels, 1990–93 and 1996–98

Category	# Hotels						
	1990	1991	1992	1993	1996	1997	1998
5 Star	79	85	82	87	91	94	99
4 Star	42	56	49	54	65	73	74
3 Star	114	115	115	125	203	278	289
2 Star	217	233	235	237	260	308	314
1 Star	81	91	96	93	112	135	142
Heritage			19	20	32	41	46
Awaiting Classification	161	167	202	199	217	182	200
Total	694	747	798	815	980	1111	1146
Category	**# Rooms**						
	1990	1991	1992	1993	1996	1997	1998
5 Star	15090	15636	15435	16151	17853	17973	19610
4 Star	2882	3742	3543	3740	4888	5270	5450
3 Star	5953	5913	6045	6736	10645	14042	14776
2 Star	10207	8139	8740	8627	9414	10773	11136
1 Star	2604	3097	3482	3506	3926	4607	4912
Heritage						1156	1292
Awaiting Classification	7669	7968	9811	9589	9681	7613	8397
Total	44405	44495	47707	48934	57386	61434	65573

Source: Annual Reports of the Department of Tourism, Government of India.

portant to get a good occupancy rate. Occupancy rates tended to be higher in hotels with a good location, with a good brand image and a higher proportion of business and airline occupants. To enhance occupancy through a build up of client loyalty, hotels started loyalty programs whose members obtained preferred hotel rooms, lower rates, and other benefits.

Location Location was considered important but the degree of its importance depended on the target audience. Hotels located close to airports, for instance, tended to have airline crew, transit passengers and tourists as their dominant clientele; those situated in business districts tended to have business clientele due to their proximity to probable places of business interactions; while those situated in quiet locations attracted conventions and conferences. The cost of property generally being the lowest in the first category, these hotels could also offer larger discounts to their clients.

Brand image The image of a hotel in terms of service orientation, status commanded, expense category, overall ambience, customer types, and progressiveness affected the nature of customers and the demands made by them on the hotel. Hotels tended to build this brand image through advertisements in TV, news papers, magazines (especially in flight magazines and travel guides) and direct mailing to prospective clients and corporate managers dealing with hotel bookings. The hotels also tried to build relationships with administrative staff of corporations through personal visits and presentations. The idea was to create a pull from the occupants to prefer the hotel rather than another.

Alliances Forming alliances, with related activity or service providers, was another instrument to drive business. Alliances with other companies provided mutual benefits. The most common alliance was with airlines, with the hotel giving a discount, or a free extra night stay (especially over a weekend) on production of a boarding pass, and the airline giving bonus points to its frequent fliers for staying at their partner hotels. Other alliances were with other hotels and trading establishments for discounts on production of their "club" cards.

Real Estate Real estate costs constituted a very significant cost in the overall cost structure of any hotel. This made the hotel industry highly capital intensive. The maze of land regulations made expansion through green field projects very time consuming, and their eventual outcome, highly uncertain. The tariffs of hotels, especially five star hotels in India were among the highest in the world, even higher than in many western cities for comparable hotels. The most important reason for this was the very high cost of urban real estate, leading to a cost of construction of ₹5 million and more per room. The costs, of course, varied a great deal depending on location. Thus choosing a location and control over cost of construction and the time taken for construction were very critical factors determining the profitability of a hotel.

Competitors to The Park, Calcutta

In Calcutta, there were four five star/five star deluxe hotels that competed with The Park. These were Hotel Airport Ashok, Hotel Oberoi Grand, Hotel Hindustan International, and Hotel Taj Bengal. The profiles of these hotels are given below.

Hotel Airport Ashok

This was one of the hotels under the Ashok chain, and was a State Enterprise under ITDC. Located just near the airport, its prime targets were the transit traveler and airline crew (distance from the airport to the city was 20 km and it took about an hour and half to get to the business centres of the city during business hours). Its service quality was considered to be less satisfactory than the other four hotels. It could attract PSU executives, government officials, and transit passengers.

Hotel Oberoi Grand

This belonged to the Oberoi chain of hotels, reputed for its professionalism and quality of service. The group had its hotels in major business and tourist places of India. It also had set up hotels in other countries. The group had pioneered the introduction of unique services like room service. Hotel Oberoi Grand, located near the business district, was established in 1933 as Eastern India Hotel. It had an image of exclusivity, and commanded high brand loyalty. Its property was classified as "heritage property" and had an old world atmosphere about it. However, it was considered to be rigid in the policies and rules, and the service was considered by the younger executives to be staid and slow. It had just renovated its rooms and was attempting to project itself as a modern, dynamic hotel. It pursued quite different pricing policies during the lean and peak seasons. It gave steep discounts during off-seasons as well as to corporate clients, especially executives from State Enterprises, but was quite flexible in its target marketing. Its competitive strategy in future, according to the executives of The Park, would be through upgrading of its facilities and service.

Hotel Taj Bengal

This was a relatively a new comer to Calcutta, starting in 1988. This hotel belonged to the Taj Group, which had an excellent reputation for the quality of service. It had its hotels in all the major cities in India and had a reputation for consistency of service among all the units. It had an excellent brand equity abroad and was frequently chosen by foreign tourists. Its reservation system, both in India and abroad, was considered excellent. Recently it had launched a major campaign stressing its competence, professionalism, a "caring" attitude and quality of service.

Though Taj Bengal was located about 9 km away from the business district, many private sector executives had Taj Bengal as their first choice, and so did pilots. To reinforce the premium image, it provided Mercedes cars for airport transfers for its deluxe clients. It was considered the first choice for prestigious marriage parties and, till recently, it had the largest banquet hall capacity. Thus, its targeting was very broad: international tourists, top business executives, and prestigious marriages. However, it was also believed to give sizeable discounts to its clients and had in fact started price wars. Its likely strategy, according to The Park executives, would be to capitalise on its image by capturing international travellers and conferences, high-end marriages and airline crew, especially of foreign airlines.

Hotel Hindustan International

This hotel was established in 1975. It was struggling to keep itself afloat, and was believed to offer the steepest discounts to ensure occupancy. It did not have a clear image in any segment, and nor did it have any particular reputation for quality of its service. It had essentially targeted relatively low budget clients. Recently, it was attempting a turn around by upgrading its services and modernization of its facilities.

ITC Welcom Group

This group, with its highly reputed hotels in all major cities, had no representation in Calcutta. It had started the construction of a new hotel with about 250 rooms, located mid way between the airport and the city at the Eastern Metropolitan Bypass overlooking the science city. The estimated cost of this property was ₹2500 million. It was reported that it had plans to expand the capacity to 1000 rooms at a later date. The headquarters of ITC Ltd., the promoting company of ITC Welcome group of hotels was in Calcutta.

The Hyatt Group

Hyatt was an international chain reputed for its high quality of service. This chain was also in the process of constructing a new hotel with about 250 rooms at a cost of ₹1000 million, also at the Eastern Metropolitan Bypass near the Salt lake Stadium.

A comparison of the facilities at The Park vis-à-vis its competitors may be seen in Exhibits 5 (A) and 5 (B). The hotels vied with each other to get a share of limited market. The market was not growing because the economy of West Bengal had not picked up. The companies with headquarters in Calcutta like ICI India, Philips India, Bata India, Hindustan Motors, and Dunlop were not doing well. Either their activities had declined or they had shifted their operations to other locations. Brooke Bond India Limited, for example, had shifted its headquarters to Bangalore. The business from the coal sector was also stagnant. The hotels therefore, relied on local activities like marriages and conferences to drive business.

Exhibit 5(A) Comparison of The Park with its competitors

	Hotel Oberoi Grand	Hotel Taj Bengal	Hotel Hindustan International	The Park
Particulars of rooms				
Total # rooms	213	229	186	149
Deluxe suites	3	11		17
Executive suites	3	-	8	
Deluxe	48	147 (luxury)	26	7
Garden facing	29	-	-	
Superior	130	-	9	125
Standard	0	71	56	
Room Revenues (1998) (₹Million)	124.2	146.3	65.0	92.7
Restaurants: (The numbers indicate the number of guests who can be accomodated)				
Coffee shop	80 (La Terrase)	86 (Esplanade)	132 (Palm Court)	66 (Atrium)
Oriental restaurant	58 (Baan Thai)	87 (Chinoisserie)	84 (Oriental)	63 (Zen)
Indian restaurant	74 (Gharana)	120 (Sonargaon)	100 (Kalash)	76 (Saffron)
Bar	50 (Chowringhee)	55 (Junction)	30 (Covers)	25 (Someplace Else)
Discotheque		75 (Incognito)	26 (Anti Clock)	50 (Tantra) (night club cum disco)

Source: Data given by The Park.

@ Covers can vary depending on the type of banquet. Whether sitting or standing or buffet.

Exhibit 5(B) Banquet facilities

Hotel Oberoi Grand	Hotel Taj Bengal	Hotel Hindustan International	The Park
Ball room 840	Crystal 700	Silver Cup 150	Rosewood 125
Cooch Behar 50	Portico 40	Regency 100	Ebony 50
Burdwan 50	Mandarin 40	Camelot 30	Banyan 35
La Rotesserie 80	Oriental 25	Poolside 200	Pine 175
	Terrace 700	Lord Clive Chamber 15	Business Center 25
	Poolside 400		The Willow 25
			The Birch 40

Source: Information supplied by The Park.

Note: The numbers represent the number of guests who can be accommodated.

For its restaurants business, the hotel faced competition from independent restaurants that served Chinese and North Indian cuisine. Competition also came from Gymkhanas and clubs whose members were corporate executives and officers from civil services.

THE PARK AND ITS BACKGROUND

The Park, Calcutta belonged to a chain of four premium boutique hotels belonging to the Apeejay Surrendra Group whose shares were closely held by the Paul family. The Apeejay Group, established in 1910, had interests in a number of businesses such as hotels, trading, real estate, construction, tea and steel, and in all the businesses the shares were closely held by the Paul family. The hotel business was managed under The Park name for all the hotels in the chain. Besides the Calcutta property, the chain had four other properties located at Visakhapatnam, Delhi, Bangalore, and Chennai. Among them, The Park, Calcutta was the oldest and it had opened for business on November 1, 1967 with 150 rooms. The Park, Visakhapatnam was opened in 1968; The Park, Delhi in 1987 and The Park, Bangalore in 1999. The property at Chennai had recently been acquired and after the needed work to upgrade it to the standards required, it was expected to be commissioned by early 2002. A 100 room hotel was under development in Navi Mumbai. When completed, this would become the sixth member in the chain. This would make the chain the fourth largest Indian chain in the five star category, the three larger chains being the Taj, ITC, and Oberoi.

Each of the properties in The Park chain had its own clientele, its own tariffs, and its own décor. The décor and even the general appearance of each property, and even of different floors in the same property, were strikingly different. Each property was managed largely independently, although certain activities and policies had been made uniform across the chain. There was no corporate headquarters for the chain as such, but Ms. Priya Paul, a member of the Paul family, who was managing the hotel business, coordinated across the properties. Manuals and operating procedures were formulated for various departments such as human resources, housekeeping, food and beverage service and adopted and implemented by all hotels. Exchange of ideas and information among different hotels of the chain took place through periodical meetings among the executives of the different properties. Within broad parameters, there was considerable freedom for each property to introduce changes and practices.

The Park, Calcutta was located on the Park Street near the busy arterial road of Chouringee. It was a landmark in the city. In the 1960s, The Park was a very up-market hotel, with the "world staying there": certainly many celebrities had The Park as their favorite hotel. In the 1980s, it attracted a substantial part of its clientele from the public sector undertakings that had their marketing or regional offices in Calcutta. It also attracted some clients from multinational corporations that had their corporate headquarters in Calcutta. The clientele in both the above categories was largely middle management level executives. The hotel's name was changed from The Park to The Park Hotel; its image also changed to one of a centrally located, reasonably comfortable and affordable hotel for middle management executives and budget travelers.

According to an executive who was with the hotel from the 1980s, during the 1980s the business became largely assured, and this assurance bred complacency and slackness in the management. The standards of service declined. With the increasing sickness of PSUs and the decline of industrial activities in the Eastern belt, the business from corporate clients tended to decline. Coupled with this, the hotel had to contend with an aging staff. New competitors entered, both in the five star and other segments, the most formidable among them being the Taj Bengal belonging to the Taj Group. The future of the Park chain looked bleak.

At this time, in 1990, Ms. Priya Paul, a member of the family that owned the business, took over the management of the family's hotel business. A graduate in Economics from Wellesley College, USA, Ms. Paul had a very keen interest in hotel business (Refer to Exhibit 6). She decided to revamp the hotel's image, operations and standards of service. She was aware that the hotel, despite its prime location, had a basic problem that it could not expand to any great extent. It could thus, not become a large-sized hotel, not in the short run, at any rate. She was also aware of the difficulty in truly differentiating a hotel from its competitors, unless a new concept was evolved to position it. She, therefore, devised a new strategy of positioning the hotel as a "boutique" hotel and was instrumental in providing The Park with a new direction. She recruited Mr. Vijay Dewan, who had earlier worked with Oberoi Hotel in Iraq, to assist her and head The Park, Calcutta, as the General Manager and the Chief Executive (Refer Exhibit 6).

Exhibit 6

Ms. Priya Paul

Ms. Priya Paul, the President of The Park group of hotels, has a bachelor's degree from Wellesley College, US She started her career under her father, the late Mr. Surrendra Paul, as the marketing manager of The Park, New Delhi in 1998. She succeeded her father as the president of the hospitality division of the Apeejay Surrendra Group at a relatively young age.

Despite her young age, Ms. Paul quickly established a reputation as a dynamic business woman, forthright and adventurous. The placing of The Park chain as a collection of boutique hotels was essentially her idea. In recognition of her achievements in the hospitality industry, the Federation of Hotels and Restaurant Associations of India (FHRA) awarded her the accolade of "Young Hotel Entrepreneur of the Year 2000", the first recipient of the award.

An active participant in several industry associations, Ms. Paul holds several posts including The Vice President, Hotel Association of India, Member, PATA Environment and Eco-Tourism Committee and Founder Member, World travel Tourism Council, Asia Chapter, and The Young Presidents' Organization (YPO).

Ms. Paul has a great deal of interest in arts and is a very keen patron of arts. She is a trustee of the India Foundation of Arts (IFA). She puts very strong emphasis on contemporary design in her hotels. Her other interests include cuisine and their histories, meditation and reading.

Mr. Vijay Dewan

Mr. Vijay Dewan is the Vice President of The Park Hotels, where he is responsible for hotel operations, business strategy formulation, overseeing marketing operations and planning sustainable growth for the hotels. Mr. Dewan has a Masters Degree in Organic Chemistry and a post Graduate Diploma in Hotel Management from The Oberoi School of Hotel Management. He started his career with The Oberoi Hotel, Delhi in1984 as Assistant Manager. In 1987, he moved to The Oberoi Palace, Srinagar as the Food and Beverage Manager and then was posted as Front Office Manager at The Babylon Oberoi, Baghdad, Iraq. He was soon promoted to the post of Rooms Division Manager.

In 1991, Mr. Dewan moved to The Park Hotels and was located at Calcutta, where he took over as General Manager a year later. He was appointed Vice President of The Park Hotels in 1994. Sixteen years in the industry has given Mr. Dewan an in-depth perspective on the needs of the modern day traveler.

He believes in constantly updating his skills, and has participated in several professional courses including a General Manager's Program from Cornell University in 1995, a course on Leadership for Change from the London Business School in 1997, and one on Strategic Marketing Management from The Harvard Business School in 2000.

Mr. Dewan is also involved in several industry forums and is currently a Managing Committee Member of the Federation of Hotels & Restaurants Association of India (FHRAI) and the Chairman of the Hotel Association of India (HAI) in West Bengal.

Based at Calcutta, Mr. Dewan is an avid golfer and finds it the ultimate relaxant.

The "Boutique" Concept

Boutique hotels were different from the conventional luxury hotels in that they offered a richer, more classy and more intimate experience. According to Mr. Vijay Dewan, Vice President of The Park, Calcutta, who also acted as the CEO of the property, boutique hotels are "those providing a distinctively different and more personalised service, amenities and style". Style was the essence. Nothing was laid down as such, but each item: lobby, rooms, the restaurants and so on, was to reflect the distinctiveness and the style. This also involved conveying an image of "a place in which things happen", and needed constant search for new ideas and for being the pioneer in giving new and distinct facilities. Mr. Dewan continued:

This positioning was through our own judgement. It was not through any systematic study. We needed a product that was totally different. Hence, what we were doing was to create a new concept, and a new brand.

According to Ms. Salmoli Ghosh, Deputy Manager, Public Relations:

The main thing about the boutique concept is the design. Boutique hotels in the West are different from the large five star luxury hotels. They tend to be smaller, but offer a friendlier service, homelier so to speak, but otherwise they have all the features and facilities of a large five star hotel. They are classy, stylish, design driven, trendy, sophisticated, upmarket and exclusive. So the ambience, service, everything are meant to make the customers feel more at home.

A boutique hotel is also a trendy, designer and niche hotel, where things are "happening". Service will not be formal, but customer friendly, close to the customer. Each of our properties has a root of its own. Our Calcutta property is art oriented. Delhi is more architecture oriented. Rooms at Delhi and Calcutta are quite different. Even rooms of different floors are different. The designs of The Residence (the executive floor) rooms and the suites are different.

The idea of positioning the Hotel as a boutique hotel originated from Ms. Paul and Mr. Dewan. They felt there was a need for such a hotel in India. There were the traditional five star hotels, and the budget hotels, but we were different from both. We targeted at a group of customers who were young, trendy, who are aware of good things, and who might have stayed at such boutique hotels abroad.

The vision of the hotel was restated as "leadership through differentiation". A mission and vision statement was made in 1997 and circulated among the employees; it was also displayed at all prominent places in the hotel including the back room work areas (Refer Exhibit 7 for the Mission and Vision Statement). The difficult question was how to differentiate, and how to make this differentiation effective. It involved looking again at each of its facilities and services. Exhibit 8 gives a summary of the various steps taken, which we describe below in detail.

Exhibit 7 The Park: Vision and mission

The Hotel has a vision and mission statement, which reads as follows:

Our Vision

Leadership through differentiation.

Our Mission

We will operate a collection of premium boutique hotels and restaurants, establishing global standards of product quality and service excellence.

We will make customer satisfaction the purpose of every action we take and every job we do.

We believe our strength is our people and we will encourage their development. We respect them as individuals and believe that teamwork, commitment and integrity are values that lead us to success.

We will ensure the profitability and growth of the company for the long-term benefit of our shareholders, our customers and our employees.

We believe that it is essential to be a good corporate citizen and serve the community that sustains us.

Source: The Vision and Mission Statement of The Park, reproduced verbatim.

Exhibit 8 Significant changes introduced in The Park During the last five rears

1. The décor of the hotel was changed to give it a new elegant look. All the rooms were renovated. A separate floor was earmarked and converted into deluxe suites called The Residence. The Residence suites had a separate express check-in and a separate reception. A Butler Pantry and a special lounge were located on this floor.
2. All the rooms were well furnished and equipped with the latest basic amenities: a telephone, a television, minibar, hair-dryers and a telephone connection in the bathroom, to name just a few.
3. A special Oriental restaurant called **Zen**, which was the only one of its type in Calcutta, was started. It offered exquisite cuisine from 7 different oriental countries. An Indian restaurant **Saffron** with the central theme décor of a cosmic restaurant was started.
4. A pub cum discotheque called **Someplace Else** on the ground floor of the hotel was started for the youngster crowd to have fun. This idea was also an original one. The concept was to provide one-stop entertainment to the youth.
5. In December 1999, Someplace Else was made into a bar with live band; a new night club cum disco was opened, named **Tantra.** This was a trendy international night club with split levels, reflecting Indian traditions. Tantra has "redefined the night life of Calcutta with its exclusive clientele, innovative concepts and events, extensive stock of beverages and its pulsating music" according to an executive of The Park.
6. The hotel provided its guest with a 24-hour coffee shop called "**The Atrium Café**". This coffee house was lit naturally during daytime, and provided a wonderful view of sky at night. It was equipped to serve breakfast, lunch and dinner along with a choice of 25 different varieties of coffees - the only coffee shop in Calcutta to offer such a wide variety.
7. The banquet halls were re-furnished and in 2000, two new halls were added to the two existing halls, taking the capacity of banquet halls from 410 to more than 1200. The aim was to increase the banqueting space in the hotel and to provide the discerning section of the clientele the advantages of premium banqueting. The décor, ambience, food, facilities and equipment provided in these two new halls were targeted at the premium market.
8. A swimming pool was set up. This was connected by a private bridge for use by the room guests. The health club/gymnasium was equipped with the latest equipment.

The hotel organized food festivals, which were very different from the usual ones held at other hotels. For example, The Park had a Croissant festival, a coffee festival called Coffee World Tour featuring different flavors of coffee from all over the world and a Burmese food festival.

Source: Data given by The Park.

The Facilities and the Changes Brought In

Rooms

View of the Superior Room

View of the Residence suite

View of the Residence Suites

Zen

Saffron

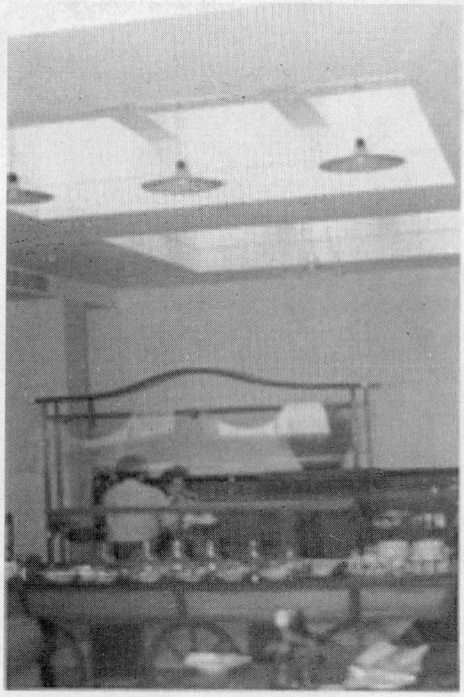

Atrium showing skylight

Tantra

The Spa

Atrium showing the plasma TV

Banquet Hall

Someplace Else

In 2001, The Park, Calcutta had a total of 150 rooms. The décor of all the rooms was changed. All rooms were equipped with multi-channel TVs, centralized air conditioning with individual temperature control for each room, individual refrigerator cum mini bar, computer and fax link ups, digital safes, voice mail and email link ups (refer Picture 1). Even though now these were comparable to the facilities in other five star hotels, at the time of their introduction, The Park had the distinction of being the first in many of the facilities. The hotel had also the usual facilities available in all five star hotels such as 24 hours business centre, 24 hours currency exchange, baby sitting facility, book shop, gift shop, doctor on call, laundry and access, and special rooms for the physically challenged people.

Of the 150 rooms, 17 were deluxe suites and 7 were deluxe rooms. The rooms and suites were in a floor that constituted The Residence floor. It was redesigned and equipped with new facilities. The floor provided better service, separate express check-in and check-out counters located at the floor, computer on request, personal fax, personal video cassette player and music system, an audio and video library located in The Residence lounge and jacuzzis[3]. Even in 1999, when we visited the hotel first, jacuzzis were a unique feature of this hotel though afterwards other hotels had also introduced it. The hotel had kept up its introduction of new facilities such as two line telephones. See Pictures 2 and 3 for a view of the Residence suites.

Similar changes were introduced in the other properties as well. For example, a program for major improvement of rooms was undertaken for the Delhi property. The rooms in the Bangalore property, after its acquisition in 1999, were redesigned with classical materials like wood for flooring. leather for the upholstery, silk for the curtains and furnishings and white marble for the bath rooms. The idea was to convey a central message of being similar, yet different. All rooms in The Residence were equipped with computers, high speed internet connectivity, net access through TV and two line telephones.

The Restaurants and Cafe

In 2001, The Park, Calcutta had two restaurants: Zen and Saffron. Both these had been totally redesigned and repositioned. Zen, an oriental restaurant was the first of its kind in Calcutta, served cuisine from seven Asian countries (Thailand, Hong Kong, Singapore, Indonesia, China, Malaysia and Japan). The restaurant was designed to convey a very tranquil and exotic ambience (see Picture 4). Saffron, earlier called Sujata, was also completely redesigned to convey a "cosmic" appearance (Picture 5). It served Indian food from all the regions of the country. Both these restaurants had their interiors designed by specially commissioned interior decoraters and had very contemporary decors.

An ultra modern coffee shop called The Atrium Cafe, fitted with a glass top so that it was lighted naturally during day, served buffet breakfast, lunch and dinner besides a la carte orders (See Picture 6). It boasted of a plasma wall-mounted TV (See Picture 7), the first of its type in Calcutta. Besides serving buffet breakfast, lunch and dinner, Atrium took pride in offering 25 varieties of coffee from all over the world, the largest selection among any hotel in India.

Discotheque, Health Club, and Internet Club

The Park had a pub-cum-discotheque named "Someplace Else"[4] that served authentic British pub food. It attracted youth from the city. Till last year, after 9 p.m., it was a nightclub open only to members and hotel guests. Last year, the night club was shifted to a separate area, the new facility being named "Tantra". Thereafter, "Someplace Else" became a full fledged pub cum discotheque (refer Pictures 8 and 9) offering live bands every evening as a unique feature. Tantra a night club-cum-bar and was in split levels, each with a different décor (Picture 10). The lower level was open to everyone, while the upper level was only for members. The first floor was an exclusive meeting place for the elite in Calcutta and tried to live up to this image by serving single malt whiskeys, a range of expensive cognacs, wines and cigars. The hotel also set up an ultra modern health club called The Spa. The Spa had a swimming pool and a gymnasium with the latest equipment for exercising (resistance training, stationary run/cycling, etc.). The facilities were considered by the users to be the best in the city. The Spa was open to room guests and members (See Pictures 11 and 12).

Banquet Halls

The hotel had earlier four large banquet halls, named The Pine hall, The Rosewood Hall, The Ebony Room and The Banyan Room. In the year 2000, two more premium banquet halls named The Birch and The Willow were added, with the state-of-the-art facilities, taking the total capacity to more than 1200. These halls introduced the concept of premium banqueting in the city and were claimed to be ideally suited for catering to the city's premium banqueting, day conferencing as well as evening cocktails and theme dinners. With well-designed partitions the halls could be divided into smaller rooms that could serve as conference rooms. The locals used the halls for hosting wedding receptions and organizing conferences. These facilities constituted the largest banqueting facility in the city. (refer to Picture 13).

Transition of The Park to a New Position: The Intangibles

The process of The Park's repositioning itself as a "boutique hotel" was by no means painless. In the 1960s, the hotel had a personalized service where the staff knew most of the frequent customers and their tastes well. "The hotel developed a reputation for courtesy and personalized attention, and had a loyal customer base not only from the public sector but also from the private", said a manager who was with the Hotel from 1968 in an interview to the case writers[5].

An executive shared the changes in the profile of the hotel over the years in the following words:

We did quite well till the eighties. Our service conditions were good. We built a reputation for ourselves in the eastern corporate world. We had created a good image for ourselves. A number of celebrities and film personalities such as Raj Kapoor and Sanjeev Kumar had our hotel as their first choice (Now, however, such celebrities prefer Taj, he added). We really reached excellent standards of service. Sometime in the early eighties, our standards started declining. Maintenance, cleanliness, levels of service, all declined. In the meanwhile our staff had started becoming old: we had (and still have) a higher proportion of older staff as compared to our competitors. Even in the area where we were strong, namely, identifying and quickly responding to customer problems, we fell behind.

From 1990 onwards, the management started a drive for revival. The revival started with the renovation of physical facilities: front areas such as lobby, rooms, restaurants as well as back room facilities such as the kitchen, boilers, laundry and other facilities. The laundry was modernized by installing new imported equipment such as automatic ironing equipment, dry cleaning machines, dryers and washing units.

Simultaneously, The Park initiated a program of retraining. The hotel had old timers who were good at one time but had got used to sloppy ways of working. Still the hotel did not want to lose them. An executive said, "They could again become assets—providing a service with an old world charm—if we could train them". No one was forcefully retrenched. A voluntary retirement scheme (VRS) was offered but it was not a success, as only a few employees opted for it.

It was the opinion of The Park executives that the younger generation of guests and people frequenting the bar, night club etc. preferred a more informal style. Especially in Someplace Else and Tantra, many guests liked striking an informal note with the staff, especially the managers. Hence the Hotel selected such people who would have the natural ability to get across to the younger generation informally, yet without generating an impression that they were getting too personal. They were also trained in handling such customers. As a manager in charge of Someplace Else explained: "You must enjoy being with these people, genuinely. Otherwise it will not work. I know many of our regular customers by name and I know many of them would like to be addressed by their names. You must exercise judgement in these things".

The renovation of facilities was supported by a clear definition of the clientele. An executive explained:

We also realized the need for defining our clientele. We wanted higher level executives, business travelers and people with higher paying capacities. We thus got our Residence Floor ready with up-to-date facilities. We were the first to introduce facilities like fax and Jacuzzis in each room. This has started paying off. We also defined ourselves as a boutique hotel—smaller than a glittering five star hotel but with all facilities and a unique and stylish décor.

Said another executive from Public Relations[6]:

We took some time in putting this boutique concept into practice—we got international designers to tastefully decorate our rooms; we purchased many new paintings. We commissioned renowned artists to paint murals. Our hotel developed a very distinctive look and décor.

Being a boutique hotel meant that The Park had to communicate the image of being young and trendy. It had to promote individualism and innovation. An executive remarked: "Not only do we encourage individualism but also thrive on it".

Being a boutique hotel meant that the rooms and facilities be continuously upgraded and made contemporary. Said Ms. Indrani Sanyal, Executive House Keeper:

We have to plan for continuous renovation of rooms. We are now changing all the bath room fittings and room furniture.

To keep rooms in a top condition, maintenance is very important. At a time, we usually keep two rooms free for preventive maintenance from 9 a.m. till 6 p.m. During this period, everything is checked and repaired if necessary. But we see to it that there is no loss in revenue. If the rooms are fully booked, we may skip this for a day or two. But we can always catch up on Saturdays and Sundays when the rooms are available.

One of the difficulties faced in making the transition was that different hotels in the Apeejay chain were being managed independently, and hence there was no commonality of strategies. Ms. Paul recognized the issue and initiated efforts to co-ordinate across the hotels. Manuals were shared and wherever possible, made common across different properties. Frequent meetings were arranged to enable the executives to meet and share their ideas, and the steps taken at improvement. The hotel group was in the process of introducing an integrated reservation system.

Use of Information Technology

One of the planks of The Park's boutique strategy was to achieve a superior and a distinctive level of customer service. For this, it had employed Information Technology (IT) in a big way. A software package covering purchase, accounts, and staff database and front line operations had been introduced. The most important among these, from the point of view of customer service, was the database built for the front line operations. Each guest, at the time of registering, was put on the database, and during his stay, all his/her orders (room service) and preferences were recorded. When the guest booked a room the next time, the front desk, house keeping and room service were alerted about his/her past history through an "expected arrival report", so that the right questions could be asked confirming his/her preferences, as for example, for rooms. This quite often pleasantly surprised the guests. The housekeepers were also informed about the preferences.

All complaints and requests were registered in the computer (usually guests phoned up either front desk or house keeping for complaints) and then passed on to the appropriate branch (e.g., electrical). These would indicate the time of booking of the complaint as well as the time it was attended to; subsequent delays if any; and the time it was finally set right. The house-keeping manager reviewed these data every morning and all cases of undue delays were investigated.[7]

Besides, the above follow up, a system introduced by The Park ensured that the complaints registered by a guest would go into the guest's history also, and the next time the guests checked in, the concerned departments were informed about the problems faced by the guest during his/her last stay. The idea was to ensure that the same problem did not occur the next time that guest checked into the hotel. For example, if on the last occasion, the guest had complained about nonfunctioning of TV, or the coffee being cold, the electrical/room service would be specially alerted so that this particular complaint did not recur, definitely not to the particular guest. This was given special emphasis is in the case of frequent guests, e.g. airline crews and corporate guests. For example, if a frequent guest was observed to put the flower vase in his room at a particular location, the next time he arrived, he would be surprised to find it already put at that location.

The staff database showed the training received by each employee and his/her strengths and weaknesses that would indicate areas for further training and development.

The purchase/inventory package was considered to be sophisticated and would track the stock and order position of each item, indicating the need for reordering (food items were ordered and tracked separately). The Hotel thought it had an advantage in terms of cost management of supplies as compared to all its competitors.

For streamlining the back office operations, The Park had just introduced an integrated package called Prologic which would integrate materials management and Food & Beverages (F&B). It was in the process of implementing the same.

The Park hotel group had a website which gave descriptions of it facilities. The Park, Calcutta had a link with its own home page, just as the other properties had their own. Customers could make on line reservations where they could indicate if they were members of the "Preferred at The Park" loyalty program (see below) or whether their organizations were privileged members (getting special rates). The confirmations were, however, done through e-mail manually. The Park was considering packages such as Fidelio, which were large integrated packages that could handle a variety of functions such as front office, sales, catering, and yield management. The site could do reservations across properties also from the same site.

Yield management was becoming an important weapon in the hotel industry. These packages gave optimal rates to be quoted given a season and a lead time. Essentially it was similar to the packages existing in airlines where fares were quoted on a continuous basis to maximise the yield. None of the hotels in India had yet adopted such packages, including The Park.

Human Resource Development and Repositioning Strategy

The new initiatives launched by the hotel needed to be supported by matching initiatives in the HR Department. Though the management had developed a mission statement and gave it wide publicity, the difficulty lay in carrying the mission to people at all levels. According to Mr. Siraj Mukherjee, Manager, Training: "The problem is how to make people understand this statement. I don't think it is really understood by many people"[8]. Concurred Ms. Malaya Das, Head, Department of HRD: "How we can make people understand our mission and vision down the line continues to be a major problem. By and large everybody understands differentiation, but they have to still understand the true spirit of differentiation". Ms. Mahua Mukherjee, Manager, Training and HRD thought that translation of the ideas contained in the new strategy and the mission statement involved all aspects of HR recruitment, training compensation and performance appraisal[9]. She explained the steps taken by the HR department in this context:

While we have a large number of older people, we recognize the importance of having a younger team. We have been recruiting people who are dynamic, having an urge to do new things, are creative, are good learners and have also the ability to work hard. We give a lot of weightage for creativity, innovativeness, and initiative in our appraisals.

We are laying great emphasis on goal setting and direction at each level. We have allocated responsibilities and targets for each department. Many of the departments are now run as independent profit centres. For example, the restaurants, the Spa (the health centre) and Someplace Else are profit centres. Others are given performance targets.

Increasingly, we are linking our promotions and compensations to the results achieved. This is creating a lot of stress and discomfort, particularly to the older group, who are not used to such appraisals, but we have to take these measures. Systematic training has also helped us a lot. The training, performance appraisal and goal setting are all linked. During appraisal sessions, people are frankly told about their positive and negative points, so that they can take corrective action themselves.

Mr. Rahul Guha from the HR Department told the authors:

The working conditions in a hotel are not among the best. We have long working hours and the pay in the industry is generally low.... Hence we have to find ways to retain staff. We have introduced a number of welfare measures. We have introduced bunkers for employees to take rest in between shifts if they cannot go home. We give good birthday gifts. We give a month's pay as a gift when the employees get married. We have introduced scholarships for employees' wards, Mediclaim insurance for all permanent employees and reserved seats for the wards of employees in Apeejay School, which is a good school. We hope to retain more employees and keep their morale high through these measures.

Mr. Malaya Das explained the efforts made to translate the mission into actual practice at all levels:

Our pay structure was earlier uncompetitive. We have revised our pay structure. Now our salaries are competitive with the others in the hotel industry. We are now conducting industry surveys with regard to salary levels.

We take our fresh trainees mostly from hotel management institutes. For front line people, we take also fresh graduates. We look, in a candidate, for:

(i) A service attitude: what is their capacity to smile? A real genuine smile, I mean? This is especially important for front desk people.
(ii) A hotel management background, especially for F & B people.
(iii) A good disposition.
(iv) An ability to communicate in English and in the vernacular.
(v) The family background and interests.
(vi) We have not yet started administering psychometric tests, but we shall be introducing them soon.

For all recruits, training is centered around our mission and core values. We manage many of our operations through a contract trainee system. Under this system, we train a person for three years without any guarantee of employment. During training, we watch the people closely, and only those who are really good are absorbed into the hotel as permanent supervisors. They have also to undergo an examination before confirmation. The percentage of people thus absorbed varies with the departments and requirements, but the average rate is around five percent for these contract trainees. But the employability of our trainees is very high. They are given a lump sum when they leave, and they find it very easy to get a position in Taj and Oberoi. Many employees discovered that after our upgradation to the five star deluxe category, their employability also went up.

Our turnover is now quite low. The overall turnover rate is about 20 percent, but this is due to the high turnover of trainees, many of whom we do not confirm. Our retention at senior levels is quite good.

Attempts were being made to equip employees with a greater variety of skills, both for their own benefit and for that of the Hotel. For example, room boys and butlers were taught the elements of repairs of TV sets, so that they can quickly repair TVs in case of minor complaints rather than getting the electricians. The mechanics might or might not be available. But said Ms. Indrani Sanyal, Manager (House Keeping): "Multi Skill development has so far not been much of a success"[10].

A great deal of stress was laid on training at all levels. Training needs had been identified for each employee and a number of training courses organized, including for senior level executives. Front line staff, waiters, room boys and others had to undergo compulsory refresher courses where the "right way" of doing things was reinforced. The hotel spent about four percent of its revenues on training, which was considered much higher than the industry average. The Park also sent its executives to various international institutions for training such as The Institute of Hotel Management at the Cornell University, Harvard Business School, National University of Singapore, and London Business School for various programs.

When asked for the details of how exactly this training was conducted, through an example of a particular function, Ms. Indrani Sanyal, Executive Housekeeper took the example of room boys and supervisors:

We give a full training in each activity involved in the cleaning of a room: cleaning procedures, equipment to be used, setting up store cupboards, arranging the room and the bath room, etc. They are also told how to ask for supplies and linen.

We consider the training of supervisors as extremely important. Each new supervisor does 25 to 30 days of independent room cleaning herself. She has to give a perfect room before she can actually supervise. We also give theory classes in which the housekeeping standard operating procedures manuals are discussed and explained in detail. They are also tested on how much of the SOPs and instructions have been understood and assimilated by them.

During the last one year, a number of initiatives had been taken to assess the competency profiles and the training needs of the employees. Each employee had the competency gaps mapped and the training needs assessed. A software called Peoplesoft was planned to be introduced to enable a more scientific assessment of competencies backed by psychometric tests[11]. Mr. Manohar Agrawalla, Manager, IT services, said that this software would enable the progress and performance of each employee to be tracked continuously and systematically.

Asked how she would rate the quality of her manpower, Ms. Malaya Das replied:

About 15 percent of our employees will be above par in the hotel industry. About 70 percent will be at par. The rest could be below par.

Mr. Dewan summed up the efforts at improving the HRD practices:

We conducted an employee satisfaction survey by a reputed agency in India. The results revealed a lot of dissatisfaction regarding salaries and some of the facilities. We took immediate steps to improve and strengthen our salary structure to a competitive market rate. In fact, our salary structure is now better than the Taj Group of Hotels and the salaries offered are among the best in the industry. Employee facilities have been upgraded on, in terms of lockers and dining rooms facilities. There is emphasis on competency mapping, career planning and development of each employee. Today we run one of the best hotel management training programs in the country. All these efforts have changed the image of the hotel itself in the eyes of the job aspirants and made The Park an exciting place to work in.

Marketing, Selection of Target Clientele, Sales and Public Relations

The entire effort of marketing in The Park was designed to link with its concept of a boutique hotel. It had identified its target group as the "Values and Life Style Group", which, according to the Hotel, consisted of four distinct subgroups, each with its own needs and priorities.[12]

(a) Achievers who were middle-aged and prosperous; essentially higher and higher-middle management of large companies and individual businessmen with a life style and spending capacity. These people tended to associate with status and were open to trying new things.
(b) Emulators who were youthful and ambitious with spending capacity and a love for "showing off".
(c) I-am-me people who were still very young but were into a stage of transition into higher levels of management and social status, highly ego conscious and sensitive.
(d) Socially conscious integrated individuals who were leaders, mature, and successful with very strong and clear preferences. They were generally the top management.

Activities, promotions and other personalised approaches were tailored for each segment. For example, youthful events with young celebrities tended to be addressed to the I-am-me group while a get-together with a senior political or business leader would be addressed to Group (d) above.

The Park had been concentrating of late on the corporate segment. The average revenue per room depended on a judicious selection of the mix of clientele. Presently, corporate clientele accounted for 65 percent of the number of person days of occupancy. Said Mr. Rahman, Regional Manager, Sales & Marketing:

The corporate is our area of concentration. The growth in this segment for us has been about 20 percent per year. The public sector has come down; so has airline crew. In fact we have not had air line crew for the last two years.

A common strategy among hotels was to link the tariffs offered to each customer to the volume of business generated. The negotiations were usually based on commitments on both sides: for a fixed tariff rate for the year on the part of a hotel; and to assure the hotel a certain number of room days in a year by the customer. The discount depended on the volume of this commitment.

The gross average revenue per available room (ARR) for The Park was ₹3,300, and the revenue per available room (REV PAR) was ₹2,450. The REV PAR was the highest among all the hotels of the city, according to the executives of The Park[13].

The Park struck an alliance with Jet Airways, the largest private sector operator in India and the second largest domestic airline. Jet Airways was a young airline launched in the early 1990s, and was considered to be a well managed airline, a story of successful privatization. Jet Airways had a market share of about 36 percent in Indian market, and was reputed for its quality of service. It had a loyal clientele among corporate travelers, and its frequent flier program was considered to be very efficient and well designed. As per the terms of this alliance, Jet Airways would give write ups in its in flight magazines, and sell some miles to The Park, which the hotel would award to each guest who checked in, on production of a boarding pass. During certain promotions, The Park would give discounts and free family stay for Jet Airways travelers.

Marketing was largely a Head Office activity, with packages and promotions decided there. Marketing was in two different categories: one for the corporate and the other, to individuals at large. The former was essentially a business to business relationship, with emphasis on relationship building with key executives and decision-makers in the client organizations. Promotion materials were also directed at the corporate as well as to their frequently staying executives. This was supplemented by sales people who kept up their contacts and ensured their share of bookings from each corporate.

The businesses to customer relationships were through advertisements and personal contacts. The Park placed high quality advertisements in up-market magazines and in-flight reading materials of airlines. These advertisements were handled by advertising agency which worked with the Public Relations Department of the Hotel. Four main campaigns had been conducted during the last three years: one was a "The Park" campaign in print media and magazines; the second was a campaign for The Residence in the print media and life style magazines such as *Elle*, *Cosmopolitan*, and *Society*; the third was a TV campaign on The Park; and the fourth was a print media campaign for the "Preferred at The Park" loyalty program. Copies of the advertisements by The Park may be seen in Exhibit 9.

An important component of the strategy of The Park was its organization of events and festivals. Food festivals were organized by the restaurants. In 1999, The Park organized an Indonesian and a Burmese food festival at Zen, Awadhi and Hyderabadi festivals at Saffron, and a Mexican and a Mauritian festival at The Café Atrium. Atrium had also organized a croissant festival and a coffee world tour festival, featuring different types of croissants and coffee from various parts of the world. The restaurants also organized events to coincide with occasions such as Diwali, cricket matches, etc. during which the hotel organized interesting contests and give always so that the guests would find it memorable.

Exhibit 9 Advertisements of The Park

The Hotel, mainly through Someplace Else, also organized other events on a larger scale. It also organized get-togethers with celebrities, a number of fashion shows involving well known designers like Suneet Verma, Tarun Tahiliani, and Rohit Bal, theatre shows, French operas, cinema shows, especially of the latest films that had not yet been released in Calcutta, and dialogue events between the invited public and well known social/thought leaders. Last year it had well known film actor and a heartthrob of the younger generation, Hrithik Roshan coming and dancing at The Park. It had also organized an off beat "Sadie Hawkins" event where girls could propose to boys. All these events and activities were well received and the Hotel management hoped that it would have generated adequate awareness in the minds of public about the property.

From the Public Relations Department, Ms. Salmoli Ghosh remarked:

> *One thing about this place is that we have a lot of fun organizing these events. A lot of freedom is there with us to decide and organize events that we think fit with The Park's image. I, for one, have great fun. But a very important thing is that in this kind of place, you must be the kind of person who enjoys doing these things.*

To achieve effective tracking of customer preferences, special requests and customer complaints, the hotel had launched a project called The Care Project. This would involve the front office (reception, lobby desk, Residence Floor Reception, cashiers, bill desk and telephone exchange), housekeeping, engineering, butlers and room service. The customer preferences generated at different points and related to food and drink, room-related preferences, time routines, business related preferences and travel-related preferences were recorded into database. When the guest checked in next time, all departments were given a copy of these preferences and past complaints.

Preferences were arrived at by (i) repeat requests (ii) explicit preference requests followed by a confirmation, (iii) a preference form at the time of booking and before arrival (iv) feed back form and (v) bits of information picked up by room boys, butlers and other staff during conversation with guests and even observance of their behavior.

The Park had recently got a customer satisfaction survey conducted by Gallup. This revealed a number of areas which produced dissatisfaction among customers, e.g., check-in, response time for complaints, and food quality. According to Mr. Dewan, these were addressed and significant improvements could be made. Now The Park had engaged Gallup to do a continuous survey.

The Park had become a member of the "Small Luxury Hotels of the World" which was a "select group of hotels used by a select group of travelers", according to Mr. Dewan. The membership was $25,000 p.a. plus a fee for each room booked through one of the 15 sales offices of the group all over the world, or through the website of this group. The group allowed international reservation with facility for confirmations. According to Mr. Dewan, the membership was highly beneficial to The Park, with a number of overseas bookings coming through this program.

The Gallup Survey of Customers

To get an idea of what the customers thought about The Park and the image the hotels of the chain had in the minds of the customers, The Park commissioned a customer survey by Gallup Organization, New Delhi. It was found that about 13 percent of the respondents gave a top of the scale (5 out of 5) to overall satisfaction, and 64 percent gave either a 4 or 5 in the case of superior rooms. In the case of Residence, it was substantially higher: 23 percent gave 5 and 67, either 4 or 5. Similar polls were conducted with respect to the restaurants, banquet halls, the night clubs and The Spa. The details may be seen in Exhibit 10.

Exhibit 10 Results of customer satisfaction survey

Item	% respondents giving a rating of	Superior rooms	Residence rooms	Atrium	Saffron	Zen	Banquets	Tantra	Someplace Else	The Spa
Overall satisfaction	5	13	23	25	36	12	7	18	14	3
	4 or 5	64	67	64	76	86	68	62	70	60
Loyalty	5	26	30	23	32	18	7	40	27	10
	4 or 5	62	67	54	70	62	59	72	62	57
Advocacy	5	23	30	27	34	28	16	41	28	13
	4 or 5	65	70	58	70	72	71	76	71	63

Source: Data supplied by The Park, Calcutta.

Note: These data apply only to the Calcutta property.

"Preferred at The Park" Loyalty Program

Last year, The Park had introduced a loyalty program. The members of this program were called "preferred" members. The membership could be either for dining only or for dining plus room. The membership was through payment of ₹500 per year for the dining-cum-room membership and a one time membership fee of ₹3000 for dining membership. Renewal fee for room membership was ₹400 per year, or 500 points, which could be earned by an expenditure of ₹10,000. The members were given a smart card that identified them as "Preferred at The Park" category members, and it contained details of the member such as the name, visit details, account to which debits should be raised and the points accumulated till date. Room members were guaranteed room availability. Room and dining members could get the following facilities at all the properties of The Park Hotels:

- Early check in and late check-out.
- Complimentary access to The Residence Lounge (irrespective of the category of room the guest is staying in) and the health club.
- Complimentary stay for spouse.
- Deluxe amenities in the room.
- Complimentary use of the meeting room for half a day for 6 persons (subject to availability).
- One complimentary drink served in the bar.

Dining members could get discounts of between 50 percent (for one guest) and 15 percent (for 10 guests) on food.

The cards were valid for all The Park properties. Each time a member used a card for stay and/or food, for every ₹20 spent, he/she got one point, worth about ₹0.93. These points could be redeemed for a variety of items such as travel, life style purchases, consumer durables and so on. The Park was the first hotel in India to introduce the smart card technology for which they received the Golden Peacock award in 1999 for introducing the best technology in the hotel industry.

The Question of Centralization

As noted earlier, the The Park chain of hotels functioned largely independently. With the introduction of the boutique concept, the question of what functions needed to be dealt with centrally so as to ensure uniformity across the various hotels of the chain had assumed central importance. Presently, the different properties designed their own décor but conforming to the overall boutique concept. The advertisement and promotions had been centralised, but the question of discounts to be offered by the different properties had often cropped up during discussion among the executives. With the creation of a web site, the need for ensuring a consistent message was evident, but how to implement this without encroaching upon the freedom of the property managers was not clear.

Marketing and sales also needed a relook. To what extent should it be left to the individual property managers? Being in constant touch with the important clients was very important, and –clearly much could be said to encourage properties to manage this in the way they saw best. But the possibility of contradictory messages had to be taken into account. Similarly, the HRD function also needed to be looked at. Was there a need to centralise all training? Or the curriculum development could be done at one place, the implementation being left to the properties? What about the management of a common culture? With the boutique concept, and the web based booking that encouraged booking at different properties in one stroke, would the customer expect a certain commonality of the levels of service, the quality and the way the staff behaved to the customers? Should this aspect be centralised also?

A larger question that needed to be tackled quite soon was: Had it become necessary to have a corporate office, distinct from the properties? If so, what should this office do? What functions should be centralised, and what functions to be decentralised?

THE TASK AHEAD: CONCERNS OF THE TOP MANAGEMENT

Though the Hotel had turned around and was in fact profitable (refer Exhibit 11 for the financials of The Park between 1996–97 and 1999–2000), the top management was still concerned about the strategic direction of the Hotel. The following were the key concerns:

- Was the concept of a boutique hotel sustainable? Was it enough to differentiate it from its competitors?
- If the answer to above were "Yes", what would be the implications for further action? More specifically,
- Is the concept of a boutique hotel sufficiently clear to its own people? How effective have the efforts of the hotel been in conveying the idea to the customers?
- Have the steps taken by the hotel been adequate and enough to give the hotel a sustainable competitive advantage? Was the transition from "A centrally located comfortable hotel with lower tariffs, mainly for State Enterprise executives" to a "small luxurious boutique hotel for trendy and successful people" complete?
- What were the unfinished tasks? How should these tasks be taken care of? To what extent can the steps and the boutique concept be easily imitated by its rivals?
- If the answer to first question is "No", what new direction should the hotel define for itself?

Exhibit 11 Performance of The Park, 1996–1997 to 1999–2000

A. The Balance Sheet

SOURCES OF FUNDS	**1999–2000**	**1998–99**	**1997–98**	**1996–97**
	₹	₹	₹	₹
SHAREHOLDERS FUNDS:				
Share Capital	4,000,000	4,000,000	4,000,000	4,000,000
Reserves & Surplus	162,970,813	141,967,935	124,146,855	85,191,390
	166,970,813	145,967,935	128,146,855	89,191,390
LOAN FUNDS				
Secured Loans	4,770,895	14,467	694,011	3,365,909
Unsecured Loans	0	0	34,439,818	**40,121,507**
	4,770,895	14,467	35,133,829	43,487,416
TOTAL	171,741,708	145,982,402	163,280,684	132,678,806
APPLICATION OF FUNDS				
FIXED ASSETS				
Gross Block	358,888,382	313,951,278	291,280,121	242,347,027
Less: Depreciation	181,066,964	159,711,461	141,456,109	121,732,398
Net Block	177,821,418	154,239,817	149,824,012	120,614,629
Capital Work–in procsss	10,909,553			3,342,017
	188,730,971	154,869,131	149,824,012	123,956,646
INVESTMENTS	967,350	967,150	967,150	1,389,150
CURRENT ASSETS, LOANS AND ADVANCE				
Inventories	23,240,067	23,109,224	23,310,424	21,302,277
Sundry Debtors	24,338,154	22,336,312	68,962,184	43,577,715

Cash & Bank Balances	3,808,150	4,505,635	5,147,300	5,921,237
Loans & Advances	208,068,814	127,460,586	68,244,883	36,986,468
Interest Accrued on Investment		540,000	540,000	540,000
	259,455,185	**177,951,757**	**166,204,791**	108,327,697
LESS: CURRENT LIABILITIES AND PROVISIONS	277,411,798	187,805,636	153,715,269	100,994,687
NET CURRENT ASSETS	(17,956,613)	(9,853,879)	12,489,522	7,333,010
TOTAL	171,741,708	145,982,402	163,280,684	132,678,806

B. Profit and Loss Account

INCOME	1999–2000 ₹	1998–99 ₹	1997–98 ₹	1996–97 ₹
Rooms, Rent, Food & Beverages	249,167,405	226,187,375	221,882,698	173,473,400
Other Income	5,620,801	16,503,332	25,618,570	9,349,982
	254,788,206	**242,690,707**	**247,501,268**	182,823,382
EXPENDITURE				
Expenses	193,326,473	186,031,477	177,836,829	149,996,869
Interest	9,074,773	6,659,619	610,645	4,729,326
Depreciation	21,384,082	18,255,352	17,630,373	13,480,174
Less: Depreciation on Revalued Amount	1,641,559	1,728,066	1,819,143	1,915,035
Net depreciation	19,742,523	16,527,286	15,811,230	11,565,139
Sub total expenses	222,143,769	209,218,382	194,258,704	166,291,334
Profit\(Loss) for the year	32,644,437	33,472,325	53,242,564	16,532,048
Profit as per last account	52,409,040	38,630,696	6,715,842	(3,515,468)
Adjustments		(4,601,679)		
	85,053,477	67,501,342	59,958,406	13,016,580
APPROPRIATIONS				
Investment Allowance Reserve written back			--	1,507,282
Provision for Taxation	(10,000,000)	(9,321,500)	(12,494,273)	(5,256,000)
Income relating to earlier year			26,317	--
Foreign Exchange Earnings Reserve	3,421,998	(5,770,802)	(8,859,754)	(2,552,020)
Balance carried to Balance Sheet	71,631,479	52,409,040	38,630,696	6,715,842

Source: Annual Reports of the Hotel furnished to us by the Hotel.

NOTES

1. "Small Luxury Hotels of the World" was a group of hotels answering to the description implied in the title. Belonging to this group put The Park in the company of a number of well known hotels all over the world.
2. A "boutique" hotel was one with a distinct, contemporary and trendy décor, with attractive art work, offering a personalised service, and generally relatively small. A further explanation of the boutique concept is given later in the case.
3. Jacuzzi was a set of small shower sprays fitted along the bathtubs at its sides. One could relax in this facility while reading, listening to music etc.
4. The discotheque in The Park, Delhi also had the same name.
5. Interview with Mr. R. Mehrotra, Manager, Marketing & sales.
6. Interview with Ms. Salmoli Ghosh, Deputy Manager, Public Relations
7. Interview with Mr. V.K. Ramalingam, Executive, House Keeping
8. Interview with Mr. Siraj Mukherjee.
9. Interview with Ms. Mahua Mukherjee.
10. Interview by case writers
11. Interview with Mr. Manohar Agrawalla, Manager, IT services.
12. Information given to us by The Park
13. Interview with Mr. Rahman, Regional Manager, Sales and Marketing.

Kanpur Confectioneries Private Limited (A)

CASE

5

Mukund Dixit and Vandana Dixit

On September 10, 1987, Mr. Alok Kumar Gupta, 47, Chairman and Managing Director of Kanpur Confectioneries Private Limited (KCPL), was in a meeting with his brothers, Vivek, 42, and Sanjay, 33, to decide their response to the proposal of A-One Confectioneries Private Limited (APL) that KCPL might consider becoming its contract manufacturer. APL was a leading national player in the confectionery industry. It had desired to expand its supply to the market by subcontracting orders to other manufacturers. It had also desired to retain full control over the quality and production processes. It had promised to the subcontractors that it would compensate them adequately in terms of volume of business and conversion charges. To KCPL the advantages were in getting an assured return on its investment and access to APL's manufacturing expertise but the disadvantages were in the possible loss of independence in decision making, dilution of company's own brand, "MKG", and family prestige.

KCPL AND ITS BACKGROUND

KCPL was started in 1945 by Mohan Kumar Gupta, then 28, in Jaipur, Rajasthan to sell sugar candies under the brand "MKG". Earlier, he was a worker in a candy unit in Jaipur. He started his own business with the dealership of candies produced by others. With the experience gained he set up a production unit in Jaipur in 1946. Between 1946 and 1950 thirty units were set up in the unorganised sector in Rajasthan to sell a variety of candies. As the competition increased the margins came down. KCPL could not compete on costs as its costs were higher than the other manufacturers. Mohan Kumar faced a financial crisis. He decided to shift the production to another state and reduce costs. In 1954, he bought one and a half acres plot in Radha Industrial Estate, Kanpur, Uttar Pradesh (UP) and set up a candy making unit. He became the first entrepreneur to set up a candy making unit in UP. He appointed three sales representatives to cover the entire state, establish dealership, and promote "MKG" as a leading brand. He advertised "MKG" in the vernacular newspapers and on hoardings located at crossroads. To build further on his success, he established a dealer's network in the neighbouring states of Bihar and Madhya Pradesh. By the end of 1960s he was a market leader in candies in the northern region. He decided to invest his surplus cash to diversify into making glucose biscuits and selling them under the "MKG" brand. In 1970, there were two large national and six regional manufacturers. The demand was growing at more than 15% per annum. The margins were

Prepared by Professor Mukund Dixit and Mrs. Vandana Dixit. The names of places, products and people are disguised. The case writers express their gratitude to the members of the family that co-operated with them in writing this case.

attractive. He saw the biscuits' venture as an extension of the candy business. The process was simple and the equipments were available indigenously. Sugar was the common raw material. However, he had to arrange for regular supply of other raw materials like maida (refined wheat flour) and vegetable oil (vanaspati). He tied up with local merchants and commenced production in 1970. He rented depots in key towns for stocking the biscuits. He continued to advertise the brand in vernacular newspapers. He also advertised the brand at retail shops. The business was profitable but the acceleration of production was constrained by the scarcity of ingredients like maida, sugar and vanaspati. He extended his range and offered cream, salt and Marie biscuits under the "MKG" brand.

In 1973–74, KCPL reached the number two position in the market with a monthly sale of 110 tonnes (1 tonne=1000 kg). Prince Biscuits, promoted by Ghanshyam Das in 1960, was the leader with a monthly sale of 130 tonnes. His plant, located at Agra, Uttar Pradesh, had a monthly capacity of 150 tonnes. International Biscuits Ltd. held the third position with a sale of 100 tonnes per month. Its plant located at Mumbai, Maharashtra, had a capacity of 800 tonnes per month. It was a leading player in western and eastern regions. A-One Confectioneries Limited, an overall national leader with a total capacity of 900 tonnes per month, did not have a significant presence in the North. However, it had a leading position in the South.

In 1980–81, KCPL's turnover in biscuits' business was ₹2 crore, an increase of 15 per cent over 1979–80. Its net profits were ₹20 lakh, an increase of 12 per cent over the previous year. In 1980–81, KCPL doubled its capacity from 120 tonnes per month to 240 tonnes per month. In 1983–84, its sales increased to ₹3 crore and net profits to ₹25 lakh.

Technology and Operations in 1987

Biscuit making involved preparation of dough by mixing maida, sugar syrup, vanaspati and certain preservatives in a given proportion, stamping the dough to get various shapes and sizes, and baking the shapes to get ready to eat biscuits. It is the proportion of ingredients that enabled the company to develop a secret formula. The quality of materials received was checked in a laboratory for impurities and existence of metal particles. Maida was cleaned and fed to the mixing unit manually. The sugar crystals were converted into sugar syrup by dissolving the crystals in water and heating the solution. The hot solution was cooled to room temperature and stored in cylinders. The syrup was mixed with maida and vanaspati in small mixers. The mixed dough was fed to the stamping unit and the stamped wet biscuits were fed to the oven for baking. The temperature needed for baking varied from stage to stage. The quality of biscuits depended on the care with which the temperature was maintained at different phases of baking. The ready to eat biscuits were sent to the packing department. The biscuits were manually packed in packets of 100 grams.

In 1986–87 the average monthly production of "MKG" biscuits was 120 tonnes. KCPL depended on both permanent and casual workers for its operations. In all there were ninety permanent employees. The monthly salary bill was ₹2.75 lakh. Casual workers were employed on daily basis to support activities in the packing and material-handling department. The size of casual work force depended on the volume of production. On an average, six casual workers were employed to support one tonne of production. The daily wage rate was ₹50. The workers were from the local region. The prime problem in operations was absenteeism. The workers used to abstain from work without notice. The absenteeism was as high as fifty percent. This had led to uneven production. The daily production varied between 2 tonnes per day to 6 tonnes per day. The company sought the advice of technical consultants on issues relating to capacity expansion, equipment selection and productivity improvements. The overall operations were supervised by Arun Kapoor, Manager (Operations). He was a graduate in science from a local college.

KCPL bought maida in bags of 50 kg, sugar in bags of 100 kg and vanaspati in tins of 15 kg, from local suppliers and stocked them near the mixing unit.

Induction of Family Members

Mohan Kumar had six sons. Alok Kumar, the eldest son, joined the business in 1960 after completing his graduation in commerce. Vivek, the second son, joined the company in 1965 after completing his graduation in mechanical engineering. Sanjay, the youngest son, joined the business in 1974 after completing his graduation in arts. The other three sons started their own trading concerns to trade in metal parts and containers. In 1982, Mohan Kumar handed over the leadership of KCPL to his eldest son. The sons of Alok were studying in school.

The allocation of responsibilities among the family

members was clear. Alok Kumar looked after finance and liaison functions. Vivek looked after human resource management and manufacturing, and Sanjay was responsible for marketing, logistics and administration. They did not interfere in each other's areas. The family members met on the fifth of every month to review the operations and performance of the businesses, and think through the issues for the future. Decision making within the family was seen by them as participative. The family members could disagree on issues without disrespect to the fraternal hierarchy.

The management principles laid down by the family were: respecting the laws of the land, not exploiting labour, running business on ethical lines, treating the consumer as king, and not evading taxes.

Funds Management

The banker to the company was State Bank of India. KCPL was associated with this bank since 1954. The company believed in the policy of ploughing back the surplus. The family members earned a salary.

"MKG" Brand

"MKG" was a popular brand in the northern region. "MKG" biscuits were known for their quality, crispness and affordable price. The brand was advertised in the vernacular dailies and weeklies. It was also advertised on hoarding on crossroads and at the point of sale in "Kirana" shops located in residential colonies. The biscuits were available in standard packs of 100 grams. KCPL did not sell loose biscuits. The Kirana shop owners broke the pack and sold them loose whenever needed. The consumers were middle class families in urban and semi urban areas. The families in metropolitan cities preferred A-One or International.

Canteens of institutions bought biscuits by floating competitive tenders. They placed orders with the lowest bidder. In 1986–87 KCPL had sold 360 tonnes to small and medium sized institutions. The total demand from these institutions was estimated to be around 2400 tonnes. The large institutions preferred the other three brands.

Competition and KCPL's Performance

In 1973–74, glucose biscuits were a growing segment of the biscuit industry. Only two national players, A-One Confectioneries Private Limited and International Biscuits Limited, dominated the industry. However, competition increased with the setting up of seventy units in the unorganized sector between 1975 and 1980. Some of them were set up in the backyards of entrepreneurs under less hygienic production conditions. They either sold unbranded biscuits or sold them with brand names sounding similar to the leading brands. They even imitated the packaging style of the leading brands. It was apprehended by the industry that the units in unorganized sector avoided payment of taxes. The manufacturers had to pay an excise duty of 15% and sales tax of 7% of sales value. During the same period 8 new units were set up in the organized sector in Uttar Pradesh.

In the new competitive environment, KCPL got stuck in the middle. It could not increase its prices to take care of rising costs of labour and material. It did not have the national scale to reduce costs considerably nor did it have the premium image to get a higher price. It could not withstand the competitive pressure. Between 1983–84 and 1986–87 its sales declined. Its capacity was rendered surplus. It incurred a loss. See Exhibit 1 for details of monthly operating performance of "MKG" operations in 1986–87.

The candy business was on the decline. Owing to increased competition from both organized and unorganized players the margins were under pressure. The business had become unattractive and uncompetitive. The family members decided to close the candy line.

Exhibit 1 Details of MKG's monthly operations in 1986-87

Dimension	"MKG"	APL
Sale Per Month (Tonnes)	120	1200 National (200 North)
Price Per Tonne (₹)	18,100	19,000
Consumption of Maida per tonne (in Kg)	750	700
Consumption of Vanaspati per tonne (In Kg)	150	140
Consumption of Sugar per tonne (In Kg)	200	190
Price of Maida per bag of 50 Kg.	500	490
Price of Vanaspati per tin of 15 Kg	520	500
Price of Sugar per bag of 100 Kg	1200	1150
Preservatives and Packaging costs per tonne	1,000	1,000
Casual Labour cost per tonne (₹)	300	400
Wage Rate	50	80
Permanent Salary Bill Per Month (₹ lakhs)	2.75	NA
Interest Per Month (₹)	10,000	NA
Other fixed Commitments	60,000	NA

The data relates to "MKG" biscuits operations. They do not cover the impact of Pearson contract.

Source: Discussion with company executives and trade.

Arrangements with Pearson Health Drinks Ltd.

In 1985 Pearson Health Drinks Limited (Pearson), a multinational company selling "Good Health" nourishing health drink, decided to diversify into health biscuits by building on its good will in health drink market. It also decided that it would not set up its own manufacturing facility. It would outsource the supply from small and medium scale units by providing technical support. Mr. Ramakant Joshi, a consultant to KCPL, recommended KCPL's case to Pearson. He had worked with Pearson before starting his consulting company. Pearson promised a load of 100 to 125 tonnes per month and a conversion rate of ₹3 per kilo after reimbursing fully the cost of materials. It also agreed to allow KCPL to run its existing line of business. KCPL saw an opportunity to utilize its surplus capacity. It also hoped to learn new skills of quality management. It did not see Pearson as a competitor to KCPL. The agreement with Pearson was signed at its corporate office in Paris in May 1986. The initial order from Pearson was for 50 tonnes per month between May 1986 and March 1987. Pearson relied on the expertise of KCPL. It did not provide any technical guidance. Its officers inspected the quality of the biscuits before dispatch.

The market response to Good Health biscuits was not very encouraging. They were seen as high priced biscuits without any additional benefits. The customers had perceived the A-One biscuits as health and energy providing biscuits. The price of A-One biscuits was two-thirds of "Good Health" biscuits. APL had stressed in its advertisements that its biscuits contained milk solids.

Offer of APL

On September 8, 1987 Mr. Bharat Shah, Chairman of APL, mentioned in the meeting of Confectioneries Manufacturers Association of India (CMAI) that his company was interested in augmenting its supplying capacity by promoting contract manufacturing units (CMU) that made biscuits for APL according to the specifications developed by APL. He also mentioned that his company would provide technical guidance to the CMUs and offer fair conversion charges. Mr. Alok Kumar Gupta met Mr. Shah after the conference and enquired whether he was serious in his proposal. Mr. Shah answered in the affirmative.

To APL, CMU route was an attempt to reduce its cost of manufacturing. APL was an overall national market leader with a reputation for quality and price competitiveness. It had not changed its prices in the last three years. It had its plants in Chennai, Tamil Nadu. Its monthly capacity in 1986–87 was 1200 tonnes. It had mechanized most of its operations and reaped benefits of large scale economies. It had introduced quality control procedures based on Japanese practices. These practices had enabled the company to minimize wastage and improve responsiveness to customer's orders. It competed with both national and regional players in various biscuit segments. It had aspirations of becoming a leader in each of the regional segments. It had entered the northern region in 1973–74. By 1986–87, it had become a leading player in the segment with a monthly sale of 200 tonnes.

The Proposal

APL offered to place an initial order for producing seventy tonnes of glucose biscuits per month. It also offered to supply the pre printed packing material with APL name. It would inspect the production processes of KCPL and recommend changes in processes and equipments, if needed. The changes needed to be carried out by KCPL at its own cost. APL would post two quality control officers at KCPL plants and enable KCPL to adhere to quality procedures. It would supply the "APL secret ingredient" to KCPL but KCPL would be required to buy the other ingredients like sugar, maida and vanaspati oil from one of the authorized suppliers of APL. It offered to reimburse the raw material expenses as per its norms and pay a conversion charge of ₹1.50 per kg to cover the expenses on labour, overheads and depreciation. The initial contract was to be for three years. Shah had hinted that the off take would be increased if KCPL rose to the expectations of APL. In terms of control, KCPL would be required to send daily production and raw material consumption report to APL.

Discussion in the Family

Alok Kumar presented the proposal of APL to his brothers. There were both advantages and disadvantages. A clear advantage was in terms of avoiding marketing, brand building and distribution expenses, and minimizing the business risks. It would also help them utilize the surplus capacity. The disadvantage was in the possible loss of independence. It was also feared that they might not be able to concentrate on strengthening the "MKG" brand built over the years. In fact, the family name was dependent on the success of the biscuit line. In the early years of its growth, Mohan Kumar had the vision of emerging as a leading national brand and competing successfully with APL.

There were also anxieties in terms of how the relationship with APL would work out and how APL's experience of managing large plants in Chennai would help in running a small plant in Kanpur. Would there be interference? Would they be asked to make additional investments in manufacturing? Was the conversion charge fair? How would Pearson view the venture was another issue.

The other questions were: What did the family members want from their business ventures? What would they like to give to their sons when they grew up? They had to decide soon as they were not sure whether other biscuit manufacturers were also interested in the opportunity and would out beat KCPL in approaching APL.

CASE 6

Kanpur Confectioneries Private Limited (B)

Mukund Dixit and Mrs. Vandana Dixit

On July 5, 2001, Mr. Alok Kumar Gupta, Chairman and Managing Director of Kanpur Confectioneries Private Limited (KCPL), was in a meeting with his brothers, Vivek and Sanjay, and his son Kunal to review the progress made since signing the agreement with A-One Confectioneries Limited on December 10, 1987, and develop a course of action for future.

The Company

Kanpur Confectioneries Private Limited was started in 1945 by Mohan Kumar Gupta in Jaipur, Rajasthan, to produce and sell candies under the brand name MKG. In 1954, he bought one and a half acres plot in Radha Industrial Estate in Kanpur, Uttar Pradesh, and shifted his manufacturing operations there. He diversified into making glucose biscuits under the brand "MKG" biscuits in 1970. He saw the venture as an extension of the candy business. The process was simple and the equipment were available indigenously. Over the years he extended his range of biscuits and offered cream, salt and marie biscuits under the same brand. (See Kanpur Confectioneries Private Limited (A) for details.)

MKG Brand

MKG was a popular brand in the northern region. MKG biscuits were known for their quality, crispness and affordable price. The brand was advertised in the vernacular dailies and weeklies. It was also advertised on hoardings at crossroads and at the point of sale in "kirana" shops located in residential colonies. The biscuits were available in standard packs of 100 grams. KCPL did not sell loose biscuits. The "kirana" shop owners broke the pack and sold them loose whenever needed.

Competition

At the time of entry, glucose biscuits were a growing segment of the biscuit industry. Only two national level players, A-One Confectioneries Private Limited, (ACPL) and International Biscuits Limited (IBL), dominated the industry. Between 1970 and 1974 the price of biscuit making ovens declined and they became easily available. As a result, there many biscuit making units mushroomed in the organized and unorganized sectors. About 70 units came up in the unorganized sector

Cases of the Indian Institute of Management, Ahmedabad, are prepared as a basis for class discussion. Cases are not designed to present illustrations of either correct or incorrect handling of administrative problems.
Prepared by Professor Mukund Dixit and Mrs. Vandana Dixit. The names of places, products, and people are disguised. The case writers express their gratitude to the members of the family that cooperated with them in writing this case.

between 1975 and 1980. Some of them were set up in the backyards of entrepreneurs under less hygienic production conditions. They either sold unbranded biscuits or sold them with brand names sounding similar to the leading brands. They even imitated the packaging style of the leading brands. Entries were also made in the organized sector. In Uttar Pradesh alone eight new units were set up in the organized sector between 1970 and 1985.

In the new competitive environment, KCPL got stuck in the middle. It could not increase its prices to take care of rising costs of labour and material. It did not have the national scale to reduce costs considerably nor did it have the premium image to get a higher price. It could not withstand the competitive pressure.

Arrangement with Pearson Health Drinks Ltd.

In 1985, Pearson Health Drinks Ltd. (PHL), a multinational company selling "Good Health" nourishing health drink, decided to diversify into health biscuits by building on its goodwill in the health drink market. It also decided that it would not set up its own manufacturing facility. Pearson promised a load of 100 to 125 tonnes per month and a conversion rate of ₹3 per kilo after reimbursing the material costs. It also agreed to allow KCPL to run its existing line of business. KCPL saw an opportunity to utilize its surplus capacity. It also hoped to learn new tools of quality management. It did not see Pearson as a competitor to KCPL. The agreement with Pearson was signed with their corporate office in Paris in May, 1986. The initial order from Pearson was for 50 tonnes. Pearson relied on the expertise of KCPL. It did not provide any technical guidance. Its officers inspected the quality of the biscuits before dispatch.

The market response to "Good Health" biscuits was lukewarm. They were seen as high priced biscuits with no additional benefits. The customers had perceived the A-One biscuits as health and energy providing biscuits. The price of A-One biscuits was two-third of "Good Health" biscuits. A-One had stressed in its advertisements that its biscuits contained milk solids.

Decision to Associate with A-One Confectioneries Ltd.

On September 8, 1987 Mr. Bharat Shah, Chairman of A-One Confectioneries Limited, mentioned in the meeting of Confectioneries Manufacturers Association of India (CMAI) that his company was interested in augmenting its supplying capacity by promoting contract manufacturing units (CMU) that made biscuits for A-One according to the specifications developed by A-One. He also mentioned that his company would provide technical guidance to the CMUs and offer fair conversion charges. Mr. Alok Kumar Gupta met Shah after the conference and enquired whether he was serious in his proposal. Shah answered in the affirmative.

For A-One, the CMU route was an attempt to reduce its cost. A-One was an overall national market leader with reputation for quality and price competitiveness. It had not changed prices of its biscuits in the last three years. It had its plants in Chennai, Tamil Nadu. It had mechanized most of its operations and reaped benefits of large-scale economies. It had introduced quality control procedures based on Japanese practices. These practices had enabled the company to minimize waste and reduce cost.

Discussion in the Family

The discussion among the family members was emotional and rational. They were proud of their brand name and the quality of their biscuits. Would they be required to discontinue their brand one-day or the other? Would they be able to maintain their managerial independence? At some point they had seen themselves emerging as a leading national brand and competing successfully with A-One. A contract with A-One would put an end to all such aspirations. "What was the value of holding on to aspirations when the unit was stuck in the middle between large players with advantages of costs from economies of scale and the small un-organized players, also with cost advantages?" was another argument. Given the financial position of the unit, it was worth going in for contract manufacturing if the conversion charges left a surplus for covering the overheads. There were advantages of imbibing new technology practices of A-One and transferring them to run the MKG lines. One of the family members posed the issue as a survival issue. If KCPL did not take the initiative other biscuit manufacturers would and strengthen the competitive advantage of A-One. It could be squeezed from both, the stronger A-One brand and the unorganized units. Since KCPL did not have any distinctive advantage in the industry, there was a threat of being wiped out sooner or later.

After considering the advantages and disadvantages, the family decided to approach A-One and sign an agreement to be a contract manufacturer. It had its first round of discussions in Chennai in September 1987. On

December 10, 1987 Vivek interacted with Bharat Shah and signed the agreement. There were anxieties till the last minute, to the extent that Vivek called Alok five minutes before signing the agreement and enquired whether he should change his mind.

KCPL signed a contract with A-One for three years. It became the first CMU of A-One and was referred to as the mother CMU. Pearson did not object to the agreement. The marketing manager of Pearson mentioned to Alok Kumar that KCPL was able to conclude the agreement because of its association with Pearson.

Changes Introduced by A-One

The production for A-One started in January, 1988 with an order of 69 tonnes per month. This load continued for six months. KCPL maintained all the three lines of production—"MKG", Good Health and A-One. Initially A-One had difficulty in seeing a small-scale unit's operations from the experience of large-scale operations. It had to learn and then develop suggestions for adopting their practices. It took eight months to iron out the issues and develop a viable set of practices. It sent its engineers to KCPL to study the processes and suggest modifications. It also sent its engineers to learn from KCPL's operations. A-One posted two site officers to provide technical guidance to KCPL and play a liaison role between A-One and KCPL. The site officers were paid by A-One but their office space was provided free of charge by KCPL.

A-One released a monthly requirement order against which KCPL developed a daily production schedule. KCPL was required to send a daily production data to A-One. A courier was employed to send the daily production data. With the advent of the Internet in 1998, the information was sent by e-mail. A-One supplied raw material (maida, sugar, and preservatives) and A-One mixture, a unique combination of chemicals that gave a distinct taste to the biscuits, to KCPL according to a production plan. A-One also supplied cardboard boxes, packaging material, plain paper and printed paper. Initially the biscuits were made in pack sizes of 100 grams. In 1998, the pack sizes were extended to 50 grams and 25 grams.

Vivek and Sharma, Manager (Operations) brought about changes in operations through training. Sharma supervised the overall operations. Vivek and Sharma attended training courses organized by the business development department of A-One in Bombay, Bangalore, Ahmedabad and Goa. There, they were exposed to concepts of quality circle, human resources development and effective shopfloor management. They initiated similar training sessions at KCPL to reduce wastage, rejections, enhance hygiene, and improve labour relations. As a result, absenteeism came down from 50 per cent to 2 per cent. The involvement of casual workers was reduced to none. Earlier KCPL depended on both permanent and casual workers for its operations. The casual workers were employed on a daily basis to support activities in the packing and material-handling department. The size of casual workforce depended on the volume of production. The size varied between 20 and 40. The workers were from the local regions. The prime problem in operations was absenteeism. The workers used to abstain from work without notice. This had led to uneven production. Mr. Sharma commented:

> *In 1989 there was utter confusion on the shopfloor. There were problems in absenteeism. On the plant side automation was low. Our workers were not quality conscious. Cleanliness was below expectation. We worked from basics and changed all that.*

The improvements were in automation in cleaning, mixing, loading, baking and packing. One of the innovations was the development of maida filters. Earlier maida was cleaned and fed manually. Eight to ten workers were needed in the operation. In the new system, an automatic filtering and feeding unit cleaned the maida eight times and fed it into the mixing unit directly. The idea was borrowed from the visit to a cold drink bottling plant where sugar was fed through the gravitational pull. A dough lifter was developed to transfer the dough from the mixing unit to the baking unit. Ventilation and airflow in the baking unit were improved. Vanaspati storage was shifted from tins to silo system. Earlier vanaspati was brought in tins and tins were emptied into the mixing unit. This created delay and clutter on the shop floor. In 1992, this was replaced by a system where vanaspati was stored in silo and drawn into the mixing unit as and when needed. The storage silo received vanaspati from tankers.

The emphasis was on documentation and clear visibility of instructions. Each equipment was identified in Hindi, the vernacular language, and the instructions for material and equipment handling were also in Hindi. The company had adopted the "learn and teach" concept where each one was required to teach the colleagues in formal sessions. A-One helped KCPL to introduce the 5S concept in managing the shop floor in 1998. See Exhibit 1 for an idea of the 5S practice. KCPL initiated a process of extending the 5S practice to the residences of employees. The company executives volunteered to visit the residences of the employees and teach the 5S concept.

Exhibit 1 What is 5S?

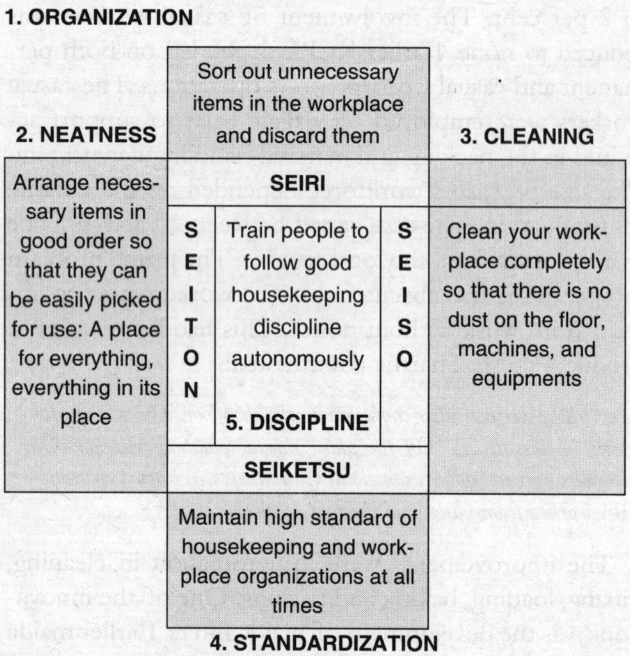

Source: Company records.

A-One monitored the performance of KCPL on cleanliness in housekeeping, rejections, dispatch, and employee productivity management. It insisted on continuous upgradation of equipment and improvements in shopfloor practices. It encouraged active interaction among the 22 CMUs set up by it. Every year the CMU entrepreneurs and their managers were encouraged to visit one another's plants and learn from the innovations introduced. Initially, there were resistances to such visits. Once the advantages were known it became a welcome practice. It was referred to as 'teerthyatra' (pilgrimage). There wasn't any sense of competition as each one received orders to utilize his capacity fully. A-One held annual workshops of CMUs to review their progress and concerns. In 1993–94, A-One decided to adopt its own standards of quality beyond those of Bureau of Indian Standards. CMUs were asked to adopt these standards at the earliest.

KCPL constituted a committee called "Jagruti Committee" (Vigilance Committee) consisting of representative of employees in 1998, to monitor the performance of the company and recommend changes on a continuous basis to improve performance. This idea was picked from A-One.

KCPL tried to operate on just in time mode as far possible. It maintained three months stock of maida, vanaspati and sugar. A-One identified the suppliers and fixed the terms of payments. KCPL contacted the suppliers directly and obtained the supplies. The biscuit bundles packed in boxes supplied by A-One were dispatched to C&F the agents of A-One in Kanpur and Lucknow according to the agreed weekly allocation schedule.

Computers were introduced in 1998 for accounting use. After that five more computers were installed in the company. The usage was as follows:

Location	Usage
MD's cabin	Financial management and accounting
Director's cabin	Interaction with A-One through e-mail
Receptionist	Correspondence
Dispatch Department	For inventory and stores management
Laboratory Department	Material analysis and reporting

In four months it was clear to KCPL that A-One was very keen on building a healthy relationship with contract manufacturers. It was very soft and very fair. There were no problems with payments. It paid 80 per cent of the conversion charges on the production of an interim bill by the end of the month and the balance 20 per cent by the 20th of the following month. Over the years, the tonnage expanded from 300 to 400, 700, and finally to 1000 tonnes per month. KCPL realized that A-One had bigger plans and its conversion charges were based on a load of 1000 tonnes. At this load the unit made very healthy profits.

In 1993–94, A-One asked KCPL to produce orange cream biscuits as well. It supplied the cream for making cream biscuits. The base biscuits were made in the existing oven and sandwiching was done in a separate section set up for the purpose.

As the load from A-One increased, the time and resources needed to meet A-One's requirements of quality inspection, production planning and control, dispatch and logistics management increased. KCPL was not able to pay attention to both, contract manufacturing and promotion of its own brand. Besides, the venture with A-One turned out to be more exciting and rewarding than their own branding and distribution.

Discontinuing other Lines

Till September 1990, KCPL operated one line each for MKG, A-One and Pearson. Pearson had promised a monthly load of 100–150 tonnes per month. As the planned sales of "Good Health" biscuits did not materialize, KCPL did not receive the promised orders. The company decided not to continue with Pearson. In September 1990, the company decided to close all other lines and focus on contract manufacturing for A-One. Pearson was unhappy with the developments. It developed alternative suppliers in Andhra Pradesh and West Bengal.

Employee Profile and Industrial Relations

The number of employees increased from 98 in 1990 to 175 in 2001. Typically, the employees were 10th to 12th standard pass. Seven employees were graduates. The supervisors had risen from the ranks. The shift-in-charge was a science graduate and the operations-in-charge was a postgraduate. Mr. Sharma, Manager (Operations), had joined the company in 1989 as a mixing supervisor after completing his postgraduation in science from Kanpur University. Mr. Tewari, logistics-in-charge, had joined the company in 1988 as a clerk.

The company did not have any problems with employee relations. It did not have a union. The management referred to the community of employees as the KCPL Pariwar. Gifts were given to children of employees in recognition of their scholastic achievements.

Performance

KCPL could make profits from the conversion charges by managing its costs better. Management of costs was considered critical because A-One itself was facing a competitive situation and had not increased the price of A-One biscuits in the last four years. KCPL minimized investments in plant and machinery, saved on power and fuel, and wages and salaries. A-One did not interfere in the decisions on the appointment of people and their compensation.

The company won several awards for quality maintenance and people initiatives from A-One. In 1994–95 it won the National Productivity Council award for the second best productivity performance in consumer edible products. It received an appreciation award for outstanding technical innovation in the process of manufacturing of biscuits in 1993–94. It received an appreciation award for implementation of the 5S concept in 1999–2000.

Future Concerns

KCPL moved into a new office building in February 2001. It was happy with the progress so far. One of the family members opined that the decision to associate with A-One was a "star" decision. The alignment with A-One had worked very well. KCPL had prospered in terms of tonnage and profitability. Uncertainties regarding the survival of business had disappeared. The unit was able to invest in building a new office with facilities for training and conducting conferences for a group of 15 participants. Further investments were planned for landscaping and creating car parking. Nonetheless, there were several concerns regarding the future.

Despite better performance, the question was whether all the family members would be gainfully employed in contract manufacturing. The third generation of the promoter's family had started joining the business to share managerial responsibilities. Kunal Gupta, son of Alok Kumar, had joined the business in 1993 to provide support for finance and HR functions. He was a commerce graduate. Anil, son of Vivek, was expected to join the company after completion of his engineering studies and provide technical support to his father. With the new generation of successors coming in, the managerial workload got distributed. Professional managers like Sharma and Tewari had risen in the managerial hierarchy and developed capabilities to manage day-to-day operations. Would there be meaningful work for all? Should the family think of new business lines?

The location at Radha Industrial Estate, Kanpur, had enough space to double the capacity. The company could set up one more plant if A-One promised a higher offtake. Already the family had diversified into leasing and finance, rubber products processing, information technology products, and wind power. In 1993–94, the company diversified into leasing of industrial equipment and four wheelers. The leasing industry was in the boom phase. The motive here was to utilize the surplus cash from biscuit operations. The opportunity was lucrative if an initial base of customers could be established. This did not happen and the leasing business did not take off as expected. Another diversification was into the rubber component business. This was through the acquisition route. The BDK unit, a leading unit in Kanpur, was looking for a partner who would buy their rubber component business. The family saw the rubber component business as equivalent to the franchising operations and bought the unit. The unit entered into an agreement with Alfa Lavel of Pune to supply components. In 1998, it entered into an agreement with Pentafour Communication Ltd, a software developing company, to retail its ERP and Accounting software in Uttar Pradesh. The software provided support to the management of hospitals, bank branches and small offices. The family also entered into the wind energy business to take advantage of tax concessions. It had set up a wind farm in Madhya Pradesh to supply power to the Madhya Pradesh Electricity Board. Payment for the power supplied was obtained promptly as the Association of Wind Power Suppliers in Madhya Pradesh was strong.

In the context of the above, the family members had to review the progress made since the A-One decision and develop directions for the future.

CASE 7

Aravind Eye Care System: Giving the Most Precious Gift

S. Manikutty and Neharika Vohra

In 1976 when Padmashree Dr. G. Venkataswamy,[1] or Dr. V as he was popularly known, retired from the Government Medical College, Madurai,[2] as head of the Department of Ophthalmology, he was determined to continue his work of providing quality eye care to the rich and poor alike—the work he had started at the Government Medical College, Madurai. His work involved organizing rural eye camps where vision was checked and corrective glasses were prescribed, cataract was diagnosed, and corrective and preventive measures for proper eye care were explained to patients. Dr. V was seized with the passion of eradicating needless blindness, first from his home state Tamil Nadu, and then the country. He made this his life mission. It deeply pained him that an estimated 45 million people worldwide and 10 million in India had lost the precious gift of sight, most often quite needlessly. To carry out his mission, after retirement, Dr. V formed a non-profit organization, which he named Govel Trust, investing all his life savings in it[3]. He was the Chairman of the trust and his two brothers, two sisters and their spouses became the trust members (Dr. V remained a bachelor throughout his life). The President of Madurai Main Rotary was taken in as an ex officio member. In 1976, the Govel Trust set up a modest 11-bed hospital, named Aravind Eye Hospital (AEH), in the house of one of Dr. V's brothers at Madurai. In this hospital, five beds were for paying patients and six were reserved for free patients.

By 2003, the humble 11-bed hospital had grown to become the Aravind Eye Care System (AECS) comprising a chain of hospitals; a centre for manufacturing synthetic lenses, sutures, and specific eye pharmaceuticals; an institute for training; an institute for research; an international eye bank; a women and child care centre; a post-graduate institute of ophthalmology; and a centre for community outreach programmes (Exhibit 1). In a span of 23 years, AEH in Madurai had become a 1500 bed hospital that performed nearly 95,000 eye surgeries every year. In addition, there were four more AEHs located in Tirunelveli, Coimbatore, Theni, and Pondicherry (Puducherry, refer to Case 2, Exhibit 1). The five hospitals together performed a total of 190,000 surgeries every year, or about 45 per cent of all eye surgeries done in Tamil Nadu and five per cent in India. The persons at the helm of this system were Dr. V, his sister, Dr. G. Natchiar, and her husband, Dr. P. Namperumalsamy (Dr. Nam).

Case material of the Indian Institute of Management, Ahmedabad. Cases of the Indian Institute of Management, Ahmedabad are prepared as a basis for class discussion. Cases are not designed to present illustrations of either correct or incorrect handling of administrative problems. The authors wish to thank Dr.V, Dr. Nam, Dr. Natchiar, Dr. S. Aravind, Mr. G. Srinivasan, Dr. Viji, Dr. Murali, Mr. Thulasiraj, and other doctors and staff of different AEHs, and other units of Aravind Eye Care System for their help and cooperation. The Confederation of Indian Industry (CII), Southern Region, Chennai, helped with initial contacts and bore the case writing cost.

Exhibit 1 Aravind eye care system

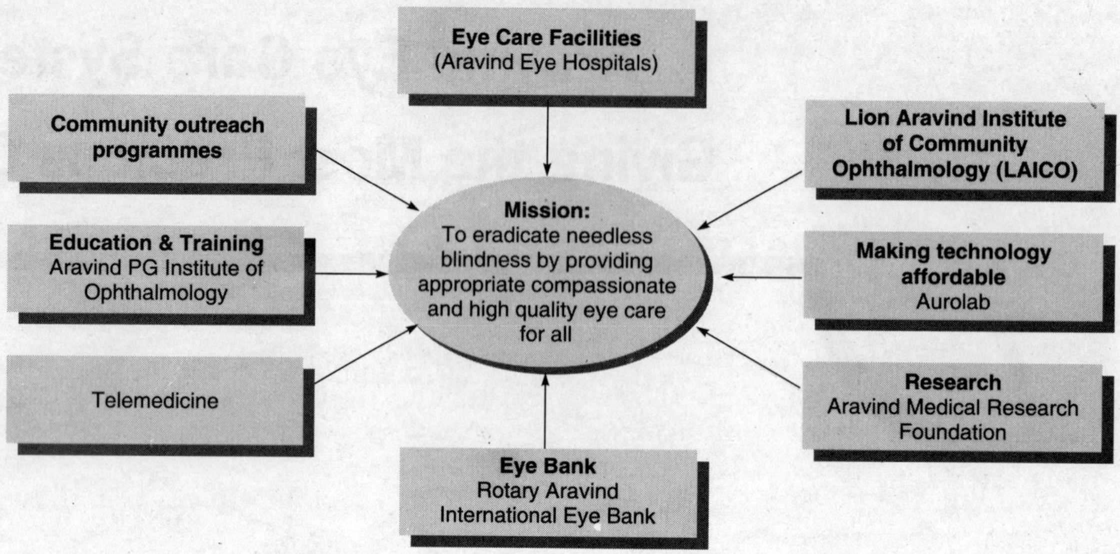

Source: Aravind Eye Care System.

In March 2003, one of the case writers met Dr. V, Dr. Nam and Dr. Natchiar in Dr. V's office. It was 8.30 in the morning and Dr. V, then 85, was busy planning his day's schedule. Dr. V began the interview by saying:

Despite all our efforts, so many people with vision problems with their still have no access to hospitals. Much of the blindness can be corrected through surgery. But they are afraid of operations. So we have to increase the awareness of the causes of blindness and the need for early treatment. Even in villages where we conduct eye camps, only seven per cent of people with eye problems turn up. We have to do more to create demand.

Most of this blindness is needless and curable. We have to eradicate all needless blindness…

Dr. Nam was equally enthusiastic about this vision:

At present we do about 3.6 million eye surgeries in India. If this can be increased to 5 million, needless blindness can be eradicated. We do about 2,600 surgeries per doctor per year in our Aravind Eye Hospitals. The all India average is about 400. It is possible for other hospitals to come up to our level of productivity. We are willing to help them to do so.

Dr. Nam further added:

We perform 95 per cent of our cataract surgeries with insertion of intraocular lenses (IOL).[4] *The all India average of IOL surgeries is only 60 per cent and in some states like Bihar, it is only 30 per cent. We have to raise this percentage through training of doctors.*

Dr. Natchiar said:

All our systems are oriented towards enabling the doctors to be at their productive best. We support them through well-trained paramedical staff. Community outreach programmes are central to our mission, since most of the blind are poor and are in rural areas.

History

Dr. V was born in 1918 in a small village near Madurai. His father was a reasonably well-to-do farmer. Dr. V studied in the local school and then went to Chennai to do medical studies. He completed his M.B.B.S. in 1944 from Madras University and joined the Army Medical Corps in 1945, but was discharged in 1948 after he developed severe rheumatoid arthritis. Arthritis incapacitated him to such an extent that he could not hold even a pen. However, with sheer perseverance and will power, he not only started to write but was also able to wield the surgeon's scalpel.

He then joined Government Medical College, Madurai as an ophthalmic surgeon and rose to become the Head of the Department of Ophthalmology in1956. In 1961, Dr. V pioneered a state-level programme of outreach eye camps to address the problem of blindness in the state. People living in distant villages came to these eye camps to get their eyes tested, diagnosed, and treated. In 1965 Dr. V visited the United States to attend a conference on the rehabilitation of the blind. It was at this conference in New York that he struck a life-long friendship with Sir John Wilson, the founder of the Royal Commonwealth Society for the Blind (now known as Sight Savers International), an organization that had been supporting eye camps in India. Dr. V and Sir John Wilson met the then Prime Minister of India, Mrs. Indira Gandhi, to seek support for setting up a national organization to control blindness. Dr. V had also attended the then Chief Minister of Tamil Nadu, Mr. M. Karunanidhi, who supported government-sponsored eye camps all over Tamil Nadu spearheaded by Dr. V. Thus, even before he retired, Dr. V was overseeing the growing network of eye camps in the state. He had also developed a network of friends and well wishers across India who empathized with his passion for providing good quality affordable eye care.

In 1976, when the Govel Trust was founded, Dr. V's sister Dr. G. Natchiar, and her husband Dr. Nam were also ophthalmologists at the Government Hospital, Madurai. So when Govel Trust decided to set up Aravind Eye Hospital (AEH) in Madurai, Dr. V persuaded them to join the hospital. Over the years other family members (all doctors) joined to head different specialties. Many (including Dr. V, Dr. Nam, and Dr. Natchiar) received training in the United States and were highly competent surgeons.

Dr. V was profoundly influenced by Mahatma Gandhi and Sri Aurobindo Ghosh, the sage philosopher who had founded the ashram in Pondicherry. He always felt a strong urge to do something for the society (rather than take from it). In an article in 2001 Dr. V wrote:

> *Many people often ask me: What made me take up a task of such magnitude at the age of 58? I guess I drew my inspiration from the legacy of our great forefathers… Besides, there were inspirational leaders like Mahatma Gandhi and Sri Aurobindo whose philosophy and way of life influenced many. Naturally I felt impelled to give something back to this great land of ours.*[5]

He named the hospital after Sri Aurobindo as a tribute to the great sage.

Initial Growth

In 1976, Dr. V put in his personal savings to set up AEH, Madurai. However, for cataract surgeries of poor patients from eye camps AEH received partial government support.[6] From the beginning, Dr. V had insisted on following the policy of taking both paying and free patients. The paying patients were charged moderately, same as other comparable hospitals in the city. There were to be no "five star" customers to cross-subsidize poor patients. Dr. V was certain that high productivity and large volumes were necessary for the hospital to become viable, and also to generate a surplus for providing funds for expansion.

As a result, the AEH, Madurai started generating a surplus from the very beginning, and within one year, it opened another 30 bed hospital. In 1978, an exclusive 70-bed hospital was built for free patients. The hospital presently used for paying patients was built in 1981 with 250 beds in a five-storeyed building of 80,000 sq. ft. Dr. V and his team initially focused only on cataract surgery, but other specialties such as retina, cornea, glaucoma, paediatric ophthalmology, neuro-ophthalmology, uvea, low vision, and orbit were gradually added. No compromises were ever made on equipments: they were of the best quality and many were imported. However, the waiting halls, examination rooms, and doctors' chambers were spartan and utilitarian.

In 1984, a new 350 bed hospital was opened to cater exclusively to free patients in Madurai. The top floor of this building housed the nurses' quarters. From the beginning, AEH had the policy of not conducting surgeries at eye camps as was the common practice at that time.[7] The eye camps were for poor patients. Everyone who came to these camps was checked free, and those who needed surgery were brought to the main hospital. Patients did not have to pay for the surgery but they had to bear the cost of the intra ocular lens (IOL). The cost of IOLs was quite high. So in 1992, a new manufacturing facility, Aurolab, was set up to produce IOLs at an affordable cost. These lenses brought down the cost of IOL implant surgery to about ₹500 (which covered the cost of IOL, special sutures, and medication). AEH also took up intense counselling on IOL implant surgery and health education for both the walk-in free patients at the base hospital and those attending eye camps. Though these patients were required to pay ₹500 for IOL implant, in deserving cases, the doctor in charge at the Outpatients Department had the power to waive even that cost. Later, in 1995, when the Indian Government launched a cataract blindness control programme with World Bank funding and offered a subsidy for the camp patients, who were not charged this amount. In stages, the number of free beds increased to the present number of 1,468 beds (1200 free and 268 paying) in the hospitals in Madurai.

By the end of 1990s, Govel Trust had ventured into other towns of Tamil Nadu. An 874 bed hospital was set up in 1997 in Coimbatore, the second largest city in Tamil Nadu. In 1985, a 100 bed hospital was opened at Theni, the birth place of Dr. Nam, a small town 80 km west of Madurai. Theni catered to additional eye camp patients. In 1988, another hospital with 400 beds was opened at Tirunelveli, a town 160 km south of Madurai. Then to cater to the people of north Tamil Nadu, in 2003, a 750 bed hospital was set up in Pondicherry. Though Pondicherry was a Union Territory, it came within the geographical area of Tamil Nadu and it was also the town where Aurobindo Ashram was located. As of 2003, the five hospitals of AECS among them had a total of 3,649 beds, of which 2,850 were for free patients and 799 were paying beds (Refer Exhibit 2).

Exhibit 2 Aravind eye care system: number of beds in different hospitals

(As on 2003)

Unit	Free	No. of beds Paying	Total	Operation Theatres/Tables
Madurai	1100	315	1415	13/45*
Tirunelveli	300	130	430	3/9
Theni	150	30	180	1/3
Coimbatore	700	174	874	8/25
Pondicherry	600	150	750	8/25
Total	2850	799	3649	33/107

* Consisting of 25 tables in free hospitals and 20 in paying hospitals.
Source: Aravind Eye Care System.

From Hospital to Eye Care System

Initial focus of the Govel Trust was on building hospitals and reaching out to the poor with quality surgery. However, Dr. V soon realized that to achieve the ultimate goal of eradicating needless blindness through affordable and quality eye care AEHs, would have to undertake several other activities. Thus, over the years, AEHs evolved to become Aravind Eye Care System (AECS). AECS went into manufacturing of lens, undertook research and training activities, got involved in community health, etc. In 2003,the main divisions of AECS 2003 were Aurolab for manufacturing intraocular lenses; Lions Aravind Institute of Community Ophthalmology (LATCO), a training centre; Aravind Medical Research Foundation, a centre for ophthalmic research; Aravind Centre for Women, Children and Community Health, a research centre for women and children; and the eye bank, the Rotary Aravind International Eye Bank.

Blindness in India

Blindness can be classified into different categories (Exhibit 3). In India, about 12 million people were bilaterally blind and another 8 million were blind in one eye. About 36 million had low vision, needing regular monitoring.

State wise variation in blindness across country was considerable. For example, in the age group of 50 years and above (this group accounted for 90 per cent of country's blindness which was about 16 per cent of the population), it varied from 4.3 per cent in Kerala to 13.7 per cent in Karnataka.

Exhibit 3 Categories of blindness

Category	Definition	Prevalence in the 50 years and older age group	
		India	Tamil Nadu
Bilateral blindness	Both eyes < 6/60 – NPL	8.5	6.0
Social blindness	Both eyes <3/60 – NPL	5.3	4.0
Economic blindness	One eye < 6/60 – 3/60; Fellow eye < 6/00 – NPL	3.2	2.1
Unilateral blindness	One eye < 6/60; Fellow eye > = 6/18	5.1	6.8
Low vision	One eye < 6/18 – 6/60; Fellow eye < 6/18 – NPL	23.8	28.5

Source: National survey on blindness—2001-2002, summary, Quarterly Newsletter of National Programme for Control of Blindness & Vision 2020: The Right to Sight Initiative, 1(2), July-September 2002.

Cataract was the most common cause of blindness, accounting for 62.6 per cent, followed by uncorrected refractive errors (19.7 per cent). The other important causes for bilateral blindness were glaucoma (5.8 per cent) and posterior segment pathology (4.7 per cent).

Exhibit 4 gives a cross-section of the human eye, and a brief description of the common diseases and their treatment. Every year around 9000 ophthalmologists undertook an estimated 3.7 million cataract surgeries in India. In Tamil Nadu (population as per Census 2001: 62,110,839), 370,031 cataract surgeries were done in 2001–2002. Government hospitals did about 7.17 per cent of these; 10.16 per cent were done in eye camps, 7.86 per cent in private clinics, and the rest (74.82 per cent) by non-profit organizations like AEH.[8] Other major private eye hospitals in Tamil Nadu and the number of surgeries done by them per year, as per the information given by Aravind Eye Care System, were as follows:

Exhibit 4 The human eye and its diseases and cross section of human eye

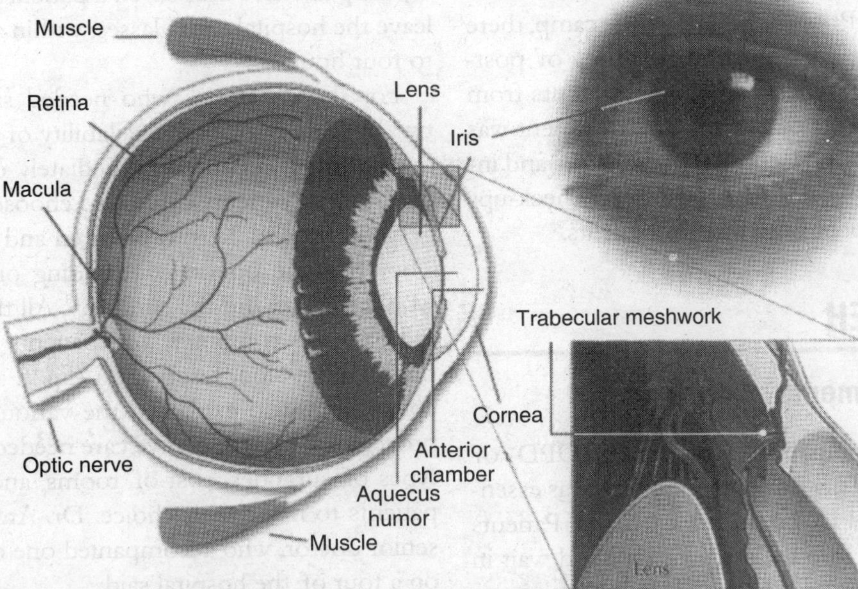

Cross section of the eye

Source: Taken from *Jetwings*, March 2003- p 132.

Common Eye Diseases

Cataract is a medical condition in which the lens of the eye becomes progressively opaque and the vision gets blurred. The degeneration takes place over five to ten years. Earlier, the surgical procedure was to remove the lens after it had become fully opaque (when it reached maturity) and in its place the patient was prescribed to wear spectacles commonly known as aphakic glasses which had thick, positive power lenses. The new technique was to insert a tiny artificial intra-ocular lens (IOL) inside the eye in place of the natural lens. In IOL surgeries, patients did not require long hospitalization, the post-operative recovery was faster, and sight was restored in a short span (in a week to ten days). Further improvement was the availability of IOL lens that could be "folded" and inserted into the eye through a small opening. Once placed inside, it "opened out". These lenses required very small incision and hence recovery period was also short. With multi-focal lenses it became possible to take care of both distant and near vision. However, till as late as 2003, about 40 per cent of cataract surgeries in India followed the traditional procedure using aphakic lenses.

Another major breakthrough in ophthalmic surgery came with the introduction of phaco emulsification technique, wherein the opaque natural eye lens was first pulverized using ultrasonic beams and then extracted by suction. IOL was then inserted as usual. This technique enabled a patient to return home two to three hours after the surgery.

IOL insertion required advanced training of surgeons in microsurgery. In trained hands, the time taken to conduct the actual surgery, IOL and non IOL were same: about 12–15 minutes. Phaco surgery required both highly trained doctors and special and expensive equipment. Minimum cost of a good equipment to do phaco surgery was ₹600,000.

Glaucoma is the second common cause of blindness. It is caused when the level of aqueous humor, the fluid in the anterior chamber of the eye, increases as a result of a blockage of the exit passage, which leads to pressure build up in the eye. In severe cases it can damage the retina and the optic nerve. Unlike cataract, glaucoma is a silent killer of vision. The patient would get no symptoms or warnings. Diabetics are prone to glaucoma. While cataract is usually age related, glaucoma can attack a person at any age. Because of its insidious nature, the preventive measure is regular eye check up.

Pathology of the posterior segment include the cornea and retina. These involve highly skilled surgeries. Retinal surgeries can be done using lasers. Corneal surgeries involve quite a variety of surgeries, including eye transplants.

Uncorrected refractive errors are usually corrected by spectacles and later on by contact lenses, but recently LASIK surgeries involving laser incisions to alter the shape of the eye ball are becoming common. With small powers, LASIK surgeries could eliminate the need for spectacles/contact lenses; with higher powers, it could substantially reduce the power.

Sankara Nethralaya, Chennai	25,000
Joseph Eye Hospital, Tiruchirapalli	27,000
Sankara Eye Society, Coimbatore	30,000
K.G. Eye Hospital, Coimbatore	6,000

As on 2003, the all India average of IOL implantation surgery was 65.4 per cent of which Tamil Nadu with 91 per cent surgeries was at the top followed by Andhra Pradesh (79.7 per cent), Orissa (79.3 per cent), and Maharashtra (71.5 per cent).[9]

Eye camps were a popular way to reach out to rural population. Generally charitable trusts or individuals sponsored eye camps. Prior to the date of the camp, there would be a publicity campaign through pasting of posters, distribution of pamphlets and announcements from moving vehicles. The cost of surgery and treatment was supported by the State and Central Governments and institutions such as the World Bank. Eye camp check-ups and subsequent treatment were free for patients.

Work Flow at AEH

Outpatient Departments

The workflow at the outpatient departments (OPD) of different units of AEHs, both paying and free, was essentially the same[10]. All OPDs began work at 7 a.m. Patients would gather much before the starting hour and wait in the designated waiting areas. Sharp at 7 a.m., the registration process would begin. The computerized registration took about one minute per patient. After registration, patients would move to the case counter located adjacent to the waiting hall. The case history of the patient would be taken by the staff and a computerized case sheet would be given to the patients. Then they would be escorted to the designated doctor. Three computers were kept for recording new cases and one for old cases. These computers could handle around 200 cases per hour. Trained paramedical staff did the preliminary checks of patients, and paramedics trained in refraction testing conducted the basic refraction tests. There were four to five examination stations where the resident doctors examined the patients. They would record their diagnoses and recommendations. After this, a permanent doctor of the hospital would examine the patient, check the diagnosis and the recommendations of the resident doctor, and confirm the diagnosis and treatment, or modify them, as needed. The whole process usually took about two hours but it could vary depending on the tests needed. The OPD in the paying units examined around 1000 patients a day, six days a week.

Patients who were advised glasses after the refraction tests had the option of going to one of the spectacle shops located in the hospital. These shops were run as a separate profit centre. These shops sold spectacles at a price lower than the market rate. Both free and paying hospitals had separate shops but the prices of similar spectacles were the same. Patients received the spectacles the same day because the grinding of the glasses and fitting was done in-house. The system of in-house spectacle shop at AEH thus saved a patient's time. They would leave the hospital with glasses, within a time slot of three to four hours.

For those patients who needed surgery, there were two options. Subject to availability of rooms, they could decide to get admitted immediately or schedule a later date. Paying patients could also choose the mode of surgery, the type of lens to be fitted and the type of room. They had the option of deciding on the doctor who would to carry out the surgery.[11] All these requests were fed into the computer, and patients would be handed out an admission/reservation slip.[12]. AEH had a set of counsellors who explained the various options, surgical procedures, post-operative care needed, cost of different types of surgeries, cost of rooms, and generally helped patients to make their choice. Dr. Aravind Srinivasan, a senior doctor, who accompanied one of the case writers on a tour of the hospital said:

> *In many hospitals, many of these functions (especially refraction testing) are carried out by doctors. We seek to maximize the doctors' contribution by helping them to devote their time mainly to medical advising. Tests that can be done by paramedical staff are assigned only to them. Our counsellors are highly trained to help patients to take informed decisions, so that doctors are not required to spend their time on such matters.*

The flow of patients was smooth. They received clear directions and paramedical personnel were stationed at critical places for directing people, thus avoiding confusion and crowding. As a result the waiting halls were not crowded—quite unusual in a hospital of this size in India.

All surgeries were done in the morning. Afternoons were for attending OD. The doctors were rotated between free and paying hospitals, so that both categories of patients received similar quality of medical attention.

Surgical Wards

The workflow in the surgical wards in Madurai was equally smooth and efficient. At 6.45 a.m., one of the case writers was picked up by Dr. Aravind Srinivasan to observe the procedure for cataract surgery.

At 7 a.m., the doctor and the case writer were in their surgical gowns and masks. The names of patients undergoing surgery during the day had been put up in each operation theatre. This scheduling was done by using a software that incorporated the patient's preferences for a particular doctor. The nursing staff reported at 6.30 a.m., and the patients for the day were already in the ward adjacent to the operating theatres. The patients who were to be operated were administered local anaesthetic injections, and their eyes were washed and disinfected. At 7.15 a.m., when the case writer accompanied Dr. Srinivasan inside the operation theatre two patients were on two adjacent operating tables. Most hospitals avoid two operating tables in the operation theatre because of high risk of infection. However, AEH had been following this system from its inception and had not had any problems, perhaps because, generally eye patients were otherwise healthy and the chance of cross infection was considered to be very small.

The operation theatre had four operating tables, laid side by side. Two doctors would operate, each on two adjacent tables. Dr. Aravind's first patient was already on the first table, with microscope focused, instruments ready and the nurses fully attentive. The case writer watched Dr. Srinivasan carry out a phaco procedure on the TV screen; the procedure was being transmitted through a camera attached to the microscope. The doctor kept giving a description of what he was doing for the benefit of the case writer. The entire procedure took about 12 minutes; the team consisted of one doctor and four nurses.

By the time the first operation was over, the second patient was ready to be operated on with the microscope focused on the eye. Dr. Srinivasan moved straight to the second table. Meanwhile, the first patient was bandaged by the nurses and moved out. The third patient walked in and was sitting on a bench in the theatre. As soon as the first patient moved out, the third patient was put on the first table and was readied for the operation.

The case writer observed that, as soon as the second surgery was over, the doctor moved back to the first table with virtually no loss of time. He was constantly moving between the two tables with hardly any break. In the same way, another doctor operated on the third and the fourth tables. After the day's surgeries Dr. Srinivasan said:

I work like this the entire morning from 7 a.m. till 1 p.m. or 1.30 p.m., or even later, if there are a large number of patients to be attended to. Most doctors take a short time off for breakfast and a brief five to ten minutes break for tea. I usually do about 25 surgeries in a half-day session. Most do this number.

In the afternoon, the operating theatres were scrubbed and cleaned and instruments sterilized. The patients who had already been operated on were moved back to their wards.

The procedure in the hospitals at Theni and Coimbatore was similar. AEH, Coimbatore was a newer and a better, well-designed and integrated hospital. It had all the specialties and facilities needed for conducting the Dip NB (equivalent to MS) programme. It also conducted short-term specialized programmes for doctors from other developing countries. The basic workflow for outpatients and surgeries was the same as it was in Madurai. AEH Theni was smaller than other hospitals and did not do paediatric and retinal surgeries.

Exhibit 5 gives the details of number of surgeries done and outpatients attended to from 1997 to 2003 by all hospitals under the AECS. Even in a small hospital like Theni, the three doctors stationed there performed 6,000 surgeries every year. We were told that in most eye hospitals, a surgeon did about 300 surgeries per year, while in AEHs they did about 2,500 surgeries per year. Exhibit 6 gives details of out patients' visits and major surgeries done in each hospital of the AECS.

Exhibit 5 Surgeries done and OP visits, 1997–2003

Year	Paying		Free including Camp		Total	
	OP visits	Surgery	OP visits	Surgery	OP visits	Surgery
1997	401,518	42,808	574,350	80,287	975,868	123,095
1998	465,496	49,275	697,649	108,552	1,163,145	157,827
1999	530,253	55,460	752,819	127,708	1,283,072	183,168
2000	567,105	58,267	763,888	134,498	1,330,993	192,765
2001	603,800	63,265	725,210	127,893	1,329,070	191,158
2002	650,047	68,055	749,324	128,384	1,399,371	196,425
2003	758,991	78,487	688,584	123,579	1,447,575	202,066

Source: Aravind Eye Care System.
Note: The above figures are for all the hospitals of the AECS.

Exhibit 6 Patient statistics for different units of the aecs, 2003

	Madurai	Tirunelveli	Theni	Coimbatore	Pondicherry	Total
Outpatient Visits						
Paying	288,709	147,900	45,043	211,672	65,667	758,991
Free (Direct & Camp)	273,926	116,979	38,579	217,518	41,582	688,584
Of the above:						
Hospital OP visits	415,995	198,849	63,937	293,317	86,883	1,058,981
Eye camp OP visits	146,640	66,030	19,685	135,873	20,366	388,594
Total	562,635	264,879	83,622	429,190	107,249	1,447,575
# eye camps	379	268	63	386	62	1,158
Surgery						
Paying	37,377	14,097	2,224	19,024	5,765	78,487
Free (Direct & Camp)	60,273	18,403	5,711	32,658	6,534	123,579
Total	97,650	32,500	7,935	51,682	12,299	202,066
Some major types of surgeries						
ECCE without IOL	1,075	267	62	836	185	2,425
ECCE with IOL	28,358	4,607	6,448	8,276	978	48,667
ECCE IOL with phaco	11,760	16,133	377	7,117	2,340	37,727
Small incision cataract surgery with IOL	29,696	2,693	0	23,478	5,463	61,330
Laser photocoagulation	6,885	3,503	160	3,652	1,005	15,205

Source: Aravind Eye Care System.

Dr. Aravind Srinivasan explained:

We work like this for six days a week. On most Sundays we go out to eye camps and spend at least half a day testing patients. Sometimes if one is lucky, one may get one Sunday off in a month.

He continued:

Besides surgery, we do outpatient work, and many do research as well. To us, this hospital is our life. We have dedicated our lives for this one mission.

The paying wards had regular beds but the free wards had "beds" in the form of mats placed on the floor. Two types of mats were used to distinguish eye camp patients from walk-in free patients. The use of mats enabled better utilization of floor space—about 30 patients could be accommodated in one room.

AEH, Madurai, had an excellent IT system that kept track of all patients. The system generated daily schedules taking into account the load on that day, patients' preference for any doctor, and pending work. This enabled the hospital administration to keep track of the workload in different units. Details of complications in terms of categories of patients and surgeons were maintained. Abstracts of medical records of patients were entered into the system, including their past clinical visits, and this enabled a history sheet to be generated for an old patient quickly.

The data on the complication rates of AECS' hospitals revealed that quality of surgery was given high priority. AECS management kept a very close track of the intra-operative as well as post-operative complication rates. According to AECS doctors, the major complications were under control and the figures for complications were considered highly satisfactory. All the same, each case of complication was traced to the operating team that had performed it and the reasons identified. Corrective action, including training of whoever was found deficient, was undertaken. Exhibit 7 gives the complication rates of AEH, Madurai, in 2002. Exhibit 7a provides complication rates of AEH, Coimbatore, and that of the Royal College of Ophthalmologists, UK.

Eye Camps and Community Outreach Programmes

The AECS considered its community outreach programmes to be absolutely vital to its mission. The only way people in most rural areas could get access to eye care was through eye camps. These camps were organized by different agencies and conducted differently. AECS conducted about 1500 eye camps every year.

Each of the hospitals of AECS had its own set of camp organizers who planned their activities for each calendar

Exhibit 7 Free section complication details, AEH, Madurai, 2003

Name	Intra-operative		Post-operative		Total	
	#	%	#	%	#	%
A/C Shallow	1	0.00	17	0.02	18	0.02
Blood Clot	0	0.00	53	0.08	53	0.08
Cornea Oedema	0	0.00	152	0.23	152	0.23
Cortex	0	0.00	2	0.00	2	0.00
Endopthalmitis	0	0.00	59	0.09	59	0.09
Hyphema	0	0.00	38	0.05	38	0.05
Hypopyon	0	0.00	63	0.09	63	0.09
Iridodialysis	0	0.00	1	0.00	1	0.00
Iris Prolapse	0	0.00	2	0.00	2	0.00
Posterior Capsular Rent with IOL	670	1.02	1	0.00	671	1.02
Posterior Capsular Rent (No IOL)	87	0.13	0	0.00	87	0.13
Striate Kerotopathy	0	0.00	70	0.10	70	0.10
Vitreous disturbance	695	1.06	0	0.00	695	1.06
Zonular Dialysis	86	0.13	0	0.00	86	0.13

Total surgeries done: 65,180

Source: Aravind Eye Care System.

Exhibit 7(a) Medical complications at AEH, Coimbatore and the Royal College of Ophthalmologists, UK.

Adverse Events During Surgery			Adverse Events Within 48 hours of Surgery		
Event	Aravind, Coimbatore N=22,912	UK National Survey N=18,472	Event	Aravind, Coimbatore N=22.912	UK national Survey N=17,257
Capsule rupture and vitreous loss	2.0%	4.4%	Corneal Oedema	8.0%	9.0%
Incomplete cortical clean up	0.75%	1.00%	Uveitis more than expected	5.0%	5.6%
Iris trauma	0.3%	0.7%	Peri-ocular bruising and edema more than expected	1.0%	1.4%
Persistent iris prolapse	0.01%	0.07%	Weak leak/rupture	0.67%	1.2%
Anterior chamber collapse	0.3%	0.5%	Hyphaema	0.9%	1.1%
Loss of nuclear fragment into vitreous	0.2%	0.3%	Retained lens material	0.87%	1.1%
Wounds	0.30%	0.25%	Vitreous to section	0.1%	0.3%
Choroidal haemorrhage	------	0.07%	Endophthamitis	0.05%	0.03%
Loss of intra ocular lens into vitreous	0.01%	0.16%	Hypopyon	0.04%	0.02%
			Other*	0.7%	1.5%

Source: The Aravind eye care system: delivering the most precious gift in C.K. Prahalad (2004), *The Fortune at the Bottom of the Pyramid.* N.J.: Wharton Publishing.

year, and these were coordinated from Madurai. Generally each district had a camp organizer who would set a target for the year based on the population, estimated percentage of blind people, estimated turnout at the camps, and percentage needing surgeries. The camp organizers then had to find sponsors. However, finding sponsors was not a problem. They comprised local NGOs, Lions and Rotary Clubs, local industrialists and businessmen, and philanthropists. Sponsors took care of the expenses connected with the publicity such as pamphlets, banners, and announcements from moving vehicles using a public address system, and the organization of the camps (usually in some school or public place). The camps were held usually on Saturdays and Sundays and started early in the morning. Lunch arrangements were made for those who had to undergo surgery at the base hospital. These expenses were also borne by the sponsors. The sponsors provided free transportation to and from the hospital to the patients. The hospital, in turn, met the cost of surgery, stay, and food in the hospital. It also provided free post operative medication for 40 days.

Doctors (mostly post-graduate residents) and paramedical staff usually reached the camp site previous evening to supervise the arrangements and, depending on the distance, would camp for the night. In the morning, patients were first registered with the help of local volunteers, and then given a case sheet and an identity card. The identity cards helped in future follow-ups. The paramedical staff conducted the preliminary tests for refraction, and patients above 40 years of age were tested for intraocular pressure to screen for glaucoma. Senior doctors evaluated the test findings, carried out final examination, reviewed patient records, and then made the final diagnosis and prescribed treatment. An optician also accompanied the team, with a large stock of spectacles with commonly prescribed powers. Thus, those who were advised glasses could purchase them on the spot and the glasses would be delivered to them within one hour. About 75 to 90 per cent opted to purchase spectacles at the camp site and over 85 per cent got them immediately. The rest got them the following week at the same campsite, or they were couriered to them at AECS' cost. This innovation of having a mobile optical shop at campsite was decided after a study of barriers to refractive correction. Mr. R.D. Thulasiraj, Executive Director, LAICO, (who was earlier the administrator of AEH, Madurai) explained:

We found that the cost associated in procuring a pair of glasses (which included a couple of visits to the shop, a second visit to the doctor for a final check up, etc.) was higher than the actual cost of the pair of glasses. If the cost of time, travel, and other incidental expenses were put together, getting a pair of glasses became prohibitively expensive. As a result, we found out that many people who were checked at the camps did not bother to get their glasses and the cycle of needless blindness/poor sight continued.

We decided that if this cycle had to be circumvented, it was important to be able to provide glasses to eye camp patients soon after the refractive errors had been detected. An analysis of the data revealed that the most time-consuming part of readying the spectacles was preparing the glasses correctly as per prescription. Based on the large data AEH had of the probable refractive needs of patients, a forecast was made before each eye camp as to how many lenses in each power should be taken to the camp to meet the projected need. The fitting of the glass to the frame was done at the camp site and spectacles were provided there and then to patients. However, patients did have the choice of not buying the spectacles at the camp.

In the advertisement of the camp, patients coming for the check-up were usually advised to come prepared to go to the base hospital for surgery, if necessary. Thus, most of them came with their bags and, often, with relatives who could accompany them. Persons needing and willing to undergo surgery were then counselled about the procedure, length of stay, and facilities at the base hospital. If they agreed to surgery, then they were taken to the base hospital after lunch. They would be operated upon either the next day or the day after depending on the workload. Their basic needs such as food during their stay were taken care of by AECS.

Generally people from the same or adjoining villages travelled together, were operated on the same day, and stayed together in the hospital. They thus formed a support group. This group of patients and relatives returned after about three days in a transport provided by the hospital. The hospital also met the cost of surgery including cost of IOLs, sutures, and post-operative medication for forty days, of which the government reimbursed to the extent of ₹500 per patient.[13] The cost of the doctors' travel to and from the campsites was mostly met by the hospital.

The cost of an eye camp to the sponsor varied depending on the nature of the camp. A small camp with 300 outpatients (leading to about 60 surgeries) generally cost ₹6,700 while a large camp with 1,000 outpatients and 200 surgeries could cost ₹42,500 to the sponsor.

The Theni hospital conducted eye camps in two districts in the adjoining state of Kerala and AEH Pondicherry was expected to reach out to some of the villages in the neighbouring state of Andhra Pradesh.

Exhibit 8 gives the number of camps organized by AECS from 1998 to 2002 and the numbers of patients treated from camps (apart from "walk-in" free patients at the hospitals).

Exhibit 8 Eye camps organized and patients treated, 1997–2003

Year	No. of Camps Organized	Patients Seen	Surgeries of "Camp" Patients
1997	1041	287,571	40,389
1998	1346	373,997	65,926
1999	1488	413,580	87,084
2000	1548	426,350	93,519
2001	1480	422,373	88,585
2002	1549	461,762	92,372
2003 (incl.Pondicherry)	1158	388,594	81,357

Source: Aravind Eye Care System.

Other Community Outreach Programmes

Diabetic Retinopathy Management Project

This project was initiated in 2000 with the aim to create awareness about diabetic retinopathy in the rural communities. In 2002, 46 eye camps were organized in which 11,644 persons were examined. Of these, 3,443 were diabetic, who were screened for retinopathy, and of these 533 were found to have retinopathy. Some of them were advised surgery. Extensive campaigns were also conducted through leaflets, posters, and booklets on diabetes and its effect on the retina.

Community Based Rehabilitation Project

In 1996, Theni hospital, with the support of Sight Savers International, undertook the rehabilitation of incurably blind people by providing community based support. House-to-house identification of eye problems and screening camps were organized and patients with eye problems were treated. Rehabilitation consisted of teaching the incurably blind people skills in orientation, mobility, and activities of daily living. Some were economically rehabilitated through building of appropriate skills.

Eye Screening of School Children

In this project, teachers were trained to detect eye defects in children to take early corrective measures. They were also taught to measure visual acuity, identify signs of squint and vitamin deficiency. The children were then tested by ophthalmic assistants and later by ophthalmologists. In 2002, 68,528 children in 80 schools were screened and 3,075 were given glasses to correct refractive errors.

Use of IT Kiosks for Tele Advice

This initiative was launched with the help of the Indian Institute of Technology (IIT), Chennai. Under the guidance of Dr. Ashok Jhunjhunwala, a faculty member of the institute, a number of IT kiosks were put up all over Tamil Nadu by a company called n-Logue. In one cluster of villages near Melur, about 40 km. from Madurai, the IT kiosks were provided with web cameras that enabled patients to screen the picture of their eyes and email them along with a voice description of the problem to doctors at AEH, Madurai. One doctor was nominated to take care of these emails. The doctor would make the diagnosis based on the description given by the patient and the picture sent and advise the patient suitably. This was, however, not an on-line service.

Other Units and Activities of AECS

Aurolab

The cost of surgery was always a central concern at AECS. As explained earlier, AECS had decided on adopting the IOL implant surgery as the standard operative procedure for all cataract cases. However, the cost of IOL lenses which had to be imported was very high, about $80–100, and this made the cost of surgery quite high. In 1991, AECS set up Aurolab as a separate non-profit trust to manufacture lenses. Its mission was to achieve "local production at an appropriate cost". Some of the members of the Aurolab Board were also members of the Govel Trust. The technology was obtained from IOL International, Florida, USA, for a one-time fee for technology transfer along with a buyback arrangement. This helped in maintaining quality. This venture was also supported by Seva Foundation, Sight Savers International, the Combat Blindness Foundation, USA, Canadian International Development Agency (CIDA) through Seva Service Society, and David Green, an Ashoka Fellow and Executive Director of Project Impact Inc. in California.

Out of the 220 employees of Aurolab, 10 per cent were diploma or graduate engineers, pharmacists, and marketing personnel; and 90 per cent were women technicians. Girls from rural areas with 12 years of formal education were selected and given the same training that was given to ophthalmic assistants, for a period of six months. Then for the next 18 months, they were given specialized training in manufacturing of lenses.

Raw material for lenses was imported from US/UK. Soon Aurolab was selling the rigid IOL lenses for less than US $5. By 2002, it was producing about one-sixth of the total number of low-end lenses produced in the world. However, it also produced the foldable and the superior category acrylic lenses. It was able to get the CE Mark (a mark of quality) and ISO 9002 certification. In 2003, by working single shift, Aurolab was producing around 600,000 lenses per year. Large NGOs such as CBM, Lions, and Rotary bought IOL lenses from Aurolab, and supplied them to various eye hospitals all over the world. This increased sales worldwide, and 33 per cent of the lenses produced by IOL were exported. Of the remaining 67 per cent, 20–25 per cent were consumed by AEH and the rest were sold in the open market in India. Since its inception, Aurolab had supplied more than 2 million lenses to NGOs in India and about 120 countries world over.

While the cost of lenses came down, the price of sutures remained high. This now became a need to be addressed. In 1998, Aurolab diversified into manufacturing of sutures used in IOL surgery. It set up the Sutures Division. The sutures are made from silk and nylon and come attached to a tiny stainless steel needle. The cost of sutures produced at Aurolab was one-fourth the price of imported ones.

The Managing Director of Aurolab, Dr. Balakrishnan, Ph.D., said with pride:

> *Aurolab was responsible in driving down the prices of IOL all around the world. Our lenses are of high quality, but priced low; that takes us nearer to our goal of eliminating needless blindness.*

Thereafter, Aurolab decided to diversify further and started two new Divisions: Pharmaceutical Division and the Spectacle Lens Division.

The Pharmaceutical Division produced pharmaceuticals used in cataract surgery and other eye-related ailments at a reasonable cost. These pharmaceuticals were either not easily available or available at a high cost. In 2002, it formulated 25 drugs and was the sole Indian manufacturer for Econazole, Coltrimazole, and Prednisolone Sodium Phosphate eye drops.[14] Aurolab pharmaceuticals and suture needles were covered under the Indian Drug Control Act and were WHO GMP certified. The international certification also made it possible to sell the formulations in the international market.

The Spectacle Lens Division set up in 1999 provided technical support services to AECS' in-house spectacle shops for the production of spectacles, quality control, and training of personnel. Ever since World Health Organization (WHO) had identified detection and correction of refractive errors through spectacle lenses as a major requirement for reducing avoidable blindness, the division focussed its attention on this aspect. A laboratory with plastic lens surfacing and computerized edging facility was established to research and refine the process. Lens edging facilities were established close to the optical shops for quicker delivery. Technology for applying hard coating to both sides of the lens to make it scratch resistant and for providing colour tints to lenses to satisfy the needs of low vision patients had also been acquired.

Lions Aravind Institute of Community Ophthalmology (LAICO)

In the early 1990s, AECS started collaborating with Lions Club International Foundation, a voluntary organization for community service. In 1992, with the support of Lions Club International Sight First Programme and Seva Sight Programme, AECS established Lions Aravind Institute of Community Ophthalmology (LAICO). The objective of LAICO was to improve the planning, efficiency, and effectiveness of eye hospitals with a special focus on developing countries. It contributed to eye care through teaching, training, research, and consultancy. It offered long term courses in hospital management as well as short duration skill development courses in the area of community outreach, social marketing, and instruments maintenance. These courses were offered at very reasonable fees. The list of courses, duration, and fees charged in March 2003 are given in Exhibit 9. Till 2003, LAICO had already worked with 149 eye hospitals in India, Africa, and South East Asia. It was Asia's first international facility for training blindness prevention workers in India and other parts of the world.

LAICO also provided capacity building services to other hospitals. Its staff would first visit the hospitals requesting support, assess and identify their problems, bottlenecks, and constraints. Then it would invite some personnel from these hospitals for training at LAICO. Training consisted of visiting the hospitals under AECS and the outreach camps to study the workflow. At the end of the training, the participants would have to pres-

Exhibit 9 Training courses offered at LAICO and course fees

Courses	Duration	Course Fee for participants from India/Nepal* (₹)	Course Fee for overseas participants ($)
Management Training for **Heads of Eye Hospitals**	One week	10,000	330
Management Training for Eye Care **Programme Managers**	Two weeks	15,000	500
Management Training & Systems Development for **Hospital Administrators/Managers**	One month	15,000	500
Certificate Course for Clinical & Supervisory Skills Development in **Ophthalmic Paramedical Personnel**	Three months	25,000	850
Community Outreach Course	Four weeks	7,500	250
Instruments Maintenance Technicians Course	Six weeks	10,000	325
Instruments Maintenance Ophthalmologist Course	Five days	2,000	70

* Fee does not include lodging and boarding
Source: Aravind Eye Care System.

ent a full action plan, implement it, and the progress would be assessed after six to nine months.

Till 2003, LAICO had made interventions in UP, West Bengal, Orissa, Delhi, and a few other states in India. Its international intervention included Malawi, Kenya, Zimbabwe, and Zambia. In some countries, in addition to training doctors, nurses from AECS were sent for a month to impart rigorous training to the nursing staff there. Dramatic improvements were recorded in functioning wherever LAICO had intervened. Mr. M. P. Saravanan, a faculty member of LAICO, narrated the following intervention experience in Chitrakoot:

> *In Chitrakoot, they were doing 20,000 to 25,000 surgeries a year. Ninety per cent of this was done in a three-month period. Of the surgeries, 70 to 80 per cent were non-IOL surgeries. Only in slack periods would they take up IOL. After our intervention, they were able to do 25,000 to 30,000 surgeries a year; all IOL. Our aim in such interventions was to enhance not only their capabilities but also their skills.*

The performance of hospitals before and after intervention is presented in Exhibit 10. Data are for 40 hospitals two years after intervention.

Exhibit 10 Result of aravind's intervention in other hospitals

	# Surgeries Done		
	IOL	Non IOL	Total
1 year prior to intervention	18558	33948	52506
1 year after intervention	40055	36940	76995
2 years after intervention	51291	40154	91445

	# Hospitals Performing Surgeries	
	1 year before intervention	2 years after intervention
< 1000 surgeries	21	9
1000 – 2999 surgeries	16	20
3000 – 4999 surgeries	3	8
> = 5000 surgeries	0	3

Cost Recovery Percentage (Income/Expenditure) # Hospitals		
	1 year before intervention	2 years after intervention
< 60%	10	4
60 – 79%	4	6
80 – 99%	6	5
> = 100%	5	10

Source: S. Saravanan (2003), Organizational capacity building: a model developed by aravind eye care system," *Illumination,* 3(1) January-March, .20-21.

LAICO, in collaboration with the International Agency for Prevention of Blindness (IAPB), had committed itself to the global initiative of "Vision 2020: The Right to Sight" Mr. Thulasiraj was the regional chairman of the IAPB, Southeast Asia Region, and was, thus, involved in the policy making for eradicating blindness at the national and international levels.

Aravind Medical Research Foundation (AMRF)

AMRF coordinated all the research undertaken by different units of AECS. Several clinical studies, population based studies, and social and health systems researches were conducted using the data readily available in the hospitals and the community outreach programmes. Many of these research projects were supported by different agencies and some by AEH itself. Research covered a variety of fields like clinical trials to evaluate alternate surgical techniques and drug therapies, impact of vitamin supplements on morbidity and mortality of infants and children, beneficiary assessment, impact assessment of cataract intervention, barriers experienced by patients in accessing eye care sources, and infrastructure utilization in eye care. Dr. VR. Muthukkaruppan, who was earlier Professor of Immunology at the Madurai Kamaraj University, and the former Vice Chancellor of Bharathidasan University, Tiruchirapalli, had been appointed to provide leadership to the research efforts of AMRF.

Exhibit 11 gives details of ongoing and completed research projects.

Exhibit 11 Major research projects

Major Projects Completed

1984	Study of Eales' disease
1986	Operations research for effective delivery of cataract services
1986	Rapid survey techniques for blindness and cataract assessment
1987	Effect of small doses of vitamin A in children under five years of age
1989	Safety and efficacy of vanadium stainless steel (VSS) sutures in cataract surgery
1989	Study on salt pan Keratitis
1992	Madurai IOL study
1993	Childhood cataract in South India
1994	Aravind comprehensive eye survey
1994	Series of drug trial with Ofloxacin on patients with suppurative Keratitis
1998	Vitamin A supplementation in newborns (VASIN) study.

Major Ongoing Projects

1995	Molecular genetics of congenital cataracts in man and mouse
1997	Newly recognized presumed Trematode induced ocular inflammation in children
1998	1. Role of antioxidants in prevention of cataract
	2. Vitamin A supplementation in newborns (VASIN) study
1999	Value of culture and serology in ophthalmic complication of leptospirosis
2000	1. Diabetic retinopathy (action research project)
	2. Molecular genetics for hereditary glaucoma
	3. Paediatrics parasitic eye diseases
	4. Trial study of lensectomy vs. lens aspiration and primary capsulotomy in children
	5. Culture of rubella virus from proven cases of congenital rubella syndrome
	6. Molecular and genetic basis of congenital contract
	7. Trials on paediatric glaucoma
	8. Certain drug trials in corneal ulcers and conjunctivitis
2001	1. Molecular genetics of juveline onset primary angle glaucoma
	2. Genetics and structural analysis of myocillin protein involved in juvenile onset primary angle glaucoma
	3. Aetiology and pathology mechanism of leptospirosis uveitis
	4. Improving child health through health education project
2002	1. Corneal epithelial stem cells for clinical and toxicological applications
	2. Prevention of traumatic corneal ulcer: A multicenter intervention project in South East Asia

Source: Promises to Keep..., Annual Report (2001) Madurai: Aravind Eye Care System, .40-42.

Aravind Centre for Women, Children, and Community Health (ACWCCH)

The centre was started in 1984 with the aim of reducing nutrition-related blindness in children through preventive health care. It worked with government's public health programmes of immunization, education programmes on nutrition, and training programmes to create awareness. It conducted regular village health programmes and training programmes for village health care workers.

Rotary Aravind International Eye Bank (RAIEB)

RAIEB was established in 1998 and was one of the four eye banks in the country affiliated to the International Federation of Eye Banks. Till 2003, the bank had processed 4,383 eyes and AECS had conducted 2,181 transplants.

Aravind Post-Graduate Institute of Ophthalmology

As part of its efforts to train ophthalmologists, in 1982 AECS introduced post graduate residency programme at its Madurai unit, and with this, the name of the hospital was changed to Aravind Eye Hospital and Post-Graduate Institute of Ophthalmology (AEH&PGIO). As of 2003 AEH&PGIO had admitted around 30 resident doctors. Admission was strictly on merit. No capitation fee was ever collected even when the going rate in 2003 was about ₹1.5 to 2 million at other private teaching hospitals. It was affiliated to Dr. MGR Medical University, Chennai, and offered Diploma in Ophthalmology (DO), and MS in Ophthalmology (MS). In 2001, eight candidates had earned their DO and four graduated with MS. In 2002, six graduated in DO and four in MS. In affiliation with the National Board of Examination, New Delhi, the AECS also offered the Diplomate of the National Board. Nine students qualified in 2001, and 13 in 2002. In affiliation with the Royal College of Ophthalmologists, London, membership of the Royal College of Ophthalmologists (MRCOpth) and FRCS were offered. Four candidates passed Part 1 of the MRCOpth in 2002[15] and four candidates received their FRCS. It also took fellows for super specialization in fields of retina-vitreous, cornea, paediatric ophthalmology, glaucoma, anterior chamber, and uvea. In addition, it conducted various short-term courses for practising ophthalmologists.

Recruitment and Training

AEH laid great stress on the kind of people it recruited. Dr. Natchiar, who was in charge of training of paramedical staff, told the case writers:

We have a ratio of about 1:6 between doctors and nurses. Then we have also about 40 counsellors. We have about 900 girls between our four hospitals and Aurolab. We generally recruit girls from rural background. We do not prefer urban girls. We take girls in the age range of 17 to 19; very rarely more than 19. We look for girls with right attitude from large families, preferably farmers' families. Knowledge and skills are important, but they come second. We never advertise. Once a year, we put up a notice for recruitment in our hospitals and word of mouth carries the news. We receive around 400–500 applications and we take about 60–100 girls per year. Selection for all the hospitals is done at Madurai and Tirunelveli. I along with Dr. Usha (a younger ophthalmologist and a member of the family who was being groomed to head the recruitment and training of nurses) and the head nurse are involved in all selections. Parents are always called for the interview.

We look for the right kind of person. We do not give any consideration to any letters of recommendation.

After recruitment, we give them two years' training. The training is considered to be excellent and is recognized in the USA, and the Government of India is considering adopting our training syllabus for nurses' training. During the training period, we rotate them among different units of our different hospitals.

In the first four months, they were given training in basic sciences and human anatomy and physiology. The trainers and Dr. Usha, who headed the training of nurses, would select ophthalmic assistants from this group. They would be further trained to work in the outpatient department, operation theatre, counselling, etc. Though the criteria for making such decisions were not clearly articulated, they were well understood by the team. In the next eight months, they received special training for the department they were chosen for. Following this, another six months were spent in apprenticeship under a trainer nurse working in the same department. There was one-on-one training at each step. During the last six months, they worked on their own with some guidance from senior nurses and doctors. The medium of instruction was essentially Tamil (the language spoken in the state); they were also taught some basic medical terminology in English and were given training in basic conversational English.

The nurses' training was designed after the training programme of ophthalmic assistants that Dr. V had coordinated in 1973 for the rehabilitation work funded by the USAID. The training programme did not lead to a degree. However, there were efforts underway in February 2003 to formalize the programme and the training modules were being upgraded with the help of qualified volunteers from the USA.

Dr. Natchiar added:

At the end of two years, we take parents' consent before absorbing the girls permanently. In our experience, 99 per cent of the trainees stay on with us. Those who we consider to be unsuitable, mainly because of their attitude, are not given job offers.

During the three years of their service as permanent employees, ophthalmic assistants were also imparted training in cooking, housekeeping, tailoring, etc. This helped them to be prepared for becoming good housewives in the future. The cost for these programmes was borne by AECS. Voluntary bhajan (devotional songs) and yoga sessions were organized in the evening. The nurses were encouraged to be always kind to patients and approach them with gratitude for providing them an opportunity to serve. The nurses were asked to save a part of their salary, so that they had a sizable sum for their marriage.

According to Dr. Natchiar:

More than salaries, it is the recognition that they get in society. They get a lot of respect. Not only do they get very good training and experience, they also have an opportunity to go abroad, even if it is for short periods. All these are seen as positive factors.

The nurses too corroborated Dr. Natchiar's views. One of the senior nurses said:

I work harder than the government hospital nurses and I get paid a little less or the same as them, but I get much more respect in society. When I travel in the bus, someone generally recognizes that I work in Aravind Eye Hospital and would offer me a seat, or be nice to me. I really feel happy about it.

Both Dr. Usha and Dr. V stressed that ophthalmic assistants were at the core of AECS' success. Their contribution to the smooth functioning of the hospitals of AECS was immense. The senior assistants appreciated the atmosphere of peace and efficient functioning of the hospitals and set an example for the junior staff.

All AECS hospitals abounded in photographs of Sri Aurobindo and Mother, and staff members were expected to imbibe the values of service. When the new unit was opened in Pondicherry, two old time "founder" sweepers from Madurai were sent to inculcate the right attitude and values in the new cleaners. One of the doctors very succinctly described the ethos of AEH:

We have a unique culture based on service. All the doctors speak softly to patients and nurses. No one shouts. If a doctor behaves in an unacceptable manner, word goes around the hospital in no time, and the doctor is in trouble. We believe mutual respect to be our core value.

Doctors were crucial at AEH. Most were inducted as residents. About 30 MBBS doctors were taken in the three-year residency programme which led to a masters' degree in surgery (MS). During the residency period they received a stipend. The residents were given training in all branches of ophthalmic surgery. At the end of the training, many were offered jobs as permanent medical officers in different AEHs, and most accepted the offer.

AEH also offered a Fellowship Programme for doing super specialization after an MS degree in areas like, retina-vitreous, cornea, paediatric ophthalmology, glaucoma, uvea, and orbit. Duration of the programme was 18 months and it did not lead to any degree. During the course of the programme, the Fellows received a stipend. There were 15 fellows pursuing different specializations in 2003.

The case writers interviewed some of the Fellows. They felt that in their MS course in other colleges they did not get adequate exposure to surgery. They also felt that AECS gave them wider choice in specialization. To quote one Fellow:

We did not get adequate surgical exposure in MS. This is usually the case with many colleges, especially in north India. Here I have been exposed to not only different kinds of IOL surgeries but even in plastic surgery. In Delhi, where I had studied, we did not have so many different cases. The college did not even have a phaco machine. We used to do about one or two cases of surgery a month whereas here we do around 30 a day!

A large number of Fellows were from other parts of India and so they went back to their home states after completion of training. Those who joined AEHs were largely locals.

Unlike many large hospitals AEH employed only full time doctors and did not allow any doctors to do private practice. Dr. V clearly stated:

We do not think part time or external doctors can develop institutional loyalties. They also may not develop the skills we need.

On an average, AECS doctors (at Madurai) spent 60 per cent of their time in clinical work, 20 per cent teaching, and 20 per cent in research. But this varied considerably among doctors. Though doctors were not allowed to miss surgical work, they could take time off from OPD to pursue research. They could apply for research grant from AECS which in turn would channel the fund through Aravind Medical Research Foundation or get from outside funding agencies. They were also encouraged to teach at LAICO.

AECS ensured professional growth of all the doctors. They regularly organized Journal Rounds, which all medical officers and Fellows were required to attend. At this forum, a doctor or a Fellow would pick up an article of interest from a journal and present it to others. In the Grand Rounds, doctors from different AEHs would have a tele-discussion on a particular topic.

One of the medical officers explained the advantages of being at AEH:

I see the following plus points here. I am at my home place. We get a very good exposure to the latest surgical techniques. We also get opportunities to practice tele-medicine with eminent people.[16] *If you want to be abreast of latest techniques in ophthalmology, this is the best place. We get opportunities to do research, attend international conferences and present papers. We can attend one or even more than one conference each year.*

I am in charge of the newly set up Vision Rehabilitation Centre. My long term mission is to develop this centre using new techniques such as magnifying devices. By developing skills for the visually handicapped, I'll be able to improve the quality of their life. I plan to set up similar rehabilitation centres in other hospitals too.

Asked whether he found time for research in the midst of all these activities, he said:

Time is not a problem. Those interested can find time.

But this view was not shared by all. To some, this heavy work load was not conducive for research:

It is all right to say you have a lot of opportunities to do research. But after a long day of 12 or 13 hours, how many can find the energy to do research? Every day is a full day here.

Another doctor had this to say:

We do commit ourselves totally to the cause of eradication of avoidable blindness. That means we have to do a certain number of surgeries every day. But subject to this, we have quite a lot of flexibility.

There was good understanding between medical officers and ophthalmic assistants. This bonhomie developed as a result of frequent visits to eye camps where they worked closely as a team.

Quality was strictly monitored at AECS. Morbidity meetings were organized every week in a non-threatening manner. Complication rates of individual surgeons as well as that of the hospital were calculated every month. Dr. V and others gave a lot of stress on the quality of eye care. According to Dr. Nam:

Our destination is "good sight". We provide our doctors with the best that is available in the world. We train them through exchange programmes with prestigious medical schools all around the world. We have set up very rewarding collaborative research programmes with several universities.

One of the case writers met a resident who had come from Harvard Medical School. He told the case writer:

I've had more clinical experience here than any of my classmates at Harvard. In Harvard, I would only read about rare eye diseases; here I get to see them.

However, AECS did face the problem of retention of doctors. According to Mr. Thulasiraj, Executive Director of LAICO:

Doctor turnover is a problem. The retention is only for about three to four years. Every year we lose 20 to 25 doctors. India produces about 800 ophthalmologists a year. Can we get from that pool? We also have the fellow pool of about 25 or so.

However, both Dr. Nam and Mr. Thulasiraj were confident that this was not a serious issue because, though earlier, doctors at AECS were paid less than the market rate, it was not so any more. Their salaries were now at par with those from other hospitals. The only difference was, at other places, with private practice, they could make more money.

However, Mr. Thulasiraj added:

What we can offer is a good work environment, a good name, and a status based on our high integrity. We also offer good salaries and opportunities for personal growth. With this we should be able to retain enough doctors.

FINANCIALS

Though majority of the patients were treated free, AECS had always been financially self-supporting. Right from its inception, it did not take any government grants or donations (except for the support given by the government towards eye camp patients), and till today it had not applied for any other government grants for service delivery. Exhibit 12 gives the income and expenditure from 1997–98 till 2001–2, Exhibit 13 gives the income and expenditure statement of 2001–2.

Exhibit 12 Income and expenditure, 1997–98 to 2002–03

(₹ million)

	Income	Expenditure	Surplus
1997–98	180.3	81.7	98.6
1998–99	239.5	123.2	116.3
1999–2000	276.3	143.2	133.1
2000–2001	340.4	156.6	183.8
2001–2002	388.0	177.5	210.5
2002–2003	423.7	204.7	219.0

Exhibit 13 Income statement, 2002–2003

(₹ million)

Medical service	16.21
Operation charges	254.32
Treatment charges	22.84
Consulting fees	23.73
X Ray & Laboratory charges	4.32
Tuition fees and course fees	4.79
Grants in aid	37.80
Donations	3.74
Interest received	45.92
Dividends received	2.50
Miscellaneous income	1.93
Total	418.10

Expenditure

Staff Salary	41.22
IOL cost	39.74
Medicines	15.97
Electricity	15.40
Hospital linen	1.02
Camp expenses	6.57
Interest expenses	0.15
Library books	0.29
Water supply	1.31
Depreciation	46.00
Miscellaneous expenditures	37.04
Excess of income over expenditure	213.39
Total	418.10

Source: Aravind Eye Care System.

Mr. G. Srinivasan, brother of Dr. V, and the Founder-Secretary of the Govel Trust looked after the entire finance and accounts of AECS. In the initial years, Govel Trust had borrowed some funds from the State Bank of India by pledging the properties of the trustees. The hospital or the trust did not try to raise any funds through donation. AEH Madurai was self-supporting right from the beginning and was able to meet all its recurring expenditure. After five years, it accumulated adequate surplus for its own development and also for the establishment of new hospitals in Theni, Tirunelveli, Coimbatore, and Pondicherry. The rates charged by AECS for surgery and hospital stay were quite moderate. Exhibit 14 gives the details of the rates charged at AEH Madurai. Other AEHs too met all their operational costs through patient revenues and generated surplus to contribute to the development of subsequent hospitals. Though donations were accepted and welcome, the hospital consciously chose to remain financially viable essentially through patient revenues for its core activities of patient care, community work and training. Mr. G. Srinivasan stated, 'Tight financial control, on time accounting, coupled with appropriate pricing and transparency are the reasons for this financial success.'

Exhibit 14 Rate card of AEH, Madurai (`)

Cataract with IOL	Surgery	Two days' room rent	Medicines	Total Cost
Suite AC	5500	2000	700	8700
Deluxe AC	4500	1200	700	6600
A Special	4500	600	700	6600
A	4000	300	700	5300
B	3250	200	700	4400
C	2750	60	700	3800

Phaco with IOL	Surgery	Two days' room rent	Medicines	Total Cost
Suite AC	6500	1500	700	8900
Deluxe AC	6000	800	700	7700
A Special	6000	400	700	7300
A	5500	240	700	6700
B	5000	160	700	6100
C	4750	60	700	5700

Phaco with Foldable IOL	Surgery	Two days' room rent	Medicines	Total Cost
Suite AC	9500	1500	700	11900
Deluxe AC	8500	800	700	10200
A Special	8500	400	700	9800
A	8500	240	700	9700
B	8500	160	700	9600
C	8500	60	700	9500

Phaco with Acrylic 3 Piece IOL	Surgery	Two days' room rent	Medicines	Total Cost
Suite AC	12500	1500	700	14900
Deluxe AC	11500	800	700	13200
A Special	11500	400	700	12800
A	11500	240	700	12700
B	11500	160	700	12600
C	11500	60	700	12500

Cataract without IOL	Surgery	Two days' room rent	Medicines	Total Cost
Suite AC	3500	1500	700	5900
Deluxe AC	2000	800	700	3700
A Special	2000	400	700	3300
A	1500	240	700	2700
B	1250	160	700	2300
C	1100	60	700	2100

Source: Aravind Eye Care System.

Both Dr.V. and Dr. Nam stressed that not only was AECS self-sufficient in terms of operational income and expenditure, but it also took care of capital expenditure for all expansion and new units. Dr. V told the case writers:

> *You management people will tell me, why don't you go to the bank, take loans and grow faster? Cost of debt is low. But we, as a policy, will not go to the bank for loans, since it will compromise our freedom.*

At AECS, they believed in gradual growth. Expansion would take place only after enough funds had been accumulated. Dr. V saw no conflict between his objective of speedy eradication of blindness and the policy of gradual growth. He felt:

It is important to preserve our financial self-sufficiency. Also there is a limit to the rate at which we can grow effectively without compromising on the basic values of the organization.

ORGANIZATION STRUCTURE

AECS worked under the Govel Trust of which Dr. V was the Chairman, Dr. Nam the Director, and Dr. Natchiar the Joint Director. Exhibit 15 gives the organization structure.All AEHs reported to Dr. Nam. The heads of different units or clinics in AEHs who were generally senior medical officers reported directly to Dr. Nam. Post-graduate and Fellow students were under the respective clinic heads. However, nursing and other paramedical staffs were under the Joint Director. Heads of other units like LAICO too reported to Dr. Nam.

There were weekly meetings of all the heads of the hospitals, in which all operational and strategic matters were discussed. Dr. Nam would either visit other AEHs or talk to the heads on telephone.

AECS functioned in an open and transparent manner. Information was freely shared with everyone. The top management believed in "leading by doing". Once one of the case writers found Dr. V and Dr. Aravind Srinivasan picking up pieces of paper from the floor and handing them over to the first sweeper they met. They did not shout or get upset with the sweeper but by their action demonstrated the value of cleanliness and humility.

There was a conscious attempt to imbibe the workplace with spiritual ethos. AEH Madurai had a meditation room where some of the personal belongings of Sri Aurobindo had been kept. Dr. V visited this room every day. And though no one was compelled to go to the meditation room; many staff members and patients went there on their own accord. In Dr. V's words, "There is an atmosphere of spirituality in the hospital."

AEH in Madurai also had a small crèche for the very small children of the staff. Same care was given to all children irrespective of their parent's position in the organization, including doctors.

As on February 2003, the staff strength of AEH Madurai was 762. For about 113 doctors, there were 307 nurses, 38 counsellors, and 304 other staff. The pattern of staffing in other units was broadly similar. Exhibit 16 gives the break-up of staff strength for different units of AECS.

Exhibit 15 Aravind hospital: organization structure (medical)

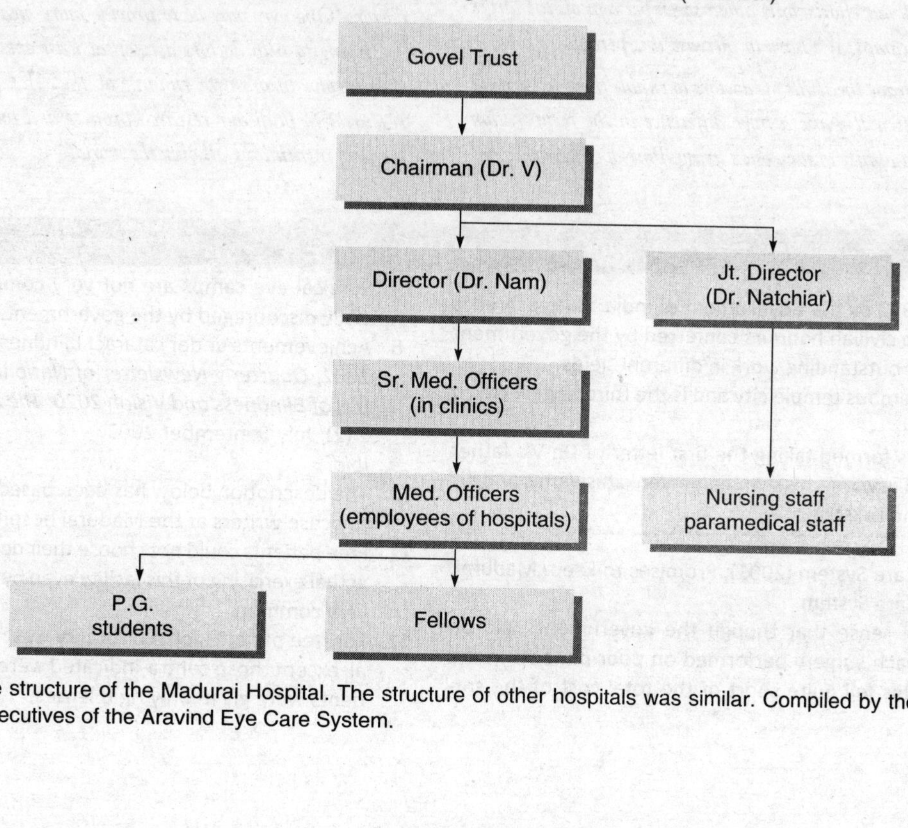

Note: The above is the structure of the Madurai Hospital. The structure of other hospitals was similar. Compiled by the case writers after discussions with the executives of the Aravind Eye Care System.

Exhibit 16 Break-up of staff strength in different units of AEHS (2003)

Category	Madurai	Theni	Tirunelveli	Coimbatore	Pondicherry
Medical Officers	38	2	10	22	13
Fellows & PGs	62	3	16	23	3
Paramedics	259	21	100	148	56
Counsellors	34	2	16	17	7
Others	310	18	59	72	58
Total	703	46	201	282	137

Source: Data supplied by Aravind Eye Care System.

FUTURE DIRECTIONS

Though happy and satisfied with his achievements so far, Dr. V felt he had a long way to go. His vision was no longer focused just on the functioning of AECS, but on the larger issue of how to make a lasting impact on the problem of blindness. Dr. V said:

I am now seriously wondering how to develop sustainable systems. Only by strengthening the existing hospitals this can be achieved. I feel doctors in India are heavily underutilized. They are engaged in activities unrelated to their work. We have to find a way to improve the functioning of hospitals so as to increase the productivity of doctors. Moreover, despite all our efforts, only about seven per cent of the target population come to camps. We have to increase this percentage too.

We also have to upgrade the skills of doctors to enable them to perform IOL surgeries. This will make a huge difference in the recuperation time and subsequent ability to earn one's living. Post-operative care has to be improved; counselling needs to be improved. It is in these areas that we hope to make a difference.

Mr. Thulasiraj added:

I can see many management issues coming up. There is going to be a need to restructure ourselves. There is considerable geographical spread as well as functional diversity. How should we restructure?

We are still too centralized in our decisions. Too many decisions are taken here in Madurai. We also have to broad base our leadership. Too much energy is coming from Madurai. How do we stimulate similar efforts from other units?

A lot of our strength comes from what I call "unconscious competence." Our strength is really not our technical skills or equipment. This can be easily replicated. Values are our unique strength. Values are the real reason for efficiency. We must find ways of sustaining and strengthening our values and culture. Integrating the culture of all our units is very important.

Integrity is a hallmark of this place. We never give commissions to other doctors, chemists, or other hospitals for special tests. We tell other diagnostic facilities what they should charge a poor patient sent from AECS for a particular test (e.g. MRI or CT scan) and they oblige. We have been able to have our way. We should be able to keep this integrity intact.

Dr. Aravind Srinivasan said:

One of our key strategic future steps is to develop dual specialties among our doctors. We would like to retain and get the best out of our doctors. One way may be to provide more meaning to their work. We are trying to help doctors develop at least one other specialty. We can then involve them in the running of the AECS. We also need to find resources to fund our research projects and build more linkages with eye care institutions all over the world.

NOTES

1. Awarded in 1972 by the Government of India. Padmashree is one of the top civilian honours conferred by the government every year for outstanding work in different fields.
2. Madurai is a famous temple city and is the third largest city in Tamil Nadu.
3. The name was formed taking the first letter of Dr. V's father name, Govind aswamy, his own name Venkataswamy, and his mother's name Lakshmi.
4. See later.
5. Aravind Eye Care System (2001), Promises to keep. Madurai: Aravind Eye Care System.
6. Partial in the sense that though the government paid an amount for each surgery performed on poor patients in the eye camps, this fell quite short of the total cost of the surgery.
7. Surgical eye camps are not very common now and are officially discouraged by the government.
8. Achievements under cataract blindness control project: 1994-2002, *Quarterly Newsletter of National Programme for Control of Blindness and Vision 2020: The Right to Sight Initiative*, 1 (2), July-September 2002.
9. *Ibid.*
10. The description below has been based on the observations of the case writers at the Madurai hospital.
11. Free patients could not choose their doctors. We were told that actual exercising of this facility even by paying patients was not very common.
12. For free patients, phaco surgery was not available. Of course, all except those contra-indicated were given IOLs, but free patients were given only rigid lenses.

13. Actually, this was reimbursed based not on the number of patients operated but who turned up at the follow-up camp. Since many did not turn up in these camps, the hospitals were denied reimbursement to that extent.
14. Aravind Eye Care System (2001) *Activities Report*. Madurai: AECS.
15. In 2002, out of 11 candidates who appeared from India, five were from AECS. . Out of the 7 candidates who cleared that year, four were from AECS.
16. More specifically, primary open angle glaucoma. There are other types of glaucoma, the incidence of which is rare.

CASE 8

ITC Limited, Bangalore (A)

Ajeet Mathur

The Board meeting that Tuesday generated a lot of discussion. The Member (Technical), J.M. Khanna, had himself headed the Company's Bangalore operations until the previous year and was well conversant with what he presented. Rolling back the flipcharts prepared for the meeting, he concluded, "Limits to our diversification strategy are real and need about three years" time to resolve. According to Ram, (Ram Laxman, Member, Marketing) market research indicates that demand for products in our traditional businesses is twice the production levels. But factories are not taps that can be opened wider to expand supply without a time lag. Do we have a vision? Do we have the patience and determination? If yes, gentlemen, approve my proposal for the capital investments needed for the expansion and we can achieve conversion cost reductions of sixty per cent."

"Three years is a long wait for a golden opportunity to treble contributions to profit ! Why not expand by stealth, chip away the inefficiency bottlenecks and negotiate new arrangements with workers now? Bangalore has the least unit cost of production. There is something to gain if cost can be reduced but nothing to lose if production expands even at the same unit cost", D.P. Barua Member (Finance) thought aloud.

The stream of questions seemed unending. Can it be done? Who would lead this? What are the risks? The Board resolved to let Member (Technical) Khanna and Member (Personnel) Vinod Suri discuss with the Bengaluru team headed by K.V. Krishnamurthy and deferred the strategic decision for due consideration the following month.

The Company

ITC Limited was incorporated in Calcutta in 1910 as Imperial Tobacco, an Indian subsidiary of the BAT Group, bringing together the Peninsular Group of companies and the Imperial Group of companies responsible for production since 1905 and marketing respectively, along with a host of trade investments in related businesses. In 1979, BAT industries had a worldwide presence in packaged foods, garments, cigarettes and smoking tobaccos, hotels, paper and financial services. The Indian subsidiary had become a widely held company after repeated rounds of dilution of foreign shareholding. In 1979, BAT held less than 39 per cent equity in ITC Limited. The ITC Board had two BAT nominee representatives and other executive directors, including the Chairman were employees of ITC. Many directors had begun their careers in ITC and grown with the Company. By 1980, the Company marketed more than eighty different branded products, and had made successful forays into merchandising of sports accessories

Prepared by Prof. Ajeet Mathur, Indian Institute of Management, Ahmedabad.

and sportswear. ITC's diversification into marine foods had been a disaster and growth in garment exports remained lacklustre. The printing and packaging division under Y.C. Deveshwar was beginning to draw external customers other than catering to in-house demand and a separate company had been created for the paperboards business (Bhadrachalam). The hotels division under the banner "Welcomgroup" was expanding well, with owned properties as well as managed properties. The collaboration with Sheraton had shown what could be achieved if cash flows from traditional businesses in paper and paperboards, printing and packaging, and cigarettes and smoking tobaccos could be augmented to fund this diversification. The Company's main business division produced more than 75 per cent of its profits and five factories were located in Monghyr, Saharanpur, Bangalore, Kolkata and Mumbai.

According to the Industrial Engineering Department, the Company was working to full production capacity in all factories as per column 1 in Table 1.

Table 1 ITC Limited, Bangalore: key indicators 1978

Factory	Production units in mins per day	Conversion Cost per unit in Rs per thousand	Average gross price (incl. excise) per unit for brand mix per packet of tens	Employee numbers
Monghyr	19	2.38	4.25	2315
Bangalore	33	1.95	6.80	2450
Saharanpur	26	2.05	5.15	2200
Kidderpore	10	2.78	4.50	1400
Parel (Mumbai)	12	2.95	4.95	1152
All India Demand forecast (1980–90) for Company's brands	220			

The Bangalore factory, established since 1912 had the widest product mix, the latest machines, blending experimentation was housed in nearby Peenya the Company's in-house research centre and the green leaf threshing plant was in the process of being moved to Hosur. The Company stored three years' of green leaf stock as inventory in the 22 godowns inside the Bangalore factory premises. The factory had a rail siding connected with Bangalore Cantonment Railway Station and with the Broad Guage Bangalore–Chennai Railway line. The first contained shipment for exports in India had been inaugurated at ITC's Bangalore Factory in 1978.

The following additional information was available to the Board:

1. An increase of 50 per cent in output on present norms would require nine more high speed packaging units, each of which could be ordered from abroad or ordered from a domestic manufacturer in Chandigarh.
2. Each high speed machine (HSM) needed a crew of "one operator" and three semi-skilled persons called "attendant". The only other type of machine the slow speed machine (SSM)—required a crew of one "operator" and one "attendant". Further, a "Mechanic" was allocated for every 3 SSMs/2 HSMs, and a "Technician" was provided per 4 HSMs/6 SSMs. This was necessary because the machinery required high precision settings and needed frequent adjustments.
3. There were 12 slow speed machines and 6 high speed machines installed since the last modernization in 1974.
4. Speciality preservative foils for packaging additional output were not immediately available in India but the company's purchase department had identified sources of supply and vendors could be developed in India or abroad. It was likely that a specific joint venture for in-house needs and sales could be set up and this could also be at the same site since there was plenty of land in the Bangalore factory premises that was not used.
5. The factory worked three shifts of 8 hours, 8 hours, and 6.5 hours (night shift). The number of employees working as crews in the manufacturing departments was 712. There were 10 technicians, 19 mechanics, 80 operators and 180 attendants. The other employees consisted of clerical and unskilled categories.
6. About 30 per cent of employees were due to retire on reaching the age of 58 in the next three years.
7. Absenteeism was about 20 per cent, including paid leave. An absentee cover of 25 per cent for technically skilled persons was considered necessary.
8. The Company traditionally allowed heirs of retiring and deceased employees to be recruited at the junior most unskilled levels. Since career progression and growth from within was a policy of the Company, this had caused much technical

erosion. Operators were eligible for promotion to "Mechanic" and mechanics to "Technician". Fitter trades from engineering department were also occasionally considered for promotion to positions of "Mechanic" and "Technician". There was a shortage of fitters in engineering department.

9. The company had always encouraged collective bargaining with its employees and periodically entered into three year long term agreements with recognised trade unions on the principle "one unit one union". Each such agreement was a factory wide settlement for three years. The last such agreement with ITC Workers Union was made in 1976. All office bearers of the ITC Workers' Union were from amongst employees. A second union had recently formed under the Presidentship of Shri Surya Narayana Rao who had lost the election to the State Legislature. Any seven persons could form a union according to law but the Company believed that it was not obliged to recognize all such unions.
10. The management team at Bangalore consisted of about thirty senior managers in various functions such as manufacturing, commercial, purchase, engineering, finance, personnel supported by supervisory staff and office staff in administrative positions numbering about sixty. It was the policy of the company to periodically transfer all senior managers between its various offices and also between functions and divisions. There were five human resources specialists in the personnel team at Bangalore. The personnel team was headed by Ashit K. Sarkar, who had served the company with distinction for more than 25 years at various locations with a proven track record in manufacturing and in industrial relations. The other four members consisted of a Barrister from the Inner Temple in the UK for whom this was her first factory assignment, an IIM alumnus with specialisation in organisation behaviour and economics, a statutory Welfare Officer from the region who had served in that role for more than fifteen years, and a social worker from Tata Institute of Social Sciences who had been inducted a month ago for her factory internship. She was from Kerala and was learning the Kannadiga language. Sarkar was optimistic that much could be done if management credibility could be communicated and gains shared among all contributing constituents so that everybody had something to gain from change.

As Vinod Suri paced up and down the corridor on the third floor of Virginia House waiting for others to arrive in the Boardroom, he felt greatly troubled. He wondered how would they temper the risks in blending the regard for conventional wisdom and how would the Board distribute responsibilities for strategy formulation and implementation in this case where spillovers were unpredictable? Being a new Board Member and not yet confirmed in his position, he was also acutely aware that this could make or break his career.

CASE 9

ITC Limited, Bangalore (B)

Ajeet Mathur

A mood of nostalgia hung over Virginia House that evening in Kolkata. The farewell party for Keki Randeria, Member (Personnel), seemed like unending. All personnel managers of the company from every division were there to give him a warm send-off. Keki was leaving the company and relocating to Mumbai for new responsibilities with another multinational firm. He had served the company for over two decades. Keki had joined ITC as a welfare officer in Mumbai after leaving the Indian Air Force and moved up to eventually head the personnel function at the board level. During Keki's tenure, the company had witnessed new and important policy transitions in human resource management and industrial relations. These included new terms and conditions for management staff (the company moved away from a perquisite-based compensation system to more cash based remuneration), extensive rationalization of manpower across all divisions through voluntary retirement schemes, and the creation of a cost and profit centre for training and development. He was particularly remembered for proposing the abolition of the personnel department in one of his first company-wide circulars signed as Member (Personnel) in 1976.

Vinod Suri, Keki's successor, seemed inconsolable despite three stiff doses of the best that the two renowned Scotsmen Haig & Haig had to offer. Valiantly trying to drown his sorrows, he was sweating over a strategic decision that needed to be made that evening. Should the company risk a strike at its largest manufacturing complex in Bangalore and lose ₹10 million a day in output value from tomorrow, or avoid the strike by accepting unreasonable demands that could cripple the restructuring of ITC's traditional businesses, reducing cash flows needed for diversification to a trickle, jeopardizing the whole corporate strategy?

ITC Limited was incorporated in Calcutta (now renamed Kolkata) in 1910 as Imperial Tobacco Company Limited, an Indian subsidiary of the BAT Group of Industries, bringing together the Peninsular Group of companies and the Imperial Group of companies responsible since 1905 for production and marketing respectively, along with trade investments in related businesses. In 1979, BAT industries had a worldwide presence in packaged foods, garments, cigarettes and smoking tobacco, hotels, paper, and financial services. By 1977, the Indian subsidiary had become a widely held company af-

Cases of the Indian Institute of Management, Ahmedabad, are prepared as a basis for class discussion. Cases are not designed to present illustrations of either correct or incorrect handling of administrative problems.

Prepared by Professor Ajeet Mathur, Indian Institute of Management, Ahmedabad.

The case forms part of the narration in the book titled *Industrial Restructuring and Union Power* (ILO-ARTEP, World Employment Programme, 1991). Permission received from J.N. Sapru, Chairman, ITC Limited is gratefully acknowledged.

ter repeated rounds of dilution of foreign shareholding. In 1979, BAT held less than 39 per cent equity in ITC Limited. The ITC Board had two BAT nominees. Other executive directors, including the Chairman A.N. Haksar, were employees of ITC. Most of the directors had begun and grown with the company, and it was customary to end a career in ITC only upon retirement. ITC embarked on diversification in the 1970s in a bid to move away from the long term uncertainties associated with smoking and health concerns likely to affect its traditional businesses. Opportunities and advantages of growth through diversification through the pooling and syndicating of corporate functions across a portfolio appealed as a viable route for sustainable growth and value creation.

The company marketed more than eighty different branded products, and had made successful forays into merchandising of sports accessories and sportswear. ITC's diversification into marine foods had been a disaster and growth in garment exports remained lacklustre. The printing and packaging division under Y.C. Deveshwar was beginning to draw external customers other than catering to in-house demand and a separate company had been created for the paperboards business (Bhadrachalam). The hotels division under the banner Welcomgroup was expanding well, with owned properties as well as managed properties. Its latest hotel Windsor Manor was under construction in Bangalore. The collaboration with Sheraton had shown what could be achieved if cash flows from traditional businesses in paper and paperboards, printing and packaging, and cigarettes and smoking tobacco could be augmented to fund this diversification. The company's main business division produced more than 75 per cent of its profits and its five manufacturing units were located in Monghyr (Bihar), Saharanpur (UP), Bengaluru (Karnataka), Kolkata (West Bengal), and Mumbai (Maharashtra). The Bangalore factory was the largest production complex of the company.

Operating since 1912, ITC, Bangalore, had the widest product mix and the latest machines. The blending unit was housed in nearby Peenya at the company's in-house research centre. The green leaf threshing (GLT) plant located at the factory site supplied leafstock to ITC's Bangalore and other factories. GLT was in the process of being moved to Hosur but the move had not yet taken place. The company stored three years' of green leaf stock as inventory in 22 leaf godowns inside the Bengaluru factory premises some of which also supplied higher grades to four other factories. The factory had a railway siding connected to the broad gauge Bangalore–Chennai main railway line. This had enabled ITC, Bengaluru, to become the first company in India to pioneer containerized shipment of exports from India.

Market research indicated that demand for ITC products in its traditional businesses was twice the current production level. A year ago, the company had decided to expand production and restructure the socio-technical system in Bangalore. It was believed that this expansion could be achieved with very little new capital investment. Higher output levels were considered achievable by rationalizing manpower costs and increasing productivity norms to generate savings from improved operations management and work practices. The rated capacity of the plant was 52 million units a day whereas actual production was about 33 million units a day. The nucleus of young MBAs at ITC, Bengaluru, privately speculated that the rated capacity of 52 million was itself a gross underestimation and that the factory could produce over 60 million units a day with machines that were already commissioned.

ITC was renowned for its excellent human resource management and industrial relations. The company had won the Federation of Indian Chambers of Commerce and Industry (FICCI) award and declared the best company in India for human resource management and harmonious industrial relations. The company's human resource development policy required that external selection in managerial, administrative, and technical cadres for any position was limited to those with potential to grow into responsibilities at least two levels higher than the job level at which they were recruited. The company also encouraged collective bargaining with its unionized employees and periodically entered into three year long term agreements with recognized trade unions based on the principle "one unit one union". Each such agreement was a factory wide settlement for three years. The last such agreement with the ITC Workers' Union (Reg. No.2) was made in 1976. All office bearers of the ITC Workers' Union were from amongst employees. A second union, ITC Employees Association (Reg. No.49), had recently been formed with Shri Surya Narayana Rao as its President. Rao, a Communist Party politician, had been defeated in elections to the state legislature of Karnataka.[1]

The management team in Bangalore consisted of about thirty senior managers in various functions such as manufacturing, commercial, purchase, engineering, finance, and personnel, supported by supervisory staff and office staff in administrative positions numbering about sixty. It was the policy of the company to periodically transfer all senior managers among its various offices and also between functions and divisions. There were five human resource specialists in the personnel team in Bangalore. The personnel team was headed by Ashit K. Sarkar, who had served the company with distinction for more than twenty-five years at various locations with a proven track record in manufacturing and industrial relations. Sarkar was optimistic that management credibility could be communicated and gains shared among all contributing constituents so that everybody had something to gain from change.

The other four members consisted of Amrit Sujan, a barrister from the Inner Temple in the UK for whom this was her first factory assignment, Narain, IIM alumnus with specialization in organization behavior and economics, Rudrappa, (a Kannadiga from Karnataka), the statutory welfare officer, who had been in this position for more than fifteen years, and Bina Antony, a social worker, inducted from the Tata Institute of Social Sciences, a month ago. Bina, originally from Kerala, was educated in Mumbai and was new to Bangalore and learning the Kannada language. With her induction, it was hoped that social welfare measures for workers and their families would be strengthened and a counselling service for workers introduced.

T.P. Jose, one of the production managers in the intermediate processing department told the case writer, "My department cannot increase output without getting more mechanics and technicians required for the precision settings of Mark 8 machines and their PA7RO attachments. Machine operators keep putting a shim here and a shim there to avoid shutting down poorly set machines and that leads to downtime and considerable wastage and is hardly a solution."

According to T.V. Ramaswamy, production manager of the final processing department, "The main constraint in my department is the acute shortage in the highly skilled categories of mechanic and technician for operating high-speed duplex packing machines."

This technical skills constraint could not be quickly mitigated without direct external recruitment to these positions. The only external recruitment previously done had been into the grade of Fitter in the engineering department. There were two levels of Fitters: Fitter I and Fitter II. Fitter I level workmen were typically skilled senior experienced fitters promoted from the ranks of Fitter II after qualifying in a promotion test on completion of five years' service. Fitter II level workmen were recruited from the stock of diploma holders in mechanical engineering and skilled tradesmen from vocational and technical training institutes such as Industrial Training Institutes (ITI). The company philosophy of "growth from within" ran counter to the notion of direct external recruitment. Any such move was likely to be opposed by union employees, who would see it as loss of their promotion opportunities.

Another problem was that the current long term agreement (LTA) did not end until about another year. Discussions could not normally be initiated for the next long term wage agreement where new work arrangements, norms, practices, etc. would be discussed. Moreover, it could take some time before a new charter of demands from the union representing workmen could be negotiated for a new long term agreement. In the past, this process had taken one to two years after commencement of negotiations.

Because of learning curve effects and loose past work practices, it was common knowledge that there was considerable slack in the system and also excess manpower in a number of departments in the semi-skilled categories. Some of this could be redeployable in an expansion under new rationalized norms. The company had successfully shed excess manpower through voluntary retirement schemes since the early 1970s (the first company in India to do so). There had been an embargo on recruitment since 1976 (despite natural wastages such as deaths, resignations, retirement) as part of what was euphemistically termed the "numbers' game". ITC's diversification strategy had gathered momentum by the end of 1970s. There was a need to squeeze resources from the "cash cows" of traditional businesses. Significantly, traditional businesses had not lost their "star" status and the market was buoyant also for their products.

The company decided to take the risk of restructuring and rationalization of work practices at the Bangalore complex without waiting for the next long term agreement. In consultation with office bearers of the ITC Workers' Union, a set of management proposals was presented by each department to its sectional union representatives. Workmen were encouraged to identify savings they could generate through reduction of machine crews, handing and taking over of running machines, continuous shifts, improved throughput coordination between making and packing, better work methods, new information systems, preventive maintenance, etc. Workmen were promised one-third of any savings in money they agreed to create which would be computed in money and immediately ploughed back into their salaries as personal allowances, while one-third would go towards company profits and another one-third be passed on to the consumer. This formula appealed to workmen and almost every department came up with savings. Supplementary "mini-agreements" were then signed between the union and management departmentally to implement these new productivity norms.

A new group incentive scheme—PIP (Productivity Index Payments)—was additionally introduced whereby each workman would earn a PIP payment corresponding to his job based on a consolidated PIP index. The PIP index would be computed monthly for the whole factory based on the number of final containers produced in that month aggregating the agreed weighted average for the various products.

Direct external recruitment, however, remained a thorny issue. The office bearers and some members were able to understand the non-availability of mechanics and technicians for the precision setting required by the machines as the bottleneck holding down factory production and productivity but remained reluctant to agree to inducting talent from outside. As a quid pro quo, the company offered to recruit a certain number of sons of retiring employees in anticipation of needs for unskilled work arising in the course of expansion. In biting this bait, office bearers of the ITC Workers Union (Reg. no. 2) agreed not to make a noise if fair opportunities were also given through testing to internal candidates from amongst operators and attendants. The company created a new pool of junior workers and recruited unskilled employees from among retiring employees' nominees on the basis that every retiring employee could nominate as many of his progeny as he wished and the company would then select one from among them to be employed as a junior worker. Promotion tests to posts of mechanics were conducted and eight operators found suitable to be trained as mechanics were promoted and sent for training to the Technical Training Centre. To begin filling the remaining vacancies, the company conducted a nation-wide talent search. Besides hiring from competitors in the same industry in Maharashtra and Gujarat, this included tapping into the Indian Air Force pool of technical airmen retiring after 15 years' service and the engineering and technical branches of the Army by building lists on a nation-wide basis. Assessment centres were then convened at the Technical Training Centre of the Bangalore factory. Selections were completed and the first round of letters of employment were issued to nine technicians and twelve mechanics. The list of selected candidates is presented in Exhibit 1 (the names have been changed for the sake of privacy and personal data protection).

Exhibit 1 (Names have been changed without alteration of profile)

Technicians appointed

1. V.K. Mahadevan, age 35, Weapon Armourer, ex-Indian Army, married, one child.
2. Mathew Verghese, age 34, Airframe Fitter, ex-Indian Air Force, bachelor.
3. Jacob Abraham, age 33, Engine Fitter, ex-Indian Air Force, married, two children.
4. T.S. Eranyanathan, age 39, Dip. Mech Engg, 18 years' industry experience, married.
5. V.K. Chockalingam, age 37, Dip. Mech Engg, 15 years' industry experience, married.
6. K.K.P. Nair, age 34, Airframe Fitter, ex-Indian Air Force, married, three children.
7. A.P. Amritalingam, age 35, Weapon Armourer, ex-Indian Army, married.
8. T.K.P. Unnikrishnan, age 34, Airframe Fitter, ex-Indian Air Force, married, three children.
9. S.G. Krishnan, age 37, Dip. Mech Engg, 15 years' industry experience, married.

Mechanics appointed

1. A.K. Parikh, age 40, ITI Fitter, 15 years' experience with GTC Baroda, married, one child.
2. T.K. Singh, age 39, ITI Fitter, 16 years' experience with NTC Kolkata, married, one child.
3. K.P. Kutty, age 34, Engine Fitter, ex-Indian Air Force, married, two children.
4. A.M. Nair, age 33, Millwright Mechanic, 14 years' industry experience, married.
5. I.K. Abraham, age 33, Weapon Armourer, ex-Indian Army, married.
6. Mohd. Kallivayalil, age 33, Airframe Fitter, ex-Indian Air Force, bachelor.
7. R.K. Iyer, age 40, ITI Fitter, 15 years' experience with GTC Baroda, married, one child.
8. G. Ganapathi, age 38, Millwright mechanic, 20 years' industry experience, married.
9. John Abraham, age 37, Airframe Fitter, ex-Indian Air Force, married, two children.
10. D.K.P. Nair, age 34, Airframe Fitter, ex-Indian Air Force, married, two children.
11. A.S. Koshy, age 35, Weapon Armourer, ex-Indian Army, married.
12. T.T. Manikutty, age 38, Dip. Mech Engg, 17 years' industry experience, married.

There was a sharp reaction from workers as soon as the external technical recruitment was announced. Some workers, particularly operators and attendants, who had failed the promotion tests felt betrayed by the ITC Workers' Union (Reg. no. 2). On their part, office bearers of the ITC Workers' Union now felt unable to admit that they had been consulted and this was part of a negotiated deal (although the agreement had not been made in writing). Under pressure from workers, the ITC Workers' Union (Reg. no. 2) now presented the company with a strike notice. The strike notice demanded that appointment letters to the new external recruits into positions of mechanics and technicians be cancelled and their appointments revoked, threatening an indefinite strike from the very next day if their demand was not met.

In a curious twist to this situation, the ITC Employees' Association (Reg. no. 49), a union not recognized by the company as a bargaining agent representing workmen, launched a vigorous campaign against the strike notice and propaganda of the recognized union. Office bearers and committee members of the ITC Employees' Association (Reg. no. 49) conducted gate meetings at the beginning and closing times of all three shifts and urged workers to kick out the Union that had betrayed the interests of workmen long ago and all along. They pointed out that everybody knew that external candidates were coming to the factory for being tested and interviewed for the past many months and this was done openly and was not a secret. The ITC Employees' Association (Reg. no. 49) also pasted posters on the walls of the factory highlighting betrayal by the ITC Workers' Union (Reg. no. 2), emphasizing that there was no need at this late stage to lose wages over an unjustified and illegal strike. The unrecognized union further promised full protection to all workers who would want to work and not participate in a futile protest action. This made sense to large sections of workers. Yet, it was difficult to know whether the majority of workers supported or opposed the proposed strike.

Should the company risk its reputation for harmonious and strike-free industrial relations and face up to the strike threat called by the ITC Workers' Union (Reg no. 2)? Is it possible to avoid losing ₹10 million a day in output value? Or should the company avoid the strike by accepting the union demands to keep the wheels of production moving? There was also a question about the credibility of the company's contracts of employment that had been signed and delivered to the new employees who were about to join their duties.

The managers of the Bangalore factory were perplexed. The situation required a quick decision. Despite its immediacy, whatever the Bengaluru decision, it was certain to reverberate with strategic consequences—intended and unintended—for the whole company for a long time to come.

The conclave of those assembled at the farewell party included almost all the human resource experts of the company and the entire board of directors. Vinod Suri let the two Scotsmen quench his thirst for the fifth time. As he puffed on one of ITC's premium brands and blew smoke rings through the alcoholic haze that clouded him, he wasn't able to make up his mind. He was wondering whether it would be appropriate to disrupt the party spirits and take aside and consult his colleagues or inform them that the Bangalore team was in a quandary and had a strategic decision to make that night.

NOTES

1. Any seven persons could form a union according to law but the company believed that it was not obliged to recognize all such unions.

CASE 10

The Living Room: Redefining the Furniture Industry

Sowmya Kolluri and N. Ravichandran

Introduction

Mr. Jehangir Nagree, graduated in Civil Engineering from Veermata Jijabai Technological Institute, Mumbai, in 1971. The economic depression of the early 1970s and his uncanny love for wood, kindled the entrepreneur in him leading to the formulation of "The Living Room" (TLR) in 1971. In 2004–2005, the company recorded a sales turnover of ₹178 lakh, with a net profit of ₹20.88 lakh. TLR as a business was operational, along with Jehangir's brother, but a family split occurred in 2003.

TLR started with a showroom in Mahim, Mumbai along with a workshop in the vicinity, where skilled local carpenters made the furniture. "The Living Room" was positioned as a substitute for the family carpenter who offered a product that was easy to purchase, good in design, genuine and trustworthy in quality.

Jehangir quickly realized the constraint of living space in Mumbai apartments and houses, which prevented typical families from using a wide range of quality furniture. He designed the "sofa-cum-bed" which, as the name suggests, was a 3-seat sofa that could be converted into a bed, by pulling the base. This was named "Super Wondrette". This innovation became an instant hit and helped "The Living Room" establish itself as a brand in Mumbai.

TLR was jointly managed by the founder, Jehangir and his wife, Shakera. Jehangir was a man driven by a passion for this business. His contagious enthusiasm and commitment served as a motivation to his employees. Both Jehangir and Shakera personally spent time in the retail outlets, interacting with customers, employees, and visitors with warmth.

The couple has two daughters, both well-educated, married and working in reputed Investment Banks in the USA. As a very well-to-do family, they maintained good relations in the society. They traveled abroad frequently, especially to trade fairs in Italy, to understand the upcoming designs and styles in furniture.

Products

The Living Room made a wide range of home furniture. The sales composition comprised sofa sets: 30 percent; beds, wardrobes, dressing tables and other accessories: 25 percent; dining sets: 20 percent; kitchen cabinets, wall units and study tables: 25 percent. In August 2005, TLR had also introduced office furniture like workstations, office tables, chairs, running tables, side runners, etc. TLR typically catered to small offices, which did not have the sufficient volumes to buy from institutional sellers.

Cases of the Indian Institute of Management, Ahmedabad, are prepared as a basis for class discussion. Cases are not designed to present illustrations of either correct or incorrect handling of administrative problems.

It is based on an earlier version of a case prepared by Sowmya Kolluri and Gopal Putrevu under the direction of Professor N.Ravichandran, for Confluence 2005.

Quality and long life of the furniture were the core strengths of all TLR products. This was ensured by high standards in manufacturing, workmanship and quality components.

TLR had a large variety of models in all its products. For example, TLR, recognized as a pioneer in sofa-cum-bed, introduced new models in this product category. The designing was done in-house after considering the market trends and customer feedback. The designs were mostly standardized. However, product dimensions could be changed to suit customers' requirements. Typical price range of the products is given in Exhibit 1.

Exhibit 1 Price ranges of products

Product	Range (₹)
Sofa-cum-beds	14,950–24,200
Single beds	7,450–16,000
Double beds	9,500–24,200
Wardrobe	13,850–44,000
Wall-unit	13,450–25,200
Sofa-sets	19,960–84,500
Centre-tables	2,250–8,500
Shoe racks	3,200–6,500
Kitchens starting from	26,750
Office tables from	5,750

All the above prices included VAT, delivery, fitting and one year warranty

Besides style, utility was the most important aspect in the design of TLR products such as wardrobes, kitchen sets, etc. Innovative designs were made for maximizing space utilization.

Brand

Jehangir had a vision to build a *brand* for TLR products to compete effectively in the highly unorganized furniture market in India. In the early days the brand name was not important. The product sold based on its unique design. Over the years, the brand "The Living Room" became synonymous with quality, trust and value for money (VFM).

In order to reinforce this image, TLR insisted on transparency in all its processes related to customers. The prices were set at a reasonable level and disclosed at the very beginning of the communication. There were no hidden costs. There were no discounts and bargains. TLR believed, value for money was not giving cheap products but giving the customers the best quality, style, and design for the price that they pay–be it for a sofa-cum-bed priced at ₹15000 or a sofa set priced at ₹45000.

Over the years the expectations from the brand had changed owing to greater competition and more choices becoming available to the consumers in Mumbai. In addition to VFM, TLR added different style dimensions to meet the changing customer tastes. However, changing customers' perception was a concern. The traditional logo of TLR [Exhibit 2(a)] had been changed in late 2004, to bring about a change in consumer perception of the brand. The new logo [Exhibit 2(b)], was considered to be trendy and contemporary.

Exhibit 2(a) The old logo

Exhibit 2(b) The new logo

Customers

TLR had four showrooms in Mumbai and one each in Goa and Surat. Customer profile of TLR varied widely (Exhibit 3, Appendix 2).

According to a typical customer,

> *I would not come here (TLR) for contemporary designs, to be showcased in my living room, but only for functional, basic furniture like bed, wardrobe, etc.*

Exhibit 3 Profile of customers at five showrooms

Location	Showroom Area in sq.ft.	Profile
Mahim	6000	The oldest store. Predominantly upper middle class customers. Customers are more conservative in spending. Products like sofa-cum-bed are sold most.
Malad	10000	Situated in a locality with high end residential and commercial constructions. Has office furniture to cater to the BPO offices coming up. Targets the higher end customers with the imported collection and similar products.
Mulund	8000	A mix of upper middle class and upper class customers. The store is surrounded by several competitors in close proximity.
Kandivili	8000	Upper class customers. The locality consists of high end residential buildings that were being constructed when the showroom opened. It was the only player in the locality till recently.
Vashi	7000	Upper middle class customers with conservative spending. The area is dominated by a strong presence of unorganized players.

In the initial years of TLR, there was a certain amount of aspiration value attached to its products. Hence, the customer segments were upper middle class families and middle class families who would have saved money to buy good furniture for their home.

According to Shakera, in those days the typical TLR customers were of two types. One was those who had been buying the brand for many years or whose parents had bought TLR products before. They bought it because of the trust they had in the quality and longevity of the product. The second consisted of customers who belonged to the younger generation–young couples with a combined income of over ₹50,000 per month, setting up a new home, and willing to spend a considerable amount on furniture. These people came to TLR not only for the quality but also for the innovative designs and variety. Most customers, however, looked at all other offers prevalent in the market before making the purchase. According to the Kandivli showroom manager,

Here, four customers could bring a business of ₹4–5 lakhs, whereas in Mahim, it needs more than 15 customers to bring comparable size of business.

For a brand in the highly unorganized furniture market, TLR, was the first furniture company to advertise on television, in 1974. However, in 2005, most of the advertising was done through newspapers in the form of inserts, advertisements, etc. *The Times of India* (*Bombay Times*) and The Hindu newspapers were most frequently used. Hoardings were also put up routinely in several places in Mumbai.

The advertisements carried pictures of the products available at various showrooms with their prices. Mentioning price was considered important to ensure transparency when the customers visited the showroom and saw the same price. It also emphasized on the competitive prices offered by TLR, reinforcing its image as a "value for money" brand. In some advertisements, TLR tried to communicate as being a one-stop shop for furniture.

TLR did not undertake many promotions. Discounts were rarely given and all offers were explicit and transparent. TLR made two types of offers–exchange offers (a fixed percentage discount in exchange for old furniture) and package offers (a 5 percent discount upon purchasing a certain set of products bundled together). The competitors, at the same time, tried to attract customers with discounts as high as 60 percent. TLR offers also included accessories like mattresses, bed sheets, pillows, etc. and other gifts like a gold figurine of Ganesha, a Persian carpet or a silver coin.

Promotional offers were advertised extensively. In exchange offers, all prices (pre and post discount) were published in the advertisements, to make it transparent and ensure the customer about the genuineness of the offer. Shakera also appeared on a Television show (Sweet Home) talking about interior decoration. Word of mouth publicity, based on the goodwill the brand had earned over the years, also played a major role in communication.

TLR aimed at creating a unique retail experience for its customers, as it was an essential part of connecting to the brand. Products were arranged in the setup of a living room, or a bedroom, etc. Fast moving items were put at the furthermost corner of the showroom to ensure that every customer was routed in such a way so as to maximize the product exposure. Store managers sensed what the customer was looking at and based on his observation changed the setting periodically to suit the local customer tastes. Store managers shared their experiences with other colleagues in their weekly meetings.

The showrooms were located at street corners to increase visibility. The outside signage was still the old logo, brightly illuminated.

Jehangir did not want to focus too much on increasing the customer base to increase sales, but aimed at increasing sale per customer. In 2004–05, regular items constituted 80 percent of total sales, and expensive items 20 percent. Jehangir was concerned about increasing this from 20 percent to 40 percent.

Sales of individual items were tracked both in the *regular* and *expensive* category in the meetings every Tuesday. "Sales per customer" was a key performance parameter and efforts were made to achieve it through packaged deals.

In 2003, TLR had ventured into Pune by opening a showroom in the franchise model. However, it was unsuccessful because the franchisee was unable to maintain exemplary customer service, thus adversely affecting the brand. The franchisee also stocked their own or local products in the same outlet. Based on this experience, TLR served the Pune market through a different model. Purchases were made at the Mumbai showrooms and goods were delivered to Pune free of charge.

THE BUSINESS MODEL

Organization

The organization structure of TLR is shown in Exhibit 4.

Showroom

At the showroom the store management, layout and arrangement of products, etc, was done by the Showroom Manager. In some showrooms, there was an Assistant Manager.

Factory

At the Factory, the Assistant Factory Manager looked after production and quality control. The Hardware Control Manager ensured the proper utilization of raw material, which accounted for 60 percent of the cost of manufacture, and continuously aimed at reducing the wastage.

Administration

Finance and accounts were handled in the Mahim office. All transactions were entered into a computer and communicated to the Mahim office. Recruitment was done centrally and was personally supervised by Jehangir and Shakera. The requirement of manpower was communicated to the Head Office (Mahim office), which then took the decision.

Processes

Employees and Training

The sales people were trained extensively on the technical aspect of furniture as well as in the method of interaction with customers. TLR believed in long term relationship with customers and gave genuine advice even if it meant loss of sale. This helped in building trust and relationship with customers so much that most customers asked for the salespeople by name. Training programs were organized once a month. The top management also regularly interacted with employees. All employees at the store were rotated across outlets once in two years. This was done to encourage free flow of ideas and information across outlets.

Management Control

One of the five offices was chosen for the weekly Tuesday meetings, attended by the top management and the store managers along with a salesperson (from each of the other showrooms) to review the weekly sales performance. The objective of these meetings was to

Exhibit 4 The organization structure of TLR

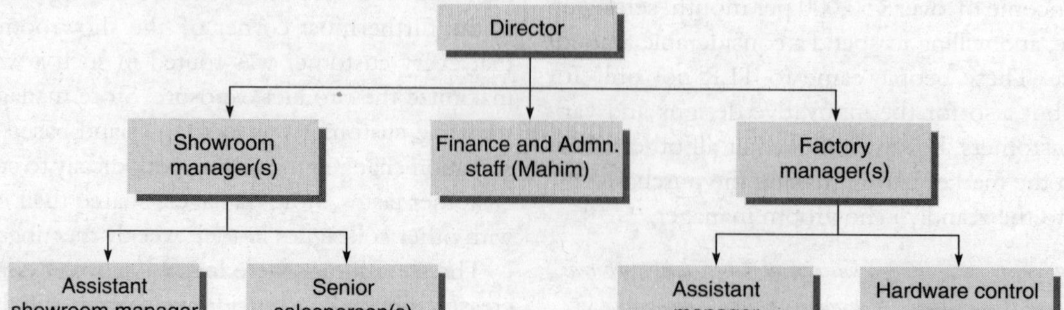

analyze sales performance, customer feedback, product portfolio decisions, etc. This communication reduced the response time for incorporating customer preferences in newer models and replicating the success factors of one showroom in another.

Manufacturing

TLR had four manufacturing units in Mumbai and one in Goa. The factory in Goa was the largest and worked as an assembly line system. Others facilities, located in Mumbai, manufactured a mix of all the other products. The manufacturing units in Mumbai catered to large variety (customization) and small volume products. This ruled out the possibility of assembly line operations. Manufacturing was also done by certain units not owned by TLR, on a contractual basis.

Being one of the oldest players in Mumbai, TLR enjoyed long term relationship with a large number of skilled carpenters. TLR recruited from this labor pool depending on the work load and paid them on a piece rate. Access to skilled labor gave TLR the flexibility to provide customized products. Typically, customization happened at two levels–product and project. Product customization involved changes in the design, wood, upholstery and related peripherals. Project customization meant changing the fitment and measurement of the product to the customer's requirements.

Logistics and Distribution

All imported products were first sent to Bhiwandi[1] warehouse. These were then sent to the Kandivli warehouse and finally to showrooms. Products which were manufactured in the Goa factory and were to be sold in Mumbai, were sent to the Kandivli warehouse while the products to be sold outside Mumbai (to places like Pune) were sent directly to the customers' sites, primarily to save octroi[2], etc. Refer Exhibit 5.

The Industry and Competition

The furniture industry in India in 2005 was primarily considered unorganized due to the long reliance on local skilled carpenters. However, the face of the sector was slowly changing with the effect of several factors like growth of organized retail, international exposure of customers, entry of foreign players, greater affinity for branded products, shifts in customer tastes and convenience seeking behavior. The outlook of the sector was quite optimistic. Durables purchases peaked in the 20-34 years age group–double-income couples setting up households were the driving force. The neighborhood carpenter or the upgraded craftsman who designed with an eye on foreign magazines no longer satisfied the consumer[3].

India had a huge middle-class population (an estimated 300 million[4] in 2005) whose spending was on the rise. The average Indian expenditure had gone up by more than 10 percent CAGR in the last 10 years. However, the percentage spent on furniture was still lower in India as compared to other developed countries.

Competitive Landscape

At one end of the spectrum of offering in this industry was the local neighborhood carpenter, who made products as per the customer's order, design and desire. Moving ahead, there were some players who employed these carpenters and sold to the customers. They being unorganized, had the cost advantage of retail space rental, sales taxes, etc. In the organized furniture retail, one segment catered to office furniture, while the other catered to home furniture. The Indian market in 2005, comprised players like Style Spa (earlier Gautier), Durian, The Living Room, Furniturewalla, @Home, Off the Shelf, etc. (Refer to Appendix 1). At the other extreme of the spectrum were the interior decorators

Exhibit 5 Distribution structure

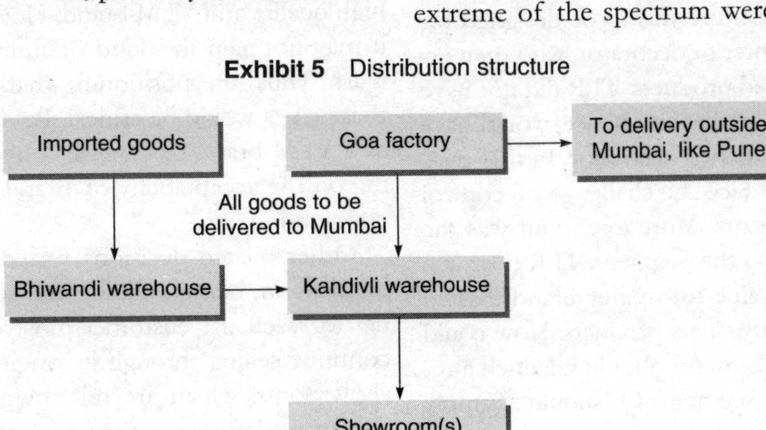

who provided the customer with personalized furniture. Interior decorators usually had a team of dedicated carpenters.

By 2005, the big retail chains had not developed their own private labels in furniture retail. Some of the reasons identified were the differences in local tastes, neighborhood carpenter dominance, complexity in design, etc. However, the threat of the private labels remained as some of the chains aimed to provide a "one-stop" shopping experience to the customer.

On the survival of local carpenters, Jehangir said, "Organized furniture retail might grow, but the local carpenter would continue playing a big role in the Indian context."

Growth Options

Jehangir realized the tremendous opportunity available in the Indian furniture industry. The industry was fast changing from a localized unorganized industry to one with successful national brands. With the FDI regulations expected to liberalize, huge foreign investments were also likely. It was clearly evident that the furniture industry was booming. Jehangir was seriously evaluating the growth options available for TLR in this context.

Expansion of Product Portfolio

TLR could extend its presence in the product spectrum, catering to lower or higher value products. Moving lower would mean direct competition with the local players, solely competing on price. In this case, it would not be economical to provide the same product quality and after sales service that TLR currently provided. Not providing the same, on the other hand, could seriously dilute the brand.

TLR also had the option of moving up to high value products. The method of selling of these products was very personalized. The furniture was to be designed for each of the homes by an interior decorator, who then ordered the highly customized products. TLR did not have adequate exposure in this market and hence, would have to use the services of an interior decorator. In this case, the company was likely to face the challenge of control of relationship with its clients. More important was the challenge of acceptability in this segment. TLR now was strongly entrenched as a value-for-money brand trusted for the quality and longevity of its products. How could it reposition itself in this segment? Should it launch a related brand to cater to this segment? Or should it simply change the communication?

Jehangir from his experience in the industry realized that there was another class—the aspiration driven upper end of the middle class segment. They would like to possess the upper class furniture and acceptability of the brand would not be an issue. TLR could upgrade to this segment by offering furniture that was value for money.

In 2005, TLR had entered the office furniture market. It catered to small enterprises, which did not have the volumes to go in for institutional sellers. With the increase in the number of BPO and IT firms, the market for office furniture was also growing. TLR could venture into this market, increasing its customer base to a larger clientele. However, the kind of selling required for institutional buyers was very different from the traditional approach of TLR, which was primarily direct sales supported by transparency and single-price.

Future Expansion

With the increasing number of Information Technology Enabled Service companies, the resident profile of many cities in India was rapidly changing. These cities recorded a high percentage of young and immigrant population, with dual income households and rising levels of average disposable income. Thus, TLR saw great opportunities in cities like Bangalore, Hyderabad, Ahmedabad, Lucknow, Surat, Indore, and Gurgaon (Appendix 3). However, TLR had no plans to set up manufacturing facilities in these cities.

In the cities where organized furniture retail was prevalent, the challenge would be competition. However, in smaller cities, the furniture market was still dominated by the unorganized sector. The challenge would be to create a brand, upgrade the customers and entice them to pay premium price for a branded product.

In Mumbai, TLR made a breakthrough with the sofa-cum-bed. It leveraged this image to succeed as a trusted, high quality and VFM brand. However, in the new cities, it may not gain this kind of immediate acceptance and trust. Thus, the positioning that TLR chose in any of these cities would be critical. Possible options are to stay as a VFM brand or enter as a high end player, depending on the acceptability of branded products, nature of competition, etc.

Other related decisions would involve market communication, brand building and selection of retail channel to reach the customer most effectively. TLR could continue selling through its original model of exclusive showrooms, which are fully owned or franchised outlets. In the latter case, the issues of control of franchises would be important, as evidenced in the Pune attempt. TLR can also forming partnerships with existing players in the cities. At the other extreme, TLR could substitute the "brick and mortar" model by a web enabled business model. It could give the customers the additional benefit of designing their furniture online. The showrooms could source the components centrally and assemble it at the front end.

On product offering, TLR should decide either to standardize its offering across the cities or make it more localized responding to the culture and preferences. What would be the ideal mix of centralized and local elements to leverage TLR's current efficiencies, experience and scale?

CONCLUSION

As he considered the options, Jehangir was aware of the advantage he had over competition—the access to a skilled carpenter pool—which gave him the flexibility to customize products. He wondered if he could offer this customization on a mass scale. Such a strategy would give him a unique positioning which may not be copied easily by competition.

Although Jehangir believed in the growth of TLR, an important concern for him was the scalability of the current processes and systems. He realized that each decision that he took had to be in tune with the strengths of his processes and at the same time recognizing its limitations. Can the processes of The Living Room be made self-sustaining?

Appendix 1 Competitor profile

@Home

@Home has a set of showrooms owned by Nilkamal Plastics Ltd. It offered a wide range of imported home furniture targeting the middle and upper middle class customers. @Home currently has showrooms in Mumbai, Ahmedabad, Pune and a few other towns.

Products

The showroom had the regular products like sofasets, beds and bedroom accessories, dining sets, computer and study tables, TV cabinets, side tables, shoeracks, and bunk beds and other innovative products.

In addition to furniture, a part of the showroom—"home accents" housed other related products like bedroom furnishing, cushions, clothes baskets, etc.

Showpieces of a very affordable range including artificial flowers, vases, photo frames, a wide range of candles. Small range of office furniture

The prices of all the products were on display. No discounts were offered. Many of the products of TLR were priced just below 49,900 to avoid the 50K barrier in the consumer mind.

Besides having a wide product range, the showroom had a great variety of designs in each product. Most of the designs were available in different colors. Each product had a card specifying the details of the product—material, piece wise price, colours available, etc. This decreased the dependence on the sales person.

Ambience

The showroom in Ahmedabad had 2 floors. It had a pleasant ambience. There were no huge spaces with furniture around, the halls mostly had divisions having smaller spaces for furniture. They also had a Café Coffee Xpress vendor.

Other Information

@Home is planning to introduce:

- An alliance with a paint company to offer paints, designs and textures to the walls.
- Software, which upon giving dimensions of the room, suggests the best set of furniture from their range that will go in it, along with the arrangement.

Furniturewalla

The brand offered high end furniture, targeted the upper class consumers. It had nine showrooms in Mumbai, Bangalore, Chennai, Pune, Hyderabad, Delhi, Kolkata and Ahmedabad. They planned to open a second store in Mumbai in 2006.

More than 90 percent of its furniture was imported from countries like Malaysia, Spain, Italy, etc.

Products

They offered to the consumer quality and style, with exclusive designs. They had only home furniture including sofa sets, beds and other bedroom products, dining sets, wall hangings, mirrors, etc.

They stocked only readymade furniture, with no customization of any form. These were stocked in the showroom itself and upon sale a new item was got from Mumbai.

Other Information

They advertised in newspapers and hoardings, but were also planning on shows etc.

Average spend per customer was about ₹50,000–₹60,000.

All the nine showrooms were owned by the company with appointed Showroom Managers.

They had an informative website with all the designs of furniture they offered, categorized into modern and traditional.

Durian

The brand Durian, with more than 44 (16 were on franchise) outlets in the country provided 100 percent imported furniture in the home and office segment. 10 more outlets are to be opened soon.

They also had a separate setup in the US for selling imported furniture for the home segment in New Jersey and for the new office segment in Los Angeles.

Products

The product range included sofa sets, bedroom sets, dining sets, wall units, computer tables and other innovative products like shoeracks, trolleys, etc. They had plans to introduce kitchen sets soon. Durian offered a wide variety of models across different price ranges. For instance, Durian offered sofa sets and dining tables ranging from ₹14,000 to 3 lakhs.

Promotion and advertising

Durian spent aggressively on product promotion and advertisements. They advertised on popular channels like Discovery and NGC, (both English and Hindi) Discovery Travel and Living, History, Animal Planet, Sanskar, AXN, CNBC TV18, CNBC Awaaz, Zee Cinema and Zee Music.

Appendix 2 Survey analysis

They used popular film stars and models as brand ambassadors each year. Some of them included Katrina Kaif, Ria Sen and Koena Mitra.

A survey was conducted over a period of 15 days in the 4 showrooms of TLR in Mumbai. The customers were requested to fill in questionnaires placed in the showrooms. The total number of responses received was 100: Mahim—37, Malad—25, Kandivili—28, Thane—10.

Survey objectives

- To understand the profile of the customers of TLR. Variables captured included—income, occupation, marital status, family size, number of earning members, mother tongue, location and ownership of residence
- To understand consumer behavior in terms of ownership, use and purchase of furniture. This included –
  - Frequency of purchase of furniture
  - Items currently owned
  - Reason for their current purchase
  - Probable item in the next purchase
  - Number of showrooms they have visited before TLR
  - Importance of discounts and offers
  - The salesperson's inputs on the knowledge of the customer on the product purchased
- To understand consumer perception towards TLR
  - First source of awareness about TLR
  - History of any previous purchase from TLR
  - Ratings for TLR on the attributes of style, quality, variety, price, service, ambience, display and any other attribute they thought was relevant. The ratings were to be on a scale of 1–10, with 10 being the most preferred rating
  - If the customer would recommend TLR to others, and if so, for what products

Results

Problems faced

As the survey was to be conducted in-store, the questionnaire was placed in the showrooms.

- Low number of responses, as it was voluntary
- Many incomplete forms
- Inappropriate comprehension of questions

Profiling the customer

- The distribution of household income per month was almost uniform from ₹20000 to 50,000 and above.
- Distribution of age was also uniform from 20–67 years.
- Nuclear families with 1–4 members were prominent.

Other findings

- Newspaper advertisement was the most common source of awareness about TLR (49 percent) followed by information from friends and family (28 percent).
- Reasons for purchase: To replace old furniture (35 percent), moving into a new house 21 percent don't have the product at home 18 percent.
- The customers also seemed to be reluctant to answer the question on offers at other stores, with only 50 responses to the question. 35/50 respondents noted the existence of discounts in the other stores.
- The customers were asked to rate TLR on a set of attributes. The findings were as follows:

Descriptive statistics

	Responses	Min.	Max.	Mean	Std. Deviation
Style	78	2	10	7.00	1.713
Quality	75	2	10	7.76	1.601
Variety	77	4	10	6.95	1.423
Price	74	1	9	6.35	1.786
Service	66	2	10	7.77	1.699
Ambience	74	2	10	7.51	1.665
Display	74	3	10	7.47	1.546
Valid N (listwise)	61				

The profile of the customer and responses were more or less uniform across all the four showrooms.

Appendix 3 City data

Table 1

Parameter	Bangalore	Ahmedabad	Surat	Lucknow	Nagpur	Indore	Chandigarh
Population growth (1991-2001)%	61.4	22.2	62.4	36.3	26.3	46.3	40.5
Population Density (Person/sq.km.)	18975	18424	21730	7120	9427	12272	7095
Significant Sectors of Employment (1999-2000) :%							
Manufacturing	32.3	32.1	53.5	14.1	15.4	25.2	17.7
Services	27.2	16.6	10.6	32.2	18.4	27.7	40.1
Trade, Hotels & Restaurants	20.3	33.3	24.1	31.3	36.3	23.2	28.2
Construction	11.4	6.2	7.1	4.6	10.6	6.3	6.5
Transport	7.3	9.6	4.6	12.6	17.6	9.1	4.5
Sectors of Investment	Engg.,Electronics, Software, Power, Roads	Pharma, Textile, Power, Roads	Chem., Engg, Power, Roads	Hospital Roads	Foods, textile, Roads, Industrial Estate	Engg., Hotel, Power, Telecom, Roads	Software Parks
Estimated Median Household Income (Rs/*annum*)	47351	41200	21079	29666	34195	33414	65564

Source: City Monitor 2002, Inter-city comparisons of quality of life in seven cities by Dr. Prem Pangotra, Director, P&M research services (P) Ltd.

Table 2 Market Potential Value range for select cities

Mumbai	600–1000	Surat	80–130	Chandigarh	50–70
Delhi	600–1000	Nagpur	80–130	Coimbatore	50–70
Hyderabad	200–260	80-130	80–130	Kochi	50–70
Bangalore	200–260	Kanpur	80–130	Indore	50–70
Ahmedabad	200–260	Jaipur	80–130	Madurai	50–70
Pune	200–260	Lucknow	80–130	Patna	50–70
				Vizag	50–70

Source: R.K. Swamy BBDO, "Guide to Urban markets" gives a rating for 784 towns with a population of above 50,000. They use a composite index called Market Potential Value which is calculated based on factors such as:

- Means (Per capita income, Per cap. Bank deposit, etc.)
- Consumption (Ownership of durables, telephone, consumption of FMCG)
- Awareness (Usage levels of Print media, TV and Radio, Female Literacy)
- Market Support(Employment in trade and transport, Bank credit in trade and transport)
- Size (Population)

Notes

1. A place near Mumbai, which is an octroi and cess free zone.
2. A tax on various goods brought into a town.
3. KSA Technopak Consumer Outlook Survey.
4. http://www.ndu.edu/library/docs/crs/crs_rs21502_10feb05.pdf.

CASE

11

Cognizant: Preparing for a Global Footprint

Madhukar Angur, S. Manikutty and Prasad Nukala

It was the last week of April 2008 when Cognizant joined the esteemed *Fortune* 1000 club. Based on overall revenues of $2.135 billion in 2007, it secured a position on the *Fortune* 1000 list at #859. Cognizant Technology Solutions (NASDAQ:CTSH), a US-based information technology services company, with significant operations in India, served several *Fortune* 1000 companies across multiple domains by providing information technology, consulting, and business process outsourcing services. It leveraged its onsite/offshore delivery model and 40 plus delivery centres[1] spread across the globe with a 59,500 strong employee base. Its turnover had grown to $2.135 billion in 2007, an increase of 49.9% over the previous year.[2] The company recorded an operating profit of about $380 million in the fiscal year 2007, an increase of 47.3% over 2006. Net profit for the year 2007 was $350 million, an increase of 50.4% over that of 2006. Refer Exhibit 1 for the financial performance of the company. Cognizant executives believed that this growth was achieved by a combination of its unique onsite/offshore model across several industries, infusion of a strong culture of customer satisfaction, and a fairly good penetration into European markets.

Despite its growth and continued good performance, Cognizant's CEO, Francisco D'Souza, confronted many challenges that included expanding its worldwide delivery while maintaining its high level of customer responsiveness, maintaining their current work culture and developing new service areas successfully to hedge against the reliance on revenues from a limited number of sectors. With strong competitors like IBM, Accenture, and Indian giants such as TCS, Wipro, and Infosys, D'Souza wondered whether a new management strategy/approach involving entry into more verticals, a larger number of clients, and modifications to its unique onsite/offshore delivery model, its so called two-in-a-box model, were called for.

IT Worldwide Trends

The software industry involved development and maintenance of software along with services such as training and consultancy. Technology innovation and global implementation required that service provider companies kept pace with the latest developments. To facilitate faster response and reduced cost to the customers, companies worked with outsourcing providers who offered technology and services. New products, technologies, and applications had shown strong growth in 2007,[3] with the United States and Japan in leading positions; India and China were seen rising up to the challenge and as likely future com-

Cases of the Indian Institute of Management, Ahmedabad, are prepared as a basis for class discussion. Cases are not designed to present illustrations of either correct or incorrect handling of administrative problems.

Written by Professor Madhukar Angur, University of Michigan, Flint School of Management; Professor S. Manikutty, Indian Institute of Management, Ahmedabad; and Mr. Prasad Nukala, Cognizant Technologies.

Exhibit 1 Financial performance of Cognizant, 2003–2007

	Year Ended (December 31)				
	2007	2006	2005	2004	2003
	($ 000, except per share data)				
Consolidated Statement of operations Data					
Revenues	2,135,577	1,424,267	885,830	586,673	365,656
Revenues-related party					2,575
Total revenues	2,135,577	1,424,267	885,830	586,673	368,231
Operating costs (exclusive of depreciation and amortization expense shown separately below)	1,206,035	787,923	479,915	319,810	199,724
Selling, general and administration expenses	494,102	343,238	206,899	132,796	84,259
Depreciation and amortization expense	53,918	34,163	21,400	16,447	11,936
Income from operations	381,522	258,943	177,616	117,620	72,312
Other Income(expense) net					
Interest Income	29,560	17,615	8,982	4,389	2,128
Split–off costs					2,010
Other income (expense), net	3,274	1,253	1,326	86	199
Total other income (expense), net	32,834	18,868	7,656	4,475	81
Income before provision for income taxes	414,356	277,811	185,272	122,095	72,231
Provision for income taxes	64,223	45,016	19,006	21,852	14,866
Net income	350,133	232,795	166,266	100,243	57,365
Basic earnings per share	1.22	0.83	0.61	0.38	0.23
Diluted earnings per share*	1.15	0.77	0.57	0.35	0.21
Weighted average number of common shares outstanding —Basic	288,155	281,715	272,988	261,980	250,022
Weighted average number of common shares outstanding —Diluted	303,593	301,124	293,790	285,113	271,628
Consolidated Statement of Financial Data					
Cash and cash equivalents	339,845	265,937	196,938	199,296	144,371
Working capital	901,495	790,888	509,628	340,189	220,873
Total assets	1,838,306	1,325,981	869,893	572,745	365,300
Stockholder's equity	1,468,210	1,073,499	714,145	453,529	274,070

Source: Company Reports 2007.

*Earnings per share (EPS) include common stock, preferred stock, unexercised stock options, unexercised warrants, and some convertible debt. In companies with a large amount of convertibles, warrants and stock options, diluted earnings per share are usually a more accurate measure of the company's real earning power than earnings per share.

petitors. Mexico was heavily investing in the IT industry, realizing the need for better resources, and for overcoming language barriers in order to be in the race. Russia and Eastern Europe, with their cheaper labor costs and quality education systems in place, were improving their talent pool and hence, many US based companies were considering them also as alternatives for their expansion. It would not be long before China also caught up on the IT industry. Canada, with no language barriers, was also expanding its IT export business.

COGNIZANT: THE COMPANY'S ORIGIN

Cognizant was a US-based provider of information technology, consulting, and business process outsourcing services. Headquartered in Teaneck, New Jersey, USA, Cognizant had developed many centres across several states in India, and in international locations such as Canada (Toronto), Europe (London, Amsterdam, Budapest), China (Shanghai), and South America (Buenos Aires). It was incubated in 1994 as DBSS, a joint venture between Dun & Bradstreet Corporation (D&B) and Satyam Computer Services, with the objective of serving as the technology development centre for D&B and its affiliates in Chennai, India. DBSS, with the new initiative, had to initially compete with the existing vendors of D&B (Please refer Exhibit 2 for the company milestones).

While working as an offshore company in India was an advantage for DBSS, so was it for every other company. Competition was stiff, and DBSS realized the need to be different from others. The company studied the "Big 5" consulting firms and realized that to be a differentiator in the market place, the difference had to be created by providing excellent customer service. The goal was defined as providing customers with the experience and delivery of a service at par or better in quality than its competitors, but at offshore prices. D&B subsequently bought out Satyam's 24% stake and named it *Cognizant Technology Solutions*. D&B itself underwent a major restructuring, leading to its splitting up into multiple divisions. Cognizant was born out of one such division in 1996. The new company was free to decide its own goals, but imbibed some lessons learnt from the parent company such as the significance of size, integrating culture within the organization, and using limited measures of performance such as customer satisfaction and retention for success.

Cognizant realized the need and importance of the transition. The transition was from an IT technology development centre for D&B, to an independent service provider for clients. Gordon Coburn, the CFO, stated to the case writers that the transition was much easier because of the existing systems of D&B. Steered by Lakshmi Narayanan who was President during that time, and subsequently became its CEO, Cognizant was listed in NASDAQ in 1998 as the first software and services company with major operations in India. The NASDAQ listing not only brought about a sense of security, belonging, ownership, and a promise of a big future for the employees, but also provided visibility for the company's performance to customers.

Within a span of 12 years after its inception, Cognizant achieved a turnover of $1 billion in 2006 and its turnover surpassed the projected revenues of $2.11 billion by 2007. By the end of 2007, its revenue grew to $2.135

Exhibit 2 Milestones of Cognizant

Year	Milestones
1994	Incubated as the technology arm of Dun & Bradstreet Corporation
1996	Started looking at third party clients and began servicing the best across industry segments
1998	Became the first IT company leveraging India to get listed on NASDAQ
2002	Became the first company assessed enterprise-wide against mature industry process certifications such as P-CMM5, BS7799, SEI-CMMi Level 5
2004	Acknowledged as a leading provider of IT services by industry analysts such as Gartner, Forrester, AMR and IDC
2004	Added to the prestigious NASAQ 100 index among companies that defined newer business paradigms.
2006	Became the fastest IT services company globally to clock a $1 billion run rate in nearly 12 years.
2007	Added to the prestigious S&P 500 membership

Source: Cognizant documents.

Exhibit 3(a) Cognizant: revenues, operating income, and stockholder's equity

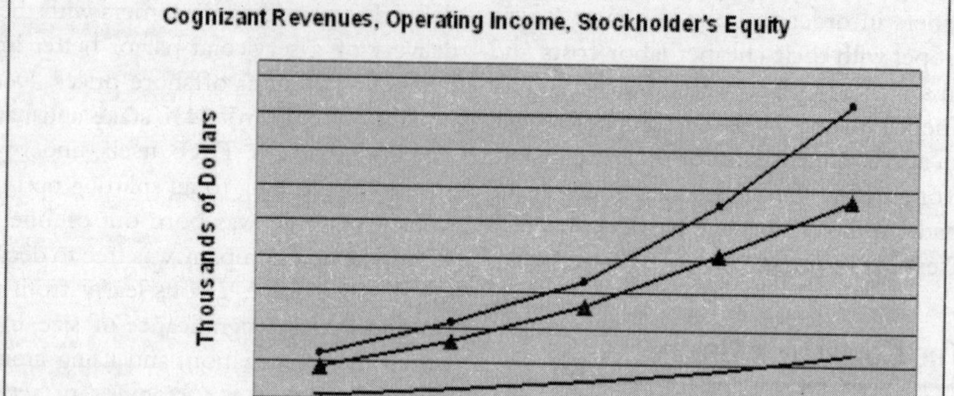

	2003	2004	2005	2006	2007
Revenues	362831	586673	885830	1424267	2135577
Operating Income	72312	117620	177616	258943	381522
Stockholder's Equity	274020	453529	714145	1073499	1468210

Exhibit 3(b) Employee strength of Cognizant

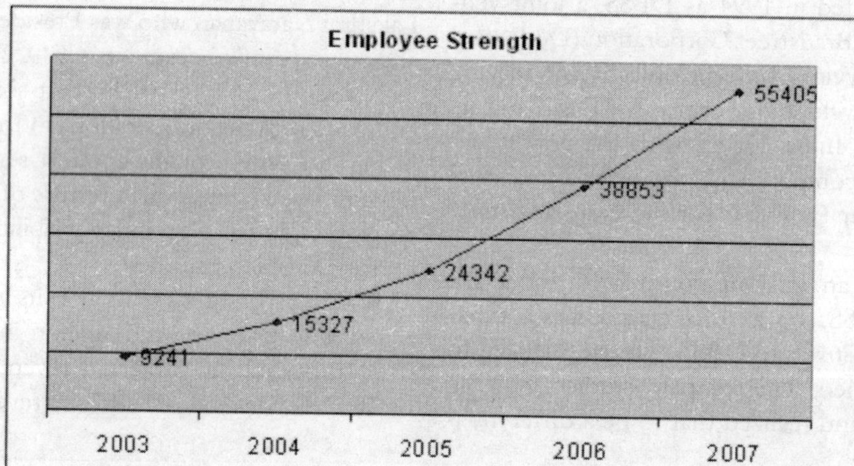

billion, posting a growth rate of around 50% year on year. Its 2008 first quarter revenue of $643.1 million was indicative of the continued growth rate the company had maintained (Please refer Exhibit 3a for the company revenues, operating income, and stockholder's equity; and Exhibit 3b for the strength of employees).

Under the leadership of Lakshmi Narayanan, Cognizant entered the top tier of the Indian software and services companies. The core competencies of the company included web-centric applications, data warehousing, component based development, and legacy and client-server systems.

COGNIZANT: GROWTH AND DIVERSIFICATION

Cognizant grew steadily. While it took 12 years to reach $1 billion in sales, Cognizant had achieved a turnover of $2.14 billion by 2007. It had become a *Forbes* Global 2000 company, and found a place in the NASDAQ 100 index, S&P 500 index, and *Fortune* 1000 companies. It was also among the top 10 of *BusinessWeek's* Hot Growth Technology Companies, and was the #1 ranked IT services company on the list (Please refer Exhibit 4 for the accolades received by Cognizant).

Exhibit 4 Accolades received by Cognizant

Magazine/Journal	Accomplishments
Red Herring, July, 1999	Cognizant Technology Solutions named one of the top 25 technology IPO's of 1998
Forbes, November, 1999	Cognizant Technology Solutions named "Best Small Company in America"
BusinessWeek, May, 2000	Cognizant Top Solution Provider in *BusinessWeek's* list of Hot Growth Companies
Investor's Business Daily, June 2001	Cognizant chosen as "Best IPO" for companies that have come public in the last three years
BusinessWeek, June 2002	Cognizant Top Tech Company in *BusinessWeek's* List of "Hot Growth Companies"
Business 2.0, October, 2002	Cognizant ranked 16 in the fastest growing 100 tech companies list published by *Business 2.0*
Forbes, October, 2002	Cognizant Top Tech Company in the Forbes 200 Best Small Companies List
Forbes, April, 2003	Top IT Services Company in 25 fastest growing tech companies 2003
BusinessWeek, June 2003	Cognizant Top Tech Company in *BusinessWeek's* List of "Hot Growth Companies"
Forbes, October, 2004	Cognizant named best small company in America
Business 2.0, October, 2005	Cognizant Top US Outsourcing Firm on *Business 2.0* Magazine's Annual "B2 100" Ranking of the Fastest Growing Technology Companies
The Economic Times, September 28, 2005	Cognizant founders chosen for "Entrepreneur of the Year" Award
Forbes, October, 2005	Cognizant the Top IT Services Company in the *Forbes* 200 Best Small Companies List
Institutional Investor, February, 2006	Cognizant one of the most shareholder friendly companies in America
Wall Street Journal, February 27, 2006	Cognizant named one of the best 5 year stock performers in WSJ's "Shareholder Scoreboard"
BusinessWeek, June 5, 2006	Cognizant named rank# 16 among *BusinessWeek's* 100 Hot Growth Companies for 2006
Fortune, September, 2006	Named among "100 Fastest Growing Companies" for the 4th Consecutive Year
BusinessWeek, December 2006	Cognizant ranked #6 in 2006 "Tech Hot Growth 50" and #1 IT Services Company
Consumer Goods Technology Magazine, January 2007	Cognizant ranked #5 in the 7th Annual Reader's Choice Rankings
BusinessWeek, March, 2007	Ranked #12 among the Best Performers
Business 2.0, June, 2007	Cognizant Ranks among 100 Fastest Growing Tech Companies
BusinessWeek, June 2007	Cognizant Ranks #15 among *BusinessWeek's* 100 Hot Growth Companies for 2007
BusinessWeek, July, 2007	Cognizant Leaps in Rankings of *BusinessWeek's* InfoTech 100
Forbes, February, 2008	Cognizant Hits #6 on *Forbes* Fastest Growing Tech Companies List
BusinessWeek, March 27, 2008	Cognizant Recognized in *BusinessWeek 50*

The Forrester Wave graphic in Exhibit 5 depicts how Cognizant effectively competed with biggies such as IBM, Accenture, TCS, Infosys (INFY), and Wipro (WIT) in the outsourcing space in North America. This was of great significance as North America was the largest market for IT outsourcing. In addition to the financial parameters, Cognizant measured success particularly in terms of customer satisfaction and customer retention matrices. A third party Customer Interactive Management Application (CIMA) company would perform the customer survey on several parameters that included both quantitative and qualitative feedback about the performance of the company.

Cognizant's operations consisted of delivery teams in India and client-facing management personnel in the US. While the process was more customer-driven, it also created challenges in execution due to the sizeable employee population in India. Cognizant realized the need for a balance between client management and project execution, and framed a strategy to move away from micro managing the project and trusting the employees. Entrusting and empowering were the key aspects of this strategy. Cognizant concentrated on choosing the right people for the job and entrusting them with special assignments such as development of new centres or sales offices, or playing a vital role in building an industry ver-

Exhibit 5 Competition

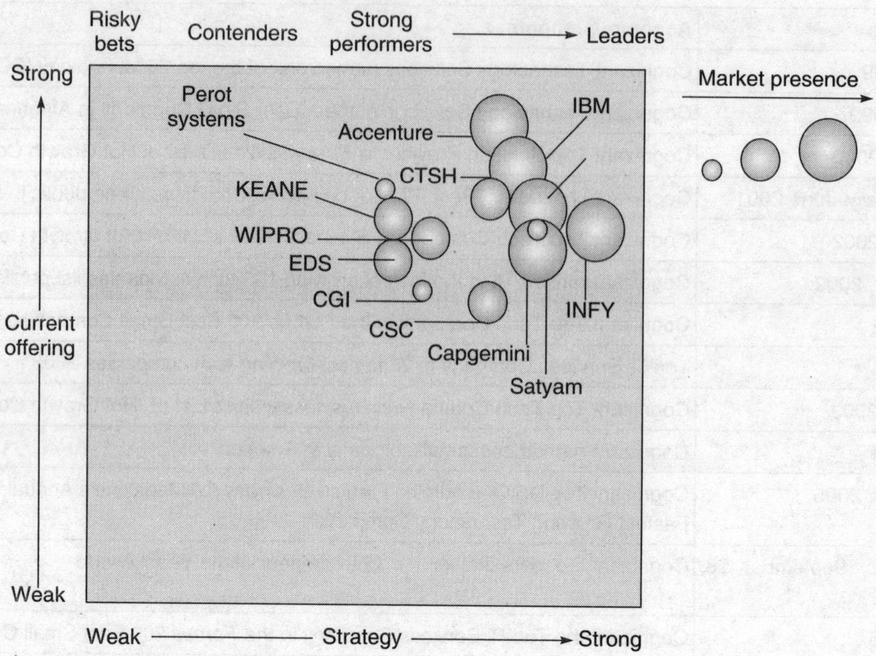

tical. The strategy worked wonders because empowering the employees not only brought out the best results both for the client and the company, but also challenged the employee's capabilities, leading to better motivation and satisfaction to the teams and the individuals. As a consequence, employees not only delivered quality work, but also had a scope for personal growth along with growth of the organization. Successful in its initial challenge, Cognizant decided to reorganize the structure aligned to industries in a phased manner. Initially, the delivery operations in India were organized based on its industry segments, while the customer-facing teams were geography centric. This model created conflicts related to issues of job responsibility. The delivery teams were holding the onsite teams responsible for finding clients. However, the onsite teams exploited the opportunity of finding clients irrespective of whether the client belonged to that particular industry segment or not in order to meet their targets. This scenario challenged the delivery teams and resulted in conflicts. To leverage the delivery team's orientation to industries, the onsite client relationship teams started shifting more towards verticals and no longer focused on geography. While the targets led to a better clientele, the exercise raised questions from Cognizant's management about the required industry experience and other issues in those domains. This explicit conflict led to further restructuring.

Cognizant's leaders had been part of the organization's growth; however industry specific experience and domain expertise were lacking to head such new initiatives. The executive leadership team, after due consultation with the senior managers, decided to hire domain experts in the respective fields. Focus on industry expertise led to building better solutions. For instance, Cognizant's retail and manufacturing industry unit worked for Ford Japan's *Yardelligent* project, a port management system, providing solutions with special functions that Ford did not find elsewhere. Such successful implementations made way for bigger clientele and business partners such as SAP, leading to further success. Cognizant provided testing services to SAP; and ERP development, maintenance, and extension services to clients.

Cognizant was fairly unique as compared to Indian IT companies, considering the fact that it generated some 80% of its revenues from the United States.

Business Segments

Cognizant's operations were aligned along industry segments: Financial Services, Manufacturing/Retail and Logistics, Healthcare, and others including Communications, Media and Information Services, and High Technology. These industry-based segments were called verticals. Here the domain knowledge was critical. Horizontals, on the other hand, were different service offerings across segments that were varied, such as consulting and business process outsourcing. Here knowledge in one vertical would be leveraged into another vertical, and a broader, application-based knowledge was what was more important in operating horizontals effectively. Data warehousing, infrastructure management services, and testing, were some of the key horizontal service offerings to the customers. Exhibit 6 shows Cognizant's verticals and horizontals and their linkages.

Along the verticals, the financial service offerings to customers comprised the following industries:

Capital Markets Concentrating on asset management firms, brokers/dealers, depositories, clearing organizations and exchanges.

Banking Concentrating on traditional retail and commercial banks, and diversified financial enterprises in areas such as consumer lending, cards and payments, wholesale banking, risk management, investment management, corporate service, and retail banking.

Insurance Focus on property and casualty insurance, life insurance, and reinsurance.

The financial services segment contributed the highest, approximately 48%, of the total revenues in 2006, and 47% in 2008. The healthcare segment contributed approximately 23% of the total revenues in 2006, improving to 24% in 2008, servicing industries in healthcare and life sciences. The manufacturing segment represented about 15% of total revenues in 2006, and remained the same in 2008. The other business segments represented 14% of the total revenues in 2006, and maintained the same position in 2008 as well. Telecommunications, information services, media, and high technology, formed the "others" category. Exhibit 7 shows the revenues earned by Cognizant in various industry segments along the verticals. Cognizant worked as much on improving its strengths in horizontals as in its verticals. The horizontals

Exhibit 6 Alignments of horizontals along industry horizontals (in year 2007)

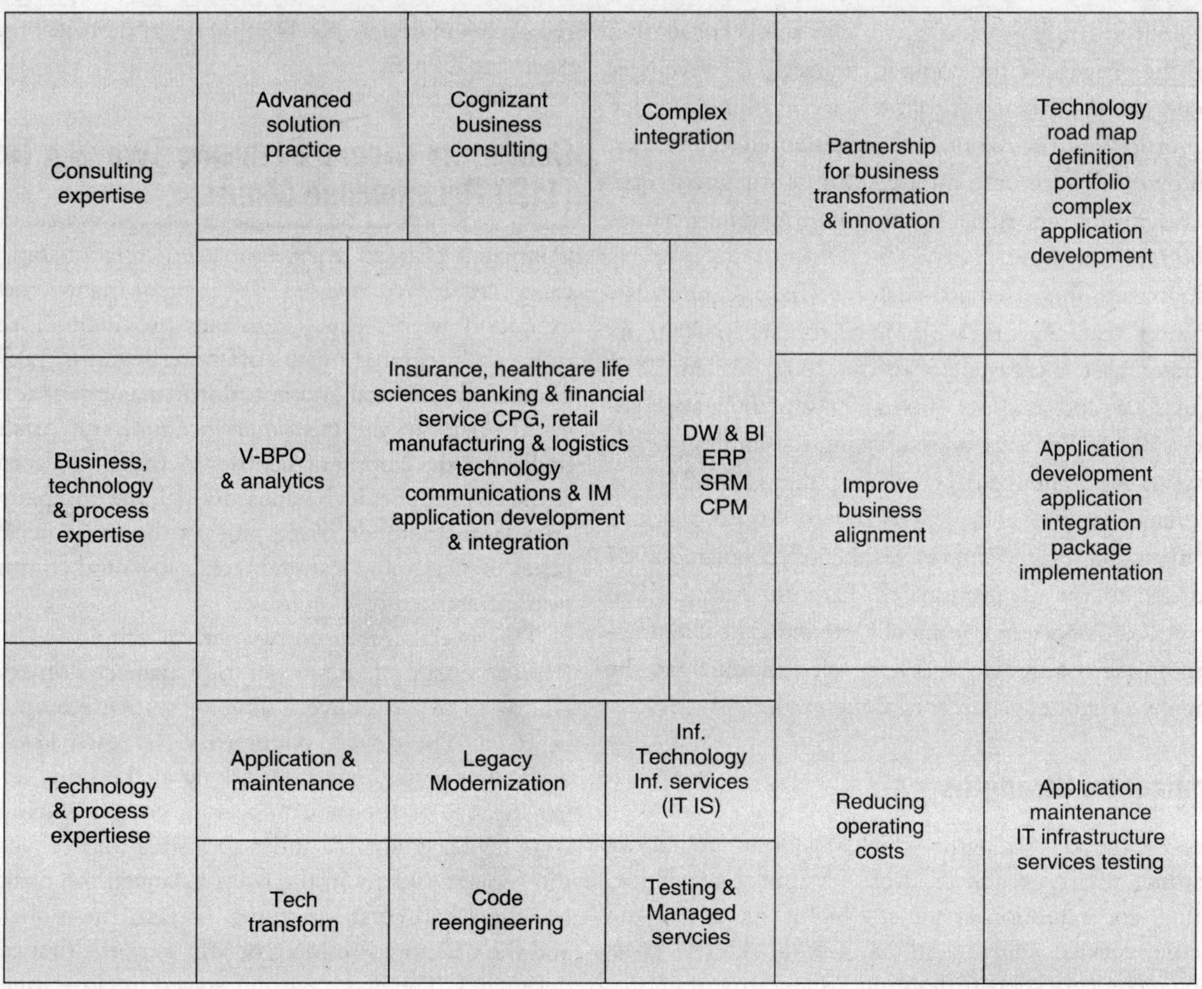

Source: Company reports 2007

Exhibit 7 Revenue distribution for three years along to verticals

(Dollars in thousands)	2007	2006	2005	2007		2006	
Revenues				Increase	%	Increase	%
Financial services	$1,001,420	$679,901	$440,958	$321,519	47	$238,943	54.19
Healthcare	504,504	330,860	176,102	$173,644	52	$154,758	87.88
Manufacturing/Retail/Logistics	320,116	209,703	152,536	$110,413	53	$57,167	37.48
Other	309.537	209.803	116.234	$99,734	48	$93,569	80.5
Total revenues	$2,135,577	$1,424,267	$885,830	$711,310	50	$538,437	60.78
Segment Operating Profit							
Financial services	$355,696	$254,115	$153,542	$101,581	40	$100,573	65.5
Healthcare	198791	135,374	71,226	$63,417	47	$64,148	90.06
Manufacturing/Retail/Logistics	108480	79,443	46,210	$29,037	37	$33,233	71.92
Other	111319	63,667	39,100	$47,652	75	$24,567	62.83
Total segment operating profit	$375,286	$526,589	$310,078	($151,303)	–29	$216,511	69.82

Year Ended December 31, 2007 compared to Year Ended December 31, 2006

Source: Company Reports 2007

were split into units that aligned with the verticals that aided the growth of the company's margin on revenues. In other words, Cognizant followed a consulting practice with verticals and horizontals complementing each other. With diversification into multiple industry aligned verticals, Cognizant reported a significant growth in revenues in 2008 third quarter.

Cognizant increased its customer base significantly year after year. Starting with 90 customers in 2000, its customer base increased to 100 in 2001, 115 in 2002, 250 in 2005, and to about 400 in 2006. In 2007, approximately 100 clients were added, taking the number of its clients to 500. The top 10 clients accounted for 34% of its revenue in 2007 and 33% in 2008 (till third quarter). The big increases in clients in years 2005, 2006, and 2007 were due to the acquisitions of Fathom, Aimnet, and Market Rx. Cognizant continually expanded its client engagement across the globe (Please see Exhibit 8 for the company's client engagements along verticals).

Cognizant's Strengths

Some of the key strengths which Cognizant relied on, according to its executives, were its robust recruiting, training, and retention systems; a highly successful and effective service delivery model; a wide referral base; strong technical expertise; continuous investment in process improvement and knowledge capture; investment in research and design (R&D); pricing; and project management capabilities.

Cognizant Global Delivery: Two in a Box (TIB) Relationship Model

Cognizant claimed a superior client relationship model called *two in a box model (TIB)* for client management and execution of projects. Cognizant provided IT services using an integrated onsite/offshore business model that combined technical and account management teams located onsite at the customer location, and offshore at dedicated development centres in India and across the globe. To support its business model, the company needed a larger number of employees than was needed for other IT firms, and a sound technology and communication infrastructure.

The model employed two sets of employees, starting from an onsite client partner to manage customers in the US, to an offsite delivery director to oversee operations in India. There were counterparts at each level. They worked as a single team. Working at the same level and irrespective of their location, both groups of employees were held accountable and responsible for the success of the project. Others in the team balanced the onsite relationships and offshore teams. In fact, the global COO and the offshore President & MD were the first two TIB designates. The client partner stayed in close touch with the client and adapted to the client's culture, operational

Exhibit 8 Client engagement along verticals

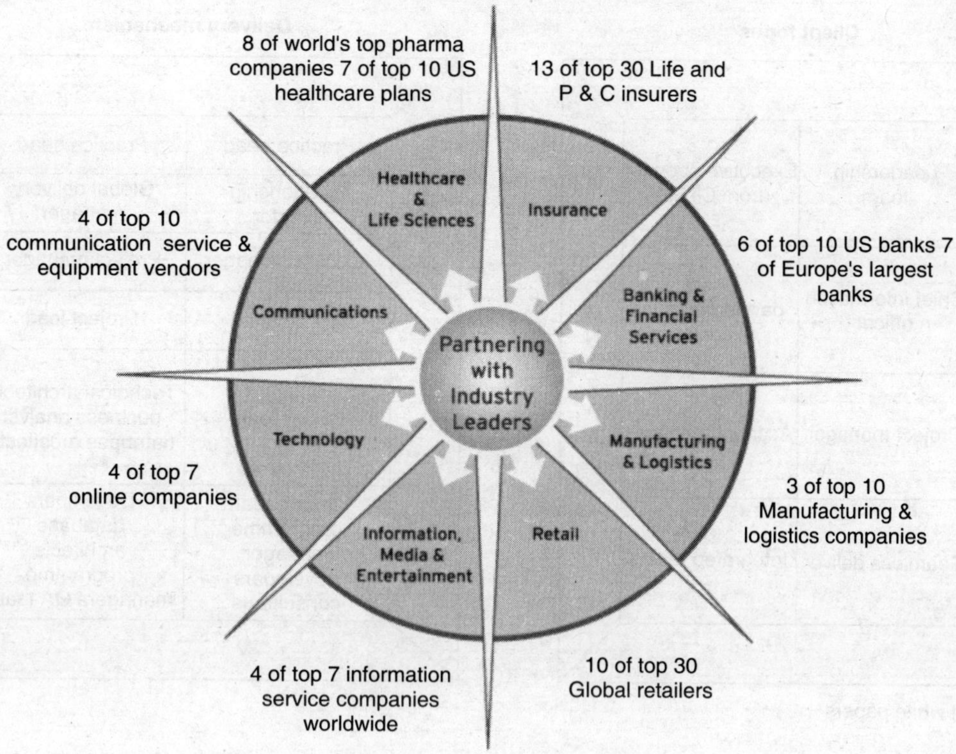

Exhibit 9 Client developments in 2007

Clients	Services by Cognizant
Merck & Co	Application outsourcing, IT infrastructure management, Business process outsourcing
Kimberly Clark	IT applications outsourcing
Rabobank, Netherlands	IT outsourcing
California State Automobile Association	Business consulting, software services and implementation
Simon & Schuster, Inc. Media & Entertainment	End to end IT infrastructure management

processes, challenges, and business goals. These client partners were extremely conversant with the company's service offerings and suggested to the customer areas where Cognizant could help. The client partner also worked consistently with the offshore delivery director to ensure that the client requirements were translated effectively as services back to the client (Please see Exhibit 10 for the TIB model). This process concentrated more on people than on geography; and it did not matter that the delivery director delivered from India while the client partner was in the US or Europe. Empowering both partners made the individuals responsible and accountable for their roles. At the same time, the success of the project was defined in the same terms for both the leaders to ensure successful project delivery to the client. The two in a box model was considered as bringing a balance to the onshore relationship and the offshore delivery. The roles of the onsite and offshore leaders were spelt out clearly. The offshore delivery leader had the responsibility of delivery, competency, revenues and profits; while the onsite person was held responsible for client relationship management, customer satisfaction, revenues and profits, and meeting the business objectives. Diversification and integration went hand in hand in this model.

Cognizant's relationship model claimed transparency to the client. It was not tied to any single delivery centre; delivery could be connected from any part of the globe to any other centre. While most of the IT companies used the *pass the baton model* or *thrown over the wall* models, Cognizant differed by offering a hybrid model. This blended the traditional consulting firm's onsite resources

Exhibit 10 Global delivery model (TIB–two in a box model)

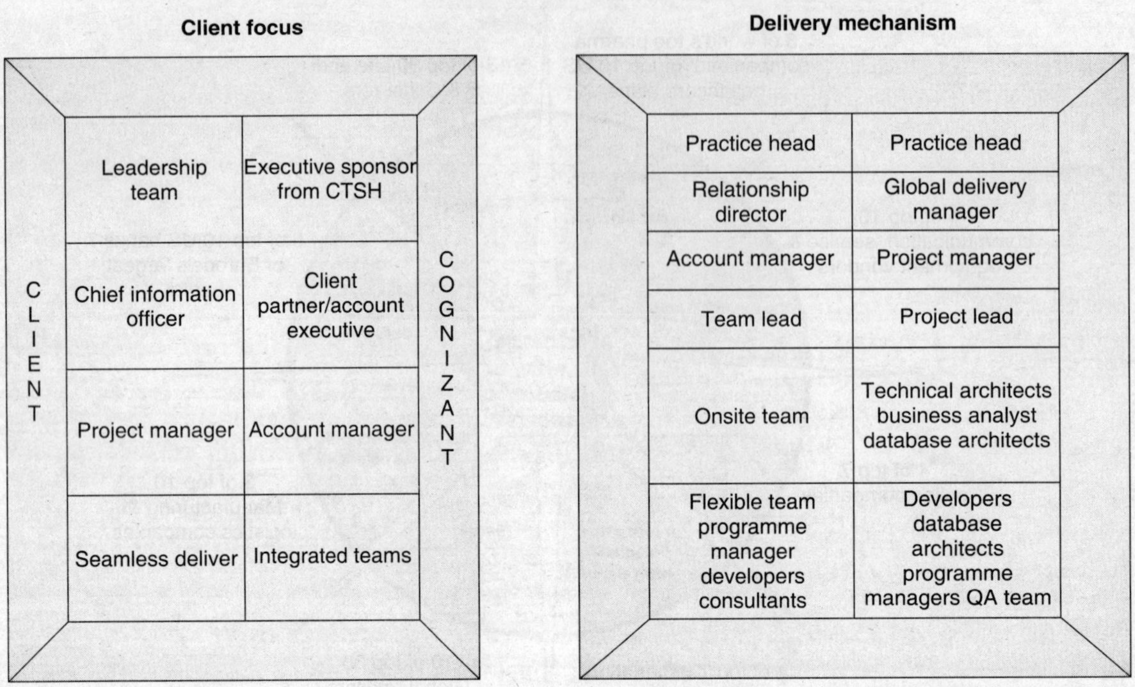

Source: Cognizant white papers

for project planning and management with the cost advantages of offshore delivery. The model was very well established and embedded in Cognizant's DNA, organizational hierarchy, and in its culture.

TIB also reduced the operational difficulties of staying late night or early morning for conference calls in order to discuss project milestones, challenges, and other issues. Once the project delivery was achieved, Cognizant followed the *transform while perform* (TwP) framework in conjunction with the TIB, to provide a better return on investment for its clients. Cognizant's TwP delivered cost savings by swapping in-house personnel with lower cost offshore talent and taking over the client's process first, and then using the savings from outsourcing to transform it into something better. The twin TIB with TwP offered programme and project management and best practices in IT services delivery, in addition to technology and domain expertise.

PERFORMANCE MANAGEMENT AND REWARDS

Francisco D'Souza, CEO of Cognizant, stated to the case writers that while the conceptualization was easy, it took a good four years for Cognizant to implement the TIB model. Unlike the sequential process management models used by other Indian IT and global majors, such a relationship model helped Cognizant in better execution and delivery. While the two in a box model helped to reach the organization's goals effectively, it was critically dependent on the capabilities of its employees to execute this model. Hence, Cognizant recognized the importance of the employees, and the need to assess and reward the employees who executed the projects onsite and offshore. Cognizant focused on the performance appraisal and a suitable incentive process to encourage the employees. The assessments varied from a pure technical competency for junior levels to comprehensive relationship management skills for senior levels. Cognizant also allowed the employee to disagree with the managers' evaluation and provided a chance to reach the next level up for review. The rewards included promotions and higher-level responsibilities in the same or different groups. The management used the same metrics for both the onsite and offshore employees. Client satisfaction, employee satisfaction, revenue, and profitability were the four dimensions by which the seniors were assessed and ranked, while the others were further categorized according to their performance. The top performers got superior compensation in terms of bonus (only employees at senior level were awarded with stock options), equity grants, and allowances. Apart from the individual benefits, Cognizant institutionalized awards such as *Global Project of the Year, Associate of the Year, Trainer of the Year, and leadership awards*. Cognizant's message to its employees was: "The better the employee performance, the better the incentives." Cognizant provided an excellent platform for young people thereby, attracting the best talent in the industry at senior level.

Cognizant thought that the most important success factors for its services were performance and reliability, quality of technical support, training and services, responsiveness to customer's needs, reputation, experience, financial stability, and competitive pricing of services. According to Malcolm Frank, Senior Vice President, Strategy and Marketing, Cognizant employed both external and internal perspectives. The external approach concentrated more on general trends in economy, technology, and competition that would deal with the performance of the companies, client satisfaction, and scope for improvement. The internal approach dealt with the core competencies of the organization, strengths, employee satisfaction, and establishment of internal processes. The above two-pronged approach was pursued across all the three geographies, services and industry. The focus was to map the internal and external approaches to ensure that the overall management approach was successful.

Quality Delivery and Research and Development

Cognizant had built effective proprietary processes for onsite and offshore integration. This ISO 9000 certified *Q* view* software engineering process was made available to all the Cognizant programmers around the world. This process was used for assessments of projects throughout the lifecycle, from risk management to ensuring quality delivery to the clients. In addition, all the Cognizant development centres had been assessed by KPMG at CMM level 5, the highest in quality delivery.

The company believed in exploring new areas continuously and expanding its areas of service offerings through its research and development services. Service offerings in various technologies reduced the dependency on any one technology that would attract broader customer relationships. In order to cater to the needs of the customers quickly, Cognizant focused on the flexibility of employee's technical ability. Most of the Cognizant programmers were trained in different architectures and technologies. Large investments were made in R&D activities to keep abreast of the emerging technologies. Cognizant believed that the ability to work in multiple technologies led to creation of new customers and satisfaction of the existing ones. Some of the areas of development included IT systems, portfolio analysis, technology architecture, programme management, legacy restoration, digital security, and forensics (Please refer to the Exhibit 8 on existing clientele and Exhibit 9 on client engagements in 2007). Cognizant did not possess any patents or specific copyrights, but the company protected its intellectual property by a combination of intellectual property laws, contracts, trade secrets, and confidentiality agreements.

Infrastructure and Training

Cognizant had made significant investments in infrastructure, in terms of providing the best in facilities, communication equipment, and technologies. The geographic limitations were overcome by providing team members with access to all project information. Effective off-peak usage of customers' technical resources (due to global time differences) and parallel processing of units within a larger project shortened delivery times and speeded up completion of projects.

In terms of training, Cognizant's in-house university called *Cognizant Academy* offered educational programs in a broad range of disciplines and trained in the necessary technical, domain or project management skills. The academy kept its employees abreast of latest technologies and maintained consistently high performance standards. In 2008, Cognizant academy offered over three million hours of courses.

Cognizant also provided onsite opportunities for the junior employee in order to learn about the multicultural settings. The *Personal Development Centre* trained its personnel on adaptation and behavior management of the individuals.

Unlike other IT companies, Cognizant focused neither on services nor on product space, *per se*. It stood by its *solutions framework* that offered pre-built solutions for particular problems in an industry that utilized deep domain expertise. These pre-built solutions saved time and could be priced at a good market rate.

Acquisitions

Cognizant targeted acquisitions in three ways. First, it looked for companies in geographical areas where the company lacked strength. Second, it looked for acquisition of new and complementary technological skills. Third, it looked for companies to build domain knowledge in verticals. The acquisition history gives an idea of how Cognizant went about on its acquisitions.

In April 2007, the company and Ordina NV announced a strategic alliance. Under the terms of this agreement, the company became Ordina's primary strategic partner in the Benelux region for providing offshore solutions. The two companies jointly offered global delivery solutions for Ordina's major customers in the financial services, public, industrial, and telecommunications markets.

In October 2007, Cognizant acquired Market Rx, a leading provider of analytics and related software services to global life sciences companies in the pharmaceutical, biotechnology, and medical devices industries. With a strong domain expertise in the areas of healthcare, data analytics and offices located in the US and India, Rx (SVC) joined the global delivery network of Cognizant.

In June 2008, the California-based Strategic Vision Consulting Inc,[4] a management and technology-consulting firm with over 60 employees, was acquired to expand Cognizant's media and entertainment industry.

Francisco D'Souza said in a press release: "The combination of SVC's strong relationships in the entertainment industry and Cognizant's global delivery model, positions CTSH as a service leader within the fast growing media and entertainment industry." According to SVC's co-founder and Managing Principal, Frank Leal, "We found a great cultural fit between both companies in terms of commitment to unparalleled client satisfaction, entrepreneurial spirit, corporate culture and overall vision for the future of the global services industry." Please refer Exhibit 11 for other mergers and acquisitions of Cognizant.

Ramon F Baez, Chief Information Officer, Kimberly-Clark reportedly said: "Cognizant has delivered on its commitment to provide Kimberly-Clark with a suite of global IT services and has high standards of customer satisfaction and also demonstrated capabilities in driving transformational outsourcing programs. We are pleased to have been instrumental in helping Cognizant become a major presence in Buenos Aires, while taking our IT function to the next level."[5]

COMPETITION

The IT services market was highly competitive with a large number of participants and was subject to rapid change. The participants were from different market segments that included system integration firms, contract programming companies, application software companies, internet solution providers, providers of professional services, computer equipment companies, and facilities management and outsourcing companies. The major competitors of Cognizant were IBM, Accenture, Infosys, Wipro, TCS, HCL, and Satyam.

The challenges stemmed from the entry/expansion of such companies as IBM, HP (especially with EDS acquired) and Accenture into the Indian market where Cognizant had successfully pursued its strategy of an on-site/overseas offshore delivery model. Their expansion into India threatened Cognizant's position there because these companies were larger and had greater resources in terms of financial, technical, and marketing resources, and greater name recognition. These competitors were also recruiting from the local talent pool including Cognizant employees; were capturing Indian clients; and were mitigating the cost advantages Cognizant had in the overseas market.

Exhibit 11 Alliances/mergers and acquisitions

Year	Acquired Company/Alliance
Jun-02	Partial assets of United Healthcare Ireland Limited
Oct-02	Assets of Silver line related to the Software services to American Express travel related services company
Apr-03	ACES International, CRM Company in California
Dec-03	Infopulse, Netherlands based company servicing capital markets on European stock exchange
Apr-04	Ygyan, SAP enterprise software company
Apr-05	Fathom solutions LLC, consulting company in Chicago
Sep-06	Aim Net, MA infrastructure management and consulting company
Apr-07	Alliance with Ordina, offshore service provider
2007	MarketRx Inc,
Mar-08	Alliance with T-Systems, Inc
Jun-08	SVC international, a media and communications industry firm

Exhibit 12 Kimberly-Clark's experience with Cognizant

Kimberly-Clark's Experience

Mention the concept of TIB to a Cognizant client, and the words may or may not resonate. But after some gentle prodding and a quick mention of its operational attributes, clients begin to recite TIB's benefits -- chapter and verse. The concept may be so intuitive that its underlying principles have become transparent to clients that have worked with Cognizant through at least one phase of an engagement.

Take Kimberly-Clark Corporation (NYSE: KMB), the multi-billion-dollar premiere health and hygiene company that recently extended its IT services partnership with Cognizant to include all applications development and maintenance under a multi-million-dollar pact. The Cognizant engagement, according to Kimberly-Clark, is a critical element in the company's attempt in re-inventing its IT footprint

The potential of the TIB methodology was clear to Kimberly-Clark during the contract bidding process, according to the company. Kimberly-Clark was impressed with the Cognizant team's understanding of its business and technological requirements.

That understanding has deepened throughout the engagement's transition phase. The Cognizant Client Partner (CP) has built a solid relationship not only with senior IT and business strategists throughout Kimberly-Clark, but also with a few members of the executive leadership team of the company. The CP is fully aware of Kimberly-Clark's business challenges, the competitive landscape and the company's progress against strategic goals.

And that deep-seated understanding is percolating throughout the Cognizant portion of the team. When issues arise, the onsite Cognizant team makes sure that everyone -- including SAP® developers in Buenos Aires -- is on the same page.

Moreover, K-C wants to make sure that Cognizant's strategic input isn't limited to the tasks at hand. K-C is encouraging Cognizant to provide far-reaching innovation and assessments on how to improve existing applications and leverage new technology to help fuel the company's transformational endeavors.

Source: Press release by Kimberley-Clark.

Competition from Some Major Indian Companies

Infosys Technologies Limited[6]

Infosys Technologies Limited (Infosys for short) was one of the largest Indian IT firms with service offerings in the areas of consulting, development, and maintenance, and BPO and engineering services. Infosys reported annual revenues of $4.176 billion[7] in 2008 and over $3.090 billion in 2007.

Infosys serviced its clients globally with a low risk delivery model that provided a competitive advantage to the company. The model worked on the basis of project allocation to a location that made best economic sense and one that had the best resources. Infosys was the first company to attain the SEI–CMMI5 status for both its onsite and offshore operations. The proven global delivery model delivered high quality solutions in reduced timeframes and scalable services by integrating its onsite and offshore capabilities. The company had been making huge investments in order to improve the delivery model. Infosys reported that its *modular global solutions framework* addressed the changing dynamics and provided maximum efficiency to the client processes. The modular framework reduced the client's internal business processes and applications into segments, and outsourced these segments on a modular basis to reduce risk and provide cost effectiveness to the clients. This approach helped Infosys retain its leadership position among the other IT outsourcing companies.

Its high quality delivery and strong domain expertise made every client relationship a long term one for Infosys. For instance, approximately 97% of Infosys' revenues came from existing clients largely due to its high standards of client relationship and management.

Infosys aimed to expand its clientele by providing broader service offerings to them. In addition to the service offerings, Infosys also concentrated on giving a very good first impression to the new clients. The new clients were briefed about the offshore model during their first engagement with the company. Infosys undertook smaller projects initially for minimizing client's risk and for demonstrating the superior performance and delivery of the company. Infosys also improved its portfolio by concentrating on new technologies, emerging trends, specific industries, and specific business issues faced by clients.

In 2007, Infosys had invested $10 million in China and in Australia. Geographic expansion was through the new sales and marketing offices and by the global development centres around the world. The expansion intended to serve clients locally and globally. In 2008, Infosys had a global footprint of 44 development centres, out of which 24 were in India and the rest were distributed worldwide. Infosys was finding robust growth in Europe with 27% of its revenues being from Europe compared to 63% from the United States in the year 2007 (See Exhibit 13 for revenues by geography, industry segments and service offerings).

Exhibit 13 Infosys revenues by geography and industry segments

Revenues by Geography

	2007
North America	63.3
Europe	26.4
India	1.6
Rest of the world	8.7
Total	100.0

Revenues by Industry Segments

	2007
Manufacturing	13.5
Banking, financial services and insurance	37.4
Banking and financial services	30.2
Insurance	7.2
Telecom	19.3
Retail	10.0
Energy and utilities	5.3
Transportation	2.4
Others	12.1
Total	100.0

Revenues by Service Offerings

	2007
Services	
Development	21.0
Maintenance	29.3
Package implementation	17.5
Testing	6.9
Re-engineering	2.1
Consulting	3.6
Business process management	4.7
Engineering services	1.6
Other services	9.4
Total services	96.1
Produces	3.9
Total	100.0

Infosys believed in meritocracy and the innovation of its employees. The total employee strength in India at the end of 2007 was 59,831 up from 44,658 at the end of 2006, with an attrition rate of 13.7% in 2007 compared to 11.2% in 2006. In 2008, Infosys had over 91,000 employees across the globe.

Talking about the huge workforce, V. Balakrishnan, the CFO of Infosys said, "If employees leave the organization at a higher pace; it might affect the company's growth plan." [8]

Infosys kept attrition under control by selective wage increases in a year. With the rising labor cost in India, Infosys expected to face competition from the countries with lower personnel costs. To attract highly talented professionals globally, Infosys worked on its branding. To enhance the brand visibility, Infosys had associated with the Wharton School at the University of Pennsylvania, and awarded the Wharton Infosys Business Transformation award to recognize the visionaries and organizations that transformed the technology space with innovative solutions.

Wipro

Wipro was a leading provider of IT services, BPO, and product engineering services, globally. Its combined IT business revenue exceeded $4.3 billion in 2007, and grew by 43% over the previous year. Its IT revenue accounted for $2 billion from the US, $1 billion from Europe, and $1 billion from India, the Middle East, and APAC. Wipro claimed to have a simple strategy of making the customers successful and believed that the rest would follow. Differentiated service lines, acquisitions and partnerships, concentration on emerging markets, global delivery, and transformational outsourcing were considered to be the strong areas of Wipro.

A major portion of Wipro's 2007–2008 revenue (52%) was reported to be from application and maintenance services. Next in line, was the technology and infrastructure industry at 17%, BPO 8%, testing 11%, and package implementation 12%. Wipro's vertical offerings included telecom service providers, financial services, retail, energy and utilities, manufacturing, technology, media and transportation services (Please see Exhibit 14 for its performance across verticals).

Wipro's recent acquisition of Info Crossing, a NASDAQ listed US company, strengthened the company's infrastructure sector. The company provided technology driven solutions, and had a global footprint over 35 countries with 743 global clients as of March 2008, and 184 global 500/*Fortune* 1000 clients.

Wipro[9] sought seamless delivery through its global delivery model. The company invested significantly in utilizing quality initiatives such as Lean and Six Sigma principles, to software engineering and ISO and PCMM, for excellence in project delivery. Wipro had MEGA partnerships with other giants like Oracle, EMC, Microsoft, and SAP for building an eco-friendly tomorrow, showing its ability for co-innovation and for joint solution offerings for the emerging markets. This was apart from the strong services presence in India and the Middle East. Wipro understood that happenings around the globe such as the sub-prime crisis in the US and a lower GDP growth would challenge clients to seek more effective business models. The challenges would lead to managing larger scale, broader, and unique services and solutions for clients in terms of transformational and solution based global delivery services. However, with six decades of experience, Wipro was confident about future growth, undeterred on sustenance, and aware of the impact of the economic slowdown.

The company's confidence stemmed from the business environment, innovation, strategic initiatives, depth of leadership, business portfolio, and the passion for success. With 60 centres of excellence across different technologies and verticals, Wipro innovated to create solutions in the emerging areas of technology and new industry practices.

That Wipro had over 94,000 employees across 56 nations, showed the company's strong resourcing process to attract top talent. The Joint–CEO structure, which Wipro called the "power of two", was a step towards strong leadership in the IT business; and the Mission-10X, a quality improvement program for the faculty (over 10,000 in almost 1500 engineering colleges), to train graduating engineers, were Wipro's visions for the future.

Some Indian companies such as Infosys, TCS, IBM, and Satyam were competing for a piece of the pie in the increasingly important and growing domestic Indian IT market, with a view to spread their bases of operations.

Exhibit 14(a) Revenues by geography–Wipro

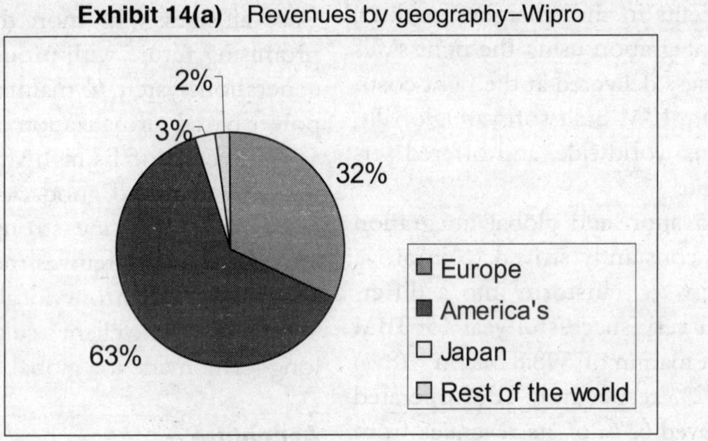

Exhibit 14(b) Wipro verticals

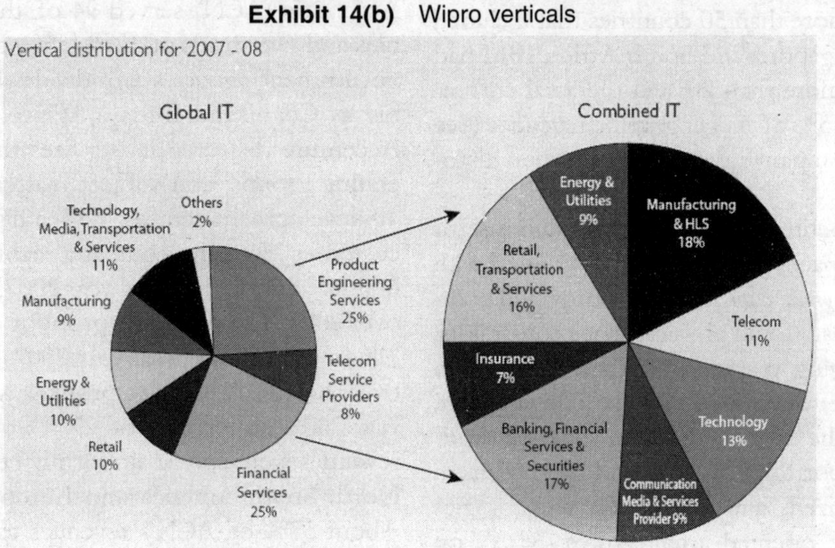

These companies, for example, had bid for contracts in the recently announced Indian Railways IT outsourcing deal. New, but serious threats to Indian companies came from other developing nations such as Eastern Europe and South America. All national players were exploring various locations globally for their operations. TCS had made acquisitions in Chile and expansions in Budapest, Hungary and China; Infosys explored Shanghai, Mauritius, and Czech cities; while Wipro explored Shanghai and Beijing. Accenture could soon be a threat to the Indian IT industry for offshoring.

International Competition

IBM

In the international arena, IBM was the largest IT outsourcing company in the world with 15% of the global outsourcing market. IBM's new global model called *globally integrated enterprise* was considered to be highly promising. With huge investments in the emerging markets, IBM focused on global integration using the right skills in the right areas of business delivered at the right costs. With a global supply chain, IBM built software globally, networked R&D functions worldwide, and offered services on a truly global scale.

Strategically, with innovation and global integration as key imperatives, IBM constantly strived to improve efficiency and productivity to transform into a different company. 2007 was a very successful year for IBM with revenues and a profit margin of $98.8 billion[10] (8%) and a growth rate of 42.2% respectively. IBM operated in 170 countries and enjoyed 63% of its revenues from its non-US operations, of which nearly 26% was from BRIC countries. In more than 50 countries that included Poland, Malaysia, Singapore, and South Africa, IBM had gained revenues of more than 20% in the local currencies contributing to 15% of its geographic revenues (See Exhibit 15 for the company's geographic revenue distribution).

While most competitors were building solutions for their infrastructure space, IBM was well positioned with its invention of the *green data centre* that provided solutions on power, real estate and physical space constraints, etc. With the emerging markets installing their green data centres and other developed nations following suit, IBM was ready for the new clients. The superior product and technology portfolio of IBM had been built on networked, modularized, and embedded technologies that included service oriented architectures (SOA); on demand, and open modular systems, to name a few. Its product portfolio had software products such as Lotus, Web-sphere, and Rational hardware such as e-servers, and mainframes. Its numerous patents had helped provide end-to-end solutions for its customers and businesses of all sizes. With more than 3000 patents, IBM had a promising future with product innovations such as next generation system Z mainframes, System P servers, and power based virtualization offerings.

Exhibit 15 Revenues by geography–IBM

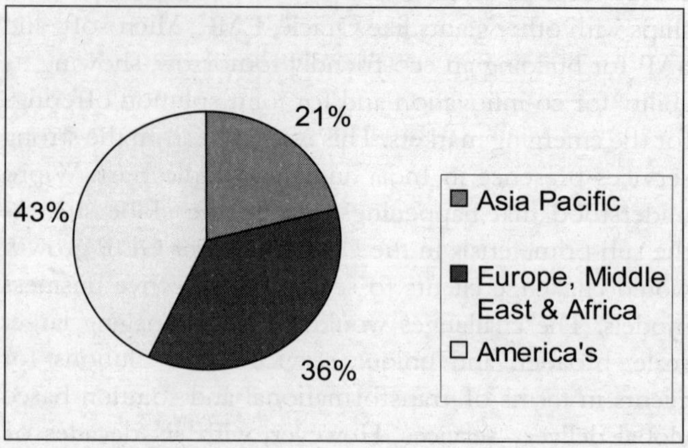

Source: Annual Reports.

As a result of its high value offerings, IBM had profitable growth and good cash earnings that enabled the company to provide strong returns to the shareholders, and towards reinvestments for a prospective 2008. IBM's belief in strong local engagement, building trust, and knowing the client's culture and commitment for the long term, made it a global leader.

Accenture

Accenture (ACN) served 94 of the *Fortune* 100 companies and two thirds of *Fortune* 500 companies and several government agencies worldwide. Its size was nearly as big as Cognizant, Infosys, Wipro, and TCS combined. Accenture delivered its services through combined operating groups, and subject matter experts spread over 40 development centres. With a high-end and long-term customer base, the company recorded revenues of $21 billion[11] during the fiscal year 2007, an increase of 17.7% over 2006. The operating profit of the company was $2.4 billion during the fiscal year 2007, an increase of 35.4% over 2006; and the net profit was $1.2 billion in fiscal year 2007, an increase of 27.7% over 2006. Accenture's revenues were spread uniformly between revenues from North/South America and Europe/Africa/Asia/Pacific. About 57% of ACN's revenues came from outside the

Americas. It derived about 22% of its revenues from the financial services.

With the high performance business strategy, ACN focused on the current marketplace and its client needs. Huge investments on innovation for unique service offerings and people were the backbone of Accenture's performance and execution. In 2007, ACN added 60,000 new employees to take its total strength of employees to 170,000 (nearly 30% increase) compared to a total of 58,000 employees at Cognizant as of March 31, 2008. Further, ACN spent over $776 million on its employee training and development during 2007.

A unique blend of research and unparalleled customer experience made ACN a world leader in management, technology, and outsourcing. To help clients to adapt to the new market, Accenture provided sales support, service marketing, transformational services, and consulting beyond the in-house R&D. It encouraged collaboration with universities for latest ideas and capitalized on *customer led innovation,* leveraging client's product and service ideas. Accenture planned to deploy 2000 consulting professionals by the end of 2008 as part of its expansion in India. An Accenture study revealed that the emerging markets would take over half of global consumption. Also, by 2010, India and China together would contain 123 million middle class households. That was more than the total number of households in the United States. To the client, serving the emerging market meant new business, new products and services. Accenture planned to serve the emerging markets with its expansion and mature presence in BRIC countries, while its competitors were still entering the market.

Accenture had a global delivery network with the most advanced and secure IT infrastructure to unify the clients and their personnel in multiple centres. The company's ability to weave a fabric of the customer's unique needs and its own rich experience in business consulting, apart from system integration, provided several leads for IT and outsourcing services.

Accenture and IBM had penetrated very well into European markets. This had been a key success factor for these companies considering the strength the euro had gained over the dollar recently.

Key Challenges for a Global Footprint

The biggest challenge in the consulting and outsourcing business was the recruiting and retaining of quality human resources. It was a challenge because of the availability of a number of consulting firms in addition to the difficulty in finding qualified and experienced resources. Cognizant had employee strength of around 59,500 as of September 30, 2008, and the company believed that the existing clients and new clients could be serviced with the available resources. Further recruitment was a device to address the problem of attrition rates that could disturb the future revenue growth.

Practice Leader and Senior VP for Advanced Solution Practice and Testing Services, Allen Shaheen, said, "The key challenge that haunts Cognizant is the management approach to employment considering the expected growth and size of the organization. Moving to the next level in terms of growth and size, invigorating the employees about the purpose of the organization, and ensuring that the culture of the organization is not diluted, is going to be a difficult task."

Cognizant reported excellent customer satisfaction based on metrics such as customer satisfaction surveys and employee satisfaction surveys. The annual customer satisfaction survey [12] reported that, of the 1300 customers who provided feedback, 89.3% reported high and extremely high customer satisfaction.

By the end of 2007, Cognizant operated with 40 global delivery centres across North America, Europe, Asia, and Latin America. The main focus of Cognizant's strategy was to identify the choice of geography in terms of the territory on which to focus, such as Europe or Asia Pacific, to aid future growth. The company reported that it had expanded its global footprint on both the demand and supply sides. The demand for Cognizant's services provided solid growth beyond the well-established US markets. The global delivery on the supply side had been expanded to China and Latin America. With a significant increase in the headcount, over a dozen clients received a portion of the services from China. In addition to this, Cognizant currently had underway a $330 million expansion of its facilities throughout India that would add another 4.3 million square feet of capacity. In the next section, we give a brief overview of the global delivery centres in India and Europe.

However, Cognizant's Senior Vice President of Strategy & Marketing, Malcolm Frank, felt that the concept of global delivery was still young. For the last two years, Cognizant had been working on a global delivery platform named *Cognizant 2.0* that divided the work in atomic levels and smaller processes across the globe, wherein smaller groups dispersed across the globe worked together for an end to end solution. These sub units were distributed across different locations, based on talent, knowledge base, experience and requirements that were

Exhibit 16 Engagement governance model

Client Engagement Governance Model

Level 1 – Steering Committee

Executive sponsorship and oversight
Ensure business goals and engagement goals alignment
Align & sell engagement objectives to stakeholders
Ensure tangible results and demonstrate values
Communicate change
Continuously educate & report executive leadership on the critical success factors of engagement

Level 2 – Program Management Office

Plan & implement change
Establish performance metrics aligned to goals
Review project scope, timelines &budget and monitor project progress
Communication, Status reporting & escalation to steering committee
Manage cross team dependencies
Identify, initiate & institutionalize process Improvements
Oversee reuse, repeatability & tools usage and creation
Oversee knowledge repository building

Level 3 – Project Delivery Team

Project Management
Quality Management
Risk Management
Resource Management
Schedule Management
Communication &Reporting
Knowledge Management
Method Tools & Standards Management
Change Management
Issue Management
Configuration Management
Monitor & measure knowledge transfer process
Ensure Successful Engagement Startup
Incorporate industry best practices

SoW Structure
(Key items covered)

- Clearly defined scope
- Solution & entitlements
- Dependencies & assumptions
- Engagement governance & review process
- Metrics & reporting
- Roles & responsibilities

Engagement reviews

- Daily ops reviews
- Weekly project level operational reviews
- Monthly programme management reviews (Internal & with customer)
- Quarterly steering committee meetings
- Annual executive review

Source: Company reports 2007

reassembled to provide end-to-end solutions that were no longer dependent on geography. This process focused to provide the best talent from the available pool instead of limiting the resources based on their geographic locations. This platform integrated the global knowledge base and the teams worldwide in order to provide a real-time view of the global work for the clients. The company called them *virtual delivery centres*. These centres were already servicing clients with tailor made solutions that had more impact than geography based outsourcing. Because of these global delivery centres, Cognizant was able to provide more efficient and higher quality services than those companies that delivered in a discrete fashion.

The company also planned to add clients and its business partners to create a better global delivery system. Cognizant's regional delivery centres would fully leverage Cognizant 2.0. This platform aimed to connect Cognizant global, regional, and local development centres virtually through one central platform using the web 2.0 technologies to deliver significant time to market, and cost, and transformational value to clients.

While talking about the regional delivery centre at Argentina, the CEO and President Francisco D'Souza, said:

> *Our DNA of having a strong local relationship management and global outsourcing capabilities will be strengthened by the new Argentina centre. Our investments in newer global, regional, and local delivery centres will enable our clients to seamlessly harness optimal talent globally for providing differentiated values to their end customers.*

Cognizant also focused on widening its portfolio of sectors in services in addition to application development and maintenance. Other service sectors included IT infrastructure management, business process outsourcing (BPO), and knowledge process outsourcing (KPO), all seen as high growth areas. Also, focus was on selecting the industry that would lead to better revenues, such as infrastructure services that were supposed to grow to three times the size of application development. The IT infrastructure management handled clients in the areas of Server Management, Database Administration and Management, Middleware and Application Server Management, Enterprise Messaging Management Services, Storage Management, Network Management, Managed Security Services, End-user Computing Support, Vendor Management, Risk mitigation, and Flexibility and Global consistency. With the acquisition of AimNet in 2006, Cognizant had built a global infrastructure operations centre that combined onsite, near-shore and offshore activities that would be easily integrated with the client's existing environment.

Cognizant Business Consulting (CBC) group, with around 1700 consulting professionals, provided advice to clients in critical areas such as IT strategy, outsourcing strategy, business process redesign, solutions evaluation, and design, as well as in numerous other strategy, domain and functional consulting areas.

There was significant progress in the BPO area. Cognizant had established centres of Excellence for BPO on various functional sectors across different industrial sectors. With its strong domain expertise, Cognizant was able to handle business critical processes for their clients such as managing clinical trials in life sciences and claims administration in the insurance industry. Not only did this process ensure enhancement of the client's capabilities, but it also created deeper domain experts within the organization. Another area of growth was SAP that offered end-to-end solutions for SAP applications producing business solutions that integrated such functions as materials management, finance, sales & marketing, and human resources on a global scale. Please refer to Exhibit 16 for the company's client governance model.

Cognizant's Global Delivery Centres

Cognizant India[13]

This was one of the major global delivery centres of Cognizant Technology Solutions. Cognizant India played a significant role in business outsourcing services in India and managed its operational services in India itself. In 2007, Cognizant India was ranked 15th among 100 "hot growth" companies. It was also ranked 6th in India in providing quality services at a significantly lower cost. According to Malcolm Frank, Senior Vice President of Strategy & Marketing, Cognizant was behind its competition in the Indian IT market space despite being aggressive in the beginning. He added: "Overall, Cognizant faces strategic problems though the company is operationally well placed because of the established processes." With an established operational base in India, Cognizant did not anticipate major competition from new entrants because of the many operational issues involved in setting up an India delivery centre. Bhaskar Das, Vice President of Human Resources in Cognizant, said, "We are not only planning to expand numbers, but also to widen the recruiting pool, from engineers, managers and scientists for various activities, to doctors, chartered accountants, and lawyers."

However, there were some issues that Cognizant India had to consider deeply. Cognizant relied primarily on Indian nationals for its onsite projects. The visa requirements for employees to work in the US and the restrictions on those visas were of primary concern. This dependence on Indian staff for onsite projects curbed the growth, though temporarily. Additionally, the exchange rates had a significant impact on operating margins. Considering the rising labor cost in India and a shortage of skilled labor, whether India could continue to be an outsourcing destination remained as a legitimate question.

Cognizant Europe

In 2007, Cognizant experienced its fastest growth in Europe. Revenue from European operations grew at 89% in 2007, and represented 16.1% of its total revenue, up from 12.9% in 2006. Most of the demand in the UK, Benelux, and Switzerland came from customers in financial services, life sciences, and manufacturing. Penetration into European markets was a reflection of Cognizant's investment strategy towards global delivery. In March 2008, Cognizant reported an initiative of forming a joint venture with T systems, the enterprise customer division of Deutsche Telecom (DT). This unique partnership was a global sales and delivery approach for system integration services. The joint venture provided the European customers with access to the systems integration capabilities of DT, a giant in the local market along with the global delivery capabilities of Cognizant. This deal was expected to increase the market share and reduce costs for both the companies. From Cognizant's point of view, it gained one more offshore client, and the opportunity to sell its application development and maintenance capabilities to the customers of T Systems because it was included in the delivery chain.

Exhibit 17 Revenues according to geography

	North America	Europe	Asia	Total
2007				
Revenues	$1,768,763	$342,866	$23,948	$2,135,57
Long Lived Assets	$12,860	$1,873	$341,314	$356,047
2006				
Revenues	$1,227,641	$183,868	$12,758	$1424267
Long Lived Assets	$9224	$1,392	$209,538	$220,154
2005				
Revenues	$772,725	$103,707	$9348	$885,830
Long Lived Assets	$8,185	$281	$138,550	$146,982

Source: Annual Reports.

Exhibit 17 gives the revenues of Cognizant from different geographic regions of North America, Europe, and Asia. Cognizant expected to see further growth in Europe. Reports[14] indicated that, geographically, Europe had continued the strong trend with growth being approximately 87% year over year. For 2008, the expected revenues were approximately $2.81 billion, a growth of over 23% as compared to 2007.

Conclusion

There was no question that IT in general, and outsourcing in particular, was the growth engine of the future. The Gartner's Forecast for Worldwide IT Outsourcing for 2004–2009 reported that the worldwide IT outsourcing spending would rise from $193 billion in 2004 to $260 billion by 2009. The BPO market was also expected to grow from $111 billion to $172 billion during 2004–2009, according to the *Gartner Dataquest* report. Technology companies were recognizing the benefits of offshore technology service providers in software R&D, and related support functions. They were outsourcing a greater portion of these activities, making the outsourcing industry much more competitive.

Cognizant had gained a strong momentum in growth. Given the economic indicators in the United States and other parts of the world, whether Cognizant could sustain its growth remained a question. It had to manage its growth, preserving its unique culture and the competencies. How should the company plan to manage the loss of talent and in turn prevent the entry of non-competent or non-ethical workforce that might disrupt the culture? How and what elements to conserve and reinforce in the Cognizant culture, which was the DNA of the company's success so far? How should the company plan to handle currency and interest rate fluctuations, and the impact of those on the operating margins? How should Cognizant see taxation changes in different countries? What other skills should Cognizant acquire to manage an increasingly wider global footprint?

NOTES

1. As on September 2008.
2. Companies and Markets, News Report, 2008.
3. Market Avenue, Reports, 2007.
4. Press release, 2008 (Internet).
5. Cognizant Press Release.
6. Infosys Annual Report, 2006-2007.
7. 20 – F, SEC Filing, Infosys, 2008.
8. "Inside Infosys: A chat with the CFO", *CFO Magazine*.
9. Wipro Annual Report, 2007-2008.
10. IBM Annual Report, 2007-2008.
11. Accenture Annual Report, 2007–2008.
12. Cognizant White Paper.
13. Cognizant Annual Report, 2007.
14. Internet: Silicon India, News, February, 2008

One Mission, Multiple Roads: Aravind Eye Care System in 2009

CASE 12

S. Manikutty

How do we grow keeping at par with the best eye hospitals in the world, yet keeping our mission? That is our challenge now.

– Dr. P. Namperumalsamy

The year 2008–2009 was one Aravind Eye Care System (AECS) could be proud of. AECS had received the prestigious Bill & Melinda Gates Award for Global Health; for the first time this award had been given to an organization not working in the realms of communicable diseases or population control. AECS had also been acknowledged by the Clinton Global Initiative in its Annual Meeting held in September 2008 when the former US President, Bill Clinton, personally introduced AECS's work in the field of Diabetic Retinopathy (DR). Thought leaders like C.K. Prahalad had recognized its contribution in bringing out an innovative and influential model to deliver quality eye care to the bottom of the pyramid in his highly acclaimed book, *The Fortune at the Bottom of the Pyramid*[1]. The hospitals under the Aravind Eye Care System had done a total of 309,015 surgeries in 2008–09, the highest in its 33 year-old history. Of these, 162,809 were for free patients.

When the case writer revisited AECS in 2009, nearly six years after writing the first case on it[2], he found that much had happened besides sheer growth. Its legendary founder, Dr. G. Venkataswamy (Dr. V) was no more (he passed away on July 7, 2006). The Pondicherry hospital had become fully functional. A new research facility, Dr. G. Venkataswamy Eye Research Institute had been commissioned on October 1, 2008. Another new facility was nearing completion in Madurai where the existing clinics, operation theatres and in-patient wards would be shifted; the old building would be for outdoor patients and administrative services. Its manufacturing arm, Aurolab, had moved into a sparking new facility, in anticipation of future growth. AECS had set up 31 Vision Centres and five Community Eye Clinics in different parts of rural Tamil Nadu as part of its outreach programme. It had also started an initiative, in a limited way, called Aravind Managed Eye Care Services (AMECS) to manage other hospitals without owning them.

These actions and initiatives were in response to certain fundamental changes in the environment. Its mission, articulated by Dr. V in the simple but powerful statement, "Elimination of needless blindness" continued to be the same, and all the key people at AECS were in agreement that this should continue. But, as seen from the quote at the beginning of this case, Dr. P. Namperumalsamy (Dr.

Prepared by Prof. S. Manikutty, Indian Institute of Management, Ahmedabad as a basis for class discussion.
The case writer wishes to place on record his gratitude to Dr. Namperumalsamy, Dr. Natchiar, Mr. Thulasiraj, Dr. S. Aravind, Dr. Kim, Ms. Dhivya and Ms. Veni of the Aravind Eye Care System for their enthusiasm and cooperation that made this case possible.

Nam), who had succeeded Dr. V as the Chief Executive, was faced with the challenge of choosing the path that would help them to move closer towards achieving the mission, ensure further growth and enable them to deliver high quality eye care.

ARAVIND EYE CARE SYSTEM: HISTORICAL PERSPECTIVE

Aravind Eye Care System had its beginnings in 1976 when Dr. V started a modest 11-bed hospital, named Aravind Eye Hospital at Madurai, the temple town in Tamil Nadu, India. Dr. V was a remarkable person. He had joined the Army Medical Corps after securing a MBBS degree in 1944, but was discharged in 1948 due to arthritis. Rheumatoid arthritis had crippled his fingers completely. However, by sheer perseverance and will power, he not only started to write but also started wielding the surgeon's scalpel again. He then joined the government service as an eye surgeon and rose to become the Head of the Department of Ophthalmology at the Government Medical College, Madurai. During his service, he pioneered state level programmes to address blindness through mobile eye camps. Despite his arthritic fingers, he trained himself to do microsurgery and in the technique of Intraocular Lens (IOL) insertion.

After his superannuation (retirement) in 1976, he started a modest 11-bed hospital with his personal savings. From the beginning, a policy was put in place—there would be paying as well as free patients. Paying patients would be charged only moderately and not more than comparable hospitals in the city. Viability was ensured through close control of costs, high productivity of doctors and achieving high volumes.

Dr. V was profoundly influenced by Mahatma Gandhi and Sri Aurobindo Ghosh, the sage philosopher who founded the famous ashram in Pondicherry. A strong need to give to society was imbibed in Dr. V. The name "Aravind" in the Aravind Eye Hospital was chosen to honour Sri Aurobindo. Dr. V once wrote:

> *Many people often ask me: What made me take up a task of such magnitude at the age of 58? I guess I drew my inspiration from the legacy of our great forefathers... Besides, there were inspirational leaders like Mahatma Gandhi and Sri Aurobindo whose philosophy and way of life influenced many. Naturally I felt impelled to give something back to this great land of ours.*[3]

Values and a certain degree of spirituality were vital components of AECS. All doctors, nurses and staff were expected to show politeness to patients, visitors and whoever they interacted with, as also among themselves. No matter how poor a patient was, he/she had to be treated with respect. The pictures of Aurobindo and the Mother were ubiquitous, and the hospital also had a meditation room. Aurobindo's teachings were continuously disseminated and reinforced, and as Mr. R.D. Thulasiraj, the Executive Director of Lions Aravind Institute of Community Ophthalmology (LAICO) and IT and Systems Director, Corporate Office, observed:

> *Our operational model is heavily dependent on work culture and values. The systems are built in our basic values.*

AECS had developed a unique approach to meet its mission. Since the majority of incidence of blindness was due to cataract, it focused on cataract surgery. They found this procedure to be amenable to a high degree of standardization, and established a unique two-bed system of operation in which the surgeon moved between two beds (for details see the earlier case, "Aravind Eye Care System: Giving the Most Precious Gift"[4]) had been developed at AECS. By this system, AECS could achieve a consistent productivity rate of 25 surgeries/day/doctor[5], when the general rate in other hospitals was just about 5–6. Though its patient rooms, doctors' rooms, outpatient (OP) area, etc., were spartan but functional, the medical and surgical equipment used at AECS were of the highest quality. Its success in bringing down the cost of surgeries was also due to its success in manufacturing IOLs in-house. The cost of imported lens was $80 whereas the ones manufactured by Aurolab cost only $5.

Due to its two-bed system of surgery and low cost of IOL, AECS could conduct surgeries at a very competitive price, and do about 60 percent of its surgeries free or almost free[6]. In 2003, the cost for a base level IOL cataract surgery was only ₹3,800 (or $80). Even with a phaco-emulsification procedure, and with foldable acrylic three piece IOL (these were optional), the cost was only ₹12,500 if the patient chose to stay in the general ward, and ₹14,900 if they chose an air conditioned room. Recent trends were for the patients to opt for surgery as outpatients.

AECS gained a name quickly and grew fast. By 1997, it was performing 123,095 surgeries per year, and had 975,868 outpatient visits. By 2003, these figures were 202,066 and 1.45 million[7], of which 123,579 in surgery and 688,584 outpatients (including camp outpatients) were treated free.

Despite such a high percentage of free patients, AECS had been creating a sizeable surplus, the net surplus being about 50 percent of the total income. For example, in 2002–03, it had a surplus of ₹219 million out of an income of ₹423.7 million. AECS's growth was fully funded by the accumulated surplus; AECS never needed to go to banks for financing its expansion[8] except in the initial years when personal properties were pledged to get a bank loan for building the first hospital.

Its expansion was spectacular. In 1977, a 30-bed hospital was opened. In 1978, a 70-bed hospital exclusively meant for free patients was built. The hospital presently used for paying patients was built in 1981 with 250 beds (80,000 sq. ft. over five floors) and all the clinics were housed there. In 1984, a new 350 bed free patient hospital was built, and AEH, Madurai progressively expanded to house 1100 free beds and 415 paying beds by 2003. In 1985, a 100 bed hospital was built at Theni, Dr. Nam's birth place; in 1988, a 400 bed hospital at Tirunelveli; in 1997, an 874 bed hospital at Coimbatore; and in 2004, a 750 bed hospital at Pondicherry. By 2003, AECS hospitals had a total of 3,649 beds between the five units (Madurai, Theni, Tirunelveli, Coimbatore, and Pondicherry), of which 2850 were for free and 799 were for paying patients. After the Pondicherry hospital, AECS did not build any new hospitals or increase the bed capacity till 2009. Then it set up a new free patients' unit in Tirunelveli and a new paying patients' hospital was being built at Madurai. In both instances, the beds from the existing units were to be shifted to the new units thus releasing space to expand the outpatient services. Thus, as on 2009, the bed capacity had not changed much from 2003. Exhibit 1 gives the number of beds in different units, as on 2009.

Exhibit 1 Aravind eye care system: Number of beds in different hospitals, 2009

Unit	Free/ Subsidized beds	Paying beds	Total	Operation Theatres/ Tables
Madurai	900	325	1225	13/49
Tirunelveli	482	158	640	5/16
Theni	123	40	163	2/8
Coimbatore	580	176	756	11/20
Pondicherry	600	136	736	8/21
Total	2685	835	3500	39/114

Source: Data supplied by Aravind Eye Care System.

It may be noted that AECS did not consider the number of beds to be an important parameter, since most cataract patients were now discharged the same day, and treated as out patients. Over the years, the mats (counted as beds earlier) in the free patients' hospital had been converted to regular cots, and the average length of stay of a patient had reduced. Many patients even opted for surgeries as outpatients. Hence, for AECS, the number of surgeries done was a more meaningful indicator of its impact than the mere number of beds. Exhibit 2 gives the number of surgeries done and the number of paying and free outpatients from 1997–2009.

Exhibit 2 Number of surgeries undertaken and the number of outpatient visits of paying and free patients, 2003–2009

Year	Paying		Free including Camp		Total	
	OP visits	Surgery	OP visits	Surgery	OP visits	Surgery
2003	758,991	78,487	688,584	123,579	1,447,575	202,066
2004	870,171	85,745	765,860	141,690	1,636,031	227,435
2005	928,785	93,134	793,113	154,101	1,721,898	247,235
Jan 2006 till March 2007	1,140,764	104,108	1,037,572	147,989	2,178,336	252,097
April 2007 to March 2008	1,101,154	114,464	1,073,614	148,202	2,174,768	262,666
April 2008 to March 2009	1,182,137	131,295	1,273,811	138,282	2,455,948	269,577

Source: Data supplied by Aravind Eye Care System.

Notes: 1. The above figures are for all AEHs.

2. The figures for surgery in April 2008 to March 2009 exclude laser procedures.

In consonance with its mission, AECS conducted a number of outreach activities. Of these, eye camps were the most important for they symbolized the organization's determination to reach out to the people in the villages. The eye camps were of different types, but the most important were the comprehensive eye camps, where complete examination of eyes was done, spectacles prescribed and delivered on the spot in about 70 percent of the cases, in addition to checking for diabetes and giving nutrition advice. In 2009 (April 1, 2008 to March 31, 2009), AECS conducted 1,319 such camps, wherein 314,780 patients were examined. Those needing surgeries were brought to the main hospitals in buses (AECS did not conduct any surgeries at the camp site), and after the surgery and recuperation, the patients were dropped back in their villages in buses. To enable delivery of spectacles on the spot, a stock of spectacles with commonly prescribed powers, was taken to the camps. For glasses that could not be delivered on the spot, they were made in Madurai and sent to them by courier[9]. In 2008–09, out of the 299,923 patients examined, glasses were advised to 59,248 persons, of whom 49,112 were ordered by the patients. Of these, 37,348 were delivered on the spot.

AECS also organized diabetic retinopathy (DR) camps refractive error camps, eye screening camps for school children, paediatric camps, and mobile van DR screening camps. Exhibit 3 gives the details of these camps conducted from 2003 to 2009.

Exhibit 3 Eye camps conducted, 2003–2009

Year (calendar years)	No. of Camps Organized	Patients Seen	Surgeries of "Camp" Patients
2003	1,158	388,594	81,357
2004	1,271	433,502	95,249
2005	1,335	437,224	98,326
2006	1,442	412,683	92,346
2007	1,448	377,377	87,667
2008	1,302	320,563	69,580
2009	1,319	314,780	71,869

Source: Data supplied by Aravind Eye Care System.

In 1982, AECS had set up its own training institute, Aravind Post-Graduate Institute of Ophthalmology (APGIM), which offered a Resident (Post Graduate) Program, a Fellowship Program for super specialization, and an Ophthalmic Assistants' Training. Its affiliation to different universities enabled it to give degree certificates in some of the programs. Its manufacturing arm, Aurolab, produced IOLs and medical consumables for eye care, like sutures and medications at low cost. Right from the beginning, these products were made available to eye hospitals and ophthalmologists outside AECS. This enabled it to achieve the needed economies of scale. It was also in consonance with its mission of elimination of needless blindness. It enabled many hospitals, not only in India, but also in other developing countries, to conduct surgeries at a much lower cost. Aurolab's products were exported to many countries. Every year it also developed a number of pioneering products. In 2009, the important new products were Auroflex–EV, negative aspheric IOLs that gave increased contrast and better visibility in low light conditions, absorbable sutures and a green laser photo coagulator, especially useful in coagulation of the tiny blood vessels of the retina.

The Aravind Medical Research Foundation expanded its research activities dramatically, especially with the commissioning of the Dr. G. Venkataswamy Research Institute on October 1, 2008. It was engaged in cutting edge research in all the areas connected with eye diseases. Some idea of the ongoing research at this institute can be obtained from Exhibit 4. Many research scholars from other parts of India and abroad came to study here. During his visit, the case writer met three scholars from different countries who had come to pursue their research taking advantage of AECS's facilities, research staff, and data.

AECS' training arm, the Lions Aravind Institute of Community Ophthalmology (LAICO), offered training programmes to outside hospitals to improve their practices. LAICO offered programmes both in techniques of surgery and in management to doctors, hospital managers and paramedics. LAICO offered training programmes both at its facilities at Madurai and at customers' sites, and also in the number of foreign countries. In all, as on 2009, LAICO had provided its services to 252 eye hospitals in India and abroad. It also undertook consultancy for improving the performance of hospitals, with need assessment, vision building workshops, follow-up visits, and monitoring. LAICO worked in collaboration with a number of voluntary organizations such as Lions Club, Sight Savers International, Seva Foundation and World Health Organization. Exhibit 5 gives some idea of LAICO's activities.

AECS also had an eye bank established with the support from Rotary International. It was set up in 1998 at Madurai, and by 2009, AECS succeeded in establishing collection centres in its hospitals at Tirunelveli, Coimbatore and Pondicherry. A total of 3,626 eyes were received in 2009, of which 1,070 were suitable for transplant, and these were all used.

Exhibit 4 Research at Dr. G. Venkataswamy eye research institute

There were a large number of research projects going on at the Eye Research institute. They were broadly categorized as follows:

Basic Research There were 25 projects under this category currently underway. Some of these have been listed below:

- Molecular genetic analysis of corneal endothelial dystrophies
- Identification of genetic defects occurring in Indian oculocutaneous (OCA) and ocular albinism (OA) families
- Association studies on diabetic retinopathy with type 2 diabetes in South Indian population
- Genetic study on congenital hereditary cataract
- A genetic component to the INDEYE study of cataract in India

Clinical Research, Vision Rehabilitation

- The study of low vision children in blind school
- Impact of the low vision devices and rehabilitation services on the quality of life

Clinical Research, Glaucoma Studies There were 22 projects under this category. Some of these were:

- Safety and efficacy of manual small-incision cataract surgery combined with trabeculectomy: comparison with phacotrabeculectomy
- Surgical outcome of phacotrabeculectomy in eyes with small pupils—A prospective study
- Correlation of central corneal thickness and retinal nerve fibre layer in POAG
- Comparison of intraocular pressure measured by Pascal dynamic contour tonometry and Goldmann applanation tonometry

Clinical Research, Retina Services and Drug Trials There were 36 projects under this category, a sample of which can be seen below:

- Efficacy and safety of posterior juxtascleral administrations of anecortave acetate for depot suspension (15mg or 30mg) versus sham administration in patients at risk for progressing to exudative Age-Related Macular Degeneration (AMD)
- A six-month, phase 3, multicenter, masked, randomised, sham-controlled trial (with six-month open-label extension) to assess the safety and efficacy of 700 μg and 350 μg dexamethasone posterior segment drug delivery system (DEX PS DDS) applicator system in the treatment of patients with macular oedema following central retinal vein occlusion or branch retinal vein occlusion
- A safety and efficacy assessment of vitreosolve® for ophthalmic intravitreal injection for inducing posterior vitreous detachment in non-proliferative diabetic retinopathy subjects

Clinical Research, Orbit and Oculoplasty There were 7 projects under this category. Some have been listed below:

- Randomised, double blind, active controlled study of the efficacy, surgical outcome and complications of Silicone Rod Sling in frontalis sling suspension surgery
- Socket reconstruction using bio-engineered autologous oral mucosal epithelium
- Corneal surface reconstruction using bio-engineered autologous oral (Buccal) mucosal epithelium
- Factors responsible for the generation of epithelial sheet rich in stem cells under ex-vivo conditions from the limbal and buccal biopsy

Clinical Research, Cornea Clinic

- Outcome and safety of supratarsal injecton of triamcinolone acetonide in improving the quality of life in patients with refractory vernal keratoconjunctivitis.
- Steroids for Corneal Ulcers Trial (SCUT)
- Mycotic Ulcer Treatment Trial (MUTT)
- Comparison of accuracy of IOL master and conventional A-scan biometry in IOL power calculation in high myopes

Clinical Research, Cataract and IOL Services There were 12 projects under this category, following are some of the ongoing projects:

- Comparison of accuracy of IOL master and conventional A-scan in IOL power calculations
- Study of visual outcome and complications following posterior capsular rupture during IOL surgery
- Capsule wash for pediatric eyes
- Role of CTR on anterior capsular contraction in patients with retinitis pigmentosa
- Contralateral eye study to compare the incidence of PCO between square edge PMMA IOL and round edge PMMA IOL and between square edge PMMA IOL and acrysof IOL

Clinical Research, Uvea Services There were three projects under this category:

- Posurdex—intermediate and posterior uveitis study
- HLA-DR determination of Vogt-Koyanagi-Harada syndrome and sympathetic ophthalmia in South Indian patients

- A double-masked, placebo-controlled, multicentric, parallel group, dose ranging study to assess the efficacy and safety of LX211 as therapy in subjects with non-infectious intermediate, anterior and intermediate, posterior or pan-uveitis

Clinical Research, Paediatric Ophthalmology Services There were 7 projects under this category. To name a few:

- How valid (sensitive and specific) is teacher's screening for refractive errors as compared to that done by trained refractionists?
- Clinical profile with ocular and oculocutaneous albinism at a tertiary care centre

Operations Research The four projects under this category were:

- Investigating gender equity in the utilisation of cataract surgical services in Aravind Eye Hospital, Madurai—SEVA Canada
- Uptake of spectacles for refractive errors across different delivery systems
- Assess the prevalence and socioeconomic burden of near visual impairment caused by uncorrected presbyopia
- HR practices which influences employee satisfaction and patient satisfaction

Aurolab Clinical Trials

- Posterior capsular opacification after implantation of square edge PMMA, round edge PMMA and acrysof intraocular lenses: A prospective, randomised comparative trial
- Clinical evaluation of hydrophobic foldable IOLs
- Effect of square edge PMMA IOL in preventing lens epithelial cell migration in paediatric cataract surgery: A randomised controlled trial
- Randomised controlled trial of Aurolase 532-I-1 with already available green laser (Iridex) in proliferative diabetic retinopathy
- Clinical evaluation of aspheric intraocular lenses

Source: Dr. G. Venkataswamy Eye Research Foundation Annual Report, 2008–09. Madurai: Aravind Eye Care System.

Exhibit 5 LAICO's activities

LAICO has, as its mission, been contributing to the prevention and control of global blindness through teaching, training, consultancy, advocacy and research in eye care delivery. It was involved in the development and training of ophthalmic personnel both in India and abroad. A major part of its activities centred around enhancing the capacity of existing and new eye hospitals worldwide through comprehensive organizational development by sharing the best practices across hospitals. It worked in collaboration with international voluntary organizations such as Lions Club International, Sightsavers International, Chirstoffel Blinden Mission, International Eye Foundation, Right to Sight, Seva Foundation, ORBIS International, and the World Health Organization.

Consultancy was done in phases: needs assessment visits, vision building workshops, follow up visits, monitoring, and final situation analysis. LAICO so far had provided this service to 252 eye hospitals in India and other countries.

Countries supported in this manner included Bangladesh, Cameroon, Ethiopia, Rwanda, Paraguay, etc. Lions SightFirst Eye Hospital, Nairobi, Kenya; Grameen GC Eye Hospital, Bogra, Bangladesh; Shalin Hospital, Congo; and Nkhoma Eye Hospital, Nkhoma, Malawi are examples of hospitals supported by LAICO.

LAICO's Teaching and Training Division was involved in conducting workshops and seminars on various topics. These workshops imparted technical and skills training, and management training to enhance the management capabilities of the hospitals.

LAICO's Projects Division provided end-to-end project management systems and processes, development and enhancement of project management capability, and sharing of best practices.

Its Research Division aimed to develop the capability of organizations to undertake scientifically rigorous and relevant research. It conducted regular workshops on research methodology. Its biostatistics department provided support in data entry, management, and analysis of data of projects.

LAICO's Information Technology and Systems Division provided maintenance and support for all applications and technologies, and assisted in the development of new technologies. It had developed an integrated Hospital Management Software (IHMS), which they planned to use in AECS' Vision and Community Centres.

To enhance the knowledge base of its doctors and personnel, AECS had set up a Tele-ophthalmology Network in 2002, which enabled the sharing of ideas, knowledge and experiences among its staff. A total of 435 video conferencing sessions were conducted between April 2008 and March 2009, each of nearly 90 minutes duration. They consisted of grand rounds of academic interests, journal clubs for research and management articles, clinical meetings, and special lectures. Classes for Post Graduate and Mid Level Ophthalmic Personnel and paramedics were also conducted through this medium.

Changes in the Environment

The environment had changed considerably since the last visit of the case writer in 2003. The following paragraphs describe the key changes.

Incidence of Cataract as the Major Cause for Blindness.

In 2003, cataract accounted for 62.6 percent of blindness in India, total or partial[10]. Due to a variety of reasons, notably the sharp increase in the number of cataract surgeries done as a result of higher awareness, this percentage was believed to have come down[11]. The number of cataract surgeries done per million population, the so called cataract surgery rate (CSR) was about 9,000 in Tamil Nadu, compared to the average rate of India of about 5,000. In states like Bihar, it was only 600, thus pointing to the magnitude of work that still had to be done (In USA, the CSR was about 5000). Despite the strides made, there still continued a considerable backlog of people needing cataract surgery. Though the incidence of cataract cases would continue to rise with aging population, the increasing awareness was expected to result in early surgeries, thus pushing up the demand for cataract surgeries. But even so, the demand for cataract surgeries seemed to be reaching a plateau. This was because of the progressively greater difficulty in accessing the people needing attention. A welcome development was the increase in the percentage of IOL surgeries in India to about 98 percent in 2009 as compared to about 65 percent in 2003.

As a result, though, in absolute numbers, AECS's cataract surgeries were going up every year, this number, as a percentage of the total surgeries done, was coming down. In 2008–09, this percentage had come down to 66 percent. Exhibit 6 provides the composition of surgeries done at AECS in 2008–09. This had important implications for the organization, since it had built a system with a high degree of operational efficiency based on the relatively standardized procedure for cataract surgeries[12]. This standardization and the resulting high productivity of its doctors had also kept the costs down, and in turn, enabled AECS to provide free surgeries to as much as 60 percent of its patients.

Exhibit 6 Types of surgeries done at AECS, 2008–09

Category of surgery	# Surgeries	Percentage
Cataract	204,672	66.23
Laser procedures	57,958	18.76
Retina & Vitreous surgery	8,393	2.72
Trab & combined procedures	7,099	2.30
Lacrimal surgeries	5,218	1.69
Other Orbit & Oculoplasty surgeries	6,336	2.05
Ocular injuries	1,164	0.38
Pterygium	3,565	1.15
LASIK refractive surgery	3,459	1.12
Squint correction	1,693	0.55
Other surgeries	9,458	3.06
Total surgeries	309,015	100.0

Source: Aravind Eye Care System (2009), Activity Report, 2008–09. Madurai: Aravind Eye Care System, p.11.

Explanation: LASIK (Laser Assisted in situ Keratomileusis) is a surgical procedure that uses a laser to correct nearsightedness, farsightedness, and/or astigmatism. In LASIK, a thin flap in the cornea is created using either a microkeratome blade or a femtosecond laser. The surgeon folds back the flap, and removes some corneal tissue underneath using an excimer laser. The flap is then laid back in place, covering the area where the corneal tissue was removed.

With nearsighted people, the goal of LASIK is to flatten the too-steep cornea; with farsighted people, a steeper cornea is desired. LASIK can also correct astigmatism by smoothing an irregular cornea into a more normal shape.

Reduced Demand for Free Services

There was a general improvement in the living conditions and so the percentage of people who needed free medical service was coming down. On the other hand, the expectations of patients were going up. This was reflected in the improvement in facilities provided by all AEHs. For example, all AEHs now provided cots to its free patients (as compared to mats earlier), resulting in the reduction in the number of patients who could be accommodated as cots occupied more floor space. Dr. Natchiar summarized these changes:

> *Now patient expectations have gone up. They do not want to stay long in hospitals. The number of patients demanding private rooms has gone up, while the number of those willing to share accommodation has come down.*

There were also multiple insurance schemes, both private and state sponsored, that enabled patients to cover their costs. AECS's policy remained the same: to treat everyone who came to the free patients' unit free of cost. Details of patients treated under different categories can be seen in Exhibit 7.

Exhibit 7 Patient statistics for different units of the AECS, April 2008 to March 2009

	Madurai	Tirunelveli	Theni	Coimbatore	Pondicherry	AMECS	Total
Outpatient Visits in hospitals							
Paying	437,906	201,082	68,564	286,624	187,961	188,892	1,371,029
Free	137,486	63,218	19,803	97,357	55,778	--	373,642
Outreach							
Comprehensive free eye Camps	100,767	45,362	24,049	73,927	55,818	83,686	383,609
School eye screening: Base hospitals	68,160	38,182	15,831	33,600	46,956	7,410	210,139
School eye screening: Vision Centres	11,275	2,650	50,962	2,350	-	-	67,237
Refraction camps	8,242	7,530	5,805	14,686	8,351	12,280	56,894
Diabetic retinopathy camps	9,857	13,456	4,449	21,824	2,833	-	52,419
Vision Centres	36,637	26,192	31,105	13,436	15,828	-	123,198
	Madurai	**Tirunelveli**	**Theni**	**Coimbatore**	**Pondicherry**	**AMECS**	**Total**
Community Clinics	35,165	25,934	13,770	25,380	-	-	100,249
Other outreach patients							132,998
Total outpatient visits	846,806	425,925	234,693	574,501	374,023	292,268	2,748,216 (2,455,948 without AMECS)
Surgeries							
Paying	57,484	19,556	4,541	33,112	16,602	14,911	146,206
Free (direct & camp)	54,152	20,450	4,772	39,663	19,245	24,527	162,809
Total	111,636	40,006	**9,313**	**72,775**	**35,847**	39,438	**309,015 (269,577 without AMECS)**

Source: Aravind Eye Care System (2009), Activity Report, 2008–09. Madurai: Aravind Eye Care System, p.11.

Exhibit 8 Causes for blindness in India, 2003

	Percentage
Cataract	62.6
Refractive errors	19.7
Corneal blindness	0.9
Glaucoma	5.8
Others	11.0

Projections of Incidence of Diabetes and DR, 2020

	2003	Est. 2020
Population estimates in million	1000	1250
Prevalence of diabetes	2%	5%
Estimated number of DR patients (millions)	5	15.6
Estimated number of DR patients who are blind	150,000	470,000

Source: Vision 2020 Document.

Changes in the Demand and Need for Other Areas if Eye Care

Though there was a decline in the cataract surgery in AECS, other areas of eye care had begun to emerge needing attention. Among these, the most important were diabetic retinopathy (DR) that included control of diabetes, refraction correction, and prevention and treatment of glaucoma. It was expected that soon many of the activities of AECS will get directed towards these areas (Exhibit 8).

Unlike cataract, diabetic retinopathy was preventable; however, if not treated in time, the damages it caused to retina were usually irreversible. Hence, the focus here had to be more on prevention and early attention than cure, and the attention needed to be directed towards education of population, effective screening for diabetes, and monitoring of the patients. It was estimated that in 2003 about two percent of India's population (nearly 20 million) were diabetic. Out of this number, about 5 million were DR patients and 1.5 million needed treatment. Further, about 150,000 of these were blind. What was more disturbing was that the trends were expected to worsen. According to the Vision 2020 document, the percentage of the diabetics was expected to increase to 5 percent by 2020, which would mean 62.5 million patients. It was estimated that of these, 15.6 million would have DR, and 4.7 million would need treatment[13]. AECS felt that to treat diabetes and DR it would have to adopt a highly non standard approach, with high uncertain outcomes.

Glaucoma if left untreated also led to blindness. About four percent of India's population was estimated to have glaucoma[14].

Refraction correction too had become an important area of concern. A survey conducted in Delhi indicated that one percent of children aged 5 to 15 years had VA of less than 6/18 in the better eye[15]. In 2008–09, out of the patients examined in refractive error camps, 29 percent had to be prescribed glasses; in the screening camps organized for school children, the figure was around 6–8 percent; in paediatric camps, this was 1.1 percent[16]. There was increased demand for laser and LASIK surgeries for reducing or eliminating myopia, for DR, Glaucoma and for treating conditions following cataract operations. In 2008–09, out of 309,015 surgeries conducted in all hospitals of AECS, 57,958 were laser procedures for other than refractive errors, and 3,459 were LASIK procedures for refractive corrections (Exhibit 6). Thus, about 20 percent of all surgeries of AECS were laser/ LASIK surgeries. Said Dr. Nam:

Earlier, we used to do about 1000 laser surgeries p.a. for diabetic retinopathy. Now we are doing about 20,000 in Madurai alone, and about 55,000 in all our hospitals. Probably 100,000 surgeries will be needed in our hospitals. We have, in India, about 46 million diabetics, of whom about 5 million or nearly 11 percent will have DR. Of these, 30 percent will also need laser procedures. Thus, laser surgeries are emerging as a very crucial area for us.

The challenge here is to bring down the cost of laser equipment from the present ₹2.5 million to at least about ₹0.8 million. Aurolab is presently working on this.

At present, most of these surgeries are done by specialists. We need to train the ophthalmologist in this procedure. The nature of these surgeries varies considerably from case to case, with many categories of retinopathies. The surgeons need to get acquainted with them.

Expectations from Doctors and Other Staff

Doctors' salaries were becoming highly competitive. But they were also looking for opportunities to establish their own names among peers, and in particular, looking for opportunities to do research, publish papers, to take part in conferences and network among peers. It was thought that such activities would directly increase doctors' competences, and increase the visibility and awareness of the hospitals the doctors belonged to.

Competition

Competition from other hospitals was also increasing sharply. New hospitals were coming up, and they generally looked better than at least the old building of AEH, Madurai. They provided better room and food facilities as compared to AEHs, which were seen as functional, no-frills chain of hospitals. These new hospitals enticed doctors with better pay. One of the doctors the case writer interviewed remarked that many of the doctors in other private chain of eye hospitals located in different cities of Tamil Nadu were ex-AECS personnel[17]. Many of the corporate hospitals too had doctors who had been with AECS earlier. In fact, AECS doctors were always in high demand due to their excellent training, exposure to a wide variety of diseases and good work ethics. But none of the competing hospitals, according to this doctor, offered comparative scope for professional advancement, as did AECS.[18]

Continued Incidence of Blindness in India

Of the total estimated 45 million blind people (VA< 3/60 in the better eye) in the world, 7 million were in India[19]. There were 12 million bilaterally blind persons in India with VA less than 6/60 in the better eye (the definition used in India).

There were about 11,000 eye surgeons in India, or about one surgeon for about 100,000 people. This ratio varied enormously between urban and rural areas: 1:20,000 as against 1:250,000. Even of these, about 50 percent qualified eye surgeons were "non-operating" surgeons, i.e., not doing any surgeries. The quality of the "operating" surgeons varied: many could not perform IOL surgeries. This had an impact on the overall effectiveness of the anti-cataract campaign: a study conducted in 1998 indicated that while nearly 40 percent of patients who had traditional surgery had poor visual outcome, less than 10 percent following IOL surgeries had a poor outcome. Hence, there was an imperative need to train more surgeons in IOL surgery. Paramedics were also in short supply, leading to a situation where surgeons had to perform jobs like refraction testing and pre-operative care.

The Government of India's Vision 2020 envisaged an increase in CSR to 5,000 by 2010; 5,500 by 2015; and 6,000 by 2020, and increase in the proportion of IOL surgery to 100 percent by 2010. It also indicated the further need to train eye surgeons in micro surgery, laser surgery, etc.

Paediatric blindness was also an area that had to be addressed. About 0.8 per 1000 children were estimated to have serious vision problems in India, mostly due to posterior segment problems, ocular trauma and refraction errors. These could be addressed by school eye screening programmes, vitamin A supplementation and improved general nutrition.

Vision 2020 document had outlined several areas of action in prevention, treatment, better techniques, creation of HR and infrastructure, and financial outlays needed. Mr. Thulasiraj was one of the members of the Working Group under the National Programme for Control of Blindness.

Aravind Eye Care System's Responses

AECS had responded to these challenges on a number of fronts such as the following:

Reduced Percentage of Cataract Surgeries and Expansion into Other Areas

Due to its emphasis on undertaking other surgeries besides cataract, the mix of AECS's surgeries had altered. Cataract surgeries had decreased in terms of percentage of all surgeries (though in absolute terms they were still increasing). The laser and LASIK surgeries had increased steeply and now constituted to around 20 percent of AECS's surgeries. They were being performed even in smaller units such as Theni and Tirunelveli. The laser surgery was also expected to gain further importance. The other areas gaining in importance were Trab and combined procedures, retina and vitreous surgeries, lacrimal surgeries, and other orbit and oculoplasty surgeries.

Mr. Thulasiraj, Head, LAICO told the case writer:

> *This shift is an outcome of a strategic decision to focus on sub speciality services as areas of rapid growth while continuing to maintain the leadership in cataract services.*

Reduction in Eye Camps

The number of eye camps conducted by AECS had levelled off and the number of patients seen in these camps was coming down (Exhibit 3). The eye camps were now of four types: the traditional comprehensive eye camps, diabetic retinopathy (DR) screening camps, refraction camps, and school eye screening camps. There was also a new mobile van screening camp, mainly for DR screening.

It was not clear that the need for eye camps by AECS was coming down. Eye camps did provide a quick way to check a relatively large number of people and other hospitals and private surgeons continued to organize eye camps. It was estimated that still only about eight percent of those who needed screening were in fact getting themselves screened.

Establishment of a Network of Vision Centres and Community Eye Clinics

AECS had also established Vision Centres (VC) and Community Eye Clinics (CEC) in rural areas. VCs were small units staffed with an ophthalmic technician and had telemedicine support from the base hospital. It also had an administrative support person. The doctor was in the base hospital but was linked or "on duty" on video with the VC. He or she offered consultation to patients via webcams and computer screens. If needed, the patient would be advised to go to the hospital, with a briefing given by the VC.

Patients were charged ₹20 per consultation, and the charges were collected on the spot at these centres. At the time of writing this case, there were 31 VCs. Each centre served a population of about 50,000. They were all operating from rented buildings.

Dr. Nam told the case writer: "We plan to increase our Vision Centres to about 50. They provide rural patients an easy access to our facility." In response to a question by the case writer, he replied, "Only a few cannot afford even ₹20 that we charge as consultation fees. We treat these patients free." If a patient needing surgery was not able to afford the low subsidized rates, he or she was given free surgery or admitted through an eye camp.

The CECs were larger than VCs, but smaller than the hospitals. Every day a doctor from the nearest base hospital would visit the CEC. All CECs had an optician, a field organizer, an optical shop person and a nurse. They did not have facilities for surgery but could diagnose eye problems and diabetics, and prescribe and deliver spectacles.

There were five CECs; around 60 to 70 patients visited each centre every day and each CEC served a population of about 300,000. The patients were charged ₹20 per consultation.

Exhibit 9 Vision and community eye centres: Patients treated

	Madurai	Tirunelveli	Theni	Coimbatore	Pondicherry	Total
Vision Centres						
Number of centres	8	5	8	4	5	30
Patients treated, new + repeat	36,637	26,192	31,105	13,436	15,828	123,198
Patients per day per vision centre	17	19	16	13	10	15
Community Clinics						
Number of centres	2	1	1	1	-	5
Patients treated, new + repeat	35,165	25,934	13,770	25,380	-	100,249
Patients per day per vision centre	56	83	44	81	-	64

Source: Aravind Eye Care System (2009), Activity Report, 2008-09. Madurai: Aravind Eye Care System, p.14.

Note: The patients treated by AMECS not included in the above.

If a surgery was required, the patient would be sent to the respective main hospital. In 2008–09, 100,249 patients had visited the CECs, and 123,198 the VCs.[20] Exhibit 9 shows the attendance at the VCs and CECs.

AECS was planning to convert some of the CECs to small Surgical Centres (smaller than AEH, Theni) where simple surgeries would be undertaken. The two CECs at Tuticorin and Tirupur were being converted into surgical centres.

Other Outreach Activities

AECS had expanded the scope of its eye screening activities for school children, both in its base hospitals and in VCs. It had screened 210,139 students in the base hospitals and 67,237 in the VCs.[21] It held separate paediatric eye screening camps for children to identify vision problems in infants and babies. It also conducted separate refraction camps and mobile-van screening camps to expand its outreach (Exhibit 10).

Aravind Managed Eye Care Services (AMECS)

Pursuing its mission of eradicating needless blindness, AECS had been engaged, through LAICO, in training doctors in other hospitals to improve their efficiency (refer Case 7). This was, however, a limited activity. It was cautiously venturing into managing other hospitals without owning them. AECS had entered into a partnership with some socially conscious organizations. At the time of writing this case, it was managing four such hospitals: one at Amreli, Gujarat in collaboration with Sun Pharmaceuticals Group; one at Kolkata in collaboration with MP Birla Group; and one each at Amethi and Lucknow, UP in collaboration with the Rajiv Gandhi Charitable Trust. While the Amreli hospital was managed by the AEH, Coimbatore; the rest were managed by AEH, Madurai.

In these hospitals, AECS neither provided any facilities and nor had it made any investments. It sent selected personnel from its respective units to supervise their activities. These employees were from the area where the hospital was located. They were selected by AECS and trained at respective AEH. The managed hospitals retained their own name though they had indicators to show they were being managed by AECS. The top management of AECS was very cautious with their brand equity and was not yet ready to lend its brand to these units.

The experience with these AMECS so far had been mixed. AECS executives attributed the difficulties to the cultural differences between Tamil Nadu and the northern states of the country. Dr. Nam said:

Managing by remote control is always difficult. We still have our doubts regarding transmission of our core values such as compassionate care.

Mr. Thulasiraj added:

Our operations model is heavily dependent on work culture and values. Our systems are built on trust. If the work culture and values are not there this system will not work well.

Dr. Natchiar corroborated:

We shall select future AMECS more carefully. We also have an exit policy.

Exhibit 10 Number of camps conducted and patients screened, 2009

	Madurai	Tirunelveli	Theni	Coimbatore	Pondicherry	AMECS	Total
Regular Comprehensive Eye Camps							
Camp(nos.)	335	264	88	342	248	441	1,718
Patients examined	100,767	45,362	24,049	73,927	55,818	83,686	3,83,609
Glasses advised	18,393	9,116	6,436	12,976	12,327	10,769	70,017
Glasses ordered	15,702	7,316	5,877	10,555	9,662	7,437	56,549
On the spot deliveries	12,264	5,308	4,454	8,852	6,470	333	37,681
Percentage	78%	73%	76%	84%	67%	4%	67%
DR Screening Camps							
Camp(nos.)	40	78	20	135	13	-	286
Patients screened	9,857	13,456	4,449	21,824	2,833	-	52,419
Diabetics identified	4,617	3,946	1,234	4,787	902	-	15,486
DR patients identified	659	590	213	1,110	140	-	2,612
Refractive Error Camps							
Camp(nos.)	30	38	25	58	30	88	269
Patients examined	8,242	7,530	5,805	14,686	8,351	12,280	56,894
Glasses advised	3,113	2,204	1,552	3,339	3,162	3,179	16,549
Glasses ordered	2,745	1,894	1,362	3,003	2,735	2,528	14,267
On the spot deliveries	1,780	1,379	956	2,565	1,785	887	9,352
Percentage	65%	73%	70%	85%	65%	35%	66%
Eye Screening of School Children: Base Hospitals							
School(nos.)	58	29	10	27	36	20	180
Teachers trained	397	232	60	54	135	61	939
Children screened	68,160	38,182	15,831	33,600	46,956	7,410	210,139
Children with eye defects	4,771	2,440	1,329	5,142	33,25	1,094	18,101
Eye Screening of School Children: Vision Centres							
Schools(nos.)	13	2	160	3	-	-	178
Teachers trained	49	8	0	6	-	-	63
Children screened	11,275	2,650	50,962	2,350	-	-	67,237
Children with eye defects	603	148	3,034	147	-	-	3,932
Paediatric Camps							
# Camp(nos.)	4	3	0	3	2	-	12
Children examined	1,311	334	0	260	498	-	2,403
Refractive error	179	35	0	27	47	-	288
Glasses prescribed	130	26	0	5	41	-	202

	Madurai	Tirunelveli	Theni	Coimbatore	Pondicherry	AMECS	Total
Glasses ordered	117	20	0	0	33	-	170
Other defects identified	70	21	0	24	51	-	166
Mobile Van DR Screening Camps							
Camp(nos.)	0	12	1	29	-	-	42
Patients screened	0	1985	355	5057	-	-	7,397
Diabetics identified	0	837	108	1332	-	-	2,277
DR patients identified	0	198	6	302	-	-	506

Source: Aravind Eye Care System (2009), Activity Report, 2008-09. Madurai: Aravind Eye Care System, p.14.

The agreement was usually for five years and it was understood that during this period AECS would gradually reduce its staff at these hospitals. The agreement's exit policy allowed AECS to review the agreement periodically. Essentially this step was seen as a means to expand quickly without too much upfront investment.

Upgrading of Facilities

AECS had started upgrading its facilities. Dr. Natchiar told the case writer:

Patient expectations are going up. Patients do not want common rooms; there is a growing demand for more and better private rooms.

Hence it constructed a whole new block at AEH, Madurai without significantly adding to the overall number of beds. As already stated, the floor mats for free patients had been replaced with cots. There were also improvements on the look and feel of the hospitals, and the patient rooms.

However, AECS still wanted to be seen as a hospital affordable for all classes of patients, be they poor or rich. Said Dr. Kim, Head, Retina-Vitreous Clinic:

We have an image of a common man's hospital that caters to the poor sections of the society. We want it to continue. We continue to ask for every new project, how does this project benefit the patient? We always try to see it from the patients' point of view and not just how it benefits the institution. This is a strong underlying motivator.

He added:

We need to keep OP attractive. Ours is a surgery oriented organization. But we need to keep charges affordable. Otherwise patients could get overawed.

AECS had always designed its services around patients. To further enhance its patient-centred care, it was endeavouring to make the patient an active partner—one who would understand his/her condition better, adhere to the treatment decided upon, and also motivate his community to access eye care. To do this, AECS' Centre for Patient Empowerment intended to improve eye care awareness in the community and also find ways to enhance patient experience within the service delivery system.

Emphasis on Research

Research had always been an important activity at AECS. It served to maintain a strong knowledge base that translated into better and more efficient medical care. For example, a number of research projects were connected with diabetes and its impact on blindness, and these projects could lead to better ways to control DR. Research on transplantation of cells had led to better means of tissue reconstruction, as for example, with corneal tissue. With increased categories of surgeries and number of non cataract surgeries, this research was expected to give AECS an edge over its competitors.

Research was also a means for giving opportunities to doctors for self development. The doctors could take any one day per week off from their work in pursuit of research. This gave doctors an opportunity to attend international conferences and gain peer recognition. Dr. Nam observed: "This is also a retention strategy." Research was also a source of funds: about ₹15 million was received as research grants during 2008-09. Exhibit 11 gives details of ongoing sponsored research projects at Aravind Medical Research Foundation.

To pursue a comprehensive research programme on eye care, AECS had built a brand new research facility, Dr. G. Venkataswamy Eye Research Institute, in the memory of its founder, at a cost of ₹290 million. It was inaugurated on October 1, 2008 by Dr. A.P.J. Abdul Kalam,

Exhibit 11 Sponsored research projects at Aravind Medical Research Foundation, 2009

S.No	Name of the study	Investigator	Duration	Funded by
1	Studies on the proangiogenic and vascular growth factors in relation to the pathogenesis of Eales' disease and Diabetic Retinopathy	Dr.V.R.Muthukkaruppan Dr.P.Namperumalsamy Dr.Dhananjay Shukla Dr.R.Anand Rajendran	2005–2009	Department of Science and Technology
2	Corneal surface reconstruction using bio-engineered autologous oral mucosal epithelium	Dr.V.R.Muthukkaruppan Dr.N.V.Prajna Dr.Usha Kim Dr.M.Srinivasan	2006–2009	Defence Research & Development Organization
3	Identification of Genetic defects occuring in Indian Oculocutaneous (OCA) and Ocular Albinism (OA) families	Dr.P.Sundaresan Dr.P.Vijayalakshmi Dr.Asim Kumar Sil	2006–2009	Department of Biotechnology
4	Genetic and functional analysis of Fuch's Endothelial Corneal Dystrophy (FECD) and Congenital Hereditary Endothelial Dystrophy (CHED) in Indian patients	Dr.P.Sundaresan Dr.M.Srinivasan Dr.Arunkumar	2007–2010	Department of Science and Technology
5	Pathogen host interaction in human mycotic keratitis	Dr.N.V.Prajna Dr.K.Dharmalingam Dr.Lalitha Prajna	2007–2010	Department of Biotechnology
6	Standardization and application of Multiplex PCR in the detection of infectious agents in the intraocular fluid of patients with retinochoroiditis	Dr.Lalitha Prajna Dr.S.R.Rathinam Dr.Kim	2007–2010	Indian council of Medical Research
7	TIFACCORE in Diabetic retinopathy	Dr.Kim Dr.V.R.Muthukkaruppan Dr.P.Sundaresan	2007–2008	TIFACCORE
8	Genetic and functional dissection of FOXL2 gene involved in the pathogenesis of the blepharomosis syndrome (BPES)	Dr.P.Sundaresan Dr.Usha Kim Dr.Reiner Veitia	2008–2010	ICMR-INSERM
9	A Genetic component to the INDEYE study of cataract and age related macular degeneration in India	Dr.P.Sundaresan Dr.Dorothea Nitsch Dr.Liam Smeeth Dr.Astrid Fletcher	2008–2010	Wellcome trust
10	Molecular genetics on keratoconous	Dr.P.Sundaresan Dr.M.Srinivasan Dr.N.V.Prajna	2008–2011	ALCON Anterior Segment
11	Screening of LOXL1 gene mutations in exfoliation glaucoma patients	Dr.P.Sundaresan Dr.S.R.Krishnadas Dr.G.Haripriya Dr.George V. Puthuran	2008–2011	ALCON Anterior Segment
12	Elucidating the virulence genes involved in the pathogenesis of corneal ulcers by Aspergillus sps and the study of host response via the expression of Toll-like receptors	Dr.Lalitha Dr.N.Venkatesh Prajna Prof.K.Dharmalingam	2008–2011	ALCON Anterior Segment
13	Molecular insights into the etiology of infectious uveitis	Dr.Lalitha Prajna Dr.S.R.Rathinam	2008–2011	DBT
14	Antigenic Mimicry between Leptospiral and Human Lens proteins	Dr.Gowri Priya Dr.S.R.Rathinam Dr.VR.Muthukkaruppan	2008–2011	ALCON Anterior Segment

S.No	Name of the study	Investigator	Duration	Funded by
15	Cytokine profile in Aqueous humor of Trematode-induced Granuloma	Dr.Gowri Priya Dr.S.R.Rathinam Dr.V.R.Muthukkaruppan	2008–2011	ALCON Anterior Segment
16	Developing Xenobiotic—free culture conditions to generate stem cell rich epithelium for corneal surface reconstruction	Dr.Gowri Priya Dr.V.R.Muthukkaruppan Dr.N.V.Prajna	2008–2011	ALCON Anterior Segment
17	Factors responsible for the generation of epithelial sheet rich in stem cells under exvivo conditions from the limbal and buccal biopsy	Dr.Gowri Priya Dr.N.V.Prajna Dr.Usha Kim	2008–2009	Champalimaud Grant
18	Evaluation of a suitable invitro model for diabetic retinopathy	Dr.S.Senthilkumari	2008–2009	Champalimaud grant
19	Transcriptome and proteome analyses of ALR2 and its involvement in the pathogenesis of diabetic retinopathy	Dr.P.Sundaresan	2009–2012	Department of Biotechnology

the former President of India. It had immunology, molecular genetics, genetic susceptibility, stem cell biology, proteomics, and translational research as thrust areas. It was recognized as a centre of National Retinoblastoma Registry by the Indian Council of Medical Research and a centre for Diabetic Retinopathy by TIFAC-CORE, Department of Science and Technology, Government of India.

Exhibit 12 Articles published by AECS' staff in international and national peer reviewed journals, 2004–08

Aravind Eye Care System	
Year	**No of Publications**
2004	46
2005	49
2006	70
2007	65
2008	73
Total	303

Note: This includes the papers shown in Exhibit 13.

Breakup of the Above in Terms of Staff from Different Units of AECS

AEHs (5 hospitals)	238
LAICO	31
Dr. G.V.Eye Research Foundation (Research articles)	34[1]
	303

Source: Data supplied by AECS.

Its scholars and students attended and presented a number of papers at international conferences and published papers in peer reviewed journals (See Exhibit 12 for details). They also had to their credit a number of publications in journals (See Exhibit 13 for details). As on 2009, it had 25 research scholars working on different projects under the guidance of AECS doctors. Many research scholars from different countries regularly visited this institute to enhance their understanding of certain types of eye diseases, especially in the tropical conditions. They also used AECS' formidable data bank developed from different projects. During his visit, the case writer met three foreign scholars who were pursuing their research there.

Exhibit 13 Number of published research articles by staff of Dr. G.V. Eye research foundation, 2004–08

2004	:	4
2005	:	2
2006	:	8
2007	:	8
2008	:	12
Total	:	34

Issues in Future Directions

AECS had always produced a healthy financial surplus, and funds had never been a problem. Exhibit 14 shows that AECS had produced a surplus continuously for the last ten years (it produced surpluses even in the earlier years). Exhibit 15 gives the Income and Expenditure Statements of AECS for the year 2008–09. So, though finance was not a serious issue, there were other issues which AECS needed to look into and determine its future direction.

Exhibit 14 Income and expenditure, 1997–98 to 2008–09

(₹ million)

Year	Income	Expenditure	Surplus
1997–98	180.30	81.70	98.60
1998–99	239.50	123.20	116.30
1999–2000	276.30	143.20	133.10
2000–2001	340.40	156.60	183.80
2001–2002	388.00	177.50	210.50
2002–2003	423.70	204.70	219.00
2003–2004	454.30	259.20	195.10
2004–2005	511.40	284.70	226.70
2005–2006	661.30	323.50	337.80
2006–2007	750.10	429.30	320.80
2007–2008	800.50	474.90	325.60
2008 - 2009	1,161.60	594.50	567.10

Source: Data provided by AECS.

Exhibit 15 Income and expenditure statements, 2008–09

(₹ million)

Income statement, 2008–2009

Particulars	Amount
Medical service	63.50
Operation charges	605.30
Treatment charges	65.80
Consulting fees	48.30
X Ray & laboratory charges	16.10
Tuition fees and course fees	21.80
Grants in aid	75.50
Donation	9.70
Interest received	179.80
Dividends received	0.50
Miscellaneous income	0.60
Vision Centre income	2.40
Research study and consultancy	15.50
Sale of applications	0.40
Sale of Ophthalmic books	1.30
Building amenities	4.60
Royalty	3.40
Award	42.80
Profit on sale of assets	1.00
Mess revenue	3.30
Agriculture income	0.01
Total	1,161.61

Expenditure statement, 2008–2009

Particulars	Amount
Staff salary	133.90
IOL cost	112.00
Medicines	95.80
Electricity	33.00
Hospital linen	2.00
Camp expenses	11.60
Interest expenses	0.01
Library books	0.20
Water supply	3.10
Depreciation	55.60
Miscellaneous expenses	1.50
Drs. consultancy charges	48.20
Contribution to RAI Eye Hospital	1.50
Project expenses	6.20
Instrument equipment maintenance	20.60
Building repairs	11.50
Electrical Item	11.60
Vehicle maintenance	2.90
General maintenance	0.90
Cleaning and sanitation	7.00
Printing and stationary	7.00
Postage and telegram	4.50

Security charges	2.70
Travel	6.20
X ray and photography	0.40
Hospital expenses	1.40
Building rent	0.10
Subscription	0.80
Academic expenses	0.40
Advertisement	0.30
Donation paid	10.80
Tax and legal fees	0.60
Audit fees	0.20
Total	594.51
Excess of income over expenditure	567.10

Source: Data supplied by AECS.

To get different perspectives on AECS' future direction the case writer interviewed a number of its key personnel. These views have been grouped by the case writer under some broad categories and are presented below:

The Basic Vision for AECS

Though there was complete agreement on AECS' basic mission of eradicating needless blindness, there were differences on where they should focus. Dr. Nam felt:

Our emphasis is to be at par with the best eye hospitals in the world without diluting our vision… We see our activities in four broad areas: paediatric eye care, cataract, retinopathy, glaucoma, and refraction.

Dr. S. Aravind, a senior doctor, who was also the administrator of the hospital, said:

We are looking at how our vision is to be attained… I sometimes wonder whether our mindset has become incremental. Earlier, we had a lot of constraints, and we learnt to work within constraints. Now we have resources, and many options are available.

According to Dr. Kim:

We are a highly mission driven set of people. Resources are not the only consideration in deciding the direction of growth.

Growth: Directions

There were a number of directions that AECS could take; the real problem was one of prioritization.

Dr. Nam said:

Diabetes is a challenge. We have 46 million diabetics in India. To reach them, innovative methods are needed; for example, greater use of paramedics in the campaign against diabetes. We need to create awareness among patients and even among doctors on this issue, because blindness from diabetes is fully preventable, though diabetes itself is not. DR follow up systems need to be initiated.

In another ten years, cataract prevention and taking care will become equal in importance.[22] *Glaucoma, macular degeneration with age, etc. will also become important. We need to move in multiple directions.*

We have set up the Vision Centres. We have 31 of them: we plan to go up to 50. We are also developing Community Centres. Is this the way to go? This is an extremely decentralized model. There are serious control issues.

Refraction is another major area. Laser surgeries are gaining ground fast. Probably 100,000 laser surgeries per year are needed. How do we tie this up with spread in education? We are now training teachers to identify children who need eye testing and correction, and we have devised a rough and ready system to identify defective vision.[23] *We have devised a half day training module and we are training teachers. We are also involving voluntary organizations in this exercise.*

Mr. Thulasiraj said:

We have a tremendous opportunity in the treatment of refractive errors. These services are characterized by non availability especially in rural areas; they are concentrated in urban areas. We can set up a network of Refraction Centres.

He also saw big opportunities in training:

We have tremendous opportunities in LAICO. We are now working with voluntary sector and have done a lot of work. We are looking at working with private and government doctors. We are into quite interesting activities. For example, we offer a range of IT products, like online patient care management.

We shall have a Projects Division to manage research projects.

According to Dr. Aravind:

Resources are not a problem. The challenge today is our aspiration, not our resources. How do you retain the same hunger and the same passion? Earlier, if we failed, the price was small. Now the stakes are higher. There is a tendency to play safe.

Concurred Mr. Thulasiraj on some of the above points:

Resources are not a problem. Financially, all our hospitals are viable. We can bankroll new hospitals every year. We can thus grow rapidly if we adopt a pure hospital growth format.

We have to address mindset issues. We are diffident about moving out of our comfort zone. We have been essentially in Tamil Nadu and we have limited, very limited experience outside Tamil Nadu. But we have before us national and global opportunities.

Geographic Expansion

There were different views on whether and how to grow beyond Tamil Nadu. Dr. Nam felt:

Expansion to other Indian states is an issue. Culture is an important issue for us. Culture in North India is quite different. Managing by remote control is difficult. We want to protect our own distinctive culture.

We still have our doubts on the feasibility of transmission of values like compassionate care. So our involvement with AMECs is really an experiment. We think it will take enormous efforts to expand these.

Concurred Dr. Kim:

Yes. We need to be very careful about the cultural aspect. Should we move into states like Bihar?

Business models should not obscure our hospital's growth model. These are different definitions and paths to growth.

Mr. Thulasiraj added:

Our operational model itself is heavily dependent on our work culture and values. Our systems have an underlying foundation of value systems. They are based on trust. If this work culture and values are not there, this system will not work. So this could pose problems for growth.

AECS executives saw opportunities to expand globally in certain activities. According to Dr. Nam:

DR (Diabetes Retinopathy) can be studied adopting a global approach. We need more research, and develop more knowledge. Hence our research centre has to become important.

Dr. Kim added:

We are moving more into research, especially in specialties. We have to give new services that are currently not available but necessary for eye care to stay ahead of competition.

Mr. Thulasiraj said:

We have a global opportunity. There are 135 countries in the world with a population of less than 20 million each. They cannot develop their own specialty competencies. We are, on the other hand, developing more specialties. We can thus give our knowledge and offer our services to many of these countries. We can even expand our manufacturing to make them offshore. So many innovations are possible.

HR Issues

Another major challenge was developing a large cadre of competent doctors, nurses and paramedics, especially because they also had to be imbibed with the right values. Dr. Nam summarized these challenges:

Now many non cataract operations, as for example, the DR operations, are done by specialists. We need to train more ophthalmologists in these surgical procedures.

Knowledge management is important. We are doing this through our Virtual Academy. We have SAT connectivity with all hospitals, and we organize lectures every day and share our experiences over the entire AECS system. But we should be able to talk to other ophthalmologists also across the country.

Dr. Natchiar explained:

We concentrate on empowering people in existing facilities, and recruit new people in new facilities. But our policy of sending core people from older units will continue.

Dr. Kim added:

We have developed a good training programme for our own staff. In fact our personnel are in great demand and are well regarded. We do Mid Level Ophthalmic Personnel (MLOP) training for other hospitals. This is becoming an important activity.

Dr. Aravind saw an issue in getting the next generation ready. He said:

The older generation is now in the sixties. And except for a few, the younger generation is in the forties. There could be a situation when the younger generation would have to take over responsibilities before they are fully ready.

Mr. Thulasiraj added:

LAICO is developing a cadre of managers for AECS. For example, those with a Masters in Hospital Management, we give one year training in our Fellow Programme in Management. After one year, they are absorbed as managers.

The case writer found it remarkably interesting that with such a high degree of convergence across its executives regarding its basic mission, there could still be such widely different perspectives regarding how this should be achieved.

NOTES

1. Prahalad, C.K. (2004), *The Fortune at the Bottom of the Pyramid: Eradicating Poverty through Profits*. New Jersey: Wharton Publishing.
2. Manikutty, S. and Vohra, N. (2004), "Aravind Eye Care System: Giving the Most Precious Gift". Case material, Indian Institute of Management, Ahmedabad, Case # BP0299.
3. Aravind Eye Care System (2001). "Promises to Keep." Madurai: Aravind Eye Care System.
4. *Op. Cit.*, Case BP0299.
5. Actually, per half day, from 7 a.m. to 1 p.m. No operations were conducted in the afternoons.
6. For eye camp patients brought to the hospitals, the treatment was fully free, but the Government gave a certain grant (₹500 per patient in 2003; ₹750 now), but in large number of cases the process and paperwork needed to avail this grant posed a major hurdle. For the walk-in free patients, there was a nominal charge of ₹500 per patient in 2003 (now ₹750).
7. All figures from data given by AECS. See also the earlier case on Aravind Eye Care System, BP0299, Exhibit 5.
8. AECS was wholly owned and operated by a non profit organization, Govel Trust. Hence the surplus could go only to fund AECS's activities.
9. For details of how these eye camps were operated, see the case BP 0299, pp.10–12.
10. Case BP0299, p.5.
11. Latest data not available.
12. For details, see case BP 0299, pp.8–9.
13. *National Programme for Control of Blindness-India: Vision 2020 Plan of Action*. (2003). New Delhi: Ophthalmology/Blindness Control Section, Directorate General of Health Services, Ministry of Health and Family Welfare, Government of India, p.1. This document is hereafter referred to as the Vision 2020 Document.
14. Ibid. p.1.
15. Ibid., p.1.
16. Compiled from Aravind's Activity Report, 2008-09, p.14.
17. Interview with Dr. Kim, Head, Retina-Vitreous Clinic.
18. Interview with Dr. Kim.
19. Vision 2020 document, p.1.
20. Aravind Eye Care System (2009), Activity Report 2008-09, p.11.
21. Ibid.
22. Though at present cataract was not preventable, a lot of research was going on in this area and a breakthrough on how to prevent cataract was highly likely.
23. AECS had devised a "string and board" system by which a patient could sit at a fixed distance from a board with letters of different size written on it.

CASE 13

Wal-Mart Stores, Inc. (WMT)

Francine Barley, David Bragg, Misty Dawson, Hammad Shah, Brian Sillanpaa, Nathan Sleeper Dominik Steinkuler, Lutz Kaufmann, Daniel Schmidt
Arizona State University

Lee Scott ignored his fear of public speaking as he prepared to step in front of 20,000 people at the Bud Walton Arena in Fayetteville, Arkansas, on June 1, 2007.[1] For his seventh year as Wal-Mart CEO, Scott addressed his company's shareholders at its annual meeting.

Outside the building, the local "Against the Wal" protesters were back for the fourth year in a row, clutching a list of seven demands: "living wage," "affordable health care," "end discrimination," "zero tolerance on child labor," "respect communities," "respect the environment," and "stop union busting."[2]

Inside the arena, shareholders had their own concerns, with declining share prices and 11 shareholder proposals—all opposed by the company.[3] Since Scott became CEO in 2000, Wal-Mart's stock price has dipped about 27 percent, from \$64.50 to the \$47 range.[4]

In the same timeframe, competitor Costco's stock price has appreciated roughly 20 percent, and Target's has climbed more than 70 percent[5] (see Exhibit 1). Analysts

Exhibit 1 Changes in stock price: Wal-Mart, Target, and Costco, January 3, 2000, through May 14, 2007

Source: 2007, *Yahoo! Finance*, http://finance.yahoo.com/charts#chart6:symbol=wmt;range=20000103,20070518;compare=cost+tgt;indicator=volume;charttype= line;crosshair=on;logscale=on;source=undefined, May 17.

Exhibit 2 Wal-Mart retail units and sales, 1997–2007

	2007	2006	2005	2004	2003	2002	2001	2000	1999	1998	1997
Number of retail units											
Wal-Mart Stores	1,074	1,209	1,353	1,478	1,568	1,647	1,736	1,801	1,869	1,921	1,960
Supercenters	2,257	1,980	1,713	1,471	1,258	1,066	888	721	564	441	344
Neighborhood Markets	112	100	85	64	49	31	19	7	4	0	0
SAM'S Clubs	579	567	551	538	525	500	475	463	451	443	436
US Stores Total	4,022	3,856	3,702	3,551	3,400	3,244	3,118	2,992	2,888	2,805	2,740
International Stores	2,760	2,181	1,480	1,248	1,163	1,050	955	892	605	568	314
Total Stores	6,782	6,037	5,182	4,799	4,563	4,294	4,073	3,884	3,493	3,373	3,054
Percentage of total retail units											
Wal-Mart Stores	26.7%	31.4%	36.5%	41.6%	46.1%	50.8%	55.7%	60.2%	64.7%	68.5%	71.5%
Supercenters	56.1%	51.3%	46.3%	41.4%	37.0%	32.9%	28.5%	24.1%	19.5%	15.7%	12.6%
Neighborhood Markets	2.8%	2.6%	2.3%	1.8%	1.4%	1.0%	0.6%	0.2%	0.1%	0.0%	0.0%
SAM'S Clubs	14.4%	14.7%	14.9%	15.2%	15.4%	15.4%	15.2%	15.5%	15.6%	15.8%	15.9%
International	40.7%	36.1%	28.6%	26.0%	25.5%	24.5%	23.4%	23.0%	17.3%	16.8%	10.3%
Sales by segment											
Wal-Mart	$226,294	$209,910	$191,826	$174,220	$157,120	$139,131	$121,889	$108,721	$95,395	$83,820	$74,840
SAM'S Clubs	$41,582	$39,798	$37,119	$34,537	$31,702	$29,395	$26,798	$24,801	$22,881	$20,668	$19,785
International	$77,116	$59,237	$52,543	$47,572	$40,794	$35,485	$32,100	$22,728	$12,247	$7,517	$5,002
Total	$344,992	$308,945	$281,488	$256,329	$229,616	$204,011	$180,787	$156,250	$130,523	$112,005	$99,627
Percentage of sales by segment											
Wal-Mart	65.6%	67.9%	68.1%	68.0%	68.4%	68.2%	67.4%	69.6%	73.1%	74.8%	75.1%
SAM'S Clubs	12.1%	12.9%	13.2%	13.5%	13.8%	14.4%	14.8%	15.9%	17.5%	18.5%	19.9%
International	22.4%	19.2%	18.7%	18.6%	17.8%	17.4%	17.8%	14.5%	9.4%	6.7%	5.0%
Percentage of sales											
Domestic	77.6%	80.8%	81.3%	81.4%	82.2%	82.6%	82.2%	85.5%	90.6%	93.3%	95.0%
International	22.4%	19.2%	18.7%	18.6%	17.8%	17.4%	17.8%	14.5%	9.4%	6.7%	5.0%
Percentage change in sales											
Domestic	7.3%	9.1%	9.7%	10.6%	12.0%	13.3%	11.4%	12.9%	13.2%	10.4%	2.0%
International	30.2%	12.7%	10.4%	16.6%	15.0%	10.5%	41.2%	85.6%	62.9%	50.3%	25.9%
Percentage sales change											
Domestic	50.4%	75.6%	80.2%	74.6%	79.3%	85.4%	61.8%	59.3%	74.5%	79.7%	
International	49.6%	24.4%	19.8%	25.4%	20.7%	14.6%	38.2%	40.7%	25.5%	20.3%	

Source: 2007, 2002, Wal-Mart Annual Reports.

Exhibit 3 Wal-Mart income, 1997–2007

	Income Statement (figures in $millions; fiscal year ends 1/31)										
	2007	**2006**	**2005**	**2004**	**2003**	**2002**	**2001**	**2000**	**1999**	**1998**	**1997**
Total Operating Revenue	$348,650	$312,101	$284,310	$252,791	$226,479	$201,166	$178,028	$153,345	$129,161	$112,005	$99,627
Cost of Sales	$264,152	$237,649	$216,832	$195,922	$175,769	$156,807	$138,438	$119,526	$101,456	$88,163	$78,897
Gross Operating Profit	**$84,498**	**$74,452**	**$67,478**	**$56,869**	**$50,710**	**$44,359**	**$39,590**	**$33,819**	**$27,705**	**$23,842**	**$20,730**
Gross Margins	24.2%	23.9%	23.7%	22.5%	22.4%	22.1%	22.2%	22.1%	21.4%	21.3%	20.8%
Operating, Selling, G&A Exp.	$64,001	$55,739	$50,178	$43,877	$39,178	$34,275	$29,942	$25,182	$21,469	$18,831	$16,437
Operating Income	**$20,497**	**$18,713**	**$17,300**	**$12,992**	**$11,532**	**$10,084**	**$9,648**	**$8,637**	**$6,236**	**$5,011**	**$4,293**
Net Interest Expense	$1,529	$1,178	$980	$825	$930	$1,183	$1,194	$837	$595	$716	$807
Income Before Taxes	$18,968	$17,535	$16,320	$12,167	$10,602	$8,901	$8,454	$7,800	$5,641	$4,295	$3,486
Taxes	$6,365	$5,803	$5,589	$3,071	$2,662	$2,183	$2,008	$2,218	$1,432	$871	$508
Effective Tax Rate	33.6%	$33.1%	34.2%	25.2%	25.1%	24.5%	23.8%	28.4%	25.4%	20.3%	14.6%
Net Income from Opera-	$12,603	$11,732	$10,731	$9,096	$7,940	$6,718	$6,446	$5,582	$4,209	$3,424	$2,978
Other Items	$(894)	$(177)	$(215)	$(42)	$15	$(126)	$(211)	$(258)	$188	$80	$64
Net Income	$11,709	$11,555	$10,516	$9,054	$7,955	$6,592	$6,235	$5,324	$4,397	$3,504	$3,042
Shareholder Income											
EPS (diluted) ($dollars)	$2.71	$2.68	$2.41	$2.07	$1.79	$1.50	$1.44	$1.25	$0.94	$0.76	$0.65
Dividend ($dollars)	$0.67	$0.60	$0.52	$0.36	$0.30	$0.28	$0.24	$0.20	$0.16	$0.14	$0.11

Source: 2007, 2002, Wal-Mart Annual Reports.

are saying Wal-Mart's "glory days are over" and its stock is "dead money."[6] Some observers are speculating that Scott's days as CEO may be numbered if he is unable to get the company back on track soon.

It is a big company to change. From its humble origins 45 years ago as a single shop in the Ozarks, Wal-Mart has grown to 1.8 million employees supporting more than 6,700 stores in 14 countries, serving 175 million customers per week and pulling in an average of $6.6 billion in weekly sales.[7] Over the past decade, Wal-Mart doubled its store count, tripled its revenue, and nearly quadrupled its net income[8] (see Exhibits 2 and 3). Wal-Mart earned more in its first quarter of fiscal 2007 ($78.8 billion) than Target made all year ($59.5 billion).[9] Wal-Mart's revenue gave it the No. 1 spot on *Fortune's* April 2007 list of America's largest corporations.[10] By contrast, its profit as a percentage of revenue came in at 3.2 percent, and its total return to investors was 0.1 percent, earning Wal-Mart sub-par ranks by those measures (no. 354 and no. 355, respectively).[11]

Over the past several years, Wal-Mart has stumbled upon a variety of compounding difficulties. Opposition has been mounting against not only Wal-Mart's practices, but also its very presence, due to multiple relationship issues with employees, communities, and governments.[12] It is increasingly challenging for the company to expand at its current rate, both in the United States and abroad. Meanwhile, key competitors have been "growing two to five times faster than Wal-Mart" in same-store sales.[13]

As a result, the company has gradually been losing some of its luster, even in the eyes of its former admirers. In 2004, Wal-Mart had been number one on *Fortune* magazine's list of "America's Most Admired Companies" for the second year running, notwithstanding "a year of bad press and lagging stock price."[14] In 2007, by contrast, Wal-Mart was tied for number 19, behind Costco (no. 18) and Target (no. 13).[15]

What had worked in the past was no longer sustainable in the current competitive environment. Scott wondered whether the change efforts he had started over the past few years would begin to have a positive effect or whether he should somehow adjust Wal-Mart's course.

COMPANY HISTORY

Origins

Before founding Wal-Mart, Sam Walton accumulated experience in variety store retailing as a JCPenney management trainee and a franchisee of Ben Franklin stores.[16] Anticipating discount market growth, Walton opened his first Wal-Mart store in Rogers, Arkansas, in 1962, the same year Kmart and Target were founded.[17] Wal-Mart opened 24 more stores by 1967.[18] This start was slow compared with Kmart, which had already opened 162 stores by 1966.[19] Wal-Mart went public in 1970, giving it access to the financial resources needed to begin a decades-long expansion campaign that led to the opening of 3,800 stores by 2005.[20] Wal-Mart opened its first Sam's Club warehouse in 1983 and its first international store in 1991, and the company's national and international multiplatform expansion continues[21] (see Exhibit 4).

Recent History

Wal-Mart's growth soared in recent years, with the company adding nearly one new store every day (since 2006).[22] The company's rapid expansion brought its total retail store presence to 6,782 units worldwide as of February 8, 2007.[23] Wal-Mart spread with a missionary zeal, to "save people money so they can live better."[24] As Wal-Mart's presence continued to grow, so did its sales, to a record $345 billion in the fiscal year ended January 31, 2007 (hereafter referred to as 2007).

The company's massive growth brought with it massive controversies, however. Wal-Mart faced multiple accusations, charges, and lawsuits, many resulting in fines, including environmental violations, child labor law violations, use of illegal immigrants by subcontractors, and allegedly poor working conditions for associates.[25] Side effects of these issues include communities rejecting expansion of Wal-Mart stores into their neighborhoods.[26] Anti-Wal-Mart press is also on the rise, with books such as *How Wal-Mart Is Destroying America and the World: And What You Can Do About It* by Bill Quinn, and Robert Greenwald's film, *Wal-Mart: The High Cost of Low Price.* By one estimate, Wal-Mart's reputation issues have cost it $16 billion in market capitalization and an unknown amount of lost business in each store category or business segment.[27]

Business Segments

Wal-Mart's three business segments are Wal-Mart Stores, Sam's Club, and Wal-Mart International.[28] The Wal-Mart Stores segment includes walmart.com and three retail store formats in all 50 of the United States, including 2,257 Supercenters, 1,074 Discount Stores, and 112 Neighborhood Markets.[29] The Neighborhood Markets

Exhibit 4 Wal-Mart key events, 1962–2004

1960s	
1962:	Company founded with opening of first Wal-Mart in Rogers, Arkansas.
1967:	Wal-Mart's 24 stores total $12.6 million in sales.
1968:	Wal-Mart moves outside Arkansas with stores in Missouri and Oklahoma.
1969:	Company incorporated as Wal-Mart Stores, Inc., on October 31.
1970s	
1970:	Wal-Mart opens first distribution center and home office in Bentonville, Arkansas. Wal-Mart stock first traded over the counter as a publicly held company. 38 stores now in operation with sales at $44.2 million. Total number of associates is 1,500.
1971:	Wal-Mart is now in five states: Arkansas, Kansas, Louisiana, Missouri, and Oklahoma.
1972:	Wal-Mart approved and listed on the New York Stock Exchange.
1973:	Wal-Mart enters Tennessee.
1974:	Wal-Mart stores now in Kentucky and Mississippi.
1975:	125 stores in operation with sales of $340.3 million and 7,500 associates. Wal-Mart enters ninth state: Texas.
1977:	Wal-Mart enters its 10th state: Illinois.
1979:	Wal-Mart is the first company to reach $1 billion in sales in such a short period of time: $1.248 billion. Wal-Mart now has 276 stores, 21,000 associates and is in its 11th state: Alabama.
1980s	
1981:	Wal-Mart enters Georgia and South Carolina.
1982:	Wal-Mart enters Florida and Nebraska.
1983:	First Sam's Club opened in April in Midwest City, Oklahoma. Wal-Mart enters Indiana, Iowa, New Mexico, and North Carolina. For eighth year straight Forbes magazine ranks Wal-Mart No. 1 among general retailers.
1984:	Wal-Mart enters Virginia.
1985:	Wal-Mart has 882 stores with sales of $8.4 billion and 104,000 associates. Company adds stores in Wisconsin and Colorado.
1986:	Wal-Mart enters Minnesota.
1987:	Wal-Mart's 25th anniversary: 1,198 stores with sales of $15.9 billion and 200,000 associates.
1988:	First Supercenter opened in Washington, Missouri.
1989:	Wal-Mart is now in 26 states with the addition of Michigan, West Virginia, and Wyoming.
1990s	
1990:	Wal-Mart enters California, Nevada, North Dakota, Pennsylvania, South Dakota, and Utah.
1991:	Wal-Mart enters Connecticut, Delaware, Maine, Maryland, Massachusetts, New Hampshire, New Jersey, and New York. International market entered for first time with the opening of two units in Mexico City. Wal-Mart has entered 45 states with the addition of Idaho, Montana, and Oregon. Wal-Mart enters Puerto Rico.
1993:	Wal-Mart enters Alaska, Hawaii, Rhode Island, and Washington.
1994:	Three value clubs open in Hong Kong. Canada has 123 stores and Mexico has 96.
1995:	Wal-Mart Stores, Inc., has 1,995 Wal-Mart stores, 239 Supercenters, 433 Sam's Clubs, and 276 International stores with sales at $93.6 billion and 675,000 associates. Wal-Mart enters its 50th state, Vermont, and builds three units in Argentina and five in Brazil.
1996:	Wal-Mart enters China through a joint-venture agreement.
1997:	Wal-Mart replaces Woolworth on the Dow Jones Industrial Average.
1998:	Wal-Mart enters Korea through a joint venture agreement.
1999:	Wal-Mart has 1,140,000 associates, making the company the largest private employer in the world.
2000s	
2000:	Wal-Mart ranked 5th by Fortune magazine in its Global Most Admired All-Stars list.
2001:	Wal-Mart named by Fortune magazine as the third most admired company in America.
2002:	Wal-Mart ranked #1 on the Fortune 500 listing.
2002:	Wal-Mart has the biggest single day sales in history: $1.43 billion on the day after Thanksgiving.
2003:	Wal-Mart named by Fortune magazine as the most admired company in America.
2004:	Fortune magazine placed Wal-Mart in the top spot on its "Most Admired Companies" list for the second year in a row.

Source: 2007, The Wal-Mart Timeline, Wal-Mart Facts, http://www.walmartfacts.com/content/default.aspx?id=3, April 1.

have the smallest format, with an average size of 42,000 square feet, and a primary focus on grocery products.[30] Wal-Mart's Discount Stores "offer a wide assortment of general merchandise and a limited variety of food products" within 107,000 square feet of selling space.[31] Supercenters average 187,000 square feet and add a full line of food products to Discount Stores' typical selection.[32] Wal-Mart converted 147 Discount Stores into Supercenters in 2007.[33] Overall, Wal-Mart Stores opened 303 new units in 2007 (276 Supercenters, 15 Discount Stores, and 12 Neighborhood Markets).[34]

Membership-based Sam's Club operates in a retail warehouse format, as well as online at samsclub.com. The segment's 579 clubs average 132,000 square feet, and provide "exceptional value on brand-name merchandise at 'members only' prices for both business and personal use."[35] Sam's Club opened 15 new units in 2007.[36]

Wal-Mart International added 576 (net) new stores in 2006—on its way to doubling its total retail unit count over the past few years.[37] Wal-Mart now operates 2,760 stores outside the United States in various formats, under diverse brand names, in 13 foreign countries and territories.[38] Wal-Mart International includes "wholly owned operations in Argentina, Brazil, Canada, Puerto Rico, and the United Kingdom; the operation of joint ventures in China; and the operations of majority-owned subsidiaries in Central America, Japan, and Mexico."[39] In 2006, Wal-Mart divested its operations in Germany and Korea.[40] Mike Duke, vice chairperson of Wal-Mart Stores and head of the International Division, commented that it had "'become increasingly clear that in Germany's [and South Korea's] business environment it would be difficult to obtain the scale and results we desire.' Wal-Mart seeks markets where it feels that there is potential for it to become a top three retailer, an opportunity that did not exist for it in Germany [or South Korea]."[41] Wal-Mart International's UK-based Asda subsidiary brings in the largest share of the company's international revenue, at 37.4 percent.[42] Wal-Mart de Mexico provides the next largest share, at 23.6 percent of Wal-Mart International sales[43] (see Exhibit 5).

Exhibit 5 International Wal-Mart retail units and banners, 2007

2,760 total units		
Country	**Retail Units**	**Date of Entry**
Mexico	889	November 1991
Puerto Rico	54	August 1992
Canada	289	November 1994
Argentina	13	November 1995
Brazil	302	May 1995
China	73	August 1996
United Kingdom	335	July 1999
Japan	392	March 2002
Costa Rica	137	September 2005
El Salvador	63	September 2005
Guatemala	132	September 2005
Honduras	41	September 2005
Nicaragua	40	September 2005

Sources: 2007, International Data Sheet, Wal-Mart Stores, http://walmartstores.com/Files/Intl_operations.pdf, February 8; 2007, Wal-Mart Annual Report, 24.

One of the challenges for each of Wal-Mart's segments is determining the appropriate product offerings for each location.

Product/Service Diversification

Wal-Mart continues to build on the discount general-store concept that reflects founder Sam Walton's ideals: "a wide assortment of good quality merchandise; the lowest possible prices; guaranteed satisfaction with what you buy; friendly, knowledgeable service; convenient hours; free parking; [and] a pleasant shopping experience."[44]

The company's Neighborhood Market locations provide an average of 29,000 items per store; its Discount Stores offer 120,000 items in each store; and its Supercenters stock more than 142,000 different items. Walmart.com offers customers 1 million SKUs (stock keeping units or items in stock), multiple times the number offered in Wal-Mart's retail stores.[45] Sam's Club features appliances, electronics, furniture, jewelry, and office products, plus healthcare, business, personal and financial services.[46] Interestingly, Wal-Mart "caters heavily to customers with little or no access to banking services, often described as the 'unbanked.'"[47] This category fits 20 percent of Wal-Mart's customer base and, as such, Wal-Mart provides substantial financial services for this customer segment by providing services such as check cashing. It has 170 money centers in its approximately 4,000 US stores.

Product and service offerings are just one of the many complex decisions that Wal-Mart's strategic leaders have to make.

Strategic Leaders

Ultimate leadership control has remained in the Walton family, with chairmanship changing hands only once, from father to son. Successors to the highest executive positions at Wal-Mart have always come from within the company. After eight years as CFO and executive vice president, David Glass succeeded Sam Walton as president and later as CEO.[48] H. Lee Scott joined Wal-Mart in 1979 and was named CEO by David Glass in 2000[49] (see Exhibit 6).

Decision Makers

Twenty-five senior Wal-Mart officers meet via weekly videoconferences "to review the Company's ongoing performance, focus on initiatives to drive sales and customer service, and address broader issues"[50] (see Exhibit 7). Eight of these senior officers currently have the most critical roles.

The most powerful among them is S. Robson (Rob) Walton, first son of Sam Walton and chair of the board of directors since 1992.[51] Rob Walton was initiated into the fledgling family business one night in the early 1960s after he earned his driver's license when Sam recruited him to truck goods from a garage in Bentonville to a Wal-Mart store.[52] Rob officially joined the company in 1969, shortly after graduating from law school, worked his way up to the vice chair position, and became board chair in 1992 after his father died.[53] "We lead when we embrace my dad's vision," according to Rob, "to improve the lives of everyday people by making everyday things more affordable."[54] Rob now lives in Colorado, where he races bicycles and sports cars in his spare time, and flies the company jet to his Bentonville office.[55] He continues to serve as the primary conduit for Walton family input related to company proceedings.[56]

Exhibit 6 History of leadership succession at Wal-Mart

	History of Leadership Succession at Wal-Mart		
Year	**President**	**CEO**	**Chairman**
1962	Sam Walton	Sam Walton	Sam Walton
1984	David Glass	Sam Walton	Sam Walton
1988	David Glass	David Glass	Sam Walton
1992	David Glass	David Glass	Rob Walton
2000	H. Lee Scott	H. Lee Scott	Rob Walton

Sources: 2007, The Wal-Mart Timeline, Wal-Mart Facts, http://www.walmartfacts.com/content/default.aspx?id=3, April 1; D. Longo, 1998, Wal-Mart hands CEO crown to David Glass, *Discount Store News*, February 15.

CEO Lee Scott "rose through the ranks by excelling at the mechanical aspects of retailing, playing an indispensable part in Wal-Mart's technology-induced rebound in the latter half of the 1990s."[57] The son of a gas station owner and a music teacher in small-town Kansas, Scott worked factory night shifts to pay for college, while he, his wife, and their baby lived in a mobile home.[58] He put his business degree to use in logistics, first as a dispatcher for Yellow Freight, then as a "headstrong," "aggressive, even abrasive" Wal-Mart transportation manager.[59] His skill in reducing costs helped him ascend to senior logistics jobs, then into the top merchandising post, where he cut billions in excess inventory in the late 1990s.[60] Next Scott ran the 2,300-unit Wal-Mart Stores Division for a year before becoming Wal-Mart's chief operating officer and vice chairperson in 1999.[61] He became CEO in January 2000.[62]

Mike Duke, an industrial engineer who had 23 years of experience with Federated and May Department Stores, followed Scott's path, climbing the distribution and logistics ladder to the leadership of Wal-Mart Stores Division.[63] Now he oversees international operations as vice chairperson.[64]

John Menzer, who joined Wal-Mart in 1995 after 10 years with Ben Franklin Retail Stores, served as Wal-

Exhibit 7 Wal-Mart senior officers, May 2007

Eduardo Castro-Wright Executive Vice President and President and Chief Executive Officer, Wal-Mart Stores Division **M. Susan Chambers** Executive Vice President of People Division **Patricia A. Curran** Executive Vice President, Store Operations, Wal-Mart Stores Division **Leslie A. Dach** Executive Vice President, Corporate Affairs and Government Relations **Linda M. Dillman** Executive Vice President, Risk Management and Benefits Administration **Michael T. Duke** Vice Chairman, Responsible for International **Johnnie C. Dobbs** Executive Vice President, Logistics and Supply Chain **John E. Fleming** Executive Vice President and Chief Merchandising Officer, Wal-Mart Stores Division **Rollin L. Ford** Executive Vice President, Chief Information Officer **Craig R. Herkert** Executive Vice President and President and Chief Executive Officer, The Americas, International **Charles M. Holley, Jr.** Executive Vice President, Finance and Treasurer **Thomas D. Hyde** Executive Vice President and Corporate Secretary	**Gregory L. Johnston** Executive Vice President, Club Operations, SAM'S CLUB **Thomas A. Mars** Executive Vice President and General Counsel **C. Douglas McMillon** Executive Vice President and President and Chief Executive Officer, SAM'S CLUB **John B. Menzer** Vice Chairman, Responsible for US **Stephen Quinn** Executive Vice President and Chief Marketing Officer, Wal-Mart Stores, Inc. **Thomas M. Schoewe** Executive Vice President and Chief Financial Officer **H. Lee Scott, Jr.** President and Chief Executive Officer **William S. Simon** Executive Vice President and Chief Operating Officer, Professional Services and New Business Development **Gregory E. Spragg** Executive Vice President, Merchandising and Replenishment, SAM'S CLUB **S. Robson Walton** Chairman of the Board of Directors of Wal-Mart Stores, Inc. **Claire A. Watts** Executive Vice President, Merchandising, Wal-Mart Stores Division-US **Steven P. Whaley** Senior Vice President, Controller, Wal-Mart Stores Inc. **Eric S. Zorn** Executive Vice President and President, Wal-Mart Realty

Source: 2007, Senior Officers, WalMartStores.com, http://walmartstores.com/GlobalWMStoresWeb/navigate.do?catg=540, May 25.

Mart's chief financial officer before becoming CEO of Wal-Mart International in 1999.[65] He led the acquisitions of Seiyu (a majority-owned subsidiary in Japan) and Asda.[66] Now as vice chairperson, Menzer is responsible for Wal-Mart Stores and various corporate functions, including strategic planning.[67]

A native of Ecuador, Eduardo Castro-Wright leads the Wal-Mart Stores Division in the United States after leading Wal-Mart de Mexico from 2001 to 2005, following a distinguished career with Nabisco in the Latin America and Asia-Pacific regions.[68]

Doug McMillon became president and CEO of Sam's Club after a 15-year career with Wal-Mart, first as a buyer, then as a merchandising manager and leader.[69]

Nineteen-year Target veteran John Fleming ascended through Walmart.com in the early 2000s to become Wal-Mart Stores' chief marketing officer, prior to his January 2007 induction as chief merchandising officer for Wal-Mart Stores.[70]

After 13 years in marketing roles with PepsiCo, Stephen Quinn joined Wal-Mart as senior vice president of marketing in 2005, and then in January 2007 took over Fleming's former position as chief marketing officer for Wal-Mart Stores.[71]

These eight leaders are supported and monitored by the board of directors.

Board of Directors

Wal-Mart has an active, high-caliber, 14-member board of directors that may soon get even more powerful. "The Board has been instrumental in encouraging the company to more quickly address critical issues, and I am extremely pleased that they are not reticent about sharing their opinions," Rob Walton recently wrote, adding: "Today's Board is the furthest thing from a rubber stamp."[72] Two out of three board members have held CEO po-

Exhibit 8 Wal-Mart Board of Directors, May 2007

Aida M. Alvarez, 57 Former Administrator of the US Small Business Administration; joined board in 2006 **James W. Breyer, 45** Managing Partner of Accel Partners; joined board in 2001 **M. Michele Burns, 49** Chairman and CEO of Mercer Human Resources Consulting; joined board in 2003 **James Cash, Jr., Ph.D., 59** Retired Professor of Business Administration at Harvard Business School; joined board in 2006 **Roger C. Corbett, 64** Retired CEO and Group Managing Director of Woolworths Limited; joined board in 2006 **Douglas N. Daft, 64** Retired Chairman of the Board and CEO of The Coca-Cola Company; joined board in 2005 **David D. Glass, 71** Former President and CEO of Wal-Mart Stores, Inc.; joined board in 1977 **Roland A. Hernandez, 49** Retired Chairman and CEO of Telemundo Group, Inc.; joined board in 1998	**Allen I. Questrom, 67** Former Chairman and CEO of JCPenney Company; Barneys New York, Inc.; The Neiman Marcus Group, Inc.; and Federated Department Stores, Inc.; standing for election in June 2007 **H. Lee Scott, Jr., 58** President and Chief Executive Officer of Wal-Mart Stores, Inc.; joined board in 1999 **Jack C. Shewmaker, 69** Retired Vice Chairman of Wal-Mart Stores, Inc.; joined board in 1977 **Jim C. Walton, 58** Chairman of the Board and CEO of Arvest Bank Group, Inc.; joined board in 2005 **S. Robson Walton, 62** Chairman of the Board of Directors of Wal-Mart Stores, Inc.; joined board in 1978 **Christopher J. Williams, 49** Chairman and CEO of The Williams Capital Group, L.P.; joined board in 2004 **Linda S. Wolf, 59** Former Chairman of the Board and CEO of Leo Burnett Worldwide, Inc.; joined board in 2005

Sources: 2007, Board of Directors, Wal-Mart Stores.com, http://walmartstores.com/GlobalWMStoresWeb/navigate.do?catg=502, May 25; 2007, Wal-Mart Stores, Inc., Form DEF 14A, Proxy Statement, Notice of 2007 Annual Shareholders' Meeting, US SEC, April 19.

sitions and/or chaired the boards of various companies. Retail turnaround guru Allen Questrom, who overhauled JCPenney, joined the board in June 2007.[73] Questrom recently told *Women's Wear Daily*: "[Wal-Mart is] never going to be a leader in fashion apparel. That's not their calling. But can they improve on that, sure they can."[74] The most famous former board member is New York Senator and Democratic presidential candidate Hillary Rodham Clinton, who served on the Wal-Mart board from 1986 to 1992 as a "loyalist reformer"[75] (see Exhibit 8).

Several board members are among the largest shareholders in the company.

Shareholders

Of the 4.1 billion Wal-Mart shares outstanding, insiders and beneficial owners hold 42 percent, while institutional investors and mutual funds hold 37 percent.[76]

The Walton family owns almost 1.7 billion shares through its holding company, Walton Enterprises, LLC, whose directors were five of America's ten wealthiest individuals in 2005: Sam's three sons, Rob Walton, director Jim C. Walton, and John T. Walton (d. 2005); daughter Alice L. Walton; and widow Helen R. Walton (d. 2007).[77]

Top non-Walton inside shareholders include CEO Lee Scott (1.2 million shares), director David D. Glass (1.2 million shares), director Jack C. Shewmaker (557,674 shares), Mike Duke (413,213 shares), and John Menzer (401,883 shares).[78]

Some 1,127 institutions own Wal-Mart stock.[79] Nearly 536 million Wal-Mart shares are owned by 785 mutual funds.[80]

In total, as many as 312,423 shareholders held common stock in Wal-Mart on March 16, 2007, when the company finalized its annual report for fiscal 2007.[81]

Financial Results

Fiscal 2007 and Recent Years[82]

Over the past 10 years, Wal-Mart's net income has nearly quadrupled, from $3 billion in 1997 to $11.7 billion in 2007. Revenues have more than tripled, from $100 billion to $345 billion. Meanwhile, operating, selling, and general administration expenses have quadrupled, outstripping the increase in revenue and net income, averaging 14.6 percent of sales. Despite the increase in expenses, steadily higher gross margins have boosted operating income (refer to Exhibit 3).

Exhibit 9 Wal-Mart balance sheet, 1997–2007

	Balance Sheet (all figures in $millions; fiscal year ends 1/31)										
	2007	**2006**	**2005**	**2004**	**2003**	**2002**	**2001**	**2000**	**1999**	**1998**	**1997**
Assets											
Inventories	$33,685	$31,910	29,419	26,263	24,098	21,793	20,710	18,961	16,058	16,005	15,556
Other Current Assets	$12,903	$11,915	$8,494	$7,285	$4,769	$4,122	$4,086	$4,021	$3,445	$2,584	$1,829
Total Current Assets	$46,588	$43,825	$37,913	$33,548	$28,867	$25,915	$24,796	$22,982	$19,503	$18,589	$17,385
Net Property, Equipment &Leases	$88,440	$77,865	$66,549	$57,591	$50,053	$44,172	$39,439	$34,570	$24,824	$23,237	$19,935
Goodwill & Other Long-term Assets	$16,165	$13,934	$12,677	$11,316	$11,309	$9,214	$10,082	$9,738	$2,739	$2,395	$1,251
Total Assets	$151,193	$135,624	$117,139	$102,455	$90,229	$79,301	$74,317	$67,290	$47,066	$44,221	$38,571
Return on Assets	8.8%	9.3%	9.8%	9.7%	9.6%	9.0%	9.3%	10.1%	9.6%	8.5%	8.0%
Liabilities & Shareholder Equity											
Current Liabilities	$51,754	$48,348	$42,609	$37,308	$31,752	$26,309	$28,096	$25,058	$15,848	$13,930	$10,432
Long-Term Debt	$27,222	$26,429	$20,087	$17,088	$16,545	$15,632	$12,453	$13,650	$6,875	$7,169	$7,685
Long-Term Leases	$3,513	$3,667	$3,073	$2,888	$2,903	$2,956	$3,054	$2,852	$2,697	$2,480	$2,304
Other Liabilities	$7,131	$4,009	$1,974	$1,548	$(432)	$(788)	$(693)	$(148)	$505	$2,123	$999
(minority interest, discontinued ops, deferred taxes)											
Total Liabilities	**$89,620**	**$82,453**	**$67,743**	**$58,832**	**$50,768**	**$44,109**	**$42,910**	**$41,412**	**$25,925**	**$25,702**	**$21,420**
Shareholder Equity	$61,573	$53,171	$49,396	$43,623	$39,461	$35,192	$31,407	$25,878	$21,141	$18,519	$17,151
Return on Equity	22.0%	22.9%	23.1%	22.4%	21.8%	20.7%	23.0%	24.5%	22.0%	19.6%	18.8%

Source: 2007, 2002, Wal-Mart Annual Reports.

Exhibit 10 Wal-Mart financial ratios, 1997–2007

	2007	**2006**	**2005**	**2004**	**2003**	**2002**	**2001**	**2000**	**1999**	**1998**	**1997**
Stability											
Debt Ratio	59.3%	60.8%	57.8%	57.4%	56.3%	55.6%	57.7%	61.5%	55.1%	58.1%	55.5%
Stockholders Equity to Assets	40.7%	39.2%	42.2%	42.6%	43.7%	44.4%	42.3%	38.5%	44.9%	41.9%	44.5%
Leverage	2.50	2.46	2.36	2.32	2.27	2.31	2.47	2.43	2.30	2.32	n/a
Debt to Equity Ratio	1.46	1.55	1.37	1.35	1.29	1.25	1.37	1.60	1.23	1.39	1.25
Debt to Capitization Ratio	0.38	0.39	0.34	0.33	0.33	0.34	0.32	0.39	0.32	0.39	0.39
Liquidity											
Current Ratio	0.90	0.91	0.89	0.90	0.91	0.99	0.88	0.92	1.23	1.33	1.67
Quick Ratio	0.25	0.25	0.20	0.20	0.15	0.16	0.15	0.16	0.22	0.19	0.18
Profitability											
Operating Profit Margin	5.9%	6.0%	6.1%	5.1%	5.1%	5.0%	5.4%	5.6%	4.8%	4.5%	4.3%
Operating Ratio	18.4%	17.9%	17.6%	17.4%	17.3%	17.0%	16.8%	16.4%	16.6%	16.8%	16.5%
Net Profit Margin	3.3%	3.6%	3.6%	3.6%	3.5%	3.3%	3.5%	3.5%	3.4%	3.1%	3.1%
Total Asset Turnover	2.4	2.5	2.6	2.6	2.7	2.6	2.5	2.7	2.8	2.7	n/a

Source: 2007, 2002, Wal-Mart Annual Reports.

Wal-Mart had assets totaling $151 billion in 2007, up from $39 billion in 1997. Concurrent with the increase in assets, liabilities have grown 319 percent over the same period, from $21.4 billion to $89.6 billion. Shareholder return on equity measured 22 percent in 2007, close to its 10-year average. Total shareholder equity rose from $17.2 billion in 1997 to $61.8 billion in 2007 (see Exhibit 9).

Wal-Mart has improved its profitability over the last several years. Compared with an average operating profit margin of 5.1 percent in the prior three-year period, Wal-Mart has averaged 6.0 percent in the past three years. In 1997, Wal-Mart's operating profit margin was 4.3 percent. From a debt perspective, Wal-Mart has fluctuated up and down, with a debt ratio between 55.1 percent and 61.5 percent over the last 10 years. As of 2007, it measured 59.3 percent, 150 basis points over its 10-year median (see Exhibit 10).

Comparative Revenue[83]

Sales by Region Of nearly $345 billion in total sales in 2007 (not including Sam's Club fees), domestic US revenues totaled nearly $268 billion, or 77.6 percent of sales, while international revenues were $77 billion, or 22.4 percent of sales. International operations are becoming increasingly important to the company. Driving Wal-Mart's overall growth, international sales growth has averaged 33.6 percent over the past 10 years, whereas domestic sales have grown an average of only 11.0 percent in the same period. In the last three years, domestic sales growth has averaged 8.7 percent versus average international growth of 17.8 percent (refer to Exhibit 2). Wal-Mart has experienced varying rates of growth in international markets. Nonetheless, international revenue has been a constant source of sales growth for Wal-Mart, outpacing the revenue contribution from the Sam's Club segment since 2001.

Sales by Segment Wal-Mart Stores brought in 65.6 percent of all sales in 2007, down from 75.1 percent of sales in 1997. Wal-Mart International was responsible for 22.4 percent of sales, up from 5.0 percent a decade earlier, while Sam's Club accounted for 12.1 percent of sales in 2007, down from 19.9 percent in 1997 (refer to Exhibit 2).

Sam's Club has suffered against rival Costco for years, losing the battle for comparable-store sales in "64 of the past 73 months," according to one researcher, as well as the battle for membership renewals.[84] Average annual sales per warehouse were $73 million for Sam's Club versus $135 million for Costco in fiscal 2006.[85]

Wal-Mart's online business has not been a significant source of revenue, bringing in an estimated $135 million in sales in 2002, the same year JCPenney.com had sales of $324 million and Amazon.com reached sales greater than $3 billion.[86]

Wal-Mart Supercenters drove 56.1 percent of the company's sales, reflecting the company's competitive strength in traditional nonmembership discount formats.

Results Relative to Competitors

Market Leadership Wal-Mart is the number one retailer in 77 of the 100 largest general merchandise markets in America, squaring up against Target or Costco in all but 11 of these markets.[87] Either Wal-Mart, Costco, or Target holds the top position in 91 of the top 100 largest general merchandise markets in the United States.[88] Geographically, Wal-Mart is the dominant retailer in the South and throughout midsized and small-town markets, while Costco is the leader in California and Washington.[89] According to ACNielsen, (the world's leading marketing information company), in the United States, Wal-Mart "controls 20 percent of dry grocery, 29 percent of nonfood grocery, 30 percent of health and beauty aids, and 45 percent of general merchandise sales."[90] It also controls 45 percent of the retail toy segment.[91] However, Target, Kroger, and Family Dollar Stores are all growing revenue faster than Wal-Mart, threatening its dominance (see Exhibit 11).

Financial Ratios From a competitive profitability perspective, Wal-Mart's 5.87 percent operating margin and 3.23 percent net margin put it in the middle of the pack relative to its key competitors (refer to Exhibit 11). Target enjoys higher margins, closer to those of JCPenney, while Costco has lower margins, closer to those of Dollar General and Kroger. Wal-Mart's margins are nearest those of Family Dollar Stores and Sears Holdings (Kmart and Sears). Wal-Mart's profit margin may be held down somewhat by its presence in the lower margin grocery business, especially in its Neighborhood Markets format.[92] In Supercenters, groceries serve a larger role of driving store traffic and drawing customers toward higher margin products. From a management effectiveness standpoint, Wal-Mart is creating a return on equity that is higher than Target's and much higher than Costco's and a return on assets that is nearly identical to Target's and higher than Costco's.

Exhibit 11 Comparison of financial ratios

	Financial Ratios of Select Retailers (sorted by revenue growth, as of May 26, 2007)					
	Quarterly Growth (yoy)		Profitability (ttm)		Management Effectiveness (ttm)	
	Revenue Growth	Earnings Growth	Net Profit Margin	Operating Margin	Return on Assets	Return on Equity
Amazon.com, Inc.	32.30%	117.60%	2.18%	3.74%	10.37%	73.86%
Target Corporation	16.30%	19.20%	4.69%	8.52%	8.93%	18.68%
Kroger Co.	14.50%	36.50%	1.69%	3.47%	7.10%	23.95%
Family Dollar Stores, Inc.	12.20%	66.00%	3.49%	5.70%	9.44%	17.68%
Wal-Mart Stores, Inc.	9.60%	8.10%	3.23%	5.87%	8.81%	21.80%
Costco Wholesale Corp.	7.50%	–15.80%	1.73%	2.55%	6.25%	12.07%
J.C. Penney Corporation	3.10%	13.30%	5.90%	9.73%	9.57%	26.43%
Dollar General Corp.	3.00%	–65.50%	1.50%	2.67%	5.24%	7.96%
Sears Holdings Corporation	1.30%	26.50%	2.81%	4.59%	5.06%	12.25%

Sources: 2007, Key Statistics, Capital IQ, A Division of Standard & Poor's, Yahoo! Finance, http://finance.yahoo.com/q/ks?s=WMT, http://finance.yahoo. com/q/ks?s=TGT, http://finance.yahoo.com/q/ks?s=COST, http://finance.yahoo.com/q/ks?s=KR, http://finance.yahoo.com/q/ks?s=DG, http://finance.yahoo. com/q/ks?s=FDO, http://finance.yahoo.com/q/ks?s=SHLD, http://finance.yahoo.com/q/ks?s=JCP, http://finance.yahoo.com/q/ks?s=AMZN, May 26.

First Quarter, Fiscal 2008 (Quarter Ending April 30, 2007)

Wal-Mart had a difficult first quarter. Revenue and earnings "were not where we would have expected [them] to be, nor where we believe they should be," according to CEO Scott.[93] "Quite honestly, we're not satisfied with our overall performance."[94] Wal-Mart increased company sales (not including Sam's Club fees) by 8.3 percent in the first quarter to $85.3 billion.[95] Overall operating income increased 7.9 percent year-over-year, with nearly 53.1 percent of the change coming from Wal-Mart's international operations[96] (see Exhibit 12).

Closing out the first quarter on a down note, Wal-Mart's April same-store sales decrease was the worst ever recorded in 28 years of tracking: an overall US comparable-store sales slide of 3.5 percent for the month, with a 4.6 percent drop at Wal-Mart Stores offset by a 2.5 percent increase at Sam's Clubs.[97] Much of the April decline was blamed on the apparel business, which constitutes 10 percent of Wal-Mart's sales.[98] Recent failed forays into fashion appear to have dragged down overall same-stores sales.[99] Wal-Mart wasn't the only retailer to have a bad April. The International Council of Shopping Centers reported an average 2.3 percent drop in same-store sales across 51 chains.[100] Against the trend, Costco posted a 6 percent same-store sales gain in April (see Exhibit 13).

The financial situation might be better considered with an understanding of the competitive situation in Wal-Mart's industry.

Competitive Situation

We face strong sales competition from other discount, department, drug, variety and specialty stores and supermarkets, many of which are national, regional or international chains, as well as internet-based retailers and catalog businesses. Additionally, we compete with a number of companies for prime retail site locations, as well as in attracting and retaining quality employees ("associates"). We, along with other retail companies, are influenced by a number of factors . . . cost of goods, consumer debt levels and buying patterns, economic conditions, interest rates, customer preferences, unemployment, labor costs, inflation, currency exchange fluctuations, fuel prices, weather patterns, catastrophic events, competitive pressures and insurance costs. Our Sam's Club segment faces strong sales competition from other wholesale club operators, catalogs businesses, internet-based and other retailers."

—2007 Wal-Mart Annual Report, 28–29

Exhibit 12 Wal-Mart fiscal 2008 first quarter results versus target

Wall-Mart Stores, Inc. Fiscal 2008 First Quarter Results Quarters Ending 4/30, all figures in $millions			
Income	**Q1 2008**	**Q1 2007**	**YoY% Chng**
Total Operating Revenue	$86,410	$79,676	8.5%
Cost of Sales	$65,311	$60,237	8.4%
Gross Operating Profit	**$21,099**	**$19,439**	8.5%
Gross Margins	24.4%	24.4%	
Operating, Selling, G&A Exp.	$16,249	$14,944	8.7%
Operating Income	**$4,850**	**$4,495**	7.9%
Net Interest Expense	$392	$368	6.5%
Income Before Taxes	$4,458	$4,127	8.0%
Provision for Taxes	$1,532	$1,388	10.4%
Effective Tax Rate	34.4%	33.6%	2.2%
Net Income from Operations	$2,926	$2,739	6.8%
Other Items	$(100)	$(124)	
Net Income Shareholder Income ($dollars)	**$2,826**	**$2,615**	8.1%
EPS (diluted)	$0.68	$0.63	7.9%
Dividend	$0.67	$0.60	
Comparable-Store Sales Growth	0.6%	3.8%	
Wal-Mart Stores	–0.1%	3.8%	
Sam's Club (excl. fuel)	4.7%	4.3%	
Segment Breakdown Revenue by Segment			
Wal-Mart Stores	$55,437	$52,499	5.6%
Sam's Club	$10,323	$9,775	5.6%
International	$19,627	$16,561	18.5%
Total (excludes other income)	$85,387	$78,835	8.3%
Operating Income by Segment			
Wal-Mart Stores	$3,927	$3,858	1.8%
Sam's Club	$363	$303	19.8%
International	$903	$757	19.3%
Total (excludes other income)	$5,193	$4,918	5.6%
Operating Margins by Segment			
Wal-Mart Stores	7.1%	7.3%	–3.6%
Sam's Club	3.5%	3.1%	13.4%
International	4.6%	4.6%	0.7%
Total (excludes other income)	6.1%	6.2%	–2.5%
Cash Flows			
Net Income	$2,826	$2,615	
Change in Inventories	$(1,280)	$259	
Accounts Payable	$(1,115)	$(442)	
Accounts Receivable	$62	$219	
Cash Flows from Operating Activities	$493	$2,651	

Total Operating Revenue*	$14,041	$12,863	9.2%
Cost of Sales	$9,186	$8,473	8.4%
Gross Operating Profit	**$4,855**	**$4,390**	10.6%
Gross Margins	34.6%	34.1%	
Operating, Selling, G&A Exp.**	$3,655	$3,373	8.4%
Operating Income	**$1,200**	**$1,017**	18.0%
Net Interest Expense	$136	$131	3.6%
Income Before Taxes	$1,064	$886	20.2%
Provision for Taxes	$413	$332	24.5%
Effective Tax Rate	38.8%	37.5%	3.6%
Net Income from Operations	$651	$554	17.6%
Other Items	$-	$-	
Net Income Shareholder Income ($dollars)	**$651**	**$554**	17.5%
EPS (diluted)	$0.75	$0.63	19.6%
*includes sales and net credit card revenues			
**includes SG&A, credit card expenses, depreciation and amortization			
Comparable-Store Sales Growth	**4.3%**	**5.1%**	

Sources: 2007, Wal-Mart Stores, Inc., Form 8-K, US SEC, May 15; and 2007, Target Corporation, Form 8-K, US SEC, May 23.

Exhibit 13 April 2007 same-store sales growth

April 2007 Same-Store Sales Growth	
Discounters	
Wal-Mart	–3.5%
Costco	+6.0%
Target	–6.1%
Dollar General	–2.4%
Department Stores	
Federated	–2.2%
JCPenney	–4.7%
Nordstrom	+3.1%
Dillard's	–14.0%
Neiman Marcus	+1.0%
Saks	+11.7%
Apparel	
TJX	–1.0%
Kohl's	–10.5%
Gap	–16.0%
Limited	–1.0%
AnnTaylor	–12.8%
Teen Apparel	
Abercrombie & Fitch	–15.0%
American Eagle Outfitters	–10.0%

Source: J. Covert, 2007, Retail-sales slide fuels concern: Decline of 2.3% in April among worst on record; even Wal-Mart slipped, *Wall Street Journal*, May 11, A3.

Competitors

Target Target Corporation operates 1,318 general merchandise stores and 182 SuperTarget stores in 47 states, in addition to its online business, target.com.[101] Target describes itself as "an upscale discounter that provides high-quality, on-trend merchandise at attractive prices in clean, spacious and guest-friendly stores."[102] Target has grown revenue from $33 billion in 2001 to more than $59 billion in 2006, a compound annual growth rate of 12.5 percent.[103] Profits have risen as well, as earnings from continuing operations averaged an annual growth rate of 20.4 percent over the same period[104] (see Exhibit 14).

Costco Costco Wholesale Corporation runs 510 warehouses, averaging 140,000 square feet, in 38 states, six foreign countries (Canada, Mexico, the United Kingdom, Taiwan, Korea, and Japan), and Puerto Rico.[105] Costco offers three kinds of membership and roughly 4,000 products, 10 to 15 times fewer than many competitors, according to the company.[106] Costco benefits from a limited number of products sold in high volumes, high inventory turnover, low costs via purchasing discounts and a no-frills approach, and favorable real estate locations. Gross margins have averaged about 10.6 percent over the past five years, and operating income has increased an average of 10.5 percent over the same period[107] (see Exhibit 15).

Kroger The Kroger Co. is "one of the nation's largest retailers, operating 2,468 supermarket and multi-department stores under two dozen banners including Kroger, Ralphs, Fred Meyer, Food 4 Less, King Soopers, Smith's, Fry's, Fry's Marketplace, Dillons, QFC, and City Market."[108] Kroger's operating income fell 13.1 percent between 2002 and 2006, from $2.8 billion to $2.2 billion, despite an increase in revenue of 27.7 percent.[109] Operating margins have averaged 24.8 percent over the last three years, up from 15.7 percent in the three years prior[110] (see Exhibit 16).

Other General Discount Competitors Sears Holdings (Kmart and Sears) offer some additional US competition in general merchandise, while Tesco of Britain and Carrefour of France compete with Wal-Mart internationally. Carrefour is the second-largest retailer in the world (after Wal-Mart) and is probably its closest international competitor from a strategy perspective, as it focuses on hypermarkets (similar to Supercenters), in addition to a variety of other formats.[111] Tesco emphasizes convenience and competes primarily in groceries, but also in general merchandise against Wal-Mart's UK subsidiary Asda.[112] Tesco is looking to expand to the West Coast of the United States in 2007.[113] Amazon.com adds another level of global competition for Wal-Mart due to its high number of SKUs and its convenience.

Exhibit 14 Target performance, 2001–2006

Target	2001	2002	2003	2004	2005	2006
Revenue	$33,021	$7,410	$42,025	$46,839	$52,620	$59,940
COGS	$23,030	$25,948	$28,389	$31,445	$34,927	$39,399
Gross Margin	$9,991	$11,462	$13,636	$15,394	$17,693	$20,541
Gross Margin %	30.3%	30.6%	32.4%	32.9%	33.6%	34.3%
Operating Income/ EBIT	$2,246	2,811	3,159	3,601	4,323	5,069
		25.2%	12.4%	14.0%	20.0%	17.3%
Net Income	$1,101	$1,376	$1,619	$1,885	$2,408	$2,787
Net Income % chg		25.0%	17.7%	16.4%	27.7%	15.7%

Note: $in millions

Source: 2006, Target Corporation Annual Report.

Exhibit 15 Costco performance, 2001–2006

Costco	2001	2002	2003	2004	2005	2006
Revenue	$34,137,021	$37,994,608	$41,694,561	$47,148,627	$51,879,070	$58,963,180
COGS	$30,598,140	$33,983,121	$37,235,383	$42,092,016	$46,346,961	$52,745,497
Gross Margin	$3,538,881	$4,011,487	$4,459,178	$5,056,611	$5,532,109	$6,217,683
Gross Margin %	10.4%	10.6%	10.7%	10.7%	10.7%	10.5%
Operating Income/ EBIT	$992,267	1,131,535	1,156,628	1,385,648	1,474,303	1,625,632
		14.0%	2.2%	19.8%	6.4%	10.3%
Net Income	$602,089	$699,983	$721,000	$882,393	$1,063,092	$1,103,215
Net Income % chg		16.3%	3.0%	22.4%	20.5%	3.8%

Note: $in thousands
Source: 2006, Costco Wholesale Corp. Annual Report.

Exhibit 16 Kroger performance, 2001–2006

Kroger	2001	2002	2003	2004	2005	2006
Revenue	$49,000	$51,760	$53,791	$56,434	$60,553	$66,111
COGS	$36,398	$37,810	$39,637	$42,140	$45,565	$50,115
Gross Margin	$12,602	$13,950	$14,154	$14,294	$14,988	$15,996
Gross Margin %	25.7%	10.6%	10.7%	25.3%	24.8%	24.2%
Operating Income/EBIT	$2,359	$2,573	$1,374	$843	$2,035	$2,236
		9.1%	−46.6%	−38.6%	141.4%	9.9%
Net Income	$877	$1,202	$285	$(104)	$958	$1,115
Net Income % chg		37.1%	−76.3%	−136.5%	$1021.2%	$16.4%

Note: $in millions
Source: 2006 The Kroger Co. Annual Report.

Niche Competitors Other retailers compete with Wal-Mart at the department level, including Safeway, Best Buy, Circuit City, Home Depot, Ace Hardware, Lowe's, Kohl's, Mervyn's California, Barnes & Noble, and Borders, among others. In order to provide lower prices than its competitors, Wal-Mart has developed a unique relationship with its suppliers.

Suppliers

Wal-Mart's 1,600-member Global Procurement Services team, based in 23 countries, buys merchandise from suppliers in more than 70 countries, including 61,000 suppliers in the United States.[114] Leveraging its size, "Wal-Mart not only dictates delivery schedules and inventory levels but also heavily influences product specifications. In the end, many suppliers have to choose between designing goods their way or the Wal-Mart way."[115] In return, companies with a streamlined product and supply chain can benefit greatly. "If you are good with data, are sophisticated, and have scale, Wal-Mart should be one of your most profitable customers," says a retired consumer-products executive.[116] "Wal-Mart controls a large and rapidly increasing share of the business done by most every major US consumer products company," about 28 percent of the total sales of Dial and almost a quarter of the sales of Del Monte Foods, Clorox, and Revlon.[117]

Customers

Wal-Mart attracts 175 million people to its stores each week.[118] According to ACNielsen (the world's leading marketing information company), the typical Wal-Mart shopper has an annual household income of $10,000 to $50,000.[119] These shoppers account for 54 percent of Wal-Mart's sales.[120] Wal-Mart also attracts an affluent segment (with household incomes of at least $75,000) that accounts for 26 percent of its customer base.[121] The affluent segment cross-shops the most with Costco (27 percent) and Target (28 percent).[122] These upscale shoppers likely have lower price elasticity, a relatively lower switching cost, but a higher sensitivity to brand reputation.

Even though Wal-Mart recently hired some well-known public relations experts and ended its relationship with its Ad Agency of 32 years in hopes of creating a more positive image, according to a 2004 study, "2 to 8 percent of Wal-Mart consumers surveyed have ceased shopping at the chain because of 'negative press.'"[123] Shoppers interviewed by the authors of this case have strong opinions about Wal-Mart (see Exhibits 17 and 18).

Wal-Mart's recent struggles with bad press and lawsuits have created urgency to find a way to protect its market share from potential entrants or substitutes.

Other Sources of Competition

Customers have many alternatives for each of the products and services that Wal-Mart provides, but few alternatives exist for the large-scale discount superstore or warehouse shopping experience. The same products can be purchased at different types of retailers, but it is difficult to replicate the convenience, price, and diversity of merchandise found at a Wal-Mart. Also, new potential market entrants with similar scale would have difficulty competing in any substantial volume on price across a wide array of merchandise. Other large incumbents such as Target and Costco have also built economies of scale that would be difficult for a start-up to replicate. Supply chains must be extensive and very efficient. Product differentiation is usually minor in discount store merchandise. However, switching retailers would be easy for customers in well-served areas.

Beyond these retail industry forces, more general external trends also influence Wal-Mart's competitive situation.

External Trends

Government Wal-Mart has become a "poster company" on political issues related to trade, health care, the environment, discrimination, worker pay, and general anticorporate sentiment. Many activists even contend that Wal-Mart is breaking antitrust laws by using its "power to micromanage the market, carefully coordinating the actions of thousands of firms from a position above the market."[124] Concerns about Wal-Mart's handling of hazardous waste have prompted local, state, and federal officials in the southwestern United States to initiate official actions. In addition to activists and union groups, US political figures are lashing out against Wal-Mart. Democratic presidential candidates are "denouncing Wal-Mart for what they say are substandard wages and health care benefits."[125] Wal-Mart's political action committee's contributions to candidates (even to a former board member) are being returned as a sign of protest.[126] This sentiment is not only surfacing nationally, but locally as well. Governments in Inglewood, California, Cedar Mill, Oregon, and Vancouver, Canada, have rejected Wal-Mart expansion plans.[127]

Exhibit 17 Wal-Mart shopper profile

Income	
	% of sales
<$50,000	54%
$50-$75000	20%
$75,000 +	26%
Education	
	% of sales
Less than a High School Diploma	20%
High School Diploma (incl. some college)	57%
Bachelor Degree and above	23%
Leisure Pursuits—Typical Customer	
	% of customers
Tend Their Garden	43%
Listen to Country Music	30%
Like Auto Racing	17%
Go Fishing	17%
Go Camping	19%
Leisure Pursuits—Affluent Customer	
	% of customers
Listen to Talk Radio	34%
Go to a Theme Park	32%
Listen to Contemporary Music	25%
Go to the Museum	21%
Go to the Zoo	18%

Source: S. Kapinus, 2006, Rollback sushi and discount organics: What Wal-Mart's push to upscale consumers means to you, *ACNielsen Consumer Insight Magazine*, http://us.acnielsen.com/pubs/2006_q2_ci_rollback.shtml, Q2.

Exhibit 18 Interviewee perspectives on Wal-Mart, 2007

The environment steps are baby steps at the moment. We hope they will take substantive and [significant] action around the critical issues of the environment. Sadly, in the past, much of their efforts have been about publicity and positive spin, not about substance. We will wait to see what level of real commitment they will make around the environment.

—Robert Greenwald, producer/director,
Wal-Mart: The High Cost of Low Price (2007, e-mail interview, May 22)

[Wal-Mart has] a problem with blight. They leave behind in some cases blight by opening a new Supercenter and leaving their old stores empty. They need to have a plan for communities and not leave those huge buildings empty. In Hood River, the community didn't want Wal-Mart to open a Supercenter because they would leave the old store vacant, and Wal-Mart listened. They didn't open the Supercenter.

—Fred G.,
55, suburban Wal-Mart shopper (2007, personal interview, May 21)

[B]eing the low-cost provider loses some of the service, the pleasure of going shopping. Target has wider aisles, and less product on the shelf. In contrast, Wal-Mart bombards you with tons of products.

—Oliver Davis,
Target shopper (2007, personal interview, May 21)

There was a long time I didn't shop at Wal-Mart, and that had to do with the store's image of ruthlessness when it came to destroying the competition. To be honest, I feel a certain amount of shame at shopping there. As a mother, though, I'm afraid budget and convenience rule. In other words, I've sold out.

—Lili N.,
34, affluent shopper (2007, e-mail interview, May 19)

I shop at Wal-Mart for convenience-type items, but if the item I need is over $100 or is something that I need of quality, I will shop elsewhere. . . . I do not believe that Wal-Mart is capable of becoming related to quality items in the near future like Target and I do not believe that they will be successful at both discount and high quality.

—Andre S.,
26, budget-conscious shopper (2007, personal interview, May 20)

The [Wal-Mart] store itself is a little overwhelming—too many people, parking is usually tight, and the lines at the check-out are long. Also, there are so many [unfamiliar] employees working in a single Wal-Mart, that my shopping experience has no personal touch. I enjoy going to my neighborhood HEB [grocery store] because I see familiar faces—both at the check-out and in the aisles. If Wal-Mart would be willing to downsize a bit and have more of a neighborhood feel to it, I might consider stopping in more often.

—Angie R.,
29, affluent shopper (2007, e-mail interview, May 20)

Wal-Mart . . . lets you stay in their parking lot overnight. Friends stay at the "Wally-World" when we go windsurfing in Hood River. You can use their facilities and treat the parking lot like a campground. I like to shop there because of that corporate policy.

—Fred G.,
55, suburban Wal-Mart shopper (2007, personal interview, May 21)

I shop at Wal-Mart very infrequently because I find it hard to find things, [and the store is] often not very clean. There doesn't seem to be well-laid-out aisles like Target; it is more of a jumbled maze. However, one plus is the live fish they have. Kids love to go by and see them! And they usually have better prices. If I am looking for a particular item, like a kids' outdoor toy/sandbox, that is what usually gets me there, because you can find it cheaper.

—Crystal B.,
35, affluent shopper (2007, e-mail interview, May 21)

Wal-Mart neighborhood grocery is OK if you just need staples—it'll be cheap. I won't go into the 24-hour Supercenter down here. I think that was the store that had a stabbing over a Black Thursday laptop deal or something like that. SuperTarget is almost as bad during midday Sunday, but at least the store is cleaner and the meat looks a little better.

—Michael C.,
35, Wal-Mart shopper (2007, e-mail interview, May 21)

When I was an Operations Manager for a Fortune *500 company, we were having a yearly employee appreciation picnic . . . [so] my secretary and I hopped into a company van, shot down to Sam's Club, loaded up four shopping carts of hamburgers, hotdogs, beverages, and all the fixings, got to the checkout, pulled out my Visa, and then found out that Sam's club didn't accept Visa. After a few minutes of arguing with an unhelpful and unsympathetic manager, I left all four carts at the checkout and have never been back since.*

—Brian S.,
former Sam's Club member (2007, discussion-board posting, May 22)

Wal-Mart has been such a negative experience that it would be hard for me to go back. I have been hesitant to go to a neighborhood Wal-Mart because of my poor shopping experiences around the country at different big-box Wal-Marts. The Wal-Mart I am closer to is a lower socioeconomic neighborhood, and I drive past it to go to Target because I perceive it as being safer and I feel that I am getting a higher quality product.

—Oliver Davis,
Target shopper (2007, personal interview, May 21)

[Wal-Mart] will continue to grow, and will make many changes in that time. Some are for the better and some are not. Unfortunately, sometimes plans that are not well [thought-out] are implemented and mandated, which only causes frustration/irritation. Other times workers are stuck in [their] ways and don't want to change.

—Anonymous
Wal-Mart manager (2007, e-mail interview, May 21)

[Wal-Mart needs better] price marking, more UPC scanners in the store. I see something and the price is ambiguous. They don't mark the prices. They can also make checkout faster. Why is it so slow? I don't go to Kmart anymore because a lot of times the UPC of something doesn't ring up at the cash register. It isn't in their system. If it is on the shelf, the UPC should be in the computer. Wal-Mart is also getting worse at this.

—Fred G.,
55, suburban Wal-Mart shopper (2007, personal interview, May 21)

[Wal-Mart] does offer a big variety [of benefits for associates], some much better than other companies and some not so good in my opinion. Some examples of good discounts are 10% discount on most items (excludes grocery, clearance, and a few other items—biggest complaint on this is that tax in most areas eats up most of the discount), vacation (depends on variety of factors, but generally 2 weeks for full time and 1 week for [part-time] 1st year, and increases thereafter), personnel days (day off with pay—earned up to a certain # each year (average 2)), sick days, holiday pay, etc. On the other side of the coin, [I] think much more needs to be done to provide better health care for its workers, and a goal should be done to improve this every year. Many co-workers I know have dropped [their] coverage or rely on state assistance programs. Wal-Mart also did away with some of its [benefits], such as Christmas bonuses, unless you are grandfathered in (must have been hired before the change was made).

—Anonymous
Wal-Mart manager (2007, e-mail interview, May 21)

We have an Associates Fund that everyone chips into in case someone is in critical need. For example, if a cashier were to, heaven forbid, have their house burn down, the fund would immediately come to help out by supplying a place to stay, warm clothes, and food, pretty much everything that the associate would need to get back on her feet, up to and including a replacement house, if that's what it takes. . . . A happy associate is more productive.

Sergio Jimenez,
Wal-Mart store co-manager (2007, personal interview, May 20)

Wal-Mart takes care of their people in dire situations. When my friend's wife died, they brought them groceries and really took care of them.

—Wendy S.,
46, friend of Wal-Mart associate (2007, personal interview, May 20)

One thing the company does . . . every year is [to] hold [grassroots] meetings for associates to come and vent about things they don't like, in the hope that something will change. Sadly, most associates (workers) feel that they are allowed to vent, but not without [retaliation] any more, or at best [their] input will not change anything. I think the company should not just write down the input they are being given, but act on it when possible. If they would do so it would boost morale, and more effort would be given, [causing] customer satisfaction to go up and sales to boost as well.

—Anonymous
Wal-Mart manager (2007, e-mail interview, May 21)

If I [were] to change Wal-Mart, I would reduce product on the shelves and change the lighting, and widen the aisles. [T]he bouncing ball for Wal-Mart gives it a cartoon-ish edge, whereas Target does an ad that goes coast to coast, with a heavy CGI aspect that it isn't cartoon-y. It has a big-city feel whereas Wal-Mart has a small-town middle America feel. I am partial to bigger cities. . . . Smaller towns that have limited options [make] me feel constrained, which is one of the reasons I like Target, which has hip trends, whereas Wal-Mart just has the bouncy smiley face. [T]he smiley face reduces [Wal-Mart's] seriousness. I would go to more subtle references to being the low-cost provider, and pitch one-stop shopping, but push the option to have your own personal brand, and reduce the number of SKUs on the walls so you don't feel overwhelmed by the experience there.

—Oliver Davis,
Target shopper (2007, personal interview, May 21)

I would LOVE a coupon for a certain amount off any item the store. Sort of what Michael's has (40% off any item) or Bed Bath and Beyond has (20% off). I also find Target's returns the most convenient I've ever experienced: they can locate the item you purchased by sliding your credit card through the reader so you don't have to go searching for your receipt. I appreciate that kind of convenience.

—Lili N.,
34, affluent shopper (2007, e-mail interview, May 19)

Legal Class-action lawsuits against Wal-Mart have become commonplace. In *Savaglio v. Wal-Mart Stores, Inc.*, the "plaintiffs allege that they were not provided meal and rest breaks in accordance with California law, and seek monetary damages and injunctive relief."[128] A jury ruled in favor of those plaintiffs and awarded them a total of $198 million.[129] In *Dukes v. Wal-Mart Stores, Inc.*, currently pending on behalf of all present and past female employees in all of Wal-Mart's retail stores and warehouse clubs, Wal-Mart is alleged to have "engaged in a pattern and practice of discriminating against women in promotions, pay, training, and job assignments."[130] These lawsuits are providing ample fodder for Wal-Mart opponents to inflict ongoing reputation damage.

Global The globalization trend that began in the 1990s persists. As trade barriers continue to come down around the world and as technology enables greater access to information, the world is becoming one mega-market of labor, capital, goods, and services. Bilateral and multilateral free trade agreements are continuing to shape markets.

Technology The development of radio frequency identification (RFID) is expected to play a major part in the next evolution of supply chain management in the retail industry. This technology may better enable retailers to track inventory locations, store shelving status, packages en-route to and from suppliers, warehouses, shelves, and even shoplifting.[131] Recent developments in the technology include a movement toward "common standards and practices that could make RFID as ubiquitous as bar codes," and a push to lower the cost per RFID tag from the current 10-cent mark to the Wal-Mart target of 5-cents.[132] RFID chips are increasingly "able to hold much more information and fit into different shapes and sizes—woven inside clothing, slipped into a paper-thin tag or molded inside a key chain."[133]

Another technology development impacting the retail industry is the unabated growth of electronic commerce, and the increasing pervasiveness of broadband Internet access in most developed countries. As consumers at various socioeconomic levels come to rely more on the Web for information, entertainment, and shopping, retailers are discovering the need to use their online presence not just to spur online sales, but to drive traditional-format sales as well.

Demographics Americans, like those in many developed nations, are getting older. The Census Bureau estimates the number of those aged 65 and up will rise from approximately 35 million in 2000 to 86.7 million by 2050. The age 65 and up cohort made up 12.4 percent of the total US population in 2000; by 2050, it will make up 20.7 percent of a projected population of nearly 420 million.[134]

The country is also becoming more diverse.[135] Ethnic and gender diversity in the US workforce is on the rise. In 1995, whites/non-Hispanics made up 76 percent of the workforce, but this is projected to decrease to 68 percent in 2020. According to the US Department of Labor, women comprised 46 percent of the labor force in 2006.[136] The percentage of women over the age of 16 in the labor force has risen 23 percent in 44 years to 59 percent in 2004.[137]

The distance in America between the "haves" and the "have-nots" is growing. Increasing returns to education have created a bifurcation in income distribution.[138] The bottom quintile has seen its mean income increase 34.5 percent in real terms from 1967 to 2005, whereas the top income quintile had an increase in mean income of 80.8 percent over the same time period.[139] Average income growth for the bottom three quintiles was only 30.4 percent. The typical Wal-Mart customer is in the middle-income quintiles.

As Wal-Mart's competitive landscape continues to evolve, the company is taking its strategic cues from Sam Walton's words of wisdom: "Everything around you is always changing. To succeed, stay out in front of that change."[140]

Current Strategies

To manage its competitive environment, Wal-Mart is currently deploying a variety of strategies, most of which stem from its relentless core generic strategy of cost leadership, but some of which represent beyond-cost approaches. "Our everyday low price position is the basis for our business," wrote Rob Walton in Wal-Mart's 2006 annual report.[141] He added, "While this core principle is critical to our growth and business strategy, by itself it is not enough anymore."[142] According to Scott in this year's shareholder letter, Wal-Mart is confronting "a period of perhaps the most rapid and profound change in our Company's history. With our transformation plan, we are committed to staying 'Out in Front' of the changes around us."[143] The corporate plan, encompassing previous change initiatives as well as newer ones, rests on "five pillars": "broadening our appeal to our customers, making Wal-Mart an even better place to work, improving operations and efficiencies, driving global growth, and contributing to our communities.[144]

Strategies to Deal with External and Reputational Challenges Wal-Mart is pursuing two key strategies that will help them overcome external issues affecting the company, including environmental and community-impact issues, among others. These strategies include sustainability efforts and localized charitable giving to help portray it as being a responsible corporate citizen and a good neighbor. Wal-Mart launched its global environmental sustainability initiative in 2004 and has since taken action toward several sustainability goals: sell 100 million compact fluorescent bulbs by 2008; reduce packaging by five percent by 2013; buy fish from certified fisheries; sell "more organic and environmentally friendly products"; and make company facilities and trucks more energy-efficient.[145] The Wal-Mart Foundation in 2006 gave "more than $415 million in cash and in-kind merchandise to 100,000 organizations worldwide," making it the "largest corporate cash contributor in America."[146] The Foundation "gave most of the money at the local level where [it] can have the greatest impact."[147]

Wal-Mart has beefed up pro-community, pro-sustainability, pro-health care information on its Web site, on its television ads, and in its annual report. The company recently launched *In Front with Wal-Mart*, a 30-minute television show airing on the Lifetime and USA networks that "gives [Wal-Mart] a chance to showcase [its] incredible associates and the variety of ways they give back to their communities, bettering the lives of America's working families" and "sheds light . . . on some of [Wal-Mart's] eco-friendly practices."[148] Wal-Mart created an interactive Web site on sustainability, dedicated a page of its 2007 annual report to sustain-ability, and will soon publish a separate Sustainability Report.[149]

In its public outreach, Wal-Mart also stresses its benefits to suppliers and communities, as well as its commitment to providing affordable health care and competitive wages for its associates.[150] These efforts tie into its supply-chain innovation and people strategies.

Supply-Chain Innovation and People Strategies

As previously mentioned, Wal-Mart creates value for customers with a highly efficient and innovative supply-chain management operation. This operation combines tough, low-cost procurement tactics, leading-edge information systems and "rocket-science" logistics.[151]

There's not much negotiation at all. The manufacturer walks into the room. I've been in these little cubicles, I've seen it happen. The buyer says, "Look, we want you to sell it to us for 5 percent on a dollar—at cost—lower this year than you did last year." They know every fact and figure that these manufacturers have. They know their books. They know their costs. They know their business practices—everything, you know? So what's a manufacturer left to do? They sit naked in front of Wal-Mart. You know, Wal-Mart calls the shots. "If you want to do business with us, if you want to stay in business, then you're going to do it our way." And it's all about driving down the cost of goods.

—Former Wal-Mart store manager Jon Lehman on *Frontline* in 2004[152]

All Wal-Mart suppliers must participate in Retail Link, a computerized system in which they "plan, execute, and analyze their businesses."[153] Along with electronic data interchange, suppliers receive purchase order information and supply invoices electronically, thereby lowering expenses and increasing productivity. Suppliers must meet Wal-Mart's strict lead-time and shipping requirements by using the technology and complying with operating procedures. The Wal-Mart logistics team uses an Internet-based Transportation Link system that complements a Backhaul Betty telephone voice-response system to help them move goods. In one year, Wal-Mart estimated nearly 1 million loads of general merchandise moved to Distribution Centers throughout the country.[154] Store-bound shipments travel by the company's 7,000 trucks, one of the largest fleets in the world.[155] The company relentlessly strives to develop its supply-chain process. For example, "[t] o ensure greater supply chain visibility, satellite-based tracking technology is being installed in the Company's entire fleet of over-the-road trailers. The data generated . . . increases productivity, reduces costs and enhances security."[156]

In the stores, Wal-Mart's legendary inventory management capability is driven by its advanced Texlon barcode system. In addition to tracking the sales price, inventory levels of each product, and a history of quantities sold, Texlon can record trends and predict future needs. Quantities sold can be traced to specific weeks, days, or even hours of each day. Seasonal projections can be documented, and shopping habits are noted. Information is sent daily at midnight to the warehouses, so depleted products are restocked the following night. Reliance on this kind of technology to drive the supply chain enables Wal-Mart's suppliers to use "pull production" instead of "push production." The barcode system will eventually be replaced by an RFID-based system, technology Wal-Mart is driving.

Wal-Mart's technological supply-chain sophistication is intended to provide "value for customers, associates, and shareholders."[157] The system depends on Wal-Mart's 1.8 million associates to provide the final link in the value chain to customers. Wal-Mart's people strategy involves "[g]iving our associates the tools and opportunities they need to be as productive as possible," which has enabled "workforce productivity gains in every quarter of the last two years."[158] Associates who feel overworked may create a weak link in the value chain.

> *I would say that some customers are happy, but most are not. . . . [M]any workers feel they are being overworked due to mainly understaffing issues, which causes workers to treat the customers worse, then causing customers to become upset. Many customers have at one time been [Wal-Mart] associates and understand how things are handled at each store level and can relate. Personally, [I] believe that overall morale a few years ago was much higher with workers, and that attitude was passed along to the customers. Today many customers feel that [Wal-Mart] only wants them for [their] money, and does not care about them."*
>
> **—Anonymous Wal-Mart manager (2007, e-mail interview, May 21)**

Reassuring its "valued long-term associates" that the company "is listening to them," Wal-Mart "again increased [its] average full-time hourly wage in the United States."[159] The company is against unionization of its associates.

Wal-Mart's operational effectiveness goals of improving return on investment, comparable-store sales, and working capital productivity are setting the agenda for its business-segment strategies.[160]

Wal-Mart Stores Segment Strategies

The Wal-Mart Stores segment is in its second year of a three-year strategic plan to improve ROI, people development, and customer relevancy.[161] Customers have become the prime focus since January 2007, when Wal-Mart Stores elevated its new marketing and merchandising chiefs and completed its management reshuffle.

In 2006, Wal-Mart Stores rolled out a $4 generic prescription program, a clear opening-price-point approach. Merchandising has been characterized by the product-focused "opening price point" strategy, which relied on attractive low prices on entry-level items in every category to set the stage for higher-margin prices on more desirable items.[162] This single strategy has served to focus each of the two dozen departments at a typical Wal-Mart Supercenter (see Exhibit 19). Wal-Mart stores often offer retail space to other vendors that provide services, such as nail salons, hair salons, coffee shops, food and beverage vendors (e.g., McDonald's and Subway), full-service banks, and even employment agencies in some locations.

Recently, Wal-Mart Stores "realigned [its] merchandising . . . around five key power categories—entertainment, grocery, health and wellness, apparel, and home."[163] Global Procurement meanwhile is "establishing groups of technical experts—specialists that focus on the many important dynamics of a particular category purchase."[164]

Exhibit 19 List of departments in Wal-Mart

Wal-Mart Departments	
Grocery	Pharmacy
Bakery	Health & Beauty
Produce	Vision Center
Deli	Jewelry
Frozen Foods	Lawn & Garden
Apparel	Portrait Studio
Housewares	Photo Lab
Entertainment	Hardware
Electronics	Furniture
Tire & Lube Express	Sporting Goods
Automotive	Toys & Games
School Supplies	Office Products & School Supplies

Source: http://www.walmart.com.

The Wal-Mart Stores customer segmentation and merchandising strategies have been in flux over the past few years, with three different strategies in play to move Wal-Mart Stores toward a more customer-focused position.

The first customer-focused strategy—mimicking Target's upscale, fashion-forward appeal—flopped. "In working to broaden our appeal to our customers, we moved too quickly in the rollout of some of our fashion-forward apparel in the United States," according to Scott.[165] Wal-Mart Stores has at least partially retreated from this strategy.

The second customer-focused strategy—localizing selections based on store-neighborhood demographics—continues to drive various store changes, though it may be waning. In 2006, Wal-Mart "launched six different types of customized stores to attract different demographics, from inner-city residents, to affluent suburbanites, to rural shoppers."[166] With these stores, Wal-Mart attempted to target African-Americans, Hispanics, empty-nesters, suburbanites, rural residents, and the affluent. Wal-Mart expanded and empowered regional marketing teams, moving many executives away from headquarters into regions to better understand Wal-Mart's wide customer base.[167] These changes were inspired by localized merchandizing selection in Wal-Mart de Mexico stores aimed at different mixes of inventory for different income levels.[168] For example, the localization strategy expanded the mix of hip-hop, gospel, and R&B music in a store outside Chicago and led to plans for larger pharmacy sections and fewer children's clothes at a store geared toward empty-nesters.[169] In his March letter to shareholders, Scott wrote, "We continue to strive to make sure every Wal-Mart store is a 'Store of the Community'—one that reflects the individual needs of each neighborhood we serve".[170]

The third customer-focused strategy—appealing to the three universal types of low-price-seeking customers who currently shop at Wal-Mart—now guides merchandising and marketing decisions. According to Fleming and Quinn, the three types are "'brand aspirationals' (people with low incomes who are obsessed with names like Kitchen Aid), 'price-sensitive affluents' (wealthier shoppers who love deals), and 'value-price shoppers' (who like low prices and cannot afford much more)."[171] For these types, the Wal-Mart Stores segment is concentrating on developing unique, innovative products and providing distinguished brands (such as the recently added Dell desktop computers) to better appeal to its core customers as the low-price leader on well-known brands.[172]

> *This is a much better strategy for Wal-Mart than the store segmentation strategy path . . . they were going down before . . . because it aligns with their basic brand proposition (EDLP) and basic consumer rather than trying to attract a new consumer by adding high-end fashion and complicated assortments. For the same reason, it aligns better with Wal-Mart's supply chain strength. It's far easier to roll out a national brand in stores nationally than it is to ship different assortments to different stores within a region without disrupting the cost efficient supply chain that is Wal-Mart's core competitive advantage. I'm not sure what took them so long but it looks like Wal-Mart is back to a strategy that is sustainable and executable for them.*
>
> **—Forrester Research senior analyst Lisa Bradner**[173]

Sam's Club Segment Strategies

Sam's Club, meanwhile, is focused on three areas: "reinvigorating the brand" by broadening products and services; improving inventory management and other performance measures; and optimizing the "in-club experience."[174] Sam's Club stores offer members products such as frozen and dry food goods in bulk, electronics, computer equipment, clothing, books, electronic entertainment, and general merchandise. Sam's Club recently restructured its management layers to give stores additional flexibility and to boost service.[175] Rumors have circulated that Sam's Club may spin off from Wal-Mart, in part to set its own direction in attracting and retaining members and associates, two key groups who are generally less loyal to Sam's Club than to its rival Costco.[176]

Wal-Mart International Segment Strategies

Wal-Mart International's strategy is to prioritize "where the greatest growth and greatest returns exist," what the segment calls "majoring in the majors."[177] The majors appear to include the Americas primarily, followed by the United Kingdom and Japan, as well as China and India over the long term.[178] Wal-Mart International is labeling this strategy "focused portfolio execution."[179] Its second strategy is global leverage, or "taking full advantage of our worldwide assets, including formats, information systems, purchasing organizations, category expertise, and shared best practices."[180] In the past year, it has concentrated on turning around Asda in the United Kingdom through "improved execution in all phases of customer service, differentiation with competitors, and development of new channels and formats."[181] To better compete against UK leader Tesco, second-largest Asda reportedly may be considering acquiring the third-largest UK retailer, the J. Sainsbury chain of grocery and convenience stores.[182] Wal-Mart's international stores are varied in their mix of products and services, and they stick to the motto of "offering working families the things they need at the prices they can afford."[183]

Just as the business segments are looking to focus on the right challenges for their short- and long-term success in the marketplace, the company must ensure it is applying its greatest resources against its greatest strategic challenges across the enterprise.

Strategic Challenges

The challenges Wal-Mart faces today are actually not much different from what they have been for the past several years. These following quotes come from an article in April 2003: "Even though it is the nation's largest apparel retailer with more than 12 percent of the market, Wal-Mart could be doing better in this category"; "It would like to be a fashion retailer and take on Target with good quality at a low price-point, but it hasn't convinced the American consumer it should be a destination for casual fashion"; "Wal-Mart is . . . looking abroad for future sales growth"; "Wal-Mart will need to struggle against the urge to centralize operations and eliminate decision making from the front-lines where managers have face-to-face contact with customers"; and "The only area in which Wal-Mart has not been able to pummel its competition is against Costco."[184] One of the company's challenges may be to stop proliferating nearly identical sets of challenges each year. Like the stock price, the challenges appear to be stuck in a holding pattern.

One key new challenge is the sluggishness of same-store sales relative to Wal-Mart's competitors. According to *BusinessWeek,* Wal-Mart faces "the diciest conundrum in retailing today . . . can it seduce . . . middle-income shoppers into stepping up their purchases in a major way without alienating its low-income legions in the process?"[185]

Another growing challenge is the difficulty of expanding in the domestic market, whether because of community opposition or geographic saturation (see Exhibits 20 and 21).

These and other strategic challenges are weighing on the minds of Wal-Mart's shareholders, especially on the two with the most responsibility for the company's fate.

Questions Wal-Mart Leaders Must Address

CEO Lee Scott and Chairman Rob Walton are grappling with some vexing questions as they head into the 2007 Wal-Mart Annual Shareholders' Meeting:

- How can Wal-Mart Stores and Sam's Club increase same-store sales?
- How should the company capture share of middle-and upper-income wallets?
- Should Wal-Mart Stores fully retreat from fashion-forward merchandising and marketing? Will its neighborhood-store-localization strategy increase sales enough to offset the associated costs? What should it do to make its new three-types-of-custom-ers segmentation strategy work?
- Should the company spin off Sam's Club? If not, what should it do to compete more effectively against Costco?
- Is Wal-Mart expanding the right kind of new stores at the right pace and in the right places? How and where should the company continue to grow internationally? Should Asda buy J. Sainsbury?
- What will it take to restore the company's reputation in America?
- Should Lee Scott change Wal-Mart's course? If so, how?
- Should Rob Walton replace Lee Scott? If so, when and with whom?

Exhibit 20 Spread of Wal-Mart stores, 1970–1995

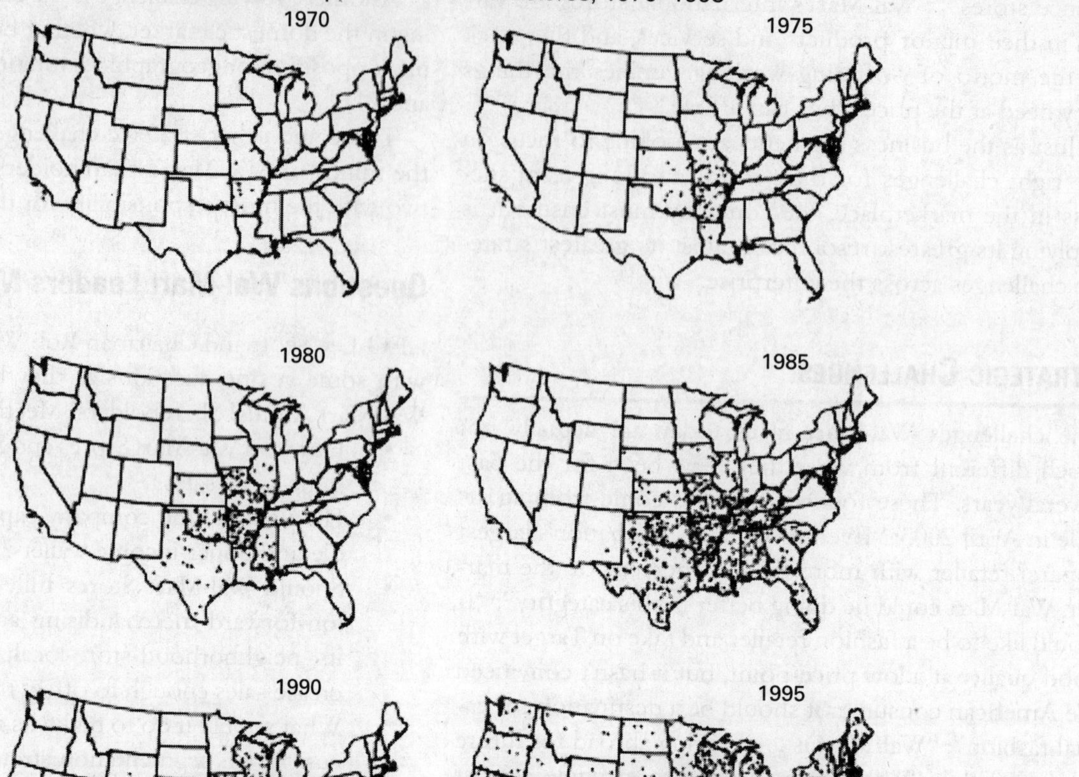

Source: E. Basker, 2004, Job creation or destruction? Labor-market effects of Wal-Mart expansion, University of Missouri, January, Figure 1, 28.

Exhibit 21 Number of countries having a Wal-Mart Store, 1963–2006

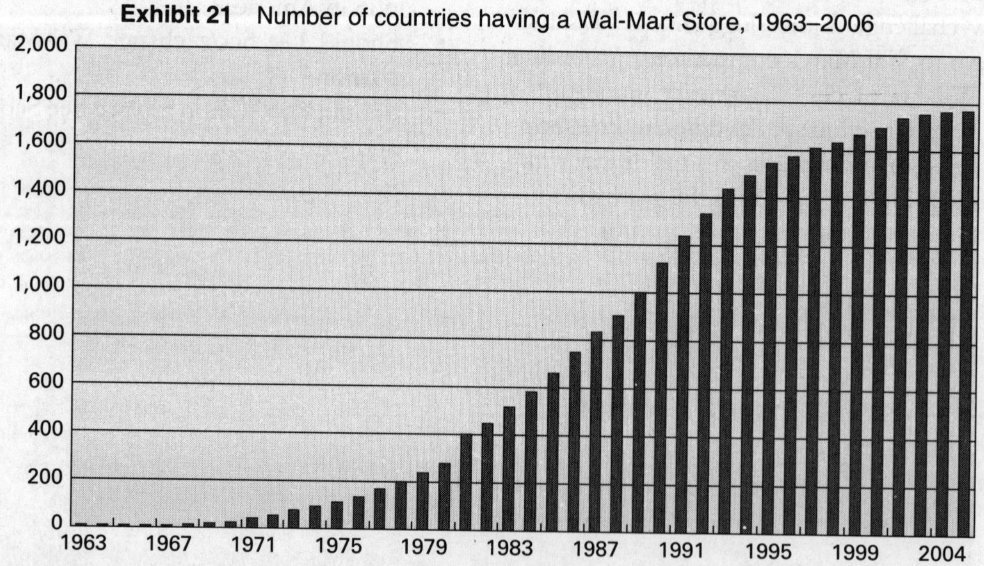

Source: 2005, The economic impact of Wal-Mart, Global Insight, Business Planning Solutions, Global Insight Advisory Services, November 2, Figure 4, 33.

NOTES

1. A. Bianco, 2006, *The Bully of Bentonville: The High Cost of Wal-Mart's Everyday Low Prices*, New York: Doubleday Publishing, 1.
2. 2007, 7 demands for change, Against * The * Wal, http://www .againstthewal.net/7demands.html, May 18.
3. 2007, Notice of 2007 Annual Shareholders' Meeting, DEF 14A, Proxy Statement, Wal-Mart Stores, Inc., US SEC, April 19, 52–68.
4. A. Bianco, 2006, *The Bully of Bentonville: The High Cost of Wal-Mart's Everyday Low Prices*, 267; 2007, *Yahoo! Finance*, http:// finance.yahoo.com/charts#chart6:symbol=wmt;range=20000103, 20070518;compare=cost+tgt;indicator=volume;charttype=line; crosshair=on;logscale=on;source=undefined, May 17.
5. 2007, *Yahoo! Finance*, http://finance.yahoo.com/charts#chart6:sym bol=wmt;range=20000103,20070518;compare=cost+tgt;indicator= volume;charttype=line;crosshair=on;logscale=on;source=undefine d, May 17.
6. A. Bianco, 2007, Wal-Mart's midlife crisis, *BusinessWeek*, April 30, 46–52.
7. 2007, Wal-Mart Data Sheet, http://walmartstores.com/Files/US_ operations.pdf, February 8.
8. 2007, Wal-Mart Annual Report.
9. 2007, Wal-Mart Stores, Inc., Form 8-K, US SEC, May 15; and 2007, Company Overview, Target.com, http://investors.target.com/ phoenix.zhtml?c=65828&p=irol-homeProfile, May 25.
10. L. Michael Cacace & K. Tucksmith, 2007, Fortune 500 largest US corporations, Fortune, April 30, F2.
11. Ibid.
12. A. Bianco, 2007, Wal-Mart's midlife crisis, 49–52.
13. A. Bianco, 2007, Wal-Mart's midlife crisis, 46.
14. 2004, Wal-Mart Tops Fortune's List of America's Most Admired Companies, *Fortune*, http://www.timeinc.net/fortune/information/ presscenter/fortune/press_releases/02232004AMAC.html, February 23.
15. 2007, America's Most Admired Companies 2007, *Fortune, CNNMoney.com*, http://money.cnn.com/magazines/fortune/ mostadmired/2007/top20/, May 18.
16. W. Zellner, 2004, Sam Walton: King of the discounters, *BusinessWeek*, August 9.
17. Ibid.
18. Ibid.
19. A. A. Thompson & A. J. Strickland, *Strategic Management, Concepts & Cases*, 10th ed., New York: Irwin/McGraw-Hill.
20. 2007, The Wal-Mart Timeline, Wal-Mart Facts, http://www .walmartfacts.com/content/default.aspx?id=3, April 1; D. Longo, 1998, Wal-Mart hands CEO crown to David Glass, Discount Store News, February 15, 1988.
21. 2007, Wal-Mart Annual Report, 19; 2007, The Wal-Mart Timeline, Wal-Mart Facts, http://www.walmartfacts.com/content/default. aspx?id=3, April 1.
22. A. Bianco, 2007, Wal-Mart's midlife crisis, 46–54.
23. 2007, Data Sheet, Wal-Mart Stores, http://walmartstores.com/Files/ US_operations.pdf, February 8, May 25; and 2007, International Data Sheet, Wal-Mart Stores, http://walmartstores.com/Files/ Intl_operations.pdf, February 8, May 25.
24. 2007, Wal-Mart Annual Report, 1.
25. A. Biesada, 2007, Wal-Mart Company Overview, Hoovers Online, http://premium.hoovers.com, May.
26. Ibid.
27. P. Engardio, 2007, Beyond the green corporation, imagine a world in which eco-friendly and socially responsible practices actually help a company's bottom line. It's closer than you think, *BusinessWeek Online*, January 29.
28. 2007, Wal-Mart Annual Report, 18-19.
29. 2007, Wal-Mart Annual Report, 31.
30. 2007, Wal-Mart Annual Report , 28.
31. Ibid.
32. Ibid.
33. 2007, Wal-Mart Annual Report, 31.
34. Ibid.
35. 2007, Wal-Mart Annual Report, 28.
36. 2007, Wal-Mart Annual Report, 36.
37. 2007, Wal-Mart Annual Report, 32.
38. 2007, International Data Sheet, Wal-Mart Stores, http://walmartstores .com/Files/Intl_operations.pdf, February 8.
39. 2007, Wal-Mart Annual Report, 32.
40. 2007, Wal-Mart Annual Report, 51-52.
41. 2006, IGD looks at Wal-Mart's decision to pull out of Germany, http://www.igd.com/CIR, March 8.
42. 2007, Wal-Mart Annual Report, 32.
43. 2007, Informe Annual 2006, Wal-Mart de Mexico, http://library .corporate-ir.net/library/19/194/194702/items/231792/AR06.pdf, May 21; and 2007, CIA World Fact Book, Mexico, https://www.cia .gov/library/publications/the-world-factbook/geos/mx.html#Econ, May 21.
44. 2007, Wal-Mart Facts: The Wal-Mart Story, http://www.walmartfacts .com/content/default.aspx?id=1, April 1.
45. 2006, CNBC Interview with Carter Cast, http://www.hoovers.com/ global/co/interviews/player.xhtml, November 7.
46. 2007, About Sam's Club, Samsclub.com, http://pressroom.samsclub .com/content/?id=3&atg=524, March 1.
47. K. Hundson, 2007, Wal-Mart Pushes Financial-Services Menu, *Wall Street Journal*, June 6, A3.
48. 2007, The Wal-Mart Timeline, Wal-Mart Facts, http://www .walmartfacts.com/content/default.aspx?id=3, April 1; D. Longo, 1998, Wal-Mart hands CEO crown to David Glass, Discount Store News, February 15.
49. 2007, The Wal-Mart Timeline, Wal-Mart Facts, http://www .walmartfacts.com/content/default.aspx?id=3, April 1.
50. 2007, Wal-Mart Annual Report, 14; 2007, Senior Officers, Wal-Mart Stores, http://walmartstores.com/GlobalWMStoresWeb/navigate .do?catg=540, May 6.
51. 2007, S. Robson Walton, Wal-Mart Stores, http://

walmartstores .com/GlobalWMStoresWeb/navigate.do?catg=540&contId=15, May 6; 2005. Forbes: America's richest 400, MSN Money, http:// moneycentral.msn.com/content/invest/forbes/P129955.asp, September 23.

52. A. Bianco, 2006, *The Bully of Bentonville: The High Cost of Wal-Mart's Everyday Low Prices*, 61.
53. 2007, S. Robson Walton, Wal-Mart Stores.
54. 2007, Wal-Mart Annual Report, 13.
55. A. Bianco, The Bully of Bentonville: The High Cost of Wal-Mart's Everyday Low Prices, 104.
56. Ibid.
57. A. Bianco, The Bully of Bentonville: The High Cost of Wal-Mart's Everyday Low Prices, 79.
58. Ibid.
59. A. Bianco, *The Bully of Bentonville: The High Cost of Wal-Mart's Everyday Low Prices*, 80.
60. A. Bianco, *The Bully of Bentonville: The High Cost of Wal-Mart's Everyday Low Prices*, 81.
61. 2007, H. Lee Scott, Jr., Senior Officers, WalMartStores.com, http://walmartstores.com/GlobalWMStoresWeb/navigate.do?catg=540&contId=17, May 25.
62. Ibid.
63. 2007, Michael T. Duke, Senior Officers, WalMartStores.com, http://walmartstores.com/GlobalWMStoresWeb/navigate.do?catg=540&contId=22, May 25.
64. Ibid.
65. 2007, John B. Menzer, Senior Officers, WalMartStores.com, http://walmartstores.com/GlobalWMStoresWeb/navigate.do?catg=540&contId=19, May 25.
66. Ibid.
67. Ibid.
68. 2007, Eduardo Castro-Wright, Senior Officers, WalMartStores.com, http://walmartstores.com/GlobalWMStoresWeb/navigate .do?catg=540&contId=41, May 25.
69. 2007, C. Douglas McMillon, Senior Officers, WalMartStores.com, http://walmartstores.com/GlobalWMStoresWeb/navigate .do?catg=540&contId=33, May 25.
70. 2007, John E. Fleming, Senior Officers, WalMartStores.com, http://walmartstores.com/GlobalWMStoresWeb/navigate.do?catg=540&contId=42, May 25.
71. 2007, Stephen Quinn, Senior Officers, WalMartStores.com, http://walmartstores.com/GlobalWMStoresWeb/navigate.do?catg=540&contId=6396, May 25.
72. 2007, Wal-Mart Board of Directors, Walmart.com, June 28.
73. M. Halkias, 2007, Questrom nominated to Wal-Mart board, Dallas Morning News, http://www.dallasnews.com/sharedcontent/dws/bus/ industries/retail/stories/042507dnbusquestrom.36b21ad.html, April 24.
74. Ibid.
75. S. Braun, 2007, At Wal-Mart, Clinton didn't upset any carts, *Los Angeles Times*, http://www.latimes.com/news/nationworld/nation/ la-na-hillary19may19,0,5168474.story?coll=la-home-center, May 19.
76. 2007, Morningstar, Wal-Mart Stores (WMT), http://quicktake .morningstar.com/StockNet/powerbrokers.aspx?Country=USA& Symbol=WMT&stocktab=owner, May 6; 2007, Wal-Mart Stores Inc. (WMT), Major Holders, *Yahoo! Finance*, http://finance.yahoo. com/q/mh?s=WMT, May 6.
77. 2007, Wal-Mart Stores Inc. (WMT), Major Holders, *Yahoo! Finance*, http://finance.yahoo.com/q/mh?s=WMT; May 6; and 2005, Forbes: America's richest 400, MSN Money, http://moneycentral.msn.com/ content/invest/forbes/P129955.asp, September 23; 2002, Proxy, Wal-Mart Stores, http://www.walmartstores.com/Files/proxy_2002/ proxy_pg05.htm; M. Weil and M. Barbaro, 2005, John T. Walton, 58; Heir to Wal-Mart Fortune, The Washington Post, http:// www.washingtonpost.com/wp-dyn/content/article/2005/06/27/AR2005062701471.html, June 28; 2007, Associated Press, Washington Post, Helen R. Walton; Philanthropic wife of Wal-Mart chief, http://www.washingtonpost.com/wp-dyn/content/ article/2007/04/20/AR2007042002060.html, April 21.
78. 2007, Wal-Mart Stores Inc. (WMT), Insider Roster, *Yahoo! Finance*, http://finance.yahoo.com/q/ir?s=WMT, May 6.
79. 2007, Wal-Mart Stores Inc. (WMT), Major Holders, *Yahoo! Finance*, http://finance.yahoo.com/q/mh?s=WMT, May 6.
80. 2007, Morningstar, Wal-Mart Stores (WMT), http://quicktake .morningstar.com/StockNet/powerbrokers.aspx?Country=USA&Sym bol=WMT&stocktab=owner, May 6.
81. 2007, Wal-Mart Annual Report, 64.
82. 2007, 2002 Wal-Mart Annual Reports.
83. Ibid.
84. 2007, Sam's Club vs. Costco: Battle of the brands, BloggingStocks, *AOL Money & Finance*, http://www.bloggingstocks. com/2007/04/12/sams-club-vs-costco-battle-of-the-brands/, April 12.
85. T. Otte, 2007, Spinoff in Bentonville revisited, Value Investing, *MotleyFool.com*, http://www.fool.com/investing/value/2007/05/07/ spinoff-in-bentonville-revisited.aspx, May 7.
86. M. Wagner, 2003, Where's Wal-Mart: Wal-Mart's web revenue hardly registers on its ledger, *Internet Retailer*, http://www.internetretailer .com/internet/marketing-conference/70624-wheres-wal-mart.html, April.
87. D. Pinto, 2005, Mass market retailers, http://www .mass-marketretailers.com/articles/Every_winner.html, May 16.
88. Ibid.
89. Ibid.
90. A. Bianco, 2007, Wal-Mart's, midlife crisis, 48.
91. D. Pinto, Mass market retailers.
92. M. Holz-Clause & M. Geisler, 2006, Grocery Industry, Grocery Retailing Profile, *AgMRC*, http://www.agmrc.org/agmrc/markets/ Food/groceryindustry.htm, September.
93. 2007, Wal-Mart F1Q08 (Qtr End 4/30/07) Earnings Call Transcript, SeekingAlpha.com, http://retail.seekingalpha.com/article/35633, May 15.
94. Ibid.
95. 2007, Wal-Mart 1st Quarter 2008 Earnings Release, May 10.
96. Ibid.
97. 2007, Wal-Mart April Sales News Release, May 10.
98. R. Dodes & G. McWilliams, 2007, Fashion faux pas hurts Wal-Mart, *Wall Street Journal*, May 21, A8.

99. G. McWilliams, 2007, Wal-Mart net rises as weakness persists, *Wall Street Journal*, May 16, C6.
100. J. Covert, 2007, Retail-sales slide fuels concern: Decline of 2.3% in April among worst on record; even Wal-Mart slipped, *Wall Street Journal*, May 11, A3.
101. 2007, Target Corporation, Form 8-K, US SEC, May 23; 2007, Company Overview, *Target.com*, http://investors.target.com/ phoenix.zhtml?c=65828&p=irol-homeProfile, May 25.
102. Ibid.
103. 2006, Target Annual Report, 2.
104. Ibid.
105. 2007, Company Profile, Costco Wholesale Investor Relations, http://phx.corporate-ir.net/phoenix.zhtml?c=83830&p=irol-homeprofile, May 5.
106. 2006, Costco Annual Report, 9.
107. 2006, 2002, Costco Annual Report.
108. 2007, The Kroger Co., Form 10-K, US SEC, April 4.
109. Ibid.
110. Ibid.
111. 2007, Carrefour profile, Hoovers, Lexis/Nexis Academic, May 8.
112. 2007, Tesco profile, Hoovers, Lexis/Nexis Academic, May 8.
113. Ibid.
114. 2007, Global Procurement, WalMartStores.com, http://walmartstores.com/GlobalWMStoresWeb/navigate.do?catg=337, May 26.
115. A. Bianco & W. Zellner, 2003, Is Wal-Mart too powerful? *BusinessWeek*, http://www.businessweek.com/magazine/content/03_40/b3852001_mz001.htm, October 6.
116. Ibid.
117. Ibid.
118. 2007, Wal-Mart Facts, http://www.walmartfacts.com/FactSheets/3142007_Corporate_Facts.pdf, March 14.
119. S. Kapinus, 2006, Rollback sushi and discount organics, ACNielsen Consumer Insight, http://us.acnielsen.com/pubs/2006_q2_ci_ rollback.shtml, Q2.
120. Ibid.
121. Ibid.
122. Ibid.
123. Barney Gimbel, 2006, Attack of the Wal-Martyrs, http://money.cnn .com/magazines/fortune/fortune_archive/2006/12/11/8395445/ index.htm, November 28.
124. B. C. Lynn, 2006, It's time to enforce antitrust law and break up Wal-Mart, *Harper's Magazine*, July.
125. A. Nagourney & M. Barbaro, 2006, Eye on election, Democrats run as Wal-Mart foe, *New York Times*, August 17.
126. Ibid.
127. 2006, Beaverton council rejects Cedar Mill Wal-Mart plan, Beaverton Valley Times, August 8; 2005, No Wal-Mart for Vancouver, CBC News, June 29; 2004, Inglewood Wal-Mart proposal defeated, http://www.laane.org/pressroom/stories/ walmart/040407CityNewsService.html, April 6.
128. 2007, Wal-Mart Annual Report, 56.
129. Ibid.
130. Ibid.
131. C. Harrison, 2003, Commitment from Wal-Mart may boost tracking technology, Dallas Morning News, July 15.
132. Ibid.
133. Ibid.
134. 2004, US Census Bureau, Interim Projections Consistent with 2000 Census, http://www.census.gov/population/www/projections/ popproj.html, March.
135. Ibid.
136. 2007, US Department of Labor, Women's Bureau: Statistics & Data, http://www.dol.gov/wb/stats/main.htm, May 14.
137. E. L. Chao & K. P. Utgoff, Women in the labor force: A databook, US Bureau of Labor Statistics, May 2005, 1.
138. G. Becker & K. Murphy, 2007, The upside of income inequality, *The American*, May/June, 24–28.
139. 2007, US Census Bureau, Historical Income Inequality Tables, http:// www.census.gov/hhes/www/income/histinc/ineqtoc.html, May 21.
140. 2007, Wal-Mart "Out in Front," Fact Sheets, WalMartFacts.com, http://www.walmartfacts.com/FactSheets/4112007_Wal-Mart__Out_ in_Front_.pdf, April 11.
141. R. Walton, 2006, Wal-Mart Annual Report, inside cover.
142. Ibid.
143. H. L. Scott, 2007, Wal-Mart Annual Report, 10.
144. 2007, Wal-Mart "Out in Front."
145. 2007 Wal-Mart Annual Report, 5, 12; and Wal-Mart Stores Overview, http://walmartstores.com/GlobalWMStoresWeb/navigate .do?catg=345, May 25.
146. 2007 Wal-Mart Annual Report, 8, 12.
147. Ibid.
148. 2007, In Front with Wal-Mart, Wal-Mart Stores, Inc., http://www .infrontwithwalmart.com/about.aspx, May 20.
149. 2007, Wal-Mart Annual Report, 5.
150. 2007, Wal-Mart Annual Report, 11.
151. 2003, Knowledge@Wharton, The Wal-Mart Empire: A Simple Formula and Unstoppable Growth, Research at Penn, http://www. upenn.edu/researchatpenn/article.php?631&bus, April 9.
152. 2004, FRONTLINE co-production with Hedrick Smith Productions, Inc., WGBH Educational Foundation, http://www.pbs.org/wgbh/ pages/frontline/shows/walmart/etc/script.html.
153. 2007, Wal-Mart supplier requirements and processes, http:// walmartstores.com/GlobalWMStoresWeb/navigate .do?catg=331, May 19.
154. Ibid.
155. 2007, Wal-Mart Sustainability, http://walmartstores.com/microsite/ walmart_sustainability.html, May 19.
156. 2007, Wal-Mart Annual Report, 16.
157. Ibid.
158. 2007, Wal-Mart Annual Report, 11.
159. Ibid.
160. 2007, Wal-Mart Annual Report, 21.
161. 2007, Wal-Mart Annual Report, 18.
162. S. Hornblower, 2004, Always low prices: Is Wal-Mart good for America? Frontline, http://www.pbs.org/wgbh/pages/frontline/ shows/walmart/secrets/pricing.html, November 23.
163. 2007, Wal-Mart Annual Report, 18.
164. 2007, Wal-Mart Annual Report, 17.
165. H. L. Scott, 2007, Wal-Mart Annual Report, 11.

166. B. Helm & D. Kiley, 2006, Wal-Mart leaves draft out in the cold, *BusinessWeek*, http://www.businessweek.com/bw-daily/dnflash/ content/dec2006/db20061207_540888.htm?campaign_id=rss_ innovate, December 7.
167. A. Zimmerman, 2006, To boost sales, Wal-Mart drops one-size-fits-all approach, *Wall Street Journal*, http://online.wsj.com/ article/SB115758956826955863.html?mod=hps_us_pageone, September 7.
168. Ibid.
169. Ibid.
170. H. L. Scott, 2007, Wal-Mart Annual Report, 11.
171. M. Barbaro, 2007, It's not only about price at Wal-Mart, *New York Times*, http://www.nytimes.com/2007/03/02/ business/02walmart.ht ml?ex=1330491600&en=5a72ddc69030ce62&ei=5088&partner=rssnyt&emc=rss&pagewanted=print, March 2
172. 2007 Wal-Mart Annual Report, 17; P. Svensson, 2007, Dell to sell computers at Wal-Mart, Associated Press, *Yahoo! Finance*, http:// biz.yahoo.com/ap/070524/dell_wal_mart.html?.v=11, May 24.
173. T. Ryan, 2007, From RetailWire: Wal-Mart classifies customers for growth, Supply Chain Digest, http://www.scdigest.com/assets/ newsViews/07-03-27-2.php?cid=977, March 27.
174. 2007, Wal-Mart Annual Report, 19.
175. 2007, Wal-Mart cutting managers at Sam's Club, *Reuters*, http:// www.reuters.com/article/businessNews/idUSN2628417520070426?f eedType=RSS, April 26.
176. T. Otte, 2007, Spinoff in Bentonville revisited, value investing, *MotleyFool.com*, http://www.fool.com/investing/value/2007/05/07/ spinoff-in-bentonville-revisited.aspx, May 7.
177. 2007, Wal-Mart Annual Report, 19.
178. Ibid.
179. Ibid.
180. Ibid.
181. 2007, Wal-Mart F1Q08 (Qtr End 4/30/07) Earnings call transcript, retail stocks, SeekingAlpha, http://retail.seekingalpha.com/ article/35633, May 15.
182. 2007, Wal-Mart evaluating options in possible bid for the UK's J. Sainsbury chain, *Supply Chain Digest*, http://www.scdigest.com/ assets/newsViews/07-03-27-3.php?cid=978, March 27.
183. 2007, Wal-Mart Retail Divisions, http://www.walmartfacts.com/ articles/2502.aspx, April 4.
184. 2003, The Wal-Mart Empire: A simple formula and unstoppable growth, *Knowledge@Wharton*, http://www.upenn.edu/ researchatpenn/article.php?631&bus, April 9.
185. A. Bianco, 2007, Wal-Mart's midlife crisis, 56.

Apple Computer, Inc.: Maintaining the Music Business While Introducing iPhone and Apple TV*

CASE 14

Robin Chapman, Robert E. Hoskisson
Arizona State University

"This will go down in history as a turning point for the music industry," said Apple Computer CEO Steve Jobs. "This is landmark stuff. I can't overestimate it!"[1] Jobs was referring to the April 2003 debut of Apple's iTunes Online Music Store, the first legal online music service to have agreements with all five major record labels. Although initially available only for Macintosh users, iTunes sold more than 1 million songs by the end of its first week in operation. Not only did iTunes change the nature of the music industry, it also added greatly to Apple's revenues by way of promoting the purchase of the iPod—a portable digital music device that can store downloaded iTunes songs. In 2007, Apple controlled more than 70 percent of the digital music market,[2] and its net income was $3.5 billion (see Exhibits 1 and 2). Jobs hopes further that the success of iTunes will flourish with the launch of Apple TV and iPhone in 2007. In May 2007, Apple was named by *BusinessWeek* as the most innovative company for the third year in a row. Apple's focus on innovation has helped it maintain a competitive advantage and marketing prowess over other industry players that have historically been much stronger than Apple.[3] However, Apple must beat the competition on a number of levels. iTunes faces stiff competition from new and existing online music and video download services both legal and illegal. The iPod, Apple TV, and iPhone all face the threat of lower-priced rivals and possible substitutes. Apple's innovative ability and the quality of its marketing strategy will likely determine the outcome of the company's foray into the music, mobile phone, and video-on-demand businesses.

Early Company History

On April 1, 1976, Steve Jobs and Stephen Wozniak began the partnership that would eventually become Apple Computer. Both electronics gurus, Jobs and Wozniak had known each other since high school and had worked together previously on other projects.[4] In early 1976, Wozniak had been working on combining video monitors with computers. His idea was to invent a user-friendly computer that ordinary consumers could buy. Wozniak,

* This case is intended to be used as the basis for class discussion rather than to illustrate effective or ineffective handling of an administrative or strategic situation. We appreciate the previous input on an earlier case focused only on the music industry by Jeff Berrong, Marilyn Klopp, Max Mishkin, Jimmy Pittman, and Adrian Ray under the direction of Professor Robert E. Hoskisson.

who worked for Hewlett-Packard (HP) at the time, decided to approach his employer with his idea. HP, however, did not see a future for personal computers (PCs) and soundly rebuffed him. At that point, Steve Jobs told his friend Wozniak that they should go into business together and sell computers themselves.[5]

Their first computer, the *Apple I*, was built in the garage of Jobs's parents (see Exhibit 3). Known as a "kit computer," the original Apple consisted merely of a circuit board and did not even have an exterior casing. It was intended to be sold to hobbyists only. Jobs called the computer an "Apple" in honor of his days working at an orchard while seeking enlightenment—and because neither he nor Wozniak could come up with a better name.[6] The *Apple I* received mixed responses from hobbyists, and the duo decided it was time to expand the market for personal computers by building a more attractive and useful machine, the *Apple II*.[7]

GROWTH

After taking on new partners to fund expansion plans, the company officially became Apple Computer, Inc., in early 1977.[8] Within months, the recapitalized company introduced the *Apple II*, the first computer to come with a sleek plastic casing and color graphics.[9] Annual sales increased dramatically to $10 million, and the company began to grow quickly in size, adding thousands of employees.[10] On December 12, 1980, Apple became a public company. On the first day of trading, its share price increased from an initial $22 offering to $29.[11] By the end of the year, Apple reached $100 million in annual sales.[12] The fledgling company, however, soon faced some experienced competition.

In 1981, IBM released its first personal computer. IBM's sheer size ensured its domination of the young PC market. Steve Jobs realized that Apple would have to move fast in order to remain a viable company. Over the next few years, the company released several new computer models, most notably the *Apple III* and the *Lisa*. Neither of these models sold particularly well.

In 1983, Jobs recruited Pepsi-Cola CEO John Sculley as Apple's president and CEO. Jobs hoped that this change would bring more structure and organization to the young company.[13] Apple's biggest computer achievement, the Macintosh (Mac), was released. After initially opposing it, Jobs had personally taken on the task of developing the Mac, which became the first PC featuring a graphical interface and a mouse for navigation. Apple first presented the now-famous Macintosh computer with a riveting January 1984 Super Bowl commercial. The memorable commercial featured an Orwellian *1984* world filled with stoic human zombies, all watching a large-screen image of "Big Brother." A young woman rushes into the room and dramatically destroys the screen. Apple used this *1984* imagery to depict IBM's computer dominance being destroyed by the new Macintosh.[14] With features that made the Mac easy to use for publishing and a marketing strategy that concentrated on universities, the new computer sold very well, pushing Apple's fiscal 1984 sales to an unprecedented $1.5 billion.[15]

Exhibit 1 Consolidated statements of cash flows

(In millions)	Three Fiscal Years Ended September 29		
	2007	**2006**	**2005**
Cash and cash equivalents, beginning of the year	$6,392	$3,491	$2,969
Operating Activities: Net income	3,496	1,989	1,328
Adjustments to reconcile net income to cash generated by operating activities:			
Depreciation, amortization, and accretion	317	225	179
Stock-based compensation expense	242	163	49
Provision for deferred income taxes	78	53	50
Excess tax benefi ts from stock options	—	—	428
Gain on sale of Power School net assets	—	(4)	—
Loss on disposition of property, plant, and equipment	12	15	9
Changes in operating assets and liabilities:			
Accounts receivable, net	(385)	(357)	(121)
Inventories	(76)	(105)	(64)
Other current assets	(1,540)	(1,626)	(150)
Other assets	81	(1,040)	(35)
Accounts payable	1,494	1,611	328
Other liabilities	1,751	1,296	534
Cash generated by operating activities	5,470	2,220	2,535

Source: Apple's 2007 Fiscal Year 10K, www.apple.com/investor.

SHAKE-UP

By 1985, however, Jobs and Sculley began to disagree over the direction they wanted the company to take. After Jobs's attempt to remove Sculley failed, Jobs left Apple in May to start his own new business, NeXT Computers. Meanwhile, Microsoft benefited from Apple's poor negotiation of a contract that cleared the way for successive versions of the Windows operating system to use graphical user interface (GUI) technology similar to that of the Mac. With this agreement, "Apple had effectively lost exclusive rights to its interface design."[16]

In 1990, Microsoft released Windows 3.0, the first universal software that could run on nearly every PC regardless of the manufacturer. Although Apple's worldwide sales had reached $7 billion by 1992, Apple soon found itself fighting an uphill battle against the movement toward standardized software. More and more businesses and consumers wanted compatible operating systems, but the Macintosh still ran exclusively on Mac OS, a system not available to other computers. By 1993, Apple's board of directors replaced Sculley as CEO. Apple moved through two CEOs over the next five years.

Exhibit 2 Apple computer, fourth-quarter fiscal 2007 10Q report

Net Sales (net sales in millions and unit sales in thousands)	**Three Months Ended**		
	12/29/07	**12/30/06**	**Change**
Net Sales by Operating Segment:			
Americas net sales	$4,298	$3,521	22%
Europe net sales	2,471	1,712	44%
Japan net sales	400	285	40%
Retail net sales	1,701	1,115	53%
Other segments net sales (a)	738	482	53%
Total net sales	$9,608	$7,115	35%
Unit Sales by Operating Segment:			
Americas Macintosh unit sales	841	625	35%
Europe Macintosh unit sales	705	491	44%
Japan Macintosh unit sales	91	70	30%
Retail Macintosh unit sales	504	308	64%
Other segments Macintosh unit sales (b)	178	112	59%
Total Macintosh unit sales	2,319	1,606	44%
Net Sales by Product:			
Desktops (c)	$1,515	$955	59%
Portables (d)	2,037	1,455	40%
Total Macintosh net sales	3,552	2,410	47%
iPod	3,997	3,427	17%
Other music-related products and services (e)	808	634	27%
iPhone and related products and services (f)	241	—	NM
Peripherals and other hardware (g)	382	297	29%
Software, service, and other sales (h)	628	347	81%
Total net sales	$9,608	$7,115	35%
Unit Sales by Product:			
Desktops (c)	977	637	53%
Portables (d)	1,342	969	38%
Total Macintosh unit sales	2,319	1,606	44%

Net sales per Macintosh unit sold (i)	$1,532	$1,501	2%
iPod unit sales	22,121	21,066	5%
Net sales per iPod unit sold (j)	$181	$163	11%
iPhone unit sales	2,315	—	NM

(a) During the third quarter of 2007, the Company revised the way it measures the Retail Segment's operating results to a manner that is generally consistent with the Company's other operating segments. Prior period results have been reclassified to reflect this change to the Retail Segment's operating results along with the corresponding offsets to the other operating segments. Further information regarding the Company's operating segments may be found in Notes to Condensed Consolidated Financial Statements at Note 7, "Segment Information and Geographic Data."
(b) Other Segments include Asia Pacific and FileMaker.
(c) Includes iMac, eMac, Mac mini, Mac Pro, Power Mac, and Xserve product lines.
(d) Includes MacBook, iBook, MacBook Pro, and PowerBook product lines.
(e) Consists of iTunes Store sales, iPod services, and Apple-branded and third-party iPod accessories.
(f) Derived from handset sales, carrier agreements, and Apple-branded and third-party iPhone accessories.
(g) Includes sales of Apple-branded and third-party displays, wireless connectivity and networking solutions, and other hardware accessories.
(h) Includes sales of Apple-branded operating system, application software, third-party software, AppleCare, and Internet services.
(i) Derived by dividing total Mac net sales by total Mac unit sales.
(j) Derived by dividing total iPod net sales by total iPod unit sales.

Source: Apple Company, 2007 4Q Form 10Q, www.apple.com/investor, 22.

Exhibit 3 Select apple product releases

1976	Apple I
1977	Apple II
1980	Apple III
1983	Lisa
1984	Macintosh Graphical user interface (GUI)
1986	Macintosh Plus
1987	Macintosh II
1991	Macintosh Quadra PowerBook 100
1994	PowerMac 6100
1997	PowerBook G3
1998	iMac
1999	iBook
2001	iTunes iDVD iPod
2003	iLife suite iTunes 4 (online music store w/200,000 downloadable songs)
2004	iPod Mini eMac iPod (Click Wheel) iPod (U2 Special Edition) iPod Photo
2005	iPod Shuffl e iPod nano iPod color iPod with video
2006	MacBook Mac mini
2007	Apple TV iPhone

Source: www.apple-history.com.

During this time, Apple partnered with IBM and Motorola to produce the PowerPC chip, which would run the company's new line of PowerMacs, allowing it to outperform computers powered by Intel microprocessors.[17] Despite this and Apple's attempts to reorganize, losses mounted in 1996 and 1997. In December 1996, Apple acquired NeXT, with the plan of using its technology as the basis for a new operating system. After being gone for more than a decade, Jobs returned to the company he had originally cofounded with Wozniak.

JOBS'S RETURN

One of the first problems Steve Jobs moved to fix was the ongoing dispute between Apple and Microsoft over the Windows graphical user interface (GUI). Microsoft not only paid an undisclosed amount to Apple, but also made its Office 98 suite compatible with Macintoshes.[18] Jobs then proceeded to change the company's sales strategy in 1997 to encompass direct sales—both online and by phone. In a flurry of product releases, Apple introduced the new generation of PowerMacs, PowerBooks, and the highly anticipated iMac and iBook, which were less expensive computers aimed at the low-end computer market. After an entire year without showing a profit, the first quarter of 1998 began three years of profitable quarters for Apple.[19]

Jobs stated that he wanted to transform the company by making the Mac "the hub of [the consumers'] digital lifestyle." To do this, Apple introduced iLife in 2002, a software suite including applications such as iPhoto, iMovie, iTunes, and eventually the iPod. With the advent of Napster and peer-to-peer music sharing, Apple saw a way to capitalize on the emerging trend of cheap music downloads by creating a legal online music distribution network. iTunes would be the key to exploiting this market. Once downloaded by way of iTunes, music could then be transferred only to an iPod (due to encryption). With iTunes, Apple has quite possibly revolutionized the distribution of music and hopes to do the same with the distribution of movies on demand. Similar changes may be expected with the iPhone in the mobile or smartphone industry segments and with Apple TV in the mobile media and set-top box industry segments.

iTunes: Apple's Online Music Store

Apple ventured into the market of legal downloads with the introduction of its iTunes Music Store.[20] iTunes offers downloads at a specified price without requiring a subscription or monthly fees. Originally offered exclusively on Apple's own Mac, iTunes can now be installed on PCs as well. The idea behind iTunes was to provide a solution to the illegal pirating of music and software from rival sources such as Kazaa.

iTunes offers its users a selection of more than 6 million songs, with new songs continually added.[21] Titles are from just about every genre of music. Users can perform a search by type of music, artist name, or title of track or album. Each song available can be previewed without making a purchase. Purchasers have the option of purchasing an entire album or single songs. Each song is \$0.99, and a complete album starts at \$9.99. Downloads can be made not only to a Mac or PC, but also directly to an iPod. All new song additions are encoded in AAC format, which many say is superior to MP3, although iTunes does still carry the MP3 format on some of its older selections.

Once songs are downloaded, they are stored as a digital music library. As this collection grows, this list of songs can be arranged in many different ways. Songs can be arranged by personal rating, artist, or genre. This feature allows for a customizable playlist for playback or burning to a CD.

In addition iTunes offers a collection of more than 10,000 audiobooks ranging in price from \$2.95 to \$15.95, including many different language lessons. Also available are downloadable versions of public radio shows. Gift certificates are also available in different denominations and can be sent electronically through e-mail.

As previously mentioned, in its first week of existence, the number of downloads from iTunes surpassed the 1 million mark. This feat is amazing considering that at the time of iTunes' introduction, the download service was available only for the Mac. In addition, at that time, Mac users comprised less than 5 percent of US computer users.[22] When iTunes became available for use on the PC, sales increased even more rapidly. iTunes PC downloads reached the 1 million mark in three days, less than half the time it took for the Mac version. But the success of iTunes is not measured in number of downloads sold per day or week, since after paying royalties, Apple makes only approximately 10 cents per song. iTunes is simply used as a means to boost the sale of iPods, iPhones, and Apple TVs, which generate a substantial profit per sale. For example, the iPod has been labeled "the profit machine" for Apple, as it tends to produce a 50 percent profit margin, per unit, before marketing and distribution costs.[23]

iTunes, iPod, iPhone, and Apple TV

iPod

For music lovers, the iPod is the greatest invention since the Walkman. With up to 160 GB of storage, it allows users to carry up to 40,000 songs or 200 hours of video wherever they go.[24] There are currently four different iPod styles: the iPod shuffle, iPod classic, iPod nano, and iPod touch. iPod owners can purchase accessories such as the armband, the radio remote, and the universal dock and remote to make using the iPod even more enjoyable. In 2007, with more than 100 million products sold, the closest competitor to Apple's iPod had only 8 percent of the market share, leaving Apple with the vast majority. While others are seeking to simply duplicate the complementary and innovative relationships between iPod and iTunes, Apple continues to innovate with new products such as the iPhone and Apple TV.[25] (See Exhibit 4 for more details about the iPod products.)

iPhone

In first-quarter 2007, Apple launched its "revolutionary" product, the iPhone. The iPhone combines three concepts popular with consumers: a mobile phone, a widescreen iPod, and an Internet communication device. The iPhone brags "an entirely new user interface based on a large multi-touch display and pioneering software," which users can control with just their fingers.[26] The iPhone's default Internet browser will be Apple's own Safari,** but it is open to other software as well.[27] The iPhone allows for 8 hours of talk time, 24 hours of audio playback time, and 10 days of standby time.[28] Apple sold 1 million iPhones less than three months after this product was available to consumers. Apple expects this trend to continue during 2008 and to reach sales of 10 million iPhones, stealing 1 percent of the mobile phone market share.[29]

Apple TV

In addition to the iPhone, Apple also introduced the Apple TV in 2007. With this product, Apple intends to revolutionize the Internet video industry, as it did with the music download industry. Users can download movies and TV shows via the iTunes online service or via YouTube as well as view digital photos and home videos.[30] Some negative hype claims that the Apple TV will be a flop just like the Apple III and the Power Mac Cube. Some of the features that made the first edition unpopular include the following:

- Users are not able to download a movie from iTunes directly to their TV; they have to download it to their PC first.
- It requires an HDTV, but the movies that can be downloaded are of such low resolution that the picture looks fuzzy and old-fashioned.
- It has no DVD drive.

Steve Jobs announced at the Macworld Conference & Expo in January 2008 that the upgraded version of Apple TV will allow owners to order movies directly from the TV rather than having to download to the PC.[31] Also, critics do compliment the fact that the Apple TV plays a slideshow of digital photos.[32]

The price to rent a movie using Apple TV is $2.99 for library titles, $3.99 for new releases, and $1 extra to view the movie in high definition.[33]

One key component that must be in place to have good media content for the three products mentioned is the relationship that Apple has with each of its media and phone service suppliers.

Service Suppliers: iTunes, Apple TV, and iPhone

iTunes

iTunes has agreements with all five major record labels (BMG, EMI, Sony Music Entertainment, Universal, and Warner Bros.) as well as more than 200 independent labels. These agreements allow iTunes to sell the music owned by these labels and pay the record label each time a song is downloaded. This deal is considered a reseller agreement, meaning that Apple is not licensing content from these labels, but rather buying it wholesale and reselling it to consumers.[34] Apple gets to keep its share, while the portion the label receives must be divided among many parties including artists, producers, and publishers. Labels earn approximately 70 cents per song sold on iTunes. This figure may seem small, but it is still greater than losing money to the millions of illegal downloads that nearly crippled the music industry.

The revenues for record label companies have been dropping in the past year due to tough market conditions, and Apple has introduced a strategy that may help increase revenues by at least a small percentage. It has already contracted with EMI to make its entire catalog available to iTunes' users in two formats, the traditional download option, which includes the Fair-play digital rights management (DRM) software and DRM-free versions. The DRM software limits the number of times a song can be copied, which decreases the quality of the song. The DRM-free versions would deliver greater quality music but would require a higher price tag. iTunes will start the DRM-free songs at $1.29 per song versus the traditional $0.99 per song. Other record labels may enter into the same agreement with Apple depending on how successful this strategy is with EMI.[35]

NBC recently cancelled its agreement with Apple to provide its TV shows on iTunes due to pricing disputes. Walt Disney Studios previously offered its new releases, and Paramount, Metro-Goldwyn-Mayer (MGM), and Lionsgate allowed older library titles to be purchased on iTunes, but the supplier agreements have changed with the launch of Apple TV.[36]

Apple TV

Apple did not have an easy time finalizing with movie studios contracts that will allow Apple to sell movies on

** Safari is Apple's Internet browser that was introduced in 2003. It is part of Apple's strategy to gain more market share by having both hardware and software products. Apple suggests that Safari is the fastest browser available. It blocks pop-up advertising and has a built-in text reader that reads the site pages aloud. In addition to being the default browser for the iPhone, it is the default browser for the iPod Touch and the Mac computer. Safari's user share was estimated to be 6 percent in early 2008. (P. Festa, 2003, Welcome to the browser jungle, Safari, *CNET News*, www.news.com, January 7; 2008, *Wikipedia*, http:// en.wikipedia.org.)

iTunes for use on the iPod and Apple TV. Not only were the studios concerned about losing significant revenues from the sales of DVDs and Blu-ray discs, but some studios urged Apple to require a watermark on digital video for it to play on its devices. Their concern is heightened given the pirating experienced in the music download business. One movie-studio executive said, "Our position is, if you want our content, you have to protect our business." Apple, however, responded that it trusts its consumers not to play pirated movies.[37]

The limited number of movie downloads available on iTunes would significantly diminish the success of Apple TV. Thus, Apple's CEO was persistent in his negotiations with the movie studios. Jobs announced at the Macworld Expo in 2008 that Apple had reached agreement with each of the following major studios: Twentieth Century Fox, The Walt Disney Studios, Warner Bros., Paramount, Sony Pictures Entertainment, MGM, Lionsgate, and New Line Cinema.[38] Despite NBC's issues with Apple concerning TV shows, Universal Pictures (owned by NBC and General Electric) has agreed to allow Apple to rent its movies via iTunes.

The supplier agreement between Apple and the movie studios is that new movies will not be available for rent until 30 days after the DVD is distributed. Within a 24-hour period, customers will be able to watch a film as many times as they like once the movie is started. Movies that are downloaded but not started will not be available for viewing after 30 days.[39]

iPhone

Cingular was selected as the exclusive wireless carrier for the iPhone in the United States because, according to Steve Jobs, Cingular is the best and most popular carrier in the United States.[40] Together these companies developed the Visual Voicemail feature that allows users to listen to the voicemails they prefer rather than having to listen to all messages in succession. Since the agreement was made between Cingular and Apple, Cingular was acquired by AT&T. iPhone owners are required to sign a two-year service agreement with AT&T. AT&T offers four different plans, with monthly fees ranging from $59.99 to $119.99. All plans include the visual voicemail, unlimited access to the Internet, and rollover minutes.[41]

Hardware

Concerning its hardware suppliers, Apple is usually not forthcoming with this information. However, a disassembled iPhone reveals that the microprocessor chip is supplied by Samsung; Philips, Texas Instruments, and Linear Technology all play a role in providing the batteries, and many other companies provide chips that are central to the camera, display, and motion sensor.[42]

Many companies have expressed frustration in working with Apple because Steve Jobs is very clear on his vision for his products and can tend to be controlling. Maintaining good supplier relationships and keeping enough control to provide the quality of products expected of Apple is a balance that Apple will have to find in order to stay ahead of its competitors.

Competitors

iTunes

Since the October 2003 launch of iTunes.com for Windows, Apple has faced a multitude of competitors. During the late 1990s, the emergence of music sharing came about with Napster, a freeware program offering free downloads using peer-to-peer transfers. Peer-to-peer transfers allow users to connect directly with other users without the need for a central point of management.[43] However, in recent years due to legal proceedings, Napster and all other competitors have become a subscription service similar to iTunes.

Napster In May 1999, 19-year-old Shawn Fanning created Napster while studying at Northeastern University. The name Napster came from the Internet "handle" he had used as a programmer. He created a type of software that allowed music fans anywhere to "share" MP3s in one forum. During the first year of service, Napster was obtaining more than 250,000 new users a week while maintaining a free service.[44] This software creation led to the ever-growing controversy of the availability of MP3s on the Internet. Music sharing exploded in the late 1990s, and Napster's servers were overloaded with millions of requests a day for media downloads. Music artists considered this new "sharing" forum to be a continuous copyright violation. Fanning soon became the target of their animosity and became one of the most disliked people in the music industry.

During 2000, Napster was in and out of court and was finally slated to shut down on July 26, 2000. The decision was reversed two days later on July 28, 2000.[45] In 2001, Konrad Hilbers, a 38-year-old German, became CEO of the rapidly declining music file-sharing site. In June 2001, Napster had more than 26 million users, but growth was

Exhibit 4 iPod product descriptions

	iPod shuffle		iPod nano		iPod classic		iPod touch	
Capacity[1]	1GB	Up to 240 songs	4GB	Up to 1,000 songs, up to 3,500 photos, up to 4 hours of video, or some of each	80GB	Up to 20,000 songs, up to 25,000 photos, up to 100 hours of video, or some of each	8GB	Up to 1,750 songs, up to 10,000 photos, up to 10 hours of video, or some of each
	2GB	Up to 500 songs	8GB	Up to 2,000 songs, up to 7,000 photos, up to 8 hours of video, or some of each	160GB	Up to 40,000 songs, up to 25,000 photos, up to 200 hours of video, or some of each	16GB	Up to 3,500 songs, up to 20,000 photos, up to 20 hours of video, or some of each
							32GB	Up to 7,000 songs, up to 25,000 photos, up to 40 hours of video, or some of each
Price	1GB 2GB	$49 $69	4GB 8GB	$149 $199	80GB 160GB	$249 $349	8GB 16GB 32GB	$299 $399 $499
Color display			2-inch		2.5-inch		3.5-inch Multi-Touch	
Wireless data[2]							Wi-Fi (802.11b/g)	
Battery life[3]	Up to 2 hours of audio		Up to 24 hours of audio Up to 5 hours of video		Up to 40 hours of audio Up to 7 hours of video		Up to 22 hours of audio Up to 5 hours of video	

1. 1 GB = 1 billion bytes; actual formatted capacity is less. Music capacity is based on 4 minutes per song and 128-Kpbs AAC encoding; photo capacity is based on iPod-viewable photos transferred from iTunes; video capacity is based on H.264 1.5-Mbps video at 640-by-480 resolution combined with 128-Kbps audio; actual capacity varies by content.
2. Internet access is required; broadband is recommended; fees may apply.
3. Testing was conducted by Apple in August 2007 using preproduction hardware and software. For audio playback, the playlist contained 358 unique audio tracks consisting of content imported from CDs using iTunes (128-Kbps AAC) and content purchased from the iTunes Store (128-Kbps AAC); all settings were default except that Ask to Join Networks was turned off for iPod touch. For video playback, video content was purchased from the iTunes Store; all settings were default except that Ask to Join Networks and Auto-Brightness were turned off for iPod touch. Battery tests are conducted with specific iPod units; actual results may vary. Rechargeable batteries have a limited number of charge cycles and may eventually need to be replaced (see www.apple.com/support/ipod/ service/battery). Battery life and number of charge cycles vary by use and settings. See www.apple.com/batteries for more information.

Source: www.apple.com/ipod/whichipod.

declining fast, going from 6.3 billion to 2.2 billion minutes used a day. On March 7, 2002, Napster closed its servers while opting to implement a fee-based service to comply with the federal judge's decision. On June 3, 2002, Napster filed for Chapter 11 bankruptcy in an effort to secure court-ordered protection from creditors. This move was part of the overall financial restructuring strategy of Bertelsmann AG, which was proceeding with its takeover of the once popular file-sharing system. By July 2003, Roxio, Inc., had acquired Napster and was planning a Napster 2.0 launch for December 2003. Napster 2.0 is a successful, legal fee-based service.[46]

Through restructuring and quality legal representation, Napster finally has a legal base that is expected to stand. Currently, Napster 4.0 is online with content agreements from five major record labels and hundreds of independent labels; therefore, its library is made up of more than 5 million songs. Members have unlimited access to the library for $12.95 per month. Napster 4.0 now accommodates the use of its software for Mac and Linux users.

Kazaa Sharman Networks Limited was founded in January 2002 as a private limited company. Sharman Networks develops and markets world-class Internet applications. Kazaa Media Desktop and Kazaa Plus are products of Sharman Networks. Sharman Networks earns revenue by soliciting companies to advertise on its software. Users that prefer ad-free use of the software can purchase an upgrade, Kazaa Plus for $29.95. This upgrade will also allow for greater search capabilities and more download sources.[47]

Being Australian-based, the company avoided legal intervention in allowing the file sharing, but in 2005, the Federal Court of Australia ruled that Kazaa had knowingly allowed users to illegally download copyrighted songs. The company was charged to change its software to prohibit copyrighted music or videos from being shared.[48] Kazaa owners agreed to pay the four major record labels (Universal Music, Sony BMG, EMI, and Warner Music) $100 million.[49]

Kazaa Media Desktop is a program rumored to be littered with spyware and ad-based programs that "infect" consumer systems; thus many users have become wary of accessing Kazaa's site.[50]

RealNetworks, Inc RealNetworks, through its RealPlayer Music Store, sought a price war with Apple by dropping the price to $0.49 per song and $4.99 per album compared to Apple's price of $0.99 and $9.99, respectively. Analysts indicated that RealNetworks was pricing below the cost of purchasing the music from the record companies, and eventually it did increase its price to $0.99 per song; however, it still offers, select songs for $0.49 a track. As part of its battle to reduce Apple's market share, RealNetworks launched technology called Harmony, which allows RealNetworks users to translate songs purchased from RealPlayer Music Store into a format that can be played on an iPod. It also allows RealNetworks music to be played on Microsoft formats.[51] RealPlayer is a RealNetworks medium through which it competes in the video-on-demand market. Video can be downloaded from the Web to an iPod, PC, CD, and DVD. RealPlayer customers can subscribe to its SuperPass membership, which combines the benefits of RealPlayer and the RealPlayer Music Store. The $14.99 monthly fee provides subscribers with $10.00 worth of music downloads and full-length movies per month.

Sony Sony started a music download service called Connect in the spring of 2004. Despite its efforts to compete in the music downloading market, it did not realize significant success; thus, Connect closed at the end of March 2008.[52] Instead, Sony is focusing its attention on gaining market share in the video download segment.[53]

Virgin Media Virgin offers more than 15,000 record labels in addition to computer games and videos and Blockbuster movies. Similar to iTunes, customers can listen to a 30-second sample before purchase and download exclusive tracks through Virgin's V2 music label before the tracks are released to the general public.[54]

Wal-Mart Wal-Mart launched its own online music store. It is currently the number-one music retailer in the nation, followed by iTunes.[55] Initially Wal-Mart offered music in MP3 format for $0.88 per song, $0.11 cheaper than Apple, but currently it offers songs for $0.94 and albums starting at $7.88.[56]

Yahoo! Music Unlimited Subscribers to Yahoo! Music Jukebox have access to more than 2 million songs. Users can listen to 150 LAUNCHcast radio stations or download songs to any PC. After paying a monthly $6.00 fee, subscribers pay only $0.79 per song. Nonsubscribers can also download songs for $0.99 each.[57] At this time, Yahoo! offers only music on its site; video and TV shows are not available.

Apple TV

Amazon Unbox The Amazon Unbox was introduced in 2006. Users download films or TV shows to the Amazon

Unbox Player or on Windows Media Player. In addition, Amazon established a partnership with TiVo in 2007 that allows consumers to purchase movies or TV shows through Amazon's Unbox and send it to the TiVo machine to view. Amazon's service is similar to its competitors in that once a movie or show is downloaded, it must be viewed within 30 days and once it is started, it must be viewed within 24 hours. Amazon also has agreements with most of the major movie studios such as Paramount Pictures, Universal Studios, Warner Bros., CBS, and Fox.[58] NBC contracted with Amazon to offer its TV shows for download after NBC cancelled its agreement with Apple for the iTunes service.[59]

CinemaNow This company seemed to have been ahead of the game, entering the video download market in 1999. It was the first to offer pay-per-view movies from the major Hollywood studios, the first to offer Download-to-Own services, and the first distributor of Burn-to-DVD movies. It is headquartered in Marina Del Rey, California, and its library consists of more than 10,000 movie titles, television programs, music concerts, and shorts. It has enabled users to download movies to the Microsoft Xbox 360 video game console as part of its strategy of providing multiple platforms on which to download movies. It has recently been creating joint ventures to differentiate itself in the industry. It originated as a distributor of videos via the Internet and has progressed most recently to wireless Internet "infotainment," a new feature available in select new car models. Its agreement with USTelematics, Inc. will allow it to offer a package of features and functions, including the creation of a mobile Wi-Fi Internet hotspot to enable online computer usage in the car, as well as DVD, movies, TV, Xbox, and other computer games.[60]

Disney Disney, through an agreement made with Microsoft in 2007, offers movie download service for use on the Xbox 360. This service is one of the few that offers movies in high-definition format. Consumers have access to the Walt Disney Studios library, including titles from Walt Disney Pictures, Touchstone Pictures, Hollywood Pictures, and Miramax Films.[61]

HP HP announced at the beginning of 2008 that it had reached an agreement with Sony Pictures Home Entertainment (SPHE) to deliver movies on demand. HP's manufactured-on-demand service will produce a DVD of any movie, TV show, or other content offered through SPHE. HP believes this service will aid movie studios in trying to match supply and demand for movies it sells on DVD. The current list of items available for order are classic TV shows never released on DVD, foreign movies, specialty cable programming, independent movies, specialty genres such as religion and education, and recently broadcast TV shows.[62]

Movielink Recently acquired by Blockbuster, Movielink began in 2002 and was owned by five of the top movie studios: Universal Studios, Paramount Pictures, Sony Pictures, MGM, and Warner Bros. It operates as a subsidiary of Blockbuster and offers 3,300 movie titles.[63] Consumers who purchase a movie from Movielink must view it using a computer, a TV connected to a computer, or an Xbox 360 game console or via a set-top box company.

Netflix Like many of its competitors, Netflix has teamed up with a technology company, LG, to become a stronger player in the video-on-demand market. In January 2008, Netflix announced that through LG's set-top box, customers can stream movies directly on their TVs. The device is expected to be available in the second half of 2008.[64] In the meantime, Netflix subscribers can stream to their PC an unlimited number of movies per month, unconstrained by hourly limits, for a monthly fee with plans starting at $8.99 per month. The on-demand library offers viewers the option of 6,000 titles of movies and TV shows.[65]

Sony In the United Kingdom and Ireland, Sony offers video-on-demand service through its PlayStation Portable device. It has partnered with British Sky Broadcasting to provide the movies.[66] It also offers this service in Japan, but it is currently not available in the United States.

Vudu Vudu, headquartered in Santa Clara, California, entered the video-on-demand market in April 2007.[67] Vudu's black box connects to the TV and Internet, and the built-in hard drive gives users the option of viewing 5,000 movie titles instantly. The box costs $400. The service has no monthly service charge, but a rental costs $2.00 to $4.00 per movie. As such, Vudu claims to be the cure-all for the movie rental business; it saves customers from running back and forth from the video store or waiting for the movie to come in the mail from Netflix or Blockbuster; it offers more movie titles than video-on-demand providers; and it is more functional than Internet download services because it does not require a PC. Similar to Vudu's competitors, once a movie is downloaded, it must be viewed within 24 hours.

Vudu offers movies from all major Hollywood studios. But since it is subject to the distribution windows, the time frame in which select movies are available may not match consumer demand. Only some movies have previews, and some are available only for purchase and not for rent.[68]

Wal-Mart In December 2006, Wal-Mart entered the movie download segment of the entertainment industry, but only a year later it exited the business because it had not caught on with consumers. Raul Vasquez, Wal-Mart's CEO for walmart.com, stated that the download service was an experiment. "We want to understand what the customers want. And I think what we learned is that the initial experience of buying and downloading content needs to be better. We thought it was going to be easier for the customer to understand."

iPhone

Motorola Motorola has been a long-time leader in mobile phone sales in the United States. However, since Apple's iPhone and Research In Motion's (RIM) Blackberry have been gaining ground, the leader is falling hard and fast. Motorola's RAZR phone has lost its popularity, and its smartphone made in partnership with Microsoft, the Motorola Q, has not performed as expected. Motorola announced in January 2008 that it is seeking alternatives for its handset business, most likely a divestiture.[69]

Palm Despite the fact that Palm sold 689,000 Treos in the first quarter of 2007, a 21 percent increase from the previous year, Palm is struggling to remain a major player in the smartphone market amid the success of the Blackberry and the iPhone. The competition with the iPhone is especially fierce since AT&T is the phone service provider for both products. Palm introduced its Centro in October 2007 as a low-cost strategy to increase market share. Although the Centro sells for $99, it does not have all of the features of the iPhone. But cost-conscious consumers may choose it over the iPhone given the iPhone's $399 price tag.[70]

Research In Motion The Blackberry created by Research In Motion (RIM) has been a popular product among corporate consumers who mainly needed e-mail service and a calendar. To stay in the competitive game, however, RIM has been adding features to make its product more appealing to users who want the fun features in addition to the features that aid in their work. Blackberrys now have cameras and can play music. There is a rumor that RIM is going to introduce a Blackberry 9000, which will have a touch-sensitive screen, making it similar to the iPhone.[71] Conversely, Apple has recently released tools that make its iPhone more corporate-user friendly, and it will now be compatible with Microsoft's Exchange platform.[72]

Exhibit 5 illustrates a comparison of the product features for the iPhone relative to its key competitors.

iPod

Some of the iPod's major competitors include Rio Karma, Dell Digital Jukebox DJ, Samsung Napster YP-910GS, and the Gateway Jukebox Player DMP-X20 (see Exhibit 6).[73] Some of the differences from the iPod include a longer battery life, such as a 16-hour battery life for the Dell MP3 player. The weight also varies from one competitor to the next, ranging from 7.7 ounces to 5,5 ounces. (For a detailed list of the major competitors' specifications, see Exhibit 7.)

The Microsoft Zune premiered in the fall of 2006. Due to its lack of tremendous success, in the fall of 2007, Microsoft exerted great energy in combating the success of the iPod with its improved Zune. The Zune offers options of 4, 8, or 80 gigabytes of storage with prices ranging from $150 to $300. The newest edition of the Zune is smaller, has a better viewing screen, and allows users to wirelessly synchronize the gadget with the music on their computers. It also includes a touch-sensitive pad that allows users to navigate through songs with more precise control than the iPod, according to Microsoft executives.[74] But critics suggest that the Zune does not pose a significant threat to the iPod because it does not offer any significant technological breakthroughs.[75] Only 1.2 million Zunes sold during 2007 while Apple sold more than 41 million iPods. Apple's success can likely be attributed to its marketing competency.

Marketing

Up until this point, Apple's marketing endeavors have earned it awards, product sales, and a devoted base of customers, both new and old. In 2003, Apple was awarded *Advertising Age's* Marketer of the Year for its upbeat, original, and (most importantly) memorable advertisements for both its iPod and iTunes.[76] Apple has been hailed as one of the best marketers by many different sources and has had a reputation over the years of being a brand that can gain customers through its well-thought-out and carefully executed marketing strategies.

Marketing has been one of Apple's strengths; however, staying on top of the game will become more difficult as Apple develops a broader range of products and markets them to the mainstream customer rather than just the "tech-savvy fanatics" in fields such as education and design.[77] "The customer base is now more diverse, including students and mainstream consumers, and it's harder to satisfy as a whole," says Lopo L. Rego, a marketing professor at the University of Iowa.[78] Business lead-

Exhibit 5 iPhone properties and its competitors

Apple iPhone—$499 to $599	Moto Q—$499	BlackBerry Pearl—$299	Palm Treo 750—$649
N/A	FM Radio with Software Sold Separately	No	FM Radio with Software Sold Separately
Bluetooth Wireless Technology v2.0 + EDR	Bluetooth Wireless Technology v1.2	Bluetooth Wireless Technology v2.0	Bluetooth Wireless Technology v1.2
N/A but most likely	Video Capture/Camcorder QCIF-quality	N/A	Video Capture/Camcorder QCIF
Full QWERTY Soft Keyboard	QWERTY Keyboard Backlit with thumbwheel	QWERTY Keyboard	QWERTY Keyboard Backlit
N/A	Infrared Port	No	Infrared Port
N/A	Use Phone as Modem via USB Cable, Bluetooth, or IR	Use This Phone as a Modem	Use Phone as Modem via USB Cable, Bluetooth, or IR
iSynch via Bluetooth or Wi-Fi Mac or PC	PC Synch via Cable: Infrared or Bluetooth: Active Sync	PC Synchronization	PC Synch via Cable: Infrared or Bluetooth: Active Sync
Full Color Display 3.5" 320 × 480 Pixels at 160 ppi	Color Display 320 × 240 Pixels, 65K Colors, QVGATFT	Color Display 240 × 260 Pixels, 65K Colors	Color Display 320 × 320 Pixels, 65K Colors, TFT
Multi Touch Screen	No	No	Touch Screen
Speakerphone	Speakerphone	Speakerphone	Speakerphone
Widgets	To-Do List, Alarm, Calculator, Calendar, etc.	To-Do List, Alarm, Calculator, Calendar, etc.	To-Do List, Alarm, Calculator, Calendar, etc.
N/A	Voice Memo	N/A	Voice Memo
N/A	Vibrate	Vibrate	Vibrate
N/A	Voice recognition	Voice-activated Dialing	No
Predictive Text Entry with corrector	N/A	Predictive Text Entry	No
Advanced Sensors for Rotation Detection	No	No	No
Messaging & Internet Features	**Messaging & Internet Features**	**Messaging & Internet Features**	**Messaging & Internet Features**
Safari Full Rich HTML Browser	Pocket Internet Explorer HTML	Full HTML Web Browser	Blazer Browser Supports
N/A	MMS	MMS	MMS
SMS	SMS	SMS	SMS
POP3/IMAP Push Email services	Pocket Outlook Supports POP, IMAP, APOP, ESMTP	Push Email POP3, IMAP, SMTP	Pocket Outlook Supports POP, IMAR, APOP, ESMTP
Google Maps Built in	No	No	No
Widgets	No	No	No
Visual Voice Mail	No	No	No
N/A	IM	IM	IM
Technical Specifications	**Technical Specifications**	**Technical Specifications**	**Technical Specifications**
OSX	Windows Mobile 5.0 + BREW	BlackBerry OS with Intel XScale Processor + Java	Palm OS 5.4 with Intel 312 Mhz XScale Processor
Data Download Speed—EDGE + WiFi (802.11 b/g)	Data Download Speed—EV-DO and 1xRTT	Data Download Speed—EDGE	Data Download Speed—EV-DO and 1xRTT
GSM Quad Band 850, 900, 1800, 1900	GSM Quad Band 850, 900, 1800, 1900	GSM Quad Band 850, 900, 1800, 1900	GSM Quad Band 850, 900, 1800, 1900
Built-in Memory—4GB or 8GB Available	Built-in Memory—64 MB Available	Built-in Memory—64 MB Plus Online Photo	Built-in Memory—123 MB Available
None	SecureDigital (SD) Card Format Compatible Slot	MicroSD Card Format Compatible Slot	SecureDigital (SD) Card Format Compatible Slot
Dimension—115 × 61 × 11.6mm	Dimension—116 × 63 × 11.5mm	Dimension—107 x 50 x 14.5mm	Dimension—111.8 x 58.4 x 20.3mm
Weight—4.8 oz	Weight—6.40 oz	Weight—3.2 oz	Weight—6.40 oz
Battery Life	**Battery Life**	**Battery Life**	**Battery Life**
Up to 300 Minutes Talk/Video/Browsing	Talk Time—Up to 240 Minutes	Talk Time—Up to 210 Minutes	Talk Time—Up to 282 Minutes
N/A	Standby Time—Up to 192 Hours	Standby Time—Up to 360 Hours	Standby Time—Up to 300 Hours
Up to 16H Audio Playback	N/A	N/A	N/A
No	Removable	Removable	Removable

Exhibit 6 Products of competitors to iPod

Creative Nomad
Jukebox Zen NX (20 GB)

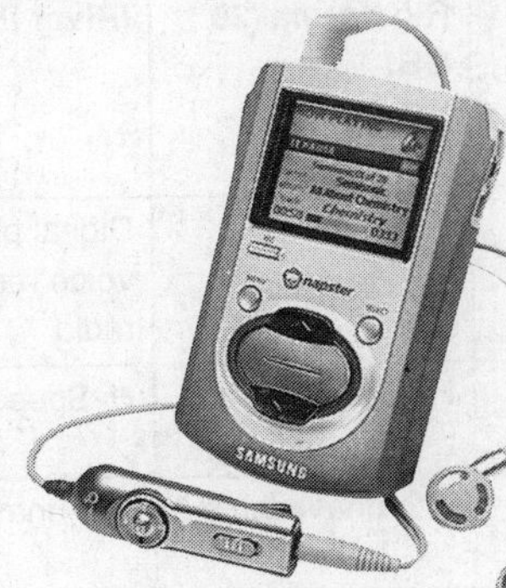

Samsung Napster
YP-910GS (20 GB)

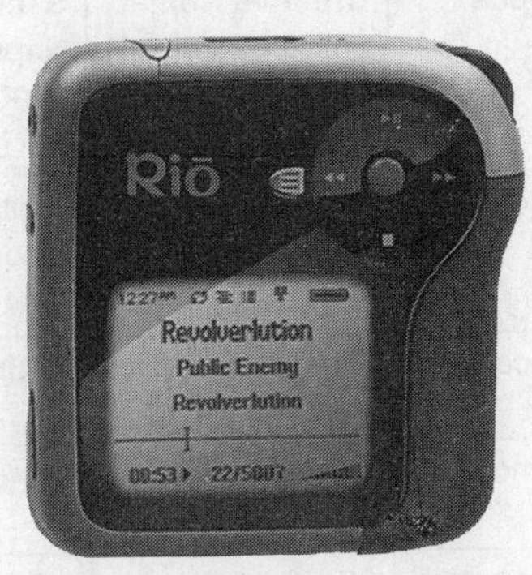

Rio Karma (20 GB)

iRiver iHP-120

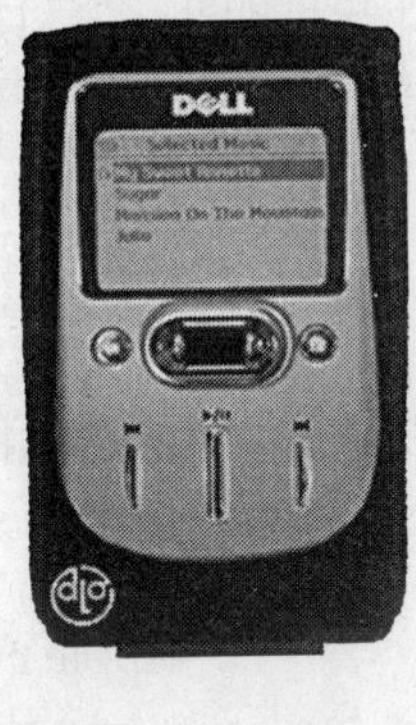

Dell Digital Jukebox
DJ (20 GB)

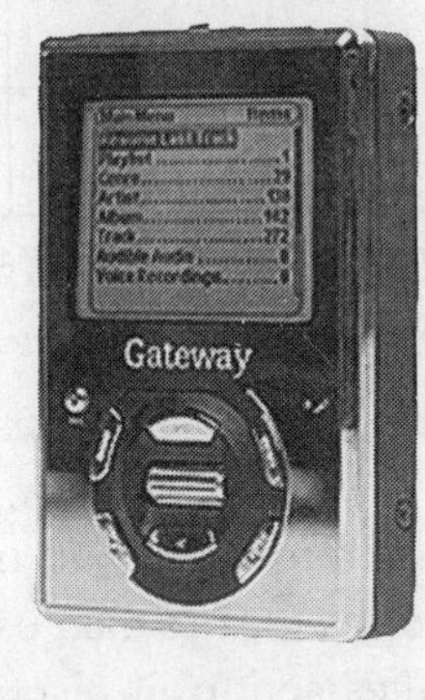

Gateway Jukebox Player
DMP-X20 (20 GB)

Source: http://reviews.cnet.com/4520-6497-5093864.html.

ers today have a daunting job in balancing shareholder demands and running a successful company. Businesses want to market new products aggressively to try and ensure their products' success. Apple heavily promoted the iPhone when it was introduced in July 2007. Customer and investor expectations, due to Apple's reputation, boosted the stock price. But when customers don't believe that the marketing promises have been delivered, stock price, brand equity, and investor confidence are significantly affected.[79] Apple's success lies in a carefully thought-out plan.

Marketing Plan

A marketing plan begins with design of the product.[80] In an industry of low profit margins and cost cutting, Apple takes a different approach to the design of its products. While competitors are doing everything they can to keep costs down, Apple does what it can to make its product different. In 2007, for the third year in a row, Apple was named as the Most Innovative Company by *BusinessWeek*.[81] Its CEO, Steve Jobs is "a legend for his design sense."[82] Even employees of one of Apple's biggest competitors, Microsoft, have recognized Apple's dominance in the design of eye-catching products. The employees created a mock promotion for the iPod had it been created by Microsoft and circulated it on YouTube.[83]

Steve Jobs is essential to the public relations and promotional aspect of Apple, especially with the iPod.[84] He maintains relationships with the media and has been called the "public face and champion of the brand."[85] He is an expert when it comes to talking with the press,

Exhibit 7 Details of products of competitors to iPod

Basic Specs	Creative Nomad Jukebox Zen NX (20 GB)	Samsung Napster YP-910GS (20 GB)	Rio Karma (20 GB)	iRiver iHP-120	Dell Digital Jukebox DJ (20 GB)	Gateway Jukebox Player Product DMP-X20 (20 GB)
Product type	Digital player	Digital player/ recorder/radio	Digital player	Digital player/ voice recorder/ radio	Digital player/ voice recorder	Digital player/ voice recorder/ radio
PC interface(s) supported	Hi-Speed USB	Hi-Speed USB	Hi-Speed USB	Hi-Speed USB	Hi-Speed USB	Hi-Speed USB
Flash memory installed	8 MB	Info unavailable	Info unavailable	Info unavailable	Info unavailable	Info unavailable
Storage capacity	20 GB	20 GB	20 GB	20 GB	20 GB	20 GB
Digital formats supported	MP3	MP3	MP3	MP3	MP3	MP3
Weight	7.2 oz	6 oz	5.5 oz	5.6 oz	7.6 oz	7.7 oz
Resolution	132 X 64	Info unavailable	160 X 128	Info unavailable	160 X104	160 X 128
Battery technology	Lithium ion	Lithium polymer	Lithium ion	Lithium polymer	Lithium ion	Lithium ion
Mfr estimated battery life	14 hour(s)	10 hour(s)	15 hour(s)	16 hour(s)	16 hour(s)	10 hour(s)
Software included	Creative MediaSource	Drivers & Utilities	Drivers & Utilities	Drivers & Utilities	Drivers & Utilities	Drivers & Utilities

Source: http://reviews.cnet.com/4520-6497-5093864.html.

maintaining relationships with magazine editors, and continually creating new relationships.[86] Because of his dynamic, high-energy personality, he usually holds a new idea that he is energetic about and is always ready and willing to share the idea to gain exposure.

Jobs also takes action in response to customer feedback to show that he is listening and concerned. For example, three months after the iPhone was available in stores, Apple cut the price of this product by one-third. This was a strategic move to increase demand and meet sales goals; it was not the result of a faulty product. Consumers who had purchased the iPhone in the first three months for the higher price expressed great dissatisfaction. Jobs responded by promising these consumers a $100 Apple store credit.[87]

A more recent advantage in Apple's marketing strategy is its retail stores. Apple has opened more than 200 retail stores located worldwide. At the time that Apple opened its first retail store in 2001, analysts predicted that Apple would report huge losses and shut the store within two years. At the time, no computer manufacturer had proved profitable in running its own branded store.[88] However, Apple's retail stores contributed an estimated $200 million, 15 to 16 percent of its profits during the past two years (see Exhibit 8).[89] Apple's philosophy behind the stores is brand exposure. Apple believes that the more people can touch an Apple product and see what it can do with their own eyes, the greater the potential market share.[90] In addition, the stores provide free group workshops, personal training, and personal assistance for Apple customers.[91]

Apple offers a One-to-One program for an annual fee of $99; subscribers can attend a tutorial session with an Apple expert for an hour once a week for one year. Apple customers can also consult with the staff at the "Genius Bar" by appointment. The Genius Bar is where Apple product users meet face-to-face with Apple's "geniuses" for answers to technical questions and for problem troubleshooting. In addition, customers wanting to purchase a new computer or other equipment can schedule an appointment with a shopping assistant, who helps ensure that the customer selects the right equipment for his or her needs. Apple has apparently struck a chord with customers because its staff conducts more than 50,000 training sessions per week.[92] "Apple has become the new gathering place," said Steven Addis, chief executive of Addis Creson, a brand strategy and design firm in Berkeley. "You can't help but get caught up with it when you first walk in."[93]

As so eloquently stated in a *USA Today* article, "Apple's arsenal of attention-getting tools holds lessons for any company: design cool, innovative products. Have

Exhibit 8 Retail sales as a contribution to overall Apple revenue

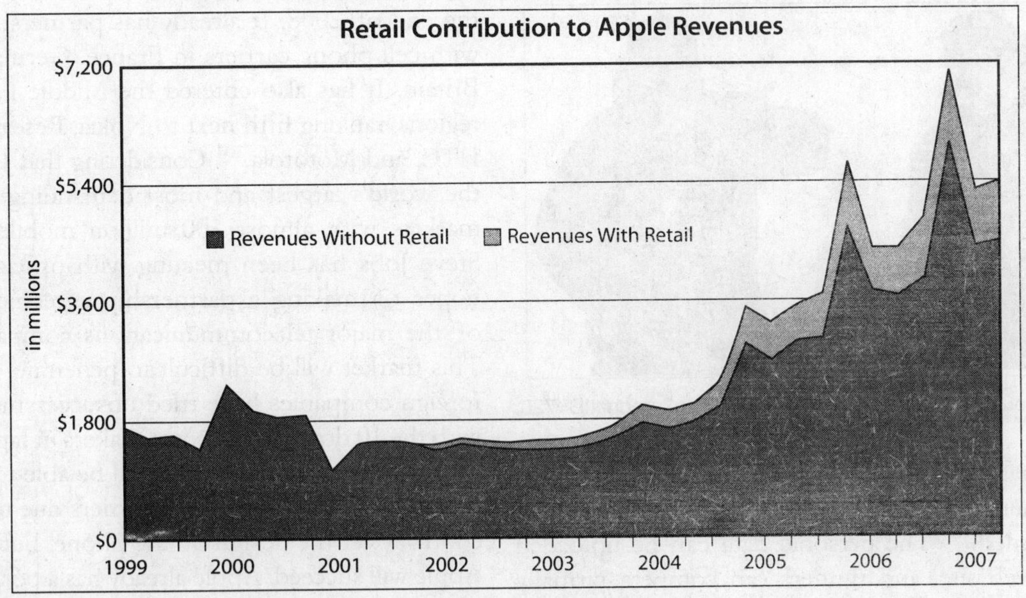

Source: 2007, Retail Stores' Importance Highlighted, http://ifoapplestore.com, August 17.

a streamlined product line. Invest in memorable ads. Work your customer base to make customers feel special and create word-of-mouth agents. Most important: keep the world and media surprised, to generate gobs of attention."[94]

Finally, Apple has garnered major success for iPod and iTunes by way of strategic partnerships with other well-known brands. Apple has created marketing agreements with Volkswagen of America, Burton Snowboards, Nike, and Starbucks. By affiliating itself with different brands, Apple gains consumer confidence as well as exposure through marketing partner advertisements.

Strategic Agreements

All of the strategic agreements that are currently known by the public are agreements related to the iPod. It remains to be seen what alliances or joint ventures Apple enters in order to create awareness for the iPhone and Apple TV.

Volkswagen In early 2003, Volkswagen of America (VW) offered a free iPod to customers who purchased a 2003 hardtop Beetle 10. The ad campaign was aptly named "Pods Unite."[95] The deal brought iPod enthusiasts (and people who just wanted to learn more about the iPod) into the Volkswagen stores, and both products benefited from the advertisement. For three months, iPods were shown in Volkswagen showrooms.[96] Also, the Volkswagen sold iPod connectivity wiring and a cradle for the iPod to be used in the new VW Beetle.[97] Because both brands are known for unique design, it is likely that the promotion brought in consumers who highly value the design aspect of a product, whether it is a car or a digital music player.

In the fall of 2007, rumors came out that Apple and VW were in discussions about furthering their relationship to create an iCar. This car would feature products that Steve Jobs fashioned. No details have been specified by either company's leaders.[98]

Burton Snowboards In January 2004, Burton released a snowboarding/snow-skiing jacket made especially for use with the iPod (Exhibit 9). The jacket has a built-in iPod control electronic system on the sleeve of the jacket so that the wearer can operate the iPod without removing gloves, digging in pockets, or fumbling with zippers.[99] The iPod rests in a protected chest pocket in the inner lining of the jacket. With this jacket, Apple places a product into the hands of those who use iPods and creates exposure for the iPod by way of young snowboarders and skiers showing off and wearing the special jacket.

Nike Nike and Apple have teamed up to create a smart running shoe. When runners combine a pair of Nike athletic shoes, an iPod nano, and the iPod Sport Kit, they are able to track their run in real time, with time, distance, pace, and calories burned displayed on the iPod. The iPod Sport Kit became available in 2006. Users' playlists can be selected based on the desired workout. If runners need a sudden burst of energy, they can press the Power Song button. An additional feature is the voice

Exhibit 9 Complementary product advertised with iPods

Source: www.burton.com/Burton/gear/products.asp?productID=728.

feedback that tells runners when they reach a personal best, whether it is in regard to pace, distance, time, or calories burned.[100] The personal data can be uploaded to Nike's Web site, and runners can compete virtually against one another.[101] The most recent partnership between Nike and Apple will shift to the gym. Teaming up with gym equipment makers and 24-Hour Fitness and Virgin Athletic Clubs, Apple and Nike will allow club members to plug their iPod nanos into the cardio equipment to track workouts, upload the information to Nike's Web site, and set goals based on personal history or to compete with others tracked on the Web site.[102]

Starbucks In September 2007, Starbucks and Apple announced a joint venture that allows Starbucks customers to access (at no cost) the iTunes Wi-Fi Music store at more than 600 participating Starbucks locations. Customers can browse, search, and preview all songs available on the iTunes store, including the "Now Playing" service, which displays the name of the song playing at that moment in Starbucks. "Getting free access to the iTunes Wi-Fi Music Store and the 'Now Playing' service at Starbucks is a great way for customers to discover new music," said Steve Jobs.[103] If customers have to leave the Starbucks store before the download of a song is complete, their personal computer will complete the download automatically at a later time. Every song purchased in a Starbucks participating location syncs back to the users' computer the next time they connect. In addition to these agreements with domestic companies, Apple is seeking opportunities to create demand for its products in the global market.

Going Global

To stay on top of its game, Apple is pursuing opportunities to sell the iPhone globally. Apple has a goal of capturing 1 percent of the global cell phone business by the end of 2008. It already has partnership agreements with cell phone carriers in France, Germany, and Great Britain. It has also entered the Middle East and Africa regions, ranking fifth next to Nokia, Research In Motion, HTC, and Motorola.[104] Considering that Japan is one of the world's largest and most demanding mobile phone markets with almost 100 million mobile phone users, Steve Jobs has been meeting with officials in Japan in hopes of making a partnership agreement with some of the major telecommunications companies in Japan. This market will be difficult to penetrate, as many other foreign companies have tried unsuccessfully to compete with the 10 domestic handset makers in Japan. Some analysts wonder whether Apple will be able to develop a relationship with the Japanese carriers due to Apple's tight control over the design of the phone, but others believe Apple will succeed. Apple already has a positive brand image in Japan related to the Macintosh computer and the iPod and has seven Apple retail stores already in place.[105]

Stephen Kobrin, a Wharton Multinational management professor explained in a recent interview that companies that are high-tech and driven by technology that demands that they expand into many countries simultaneously are "born global." He clarifies by further stating, "Companies that are born global 'tend to have high-tech products that immediately find acceptance in many different cultures and societies.'"[106] Thus, it is likely that the iPhone will experience success in many different markets, as will the Apple TV and other new products that Apple may launch when they become part of its global strategy.

Future Opportunities and Challenges

As Apple tries to expand its product line to include media and software in addition to hardware and as it tries to reach many different consumers rather than its traditional niche of "cult followers," the tech-savvy consumers who work in fields such as education and design, the company will find it more difficult to keep a positive brand image among all consumers. The technology and entertainment industries are constantly and rapidly changing. Will Apple be able to keep its reputation related to innovative design and continually launch products that will be the "latest hit"? Competition has become extremely fierce in the technology sector, and Apple needs to be concerned not only about major competitors, but also about start-up companies. For example, in relation to the iPhone, GotVoice is a Web-based company that allows subscribers to record voicemail messages in MP3 format and send those messages to their e-mail account to view the subject line and the message length. This capability rivals Apple's Visual Voicemail on the iPhone, and the service is free unless users prefer to pay $10 to avoid ad pop-ups.[107]

Interestingly, GotVoice has an advantage over Apple's Visual Voicemail in that it works not only with cell phones, but also with home and work phones.[108] It will be a challenge for Apple to maintain its competitive advantage in new product hardware and to create strong relationships with powerful suppliers of media and other services as well as fend off startups such as GotVoice in software and other areas.

NOTES

1. D. Leonard, 2003, Songs in the key of Steve, *Fortune*, April 28.
2. D. Chmielewski & M. Quinn, 2007, Technology; Movie studios fear the sequel to iPod; They see risk that new Apple TV signals effort to control distribution, *Los Angeles Times*, June 11, C1.
3. R. E. Hoskisson, 2007, Strategic Focus: Apple: Using innovation to create technology trends and maintain competitive advantage, Hitt, Ireland, & Hoskisson, *Strategic Management: Competitiveness and Globalization*, 8th Edition.
4. Ibid.
5. Apple history, www.apple-history.com/frames.
6. Ibid.
7. L. Kimmel, 1998, Apple Computer, Inc.: A History, www.geocities .com/Athens/3682/applehistory.html.
8. Ibid.
9. http://apple-history.com.
10. Apple Computer History Weblog, http://apple.computerhistory.org.
11. L. Kimmel, 1998, Apple Computer, Inc.: A history.
12. Apple Computer History Weblog.
13. http://apple-history.com.
14. Ibid.
15. Apple Computer History Weblog.
16. http://apple-history.com.
17. Ibid.
18. Ibid.
19. Ibid.
20. http://www.apple.com/itunes.
21. 2008, iTunes store, www.apple.com/itunes/store/, January 8.
22. P. Hardy, 2003, Apple launches Windows-based iTunes, *Music & Copyright Magazine*, October 29.
23. A. Hesseldahl, 2005, Unpeeling Apple's Nano, *BusinessWeek*, www.businessweek.com, September 22.
24. 2007, www.apple.com.
25. R. E. Hoskisson, Strategic Focus: Apple.
26. 2007, Apple reinvents the phone with iPhone, Apple Inc. press release, www.apple.com/pr/library/2007/01/09iphone.html, January 9.
27. K. Allison, 2007, Apple encroaches on Window's turf, *The Financial Times*, www.ft.com, June 11.
28. 2007, iPhone delivers up to eight hours of talk time, Apple Inc. pressrelease, www.apple.com/pr/library/2007/06/18iphone.html, June 18.
29. 2007, In three months, iPhone sales top a million, *New York Times*, www.nytimes.com, September 11.
30. Ibid.
31. M. Quinn & D. C. Chmielewski, 2008, Studios join Apple's movie-rental service, *Los Angeles Times*, www.latimes.com, January 16.
32. B. Schlender, 2007, The trouble with Apple TV, *Fortune*, June 11,155(11): 56.
33. 2008, www.apple.com/appletv/rentals.
34. W. Cohen, www.rollingstone/news/newsarticle.asp?nid=18075.
35. K. Regan, 2007, EMI revenue falls but DRM-free iTunes sales promising, *Ecommerce Times*, www.ecommercetimes.com, August 6.
36. M. Garrahan & K. Allison, 2007, Apple signs film deal with Fox studio, *Financial Times*, www.ft.com, December 27.
37. D. C. Chmielewski & M. Quinn, 2007, Technology; Movie studios fear the sequel to iPod; They see risk that new Apple TV signals effort to control distribution, *Los Angeles Times*, June 11, C1.
38. 2008, Apple premieres iTunes movie rentals with all major film studios, Apple press release, www.apple.com/pr/library, January 15.
39. M. Quinn & D. C. Chmielewski, Studios join Apple's movie-rental service.
40. 2007, Apple chooses Cingular as exclusive US carrier for its revolutionary iPhone, Apple Inc. press release, www.apple.com/pr/ library/2007/01/09cingular.html, January 9.
41. 2008, www.apple.com/iphone.
42. A. Hesseldahl, 2007, Take the iPhone apart, *BusinessWeek*, www.businessweek.com, July 2.
43. 2001, Napster's History, http://w3.uwyo.edu/~pz/nap2.htm.
44. 2001, The history of the Napster struggle, www .theneworleanschannel.com/news/457209/detail.html.
45. 2003, Napster 2.0 to launch by Christmas, www.roxio.com/en/ company/news/archive/prelease030728.jhtml.
46. Ibid.
47. J. Ketola, 2003, Kazaa Plus service launched, www.afterdawn.com, August.
48. 2008, Wikipedia, http://en.wikipedia.org/wiki/kazaa.
49. 2006, Kazaa settlement, *BBC News*, http://news.bbc.co.uk., July 27.
50. 2003, Kazaa Usage Map, http://tools.waglo.com/kazaa.
51. N. Wingfield, 2004, Price war in online music, *Wall Street Journal*, www.wsj.com, August 17.
52. 2008, http://musicstore.connect.com.

53. Y. I. Kane, 2007, Sony to challenge Apple in TV, movie downloads, *Wall Street Journal*, www.online.wsj.com, September 4.
54. 2008, www.virgin.com/VirginProducts/Shopping/Musicdownloads .aspx.
55. 2008, iTunes now the number two music retailer in the United States, Apple press release, www.apple.com/pr/library.
56. 2008, http://musicdownloads.walmart.com.
57. 2008, http://music.yahoo.com.
58. B. Stone, 2007, Amazon and TiVo in venture to put downloaded movies on TV, *New York Times*, www.nytimes.com, February 7.
59. G. Sandoval, 2007, NBC says goodbye to Apple, hello to Amazon, www.news.com, September 4.
60. 2008, CinemaNow Inc., *BusinessWeek*, http://investing.businessweek.com, March 14; 2008, www.cinemanow.com; 2008, Wikipedia, http://en.wikipedia.org; A. Gonsalves, 2007, *Information Week*, www.informationweek.com, July 18.
61. 2007, The Walt Disney Studios to offer movie rentals on demand through Xbox Live starting now, *MicrosoftNews*, www.microsoft .com/presspass, July 10.
62. 2008, HP and Sony Pictures Home Entertainment announce manufactured-on-demand content licensing agreement, *HP News Release*, www.hp.com/hpinfo/newsroom, January 24.
63. 2007, Blockbuster acquires Movielink, *New York Times*, www .nytimes.com, August 9.
64. 2008, Netflix and LG unveil video-on-demand service, *Appliance Magazine*, www.appliancemagazine.com, January 7.
65. 2008, Netflix now offers subscribers unlimited streaming of movies and TV shows on their PCs for the same monthly fee, Netflix press release, www.netflix.mediaroom.com, January 14.
66. Leipzig, 2007, PSP (PlayStation Portable) video download service, Sony Computer Entertainment Europe press release, www.scei .co.jp/corporate/release, August.
67. 2008, Wikipedia, http://en.wikipedia.org.
68. D. Pogue, 2007, High-speed video store in the living room, *New York Times*, www.nytimes.com, September 6.
69. J. Goldman, 2008, Motorola hangs up on handsets, www.cnbc .com, January 31; A. Hasseldahl, 2008, Blackberry vs. iPhone: Who wins? *BusinessWeek*, www.articles.moneycentral.msn.com, January 3.
70. E. M. Rusli, 2007, Palm wilts, *Forbes*, www.forbes.com, October 2.
71. A. Hesseldahl, 2008, Blackberry vs. iPhone: Who wins?
72. J. Goldman, 2008, iPhone vs. Blackberry: Apple launches new software, www.cnbc.com, March 6.
73. www.reviews.cnet.com/html.
74. N. Wingfield, 2007, Microsoft tunes its Zunes to catch up with iPod, *Wall Street Journal Online*, www.wsj.com, October 3, D8.
75. Ibid.
76. A. Cuneo, 2003, Apple transcends as lifestyle brand, *Advertising Age*, December 15.
77. 2007, A bruise or two on Apple's reputation, *BusinessWeek*, www .businessweek.com, October 22.
78. Ibid.
79. J. Quelch, 2007, How marketing hype hurt Boeing and Apple, *Harvard Business*, http://discussionleader.hbsp.com, November 2.
80. Ibid.
81. J. Smykil, 2007, *BusinessWeek* names Apple most innovative, http://arstechnica.com, May 6.
82. L. Gomes, 2006, Above all else, rivals of Apple mostly need some design mojo, *Wall Street Journal*, May 24, B1.
83. Ibid.
84. Cuneo, Apple transcends as lifestyle brand.
85. Ibid.
86. Ibid.
87. 2007, In 3 months, iPhone sales top a million.
88. R. Stross, 2007, Apple's lesson for Sony's stores: Just connect, *New York Times*, www.nytimes.com, May 27.
89. Ibid.; 2007, Retail stores' importance highlighted, http:// ifoapplestore.com, August 17.
90. Cuneo, Apple transcends as lifestyle brand.
91. www.apple.com/findouthow/retail/.
92. J. Boudreau, 2008, Apple tutorial classes help create bond with customers, *The Mercury News*, www.mercurynews.com, March 3.
93. Ibid.
94. J. Graham, 2007, Apple buffs marketing savvy to a high shine, *USA Today*, www.usatoday.com, March 3.
95. Wong.
96. Ibid.
97. Ibid.
98. C. Campellone, 2007, Apple and Volkswagen team up for possible iCar, http://media.www.theloquitur.com, September 20.
99. Ibid.
100. www.apple.com/ipod/nike/run.html.
101. E.C. Baig, 2006, Apple, Nike exercise iPods to track workouts, *USA Today*, www.usatoday.com, May 23.
102. 2008, Nike, Apple plug iPods into gym equipment, *USA Today*, www.usatoday.com, March 4.
103. 2007, Apple and Starbucks announce music partnership, Apple press release, www.apple.com/pr/library, September 5; http://www .apple.com/itunes/starbucks.
104. N. Gohring, 2008, Apple beats Microsoft and Motorola in 4Q phone sales, IDG News Service, February 6.
105. Y. I. Kane & N. Wingfield, 2007, For Apple iPhone, Japan could be the next big test, *Wall Street Journal Online*, www.wsj.com, December 19, B1.
106. 2007, What makes a global leader? *India Knowledge at Wharton*, http://knowledge.wharton.upenn.edu/india, October 4.
107. M. S. Lasky, 2007, iPhone versus your phone: Tips to avoid iPhone envy, *PC World*, www.pcworld.com, June 27.
108. 2008, www.gotvoice.com.

CASE 15

A Horror Show at the Cinemaplex?

Steve Gove
Virginia Tech
Brett P. Matherne
Loyola University of New Orleans

If the motion picture industry's performance in 2007 were a feature presentation, the marquee would read "Massive Box Office: Smashing Records—the Sequel!" At $9.63 billion, box office revenue set another record in 2007, a full 5 percent above the record set in 2006.[1] An astonishing 1.4 billion tickets were sold in 2007. But beyond the headlines, the industry is a study in contradictions:

- The number of theaters is declining, but the number of screens is at an all-time high.
- Revenues are up, but attendance is largely flat—1.4 billion tickets sold is little improved from 1997, when 1.35 billion tickets were sold, and is a fraction of the 4 billion sold in 1946. In 1946, the average person attended 28 films a year. Today, it is 6.[2] (see Exhibits 1 and 2).
- The US population is increasing, but the size of the market in the core demographic group is growing more slowly (see Exhibit 3).
- Americans spend more time than ever on entertain-ment—3,500 hours annually—but only 12 of those hours are spent at the movies.[3] The average person watches that much television every three days.

Movies remain as popular as ever, but opportunities for viewing outside the theater have greatly increased. While motion picture studios increased revenues through product licensing, DVD sales, and international expan-

Exhibit 1 Domestic tickets sold and box office gross

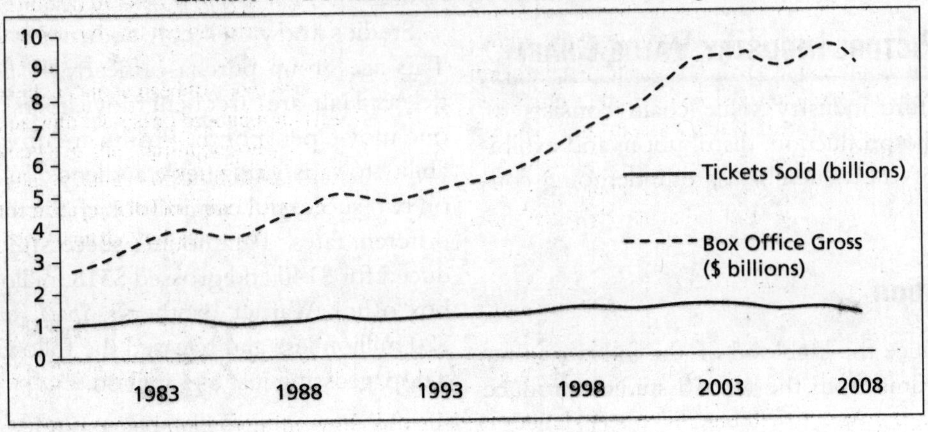

Source: http://boxofficemojo.com & US Census.

Exhibit 2 Average movie ticket price

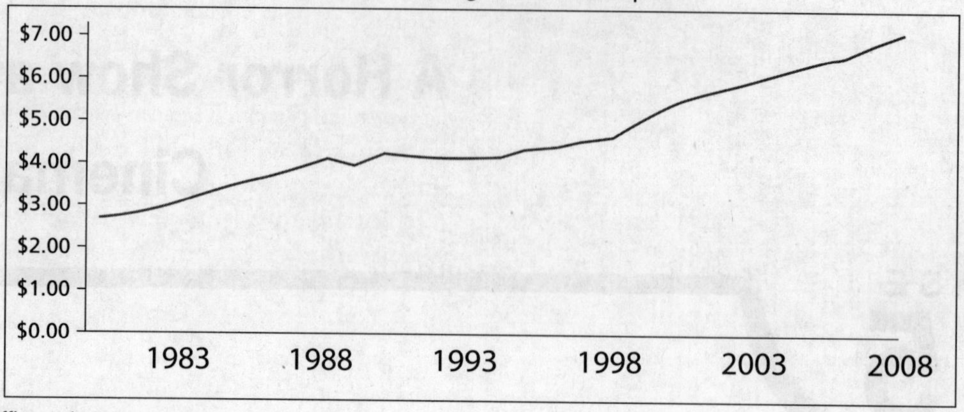

Source: http://boxofficemojo.com.

Exhibit 3 Population trend among 14 to 17 and 18 to 24 age groups (Millions)

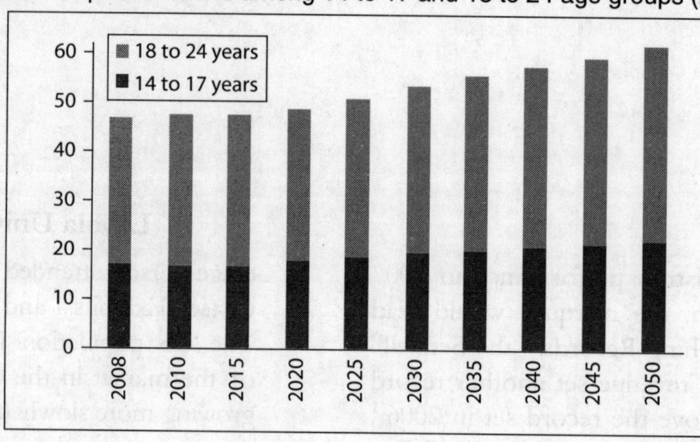

Source: US Census.

sion, the exhibitors—movie theaters—have seen their business decline. Movies are more available than ever, but fewer are venturing to the theater to see them. Many theaters have ceased operation, driven from the market by consolidation and a lack of patrons.

Will the marquee at the local theater soon change to: "A Horror Show at the Cinemaplex?" How has this come to be? What can exhibitors do to respond?

The Motion Picture Industry Value Chain

The motion picture industry value chain consists of three stages: studio production, distribution, and exhibition. All stages of the value chain are undergoing consolidation.

Studio Production

The studios produce the lifeblood of the industry; they create content. Films from the top 10 studios produce over 90 percent of domestic box office receipts (see Exhibit 4). Studios are increasingly part of larger corporations, managed as any other profit center. Management is a challenge as investments are large and there is no one formula for success. Because of this, profitability swings wildly. The cost of bringing a typical feature to market is more than $100 million, up 25 percent in the past five years.[4] Typically, marketing expenses are a third of these costs.

Studios know their core audience is 12 to 24 years old. This age group purchases nearly 40 percent of theater tickets. Half are "frequent moviegoers" attending at least one movie per month. Profits are driven by the studios' ability to satisfy this fickle audience. In 2008, films based on two successful comic book characters met with wildly different fates.[5] Paramount's successful *Iron Man* was produced for $140 and grossed $318 million at the domestic box office. Warner Brothers's *Speed Racer*, produced for $20 million less and released the following weekend, was a flop, grossing just $44 million.

Exhibit 4 Market share of film production (2007)

Studio Parent & Label	2007 Combined Share (%)
Time Warner (Warner Brothers & New Line)	19.8
Sony (Sony & MGM)	16.7
Viacom (Viacom & Paramount)	15.5
Disney (Disney, Buena Vista Pictures, & Miramax)	15.4
Universal Studios	11.4
News Corp. (20th Century FOX)	10.5
Lions Gate	3.6
DreamWorks SKG*	0.0
	92.9

Note: *DreamWorks share in 2005 was 5.7%.
Source: Adapted from Mintel Report: Movie Theaters, United States, February 2008.

Demographic trends are unfavorable. The US population will increase 17 percent by 2025, an increase of 54 million people. However, the number of 12- to 24-year-olds is expected to increase only 9 percent—just 4 million more potential viewers. Based on the current number of theaters and screens, this is an increase of less than 700 additional viewers per theater, or roughly 100 per screen.

Distribution

Distributors are the intermediaries between the studios and exhibitors. Distribution entails all steps following a film's artistic completion, including marketing, logistics, and administration. Exhibitors negotiate a percentage of gross from the studio or purchase rights to films and profit from the box office receipts. Distributors select and market film to exhibitors, seeking to maximize potential attendees. Distributors coordinate the manufacture and distribution of the film to exhibitors. They also handle collections, audits of attendees, and other administrative tasks. There are over 300 active distributors, but much of this work is done by a few major firms, including divisions of studios. Pixar, for example, co-produced *Finding Nemo* with Disney and distribution was handled by Disney's Buena Vista.

Exhibition

Studios have historically sought full vertical integration through theater ownership, allowing greater control over audiences and capturing exhibition profits. A common practice was for the studio to use their ownership to reduce competition by not showing pictures produced by rivals. This practice ended in 1948 with the Supreme Court's ruling against the studios in *United States v. Paramount Pictures*. Theaters were soon divested, leaving them to negotiate with studios for film access and rental.

Theaters are classified according to the number of screens at one location (Exhibit 5). Single-screen theaters were the standard from the introduction of film through the 1980s. They have since rapidly declined in number, replaced by theater complexes. These include miniplexes (2 to 7 screens), multiplexes (8 to 15 screens), and megaplexes (16 or more screens). The number of theaters decreased more than 15 percent between 2000 and 2007, but the number of screens increased because of growth in megaplexes. Nearly 10 percent of theaters are now megaplexes, and the number of screens is at a historical high of 40,077.[6] Many analysts argue the industry has overbuilt and too many theaters and screens exist to make the business profitable.

Movie attendance usually increases as the economy declines. In 2008, there were rapid increases in gas prices, a large stock market decline, and significant layoffs. One summer movie patron commented, "There's not a whole lot you can do for $10 anymore."[7] Movies do remain a bargain in the entertainment business. Four tickets to a movie can cost under $27 (depending on the time of day and location) compared to $141 for an amusement park or $261 for a pro football game.[8] For many, the air-conditioned comfort of a dark theater and the latest Hollywood release offer a break not just from the summer heat, but from reality. "It's escapism, absolutely. It's probably a subconscious thing, and people don't realize it. But there's just so much going on, with people trying to pay their mortgages and get by. It's an escape for a couple of hours."[9]

Exhibit 5 Number of theaters by complex size

	2000	2007	%Change
Single Screens	2,368	1,748	−26.18%
Miniplexes (2–7 Screens)	3,170	2,296	−27.57%
Multiplexes (8–15 Screens)	1,478	1,617	9.40%
Megaplexes (16+ Screens)	405	616	52.10%
Total	7,421	6,277	−15.42%

Sources: Developed by author from: Entertainment Industry, 2007 Report, Motion Picture Association of America, and Mintel Report "Movie Theaters, United States, February 2008."

Exhibit 6 Exhibition market leaders

Company	Theater Brands	# US Theater Locations	# US Screens	Avg. Screens per Theater
Regal	Regal, United Artists, Edwards	526	6,355	12
AMC	AMC, Loews	315	4,585	14
Cinemark	Cinemark, Century	284	3,606	12
Carmike	Carmike	280	2,412	8
	Total for four leading companies	1,405	16,958	
	Industry total	7,421	40,077	

Source: Mintel Report "Movie Theaters, United States, February 2008," SEC filings and author estimates.

Declining ticket sales and the increased costs associated with developing megaplexes led to a wave of consolidation among exhibitors. There are now four dominant exhibitors: Regal, AMC, Cinemark, and Carmike. While operating 1,405 theaters in the country (just 19 percent), these companies control 42 percent of screens. This market share provides these exhibitors with negotiating power for access to films, prices for films and concessions, and greater access to revenues from national advertisers.

There is little differentiation in the offerings of the major theater exhibitors—prices within markets differ little, the same movies are shown at the same times, and the food and services are nearly identical. Competition between theaters often comes down to distance from home, convenience of parking, and proximity to restaurants. Innovations by one theater chain are quickly adopted by others. The chains do serve different geographic markets and do so in different ways.[10] Regal focuses on mid-size markets using multiplexes and megaplexes. Regal's average ticket price of $7.43 is the highest among the leaders. AMC concentrates on urban areas with megaplexes and on large population centers, such as those in California, Florida, and Texas. Cinemark serves smaller markets, operating as the sole theater chain in over 80 percent of its markets. Cinemark's average ticket price last year of $5.11 was the lowest of the majors. Carmike concentrates on small to mid-sized markets, targeting populations of less than 100,000 that have few other entertainment options. Carmike's average ticket price in 2007 was $5.89, but at $3.05, their average concession revenue per patron is the highest among the majors.

The different approaches of the companies are reflected in the cost of fixed assets per screens. These costs result from decisions made on how to serve customers, such as the level of technology and finish of the theater—digital projection and marble floors cost more than traditional projectors and a carpeted lobby.[11] Despite multi- and megaplex facilities, Regal's cost per screen is the highest at $430,000. Carmike, the rural operator, is the lowest at just $206,000. Cinemark is in the middle at $367,000. Data is not available for AMC, but costs are thought to be near or above those of Regal.

The Business of Exhibition

There are three primary sources of revenue for exhibitors: box office receipts, concessions, and advertising. Managers have low discretion; their ability to influence revenues and expenses is limited. Operating margins among exhibitors average a slim 10 percent. This is before significant expenses such as facility and labor costs. The result is marginal or negative net income. Overall, the business of exhibitors is best described as loss leadership on movies: the firms make money selling concessions and showing ads to patrons who are drawn by the movie.

Box Office Revenues

Ticket sales constitute two thirds of exhibition business revenues. The return on these receipts, however, is quite small. A power imbalance results in contracts that return the vast majority of box office receipts to the studios. The record-setting revenues at the box office have been the result of increases in ticket prices and have flowed back to the studios.

Concessions

Moviegoers frequently lament the high prices for concessions. Concessions average 25 to 30 percent of revenues. Direct costs are less than 15 percent of the selling price, making concessions the largest source of exhibitor profit. These are influenced by the three factors: attendance, pricing, and material costs. The most important is attendance: more attendees equal more concession sales. Sales per patron are influenced by prices. The $3.75 price point for a large soda is not by accident, but the result of market research and profit-maximization calculation. Costs are influenced by purchase volume, with larger chains able to negotiate better prices on everything from popcorn and soft drinks to cups and napkins.

Advertising

Exhibitors also generate revenue through pre-show advertising. Though this constitutes just 5 percent of revenues, it is highly profitable. Mintel reports that advertising revenues among exhibitors are expected to increase at a rate of approximately 10 percent over the coming decade.[12] Audiences signal consistent dislike for advertising at the theater. Balancing the revenues from ads with audience tolerance is an ongoing struggle for exhibitors.

Overall, the exhibitor has limited control over both revenues and profits. Box office receipts are the bulk of revenues, but yield few profits. Strong attendance numbers allow for profitable sales of concessions and advertisements, but there are significant caps on the volume of concession sales per person and selling prices seem to have reached their maximum. Advertising remains an attractive avenue for revenues and profits, but audiences loathe it.

The Process of Exhibition

The fundamentals of film exhibition have changed little since the early 1940s. To show a picture, each theater receives a shipment of physical canisters containing a "release print" from the distributor. Making these prints requires $20,000 to $30,000 in up-front costs and $1,000 to $1,500 for each print. Thus, a modern major motion picture opening on 2,500 screens simultaneously requires $2.50 to $3.75 million in print costs. This is borne by the studios, but paid for by movie attendees.

Each release print is actually several reels of 35-mm film, which are manually loaded onto projector reels, sequenced, and queued for display by a projector operator. The film passes through the projector, which shines intense light through the film, projecting the image through a lens that focuses the image on the screen. A typical projection systems costs $50,000, with one needed for each screen.

Digital cinema is becoming economically viable. Digital cinema involves a high resolution (4096 × 2160) digitized image projected onto the screen. Basic digital systems cost $150,000 to $250,000 per screen. Conversion of an existing eight-screen theater to digital thus involves an investment of $1.2 to $2 million. The costs for digital "release prints" are far lower than traditional film, but these costs savings most directly benefit the studio whereas the exhibitors must pay any costs to convert theaters. The number of digital theaters is expanding rapidly. In 2004, there were less than 100, and there are now approximately 4,600, or 12 percent of screens. Because of the cost involved, most theaters use a mixture of technologies, with a minority of screens in any one facility featuring digital projection.

The Theater Experience

For a significant number of moviegoers, the draw of the theater is far more than what film is showing. Moviegoers describe attending the theater as an experience, with the appeal based on:[13]

- the giant theater screen
- the opportunity to be out of the house
- not having to wait to see a particular movie on home video
- the experience of watching the movies with a theatrical sound system
- the theater as a location option for a date

The ability of theaters to provide more than what audiences can experience at home appears to be diminishing. Of the reasons why people go to the movies, only the place aspects—the theater as a place to be out of house and as a place for dating—may be immune from substitution. Few teenagers want to watch a movie and eat popcorn with their date at home with their parents next to them on the sofa.

The overall "experience" currently offered by theaters falls short for many. Marketing research firm Mintel reports the reasons for not attending the theater more frequently are largely the result of the declining experience. Specific factors include the overall cost, at-home viewing options, interruptions such as cell phones in the theater, rude patrons, the overall hassle, and ads prior to the show.[14] A recent *Wall Street Journal* article reported on interruptions ranging from the intrusion of soundtracks in adjacent theaters to cell phones. "The interruptions capped a night of moviegoing already marred by out-of-order ticketing kiosks and a parade of preshow ads so long that, upon seeing the Coca-Cola polar bears on screen, one customer grumbled: 'This is obscene.'"[15] Recounting bad experiences is a lively topic for bloggers. A typical comment: "I say it has gotten worse. I hate paying $9.00 for a ticket and the movie is 90–100 minutes long, people talking on the cell phone, the people who work at the theaters look like they are bored, and when you ask them a question, the answer is very rude. I worked as an usher in the late '60s and we had to wear uniforms and white gloves on Friday and Saturday nights, those days are long gone."[16]

A trip to the local cinemaplex can be eye opening even for industry insiders. In 2005, Toby Emmerich, New Line Cinema's head of production, faced a not-so-common choice: attending "War of the Worlds" in a theater or in a screening room at actor Jim Carrey's house. Said Emmerich in an *LA Times* article, "I love seeing a movie with a big crowd, but I had no idea how many obnoxious ads I'd have to endure—it really drove me crazy. After sitting through about 15 minutes of ads, I turned to my wife and said, 'Maybe we should've gone to Jim Carrey's house after all.'"[17]

The unique value proposition offered by movie theaters—large screens, the long wait for DVD release, and advantages of theatrical sound systems—also appears to be fading. Increasingly larger television sets, DVD content, and the adoption of high-definition technology are all part of this change. One blogger posts, "Whereas the electronics industry has been innovating to create immersive experiences from the comfort of our own home, the US theater industry has been dragging their feet."[18]

Home Viewing Technology

Home television sets are increasingly large, high-definition sets coupled with inexpensive, yet impressive audio systems. In 1997, the screen size of the average television was just 23 inches. Currently, almost half of LCD televisions sold have screens 36 inches or larger.[19] Because set size is measured as the diagonal screen size, increases in viewable area are greater than the measurement suggests. In recent years, the viewing area of sets doubled from 250 inches to 550 inches.

The FCC requirement that all broadcasters convert to digital broadcasts by June 12, 2009, is widely credited with starting a consumer movement to upgrade televisions. Since the 1950s, television transmissions were formatted as 480 interlaced vertical lines (480i) of resolution. The new digital format is high definition (HD), providing up to 1080 vertical lines of resolution (1080p).[20] Three quarters of all televisions sold since 2006 are HD capable.

As LCD technology became the standard for both computer and television screens, manufacturing costs declined. Wholesale prices for televisions fell 65 percent from the late 1990s to 2007.[21] In 2006, the average television retailed for $29 per diagonal inch of set size. This is expected to decrease to $22 within five years.[22] Consumers, however, are actually spending more on every television, consistently electing to purchase larger sets to achieve a better viewing experience. Sharp, a leading manufacturer of televisions predicts that by 2015 the average screen will reach 60 inches.[23]

Large screen televisions, DVD players, and audio and speaker components are commonly packaged as low-cost home theaters. The average DVD player now costs just $72[24] and high-definition DVD players are beginning to penetrate the market. Retail price wars during the 2008 Christmas season led to HD Blu-Ray players dropping below $200. These home theater systems offer a movie experience that rivals many theaters, all for $1,000 to $2,000. Says Mike Gabriel, Sharp's head of marketing and communications: "People can now expect a home cinema experience from their TV. Technology that was once associated with the rich and famous is now accessible to homes across the country."[25]

Content Availability and Timing

Even the best hardware offers little value without content for display. Rental firm Netflix advertises a selection of more than 100,000 titles extending well beyond new and classic films to include television shows, sports, and music performances. HD content is increasingly available to maximize the experience offered by those HD televisions. Satellite and cable television providers have engaged in a game of one-upmanship to provide the greatest percentage of HD content available to subscribers. By the end of 2009, 2,000 movies were available on Blu-Ray DVD.[26]

Movie fans no longer have to wait long for the summer's blockbuster to appear on DVD. The time period between theatrical and DVD release has declined 40 percent since 2000. The top five films in 2000 were released on DVD an average of 37 weeks after their box office opening. In 2007, the lag was just 23 weeks. And, studios are experimenting with simultaneous releases to theaters, pay per view, and DVD.

Overall, the visual and audio experience available in the home is rapidly converging with that available at the movie theater. As a blogger on the movie fan site Big Picture posted:

I used to go to the movies all the time—even my blog is called the Big Picture. Then I started going less—and then less still and now—hardly at all. My screen at home is better, the sound system is better, the picture is in focus, the floors aren't sticky and the movies start on time. My seat is clean. And there's no idiot chattering away 2 rows behind me, and (this is my favorite) THERE'S NO CELL PHONES RINGING. EVER.[27]

Is this a horror show at the cinemaplex?

NOTES

1. Motion Picture Association of America (MPAA), 2007, Entertainment industry market statistics.
2. A. Serwer, 2006, Extreme makeover: With big screens and high-def in more and more living rooms, movie theaters are taking radical new measures to woo filmgoers, *Fortune*, 153: 108–116.
3. Mintel Report, 2008, Movie theaters—US, February.
4. MPAA, 2007, Entertainment industry market statistics.
5. All data on these two films from http://www.boxofficemojo.com.
6. Developed by author from: Entertainment Industry, 2007 Report, Motion Picture Association of America.
7. J. Woestendiek & C. Kaltenbach, 2008, $10 is small price for a big escape: Movie box office figures are flourishing despite, or because of, economic worries, *Baltimore Sun*, July 8.
8. MPAA, 2007, Entertainment industry market statistics.
9. J. Woestendiek & C. Kaltenbach, 2008, $10 is small price for a big escape: Movie box office figures are flourishing despite, or because of, economic worries, *Baltimore Sun*, July 8.
10. Data on the firms, screen sizes, location, from Web sites and SEC filings.
11. All data is from SEC filings, based on net property, plant, and equipment reported in 2007 balance sheet and on the number of screens.
12. Mintel Report, 2008, Segment performance: cinema advertising, Movie theaters—US, February.
13. Mintel Report, 2008, Reasons to go to the movies over watching a DVD, Movie theaters—US, February.
14. Mintel Report, 2008, Reasons why attendance is not higher, Movie theaters—US, February.
15. K. Kelly, B. Orwall, & P. Sanders, 2005, The multiplex under siege, *Wall Street Journal*, December 24, P1.
16. Blog comment, Over the past years..., http://cinematreasures.org/ polls/22/ (accessed December 11, 2008).
17. Incident reported in Patrick Goldstein, 2005, Now playing: A glut of ads, *Los Angeles Times*, July 12, E-1.
18. Designs of the week: The Movie Theater Experience, 2008, November 23, http://www.sramanamitra.com/2008/11/23/designs-of-the-week-the-movie-theater-experience/.
19. DuBravac, 2007.
20. DuBravac, 2007.
21. DuBravac, 2007.
22. B. Keefe, 2008, Prices on flat-screen TVs expected to keep falling, *Atlanta Journal-Constitution*, March 15.
23. Average TV size up to 60-inch by 2015, says Sharp, TechDigest, http://www.techdigest.tv/2008/01/average_tv_size.html (accessed December 11, 2008).
24. MPAA, 2007, Entertainment industry market statistics.
25. Average TV size up to 60-inch by 2015, says Sharp, TechDigest, http://www.techdigest.tv/2008/01/average_tv_size.html (accessed December 11, 2008).
26. http://www.movieweb.com.
27. The Big Picture, Why is movie theatre attendance declining?, http://bigpicture.typepad.com/comments/2005/07/declining_movie .htm (accessed December 11, 2008).

JetBlue Airways: Challenges Ahead

CASE 16

Theodore Bosley, Christopher Calton, Jeffrey Deakins, Tomoko Nakajima, Sally Orford, Robin Pohl, Robin Chapman
Arizona State University

INTRODUCTION

We're going to bring humanity back to air travel.

—David Neeleman Founder and Chairperson

David Neeleman, JetBlue's founder and chairperson, sought to "bring the humanity back to air travel."[1] Since launching operations in February 2000, JetBlue distinguished itself from its competitors by providing superior customer service at low fares. The JetBlue experience included brand new airplanes, leather seats, and personal satellite TV service. The firm experienced rapid early growth. In a period when most US airlines struggled in the aftermath of the September 11, 2001, terrorist attacks, JetBlue reported 18 consecutive quarterly profits.

Then in 2005, JetBlue announced its first net loss of $20 million. The disappointing results were attributed to spiraling fuel prices, aggressive competition, and increasing operating costs. Global events such as war, political turmoil, and natural disasters contributed to the rise in fuel prices. The average price for a barrel of oil in 2003 was $30, by the summer of 2005 prices had climbed above $60 per barrel. The legacy airlines were becoming more competitive after exiting bankruptcy and streamlining their operations to benefit from economies of scale.[2] Analysts speculated that JetBlue was experiencing growth pains:, their maintenance costs on aging planes were increasing, employees were becoming more senior, and new profitable routes were harder to obtain.[3] The company continued to lose money in 2006. While major competitors, such as AMR, the parent company for American Airlines, and Continental, reported higher than expected returns, JetBlue announced a narrow third-quarter loss of $500,000. Following its third-quarter loss, JetBlue announced plans to slow down growth by delaying deliveries of some aircraft, selling others, and eliminating some cross-country flights.[4] Despite these actions, in a recent interview Neeleman insisted, "We're still a growth airline."[5] It remains to be seen how JetBlue will continue to grow in the face of increasing strategic challenges.

HISTORY

Founding History of JetBlue

David Neeleman founded JetBlue Airways Corporation in 1999, after raising $130 million in investment capital. Building on his past experiences, Neeleman hired talented executives, such as David Barger, previous vice president of the Newark, New Jersey, hub for Continental, and John Owen, previous vice president of Operations Planning and Analysis for Southwest.[6] JetBlue chose John F. Kennedy International Airport in New York as its hub and initially obtained 75 takeoff and landing slots.

The authors would like to thank Professor Robert E. Hoskisson for his support under whose direction the case was developed. The authors do not intend to illustrate either effective or ineffective handling of a managerial situation. The case solely provides material for class discussion.

Exhibit 1 Consolidated statement of income

JetBlue Airways Corporation (in $millions, year ended December 31)					
	2006	**2005**	**2004**	**2003**	**2002**
Operating Revenues					
Passenger	$2223	$1620	$1220	$965	$615
Other	140	81	45	33	20
Total Operating Revenues	2363	1701	1265	998	635
Operating Expenses					
Salaries, wages, and benefits	553	428	337	267	162
Aircraft fuel	752	488	255	147	76
Landing fees and other rents	158	112	92	70	44
Depreciation and amortization	151	115	77	51	43
Aircraft rent	103	74	70	60	41
Sales and marketing	104	81	63	54	27
Maintenance materials and repairs	87	64	45	23	9
Other operating expenses	328	291	215	159	127
Total Operating Expenses	2236	1653	1154	831	530
Operating Income	$127	$48	$111	$167	$105
Other Income (Expenses)					
Interest expense	(173)	(107)	(53)	(29)	(21)
Capitalized interest	27	16	9	5	5
Interest income and other	28	19	8	8	5
government compensation				23	
Total other income (expense)	(118)	(72)	(36)	7	(10)
Income (Loss) before income taxes	9	(24)	75	174	95
Income tax expense (benefit)	10	(4)	29	71	40
Net Income (Loss)	$(1)	$(20)	$46	$103	$55

Source: JetBlue Airways Corporation 2006 Annual Report.

Exhibit 2 Consolidated balance sheet

JetBlue Airways Corporation
(in $millions, except share data)

	December 31				
	2006	**2005**	**2004**	**2003**	**2002**
Assets					
Cash and short-term Investments	$699	$484	$450	$607.31	$257.85
Total receivables, net	77	94	37	16.72	11.93
Total inventory	27	21	10	8.3	4.84
Prepaid expenses	124	36	17	13.42	5.59
Other current assets, total	0	0	0	0	2.85
Total Current Assets	$927	$635	$514	$645.74	$283.06
Property/Plant/Equip, total	$3438	$2978	$2130	$1421	$997
Goodwill, net	0	0	0	0	0
Intangibles, net	32	43	54	62	68
Long-term investments	0	0	0	0	0
Note receivable long-term	0	0	0	0	0
Other long-term assets, total	446	236	99	57	30
Other assets, total	0	0	0	0	0
Total Assets	$4843	$3892	$2797	$2186	$1379

	December 31				
	2006	**2005**	**2004**	**2003**	**2002**
Liabilities and Shareholders' Equity					
Accounts payable	$136	$99	$71	$53	$46
Payable/Accrued	0	0	0	0	0
Accrued expenses	164	111	94	85	54
Notes payable/Short-term debt	39	64	44	30	22
Current port. of LT debt/capital	175	158	105	67	51
Leases					
Other current liabilities, total	340	243	174	135	98
Total Current Liabilities	$854	$676	$488	$370	$270
Long-term debt and leases	$2626	$2103	$1396	$1012	$640
Deferred income tax	136	116	121	99	39
Minority interest	0	0	0	0	0
Other liabilities, total	275	86	38	34	17
Total Liabilities	$3891	$2981	$2043	$1515	$964
Redeemable preferred stock	$0	$0	$0	$0	$0
Preferred stock-non	0	0	0	0	0
Common stock	2	2	1	1	1
Additional paid-in capital	813	764	581	552	407
Retained earnings	144	145	165	120	16
Other equity, total	(7)	0	7	(2)	(9)
Total Equity	952	911	754	671	415
Total Liabilities & Shareholders' Equity	$4843	$3892	$2797	$2186	$1,379

Source: JetBlue Airways Corporation 2006 Annual Report.

Exhibit 3 Consolidated statement of cash flows

JetBlue Airways Corporation (in $millions)					
	December 31				
	2006	2005	2004	2003	2002
Cash Flows from Operating Activities					
Net Income	$(1)	$(20)	$46	$103	$55
Operating Activities					
Deferred income taxes	10	(4)	29	69	40
Depreciation	136	101	67	45	25
Amortization	18	16	11	7	2
Stock-based compensation	21	9	2	2	
Changes in certain operating assets and liabilities					
Increase in receivables	(12)	(28)	(20)	(4)	7
Increase in inventories	(28)	(20)	(6)	(11)	(4)
Increase in air traffic liabilities	97	69	39	37	46
Increase in accounts payable and other accrued liabilities	33	54	21	38	35
Other, Net	0	(7)	10	1	11
Net Cash Provided by Operating Activities	274	170	199	287	216
Cash Flows from Investing Activities					
Capital expenditures	(996)	(941)	(617)	(573)	(544)
Predelivery deposits for flight equipment	(106)	(183)	(180)	(160)	(109)
Purchase of held-to-maturity investment	(23)	(5)	(19)	(26)	(11)
Proceeds from maturities of held-to-maturity investment	15	18	25	9	2
Purchase of available-for-sale securities	(1002)	(79)	76	(235)	(80)
Increase in restricted cash and other assets	(16)	(86)	(5)	(2)	(1)
Net Cash Used in Investing Activities	$(1307)	$(1276)	$ (720)	$(987)	$(744)
Cash Flows from Financing Activities					
Proceeds from:					
Issuance of common stock	28	178	20	136	174
Issuance of long-term debt	855	872	499	446	416
Aircraft sale and leaseback transactions	406	152		265	0.3
Short-term borrowings	45	68	44	33	150
Repayment of long-term debt	(390)	(117)	(77)	(57)	27
Repayment of short-term debt	(71)	(47)	(30)	(25)	(71)
Other, Net	–15	(13)	(19)	(9)	(34)
Net Cash Provided by Financing Activities	$1037	$1093	$437	$789	$(5)
Increase in Cash and Cash Equivalents	$4	$(13)	$(84)	$89	$129
Cash and cash equivalent at beginning of period	$6	$19	$103	$14	$117
Cash and cash equivalent at end of period	$10	$6	$19	$103	$247

Source: JetBlue Airways Corporation 2006 Annual Report.

Neeleman's vision was to provide "high-end customer service at low-end prices."[7] Although JetBlue imitated competitor Southwest Airlines with a single seat class, it did so with Airbus A-320 narrow-body jets instead of Boeing 737s. The A-320 provided wider cabins and wider seats for JetBlue passengers with more room for carry-on baggage.[8] JetBlue implemented innovative IT programs such as an Internet booking system that allowed customers to make reservations online or with a touch-tone phone, and a paperless cockpit to allow pilots to prepare for flight more quickly, helping planes to stay on schedule.[9] JetBlue also provided complementary, unlimited snacks and beverages, preassigned seating, and a selection of first-run movies available from Fox InFlight on flights longer than two hours. For further differentiation, JetBlue installed 36 channels of free DIRECTV programming.

Early in 2000, the first JetBlue flights departed from New York to Fort Lauderdale, with a fleet of two planes. JetBlue gradually increased its destinations during the year to include 12 additional airports in California, Florida, New York, Utah, and Vermont. By December, Neeleman announced the landmark of JetBlue's millionth customer and reported $100 million in revenues.

Rapid Growth in 2000–2004

The September 11, 2001, terrorist attacks on America resulted in a widespread fear of air travel, negatively impacting most of the airline industry. While other airlines announced millions in lost revenue following 9/11, JetBlue made a profit and within eight weeks expanded its network to include six more destinations and resumed IT spending to further improve services offered.[10] In February 2002, JetBlue won the 2002 Air Transport World "Market Development Award" for its successful first two years of service, and also was named "Best Overall Airline" by *Onboard Service* magazine.[11] On April 11, 2002, JetBlue announced its initial public offering (IPO) of 5.86 million shares of common stock at a price of $27 per share.[12] JetBlue grew steadily between 2003 and 2004, with annual operating revenues growing from $998.4 million in 2003, to $1.27 billion in 2004. Exhibits 1 through 3 show JetBlue's financial statements for the years 2001 to 2005.

Slowed Growth in 2005–2007

In November 2005 JetBlue decided to add nine new Embraer E190s to its fleet. JetBlue ordered the aircraft with a 100-seat configuration, bigger television screens than the Airbus A-320, and 100 channels from XM Satellite Radio. Also, in late 2005, JetBlue decided to fund $80 million of an airport expansion project at John F. Kennedy Airport, which had a total budget of $875 million. The expansion would allow for more than double the number of flights at JetBlue's hub airport within three years.[13]

However, JetBlue's quarterly financial report started to show growth saturation. Quarterly growth records of operating revenue in 2005 were 29.5 percent, 34.5 percent, 40.2 percent, and –5.2 percent, respectively. JetBlue announced a fourth quarter net loss of $42.4 million, representing a loss per share of $0.25. It was JetBlue's first quarterly net loss.[14]

In 2006, the firm announced unstable earnings, and reported a loss of $32 million, a profit of $14 million, and a loss of $0.5 million in the first three quarters, respectively.[15] Even though JetBlue served 47 destinations with up to 470 daily flights, it decided to reduce its rate of growth over the next three years by delaying the delivery of additional planes.[16] Data for destination and service commenced are listed in Exhibit 4. Effort to slow the growth rate was intended to preserve cash, enabling JetBlue to remain stable among competitors.

The first quarter of 2007 did not get off to a great start for JetBlue. Bad weather in February resulted in many cancelled flights and stranded passengers. The climax of the crisis occurred when nine airplanes full of angry passengers sat on the tarmac for six hours, because JetBlue leaders had expected the weather to clear and did not cancel flights. CEO David Neeleman received bad press for his management of the situation. Neeleman responded by humbly admitting "that his company's management was not strong enough. [It] was the result of a shoestring communications system that left pilots and flight attendants in the dark, and an undersize reservation system."[17] Rapid efforts were made to regain its brand image such that a JetBlue Customer Bill of Rights was created, a customer advisory council was formed, plans were made to cross-train crew members, and new communication strategies were put in place.[18] In addition JetBlue waived change fees and fare differences to assist customers who may be affected by additional storms throughout the winter of 2007. Despite his sincere efforts to bounce back from this predicament, Neeleman eventually had to step down as CEO in order to appease shareholders. David Barger, former COO succeeded Neeleman as CEO and needed to establish a strong position against JetBlue rivals.

Exhibit 4 JetBlue's destinations

Destination	Service Commenced
New York, New York	February 2000
Fort Lauderdale, Florida	February 2000
Buffalo, New York	February 2000
Tampa, Florida	March 2000
Orland, Florida	June 2000
Ontario, California	July 2000
Oakland, California	August 2000
Rochester, New York	August 2000
Burlington, Vermont	September 2000
West Palm Beach, Florida	October 2000
Salt Lake City, Utah	November 2000
Fort Myers, Florida	November 2000
Seattle, Washington	May 2001
Syracuse, New York	May 2001
Denver, Colorado	May 2001
New Orleans, Louisiana	July 2001
Long Beach, California	August 2001
Washington, D.C. (Dulles Airport)	November 2001
San Juan, Puerto Rico	May 2002
Las Vegas, Nevada	November 2002
San Diego, California	June 2003
Boston, Massachusetts	January 2004
Sacramento, California	March 2004
Aguadilla, Puerto Rico	May 2004
Santiago, Dominican Republic	June 2004
San Jose, California	June 2004
New York, New York (LGA Airport)	September 2004
Phoenix, Arizona	October 2004
Nassau, The Bahamas	November 2004
Burbank, California	May 2005
Portland, Oregon	May 2005
Ponce, Puerto Rico	June 2005
Newark, New Jersey	October 2005
Austin, Texas	January 2006
Richmond, Virginia	March 2006
Hamilton, Bermuda	May 2006
Sarasota-Bradenton, Florida	September 2006
Cancun, Mexico	November 2006
Island of Aruba	November 2006
Chicago, Illinois	January 2007
White Plains, New York	March 2007
San Francisco, California	May 2007

Source: JetBlue Airways Corporation Form 10-K, Fiscal year ending December 31, 2006.

COMPETITIVE ENVIRONMENT

In 1978, the Airline Deregulation Act eliminated government control over fares and routes, opening up the industry to increased competition. The airline industry is now highly competitive, consisting of 43 mainline carriers and 79 regional airlines. The US Department of Transportation (DOT) classifies airlines into three categories based on annual revenue: major (revenue more than $1 billion), national (revenue between $100 million to $1 billion), and regional/commuter (revenue less than $100 million).[19] With annual revenue of $1.7 billion, JetBlue is one of the smaller major carriers and competes primarily on point-to-point routes. Its major competitors are low-cost carrier Southwest Airlines and traditional carriers, AMR Corp, United Airlines, US Airways, Continental Airlines, and Delta Air.[20]

Southwest is JetBlue's most obvious competitor, but the traditional airlines are becoming more aggressive in the low-fare market. Following recent bankruptcies, legacy airlines are emerging with clean balance sheets and lower cost structures. As the major airlines become more competitive and expand their domestic businesses, the low-cost airlines struggle to find new markets.[21]

Competition also comes from the regional carriers, which typically partner with the major airlines to share routes, risk, and costs. For example, Mesa partners with

United Airlines and operates as United Express, with Delta Airlines as Delta Express, and with US Air as US Air Express. In exchange for an agreed proportion of revenue, Mesa operates flights on select local routes, while its partners handle reservations and marketing. In recent years, the regional airlines fared better than most, growing twice as fast as the national carriers.[22] However, as the competitive environment toughens, many of the large airlines are renegotiating the agreements, and in some cases—such as Atlantic Coast, a former partner of United Airlines—regional airlines are deciding to operate independently.[23]

The major airlines also form alliances—with each other and international carriers—to share marketing and scheduling capabilities. American Airlines partners with British Airways, Quantas, and various European airlines to form the One World Alliance, which serves 135 countries and operates a shared frequent flyer program. The Star Alliance, spearheaded by United Airlines, with Lufthansa, Scandinavian Air System, All Nippon Airways, and Air Canada, serves 157 countries.[24] Such alliances increase the market power of their members, and research has shown they increase passenger volume by an average of 9.4 percent.[25] Although the benefit is more significant for global carriers seeking to expand their network abroad, researchers observed an average improvement in number of tickets booked by 7.4 percent on short-haul flights.

Although JetBlue does not currently participate in any alliances, it has had discussions about forming one with international airlines in an effort to leverage its power at the hub in JFK. JetBlue does not want to enter a traditional agreement with other airlines, because many of these agreements include increased overhead costs. JetBlue is hoping to create an agreement that will increase traffic without increasing costs.[26]

Fare pricing is an important competitive factor within the industry. For many years excess capacity posed a significant problem, causing airlines to either leave planes on the ground or fly planes with empty seats. In order to avoid this dilemma, carriers try to increase market share by discounting tickets. Even the legacy airlines slash fares in order to compete on low-cost routes. Although low-cost airlines, like JetBlue, still offer the greatest number of discounted fares, some of the cheapest tickets are now available from traditional airlines, such as American, Delta, and United.[27]

Rumors of consolidation in the industry could change the competitive landscape. US Airways made a hostile bid for bankrupt Delta Airlines in fourth quarter 2006, but withdrew its offer in January 2007 due to the inability to reach financial agreement with Delta creditors.[28] The merger would have created the largest airline in a fragmented industry and would likely have triggered further consolidations.[29] Even though a wave of consolidation may create a more efficient airline industry with fewer major players, consolidations affect ticket prices, usually leading to higher ticket prices, and complicate the flight paths offered by airlines. Therefore, consolidations affect all competitors within the industry.

Key Competitors

Southwest Airlines

Southwest is the leading low-fare, no-frills, US carrier. The company was founded in 1967 as a Texas-based airline to serve Dallas, Houston, and San Antonio. The airline now flies to more than 63 cities across the United States. In 2006, Southwest reported a $499 million profit and net sales of $9.86 billion.[30] Exhibit 5 compares key financial data for the major airlines. In 2005, America West's CEO, Douglas Parker, described Southwest as follows: "They really were at one point the scrawny kid who was lifting weights in his basement. Now they come out and they're bigger than anybody else and stronger than anybody else."[31]

Southwest's strategy emphasizes low costs; the firm was the first to sell tickets online and to introduce unassigned seating. It operates a single aircraft fleet of 481 Boeing 737s. The company is also lauded for its unique and friendly culture and its high level of customer service.[32] However, evidence now indicates a shift in its strategy—from serving underserved routes, to competing in major markets such as Denver and Philadelphia. Southwest is now the largest US airline in terms of number of passengers (Exhibit 6), and in order to continue to grow, Southwest is competing against United in its Denver hub, and US Airways, on routes out of Philadelphia.[33]

AMR Corp.

As the world's largest airline, American Airlines (AMR's main subsidiary) offers flights to 150 destinations throughout North America, Latin America, the Caribbean, Europe, and Asia. It has had its share of success and failures; two of its planes were hijacked during

Exhibit 5 US major airlines' select financials for year ended 2006 (in $millions)

	JetBlue	UAL	SWA	Delta	Continental	US Airways	AMR Corp.
Total revenues	$2,363	$19,340	$9,086	$17,171	$13,128	$11,557	$22,563
Cost of revenues	1,653	14,114	6,311	14,430	11,007	9,049	17,659
Gross profit	570	5,226	2,573	1,694	1,453	1,814	4,904
Profit as % of revenue	24%	27%	28%	10%	11%	16%	22%
Operating income (loss)	127	23,381	934	(6,148)	468	558	1,060
Net income (loss)	$(1)	$22,386	$499	$(6,203)	$343	$304	$231
Total assets	$4,843	25,369	$13,460	$19,622	$11,308	$7,576	$29,145
Current assets	927	6,273	2,601	5,385	4,129	3,354	6,902
Total liabilities	$3,891	$23,221	$7,011	$33,215	$10,961	$6,606	$29,751
Current liabilities	854	7,945	2,887	5,769	3,955	2,712	8,505
Total owner equity	$952	$2,148	$6,449	$(13,593)	$347	$970	$(606)

Source: 2007, MSN Money Central, http://moneycentral.msn.com/investor/research/welcome.asp, July 24.

Exhibit 6 Top 10 US airlines, ranked by August 2006 domestic scheduled enplanements

Passenger numbers in millions				
August 2006 Rank	**Carrier**	**August 2006 Enplanements**	**August 2005 Rank**	**August 2005 Enplanements**
1	Southwest	8.7	1	8.1
2	American	6.5	3	6.8
3	Delta	5.4	2	7.0
4	United	5.1	4	5.0
5	Northwest	4.1	5	4.2
6	Continental	3.1	7	2.9
7	US Airways	2.6	6	3.1
8	America West	1.8	8	1.9
9	AirTran	1.8	9	1.5
10	JetBlue	1.7	13	1.3

Note: Percentage changes based on numbers prior to rounding.
Source: Bureau of Transportation Statistics, T-100 Domestic Market.

the September 11, 2001, terrorist attacks and the firm barely avoided bankruptcy in 2003.[34] In 2006, AMR Corp. reported net earnings of $231 million, an improvement over its net loss of $861 million in 2005 and other significant losses in preceding years.[35] In order to return to profitability, the firm streamlined costs and expanded its routes in Asia.

United Airlines

United also lost two planes on September 11, 2001, and after several years of financial difficulties, UAL eventually filed for Chapter 11 bankruptcy in 2002.[36] UAL emerged from bankruptcy as a more competitive firm. In February 2004, United launched its own low-cost offshoot, Ted. The firm is now looking for new ways to expand and improve profitability. Global expansion is central to UAL's strategy; in July 2006, the firm announced plans to expand its Asia/Pacific routes.[37] Recent rumors report that UAL hired Goldman Sachs to assess possible merger options.[38]

US Airways

US Airways Group is the product of a merger between US Airways and America West. CEO Parker believes this acquisition strategy is successful; when comparing the firm's post-bankruptcy performance to United, he stated, "The big difference is we were able to generate synergies that United was not able to."[39] Shareholders experienced a 45 percent increase in stock price during the first full year after the merger.[40]

Delta Air

With an 11.8% domestic market share, Delta places third among traditional airline icons.[41] Delta is strongly focused on international expansion, adding 50 new international routes in 2005–2006. Delta now serves over 450 destinations in 95 countries. Delta filed for bankruptcy and was a target acquisition by US Airways just before it emerged from bankruptcy in April 2007.

Continental Airlines

Continental targets the business traveler by serving diverse US and international routes.[42] Continental has a strong balance sheet, having recently retired $100 million in debt.[43] In the third quarter of 2006, Continental followed in the path of the other legacy airlines by reporting stronger than expected results. The positive results were attributed to greatly increased number of passengers, especially on Continental's regional and Latin American routes.[44]

As well as domestic competitors, the international airline market conditions are a factor that JetBlue must consider.

International Market Conditions

The demand for international travel has increased significantly over the past decade (see Exhibit 7). The international travel growth rate is more than double the domestic travel growth rate in the United States.[45] Travel to Southeast Asia and China increases every year by about 7.3 percent and 8.0 percent. Looking forward, the number of transatlantic plane tickets purchased is expected to grow by 4.6 percent annually. Global business transactions have contributed, as well as more discretionary income for consumers, and lower airfare resulting from greater efficiencies in international travel.

The international market is attractive to many airlines because they can include fuel surcharges in the ticket price and recover some of the costs associated with higher-priced fuel.

However, the airline industry is monitored more scrupulously by the government than any other industry conducting business internationally. The government has many regulations on when, where, and how airlines can fly, how much they can charge, and how they can market international travel.[46] Many lobbyist firms and politicians in the United States have been fighting for deregulation and less restrictions on international air travel so that the United States might be more of a force in the international market. The European airline industry, more specifically AirFrance/KLM, has taken the lead in revenues for international aviation.[47]

Not only is it important for JetBlue to consider its competitive environment, but it is also important to understand the companies/industries that supply the provisions necessary to remain competitive.

Key Suppliers

Fuel

Fuel is usually the second-highest expense for an airline next to labor.[48] Therefore, fuel price increases are a major contributor to rising operating costs in the airline industry. A Merrill Lynch analyst indicated that for every $1 increase in price for a barrel of fuel, the airline industry experiences a $450 million loss in pretax profits.[49] According to the FAA, jet fuel costs rose by 20.1 percent in 2004, 40.5 percent in 2005, and 30.4 percent in 2006.[50] In 2006, fuel costs became JetBlue's largest operating expense at 33.65 percent.[51] The FAA forecasts fuel costs will remain high for the next several years. Neeleman seriously considers fuel costs and is investigating alternative sources of energy, such as liquid coal. Because the United States has an abundant supply of coal, Neeleman is urging his customers to support a new bill to fund additional coal-to-liquid plants.[52]

Airlines engage in fuel hedging in order to manage unpredictable costs. However, the jet fuel commodities market is illiquid, and it is especially difficult for the large airlines to hedge sufficient quantities of fuel.[53] JetBlue is increasing its efforts to systematically hedge against future fuel needs. JetBlue also seeks more efficient fuel usage through the planes purchased and improved flight planning.[54]

Exhibit 7 US commercial air carriers total US passenger traffic

	Revenue Passenger Enplanements (millions)			Revenue Passenger Miles (billions)		
Fiscal Year	**Domestic**	**International**	**System**	**Domestic**	**International**	**System**
Historical*						
2000	641.2	56.4	697.6	512.8	181.8	694.6
2001	626.8	56.7	683.4	508.1	183.3	691.4
2002	574.5	51.2	625.8	473.0	158.2	631.3
2003	587.8	54.2	642.0	492.7	155.9	648.6
2004	628.5	61.4	689.9	540.2	177.4	717.7
2005	661	86.2	747.2	573.7	221.5	795.1
Forecast						
2006	660.9	89.7	750.6	577.6	232.5	810.1
2007	693.3	75.8	769.1	603.3	221.5	824.7
2008	713.8	79.8	793.6	624.6	234.5	859.0
2009	735.7	84.0	819.7	647.7	247.9	895.6
2010	758.9	88.3	847.2	671.9	262.1	934.1
2011	782.6	92.9	875.5	697.6	276.9	974.5
2012	807.7	97.6	905.2	724.5	291.9	1,016.4
2013	833.4	102.3	935.7	752.6	307.4	1,059.9
2014	860.5	107.2	967.7	782.2	323.5	1,105.7
2015	888.4	112.3	1,000.7	813.3	340.2	1,153.5
2016	917.7	117.6	1,035.3	846.1	357.5	1,203.6
2017	848.4	123.1	1,071.6	880.6	375.2	1,255.8
Average annual growth 2005–2017	2.9%	5.0%	3.1%	3.6%	5.5%	4.1%

Source: Forms 41 and 298-C, US Department of Transportation.

Aircraft Manufacturers

The aircraft industry is dominated by two companies, Airbus and Boeing. Due to the weak economy following September 11, 2001, their orders for new commercial planes fell sharply. However, as commercial business improved, the large manufacturers profited from the buoyant space and defense markets. Embraer, the number four aircraft manufacturer, has seen lackluster commercial sales, but is benefiting from increased sales in the military sector.

Typically, the low-cost airlines operate few aircraft types, reducing their maintenance, scheduling, and training costs. JetBlue currently owns two airplane models, and its growth plans include the addition of 96 Airbus A-320s and 92 Embraer E190s.[55] Cost efficiencies would be lost if JetBlue switched suppliers, exposing the firm to any problems related to either of its aircraft suppliers. But currently more pressing for JetBlue are the challenges associated with the airline industry.

General Environment

A number of new trends are emerging in air travel. After September 11, 2001, the industry saw a drop in the number of corporate travelers, but five years later this trend appeared to be reversing. According to a survey by the National Business Travel Association, 65 percent of businesses expect employees to take more flights in 2007, and 75 percent predict an increase in the amount of business travel.[56]

Another factor in the environment of air travel is the characteristics of the airport and FAA density regulations. JetBlue experiences general performance setbacks by operating in high traffic areas such as the northeastern United States, and the airport congestion hampers performance statistics.[57] The FAA regulates airport slot (a slot is a time frame allotted for takeoff and landing)[58] allocations with the intent to ease congestion problems and enhance airport capacity. For example, recent measures at New York La Guardia airport include growth limitations, regulations encouraging use of larger aircraft, and a proposal for 10-year slot reallocation.[59]

Natural disasters and annual weather patterns also affect the performance statistics for air travel. Florida is quite popular during the winter months and the western states during summer months. Air travel is also affected by winter weather in the Northeast and tropical storms along the Atlantic and Gulf coasts.[60]

In the airline industry, more than 60 percent of employees are unionized.[61] Although JetBlue is non-unionized, it can be affected by the industry environment. In June 2006, the International Association of Machinists and Aerospace Workers campaigned to represent JetBlue's ramp service workers. The bid was unsuccessful; however JetBlue's management commented, "We can expect ongoing attempts by unions to organize groups of JetBlue crewmembers."[62]

As can be expected from the general environment, JetBlue is exposed to the widespread attraction of media coverage and negative press. One recent major incident appearing in headlines is the mechanical failure of Flight 292 landing in Los Angeles.[63] On September 21, 2005, JetBlue Flight 292 left Burbank, California, bound for JFK in New York City. Soon after takeoff, the pilot acknowledged problems with the landing gear. The decision was made to have an emergency landing at Los Angeles International Airport and after circling Orange County for three hours, to burn off fuel, Flight 292 landed safely. None of the 139 passengers or six crew members was injured during the landing. Upon landing it became certain that the nose gear had rotated 90 degrees and was locked in the down position[64] (see Exhibit 8). Although the outcome was ultimately favorable, had Flight 292 crashed or lives been lost, JetBlue's image would have suffered drastically. The perceived safety of air travel is important for all airlines.

Exhibit 8 JetBlue Airbus A-320 Flight 292 with its nose landing gear jammed

Source: JetScott, 2005, http://www.aerospaceweb.org/question/planes/ q0245a.shtml, October 2.

Airlines also face a heightened sense of consumer information privacy. In 2002, JetBlue offered extensive passenger data to a data mining company, Torch, who in conjunction with the US Army, tested a customer profiling system to identify high risk passengers that might threaten military installations.[65] According to the District Court, Eastern New York, Memorandum & Order 04-MD-1587, JetBlue was responsible for the release of "each passenger's name, address, gender, home ownership or rental status, economic status, social security number, occupation, and the number of adults and children in the passenger's family as well as the number of vehicles owned or leased."[66] With increased online purchases, all airlines are publicly pressured to protect passengers' identity.

JetBlue must make a conscious effort to rise above all of the setbacks associated with the general environment and ensure that all actions are in alignment with its corporate and business strategies.

JetBlue Strategies

Because many of the other airlines play a significant role in the low-cost carrier segment within the airline industry, JetBlue competes by differentiation. The goal is to achieve an image of far superior customer service.

Superior Customer Service

JetBlue delivers this service by offering additional preflight and on-board conveniences that other low-cost carriers do not provide as a whole package. Before traveling, customers benefit from JetBlue's simple-to-use reservation system, ticketless travel, and preassigned seating. The cabin features leather seats and an additional two inches of leg room than most carriers. As previously mentioned, on board JetBlue passengers receive free DIRECTV service, and its Embraer E190 planes have XM Satellite Radio.[67] To improve the customer experience, JetBlue added healthier snacks and, as of November 2006, offers a 100 percent transfat-free selection. All snacks are complementary and unlimited.

All passengers on "shut eye" flights receive a comfort kit from Bliss, which includes earplugs, lip balm, an eye mask, and hand lotion. Crewmembers wake customers with the smell of Dunkin' Donuts coffee and offer a hot towel service.[68]

It is valuable to customers to have their flight depart as planned. To provide customers with confidence, JetBlue focuses on its completion rate, even at the expense of its on-time rate. At the end of third quarter 2006, JetBlue had a 99.6 percent completion rate. In addition, customers want to be confident that they will have their bags at the end of the flight. At 2006 year-end, JetBlue was ranked number 1 out of the 15 busiest airlines in regard to the least number of lost or mishandled bags.[69]

A critical factor in achieving superior service is employee moral. As Neeleman has stated, the crew-members are the "real secret weapon."[70] His philosophy is that if crew members are treated well, they will in turn treat the customers well.

Culture

Currently, David Neeleman, chairperson, and Dave Barger, CEO, are hands-on people who like to interact with employees and customers. Each week members of top management fly with 8 to 12 crew members and almost always attend new hire training to teach new crewmembers about JetBlue's brand, how the company makes money, and how crewmembers contribute to the bottom line. Whenever they fly, they help the crew clean the plane after the flight to ensure a quick turnaround time. In addition they have informal meetings with crew-members to learn about issues and problems as crew-members see them.[71] This management style continues to attract motivated new hires; JetBlue has a reputation as a great place to work, company profit sharing, high productivity of planes and people, and rapid advancements. In 2004 alone, JetBlue hired 1,700–1,800 people.[72]

The combined effort to provide exceptional service and instill a valued-employee culture will fulfill Neeleman's hope that JetBlue can "keep our folks fresh and keep our customers coming back."[73]

However, as proven by Delta's Song and the installation of leather seats in its planes, the "superior service" attributes can be imitated by competitors. What has also allowed JetBlue to remain one step ahead in its competitive environment is cost management.

Cost Management

JetBlue's cost-saving initiative includes electronic ticketing, paperless cockpits, and online check-in.[74] In order to achieve paperless cockpits, JetBlue supplied pilots and first officers with laptops to retrieve electronic flight manuals and make preflight load and balance calculations.[75] In the year following implementation of paperless cockpits, the company saved approximately 4,800 hours of labor.[76] One of JetBlue's more original strategies to cut costs is its telephone reservation system. Reservation agents work from their homes in Salt Lake City, using personal computers equipped with VoIP technology. VoIP stands for Voice over Internet Protocol and utilizes the Internet to make free phone calls.[77] This system gives JetBlue flexibility to handle varying call volumes without needing a costly call center.[78]

JetBlue also uses technology to manage its marketing costs. JetBlue employs Omniture software to increase efficiency of Internet searches, decreasing associated search conversion costs by 94 percent.[79] By using animation in its television ads with its advertising agency, JetBlue produced eight ads for the standard price of one.[80]

Another value-adding initiative is BlueTurn, the name for JetBlue's ground operations. In an effort to improve the overall on-time performance statistics, BlueTurn allows crewmembers to minimize ground time and decrease the turnaround time for aircraft.[81]

JetBlue operates two aircraft types and a single travel class. This simplicity reduces training, maintenance, and operating costs relative to competitors that operate multiple aircraft types.

These cost-cutting strategies follow the standard low-cost, low-fare business model, without sacrificing the ultimate strategy of providing superior customer service with happy employees.

In order to best market its services, JetBlue has carefully considered its marketing approach.

Marketing Strategy

Neeleman believes that marketing is best accomplished by word of mouth; therefore top management aims to make sure that customers are treated well and employees feel valued.[82] Yet, they have made concerted efforts to market in other ways. To establish a media campaign, JetBlue hired J. Walter Thompson (JWT) as its advertising agency.[83] To create a fresh identity, JWT found candid statements by customers on JetBlue service. Online sources were consulted such as Craigslist and Epinions. The statements, written as short stories, were used to create eight different animated ads as testimonials to JetBlue's customer service. Other forms of direct marketing were used such as leather benches and snack bins in serviced airports. JetBlue also created comical postcards and distributed to customers to mail back their comments.[84]

In order to record customers' opinions on JetBlue service, an interactive video installation called the "JetBlue Story Booth" was set up in Rockefeller Center, and is traveling around the country to other cities served by JetBlue.[85] In the one-week New York exhibit, an estimated 20,000 people participated in the installation.[86] A vehicle called Blue Betty was created to simulate an airplane cabin and showcase in-flight amenities. As it traveled to various events across the country, visitors could enter a contest (or lottery) for ticket giveaways. JetBlue also used direct marketing to target college students with a public relations team called CrewBlue. This group used unconventional methods of posters, flyers, and chalk art to educate students about various aspects of the airline's services. Other marketing efforts include "Blue Days," where students were encouraged to wear blue and were rewarded with airline tickets through drawings. A 2005 survey indicated this marketing campaign was successful and increased JetBlue awareness by 41 percent.[87]

In addition to marketing initiatives, JetBlue on a consistent basis updates its business strategy to increase growth and revenue.

Current Strategies

In the first quarter of 2006, due to operating losses, JetBlue executives announced a turnaround plan called "Return to Profitability." Items included in this initiative were revisions to fare structures, corrections to flight capacity, and reprioritizing of flight segments (short, medium, and long haul).[88]

The growth rate has been slowed. The company expects to grow between 14 and 17 percent over the next year versus the 18 to 20 percent originally forecasted.[89]

JetBlue plans to fuel this growth by adding a number of flights on existing routes, connecting new city pairs among the destinations already served, and entering new markets usually served by higher-cost, higher-fare airlines. To determine which cities JetBlue should include in its flight pattern, executives study information made available from the Department of Transportation, which outlines the historical number of passengers, capacity, and average fares over time in all city-pair markets within North America.[90] This information along with JetBlue's historical data allows them to predict how a market will react to the introduction of JetBlue's service and lower prices.

JetBlue expects to use the new Embraer fleet to create demand in many midsized markets that could benefit from its point-to-point service.[91]

In addition, as mentioned previously, JetBlue is in the midst of some discussions about creating a partnership to enter the international market. Due to the limited type of aircraft in JetBlue's fleet, an alliance is the only way for JetBlue to capitalize on the international market opportunities, because its aircraft are not large enough to fly overseas.

The firm is also optimistic that recent moves to expand distribution channels will increase revenue. In August of 2006, the company signed a five-year agreement with Sabre Holdings and Galileo International. This arrangement will allow more than 52,000 travel agencies to purchase tickets for JetBlue travelers with a single connection. These deals are an attempt to reach a broader customer base, especially business travelers.[92]

Moreover, JetBlue is constantly striving to introduce new methods of providing superior customer service. As of March 2007 the first 11 rows in the cabin feature four inches of legroom between each row rather than the previous two inches.[93] To augment its flight services, JetBlue has established complementary products and services.

Associated Products and Services

In addition to air travel, JetBlue sells combined flight and hotel packages, which it terms "JetBlue Getaways." When JetBlue Getaways launched in November 2005, Tim Claydon, vice president of Sales and Marketing, commented, "By working with the hotels directly, rather than through an intermediary, we are able to offer our customers only the finest properties at great prices. Using the latest technology to combine the lowest JetBlue airfare with the best hotel or resort rate, we are able to offer our customers a new level of value with vacations beginning and ending on JetBlue Airways—something not available on any other online travel site."[94]

An American Express card was issued in 2005 called the "JetBlue Card," which earns TrueBlue points for members.[95] Customers earn TrueBlue points when purchasing flights, movie tickets, sporting event tickets, and gym memberships. When a customer amasses 100 TrueBlue points (equivalent to approximately five medium-length round trips), the customer earns a free round-trip valid for one year. In 2006, award travel accounted for only 2 percent of JetBlue's total revenue passenger miles.[96]

In order to sustain its business and corporate strategies, JetBlue monitors its financial situation regularly.

FINANCIAL CONDITION

JetBlue's current financial situation is highlighted by its short-term liquidity, long-term stability, and company profitability. Stockholder profitability signals whether JetBlue is meeting its stockholders' expectations.[97]

Short-Term Liquidity

JetBlue's balance sheet over the past five years is shown in Exhibit 2. JetBlue has struggled with financial performance since 2005. The growth of current liabilities from 2003 to 2006 is significant, compared to the growth of current assets. However, the payables turnover ratio has been increasing, which indicates that JetBlue has been able to pay its suppliers at a faster rate even though it has not been as efficient in collecting receivables as in years past. (Liquidity ratios are shown in Exhibit 9 and turnover ratios are shown in Exhibit 10.)

Exhibit 9 Liquidity ratios

	2006	2005	2004	2003	2002
Current ratio	1.1	0.94	1.05	1.75	1.05
Quick ratio	1.05	0.91	1.03	1.72	1.03

Source: JetBlue Airways Corporation 2006 Annual Report.

Exhibit 10 Receivables and payables

Receivables	2006	2005	2004	2003	2002
Receivable turnover Days	30.6	26	47.1	69.7	38.8
to collect	11.9	14.1	7.8	5.2	9.4
Payables	**2006**	2005	2004	2003	2002
Payable turnover Days to pay	16.4	13.8	12.9	11.5	9.5
		26.4	28.3	31.7	38.5

Source: JetBlue Airways Corporation 2006 Annual Report.

Exhibit 11 Stability ratios

	2006	2005	2004	2003	2002
Debt/Asset ratio	0.8	0.8	0.7	0.7	0.7
Asset/Equity ratio	5.1	4	3.5	3.3	3.5
Debt/Equity (financial leverage)	4.1	3.3	2.7	2.3	2.3
Interest coverage ratio	0.7	0.7	2.7	8.4	7.1

Source: JetBlue Airways Corporation 2006 Annual Report.

Exhibit 12 Fuel expenses

	2006	2005	2004	2003	2002
Operating revenue	$2363	$1701	$1265	$998	$635
Aircraft fuel	752	488	255	147	76
Aircraft fuel %	31	29	20	15	12
Other Costs % Revenue					
Salaries and benefits %	23	25	27	27	26
Aircraft rent %	4	4	6	6	6
Sales and Marketing %	4	5	5	5	7
Maintenance %	4	4	4	2	1

Source: JetBlue Airways Corporation 2006 Annual Report.

Long-Term Stability

Long-term financial stability will be an issue as JetBlue toils to consistently turn a profit. JetBlue has maintained a fairly consistent debt-to-asset mix as most of the cash received from issuances has been invested in capital assets. The majority of JetBlue's issuances are floating rate bonds, exposing the firm to increases in the Federal Reserve's prime rate.[98] JetBlue's first quarter 2007 assets/equity ratio stood at 5.4 compared to the industry average of 3.[99] (See Exhibits 3 and 11 for details.)

Exhibit 13 Profitability

	2006	2005	2004	2003	2002
Gross margins	20%	27%	33%	40%	45%
Operating margins	5.4%	3%	9%	17%	17%
Net profit margins	0.4%	−1%	4%	10%	9%
Return on equity	0.97%	−2%	6%	19%	19%
Return on assets	2%	2%	3%	6%	6%

Company Profitability

JetBlue's gross margins continued to decline in recent years, which can be mainly attributed to increasing fuel charges as shown in Exhibit 12. Salaries, landing fees, and other expenses remain fairly stable as a percent of revenues (most have actually decreased, see Exhibit 1). For

2006, gross margins remained 23 percent (see Exhibit 13). As stated earlier, interest expense has a negative effect on profitability.

Stockholder Profitability

In July 2007, the stock was trading at $11.01 versus $14.90[100] at the end of April 2002. In addition to the lackluster stock movement, JetBlue has never paid dividends, so the overall return for the past four years is 5.5 percent. According to moneycentral.com and Yahoo! Finance, the average analyst recommendation is "Hold" for JetBlue. The declining return on equity and inconsistency of net income appears to be having negative implications for JetBlue.

Strategic Challenges

JetBlue faces many challenges as it continues to operate in the highly competitive airline industry. The main challenges are maintaining JetBlue's culture as it grows, dealing with the surfacing complexities of two fleet types, managing maintenance expenses as airplanes and engines begin to age, and dealing with an increasingly senior labor pool. Although fuel prices are a concern, they affect the industry in the same way, and airlines have opportunities to mitigate these risks. Southwest hedged its fuel position more effectively than other airlines, but these hedges will expire and everyone will have a more level playing field when it comes to fuel prices.[101]

Maintaining the JetBlue culture will be difficult to do as the airline grows. The explosive increase in employees may hinder the ability to sustain high utilization and maintain a positive work environment. The time that top management has to interact with individual crewmembers will decrease. Neeleman stated that he would no longer be able to respond to every crew-member's e-mail.[102] This change will hinder a popular cultural component because the chairperson and CEO may no longer be seen as accessible.[103]

Multiple Aircraft Types

JetBlue will have a challenge as it continues to integrate two different types of aircraft. The firm suffered a setback when it incorporated the Embraer E190 into its fleet. JetBlue wanted to fly the new planes 14 hours a day, similar to its A-320s. However, the airplane characteristics were different from the Airbus.[104] Both pilots and mechanics needed additional time and training to understand the new plane. These factors caused flight delays and cancellations throughout the JetBlue system.[105] JetBlue had to reevaluate its plans.

Another issue associated with two types of aircraft is that JetBlue must staff two groups of pilots and flight attendants. The different aircraft require unique training and integration procedures. JetBlue will need separate inventories, training programs, and facilities to accommodate two fleet types.[106] In addition, the pay scales are different, which requires additional support from corporate employees.

Increased Maintenance Expenses

Maintenance expense will be a significant concern for JetBlue in coming years. As with a new car, new airplanes rarely need maintenance and when they do, they are covered under warranty. In 2004, JetBlue experienced a 94 percent increase in maintenance costs.[107] The increase in maintenance costs was not as significant in 2005 and 2006 at 36 percent and 42 percent, respectively (see Exhibit 1); however, as the large fleet of new planes comes due for heavy maintenance at the same time, JetBlue will experience a significant increase in maintenance costs.

Airplane operators have A, C, and D levels of scheduled maintenance and inspection intervals. A-checks occur every 400–500 hours and are similar to an oil change on a vehicle. C- and D-checks are more extensive, more expensive, and longer. The C-check schedule is every 18 months/6,000 hours/3,000 cycles.[108] Additionally, the fourth C-check consists of more inspections, and takes 10 days, compared to just 4 days for regular C-checks.[109] Furthermore, JetBlue decided to outsource maintenance to Air Canada Technical Services in Winnipeg, and Aeroman in El Salvador. Because these operations are not co-located with any of its scheduled service, JetBlue has to spend additional money ferrying planes and paying employees to work in these facilities. JetBlue spends "seven figures" each year in ferrying planes and as much as $700 per day extra for people to monitor the quality of work.[110] As JetBlue's planes enter more extensive service, the amount of time to ferry airplanes and actual maintenance will increase.

Engine expense is another huge maintenance cost for JetBlue. In July 2005, JetBlue signed a 10-year service agreement with a German company, MTU. It covers all scheduled and unscheduled repair for all A-320 engines.[111] At year-end 2006, JetBlue had more than 90 A-320 aircraft, and with two engines per plane and a healthy spares inventory, JetBlue has a significant number of engines to maintain (including its 23 E190 airplanes and engines).[112] Typical charges for a comparable engine overhaul range from $1 million to $1.5 million per heavy visit.

In addition to engines and airframes, airplane operators have additional equipment they must maintain and arrange for contract maintenance support. They have auxiliary power units, landing gear systems, environmental systems, avionics, and flight controls.

As the number of aircraft increases, the cost to maintain will increase. JetBlue may lose economies of scale because multiple aircraft types require multiple repair facilities, and they will have to employ and house multiple sets of inventory and people.

Increased Payroll Expenses

Payroll costs will multiply at JetBlue as the company ages. During 2006 salaries, wages, and benefits increased 29 percent, or $125 million, due primarily to an increased workforce (refer to Exhibit 1).[113] According to the Bureau of Transportation (see Exhibit 15), JetBlue experienced a 212 percent staff growth and ranks third among low-cost carriers for total number of employees in the United States.

Currently, all of the crewmembers are near the bottom of the pay scales, and JetBlue enjoys a relatively low-cost labor pool. However, as these people attain seniority with the company their pay level will increase.[114] Not only will salaried employees get annual pay raises, but crewmembers are paid for each hour flown, according to type of aircraft and depending on the number of years with the company (see Exhibit 14). A more senior staff means the company will start paying higher wages.

Exhibit 14 Pay scale table

200 Year	A-320 Captain	EMB190 Captain	A-320 FO	EMB190 FO
12	$126	$89	$76	$53
11	$126	$87	$76	$52
10	$126	$85	$76	$51
9	$125	$84	$75	$50
8	$124	$82	$74	$49
7	$123	$80	$74	$48
6	$122	$79	$73	$47
5	$121	$77	$72	$46
4	$118	$76	$67	$44
3	$116	$74	$61	$42
2	$113	$72	$56	$40
1	$110	$71	$51	$37

Note: Guarantee of 70 hrs/month; above 70 hours paid at 150%.
Source: 2006, Will fly for food, http://www.willflyforfood.cc/Payscales/PayScales.htm.

Exhibit 15 Low-cost carrier full-time equivalent employees, August 2002–2006

		(Numbers in thousands)					
Rank		2002	2003*	2004*	2005*	2006	Percent Change 2002–2006
1	Southwest	34	33	31	31	32	–4.5
2	America West	12	11	11	12	13	7.0
3	JetBlue	3	5	6	8	10	212.4
4	AirTran	5	5	6	6	7	56.9
5	Frontier	3	3	4	4	5	70.6
6	ATA	7	7	7	4	3	–61.5
7	Spirit	2	2	2	2	2	–14.4
8	Independence	N/A	4	4	3	N/A	N/A
	Total****	65	71	72	71	71	9.3

*Employment numbers in 2003, 2004, and 2005 for Independence Air, which changed its business model from a regional to low-cost carrier in mid-2004, are included with low-cost carriers. The carrier did not meet the standard for filing in previous years. The airline discontinued flights on January 5, 2006.

N/A = Not applicable because carriers did not meet the standard for filing.

Source: Bureau of Transportation Statistics.

Because JetBlue desires to remain nonunionized, it will have to pay its employees well to ensure they do not become disgruntled and demand representation. Unions have not gained a foothold in JetBlue, but the Air Lines Pilot Association has JetBlue as a target. In addition to pilots, flight attendants, mechanics, ground crews, and gate agents will also receive pressure from other national unions for representation. If by chance the employees of JetBlue succumb to union pressure, union negotiators will then push for increased wages and other amenities—such as hotel requirements, time off, minimum number of flight hours per month, and so on—resulting in higher costs.

JetBlue's Challenge in Coming Years

David Neeleman started an airline based on previous experience and an entrepreneurial spirit. He knew what people wanted and how much they would pay for it. JetBlue attracted high-quality employees because of the unique culture that stressed customer service and differentiated offerings. Allowing at-home reservations agents, paperless cockpits, and crewmem-bers' easy access to executives has created an environment with which people want to associate. In addition, by purchasing brand new Airbus airplanes and having a junior staff, JetBlue has minimized labor and maintenance costs, both major operating expenses, for several years. As growth slows in the domestic market, its aircraft begin to age, and the workforce becomes more senior, the number of challenges will increase. Barger and Neeleman are faced with persistent questions about how to continue to grow the airline profitably. Does JetBlue attack Southwest, United, Delta, American, or Continental strongholds in the Midwest and/or smaller airports? Does it form an alliance in order to expand into international markets such as Europe and Asia? To minimize expenses related to airplanes, should JetBlue return to one airplane type? Finally, while unions are prevalent at every other airline, how can JetBlue maintain an environment where employees remain committed, dedicated, and satisfied?

NOTES

1. 2002, JetBlue Airways Corporation, *International Directory of Company Histories,* Vol. 44. St. James Press. 2006, Reproduced in Business and Company Resource Center. Farmington Hills, Mich.:Gale Group.
2. M. Trottman & S. Carey, 2006, Legacy Airlines may outfly discount rivals, *Wall Street Journal,* October 30, C1.
3. T. Fredrickson, 2006, Middle-aged JetBlue finds it's harder to fly; Ballooning fuel costs, intense competition turn it into a loser, *Grain's New York Business,* February 13, 22(7):4.
4. J. Bernstein, 2006, JetBlue posts quarterly loss, *Newsday,* October 25.
5. J. H. Dobrzynski, 2006, We're still a growth airline, *Wall Street Journal,* November 4, A6.
6. JetBlue Airways Corporation, http://galenet.galegroup.com.ezproxy1.lib.asu.edu/servlet/BCRC.
7. S. Overby, 2002, JetBlue skies ahead, *CIO Magazine,* http://www. cio.com, July 1.
8. 2006, Airbus, http://www.airbus.com/en/aircraftfamilies/a320/a320/.
9. S. Overby, JetBlue skies ahead.
10. Ibid.
11. 2002, JetBlue announces second quarter 2002 earnings—Low-fare carrier achieves record operating margin of 18.6%, JetBlue Airways Corporation press release, July 25.
12. 2002, JetBlue announces initial public offering of its common stock, JetBlue Airways Corporation press release, April 11.
13. 2005, JetBlue's New Terminal 5 will more than double airline's JFK capacity within three years, JetBlue Airways Corporation press release, December 7.
14. 2006, Fourth quarter of 2005, JetBlue Airways Corporation press release, February 1.
15. 2006, Third quarter of 2006, JetBlue Airways Corporation press release, October 24.
16. Ibid.
17. J. Bailey, 2007, JetBlue's C.E.O. is mortified after fliers are stranded, *New York Times,* http://www.nytimes.com, February 19; T. Keenan, 2007, JetBlue damage control, http://www.foxnews. com, February 27.
18. 2007, JetBlue announces the JetBlue Customer Bill of Rights, JetBlue Airways Corporation press release, February 20.
19. 2006, Air transportation, scheduled, *Encyclopedia of American Industries,* online ed., Thomson Gale.
20. 2006, Hoover's Company Records, JetBlue Airways Corporation, October 31.
21. R. M. Schneiderman, 2006, Legacy carriers fly back into favor, *Forbes,* http://www.forbes.com, October 20.
22. 2006, Air transportation, scheduled.
23. J. Schoen, 2006, Airline woes spark industry dogfight, http://www .msnbc.com, July 31.
24. 2006, Star Alliance, http://www.staralliance.com/en/travellers/index .html.
25. K. Iatrou & N. Skourias, 2005, An attempt to measure the traffic impact of airline alliances, *Journal of Air Transportation,* 10(3): 73–99.
26. C. Jones, 2006, JetBlue seeks international partnerships, *Deseret News,* Salt Lake City, March 16.
27. D. Rosato, 2006, How to score a cheap airline ticket, *CNNMoney,* http://www.cnnmoney.com, October 27.

28. 2007, US Airways withdraws offer for Delta Air Lines, press release, http://www.usairways.com, January 31.
29. C. Palmeri, D. Frost, & L. Woellert, 2006, Doug Parker wants to fly Delta, *BusinessWeek,* http://www.businessweek.com, November 16.
30. 2006, Southwest Airlines Co. Annual Report.
31. W. Zellner, 2005, Southwest: Dressed to kill . . . competitors, *BusinessWeek,* February 21.
32. R. E. Hoskisson, M. A. Hitt, & R. D. Ireland, 2003, *Competing for Advantage,* Mason, OH: South-Western, 24.
33. D. Reed, 2006, At 35, Southwest's strategy gets more complicated, *USA Today, July* 11.
34. 2006, Hoover's Company Reports: In-depth records, AMR Corporation, November 28.
35. 2006, AMR Corp Annual Report.
36. 2006, Hoover's Company Reports: In-depth records, UAL Corporation, November 28.
37. Ibid.
38. R. M. Schneiderman, 2006, Report: UAL looking to merge, *Forbes,* December 1.
39. C. Palmeri, D. Frost, & L. Woellert, 2006, Doug Parker wants to fly Delta.
40. 2006, USAirways Group, Inc. Annual Report.
41. 2006, Airline Domestic Market Share: September 2005–August 2006, *Bureau of Transportation Statistics—The Intermodal Transportation Database,* http://www.transtats.bts.gov/, December 6.
42. 2006, Hoover's Company Reports: In-depth records, Continental Airlines Inc., November 28.
43. R. Fozard, 2006, Continental's surprising ascent, *BusinessWeek,* July 31.
44. R. M. Schneiderman, 2006, Continental packs 'em in, *Forbes,* October 19.
45. 2006, Congressional testimony, *Congressional Quarterly, Inc.,* February 8.
46. Ibid.
47. Ibid.
48. E. Roston, 2005, Hedging their costs: Whether oil prices go up or down, smart airline companies are covered, *Time,* July 27.
49. 2005, Oil prices will prune revenue gains but Southwest, JetBlue look good, *Airline Business Report,* July 4, 23(12).
50. 2007, FAA aerospace forecast fiscal years 2007–2020, http:// www .faa.gov/data_statistics/.
51. 2006, JetBlue Airways Corporation Form 10-K, Fiscal year ending December 31, 21.
52. C. Jones, 2006, JetBlue founder pushes for alternative fuel, http:// www.timesdispatch.com, November 15.
53. K. Johnson, 2005, Fuel hedging gets tricky, *Wall Street Journal,* May 19.
54. 2005, JetBlue Airways Corporation Form 10-K, Fiscal year ending December 31, 4.
55. Ibid, 9.
56. 2006, *Wall Street Journal* (Eastern edition), November 22.
57. 2005, JetBlue Airways Corporation Form 10-K, Fiscal year ending December 31, 2.
58. 2000, http://www.house.gov/transportation/aviation/hearing/ 12-05-00/12-05-00memo.html.
59. D. Bond, 2006, The FAA's demand-management plans for LaGuardia call for bigger aircraft, market-based slot turnover, *Aviation Week & Space Technology,* September 4.
60. 2005, JetBlue Airways Corporation Form 10-K, Fiscal year ending December 31, 69.
61. S. Overby, 2002, JetBlue skies ahead.
62. S. Lott, 2006, IAM fails in first attempt to organize JetBlue ramp staff, *Aviation Daily,* July 20.
63. 2006, Significant safety events since 2000 for JetBlue Airlines, AirSafe.com, LLC, http://www.airsafe.com, May 6.
64. J. Scott, 2005, http://www.aerospaceweb.org/question/planes/ q0245a.shtml, October 2.
65. R. Singal, 2003, Army admits using JetBlue data, Wired News, http://www.wired.com, September 23.
66. 2002, United States District Court Eastern District of New York, Memorandum & Order, JetBlue Airways Corp: Privacy Litigation: 04-MD-1587 (CBA), http://www.epic.org/privacy/airtravel/jetblue/ decision_0705.pdf.
67. 2005, JetBlue Airways Corporation Form 10-K, Fiscal year ending December 31, 2.
68. 2006, JetBlue Announces 6.6 Percent Operating Margin for Third Quarter 2006, JetBlue Airways Corporation press release, October 24.
69. J. Miner, 2006, http://luxuryresorttravel.suite101.com/article/cfm./ jetblue_airways_pros_and_cons, November 13.
70. S. Salter, 2004, And now the hard part, *Fast Company,* http:// www .fastcompany.com, May, 82: 67.
71. Ibid.
72. Ibid.
73. B. Harrell, 2005, http://www.yaleeconomicreview.com/issues/ fall2005/davidneeleman.
74. 2005, JetBlue Airways Corporation Form 10-K, Fiscal year ending December 31, 3.
75. S. Overby, JetBlue skies ahead.
76. Ibid.
77. R. Valdes, How VoIP works, http://electronics.howstuffworks.com/ ip-telephony.htm.
78. S. Salter, 2004, Calling JetBlue, *Fast Company,* http://www .fastcompany.com, May, 82.
79. 2005, JetBlue soars with Omniture Research Center, Omniture, Inc., http://www.omniture.com, December 2.
80. D. Sacks, 2006, Rehab: An advertising love story, *Fast Company,* http://www.fastcompany.com, June, 106.
81. Ibid.
82. B. Harrell, http://www.yaleeconomicreview.com/issues/fall2005/ davidneeleman.
83. 2005, JetBlue Airways Corporation Form 10-K, Fiscal year ending December 31, 3.
84. D. Sacks, Rehab: An advertising love story.
85. 2006, XS Lighting & sound lights JetBlue interactive kiosks, *Prism Business Media,* http://www.livedesignonline.com, June 7.
86. K. Prentice, Your client's ad, taking it to the streets, *Media Life Magazine,* Http://www.medialifemagazine.com, May 15.

87. Ibid.
88. 2005, JetBlue announces first quarter results, JetBlue Airways Corporation press release, April 1.
89. 2006, JetBlue announces 6.6 percent operating margin for third quarter, JetBlue Airways Corporation press release, October 24.
90. 2005, JetBlue Airways Corporation Form 10-K, Fiscal year ending December 31, 10.
91. Ibid.
92. R. M. Schneiderman, 2006, JetBlue courts Corporate America, *Forbes,* August 11.
93. D. Neeleman, 2006, http://www.jetblue.com/about/ourcompany/ flightlog, December 14.
94. 2005, Introducing JetBlue getaways, JetBlue Airways Corporation press release, November 3.
95. 2005, JetBlue Airways Corporation Form 10-K, Fiscal year ending December 31, 1.
96. 2006, JetBlue Airways Corporation Form 10-K, Fiscal year ending December 31, 19.
97. Financial Accounting Module 3.
98. 2005, JetBlue Airways Corporation Form 10-K, Fiscal year ending December 31, 17.
99. 2006, Industry data from www.moneycentral.msn.com.
100. 2006, *Yahoo! Finance,* http://finance.yahoo.com/q/hp?s=JBLU&a=0 3&b=18&c=2001&d=10&e=30&f=2006&g=m.
101. K. Prentice, 2006, After backing away, some airlines turning to fuel hedging again, Associated Press State & Local Wire, September 4.
102. S. Salter, On the runway, *Fast Company,* http://www.fastcompany .com, May (82).
103. S. Salter, And now the hard part, 67.
104. D. Reed, 2006, Loss shifts JetBlue's focus to climbing back into black, http://www.usatoday.com, Feb 22.
105. Ibid.
106. M. Bobelian, 2003, JetBlue lands expansion plans, *Forbes,* http:// www.forbes.com, June 10.
107. T. Reed, 2006, TheStreet.com, http://www.thestreet.com/stocks/ transportation/10260392.html, January 6.
108. 2006, *Aircraft Technology, Engineering & Maintenance,* October/ November, 99.
109. 2005, McGraw-Hill Companies *Overhaul & Maintenance,* Magazine for MRO Management, October 2.
110. Ibid, 5.
111. 2006, JetBlue Airways Corporation, Form 10-Q, October 24.
112. *Aircraft Technology Engineering & Maintenance,* 101.
113. 2006, JetBlue Airways Corporation Form 10-K, Fiscal year ending December 31, 41.
114. T. Reed, http://www.thestreet.com.

Index